FINANCE
THEORY AND PRACTICE

4th Edition

Professor Anne Marie Ward

BA (Hons), Macc, FCA, PGCUT, PhD, FHEA
School of Accounting, Finance and Economics, Ulster University

Published in 2020 by
Chartered Accountants Ireland
Chartered Accountants House
47–49 Pearse Street
Dublin 2

ISBN: 978-1-912350-36-0

Typeset by Datapage
Printed by Grafo S.A.

For my family – Martin, Thomas, Anna, Mary, Seamus and Barry.

And one other – this book will always remind me of Kieran.

Abbreviated Contents

Detailed Contents

Appendices

Preface

This textbook focuses on topics that are considered important for anyone who is pursuing a career as a financial manager within a company. It is not geared for a person who wishes to be a trader in the markets – it would have a completely different emphasis if that were its aim. *Finance: Theory and Practice* focuses on the investment, finance and dividend decision from the perspective of internal management.

I have been teaching managerial finance on degree courses, postgraduate courses and for professional bodies since 1999. The 1st edition of this textbook was published in 2007 in response to a request from Chartered Accountants Ireland for a textbook that covered its entire syllabus and was written for an Ireland/UK audience. The 1st edition was well received by the professional body and positive feedback was received from their students. Since this time the textbook has been adopted by a number of universities and institutes of technology throughout the island of Ireland. The editions that followed have incorporated feedback from lecturers and students on courses that have adopted the book. This 4th edition has been updated in light of changes to the Chartered Accountants Ireland syllabus and feedback from lecturers. The main changes include the reintroduction of a chapter on ratio analysis (Chapter 4) and a new chapter on corporate failure (Chapter 5). As a result, some material has been removed from Chapter 6 (An Introduction to Working Capital) and the chapter on amalgamations has been renamed 'Mergers and Acquisitions'.

New topics, such as market structure (Chapter 1) and the growing influence of and products relating to sustainability (for example, green bonds in Chapter 10) have been introduced; while several topics no longer on the Chartered Accountants Ireland or the ACCA syllabi have been removed.

To improve readability, I have included several additional diagrams and updated the real world examples and added more worked examples. Finally, the Review and Challenging questions have been updated.

I hope you enjoy reading and studying with this textbook. I am always happy to receive feedback and will continue to try to improve the book in future editions.

Anne Marie Ward
July 2020

Pedagogy

Structure This text is structured into seven main **parts**. The first part, The Role of Business Finance in Strategic Management and Influences on Business Finance Decision-making, provides foundation knowledge for the rest of the text. The other parts have been structured according to the key decisions faced when dealing with the management of business finance, namely the investment, financing and dividend decisions.

Learning Objectives In each chapter the expected competencies to be gained by readers are outlined at the outset.

Chapter Clarity Each chapter begins with an introduction that explains the flow and connection between topics included in the chapter. The body of each chapter provides the detail and a conclusion sums up by highlighting key points. Diagrams are used to break up the text. They typically highlight relationships and provide key definitions.

Real World Examples Where relevant and practical, real world examples are included to provide a link between theory and the business world.

Research In some instances the views, theories and findings of research studies (performed primarily on data from the United Kingdom and/or the Republic of Ireland) are integrated into the discussion of a topic.

Newspaper Articles Reference is made to newspapers articles (mostly from *The Irish Times*, *The Belfast Telegraph*, the *Irish Independent* and the *Financial Times*), again to stress the relevance of the topic being discussed to practical business issues.

Worked Examples The worked examples increase in complexity as each chapter progresses. Each chapter ends with an examination standard question.

Key Terms When key terms are first defined in a chapter they are highlighted in **bold and in blue**. At the end of each chapter the key terms are summarised in a table. The reader should be aware of the key terms and revisit the chapter when unable to define/explain one.

Review Questions These questions are designed to assist readers in identifying and revising the key issues within each chapter. As solutions to Review Questions are provided in **Appendix B**, they are a way for readers to provide themselves with feedback on their understanding of each topic. The questions range from short, quick-fire questions, to examination standard questions.

Challenging Questions These questions are all examination standard and have been categorised as either 'Level 1' or 'Level 2'. Level 1-type questions are undergraduate or CAP1 standard. Level 2-type questions are at postgraduate or CAP2 standard. Successful completion of these questions demonstrates a thorough understanding of the issues covered in the chapter and indeed may refer to issues covered in preceding chapters. (The solutions to these questions are available from the lecturer.)

Mathematics made Simple This book does not try to derive mathematical formula or to prove existing accepted models. In each instance, the accepted approach is explained in simple terms, using narrative. A formula is provided and an example of how to calculate the outcome of the formula using input variables is given.

Financial Mathematics for Assessing the Time Value of Money A brief explanation of the formulae and approaches for adjusting cash flows to take account of the time value of money has been included in **Appendix A**. Examples are used to help readers understand the application of the formulae.

Index Tables Index tables have been provided in the appendices to save readers time when they are adjusting cash flows for the time value of money.

Bibliography The readers of this text can deepen their understanding of areas of interest to them by sourcing other authors' work. The bibliography contains textbooks, newspaper articles and academic literature that are considered relevant by the author.

Lecturers' Resources Chartered Accountants Ireland provide adopting lecturers with access to the solutions to the Challenging Questions as well as additional questions and answers and PowerPoint slides for each chapter. Contact publishing@charteredaccountants.ie for details.

PART I

THE FINANCE FUNCTION

CHAPTER

1

The Role of Business Finance in Strategic Management and Influences on Business Finance Decision-making

Learning Objectives

Upon completing this chapter, readers should be able to:
- demonstrate an understanding of strategic management;
- explain how business finance supports strategic planning;
- discuss various company objectives and explain the conflict that may arise between financial and non-financial objectives;
- describe the role of the business finance manager – including the three key decision areas;
- outline the qualities required in a business finance manager; and
- discuss internal and external influences on business finance decision-making.

INTRODUCTION

Business finance is concerned with the financial evaluation of the source and use, or intended use, of a company's financial resources. Business finance provides information that can be used to aid company decision-making. The theoretical objective of business finance is to ensure that decisions made are consistent with the overall strategic objective of a company. In this text, the strategic objective is assumed to be equity holder wealth maximisation, otherwise known as **value creation**. Having a strong business finance function within a company is vital for the successful strategic management of a company and strategic management is pivotal to the success of a company.

In recognition of the importance of strategic management to a company's success, the first part of this chapter explains strategic management, highlighting the variety of strategic objectives a company might choose to pursue. Many companies pursue a finance-orientated primary objective. The attainment of this primary strategic objective is not as straightforward as it might seem. Companies do not just pursue a single course of action without having regard for corporate strategies in respect of other areas, including non-financial issues. In many instances pursuit of secondary, non-financial objectives will restrict the extent to which a company can achieve its primary financial objective. For example, ensuring employee welfare is maintained at a high level is costly and will certainly reduce the short-term profits of a company; however, it may improve employee retention, leading to reduced recruitment costs and increased productivity. In addition, conforming to regulations and ethical codes of conduct will ultimately result in a company taking decisions that reduce profitability. However, acting ethically is usually regarded favourably by equity holders, who may act illogically by supporting a less-profitable company with strong ethical practices.

The second part of this chapter introduces business finance in the context of its role in the support of strategic decision-making. Successful business finance decision-making requires a wide variety of knowledge of various other topics, such as: financial accounting (e.g. to analyse performance); management accounting (e.g. for budgeting); maths and statistics (e.g. for assessing risk and return); law (e.g. for knowing about the legal limitations on company distributions) and economics (e.g. for determining the expected impact of interest rate movements). The business finance manager also requires knowledge of the financial environment, including financial institutions and financial markets, as these are the main sources of finance for a company.

COMPANY SUCCESS

Many large companies are complex (e.g. they might be conglomerates, have foreign subsidiaries, joint ventures and many product lines) and hence require a very well formulated management structure, one which allows relevant and reliable information to be communicated quickly from several lower level departments to the central management team – the board of directors – and vice versa. Managers at the lower levels of a company are referred to as operational managers. Operations management deals with the day-to-day running of a company. This level of management provides information to assist strategic decision-making within a company, e.g. by providing information on the expected costs and revenues of undertaking a certain action. Operational management activities also include monitoring actual outcomes against planned outcomes, taking steps to alleviate potential differences and providing feedback on the corrective action and the progress of the plan to strategic management levels (members of the board of directors).

The board of directors is headed by a single person who is responsible for the overall management of the company – the managing director. Decisions taken at board-of-directors level are termed 'strategic'. Company success is arguably related to strong strategic management and a focus on long-term sustainability. There are many studies that emphasise the importance of strong, focused strategies in the successful management of a company. Business finance is central to successful strategic management. To place business finance in context, strategic management is briefly explained.

STRATEGIC MANAGEMENT

Strategic management focuses on company policy decision-making. Strategic management aims to ensure that a company remains successful in the long term and acts to either take advantage of, or make changes to, the company's operations to ensure continued success in light of economic changes that are beyond a company's control. It does not deal with detailed issues such as operational or employee problems within a department – these types of issues are dealt with at operational management level. Strategic management takes a holistic view in respect of a company. It normally has several facets that hinge on a central core objective: the overriding aim of the company. In this textbook the assumed objective being pursued by companies is **value creation**. Long-term value creation can be achieved by a focus on **company sustainability** as positive returns from operating responsibly within environmental constraints provide value not only for the company but also for society. This can have positive implications for a company's reputation and can strengthen relations with policy-makers and finance providers. In practice, however, not all companies pursue value creation as their core objective (see the Financial Objectives section later in this chapter). In this textbook, company strategy is classified into three areas: corporate strategy, competitive strategy and operational strategy.

CORPORATE STRATEGY

A company's corporate strategy should be developed as part of a sustainable business framework that factors in the impact of the company's actions on the environment and society. Successful companies normally have a clearly defined primary objective that helps to achieve the company's mission. A company's **mission statement** encompasses the purpose, aims and ethos of the company. Formulating this statement is the most important strategic decision facing a board of directors. All other strategic and operational decision-making is angled at achieving the company's mission. Another corporate strategy issue is determining the types of business the company should operate. When a company is formed, this type of information is included as part of the objects of the company (detailed in the company's memorandum and articles of association). The board of directors has to obtain agreement from a company's equity holders before it can change the objects (business activities) of a company. Changing business activity may be achieved by acquiring another company, starting a new venture or exiting a market and selling the relevant portion of the company.

Corporate strategy also includes determining the capital structure of the company. The board of directors will have to decide on the source of finance to pursue when the company needs to obtain external funds. Related to this is another key strategic decision: the dividend policy of the company. When a company pays a dividend, it reduces the amount of funds available for investment and hence growth. The board of directors has to balance the demands for distributions from equity holders with the availability of funds for financing new profitable projects that, if undertaken, would lead to higher growth and an increase in equity share price.

Competitive Strategy

The ability to remain competitive is vital for company success. This does not necessarily mean having the cheapest price. A company can improve its competitive position by providing better quality products, a better variant of the product or a new product to do the same task. **Competitive strategy** focuses on how the company's **strategic business units** compete in particular markets, supplying the resources required to the various parts of the company that operate in different markets and deciding whether to enter new markets or exit old markets. To enable the strategic managers to undertake successful strategic decision-making, they require a sound knowledge of the industry in which they operate. This will support the strategic management team in identifying comparative advantages the company has over its competitors and putting in place a plan to exploit these advantages.

Industries are all different and the potential for companies within a particular industry to make a profit is largely controlled by competitive forces, both from within the industry and from other industries. Porter (1985) formulated a five-point list to capture competitive forces that he considers influence industry success. It is briefly summarised in **Figure 1.1**.

Figure 1.1: Competitive Forces (Porter 1985)

Threat of potential market entrants	When there are barriers to entering a particular industry (e.g. the need to invest a significant capital outlay to get started), then the potential profitability of companies within that particular industry will be higher. When a market is easily entered, more companies are likely to join, resulting in more competition (and possibly price wars). Existing companies are more likely to set competitive prices, and hence keep profitability low, in an attempt to create a barrier to entry.
Existing competition	The type of industry will also impact on industry (hence company) success. An industry with homogenous products and homogenous cost structures (those that have a high proportion of fixed costs) will be less profitable, as individual companies will find it more difficult to create a comparative advantage over their rivals, as they are evenly balanced. The extent of the market share in these circumstances will be linked to individual company success.
Pressure from substitutes	Within every industry, companies come under pressure from direct competition for market share from other companies within the same industry. However, this is not the only competition some industries face; many whole industries are exposed to competition from other industries. A good example is energy. The coal industry once dominated the energy world. Now coal has been substituted to a large extent by the oil and electricity industries, and 'fracking' and green energy sources such as wind, hydro and tidal energy are becoming a threat to the oil industry.
Bargaining power of buyers	Buyers are not as loyal as they once were. Many buyers now 'shop around' before purchasing a product. Universities frequently change their preferred suppliers after a competitive tendering process. By playing off companies within the same industry against each other, buyers ensure that individual company and overall industry profitability are reduced.
Bargaining power of suppliers	The quantity of suppliers to an industry will influence the profitability of that industry. If an industry has few suppliers, then their dominant position leaves them in a stronger position to raise purchase prices and to provide a poorer quality service, with little chance of losing business. When an industry has many potential suppliers, competition will keep the purchase price down and the quality of service high.

Operational Strategy

Operational strategy focuses on ensuring that operational- and functional-level goals and objectives are consistent with overall corporate strategies, e.g. by ensuring that the finance department supports investments that are consistent with the company's long-term future plans, even if this means not investing in projects that reap larger short-term rewards.

VALUE CHAIN ANALYSIS

As described earlier, Porter (1985) argues that industry knowledge is important for selecting the correct strategy to pursue to maximise company value. He also suggests that management should focus on key drivers (activities) that will add value to the company. He calls this **value chain analysis**. In his text, Porter identifies five key activities that are common to most firms and that should add value to the products that a company sells (see **Figure 1.2** and **Figure 1.3**), and four important support activities (see **Figure 1.4**).

FIGURE 1.2: PORTER'S VALUE-ADDING ACTIVITIES (1985)

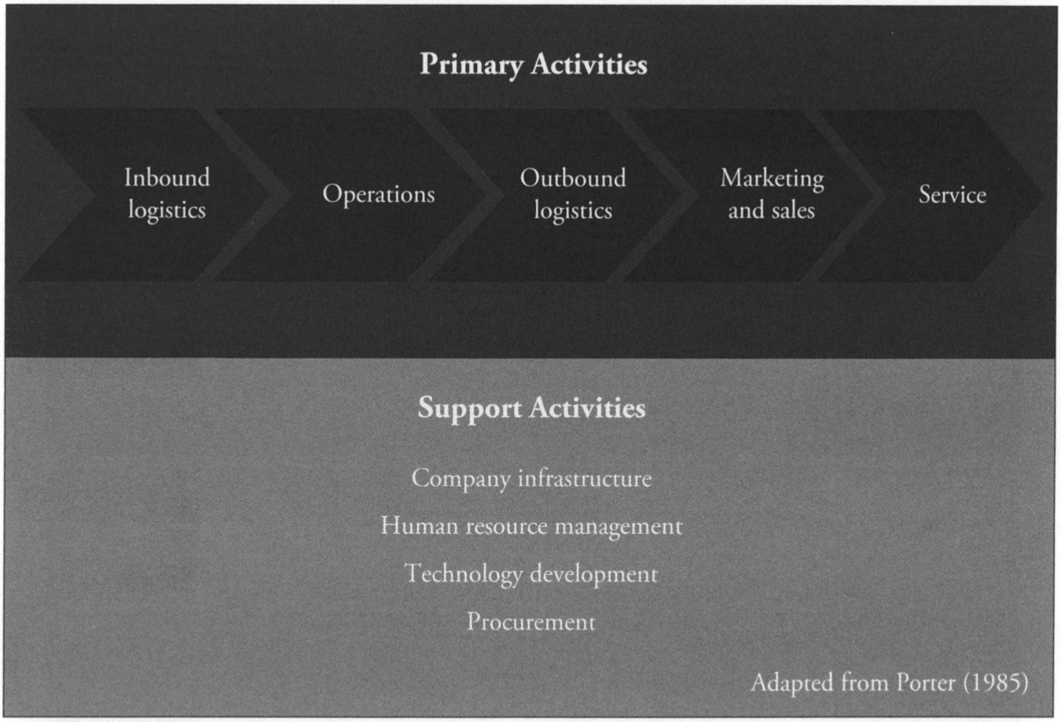

Adapted from Porter (1985)

Figure 1.3: Porter's Primary Activities (1985)

Activity	Description
Inbound logistics	The processes and procedures for receiving inventory and ensuring that it is efficiently delivered to manufacturing so that production is not affected. In the case of a retail entity, this activity will be concerned with, e.g. the ordering, receipt, storage and distribution of the goods to the shop floor.
Operations	Is concerned with ensuring that the production process is efficient with the raw materials and consumables being converted to finished goods in the most productive manner. In a large supermarket this could be baking fresh bread and packaging and presenting it in a way to better maximise sales.
Outbound logistics	Deals with the end product – the finished goods. In manufacturing entities it is concerned with the correct warehousing and distribution of the goods to customers (retailers). In retail stores, it is concerned with the proper storage, display and packaging of foods that customers purchase (including the supply of trolleys, baskets, carrier bags, etc.).
Marketing and sales	Involves the identification and service of potential customers. It determines the product-market relationship and identifies areas for growth.
Service	Focuses on quality and brand enhancement. It deals with after-sales care, e.g. installation, providing guarantees, warranties, repairs policy, returns policy, a fully trained customers' complaints team.

Figure 1.4: Porter's Support Activities (1985)

Activity	Description
Firm infrastructure	This encapsulates the culture of the company, its organisational structure (departments, etc.), control systems and lines of communication. It will determine the management information systems in place, which will in turn influence the various inbound, operational and outbound activities of the company.
Human resource management	Human resource management is concerned with staff recruitment, retention and remuneration. It also encapsulates health and safety, training, staff development and pensions.
Technology development	This involves investing in technology to ensure that the company retains competitive advantage over its competitors. It encapsulates research and development into new technologies and research into competitors' technologies and technologies being developed in the marketplace.
Procurement	Purchasing involves sourcing products that meet/exceed minimum quality thresholds and that minimise costs. The quality will depend on the market for the product, which is influenced by whether the product is a luxury item or a necessity good, and on the quality and price of competitors' products. The procurement decision will also consider issues such as outsourcing and ePurchasing.

SWOT ANALYSIS

Another commonly used strategic planning tool is SWOT analysis. The starting point is to identify an objective, such as considering a potential partnership, merger, outsourcing a particular service or introducing a new product. Then the strategists (management) analyse the company internally and identify its strengths (S) and weaknesses (W), and separately examine the external strategic environment within which the company operates to identify any opportunities (O) and any threats (T) that may have a negative impact on the company – hence the name SWOT analysis.

Strengths consider the features of a company that help it to achieve its primary objective. Examples can include brand names, patents, technical know-how, trained workforce, economical and up-to-date machines, good reputation and access to natural resources. **Weaknesses** are the features of a company that may hinder its ability to achieve its primary objective. Examples can include having a weak brand identity, not having patent protection, having high staff turnover, owning machines that are old and possibly obsolete, having poor customer relations and being reliant on imports of raw materials from a foreign country. **Opportunities** are external factors that help the company to achieve its objectives. Assuming the objectives are linked to growth and profitability, then opportunities might include: identifying a niche in the market for a new product; recognising possibilities when new technologies become available; or acting quickly to take advantage of changes in the tax laws or regulation. Finally, **threats** are changes in the external environment that may damage the company's ability to meet its objectives. These may include: carbon emission limits; advances in technology being implemented by competitors; changes in customer taste; evolution of product development in competing companies; market entrants; and changes to tax laws or regulation. Strategic planning tries to manipulate a company's strengths to enable it to avail of opportunities that have been identified. By identifying weaknesses and threats, management can take steps to protect its position and to defend against external factors that may be harmful to the company's future.

COMPANY OBJECTIVES

As mentioned in the previous section, the most important strategic decision to make is to determine a company's primary objective, i.e. its 'mission'. The expected outcome of this mission is sometimes referred to as the **vision** for the company. Company objectives are either financial or non-financial. Most companies view non-financial objectives as secondary to financial objectives. In some instances, the pursuit of non-financial objectives may actually restrict the potential to maximise financial objectives.

Financial Objectives

Financial objectives include the following.

Equity Holder Wealth Maximisation

The objective **equity holder wealth maximisation** involves making decisions that ultimately benefit the equity holders (i.e. owners) of a company. As mentioned previously, this objective is also referred to as 'value creation'. When companies pursue value creation, the focus is on undertaking sustainable, long-term investments that increase the future earnings potential and cash inflows of the company. This may mean turning down projects that have higher short-term returns. Market participants value a company based on its expected future earnings potential and the risks associated with obtaining those earnings, therefore the focus is on undertaking projects with strong long-term earnings which are not over a certain risk threshold.

Profit Maximisation

Profit maximisation usually involves pursuing projects that provide a quick return in the short term. It is argued that this may damage the long-term earnings of a company, as there is less focus on the future direction a company takes. Pursuing **profit maximisation** may also put management under pressure to expose a company to higher levels of risk in an attempt to maximise profits – higher returns are usually correlated with riskier projects. Conversely, it is argued that pursuing a profit-maximising objective will create value; hence the equity holders' objectives will also be met.

Sustainability – the enlightened shareholder value approach

In recent years there has been a refocusing on how best to achieve shareholder wealth maximisation. At a strategic level, it is argued that a general focus on long-term sustainability is the most appropriate approach. This is called the **enlightened shareholder value approach**. It focuses on long-term value creation and the interests of various stakeholders, in advancing shareholder value (O'Connell & Ward, 2020). The view is that the promotion of shareholder interests does not require ignoring the interests of other stakeholders deemed to be important to the success of the company. Boards are permitted to take different stakeholder interests into account if deemed to be congruent with long-term shareholder wealth maximisation. An enlightened approach does not extend to additional rights for stakeholders, nor does the approach prioritise other stakeholders at the expense of shareholders. However, it argues that all stakeholders benefit from a long-term view and hence the sustainability of the company. It is argued that sustainability and shareholder value maximization have the potential to be complementary undertakings that result in a virtuous circle in which "doing good" helps companies do well, and doing well provides the wherewithal to do more good (Martin, Petty, & Wallace, 2009). In support of this view, policymakers are increasing the legal requirements on corporates to publish on social and environmental matters, for example, the EU Non-Financial Reporting Directive 2014/95/EU. In addition, stock exchanges have started to require their members to comply with Corporate Governance Codes that contain requirements on disclosures of social and environmental matters (O'Connell & Ward, 2020). Moreover, the enlightened shareholder value approach is consistent with the growing numbers of institutional investors who include sustainability criteria and metrics when developing and assessing portfolios of shares (Chen & Scholtens, 2018).

Alternative Financial Objectives

In some instances, profit-making companies will not explicitly pursue earnings-related objectives as their primary objective, though they will pursue policies that have financial outcomes in mind – growth, risk reduction and efficiency are examples of this type of objective.

Growth

Growth in market share is pursued as a primary objective by some companies. Growth may bring with it economies of scale and therefore result in value creation for equity holders in the long term. Growth also reflects corporate power, and dominant management teams may pursue growth as a means of maximising their own positions. Some non-profit-making or associational organisations pursue growth as a primary objective, e.g. building societies and credit unions. Growth in these financial institutions is assumed to encapsulate a social measure – it reflects the fact that the benefits of the organisation's services are being enjoyed by a wider membership, increasing social welfare.

Risk Reduction

Some industries are exposed to more risk than others. All industries that rely on research and development for future earnings are subject to high levels of risk, e.g. the pharmaceutical industry and the oil exploration industry. Companies in these industries are likely to pursue risk-minimising objectives and have profit maximisation as a close secondary objective. The potential earnings to be obtained if the research and development turns out to be successful can be great, as will the losses if the research and development is scrapped. Risk-reducing strategies may include portfolio diversification (whereupon the company becomes a conglomerate investing in several different industries to reduce overall risk), or may spread the risk by sharing the investment with, e.g. another pharmaceutical company or a venture capital company.

Efficiency

Some entities do not generate income from the provision of goods and/or services, e.g. many public bodies. They have a budget that has to cover costs and that enables the body to achieve social and financial targets. Efficiency in the use of funds to achieve the greatest social output is usually the primary objective of these types of organisation. The ultimate goal is to provide quality services at the lowest possible cost.

Non-financial Objectives

Social Objectives

Some non-profit-making organisations and public sector bodies might pursue **non-financial objectives** as their primary focus. Examples might include growth in membership numbers, reduction in patient deaths, reduction in waiting lists or improved train punctuality.

Employee Welfare

Having **employee welfare** as a secondary objective usually increases company costs as it involves paying fair wages, providing a solid pension and good holidays, adopting a strong health and safety policy, enabling the employees to advance their skills through training and education and providing good redundancy packages and retraining initiatives, when necessary. However, there are financial benefits as employees are likely to remain in the company for longer, saving recruitment and training costs, and gain greater company-specific skills, which add value.

Trade Relationships

Another social objective might be to create and maintain quality relationships with suppliers and customers. Some large companies are in a position of power in respect of the custom they provide to small companies. They could cause damage to small companies by demanding unreasonably low prices for supplies purchased or could take long credit periods, leaving the supply companies in financial difficulty. Adhering to an agreed credit agreement will maintain a good relationship. In terms of dealings with customers, the focus might be on providing quality products, which are adequately supported by the company in terms of warranty.

Environmental Policies

Other companies pursue **environmental policies**, opting, for example, to reduce pollution by planting trees for flights taken by employees or to use recycled packaging. These steps will reduce the profitability of a company, yet help the environment.

Examples of strategies from two of Ireland's listed companies, CRH Plc and Applegreen (see **Real World Example 1.1**), show a commitment to some of the objectives mentioned above, including customer relationships and efficiency. In each case the strategies are developed further with reference to several key areas on which the companies are focusing their attention.

Real World Example 1.1: CRH Plc and Applegreen

CRH Plc's strategy

Our strategy is to continue to grow and improve our business and in doing so to maximise long-term value and deliver superior returns for our shareholders and for society.

Applegreen's strategy

The Group is focused on acquiring and developing new Service Area and Petrol Filling Station sites in each of the three markets in which it operates. The Group offers a distinctive convenience retail offering with three key elements:

- A "low fuel prices, always" price promise to drive footfall to the stores;
- A "Better Value Always" tailored retail offer; and
- A strong food and beverage focus aiming to offer premium products and service to the customer.

Sources: https://www.crh.com/about-crh/strategy-business-model/, accessed November 2019.
http://investors.applegreenstores.com/about-applegreen.aspx, accessed November 2019.

Damaging Objectives

Personal Objectives

Senior directors might support decisions which maximise their financial position by ensuring, for example, that short-term profit targets are met and bonuses obtained. When a board pursues personal aspirations, it is more likely to make decisions that increase the company's short-term profitability and to be less concerned about the company's long-term earnings potential (referred to as **short-termism**).

Satisficing Objectives

In terms of company objectives, **satisficing** would occur where a company's strategic management team pursues objectives that are aimed at keeping everyone happy by providing a satisfactory return to equity holders, and not at maximising the value of a company.

Changes in Company Objectives

The primary objective of a company can change over time. A young start-up company, for instance, may strive to achieve market share and hence pursue growth as the primary objective, changing to profit maximisation when a certain size has been reached. When a company's financial risk increases beyond a point that is deemed acceptable by the board, the primary financial objective may be to reduce gearing in the company. When a company gets into real financial difficulties and is forced into liquidation, the strategic aim might be to operate the business so as to minimise the costs of liquidation and provide the maximum return to the company's stakeholders (namely the employees, creditors, tax authorities, loan creditors, preference shareholders and equity holders) and to ensure that there is equity in the treatment of each group until the company is closed and final distribution takes place.

Business Finance – Company Objectives

In business finance theory it is assumed that the primary objective of a company is to maximise company value. By doing this, the value of equity holders' holding will be maximised. **Equity holder value** is the combination of dividends received in the past and the current market value of shares held. **Equity holder return** is the dividend received in a period plus the capital gain made on the value of equity shares held over the period. Assuming only one objective is a simplistic approach to a complicated area. There is a variety of financial and non-financial objectives, and companies do not just pursue one objective – often several are considered important, with their importance changing in light of changes in the economy, the global market, the environment and even when individual directors change. In defence of assuming the pursuit of only one objective, it is argued that market forces cause a company's directors to pursue value-creation strategies, and this happens in the real world. Decision-making that conflicts with equity holders' interests will not be tolerated by the market. Equity holders can elect to change the directors or may even sell their shares, causing company value to drop, which could result in the company becoming a target for a takeover bid (after which the directors will be made redundant). An example of where equity holder pressure caused a chief executive to resign is outlined in **Real World Example 1.2.**

Real World Example 1.2: Uber

Uber founder Travis Kalanick resigned as Chief Executive in 2017 after pressure from shareholders. The company had suffered too many controversies and scandals for the shareholders liking and they demanded that Travis Kalanick step-down. Some of the public scandals included a key manager obtaining and sharing a rape victim's medical records with other managers. This was done after the victim claimed an Uber driver had raped her. Other controversies included there being over 200 human resources complaints about harassment and bullying, sexual harassment claims, sexist remarks in a high-level meeting and a lawsuit for the alleged theft of trade secrets on driverless cars.

There is a market for top level executives, with premium salary packages being paid for executives who have a proven track record in increasing company value.

It can be argued that pursuing value creation has social benefits. The proportion of shares held by the general public is increasing, aided by the spread of the internet and cloud technologies and platforms that allow trading to take place from an individual's home. The theory is that, if all companies pursue policies to increase their wealth, then society's wealth would also increase. In addition, many insurance and pension companies hold large stakes in the stock market. If the market performs well, then retired people will get higher pensions and insurance premiums will not have to be as high, which will increase society's wealth.

STRATEGIC PLANNING AND COMPANY VALUE

The elements that a board of directors will have to consider when formulating the company's **strategic plan** will be driven primarily by the company's mission and will be influenced by secondary financial and non-financial strategic objectives. In addition to considering the overall aims of the company, policymakers should also have regard to the business environment within which they operate, both internally and externally. As recommended by *Turnbull* (discussed later in this chapter), the approach to setting a strategic plan should focus on identifying the risks faced by a company and formulating strategies to minimise those risks. The external factors that may cause risk exposure include the environment (e.g. changes to regulation and/or taxation), the economy and changes within foreign markets. Internally, cost structure, employee morale, agency costs and gearing may cause risk exposure. The interaction of these various forces on the formulation of a strategic plan is set out in **Figure 1.5**. The primary objective is the overriding driver in the formulation of the strategic business plan; however, secondary objectives and identified risk exposures will also influence the plan.

The strategic plan is denominated in financial terms. Business finance is pivotal to all stages of the preparation and implementation of a strategic plan.

FIGURE 1.5: INTERACTION OF THE STRATEGIC PLAN WITH THE OBJECTIVES AND HOW THE PLAN IS IMPLEMENTED

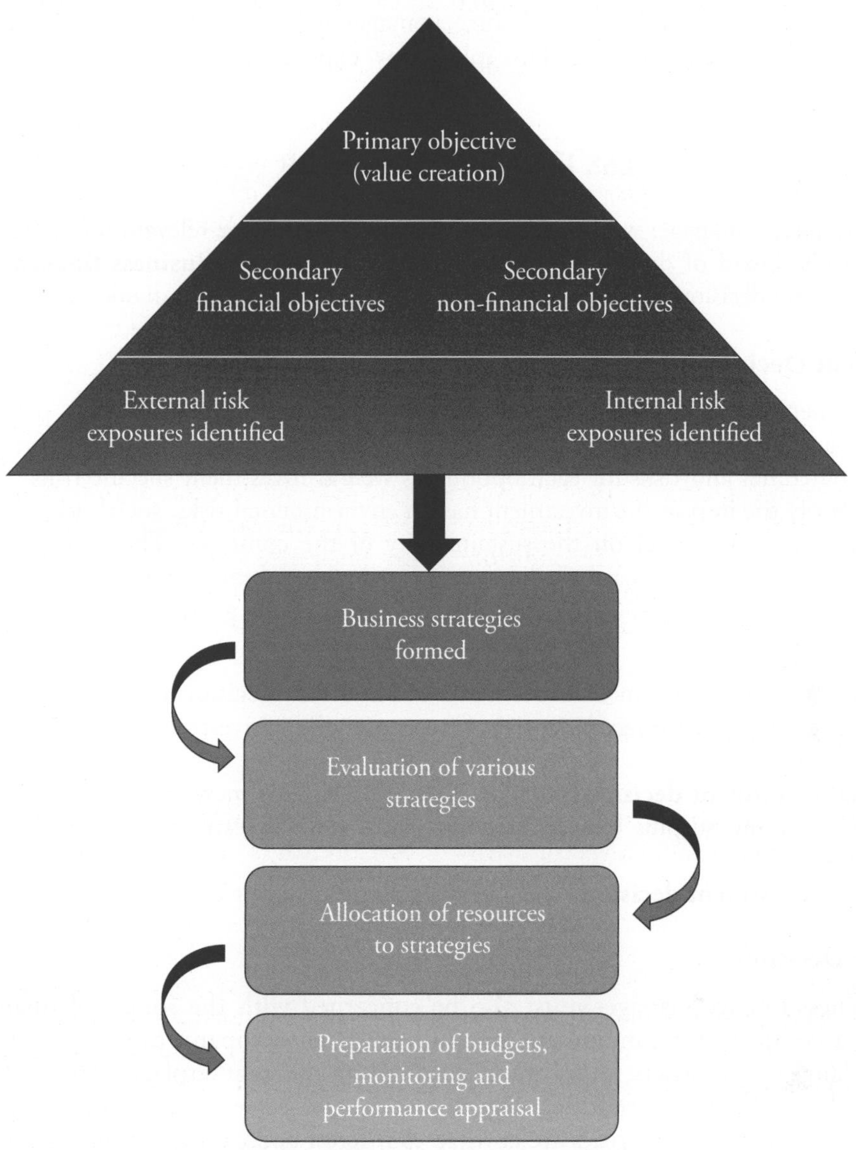

BUSINESS FINANCE EXPLAINED

Sometimes referred to as **financial management**, **business finance** is concerned with financial decision-making within a business. The decisions usually involve deciding on a course of action that will maximise the output received from a company's resources, ultimately resulting in an increase in the value of the company. Indeed, the objective of business finance decision-making is assumed to be financial planning, and raising and using resources in an effective and efficient manner to provide the maximum return to equity holders. As a company's primary objective is assumed to be value creation, the business finance objective is congruent with this aim. Most large companies have a finance function; within this department a business finance manager will have ultimate responsibility for business finance decision-making. This role is now explained.

ROLE OF THE BUSINESS FINANCE MANAGER

A business finance manager works with other managers to provide relevant information which is used by the board of directors for strategic decision-making. **Business finance** normally involves making decisions in three key areas: investment, finance and dividend decisions.

Investment Decision

The investment decision-making process involves evaluating different projects. The business finance manager usually provides meaningful reports to the board of directors detailing expected outcomes and risks for each option. As well as investment specific risks, the report should identify the impact the investment has on environmental risks, social risks and governance risks that may impact on the sustainability of the company. The appraisal methods adopted should allow the board of directors to make consistent comparisons across various options and easily identify those options that will result in the greatest value creation for the company.

Investment appraisal is deemed to be the most important decision facing a company, as it determines the future earnings potential of a company. The investment decision can be split into two types:

- **Internal investment decisions** include asset replacements, new capital projects, working capital levels and surplus cash investment (short-term investments or portfolio theory) decisions.
- **External investment decisions** include merger and takeover decisions.

Finance Decision

The business finance manager must also be concerned with the source of finance to be used by a company for funding its investments. Each company can obtain finance by selling claims to its assets and future earnings in the marketplace. These claims are formalised into financial securities, which are categorised as either debt or equity. The holders of the financial securities are entitled to interest and capital repayments, dividends and capital growth. The return required by debt-security holders is usually lower than equity-security holders as they are exposed to less risk. Debt securities rank in front of equity securities when distributions are made and on the liquidation of a company. Interest has to be paid, whereas dividends can be waived. This means that debt, though cheaper, increases the financial risks faced by a company.

The overriding aim of the **finance decision** is to obtain the cheapest source of finance without damaging overall company value. This is more complicated than it would first seem. For example, when too much debt is issued, equity holders are likely to react to the increased risk by either demanding a higher return or selling their shares. Therefore, when analysing the cost of a source of finance, the business finance manager not only has to take into account the cost of the new finance being obtained, but should also include the potential shift in the cost of the existing finance in response to the new capital structure.

Amount and timing are also important. The business finance manager has to provide the correct amount of finance: too much leaves a surplus that may not earn an appropriate return; too little exposes the investment to the risk of non-completion. If finance is received too early, it will not be utilised to earn a return, yet the financiers will have to be paid; if it is received too late, the investment will not be able to proceed as planned. Finally, in recent times investors have provided funds at favourable rates to companies that visibly pursue sustainable policies, therefore, this needs to be factored into the decision-making process.

Dividend Decision

Dividends are cash returns to equity holders. In practice, equity holders prefer a company to follow a stable dividend policy. When equity holders are happy with a company's dividend policy, they are more interested in holding shares in the company – this drives up share price, hence increasing company value. Deviations from a set dividend policy are also regarded favourably by equity holders in certain circumstances. For example, equity holders will react favourably when a company distributes surplus funds that are not being used to generate a return that is in excess of the cost of the company's capital. The distributed funds can be reinvested by the equity holders elsewhere to earn a higher return.

Relationship between the Key Decisions

Each of the key decisions cannot be taken in isolation and each decision will impact on the other two. Modigliani and Miller suggest that each company has two main sources of cash and two main uses of cash.

Figure 1.6: Yearly Sources and Uses of Cash in a Company

Company Sources	Company Uses
Profits	Dividends
Financing	Investments

Dividends and investments are uses of finance, and profits and financing are sources of finance. In all instances the sources should equal the uses. The basic relationship between the investment, financing and dividend decisions is given in a formula suggested by Modigliani and Miller:

$$P + F + D + I$$

where: P = profit
F = new financing
D = dividends/distributions
I = investment

It is argued that the interaction between the variables in the model affects company value and that the equation is constrained by various influences. For example, the availability of finance may depend on the current gearing of the company, its historical performance and its size. The variables are also related to each other, e.g. the acceptability of an investment will depend on the cost of the chosen method of financing. An investment that can only be financed using an expensive source of finance, which will not cover the rate of return received from the investment, will most likely not be accepted, even though the return from the investment exceeds the current return earned by the company and the current cost of the company's capital.

As a source of finance, retained earnings have no issue costs and are quick and easy to obtain, and as such they are the preferred source of finance by decision-makers. However, if a company uses retained earnings to finance an investment, this will reduce the amount available for dividends. Dividend policy usually influences a company's share price. Equity holders like a company to adopt a steady dividend-payout policy. Changes to the policy will affect share price and, hence, company value. A volatile policy will also reduce the attractiveness of new equity share issues to market participants. Finally, the choice of profitable investments will affect the amount of future profits available for increased dividends.

Knowledge of the potential influence of each of the key decisions on each other and the consequences for company value is required for successful business finance decision-making.

QUALITIES OF A BUSINESS FINANCE MANAGER

Business finance managers need to be strong communicators. They need to be able to transform data into information and to present this information in a meaningful manner to others. They have to attend board meetings when strategy is being discussed and to inform the board of the strengths, weaknesses, opportunities and threats in respect of each option. Collecting data about alternatives involves communicating across departments within a company, so the finance manager needs to establish communication channels with the purchasing, sales, credit control, inventory-holding, production, marketing, financial accounting and management accounting departments.

In addition to strong communication skills and internal networks, a wide knowledge is required of subjects that extend beyond finance. These areas are explained now.

Financial Accounting

Financial accounting focuses on the preparation of financial statements that portray the historical results of a company for a period (in terms of profitability and cash-generation activities) and its financial position at a point in time. The finance manager needs to be able to interpret the financial statements of a company. The statement of financial position reflects the sources of a company's finance and how that finance has been invested by the board of directors. The statement of profit or loss shows the past performance of a company. This information can be used to analyse past decisions and to predict future profitability. The statement of cash flows provides information on cash earnings and their sources, again useful information for predicting the future cash flow expectations for a company.

Management Accounting

Management accounting focuses on accounting for decision-making within a company and pays particular attention to costs and their relationship to time and to output. Management accounting information on costs can help to inform finance decision-making. The management accounting function will prepare budgets in respect of current operations and variance reports and will usually feedback reasons for variances to the board of directors. This information will be beneficial to business finance managers as it can highlight where prior finance projections were incorrect, or simply provide a better understanding of costs, leading to improved business finance decision-making in the future.

Maths and Statistics

The efficiency of a variety of options and the risk associated with these options can be formally assessed using quantitative techniques. For example, a cost minimisation model, such as the economic order quantity model, can be used to determine the optimal inventory order quantity, given a set level of demand, for a period. Expected values, standard deviations and variances can provide information on risk and return. Linear programming can help support decision-making when there is capital rationing. However, it should be stressed that these techniques usually only add weight to a business finance manager's instinctive views as to the best option to pursue when deciding amongst a variety of options.

Law

When undertaking business finance decision-making, knowledge of legislation and regulations affecting a company is mandatory. All companies have to comply with company law and public listed companies also need to comply with stock exchange rules. Legislation usually strives to protect stakeholders. For example, there are restrictions on the amount of dividends that a company can distribute. This law aims to protect loan creditors. Also, a business finance manager has to be aware of the consequences of offering assets as security for debt. If the security is fixed, then those assets cannot be sold. When equity is being raised, there is a legal requirement to allow existing equity holders to retain their current equity-holding proportion – they are given pre-emptive rights to purchase new share issues before the new issue is made available in the marketplace.

Taxation

There are different types of tax and a business finance manager needs to be aware of the different taxes as they will ultimately influence business finance decision-making. Companies pay corporation tax on net earnings, therefore changes in corporation tax rates will alter expected future cash flows. Knowing what is tax deductible and what is not is also important – e.g. depreciation is not tax-deductible, but capital allowances are. The differences in these two deductions can be material, particularly when the government gives first-year tax allowances for certain types of capital expenditure. In terms of financing, interest on debt securities is tax deductible (reducing its net cost to a company), whereas dividends are not. Given that equity holders value a company on the basis of expected future cash flows, changes to taxation will impact on company value.

As the objective of business finance is to maximise the wealth of ordinary equity holders, it is important that a business finance manager has knowledge of personal taxes. In respect of equity holdings, individuals typically face two taxes: capital gains tax and income tax. Business finance managers should keep abreast of the changes in both taxes and consideration of the changes should be reflected in dividend policy. For example, when capital gains tax rates are low, the company may feel that it would be in its equity holders' interests to retain funds, reinvest them and cause their company share price to rise. Equity holders could then sell some shares and make a capital gain, which would be taxed at a lower rate than dividend income.

Economics

The business finance manager also has to have knowledge of economics. For example, an understanding of theories on the price elasticity of demand and the allocation of scarce resources should inform decisions about new products or changes to existing products. Understanding the relationship between inflation, interest rates and foreign exchange rates and the impact of changes in these variables on the markets will inform decision-making, if sourcing finance. For example, when deciding on a loan product and the terms and type of interest rate to adopt, it is useful to have a reliable opinion on expected interest rate movements. When the business finance manager expects that these rates will fall, a flexible interest option might be preferable; conversely, when the business finance manager expects interest rates to rise, a fixed-rate loan product might be more desirable. Inflation also influences decision-making, reducing the real return earned by a company.

OTHER INFLUENCES ON BUSINESS FINANCE DECISION-MAKING

The business finance manager must be knowledgeable about the environment within which their company works. This includes knowing about the type of market structure that their company operates in, data science, conflicts that can arise between company stakeholders, good corporate governance practices, what is deemed to be ethical behaviour, the impact of government intervention on the company and globalisation. These are now discussed briefly in turn.

Market Structures

When a company decides to sell a product, they need to be aware of the specific market structure for that product. **Market structure** refers to the characteristics of a market, in particular, the number of selling and buying companies, the nature of competition, price collusion, product determination and barriers to entry and exit from the product's market. The market structure influences the price that can be set and the profit that can be generated from trading in that particular product. There are several types of market structure, but for expediency, the four main types are explained in this book. They are perfect competition, monopolistic competition, oligopoly and monopoly. The key characteristics of the different markets are presented in **Figure 1.7**.

FIGURE 1.7: CHARACTERISTICS OF DIFFERENT MARKET STRUCTURES

Market structure	Perfect competition	Imperfect competition		Monopoly
		Monopolistic	Oligopoly	
Number of sellers	Many	Many	Few (2–5)	One
Competition	Extensive	Extensive	Limited	None
Products	Homogenous	Differentiated	Differentiated but limited	Unique
Market entry and exit cost	None	Low	Medium	High
Pricing power	None	Little	Medium (incentive to collude)	High (may be regulated)
Competitive approach	Pricing	Pricing and marketing	Pricing and marketing	Advertising awareness
Product examples	Milk, carrots	Clothing, vehicles	Crude oil	Utilities

The four market structures are theoretical and are based on a number of assumptions. The assumptions and practical application of each is now outlined, in brief.

Perfect competition

The assumptions are that all companies strive to maximise profits; that there is free market entry and exit; that goods are identical; and that consumers have no preference between companies. This type of 'free' market is deemed to be good for society as companies cannot reap excess profits at the expense of society.

Monopolistic competition

The assumptions are that all companies strive to maximise profits; that there is free market entry and exit; that companies sell differentiated products; and that consumers have preference for one product over another. This type of market is also good for society so long as consumers act rationally. Excess profits can be reaped by companies from some sections of society who choose to purchase, for example, expensive brands over alternative cheaper options.

Oligopoly

The assumptions are that all companies strive to maximise profits; there are a small number of companies and they can influence prices; there are barriers to market entry and exit and products can be homogenous or differentiated. There is particular risk of price collusion in these companies and as such they typically come under the watchful eye of regulators. An example is provided in **Real World Example 1.3**.

Real World Example 1.3: Scania

In 2017 Scania, which is owned by Volkswagen, was fined €880 million by the European Commission, under their EU Antitrust Regulations, over price and emissions collusion. The truck-manufacturing company had colluded with five other truck manufacturers over a 14-year period.

Monopoly

The assumptions are that the market is made up of one company; the company aims to maximise its profits; there are high barriers to market entry and exit; and the company can set the price and control the flow of products to the market. This type of market structure would have negative societal consequences and as such regulators control the pricing behaviour of such companies, for example, utility providers have to agree their prices with regulatory bodies such as the Northern Ireland Authority for Utility Regulation (NIAUR). This body regulates the electricity, gas, water and sewage industries in Northern Ireland.

Data Science, Big Data, Data Analytics and GDPR

Data manipulation in support of decision-making is not new. However, growth in technology, data capture, data migration, data mining and analytic tools has provided insights to consumer behaviour that companies are increasingly utilising when determining their strategic policy towards markets. Business finance managers need to be aware of the opportunities that are available, the terminology used to describe the processes of data manipulation and issues arising around General Data Protection Regulation (GDPR). Four terms are explained in this book: data science, big data, data analytics and GDPR.

Data science is a term that describes the techniques used to extract, mine and cleanse information from huge databases. The techniques are typically pre-programmed and use algorithms to identify and extract relevant information. The best example is an internet search engine.

Big data is a buzzword that is used to describe the vast volumes of raw data that is available. Big data is collected by companies and governments and in recent years work on linking data from disparate sources has led to large databases of rich information. Big data is typically varied and is collected frequently, for example, if you have a Tesco Clubcard, the moment this is swiped at the till, information on your shopping habits, including shopping frequency, type of product and price of product, populates a database.

Data analytics is a term used to describe the techniques used to analyse linkages and patterns between data from different sources. Companies can use this data to tailor their marketing to particular customers. For example, big supermarkets, such as Sainsbury's and Tesco, use data collected when a customer swipes their clubcard to decide on the type and range of vouchers to issue to them. Each customer obtains vouchers tailored to their shopping habits, which keeps the customer happy. In addition, supermarkets can use it to sell products – for example, if a customer has purchased dog food, they are likely to receive emails about offers on pet insurance.

Conflict

The business finance manager has to be aware of conflicting objectives that can hinder decision-making.

Conflict between Internal Departments

Conflict can arise between different departments within a company. This conflict might be caused or accentuated by an ineffective appraisal system. For example, if the purchasing department manager is rewarded for obtaining supplies at cheap rates, this will encourage bulk purchasing to obtain discounts. However, this causes a problem for the stores department manager who has to incur extra costs trying to maintain and insure the goods. If the stores department manager is being appraised on the ability to minimise costs, conflict will arise. These sorts of issues arise in virtually every decision that impacts on more than one department. The business finance manager can introduce a more strategic viewpoint by, for example, weighing up the costs associated with having additional funds tied up in inventories and the increased costs of storing inventories against the benefit gained from the discount received. The business finance manager can inform both departments of the most appropriate course of action, thus removing conflict.

Conflict between Equity Holders and Creditors

Though the primary focus of business finance is to support decision-making that creates value for equity holders, this should not be done at the expense of other legitimate stakeholders who also have claims on company assets. Creditors/debt financiers have also invested in the company and directors have a duty of care to ensure that their decision-making does not put these financiers' claims at undue risk, even if the action would increase equity holder value. Debt financiers rank in front of equity holders when it comes to yearly distributions and on liquidation of a company; however, their return is capped, whereas the yearly and final distribution available to equity holders is not restricted. They can reap the balance of rewards available in each year and on liquidation. Conflict arises as pressure may be exerted by equity holders to distribute excessive amounts, which may cause liquidity problems and an inability to pay the debt financiers in future years.

Many debt issuers protect themselves by building covenants into debt trust deeds. These covenants might legally restrict the level of dividend that can be distributed or restrict the gearing level of a company. The ethical stance of the board of directors, in many instances, also provides protection for debt holders (ethics is discussed later in the chapter).

Agency Theory (the Equity Holder and Director Conflict)

It is one thing determining that the primary objective of a company should be value creation and getting board acceptance for this objective; it is another to encourage a board of directors to take decisions in support of this objective when the decision may cause them personal financial harm. For example, value creation will be enhanced by taking decisions that maximise the long-run earnings of the company. However, these decisions may result in the rejection of other investments that provide higher short-term returns. Directors' bonus packages may be tied into short-term profitability. In addition, low returns and cash inflows in the early years of an investment might cause the liquidity of a company to deteriorate, increasing the financial risk associated with the company. Some directors may not wish to have their single source of income (i.e. their salaries) put at risk and so may oppose decisions that are not congruent with their own personal financial goals. This conflict is referred to in the relevant literature as **agency theory**. Agency theory considers that directors are 'agents' who act on behalf of 'principals', i.e.≈the equity holders. The directors should make decisions that fulfil equity holders' needs – namely value creation.

A commonly used method to encourage congruence between the aims of directors and equity holders is to align the financial rewards available to the board of directors with those of the equity holders (i.e. bonding). The financial rewards might include setting bonuses and rewards for meeting long-term performance targets. The performance targets might include achieving a certain growth in the earnings per share over a three- to five-year period, achieving a minimum return on equity over a three- to five-year period or achieving a minimum return on assets over a three- to five-year period. Another method is to award share options to directors as part of their salary package. Share options allow the holder to purchase shares at a set price on a future date – usually in three to ten years' time. If management have performed well and taken decisions that maximise equity holder value, then share price on the exercise date will exceed the target price when the options were first issued. Management can then purchase the shares at the lower price. Recent recommendations include directors holding on to the shares they obtain through share options for a minimum period to increase the bond with the company. A problem with share option schemes is that they do not indicate whether an increased share price is due to genuine value creation caused by management decision-making or whether it is due to positive changes in the economy. Equally so, they mask good performance when there has been a general downturn.

Every company incurs a considerable amount of expenditure in trying to reduce/monitor the agency problem. These costs are termed **agency costs** and include bonding costs (i.e. costs of aligning salaries with equity holder objectives), monitoring costs (e.g. audit fees, costs associated with the remuneration committee) and residual costs (i.e. when the cost of monitoring exceeds the benefits, then monitoring to the extent required to eliminate the agency problem is not undertaken and the loss in value is accepted). If the market were considered efficient (discussed in **Chapter 10**), this would hinder managers' motivation to make decisions that conflict with equity-holders' objectives, as the actions of directors would be transparent. When directors act in conflict with equity holders' wishes, equity holders have two options: they can remove the directors or sell their shares. If sufficient numbers sell their shares, this will cause the value of the company to fall, making it a prime target for takeover. After a takeover occurs, the directors will be removed. In addition, directors operate in a competitive employment market. There is more demand for directors who have a proven track record of creating value. These directors can command high salaries.

Though equity holders are the owners of a company, they are not responsible for its governance. This responsibility falls firmly on company directors. Good corporate governance practices help to reduce agency conflicts.

CORPORATE GOVERNANCE

The Rise in the Importance of Corporate Governance

A number of high-profile company scandals and collapses in Britain (Thomas Cook, Carrillion, BHS, House of Fraser, Laura Ashley), in Ireland (Sammon Contracting, Orla Kiely) and in the United States (Hummer, Nieman Marcus) have increased the attention afforded by regulators to the corporate governance of companies. The scandals reduced public confidence in financial reporting, the audit process and the worth of regulatory watchdogs (such as the London Stock Exchange and the government). To build confidence, the London Stock Exchange set up a committee in 1991 to:

- investigate the responsibilities of executive and non-executive directors;
- determine whether an audit committee is required;
- clarify the principal responsibilities of auditors; and
- consider the responsibilities the board of directors has to other stakeholders.

This committee issued a report in 1992: the first **code of best practice** for the governance of a company. This report is known as the *Cadbury Report* after Sir Adrian Cadbury, the lead investigator. The *Cadbury Report* defined **corporate governance** as: 'the system by which companies are directed and controlled'.

The *Cadbury Report* detailed the composition of a typical board of directors in a company with good corporate governance practices and outlined the board's recommended responsibilities. These are outlined in **Figure 1.8**.

FIGURE 1.8: SUMMARY OF *CADBURY REPORT* RECOMMENDATIONS

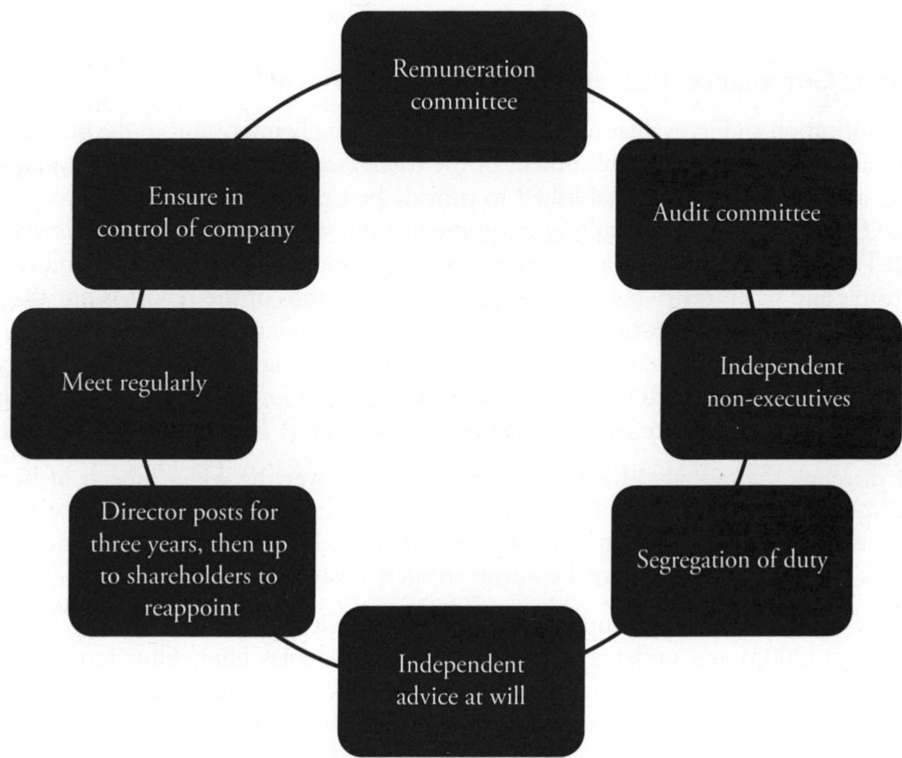

The *Greenbury Report* (1995) strengthened some of the suggestions made in the *Cadbury Report* by recommending that all members of the remuneration committee be non-executive directors, and that a remuneration report setting out all the remuneration details for each director (executive and non-executive) should be made available in the annual report of a company. A further report, the *Hampel Report* (1998), recommended that the role of the chair and chief executive be segregated and that directors receive training on corporate governance. This report recommends that directors narrow their responsibilities to their primary duty – the enhancement of equity holders value. These reports were integrated to form the *Combined Code* in 1999. Companies listed on the London Stock Exchange have to disclose the extent of compliance with the *Combined Code*. Non-plcs are not required to disclose the extent of their compliance, but it is recommended by professional accounting bodies that it be included.

Corporate Governance and Risk

Risk is inherent in virtually every strategic decision taken by a company. Company value is affected by all prior strategic decisions. The market values a company based on its expected future income and the risk associated with achieving that income. When risk is high, market participants will value a company lower than they would if risk were lower. Most boards direct specific attention to identifying the risks that a company faces and creating strategies to manage those risks. This may involve, for example, hedging transactions. The level of risk faced by a company is influenced by the nature of a business, its capital structure, foreign risk and exposures that might arise when there are changes in micro-economic conditions. For example, a manufacturing company that imports most of its supplies from one country, hires a labour force in another country and exports its products to yet another country will face far higher risks when compared to a similar company that purchases and sells its products in one country that has a stable economy. Were the future expected income from both companies the same, the latter company would be valued at a premium by the market, due to its lower exposure to the various risks.

Corporate Governance, Risk and Strategic Management

Risk identification and its evaluation have become increasingly important to the proper management of an entity. After the establishment of the *Combined Code* of practice for corporate governance, a working party was established to provide best practice guidance on how to comply with the *Combined Code*. The resulting recommendations were published in the *Turnbull Report* (1999). The report suggests that a risk-based approach should be taken when establishing internal controls and when reviewing their effectiveness. The ethos of the report is not that a company should undertake a box-ticking exercise to ensure compliance, but rather should embrace the principles of risk-based management as a means of increasing company value. This approach is captured by Sir Brian Jenkins, the Chair of the Corporate Governance Group of the ICEAW, in the preface to the guidance report *Implementing Turnbull: A Board Room Briefing* (1999):

> "for directors the task ahead is to implement control over the wider aspects of business risk in such a way as to add value rather than merely go through a compliance exercise. There is also a need to get the buy-in of people at all levels of the organisation and to focus on risk management and internal controls in such a way as to improve the business."

The *Combined Code* (1999) was updated in 2003 to include the *Turnbull Report* (1999) and the *Smith Report* (2003) and updated again (in 2005) by Douglas Flint. Flint found widespread support for the recommendations of *Turnbull*, with most companies adopting a risk-based approach to their strategic management. Indeed, the United States (US) Securities and Exchange

Commission (SEC) has identified the *Turnbull* guidance as a suitable framework for reporting on a company's internal controls for financial reporting. The US legal requirements for disclosures in relation to internal controls are set out in section 404(a) of the Sarbanes–Oxley Act (2002) and the SEC's rules. In contrast to the US's 'rule based' approach, in the UK the approach has remained 'principle based', with Flint recommending that this approach remain.

Evidence of the adoption of *Turnbull* can be found in the narrative part of most listed company's annual reports. Ryanair, Ireland's largest airline, provides an example of this and is included in **Real World Example 1.4**. (***Note***: this is only part of its policy on risk management. Full details can be obtained by using the link provided at the end of the example.)

Real World Example 1.4: Ryanair Plc Annual Report 2019 (Extract)

Risk Management and Internal Control

The Directors have overall responsibility for the Company's system of risk management and internal control and for reviewing its effectiveness. The Directors acknowledge their responsibility for the system of risk management and internal control which is designed to manage rather than eliminate the risk of failure to achieve business objectives, and can provide only reasonable and not absolute assurance against material misstatement or loss. In accordance with the Financial Reporting Council's "Guidance on Risk Management, Internal Control and Related Financial and Business Reporting", most recently revised in September 2014, the Board confirms that there is an ongoing process for identifying, evaluating and managing any significant risks faced by the Group, that it has been in place for the year under review and up to the date of approval of the financial statements and that this process is regularly reviewed by the Board.

In accordance with the provisions of the 2016 Code, the Directors review the effectiveness of the Company's system of internal control including:

- Financial
- Operational
- Compliance
- Risk Management

For the rest of the information on corporate governance and risk, see: https://investor.ryanair.com/wp-content/uploads/2019/07/Ryanair-2019-Annual-Report.pdf, pages 26 and 27, accessed November 2019.

In light of the financial crises, corporate governance came under scrutiny and the *UK Corporate Governance Code* (Financial Reporting Council, 2010) was published in May 2010 and was applicable to all listed entities with accounting periods beginning on or after 29 June 2010. The main changes were that all directors of FTSE 350 companies be subject to re-election yearly and that directors disclose how they have complied with the code and explain reasons for non-compliance, if relevant. In addition, the Code suggests that:

> "… more attention needed to be paid to following the spirit of the Code as well as its letter. Secondly, that the impact of shareholders in monitoring the Code could and should be enhanced by better interaction between the boards of listed companies and their shareholders."

To this end the Financial Reporting Council (FRC) prepared guidance on good practice for investors (*UK Stewardship Code* 2010). An updated *UK Stewardship Code* 2020 came into effect on 1 January 2020. In addition, the UK Corporate Governance Code was updated in 2018.

The UK Corporate Governance Code (2018 Code)[1] is effective for companies from 1 January 2019. This code states that the purpose of good corporate governance is to promote "transparency and integrity in business and to attract investment to the UK in the long term that benefits the economy and wider society". This wider definition emphasises the importance of: relationships with shareholders and stakeholders; having a clear purpose and strategy aligned with healthy company culture; having high-quality board composition; having remuneration which is proportionate and supports long-term success. The main changes are included in **Figure 1.9** below.

FIGURE 1.9: CHANGES INCLUDED IN THE 2018 UK CORPORATE GOVERNANCE CODE

Area	Changes
Leadership and purpose	• Workforce policies and practices should be consistent with company values and long-term sustainable success. • Monitor corporate culture and explain in annual report. • Communicate with shareholders on matters where >20% voted against a resolution. • Explain how stakeholder interests have influenced the board. • Engagement with the workforce by either appointing a director from the workforce; setting up a workforce advisory panel; or having a designated non-executive for workforce issues.
Division of responsibilities	• Chair should demonstrate objective judgement and ensure all get timely and clear information. • Non-executives given time to meet responsibilities. • Chair should be independent on appointment. • Independence of non-executives to be reviewed regularly. • Independent non-executives make up >50% of the board. • Limits to over-boarding where non-executives hold too many board positions.
Composition, succession and evaluation	• Consider the length of service of the board. • Chair tenure limited to nine years from first appointed to any position on the board. • Use external board evaluations every three years. • Nominating committee to report on the findings of the external evaluation. • Nominating committee to report on diversity.
Audit, risk and internal control	• Audit committee of small companies – two non-executives (large firms should remain at three). • Board chair cannot be on the audit committee if a smaller company.
Remuneration	• Link to strategy, long-term success. • Discretion in remuneration packages – responsibility of the remuneration committee. • Small companies need only two non-executives (large companies need three). The chair can only be on this committee if independent on appointment. • Remuneration committee remit only – review the workforce remuneration and policy. • Vesting period for share options is five years. • Executive pensions should be in line with staff pensions. • Consider remuneration risk. • Disclosures on remuneration.

[1] The full text of the 2018 Code can be found on the FRC's website at: https://www.frc.org.uk/directors/corporate-governance-and-stewardship/uk-corporate-governance-code.

ETHICS AND BUSINESS FINANCE

Business finance managers who are accountants will have to abide by the ethical standards of their accountancy body if they wish to remain members of that body. Behaving in an ethical manner will provide a defence for the business finance manager if any financial wrong-doing comes to light that may end up in court. In addition, behaving ethically will maintain the reputation of the company within the industry and with stakeholders and will not bring the accounting profession into disrepute. Common attributes of ethical behaviour are included in **Figure 1.10**.

FIGURE 1.10: THE ETHICAL ATTRIBUTES OF PROFESSIONAL ACCOUNTANTS

Integrity

Being honest and straightforward in all business and professional relationships. To act with transparency. To tell the truth and not refrain from speaking up when it is appropriate to do so.

Objectivity

Not to allow bias, conflict of interest or undue influence of others to influence professional judgements.

Professional competence and due care

Maintaining competence by having appropriate level of knowledge and skill (through attending relevant courses and studying matters that are pertinent to the role). To act with due care and skill at all times in accordance with technical and professional standards.

Professional behaviour

Complying at all times with the law and the rules of the relevant regulatory accountancy body and not to take any action that would bring the profession into disrepute.

Confidentiality

To maintain confidentiality of information obtained as a result of a professional or business relationship, unless there is a legal requirement to breach confidentiality (e.g. money laundering). Not to use information acquired from business or professional relationships for personal gain.

In many instances, having regard to ethical practices might restrict the extent to which a company can achieve its primary objective. For example, in a global economy, there is much to be gained by companies that have products that can be made in countries with no employment laws. For example, profits and company value will increase if a company is able to access cheap labour or even child labour, for next to nothing (so long as the company does not advertise its policy in this area as this may cause an adverse reaction in the stock market, as equity holders are likely to react irrationally). In these circumstances, companies justify their actions by arguing that some income to a family is better than none, or by highlighting the fact that, though the salaries paid are low, they are higher than those paid by indigenous companies. Many companies also use some of their profits for social purposes in the communities in which they are located by, for example, building schools, building churches, building hospitals or providing running water. These are all deemed to be signs of these companies acting ethically.

The use of bribery or corruption may be seen as part and parcel of normal trade within certain countries. In a global economy, when there is so much pressure to perform, directors may consider using unethical approaches to achieve a company's primary objectives. However, unethical behaviour cannot be defended on the grounds that it is normal practice in a country, nor can it be defended by the argument "if I did not do it, someone else would" or "we would lose the business to a competitor who does it".

Acting ethically in relation to company stakeholders is also in a company's long-term interest. By treating customers and suppliers correctly, future sales and supplies are being secured. Paying loan creditors the interest and capital repayments they are due on time will ensure that this source of finance can be used again in the future. Avoiding the practice of gearing the company unnecessarily, just to make returns to equity holders, builds confidence in the management of the company from creditors' perspectives. Showing concern for employee welfare (and acting on it) will ensure loyalty and increased effort from employees. By taking steps to reduce pollution, the health of employees will not deteriorate, which will reduce staff down time. In addition, the company's image will be improved and future sales may result. Equity holders should also be treated fairly; they should be kept well informed about a company's performance, future developments and strategies. Equity holders should not be surprised by the dividend that they are paid. If equity holders feel that they are being treated fairly, then the market will value the company higher and the equity-holder body is more likely to support directors' decisions in the future.

GOVERNMENT INTERVENTION

The welfare of companies within a country impacts on country wealth, therefore governments usually act to promote the growth and development of industries. Economic policy (e.g. with regard to inflation, foreign exchange policies, employment, interest rates, importing and exporting), taxation (e.g. capital gains tax rates, corporation tax rates and income tax rates and capital allowances), grants and legislative changes are the main tools used by governments to influence company business finance decision-making. Tax changes influence dividend, investment and finance policies; grants influence investment decision-making and changes to legislation enforce ethical and environmental responsibilities. For example, responsible reporting is encouraged by the Companies Acts for the benefit of stakeholders; employee welfare is protected by legislation on employment and health and safety; consumers are protected by consumer protection and consumer rights legislation; and the environment is protected by environmental legislation and grants for environmentally friendly approaches.

Governments generally try to promote free markets and competition, and try to reduce regulation. However, in some instances they will intervene if it is in the interest of the overall industry or the economy. For example, where dominant players abuse their position, regulators (the Competition Commission, for instance) will intervene to ensure that customers and smaller companies within an industry are not being treated unfairly. A prime example of government intervention is the actions taken during the financial crisis. According to the International Monetary Fund (IMF), over US$9 trillion was injected into the financial system by governments worldwide over the period 2007–2009 in the form of cash injections, lending guarantees and lending lines, in an attempt to stabilise the financial system.

GLOBALISATION

Business finance decision-making needs to consider resources and markets that exist outside the country of residence. The current business world is global in its nature. Any business that fails to consider the advantages and disadvantages associated with the global economy and markets will not be serving its equity holders' interests to the full. For example, large multinational manufacturing companies can shift their labour-intensive production facilities to parts of the world that have lower salaries and running costs (for instance, the Fruit of the Loom textile manufacturing company moved its manufacturing from Ireland to Morocco). In the past, this sort of relocation would not have been attractive as the savings to be made would have been nullified by high risks and expensive transportation costs. Now, companies spend increasing amounts of time and money building up relationships with governments and businesses in other countries. This practice helps to reduce foreign risks. Transportation costs have also fallen.

Advances in technology have been another driving force: the internet and cloud technologies have enabled quick and effective communication across the globe, cheaply. In addition, the time differences between countries mean that 24-hour working days are possible if a company has branches located across the globe. The result is that outsourcing to foreign countries is regarded as a cost-saving business technique. For example, to reduce employee costs many computer software companies use branches in India to write programming code and several telesales companies have moved operations overseas.

CONCLUSION

This chapter focuses on explaining the importance of business finance knowledge to the success of a company. Having appropriately qualified and experienced people leading a company influences its success. That is why directors in large public limited companies are awarded high salaries. These individuals determine company strategy, which is vital for company sustainability. As directors are employed by equity holders, it is assumed that the main strategy adopted, in theory, is value creation – the maximisation of financial benefits to equity holders.

Business finance has a core role to play in value creation. The three main business finance decisions influence value creation. The investment decision determines the future operating cash inflows of the company, the finance decision deals with how to finance the investments and the dividend decision focuses on how the equity holders' wealth will be influenced by the level of distributions made. These core decisions are interrelated and also impact on virtually all departments within a company (such as purchasing, sales, production, credit control, marketing and finance). Therefore, directors not only require knowledge of business finance, they also need to have a broad understanding of all the departments within a company.

As well as internal company-specific knowledge, decision-makers will also require direct knowledge of specific subject areas that may influence a decision. These include law, taxation and economics. They also require knowledge of other subject areas, such as financial accounting, management accounting, maths and statistics, to assist in the evaluation process and analysis of the impact of decisions made. The decision-makers also have to be aware of other influences, such as **business ethics** (including **agency theory** and conflicts between equity holders and creditors) and environmental responsibilities. External factors also influence business finance decision-making and the decision-makers require knowledge of the economy and the financial environment, at both national and international levels (see **Chapter 10**).

EXAMINATION STANDARD QUESTION: ETHICS

Biglab Plc, Hightech's largest UK customer, has recently approached Mr Guage expressing an interest in acquiring the entire share capital of Hightech. Public information indicates that Biglab has the capacity to complete a purchase from its existing cash balances. Mr Guage has little experience as to methods of valuing companies, and would like some guidance on the matter. You have been commissioned to provide a valuation range for Hightech.

Requirement Mr Lance, the Finance Director of Biglab, has phoned you privately to say that, in the event of a successful acquisition, you would be the natural choice for Finance Director of Hightech, at a considerably enhanced remuneration level. In the light of Mr Lance's phone call, discuss briefly the ethical implications, if any, of advising Mr Guage in relation to the valuation range and factors that may impact on it.

10 Marks

(Chartered Accountants Ireland, FAE, MABF, Extract from Autumn 1997)

Solution

The concept of independence has no direct relevance to a chartered accountant employed in industry. However, the requirement for objectivity and thus professional integrity is of equal application to all members. Without the capacity of being fully independent of an employer, it is even more important that the employed member should strive constantly to maintain objectivity in every aspect of his/her work.

An employed member should recognise the problems that may be created by financial involvements or personal relationships which, whether sanctioned by his/her contract of employment or not, could nevertheless, by reason of their nature or degree, threaten his/her objectivity. Where any doubt exists, the involvement or relationship should be disclosed to the employer.

An employed member should be aware of the difficulties that may arise from the offer of any gift or favour that may be intended to influence the recipient or that could be interpreted, by a reasonable person in full possession of the facts, as likely to have that effect.

Any report for which an employed member is responsible should be prepared with integrity and objectivity. This means, e.g. that while a report prepared by an employed member may properly present only one side of the case and may present that case to its best advantage or in the worst light, the report should be accurate, truthful and, within its scope, both complete and balanced. It should not rely on ambiguities or half-truths, but should be objectively justifiable and should not be based on unreasonable assumptions.

Key Terms

Agency costs
Agency theory
Big data
Business ethics
Business finance
Cadbury Report
Combined Code
Company sustainability
Competitive forces
Competitive strategy
Corporate strategy
Data analytics
Data science
Dividend decision
Economic environment
Employee welfare
Environmental policies
Equity holder return
Equity holder value
Equity holder wealth maximisation
Finance decision
Financial environment
Financial management
Globalisation
Greenbury Report
Hampel Report
Investment decision
Market structure
Mission statement
Monopolistic competition
Monopoly
Non-financial objectives
Oligopoly
Operational strategy
Operations management
Opportunities
Perfect competition
Profit maximisation
Satisficing
Shareholder value theory
Short-termism
Smith Report
Strategic business units
Strategic management
Strategic plan
Strengths
SWOT analysis
Threats
Trade relationships
Turnbull Report
Value creation
Vision
Weaknesses

REVIEW QUESTIONS

(See Suggested Solutions to Review Questions in **Appendix B.**)

Question 1.1

Define strategic management.

Question 1.2

Provide three examples of non-financial objectives that a company might pursue.

Question 1.3

Explain the relationship between financial and non-financial objectives.

Question 1.4

How might a government influence company business finance decision-making?

Question 1.5

Briefly explain the need for a business finance manager to have knowledge of taxation, law, mathematics and economics.

CHALLENGING QUESTIONS

(Suggested Solutions to Challenging Questions are available through your lecturer.)

Question 1.1 Objective (Level 2)

Finance textbooks generally assume that the objective of a company is to maximise equity shareholder wealth.

Requirement Discuss the reasons for this assumption, indicating THREE alternative objectives and their disadvantages where they are not consistent with the maximisation of shareholder wealth.

10 Marks

(Based on Chartered Accountants Ireland, CAP 1, Finance, Summer 2009, Extract from Q6)

Question 1.2 Objectives (Level 1)

Levfan Plc uses a range of financial and non-financial objectives to measure its performance. Levfan has been struggling to meet its financial objectives for the 12-month period ending 31 December 20X9. In advance of the year end, in an effort to improve Levfan's existing profitability and cash flow position, the finance manager has suggested that the following actions could be undertaken:

- The proposed employee pay increase of 3%, which was recently announced by Levfan and is due to take effect on 1 January 20Y0, should now be reduced to 1%;
- Payments of loan note interest should be delayed for a period of 10 days beyond the agreed due date. This should serve to improve Levfan's expected bank overdraft position at 31 December 20X9;
- A capital expenditure project on new equipment, designed to reduce company carbon emissions, should be deferred until 20Y0. Levfan had previously announced that the project would commence in October 20X9.

Requirement Outline, for **each** of the THREE measures suggested above, two reasons why implementation of each measure might result in Levfan failing to achieve its non-financial objectives.

6 Marks

(Based on Chartered Accountants Ireland, CAP 1, Finance, Summer 2019, extract from Q4)

Question 1.3 Role of Finance Manager (Level 1)

Outline briefly the role, functions and decision-making requirements of a finance manager within a company.

8 Marks

(Based on Chartered Accountants Ireland, CAP 1, Finance, Autumn 2011, Q7(b))

Question 1.4 Three Key Decisions (Level 1)

Identify *three* key decisions for a finance manager and explain how the three decision areas are related and interact.

5 Marks

(Based on Chartered Accountants Ireland, CAP 1, Finance, Summer 2012, Q5(c))

Question 1.5 Austerity (Levels 1 and 2)

Recent media reports indicate a range of fiscal austerity proposals involving increased taxation levels and/or reduced government spending. Outline the implications of such fiscal austerity for business in general.

7 Marks

(Based on Chartered Accountants Ireland, CAP 1, Finance, Summer 2012, Q3(a))

Question 1.6 Corporate Governance and Agency Theory (Level 1)

The concept of good corporate governance has been highlighted in recent times, especially in relation to the recent national and international banking crisis. Outline briefly what you understand by the following terms:

(a) corporate governance;
(b) agency theory.

5 Marks

(Based on Chartered Accountants Ireland, CAP 1, Finance, Autumn 2011, Q6(c))

Question 1.7 Non-executive Directors (Level 1)

As the window production and installation business continues to grow, Jack Plc's owners are keen to practise good corporate governance. At present, the company's board of directors consists of three executive directors. A long-term friend of one of the directors, Gerard Appleby, has recently retired after a successful and rewarding career in investment banking. The directors are considering offering him the position of non-executive director on the board of Jack Plc.

Requirement Explain the role of a non-executive director (NED).

1 Mark

Identify TWO reasons why it might not be appropriate to offer the position of non-executive director to Gerard Appleby.

2 Marks

(Based on Chartered Accountants Ireland, CAP 1, Finance, Autumn 2019, extract from Q5)

Question 1.8 Wowfactor (Levels 1 and 2)

Your client, Martina O'Shea of Wowfactor Plc, has contacted you in connection with a query from the newly appointed board of directors. They are concerned about their responsibilities in relation to the implementation of corporate governance and would like your advice.

Requirement In a briefing paper to Martina, outline the key tasks of the board of directors (executive and non-executive directors) in implementing good corporate governance.

15 Marks

(Based on Chartered Accountants Ireland, CAP 1, Finance, Summer 2008, Q4)

Question 1.9 Executive Remuneration (Level 1)

Recently, the high level of executive remuneration in the banking and finance sectors has received adverse publicity.

Requirement Outline an appropriate governance structure to determine the remuneration package of a company's chief executive officer (CEO).

8 Marks

(Based on Chartered Accountants Ireland, CAP 1, Finance, Summer 2012, Q4(a))

Question 1.10 SWOT Analysis (Level 2)

ABC Plc, a manufacturing entity with spare capacity, has always used XYZ to distribute its products to its customers. The board of directors is considering creating a new distribution company to distribute its own products to certain customers that XYZ does not service.

Requirement Perform a SWOT analysis for the above scenario.

20 Marks

Question 1.11 Fractious Energy (Level 1)

At a recent senior management meeting of Fractious Energy Plc there was strong disagreement and personal comments exchanged on two topics, as follows:

- Staff morale is suffering as budget/targets were allegedly set at a very high level to motivate better performance. However, staff were consequently failing to earn bonuses as they did not "meet or exceed expectations".
- The company offers senior executives an incentive consisting of bonuses and share options. While the company's shares are not currently listed on a stock exchange, it is expected they will be listed/quoted in about 18 months' time. The bonus is earned if annual profits exceed €/£3 million.

In the current year, the company is expecting to achieve an unusually high profit of €/£10 million, but a loss of €/£3 million is expected in the subsequent year. The chief executive has suggested that €/£6 million of expected costs from next year could be brought into the accounts for the current year. He believes this would "smooth the profits" between the two years.

Requirement Comment on the ethical and other problems apparent in the above situation.

6 Marks

(Based on Chartered Accountants Ireland, CAP 1, Finance, Summer 2012, Q7(a))

Question 1.12 Electric (Level 1)

The finance managers of Electric Products Limited are currently reviewing Electric's strategic and financial position.

Electric manufactures and distributes energy-saving kitchen appliances. All of the parts and materials used in the production of these appliances are of the highest quality and are sourced locally in Ireland. Over the past 18 months Electric's profitability has deteriorated. This is due primarily to the introduction of a new competitor into the market and the rising cost of parts and materials.

In order to improve Electric's profitability, the finance managers are evaluating two alternatives:

- *Alternative 1*: This involves the closure of Electric's manufacturing plant in Ireland and moving it to Eastern Europe, where parts, materials and labour rates are significantly cheaper than Ireland.

- *Alternative 2*: This entails making an investment of €/£500,000 in new equipment, which will improve the efficiency of the current production process. The finance managers have estimated that this will yield a positive net present value (NPV) of €/£22,000. Electric, which is currently an all equity financed company, will have to obtain loan finance from its local bank to proceed with this alternative.

Requirement

(a) Business finance managers are involved in making investment decisions and financing decisions. Explain both types of decision.

3 Marks

(b) Advise Electric's finance managers of any FOUR key issues facing the company if they decide to proceed with *Alternative 1.*

4 Marks

(c) Briefly discuss *Alternative 2* under the following headings:
   (i) Reaction of existing shareholders.
   (ii) Impact on cost of capital.

5 Marks

(d) One of the key financial objectives of a company is to achieve financial returns for its shareholders. Many companies also pursue non-financial objectives. Identify any THREE key non-financial objectives a company may pursue.

3 Marks
Total 15 Marks

(Based on Chartered Accountants Ireland, CAP 1, Finance, Autumn 2013, Q6)

Question 1.13 Tobar (Level 1)

Tobar Limited is a well-established pharmaceutical company that produces drugs to prevent, treat and cure heart disease. The financial accountant has some concerns about issues that were raised during a conversation he had with the finance director. The issues are as follows:

1. It was decided that all directors of Tobar would get a 10% bonus if profits were increased by 25% by year-end. In order to achieve this, the directors are considering investing in a new project which should generate significant profits within months. The finance director mentioned that he did not know much about the project, but that the decision to invest was made quickly over drinks after work with the other directors. The finance director did, however, say that "this new project will surely secure the director's bonuses by the end of the year".
2. The directors are also considering making a large investment in new state-of-the-art packaging equipment. This will replace all the packaging work that is currently done by hand.
3. Tobar and another Irish pharmaceutical company have been in negotiations with the government of a small South American country to supply heart medication to their local health service. The finance director said that they were considering paying the government an incentive of €/£500,000 to ensure that it gets first refusal on the contract.
4. The finance director revealed that Tobar may have to make a provision in the financial statements as the company has received a fine from the local authority regarding a 60% increase in CO_2 emissions from its manufacturing plant. While Tobar is aware that its CO_2 emissions have increased, it plans to ignore this fine.

Requirement

(a) Explain what is meant by "agency theory" and identify TWO strategies which could be used for resolving conflicts that may arise between the "principal" and the "agent".

3 Marks

(b) Discuss the implications for Tobar of the above issues (1.–4.) outlined by the finance director during his conversation with Tobar's financial accountant.

12 Marks

Total 15 Marks

(Based on Chartered Accountants Ireland, CAP 1, Finance, Summer 2013, Q6)

Question 1.14 Ethics and Market Structure (Level 1)

Paul Daly has patented an arm brace. As the sole manufacturer of the arm brace, Paul is now seeking to drive additional sales of his product. Some months ago, Paul visited the country of Meridan, a developing nation, whose government officials were very interested in acquiring the arm brace for their national health service. Contract negotiations between Paul and the government officials are now at an advanced stage.

In the last week, Paul was personally contacted by a Mr Ducas, an intermediary and employee of a high-profile businessperson based in Meridan. Mr Ducas suggested that if his employer were to make an inflated offer to Paul for the arm brace, then Paul would be in a position to negotiate a higher price from the government officials. Mr Ducas confirmed that his employer has no real interest in ultimately buying the arm brace, but suggested that Paul would stand to make significant financial benefits. In return for making the false bid, Paul has been asked to make a one-off payment of €/£50,000 to Mr Ducas' employer.

Requirement

(a) Identify the ethical issue arising in the above situation and recommend how Paul should proceed.

2 Marks

(b)

(i) Explain the difference between a monopoly and an oligopoly; and

(ii) Determine whether Paul has a monopoly or an oligopoly.

3 Marks

(Based on Chartered Accountants Ireland, CAP 1, Finance, Autumn 2019, extract from Q4)

Question 1.15 GML (Level 1)

(a) Explain what is meant by corporate governance.

2 Marks

(b) For the last few decades a number of reports on governance have been produced seeking to address various financial failures and poor governance, which has culminated in the *UK Corporate Governance Code*. List any four recommendations of the *UK Corporate Governance Code*.

4 Marks

(c) You have started work as a business finance manager in a successful manufacturing company called Go Manufacturing Limited (GML). You have just had a brief meeting with Tom, the Chief Financial Officer, on the background of the company. The following are the notes from your meeting:

(i) GML has successfully traded for 10 years and revenues and profits are increasing year on year. As a result, each year the senior management of GML always gets paid their bonuses. The bonuses are awarded as a percentage of profits and Tom has said that "the senior management work hard and do whatever it takes to get these bonuses".

(ii) Tom is also concerned that GML's corporate tax bill is rising every year but Noel, the Financial Accountant, "is good at disguising facts and figures so this year the tax bill should be fairly minimal".

(iii) GML employs 30 staff, 10 of those are management and clerical staff and 20 staff work in manufacturing. The manufacturing takes place in a warehouse that was built in the 1890s. The condition of the building is poor but Tom does not mind as the rent is very low.

(iv) GML is looking to expand its operations and is considering setting up a subsidiary company in South America. Tom said, "it's a great opportunity for the company as the raw materials can be sourced cheaply but in particular the labour costs are only a fraction of what they are here and we will not have to deal with unions."

(v) At the end of our meeting Tom mentioned that he got a letter with a fine attached from the local council in respect of dumping waste into the local river. Tom said he was just going to ignore it and hope it goes away.

Requirement Outline any possible ethical issues arising from the above notes (i)–(v).

9 Marks
Total 15 Marks

(Based on Chartered Accountants Ireland, CAP 1, Finance, Autumn 2012, Q7)

Question 1.16 Letterkenny (Level 2)

Letterkenny Plc is currently reviewing all aspects of its business in order to become more competitive. Letterkenny is involved in the production of components which are used in the healthcare industry. The Sales Director of Letterkenny, Carmel Brennan, has suggested that the company should not be worried about the quality of goods it produces. Its only aim should be to produce and sell as many products as possible, which would contribute to its real objective, which is the maximisation of shareholder wealth.

Requirement Considering a range of stakeholder and ethical perspectives, discuss critically the suggestion made by Carmel Brennan.

6 Marks

(Based on Chartered Accountants Ireland, CAP 2, SFMA, Autumn 2009, extract from Q3)

Question 1.17 Allen's Hotel (Level 2)

Background Information Allen's Hotel is a four-star hotel that has been family owned and run for three generations. The hotel is regarded for its first-class customer service provided to visitors from the United States, the United Kingdom, Ireland and mainland European countries.

The hotel is managed by John Allen, a 65-year-old veteran of the hotel trade, and his senior management team, which is composed of three members of the Allen family, who manage the hotel operations, and one non-family member, who manages the spa operation. Ownership interest in the hotel is vested with family members only. Stephen Allen is the hotel's business finance manager.

Other Matters Stephen has just received a phone call from the general manager of the All Seasons Hotel, one of the local competitor four star hotels, inviting him to accompany him for a full day at an upcoming race meeting. Stephen, a huge racing fan, is unsure whether to accept this kind invitation.

Requirement Advise Stephen on the ethical considerations of the generous offer made by the general manager of the All Seasons Hotel.

3 Marks

(Based on Chartered Accountants Ireland, CAP 2, MABF, Summer 2010, extract from Q1)

Question 1.18 Gourmet (Level 2)

Within Gourmet, there is a performance appraisal system in operation whereby all employees are evaluated on a quarterly basis against a series of predetermined metrics relevant to their specific duties. In relation to Gourmet's Regional Sales Managers, their performance is primarily evaluated based upon the total amount of sales revenue generated within their particular region in addition to a small number of other sales-related financial targets. All regional sales managers who achieve their quarterly targets in any given financial year automatically qualify for a significant bonus payment at the end of that particular year.

However, Kevin Wood, who sets the predetermined targets in conjunction with each regional sales manager, has recently become aware that one particular regional sales manager, who believed that he would not achieve his 20X5 initial quarterly sales target (i.e. January to March), informed his biggest customer at the end of March that a sales price increase was likely from early April. Consequently, the customer placed a big order at the end of March and the regional sales manager achieved his sales target. The customer was subsequently informed by the regional sales manager that the planned sales price increase had been postponed indefinitely.

Having already decided to initiate disciplinary proceedings against the regional sales manager, Kevin is unsure as to whether or not he should inform the affected customer of recent events as they continue to trade with Gourmet at their "usual" levels.

Requirement In relation to the ethical dilemma faced by Kevin Wood, outline the potential ramifications for Gourmet if he decides not to inform the affected customer of the regional sales manager's recent activities.

6 Marks

(Based on Chartered Accountants Ireland, CAP 2, MABF, Summer 2012, extract from Q1)

Question 1.19 Watt (Level 2)

It is now 20X5. Watt has impending excess production capacity. With regard to one potential solution to Watt's impending excess production capacity (and after discussing it with the remainder of the senior management team), Ann (the business finance manager) contacted a Canadian division of Pulse, called Power Inc., regarding the possibility of an inter-group trading proposal. After some initial tentative discussions, Ann was informed that Power is in the process of developing a new range of electrical components which will require the inclusion of similar components to those currently produced by Watt in its production process.

After lengthy discussions between the senior management teams of Watt and Power, it was proposed by those representing Power that both divisions should enter into an exclusive contractual arrangement in which Power would purchase all of Watt's budgeted 20X6 output on an inter-group trading basis. Assuming that no major issues arise between the divisions in 20X6, it is anticipated that Power will purchase additional quantities of output from Watt in subsequent years on a similarly exclusive but more long-term basis.

At Watt's next scheduled senior management team meeting, Ann made a presentation to the team summarising the main points to emerge from the recent negotiations with Power. There was some "lively" debate amongst those present as to the likely strategic and operational ramifications for Watt of deciding to engage in inter-group trading with Power.

Furthermore, as any decision to engage in an exclusive inter-group trading arrangement with Power may potentially have serious consequences for Watt's current customers, it was decided that, where possible, any disruption caused to the 'normal' operations of this particular group should be kept to a minimum.

Requirement Outline the primary ethical considerations that ought to be considered by Watt's senior management team regarding the inter-group trading proposal by Power and its existing customers.

6 Marks

(Based on Chartered Accountants Ireland, CAP 2, MABF, Autumn 2012, extract from Q1)

Part II

PROJECT APPRAISAL, CORPORATE PERFORMANCE AND WORKING CAPITAL MANAGEMENT

Chapters

2. Capital Investment Decision-making
3. Capital Investment Appraisal for Special Decisions and Risk
4. Ratio Analysis
5. Company Failure
6. An Introduction to Working Capital
7. Inventory Management
8. Management of Trade Receivables and Trade Payables
9. Cash Management

2

Capital Investment Decision-making

Learning Objectives

Upon completing this chapter, readers should be able to:

- identify the relevant cash flows for investment appraisal (including the effects of taxation, working capital and inflation);
- list the limitations of investment appraisal;
- evaluate different investments using the annual rate of return, the payback period, the discounted payback period, the internal rate of return, the net present value and the incremental cash flow approaches; and
- list the advantages and disadvantages of each investment appraisal method.

INTRODUCTION

There are two main types of investment decision: external investment and internal investment. **External investment** involves making decisions in respect of the acquisition of, or merger with, other companies or ventures. This falls outside the scope of this chapter. **Internal investment** involves investment in assets within a company. This can fall into two categories: the purchase of speculative investments (such as shares in the stock market) or the purchase of capital items that are used to enhance a company's operational worth. These capital investments may be similar to the current activities of a company or may be new. This chapter is only concerned with capital investment decisions. Capital investments normally involve an initial outlay or series of cash outlays, followed by a stream of cash inflows over a longer period of time.

As mentioned in the introductory chapter to this textbook, the investment decision is the most important decision facing a business finance manager. Investment decisions determine the future cash flows of a company and expected future cash flows determine company value. As is consistent with the rest of this textbook, it is assumed, when making investment decisions, that the ultimate objective of each decision is the maximisation of equity holder wealth. Regardless of how a company is financed or the level of dividend it pays out, if investment decisions are not successful, a company will not be able to service its finance or pay dividends to its equity holders. As part of the decision process, it is important that finance managers price the environment, society and governance (ESG) risk of the investment to the company.

Investment decisions are usually material and wrong decisions can be costly to a company. Capital investments are usually expensive to terminate, as they are usually tailor-made for a particular company: this reduces the investment's marketability.

An example of the negative impact of getting the investment decision wrong is the withdrawal of Tesco from the USA, as highlighted in **Real World Example 2.1**.

REAL WORLD EXAMPLE 2.1: TESCO

Tesco and its US expansion investment

Tesco has experienced capital investment failure. In 2006, Tesco entered the US market. At the time, it was the third largest retailer in the world – the largest being Wal-Mart and the second largest being Carrefour. Tesco branded its chain in the US 'Fresh & Easy'; however, it did not attract American consumers and was loss-making. In 2013, Tesco made the decision to exit the US market. Several of the stores were sold to Yucaipa Companies. In spite of this, the overall cost of restructure and other one-off costs amounted to $1.5 billion (approximately £1 billion). This highlights the importance of investment decisions.

This chapter considers some of the difficulties underlying project appraisal (i.e. the time value of money, taxation, working capital and inflation). The most commonly utilised appraisal methods are explained (accounting rate of return, payback period method, net present value method and the internal rate of return method) and the chapter concludes by identifying the most appropriate technique to be used and compares this to research findings on the use of the various techniques by companies.

DIFFICULTIES FACING PROJECT APPRAISAL

Strategic Issues: Goal Congruence

When a manager is assessing a project, it is of utmost importance that the decision is made with the 'big picture' in mind. The outcomes should be congruent with the goals of the company. This may mean sacrificing a project that makes strong short-term gains in favour of a project that will have strong long-term implications for a company. For example, Viridian Group Plc sold its software and IT subsidiary, Sx3, to Northgate Information Solutions Plc in 2005–06 for £155 million. Though the subsidiary was profitable, Viridian Group Plc was streamlining its operations to its long-term strategies.

Relevant Cash Flows

Some of the theoretical rules pertaining to management accounting decision-making are equally relevant for project appraisal. Project appraisal should only consider relevant cash flows – these are highlighted in **Figure 2.1**.

FIGURE 2.1: RELEVANT AND IRRELEVANT CASH FLOWS

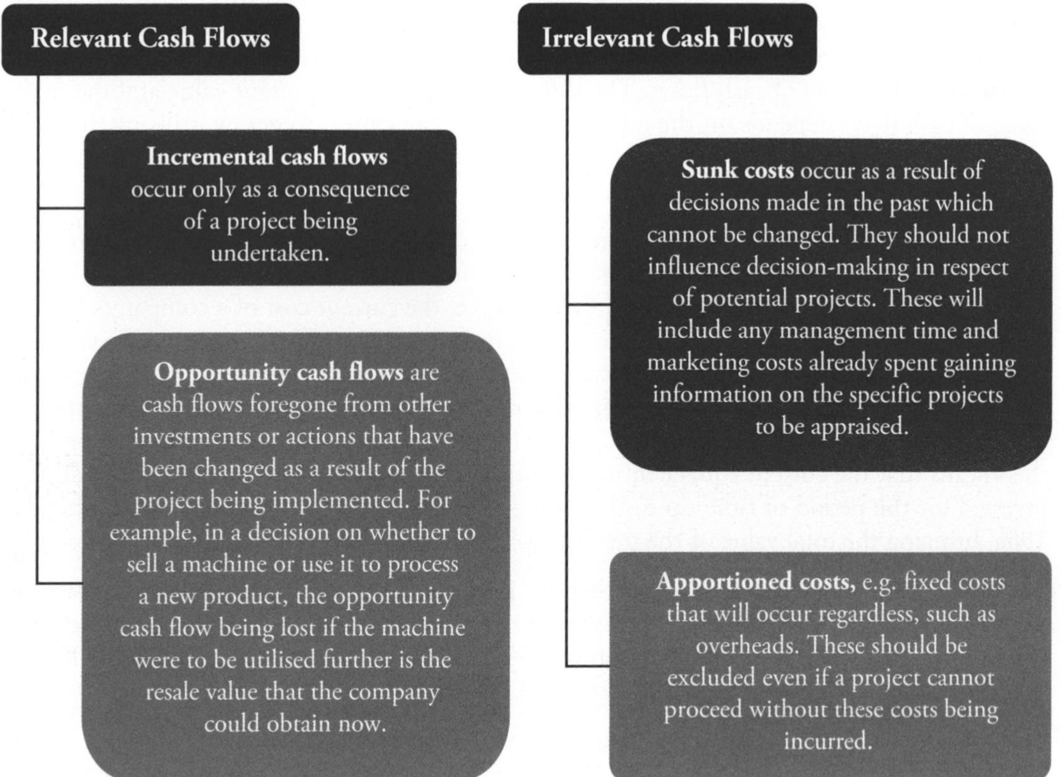

The Time Value of Money

Cash v Profit

In finance, "cash is king" and cash is very different from profit. Management performance is usually assessed using accounting ratios, which are calculated using profit figures. This may cause agency problems when project appraisal is being undertaken as the pattern of cash is more important in project appraisal than profits made. For example, when calculating profit, a project that takes five years and yields €/£5 million at the end of the period will have similar yearly profit figures (assuming that costs are evenly spread across the five years and the contract is certain) to a project that takes five years and has five €/£1 million yearly instalments for the five years ending in Year 5. In profit terms, both projects will result in the same overall performance. However, if this project were to be viewed from a finance perspective, then the latter project would be valued more highly than the former project. This is due to the impact of the time value of money. The value of money declines in line with the length of time a company has to wait to receive the money. This means that matching and accrual entries, such as trade receivables, trade payables, provisions and depreciation (to name a few), are not relevant in the investment appraisal process and have to be removed to ascertain expected cash flows.

Discount Rates

As mentioned in the previous paragraph, a company benefits from receiving money now rather than later. This money can be used either to earn a return from another investment (another project or just sitting in a deposit account) or to reduce costs (such as interest on an overdraft). To evaluate the correct worth of future cash flows, it is important to determine their current or present value. **Present value** (PV) is a term used to depict the current value of funds received in the future. The present value of cash flows will always be less than the **future value** (FV) of cash flows. The difference between the present value and the future value of cash flows depends on the return a company can expect to get by utilising the funds in the intervening period. For example, a company could use the funds to pay back its financiers, or to invest in a project.

A starting point, when evaluating the present value of a future expected cash flow, is to determine a company's required rate of return. In most instances the starting point is to use a company's **weighted average cost of capital (WACC)**, i.e. the current cost of a company's finance. This represents the return required by the current financiers. The WACC is an average weighted yield, say 10%. When a company expects to get a cash flow in the future from an investment made now, it should consider the current value of the future cash flows expected given that the current financiers require a 10% return. To do this the future cash flow is **discounted** by 10%; this means that the current equivalent of the future cash flow will be a smaller sum, which, if invested for the period of time up to the date of the future cash flow, would earn a return of 10%, bringing the total value of the present cash flow to the expected future cash flow value.

Therefore, receiving €/£1 in one year's time is deemed to be the equivalent of receiving 90.9c/p now. If the company had 90.9c/p now, it could earn a return of 9.1c/p on the funds (90.9c/p × 10%) over the year. The relationship between the present value of funds and their future value is as follows:

$$\mathbf{PV(1 + \mathit{r})^{\mathit{n}} = FV}$$

where PV is the present value, r is the **discount rate** (the rate at which the funds can be invested), n is the number of periods the cash flows will be received in the future, and FV is the future value of the cash flow. The PV of a future cash flow of €/£1 discounted at 10% is 90.9c/p ($\text{PV}(1 + 10\%)^1 = $ €/£1; hence the PV is: (€/£1 ÷ 1.1)). The above formula can be expressed in PV terms. This is as follows:

$$\mathbf{PV = FV \times \frac{1}{(1 + \mathit{r})^{\mathit{n}}}}$$

The component on the right-hand side ($1 \div (1 + r)^n$) is called the **discount factor**. It can be used for any amount of FV cash flow being analysed.

Worked Example 2.1: Present Value

Frank Ltd expects to receive cash from an investment of €/£50,000 in each year for three years starting on the last day of the first year. Frank Ltd has a weighted average cost of capital of 12%.

Requirement What is the present value of these future cash flows?

Solution

Year	Cash flows €/£	Discount factor		Present value €/£
1	50,000	$1/(1.12)^1$	0.893	44,650
2	50,000	$1/(1.12)^2$	0.797	39,850
3	50,000	$1/(1.12)^3$	0.712	35,600
				120,100

The present value of the three €/£50,000 cash inflows received at the end of Years 1, 2 and 3, discounted at 12%, is €/£120,100. This means that Frank Ltd would have to invest €/£120,100 now at 12% to receive €/£50,000 at the end of each of the next three years.

To have to calculate discount factors every time a future stream of cash flows requires discounting is time-consuming, therefore tables of **discount factors** (i.e. pre-calculated discount rates per year (for 15 years) for each rate) have been prepared. These tables are provided in **Appendix C: Present Value Discount Factors Table**.

Another short-cut to reduce calculation time is to use annuity tables. An **annuity** is a constant stream of cash flows over a set period of consecutive time. An example of an annuity is a pension. As the cash flow amount does not change, the discount factors can be added together and the sum of these applied to the constant periodic cash flows to calculate their present value. In the previous example a constant cash flow was received for three consecutive years, starting in Year 1. Therefore, an **annuity factor** equals the sum of the yearly individual discount factors, which is: 2.402 [0.893 + 0.797 + 0.712]. The present value of the €/£50,000 annuity is €/£120,100 [€/£50,000 × 2.402]. Annuity factors remain constant for given rates and given numbers of periods, therefore pre-calculated annuity factors for a range of rates and periods are presented in a table in **Appendix D: Annuity Factor Table**. Sometimes companies can receive or agree to pay a perpetuity. A **perpetuity** is a constant cash flow payable at set intervals, for example, yearly or monthly. It is calculated by dividing the cash flow by the discount rate. See **Appendix A** for further explanation.

For most companies, cash flows from projects will occur continuously throughout a year. However, to undertake daily discount calculations would be very time-consuming (although they could be performed using computer technology); therefore, for the purpose of this textbook, it is assumed that all cash flows in a year occur on the last day of the year, unless a question specifies differently. For example, a question might state that the company will acquire a machine on the first day of Year 2. This would be treated as the last day of Year 1 and discounted by one year only, as it better reflects reality.

Worked Example 2.2 provides an example that incorporates the three main time value of money approaches that may be used in investment appraisal.

Worked Example 2.2: Present Value

A company has to select between three projects.* The cash flows for each are as follows:

Year	Project 1 €/£	Project 2 €/£
1	600	800
2	600	200
3	600	300
4	600	300
5	700	300

Project 3 is expected to provide cash inflows of €/200 every year from now on.

Requirement

(a) Which project should the company choose based on the above cash flows only? The company pays interest on its overdraft at the rate of 7%.

(b) Some new information comes to light. The company is told that after Year 5, Project 2 is expected to make a steady yearly cash inflow of €/£300. Does this alter your decision from (a)?

(c) Further information comes to light. You are told that Project 1 will reap yearly cash flows of €/£100 each year for 23 years starting in Year 6. Does this alter your decision from that in (b)?

Solution

(a) *Project 1*

Year	Cash flow €/£	Discount factor @ 7%	Present value €/£
1–4	600	3.387*	2,032.20
5	700	0.713	499.10
Present value			2,531.30

* A four-year annuity at 7% (value obtained from the annuity factor table in Appendix D).

Project 2

Year	Cash flow €/£	Discount factor @ 7%	Present value €/£
1	800	0.935	748.00
2	200	0.873	174.60
3–5	300	*2.292	687.60
Present value			1,610.20

* A five-year annuity factor @ 7% – 2-year annuity factor @ 7%
= 4.1 – 1.808 = 2.292

Project 3

Perpetuity present value = cash flow ÷ discount rate

€/£200 ÷ 0.07 = €/£2,857.14 (present value)

Based on these calculations, Project 3 has the greatest present value, hence would be selected.

(b) The present value of the perpetuity on day one of Year 6 (the perpetuity formula already discounts the cash flow for Year 6 to the start of the year) is €/£300 ÷ 0.07 = €/£4,285.71. This needs to be discounted to time 0 by straight discounting using the discount factor tables. The relevant discount rate is five years at 7%. A cash flow on the first day of Year 6 is treated as having been received on the last day of Year 5. Therefore, the present value of this perpetuity is €/£4,285.71 × 0.713 = €/£3,055.71.

The overall new present value is €/£1,610.20 + €/£3,055.71 = €/£4,665.91.

After this additional information is incorporated into the calculations, Project 2 becomes the preferred option.

(c) In this instance the annuity formula is used to find the present value of this 23-year annuity at the start of Year 6. The formula for an annuity is used to calculate this (see Appendix A and Appendix D).

The formula is: $\frac{1-(1+r)^{-n}}{r}$

Where r is the discount rate and n is the number of periods.

The annuity factor is: $\frac{1-(1.07)^{-23}}{0.07} = 11.272$

Therefore, the value of the annuity at the start of Year 6 is €/£100 × 11.272 = €/£1,127.20. This needs to be discounted to time 0.

€/£1,127.20 × 0.713 = €/£803.69

The total present value is now €/£2,531.30 + €/£803.69 = €/£3,334.99

This does not change the decision: the best project, based on the cash flows in the question, is Project 2.

PROJECT APPRAISAL METHODS

There are five main methods of project appraisal: the accounting rate of return method, the payback period method, the discounted payback method, the net present value method and the internal rate of return method. These methods are now discussed using a common example to highlight differences between the methods.

The Accounting Rate of Return (ARR)

The **accounting rate of return** estimates the rate of accounting profit that a project will generate over its entire life. It compares the average annual profit of a project with the cost, or book value, of the project. This is the only investment appraisal method not to focus on cash flows. Two equations can be utilised:

$$\textbf{ARR (total investment)} = \frac{\textbf{Average annual profit}}{\textbf{Initial capital invested}} \times 100$$

$$\textbf{ARR (average investment)} = \frac{\textbf{Average annual profit}}{\textbf{Average capital invested}} \times 100$$

where the **average annual profit** is the total profit for the whole period (typically cash less depreciation) divided by the life of the investment in years, and the **average capital investment** is the initial capital cost plus the expected disposal value divided by two.

The accounting rate of return is used in practice; however, it is deemed inappropriate as the main technique to be used, due to the importance of the timing of cash flows to the success of a project (see the earlier discussion on cash versus profit). In practice, companies usually set a target accounting rate of return and consider projects that meet or exceed this target. This method is shown using the following example.

Worked Example 2.3: Accounting Rate of Return

Cow Ltd is considering three projects (each costing €/£240,000). The following cash flows are predicted:

Yearly Cash Flows

	Friesian €/£	**Aberdeen €/£**	**Saler €/£**
Year 1	160,000	120,000	238,000
Year 2	60,000	120,000	2,000
Year 3	120,000	40,000	35,000
Year 4	140,000		
Year 5	20,000		
Year 6	10,000		

Requirement

(a) Given that Cow Ltd has a target average accounting rate of return of 10% per annum (averaged over the investment period), which of the above projects should be accepted, if any? (Assume that the asset is specialised and cannot be sold at the end of the project.)

(b) How would the results be affected were you informed that the asset could be sold after three years for €/£60,000 and after six years for €/£30,000?

Solution

(a) The first step is to calculate the average profit of each project after depreciation. Therefore, the depreciation charge has to be deducted from the reported cash flow figures.

$$\text{Depreciation} = \frac{€/£240{,}000}{6} = €/£40{,}000 \text{ per year for Friesian}$$

$$\text{Depreciation} = \frac{€/£240{,}000}{3} = €/£80{,}000 \text{ per year for Aberdeen and Saler}$$

Yearly Profits/Losses after Depreciation

	Friesian	**Aberdeen**	**Saler**
	€/£	**€/£**	**€/£**
Year 1	120,000	40,000	158,000
Year 2	20,000	40,000	(78,000)
Year 3	80,000	(40,000)	(45,000)
Year 4	100,000		
Year 5	(20,000)		
Year 6	(30,000)		
Total profits	270,000	40,000	35,000
Average profits ratio	€/£270,000 / 6	€/£40,000 / 3	€/£35,000 / 3
Average profits	**€/£45,000**	**€/£13,333**	**€/£11,667**
ARR ratio	€/£45,000 / €/£120,000	€/£13,333 / €/£120,000	€/£11,667 / €/£120,000
ARR%	**37.5%**	**11.11%**	**9.72%**

The company has a target ARR of 10%. The 'Friesian' and 'Aberdeen' projects exceed the target, with reported ARRs of 37.5% and 11.11%, hence they should be accepted. Saler should not be accepted as its ARR is marginally below the target.

(b) In this instance the depreciation charge will change and is different for the 'Friesian' project, which lasts six years, relative to the other two projects (they last three years). In addition, the average capital investment will change as the asset has a residual value, which differs depending on the duration of the project.

Friesian (yearly depreciation calculation): (€/£240,000 – €/£30,000) ÷ 6 = €/£35,000
Aberdeen and Saler (yearly depreciation calculation): (€/£240,000 – €/£60,000) ÷ 3 = €/£60,000

Yearly Profits/(Losses) after Depreciation

	Friesian	**Aberdeen**	**Saler**
	€/£	**€/£**	**€/£**
Year 1	125,000	60,000	178,000
Year 2	25,000	60,000	(58,000)
Year 3	85,000	(20,000)	(25,000)
Year 4	105,000		
Year 5	(15,000)		
Year 6	(25,000)		
Total profits	300,000	100,000	95,000
Average profits ratio	€/£300,000 / 6	€/£100,000 / 3	€/£95,000 / 3
Average profits	**€/£50,000**	**€/£33,333**	**€/£31,667**
Average investment	(€/£240,000 + €/£30,000) / 2	(€/£240,000 + €/£60,000) / 2	(€/£240,000 + €/£60,000) / 2
Average investment	**€/£135,000**	**€/£150,000**	**€/£150,000**
ARR ratio	€/£50,000 / €/£135,000	€/£33,000 / €/£150,000	€/£31,667 / €/£150,000
ARR	**37.03%**	**22.22%**	**21.11%**

In this instance all three projects would be accepted as they all provide a return in excess of the 10% target.

An advantage cited for using the ARR method of investment appraisal is that it is easily understandable and closely correlates with accounting ratios that are used to assess a company's performance, e.g. the ROCE. However, it does not take into account the size of a project, the duration of a project, the cash flows and, more importantly, the time value of money. It can also be distorted by the pattern of profits, causing managers to draw incorrect conclusions. For example, if, in **Worked Example 2.3**, an extra year of use yields an extra

€/£500 profits to 'Friesian' company, this may be beneficial, causing total profits to rise to €/£300,500; however, it will mean that the average profits will fall as the total profits will be divisible by seven, hence will fall from €/£50,000 to €/£42,928 and the ARR will consequently fall from 37.03% to 31.8%. Therefore, care needs to be taken when comparing projects, as inappropriate use of the ARR may lead the decision-maker to make incorrect decisions.

The Payback Period

The **payback period method** ranks investments in order of the speed at which the initial cash outflow is paid back by subsequent cash inflows. Under this method the most attractive investment would be the one that pays back the initial outlay in the shortest time. This method focuses on cash flows, not profits, therefore depreciation and accrual accounting are ignored. This method calculates the number of years it takes for cumulative cash flows to achieve breakeven point.

Worked Example 2.4: Payback Period Method

Cow Ltd is considering three projects (each costing €/£240,000). The following cash flows are predicted:

Yearly cash flows

	Friesian €/£	Aberdeen €/£	Saler €/£
Year 1	160,000	120,000	238,000
Year 2	60,000	120,000	1,000
Year 3	120,000	40,000	36,000
Year 4	140,000		
Year 5	20,000		
Year 6	10,000		

Requirement Using the payback method, advise Cow Ltd as to the investment to undertake.

Solution

The investment in Friesian takes two years and two months to pay back the initial outlay: €/£160,000 (first year) + €/£60,000 (second year) + €/£20,000/€120,000 (which is one-sixth or two months of the third year).

The Aberdeen investment takes two years exactly to pay back the initial outlay: €/£120,000 + €/£120,000.

The Saler investment takes two years and 10 days to pay back the initial outlay: €/£238,000 (first year) + €/£1,000 (second year) + [(€/£1,000/€/£36,000) × 365] (10 days).

	Friesian		Aberdeen		Saler	
	Cash flows	Cumulative cash flows	Cash flows	Cumulative cash flows	Cash flows	Cumulative cash flows
	€/£	€/£	€/£	€/£	€/£	€/£
Year 0	(240,000)	(240,000)	(240,000)	(240,000)	(240,000)	(240,000)
Year 1	160,000	(80,000)	120,000	(120,000)	238,000	(2,000)
Year 2	60,000	(20,000)	120,000	-	1,000	(1,000)
Year 3	120,000		40,000		36,000	
Year 4	140,000					
Year 5	20,000					
Year 6	10,000					

Therefore, using the payback period method, Aberdeen is the highest ranking investment opportunity of the three on offer.

The above example highlights the shortcomings of the payback period method. The first major disadvantage is that it focuses on cash flows and ignores profitability. Both elements should be considered for project appraisal. In addition, it ignores cash flows received after the payback period, which, in the case of Friesian, is material. It also ignores the time value of money. The cash flows of Saler are more attractive relative to those of Aberdeen as most of the funds are received in the first year, yet this is not taken into account in the calculations. Were Saler to have a €/£2,000 cash inflow in Year 2 instead of €/£1,000, it would have been ranked the same as Aberdeen, yet would be deemed to be much superior if the time value of money were to be considered. In addition, the payback method does not take into account the size or relative impact of an investment. In this example the investment cash outflow in each case was the same; however, this is unlikely to be the case in practice. Use of the payback period method might lead to a small project with a short payback period being ranked in front of a large project that has a slightly longer payback period, but a much larger impact on the organisation and potentially larger net cash inflows in subsequent periods. Many companies set an initial hurdle payback period for their investment projects. Setting a period limit is regarded as subjective. It might eliminate more profitable projects that have longer lives.

On a positive note, the payback period method is a quick and simple investment appraisal technique that is particularly useful for companies that have liquidity issues and that need to recoup their cash outlay quickly. It can also be used to help decide between two projects that have similar annual accounting rates of return. Another advantage of the payback method is that it can be regarded as a risk screening technique. There is a correlation between risk and the length of time that cash flows are estimated for, in that cash flows predicted in the first couple of years are inherently less risky than cash flows that are estimated for, say, 10 years' time. Therefore, the payback method focuses managers' attention on projects that have more reliable estimates.

Discounted Payback Method

The **discounted payback period method** overcomes one of the weaknesses of the payback period method, as it takes the time value of money into consideration. This method ranks investments according to the speed at which the cumulative **discounted cash flows (DCF)** of an investment cover the initial cash outlay. An appropriate discount rate needs to be utilised. The factors affecting the discount rate to be used in investment appraisal were discussed earlier in this chapter and should be taken into account when using the discounted payback period method.

WORKED EXAMPLE 2.5: DISCOUNTED PAYBACK METHOD

Cow Ltd is considering three projects (each costing €/£240,000). The following cash flows before depreciation are predicted:

	Yearly cash flows before depreciation		
	Friesian €/£	**Aberdeen €/£**	**Saler €/£**
Year 1	160,000	120,000	238,000
Year 2	60,000	120,000	1,000
Year 3	120,000	40,000	36,000
Year 4	140,000		
Year 5	20,000		
Year 6	10,000		

Requirement Which of the above projects should Cow Ltd invest in? Cow Ltd has to borrow funds at 10%. Management decide that this is an appropriate discount rate to use and it is company policy to use the discounted payback period method for capital investment appraisal.

Solution

	Friesian			
	Yearly cash flows €/£	**Discount factor (10%)**	**Discounted cash flow €/£**	**Cumulative cash flow €/£**
Year 0	(240,000)	1.000	(240,000)	(240,000)
Year 1	160,000	0.909	145,440	(94,560)
Year 2	60,000	0.826	49,560	(45,000)
Year 3	120,000	0.751	90,120	
Year 4	140,000	0.683	95,620	
Year 5	20,000	0.621	12,420	
Year 6	10,000	0.564	5,640	

$$\text{Discounted payback period} = 2 \text{ years} + \frac{45{,}000 \times 365}{90{,}120} = 2 \text{ years and } 182 \text{ days}$$

Aberdeen

	Yearly cash flows €/£	**Discount factor (10%)**	**Discounted cash flow €/£**	**Cumulative cash flow €/£**
Year 0	(240,000)	1.000	(240,000)	(240,000)
Year 1	120,000	0.909	109,080	(130,920)
Year 2	120,000	0.826	99,120	(31,800)
Year 3	40,000	0.751	30,040	(1,760)

Investment in Aberdeen does not pay back when the time value of money is taken into consideration.

Saler

	Yearly cash flows €/£	**Discount factor (10%)**	**Discounted cash flow €/£**	**Cumulative cash flow €/£**
Year 0	(240,000)	1.000	(240,000)	(240,000)
Year 1	238,000	0.909	216,342	(23,658)
Year 2	1,000	0.826	826	(22,832)
Year 3	36,000	0.751	27,036	

$$\text{Discounted payback period} = 2 \text{ years} + \frac{22{,}832 \times 365}{27{,}036} = 2 \text{ years and } 308 \text{ days}$$

Investment	**Payback period**	**Ranking**
Friesian	2 years and 182 days	1
Aberdeen	Does not pay back	(do not accept)
Saler	2 years and 308 days	2

Therefore, Friesian is the highest ranking project using the discounted payback period method.

The highest ranking investment from the straight payback period analysis (Aberdeen) would be totally eliminated from the appraisal process were the discounted payback period method to be used, as its discounted cash inflows are insufficient to cover the initial outlay. Though this method of investment appraisal does remove one of the disadvantages associated with using the payback method, all the other disadvantages remain.

Internal Rate of Return (IRR)

The **IRR**, sometimes referred to as the **discounted cash flow yield method**, also involves discounting future cash flows to their present value. It could be considered a type of **break-even analysis**, which focuses on trying to find the discount rate at which the present value of the future cash flows (inflows and outflows combined) equals the initial investment cash outlay. It basically tries to find the return received from an investment opportunity. This is the rate which gives a NPV of zero. It is usually used by management to rank investment projects or to provide a cut-off rate for determining which projects to investigate further.

The predetermined return rate should be at least the company's target discount rate (i.e. its **hurdle rate**) for this type of project. If the IRR is greater than the target rate, then the project is expected to provide a return that is higher than the minimum return expected by management; hence it should be pursued further. When the IRR equals the target rate, the project can be accepted. When the IRR is lower than the predetermined target rate, the project should not be accepted. Where a company has to decide between a number of projects that have an IRR in excess of the target rate, then the project with the highest IRR should be accepted.

Calculating the IRR

The approach to calculating the IRR is to use trial and error and then to interpolate between two rates to find the best estimate of the IRR. The process of interpolation is portrayed in **Figure 2.2**.

FIGURE 2.2: INTERPOLATION TO FIND THE IRR

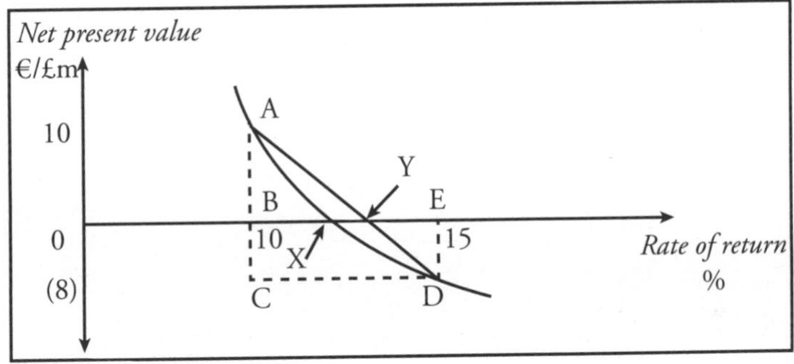

In the first instance cash flows are discounted using a 10% discount rate (this rate is selected subjectively). The result is a positive net present value of €/£10 million. As this is positive, a higher discount rate is selected for the second trial – 15%. This is again selected subjectively. The result is a negative net present value of €/£8 million. Therefore, the true rate lies between 10% and 15%. Interpolation works by assuming that the returns received from the project have a linear relationship to the rate of return. The true IRR rate is the point X; however, interpolation will use a simple mathematical equation to find the point Y, which is a close approximation to X, though not exact.

The calculation is based on the assumption that the triangle ABY, in **Figure 2.2**, is a smaller version of the triangle ACD. As the rates and NPVs are known for the larger triangle, this relationship can be used to find Y. The key is to find the proportion that BY is of the difference between C and D (i.e. the proportion of 5% (15% – 10%)). This proportion is then used to find the additional rate of return that is added to the lower value (B) to give an overall approximation for the IRR (Y). The proportion that BY is, relative to CD, can be calculated as follows:

$$\frac{BY}{AB} = \frac{CD}{AC}$$

where BY is unknown. BY represents the distance between B and Y (in terms of rates of return). AB is the distance between A and B (in terms of NPV) and so on. This process is simplified into the following formula:

$$\textbf{IRR} = \textbf{Rate 1} + \frac{\textbf{NPV 1 (Rate 2} - \textbf{Rate 1)}}{\textbf{NPV 1} - \textbf{NPV 2}}$$

Interpolation is shown in **Worked Example 2.6.**

Worked Example 2.6: IRR (Interpolation)

Cow Ltd is considering a project (costing €/£240,000). The following cash flows, before depreciation, are predicted:

	Yearly cash flows before depreciation Friesian €/£
Year 1	160,000
Year 2	60,000
Year 3	120,000
Year 4	40,000
Year 5	30,000

Requirement Calculate the IRR of the project using interpolation.

Solution

For the first trial, a discount rate of 10% is selected. At this rate the investment has a NPV of €/£91,070.

Therefore, a higher rate (30%) is selected for the second trial. At this discount rate a negative NPV of €/£4,770 results.

	Cash flows €/£	Discount factor (10%)	Present value €/£	Discount factor (30%)	Present value £/€
Year 0	(240,000)	1.000	(240,000)	1.000	(240,000)
Year 1	160,000	0.909	145,440	0.769	123,040
Year 2	60,000	0.826	49,560	0.592	35,520
Year 3	120,000	0.751	90,120	0.455	54,600
Year 4	40,000	0.683	27,320	0.350	14,000
Year 5	30,000	0.621	18,630	0.269	8,070
NPV			91,070		(4,770)

Therefore, the IRR lies between 10% and 30% and can be found using interpolation:

$$\text{IRR} = \text{Rate 1} + \frac{\text{NPV 1 (Rate 2} - \text{Rate 1)}}{\text{NPV 1} - \text{NPV 2}}$$

$$\text{IRR} = 10\% + \frac{\text{€/£}91{,}070\ (30\% - 10\%)}{\text{€/£}91{,}070 - (-\text{€/£}4{,}770)}$$

$$\text{IRR} = 10\% + 19\% = 29\%$$

The same formula can be used when two trial runs result in two positive or two negative NPVs. In this instance the formula extrapolates to find the IRR. The same example is utilised again below to provide an example of this.

Worked Example 2.7: Interpolation

Cow Ltd is considering one project (costing €/£240,000). The following cash flows before depreciation are predicted:

	Yearly cash flows before depreciation Friesian €/£
Year 1	160,000
Year 2	60,000
Year 3	120,000
Year 4	40,000
Year 5	30,000

Requirement Calculate the IRR of the project using interpolation.

Solution

For the first trial, a discount rate of 10% is selected. At this rate the investment has a positive NPV of €/£91,070.

Therefore, a higher rate (20%) is selected for the second trial. At this discount rate a positive NPV of €/£35,740 results.

	Cash flows €/£	Discount factor (10%)	Present value €/£	Discount factor (20%)	Present value €/£
Year 0	(240,000)	1.000	(240,000)	1.000	(240,000)
Year 1	160,000	0.909	145,440	0.833	133,280
Year 2	60,000	0.826	49,560	0.694	41,640
Year 3	120,000	0.751	90,120	0.579	69,480
Year 4	40,000	0.683	27,320	0.482	19,280
Year 5	30,000	0.621	18,630	0.402	12,060
NPV			91,070		35,740

Therefore, the IRR is a rate above 20% and can be found using interpolation:

$$\text{IRR} = \text{Rate 1} + \frac{\text{NPV 1 (Rate 2} - \text{Rate 1)}}{\text{NPV 1} - \text{NPV 2}}$$

$$\text{IRR} = 10\% + \frac{\text{€/£}91{,}070\ (20\% - 10\%)}{\text{€/£}91{,}070 - \text{€/£}35{,}740}$$

$$\text{IRR} = 10\% + 16.45\% = 26.45\%$$

The estimation is different from the first example due to the fact that the two chosen trial percentages are further away from the true IRR figure. This is an estimation error that increases in line with the distance the trial rates are from the true rate. The use of a linear calculation is not strictly correct, though does provide a reasonable approximation provided the trial rates are not too far away, as they were in the previous two examples.

The IRR cannot capture benefits to be received by projects that have unconventional cash flows, e.g. some projects may have negative cash flows in the future. Use of the IRR will result in two possible return outcomes. However, projects with unconventional cash flows are rare in practice. Another problem is that the IRR does not take into account the absolute cash flows to be earned, enticing the decision-maker to choose an investment based on a single rate. For example, if one project had an IRR of 15%, it would be rated higher than a project with an IRR of 14%, yet it may have less of an impact on equity holder wealth as the scale of the investment is not taken into consideration. In absolute money terms the project with the IRR of 14% may provide twice as much cash; relative to the project with the 15% IRR. For example, €/£1 million invested at 14% will increase equity holder value by more than €/£100,000 invested at 15%. The advantages and disadvantages of the IRR for investment appraisal are summarised in **Figure 2.3**.

FIGURE 2.3: ADVANTAGES AND DISADVANTAGES OF USING THE IRR FOR CAPITAL INVESTMENT APPRAISAL

Advantages

The **time value of money** is taken into consideration.

All cash flows are considered in the appraisal process.

Disadvantages

Time-consuming calculations (though these are now normally executed by a computer).

The **linearity assumption** that underlies the interpolation process.

It ignores the **scale** of projects, which may lead to sub-optimal decision-making

It is difficult to utilise when investments have **unconventional cash flows**, as more than one IRR will result.

It cannot be used when projects are **mutually exclusive**.

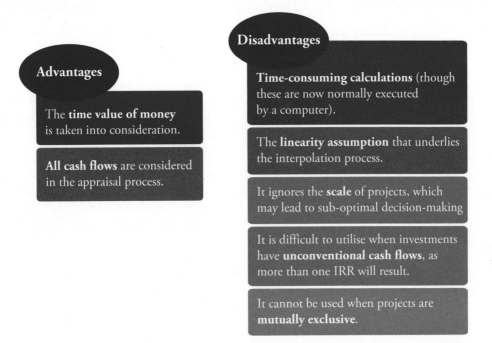

WORKED EXAMPLE 2.8: IRR FOR CHOOSING PROJECTS

Cow Ltd is considering three projects (each costing €/£240,000). The following cash flows before depreciation are predicted.

(***Note:*** the cash flows for Friesian and Aberdeen have changed from those used in previous examples.)

	Yearly Cash Flows		
	Friesian	**Aberdeen**	**Saler**
	€/£	**€/£**	**€/£**
Year 0	(24,000)	(240,000)	(240,000)
Year 1	6,000	120,000	238,000
Year 2	6,000	120,000	1,000
Year 3	10,000	40,000	36,000
Year 4	13,000	3,000	
Year 5	2,000		
Year 6	1,000		

Requirement Calculate each project's IRR and rank the resulting information for reporting to management.

Solution

Friesian investment

	Yearly cash flows €/£	Discount factor (10%)	Present value €/£	Discount factor (20%)	Present value €/£
Year 0	(24,000)	1.000	(24,000)	1.000	(24,000)
Year 1	6,000	0.909	5,454	0.833	4,998
Year 2	6,000	0.826	4,956	0.694	4,164
Year 3	10,000	0.751	7,510	0.579	5,790
Year 4	13,000	0.683	8,879	0.482	6,266
Year 5	2,000	0.621	1,242	0.402	804
Year 6	1,000	0.564	564	0.335	335
NPV			4,605		(1,643)

$$\text{IRR} = 10\% + \frac{€/£4{,}605\ (20\% - 10\%)}{€/£4{,}605 - (-€/£1{,}643)}$$

IRR = 17.37%

Aberdeen investment

	Yearly cash flows €/£	Discount factor (10%)	Present value €/£	Discount factor (12%)	Present value €/£
Year 0	(240,000)	1.000	(240,000)	1.000	(240,000)
Year 1	120,000	0.909	109,080	0.893	107,160
Year 2	120,000	0.826	99,120	0.797	95,640
Year 3	40,000	0.751	30,040	0.712	28,480
Year 4	3,000	0.683	2,049	0.635	1,905
NPV			289		(6,815)

$$\text{IRR} = 10\% + \frac{€/£289\ (12\% - 10\%)}{€/£289 - (-€/£6{,}815)}$$

IRR = 10.08%

Saler investment

	Yearly cash flows €/£	Discount factor (10%)	Present value €/£	Discount factor (15%)	Present value €/£
Year 0	(240,000)	1.000	(240,000)	1.000	(240,000)
Year 1	238,000	0.909	216,342	0.870	207,060
Year 2	1,000	0.826	826	0.756	756
Year 3	36,000	0.751	27,036	0.657	23,652
NPV			4,204		(8,532)

$$\text{IRR} = 10\% + \frac{€/£4{,}204\ (15\% - 10\%)}{€/£4{,}204 - (-€/£8{,}532)}$$

$$\text{IRR} = 11.65\%$$

In this instance the investment ranked first is Friesian, with a yield of 17.37%, followed by Saler (yield of 11.65%). Aberdeen is ranked third with a yield of 10.08%.

Net Present Value (NPV)

Due to the limitations outlined above, the IRR should be utilised with caution. A more appropriate project appraisal method to use is the **NPV method**. The NPV method of project appraisal discounts the cash inflows and outflows of an investment to their present value. Use of the correct discount rate is very important: different rates may be required for different projects depending on their risk profile (discussed earlier and in the next chapter). If the NPV is positive, then the project should be accepted as the positive amount will increase equity holder value. If the NPV is negative, then the project should be rejected as acceptance will damage equity holder value.

Worked Example 2.9: NPV for Choosing Projects

Cow Ltd is considering three projects (each costing €/£240,000). The following cash flows before depreciation are predicted:

	Yearly cash flows Friesian €/£	Aberdeen €/£	Saler €/£
Year 0	(240,000)	(240,000)	(240,000)
Year 1	60,000	120,000	238,000
Year 2	60,000	120,000	1,000
Year 3	100,000	40,000	36,000
Year 4	130,000	3,000	
Year 5	20,000		
Year 6	10,000		

Requirement Calculate each project's NPV and rank the resulting information for reporting to management. The company has a WACC of 16% and all the projects being considered are of similar risk to the current operating activities of the company.

Solution

Friesian investment

	Cash flows €/£	Discount factor (16%)	Present value €/£
Year 0	(240,000)	1.000	(240,000)
Year 1	60,000	0.862	51,720
Year 2	60,000	0.743	44,580
Year 3	100,000	0.641	64,100
Year 4	130,000	0.552	71,760
Year 5	20,000	0.476	9,520
Year 6	10,000	0.410	4,100
NPV			5,780

Aberdeen investment

	Cash flows €/£	Discount factor (16%)	Present value €/£
Year 0	(240,000)	1.000	(240,000)
Year 1	120,000	0.862	103,440
Year 2	120,000	0.743	89,160
Year 3	40,000	0.641	25,640
Year 4	3,000	0.552	1,656
NPV			(20,104)

Saler investment

	Cash flows €/£	Discount factor (16%)	Present value €/£
Year 0	(240,000)	1.000	(240,000)
Year 1	238,000	0.862	205,156
Year 2	1,000	0.743	743
Year 3	36,000	0.641	23,076
NPV			(11,025)

When the discount rate used is 16%, the only investment that should be accepted by the company is Friesian, as it covers the cost of finance (16%) and provides an excess return of €/£5,780. The other two projects have negative NPVs and, if accepted, would result in a loss of equity holder value, as they are not covering the current cost of the company's capital.

The advantages of using the NPV are highlighted in **Figure 2.4**.

FIGURE 2.4: ADVANTAGES OF USING THE NPV FOR INVESTMENT APPRAISAL

Time value of money	The time value of money is taken into consideration.
All cash flows	All relevant cash flows are considered in the appraisal process.
Adjusted for risk	The discount rate can be adjusted for risk.
Choosing amongst alternatives	When there are several alternatives, the alternative with the largest NPV will maximise equity holder value.
Variant cash flows	Unlike the IRR, when cash flows are not conventional, the NPV will provide one answer.

The main disadvantage of using the NPV for investment appraisal is that it does not provide a method of deciding which investment provides the best value for money. It considers the absolute money value that a company will end up with by the end of an investment's life; however, an investment with a small outlay and small net cash inflows may give the same NPV as an investment with a large outlay and larger inflows. The latter investment would be more risky as the amounts are larger, but using the NPV on its own as a means of selecting a project does not take this into account. For example, in **Worked Example 2.8**, the investment in Friesian is €/£24,000 and the resultant NPV when the cash flows are discounted at 10% is €/£4,605. The investment in Saler is 10 times more (€/£240,000), but when the cash flows are discounted at 10%, the NPV is €/£4,204 (which is only marginally higher than Friesian's NPV). It is clear that the Saler project is much riskier – yet had it returned a NPV of €/£4,650 it would have been the preferred project, if the decision were based purely on the NPV.

WORKING CAPITAL

Working capital is both an investment and a source and use of finance. It has cash flow implications and, where a project requires increases in working capital, this should be factored into the calculations. Likewise, when a project ends and the working capital reduces again, then the cash inflow from that process should be factored into the appraisal process. The implications of working capital investment are highlighted in the following example.

Worked Example 2.10: Working Capital

ABC Ltd is considering an investment which would require the immediate purchase of a capital asset costing €/£400,000 and working capital of €/£120,000. Net inflows will be €/£180,000, €/£160,000 and €/£140,000 for Year 1, Year 2 and Year 3. The working capital requirement will increase by 20% per year in each of the first two years. All of the working capital will be turned into cash at the end of Year 3. The company's cost of capital is 15%.

Requirement Calculate the NPV of the investment (ignore taxation).

Solution

The impact of increasing the investment in working capital on cash flows is as follows:

Time	Cash flows €/£	Working capital €/£	Net cash flows €/£	Discount factor (15%)	Present value €/£
Year 0	(400,000)	(120,000)	(520,000)	1.000	(520,000)
Year 1	180,000	(24,000)[1]	156,000	0.870	135,720
Year 2	160,000	(28,800)[2]	131,200	0.756	99,187
Year 3	140,000	172,800[3]	312,800	0.658	205,822
NPV					(79,271)

1. This represents an increase in the working capital requirement: €/£120,000 × 20%.
2. This represents an increase in the working capital requirement from Year 1: (€/£120,000 + €/£24,000) × 20%.
3. This is the total working capital that has been built up over the life of the investment, now released.

TAXATION

When appraising a project, it is important to consider all material relevant cash flows. Tax is a cash flow which is usually material.

Capital projects normally have two influences on tax cash flows: tax on profits made by the project and tax relief on capital expenditure. As tax payable is dependent on profits made, not cash flows, a separate calculation based on profits needs to be prepared to determine the tax cash flows. Depreciation is always deducted when profits are calculated. However, this expense is not allowable by the tax authorities, which have their own allowable deductions for capital investment, called **capital allowances**. Capital allowances are sometimes referred to as **written down allowances**. Depending on the jurisdiction, these may be calculated using a reducing balance or a straight line basis. In some instances the tax authorities allow a **first year allowance** or an **annual investment allowance**, which is usually up to 100% of the capital cost of an asset, though it can be higher (e.g. by giving an allowance of more than 100%, the UK government supports some industries and types of expenditure, such as research and development expenditure). In exam questions, the examiner will state the method and rate to use and students need to be flexible in their approach. Therefore, to work out the tax cash flow, profits have to be adjusted – depreciation has to be added back to profit, and capital allowances/first year allowances/balancing allowances have to be deducted and balancing charges added back. A **balancing charge** results when an asset is disposed of for a sum that exceeds the written down allowance on the date of the sale – balancing charges increase the tax charge. A **balancing allowance** results when the asset is disposed of for a sum that is less than the written down value of the asset on the date of the sale – balancing allowances reduce the tax charge. The tax cash flow will be the remaining profit multiplied by the tax rate relevant for the company (assuming the company is profitable).

The other important attribute of tax cash flows is that they do not occur in the year profits are made, but in the subsequent year. This should be assumed unless a question directs otherwise.

Worked Example 2.11: Tax Cash Flows

ABC Ltd is considering purchasing one of two capital assets for use in a particular project. The first (Fresco) costs €/£200,000, the second (Tempera) costs €/£220,000. The following information is available about the projects.

- The net yearly profits expected from the use of the Fresco asset are: €/£100,000 (in Year 1), €/£120,000 (in Year 2), €/£140,000 (in Year 3) and €/£50,000 (in Year 4).
- The net yearly profits expected from the use of the Tempera asset are: €/£120,000 (in Year 1), €/£110,000 (in Year 2), €/£120,000 (in Year 3) and €/£60,000 (in Year 4).
- The company's depreciation policy for this type of equipment is to depreciate it over three years using the straight-line basis. A blanket policy in respect of determining the residual value of machines is followed by the company whereby, from past experience, machines, on average, realise 25% of their purchase value.
- Capital allowances are 25% calculated using the reducing balance method.
- Corporation tax is 30%.
- The company's cost of capital is 15%.

Requirement Calculate the NPV of both options assuming that:
(a) Fresco is expected to be sold at the end of Year 4 for €/£40,000; and
(b) Tempera is expected to be sold at the end of Year 4 for €/£100,000.

Solution

Before preparing the NPV schedule, four workings are required. The first calculates depreciation. The second uses the information from the first step to decipher the cash flows from the project. The third calculates capital allowances. The fourth uses the information from the second and third workings to determine the tax cash flow expected.

(a) **Fresco**

Working 1: Depreciation

The residual value is €/£50,000 (25% × €/£200,000). Using the straight-line method, depreciation is calculated by:

$$\text{Depreciation} = \frac{\text{Cost} - \text{residual value}}{\text{Useful economic life}}$$

$$\text{Depreciation} = \frac{€/£200{,}000 - €/£50{,}000}{3}$$

$$\text{Depreciation} = €/£50{,}000 \text{ per year}$$

In Year 4 there will be a loss on the sale of the asset. It will have been written down to its residual value of €/£50,000, but will have been sold for €/£40,000. Therefore, this is treated as an accounting loss on the sale of the asset of €/£10,000. This will have been deducted to find the profit, hence will have to be added back to determine the cash flows in Year 4.

Working 2: Cash flows from the project

Year	**Profits**	**Depreciation/ loss on sale**	**Cash flows**
	€/£	**€/£**	**€/£**
Year 1	100,000	50,000	150,000
Year 2	120,000	50,000	170,000
Year 3	140,000	50,000	190,000
Year 4	50,000	10,000	60,000

Working 3: Capital allowances

Year	**Opening written down value**	**Workings**	**Capital allowances**
	€/£	**€/£**	**€/£**
Year 1	200,000	(200,000 × 25%)	50,000
Year 2	150,000*	(150,000 × 25%)	37,500
Year 3	112,500	(112,500 × 25%)	28,125
			Balancing allowance
Year 4	84,375	(84,375 − 40,000)	44,375

*The opening written down value in Year 2 is the opening written down value in Year 1 less the capital allowances in that period (€/£200,000 – €/£50,000).

Working 4: Tax cash flows

Year	**Cash flows**	**Capital allowances**	**Taxable cash flows**	**Taxation charge @ 30%**	**Taxation cash flow**
	€/£	**€/£**	**€/£**	**€/£**	**€/£**
Year 0	–	–	–	–	–
Year 1	150,000	(50,000)	100,000	(30,000)	–
Year 2	170,000	(37,500)	132,500	(39,750)	(30,000)
Year 3	190,000	(28,125)	161,875	(48,562)	(39,750)
Year 4	60,000	(44,375)	15,625	(4,688)	(48,562)
Year 5	–	–	–	–	(4,688)

Fresco: Net present value calculation

Year	**Machine**	**Operating activities**	**Taxation**	**Total cash flow**	**Discount factor**	**Present value**
	€/£	**€/£**	**€/£**	**€/£**	**(15%)**	**€/£**
Year 0	(200,000)	–	–	(200,000)	1.000	(200,000)
Year 1	–	150,000	–	150,000	0.870	130,500
Year 2	–	170,000	(30,000)	140,000	0.756	105,840
Year 3	–	190,000	(39,750)	150,250	0.658	98,864
Year 4	40,000	60,000	(48,562)	51,438	0.572	29,423
Year 5	–	–	(4,688)	(4,688)	0.497	(2,330)
NPV						162,297

(b) **Tempera**

Working 1: Depreciation

The residual value is €/£55,000 (25% × €/£220,000). Using the straight-line method, depreciation is calculated by:

$$\text{Depreciation} = \frac{\text{Cost} - \text{residual value}}{\text{Useful economic life}}$$

$$\text{Depreciation} = \frac{€/£220{,}000 - €/£55{,}000}{3}$$

$$\text{Depreciation} = €/£55{,}000 \text{ per year}$$

In Year 4, then, there will be a profit on the sale of the asset. It will have been written down to its residual value of €/£55,000, but will have been sold for €/£100,000. Therefore, this is treated as an accounting profit on the sale of the asset of €/£45,000. This will have been added to the operating profits to find the overall profit, hence will have to be deducted to determine the cash flows from the project in Year 4.

Working 2: Cash flows from the project

Year	Profits	Depreciation/ (profit on sale)	Cash flows
	€/£	€/£	€/£
Year 1	120,000	55,000	175,000
Year 2	110,000	55,000	165,000
Year 3	120,000	55,000	175,000
Year 4	60,000	(45,000)	15,000

Working 3: Capital allowances

Year	Opening written down value	Workings	Capital allowances
	€/£	€/£	€/£
Year 1	220,000	(220,000 × 25%)	55,000
Year 2	165,000*	(165,000 × 25%)	41,250
Year 3	123,750	(123,750 × 25%)	30,938
			Balancing charge
Year 4	92,812	(92,812 − 100,000)	(7,188)

*The opening written down value in Year 2 is the opening written down value in Year 1 less the capital allowances in that period (€/£220,000 – €/£55,000).

Working 4: Tax cash flows

Year	Cash flows	Capital allowances	Taxable cash flows	Taxation charge @ 30%	Taxation cash flow
	€/£	€/£	€/£	€/£	€/£
Year 1	175,000	(55,000)	120,000	(36,000)	–
Year 2	165,000	(41,250)	123,750	(37,125)	(36,000)
Year 3	175,000	(30,938)	144,062	(43,219)	(37,125)
Year 4	15,000	7,188	22,188	(6,656)	(43,219)
Year 5	–	–	–	–	(6,656)

Tempera: Net present value calculation

Year	Machine	Operating activities	Taxation	Total cash flow	Discount factor	Present value
	€/£	€/£	€/£	€/£	(15%)	€/£
Year 0	(220,000)	–	–	(220,000)	1.000	(220,000)
Year 1	–	175,000	–	175,000	0.870	152,250
Year 2	–	165,000	(36,000)	129,000	0.756	97,524
Year 3	–	175,000	(37,125)	137,875	0.658	90,722
Year 4	100,000	15,000	(43,219)	71,781	0.572	41,059
Year 5	–	–	(6,656)	(6,656)	0.497	(3,308)
NPV						158,247

Based on the results of these workings, ABC Ltd should invest in Fresco as it is expected to return a higher NPV of €/£162,297 relative to the NPV reported for Tempera (€/£158,247).

The relevance of tax to the value of a capital asset is illustrated by the next example.

Worked Example 2.12: Taxation

ABC Ltd is considering an investment which would require the immediate purchase of a capital asset costing €/£200,000. The company pays corporation tax at the rate of 30%, one year in arrears. The equipment is not expected to have a residual value. Capital allowances for the period of the investment are expected to be allowed at a rate of 25% on a straight-line basis. The cost of capital for investment appraisal purposes is 15%.

Requirement Calculate the NPV of the cash flows relating to the capital asset only.

Solution

The impact of purchasing a capital asset on cash flows will be an initial cash outlay followed by annual cash savings due to the tax shield on the capital allowances.

The capital allowances will be: €/£50,000 [€/£200,000 × 25%] per year for four years. This will result in a tax saving of: €/£15,000 [€/£50,000 × 30%]. As tax is payable in the year following the year in which profits are made, this cash flow advantage will have a time delay of one year. Therefore, the total present value of the cash flows that relate to the asset cost alone are as follows:

Time	Cash flows €/£	Discount factor (15%)	Present value €/£
Year 0	(200,000)	1.000	(200,000)
Year 1	–	0.870	–
Year 2	15,000	0.756	11,340
Year 3	15,000	0.658	9,870
Year 4	15,000	0.572	8,580
Year 5	15,000	0.497	7,455
NPV			(162,755)

In Year 1 the company will have been able to claim capital allowances. However, the cash benefit will not occur until the next year and is assumed to occur at the end of the year. The net cost of the asset is €/£162,755.

INFLATION

Inflation is a term used to describe the percentage increase in the cost of goods. It reflects a reduction in the purchasing power of money. Inflation has a major influence on capital investment appraisal. It impacts on the return required by a company's investors, hence the discount rate. Inflation will also impact on expected cash flows. In most countries inflation is positive, hence the expectation is that prices will increase in the future. This would not cause a problem if all the variables included in an investment were increasing at the same general inflation rate. In this instance inflation could be ignored as the discount rate would cater for the required return to cover inflation. However, inflation may impact on different variables in different ways. For example, wages may increase by a factor that is higher than inflation, sales prices may remain static due to cheap imports and rents may remain static due to a legal rental agreement covering several years. These issues cause complications for investment appraisal, particularly where cash flows extend over several years. Two approaches are utilised to deal with the problem of inflation: the gross approach and the net approach.

The Gross Approach

This involves adjusting the annual cash flows of a project by the expected rate of inflation and using a discount rate that is also adjusted for inflation. This rate is usually called the **money/market discount rate** or the **nominal discount rate** (in some instances it is also referred to as the **basic discount rate**, particularly when bank rates are utilised as they reflect the banks' prediction for expected inflation). The nominal discount rate is calculated using the following formula:

Nominal discount rate = ((1 + Real rate) × (1 + Inflation rate)) − 1

Worked Example 2.13: Calculating Nominal Interest Rates

Frank Ltd is evaluating a project where projected cash flows are estimated at future prices. Frank Ltd has a real cost of capital of 12% and inflation is expected to be 4% per annum.

Requirement What is the nominal discount rate to be used when appraising this project?

Solution

Nominal rate = ((1 + Real rate) × (1 + Inflation rate)) – 1
Nominal rate = (1.12 × 1.04) – 1
Nominal rate = 16.48%

As mentioned previously, in many instances different variables are affected in different ways when inflation changes. In these circumstances the best approach is to convert all cash flows to actual expected cash flows and to discount them, using the nominal/money rate as the discount factor. This approach is reflected in the next example.

Worked Example 2.14: NPV Including Variant Inflation

Z Ltd is considering an investment that will cost €/£500,000 now. The annual benefits for four years would be a fixed income of €/£250,000 per annum, plus savings of €/£50,000 in Year 1, rising by 5% each year due to inflation. Running costs will be €/£100,000 in the first year, but would increase by 10% each year due to inflating labour costs. The general rate of inflation is expected to be 5% and the company's required nominal/money rate of return is 20%.

Requirement Should the company invest in the project? (Ignore taxation.)

Solution

Some of the cash flows are expressed in terms of the actual amounts that will be received, whereas others will increase by a set percentage over the period. In these circumstances the cash flows will be inflated and the combined actual expected amounts calculated. When the actual expected cash flows are known, the nominal/ money rate can be used as the discount rate.

Time	Capital cost	Fixed income	Other savings	Running costs	Net cash flows	Discount factor	PV
	€/£	€/£	€/£	€/£	€/£	(20%)	€/£
0	(500,000)	–	–	–	(500,000)	1.000	(500,000)
1	–	250,000	50,000	(100,000)	200,000	0.833	166,600
2	–	250,000	52,500	(110,000)	192,500	0.694	133,595
3	–	250,000	55,125	(121,000)	184,125	0.579	106,608
4	–	250,000	57,881	(133,100)	174,781	0.482	84,244
							(8,953)

This project should not be undertaken as it has a negative NPV of €/£8,953.

The Net Method

The alternative is to exclude inflation from the calculations by adjusting cash flows accordingly to find the real cash flows, and by using a discount rate which is net of inflation. This rate is usually called the **real discount rate**. The real discount rate is found by deflating the nominal discount rate by the general rate of inflation.

Real cash flows reflect the current general purchasing power of cash flows. To obtain real cash flows, the expected monetary cash flows for each variable should be calculated (inflate using the various expected inflation rates), and then deflated using the general rate of inflation for the period in question.

Worked Example 2.15: NPV Including General Inflation

X Ltd is considering investing in a project with the following cash flows (at current prices):

	€/£
Year 0	(300,000)
Year 1	180,000
Year 2	160,000
Year 3	140,000

Inflation is currently 10% per year, and this rate is not expected to change over the lifetime of this project. The company requires a minimum return of 20% under the present and anticipated conditions.

Requirement Should the company invest in the project?

Solution

The cash flows are expressed in today's prices and all are subject to the general rate of inflation. Therefore, the correct discount rate to use is the real rate of return.

Time	**Cash flow**	**Discount factor**	**PV**
	€/£	**(20%)**	**€/£**
Year 0	(300,000)	1.000	(300,000)
Year 1	180,000	0.833	149,940
Year 2	160,000	0.694	111,040
Year 3	140,000	0.579	81,060
NPV			42,040

As the investment has a positive NPV, the company should make the investment.

Figure 2.5: Approach to take When Assessing a Project in Respect of Inflation

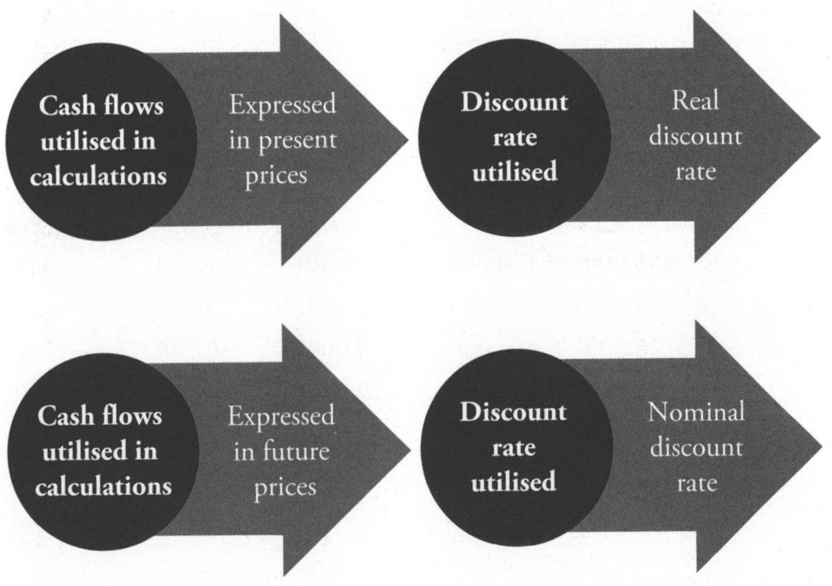

INCREMENTAL CASH FLOW APPROACH

The **incremental cash flow approach** can be used to choose between two mutually exclusive alternatives. **Mutually exclusive projects** are projects that compete with each other and only one can be accepted. For example, the investment can be in A or B (not both); the repair or replace decision is another example. The incremental approach involves subtracting the cash flows of one from the cash flows of another project: these are then discounted to present value using the company's current cost of capital. The sign of the resultant NPV is then interpreted to determine the course of action to take. This process is highlighted in the next example.

Worked Example 2.16: Incremental Cash Flows

X Ltd is considering whether to replace or repair a current asset. The company has a cost of capital of 15% and the following cash flows for each scenario have been estimated:

	Replace €/£	**Repair €/£**
Year 0	(50,000)	(20,000)
Year 1	(4,000)	(14,000)
Year 2	(6,000)	(16,000)
Year 3	(8,000)	(18,000)
Year 4	(10,000)	(20,000)
Year 5 (Realisable value)	22,000	6,000

Requirement Should the company replace the asset?

Solution

The present values of the incremental cash flows are as follows:

Time	Calculation	Cash flow	Discount factor	PV
		€/£	(15%)	€/£
0	(50,000) – (20,000)	(30,000)	1.000	(30,000)
1	(4,000) – (14,000)	10,000	0.870	8,700
2	(6,000) – (16,000)	10,000	0.756	7,560
3	(8,000) – (18,000)	10,000	0.658	6,580
4	(10,000) – (20,000)	10,000	0.572	5,720
5	22,000 – 6,000	16,000	0.497	7,952
NPV				6,512

As the investment has a positive NPV, the company should replace the asset.

CONCLUSION

The investment decisions a company undertakes are vital to its overall value. Investment decisions are the source of future income-streams to a company. Evaluating each investment correctly is very important as incorrect decisions can damage company value and are usually costly to rescind. This chapter outlines a number of techniques that can be utilised to assess different investments. The ARR ranks projects in terms of the average accounting profits generated relative to average investment. The payback period approach ranks projects in terms of the shortest period taken to recoup the initial cash outlay from future cash inflows. The discounted payback period approach is the same as the payback period approach except it takes the time value of money into consideration. The IRR approach determines the overall return that a project makes from its discounted cash flows relative to the initial investment cash outflow. It ranks projects according to the size of their return. Finally, the NPV approach ranks projects in terms of their overall absolute return in present value terms.

The NPV method is deemed to be the most appropriate by academics; the payback method (Lefley, 1994) and the IRR methods are commonly used by manufacturing companies in practice (see Arnold and Hatzopoulos, 2000; Pike, 1996; Drury, Braund, Osborne and Tayles, 1993), with the payback method being the most popular. Many companies use the payback period approach as an initial screening device and then use more sophisticated methods thereafter to differentiate between the screened projects. Arnold and Hatzopoulos (2000) found that most large and medium-sized UK companies use a combination of techniques, including NPV and IRR.

It would be easy to get carried away by the techniques on offer and to assume that the investment decision is a black or white affair. However, this is not the case. The techniques should be used in conjunction with other information. The following questions might highlight other factors that need to be considered:

- Are the selected projects consistent with the overall objectives of the company? What are the absolute values of the projects?
- Are any of the projects so large that they cause an imbalance in the diversification of projects within the company? If so, is risk affected?
- Does the company have the capacity, resources and expertise for the project?
- Can the required finance be obtained?
- Will the management be able to manage the larger entity appropriately?
- Will there be any implications for the other operating activities of the company?
- Is there any environmental, societal or governance risk associated with the project?

In addition to these more strategic issues, there are limitations to the appraisal process. Expected cash flows are estimates and the discount rate – though calculated scientifically – is subjective. Gut feeling, though completely unscientific, may play a larger role in practice than is documented. This may also be quite dangerous, as gut feeling might lead to bias in estimates that are used in project appraisal.

EXAMINATION STANDARD QUESTION: NPV CALCULATION

Sultan Ltd, an Irish manufacturing company, is currently considering an investment in a new product. The investment would involve the following costs and revenues:

1. An immediate purchase of capital equipment costing €/£1.5 million. This equipment is expected to have a residual value in five years of €/£150,000, and will be depreciated at 20% per annum on a straight-line basis. Capital allowances can be claimed at 20% per annum on a straight-line basis.
2. Sales of the new product will be €/£1.9 million for five years. Sultan earns a contribution of 45% on sales.
3. The new product would require that a project manager be recruited at a salary of €/£50,000 per annum and the company will have to make annual contributions of €/£12,000 to fund the manager's pension benefits.
4. The new product will require an investment of €/£300,000 in working capital at the start of the project, with a further €/£40,000 at the start of Year 2.
5. Annual fixed overheads relating to the new product are estimated at €/£65,000 and in addition there will be an allocation of fixed overheads of €/£50,000.
6. Research and development costs of €/£120,000 have been incurred already. Staff training costs of €/£30,000 are projected in Year 1 of the project.
7. Sultan pays corporation tax at a rate of 12.5%, payable on a current year basis.
8. Sultan has a cost of capital of 12%.
9. The new product is not similar to the company's existing product range and offers an exciting diversification opportunity for Sultan.

Requirement

(a) Indicate whether Sultan should proceed with the new product, based on the NPV criteria.

12 Marks

(b) Compute the payback period.

3 Marks

(c) Identify and comment on any other matters which should be considered in making this investment decision.

5 Marks

Total 20 Marks

(Based on Chartered Accountants Ireland, CAP 1, Finance, Summer 2012, Q1)

Solution

(a) **NPV**

NPV Schedule

Year	Equip.	Working capital	Operating cash flows (W1)	Tax (W2)	Total cash flow	Discount factor	Present value
	€/£000	€/£000	€/£000	€/£000	€/£000	(12%)	€/£000
0	(1,500)	(300)			(1,800)	1.000	(1,800)
1	–	(40)	698	(49.75)	608.25	0.893	543.2
2	–	–	728	(53.5)	674.5	0.797	537.6
3	–	–	728	(53.5)	674.5	0.712	480.2
4	–	–	728	(53.5)	674.5	0.636	429.0
5	150	340	728	(72.25)	1,145.75	0.567	649.6
						NPV	839.6

Therefore, with a positive NPV (at 12%) of €/£839,600, the project is acceptable.

W1: Cash flows from operating activities

Year	Contribution*	Manager	Overheads	Training staff	Operating cash flows
	€/£000	€/£000	€/£000	€/£000	€/£000
1	855	(62)	(65)	(30)	698
2	855	(62)	(65)	–	728
3	855	(62)	(65)	–	728
4	855	(62)	(65)	–	728
5	855	(62)	(65)	–	728

* €/£1,900,000 × 45% = €/£855,000

W2: Taxation

Capital allowances are 20% straight-line basis = €/£1,500,000 × 20% = €/£300,000 per annum for four years.

In Year 5 a further €/£300,000 is claimable, but Sultan expects to sell the asset for €/£150,000, so a balancing allowance of €/£150,000 will arise in that year.

Year	Operating cash flow €/£000	Capital allowance/ balancing allowance €/£000	Taxable cash flow €/£000	Taxation @12.5% €/£000
1	698	(300)	398	(49.75)
2	728	(300)	428	(53.5)
3	728	(300)	428	(53.5)
4	728	(300)	428	(53.5)
5	728	(150)	578	(72.25)

(b) **Payback period**

Year	Total cash flow €/£000	Cumulative cash flows €/£000
0	(1,800)	(1,800)
1	608.25	(1,191.75)
2	674.5	(517.25)
3	674.5	
4	674.5	
5	1,145.75	

$$\text{Discounted payback period} = 2 \text{ years} + \frac{€/£517{,}250 \times 365}{€/£674{,}500} = 2 \text{ years and } 280 \text{ days}$$

(c) **Other matters to be considered:**

(i) Will trained staff require a salary increase?
(ii) Has the new machinery needed extra space and have the additional costs been factored into the estimates?
(iii) How reliable are the sales and cost estimates?
(iv) The dissimilar product/diversification may alter the business risk. This may change the cost of equity with consequent change of WACC, so the 12% WACC may not represent the marginal cost of capital.

(v) Does Sultan have sufficient production/marketing skill/expertise to produce and sell this new product?
(vi) How will competitors respond to the new product – is the anticipated sale price vulnerable to price competition?

Key Terms

Accounting rate of return (ARR)
Annual investment allowance
Annuity
Annuity factor
Apportioned costs
Average annual profit
Average capital investment
Balancing allowance
Balancing charge
Basic discount rate
Breakeven analysis
Capital allowances
Discount factor
Discount rate
Discounted cash flow yield
Discounted cash flows
Discounted payback period
External investment
First year allowances
Future value (FV)
Hurdle rate
Incremental cash flows
Inflation
Internal investment
Internal rate of return (IRR)
Linearity assumption
Market discount rate
Money discount rate
Mutually exclusive projects
Net present value (NPV)
Nominal discount rate
Opportunity cash flow
Payback period method
Perpetuity
Present value (PV)
Real cash flows
Real discount rate
Relevant cash flows
Sunk costs
Time value of money
Weighted average cost of capital (WACC)
Written down allowances

REVIEW QUESTIONS

(See Suggested Solutions to Review Questions in **Appendix B**.)

Question 2.1

Outline the difficulties inherent in the evaluation of projects.

Question 2.2

List briefly the advantages and disadvantages of using the ARR method for project appraisal.

Question 2.3

List the advantages and disadvantages of using the payback period method for project appraisal.

Question 2.4

YZ Ltd is considering investing in a new machine costing €/£200,000. The machine will produce 10,000 products each year for the next five years. The company has a contract for the next five years for the sale of the products. This contract fixes the price of the product at €/£20 per item.

Production will cost €/£12 per item in the first year. This is expected to increase by 10% each year due to competition for supply. YZ's cost of capital is 12% per annum.

Requirement Should the company undertake the project? (Assume no inflation; ignore taxation.)

Question 2.5

YZ Ltd faces the same situation as outlined in Question 2.4 above, but in this instance they are informed that inflation of 5% is expected each year and the real cost of capital is 12%. The cost of capital has not been adjusted to take account of the expected inflation.

Requirement Given this additional information, should YZ accept the project?

Question 2.6

What is the difference between the nominal/money discount rate and the real discount rate?

Question 2.7 Cassanova Ltd

(a) The selection of a discount rate for project appraisal can be a difficult issue. Various methods have been put forward, as follows:
- a single company cut-off rate based on the company's overall WACC; or
- a system of multiple cut-off rates that reflects the risk of each particular investment; or
- a rate that reflects the specific cost of funding each project.

Requirement Comment on the suitability of each of the methods above and recommend which method would, in your opinion, be most suitable for appraising a new project.

7 Marks

(b) The directors of Cassanova Ltd are considering a new project. Their company policy is to select a discount rate that reflects the risk of each individual project.

The financial details of the project are as follows:

Project R123: Initial cost

	€/£
Plant and machinery	1,500,000
Equipment	500,000
Working capital	40,000
Market research	200,000

Annual pre-tax cash flows

Year 1	**Year 2**	**Year 3**	**Year 4**
€/£400,000	€/£620,000	€/£960,000	€/£1,000,000

Additional information:

1. The fee for market research has already been paid, but the company intends spreading the cost over the four-year life of the project.
2. Capital allowances are allowed at a rate of 25% per annum (straight-line basis) on all plant, machinery and equipment.
3. Corporation tax is 10% per annum and is paid one year in arrears.
4. Included in the annual cash flows is a figure of €/£15,000 per annum, which is the interest charge on the loan for financing the project.

5. The level of working capital investment is not expected to change for the duration of the project. The plant, machinery and equipment purchased for the project will be sold in Year 5 for €/£40,000.
6. The WACC of the company is 12%, but this new project is considered to be significantly more risky. A more appropriate discount rate is considered to be 18%. The project is being financed by a 9% long-term loan.

Requirement Calculate the NPV and IRR of the new project and recommend whether the company should proceed with the project, or not.

11 Marks

Total 18 Marks

(Based on Chartered Accountants Ireland, MABF II, Summer 2000, Q6)

CHALLENGING QUESTIONS

(Suggested Solutions to Challenging Questions are available through your lecturer.)

Question 2.1 Boot Ltd (Level 1)

Boot Ltd, a drug manufacturer, is considering two mutually exclusive investment projects. Both projects involve the purchase of new production machinery with an estimated five-year life. The following data are available for each project.

	Alpha €/£000	**Beta €/£000**
Cost	(808)	(280)
Government capital grant receivable at end of Year 1	30	–
Annual operating cash flows, Years 1 to 5	250	–
Year 1	–	50
Year 2	–	100
Year 3	–	150
Year 4	–	125
Year 5	–	75
Estimated residential value at end of Year 5	178	28

The company is liable to corporation tax of 15% payable at the end of each current year. The machinery qualifies for tax capital allowances at 12.5% per year (straight-line) with a balancing allowance/charge on disposal.

The company operates a straight-line depreciation policy, and discounts cash flows at 14% per annum.

Requirement

(a) Calculate for each project:

(i) The accounting rate of return (average profit : initial cost of investment).

4 Marks

(ii) The simple (undiscounted) payback period.

3 Marks

(iii) The net present value at 14% discount.

4 Marks

(b) Indicate, with reasons, which, if any, of the two projects the directors should accept.

2 Marks

(c) Outline briefly the relative advantages of the above three methods of investment appraisal.

7 Marks

Total 20 Marks

(Based on Chartered Accountants Ireland, CAP 1, Finance, Summer 2010, Q1)

Question 2.2 Violin (Level 1)

You are a financial manager in a consultancy firm that specialises in providing advice to clients in corporate finance. You have been asked to review the following query:

Violin Limited plans to invest €/£115,000 immediately in machinery for its business. The machinery will be sold for €/£45,000 in four years' time. It is expected that the machine will generate revenue of €/£55,000 in the first year of operation. This will increase by 10% per annum thereafter. The operating margin is 40%.

The machine will be depreciated at a rate of 25% per annum on a straight-line basis. Violin Limited has a target rate of return of 16%.

Requirement

(a) Calculate the accounting rate of return (ARR) for the machine and advise Violin Limited whether or not it should proceed with the investment.

6 Marks

(Based on Chartered Accountants Ireland, CAP 1, Finance, Autumn 2017, Q6)

Question 2.3 Stynes (Level 1)

Stynes Ltd is considering the purchase of a new factory for €/£1.5 million. The new factory has a useful life of 50 years and will have an estimated value of €/£1.3 million in 10 years' time. The new factory would generate net annual cash flows of €/£210,000 per annum for the next 10 years.

Stynes must also fit out the new factory and is considering whether to use second-hand equipment or purchase brand new equipment. New equipment would cost €/£600,000. This equipment has a useful life of 10 years and a nil scrap value.

Stynes can, alternatively, use second-hand equipment from another factory it owns. This equipment was purchased two years ago for €/£500,000 and now has a book value of €/£400,000. The second-hand equipment would need to be replaced if it was used in the new factory and this would cost €/£450,000. It would cost €/£50,000 to transport this equipment to the new factory.

Stynes' cost of capital is 10% per annum.

Requirement

(a) Estimate the most cost-effective method to equip the new factory.

2 Marks

(b) Calculate the net present value (NPV) of operating the new factory and recommend whether this should proceed. (Ignore tax and inflation.)

6 Marks

(c) Explain how the inclusion of taxation allowances in your calculations might have impacted on your recommendation in part (b).

3 Marks

(d) Outline two important non-financial factors that should be considered in your investment decision and comment on their significance.

4 Marks
Total 15 Marks

(Based on Chartered Accountants Ireland, CAP 1, Finance, Autumn 2011, Q3)

Question 2.4 Cleantech (Level 1)

Cleantech Ltd is considering installing alternative energy generators in its premises for 20X4.

The premises are leased, with a major rent review scheduled for five years' time. Management considers it prudent to ignore any benefits of the alternative energy generators after five years due to the uncertainties involved.

The following information is available to assist in the evaluation of the project:

1. At present the factory energy bill for 20X3 is expected to total €/£300,000 and fuel prices are expected to increase by 12% per year.
2. If the proposed alternative energy generators were to be installed, the equipment is expected to reduce Cleantech's energy bills by about 20% each year.
3. If the project goes ahead, a planning permission application will cost €/£15,000 and the generators will cost €/£145,000 installed and tested. The equipment cost of €/£145,000 would qualify for tax capital allowances of 12.5% per annum calculated on a straight-line basis and, assuming no residual value at the end of five years, a balancing tax allowance would be received.
4. Cleantech is liable to corporation tax of 20% payable at the end of the year in which the profits arise.
5. Cleantech would depreciate the costs of the generators, including the planning application costs of €/£15,000, over five years on a straight-line basis.
6. Cleantech has an estimated weighted average cost of capital of 12%.

Requirement

(a) Calculate the following:

(i) the payback period;

3 Marks

(ii) the net present value;

7 Marks

(iii) the approximate internal rate of return for the project.

6 Marks

(b) Make a recommendation as to whether the proposed project is acceptable and indicate which of the above appraisal techniques is most relevant to the decision.

4 Marks
Total 20 Marks

(Based on Chartered Accountants Ireland, CAP 1, Finance, Autumn 2008, Q1)

Question 2.5 Maple (Level 1)

Maple Ltd is evaluating a capital expenditure project, having already spent €/£32,000 on research and development. The board of directors must now decide whether to start production or not.

The details are as follows:

1. The project involves purchasing nearby old industrial premises for €/£170,000. The premises are in fairly poor condition and would probably need to be disposed of for €/£30,000 in five years' time to avoid incurring major repair costs. The premises are for sale by a firm of auctioneers, but Maple has been approached directly by the owner (Mr Twitch), who is anxious to sell and avoid paying the 2% auctioneer's fee. Also, the owner of the industrial premises has an unsecured loan to his business and wishes to use the cash proceeds from the sale of the premises to repay his loan before a likely liquidation of his company, Twitch Ltd, as the tax life of the premises is expired there will be no capital allowances available to Maple.
2. Sales are expected to be €/£190,000 per annum for the first two years, then €/£70,000 per annum for Years 3 to 5.
3. With existing spare capacity, the project would not require any additional plant or machinery.
4. Cost of sales is 50% of sales revenue.
5. The project would require working capital of €/£9,000 until the end of the five years.
6. The company is liable to 20% corporation tax, payable in the year in which the profit is earned.
7. The company estimates that its cost of capital is 10%.
8. If the development project does not proceed, it could be sold by Maple to the government of Burkistania, a foreign military dictatorship, for €/£100,000 less a customary cash fee for 'consultancy advice' of €/£70,000, payable to the ruling president's Swiss bank account.

Requirement

(a) Evaluate the project by:
   (i) Calculating the simple payback.

2 Marks

   (ii) Calculating the project's net present value at 10%.

8 Marks

(b) Outline any additional non-financial matters which need to be considered in reaching a final decision.

5 Marks
Total 15 Marks

(Based on Chartered Accountants Ireland, CAP 1, Finance, Autumn 2009, Q3)

Question 2.6 Clean 4 U (Level 1)

Clean 4 U Limited operates in the cleaning sector. Clean has decided to expand its domestic and commercial cleaning service business. Marc Ltd has offered Clean a five-year contract for cleaning their call centre offices. Clean is considering taking on this contract and its management considers the following information to be relevant:

1. New equipment costing €/£900,000 will be required by Clean at the beginning of the contract. It is expected that this equipment will have a residual value of €/£150,000 at the end of the five years.
2. The new equipment will be depreciated on a straight-line basis over the five years.
3. Clean will finance the purchase of the equipment by way of a bank loan. The loan will carry an annual interest rate of 5%.
4. Clean invests heavily in its employees and has spent €/£50,000 to date in respect of employee training. If the contract with Marc proceeds, then additional training will be required in the first year at a cost of €/£25,000.
5. Clean will earn revenue of €/£750,000 in the first year of the contract. It is expected that this will grow by 10% each year as Marc adds additional office space.

6. Consumable cleaning products will cost €/£50,000 in each year of the contract. Other variable costs will amount to 10% of annual revenue for the duration of the contract.
7. Clean will require ten new employees in the first year of the contract, and an additional two new employees each subsequent year for the duration of the contract. Each employee will initially receive an annual salary of €/£25,000. Clean's employees have negotiated a 3% salary increase each year commencing in the second year.
8. Investment of €/£100,000 in working capital will be required at the outset of the contract and a further €/£50,000 will be required at the end of the second year. It is expected that all of the working capital will be recovered at the end of the contract.
9. Proclean Ltd owns all of the ordinary share capital of Clean and charges Clean a management fee of €/£100,000 per annum.
10. Clean pays annual corporation tax of 25%. Payment is made in the same year as the liability arises. The new equipment qualifies for capital allowances on a straight-line basis over its five-year life.
11. Clean has a nominal cost of capital of 10%.

Requirement

(a) Calculate the net present value (NPV) of Clean's proposed cleaning contract. Where appropriate, explain the reason for the exclusion of any particular item.

11 Marks
Presentation 1 Mark

(b) Explain why inflation should be considered when appraising an investment project.

2 Marks

(c) Calculate, assuming an annual inflation rate of 3%, Clean's real cost of capital.

2 Marks

(d) At the conclusion of this contract, Marc plans to relocate its call centres overseas. Outline FOUR non-financial factors that Marc should consider before committing to this course of action.

4 Marks
Total 20 Marks

(Based on Chartered Accountants Ireland, CAP 1, Finance, Autumn 2019, Q2)

Question 2.7 Magenta (Level 2)

Magenta Ltd has spent the last two years developing a new type of domestic thermometer. The company has incurred expenditure of over €/£3 million to date in researching the product. The thermometer is ready for commercial production.

Magenta is now trying to decide between two mutually exclusive options for the company. The options are to both manufacture and sell the product itself or to license out the manufacture and sales of the product to a large multinational company. In each case the product will have an estimated useful life of three years.

The financial details of each option are as follows:

Option 1: Manufacture and sell the product

Sales	**Year 20X3**	**Year 20X4**	**Year 20X5**
Units (000)	50	90	160
Price per unit (€/£)	40	40	30

Materials The estimated material cost for one thermometer is €/£10. However, this is expected to fall to €/£6 in Year 3. Magenta has some existing inventory on hand that will cover 80% of the first year's production. This inventory had originally cost €/£300,000, has a replacement cost of €/£400,000, and could be sold immediately to another company for €/£325,000. If Magenta does not proceed with this venture, this material could not be used in any other project undertaken by the company.

Labour The labour force required to produce the thermometer will comprise six employees who are currently working on another project. If Magenta proceeds with the manufacturing option, this other project will be postponed and the estimated loss in contribution from postponement would be €/£50,000 per annum. The six employees are currently paid €/£28,000 each per annum. If transferred to this project, they will be awarded a pay increase of 10% per annum for each of the three years.

Capital outlay A special machine costing €/£1.2 million will be required to produce the thermometer. It will be purchased immediately, but will not be paid for until the end of Year 1. The machine is expected to be worth €/£250,000 at the end of the three years.

Working capital The total working capital investment for the period at the beginning of each year of the investment is as follows:

20X3 – €/£50,000; 20X4 – €/£70,000; 20X5 – €/£100,000

All working capital can be realised at the end of the life of the project.

Other costs Additional overheads (excluding depreciation) are estimated to be €/£0.5 million per annum. In addition, the marketing costs will be €/£500,000 per annum. There will be no money spent on marketing in Year 3. The project should also be allocated a 'fair share' (€/£20,000 per annum) of the company's general fixed administration costs, although these would not increase as a result of accepting the contract.

Capital allowances and taxation The machine will attract annual capital allowances of 20% on a straight-line basis. Corporation tax is 15% per annum and is payable one year in arrears. Corporation tax is charged on all profits.

Research and development costs It is the policy of the company to write-off research and development expenditure to the statement of profit or loss in the year in which it is incurred.

Option 2: Subcontract the manufacture and marketing of the product

Magenta could agree to another company manufacturing and marketing the product under licence. A multinational company has offered to enter into a licensing agreement with Magenta in return for a royalty fee of €/£4.50 per unit, payable at the end of each year. It is estimated that the annual number of units sold will be 10% higher if the multinational company manufactures and markets the product.

Magenta's cost of capital is 15%.

Requirement

(a) (i) Calculate the NPV for each option.
(ii) Explain, with reasons, which option should be selected by Magenta Ltd.

17 Marks

(b) Outline the principal advantages and disadvantages of using finance leases as a source of medium-term finance.

5 Marks
Total 22 Marks

(Based on Chartered Accountants Ireland, MABF II, Summer 2002, Q5)

Question 2.8 Trolak (Level 2)

Trolak Town, a club playing in a professional football league in Ireland, is considering signing the talented but eccentric goalkeeper Pablo Goodsavo, from a club in Spain. It is now the start of the new season and you have been asked to advise on the financial aspects of the transfer negotiations. At present the club, in common with many others in the same league, barely manages to break even, after expenses, in an average year. You have ascertained the following information.

Cost of Existing Players The existing players cost €/£1,450,000 in transfer fees.

'Gate' Receipts, Television Rights and Sponsorship The average home gate for the team is 15,000 people, 21 times a season and the entrance price is €/£12 per head. There is an existing squad of 22 players (some full-time and some part-time) and they earn on average €/£750 per week each. (Assume a 52-week year.)

Five of the games are normally televised live each season, earning €/£50,000 for the club on each occasion. The rights to show the delayed transmission highlights of the other games have been sold to a satellite broadcaster at €/£8,000 per game.

The directors now consider that, if an additional one-off spend of €/£200,000 is spent immediately on promotional activity, and with Goodsavo on the team, it will be possible to increase the number of spectators to 17,000 on average and to raise the entrance price to €/£14 per head.

If Goodsavo joins the club, a new sponsorship deal, to be agreed with a local company, would bring an additional €/£110,000 per annum in sponsorship revenue. In addition, the number of games televised live would increase from five to eight, but the revenue from the delayed transmission of highlights of these matches would no longer be available.

Grounds To cope with the increased attendance if Goodsavo joins, it will be necessary to spend €/£324,000 improving facilities at the grounds. This amount would be contracted for and paid immediately and capital allowances would be available on it at the rate of 25% per annum reducing balance.

Personal Terms and Further Implications Goodsavo is now 33 years old and the club proposes to offer him a three-year contract, after which he will again be a free agent, allowed to walk away from the club if he so wishes. It has been agreed with the Spanish club that the transfer fee will be paid immediately. Personal terms are yet to be agreed with Goodsavo, but his agent has indicated that he will require to be paid €/£78,000 in the first year, increasing at 5% per year compound for each of the years of his contract, plus a 'golden hello' of €/£100,000, payable immediately. The directors also estimate that the rest of the team will require a pay increase of 20% because more will now be expected of all of them.

Cost of Capital and Corporation Tax The cost of capital for Trolak is 13% and the rate of corporation tax (payable one year in arrears) is 34%.

Other Assumptions You may assume that, unless otherwise stated, all costs are to be paid in full and all revenues are received at the end of each year. Ignore the effect of capital allowances after Year 3. The 'golden hello' and the additional promotional expenditure are not tax deductible.

Requirement

(a) Assuming that the Spanish club will not accept less than €/£2,000,000 for Goodsavo, should Trolak sign him given that the decision is based on an incremental net present value analysis? Show your workings clearly.

16 Marks

(b) It is widely accepted that the payback period method of investment appraisal has little or no theoretical or academic justification as a means of investment appraisal. Yet in practice it seems that it is widely used by many companies. List briefly THREE reasons why the payback method is so popular as a method of investment appraisal, in spite of the lack of theoretical justification for its use.

6 Marks
Total 22 Marks

(Based on Chartered Accountants Ireland, MABF II, Autumn 2003, Q5)

Question 2.9 Brisk (Level 2)

You have recently been appointed Business Finance Director of Brisk Plc. The company is considering investing in the production of an electronic security device with an expected market life of four years. The previous Business Finance Director had undertaken an analysis of the proposed project. The main features of his analysis are shown below.

	Year 0 €/£000	**Year 1** €/£000	**Year 2** €/£000	**Year 3** €/£000	**Year 4** €/£000
Investment in depreciable assets	4,500	–	–	–	–
Investment in working capital	300	–	–	–	–
Sales		3,500	4,900	5,320	5,740
Materials		535	750	900	1,050
Labour		1,070	1,500	1,800	2,100
Variable overheads		50	100	100	100
Interest		576	576	576	576
Research costs		300	300	300	300
Depreciation		900	900	900	900
Total costs		3,431	4,126	4,576	5,026
Profit before tax		69	774	744	714
Taxation		24	271	260	250
Profit after tax		45	503	484	464

Additional information:

1. All of the above projected profits have been computed in terms of present-day costs and prices. However, due to inflation, variable overhead expenses and selling prices are expected to increase at a rate of 2% per annum, and material costs and labour are expected to increase by 5% per annum.
2. Capital allowances are allowed at a rate of 25% per annum on the reducing balance basis on all depreciable assets.
3. Corporation tax is 18% per annum and is paid one year in arrears.
4. The estimated scrap value of the assets at the end of Year 4 is nil.
5. The company has already incurred costs of €/£1.2 million in researching the product. The payment for this research is due in Year 1. It is the policy of the company to write off research costs to the statement of profit or loss over a four-year period.
6. The company's (nominal) required rate of return on all projects is 20%.

Requirement

(a) Calculate the relevant inflated net cash flows that would arise from this proposal for each of the four years.

12 Marks

(b) Calculate the NPV and the payback period for the investment and recommend, with reasons, whether the company should proceed with this investment.

5 Marks

(c) Outline briefly some of the limitations of the appraisal you have prepared above.

5 Marks

Total 22 Marks

(Based on Chartered Accountants Ireland, MABF II, Autumn 2004, Q5)

Question 2.10 Medicon (Level 2 – case study requiring knowledge of Chapter 13)

Background You are a partner in a 'Big 4' firm of chartered accountants that specialises in offering advice to high-growth companies, mainly in the pharmaceutical and technology sectors. One of your clients is Medicon Plc, a pharmaceutical company formed 10 years ago by a biochemistry graduate, Gerard Smith, who pioneered research into new techniques for diagnosing liver diseases. Smith subsequently patented a diagnostic kit that could be used to test for a variety of common liver complaints.

Medicon commenced trading in 20W5 (with Gerard Smith as managing director), when its testing kit received approval from the relevant health authorities in Ireland and the UK. The company grew quickly as local hospitals realised the convenience and simplicity of Medicon's product. The testing kit effectively replaced the need to send blood samples to hospital laboratories to diagnose liver illnesses, which consequently saved substantial amounts of hospital time, and resulted in significant cost savings.

Smith's ambition and enthusiasm were instrumental in driving the company forward. In 20X2 you were heavily involved in the decision to float Medicon on the stock exchange. Since then, Smith has continued to aggressively target new markets for the company's key product whilst maintaining a tight grasp on overhead costs. Medicon now provides liver testing kits to most of the main hospitals throughout Ireland and the UK. However, the company has recently become aware of plans by a foreign competitor to launch a similar liver testing kit in the Irish and UK markets within the next year.

Smith had foreseen this eventuality and, in recent years, Medicon has invested considerable resources in research and development (R&D) in an attempt to expand its innovative testing kit idea to the diagnosis of other ailments. The company will shortly introduce a new testing kit that can be used to diagnose kidney complaints. This new product is seen as a major growth area that will provide a platform for future expansion of the company.

Medicon is also considering investing in an additional new product to measure cholesterol levels. Details are now provided.

Investment Projects Gerard Smith has advised you that Medicon is currently considering investing in two separate projects, as follows:

1. New Cholesterol Testing Kit Medicon is considering commencing a new R&D project to develop a new testing kit to measure cholesterol levels. This would involve expenditure of €/£1 million per annum in the first two years (the first payment being made immediately), with a grant of €/£0.5 million to be received at the start of Year 2. The project is then estimated to generate additional after-tax profits of

€/£0.75 million per annum for the following four years. This investment is considered to have the same level of business risk as the company's existing liver testing product. Additional information in respect of Medicon is provided in Appendix I to this question.

2. Schoolweb Ltd Smith has recently held discussions with a friend, Michael Jones, who owns Schoolweb Ltd, an e-commerce company that sells a wide selection of children's schoolbooks via the internet. Schoolweb's turnover has grown rapidly since its formation in early 20X3, and Jones is keen to raise additional finance to fund a marketing campaign aimed at further increasing the awareness of its website which, in turn, should yield additional turnover. Consequently, he has offered Medicon the opportunity to invest in Schoolweb in return for an agreed shareholding in the company.

Schoolweb is considered to operate in a higher risk industry than the pharmaceutical sector and, like many similar e-commerce companies, is currently making losses. However, revenues are projected to continue to grow significantly over the next three years, with profitability likely to be achieved within that period. Jones has undertaken to provide a Business Plan showing projected earnings and cash flow over the next three years, which can be used by Smith to determine if Medicon should consider investing in Schoolweb.

Given the high-risk sector in which Schoolweb operates, Smith has asked you for advice on how to appraise the investment. In particular, he is keen to know what rate should be used to discount any projected cash flows. Additional financial information in relation to Schoolweb is set out in Appendix I to this question.

Flotation Michael Jones has indicated to Smith that he is keen to float Schoolweb at some point within the next couple of years. This would provide the long-term finance necessary to fund the increased size of operations that are projected over the coming years. However, given that the company is currently making losses and has only been incorporated for two years, Jones considers that Schoolweb currently does not have the necessary track record to contemplate undertaking a flotation. Given your experience of the flotation of Medicon and of the technology sector in general, Smith has asked you to prepare a brief report on the feasibility of floating Schoolweb.

Requirement Prepare a report to the Managing Director addressing each of the following issues:

(a) Calculate Medicon's weighted average cost of capital (WACC) and then advise on whether the company should proceed with the new R&D project to develop the cholesterol testing kit. Outline any limitations arising from the use of the WACC for the evaluation of investment projects.

23 Marks

(b) Outline briefly any significant qualitative issues that should be considered in the decision to undertake the cholesterol testing kit project.

8 Marks

(c) Determine a suitable discount rate that could be used to appraise the cash flows (to be provided by Michael Jones) relating to the investment in Schoolweb, outlining clearly the rationale for your approach.

9 Marks

(***Note:*** assume that both projects could be financed in such a way as to leave Medicon's existing financial risk unchanged, and that Schoolweb carries a similar level of gearing to Medicon.)

(d) Given Michael Jones' decision to float Schoolweb within the next couple of years, advise on whether you consider flotation feasible, outlining the specific reasons for your answer.

10 Marks

Total 50 Marks

(Based on Chartered Accountants Ireland, MABF, Autumn 2001, Q1)

Appendix I to Question 2.10

Financial Information on Medicon Plc

Extracts from Medicon Plc's Statement of Financial Position as at 31 July 20X5

	Notes	€/£000
ASSETS		
Non-current assets		20,000
Net working capital		6,500
Total assets		26,500
EQUITY, RESERVES AND LIABILITIES		
Equity and reserves		
Equity shares (3 million €/£1 shares)		3,000
Share premium		1,500
Revenue reserves		10,500
		15,000
Non-current liabilities		
10% irredeemable debenture stock	(3)	3,000
Long-term bank loan	(4)	5,000
11% preference shares	(5)	2,000
		10,000
Current liabilities		
Bank overdraft		1,500
Total equity, reserves and liabilities		26,500

Additional information for Medicon:

1. New equity could be issued in Medicon at a discount of 40c/p to the current share price of €/£5.75 (cum-div.).
2. Medicon has declared a dividend of 50c/p per equity share for the year ended 31 July 20X5, and dividends are expected to increase at an annual rate of 3%.
3. Debenture interest has just been paid and the debenture stock has a current market value of 85%.
4. Medicon currently has a 10-year bank loan of €/£5 million at a fixed interest rate of 8% per annum. Interest on any additional long-term debt would be payable at an interest rate of 9% per annum.
5. The preference shares have a current market value of 105%.
6. Medicon's overdraft is used for short-term working capital requirements and is not considered to be a long-term source of funds.
7. Corporation tax is expected to be 25% for the foreseeable future.

Additional information for Schoolweb:

1. Schoolweb is considered to operate in the internet sector with a beta risk factor of 1.7, compared to 1.2 for the pharmaceutical sector in which Medicon operates.
2. The average level of gearing in the internet industry may be assumed to be the same as Medicon's level of gearing.
3. The risk-free rate of return is currently 3% and the average market rate of return is 10%.

3

Capital Investment Appraisal for Special Decisions and Risk

Learning Objectives

Upon completing this chapter, readers should be able to:

- explain the difference between hard and soft capital rationing;
- evaluate single-period investment decisions under conditions of capital rationing (when investment projects are divisible, non-divisible and mutually exclusive);
- evaluate asset replacement decisions, including when and how often to replace assets;
- explain the difference between risk and uncertainty in the context of capital investment appraisal decisions;
- discuss factors that cause risk and uncertainty;
- explain the additional risks that are associated with investing in projects in foreign countries;
- evaluate projects that are subject to risk using sensitivity analysis and probability theory;
- list the advantages and disadvantages of each of these evaluation techniques; and
- discuss scenario and simulation analysis, including the use of information technology in assessing risk in capital projects.

INTRODUCTION

The techniques covered in the last chapter are useful when the only factor to consider during project appraisal is the project itself as a one-off event. However, in practice the economic environment may have to be taken into account – particularly when there is a shortage of finance (i.e. capital rationing), or the decision may involve investment cycles, such as asset replacement decisions, or decisions on projects with different periods that will need to be renewed several times to cover a longer period to that obtained from the first investment. The first part of this chapter considers some of the specific difficulties underlying project appraisal (e.g. capital rationing, mutually exclusive projects and multi-period projects). The second part of the chapter focuses on capital investment appraisal and risk. Capital investment appraisal techniques should play a part in an overall strategic investment plan. The techniques are mechanical and should be used as aids that inform management decision-making, not make decisions for managers. They should not lead directly to an 'accept' or 'reject' decision. A lot of background work has to be undertaken in the stages prior to a project's financial evaluation. For example, the investment ideas have to be generated and formulated into a plan. Data have to be collected about cash flows, etc. At this stage, the ideas and plan should be reviewed for viability, before more formal capital investment appraisal takes place. It is also at this stage that the risks or uncertainties in respect of estimated cash flows of a project are assessed and projects are screened before being submitted for authorisation.

This chapter explains risk and its relationship to return. The techniques that are used to account for risk in the appraisal process include manipulation of the input variables (using, for example, sensitivity analysis and scenario analysis) and the use of statistics in the evaluation of various projects with differing predicted outcomes, given the chance of the occurrence of that cash flow being known. Finally, an overview of other factors that can cause risk, particularly risk associated with foreign-based capital investments, is outlined.

CAPITAL RATIONING

The general rule when deciding on whether or not to invest in capital projects is that it is in equity holders' best interests to select all projects with a positive net present value (NPV); however, this is not always possible. **Capital rationing** occurs when a company has a restricted supply of cash available for investment purposes. In these circumstances a business finance manager has to decide which capital projects, from a pool of possibilities, to invest in. There are two types of capital rationing: hard capital rationing and soft capital rationing.

Hard Capital Rationing

Hard capital rationing occurs when the market places a restriction on the funds available for investment. External restrictions may be as a result of a company being too heavily geared. High gearing makes it difficult to raise more debt and will also make an equity issue prohibitively costly. Another influence may be the condition of the stock market. If it is low, a share issue would be undervalued; the result is that current equity-holder value would be damaged. In addition, the size of the finance requirement may negate equity as an option, as equity distributions are costly and need to be of significant size to make them worthwhile (the same applies for market bond finance). Lastly, the project itself may limit funding – if it is deemed to be very risky, potential financiers may be put off.

Soft Capital Rationing

Soft capital rationing occurs when internal management decides to place a restriction on the level of funds that should be invested in capital projects. The most common reason for placing a limit on the amount that can be invested each year is the wish of management to maintain the capital structure of the company as it is. Management may not want to raise more capital from the stock market or bond markets. Raising funds is expensive, time consuming and may have consequences for the value of a company due to changes in capital structure and risk profile. There is also the need to have controlled growth – ensuring that a project's objectives are congruent with the company as a whole and are undertaken without overtrading or over-stretching a company's resources and organisational structure.

Restrictions may also be put in place by parent companies in an attempt to maintain a portfolio of balanced projects, which can be more easily managed.

CHOOSING AMONG ALTERNATIVE PROJECTS

A common approach cannot be adopted when evaluating capital projects under conditions of capital rationing. Three different scenarios may influence the method of evaluation adopted. In the first instance projects may be **divisible**, in that it is possible to invest in a whole capital project and part of another; or they may **not be divisible**, in which case two smaller projects with a higher combined NPV will provide more added value for equity holders relative to one large project that has the highest NPV for each unit of scarce resource. Finally, projects may be **mutually exclusive**. This means that a manager has the option to invest in one project **or** another project, but not both.

Divisible Projects that are Independent of Each Other

It might seem that the most appropriate approach is to rank projects according to the size of their NPVs. However, this does not result in the most efficient use of limited funds. A more appropriate method is to maximise the NPV per scarce resource (euro/Sterling). This is represented by the following formula:

$$\textbf{PV per euro/Sterling of scarce resource} = \frac{\textbf{NPV of inflows}}{\textbf{Initial outlay}}$$

or

$$\frac{\textbf{NPV of inflows + Initial outlay}}{\textbf{Initial outlay}}$$

This ratio is calculated for each project with a positive NPV and ranked into a **profitability index**. The projects with the highest value in the index should be accepted, to the point at which the funds available for investment are exhausted.

The calculation is straightforward when appraising investments that are divisible. This is illustrated in the following example.

WORKED EXAMPLE 3.1: CAPITAL RATIONING – DIVISIBLE INVESTMENTS

Enero Ltd has a maximum of €/£800,000 available to invest in new projects. Three possibilities have emerged and the business finance manager has calculated the NPV for each of them, as follows (you are informed that the projects are divisible):

Investment	**Initial cash outlay €/£**	**NPV €/£**
X	540,000	100,000
Y	600,000	150,000
Z	260,000	58,000

Requirement Which investments/combination of investments should the company invest in?

Solution

As the funds are restricted, the normal NPV rule of accepting investments with the highest NPVs first cannot be adopted. As the projects are divisible, a profitability index can be utilised to provide the most beneficial mix of investments for the company.

Investment	Calculation	PV per €/£ (profitability index)	Ranking
X	(€/£640,000 ÷ €/£540,000)	1.185	3
Y	(€/£750,000 ÷ €/£600,000)	1.250	1
Z	(€/£318,000 ÷ €/£260,000)	1.223	2

Therefore, Enero Ltd should invest €/£600,000 into investment Y, earning €/£150,000, and €/£200,000 into investment Z, earning €/£44,615 [(€/£200,000 ÷ €/£260,000) × €/£58,000], resulting in a total NPV of €/£194,615 from the €/£800,000 investment.

Non-divisible Projects

When projects are not divisible the profitability index approach should not be adopted. Projects should be ranked in order of the size of their NPV and the combination of projects resulting in the highest overall NPV, for the limited finance that is available, should be selected. The above example is utilised again to show the result were this condition to hold.

Worked Example 3.2: Capital Rationing – Non-divisible Investments

Enero Ltd has a maximum of €/£800,000 available to invest in new projects. Three possibilities have emerged and the business finance manager has calculated the NPV for each of them, as follows (you are informed that the projects are non-divisible).

Investment	Initial cash outlay €/£	NPV €/£
X	540,000	100,000
Y	600,000	150,000
Z	260,000	58,000

Requirement Which investments/combination of investments should the company invest in?

Solution

In this instance the absolute maximum amount of total NPV that can be achieved from an investment, or combination of investments, should determine which to invest in. Two possibilities arise: either to invest in project Y, costing €/£600,000, or in both projects X and Z, costing €/£800,000. The total NPVs resulting from each possibility are detailed below.

Project	Total NPV €/£
Y	150,000
X and Z	158,000

Therefore, Enero Ltd should invest the full €/£800,000 into investments X and Z, as this will provide it with a total NPV of €/£158,000, whereas investment in project Y will yield a lower NPV of €/£150,000.

Mutually Exclusive Projects

When projects are **mutually exclusive** they are competing with each other for the funds available. For example, there may be two different machines from different suppliers that are suitable for manufacturing one product. A company seeking the investment is only interested in one machine. This company may have a budget of available investment funds for capital projects, some of which has to be used to purchase one of the two machines and the remainder invested in other projects. In this case the decision will be based on an evaluation of the mutually exclusive projects combined with the non-divisible projects. The approach to take is to compare the various combinations available and select the combination resulting in the greatest NPV. For example, four possible projects may be available, but three of these are considered mutually exclusive. In this instance the NPV of the fourth project should be combined with each of the other three and then the combination with the highest resulting NPV selected.

Worked Example 3.3: Capital Rationing – Mutually Exclusive Investments that are Non-divisible

Enero Ltd has a maximum of €/£800,000 available to invest in new projects. Five possibilities have emerged and the business finance manager has calculated the NPV for each of them as follows (you are informed that the projects are non-divisible).

Investment	Initial cash outlay €/£	NPV €/£
V	260,000	54,000
W	240,000	40,000
X	500,000	100,000
Y	560,000	140,000
Z	270,000	58,000

Requirement Which investments/combination of investments should the company invest in, given that investments V, W and Z are mutually exclusive?

Solution

In this instance the absolute maximum amount of NPV that can be achieved from an investment, or combination of investments, should determine which to invest in, given the €/£800,000 capital limit. The decision is complicated further by the fact that the company can only invest in V, W or Z.

There are four possibilities. Enero Ltd can invest in V and X, in W and X, in W and Y, or in X and Z. The combination that results in the largest NPV should be selected.

Project	Amount invested €/£	Total NPV €/£
V and X	760,000	154,000
W and X	740,000	140,000
W and Y	800,000	180,000
X and Z	770,000	158,000

Therefore, Enero Ltd should invest the full €/£800,000 in projects W and Y as this will provide it with a total NPV of €/£180,000.

PROJECTS WITH UNEQUAL LIVES

Assessing capital projects that are **multi-period** requires a special approach as an incorrect decision may be made when deciding between two projects where one has a long life and the other a short life. In these instances, the project with the long life is likely to have a higher NPV and be accepted; however, it is likely that another project will be started when the short-term project has completed. If this future project has a positive NPV, then it should influence the decision at the outset. One method to deal with unequal lives is to convert the NPV to annual equivalent present values.

Equivalent Annual Annuity Approach

The **equivalent annual annuity approach** converts the NPV of a project into an annual cash annuity that extends for the expected duration of a project. This is calculated for each project and the project with the highest annual annuity is selected. The annual annuity equivalent of the NPV of a project can be determined using the following formula:

$$\textbf{Annual annuity equivalent of the NPV} = \frac{\textbf{NPV}}{\textbf{Annuity factor}}$$

This approach can be utilised to assess projects with unequal lives, as highlighted in the next example.

Worked Example 3.4: Unequal Lives – Equivalent Annual Annuity Approach

Enero Ltd can invest in one of two competing projects. Its current cost of capital is 10%. The cash flows relating to each project are detailed as follows:

Year	Investment X cash flows €/£	Investment Y cash flows €/£
0	(50,000)	(70,000)
1	25,000	30,000
2	35,000	40,000
3	–	15,500

Requirement Which of the two projects should Enero Ltd invest in? (Ignore inflation and tax.)

Solution

In this instance the **equivalent annual annuity approach** will be utilised to choose the most appropriate investment:

	Investment X			Investment Y		
Time	**Cash flows €/£**	**Discount factor (10%)**	**Present value €/£**	**Cash flows €/£**	**Discount factor (10%)**	**Present value €/£**
0	(50,000)	1.000	(50,000)	(70,000)	1.000	(70,000)
1	25,000	0.909	22,725	30,000	0.909	27,270
2	35,000	0.826	28,910	40,000	0.826	33,040
				15,500	0.751	11,640
		NPV	1,635		*NPV*	1,950

The equivalent annual annuity is: €/£942 [€/£1,635 ÷ 1.736 (two-year annuity factor at 10%)].

The equivalent annual annuity is: €/£784 [€/£1,950 ÷ 2.486 (three-year annuity factor at 10%)].

Investment X is best as it has the highest equivalent annual annuity cash inflow of €/£942.

ASSET REPLACEMENT DECISIONS

The replacement of company assets is a more complicated decision than it would initially seem. Certain assets have the following cost and revenue life-cycle pattern: in the early years the asset is likely to be more productive, contributing more to revenue; whereas in later years the asset is more likely to require maintenance and repair, resulting in increased costs, including down time. In addition, as an asset ages, its resale value reduces. Therefore, these increasing costs have to be balanced with the cost associated with buying a new asset. An asset should be replaced when:

$$b + c < a$$

where a is the running costs associated with owning the current asset; b is the replacement cost of the asset; and c is the running costs associated with owning the new asset.

Identical Assets

When assets are being replaced with identical assets, the approach should be to identify the replacement cycle. A **replacement cycle** is the period of time an asset should be kept, before being replaced by a new asset. This can be determined using the equivalent annual cost. The **equivalent annual cost** focuses on the present value of the costs of operating the asset in yearly terms, which can be obtained using the following equation:

$$\textbf{Equivalent annual cost} = \frac{\textbf{NPV}}{\textbf{Annuity factor}}$$

When the equivalent annual cost is minimised, this is the optimum replacement cycle. This method is simple, but it cannot be used where there is inflation.

The following example shows the calculation of a replacement cycle using the equivalent annual cost.

WORKED EXAMPLE 3.5: ASSET REPLACEMENT CYCLE

Enero Ltd has a machine which produces widgets. The machine costs €/£600,000 to replace. The following yearly costs and possible re-sale values have been provided in respect of the machine for the next four years:

Year	Realisable value €/£	Repair costs €/£
1	360,000	24,000
2	300,000	34,000
3	260,000	50,000
4	200,000	60,000

Enero Ltd's current cost of capital is 14%.

Requirement When should Enero Ltd replace its machine? (Ignore inflation and tax.)

Solution

The first step is to calculate the alternative replacement cycles, ranging from one year to four years, and then to compare the outcomes using the equivalent annual cost.

	Replace yearly		*Replace every two years*		*Replace every three years*		*Replace every four years*	
Year	**Cash flow €/£000**	**NPV (14%) €/£000**	**Cash flow €/£000**	**NPV (14%) €/£000**	**Cash flow €/£000**	**NPV (14%) €/£000**	**Cash flow €/£000**	**NPV (14%) €/£000**
0	(600)	(600)	(600)	(600)	(600)	(600)	(600)	(600)
1	336	294	(24)	(21)	(24)	(21)	(24)	(21)
2			266	205	(34)	(26)	(34)	(26)
3					210	142	(50)	(34)
4							140	83
NPV		(306)		(416)		(505)		(598)
Annuity factor		0.877		1.647		2.322		*2.914*
Equivalent cost	€/£306,000 / 0.877		€/£416,000 / 1.647		€/£505,000 / 2.322		€/£599,000 / *2.914*	
Annual equivalent cost (rounded)	(€/£349,000)		(€/£253,000)		(€/£217,000)		(€/£205,000)	

The equivalent annual cost is lowest for a four-year cycle (€/£205,000). Therefore, the machine should be replaced every four years.

Different Assets

In some situations an asset will be replaced by a different asset. In these circumstances the focus is on when to replace the asset, not on how often to replace it. The first step in this decision-making process is to determine the **replacement cycle period**. Then, using the minimum cost identified, calculate the present value in perpetuity (this should reflect the cost of owning the machine). Finally, compare the present value of the costs and benefits for each time period. The asset should be replaced in the year where the present value represents the lowest cost. This is portrayed using the following example:

Worked Example 3.6: Replacement with a Different Asset

In the last example, the optimum replacement cycle for a machine was determined for Enero Ltd as being four years with an equivalent annual cost of €/£205,000. This machine is now assumed to be brand new and is considered to be the replacement for an existing machine, which is quite different. The realisable value and repair costs for the existing machine are as follows:

Year	Realisable value €/£	Repair costs €/£
0	250,000	–
1	230,000	69,500
2	150,000	77,000
3	70,000	109,000

Enero Ltd's current cost of capital is 14%.

Requirement When should Enero Ltd replace its existing machine with the new machine? (Ignore inflation and tax.)

Solution

This involves comparing the present value cost of replacing the old machine in each of the four years with the new machine and selecting the option with the lowest overall present value cost. The equivalent annual cost of the new machine was calculated in **Worked Example 3.5** as being €/£205,000. The present value of this continual expected annual outflow in perpetuity is €/£1,464,286 (i.e. €/£205,000/0.14). The optimum time to replace the current machine (which can function for three years) with the new machine is now determined by calculating the overall cost if replacement takes place immediately, after one year, after two years and after three years.

Scenario	Year	Year's cash flows €/£	Discount factor (14%)	PV cost €/£
Replace immediately	0	250,000	1,000	250,000
	1	(1,464,286)	1,000	(1,464,286)
				(1,214,286)
Replace in one year	1	(1,464,286)	0.877	(1,284,179)
	1	230,000	0.877	201,710
	1	(69,500)	0.877	(60,951)
				(1,143,420)
Replace in two years	1	(69,500)	0.877	(60,951)
	2	(1,464,286)	0.769	(1,126,036)
	2	150,000	0.769	115,350
	2	(77,000)	0.769	(59,213)
				(1,130,850)

Replace in three years	1	(69,500)	0.877	(60,951)
	2	(77,000)	0.769	(59,213)
	3	(1,464,286)	0.675	(988,393)
	3	70,000	0.675	47,250
	3	(109,000)	0.675	(73,575)
				(1,134,882)

The existing machine should be replaced with the new machine in two years' time as this results in the lowest present value for the cash flows.

RISK AND UNCERTAINTY

Future cash flows in respect of an investment are rarely known with certainty. Where cash flows are totally uncertain, the project should not proceed. When cash flows are **totally uncertain**, they cannot be assigned probabilities of occurrence, even subjective ones. Totally uncertain cash flows are different from risky cash flows. In investment appraisal, **risk** is the likelihood that any estimates or assumptions made will differ from what actually occurs. The possibilities of actual cash flows being different from those predicted are formulated into various probable outcomes, each with an assigned probability. Capital projects involve a range of estimated cash flows that can occur over a number of years. The further into the future the estimates, the greater the risk that actual cash flows will be different; therefore, the range of possible outcomes will be greater for estimates far into the future. The probabilities assigned are generally obtained from two sources, as identified in **Figure 3.1**.

FIGURE 3.1: DETERMINING THE PROBABILITIES OF OUTCOMES

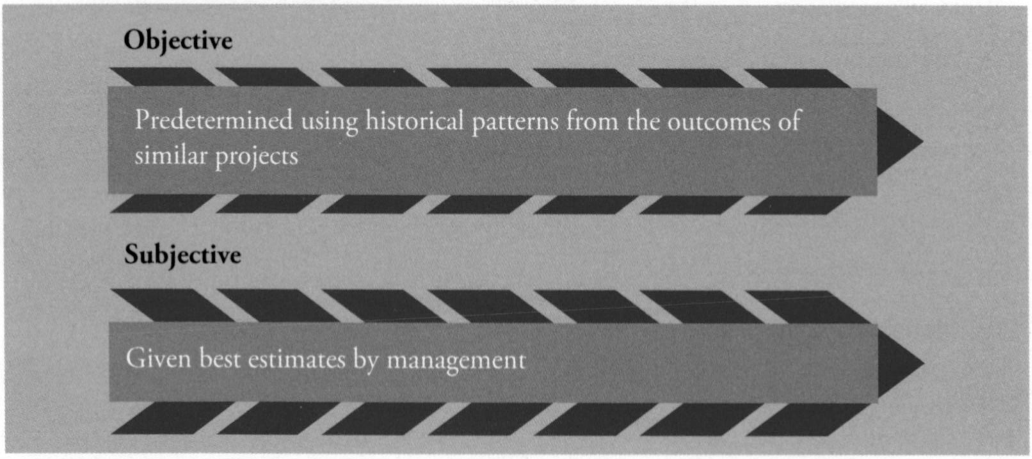

Objective

Predetermined using historical patterns from the outcomes of similar projects

Subjective

Given best estimates by management

Subjectively determined probabilities introduce an amount of uncertainty into the risk assessment of a project, but not total uncertainty.

ESG Risk

Good finance decision-making includes considering ESG (environment, society and governance) risk. Such as whether the project may be associated with an environmental risk, for example, carbon emissions or pollution; a societal risk, for example, employee or health and safety issues that may affect the community; or governance risk, for example, having insufficient expertise on the board. Moreover, if the investment is being undertaken to improve the sustainability of the business through the achievement of a specific environmental or social aim, then the finance manager should make the directors aware of the reputational opportunities associated with the investment and the potential for lower cost funding.

Influences on Risk

Economic Risk

Capital investment appraisal is subject to many forms of risk, including risks that are inherent in any economy. Cash flow estimates may be based on the expectation that the current economic climate will continue into the future; however, the economy can be volatile and, when a downturn occurs, it has the potential to occur quickly. In addition, cash flow projections can be influenced by competition from other countries. This has been exacerbated, over recent decades, by the globalisation of product markets. Predicting product prices, and hence cash outflows, is now more difficult as they may be impacted on by inflation rates in other countries affecting selling or supply prices.

Human Error

There is also risk involved in determining estimated cash flows. For example, a project's estimated costs may not have captured all the indirect costs; the purchase of a machine may involve carriage costs, duty charges, fitting and installation charges, downtime in the factory while a machine is fitted, training of staff, etc. Capturing all costs accurately may be difficult. Cash inflows are also subjective. Sales prices are affected by market forces, including the actions of competitors, the economy and technological change. In addition, the rates of taxation and capital allowances may be changed by government.

Discount Rate

There is also risk associated with predicting the discount rate to be used in the capital appraisal process. The discount rate is usually based on a company's weighted average cost of capital (WACC), which encapsulates the returns required by a company's financiers. However, the WACC is in constant flux. For instance, interest rates change, stock market prices rise and fall, a company's capital structure may alter and the company may change its business, impacting on the financiers' assessment of the risks involved in investing in the company.

Obsolescence and Technological Change

The risk of obsolescence will also impact on the investment appraisal process. At the outset, an assessment has to be made in respect of the period of time that a company will derive economic benefits from an asset or project, and this will be influenced by expected advances made by other companies. For example, a new computer system may reasonably be expected to last a company for 10 years; however, advances in software development, web programs and complementary hardware may cause the hardware to become obsolete within three years. Therefore, a point in time may come when the current project, though still capable of generating products, will no longer be viable and a new project should be pursued. This risk is more evident in high technology types of capital projects, as these are developed in a highly competitive and fast-changing environment. If a company does not keep abreast of current developments, it may lose market share.

PROJECT APPRAISAL METHODS USED TO CONSIDER THE IMPACT OF RISK

Some companies set a limit on the payback period that has to be met before a project goes ahead; others use conservative cash flows. The advantages of these methods are that they are quick and easy; however, they use arbitrary assumptions.

Another commonly used technique is to leave the cash flow predictions as they are and to build in a risk factor (margin of safety) to the discount rate. This is called a **risk-adjusted discount rate**. This technique is based on the theory that there is a relationship between expected risk and expected return; the higher the risk of an investment, the higher the required return. Therefore, if a project is deemed to be risky, a **risk premium** will be added to the normal discount rate to compensate for additional risks. The more risky a project, the higher the risk premium required. The relationship is depicted in **Figure 3.2** and is based on the theory underlying the capital asset pricing model (CAPM).

FIGURE 3.2: THE RELATIONSHIP BETWEEN RISK AND RETURN

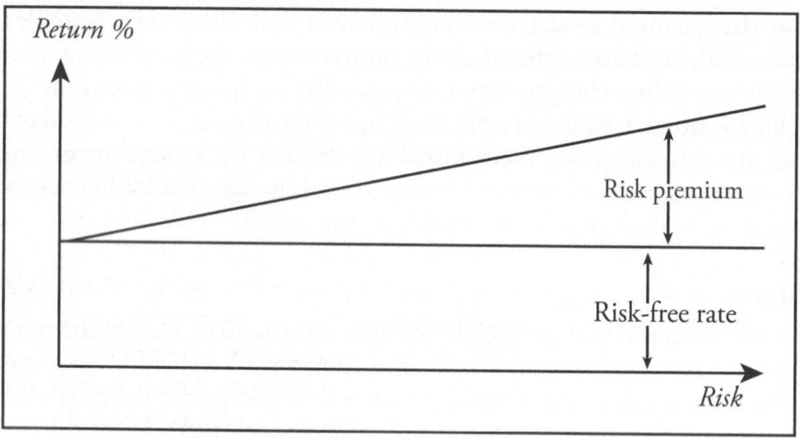

The risk premium may be determined arbitrarily or may be based on the return required for similar projects by other companies. Some companies classify projects into risk categories and have predetermined required return rates for each risk category. Again, the categorisation process is subjective, as is the premium that is required. The required rates and risk classifications may be influenced by an individual manager's views, which may not reflect the views of the equity holders (i.e. agency theory may apply). Where the project is similar in risk to the operational activities of a company, then the WACC can be used, though it may need to be adjusted if the capital structure of the company is expected to change due to a change in the method of financing.

Other more scientific methods, though time-consuming to use, provide better insight into variables that might be deemed to be most risky and the resultant outcome from variations in their estimates. This information can be obtained using sensitivity analysis. Sensitivity analysis only considers variations in one variable at a time; another method, scenario analysis, can be used to consider variations in all the variables, given the three or four likely outcomes; and simulation analysis extends scenario analysis to consider hundreds of potential outcomes. These three methods are now discussed.

SENSITIVITY ANALYSIS

Sensitivity analysis involves examining the impact of variations in key input variables on the outcome of a project. This type of analysis strives to determine the margin of safety for each key input variable, holding all else constant. The advantages and disadvantages are outlined in **Figure 3.3**.

FIGURE 3.3: ADVANTAGES AND DISADVANTAGES OF SENSITIVITY ANALYSIS

Advantages

- **Increases awareness:** provides management with an insight into the potential impact of changes in variables on a project – it makes them aware of the risks inherent in a project.
- **Critical variables:** management can identify those variables that have the smallest margin of safety.
- **Efficient use of management time:** as critical variables are identified, management can direct their attention to ensuring that estimates of these variables are more valid.
- **Other alternatives:** where the margin of safety is small, management may decide to utilise a substitute, or to change the project.
- **Management by exception:** management can focus its attention on ensuring that the critical variables remain close to its estimates.

Disadvantages

- **Subjective:** sensitivity analysis does not result in clear decision rules when trying to decide whether to 'accept' or 'reject' a project.
- **Restricted:** only one input is varied at a time.

There are two approaches to using sensitivity analysis: the first considers variations in cash flows; the second considers variations in rates used.

Sensitivity Analysis: Cash Flows

There are two approaches to calculating the sensitivity of a project to changes in input cash flows. The first uses a ratio of the NPV of a project to the PV of a variable. Therefore, the first step is to determine the total PV of the variable for which sensitivity is being tested and then to express the NPV of the project as a percentage of the PV of the variable (see **Worked Example 3.7**).

The **margin of safety** approach produces the same outcome. It determines the extent of change in a variable required before a project starts to make a negative NPV. It is calculated in the same manner as the margin of safety in break-even analysis. The margin of safety in absolute terms is calculated as:

Margin of safety = Break-even value − Estimated value

The margin of safety is sometimes expressed in percentage terms. For example, 'the variable can change by x% before the project becomes unviable'. This can be determined using the following formula:

$$\textbf{Margin of safety \%} = \frac{\textbf{Break-even value} - \textbf{Estimated value}}{\textbf{Estimated value}}$$

Worked Example 3.7: Sensitivity Analysis – Cash Flows

The business finance manager in Johnny Ltd is appraising a five-year project that has a positive NPV of €/£1 million. Wages of €/£250,000 per annum have been charged in arriving at the NPV of €/£1 million.

The company's WACC is 15% and this was deemed an appropriate discount rate to use for this project.

Requirement How sensitive is the outcome of the project to wage levels?

Solution

Step 1 Calculate the total present value (PV) of wages:

PV = FV × discount rate

where the future value (FV) of the expected wages cash flows is €/£250,000 per year for five years (assumed to be incurred at the end of each year), and the discount rate is an annuity factor representing discount rates for five years at 15%.

PV (wages) = €/£838,000 [€/£250,000 × 3.352]

Step 2 Express the NPV of the project as a percentage of the PV of the cost of wages.

The NPV of the project is €/£1 million and the present value of the wage cost is €/£838,000. Therefore, the NPV of the project is 119% of the PV of the wage cost [€/£1,000,000 ÷ €/£838,000].

This means that annual wages can rise by 119% before the project's NPV would fall to zero.

This information can also be obtained using the margin of safety approach. In this instance, the margin of safety in money terms is €/£1,162,000 [€/£1,000,000 + (€/£1,000,000 – €/£838,000)]. The annual wages can increase from €/£250,000 to €/£547,500 [calculated as €/£250,000 + (€/£250,000 × 119%)]. This has a PV of €/£1,835,220 [€/£547,000 × 3.352]. The margin of safety in percentage terms is 119% [(€/£1,835,220 – €/£838,000) ÷ (€/£1,000,000 – €/£162,000)]. The same result as that obtained when the NPV to PV percentage is utilised.

Sensitivity Analysis: Rate Changes

This approach considers the sensitivity of a project's NPV to changes in input rates, such as the discount factor, the tax rate or price per unit. This requires an interpolation approach and is best explained with the use of an example.

Worked Example 3.8: Sensitivity Analysis: Rate Changes

A manufacturing company is considering the purchase of a new machine to manufacture beach balls. The machine costs €/£550,000. It is anticipated that the machine will be used for 10 years and then scrapped. The company expects to sell the balls at 25c/p each and to sell 900,000 balls per annum. Variable costs are expected to be 5c/p per ball and fixed costs are predicted to be €/£50,000 per annum. The manufacturing company has a WACC of 15%. It is considered appropriate to use this rate when assessing this project.

Requirement Calculate the NPV of this project. How sensitive is the outcome of the project to the selling price of the balls?

Solution	**€/£**
Cost of machine	(550,000)
Cash inflows from sales: [900,000 × 25c/p × 5.019*]	1,129,275
Cash outflows for variable costs: [900,000 × 5c/p × 5.019]	(225,855)
Fixed overheads: [€/£50,000 × 5.019]	(250,950)
NPV	102,470

*Annuity factor representing discount rates of 15% for 10 years.

To assess the sensitivity of the project outcome to a change in sales price, a rate of 22c/p is selected (i.e. as the NPV is positive, the cash inflows need to fall to give a smaller NPV, therefore an arbitrary amount that is lower than the existing 25c/p is selected).

	€/£
Cost of machine	(550,000)
Cash inflows from sales: [900,000 × 22c/p × 5.019*]	993,762
Cash outflows for variable costs: [900,000 × 5c/p × 5.019]	(225,855)
Fixed overheads: [€/£50,000 × 5.019]	(250,950)
NPV	(33,043)

*Annuity factor representing discount rates of 15% for 10 years.

Interpolation is now utilised to find the selling price that will result in a zero NPV.

$$\text{Sales price} = 22\text{c/p} + \frac{-€/£33{,}043 \times (25\text{c/p} - 22\text{c/p})}{-€/£33{,}043 - €/£102{,}470} = 22.73\text{c/p}$$

Therefore, so long as the other variables are accurately estimated, this project will be viable – unless the sales price for each beach ball falls below 22.73c/p.

Sensitivity analysis involves numerous calculations (depending on the number of variables in an appraisal) that are mechanical in nature. Information technology is frequently utilised to speed up the process. Spreadsheets with pre-programmed formulae can easily determine the margin of safety percentage and perform IRR calculations for rate changes.

SCENARIO ANALYSIS

As mentioned previously, the main disadvantage with sensitivity analysis is that it only considers the impact of a change in one input variable whilst holding all others constant. Though informative, it is more likely that several variables will be impacted upon when there is, for example, a change in the economic climate. **Scenario analysis** involves changing a number of variables to provide a particular view. The most common views presented are: optimistic (best case), most likely and pessimistic (worst case) scenarios. The advantages and disadvantages of scenario analysis are outlined in **Figure 3.4**.

Figure 3.4: Advantage and Disadvantages of Scenario Analysis

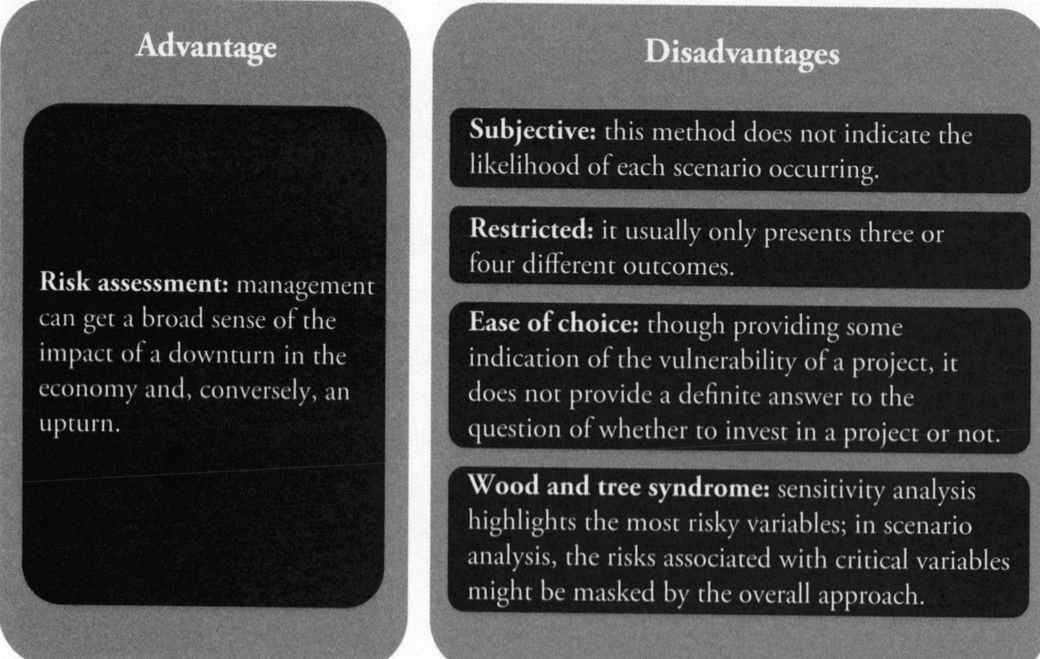

Advantage
Risk assessment: management can get a broad sense of the impact of a downturn in the economy and, conversely, an upturn.
Disadvantages
Subjective: this method does not indicate the likelihood of each scenario occurring.
Restricted: it usually only presents three or four different outcomes.
Ease of choice: though providing some indication of the vulnerability of a project, it does not provide a definite answer to the question of whether to invest in a project or not.
Wood and tree syndrome: sensitivity analysis highlights the most risky variables; in scenario analysis, the risks associated with critical variables might be masked by the overall approach.

SIMULATION ANALYSIS

Simulation analysis is performed using computer models. It is formally known as **Monte Carlo Simulation** and involves organising the variables and the influences on the variables into models and determining the various outcomes predicted for each variable, and the resultant influence of that on a project's NPV. The package runs many different scenarios, resulting in different NPVs. These are plotted to form an overall probability distribution, which can be used to determine the most likely outcomes and the risk associated with these outcomes for each project.

Though this technique is more sophisticated than scenario analysis and provides a wider range of potential overall outcomes, it is still subjective. The project appraisal manager still has to determine the probabilities of various variable changes in light of external influences and to model these into the program application. In addition, creating the initial model can be very time-consuming and the relationships between variables may be difficult to model, particularly if variables are correlated or impact on existing project outcomes.

The previous approaches (e.g. sensitivity analysis, scenario analysis) consider changes to the variables that underlie the calculation of a project's NPV. Another approach is to consider the possibility of the project having a series of different NPVs (i.e. the probability theory approach). This technique is now outlined.

PROBABILITY THEORY APPROACH (EXPECTED VALUES)

The **probability theory approach** calculates the **expected net present value (ENPV)** of the cash flows of a project, given a range of possibilities and their probable outcomes. This can be used to examine the risk associated with a project by determining the probability that the project will fail to generate a positive NPV. It can also be used to examine the worst case scenario and to determine the probability of that outcome. Statistics are used to provide an overall average or mean, or ENPV (Y in the following equation). All NPV outcomes are weighted by the probability of their occurrence. This calculation is denoted by the following formula:

$$Y = \sum_{i=1}^{n} p_i \; X_i$$

where Y is the expected value of Event X; X_i is the outcome i from event X; p_i is the probability p of outcome i occurring; and n is the number of possible outcomes. This process is shown in **Worked Example 3.10**.

Worked Example 3.10: Probability Theory Approach

A manufacturing company is considering three new projects. The project appraisal team has investigated the projects and devised a range of possible NPV outcomes and the probability of those outcomes occurring.

Project	Likelihood	NPV €/£
Project 1	Certain	4,400
Project 2	30% chance	(2,000)
	50% chance	7,000
	20% chance	8,000
Project 3	20% chance	25,000
	30% chance	16,000
	50% chance	(10,000)

Requirement Which project should be selected if risk is ignored?

Solution

Project	Probability	NPV €/£	ENPV €/£
Project 1	1.00	4,400	4,400
Project 2	0.30	(2,000)	(600)
	0.50	7,000	3,500
	0.20	8,000	1,600
			4,500
Project 3	0.20	25,000	5,000
	0.30	16,000	4,800
	0.50	(10,000)	(5,000)
			4,800

When risk is ignored, the project with the highest ENPV should be accepted, which in this case is Project 3.

The standard deviation of the resultant ENPV can be calculated for each project and used as an indication of the risk of each project: the larger the standard deviation, the riskier the project. The standard deviation σ is a statistical measure of the dispersion of outcomes (in this case NPVs) around the mean value (in this case ENPV). It is calculated as the square root of the variance σ^2. The variance is calculated as follows:

$$\sigma^2 = (X_1 - Y)^2 p_1 + (X_2 - Y)^2 p_2 \ldots\ldots (X_n - Y)^2 p_n$$

where $X_1 - Y$ is the variation of outcome one (X_1) from the mean value (Y). This is then squared, to remove the sign problem (caused by negative numbers), and multiplied by the probability of that outcome occurring. The standard deviation is calculated to allow a meaningful interpretation of the variance. This process produces an outcome that is denominated in the same scale as the expected/mean value. For example, if the mean was

€/£5 and the standard deviation was €/£2, this would mean that the average dispersal of the majority outcomes from the expected/mean value is €/£2. Therefore, most outcomes lie between €/£3 and €/£7. The smaller a standard deviation, the closer most values are to the mean, the more likely that the actual outcome will be close to the expected outcome, hence the less risky the project. The calculation of the standard deviation is provided in the following example:

Worked Example 3.11: Probability Theory Approach

A manufacturing company is considering three new projects. The project appraisal team has investigated the projects and come up with a range of possible NPV outcomes and the probability of those outcomes occurring.

Project	**Likelihood**	**NPV €/£**
Project 1	Certain	4,400
Project 2	30% chance	(2,000)
	50% chance	7,000
	20% chance	8,000
Project 3	20% chance	25,000
	30% chance	16,000
	50% chance	(10,000)

Requirement Calculate the standard deviation of the projects and recommend one project for investment, given that management are risk averse.

Solution

Project	**NPV (X) €/£**	**Probability (p)**	**Y €/£**	**$X - Y$ €/£**	**$(X - Y)^2$ €/£**	**$p(X - Y)^2$ €/£**
1	4,400	1.00	4,400	–	–	–
2	(2,000)	0.30	(600)	(6,500)	42,250,000	12,675,000
	7,000	0.50	3,500	2,500	6,250,000	3,125,000
	8,000	0.20	1,600	3,500	12,250,000	2,450,000
			4,500			18,250,000

Standard deviation $= \sqrt{18,250,000} =$ €/£4,272

Project	**NPV (X) €/£**	**Probability (p)**	**Y €/£**	**$X - Y$ €/£**	**$(X - Y)^2$ €/£**	**$p(X - Y)^2$ €/£**
3	25,000	0.20	5,000	20,200	408,040,000	81,608,000
	16,000	0.30	4,800	11,200	125,440,000	37,632,000
	(10,000)	0.50	(5,000)	(14,800)	219,040,000	109,520,000
			4,800			228,760,000

Standard deviation $= \sqrt{228,760,000} =$ €/£15,125

The three projects offer expected returns of €/£4,400, €/£4,500 and €/£4,800.

Project 3 offers the largest expected return, though it has the highest level of risk, with a standard deviation of €/£15,125. This deviation is very large, at three times the size of the mean. It is unlikely that management will find this project attractive.

Project 2 has the next largest mean value (€/£4,500) and reports a standard deviation of €/£4,272. Unlike the last project, there is a far greater chance of this project returning net cash inflows, as the standard deviation is smaller than the mean value, though it cannot be guaranteed that the project will not turn a net cash outflow of €/£2,000.

In Project 1, the expected cash inflow is certain and there is no risk involved. Though the expected value is €/£100 lower than that reported for Project 2, there is no risk, therefore it is recommended that management opt for this project.

INFLUENCES ON RISKS ASSOCIATED WITH AN INVESTMENT

Risk: Strategic Issues

When analysing a project, management cannot rely solely on the financials; there are many other influences that may impact on the success of a project. As mentioned earlier, a starting point in the process is to ensure that the project outcomes are congruent with the company's overall objectives. Management also has to consider the impact of the new project on the company. Will the new project have any impact on its current resources? Is there the expertise required for the new project? Will there be economies of scale/dis-economies of scale? Will the new project displace current sales?

Risk: Foreign Issues

Many companies try to diversify country risk by starting projects, or investing, in other countries. In addition to hedging against losses that may result from a downturn in the local economy, a company can tap into cheaper resources in other countries. For example, many labour-intensive companies have opened or relocated branches in countries with low labour costs, such as China, Bangladesh or India. When a project is being considered for a foreign country, there are additional risks that need to be factored into the assessment; these risks are now briefly outlined.

Country Risk

Country risk is the risk associated with a particular country. Factors that may heighten this risk include the policies of the local government in respect of foreign investment. Some governments encourage investment by providing grants or tax incentives; others have policies that are deemed to be discouraging. For example, they may place an additional tax on profits repatriated out of the country and, in extreme instances, may freeze bank accounts and/or expropriate assets. An example is included in **Real World Example 3.1**.

Real World Example 3.1: Country Risk

Foreign investment in Zimbabwe

In 2011, the then-President Robert Mugabe focused his attention on the mining industry. He increased exploration fees by 2,000% to $1 million and the Indigenisation and Economic Empowerment Act (2010) came into force. This Act requires all foreign companies valued at over $500,000 and all mining companies valued at over $1 to sell 51% of their shares to local people.

There are specialist agencies that advise on levels of country risk. In addition, there are a number of steps that can be taken to reduce these risks. A commonly used strategy is to form a joint venture with a local company or the government in the country being considered. Other steps include sourcing materials and labour from local companies and investing in the local communities by building schools, making donations and building hospitals.

Business Environment Risk

As well as country-specific risks, there are risks associated with trading in a different business environment. These risks are termed **business environment risks**. These risks include cultural differences and common practices in trading deals. For example, in some countries, considerable offers of hospitality are part and parcel of normal business activity, whereas in other countries this is deemed to be unethical. In addition to cultural and common practices being different, the law is also usually different. Expert advice is recommended at the planning stage of a project to determine the impact of legal and cultural differences. Consistent with country risk, business environment risk can be reduced by forging links with a local company or the government, or simply by taking on a local business person as a director of the foreign investment. These sources will provide expert local knowledge.

Foreign Exchange Rate Risk

Foreign exchange rate risk refers to the risk that the exchange rate in the future will be different from that used in the initial projections. A change in exchange rates will lead to a change in cash flows: a rise in the value of the currency of the foreign country will have a beneficial impact (each unit of foreign currency will be converted to more euro/Sterling – a stronger Dollar will mean that less Dollars are required to buy euro/Sterling, for example, €/£1 = $0.70, whereas a fall in the Dollar will mean that more Dollars are required to buy euro/Sterling, for example, €/£1 = $0.90). This may alter the feasibility of a project. There are a number of techniques to manage currency exchange rate risk, for example, opening a bank account in a foreign country and using hedging products, such as swap contracts, forward contracts and futures contracts.

Credit Risk

There is additional exposure to credit risk when dealing with customers from other countries. This is discussed fully in **Chapter 8**.

CONCLUSION

Risk is inherent in cash flow prediction for any capital investment. Where this risk can be quantified, several techniques may be utilised to analyse the impact of the risk on the decision-making outcome. Some of the techniques utilised are quite mathematical, iterative and time-consuming and lend themselves well to being handled by a pre-modelled computer package. This should help to speed up the analysis stage of the overall investment decision-making process. However, in all instances it should be remembered that computers only do what they are being told to do and the resultant NPV is still not risk free: the actual outcome is unlikely to be exactly as predicted. In all instances, capital appraisal projects should be subjected to a post-completion audit.

A **post-completion audit** monitors and evaluates the actual project's cash flows, relative to the expected cash flows. This highlights deviations, thus inciting corrective action, informs future investment appraisal decision-making processes and provides an incentive for the preparers of the appraisal cash flows to strive for accuracy in their estimates.

A survey by Cranfield School of Management in 2003 on the effectiveness of the information technology investment appraisal process found that:

> "the quality of information technology appraisal was poor, bureaucratic, inconsistent and greatly influenced by personal or political aspirations".

The respondents regarded that the assessment of cash flows relating to project appraisal was also poor. This is a significant issue, as the approving board places great emphasis on the figures it is provided with (Adams *et al.*, 2004). The Cranfield study commented on the lack of overall vision recognised by each company that responded to its survey. Investment appraisal is the most important issue facing a company. Investment should be made into projects that achieve outcomes that are consistent with the overall company mission. Alkaraan and Northcott (2006), in a study of the use of both conventional financial analysis tools and more sophisticated risk-adjusting approaches to the capital investment decision-making within large UK manufacturing companies, found little evidence of integration between strategic approaches and financial approaches, with risk-adjusting analysis tools being rarely used in practice. The authors concluded that the 'sentiment' of directors seems to be that 'simple is best' and that analysis techniques should not replace intuition and judgement.

In large companies, a separate committee or board should be established to approve projects. It could include the head of the project appraisal team, representatives of customers who will be using the products resulting from the investment process, the finance director and a director who represents the strategic views of the overall board of directors. The latter's role should be to ensure that project outcomes are consistent with the company vision. This does not mean that innovation should be stifled, but instead that innovation should be consistent with the ongoing change that a company wishes to pursue.

EXAMINATION STANDARD QUESTION: ASSET REPLACEMENT

Laytown Plc is considering the purchase of a machine which could fulfil the company's future expansion plans. In this context the company is currently appraising two machines, but only one machine may be purchased.

The Standard machine costs €/£50,000 and the Deluxe machine costs €/£88,000, payable immediately. Both machines require €/£10,000 of working capital throughout their working lives, which would be recoverable when both machines are scrapped at the end of their working lives (viz. four years for the Standard machine and six years for the Deluxe machine).

The forecast pre-tax net cash inflows associated with the two machines are as follows:

	Year 1 €/£	Year 2 €/£	Year 3 €/£	Year 4 €/£	Year 5 €/£	Year 6 €/£
Standard	20,500	22,860	24,210	23,410	–	–
Deluxe	32,030	26,110	25,380	25,940	38,560	35,100

The discount rate for the Standard machine is 12%.

The Deluxe machine has only recently been introduced to the market and has not been fully tested in operating conditions. Because of the higher risk involved, the appropriate discount rate for the Deluxe machine is believed to be 2% higher than the discount rate for the Standard machine.

If it decides to purchase one or other of these machines, the company is proposing to finance the purchase with a term loan at a fixed interest rate of 11%.

Taxation at 35% is payable on operating cash flows one year in arrears, and capital allowances are available at 25% per annum on a reducing balance basis.

Requirement

(a) For both the Standard and Deluxe machines, calculate:

(i) the payback period; and

(ii) the net present value;

and advise the company as to which machine, if either, it should purchase. **14 Marks**

(b) A survey by Pike (1996) investigated the capital investment methods of large UK companies, which yielded the following results:

Firms using:	%
Payback	94
Accounting rate of return	50
Internal rate of return........................	81
Net present value...............................	74

Suggest reasons for the widespread use of traditional techniques in the investment decision process.

8 Marks

Total 22 Marks

(Based on Chartered Accountants Ireland, MABF II, Summer 1997, Q5)

Solution

(a) (i) The payback period for the Standard machine is approximately three years: The cash flows in the first three years amount to €/£60,050 [€/£20,500 + €/£20,060 + €/£19,490]. The initial cost of the investment is: €/£60,000.
The payback period for the Deluxe machine is approximately four years.
The cash flows in the first four years amount to €/£98,033 [€/£32,030 + €/£22,599 + €/£22,016 + €/£21,388]. The initial investment is: €/£98,000.

(ii) The NPV for the Standard machine is €/£5,136.
The NPV for the Deluxe machine is €/£5,510.
(See below for workings.)

Recommendation The NPV of the Deluxe machine is greater than that of the Standard machine; initial considerations would suggest that the Deluxe machine should be preferred for this reason. However, the difference in NPV is not great and the uncertainty involved in the estimates for a five- to seven-year period is such that a small difference in NPV may not be the weightiest consideration. In favour of the Standard machine is its shorter payback period and its established reliability. Although the higher discount rate applied in the case of the Deluxe machine is intended to compensate for its greater risk, a risk-averse management board may still prefer the Standard model.

Discounted cash flow analysis of relevant cash flows – Standard machine

Year	**Non-current assets**	**Working capital**	**Cash inflows**	**Taxation (W1)**	**Net cash flow**	**Discount factor**	**NPV**
	€/£	**€/£**	**€/£**	**€/£**	**€/£**		**€/£**
0	(50,000)	(10,000)	–	–	(60,000)	1.000	(60,000)
1	–	–	20,500	–	20,500	0.893	18,307
2	–	–	22,860	(2,800)	20,060	0.797	15,988
3	–	–	24,210	(4,720)	19,490	0.712	13,877
4	–	10,000	23,410	(6,013)	27,397	0.636	17,424
5	–	–	–	(811)	(811)	0.567	(460)
						NPV	5,136

(***Note re. interest payable***: the process of discounting allows for the cost of financing the project.)

Discounted cash flow analysis of relevant cash flows – Deluxe machine

Year	Non-current assets	Working capital	Cash inflows	Taxation (W2)	Net cash flow	Discount factor	NPV
	€/£	€/£	€/£	€/£	€/£		€/£
0	(88,000)	(10,000)	–	–	(98,000)	1.000	(98,000)
1	–	–	32,030	–	32,030	0.877	28,090
2	–	–	26,110	(3,511)	22,599	0.769	17,379
3	–	–	25,380	(3,364)	22,016	0.675	14,861
4	–	–	25,940	(4,552)	21,388	0.592	12,662
5	–	–	38,560	(5,831)	32,729	0.519	16,986
6	–	10,000	35,100	(11,060)	34,040	0.456	15,522
7	–	–	–	(4,976)	(4,976)	0.400	(1,990)
						NPV	5,510

W1: Taxation cash flows

Standard machine

	Capital allowances tax effect	Tax on net cash inflows	Taxation cash flows
	€/£	€/£	€/£
0	–	–	–
1	–	–	–
2	4,375	(7,175)*	(2,800)
3	3,281	(8,001)	(4,720)
4	2,461	(8,474)	(6,013)
5	1,846 + 5,537	(8,194)	(811)

* €/£20,500 × 35% = €/£7,175

Capital expenditure on Standard machine qualifying for capital allowances:

	€/£	Reduction in tax cash flow €/£
Cost	50,000	
Year 1 25%	(12,500) × 35%	4,375
WDV:	37,500	

Year 2 25%	(9,375) × 35%	3,281	
WDV:	28,125		
Year 3 25%	(7,031) × 35%	2,461	
WDV:	21,094		
Year 4 25%	(5,274) × 35%	1,846	5,537*
WDV:	15,820*		

* It is assumed that the machine was scrapped, so there is a balancing allowance of: €/£15,820. The tax impact of this is €/£5,537 [€/£15,820 × 35%].

W2: Calculation of taxation cash flows

Deluxe machine

	Capital allowances tax effect €/£	**Inflows €/£**	**Taxation cash flows €/£**
0	–	–	–
1	–	–	–
2	7,700	(11,211)*	(3,511)
3	5,775	(9,139)	(3,364)
4	4,331	(8,883)	(4,552)
5	3,248	(9,079)	(5,831)
6	2,436	(13,496)	(11,060)
7	1,827 + 5,482	(12,285)	(4,976)

*€/£32,030 × 35% = €/£11,211

Capital expenditure on Deluxe machine qualifying for capital allowances:

	€/£	**Reduction in tax cash flow €/£**
Cost	88,000	
Year 1 25%	(22,000) × 35%	(7,700)
WDV:	66,000	
Year 2 25%	(16,500) × 35%	(5,775)
WDV:	49,500	

Year 3 25%	(12,375) × 35%	(4,331)	
WDV:	37,125		
Year 4 25%	(9,281) × 35%	(3,248)	
WDV:	27,844		
Year 5 25%	(6,961) × 35%	(2,436)	
WDV:	20,883		
Year 6 25%	(5,221) × 35%	(1,827)	(5,482)*
WDV:	15,662		

* It is assumed that the machine is scrapped, so there is a balancing allowance of: €/£15,662. The tax impact of this is: €/£5,482 [€/£15,662 × 35%].

Comment on the choice of machine using the NPV approach The application of the NPV method is complicated when a choice must be made between two or more projects, where the projects have unequal lives. It is important to consider what will happen at the end of Year 4, when the Standard machine is scrapped. This is determined using the equivalent annual cost method.

The present value of net cash flows for the Standard machine is the equivalent annual net cash flow ÷ annuity factor for four years at 12%.

€/£5,136 is equal to the equivalent annual net cash flow ÷ 3.037 (cumulative present value factors).

Therefore, the equivalent annual net cash flow is €/£1,691.

Similarly, for the Deluxe machine:

€/£5,110 is equal to the equivalent annual net cash flow ÷ 3.889.

Therefore, the equivalent annual net cash flow is €/£1,313.

Using this method, the decision rule is to choose the machine with the lower annual equivalent cost or the greater annual net cash inflow. Using this basis, the Standard machine would be selected.

(b) The survey by Pike (1996) supports the importance of unquantifiable aspects in decisions involving capital budgeting. The survey shows that 63% of respondents ranked qualitative factors as important or very important in investment decisions, while only 55% gave such ratings to sophisticated investment methods and systematic procedures. Reasons for the low ranking include:

1. Discounting is questioned in terms of relevance. A fundamental assumption underlying DCF methods is that decision-makers pursue the primary goal of maximising equity holder value. Empirically, this is questionable, with equity holder goals often given a lower priority.

2. The literature generally assumes that DCF methods are appropriate for all companies regardless of context. The employment of sophisticated tools and formal approaches to decision-making does not suit all companies. This process will vary with a company's external environment and internal characteristics. For example, DCF methods and formal risk analysis may well be appropriate in large, capital-intensive, decentralised companies operating in high technology industries and with a management that feels comfortable with analytical decision methods. Smaller companies may prefer a more interpersonal approach to management and so may find sophisticated techniques unhelpful.
3. The relevance of DCF methods is also questioned on pragmatic grounds. Management remain sceptical that the adoption of such techniques actually results in a discernible improvement in performance. Indeed, a major reason for the slow acceptance of DCF methods appears to be the paucity of evidence to show that they improve performance.
4. Another reason for disenchantment arises more from errors in application of the model than from the model itself. Frequently, there are critical errors in the way theory is applied and, generally, these errors are biased against investment.
5. The question must also be asked as to whether the **particular type of capital investment decision faced by a company** may affect the relative popularity of DCF and non-DCF techniques of appraisal.
6. Behavioural commentators suggest that a manager who believes that a particular project should be accepted will select the technique that reflects the project in the best possible light (Drury, 1996). Thus, human factors may confound scientific interpretations of the DCF/non-DCF debate.

In a study on the use of capital investment techniques in UK companies, Arnold and Hatzopoulos (2000) found that most companies employ a combination of evaluation methods. Horngren, Foster and Datar (1997) tabulated an international comparison of various capital budgeting surveys carried out by a number of authors and noted that for all the countries surveyed, ranging from the US, the UK, Australia, Canada, Ireland, Japan, Scotland and a host of other countries, with the exception of Japan and Poland, the remaining countries in the tabulation used more than one method to evaluate capital investments. The payback method remains a very popular method in all countries, particularly in Japan and Poland, where the use of DCF techniques is recorded at very low percentages. Payback method is used along with, for example, the IRR in the US and Canada, with DCF methods (IRR or NPV) in Ireland and with the IRR in Scotland. Surveys by Arnold and Hatzopoulos (2000) and by Alkaraan and Mitchell (2006) point to growth in the use of DCF techniques and an increased use of more sophisticated tools and theories from other disciplines.

The question must be asked as to whether the continuing use of traditional techniques is in any way a reflection of the tendency in a wide variety of countries to avoid relying on just one method. The traditional techniques are retained along with DCF techniques simply because no single appraisal technique can embody all the relationships and aspects of the capital budgeting decision (i.e. risk, reward, financial constraint, competing alternatives, etc.).

Key Terms

Annuity
Asset replacement decision
Business environment risk
Capital rationing
Country risk
Divisible projects
Economic risk
Equivalent annual annuity approach
Equivalent annual cost
ESG (environment, society and governance)
Expected net present value (ENPV)
Foreign exchange rate risk
Hard capital rationing
Margin of safety
Monte Carlo Simulation
Multi-period
Mutually exclusive
Objective probabilities
Non-divisible projects
Post-completion audit
Probability theory approach
Profitability index
Replacement cycle period
Risk
Risk-adjusted discount rate
Risk premium
Scenario analysis
Sensitivity analysis
Soft capital rationing
Subjective probabilities
Uncertainty

REVIEW QUESTIONS

(See Suggested Solutions to Review Questions in **Appendix B**.)

Question 3.1

Explain the difference between the term 'risk' and the term 'uncertainty'. Why are these two terms sometimes used interchangeably, even though they have different meanings?

Question 3.2

Explain the term 'margin of safety' in the context of sensitivity analysis.

Question 3.3

Why have information technology advances increased the use of simulation analysis in capital investment decision-making?

Question 3.4

Briefly suggest two steps that can be taken to reduce, or hedge, a company's exposure to country risk, when a capital project is being considered in a foreign country.

Question 3.5 Pineapple (Level 1)

At a recent meeting of the board of directors of Pineapple Limited, the chair of the board expressed dissatisfaction with the company's long-term investment strategy. He requested that the finance manager collate a portfolio of investments that Pineapple should invest in next year in order to increase its share price. The board agreed that the company can spend up to €/£3,000,000 on the investments in 20X8 as long as the shareholders receive a satisfactory return. The board agreed that the company could raise the €/£3,000,000 using debt finance. The bank has agreed to lend €/£3,000,000 to Pineapple at a fixed rate of 7% per annum.

You have identified the following projects which Pineapple could invest in:

Project	Duration	Initial outlay	Net present value
Margo	3 years	€/£1,750,000	€/£263,000
Trish	4 years and 6 months	€/£985,000	€/£154,000
Dymphna	5 years	€/£1,350,000	€/£201,350

You can assume today's date is 31 December 20X7.

Requirement

(a) Identify which project(s) Pineapple should invest in on the basis that they are:
  (i) divisible;
  (ii) indivisible.

4 Marks

(b) Capital rationing is prevalent in many companies. Discuss THREE advantages for companies practicing capital rationing.

3 Marks

(Based on Chartered Accountants Ireland, CAP 1, Finance, Summer 2017, extract from Q1)

Question 3.6 ACS (Level 1)

ACS is interested in purchasing state-of-the-art equipment to manufacture the arm brace. The equipment will cost €/£750,000. It is expected to have a useful life of four years and a scrap value of €/£125,000. Paul expects that 2,000 arm braces will be produced in each of the four years. Each arm brace will sell for €/£270 and incur variable costs of €/£132. Paul is currently negotiating the cost to rent an office and production facility for this four-year period. He anticipates that the rent will cost €/£20,000 per annum. ACS has a cost of capital of 8%. Taxation and inflation can be ignored.

Requirement

(a) Calculate the internal rate of return (IRR) of ACS' investment.

4 Marks

(b) Outline TWO advantages and TWO disadvantages of using IRR as a method of project appraisal.

4 Marks

(c) Calculate the sensitivity of the investment to a change in estimated variable costs and explain the significance of your answer.

4 Marks

(Based on Chartered Accountants Ireland, CAP 1, Finance, Autumn 2019, extract from Q4)

Question 3.7

Perro Plc is considering a project that is deemed to be risky. An initial investment of €/£200,000 will be followed by three years with the following **'most likely'** annual cash flows:

	€/£	€/£
Annual sales:		
(100,000 units × €/£4.20 per unit)		420,000
Annual costs		
Labour	210,000	
Materials	80,000	
Other direct costs	20,000	310,000
Net cash flows		110,000

The initial investment includes €/£150,000 for machines that have a zero scrap value at the end of the three-year period and €/£50,000 in working capital, which is recoverable in full at the end of the three-year period. The company's discount rate is 10%. Ignore inflation and taxation.

Requirement

(a) Calculate the NPV of the **most likely** outcome from the project being considered.

(b) State the break-even point and the percentage deviation from the **most likely** levels before break-even NPV is reached for each of the following variables: sales price, labour costs, material costs, other direct costs and the discount rate (assuming all other variables remain constant).

CHALLENGING QUESTIONS

(Suggested solutions to Challenging Questions are available through your lecturer.)

Question 3.1 Dante (Level 1)

Dante Systems Ltd is currently considering if it should invest in a project which requires equipment costing €/£120,000. The expected sales from the project are uncertain, but are estimated as follows:

Sales Units	Probability
6,000	0.10
18,000	0.20
24,000	0.45
30,000	0.15
42,000	0.10

Once the sales volume is established in the first year, it is likely to continue at the same volume in later years. The unit sale price will be €/£10 and the unit variable cost will be €/£5. Additional fixed costs related to the project will be €/£28,000 per annum. Marketing research costs of €/£12,000 have already been incurred on this project.

The project will have a life of six years, after which the equipment will be scrapped, involving a net disposal **cost** of €/£4,000.

The company's cost of capital is 10%.

Requirement

(a) Calculate the expected net present value of this project.

10 Marks

(b) Assuming the cost of the equipment and disposal costs are correct, calculate the minimum annual volume of sales required to achieve a net present value of zero.

5 Marks

Total 15 Marks

(Based on Chartered Accountants Ireland, CAP 1, Finance, Summer 2009, Q3)

Question 3.2 Zenlo (Level 1)

The directors of Zenlo Ltd are evaluating two mutually exclusive investment projects (both with a four-year life), which involve the purchase of new machinery. The following data are available:

Project	Sierra €/£	Tango €/£
Cost (immediate outlay)	(120,000)	(200,000)
Year – estimated net profit/(loss)		

1	35,000	59,000
2	(4,000)	(2,000)
3	7,000	3,000
4..	2,000	1,000
Estimated residual scrap value........................	8,000	12,000

Net profit was calculated after charging straight-line depreciation on cost less residual value. Neither project would increase the working capital requirements of the company. Tax may be ignored.

Requirement
(a) Calculate the cash flows and the payback period for each project.

6 Marks

(b) Assuming a 10% cost of capital, calculate the net present value (NPV) of each project.

4 Marks

(c) Calculate the profitability index (PI) of each project.

1 Mark

(d) Calculate the approximate internal rate of return (IRR) of each project.

4 Marks

(e) Indicate, with reasons, which (if any) of the two projects the Directors should accept.

1 Mark

(f) Outline the relative merits of NPV and payback as methods of investment appraisal.

4 Marks
Total 20 Marks

(Based on Chartered Accountants Ireland, CAP 1, Finance, Autumn 2011, Q1)

Question 3.3 Horgan (Level 1)

(a) Briefly discuss what is meant by capital rationing and distinguish between 'hard' and 'soft' capital rationing.

4 Marks

(b) Horgan's Solutions Limited has identified three viable capital investment projects, however the company only has €/£1,200,000 to invest. The details of the projects are as follows:

	Initial Outlay		Cash Flows	
		Year 1	Year 2	Year 3
	€/£000	€/£000	€/£000	€/£000
Project X	(525)	300	300	300
Project Y	(650)	350	390	490
Project Z	(700)	400	450	500

Horgan's cost of capital is 10%.

Requirement Acting as a financial advisor to Horgan, you are required to:
(a) Calculate the profitability index (PI) for each project.

6 Marks

(b) Advise Horgan which of the project(s) to accept if they are:

(i) Divisible.

2 Marks

(ii) Indivisible.

2 Marks

(iii) Mutually exclusive.

1 Mark
Total 15 Marks

(Based on Chartered Accountants Ireland, CAP 1, Finance, Autumn 2012, Q4)

Question 3.4 Oliver (Level 1)

Oliver Ltd is planning its capital budget for 20X5 and 20X6. The directors have identified five potential investments, with the following estimated cash flows in €/£000, which can be assumed all arise on the **first** day of each year:

Project	**20X5**	**20X6**	**20X7**	**20X8**
Oscar	-120	+57	+57	+57
Papa	-80	-100	+120	+140
Quebec	0	-160	+90	+110
Romeo	-100	+20	+60	+80
Sierra	-60	-40	+50	+90

None of the projects can be delayed, but they are all divisible if Oliver were to enter into joint venture agreements. The shareholders of Oliver require a minimum return of 10% per annum and a payback period of, at most, three years. The capital available for investment at the start is restricted to €/£200,000 on 1 January 20X5, but will be readily available in any amount at 10% per annum on 1 January 20X6 and subsequently.

Requirement

(a) Calculate the simple payback and the net present value of each of the five projects.

9 Marks

(b) Using the results from (a) above and allowing for the restricted capital available on 1 January 20X5, advise Oliver as to which, if any, of the five projects it should invest in.

4 Marks

(Based on Chartered Accountants Ireland, CAP 1, Finance, Autumn 2009, Q1(b))

Question 3.5 Capital Rationing (Level 1)

(a) Describe how the following factors can impact on a capital investment decision:
   (i) inflation;
   (ii) tax;
   (iii) residual value; and
   (iv) the treatment of working capital.

8 Marks

(b) A company has limited access to funds and is considering investing in the following projects, none of which can be delayed.

Project	**Now €/£m**	**Year 1 €/£m**	**Year 2 €/£m**	**NPV €/£m**	**IRR %**	**Payback years**
X	(25)	21	12	3.32	23%	1.33
Y	(20)	20	6	2.64	24%	1.00
Z	(10)	10	4	2.12	31%	1.00

The company's cost of capital is 12% and it has €/£30 million of funds available to invest now. (Ignore tax and inflation.)

(i) Assuming the projects are indivisible (i.e. it is not possible to undertake a fraction of a project), which project(s) should the company invest in, and why?

2 Marks

(ii) If the projects are divisible (i.e. it is possible to invest a fraction of the initial outlay now and receive a corresponding fraction of the NPV), which project(s) should the company invest in, and why?

4 Marks

(c) In perfect capital markets, the condition known as capital rationing should not arise. Explain briefly why capital rationing is nevertheless experienced by many companies.

4 Marks

Total 18 Marks

(Based on Chartered Accountants Ireland, MABF II, Summer 2003, Q6)

Question 3.6 Finserve (Level 1)

You have been asked by a client company, Finserve Ltd, to assist in the management of resources for its sales team. The company provides financial services to a portfolio of diverse clients.

Each salesperson is provided with a state-of-the-art laptop which costs €/£5,000. The sales director of Finserve is trying to decide on the optimum replacement cycle for the laptops. Laptop maintenance costs are payable at the end of each full year of ownership but not in the year of replacement. Finserve has a cost of capital of 14%.

Replacement	Trade-in value	Annual maintenance cost
	€/£	€/£
End of Year 1	3,000	100
End of Year 2	2,000	200
End of Year 3	1,000	300

Requirement

(a) Calculate the annual equivalent cost for each of the THREE replacement cycles and recommend when Finserve should replace the laptops.

7 Marks

(b) Outline TWO non-financial factors that Finserve should consider when determining the optimal replacement cycle.

2 Marks

(Based on Chartered Accountants Ireland, CAP 1, Finance, Summer 2019, extract from Q4)

Question 3.7 Clifton Plc (Level 1)

(a) Write a report to your managing director explaining the benefits that information technology has brought to the investment decision process.

6 Marks

(b) Clifton Plc utilises an item of capital equipment which has a useful life of four years. Recently, a new model has been launched and the company is deciding when to replace the existing equipment. To assist this decision, the following information regarding costs and residual values has been ascertained:

CURRENT MODEL

Year	Operating costs €/£000	Maintenance costs €/£000	Residual value €/£000
0	–	–	1,500
1	2,500	500	1,000
2	3,000	1,000	600
3	3,500	1,500	100
4	4,000	1,700	–

NEW MODEL

Year	Outlay €/£000	Operating costs €/£000	Maintenance costs €/£000	Residual value €/£000
0	7,000	–	–	–
1	–	1,800	200	4,000
2	–	2,200	500	3,000
3	–	2,600	900	2,000
4	–	2,800	1,200	1,000

The company's current cost of capital is 8%. Ignore taxation and inflation.

Requirement Advise Clifton Plc as to when it should replace the existing equipment.

12 Marks
Total 18 Marks

(Based on Chartered Accountants Ireland, MABF II, Summer 1996, Q7)

Question 3.8 Incremental Approach – Cleansweep (Levels 1 and 2)

Cleansweep Ltd is a profitable waste disposal company that has a four-year-old machine which is less efficient than more modern equivalent machines. The company is considering the following three proposals.

Proposal 1: Retain the Old Machine The old machine has an estimated residual life of 11 years, but its operating and maintenance costs will be €/£24,000 per year. The machine, which originally cost €/£81,500, is being depreciated at €/£5,333 per year, with an estimated scrap value of €/£1,500 in 11 years' time. This machine qualifies for tax capital allowances of 12.5% per annum for a further four years, straight-line, and has a tax written down value of €/£40,750 now after four years' use.

Proposal 2: Replace the Old Machine The company is considering trading in the old machine now for €/£8,000 and purchasing a modern machine which would cost €/£98,000 before the trade-in allowance. It is estimated that the new machine would have reduced operating and maintenance costs of about €/£11,000 per year, with an estimated residual value at the end of its 11-year useful life of €/£3,000.

Proposal 3: Overhaul the Old Machine A third possibility is to spend €/£10,000 on an immediate overhaul of the old machine. This would be an allowable expense for tax purposes. The benefit of the overhaul would be to reduce operating and maintenance costs to about €/£22,000 per year for the unchanged remaining useful life of 11 years. The overhaul would not affect the residual scrap value of €/£1,500 in 11 years' time for the old machine.

Additional information:

(i) Cleansweep is liable to corporation tax at 20%, payable at the end of the year in which the profits arise.
(ii) The company's cost of capital is estimated to be 10%.
(iii) The chief executive advises you that the board of directors normally evaluate capital projects on the basis of simple payback – requiring payback in four years.
(iv) The chief executive is disappointed that the accounting rate of return (ARR) is considered irrelevant and is not calculated. You note that his remuneration is linked to reported profits and consequently he does not favour incurring any loss on a disposal on the old machine.

Requirement Using an incremental cash flow analysis (compared to Proposal 1 above):
(a) Calculate the simple payback, after tax, on both of the above Proposals 2 and 3 (i.e. replacement and overhaul).

7 Marks

(b) Calculate the net present value of Proposals 2 and 3 (i.e. replacement and overhaul).

4 Marks

(c) Using the results from (b), calculate the sensitivity of the replacement proposal to the amount of estimated operating and maintenance costs, i.e. what is the maximum amount of such costs for the old machine that would make it profitable not to overhaul or replace the old machine?

4 Marks

(d) Following the chief executive's comments, as per notes (iii) and (iv), write a short note outlining the main objections to the use of accounting rate of return and simple payback for capital investment appraisal. Comment on the ethical acceptability of point (iv) above as a factor in selecting the best proposal. Candidates are not required to calculate ARR.

5 Marks
Total 20 Marks

(Based on Chartered Accountants Ireland, CAP 1, Finance, Summer 2008, Q2)

Question 3.9 KBL (Level 1)

The senior management of Kearney Brothers Limited has just recently approved a project to manufacture a new innovative product called the Zylex. You have been asked to evaluate the project using the net present value method. The background to the project is as follows:

1. The project is expected to last for four years.
2. KBL has carried out initial market research at a cost of €/£500,000.
3. KBL is uncertain of the number of units of the Zylex it will be able to manufacture and sell. Using the information obtained from the initial market research, KBL has determined the following probability estimates:

Units	Probability
45,000	0.3
50,000	0.2
55,000	0.4
60,000	0.1

The number of units to be manufactured and sold will remain constant over the life of the project.

4. The selling price per unit of the Zylex in Year 1 will be €/£10 per unit and this will increase by 10% each year thereafter.
5. Each unit of the Zylex requires one item of raw material, which costs €/£2.50 per unit. Due to market efficiencies the cost is expected to remain constant over the four-year period.

6. The manufacturing process generates a by-product that will have to be disposed of at a cost of €/£0.15 per unit manufactured.
7. KBL will hire skilled workers to manufacture the Zylex. Each worker will be paid €/£4.00 for each unit manufactured.
8. Existing fixed overheads amounting to €/£50,000 per annum will be allocated to the new project.
9. KBL will spend €/£70,000 per annum on advertising and marketing in Year 1 and Year 2 and €/£20,000 per annum in Year 3 and Year 4.
10. KBL will purchase a machine for €/£450,000 to manufacture the Zylex immediately. This machine will have a scrap value of €/£50,000 at the end of the project. This machine will be depreciated on a straight-line basis over the life of the project.
11. KBL will take out a loan for the purchase of the above machine and interest at a rate of 7% will be paid annually on this loan.
12. Working capital of €/£105,000 will be required at the commencement of the project.
13. The cost of capital is 10%.
14. Taxation can be ignored.
15. Assume all cash flows occur at the end of each year unless told otherwise.

Requirement Calculate the net present value (NPV) of this project and advise KBL's senior management whether or not this project is viable.

16 Marks

(***Note:*** all relevant workings should be included in your answer and marks will be awarded for a brief explanation of why any of the cash flows may be irrelevant to this investment decision.)

(Based on Chartered Accountants Ireland, CAP 1, Finance, Autumn 2012, Q1(a))

Question 3.10 Project X and Project Y (Level 2)

A company is manufacturing a consumer product the demand for which, at current price levels, is in excess of its ability to produce. The limiting factor on production is the capacity of a particular machine, which is now due for replacement.

The possibilities exist either of replacing it with a similar machine (Project X) or acquiring a more expensive machine with greater throughput capacity (Project Y).

The pre-tax cash flows under each alternative have been estimated and are given below. The company's opportunity cost of capital is 10% after tax.

Tax is payable at the rate of 12.5% one year in arrears. Assume that tax is payable on all the cash inflows, but that capital allowances are available at a rate of 25% reducing balance per annum on the cost of either machine from the accounting period in which the machine is first put into use. There are currently, and will continue to be, sufficient surplus profits in the company to absorb any excess of capital allowances or balancing allowances that may arise. Whichever machine is purchased it will be put into use at the end of 20X4. The Project X machine will be sold for €/£1,000 before the end of December 20X9, whereas the Project Y machine will have no sales value at the end of its useful life, and will be scrapped in early 20Y0.

The pertinent data are as follows:

	Project X	**Project Y**
	€/£000	**€/£000**
20X4 (cost of machine)	(27)	(40)
20X5 (cash flows generated)	–	10
20X6	5	14
20X7	22	16
20X8	14	17
20X9	14	15

Requirement

(a) Using the information above and taking into account tax information, calculate the following:
   (i) Net present value.

8 Marks

   (ii) Profitability index.

2 Marks

   (iii) Discounted payback period.

2 Marks

(b) Discuss the relevance of these calculations to the decision to be taken.

5 Marks

(c) The variables used in calculating the cash inflows on Project X are as follows:

Year	Sales/production quantity	Production cost per unit	Sales price per unit
	Units	€/£	€/£
20X5	9,000	1.5	1.5
20X6	10,000	1.5	2
20X7	40,000	1.45	2
20X8	28,000	1.4	1.9
20X9	28,000	1.4	1.9

The managing director has doubts about the accuracy of these estimates, and would like to concentrate his attention on that variable for which an error in estimating would have the most significant effect on the DCF rate of return for the project as a whole.

Calculate, in respect of Project X only, the impact of each of the following (independently) on the total pre-tax undiscounted cash flows:
(i) a 5% increase in the production cost per unit;
(ii) a 5% decrease in the selling price of the product.

In this part of the question, you may ignore taxation and capital allowances.

5 Marks
Total 22 Marks

(Based on Chartered Accountants Ireland, MABF II, Autumn 2006, Q5)

Question 3.11 SFS (Level 1)

Super Fitness Studios Limited (SFS) currently has 12 fitness gyms and studios across the country and is considering setting up a new gym with a four-year life.

The finance manager has provided you with the following financial information in relation to the set-up of a new gym by SFS:

1. SFS has received advice costing €/£100,000 from industry consultants regarding the set-up of a new gym. The consultants are to be paid immediately for this advice.
2. The consultants have estimated that the gym will attract 1,000 members in the first year. This will increase by 10% per annum thereafter. Each member will pay €/£500 per annum.
3. Before taking into account wages and salaries, the gym will earn a margin of 80% on the income it receives from membership fees each year.
4. The gym will employ eight staff members. This includes seven gym instructors and one gym manager. The gym instructors will be paid a salary of €/£30,000 per annum and the gym manager will be paid a salary €/£60,000 per annum.

5. The gym manager will get a bonus of €/£5,000 in any year that gym membership exceeds 1,100 members.
6. Fixed costs of €/£75,000 per annum will be allocated by SFS head office to the new gym.
7. The rent on the premises for the new gym will be €/£45,000 per annum for the four-year period. A premium of €/£30,000 is also payable immediately to the landlord for the premises.
8. SFS will have to purchase the gym equipment immediately for €/£120,000. Capital allowances can be claimed on the equipment cost at a rate of 25% per annum and the equipment will be sold for a residual value of €/£10,000 at the end of the four years. A balancing adjustment should be calculated on the sale of the gym equipment. Depreciation will be charged on a straight-line basis over four years.
9. SFS will take out a loan immediately to pay for the gym equipment and will pay interest at a rate of 7% per annum on the loan.
10. Specialist weight-lifting equipment will also be moved from one of SFS's current gyms to the new gym. This equipment cost €/£50,000 four years ago. This will result in lost contribution of €/£15,000 per annum in the gym from which the equipment is taken. Capital allowances have previously been claimed on these machines.
11. Tax is payable at a rate of 20% in a year in which profits arise.
12. Assume all cash flows are real cash flows (i.e. they do not include inflation) and occur at the end of the year unless otherwise stated.
13. The nominal cost of capital is 15% and the inflation rate is 4.5%.
14. All figures should be rounded to the nearest €/£000.

Requirement

(a) Calculate the net present value (NPV) for SFS of opening a new gym using the real discount factor and advise SFS's management whether or not it should proceed with this project.
(***Note:*** all relevant workings should be included in your answer and marks will be rewarded for a brief explanation of why any of the cash flows may be irrelevant to the investment decision.)

15 Marks

(b) Using sensitivity analysis, state the extent (%) by which the following items (taken separately) would have to change before the opening of a new gym would cease to be worthwhile for SFS:
  (i) the cost of the new equipment of €/£120,000;
  (ii) revenue from membership fees.

5 Marks
Total 20 Marks

(Based on Chartered Accountants Ireland, CAP 1, Finance, Summer 2013, Q1)

Question 3.12 Ringrose (Level 2)

Ringrose Ltd is a company that operates multi-storey car parks. The company's head office is in Dublin, but it operates car parks in various locations throughout Ireland.

The company is now considering the construction of a large car park adjacent to a new shopping centre, in a large town in the northwest of Ireland. The car park will provide space for a maximum of 500 cars.

The financial accountant of the company has produced the following financial projections for the proposal. The figures are based on a life of five years.

Initial costs

Construction costs	€/£5 million
Other set-up costs	€/£1.5 million

Sales It is estimated that the daily income from each car-parking space will be €/£12 in Year 1, rising thereafter by 2% per annum.

It is estimated that the car park will be open for 300 days in the year and, on average, there will be 70% occupancy of the available spaces.

Costs Variable and fixed costs of operating the car park are estimated to be €/£450,000 and €/£810,000 respectively in Year 1. Fixed costs include annual depreciation of €/£250,000 and overheads allocated from head office of €/£100,000.

Fixed and variable costs are expected to rise by 2.3% annually.

Capital allowances Expenditure on the construction of multi-storey car parks that are developed in accordance with criteria laid down by government attracts capital allowances at enhanced rates.

It is expected that the costs of constructing this car park will attract an initial allowance of 50% and an annual allowance of 4% of cost thereafter.

Capital allowances on other capital outlays will be 15% per annum, on a straight-line basis.

Corporation tax Corporation tax is expected to be 20% per annum for the foreseeable future. You may assume that corporation tax is paid in the year in which profits are earned.

Residual value It is estimated that the car park could be sold for €/£10 million at the end of the five-year period.

Discount rate The project is to be discounted at the company's current WACC of 12%.

Uncertainty One of the equity holders of Ringrose Ltd has voiced concern over the projections. He considers that they are too optimistic given the national economic forecasts for the next five years. He is concerned that, if the economy goes into recession, it could have a serious effect on the profitability of the project.

Requirement

(a) Calculate, on the basis of the figures provided, the NPV of the proposed investment.
Make your recommendations, based on your calculations, as to whether or not Ringrose Ltd should proceed with the project.

12 Marks

(b) In order to provide some comfort to the concerned equity holder, the financial accountant has decided to carry out some sensitivity analysis on the project. Assuming that none of the other inputs deviate from the estimates provided, calculate by how much each of the following inputs would need to change before the project would cease to be worthwhile.
(i) The discount rate.
(ii) The residual value.

Comment on your results.

6 Marks

(c) Outline **TWO** weaknesses in the sensitivity analysis approach to measuring risk.

4 Marks
Total 22 Marks

(Based on Chartered Accountants Ireland, MABF II, Autumn 2002)

Question 3.13 Brayshaw Plc (Level 1)

(a) Discuss **two** methods of adjusting for investment risk.

8 Marks

(b) Brayshaw Plc is currently considering a project with the following cash flows:

	Year 0	**Year 1**	**Year 2**
	€/£000	**€/£000**	**€/£000**
Initial investment	(7,000)	–	–
Variable costs	–	(2,000)	(2,000)
Cash inflows (650,000 units at €/£10 per unit)	–	6,500	6,500
Net cash flows	(7,000)	4,500	4,500

The company's cost of capital is 8%.

Requirement Calculate the margin of safety of the project with respect to changes in the following variables:

(i) Initial investment.
(ii) Sales volume.
(iii) Selling price.
(iv) Variable costs.
(v) Cost of capital.

14 Marks
Total 22 Marks

(Based on Chartered Accountants Ireland, MABF II, Autumn 1998, Q5)

4

Ratio Analysis

Learning Objectives

Upon completing this chapter, readers should be able to:

- calculate ratios to assess the financial performance, financial position and investment potential of a company;
- make suggestions for differences in reported ratios: between similar companies; for the same company over time; and relative to industry averages; and
- list the limitations of ratio analysis.

INTRODUCTION

The most common technique for assessing company financial performance is ratio analysis. **Ratio analysis** summarises the relationships between key data entries from financial statements. Trends in ratios over time are usually calculated and interpreted as being indicative of how a company will perform in the future. Ratio analysis is widely used both in-house to evaluate performance and by external parties, including investors. Ratios can provide very useful information, such as the ability of a company to survive and grow, and can be used to indicate the efficiency of management. However, care needs to be taken when interpreting ratio results as the conditions in one company may change from year to year, and no two companies are the same. Therefore, ratio analysis should be used to spark investigation, to instigate the correct questions to be asked, or to limit the investigation of changes in performance and efficiency to key areas. Ratios should not be relied on solely to explain changes in the financial performance of a company.

This chapter begins by setting out the purpose of financial statements and examines how these documents can be utilised to help determine the financial position and performance of a company over time. The chapter splits ratios that are commonly computed when analysing the financial performance of a company into three key areas that are of interest to an investor: company performance, financial position and investment potential. A proforma set of financial statements is provided at the end of the chapter and is used throughout the chapter to provide practical examples of how ratios can be used to interpret company performance, financial position and investment potential.

FINANCIAL STATEMENTS

The annual report of a company is the core document used when evaluating company performance. The annual report can range from four to five pages long for a sole trader, to over one hundred pages for Plcs. A published annual report is primarily in two parts. The first part is mostly narrative and is used by directors and management of a company (agents/stewards) to communicate information directly to equity holders in respect of how they have discharged their stewardship of the company. It also provides information on the future direction, development and plans for a company. The narrative portion of annual reports, for Plcs in particular, has expanded over the decades and now usually includes: a chair's report; an operating and financial review; a remuneration report; a directors' report; a corporate governance report; and a chair's review. Directors use these reports to reduce information asymmetry between the directors and the company's stakeholders.

Information included in narrative reports is outlined in **Figure 4.1** below. This information is both financial and non-financial in nature. The narrative part of an annual report does not form part of a company's financial statements.

Figure 4.1: Information Included in Narrative Reports

The second part of the published annual report, the financial statements, includes the historical results of a company. A company's past results are portrayed primarily in three statements:

- the statement of profit or loss;
- the statement of financial position; and
- the statement of cash flows.

An example of the typical layout of these statements is provided at the back of this chapter. The statements are accompanied by detailed notes, including accounting policies and the statement of changes in equity. In some instances, the latter might be included as a primary statement.

The financial statements provide useful information that an individual, with a reasonable understanding of business, should be able to decipher. The stewardship role of management can be assessed by reviewing the movement in the assets and liabilities of a company. Management's accountability can be assessed by reference to the statement of profit or loss, supplementary notes and the narrative reports included in the annual report, such as the chair's review or the directors' report. Ratio analysis is used to provide metrics that enable an assessment of different aspects of the business's performance.

Ratios are normally sub-divided into a minimum of three categories:

- performance;
- financial position; and
- investment potential.

Performance ratios focus on assessing the profitability of a company and the efficiency with which a company utilises its resources. Performance ratios are sometimes referred to as **operating ratios**. The financial position category examines the resources held by a company: its liquidity; solvency; and underlying financial structure. The final category, investment potential, focuses on assessing the earnings generated by a company. It investigates the extent of earnings distributed and, conversely, the amounts retained for capital growth.

Performance

The performance of a company can be analysed according to its profitability and its efficiency.

Profitability

To adequately assess company performance, it is vital to be able to interpret changes in company profitability, and indeed to compare a company's profitability to the profitability of other companies (in the same industry or in other industries). **Figure 4.2** below summarises some of the decisions that information on profitability can inform.

FIGURE 4.2: PROFITABILITY RATIOS

Determine the impact of changes in the economic resources of a company on future profitability.

Assess the ability of a company to generate cash flows from its current economic resources.

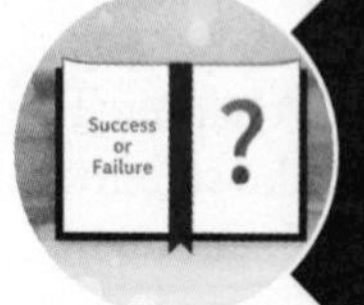

Predict the success/failure of future investment decisions made by a company.

Information on company profitability can be obtained from the statement of profit or loss (see example on page 172). The statement of profit or loss shows the income and related expenditure for a period. It is split into sections, with the first section providing information on the direct costs associated with products/services being produced – revenue less the cost of revenue. The resultant profit, or loss, is termed **gross profit**, or **gross loss**.

The second section of the statement of profit or loss deals with all overhead expenses that are not directly linked with the products being sold, these include administration and distribution expenses. These are totalled and deducted from gross profit to give **net profit**, or **profit before interest and tax (PBIT)**. Then interest is removed to give **profit before tax** and, finally, tax is removed leaving **distributable profit**.

Each of the sub-total profit entries in the statement of profit or loss provides valuable information to anyone who is trying to analyse the performance of a company (an investor). From the statement of profit or loss, an investor can see the absolute size of profits made. A quick scan of the comparatives allows an investor to determine whether profits have increased or decreased in absolute terms. The following equation can be used to determine the percentage change in profits:

$$\frac{\textbf{Current year profit}}{\textbf{Prior year profit}} \ \textbf{-1 = Growth \%}$$

Worked Example 4.1: Profit Analysis – Growth in Profitability

Using the financial statements of ABC Plc on pages 172–4, calculate the percentage growth in profits.

Solution

The percentage increase in gross profits between 20X1 and 20X2 is:

$$\frac{€/£7{,}000{,}000}{€/£6{,}200{,}000} -1 = 12.9\%$$

Profit has increased by 12.9% over the period 1 January 20X1 to 31 December 20X2.

Where the percentage change in profits is positive, this is a good sign; however, it should be interpreted with caution as this formula does not take inflation into consideration. There is only real improvement if the growth rate exceeds the rate of inflation.

Gross profit margin: a commonly used ratio to provide information on gross profit is the gross profit margin. This is calculated as follows:

$$\frac{\textbf{Gross profit}}{\textbf{Revenue}} \times \textbf{100 = Gross profit margin}$$

The **gross profit margin** is the percentage return made from each sale after direct product costs are deducted. It is sometimes referred to as the **contribution margin** – the contribution from revenue to cover a company's fixed costs and to pay financiers.

Worked Example 4.2: Profit analysis – Gross Profit Margin

Using the financial statements of ABC Plc on pages 172–4, calculate the gross profit margin for both years.

Solution

The gross profit margins are:

$$20X2: \frac{€/£20,000,000}{€/£50,000,000} \times 100 = 40.0\%$$

$$20X1: \frac{€/£17,000,000}{€/£45,000,000} \times 100 = 37.8\%$$

The gross profit percentage has increased from 37.8% of sales value to 40.0% of sales value.

The gross profit margin varies between companies, although should be reasonably similar within specific industries. For example, the margin on petrol sales is very small, circa 5%, whereas the margin on grocery sales can range from 10% to 50% (average at 30%). For products with a fast turnover (for example, bread), the gross profit margin is usually low, whereas products with a slow turnover have a higher gross profit margin (for example, jewellery). In general, a company's gross profit performance is best analysed with reference to the industry average, or with other companies selling similar products. Change in the gross profit margin from year to year within one company should not be common. Where a change in the margin does result, it may be due to:

- a change in the selling price of the product – for example, a fall in the margin may be as a result of the company reducing the selling price of its products to achieve more sales and more overall gross profit, but less gross profit per euro/pound of sale;
- a change in the purchase price of supplies – for example, from loss of discounts, wastage, theft or obsolescence of inventories;
- inflation; or
- a change in sales product mix.

Profit before interest and taxation (PBIT): the next important profit figure is the PBIT. The PBIT highlights the return made by a company from its activities before taxation and the cost of financing the company are deducted. This figure is usually analysed in two ways: the first is to provide an indication of the overall PBIT from each euro/pound of sale made (the **profit margin**); the second is to highlight the return the company has made for the financiers and owners of the company, the **return on capital employed** (ROCE).

Net profit margin (profit margin): the profit margin is calculated as follows:

$$\frac{\textbf{PBIT}}{\textbf{Revenue}} \times \mathbf{100} = \textbf{Profit margin}$$

Worked Example 4.3: Profit Analysis – Profit Margin

Using the financial statements of ABC Plc on pages 172–4, calculate the profit margin for both years using profit before interest, tax and distributions.

Solution

The profit margins are:

$$20X2: \frac{€/£8{,}500{,}000 + €/£1{,}000{,}000^{*}}{€/£50{,}000{,}000} \times 100 = 19.0\%$$

$$20X1: \frac{€/£9{,}000{,}000 + €/£1{,}000{,}000}{€/£45{,}000{,}000} \times 100 = 22.2\%$$

*€/£1,000,000 is the finance cost being added back to get PBIT.

The profit margin has fallen from 22.2% of sales value to 19.0% of sales value, over the year. This result would have been influenced by the increase in the gross profit margin (see **Worked Example 4.2**); however, this benefit has been outweighed by increases in the fixed costs of the company, namely the distribution, administration and other costs, and the reduction in other income received. These costs require further scrutiny.

The profit margin is open to more variation than the gross profit margin as it encapsulates all the costs of a company, including fixed costs. Movements in the absolute amount of gross profit will impact on the profit margin. The gross profit margin could be considered to be more variable in nature, changing with the volume of transactions; whereas the costs deducted from gross profit (administration and distribution costs) when calculating the PBIT, are more fixed in nature. In addition, exceptional one-off costs are more likely to influence this ratio. Asset sales/write-offs are posted here, as are redundancy costs, bonuses and other such one-off expenses. When all the exceptional items are removed, this ratio can provide information on economies of scale, or inefficiencies. With appropriate expenses analyses (i.e. individual expenses as a proportion of revenue), inefficient areas can be highlighted and measures put in place to reduce inefficiencies.

When analysing company performance, a holistic approach has to be taken. For example, when a company changes its product price, to generate more revenue the resultant changes in the profitability ratios might be as follows: a lower sales price is likely to stimulate more revenue; however, it will result in a lower reported gross profit margin, though higher overall profitability (net profit). Conversely, a high sales price is likely to reduce overall revenue and result in a high reported gross profit margin. However, the lower gross profit amount will result in lower overall profitability (net profit) as fixed costs will not have changed.

Return on capital employed (ROCE): the ROCE ratio is sometimes referred to as the **primary ratio** and is regarded as the most important performance ratio, as it provides information on the return earned by a company on capital invested by investors (owners and financiers). Capital invested is commonly referred to as **capital employed**. Capital employed includes:

- equity (equity share capital, reserves, share premium and other equity reserves); and
- long-term debt (debentures, loan stock, long-term debt, preference shares and any other long-term debt sources, including provisions for expenses extending beyond one year).

Capital employed can be calculated by finding the sum of the book value of equity and debt, or can be calculated using 'total assets less liabilities due within one year'. The ROCE ratio is calculated as follows:

$$\frac{\textbf{PBIT}}{\textbf{Capital employed}} \times \textbf{100} = \textbf{ROCE}$$

Worked example 4.4: Profit analysis – ROCE

Using the financial statements of ABC Plc on pages 172–4, calculate the ROCE for both years.

Solution

$$\text{20X2: } \frac{€/£8{,}500{,}000 + €/£1{,}000{,}000}{€/£40{,}500{,}000 + €/£25{,}000{,}000} \times 100 = 14.5\%$$

$$\text{20X1: } \frac{€/£9{,}000{,}000 + €/£1{,}000{,}000}{€/£29{,}500{,}000 + €/£21{,}500{,}000} \times 100 = 19.6\%$$

The ROCE has declined from 19.6% of capital employed in 20X1, to 14.5% of capital employed in 20X2. On the surface, this means that the additional investment in resources has not yielded profit levels in line with those obtained prior to the investment.

Caution: information on the timing of the increase in resources would aid interpretation of this ratio. When increases occur near the year-end, the ratio should be adjusted to remove the new capital. Indeed, assets may have been sold just prior to the end of 20X1, causing the prior year ratio to be overstated and not reflective of the return received on the capital that was invested for the whole year.

When analysing the ROCE, comparison should be made to prior year figures. The ratio should be adjusted where it is affected by exceptional items, so that like is compared with like. Obviously any increase in the reported percentage is a strong sign of performance, as the capital is producing more profit from each euro/pound invested. In addition, the ROCE should be compared to that reported by other companies in the same industry, as they will be affected similarly by changes in the economy. For example, suppose interest rates rise, causing demand for a company's products to fall. This will result in a fall in its ROCE, which the markets would react to negatively. However, so long as a company's ROCE does not fall to the same extent as in other companies from the same industry, the company's performance will be treated in a positive light. Investors will interpret the comparative results across the companies and may conclude that the lower than average fall in the ROCE is a signal of strong management who are adapting to the new economic conditions better than their competitors.

The ROCE should also be compared to the current risk-free rate of interest (bank borrowing rates, or government bond coupon rates). Investing in a company is always riskier than investing in debt; therefore, investors will assess whether the premium for investing in a company, a proxy of which might be the excess of the ROCE over the risk-free rate, is sufficient to warrant holding shares in a company. In addition, financiers will be keen to ensure that the ROCE is greater than the cost of debt. Excess returns are required not only to pay interest on debt but also to build up reserves, and to repay loan capital.

Efficiency

The ROCE provides an indication of the profitability of a company and also its efficiency in the use the company makes of funds invested in it. The ROCE is broken down into a number of other ratios that help to pinpoint the source of changes in performance or to highlight weaknesses/strengths in performance. The ratios and their interrelationship with the ROCE are highlighted in **Figure 4.3**.

Figure 4.3: Principal Operating Ratios and the ROCE

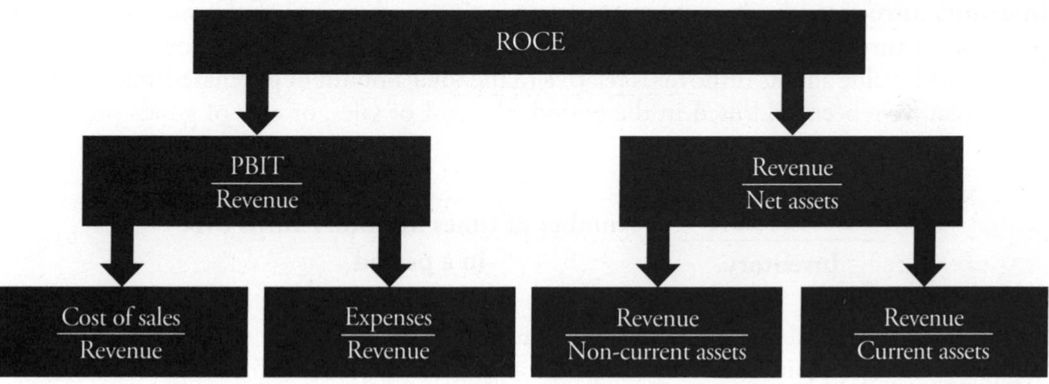

The left-hand-side ratios are considered to focus more on profitability, with those on the right-hand side regarded as indicators of management efficiency in the use of assets to generate revenue.

Non-current asset turnover: the first of the efficiency ratios, the **non-current asset turnover ratio** (revenue to non-current assets), gives an indication of the amount of revenue being generated from each euro/pound invested in non-current assets. Care needs to be taken when interpreting this ratio as the value of non-current assets in different companies may differ, depending on accounting policies adopted. For example, differing depreciation policies may also lead to differences that relate to accounting adjustments, not indicators of efficiency. In addition, the timing of additions and disposals during the year will also complicate comparison of the ratio between different years for an individual company. Aside from these pitfalls this ratio provides a good indicator of the utilisation of non-current assets by management. Where turnover is low, assets can be scrutinised to determine if they are being utilised effectively to generate revenue, this process might highlight assets that are surplus to requirements. These can be sold, with little impact on operating activities, but resulting in a cash injection to a company that can be utilised to produce more revenue.

Current asset turnover: the **current asset turnover ratio** highlights the revenue generated by each euro/pound invested in current assets.

It provides an indication of the efficiency of the utilisation of current assets in the generation of revenue. Like the non-current asset turnover ratio, its comparability is influenced by accounting policies, for example, one company might use the first-in first-out method of inventory valuation, whereas another might use the last-in first-out method. When inventory is rising or falling in price, the two methods will result in different inventory values. The determination of the provision for doubtful debts is also subjective as is any provision for a fall in inventory value. Aside from these potential discrepancies, this ratio can provide a good indicator of management efficiency. Further information can be obtained by examining the individual components making up this ratio (inventories, trade receivables, trade payables). These are now considered in turn.

Inventory turnover: the **inventory turnover ratio** is a measure of the number of times inventory is turned over in a year, on average. Inventory is valued at the lower of cost and net realisable value and its turnover is relative to the total amount of purchased/manufactured goods that have been sold/used in the period (the cost of sales, or cost of goods produced). The ratio is calculated as:

$$\frac{\textbf{Cost of sales}}{\textbf{Inventory}} = \textbf{Number of times inventory turns over in a period}$$

To find out the number of days that inventory is held for, divide 365 by the inventory turnover ratio (for months, divide 12 by the ratio; for weeks, divide 52 by the ratio). This is shown in **Worked Example 4.5**.

Worked Example 4.5: Efficiency Analysis – Inventory Turnover

Using the financial statements of ABC Plc on pages 172–4, calculate the inventory turnover rate for both years. Then calculate the number of days the inventory is held in stores.

Solution

Inventory turnover is:

$$20X2: \frac{€/£30,000,000}{€/£6,000,000} = 5 \text{ times per year}$$

$$20X1: \frac{€/£28,000,000}{€/£5,000,000} = 5.6 \text{ times per year}$$

ABC Plc's inventory turned over 5.6 times in 20X1, slowing to 5 times in 20X2. This means that inventory is held for 73 days (365÷5) in 20X2, compared to 65 days (365÷5.6) in 20X1. ABC was less efficient in its management of inventory in 20X2, hence store costs would have increased.

The type of inventory, its cost, and demand for the inventory will influence the amount held and the number of times inventory is turned over. The lower the amount of inventory held, the higher the number of times inventory turns over. A high turnover is generally considered efficient because low inventory levels result in lower costs. A minimum level of inventory is required as inventory levels that are too low might lead to stock-outs and loss of contribution. Determining the optimum level of inventory to hold is discussed in depth in **Chapter** 7.

Trade receivables period (debtors' ratio): the **trade receivables period (debtors' ratio)** measures the average number of days' credit taken by customers. It might differ from the number of days' credit given, as some customers may not pay within the agreed timescale, whereas others may avail of discounts and pay early. The ratio is calculated as follows:

$$\frac{\textbf{Trade receivables}}{\textbf{Credit sales}} \times \textbf{365} = \textbf{Number of days' credit taken by customers}$$

Determining the trade receivables days is shown in **Worked Example 4.6**.

Worked Example 4.6: Efficiency Analysis – Trade Receivables Period

Using the financial statements of ABC Plc on pages 172–4, calculate the trade receivables period for both years. Assume all sales are made on credit terms.

Solution

$$20X2: \frac{€/£8,000,000}{€/£50,000,000} \times 365 = 58.4 \text{ days}$$

$$20X1: \frac{€/£60,000,000}{€/£45,000,000} = 365 \times 48.67 \text{ days}$$

The number of days' credit taken by customers has increased from 48.67 days to 58.4 days. This may suggest that ABC Plc is allowing longer credit terms to achieve greater sales volume. Longer credit is linked to increasing bad debts, which might result in increased administration costs for the company, or the increasing credit period may simply be an indication of a weakening of the credit control procedures. This needs further investigation to highlight the main cause of the shift.

The trade receivables period is influenced by the type of industry a company operates in. Some companies trade mostly in cash (for example, supermarkets), others allow credit, stipulating a credit period. However, in these scenarios credit can be extended by the customer (for example, builders merchants, motor factors) beyond an agreed period. Other companies have strict credit and payment terms (some breweries require their customers to enter a direct debit arrangement. Therefore, the agreed credit period is rarely breached). When comparing the trade receivables ratio within an industry it is important to consider the days reported by similar companies only – not all companies in the same industry – as major differences between different types of company can occur. Like most other ratios, this ratio should not be interpreted in isolation. A reduction in the trade receivables period might seem to be efficient; however, it may have actually increased costs.

For example, the reduction may have been achieved by allowing a discount or a shorter credit period at the outset. The result in both cases might be a fall in profitability. Techniques that can be used to determine an optimum credit policy are examined in depth in **Chapter 8**.

Trade payables period (creditors' ratio): the **trade payables period (creditors' ratio)** indicates the average number of days' credit taken by a company, from its suppliers. This may differ from the number of days' credit given by suppliers, as the company may elect to pay for supplies earlier, to avail of discounts; or may choose to pay after a longer period, due to having insufficient cash to cover the payments. The trade payables period is calculated as follows:

$$\frac{\textbf{Trade payables}}{\textbf{Credit purchases}} \times 365 = \textbf{Number of days' credit taken by company}$$

The calculation of this ratio is provided in **Worked Example 4.7**.

Worked Example 4.7: Efficiency Analysis – Trade Payables Period

Using the financial statements of ABC Plc on pages 172–4, calculate the number of days' credit taken in both years. The opening inventory at the start of 20X1 was €/£5 million and all purchases are on credit terms.

Solution

The trade payables periods for 20X1 and 20X2 are:

20X2: $\frac{€/£5{,}500}{€/£30{,}000 + €/£6{,}000 - €/£5{,}000^*} \times 365 = 64.76$ days

20X1: $\frac{€/£10{,}000}{€/£28{,}000 + €/£5{,}000 - €/£5{,}000} \times 365 = 130.36$ days

*The required figure is credit purchases, where opening and closing inventory are known, purchases can be calculated from the cost of sales figure, as in this case.

The number of days' credit taken has fallen from 130.36 days to 64.76 days. This means that ABC Plc is paying its suppliers 65 days earlier in 20X2, relative to 20X1. To analyse this correctly it would be beneficial to know the agreed credit terms between the parties. It may be that in the prior year ABC Plc breached the credit terms and was losing discounts and being penalised with interest charges, or higher prices. By paying on time, ABC Plc may be availing of discounts, or a cheaper supplier. This explanation is consistent with the increased gross profit margin reported earlier in the chapter. (***Note***: figures are in €/£000s.)

Influences on the trade payables period and advice as to the optimum credit period to take are discussed in detail in **Chapter 8**.

Financial Position

The **statement of financial position** contains the primary source of information on the financial position of a company. The financial position of a company is affected by the economic resources of the company, its gearing, its liquidity and solvency and its ability to adapt to changes in its operating environment.

Economic Resources of a Company

Information on the economic resources a company controls and information on a company's ability to adapt, change and utilise these resources is vital to help an investor predict the ability of a company to generate future additional cash inflows, were they needed in the future. The **economic resources of a company** are its net assets (total assets less current liabilities). This information can be obtained from a company's statement of financial position. The statement of financial position is presented to aid interpretation of the data contained within. It has two sections. The top section details the assets of the company. Non-current assets are grouped together and are the first of the resources to be presented. The nature of these assets is highlighted as the statement of financial position splits the total into tangible, intangible and investments. Next, current assets are listed. The second section of the statement of financial position lists the equity and liabilities of a company. Equity is detailed first, followed by long-term liabilities, then current liabilities.

An analysis of the ability of a company to generate future additional cash flows from resources held can be obtained from the statement of cash flows. In a set of financial statements, the statement of cash flows is presented as a primary statement, located after the statement of profit or loss and the statement of financial position. It reports the cash flows generated by a company over a period, classified into operating, investing and financing activities. These classifications allow an investor to assess the impact of the three activities on the financial position, performance and adaptability of a company.

A proforma statement of cash flows is reproduced at the end of this chapter. The three different activities are as shown in **Figure 4.4**.

Figure 4.4: Statement of Cash Flows – Components

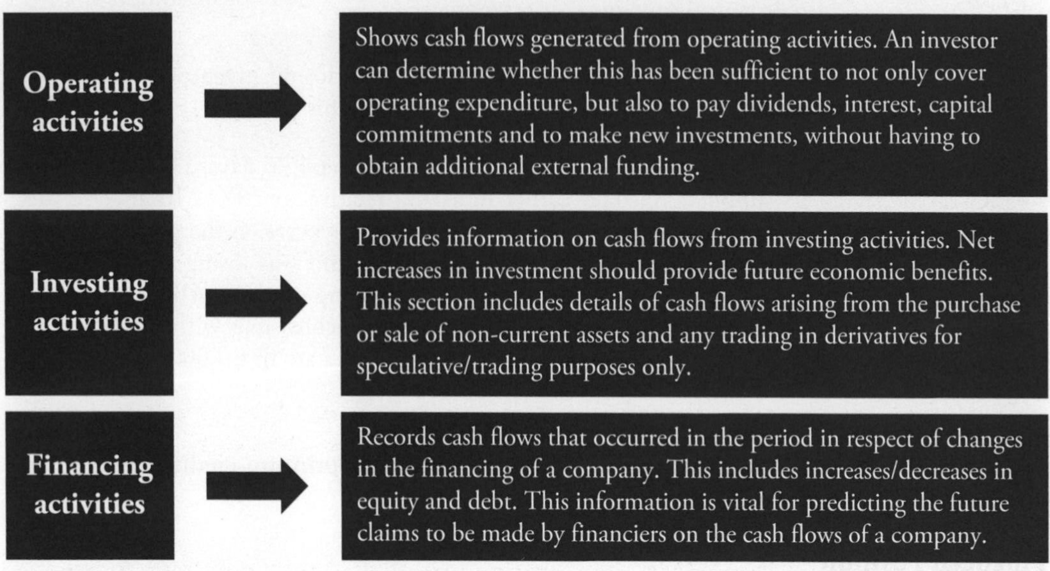

Operating activities
Shows cash flows generated from operating activities. An investor can determine whether this has been sufficient to not only cover operating expenditure, but also to pay dividends, interest, capital commitments and to make new investments, without having to obtain additional external funding.
Investing activities
Provides information on cash flows from investing activities. Net increases in investment should provide future economic benefits. This section includes details of cash flows arising from the purchase or sale of non-current assets and any trading in derivatives for speculative/trading purposes only.
Financing activities
Records cash flows that occurred in the period in respect of changes in the financing of a company. This includes increases/decreases in equity and debt. This information is vital for predicting the future claims to be made by financiers on the cash flows of a company.

Two ratios are sometimes used to compare the disclosures from the statement of profit or loss and the statement of financial position with those from the statement of cash flows. These are now explained.

Cash return on capital employed: the **cash return on capital employed** ratio is expressed as a percentage and is calculated as follows:

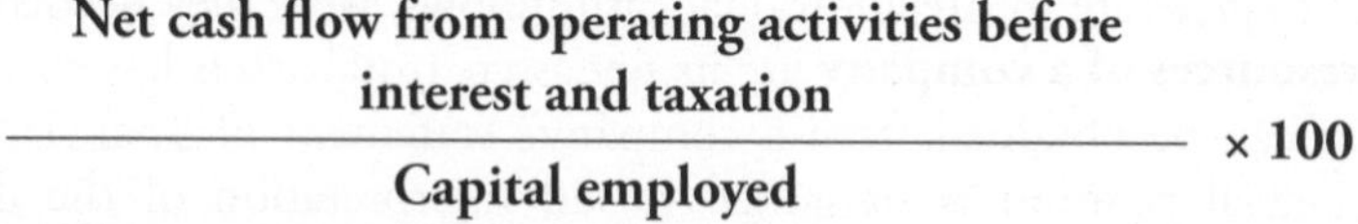

$$\frac{\textbf{Net cash flow from operating activities before interest and taxation}}{\textbf{Capital employed}} \times 100$$

This ratio provides information on the cash return on capital employed and can be compared to the profit return on capital employed to give an indication of the quality of profits earned. Calculation of this ratio is outlined in **Worked Example 4.8**.

Worked Example 4.8: Cash Flow Analysis – Cash Return on Capital Employed

Using the financial statements of ABC Plc on pages 172–4, calculate the cash return on capital employed for both years.

Solution

The cash return on capital employed ratios are:

$$20X2: \frac{€/£500,000}{€/£40,500,000 + €/£25,000,000} \times 100 = 0.76\%$$

$$20X1: \frac{€/£3,500,000^{*}}{€/£29,500,000 + €/£21,500,000} \times 100 = 6.86\%$$

*Estimate used.

In line with the reduction in the return on capital employed, the cash return from operating activities on capital employed has fallen from 6.86% in 20X1 to 0.76% in 20X2. The deterioration in cash from operating activities is a direct result of the company reducing its short-term liabilities by €/£7 million.

The problems highlighted earlier in respect of the timing of changes to capital employed are equally relevant for this ratio. Therefore, care needs to be taken when interpreting the results.

Operating cash flow to total debt: the **operating cash flow to total debt** ratio is expressed as a percentage and is calculated as follows:

$$\frac{\textbf{Operating cash flow}}{\textbf{Total debt}} \times \textbf{100}$$

This ratio provides information on the ability of a company to service its total debt from yearly cash flows. A high ratio provides a better sign of the solvency of a company. Calculation of this ratio is provided in **Worked Example 4.9.**

Worked Example 4.9: Cash Flow Analysis – Solvency

Using the financial statements of ABC Plc on pages 172–4, calculate the operating cash flow to total debt ratio for 20X2.

Solution

The operating cash flow to total debt ratio is:

$$20X2: \frac{€/£3,500,000}{€/£25,000,000+ €/£10,000,000} \times 100 = -10\%$$

This result is an indication of poor company solvency. If a company is not producing positive cash flows from its operating activities it is unlikely to be able to meet the capital claims of debt financiers in the future.

LIQUIDITY AND SOLVENCY

Liquidity is a measure of the availability of cash to a company in the near future, after taking into account the commitments and liabilities of the company in the same timeframe. The term 'near future' typically refers to a period of one year (or are already cash), and items that will cause an outflow of cash within one year. **Solvency** is a term used to denote the availability of cash in a longer timeframe to meet longer-term expected cash outflows and commitments. An analysis of the liquidity and solvency of a company will help an investor to determine the cash strength of a company in the short and long term.

Most companies use rolling cash budgets to manage their short- and long-term cash requirements. Cash budgets show the expected cash inflows and outflows, usually on a monthly basis. They can be used to highlight financing deficiencies and surpluses throughout a period. In terms of solvency, they can be used to schedule the size that long-term loan repayments should be, or to determine whether a company can purchase an asset using its own internal cash flows, or whether it should obtain external funding.

External investors do not have access to cash budgets. They have to try to gauge the liquidity and solvency of a company by analysing its statement of cash flows and performing ratio analysis on its statement of financial position. The crucial indicator of liquidity from the statement of cash flows is the extent of net cash inflows received from operating activities. In addition, two key ratios can be calculated from the statement of financial position to provide an indication of the liquidity of a company. These ratios are called the current ratio, and the quick, or acid test, ratio.

Current ratio: the **current ratio** provides a measure of the extent by which a company's current assets cover its current liabilities.

Current ratio = Current assets : Current liabilities

The calculation of this ratio is included in **Worked Example 4.10**.

WORKED EXAMPLE 4.10: LIQUIDITY ANALYSIS – CURRENT RATIO

Using the financial statements of ABC Plc on pages 172–4, calculate the current ratio for both years.

Solution

The current ratios are:

20X2: €/£19,000,000 : €/£10,000,000 = 1.9 : 1

20X1: €/£22,000,000 : €/£17,000,000 = 1.29 : 1

The current ratio has increased from 1.29 : 1 to 1.9 : 1, suggesting that ABC Plc is in a stronger liquidity position in 20X2. It now has €/£1.90 of current assets available to cover each €/£1 of current liability. This ratio would need to be compared to the industry average to determine whether the result is good, or not. If the industry average is 1.5 : 1, then a ratio of 1.9 : 1 might indicate an overinvestment in current assets – hence inefficiencies.

In textbooks, a benchmark ratio is 2 to 1 (i.e. twice as many current assets should be held relative to current liabilities). In practice, however, the ratio is industry-specific. For example, manufacturing industries usually hold sufficient inventory to ensure their production processes do not have to stop due to raw material shortages. At any point in time, they will also have work in progress and finished goods to meet orders as they fall due. Most manufacturers must trade on credit terms with their customers, so will also have a substantial amount of trade receivables. Therefore, a large current ratio is expected for manufacturing entities.

A retail company, on the other hand, will only have finished goods inventory. They usually trade on cash terms only – hence will have no trade receivables. Therefore, a much lower current ratio is expected for a retail company relative to a manufacturing company. A more meaningful evaluation of a company's liquidity position is to compare its current ratio with the average current ratio for that type of company in that industry. When a company's current ratio is less than the company-specific industry-average current ratio, this may suggest that the company is having liquidity problems; whereas when it is greater than the company-specific industry average it may indicate inefficiencies in the management of working capital, which will reduce company profits.

Quick/acid test ratio: the current ratio provides information to enable the user to determine the liquidity of the company over a period of several months to one year. The **quick/acid test ratio** is used to provide an indication of the liquidity of the company in a very short timescale as it removes the investment in inventory from the current ratio. Inventory is the least liquid current asset. Therefore, the quick/acid test ratio is a good measure of a company's ability to respond quickly when there are cash commitments to be serviced. The quick/acid test ratio is calculated as follows:

Quick/acid test ratio = (Current assets – Inventories) : Current liabilities

Calculation of this ratio is covered by **Worked Example 4.11.**

Worked Example 4.11: Liquidity Analysis – Quick/Acid Test Ratio

Using the financial statements of ABC Plc on pages 172–4, calculate the quick/acid test ratio for both years.

Solution

The quick/acid test ratios are:

20X2: (€/£19,000,000 – €/£6,000,000) : €/£10,000,000 = 1.3 : 1

20X1: (€/£22,000,000 – €/£5,000,000) : €/£17,000,000 = 1 : 1

The quick ratio has increased from 1 : 1 to 1.3 : 1. Consistent with the results of the current ratio, the quick ratio results suggest that ABC Plc is in a stronger liquidity position, in respect of its near cash assets also. It now has €/£1.30 of current assets available to cover each €/£1 of current liability. This ratio would need to be compared to the industry average to determine whether the result is good, or not.

A benchmark quick ratio outcome is commonly cited as 1 : 1, i.e. all the current liabilities being covered by the most liquid current assets. An outcome of less than 1 : 1 would be indicative of liquidity problems, as the company is unable to service its current liabilities from its current assets. A return of greater than 1 : 1 might suggest that there are inefficiencies in the management of the company's working capital, which will affect the profitability of a company.

Financial/Capital Structure

The equity invested and retained within a company and the long-term debt provided to a company make up its **financial structure**. In this text, a company's financial structure is referred to as its **capital structure**. Knowledge about the capital structure of a company is valuable when assessing a company's financial position as it can be used to predict future sources of finance that the company might acquire and to make judgements on how profits and cash flows will be distributed among financiers in the future. Information on the financial structure of a company is available from its statement of financial position. Information from the statement of profit or loss can provide guidance on risk associated with a company's capital structure.

Gearing ratio: **gearing** is the extent to which a company is financed by investors who are not owners. Information on the sources of finance obtained by a company, from investors who are not owners, can be found in its statement of financial position under the heading long-term liabilities. These sources typically include: preference shares; debentures; loan stock; long-term debt and other liabilities that extend beyond one year. The gearing ratio is calculated as follows:

$$\frac{\textbf{Long-term debt}}{\textbf{Long-term debt + Equity}} \times \textbf{100 = \% of the company financed by debt}$$

An example of the calculation of the gearing ratio is provided in **Worked Example 4.12**.

Worked Example 4.12: Financial Structure – Gearing Ratio

Using the financial statements of ABC Plc on pages 172–4, calculate the level of gearing in both years.

Solution

The level of gearing is:

$$\text{20X2:} \quad \frac{\text{€/£25,000,000}}{\text{€/£40,500,000 + €/£25,000,000}} \times 100 = 38.16\%$$

$$\text{20X1:} \quad \frac{\text{€/£21,500,000}}{\text{€/£29,500,000 + €/£21,500,000}} \times 100 = 42.15\%$$

In 20X1, 42.15% of the company was financed using debt sources; this has fallen to 38.16% by 20X2. A lower gearing ratio indicates lower financial risk. During the year the level of debt increased by €/£3.5 million, mostly as a result of an increase in long-term borrowings; however, the level of equity investment increased by a greater amount (€/£11 million). The equity increase came from two sources: a share issue provided a capital injection of €/£5 million; and €/£6 million of the €/£7 million profit made in the year was retained for future investment. Therefore, the financial structure of the company is in a stronger position at 31 December 20X2.

Like most ratios, a company's gearing should be compared to the average industry gearing level. A common rule of thumb is that a company should be able to cover its long-term debt from its equity. Management will view this ratio in a different light to external investors. When managers act to maximise equity holder value, they will seek to manipulate the capital structure of a company so as to maximise its value (see **Chapter 16** for a detailed discussion of theories on capital structure and value creation). External investors will use this ratio to highlight the financial risks associated with investing in a company. This will help them to decide if the return expected is fair given the risk involved. Debt is considered to be riskier than equity because interest has to be paid regardless of whether or not a company makes a profit, whereas dividends on the other hand, do not. The gearing ratio also informs an investor as to the potential of a company to raise future finance. If the gearing ratio is low, then a company will be able to obtain more debt. If the gearing ratio is high, the company will have difficulty raising more debt, and indeed more equity, as the equity market will require a premium for the additional risks involved with having higher gearing – making raising capital expensive.

Income gearing: if the level of debt is known, then the expected future interest and preference dividend cash outflows can be determined. The extent by which a company can service the future cost of its debt can be estimated using the **income gearing ratio**. This is calculated as follows:

$$\frac{\textbf{Debt interest + Preference dividends}}{\textbf{Profit before interest and tax}} \times \textbf{100 = \% of profit required to service debt}$$

Calculation of this ratio is shown in **Worked Example 4.13**.

Worked Example 4.13: Financial Risk Analysis – Income Gearing Ratio

Using the financial statements of ABC Plc on pages 172–4, calculate the income gearing ratio for both years.

Solution

The income gearing ratios are:

$$\text{20X2:} \quad \frac{\text{€/£1,000,000}}{\text{€/£8,500,000 + €/£1,000,000}} \times 100 = 10.5\%$$

$$20X1: \frac{€/£1,000,000}{€/£9,000,000 + €/£1,000,000} \times 100 = 10.0\%$$

The percentage of profits being used to cover debt interest has increased from 10.0% to 10.5%. The increase can be interpreted as an increase in the financial risk of the company; however, the ratio is low to start with. Debt financiers are providing about 40% of the finance for the company and only get 10% of profits. This is a strong sign for equity holders.

The income gearing ratio provides a measure of a company's ability to service its current debt. A high ratio indicates that a large proportion of the profits are required to cover the debt interest and preference share dividend, this can be interpreted as a sign of high financial risk. In addition, it would indicate that a company is limited in its ability to raise more debt as it currently has to use a high proportion of its distributable profits to cover current debt. The ratio is limited. It does not take into consideration loan repayments – a company may be able to repay interest and preference share dividends, but not capital! In addition, the ratio is only reflective of one year's situation – unless the company's profits are steady from year to year. Where a company's profits fluctuate, the ratio should be evaluated over a longer time period.

Operating leverage: **operating leverage** provides an indication of the risk associated with the extent of fixed costs in a company's operations. It is usually expressed as the '**degree of operating leverage**' and indicates the effect of a change in revenue on a company's profit before interest and tax. The higher the degree of operating leverage, the greater the increase in profits from an increase in revenue. Conversely, a reduction in revenue will have a larger impact in terms of falling profits, relative to a company that has a low degree of operating leverage. Therefore, the higher the degree of operating leverage, the riskier a company's cost structure. Operating leverage is calculated as follows:

$$\frac{\textbf{Contribution}}{\textbf{Net profits}} \times \mathbf{100} = \textbf{Degree of operating leverage}$$

Calculation of this ratio is outlined in **Worked Example 4.14**.

WORKED EXAMPLE 4.14: BUSINESS RISK ANALYSIS – OPERATING LEVERAGE

Using the financial statements of ABC Plc on pages 172–4, calculate the degree of operating leverage for both years.

Solution

The degrees of operating leverage are:

$$20X2: \frac{€/£20,000,000}{€/£7,000,000} \times 100 = 285\%$$

$$20X1: \frac{€/£17,000,000}{€/£6,200,000} \times 100 = 274\%$$

In line with the reduction in the net profit margin (see **Worked Example 4.3**), this ratio has picked up the increased risk associated with the higher proportionate level of fixed costs. The company is now in a riskier position than it was in 20X1, as the degree of operating leverage is higher, and any changes in the volume of revenue will have a larger impact now than would have occurred had the fixed cost remained consistent with last year.

INVESTMENT POTENTIAL

Potential investors need to be able to look at a company's financial statements and extract information that will allow them to make informed decisions as to the investment potential the company offers. Investors are interested in seeing their worth increase. This can be achieved by receiving dividends and/or increases in share price. Depending on their cash and tax position, some equity holders prefer dividends (low-income-band earners); others prefer to receive capital gains in the price of the share (high-income-band earners). The latter will have exhausted their income-tax-free personal allowance, but may not have utilised their capital gains tax yearly tax-free allowance. Being able to release the income from capital gains in a planned manner allows equity holders to minimise their personal tax expense. Earnings drive both dividends payable and capital growth, hence information on earnings and growth in earnings helps to inform investors about the overall return to be made from the purchase of shares. A couple of ratios are commonly calculated to provide information to an investor on a company's financial performance.

Earnings per share: the first indicator of performance is a company's **earnings per share**. This ratio is simply the earnings that are available for distribution to equity holders after loan financiers' and tax authorities' claims have been settled – reported on an individual share basis. It is calculated as follows:

$$\frac{\textbf{Earnings after tax and preference dividends}}{\textbf{Number of equity shares in issue}} = \textbf{Earnings per share}$$

An example of the calculation is provided in **Worked Example 4.15**.

Worked Example 4.15: Investment Potential – Earnings Analysis

Using the financial statements of ABC Plc on pages 172–4, calculate the earnings per share for both years. Assume that the nominal value of ABC Plc's shares is €/£1 per share.

Solution

The earnings per share are:

$$20X2: \frac{€/£7,000,000}{30,000,000} = 23.33c/p$$

$$20X2: \frac{€/£6,200,000}{25,000,000} = 24.8c/p$$

In line with the reduction in the return on capital employed, the earnings per share has fallen from 24.8c/p per share to 23.33c/p per share. Like the return on capital employed, the timing of the share issue is important. If it was not until the end of the year, the earnings per share may actually have increased to 28c/p per share (€/£7,000,000/25,000,000); this information would need to be known before a proper evaluation could take place.

The earnings per share ratio is deemed to be so important to investors that it is required to be disclosed, either on the face of the financial statements of a Plc, or in the notes to the financial statements. In general, an increase in a company's earnings per share is seen as a positive sign about a company's future, hence will lead to an increase in a company's share price. However, this is not always the case, as is highlighted by **Worked Example 4.16.**

Worked Example 4.16: Investment Potential – Earnings per Share

Fernando Plc raised €/£20 million of cheap debt at the beginning of 20X3. The company did increase its earnings per share in the year, primarily as a result of the additional return received from investing the €/£20 million raised, over and above the interest and tax that had to be paid on the additional earnings. The return, though higher than in previous years, was lower than equity holders' expectations. The following data are available for Fernando Plc just after the year-end.

	20X2	**20X3**
Earnings per share	20c/p	22c/p
Price earnings ratio	9	7.5
Share price	180c/p	165c/p

Requirement Earnings per share have risen between 20X2 and 20X3, yet share price has fallen. Why do you think this has occurred?

Solution

The fall in share price has arisen because the equity holders are disappointed in the performance of the company. Though the earnings per share have risen by 10% from 20c/p to 22c/p, this rise was not to the extent expected. Indeed, the question tells us that the increase is solely due to additional earnings being available for distribution from the investment of the new €/£20 million capital injection after all the associated costs (including interest and taxation) have been settled.

The reason for the expectation of additional earnings over and above the 22c/p is due to the increased financial risks now facing equity investors. The company has increased its debt levels by €/£20 million. Interest will have to be paid on this yearly, and the capital will have to be repaid at some point in the future. This has increased the fixed costs of the company and has moved the equity holders down the list of claimants in the event of the company being wound up - debt is always settled before equity. As a result of the higher risk, equity holders will require a higher return on their total equity investment. The return received is not higher, as expected – hence share price will fall as equity holders, unhappy with the risk return trade off, will sell their shares – driving down share price.

Price earnings ratio: the **price earnings ratio** gives an indication of the number of years it would take to recover the current share price out of current earnings of the company. The ratio is calculated as follows:

$$\frac{\textbf{Market price per share}}{\textbf{Earnings per share}} = \textbf{Price earnings ratio}$$

Calculation of this ratio is explained in **Worked Example 4.17**.

Worked Example 4.17: Investment Appraisal – Price Earnings Ratio

Using the financial statements of ABC Plc on pages 172–4, calculate the price earnings ratio for both years. The market price of the company's shares on 31 December 20X2 was 201c/p and on 31 December 20X1 was 173.6c/p.

Solution

The price earnings ratios are:

$$\text{20X2: } \frac{201\text{c/p}}{23.33\text{c/p}} = 8.6 \text{ times}$$

$$\text{20X1: } \frac{173.6\text{c/p}}{24.8\text{c/p}} = 7 \text{ times}$$

The price earnings ratio has increased from 7 to 8.6 times. This means that the market has more confidence in the future earnings of the company in 20X2 than it did in 20X1. The market must value the earnings potential of the new investment quite highly; this has increased demand for the shares and driven up share price from 173.6c/p to 201c/p. The earnings per share in 20X2 is lower than that reported in 20X1, though it may not reflect the full earnings expected from the new investment.

The current market price of a share reflects the market's expectations about the future earnings of a company. Therefore, the price earnings ratio is a measure of market confidence in a company. A low price earnings ratio suggests that the market sentiment is that a company is unlikely to maintain earnings, or have growth in earnings; whereas a high price earnings ratio suggests that the market sentiment is that a company will be able to maintain its performance and indeed improve on it. As with all ratios, care needs to be taken if using the price earnings ratio to analyse two different companies. The price earnings ratio also reflects the market's consideration of the risk associated with investing in a company – a risky company with high earnings is likely to have a lower price earnings ratio, compared to a less risky company with the same earnings. The market price will be less for the riskier company. Therefore, this ratio should not be used in isolation when deciding on whether or not to invest in a company. **Figure 4.5** outlines some factors that influence a company's reported price earnings ratio.

FIGURE 4.5: INFLUENCES ON A COMPANY'S PRICE EARNINGS RATIO

Factor	Influence
Earnings growth	Strong growth prospects will lead to an increase in the price earnings ratio.
Quality of the company's net assets and earnings	Where the market feels that a company's net assets are undervalued, a higher price earnings ratio will be reported. A stable earnings pattern also results in a higher price earnings ratio.
Financial risk	The price earnings ratio is inversely related to the gearing of a company. As gearing increases, equity holders' required return increases, hence lowering the price earnings ratio.
Stock market	The current state of the stock market will influence the price earnings ratio. Where the market is bullish, this will push up the price earnings ratio, whereas the price earnings ratio will fall in a bear market.
State of the economy	General economic and financial conditions will impact on a company's price earnings ratio.
Industry	The type of industry is also influential, as is the company's standing within the industry.
Size	Related to the prior point, size is important. Larger companies will be expected to have steadier earnings.
Marketability	Unquoted shares have restricted marketability, hence a higher return is required for investing in them. This is reflected by their having a lower price earnings ratio.

Dividend Ratios

Dividend per equity share: the **dividend per equity share** ratio calculates the annual individual monetary dividend amount that is distributed per equity share in issue. It is calculated as follows:

$$\frac{\textbf{Total equity dividend paid}}{\textbf{Number of equity shares in issue}} = \textbf{Dividend per share}$$

Worked Example 4.18 shows a practical example of the calculation of this ratio.

Worked Example 4.18: Investment Analysis – Dividend per Share

Using the financial statements of ABC Plc on pages 172–4, calculate the dividend per share for both years. Assume the dividend in the prior year was €/£800,000.

Solution

The dividends per share are:

$$\text{20X2: } \frac{\text{€/£}1{,}000{,}000}{\text{€/£}30{,}000{,}000} = 3.33\text{c/p per share}$$

$$\text{20X1: } \frac{\text{€/£}800{,}000}{\text{€/£}25{,}000{,}000} = 3.2\text{c/p per share}$$

The dividend per share has increased from 3.2c/p per share to 3.33c/p per share, an increase of 4% in the year.

Dividend policy is covered in depth in **Chapter 22**. At this early stage it is pointed out that the market usually expects a company to pay out a steady, but increasing, dividend per share. Hence, an investor would be interested in knowing the trend in the movement of this ratio over time.

Dividend yield: the **dividend yield** focuses on the value of the dividend to the equity holder. It calculates the return currently earned in the form of dividends only from an investment in the company's shares. It is calculated as follows:

$$\frac{\textbf{Dividend per equity share}}{\textbf{Market price per equity share}} \times \textbf{100} = \textbf{Dividend yield}$$

Calculation of this ratio is summarised inn **Worked Example 4.19**.

Worked Example 4.19: Investment Analysis – Dividend Yield

Using the financial statements of ABC Plc on pages 172–4, calculate the dividend yield for both years. Assume the dividend in the prior year was €/£800,000 and the market price per share was 201c/p on 31 December 20X2 and 173.6c/p on 31 December 20X1.

Solution

The dividend yields are:

$$20X2: \frac{3.33c/p}{201c/p} \times 100 = 1.66\%$$

$$20X1: \frac{3.2c/p}{173.6c/p} \times 100 = 1.84\%$$

The dividend yield has fallen from 1.84% to 1.66%. Relative to the risk-free rate of interest, this dividend yield is low; however, share price is rising, indicating that the bulk of the return being made by equity holders is capital gains.

The value of the dividend yield ratio is related to the amount of profits distributed, relative to the amount retained for growth. Normally this ratio produces a low result, which might be seen as poor given the increased risks associated with investing in equity, relative to risk-free investments. However, unless a company has a 100% payout ratio, this ratio will be low, as the additional return to equity holders will be in the form of capital growth, from the reinvestment of the profits. Therefore, it is not meaningful to analyse this ratio on its own as a determinant of company investment performance. To get a holistic view, capital growth also has to be considered.

Dividend cover: the **dividend cover** ratio indicates the extent by which profits after interest, tax and preference dividends can fall before the equity dividend is affected. The ratio is calculated as follows:

$$\frac{\textbf{Profit after taxation and preference dividends}}{\textbf{Equity dividends}} = \textbf{Dividend cover}$$

Calculation of the dividend cover ratio is provided in **Worked Example 4.20**.

WORKED EXAMPLE 4.20: INVESTMENT ANALYSIS – DIVIDEND COVER

Using the financial statements of ABC Plc on pages 172–4, calculate the dividend cover for both years. Assume the dividend in the prior year was €/£800,000.

Solution

$$20X2: \frac{€/£7{,}000{,}000}{€/£1{,}000{,}000} = 7 \text{ times}$$

$$20X1: \frac{€/£6{,}200{,}000}{€/£800{,}000} = 7.75 \text{ times}$$

Dividend cover is strong. In 20X1 profits covered dividends 7.75 times, falling to 7 times in 20X2. Even at the lower 20X2 level, profits would have to fall by 85% before the current dividend distribution would be affected.

The dividend cover ratio reflects the risk associated with a company being able to maintain its current policy in the future. If the ratio is low, then reductions in profit may compromise the ability of a company to pay out a steady, increasing dividend. Therefore, an equity holder who seeks a constant stream of increasing dividends will not be interested in a company that has a low dividend cover ratio.

Payout ratio: the **payout ratio** is related to the dividend cover ratio; it provides an indication of the proportion of funds distributed each year and therefore highlights the proportion that is being retained for growth. It is calculated as follows:

$$\frac{\textbf{Total equity dividend}}{\textbf{Earnings after taxation and preference dividends}} \times 100 = \textbf{Payout ratio}$$

Calculation of the payout ratio is shown in **Worked Example 4.21**.

Worked Example 4.21: Investment Analysis – Payout Ratio

Using the financial statements of ABC Plc on pages 172–4, calculate the payout ratio for both years. Assume the total dividend in the prior year was €/£800,000.

Solution

$$\text{20X2: } \frac{€/£1{,}000{,}000}{€/£7{,}000{,}000} \times 100 = 14.28\%$$

$$\text{20X1: } \frac{€/£800{,}000}{€/£6{,}200{,}000} \times 100 = 12.9\%$$

The payout ratio has increased from 12.9% to 14.28%. This means that a greater proportion of the profits that are available for distribution have been distributed in 20X2. Even so, distribution levels are quite low, indeed very low, for a Plc. A low payout ratio means a high retentions ratio. In this case, ABC Plc retained 87.1% (100%–12.9%) of its distributable profits in 20X1 and 85.72% (100%–14.28%) in 20X2. The stock market and equity holders will be happy with this policy where the company is retaining funds for investment or to reduce high gearing levels.

The retentions percentage is one minus the payout ratio. Alternatively, it can be calculated using one divided by the dividend cover ratio.

Where the total dividend and distributable profit figures are not available the payout ratio can also be calculated from information in respect of an individual share, as follows:

$$\frac{\textbf{Dividend per share}}{\textbf{Earnings per share}} \times 100 = \textbf{Payout ratio}$$

Though not always strictly the case, quoted companies usually have higher payout ratios relative to unquoted companies.

LIMITATIONS OF RATIO ANALYSIS

Though ratios can also be used to compare the results of different sized entities, care needs to be taken when interpreting the ratios. The following three simple examples highlight this:

1. It is easier for a small entity to achieve a higher growth figure relative to a large company, yet its actual increase in sales might be one thousand times less than the growth achieved by the large company.
2. Increased profitability might be regarded as a strong sign of performance, but closer analysis might reveal that a large part of the reported profitability came from the sale of an asset – a one-off event.
3. The profit margin might have increased, however, the return on capital employed may have reduced as the new investment is generating less profit than existing assets – the result is that investors are getting less return on each euro/pound invested in the company, even though the company is regarded as more profitable.

In addition to the risk of misinterpreting the results of ratio analysis, there are other limitations associated with the source of the data – the financial statements. The statement of financial position is a 'snapshot' of the business assets and liabilities at a point in time – the statement of financial position may not be reflective of a company's normal structure. This problem is accentuated when the company's trade is seasonal as the statement of financial position will differ greatly depending on the stage of the seasonal cycle at which the financial statements are prepared.

Ratio analysis is more meaningful in companies that have constant operations throughout a year. Even so, when a company has a constant pattern of trade, ratio analysis is limited on a stand-alone basis. Ratio analysis is most beneficial when interpreting the performance of a business over time, or when comparing the results of one company with another similar company. Different companies may adopt different accounting policies, leading to different results.

Ratio analysis is used to assess past performance and also to help with decision-making in respect of the future. In this respect ratio analysis is limited as the primary financial statements are based on historical data, which might not be the best reflection of the likely outcomes in the future. The narrative part of an annual report, which contains the financial statements, provides some information on the future developments and research undertaken by the company. This information, however, is general, usually has little detail, and is not subject to audit. For example, details of key individuals might be provided, but other important information such as staff turnover, staff morale levels and the efficiency of staff, is not provided.

CONCLUSION

Along with reading financial statements, ratio analysis is the most commonly used technique to evaluate the financial performance, position, adaptability and investment potential of a company. Ratios examine the relationship between the elements within a set of financial statements to allow the reader to make more informed decisions as to the profitability, efficiency, liquidity, solvency, financial risk and investment potential of a company, than would be possible from just viewing the statements. Ratios can be used to examine: the performance of a single company over time; the performance of a company relative to its budgeted/ expected performance; and how a company has performed relative to other companies in the same industry. It can also be used to compare the results of different sized entities, though care needs to be taken when interpreting the results.

Indeed, interpreting ratios always needs to be undertaken with care. Though the limitations of ratio analysis for investment appraisal are many, they are known; hence an investor will still find them useful. The key is to use a holistic approach to the appraisal of a company, wherein a combination of analysing the financial statements using analytical review, reading the narrative parts of the annual return, calculating ratios, reading the press in respect of the company and, if privileged enough, interviewing management, will provide a good foundation to inform decision-making.

EXAMINATION STANDARD QUESTION: RATIO ANALYSIS

Aragon (a bank) has recently received a request for a term loan from one of its customers, Valencia Plc, a company listed on the Alternative Investment Market of the London Stock Exchange. Its shares are currently trading at €/£15.00 each and its debentures at 96.5%. Valencia Plc's directors have requested a further €/£6 million (five-year floating rate) term loan at an initial interest rate of 12% per annum, in order to purchase new equipment. The equipment will not materially change the company's current average percentage return on investment. Valencia Plc's turnover increased by 9% during the last financial year. Prior to receiving the request the regional commercial manager of Aragon had conducted a review of Valencia Plc's financial position, and had decided to ask Valencia Plc's management to reduce the company overdraft by 25% within the next six months.

Statement of Financial Position Valencia Plc for the Year Ended

	20X2 €/£000	20X1 €/£000
ASSETS		
Non-current assets		
Property, plant and equipment (property revalued)	16,060	14,380

Current assets		
Inventories	31,640	21,860
Trade receivables	24,220	17,340
Investment	8,760	10,060
Cash and cash equivalents	1,700	960
	66,320	50,220
Total assets	82,380	64,600
EQUITY AND LIABILITIES		
Equity		
Share capital	3,800	3,800
Retained earnings	16,900	13,500
	20,700	17,300
Non-current liabilities		
Long-term borrowings	6,000	–
Debentures	16,000	16,000
	22,000	16,000
Current liabilities		
Overdraft	16,340	13,220
Trade and other payables	20,920	15,280
Current taxation	2,420	2,800
	39,680	31,300
Total liabilities	61,680	47,300
Total equity and liabilities	82,380	64,600

Extract Information from the Income Statement of Valencia Plc

	20X2
	€/£000
Revenue	99,360
Profit before interest and taxation	10,760
Finance costs	(3,840)
Profit before tax	6,920
Income tax expense	(2,420)
Profit for the period	4,500
Dividend paid in the year	1,100

Comparative Ratio Information for Valencia Plc's Industry (Averages)

	20X2
Share price	€/£51.20
Dividend yield	2.5%
Dividend payout ratio	50%
Gross asset turnover	1.4 times
Earnings per share	17.8c/p
Gearing	52.4%
Acid test	1:1
Interest cover	4 times
Return on revenue (PBIT)	9%
Return on investment	16.5%

Requirement You are a consultant for Aragon. You are required to produce a reasoned case:

(i) Explaining why the bank should request a 25% reduction in the company's overdraft.
9 Marks

(ii) Explaining why the company should obtain a new term-loan.
7 Marks

(iii) Making recommendations to the board of Valencia Plc in respect of how you think the company's financial position might be improved.
9 Marks
Total 25 Marks

(Clearly state any assumptions made. All assumptions must relate to all parts of the question.)
(Chartered Accountants Ireland, 1998)

Solution

Profitability	**20X2** €/£000	**20X1** €/£000	**Industry**
Return on investment	$\frac{10,760}{42,700 + 16,340^*}$ = 18.22%	–	16.5%
Return on revenue	$\frac{10,760}{99,360}$ = 10.83%	–	9%
Asset turnover	$\frac{99,360}{82,380}$ = 1.21 times	$\frac{91,156^{**}}{64,600}$ = 1.41 times	1.4 times

Liquidity					
Current ratio	$\frac{66,320}{39,680}$	= 1.67:1	$\frac{50,220}{31,300}$	= 1.60:1	–
Acid test ratio	$\frac{66,320 - 31,640}{39,680}$	= 0.87:1	$\frac{50,220 - 21,860}{31,300}$	= 0.91:1	1:1
Trade receivables period	$\frac{24,220 \times 365}{99,360}$	= 88.97 days	$\frac{17,340 \times 365}{91,156}$	= 69.43 days	–
Inventory holding period (using sales)	$\frac{31,640 \times 365}{99,360}$	= 116.23 days	$\frac{21,860 \times 365}{91,156}$	= 87.53 days	–
Trade payables period (using sales)	$\frac{20,920 \times 365}{99,360}$	= 76.85 days	$\frac{15,280 \times 365}{91,156^{*}}$	= 61.18 days	–
Solvency					
Gearing	$\frac{22,000}{22,000 + 20,700}$	= 51.5%	$\frac{16,000}{16,000 + 17,300}$	= 48%	52.4%
Interest cover	$\frac{10,760}{3,840}$	= 2.8 times	–		4 times
Investment ratios					
Earnings per share	$\frac{4,500}{3,800}$	= 118.42 c/p	–		–
Dividend per share	$\frac{1,100}{3,800}$	= 28.95 c/p	–		–
Price earnings ratio	$\frac{1,500}{118.42}$	= 12.67 times	–		20 times

* From the bank's perspective, the overdraft is part of its investment in the company.
** €/£99,360,000/1.09 = €/£91,156,000 (rounded)

Bank's perspective

(a) Reasons for requiring a reduction in the bank's overdraft include:
  (i) The bank has a large risk exposure in respect of the overdraft and term-loan. The overdraft has increased substantially in the past year from €/£13.22 million to €/£16.34 million. If the overdraft is unsecured, then the risks are even higher.

(ii) Valencia Plc is highly geared, with long-term debt representing 51.5% of the company's total long-term financing. This has increased from the prior year due to long-term borrowing, though still below the industry average of 52.4%. However, it might be more appropriate to assume that the overdraft is a long-term source of finance as it is unlikely that Valencia Plc can repay it in the short term, or on demand. If the overdraft is included, this ratio increases to 89.79%. This means that Valencia Plc is seriously over-geared.

(iii) Valencia Plc's liquidity ratios are also not strong. The current ratio has increased from 1.6 : 1 to 1.67 : 1, however the more liquid measure, the acid test ratio, has fallen from 0.91 : 1 to 0.87 : 1. This ratio is lower than the industry average of 1 : 1.

(iv) The working capital ratios have all deteriorated, suggesting that inefficiencies are occurring. The trade receivables period has increased from 69.4 days to 88.97 days – nearly three weeks' extra credit being allowed. This means that more cash is tied up in trade receivables. In addition, a longer credit period may lead to a larger proportion of bad debts. The inventory holding period has also increased from 87.5 days to 116.23 days. More cash is tied up in inventories this year relative to last year. Given the company's debt position, this is unacceptable. Inventories are being held for about three months. Holding inventory for longer means that higher levels of inventory are held, this leads to increased storage costs, as well as there being a higher risk of damage, or obsolescence. Suppliers are being paid within 76.85 days, an increase of 15 days on last year's average of 61.18 days. This increase in the credit period taken will be a source of cash to the company. However, taking extended credit periods without agreement will negatively affect any goodwill that exists between Valencia Plc and its suppliers. This may cause Valencia Plc to lose discounts and to fall down the suppliers' list of customers that they provide a quality service to.

(v) The investment in trade receivables has increased by €/£6.88 million, the investment in inventory by €/£9.78 million and the level of trade payables has increased by €/£5.64 million. This means that an additional €/£11.02 million is tied up in working capital. Were the levels of working capital in line with the increase in revenue, then the additional investment should only have been a further €/£2.152 million [(€/£17.34 million + €/£21.86 million – €/£15.28 million) × (€/£99.360 million ÷ €/£91.156 million)]. Therefore, the increase in the overdraft (€/£3.12 million) and the long-term loan (€/£6 million) would not have been necessary.

(vi) The asset turnover ratio has also fallen from 1.41 to 1.22 over the past year. The industry average was also 1.4. This decline suggests that the assets this year are not being utilised as effectively as they were last year as each euro/pound invested in assets is yielding less revenue.

(vii) The market is also pessimistic about Valencia Plc's future, as indicated by the low price earnings ratio of 12.67 times, relative to the industry-average price earnings ratio of 20 times.

To summarise, Valencia Plc should reduce its overdraft as it seems to have arisen due to inefficiencies in the management of working capital and assets. The bank is currently overexposed with a very high debt-to-equity mix (when the overdraft is taken into consideration).

(b) Reasons for granting a further €/£6 million five-year floating rate term-loan at an initial interest rate of 12% per annum to purchase new equipment include:

(i) Valencia Plc is more profitable than the average company within the industry. It provides a return on investment of 18.22% compared to the industry average of 16.5% and a return on sales of 10.83% compared to the industry average of 9%. Comparative figures were not available, though should be sought as the pattern of profitability would help to inform the decision-making process.

(ii) The new loan will cost the company 12%, this is less than the return currently being earned by the company on the investment to date (18.22%); therefore, if the new assets are to generate a return similar to that currently being generated, company value should increase as should the price earnings ratio.

(iii) The machinery that the company proposes to purchase may be offered as security for the additional loan; this will reduce Aragon's credit exposure.

(iv) The gearing ratio has been calculated using book values; it could be argued that a more appropriate means of valuing the components of the gearing ratio, would be by using market values. Using market values, gearing would be 27.33%, and when overdraft is taken into consideration it increases to 39.86% (see calculations 1 and 2 below). This revised gearing ratio shows the bank's exposure to be much lower than reported when book values are used (the ratios were 51.5% for gearing without the overdraft and 89.79% with the overdraft).

1. Calculation of gearing without the overdraft:

Market value of debentures = €/£16 million × €/£96.5 ÷ €/£100
= €/£15.44 million

Total market value of debt = €/£6 million + €/£15.44 million
= €/£21.44 million

Market value of equity = 3.8 million × €/£15.00 = €/£57 million

Gearing = €/£21.44 million/(€/£21.44 million + €/£57 million) = 27.33%

2. Gearing with the overdraft:

Total debt = €/£21.44 million + €/£16.34 million = €/£37.78 million

Gearing = €/£37.78 million/(€/£37.78 million + €/£57 million) = 39.86%

(c) The following points are suggested to help Valencia Plc improve its financial position:

(i) The management of working capital needs to be reviewed. There appears to be plenty of opportunity to reduce trade receivables, inventory and cash levels. The period of credit taken from suppliers should not be increased any further, indeed a review of the impact of the increase in the credit period taken over the past year should be undertaken to determine if the discounts lost exceed the opportunity cost of retaining the funds for the 15 days longer before payment.

(ii) The funds generated from the reduction in working capital levels could be used to reduce the overdraft or to finance the purchase of the new machine. When deciding on this, it is important to compare the cost of the overdraft at present with the cost of the new loan (12%). The flexibility of the overdraft should be taken into consideration. Valencia Plc is making good profits and should be able to generate cash quickly; therefore, having the ability to repay debt quickly might be a reason to opt for keeping the overdraft and using the cash from the reduction in working capital to finance the purchase of the new machinery. However, before this decision can be made, a cash flow projection should be prepared and the pattern of cash requirements and surpluses for the coming five years ascertained.

(iii) Valencia Plc could consider a further input of equity. However, this is an option for the future. At the present time, Valencia Plcs shares might be undervalued (given the low price earnings ratio). Were the efficiencies in working capital to come to fruition, the market might regard the company's expected performance with more confidence, causing the price earnings ratio to rise, and share price to rise. Shares could be issued when the share price has reached an acceptable level.

Key Terms

Acid test ratio
Capital employed
Capital structure
Cash return on capital employed
Current asset turnover ratio
Current ratio
Degree of operating leverage
Dividend cover
Dividend per equity share
Dividend yield
Earnings per share
Economic resources of a company
Financing activities
Financial structure
Gearing
Gross profit margin
Income gearing ratio
Inventory turnover ratio
Investing activities
Liquidity
Net profit margin
Non-current asset turnover
Operating activities
Operating cash flow to total debt
Operating leverage
Payout ratio
Price earnings ratio
Primary ratio
Profit before interest and tax
Quick ratio
Ratio analysis
Return on capital employed
Solvency
Statement of cash flows
Statement of financial position
Statement of profit or loss
Trade payables ratio
Trade receivables ratio

PROFORMA FINANCIAL STATEMENTS

Statement of Profit or Loss for ABC Plc
for the year ended 31 December 20X2

	20X2	20X1
	€/£000	€/£000
Revenue	50,000	45,000
Cost of sales	(30,000)	(28,000)
Gross profit	20,000	17,000
Other income	1,000	2,000
Distribution costs	(5,000)	(4,000)
Administration costs	(6,000)	(5,000)
Other expenses	(2,000)	(1,000)
Finance costs	(1,000)	(1,000)
Share of profit of associates	1,500	1,000
Profit before tax	8,500	9,000
Income tax expense	(1,500)	(2,800)
Profit for the period	7,000	6,200

Statement of Financial Position for ABC Plc
as at 31 December 20X2

	20X2	20X1
	€/£000	€/£000
ASSETS		
Non-current assets		
Property, plant and equipment	50,000	40,000
Goodwill	1,000	1,000
Other intangible assets	3,000	3,000
Investments in associates	2,000	2,000
Available-for-sale investments	500	–
	56,500	46,000

	20X2	20X1
	€/£000	€/£000
Current assets		
Inventories	6,000	5,000
Trade receivables	8,000	6,000
Other current assets	2,000	3,000
Cash and cash equivalents	3,000	8,000
	19,000	22,000
Total assets	75,500	68,000
EQUITY AND LIABILITIES		
Equity		
Share capital (€/£1 shares)	30,000	25,000
Other reserves	1,000	1,000
Retained earnings	9,000	3,000
	40,000	29,000
Minority interest	500	500
	40,500	29,500
Non-current liabilities		
Long-term borrowings	20,000	15,000
Deferred tax	2,000	3,000
Long-term provisions	3,000	3,500
	25,000	21,500
Current liabilities		
Trade and other payables	5,500	10,000
Short-term borrowings	1,000	2,000
Current portion of long-term borrowings	2,000	2,000
Current tax payable	500	1,000
Short-term provisions	1,000	2,000
	10,000	17,000
Total liabilities	35,000	38,500
Total equity and liabilities	75,500	68,000

STATEMENT OF CASH FLOWS FOR ABC PLC
for the year ended 31 December 20X2

	20X2	
	€/£000	**€/£000**
Cash flows from operating activities		
Cash receipts from customers	48,000	
Cash paid to suppliers and employees	(47,500)	
Cash generated from operations	500	
Interest paid	(1,000)	
Income tax paid	(3,000)	
Net cash from operating activities		(3,500)
Cash flows from investing activities		
Purchase of property, plant and equipment	(12,500)	
Proceeds from sale of equipment	2,000	
Interest received	200	
Dividends received	800	
Net cash used in investing activities		(9,500)
Cash flows from financing activities		
Proceeds from issue of share capital	5,000	
Proceeds from long-term borrowings	5,000	
Payment of finance lease liabilities	(1,000)	
Dividends paid	(1,000)	
Net cash used in financing activities		8,000
Net increase in cash and cash equivalents		(5,000)
Cash and cash equivalents at the start of the year		8,000
Cash and cash equivalents at the end of the year		3,000

(***Note:*** comparatives are also provided in financial statements allowing the reader to determine changes in the generation of cash flow and its use over a two-year period.)

QUESTIONS

(See Suggested Solutions to Review Questions in **Appendix B**.)

Question 4.1

How does inflation affect ratio analysis?

Question 4.2

What is the difference between solvency and liquidity?

Question 4.3

The following are the summarised financial statements of Alpha and Omega, two companies that operate in the same industry.

Summarised Statements of Financial Position

	Alpha €/£m	**Omega** €/£m
ASSETS		
Non-current assets	790	1,000
Current assets		
Inventories	1,200	1,800
Trade receivables	720	1,200
Bank	190	–
	2,110	3,000
Total assets	2,900	4,000
EQUITY AND LIABILITIES		
Equity and reserves		
Capital	1,160	1,756
Profits	340	404
	1,500	2,160
Non-current liabilities		
Loan	500	–
Current liabilities		
Trade payables	900	1,040
Bank overdraft	–	800
	900	1,840
Total liabilities	1,400	1,840
Total equity and liabilities	2,900	4,000

Summarised Statements of Profit or Loss

	Alpha		Omega	
	€/£m	€/£m	€/£m	€/£m
Revenue		6,000		7,200
Cost of goods sold				
Opening inventory	(1,000)		(1,500)	
Add: purchases	(4,760)		(5,916)	
	(5,760)		(7,416)	
Less: closing inventory	1,200	(4,560)	1,800	(5,616)
Gross profit		1,440		1,584
Expenses				
Overhead expenditure		(1,100)		(1,180)
Net income		340		404

Requirement

(a) Using ratio analysis, comment on the profitability, efficiency, liquidity and gearing of BOTH companies.

17 Marks

(b) List three limitations of ratio analysis for the purposes of interpreting financial statements.

3 Marks

Total 20 Marks

CHALLENGING QUESTIONS

(Suggested Solutions to Challenging Questions are available through your lecturer.)

Question 4.1 Ratio Analysis (Level 1)

A company has profit after taxation of €/£580,000. It has 2 million equity shares in issue and a price earnings ratio of 10.

(a) What is the company's EPS?
(b) What is the market price per share?

The company has 100,000 debentures currently trading at €/£120.

(c) What is the company's gearing ratio?

The company decides to pay out a dividend of 5c/p per share.

(d) What is the dividend cover?
(e) What is the company's retention policy?

Question 4.2 Company Evaluation (Level 2)

Describe what the following company has experienced.

Statement of Financial Position for the Years Ended

	20X1	20X2
ASSETS	**€/£**	**€/£**
Non-current assets	320,000	420,000
Current assets		
Inventories	120,000	300,000
Trade receivables	128,000	270,000
Bank and cash	2,000	–
	250,000	570,000
Total assets	570,000	990,000
EQUITY AND LIABILITIES		
Equity and reserves		
Equity share capital	100,000	100,000
Revenue reserves	320,000	330,000
	420,000	430,000
Current liabilities		
Overdraft	50,000	160,000
Trade payables	100,000	400,000
	150,000	560,000
Total equity and liabilities	570,000	990,000

Question 4.3 Safe (Level 1)

Safe Plc is a long-established Irish-based company and has recently enjoyed a best-in-class reputation in its industry. Safe Plc has just paid an ordinary dividend of 15c/p per share. Tax on profits is paid at an annual rate of 20%. Extracts from Safe Plc's statement of profit or loss account and statement of financial position are set out below.

Safe Plc – Profit or Loss (Extract)
for the year ended 31 December 20X0

	€/£000
Profit before interest and tax	8,000
Interest	(560)
Profit before tax	7,440
Tax	(1,488)
Profit for the year	5,952

Safe Plc – Capital Structure
as at 31 December 20X0

	€/£000
Equity	
Ordinary share capital (€/£0.50 per share)	10,000
Retained earnings	9,000

8% loan notes 20Y2	7,000
9% preference shares	4,000
	30,000

Safe Plc has identified an attractive investment opportunity, which it feels can add to its overseas product offering. An initial investment of €/£12 million is required. Safe has decided to finance this through the issue of 7% loan notes, which will be redeemed in nine years' time. The loan notes will be secured on the non-current assets of Safe. The directors of Safe have estimated that the overseas investment will increase profit before interest and tax by 15% in the financial year ending 31 December 20X1. Safe also expects dividends to increase by 5% in the year ending 31 December 20X1.

Average ratios for the industry in which Safe operates include:
- Interest cover: 9 times
- Gearing: 45%

(***Note:*** gearing is calculated as the book value of debt divided by the book values of debt and equity.)

Requirement

(a) Calculate the following ratios of Safe based on its 31 December 20X0 year-end financial information:
- Interest cover; gearing; and earnings per share.

3 Marks

(b) Calculate the following expected ratios of Safe for the year ending 31 December 20X1, assuming it proceeds with the new investment opportunity as outlined above, and the existing business performs in line with 20X0:
- Interest cover; gearing; and earnings per share.

3 Marks

(c) Discuss, based on your calculations in parts (a) and (b) above and any other relevant information, how the new investment opportunity may be interpreted by Safe's investors.

5 Marks

(d) Briefly explain how any TWO of the above ratios would change if the €/£12 million finance was raised by way of a share issue rather than the issue of the loan note. Calculations are not required.

3 Marks

(e) Outline TWO advantages and TWO disadvantages of using debt as a form of long-term finance.

4 Marks

(f) Explain, using the information provided above, TWO factors which may have resulted in the decrease in Safe's loan note coupon rate from the 8% loan note currently in issue to the 7% loan note being considered.

2 Marks
Total 20 Marks

(Based on Chartered Accountants Ireland, CAP 1, Finance, Summer 2019, Q5)

Question 4.4 Sesco (Level 2)

Sesco Plc operates 37 supermarket stores selling food and other household supplies in the domestic market.

There is considerable competition between the various supermarket chains operating in Ireland. In recent years there have been examples of too many supermarkets attempting to operate in some catchment areas, where the size of the customer base was too small to support the number of outlets.

Also, there have been examples of national and local price wars breaking out (between Sesco and its competitors) as a result of one or more operators attempting to increase market share.

Control and performance evaluation within Sesco are primarily exercised by:
- Review of league tables of profitability.
- Review of key ratios and indicators.

Stores that are not affected by price wars or increased competition usually experience sales growth of no more than 3% per annum excluding inflation. Cost controls permit only limited discretion to local management.

The management of Sesco have noticed that there is significant divergence in performance across the stores in the group. Hence, there is a need to review the systems and criteria used for control and performance evaluation. Profitability ratios and indicators per store are compared within the company rather than with industry benchmarks.

Corporate tax is at the rate of 25%.

Summary financial data and selected data for Stores A, B, C gathered by internal audit for Sesco are set out in Appendix 1 in respect of the year ended 30 April 20X2 and in Appendix 2 in respect of the year ended 30 April 20X1.

APPENDIX 1
SUMMARY DATA FOR SESCO
for year ended 30 April 20X2

	Store A	**Store B**	**Store C**	**Group (Total 37 Stores)**
Floor area (square metres)	1,200	1,000	1,100	31,500
Number of employees	72	70	67	1,785
Number of competitors in catchment area	8	4	5	
Average number of customer complaints	115	106	98	
Number of coding errors per 1,000 transactions	12	9	4	

	€/£000	**€/£000**	**€/£000**	**€/£000**
Revenue	7,680	7,200	7,370	192,450
Gross profit	1,698	1,744	1,738	43,100
Labour	(917)	(907)	(886)	(21,700)
Other costs	(731)	(647)	(692)	(16,400)
Total costs	1,648	1,554	1,578	38,100
Profit from operations	50	190	160	5,000

Note: gross profit is calculated after wastage.

	%	%	%	%
Gross profit pre-wastage	24.4	25.6	25.5	24.2
Wastage	(2.3)	(1.4)	(1.9)	(1.8)
Gross profit	22.1	24.2	23.6	22.4

Simplified capital employed in Sesco supermarkets at 30 April 20X2 is as follows:

	€/£000	€/£000	€/£000	€/£000
Inventory	324	329	343	8,500
Less: Payables	(1,241)	(1,164)	(1,191)	(31,100)
Other assets	720	940	1,122	27,400
Net assets	(197)	105	274	4,800

There are no significant receivables.

Appendix 2
Summary Data for Sesco
for year ended 30 April 20X1

	Store A	Store B	Store C	Group (Total 37 Stores)
	€/£000	€/£000	€/£000	€/£000
Revenue	8,320	6,963	7,038	186,950
Gross profit	1,947	1,693	1,655	42,050
Profit from operations	317	232	152	5,700
Number of competitors in catchment area	6	4	5	
Average number of customer complaints	99	107	101	
Number of coding errors per 1,000 transactions	8	8	3	

Requirement

(i) Explain, with reasons, which key ratios you, as Management Accountant of Sesco, would recommend be used for operational control and performance evaluation of existing stores.

(ii) Comment on the performance of stores A, B, and C, using the available information.

22 Marks

(Based on Chartered Accountants Ireland, CAP 2, SFM, Summer 2009, extract from Q1)

Question 4.5 McMahon (Level 2)

Background

McMahon Industrial Ltd is a tool manufacturer based in Dublin. It is a family business, founded in 1978 by Alex McMahon. Paul McMahon (Alex's son) inherited the business last year on the death of Alex. Paul is an engineer and has never worked in the company. Paul has asked a firm of consultants to advise him on whether he should sell or retain the business.

Future Direction

Alex McMahon was an energetic and innovative businessman and the business has grown substantially over the past four decades. However, in the years prior to his death, Alex spent less time working in the business, spending much of each year in his holiday home in Portugal. As a result the performance of the business has suffered. Extracts from McMahon's financial statements and other relevant information is provided in Appendix I. If Paul wants to retain the business, he will need to understand the reasons for this underperformance and develop a strategy to address these.

Paul has received an offer from a competitor who has indicated that he is willing to pay €/£4 million for the equity in McMahon. Paul is considering whether he should sell the company. If this sale goes ahead, it would occur on 1 January 20X8.

Ignore any personal taxation issues in your analysis.

Requirement

(a) Using the information provided in Appendix I, assess the financial performance and position of McMahon Industrial Ltd. Your analysis should address profitability, efficiency, gearing and liquidity **and** include a consideration of changes in performance:
  (i) over time; and
  (ii) in comparison to the peer data provided.

14 Marks

(b) Based on your analysis, advise McMahon Industrial Ltd of FOUR aspects of the business that a strategy to improve its financial performance and/or position should focus on.

4 Marks

Appendix I

McMahon Industrial Ltd's Statement of Profit or Loss Forecast (Extract)

	20X7 €/£000	20X6 €/£000	20X5 €/£000
Turnover (note 1)	6,516	6,452	6,325
Cost of sales (note 1)	(3,388)	(3,161)	(2,720)
Gross profit	3,128	3,291	3,605
Expenses			
Wages and salaries	(693)	(668)	(635)
Advertising and marketing	(31)	(25)	(28)
Directors' remuneration	(250)	(239)	(235)
Depreciation and amortisation	(707)	(586)	(601)
Interest	(210)	(168)	(194)
Other expenses	(365)	(309)	(286)
Profit before tax	872	1,296	1,626
Tax	(262)	(389)	(488)
Net profit	**610**	**907**	**1,138**
Dividend	214	317	398

Additional information:

1. All purchases and sales are on credit.
2. The risk-free rate is currently 1% and the market risk premium is estimated to be 5.5%. A beta of 1.1 would be appropriate for McMahon. Net profit is expected to grow by 2% for the next three years and at 2.5% thereafter. McMahon's dividend as a percentage of net profit is expected to remain at the current level indefinitely.
3. Public companies in the same industry as McMahon have been trading at an EPS multiple of 9.5. Private companies are generally valued using a discount of 20% to public company earnings ratios. McMahon has 200,000 shares issued.

Peer group data	**Forecast 20X7 Ratios**
Sales growth rate	11%
Net profit margin	22%
Gross profit margin	52%
Return on assets	16%
Gearing (long-term debt to equity)	50%
Quick ratio/acid test	1
Non-current asset turnover	1.5
Inventory turnover	7
Trade receivables days	30

(Based on Chartered Accountants Ireland, CAP 2, Autumn 2017, extract from Q1)

Question 4.6 Camelot (Level 2)

Company Background Much of the success of Camelot was due to John Thorton's native business acumen, his ability to spot and realise an opportunity, the hard work of company employees and a degree of good fortune. Over 15 years, Camelot had grown from a one-van haulage company into a transport and logistics company employing 145 people with an annual turnover of €/£25 million, building a reputation for providing progressive, top quality and reliable services.

Recent Performance The most recent performance for the financial year ended 30 June 20X5 is presented in Appendix I.

Haulage Business The haulage business of Camelot started with one van. This has grown to 50, each with its own in-house driver. Camelot's main hub, which is owned freehold, is located near a multinational manufacturing site in the west of Ireland. Camelot was one of the first companies to invest in refrigerated vans to service an emerging frozen-food sector when companies five times its size were hesitating. The business was historically profitable, but recently margins have deteriorated and in the latest financial year, the business broke even, despite a small increase in revenue. The haulage services manager is very disappointed with this performance, feeling they have always 'gone the extra mile' to service customers, a fact noted and appreciated by customers.

Warehousing Business The warehousing business developed as a spin-off from the haulage business. Camelot initially provided a simple warehousing service. The business grew into a separate revenue stream and Camelot began to offer additional value-added services, such as inventory management, invoicing, order assembly and order tracking services for which customers were prepared to pay a premium. The business has been very profitable and sales grew by 15% from the prior year.

The warehouse manager has indicated that the IT equipment needs an immediate upgrade at a cost of €/£300,000. The warehouse manager estimates that additional maintenance costs of €/£20,000 per annum would be incurred, but that savings of €/£100,000 per annum would also accrue, both commencing next year. The upgrade will have a useful life of five years and capital allowances are available at a rate of 25% per annum straight-line. All investments in Camelot must earn a return after tax of 10% and the company has an effective rate of corporation tax of 20%, paid one year in arrears.

Requirement

(a) Analyse and comment on the performance and position of Camelot and each respective business for the year ended 30 June 20X5 from a financial perspective.

8 Marks

(b) Determine whether Camelot should invest in the new warehousing business IT equipment from a financial perspective and identify three additional factors that Camelot should consider.

12 Marks

Total 20 Marks

(Based on Chartered Accountants Ireland, CAP 2, MABF, Autumn 2011, extract from Q1)

APPENDIX I

STATEMENT OF PROFIT OR LOSS
for the Year Ended 30 June 20X5

	Haulage	**Warehousing**	**Packaging**	**Total**
	€/£	**€/£**	**€/£**	**€/£**
Sales	12,500,000	11,250,000	1,250,000	25,000,000
Less: Direct costs				
Personnel	4,825,000	4,500,000	855,000	10,180,000
Maintenance	844,375	270,000	22,500	1,136,875
Utilities	603,125	900,000	90,000	1,593,125
Fuel and transport	3,618,750	0	0	3,618,750
Insurance	603,125	720,000	22,500	1,345,625
Depreciation	1,206,250	900,000	67,500	2,173,750
Other	361,875	1,710,000	67,500	2,139,375
Operating margin	437,500	2,250,000	125,000	2,812,500
Less: Support costs				
Finance	375,000	150,000	75,000	600,000
Human resources	62,500	20,000	17,500	100,000
Earnings before interest and tax (EBIT)	0	2,080,000	32,500	2,112,500

STATEMENT OF FINANCIAL POSITION

	Haulage	**Warehousing**	**Packaging**	**Total**
	€/£	**€/£**	**€/£**	**€/£**
ASSETS				
Non-current Assets				
Land and buildings	7,500,000	8,415,000	500,000	16,415,000
Plant and machinery	1,000,000	3,712,000	750,000	5,462,000
Motor vehicles	1,500,000	247,500	0	1,747,500
	10,000,000	12,374,500	1,250,000	23,624,500
Current Assets				
Receivables	1,562,500	937,500	234,375	2,734,375
Cash	500,000	1,000,000	250,000	1,750,000
	2,062,500	1,937,500	484,375	4,484,375
Total Assets	12,062,500	14,312,000	1,734,375	28,108,875

EQUITY AND LIABILTIES	
Equity	
Equity	5,000,000
Reserves	8,250,000
	13,250,000
Non-current Liabilities	
Secured bank loan 7% (rollover December 20X6)*	13,500,000
Current Liabilities	
Trade payables and accruals	997,375
Corporation tax	361,500
	1,358,875
Equity plus total liabilities	28,108,875

* Secured on land and buildings.

5

Company Failure

Learning Objectives

Upon completing this chapter, readers should be able to:
- explain the main causes of company failure;
- use ratios to identify whether a company is experiencing financial distress;
- discuss the symptoms and remedies of overtrading;
- identify courses of action to take when a company faces temporary or permanent cash flow problems;
- explain the different types and reasons for divestment; and
- calculate the cash distribution payable to stakeholders when a company goes into liquidation.

INTRODUCTION

Company failure is a drastic event that affects all the stakeholders of a corporate. Investors, including shareholders and financial institutions, lose their investment; employees and management lose their jobs and main source of income; suppliers have to write-off amounts owing from the failed corporate, possibly putting the survival of their businesses at risk; customers have to seek supplies from elsewhere; the government loses tax revenue; and morale in the community is adversely affected.

The severity of the consequences of company failure means that management must not make decisions that cause company failure. This means that management need to be aware of factors that can cause company failure and to recognise red flags that suggest that the corporate is heading in the wrong direction. If identified well in advance, then management have a greater chance of steering the company in the right direction, resulting in rehabilitation and success. If a corporate becomes financially distressed, management should ensure that they do everything in their power to minimise the loss to the stakeholders. Finally, management need to be aware of bankruptcy and liquidation. Management may have to deal with customers and suppliers that get into financial difficulty and they may have to either voluntarily liquidate the company or wind up the company under a court order.

Companies in difficulty normally have to restructure their financing. **Chapters 10–14** deal with the different forms of financing that are available and the appropriate finance mix to use. Companies in difficulty also may have to take action in terms of company reconstruction by spin-off, sell-off, de-merger, asset restructuring (such as a sale and leaseback) or even overall company sale.

POSSIBLE CAUSES OF COMPANY FAILURE

In **Chapter 2**, we learned that the value of a company is the present value of its future expected cash flows. However, though theoretically sound, this view is restrictive; corporate failure is more than just running out of cash. It is widely accepted that several factors can cause company failure. Some of these are listed in **Figure 5.1**.

FIGURE 5.1: FACTORS THAT INFLUENCE COMPANY FAILURE

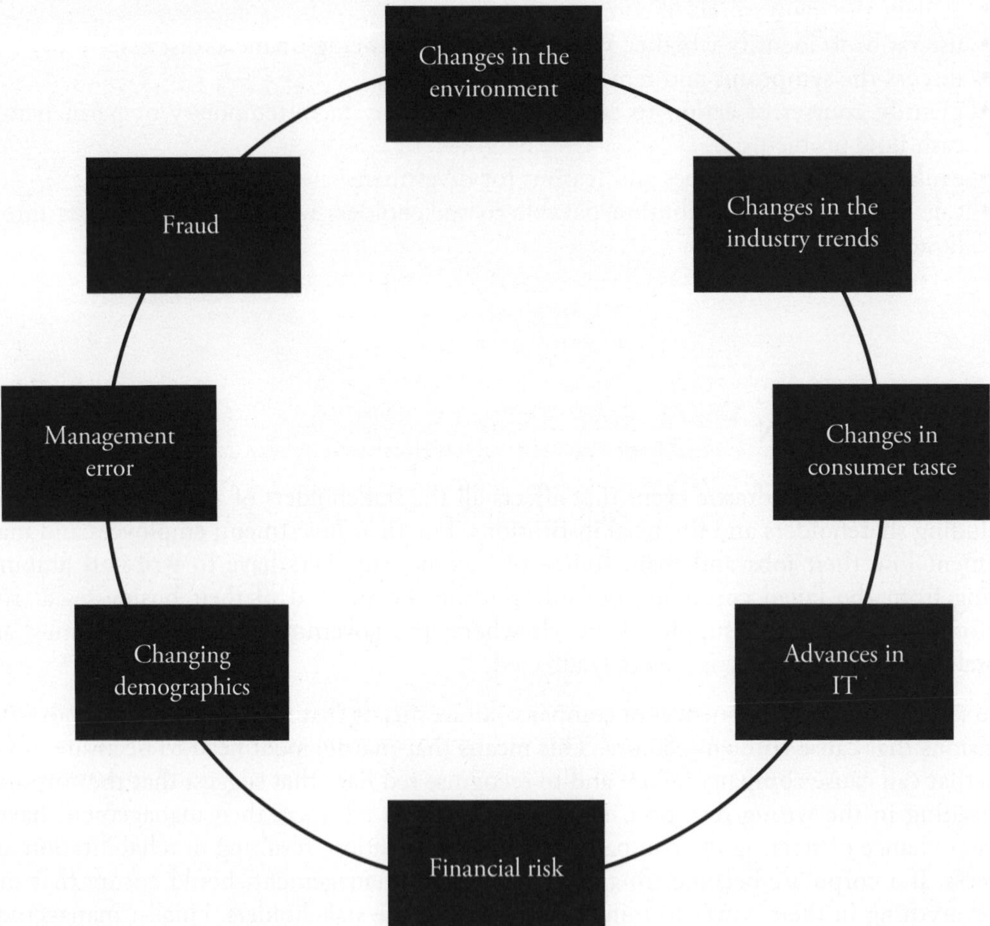

In many instances, company failure occurs due to the combination of several contributing factors, making survival difficult. **Figure 5.2** identifies seven of the largest company failures in the world.

FIGURE 5.2: SEVEN WELL-KNOWN COMPANY FAILURES

Name	Business	Assets	Year	Main reason
Lehman Brothers	Investment bank	$691.1 billion	2008	Financial crisis: over-investment in subprime mortgages.
Washington Bank	Savings and investment bank	$327.9 billion	2008	Financial crisis: 10-day run on the bank.
World Com	Telecom provider	$103.9 billion	2002	$4 billion accounting scandal.
General Motors	Motor vehicle manufacturer	$91 billion	2009	Debt and unfavourable trade union deals.
CITI group	Investment bank	$81.4 billion	2009	Failed to secure funding.
PG&E	Natural gas and electricity	$71.39 billion	2019	Liabilities from natural fires spanning two years.
Enron	Energy trading	$65.5 billion	2001	Fraud.

In some instances, the consequences of company failure are so great that the government intervenes. For example, the US government provided funding to General Motors and Chrysler, both of which subsequently went through bankruptcy proceedings, but they avoided having to liquidate their assets. The companies continue to manufacture vehicles and to employ large numbers of people. A similar situation happened in the UK where the government bailed out the Royal Bank of Scotland and the Nationwide Building Society; and in Ireland where the government bailed out the Allied Irish Bank and the Bank of Ireland.

Good corporate governance is a key determinant of a company's success, particularly when it is experiencing financial distress. Governing boards should be aware of the different causes of company failure and the indicators of corporate failure. They should also be able to interpret ratio analysis as ratios typically enable problems to be identified in advance of the firm failing.

Some of the more commonly used profitability, liquidity and gearing ratios are outlined in **Figure 5.3**.

FIGURE 5.3: RATIOS TO AID INTERPRETATION OF AN ENTITY'S PROFITABILITY, LIQUIDITY, BUSINESS RISK AND FINANCIAL RISK

Ratio	Formula	Interpretation
Profitability		
Gross profit % =	$\frac{\text{gross profit} \times 100}{\text{sales revenue}}$	The gross profit percentage is the percent return made from each sale after direct production costs are deducted. It is impacted on by sales price, sales mix, trade discounts, purchase price, carriage inwards and inventory costs.
Net profit % =	$\frac{\text{PBIT} \times 100}{\text{sales revenue}}$	This is the percentage return made after all costs, but before financing and taxation. It is impacted on by the gross profit margin, efficiency of working capital management, efficiency in overhead costs and exceptional one-off items.
ROCE =	$\frac{\text{PBIT} \times 100}{\text{capital employed}}$	This is the percentage return made by the company from the contribution by financiers to the company. Financiers can compare the return to other forms of investment (for example, the risk-free rate) to see if it is appropriate.
Business risk		
Operating leverage =	$\frac{\text{contribution} \times 100}{\text{net profit}}$	This measures the degree of operating leverage. The higher this ratio, the greater the risk associated with an entity's cost structure as it indicates a high proportion of fixed costs.
Liquidity		
Current ratio =	$\frac{\text{current assets}}{\text{current liabilities}}$	This shows the extent to which current assets cover current liabilities. A low ratio can signal liquidity issues (less than 2 : 1), a high ratio can signal inefficiency in working capital management (more than 2 : 1), but each industry is different and the industry norm should be used as the benchmark.
Acid test ratio =	$\frac{\text{current assets} - \text{inventory}}{\text{current liabilities}}$	This measure is the current ratio with the least liquid current asset, i.e. inventory, removed. It is an indication of the company's ability to respond quickly to liquidity needs. The benchmark is 1 : 1, but again, industry averages should be used as the benchmark.
Financial risk		
Gearing ratio % =	$\frac{\text{long-term debt} \times 100}{\text{long-term debt} + \text{equity}}$	This is the percentage of the financing of a company that comes from debt sources. The higher the gearing, the greater the financial risk.
Income gearing =	$\frac{(\text{interest} + \text{pref. dividends}) \times 100}{\text{PBIT}}$	This shows the percentage of the profits that have to be used to cover the yearly interest returns to financiers. The higher the income gearing, the greater the financial risk.

FINANCING AND COMPANY FAILURE

Inappropriate Financing for Growth

Overtrading occurs when a company grows too quickly with insufficient long-term finance to support the increased level of assets that should be held, given the higher level of operational activity. When a company's sales grow, so does the absolute amount of working capital that should be held. Demand is higher; therefore, inventory levels need to increase to cater for the increased demand, trade receivables increase in line with the increase in the volume of sales, and the level of trade payables increases also. In the majority of instances the increase in inventories and trade receivables outweighs the increase in trade payables, resulting in a resource requirement that needs to be financed. If no steps are taken to manage this, the company's overdraft will increase, causing liquidity problems. This can result in a situation whereby a profitable, growing company may have to go into liquidation due to cash shortages.

Overtrading is characterised by increases in turnover, current assets and possibly non-current assets. Current liabilities usually increase to a greater extent than the increase in current assets, resulting in a weakening current ratio. There usually is a large overdraft. Owners' equity or long-term debt does not increase, or increases by a small amount, hence the proportion of total assets that are financed by long-term sources reduces.

FIGURE 5.4: POSSIBLE ACTIONS TO TAKE WHEN OVERTRADING IS EVIDENT

Continue with the growth policy and take steps to obtain the correct type of long-term financing.

Sell unwanted non-current assets that are not generating sufficient income and are not critical to the business.

Examine in detail the working capital policy with a view to reducing the trade receivables and inventory holding periods and increasing the trade payables period, without harming the relationship or the prices/discounts agreed with the suppliers.

Reconsider the growth plan. If the company is getting itself into financial difficulties, then it may be better to either cancel the growth plan, or pursue it over a longer time period.

WORKED EXAMPLE 5.1: ASSESSING COMPANY GROWTH

Amarillo Ltd appointed a new marketing manager at the start of this accounting year, who has doubled the sales of the company over the past year. To stimulate growth, he reduced sales price, employed more sales staff, rented more office space, purchased additional motor vehicles and focused his attention on meeting sales targets. To this end he demanded that a higher level of inventory be stored so that sales are not disrupted by stock-outs. Amarillo Ltd has been renting additional warehouse space to meet this demand. Amarillo Ltd extended the credit period it receives from suppliers and some of them are now complaining. The overdraft limit agreed with the bank of €/£60,000 has been increased to €/£160,000. Extract information from the company's statement of profit or loss is given below, along with copies of its statement of financial position for the year prior to the marketing manager being appointed and the subsequent year, reflecting the growth achieved.

Amarillo Ltd

EXTRACT INFORMATION FROM THE STATEMENTS OF PROFIT OR LOSS
for the years ended 31 December 20X4 and 20X5

	20X4 **€/£**	**20X5** **€/£**
Revenue	2,000,000	4,000,000
Gross profit	400,000	600,000
Net income	100,000	40,000

The company provides credit on all its sales and obtains credit on all its purchases.

Amarillo Ltd

EXTRACT INFORMATION FROM THE STATEMENTS OF FINANCIAL POSITION
as at 31 December 20X4 and 20X5

	20X4 **€/£**	**20X5** **€/£**
ASSETS		
Non-current assets	320,000	420,000
Current Assets		
Inventories	120,000	300,000
Trade receivables	128,000	270,000
Bank and cash	2,000	–
	250,000	570,000
Total assets	570,000	990,000
EQUITY AND LIABILITIES		
Equity and reserves		
Equity share capital	100,000	100,000
Revenue reserves	320,000	330,000
	420,000	430,000
Current liabilities		
Overdraft	50,000	160,000
Trade payables	100,000	400,000
	150,000	560,000
Total equity and liabilities	570,000	990,000

Requirement Discuss the impact of the marketing director's policy.

Solution

Profitability In 20X5, the company's sales doubled from €/£2,000,000 to €/£4,000,000, but the gross profit margin has fallen from 20% (€/£400,000 ÷ €/£2,000,000) to 15% (€/£600,000 ÷ €/£4,000,000) and the net profit margin has fallen from 5% to 1%. This reduction in profitability is probably due to the fall in sales price and the increase in overheads resulting from the additional sales and inventory costs. These costs include: sales representatives' salaries; depreciation on sales representatives' motor vehicles; rent of additional office space and warehousing for the additional inventory; and other costs associated with holding inventory (write-offs, storemen's salaries, heat and light, etc.). In addition, there has probably been increased interest and bank charges costs associated with running a higher overdraft.

Liquidity At 31 December 20X4 the company had an overdraft of €/£50,000, €/£10,000 under the agreed limit of €/£60,000. By 31 December 20X5 this has increased to €/£160,000, which is the new agreed overdraft limit. In addition, in 20X5 the trade payables balance is 400% of the balance at 20X4, yet turnover has doubled. Inventory levels have more than doubled and inventory turnover is five days longer. Non-current assets have increased by €/£100,000. There has been no increase in the equity share capital of the company, or no long-term debt sourced.

It is clear from this analysis that Amarillo Ltd is overtrading. In fact, the company is currently at its overdraft limit. As a matter of urgency Amarillo Ltd needs to extend its overdraft facility. If Amarillo Ltd does not start to manage its liquidity appropriately and to finance its growth correctly, it may have to go into liquidation.

Other steps that Amarillo Ltd could take are to perform a cost–benefit analysis of the additional costs that were incurred in the year. Though sales have increased, profitability has fallen. Unless costs can be cut, growth does not seem worthwhile. If Amarillo Ltd can identify efficiencies in its costs and is keen to continue to pursue the growth strategy, then it should consider obtaining long-term finance, either from its equity holders or from long-term debt. In addition, management needs to consider the efficiencies that can be obtained in its inventory management and credit management to bring the conversion periods back to their 20X4 levels. Suppliers should be made aware of the steps the company is taking to improve its liquidity and their support requested in the short term. In the longer term, the credit period taken should be reduced to a level that suppliers are happy with.

Accelerated Debt Repayments

Other circumstances can lead to distressful financial situations similar to overtrading. For example, when a company repays debt, this may be done too quickly so that the cash outflow is not being adequately generated from day-to-day operational activities or from another finance source.

Inappropriate Financing for Asset Replacement

A more common situation arises when a company replaces its assets (including non-current assets) from its retained earnings. If the company does not take inflation into consideration, this may result in the company running up an overdraft, or reducing its investment in assets in real terms.

INDICATORS OF FINANCIAL DIFFICULTY

Where an investor has a more local knowledge of a company, or has been following the stories about a company in the press, then this can provide an indication of the company's financial health. Some of this information may also be disclosed in the written parts of the annual report. Information on non-financial matters that may indicate potential financial difficulties is highlighted in **Figure 5.5**.

FIGURE 5.5: GENERAL FACTORS THAT MAY INDICATE FINANCIAL DIFFICULTY

- Management infighting.
- Imbalances in management boards (for example, too many sales directors, no finance directors).
- Static view (the company is not updating its products or changing in line with advances made in other companies).
- High turnover of directors and key members of staff.
- Over-dependence on a limited number of products.
- General lack of information – a strong company is likely to advertise its strengths as a marketing tool.
- Increased competition from others in the industry and from substitute industries.
- Changes in law (for example, environmental law).
- An unusually complex capital structure.
- Pressure on managers from analysts' forecasts.
- Management's personal wealth tied up in the business.
- Pressure on debt covenants.
- Industry has a reputation for being susceptible to fraud.
- Changes of suppliers.

An analysis of the annual report and financial statements with a focus on the financial and audit-related disclosures may also provide indications of difficulties. Some signals are included in **Figure 5.6**.

FIGURE 5.6: INDICATORS FROM FINANCIAL STATEMENTS THAT MAY SUGGEST FINANCIAL DIFFICULTY

- An audit report that is not 'unqualified'.
- A change in auditor.
- Voluntary changes in accounting policies or methods (this may be motivated by window-dressing).
- One-off charges, such as restructuring.
- Significant gains or losses from non-core activities, such as the sale of stores by a retailer.
- An unusually complex capital structure.
- Use of 'special purpose vehicles'.
- The existence or increase in the use of off-balance sheet finance – this may understate the financial risk.
- Significant changes in the final-quarter figures that cannot be explained by seasonal factors – may suggest accounting manipulation.
- A defined benefit pension scheme that is underfunded.
- Arrears of VAT/PAYE/PRSI.
- Significant related party transactions.
- Evidence of accelerating or postponing discretionary expenses, such as research and development or marketing.
- Regular impairment charges being treated as exceptional – may indicate that the depreciation policies are inadequate.

HOW TO IDENTIFY AND ADVISE ON FINANCIALLY TROUBLED BUSINESSES

Failure Prediction Models

Several empirical studies have suggested that a combination of financial ratios can be used to predict business failures. Beaver (1966) suggested that failure could be predicted at least five years in advance, using financial ratios. He reported that a mixture of ratios, including profitability ratios, was more effective in predicting failure than focusing solely on liquidity and solvency ratios. Altman (1968) produced a model based on factored ratio outcomes that he claimed could be used to predict business failure (**Altman's failure prediction model**). The outcome of this model is a measure of the financial health of a business and he called the measure the **Z score**. This model is calculated as follows:

$$\mathbf{Z = 1.2A + 1.4B + 3.3C + 0.6D + 1.0E}$$

where:

A = working capital/total assets

B = retained earnings/total assets

C = profit before interest and tax/total assets

D = market capitalisation/book value of debts

E = revenue/total assets

Altman claimed that a company with a Z score of over 3 should remain solvent, whereas companies with a Z score of less than 1.8 were potential failures. Altman found that the model's prediction ability became more significant closer to the event of failure.

Worked Example 5.2: Ratio Analysis: Failure Prediction Models

ABC Plc

Statement of Profit or Loss
for the years ended 31 December

	20X5	20X4
	€/£000	€/£000
Revenue	50,000	45,000
Cost of sales	(30,000)	(28,000)
Gross profit	20,000	17,000
Other income	2,500	3,000
Distribution costs	(5,000)	(4,000)
Administration costs	(6,000)	(5,000)
Other expenses	(2,000)	(1,000)
Finance costs	(1,000)	(1,000)
Profit before tax	8,500	9,000
Income tax expense	(1,500)	(2,800)
Profit for the period	7,000	6,200

ABC Plc
STATEMENT OF FINANCIAL POSITION
as at 31 December

	20X5 €/£000	20X4 €/£000
ASSETS		
Non-current assets	56,500	46,000
Current assets	19,000	22,000
Total assets	75,500	68,000
EQUITY AND LIABILITIES		
Equity		
Share capital (€/£1 Shares)	30,000	25,000
Other reserves	1,500	1,500
Retained earnings	9,000	3,000
	40,500	29,500
Total non-current liabilities	25,000	21,500
Total current liabilities	10,000	17,000
Total liabilities	35,000	38,500
Total equity and liabilities	75,500	68,000

Requirement Using the financial statements of ABC Plc, calculate the company's Z score, using Altman's formula, for 20X5 only. Assume the market value of ABC Plc's shares is €/£2.01.

Solution

A = working capital to total assets

$$\frac{€/£19{,}000{,}000 - €/£10{,}000{,}000}{€/£75{,}500{,}000} = 0.1192$$

B = retained earnings to total assets

$$\frac{€/£9{,}000{,}000}{€/£75{,}500{,}000} = 0.1192$$

C = profit before interest and tax to total assets

$$\frac{€/£9{,}500{,}000}{€/£75{,}500{,}000} = 0.1258$$

D = market capitalisation to book value of debts

$$\frac{€/£30{,}000{,}000 \times €/£2.01}{€/£35{,}000{,}000} = 1.72$$

E = revenue to total assets

$$\frac{€/£50{,}000{,}000}{€/£75{,}000{,}000} = 0.6622$$

The Z score is then (1.2 × 0.1192) + (1.4 × 0.1192) + (3.3 × 0.1258) + (0.6 × 1.72) + (1 × 0.6622) = 2.419. Therefore, using Altman's Z score methodology, ABC Plc is not regarded as being in danger of business failure.

In the late 1970s, Taffler and Tisshaw (1977) and Taffler (1983) manipulated the model suggested by Altman to achieve a predictor model specific to UK companies. Like Altman, they gave the greatest weighting (53%) to a profitability measure (i.e. profit before tax/current liabilities) and considered financial leverage to be important (i.e. current liabilities/total assets), weighting it at 18%. They also included a liquidity measure (i.e. immediate assets minus current liabilities/operating costs minus depreciation), weighting it at 16%, and finally included a measure of the level of working capital investment in the company (i.e. current assets/total liabilities), weighting it at 13%.

Morris (1998) questions the usefulness of failure prediction models that are based on ratio analysis, suggesting that potential investors are already aware of the state of the company's affairs, and the model results add little to their decision-making processes.

FINANCIAL DISTRESS: MANAGEMENT OPTIONS

Financial distress arises when companies have insufficient cash to meet their scheduled cash outflows or when cash budgets predict cash shortages. In this situation, a company's governance team should ask itself several questions, as identified in **Figure 5.7**.

FIGURE 5.7: QUESTIONS TO ASK WHEN IN FINANCIAL DISTRESS

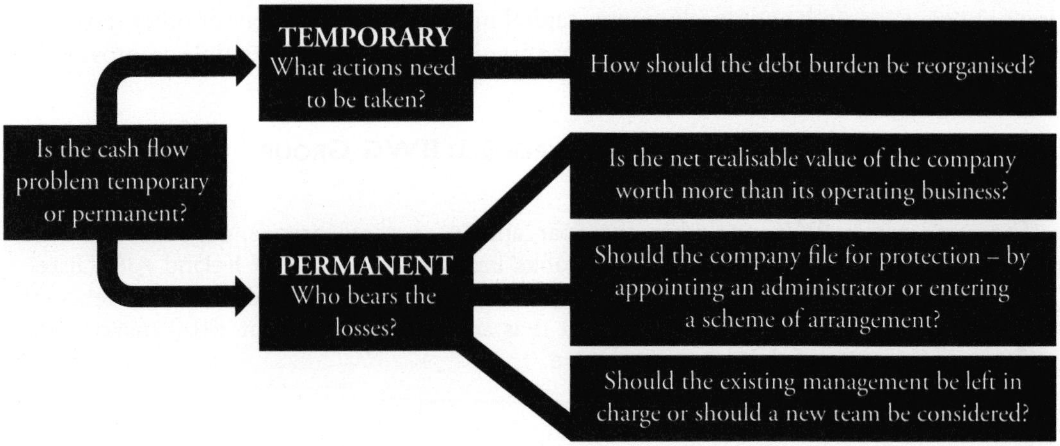

Is the cash flow problem temporary or permanent?

TEMPORARY
What actions need to be taken?

How should the debt burden be reorganised?

PERMANENT
Who bears the losses?

Is the net realisable value of the company worth more than its operating business?

Should the company file for protection – by appointing an administrator or entering a scheme of arrangement?

Should the existing management be left in charge or should a new team be considered?

Temporary Financial Problems

When the cash flow problem is temporary and the company is economically sound, the situation is salvageable with careful management. There are several options open to management to plug the temporary cash shortage, and they all involve some form of reorganisation.

Debt Reorganisation

When cash flow problems are temporary, trade creditors and loan creditors are generally willing to work with the company to help it to regain financial health. A company should get financial advice on a debt restructure plan from an agent – usually a debt-restructuring consultant or the debt advisory partner in an accountancy practice. The agent typically prepares a list of creditors with details of the debt they are owed. This includes the nature of the debt, whether it is secured or unsecured and the amount they are owed in size order. The agent then invites the creditors to a meeting. At this meeting, the company outlines the financial problems and invites the creditors to elect a small number of representatives to liaise with the company. This typically includes those creditors who are owed the most and a couple from the rest. The creditors' representative group usually numbers five or six. This is called the **committee of inspection**.

The agent may prepare a report showing the value of the company under different scenarios. One of the scenarios typically includes selling the company. This can either arise using formal liquidation or informal liquidation. Both types of liquidation show the net present value of the assets and the net present value of the liabilities. The company includes the costs associated with selling the company. In addition, the formal liquidation approach will include additional costs associated with bankruptcy. The fees are typically material. Both liquidation scenarios include the length of time the whole process is expected to take. Where the assets exceed the creditors and the costs associated with winding up the business, the surplus will be distributed to the shareholders. Where the assets do not cover the creditors and costs of winding up the business, then any debts that are secured will be paid first, with the remaining funds being distributed on a pro rata basis to the other creditors.

Other scenarios include continuing operations. The company will be emphasising what it is going to do to turn the business around. This may involve a new management team, marketing campaign, research and development, capital investment, divestment or other restructuring that is planned to improve the company going forward. An example is provided in **Real World Example 5.1**.

Real World Example 5.1: BWG Group

The retail group BWG, including the Spar and Mace retail brands, negotiated a debt restructure from a consortium of five banks including the Bank of Ireland, AIB, Ulster Bank, Bank of Scotland (Ireland) and Blackstone. The company had property debts of about €300 million before the deal and it is estimated that about €100 million was written off as part of the debt restructure.

Examinerships

To protect the company from formally receiving a bankruptcy petition, the company may appoint an examiner. **Examinerships** are court-managed restructuring procedures. The examinership process offers protection from the court to the company for a period of up to 100 days. In this period no creditor can file for bankruptcy. The management and directors remain in post. The examiner contacts the company's creditors, asking them to agree to restructuring the company's debts. The crux of the agreement is usually an extension on the time required to repay the sums owed, an agreement not to charge interest penalties and, in some instances, discounts are negotiated. The discounts may be a reduction in the amount owed by the company, an agreement to charge a lower interest rate, an agreement to take equity shares in exchange for debt repayments, or a combination of these options. A high-profile example of an Irish company that went into examinership is Eircom, as illustrated in **Real World Example 5.2**.

Real World Example 5.2: Eircom (Rebranded as 'Eir' in 2015)

In 2012, Eircom, a fixed, mobile and broadband telecommunications company that currently trades under the name 'eir', went into examinership for 54 days. When it exited the process, its €1.8 billion of debt had been restructured and the company continued trading successfully.

Receivership

In some instances, a company with financial difficulties may be subject to a **receivership**. Receiverships do not aim to dissolve a company. In receiverships, a secured creditor, e.g. a debenture holder, appoints a receiver to take over the management of the company, with the aim of ensuring that they get payment. This may involve selling the asset that the creditor's debt is secured on. The best outcome possible is that the receiver is able to pay off the debt to the creditor or come to an agreement to pay off the debt and the company continues to trade as normal. The worst outcome is that no agreement can be reached and the company goes into liquidation. In many instances the receiver negotiates the sale of the company to another company which injects cash to the business, as shown in **Real World Example 5.3**.

Real World Example 5.3: Greenstar

Greenstar, a waste management company employing 800 people, owed €83.2 million to its creditors when it was put into receivership in 2012. The receivers negotiated the sale of the company to Cerberus Capital Management, a US private equity firm. The creditors were happy with the new arrangements with the new owners. The company came out of receivership after 18 months and is trading normally.

Pre-pack Receivership

A simpler form of receivership is known as a '**pre-pack receivership**'. This is similar to a receivership except that before the formal appointment of a receiver by a creditor or group of creditors, a purchaser for the business is identified and the terms of sale are agreed for the secured assets in question. This means the business is split, with the remaining assets being left for the other creditors, many of whose debts are unsecured. This process is not as costly as receivership – see **Real World Example 5.4**.

Real World Example 5.4: Superquinn and Elverys

In 2011, Superquinn, a retailer who employed 2,400 people, found itself in financial difficulty with €400 million of debt. It was purchased by its competitor, Musgrave Group Plc, with the remaining stores rebranding as SuperValu in 2014.[1]

In 2014, sports retailer Elverys[2] was acquired by its management team backed by private investors put together by Irish company advisory group Capnua, before it entered formal receivership.

[1] https://www.independent.ie/business/irish/superquinn-and-the-strangulation-of-irelands-high-street-retailers-26806991.html; accessed April 2020.

[2] https://www.irishtimes.com/business/financial-services/pre-pack-receiverships-need-statutory-framework-1.1679530; accessed April 2020.

Pre-pack receiverships involve short receiverships that are low cost. The receiver may only be required for a few hours as everything has been decided and the receivership is established to deal with the administrative paperwork. The purchaser typically agrees to take over the nominating creditors' debts and provides a cash injection that enables the business to continue as a going concern. However, they are controversial as they lack transparency. They are not subject to judicial oversight as examinership and liquidations are. Most creditors and staff know little about what has gone on until the deal is about to be signed; moreover, the purchasing party can select the bits of the business it wants, leaving poor quality assets that may not be able to continue trading or that realise low values for the other creditors if liquidated.

Informal voluntary settlements with creditors are not as expensive as formal bankruptcy and are also simpler. Though creditors do not typically receive the full amount owed, they get more than they would have had the company gone into bankruptcy. In addition, the amounts are received sooner than they would have had bankruptcy proceedings been initiated.

Company Restructure

Company restructuring is a strategic decision that should be taken if it is expected to lead to an increase in equity holder value, but is particularly relevant when the company is in financial difficulty. Company restructuring is commonly categorised into three types: corporate, business and asset restructuring.

Corporate restructuring refers to changes in the ownership structure of a company and takes place at the strategic level. Examples of this include: when a company amalgamates with another company, or splits into two or more companies; when a company issues more shares causing a change in control; when a company repurchases its own shares or when it goes into liquidation.

Changes in the ownership structure of business units (i.e. a lower level of restructuring relative to corporate restructuring) are called **business restructuring**. Examples of this include: when a company acquires another business unit; when a company lets a business unit be taken over by its management (MBO) or by another company's management team (MBI); when a company simply sells the business unit, franchises it or forms a spin-off company; or when the company forms a strategic alliance or a joint venture with another entity. A strategic alliance or joint venture allows the individual companies in the agreement to retain their separate identities. This form of partnership is more common between companies in industries that are reliant on research, exploration and development and where the costs and risks are high. In particular, companies come together to invest in emerging economies, where the economic and political climate is unstable.

The third main type of restructuring, **asset restructuring**, is concerned with restructuring the legal ownership of a company's assets. Examples of this include: encumbering assets with debt, entering into sale and leaseback agreements, purchasing assets using leases/hire-purchase contracts, divestitures (e.g. sell-offs) and factoring debts.

Divestiture

'Divestiture', 'divestment' and 'disinvestment' are the terms used to describe the sale of an investment. Divestitures can occur at corporate level, through a demerger; at business level, when a business is separated and sold; or at asset level, when an asset/product line, etc., is sold from the rest of the company. Two forms of demerger are possible: a sell-off and a spin-off. A **sell-off** is the straightforward sale of a separate, demerged business from the parent to a third party, usually for cash. An MBO, MBI and BIMBO are examples of business sell-offs to management teams. A **spin-off** is where the business is demerged from the parent into a separate independent unit and shares in it are issued to the parent company's equity holders, in the same proportion to the holdings they have in the parent. Therefore, in a spin-off, the ownership structure stays the same. David Coatsworth explains the benefit of spin-offs in **Real World Example 5.5**.

REAL WORLD EXAMPLE 5.5: SPIN-OFFS

Various bits of research demonstrate that spun-off companies tend to outperform their former owner, at least in the early days of being a standalone business.

For example, investment bank Berenberg analysed circa 1,000 European stocks that were spun-off in the past 10 years and found that they tend to outperform the market by 11% within their first year of trading.

A study in 2003 by the Krannert School of Management found that subsidiaries spun out of companies outperformed their former parent by more than 20% over the first three years following the demerger; with most of the excess returns within the first 12 months of trading.

As a case in point, coal miner South32 (S32) was spun out of BHP Billiton in May 2015 and outperformed the latter by 6% in the first year and by four-fold over three years.

There are various exchange-traded funds which track indices of companies that have been spun out such as New York-listed VanEck Vectors Spin-Off ETF which launched three years ago. In 2016 it was up 44.7%, outperforming the S&P 500 total return index by 11.2%. So far in 2018 the ETF is up 5.6%, representing a 1.8% outperformance versus the benchmark.

Source: Coatsworth, D. (2018) "Better apart: why company break-ups can release hidden value and benefit shareholders." *Shares*, available at https://www.sharesmagazine.co.uk/article/better-apart-why-company-break-ups-can-release-hidden-value-and-benefit-shareholders, accessed 28 November 2019.

Other Motives for Divestiture

Reverse Synergies Some managers believe that reverse synergies can be obtained from splitting a business. This can be explained using a simple mathematical example. Assume a company is worth €/£7 million. This includes a business unit that is valued at €/£2 million. Management may feel that the other parts of the company will be worth more than €/£5 million if this business unit is hived-off to form a separate company.

Strategic Decision

In some instances, a company may demerge a business unit where it feels that that unit is no longer part of the company's corporate plan. In many cases it is not that this unit is unprofitable, just that the management team want to focus on core activities. It may be considered that the business is a 'poor fit' within the overall group. This was the case when GoCompare split with esure, as explained in **Real World Example 5.6**.

REAL WORLD EXAMPLE 5.6: GOCOMPARE AND ESURE

GoCompare demerged from insurer esure in November 2016. Its shares increased by 26% in the year after the split, whereas esure's increased by 38% over the same period. At the time of the demerger, esure chair Sir Peter Wood said: "Both businesses will benefit from being able to focus on their distinct strategies, with Gocompare.com operating as a leading UK price and product comparison website and esure Group as a leading UK provider of motor and home insurance."

Source: https://www.insurancebusinessmag.com/uk/news/breaking-news/shares-in-esure-fell-27-after-gocompare-demerger-39974.aspx, accessed 28 November 2019.

Figure 5.8: Advantages and Disadvantages of Divestiture

ADVANTAGES	DISADVANTAGES
• Part of a business can be sold at a profit for the benefit of its equity holders. • A risky business can be sold to reduce a group's overall business risk. • Part of the business can be sold for cash, which can be used to reduce gearing and financial risk. • Part of a business can be sold and the funds used for investment in an alternative that has a higher expected return. • Part of a business can be sold that is not a core activity, freeing up management time to devote elsewhere. • Part of an unprofitable business can be sold, reducing the burden on the group's management and on the group's resources. • A spin-off will allow investors to clearly see the performance of different parts of the company.	• There may be loss of economies of scale where the demerged business shared overheads (marketing, advertising, finance functions). • Both demerged entities may find it more difficult to raise capital in the future, as some forms of capital (particularly market-based sources of finance) are really only practical for large entities. • The individual demerged companies are more likely to be targeted for takeover by a predator company.

Improved Efficiencies

The most commonly cited motive for undertaking a spin-off in a business entity is to improve efficiency. When a company's various businesses are integrated, it is difficult to identify which parts are efficient and which parts are not. Indeed, some businesses may be supporting others. When the main businesses are separated, and tailored strategic objectives that suit the business are set, the management and organisational structure can be clearly defined and costs controlled. Efficiency and effectiveness can be improved. Consequently, investors will be in a better position to value the constituent parts of the company and can decide to remain investors, or to sell their shares.

Permanent Financial Problems

When it is deemed that the cash flow problem is permanent, management need to act quickly in the best interests of the stakeholders as all will be negatively affected. For example, employees will lose their jobs, investors – including shareholders, banks and bond holders – will lose their investment, suppliers will lose funds owed to them and future sales, customers will have to find another source for the goods or services purchased from the company, the government will lose tax revenues and the community will suffer. By acting quickly, the management team can minimise the losses incurred by the stakeholders. The different avenues open to the company are now explained.

Liquidation

In Ireland, bankruptcy is only an option for natural persons, not legal persons such as companies. The process for insolvent companies is called **liquidation**. In this instance, the company has little hope of continuing as a going concern and it is better for the stakeholders if the directors ceased the business. It usually begins when a director, creditor, shareholder or the company itself petitions the High Court to wind up the company. In this instance, the court appoints a liquidator. This process can be voluntary or forced on the company, typically by a creditor. Recent examples in Ireland are included in **Real World Example 5.7**.

REAL WORLD EXAMPLE 5.7: SETANTA INSURANCE COMPANY AND QUDOS

In 2014, Setanta Insurance Company went into liquidation. It had €93 million of outstanding claims from claimants in Ireland. A liquidator was appointed and over a four-year period, the liquidator managed payouts between the State Claims Agency, liable for Setanta's unpaid claims, and the claimants.

In 2019, another insurance company, Qudos, suffered a similar fate. The process is currently ongoing.

Liquidation provides protection for the creditor by safeguarding them against fraud by the company. It ensures that assets are taken over by an insolvency practitioner and held for the purpose of paying off the creditors. Any director found to have acted to the detriment of creditors may be held personally liable for debts caused as a result of mismanagement and may even be subject to criminal law. Liquidation also ensures that the proceeds from the realisation of a company's assets are equitably distributed between the creditors. However, formal liquidation is timely, costly and the result is that the business disappears.

In terms of cash distributions, there is a pecking order, with some creditors getting preferential treatment over others, as illustrated in **Figure 5.9**.

FIGURE 5.9: ORDER IN WHICH CREDITORS ARE PAID UNDER LIQUIDATION

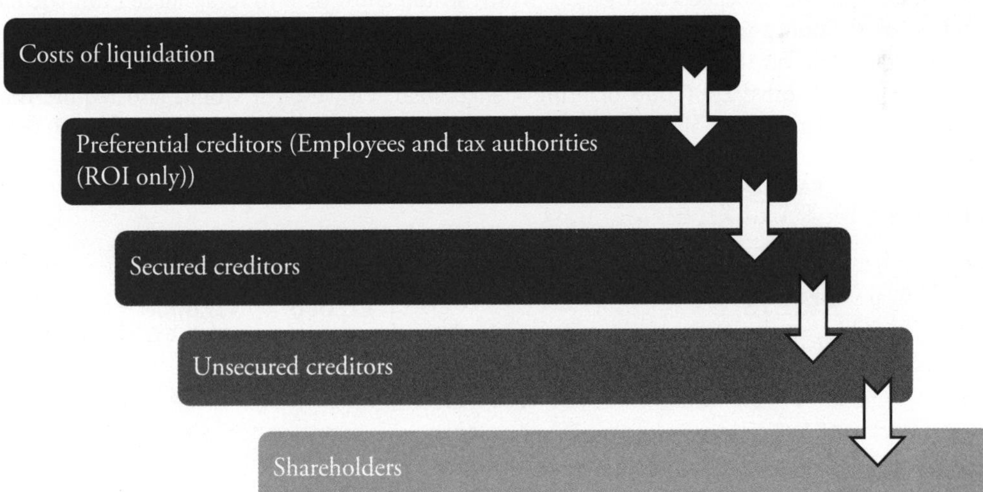

CONCLUSION

There are several factors that can contribute to a company's failure, including fraud, economic downturn, advances in IT, changes in the industry or in society. For example, the internet is awash with examples of high street retailers that have failed due to the increasing trend of customers shopping online. Management need to be aware of the possible causes. For example, inappropriate working capital management is a common cause of company failure. Overtrading and other common causes of corporate failure were outlined earlier in this chapter. Company failure can occur for other reasons also and sources of information on company performance were discussed and 'red flag' indicators of financial difficulty were outlined. Finally, the different avenues open to a corporate in financial distress were outlined, including debt restructuring, examinership, receivership, pre-pack receivership and liquidation.

EXAMINATION STANDARD QUESTION: COMPANY FAILURE

Sam Cummins established Print Media Dublin Ltd in 20X1. The corporate began printing promotional leaflets and, over time, moved into newspaper and magazine printing. The corporate's first 10 years of operation were very successful, and Print Media won contracts with some of the largest publishers in the country to print regional newspapers and magazines. However, the last few years have been very difficult for Print Media. Regional newspapers have been closing and magazines have been reducing their print runs. More recently, Print Media's situation has become critical. An annual interest payment of €/£178,000 on its bank loan is due in three months' time and Print Media will not have enough cash to meet this liability. Over recent weeks, Sam has met with his bank, which provides both Print Media's term loan and overdraft facility, and his accountant to consider the options open to him and the company. His accountant suggested two alternatives:

1. Liquidate Print Media; or
2. Sell two investment properties that Sam owns personally. This would realise €/£880,000 (after clearing the associated mortgages), which would allow Sam to recapitalise Print Media. These are the only assets of significant value that Sam owns, other than his family home. Sam's accountant believes that should he inject this capital into Print Media, the bank would be willing to write-off €/£400,000 of Print Media's loan. However, it would also require that Sam's personal guarantee of Print Media's loan be increased from €/£200,000 to €/£600,000.

Extract from Print Media's Statement of Financial Position

	20X9 (Forecast)	**20X8**
ASSETS	**€/£000**	**€/£000**
Non-current assets		
Property	775	782
Other non-current assets	1,965	2,028
	2,740	2,810

Current assets		
Inventory	130	106
Trade receivables	288	462
Cash	0	75
	418	643
Total assets	**3,158**	**3,453**
EQUITY AND LIABILITIES		
Equity		
Ordinary shares	10	10
Retained earnings	(227)	323
	(217)	333
Non-current liabilities		
Bank loan	2,659	2,659
Current liabilities		
Trade payables	365	195
Wages	80	82
Bank overdraft	96	55
Tax	175	129
	716	461
Total equity and liabilities	3,158	3,453

EXTRACT FROM PRINT MEDIA'S STATEMENT OF PROFIT OR LOSS

	20X9 (Forecast) €/£000	**20X8 €/£000**
Revenue	842	1,355
Operating profit	(426)	122

Peer corporate information

Acid test ratio	1
Operating margin	19%
Financial gearing ratio (debt / equity)	85%

Additional information

- The bank loan is secured by a fixed charge over Print Media's property and a personal guarantee from Sam Cummins in the amount of €/£200,000.
- It is estimated that should Sam liquidate Print Media, the liquidation process would incur costs of €/£118,000.

- In the event of a liquidation, it is estimated that Print Media's assets would, as a percentage of their book values, realise the following:
  - Property: 100%;
  - Other non-current assets: 40%;
  - Inventory: 35%;
  - Trade receivables: 80%.

Requirement

(a)

(i) Calculate the following THREE ratios for Print Media, for **both** 20X9 and 20X8:
- Acid test ratio;
- Operating margin;
- Financial gearing ratio (debt/equity).

(ii) Assess the financial position and financial performance of Print Media, using the ratios calculated in part (i) and the peer corporate information provided.

6 Marks

(b) In relation to the alternatives suggested by the accountant:

(i) Calculate the revised 20X9 financial position of each creditor, assuming Print Media is liquidated;

(ii) Prepare a revised 20X9 statement of financial position for Print Media following the restructuring proposed in alternative 2;

(iii) Comment, for **each** alternative, on the outcome for each creditor, including Sam Cummins.

12 Marks

(c) Advise Sam Cummins which alternative to select, based on the analysis in part (b) and other factors.

3 Marks

Total 21 Marks

Solution

(a)

	Peer corporate information	**Print Media**	
		20X8	**20X9**
Acid test ratio	1	1.16	0.40
Operating margin	19%	9%	(51%)
Gearing (debt to equity)	85%	798%	Equity negative

The table above compares the peer data provided with the same ratio computed for Print Media.

The acid test ratio measures the ability of a corporate to meet its current liabilities using the more liquid current assets (excluding inventory). Print Media's acid test ratio has declined from a comfortable level of 1.16 in 20X8 to 0.40 in 20X9. This indicates a severe and urgent liquidity problem. Trade receivables and cash have fallen very significantly; trade payables and tax have risen significantly. These movements are symptomatic of a corporate experiencing a fall in sales and cash flow difficulties.

Operating margin measures the profit (before paying interest and tax) made on each €/£ of sales. Print Media's operating margin has fallen from approximately half of the peer corporate level (0.09 relative to 0.19) to a significant loss-making position (–0.51). That is, for every €/£1 in sales Print Media is currently making an operating loss of €/£0.51. While a full statement of profit or loss is unavailable to investigate the cause of this loss is unavailable, it suggests that Print Media has significant fixed costs, which will make a return to profitability very difficult with a significant increase in sales.

The gearing ratio measures the proportion of debt to equity used to finance the corporate. The peer corporate uses 0.85 units of debt for each unit of equity. Print Media had 7.98 units of debt per unit of equity in 20X8 and in 20X9 its equity was negative and so a meaningful ratio cannot be computed. This gearing ratio is likely to be the result of accumulating losses over the past number of years rather than over borrowing per se but the result is that the company now has an unsustainable debt burden.

(b) Compare the effect of each alternative for every creditor and Sam Cummins. Your answer should include a reformulated statement of financial position following the proposed recapitalisation.

Alternative 1 – Liquidation

ASSET SALES

	Value			**Value realised**
	€/£000	**€/£000**		**€/£000**
Non-current assets				
Property	775		1	775
Other non-current	1,965	2,740	0.4	786
Current assets				
Inventory	130		0.35	46
Trade receivables	288		0.8	230
Cash	0	418	1	0
Total realised		3,158		1,837

DISTRIBUTION TO CREDITORS

	Distributed		**Residual**
	€/£000	**€/£000**	**€/£000**
Liquidation expenses			1,837
Bank			(118)
			1,719
Fixed charge	775		(775)
+ Personal guarantee	200	975	0
			944

Preferential creditors				
Tax	175			
Wages	80	255	(255)	
			689	
Unsecured creditors				% Rate
Bank	1,980	(2,659 + 96 – 775)	**582**	29.38%
Trade creditor	365		**107**	29.38%
	2,345			

Bank (final position) 1,557 (1,980 + 775 + 200)

(***Note***: in Northern Ireland from April 2020, PAYE (employee contributions) and VAT are preferred creditors but other corporate taxes are not. In the ROI, tax liabilities are ranked as preferred creditors.)

Alternative 2 – Restructure

	20X9 (Forecast)	Change	20X9 (Reformulated)
ASSETS	**€/£000**		**€/£000**
Non-current assets			
Property	775		775
Other non-current	1,965		1,965
	2,740		2,740
Current assets			
Inventory	130		130
Trade receivables	278		278
Cash	10	880	890
	418		1,298
Total assets	3,158		4,038
EQUITY AND LIABILITIES			
Current liabilities			
Trade payables	365		365
Wages	80		80
Bank overdraft	96		96
Tax	175		175
	716		716
Non-current liabilities	2,659	(400)	2,259

Equity			
Ordinary shares	10	880	890
Accumulated gains/losses	(227)	400	173
	(217)		1,063
Total equity and liabilities	3,158		4,038

Bank

Balance of loan reduced to	2,259
Net loss	400

Other creditors

Tax	No change
Wages	No change
Trade creditors	No change

Comparison of the financial position of each creditor

	Liquidation	**Recapitalisation**
	€/£000	**€/£000**
Bank (loan + overdraft)	1,557	2,355
Employees	80	80
Revenue/tax	175	175
Trade creditors	107	365
Sam Cummins*	(200)	between 0 and (1,280)*

*The final position of Sam Cummins in the recapitalisation scenario depends on the probability of Print Media failing in the future – see discussion below.

Liquidation

The liquidation expenses will be met in full.

The bank will receive €/£775,000 from the sale of the property over which it has a fixed charge. The bank will also recover 29% of its remaining €/£1,980,000 balance as an unsecured creditor. It will recover €/£200,000 from Sam Cummins on foot of his personal guarantee.

Its loss (from its nominal position pre-liquidation) will be €/£1,208,000.

As preferential creditors, Revenue and employees will have their claims met in full.

(***Note:*** in Northern Ireland from April 2020, PAYE (employee contributions) and VAT are preferred creditors but other corporate taxes are not. In the ROI, tax liabilities are ranked as preferred creditors.)

There will be a residual of €/£689,000 to meet unsecured creditors' claims of €/£2,345,000. This will be distributed between the bank (€/£582,000) and trade creditors (€/£107,000).

As there will be no residual following the distribution to unsecured creditors, Sam Cummins, as the shareholder, will receive nothing. He will have to meet an obligation of €/£200,000 to satisfy his personal guarantee to Print Media's bank.

Recapitalisation

The bank agrees to reduce its balance owed by €/£400,000. The balance owed to the bank is €/£2,355,000. Its security position is improved as it increases the personal guarantee from Sam Cummins to €/£600,000.

Employees' and Revenue's positions remain unchanged.

Trade creditors are in a much stronger position after the recapitalisation as the equity investment from Sam Cummins dramatically improves the solvency of Print Media.

Sam Cummins liquidates €/£880,000 of personal assets and invests this (in the form of equity) in Print Media. He also increases his personal guarantee of Print Media's bank debt from €/£200,000 to €/£600,000.

The combined effect of Sam's investment and the write-down of the bank debt is that the book value of equity in Print Media rises by €/£1,280,000 (from –€/£217,000 to €/£1,063,000). The net financial effect of this proposal for Sam Cummins while the guarantee is in existence is [–€/£880,000 – €/£400,000 + €/£1,280,000] = €/£0.

In the event the company fails in the future, Sam's position is –€/£880,000 – €/£400,000 = –€/£1,280,000.

(c) Liquidating Print Media will result in an immediate requirement for Sam Cummins to pay €/£200,000 to satisfy his personal guarantee on Print Media's debt. His investment in Print Media currently is effectively worthless since its liabilities are greater than its assets by a considerable margin.

Recapitalising Print Media requires Sam to inject €/£880,000 of his personal wealth into the company and increase his guarantee to €/£600,000 – the net financial effect of the recapitalisation as discussed in part (b). If there is a significant probability of the guarantee being called, the net effect for Sam of the recapitalisation is negative.

The key factor is the future performance of Print Media. Based on the information provided and the analysis in part (a), Print Media is performing extremely poorly and its cost structure and asset structure appear to be completely out of line with its ability to generate turnover. The information provided also indicates that the problems faced by Print Media are due to a declining industry rather than factors within the control of the corporate. This suggests that even if recapitalised, Print Media will continue to make significant losses. Two further years of losses on the scale that Print Media suffered last year would leave the recapitalised Print Media insolvent once again. This would be financially disastrous for Sam Cummins as his €/£880,000 investment would be lost and his €/£600,000 guarantee would be called upon.

A liquidation of Print Media is the optimal choice in the circumstances.

(Based on Chartered Accountants Ireland, CAP 2, SFMA, Summer 2019, Q4)

Key Terms

Altman's failure prediction model
Committee of inspection
Examinership
Financial distress
LBO (leveraged buy-out)
Liquidation
MBO (management buy-out)
Over-capitalisation
Overtrading
Pre-pack receivership
Receivership
Under-capitalisation
Z score

REVIEW QUESTIONS

(See Suggested Solutions to Review Questions in **Appendix B**.)

Question 5.1
What is overtrading?

Question 5.2
Explain what an examinership involves.

Question 5.3
Why do liquidations usually result in loss for the creditors and the owners?

Question 5.4
What protection can a corporate obtain from creditors if there are going concerns but need to restructure their debt?

Question 5.5
List the reasons why an MBO might result in a demerged business being more successful than it had been when it was part of the group.

Question 5.6
List potential reasons for the failure of an MBO.

Question 5.7
What questions might an investor ask when assessing whether to back a management buy-out?

CHALLENGING QUESTIONS

(Suggested Solutions to Challenging Questions are available through your lecturer.)

Question 5.1 East (Level 2)

Jane Fallon is the Managing Director and sole shareholder in East Ireland Hotels Ltd. Prior to founding East, Ms Fallon worked in hotels since finishing college and is passionate about the business. A sizeable inheritance allowed Ms Fallon to leave her job and found East. Apart from her shares in East, Ms Fallon owns a modest house and an equity portfolio valued at €/£800,000.

East owns The East Coast Hotel, which the company built in 20W4. After eight years of profitable trading, East began sustaining losses in 20X3. Losses have continued for the last three years. Trade has improved in the last two months and Ms Fallon believes that the business will return to profitability in the near future.

A loan of €/£2,500,000 was advanced to East by its bank in 20X2 to finance a renovation and to refinance the loan originally advanced for the Hotel construction. This loan is on a 10-year interest only basis at a variable rate of EURIBOR/LIBOR + 5% and is secured by way of a fixed charge on the property. East failed to meet interest payments on the loan in 20X4 and with the agreement of the bank, pending a final resolution, has been making reduced annual payments of €/£50,000 for the last three years. The remaining interest has been waived. Ms Fallon has advanced a number of directors' loans to East to support the business, totalling €/£450,000. The non-current liabilities shown in the statement of financial position below comprise the bank loan and the directors' loans.

STATEMENT OF FINANCIAL POSITION

	20X7 Forecast
ASSETS	**€/£000**
Non-current assets	
Property	1,850
	298
	2,148
Current assets	
Inventory	73
Trade receivables	185
Cash	59
	317
Total assets	2,465
EQUITY AND LIABILITIES	
Current liabilities	
Trade payables	245
Wages	49
Bank overdraft	50

Tax	106
	450
Non-current liabilities	2,950
Equity	
Ordinary shares	100
Accumulated gains/losses	(1,035)
	(935)
Total equity and liabilities	2,465

Last week the bank met with Ms Fallon and her accountant. Following this meeting, the accountant outlined two alternatives to Ms Fallon:

1. East is liquidated. It is estimated that liquidation expenses of €/£95,000 would be incurred; or
2. Ms Fallon injects €/£500,000 in additional equity capital to East. The bank agrees to write-off €/£400,000 of the loan. The remaining €/£2,100,000 will be secured by a fixed charge on the Hotel and a personal guarantee, in the amount of €/£300,000. Ms Fallon will be required to maintain a balance of €/£300,000 in her personal account at the bank for the duration of this guarantee. Ms Fallon's loan to East will be written off.

(***Note***: you should ignore any taxation implications in your analysis.)

Additional information:

- *Property* would be expected to realise 100% of book value in a liquidation.
- *Other non-current assets* would be expected to realise 35% of book value in a liquidation.
- *Inventory* and *trade receivables* would be expected to realise 30% and 75% respectively of book value in a liquidation.

Requirement

(a) Compare the outcome of the two alternatives. Your analysis should:
    (i) Calculate the final financial position of each creditor resulting from the liquidation of East.
    (ii) Prepare a reformulated statement of financial position for East following the restructuring proposed in alternative 2.
    (iii) Comment, for each alternative, on the outcome for each creditor, including Ms Fallon.

14 Marks

(b) Apart from the financial analysis in (a), outline the factors Ms Fallon should consider when deciding whether to proceed with alternative 2. Based on these factors and your analysis in part (a), advise Ms Fallon on which alternative to proceed with.

4 Marks

(c) Based on the information provided, identify three key risks you see facing East after a restructuring.

3 Marks
Total 21 Marks

(Based on Chartered Accountants Ireland, CAP 2, Summer 2017, Q4)

Question 5.2 TBB (Level 2)

You are a Chartered Accountant and have been engaged to advise Mr Teaborn, a wealthy individual and the sole shareholder in Teaborn Bakeries (TBB). TBB is a wholesale bakery business, which manufactures premium baked products primarily for sale to supermarkets. TBB expanded rapidly during the period 20W2 to 20W7, from operating a single bakery to currently operating three manufacturing plants. This expansion was funded by a term loan and overdraft facilities from BankAIR. The recession affected business badly; demand for the premium baking products it manufactures declined dramatically, leading to severe cash flow difficulties. By 20X0, TBB was unable to meet the agreed repayments on the term loan facility. The value of TBB's three manufacturing plants declined by more than 50% as a result of the fall in property prices. In 20X0 BankAIR agreed to change the facilities to an interest-only basis. This arrangement has been extended repeatedly. Demand for TBB's products has improved recently and Mr Teaborn is strongly of the opinion that the prospects for TBB are good. Mr Teaborn is examining his options for the future and three proposals are under consideration.

Option One TBB appoints a liquidator. You may assume that the creditors will approve the liquidator appointed. Liquidation costs are expected to be about €/£5,000.

Option Two Mr McCarthy, a retired businessman, is willing to invest €/£3,100,000 for 100% of the equity in TBB, subject to BankAIR writing down the term loan facility to €/£6,500,000. BankAIR has agreed to this proposal, on the condition that, immediately afterwards, €/£1,500,000 of the new equity is used to clear the overdraft and reduce the loan balance. Mr Teaborn's Personal Guarantee will be released.

Option Three Mr Teaborn invests €/£3,100,000 in TBB, subject to BankAIR writing down the term loan facility to €/£6,500,000. BankAIR has agreed to this proposal, on the condition that, immediately afterwards, €/£1,500,000 of the new equity is used to clear the overdraft and reduce the loan balance. Mr Teaborn's Personal Guarantee will be released.

Assume that TBB will continue as a going concern under options two and three.

A summary of the statement of financial position for TBB as at 31 May 20X5 is provided in Appendix I.

Ignore any tax implications.

Requirement

(a) For each of the THREE alternative restructuring proposals under consideration, outline the financial outcomes for Mr Teaborn, BankAIR **and** the other relevant stakeholders.

14 Marks

(b) Advise Mr Teaborn on which of the proposals outlined he should pursue.

3 Marks

(c) Based on the information provided, highlight TWO key long-term risks facing TBB should the business continue to operate and advise on how these may be mitigated.

4 Marks

Total 21 Marks

APPENDIX I

SUMMARY OF THE STATEMENT OF FINANCIAL POSITION FOR TBB as at 31 May 20X5

ASSETS	**Note**	**€/£000**
Non-current assets		
Property (net book value)	1	3,856
Plant & machinery	1	1,990
Fixtures and fittings	1	195
		6,041
Current assets		
Inventory	1	399
Trade receivables	1	1,651
Cash		63
		2,113
Total assets		8,154

EQUITY AND LIABILITIES		
Equity		
Ordinary shares (nominal value €/£10 per share)		100
Accumulated gains/losses		(2,101)
		(2,001)
Current liabilities		
Bank overdraft	2	1,300
Trade payables		975
Wages		175
Taxation due		95
		2,545
Non-current liabilities		
Long-term loan	2	7,610
		7,610
Total equity and liabilities		8,154

Notes:

1. In the event of liquidation, it is expected that the following could be recovered from asset sales net of selling costs (as a percentage of Book Value): property 80%, plant & machinery 50%, fixtures and fittings 30%, inventory 50%, trade receivables 60%.
2. The Term Loan facility is secured by a fixed charge over the property assets. Mr Teaborn has signed a personal guarantee, in the amount of €/£1,000,000, as security for the bank facility. No other security is in place for the loan or overdraft facilities.
3. Mr Teaborn has liquid assets in excess of €/£10,000,000.

(Based on Chartered Accountants Ireland, CAP 2, SFMA, Summer 2015, Q3)

Question 5.3 Shock (Level 2)

Shock Electric Ltd is a family-owned company that has been trading for the past 20 years. Despite the difficult recent economic environment, Shock has managed to achieve a very significant increase in its turnover in the 12 months to 31 December 20X5.

Strategic Plan When the first indications of the economic downturn appeared, Jim Jones, Managing Director of Shock, reviewed the company's strategic plan and made significant changes aimed at ensuring that Shock maintained its profitability. The revised strategy, which was implemented at the start of the recent financial period, centred on growing sales levels. To achieve this objective, Shock increased the period of credit offered to its customers from 1 January 20X5 and launched a range of promotional offers. The business is a very seasonal one, with significant fluctuations in activity at different times of the year due to seasonal promotions. Jim recognised that one of the biggest issues facing businesses in the current economic environment was a lack of credit facilities available from financial institutions.

This strategy has been extremely successful and Shock has managed to increase its revenue by almost 85% year on year. The following ratios have been extracted, comparing Shock's performance against a local competitor and the industry average.

SHOCK'S PERFORMANCE VS. INDUSTRY AND LOCAL COMPETITOR RATIO INFORMATION

	Shock Year-end 31/12/20X5	Local Competitor Year-end 31/03/20X6	Industry Average Year-end 30/06/20X6
Revenue growth	+85%	−15%	−2%
Current ratio	1.07 : 1.0	1.9 : 1.0	2.1 : 1.0
Quick ratio	0.68 : 1.0	1.1 : 1.0	1.0 : 1.0
Trade receivables	85	35	20
Trade payables days	104	50	45
Inventory turnover	6	10	12
Gross profit margin	15%	25%	25%
Profit before interest and tax	3%	12%	14%

Loan Facilities and Threat of Liquidation Shock moved into new premises in 20X5. The company had planned to sell the old premises, but in the current economic environment it has been unable to find a purchaser. It had taken out a short-term facility (i.e. a bank loan) to cover the financing costs associated with the new strategy. The facility was to be repaid in full on 31 March 20X6 out of the proceeds from the sale of the old property and the increased revenue generated by the new strategy. Shock was not in a position to repay the facility at 31 March 20X6 and, as a result, the senior loan officer of the bank has called an urgent meeting to discuss the matter. The bank is not prepared to extend any further financing and has indicated that the bank is prepared to instigate legal proceedings to recover the money due.

Proposal from Venture Capitalist Given the current difficulties, Shock is now considering a capital reconstruction as it believes that the underlying business is profitable in the medium term. A venture capitalist is considering investing in Shock and has conducted an appraisal based on the interim financial statements for the period ended 31 March 20X6 (see Appendix I below). The venture capitalist's conclusions are:

- The non-current assets of Shock are estimated to be worth €/£1.2 million less than the book values presented.
- Inventory would realise 80% of the book value.
- Bad debts are estimated at 15% of the value of trade receivables.
- All other assets and liabilities are considered to be worth the values presented in the interim financial statements.
- Costs associated with an involuntary liquidation are estimated to be 13% of the assets realised.
- If the company can be rescued, earnings after interest and tax are expected to be €/£480,000 for 20X6. A prospective P/E ratio of 12 is estimated; this is based on the average for companies in similar businesses and taking into consideration the impact of the capital reconstruction.

The venture capitalist has indicated its willingness to invest provided the following conditions are met:

- The venture capitalist will purchase new shares in the business so that its shareholding of the expanded capital will represent 30% of the issued share capital.
- The venture capitalist is prepared to pay €/£1 per share.
- The secured shareholders' loan would be written off without Shock making any further payments in respect of either interest or capital.
- The venture capitalist would hold the shares for a period of between five and seven years. At the end of this investment period (as determined by the venture capitalist), Shock would be floated on a suitable secondary stock exchange.

Invoice Collection Service A financial institution provides an invoice collection service. The terms of the service are as follows:

Flat fee	0.3% of receivables taken over
Percentage of receivables which the institution invoice collector is prepared to take over	80%
Overdraft interest rate	12%
Collection period using invoice collection service	30 Days
Collection period all other customers	80 Days

Appendix I

Shock Electric Ltd

Statements of Financial Position

	Period Ended 31 March 20X6	**Year Ended 31 December 20X5**	**Year Ended 31 December 20X4**
	€/£000	**€/£000**	**€/£000**
ASSETS			
Non-current assets			
Property	6,000	6,000	3,500
Plant & machinery	1,200	1,000	450
	7,200	7,000	3,950
Current assets			
Inventory	6,570	6,430	430
Trade receivables	11,390	11,230	2,500
Bank	0	0	400
	17,960	17,660	3,330
Total assets	25,160	24,660	7,280
EQUITY AND LIABILITIES			
Equity			
Equity share capital (nominal €/£1 each)	3,800	3,800	2,800
Revenue reserves	2,580	2,550	1,950
Total equity and reserves	6,380	6,350	4,750
Non-current liabilities			
Secured shareholders' loan	1,900	1,900	800
Current liabilities			
Trade payables	12,091	11,685	1,600
Overdraft	1,039	975	0
Tax	250	250	130
Bank loan	3,500	3,500	0
	16,880	16,410	1,730
Total equity and liabilities	25,160	24,660	7,280
Revenue for the period ended	12,227	48,230	26,070

Requirement

(a) Analyse the financial performance of Shock for the year ended 31 December 20X5. Your answer should include:
- Commentary against the competitive and industry information.
- Appropriate comments on the usefulness and limitations on the information as presented.
- An evaluation of the growth strategy identifying positive and negative aspects.
- Identification of the three key risks facing Shock and how these might be addressed.

(***Note:*** the computation of additional ratios is not required as part of your solution to this part of the question and you may assume that the ratios as presented are computationally accurate.)

35 Marks

(b) Discuss the advantages and disadvantages from the bank's perspective of forcing Shock into liquidation. Calculate how much the bank is likely to receive in a liquidation situation.

22 Marks

(c) (i) What value has the venture capitalist placed on Shock? How much cash will be injected into the business by the venture capitalist? Comment on whether this is sufficient to alleviate the current financial difficulties of the company.

9 Marks

(ii) Using two other methods of valuing the company, assess whether the venture capitalist's offer is consistent with your chosen valuation methods. Advise Shock's shareholders on whether or not they should accept the offer from the venture capitalist.

10 Marks

(d) Assess the invoice collection proposal and make a recommendation as to whether Shock should avail of this service.

10 Marks

(e) Calculate the working capital cycle in days for Shock and its local competitor. Explain the significance of these figures.

9 Marks

(***Note:*** for Shock, use year-end data for 31 December 20X5 and the local competitor year-end 31 March 20X6.)

Presentation 5 Marks

Total 100 Marks

(Based on Chartered Accountants Ireland, CAP 2, Autumn 2009, Q1)

Question 5.4 Gourmet (Level 2)

Background Gourmet Ltd is an Irish-owned mid-sized bakery that focuses on the production and sale of a range of speciality breads from its production facility in County Dublin. Gourmet was founded 15 years ago by the current Managing Director, Jane Smith, and has expanded consistently over the years to the extent that Gourmet now exports 50% of its output to England and France. The remainder of Gourmet's produce is sold throughout the island of Ireland via a network of both multinational and independent retailers.

The market for speciality breads in Ireland has become more competitive in recent years with the introduction of a number of premium European brands to the Irish market. Coupled with this, the global economic downturn has also impacted on Gourmet's recent performance and, as a result, Gourmet is continually seeking to reduce its cost base wherever possible, while at the same time attempting to increase sales revenue in its chosen market segments.

New Product Development As one means of increasing sales revenue (and ultimately profitability), Gourmet recently introduced (at the beginning of 20X5) a range of gluten-free breads ('Brown', 'Wholemeal' and 'Wholegrain') to the Irish market. According to Gourmet's Sales Director, Kevin Wood, even though the Irish market for gluten-free products has been in existence for a number of years, there still remains huge scope for expansion in the short to medium term and, hence, the decision by Gourmet's board of directors to enter this particular market segment.

The unanimous belief amongst Gourmet's board of directors was that their hard-earned reputation for quality produce at a reasonable price should allow Gourmet to capture a significant share of this potentially lucrative and expanding market in the coming years. However, the decision to enter this market was not taken lightly as it necessitated a significant capital investment, which was funded primarily by a bank loan.

Performance Measurement At the conclusion of the Board meeting that sanctioned Gourmet's entry into the Irish gluten-free bread market, it was decided that a regular (i.e. three-monthly) performance review should be conducted by the board of directors to gauge Gourmet's success or otherwise in this particular market. Jane Smith has repeatedly stressed that unless the new gluten-free products are capable of achieving Gourmet's budgetary targets in the short term, its proposed strategy for these products would have to be reviewed. Appendix I contains all of the relevant data for Gourmet's initial three months of trading in the Irish gluten-free bread market.

Financial Performance Last week David Hayes, Gourmet's newly appointed Finance Director (after a period of 18 months during which there was no Finance Director), received a letter from Gourmet's bank asking him to meet them as they were concerned that Gourmet's overdraft limit of €/£500,000 had been significantly and consistently exceeded. The bank has asked for an action plan to be prepared to address this situation.

When David Hayes informed the Board about this and outlined the consequences should the bank withdraw the overdraft facilities, the Board was shocked. While they were aware that Gourmet had been increasingly relying on its overdraft in the last year, they had been happy with its sales growth and did not see the overdraft as a significant issue. David Hayes's priority is to get a clear understanding of the financial position before meeting the bank next week to discuss the overdraft facility. To prepare for this, he has gathered some financial information on peer group companies, and this is contained in Appendix II.

Investment Appraisal Gourmet uses a range of approaches to assess new investments. Projects requiring a capital investment of less than €/£1 million can be approved by line managers without a formal analysis process. For projects requiring a capital investment in excess of €/£1 million, Gourmet rejects any projects with an expected pay-off period of greater than four years. This is used as a first-stage filter. Projects are then analysed on a net present value (NPV) basis, using Gourmet's cost of borrowing as the discount rate. If projects have a positive NPV, they are presented to the board of directors for approval.

David Hayes has seen a document outlining this investment appraisal policy and has mentioned to Jane Smith that he believes it could be significantly improved. Jane was sceptical as this policy had been in place for a long time and seemed to work fine.

Requirement

(a) Using the information provided in Appendix II, prepare an analysis of the financial performance of Gourmet over the last three years and compare this to the peer group average under the following headings:
- Profitability
- Liquidity and gearing
- Working capital management

(***Note:*** you are not required to calculate any additional ratios to those provided in Appendix II.)

12 Marks

(b) Based on your answer to part (a), prepare an action plan (to be approved by the Board of Directors before being presented to the bank at next week's meeting), which outlines how Gourmet can address the deterioration in its financial performance.

8 Marks

(c) Critically assess Gourmet's approach to investment appraisal. If you believe it is not appropriate, suggest an alternative approach.

5 Marks

(d) Using the information provided in Appendix II, calculate an appropriate discount rate for Gourmet to use in analysing projects. Highlight any assumptions that you make (after you have studied **Chapter 13**).

5 Marks

Total 30 Marks

(Based on Chartered Accountants Ireland, CAP 2, MABF, Summer 2012, extract from Q1)

Appendix I

Financial Statements For Gourmet Ltd

Statement of Profit or Loss
for Year Ended 31 December

	20X4 €/£000	20X3 €/£000	20X2 €/£000
Turnover	4,004	2,860	2,200
Cost of sales	(2,723)	(1,659)	(1,210)
Gross profit	1,281	1,201	990
Operating expenses	(641)	(400)	(264)
Directors' salaries	(250)	(150)	(100)
Operating profit	391	651	626
Interest	(284)	(74)	(59)
Profit before tax	107	577	567
Tax	(13)	(72)	(71)
Net profit	94	505	496

Statement of Financial Position
as at 31 December

	20X4 €/£000	20X3 €/£000	20X2 €/£000
Non-current assets	**8,150**	**4,145**	**3,200**
Inventories	435	280	165
Trade receivables	900	450	240
Cash and cash equivalents	12	86	100
Current assets	**1,347**	**816**	**505**
Total assets	**9,497**	**4,961**	**3,705**
Trade payables	800	550	100
Bank (overdraft)	1,160	517	80
Current liabilities	**1,960**	**1,067**	**180**
Share capital	1,000	1,000	1,000
Retained earnings	2,023	1,930	1,425
Total equity	**3,023**	**2,930**	**2,425**
Non-current liabilities (Debt)	**4,514**	**964**	**1,100**
Total equity and liabilities	**9,497**	**4,961**	**3,705**

APPENDIX II
FINANCIAL PERFORMANCE OF GOURMET LTD AND PEER GROUP AVERAGE

	Peer Group		Gourmet Ltd	
	20X4	20X4	20X3	20X2
Profitability				
Gross profit margin	40%	32%	42%	45%
Net profit margin	19%	2%	18%	23%
Return on capital employed	15%	4%	13%	17%
Liquidity/Gearing				
Current ratio	2.0	0.7	0.8	2.8
Quick ratio	1.0	0.5	0.5	1.9
Gearing ratio	0.5	0.5	0.2	0.3
Interest cover	8.0	1.4	8.8	10.6
Working Capital Management				
Non-current asset turnover	0.8	0.5	0.7	0.7
Inventory turnover	20	9	10	13
Trade receivables days	30	82	57	40
Trade payables days	30	107	121	30

(***Note:*** you may assume that all ratios are correct and have been rounded consistently.)

Additional information:
- All borrowings are advanced at an interest rate of 4.5%.
- Corporation tax is payable at 12.5%.
- The yield on short-term government debt is 3%.
- Publicly traded companies in the same sector as Gourmet have beta values ranging from 1 to 1.3.
- The historical return on the stock exchange is 11%.

Question 5.5 Qwerty (Level 2)

Background It is now June 20X5. Qwerty Limited is an Irish-based company that designs, manufactures and sells a wide range of wireless computer keyboards to retailers in both Ireland and Northern Ireland. Qwerty is co-owned by twin brothers Paul and Joe Hayes, who founded the company after graduating from their local university with undergraduate degrees in Computer Science and Electronic Engineering, respectively. Since then, Qwerty has experienced rapid sales growth (with modest but growing profitability) and now employs 55 full-time employees at its Limerick base. Paul and Joe are the only directors of the company.

Performance Measurement As a result of the ongoing difficulties experienced by Qwerty in acquiring adequate levels of credit from its local financial institutions to fund its working capital, Paul and Joe have decided, with immediate effect, that if any of their products are budgeted to be loss-making for the forthcoming year, they should be discontinued immediately in an attempt to protect the future viability of the company. Consequently, the 20X6 budgetary data for one of Qwerty's most popular (and, to date, profitable) keyboards, 'Exile', are causing Paul and Joe a lot of concern (see Appendix I for the 20X6 budgetary data on 'Exile'). In an ongoing attempt to reduce their costs, all of Qwerty's

20X6 budgetary forecasts were jointly prepared by the company's co-owners, having previously been contracted out to a small local firm of Chartered Accountants.

In addition to focusing on product profitability as a key performance indicator, Paul and Joe are also keen to consider the use of some non-financial metrics to guide them in making future strategic decisions. Having discussed the various options available, allied to the nature of the industry in which they compete, they have collectively decided on 'innovation' as the key non-financial success factor for Qwerty to focus on in the short to medium term, although they have yet to agree on any specific performance measures.

Requirement As an external financial consultant, you are required to:

(a) (i) Prepare a financial analysis of the decision to discontinue the manufacture of 'Exile' in 20X6 (see Appendix I for details). Explain your treatment of each item that comprises your analysis and state clearly any assumptions that you make.

8 Marks

(ii) Advise Paul and Joe based upon your financial analysis in (a)(i) above.

2 Marks

(b) Discuss THREE non-financial considerations that Paul and Joe should also consider prior to making their final decision as to whether or not to withdraw the 'Exile' wireless keyboard from sale in 20X6.

6 Marks

(c) Critically evaluate Paul and Joe's new proposed policy in respect of discontinuing any products which are budgeted to be loss-making within Qwerty. In addition, suggest any improvement to the proposed policy that you consider appropriate.

5 Marks

Total 21 Marks

(Based on Chartered Accountants Ireland, CAP 2, MABF, Autumn 2013, extract from Q1)

Appendix I
20X6 Budgetary Data for 'Exile'

	€/£
Total sales revenue	205,500
Expenses	
Direct material costs (Note 1)	(96,950)
Indirect variable material costs	(37,500)
Direct labour costs	(42,300)
Fixed production overheads (Note 2)	(12,750)
Variable production overheads	(8,175)
Insurance costs (Note 3)	(15,500)
Local authority rates (Note 4)	(6,600)
Depreciation (machinery) costs	(12,000)
Loan interest	(6,000)
Production Supervisor costs (Note 5)	(40,000)
Selling costs (Note 6)	(26,100)
Electricity costs (Note 7)	(5,400)
General administration costs (Note 8)	(15,350)
Cost of independent consultants' report (Note 9)	(7,500)
Total costs	(332,125)
Total budgeted loss	(126,625)

Additional information:

1. All of the direct materials needed to produce 'Exile' in 20X6 were bought by Qwerty during the second half of 20X5. If these materials are not used to produce 'Exile' in 20X6, they will be sold immediately to a rival company for €/£11,750.
2. One quarter of the fixed production overheads relate to 'Exile', while the balance represents an allocation of Qwerty's total fixed production overhead expense for 20X6.
3. 50% of the insurance costs relate specifically to 'Exile', while the remainder is company specific.
4. The local authority rates payable by Qwerty in 20X6 were calculated on the basis of the size of the company's premises.
5. The Production Supervisor who oversees the production of 'Exile' is a full-time permanent employee of Qwerty. If Qwerty decides to terminate the production of 'Exile', the Production Supervisor is expected to remain with the company (in another role) for 20X6.
6. All of the selling costs relate specifically to 'Exile'.
7. 45% of the electricity costs currently allocated to 'Exile' cannot be avoided by Qwerty if a decision is taken to terminate the production of this product.
8. The general administration costs relate to the salary of a contract employee who works exclusively on 'Exile'. She will not have her short-term contract renewed if a decision is taken to terminate the production of 'Exile', but will instead be entitled to compensation to the value of 40% of her salary, payable immediately.
9. Qwerty commissioned an independent consultant during 20X5 to devise a new marketing strategy for 'Exile'. The consultant delivered his report at the end of 20X5 and will be paid at the beginning of 20X6.

Question 5.6 Packaging Solutions (Level 2)

Background Information You have recently been appointed as the company management accountant at the head office of Packaging Solutions Ltd, a medium-sized company comprising two divisions, the Packaging Division and the Recycling Division.

Each division has its own dedicated management team responsible for operational decision-making and control. The divisions are currently managed as profit centres with all strategic investment and financing decisions taken by the board, located at head office.

Mission and Performance Targets The mission statement of the company reads as follows:

> "Packaging Solutions is committed to operating in an environmentally sustainable manner and aims to be the leading supplier of packaging and recycling solutions on the island of Ireland."

This statement has been translated into the following company performance targets for each division:

- achieve and maintain a market share of at least 25%;
- deliver an annual profit before interest and taxes (PBIT) of 15%; and
- deliver 100% customer satisfaction.

The Packaging Division The Packaging Division provides a wide range of paper packaging solutions to commercial customers on the island of Ireland. In mid-20W6, and anticipating ever increasing customer demand, plant capacity was increased substantially, financed with five-year unsecured debentures.

With the onset of the global recession in 20W8, customer demand began to weaken and suppliers began to seek price increases for their raw materials. Customer demand continued to weaken throughout 20W9 and 20X0. The division's management team has continued to express confidence to the board on the division's medium- to long-term prospects. There is some evidence to suggest that the market for packaging solutions will recommence growth by late 20X1. Secretly, the divisional management team is very concerned at their lack of experience in managing a business in temporary decline. Given the continued margin pressures, the divisional management team intends to embark on a *cost reduction programme*, one provision of which seeks to terminate and re-hire all employees in the division at substantially reduced pay rates.

Recycling Division Three years ago the company built a recycling plant and established a separate Recycling Division. The plant was initially intended to process the waste produced by the Packaging Division into high-quality raw materials for re-use or sale. An experienced operational manager and a specialist marketing manager were appointed to grow the business. Following the division's expansion into recycling under contract for third parties, it has grown rapidly.

The division is weathering the recession well. Demand has remained strong locally and management estimate that revenue could be doubled through local and/or overseas expansion, with Sweden identified as a potential growth market. Divisional management also believes that the profitability of the division could be increased by substituting the recycling it performs for the Packaging Division with third-party contracts.

Recent Financial Performance and Management Information System The board is extremely concerned about the financial performance of the company in the latest financial year, particularly in the Packaging Division. Though much of the loss in this division can be attributed to declining sales and raw material cost pressures, the board is frustrated at the inability of the division's management team to clearly explain the detailed operating factors that have contributed to this poor performance.

Details of the financial performance of both divisions over the past three years (and related market data) are included in Appendix I. The unsecured debenture holders have intimated that they do not favour a rollover of greater than 25% of their existing debt.

Strategic Proposals Given the recent financial performance, the board, now fearful for the future of the company, has arranged a meeting to consider the following three strategic proposals:

1. Cease trading and close the company

Realisable values are provided at the end of Appendix II. Additionally, this proposal would give rise to redundancy and closure costs of €/£20 million (after tax) if the company was closed, all payable before any other liabilities, except the secured variable-rate loan.

2. Sell the company to Icon Plc

Icon Plc, a large printing and packaging company, has offered €/£35 million for the company, conditional on Icon Plc taking responsibility for all liabilities of the company, excluding the unsecured debentures.

3. Continue trading and restructure the finance of the company

Under this proposal, the 20X1 unsecured debenture holders would replace 100% of their interest with 18 million new ordinary shares at €/£1 each (every €/£1 of debt replaced with €/£1 of ordinary shares). As part of the arrangement the debenture holders will give a binding guarantee not to sell their shares until 20X8. A free cash flow forecast for the company *incorporating* the proposed finance restructuring is outlined below.

The cost of equity for the entire company can be assumed at 12%.

	20X1 €/£000	20X2 €/£000	20X3 €/£000	20X4 €/£000
Free cash flow available to equity holders	1,235	1,950	4,200	5,000

Management Buy-out Alternative Following the Icon Plc offer, the existing Packaging Division management tabled a proposal with the board to buy out their division at a price to be agreed. The intention of the divisional management would be to continue to run the division as a going concern, with further development capital secured by a local venture capitalist.

Requirement

(a) From the information available, identify TWO potential ethical issues and recommend *one* action that could be taken to resolve each respective issue.

6 Marks

(b) (i) Evaluate *each* of the three strategic proposals under consideration by the board from the perspective of the existing shareholders *and* the unsecured debentures holders in the company. You are required to support your answer with relevant calculations.

Strategy 1. Cease trading and close the company.

6 Marks

Strategy 2. Sell the company to Icon Plc.

3 Marks

Strategy 3. Continue trading and restructure the finances of the company.

8 Marks

Recommendation to the board.

3 Marks

(ii) Outline briefly any FOUR pieces of additional information that would assist the board in making a decision.

4 Marks

(c) Discuss briefly, TWO potential advantages of the proposed management buy-out for the company and for the management team of the Packaging division, respectively.

4 Marks

(Based on Chartered Accountants Ireland, CAP 2, MABF, Autumn 2010, extract from Q1)

Appendix I
Packaging Solutions Ltd

	PACKAGING DIVISION			RECYCLING DIVISION		
	20W8 €/£000	20W9 €/£000	20X0 €/£000	20W8 €/£000	20W9 €/£000	20X0 €/£000
Sales	60,000	54,000	46,000	8,000	14,000	20,000
Gross profit %	30%	25%	22%	40%	42%	45%
PBIT %	8%	3%	(5%)	(10%)	5%	15%
PBIT	4,800	1,620	(2,300)	(800)	700	3,000

	PACKAGING DIVISION			RECYCLING DIVISION		
	20W8	20W9	20X0	20W8	20W9	20X0
	€/£000	€/£000	€/£000	€/£000	€/£000	€/£000
Finance cost	(1,350)	(1,500)	(1,750)	(200)	(225)	(250)
PBT	3,450	120	(4,050)	(1,000)	475	2,750
Tax	(520)	(20)	600	150	(70)	(415)
PAT	2,930	100	(3,450)	(850)	405	2,335

	MARKET DATA (Island of Ireland)					
	PACKAGING			RECYCLING		
	20W8	20W9	20X0	20W8	20W9	20X0
	€/£000	€/£000	€/£000	€/£000	€/£000	€/£000
Total market	400,000	380,000	350,000	90,000	120,000	150,000

Appendix II

Packaging Solutions Ltd

Statement of Financial Position
as at 30 June 20X0

	Packaging Division	Recycling Division	Total Company
ASSETS	**€/£000**	**€/£000**	**€/£000**
Non-current assets			
Land and buildings	24,000	6,000	30,000
Plant and machinery	28,000	7,000	35,000
	52,000	13,000	65,000
Current assets			
Inventory	2,700	900	3,600
Trade receivables	10,200	2,550	12,750
Cash	0	440	440
	12,900	3,890	16,790
Total assets	64,900	16,890	81,790
EQUITY AND LIABILITIES			
Current liabilities			
Trade payables	3,500	1,500	5,000
8% bank overdraft (unsecured)	4,900	0	4,900
	8,400	1,500	9,900
Equity			
Ordinary shares at €/£1			20,000
Reserves			30,390
			50,390

Non-current liabilities	
8% unsecured debentures (20X1)	18,000
Secured variable loan (20X4) (Current rate 7%)	3,500
	21,500
Total equity and liabilities	81,790

Realisable values: after-tax realisable values of assets if not sold as part of a going concern are estimated at:

Land and buildings	€/£15 million
Plant and machinery	€/£10 million
Inventories	€/£1.56 million
Trade receivables	€/£10.45 million

6

An Introduction to Working Capital

Learning Objectives

Upon completing this chapter, readers should be able to:

- define working capital and explain the importance of managing working capital;
- discuss the working capital cycle;
- calculate the net investment by a company in working capital;
- calculate the operating/cash conversion cycle;
- discuss the symptoms and remedies of over-capitalisation;
- use ratios to determine the finance required for working capital; and
- explain the three main working capital management strategies: aggressive, neutral and conservative.

INTRODUCTION

Most Plcs have a treasury department that manages global transactions, equity holdings and funding requirements. This department also manages a company's working capital. This involves determining the level of inventory to keep in store, the credit period to allow to customers, the credit period to take from suppliers and the cash balance to keep on hand. In most companies the amount held in these current assets and liabilities represents a major investment, tying up funds, which has a cost. Yet, the investment is necessary as otherwise normal trading activities would be disrupted, affecting profits. Information on a company's working capital can be obtained from its financial statements. Ratio analysis can be used to determine the efficiency with which management utilises its working capital. Financial statements can also inform the reader as to how working capital is being financed.

This chapter: defines working capital; explains the purpose of managing working capital; identifies the costs of working capital; discusses the type of finance to use; and the three main types of working capital management strategy: aggressive, neutral and conservative.

WORKING CAPITAL

Working capital is the net investment by a company in operating current assets (trade receivables, inventories, bank and cash) and operating current liabilities (trade payables and an overdraft). It is calculated as follows:

Working capital = Inventories + Trade receivables + Bank/cash − Trade payables − Overdraft

or

Working capital = Current assets − Current liabilities

A company usually expects its working capital components (for example, inventories and trade payables) to be realised within a short period of time, hence they are regarded as current at any one point in time. These components are required on an ongoing basis and specific items can be turned over many times in one year. Therefore, a **permanent investment** in working capital is required to enable a company to carry on its business. Working capital also includes other tied-up funds, which may be difficult to quantify (for example, intellectual capital) or are deemed to be immaterial (accruals, prepayments and VAT). Where material, these items are included as a formal part of the working capital management decision-making process.

WORKING CAPITAL MANAGEMENT

A company has to have working capital to carry on its business. Goods are purchased on credit or by cash, and form inventories. These have to be held before sales can be made. Credit usually has to be given to obtain sales. Working capital management tries to achieve an optimum balance between ensuring that: sufficient levels of working capital are held so as not to negatively impact on a company's operations; adequate liquidity levels are maintained; and costs associated with holding working capital are minimised. The interrelationship between the first two factors (the working capital elements required to ensure that operational activities are not disrupted) and liquidity are portrayed in **Figure 6.1**. This diagram also highlights the potential impact of working capital on decision-making in other areas within a company.

When more funds are tied up in the major working capital components (trade receivables, trade payables and inventory), then the amount of cash available for other business decisions is reduced. This may impact on the future profitability of a company because the company may have less cash available to invest in long-term assets that earn a higher return.

FIGURE 6.1: WORKING CAPITAL CYCLE: COMPONENTS, INFLUENCES AND SOURCES

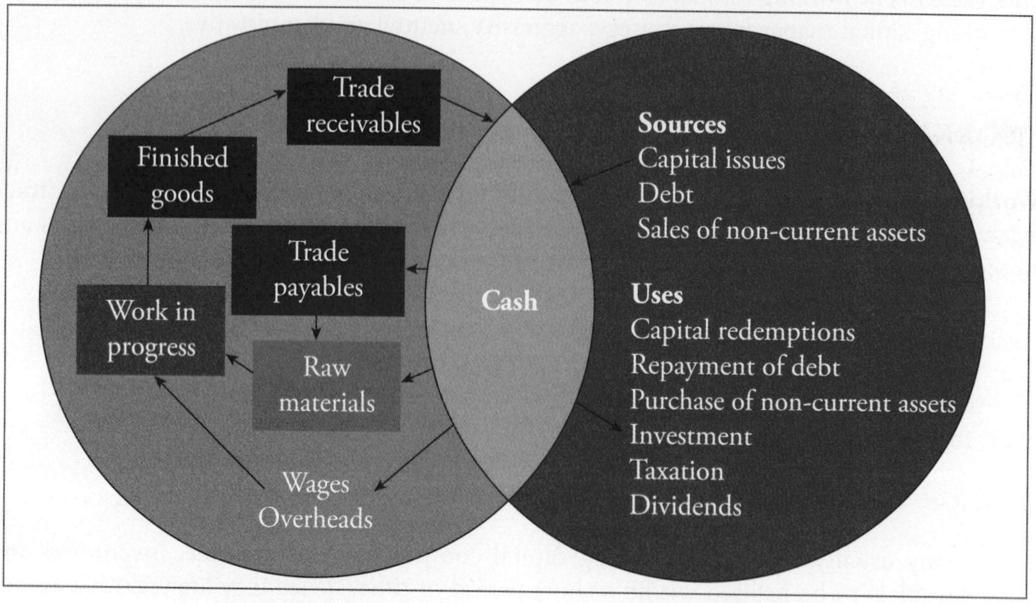

As highlighted in **Figure 6.1**, cash can be sourced from capital issues, debt or the sale of non-current assets. These sources are usually costly. Cash generated from operating activities that are supported by an optimum investment in working capital is a more efficient source of cash. This will ensure that optimum levels of cash are available to meet taxation and dividend demands, while also providing funds that can be used for long-term objectives (e.g. capital redemption, debt repayment, and capital investment). The key to this process is to ensure that the company's activities are profitable and that they generate net cash inflows.

Management of the individual working capital components should ensure that sufficient inventory is available to keep production at a level so there are no stock-outs resulting in lost sales. Yet the level should not be so high as to increase the overhead costs associated with holding inventory, including the cost of the funds tied up (this is examined in **Chapter** 7). The credit period afforded to customers should be at a level that does not result in customers transferring their custom elsewhere. This should be balanced with the costs that are associated with allowing long credit periods, such as higher levels of bad debts, higher administration costs incurred in chasing up the debts and the cost of funds tied up (examined in **Chapter 8**).

Management of purchases is also important. The majority of companies operate using credit facilities; therefore, credit is expected and should be taken. If a company purchases goods for cash, funds are tied up unnecessarily, which has implications for the company's liquidity. However, care needs to be exercised when taking credit, as payment after an agreed timescale may lead to a loss of supply, interest penalties, or loss of discounts (examined in **Chapter 8**). Cash itself needs consideration. Cash is required to pay for certain legal obligations, such as taxation and salaries, therefore a certain amount of cash is required to service running expenses, yet cash sitting in a current account does not earn a high return. A sound cash management policy is required to identify the optimum level of cash that should be held.

This may involve financing the cash requirement where there is a deficit, or establishing an investment policy in respect of any surplus (this is considered in detail in **Chapter 9**).

Industry Influence

The type and level of working capital a company holds is influenced by the industry within which the company operates. A manufacturing company will purchase raw materials and consumables. Then, using in-house costs such as wages and overheads, work in progress and finished goods are generated. Therefore, at any one point in time a manufacturing company will have four types of inventory: raw materials; work in progress; finished goods; and consumables. Its sales and purchases are usually on credit. Manufacturing companies usually hold high levels of raw material and consumable inventory as the cost of a stock-out is high, i.e. production is halted and certain costs that are used to generate products are fixed. These costs occur regardless of whether the manufacturing process is active or not, for example, supervisors' salaries, rent, rates, etc. Manufacturing entities usually operate with quite high levels of trade receivables and take credit from suppliers. The credit period is influenced by the normal trading terms for each particular manufacturing industry.

In contrast, a retailing entity usually has only one type of inventory – finished goods. Retail companies usually purchase finished goods inventory on credit. Most of their sales are for cash. Inventory levels of finished goods are generally quite high, though some retailers have a just-in-time relationship with their suppliers ensuring prompt delivery of goods straight to the shop floor, reducing the level of inventory that is required to be held in stores.

Even within the retailing sector, differences occur depending on the type and nature of the product being sold. For example, a jeweller will purchase goods infrequently and may hold inventory for over a year. This inventory will not deteriorate and may even increase in value. Whereas a greengrocer will purchase inventory frequently and will turn over its inventory every few days or even daily. A greengrocer's products are prone to deterioration and fall in value over time. Seasonality is also another factor to take into consideration. A jeweller may increase its inventory levels before Christmas and St Valentine's Day, whereas a greengrocer will not be subject to the same degree of fluctuation in the demand for its products. Individual items may be seasonal, for example, pumpkins at Halloween and brussels sprouts at Christmas.

Working Capital: Investment and Associated Finance Cost

All the components making up the working capital cycle are considered to be current in nature. However, as mentioned previously, there is never a time when an entity can operate without them. Even though the components can turn over quickly, working capital is a permanent requirement that has to be financed. Therefore, a minimum level of working capital should be held as a long-term investment (i.e. **permanent working capital**). In some instances the investment can be short-term (i.e. **temporary working capital**), for example, when an entity trades in a product that has cyclical demand, such as umbrellas or ice-cream. In these cases the levels of inventory will increase for a few months of the year and the investment requirement will be higher for this period.

Like any investment, working capital has a finance cost. This cost is the **opportunity cost** of not utilising the funds in an alternative project that would benefit the company. The opportunity cost depends on the circumstances of the company. Where the company has surplus cash, the cost is the return that could be achieved from investing the required funds in other types of investments. Where the company has to seek funding for working capital investment, the cost is the interest that is incurred on the financing. Where both situations exist, i.e. the company is in overdraft and can invest in more profitable projects, then the finance cost of having funds tied up in working capital is the higher of the two rates.

Worked Example 6.1: Operating Cost of Investing in Working Capital

Verde Ltd can increase its sales by €/£1,000,000 per annum if it increases its inventory level by €/£600,000. The company has a contribution margin of 15%. It is expected that the company's average trade receivables will increase by €/£300,000. Trade payables are also expected to increase. The company has credit terms with its suppliers, similar to those it gives to its customers. The company currently receives 12% on its investments.

Requirement Advise Verde Ltd as to whether or not it should increase its inventory levels.

Solution

	€/£	€/£
Contribution from additional sales: [€/£1,000,000 × 15%]		150,000
Financing requirement		
Additional trade receivables	300,000	
Additional trade payables: [€/£300,000 × 85%]	(255,000)	
Additional inventory	600,000	
Total finance requirement	645,000	
Finance cost: [€/£645,000 × 12%]		77,400
Increase in profits		72,600

Verde Ltd should increase its inventories as the contribution from the increased sales will more than compensate for the finance costs that will be incurred in having to invest in higher levels of working capital.

As can be seen from **Worked Example 6.1**, an increase in working capital levels within a company has a direct finance requirement (e.g. working capital increased by €/£645,000 in Verde Ltd). Alternatively, if working capital were to be managed more efficiently, reducing the investment requirement, then working capital can be seen as a source of finance.

Using Ratios to Determine the Financing Requirement

If known, the trade receivables-days ratio, trade payables-days ratio and the inventory-days ratio can be used to determine the resultant balance of trade receivables, trade payables and inventory (see **Figure 6.3** for the ratio components). This enables the investment in working capital to be determined. In **Worked Example 6.2**, projected sales increases are used to determine the expected level of working capital that requires financing.

WORKED EXAMPLE 6.2: CASH CONVERSION PERIOD

Blanco Plc expects its annual turnover to increase from €/£500,000 to €/£1,500,000. Its customers currently take 40 days' credit.

Requirement Assuming all else remains stable, determine the additional working capital requirement and finance cost of this growth. Blanco Plc can invest its surplus cash at 15%.

Solution

Trade receivables before growth: $€/£500{,}000 \times \frac{40}{365} = €/£54{,}795$

Trade receivables after growth: $€/£1{,}500{,}000 \times \frac{40}{365} = €/£164{,}383$

Therefore, the additional finance requirement is: €/£109,588 [€/£164,383 − €/£54,795]

This has an opportunity cost of: €/£16,438 [€/£109,588 × 15%]

TARGETED WORKING CAPITAL MANAGEMENT POLICIES

Many factors influence the level of working capital a company chooses to maintain, such as the company's liquidity, ease of sourcing finance, type of business, economic climate and management preferences. Depending on the individual circumstances of a company, the management may choose to finance working capital very differently from what you would expect. Three polar policies are considered to capture the range of strategies that management pursues. These are termed: conservative, neutral and aggressive. In practice, policies can lie anywhere along a continuum between the extremes of conservative and aggressive strategies. Extreme examples of statements of financial position under the three main headings are presented in **Figure 6.2** (overleaf).

Conservative

When a company operates a **conservative working capital management strategy** it is **over-capitalised**, holding high levels of current assets, including cash, and paying suppliers quickly. It usually has no liquidity problems and has a high current ratio (e.g. 7 : 1 in **Figure 6.2**), which is indicative of ineffective management of working capital and cash. When working capital is outstanding for long periods, the company is more likely to experience direct costs associated with the timescale, such as increased bad debts within trade receivables and increased obsolescence in inventories. In addition, it is generally considered that higher returns can be obtained by investing in non-current assets. For example, investment in long-term securities provides a higher yield than investment in short-term securities.

FIGURE 6.2: PRO FORMA STATEMENTS OF FINANCIAL POSITION UNDER THE THREE MAIN WORKING CAPITAL STRATEGIES: CONSERVATIVE, NEUTRAL AND AGGRESSIVE

ASSETS	Conservative €/£m	Neutral €/£m	Aggressive €/£m
Non-current assets	1	3	6
Current assets	7	5	2
Total assets	8	8	8
EQUITY AND LIABILITIES			
Equity and reserves	4	3	2
Long-term liabilities	3	2.5	–
Current liabilities	1	2.5	6
Total equity and liabilities	8	8	8
Current ratio	7 : 1	2 : 1	0.33 : 1

Investment in plant and machinery secures future yields for a company. Therefore, though a company pursuing a conservative working capital policy is in a strong liquid position and can take action on profitable speculative opportunities that may arise, there usually is an opportunity cost in terms of income foregone from not investing surplus funds optimally.

In terms of how a company is financed, companies that pursue a conservative working capital policy usually finance some of their current assets using short-term liabilities, but most of their current assets are financed by long-term sources. The level of long-term debt and equity is usually high. As a consequence of the inefficient asset mix, combined with the additional finance costs associated with having long-term debt, the percentage return on assets is usually low. This policy is best adopted when an economy is in a recession, as longer credit periods may be granted, suppliers are paid quickly at a lower cost due to negotiated high discounts and all sales can be serviced due to high inventory levels. This will provide an advantage over competitors who have to order-in the product, resulting in an increase in market share.

Neutral

When a company pursues a **neutral working capital management strategy** it holds sufficient current assets to cover its current liabilities as they fall due, with a little in reserve. This is reflected by a current ratio of between one and two to one. In the aforementioned example, the ratio is 2 : 1. Pursuing this policy usually ensures that a company keeps an efficient level of working capital with a surplus of cash that may not be sufficient to undertake speculative profitable investments that arise, but is sufficient to support the daily operational requirements and any planned finance repayments, such as loan repayments.

Under this policy, long-term sources are used to finance some (at least a half) of the current assets and all of the non-current assets. Therefore, the finance term is usually matched to the term of the assets (as explained earlier, there is a permanent demand for working capital, hence it is best to finance this using long-term means). This policy is deemed best suited to a stagnant economy. For example, additional inventories are not required as growth is not expected. This approach is also termed **moderate working capital management strategy**.

Aggressive

When a company pursues an **aggressive working capital management strategy** it keeps a minimum level of current assets, with low inventory levels and trade receivables. This results in lower working capital costs. For example, there should be minimal amounts of inventory holding costs and bad debts. Companies pursuing this policy usually have high levels of current liabilities as they take credit periods from suppliers and operate with a high overdraft. This may result in increased working capital costs, such as discounts lost and overdraft interest. This policy results in a company reporting a low current ratio – usually lower than 1 : 1. In the aforementioned example, the current ratio shows that for every 33c/p invested in current assets, the company has €/£1 of current liabilities, i.e. 0.33 : 1. Therefore, it cannot meet its current liabilities out of its cash, or near cash. In these circumstances the company usually has liquidity problems and treats its overdraft as though it were a long-term source of finance.

In terms of financing, a company pursuing this strategy usually has low levels of long-term finance and, in particular, does not hold much long-term debt. This ensures that interest costs are minimised. The current liabilities are used to finance current assets and some of the non-current assets. The investment in non-current assets is usually higher relative to the other two policies and return on assets reported is usually high. This policy works best in a boom economic climate, as demand outstrips supply and the company's performance is not adversely impacted by losing sales due to stock-outs. In addition, as a result of the excess demand in the marketplace, customers are usually happy to settle their accounts quickly in order to secure the supply. A major concern with this policy is liquidity and the reliance on suppliers as a source of finance. It is likely that suppliers may stop supplying if such poor credit terms are maintained.

THE OPERATING CYCLE/CASH CONVERSION CYCLE

To this point, the chapter has focused on the absolute amount of working capital that needs to be financed, its potential cost and the finance implications of movements in that requirement. However, this is not useful if comparing the efficiency of working capital management:

- from year to year where there are changes in operations, sales and purchases;
- relative to other companies; or
- relative to the industry average.

In particular, focusing on monetary values does not provide an indication of the efficiency of management in relation to working capital. More useful information for assessing the efficiency of management in respect of working capital can be obtained by calculating the company's working capital operating cycle/cash conversion cycle.

The **operating cycle/cash conversion cycle** represents the length of time, in days, that it takes to convert cash payable for net inputs (purchases of raw materials, etc.) into cash receivable for outputs (sales). In a manufacturing entity the operating cycle/cash conversion cycle is quite long and will include the number of days that: raw materials are held in inventories; the product is in the manufacturing process; the finished goods remain in inventory before being sold; and the number of days it takes for the customer to pay for the goods. As the purchases of raw materials are rarely for cash, the operating cycle/cash conversion cycle is reduced by the number of days of credit taken from suppliers. The type of product also influences the expected cycle length. For example, a manufacturer who makes safety pins will have a short work in progress period, whereas a whiskey manufacturer may have a work in progress period of 10 years or more.

The operating cycle/cash conversion cycle for a manufacturing entity can be calculated as follows:

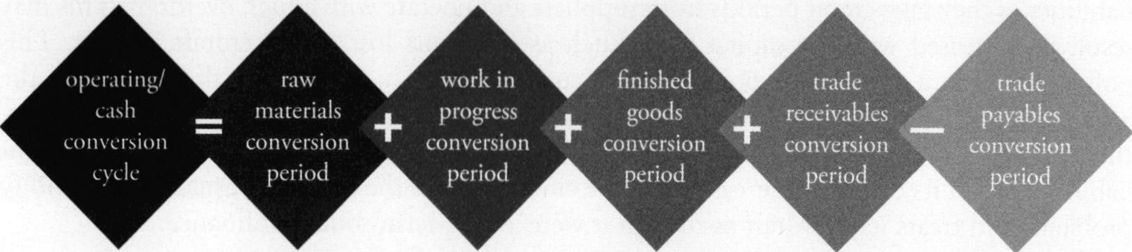

In a retail company the cycle is short and is mostly the average number of days purchased items remain in inventory, less the time taken to pay suppliers. Usually sales are in cash. Where credit is given, the cycle can be calculated as follows:

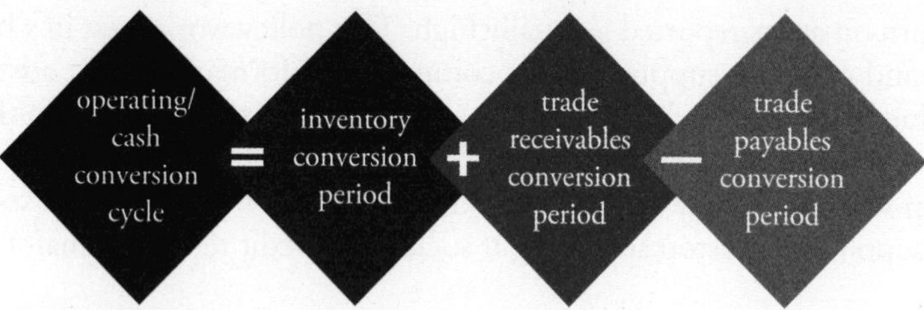

Worked Example 6.3: Cash Conversion Cycle

Marron Ltd is a wholesaler that trades in sports gear. The average inventory holding period is 30 days. Customers usually pay within 40 days and Marron Ltd has agreed to pay its suppliers within 20 days.

Requirement Calculate Marron Ltd's cash conversion cycle.

Solution

The cash conversion cycle is: 30 days + 40 days − 20 days = 50 days

Marron Ltd will have to finance the cost of the products for 50 days.

Management has to carefully balance the operating cycle/cash conversion cycle. As mentioned previously, working capital has to be financed, and hence has a cost. If the cycle is too long, this will tie up a company's resources unnecessarily and is a cost to the company that will reduce company profitability. Tying up funds in working capital unnecessarily is called **over-capitalisation**. Over-capitalisation can be identified using accounting ratios, such as sales to working capital, liquidity ratios and turnover of the individual working capital components, for example, the trade receivables period, etc. If the cycle is too short it may affect production, resulting in lost sales, poorer quality products, etc. An insufficient level of working capital is called **under-capitalisation**. Over-capitalisation can lead to liquidity problems and eventually company failure.

The operating cycle/cash conversion cycle is calculated using ratios that convert monetary values into days (see **Figure 6.3**). The information to do this can be obtained from a company's financial statements. When calculating the cycle in days for a set timeframe, the average monetary value for the year should be used; unless this information is not available, whereupon closing balances should be used.

Figure 6.3: Calculation of the Total Cash Conversion Cycle in Days

				Days
Average number of days raw material in inventories	=	$\frac{\text{Average raw material inventory value} \times 365}{\text{Purchases of raw material in period}}$	=	A
Less:				
Average number of days' credit taken on the purchase of the raw materials	=	$\frac{\text{Average value of trade payables} \times 365}{\text{Credit purchases of raw material in period}}$	=	(B)
Plus:				
Average number of days the product takes in the production process	=	$\frac{\text{Average value of work in progress} \times 365}{\text{Cost of goods produced in period}}$	=	C
Plus:				
Average number of days finished goods remain in stores before being sold	=	$\frac{\text{Average value of finished goods} \times 365}{\text{Cost of goods produced in period}}$	=	D
Plus:				
Average number of days' credit allowed on sales	=	$\frac{\text{Average value of trade receivables} \times 365}{\text{Credit sales in period}}$	=	E
Total operating/cash flow period				A to E

Notes

1. The operating cycle/cash conversion cycle can be used to assess the efficiency of a company in its use of current assets and liabilities.
2. So long as sales are not lost and production is not affected, a lower conversion period would reflect more efficient use of working capital. Indeed, in these circumstances the company should have a higher return on its assets compared with a similar entity that has a longer operating cycle/cash conversion cycle.

How these ratios interact with each other to provide an overview of the financial performance and financial strength of an entity is covered in **Worked Example 6.4**. The financial performance and financial strength ratios are covered in **Chapter 4**.

Worked Example 6.4: Cash Conversion Period

Two companies, Amarillo Ltd and Gris Ltd, manufacture shoes that they sell to retailers in Ireland. They are similar entities facing similar competition. Extract information from their statements of profit or loss and copies of their statements of financial position are available. These are as follows:

EXTRACT INFORMATION FROM THE STATEMENTS OF PROFIT OR LOSS
for the years ended 31 December 20X5

	Amarillo Ltd	**Gris Ltd**
	€/£	**€/£**
Revenue	2,000,000	4,000,000
Gross profit	400,000	600,000
Net income	100,000	40,000

Both companies provide credit on all sales and obtain credit on all purchases.

EXTRACT INFORMATION FROM THE STATEMENTS OF FINANCIAL POSITION
as at 31 December 20X5

	Amarillo Ltd	**Gris Ltd**
ASSETS	**€/£**	**€/£**
Non-current assets	320,000	420,000
Current assets		
Inventories	120,000	300,000
Trade receivables	128,000	270,000
Bank and cash	2,000	–
	250,000	570,000
Total assets	570,000	990,000
EQUITY AND LIABILITIES		
Equity and reserves		
Equity share capital	100,000	100,000
Revenue reserves	320,000	330,000
	420,000	430,000
Current liabilities		
Overdraft	50,000	160,000
Trade payables	100,000	400,000
	150,000	560,000
Total equity and liabilities	570,000	990,000

Requirement

(a) Calculate the cash conversion period for both companies.
(b) Calculate the working capital requirement for both companies.
(c) Using the results from parts (a) and (b), outline which company you believe to be more efficient in the management of its working capital.

Solution

In this question there is insufficient information to calculate separately the raw material conversion period, the production period and the length of time the product remains as finished goods within stores. Therefore, an overall inventory conversion period is calculated.

(a) **Cash conversion period**

	Amarillo Ltd €/£	Gris Ltd €/£
Inventory		
Inventory / Cost of goods sold	120,000 × 365 / 2,000,000 − 400,000	300,000 × 365 / 4,000,000 − 600,000
Inventory conversion period	27.38 days	32.20 days

Gris Ltd has its product tied up in the production and inventory holding process for almost five days more than Amarillo Ltd.

Trade payables		
Trade payables / Cost of goods sold	100,000 × 365 / 2,000,000 − 400,000	400,000 × 365 / 4,000,000 − 600,000
Trade payables conversion period	22.81 days	42.94 days

*A more appropriate denominator is credit purchases, however this information is not available from the question.

Gris Ltd takes over 20 days more credit from its suppliers compared to Amarillo Ltd.

Trade receivables		
Trade receivables / Credit sales	128,000 × 365 / 2,000,000	270,000 × 365 / 4,000,000
Trade receivables conversion period	23.36 days	24.64 days

Gris Ltd allows one day more credit to its customers than Amarillo Ltd.

Cash conversion cycle

Amarillo Ltd = 27.38 days − 22.81 days + 23.36 days = 27.93 days

Gris Ltd = 32.2 days − 42.94 days + 24.64 days = 13.9 days

(b) **Working capital requirement**

	Amarillo Ltd €/£	Gris Ltd €/£
Inventory	120,000	300,000
Trade receivables	128,000	270,000
Trade payables	(100,000)	(400,000)
Working capital requirement	148,000	170,000

(c) **Working capital efficiency**

From the overall cash conversion period calculation in (a), it would appear that Gris Ltd is more efficient as it has a shorter period. In addition, the calculations in (b) show that Gris Ltd's net investment in working capital is only €/£22,000 more than that of Amarillo Ltd, yet its sales are double. However, on inspection of the components making up the cash conversion period calculation and the working capital investment, it would seem that Gris Ltd is using its suppliers to finance its working capital. Taking nearly 43 days to pay its suppliers, 20 days more than Amarillo Ltd. This may account for the difference in the gross profit return of both companies. Amarillo Ltd is earning 20% gross profit on its sales [€/£400,000 ÷ €/£2,000,000], whereas Gris Ltd is earning 15% [€/£600,000 ÷ €/£4,000,000]. Amarillo Ltd may be availing of discounts or special price deals for its quicker payment, or Gris Ltd may be paying prices with penalties or finance costs built into them.

Gris Ltd also has its funds tied up in inventories for almost five days longer than Amarillo Ltd. This may indicate a slower production process, holding higher raw material inventory or not being able to move finished goods as quickly as Amarillo Ltd. More detailed information is required to determine exactly where the difference arises.

In terms of trade receivables, Gris Ltd takes one day longer to collect payment from its customers.

Other important information can be obtained from the extracts of financial data that are supplied in the question, which help to form an opinion on the working capital management policy in each company. In particular, it is clear from the statement of financial position of Gris Ltd that the company is reliant on its short-term liabilities (trade payables and overdraft) to finance its current assets. It has a current ratio of 1 : 1, whereas Amarillo Ltd has a current ratio of 1.67 : 1. The larger overdraft proportion may contribute to the lower overall net profit of 1% [€/£40,000 ÷ €/£4,000,000] being reported by Gris Ltd, compared to a net profit of 5% [€/£100,000 ÷ €/£2,000,000] reported by Amarillo Ltd.

It would seem then, from an analysis of the components making up the operating cycle/cash conversion cycle, profitability and liquidity of the two companies, that Amarillo Ltd has a stronger working capital policy.

WORKING CAPITAL: THE FINANCE MIX

In the previous example, two similar companies finance their working capital in different ways. Amarillo Ltd finances its working capital requirement using some current liabilities and some long-term liabilities, as is evident from the current ratio of 1.67 : 1. This ratio reflects that about 60% of the current assets are financed using current liabilities and the remainder are financed from long-term sources. Gris Ltd finances its current assets almost entirely with its current liabilities. Its current ratio is 1 : 1. The statement of financial position data suggests that Gris Ltd has potential liquidity problems. This example prompts the question: "What is the correct finance mix for working capital?"

Earlier in this chapter, it was explained that investment in working capital is mostly permanent in nature, though there may be a temporary portion due to seasonal fluctuations in demand for a company's products. A general rule of thumb in respect of financing decisions is that the finance term should match the life of the asset (see **Chapter 10** for more detail). In the case of working capital the asset requirement is permanent, therefore this portion of working capital should be financed from long-term sources, with temporary fluctuations being financed by short-term means, such as an overdraft. It would seem, then, that in **Worked Example 6.4** Amarillo Ltd is also better at financing its assets than Gris Ltd.

CONCLUSION

This chapter introduced working capital as an investment that needs financing and as a source of finance when liquidity is required. This chapter highlights the importance of having an appropriate working capital management policy. Working capital has a cost that will directly impact on a company's profitability. In addition, an insufficient investment in, or strategy for, working capital may lead to a loss of profits. For example, in a growth period, increases in working capital will result. If this increase is not funded appropriately, then a company may have liquidity problems, even though it is profitable. Inappropriate working capital management is a common cause of company failure. The next three chapters lead on from this chapter and focus on working capital management in relation to the individual components of the working capital equation: inventories; trade receivables; trade payables; and cash.

EXAMINATION STANDARD QUESTION: INVESTMENT IN, AND FINANCING OF, WORKING CAPITAL

You have been commissioned by the managing director of Amarillo Plc to determine the investment in working capital that will be required if it purchases a small business that manufactures components for motor vehicles. The target company, Violetta Plc, has an annual turnover of €/£3 million. Its costs are estimated based on the past three years' performance results as a percentage of its sales price. These costings are expected to be maintained. Direct materials cost about 30% of sales price, direct labour 25%, variable overheads 10%, fixed overheads 15% and administration is about 5%.

You are also told that similar credit terms are going to be allowed to customers, and taken from suppliers, and similar inventory levels maintained. The terms are as follows:

- Customers take, on average, three months to pay for goods purchased.
- Direct materials are paid for after two months.
- Direct labour is paid for after one week. The labour force works for 48 weeks of the year.
- Variable overheads are paid for within one month.
- Fixed overheads are paid for within one month.
- Administration overheads are paid for within half a month.
- Three months' inventory of raw materials is held.

Work in progress (approximately 50% of the finished goods) is held for about two months. Work in progress is valued using variable production costs. Assume that all of the required direct materials become part of work in progress at the start of the production process.

One month of finished goods inventory is held in store. Finished goods are valued using variable production costs.

Requirement

(a) Estimate Violetta Plc's expected annual profit.

5 Marks

(b) Compute the finance that will be required to support operational working capital requirements.

10 Marks

(c) Calculate the finance cost associated with the investment in working capital and the adjusted expected profit from the venture. Assume that Amarillo Plc has an overdraft of €/£2,000,000 on which it pays interest at the rate of 12% per year.

2 Marks

Total 17 Marks

Solution

(a) Violetta Plc's expected annual costs (**excluding finance costs**) are as follows:

		€/£
Direct materials	(€/£3,000,000 × 30%)	900,000
Direct labour	(€/£3,000,000 × 25%)	750,000
Variable overheads	(€/£3,000,000 × 10%)	300,000
Fixed overheads	(€/£3,000,000 × 15%)	450,000
Administration costs	(€/£3,000,000 × 5%)	150,000
Total costs		2,550,000

Therefore, expected profit is: €/£450,000 [€/£3,000,000 − €/£2,550,000].

(b) The working capital requirement is as follows:

Expected current liabilities		€/£
Suppliers for raw materials	[€/£900,000 × $\frac{2}{12}$]	150,000
Direct labour	[€/£750,000 × $\frac{1}{48}$]	15,625
Variable overheads	[€/£300,000 × $\frac{1}{12}$]	25,000
Fixed overheads	[€/£450,000 × $\frac{1}{12}$]	37,500
Administration costs	[€/£150,000 × $\frac{0.5}{12}$]	6,250
Total source of finance		234,375

Expected current assets		**€/£**	**€/£**
Trade receivables	[€/£3,000,000 × $\frac{3}{12}$]		750,000
Inventory:			
Raw materials	[€/£900,000 × $\frac{3}{12}$]		225,000
Work in progress:			
Raw materials	[€/£900,000 × $\frac{2}{12}$]	150,000	
Direct labour	[€/£750,000 × 50% × $\frac{2}{12}$]	62,500	
Variable overheads	[€/£300,000 × 50% × $\frac{2}{12}$]	25,000	237,500
Finished goods:			
Raw materials	[€/£900,000 × $\frac{1}{12}$]	75,000	
Direct labour	[€/£750,000 × $\frac{1}{12}$]	62,500	
Variable overheads	[€/£300,000 × $\frac{1}{12}$]	25,000	162,500
Total finance required for current assets			1,375,000

Therefore, the total finance requirement is:

€/£1,140,625 [€/£1,375,000 – €/£234,375]

(c) The additional finance cost associated with this venture is:

€/£136,875 [€/£1,140,625 × 12%]

The expected profit from the venture is adjusted to:

€/£313,125 [€/£450,000 – €/£136,875]

Key Terms

Aggressive strategy
Cash conversion cycle
Conservative strategy
Moderate strategy
Neutral strategy
Operating cycle
Opportunity cost
Over-capitalisation
Permanent investment
Permanent working capital
Temporary working capital
Under-capitalisation
Working capital

REVIEW QUESTIONS

(See Suggested Solutions to Review Questions in **Appendix B**.)

Question 6.1

What is working capital?

Question 6.2

What is over-capitalisation?

Question 6.3 Rojo Plc (Level 1)

Rojo Plc manufactures engines. The market is competitive and profits are being squeezed in many of the other engine manufacturing entities. The company's directors are reviewing its current position, relative to the expected position in the coming year. They are happy to report that profitability will be maintained at the same level. The directors ask you for your comments before they announce the good news in this difficult time to the equity holders.

Requirement Analyse the following information in light of the above comments. In particular, comment on working capital requirements. All purchases and revenue are on credit terms.

	Current year €/£000	Expected next year €/£000
Revenue	500,200	580,000
Cost of goods sold	420,050	500,000
Purchases	280,000	340,000
Working capital		
Finished goods inventory	60,000	70,000
Work in progress	45,000	80,000
Raw material inventory	80,000	150,000
Trade receivables	62,500	65,000
Trade payables	42,000	60,000

CHALLENGING QUESTIONS

(Suggested Solutions to Challenging Questions are available through your lecturer.)

Question 6.1 NML (Level 1)

You are a trainee accountant in Nortic Manufacturing Limited (NML) and have been asked to review the company's cash conversion cycle and compare it with the industry average.

The finance manager has provided you with NML's investment in working capital for 20X3 as well as the equivalent industry averages.

	NML 20X3 €/£	Industry 20X3 €/£
Sales	540,000	468,750
Purchases of raw materials	255,000	210,000
Cost of goods produced	372,000	315,000
Raw materials inventory	93,000	54,500
Work in progress	43,000	29,000
Finished goods inventory	65,500	59,000
Receivables	58,000	47,000
Payables	49,000	33,500

Both NML and the industry provide credit on 80% of their sales and obtain credit on 100% of their purchases. The degree of completion of the work in progress is 70% for both NML and the industry. Assume a 365-day year.

Requirement

(a) Calculate the cash conversion cycle in days for both NML and the industry for 20X3.

7 Marks

(b) Comment briefly on the results obtained in part (a) above.

2 Marks

(c) Discuss what is meant by overtrading and identify four ways overtrading can be alleviated.

6 Marks
Total 15 Marks

(Based on Chartered Accountants Ireland, CAP 1, Finance, Summer 2013, Q7)

Question 6.2 Strategies

Possible strategies for financing a firm's working capital requirements range from aggressive to prudent (conservative).

Requirement Explain the above two strategies and comment critically on their merits.

5 Marks

(Based on Chartered Accountants Ireland, CAP 1, Finance, Summer 2012, Q6(a))

Question 6.3 Taccor (Level 1)

Taccor Ltd wishes to finalise its expected working capital position for the year-end date of 31 December 20X1. Taccor's finance manager has recently resigned her position and the company's finance director has asked for your assistance with regard to completing the working capital projections.

Taccor's 20X1 credit sales are expected to total €/£8.4 million, while cost of sales for the same period have been estimated at €/£3.78 million. Taccor allows two month's credit to its customers and, on average, pays its trade suppliers one month in arrears.

Taccor has a current ratio of 1.4:1. Current assets consist of inventory and trade receivables, while current liabilities comprise trade payables and a bank overdraft. Taccor's working capital cycle (cash conversion cycle) is forecast to be three months.

Requirement

(a) Calculate the expected size of Taccor's bank overdraft as at 31 December 20X1.

4 Marks

(b) Calculate the expected net working capital position of Taccor as at 31 December 20X1.

2 Marks
Total 6 Marks

(Based on Chartered Accountants Ireland, CAP 1, Finance, Summer 2019, extract from Q3)

Question 6.4 Alpha (Level 1)

Alpha Ltd is a holding company. Senior management wishes to compare the performance of the two subsidiaries of Alpha Ltd, Beta Ltd and Gamma Ltd, which operate in a similar industry.

EXTRACTS FROM THE FINANCIAL STATEMENTS
for the year ended 31 March 20X5

	Beta €/£	Gamma €/£
Revenue	767,000	593,000
Cost of sales	568,000	377,000
Current assets		
Inventory	122,000	97,000
Trade receivables	124,000	136,000
Bank	6,000	8,000
Current liabilities		
Trade payables	107,000	130,000

Requirement As financial controller, prepare a memorandum for the holding company's managing director, which should include the following:

(a) A commentary on the profitability of each company.

2 Marks

(b) An estimate of the cash conversion cycle for each company.

10 Marks

(c) A list of key recommendations for improvements in the working capital management of each company based on your results from part (b).

4 Marks

(d) A discussion of two sources of short-term finance that would be suitable for the financing of working capital.

4 Marks

Total 20 Marks

(Based on Chartered Accountants Ireland, CAP 1, Finance, Summer 2011, Q2)

Question 6.5 Legacy (Level 1)

Legacy Ltd is a large manufacturing company. It is currently analysing its performance in respect of the management of its working capital. Information from Legacy's profit or loss account for the year ended 31 December 20X7, and for the comparative period ending 31 December 20X6, is presented in the table below:

	20X7 €/£000	20X6 €/£000
Sales	35,000	25,000
Purchases	13,750	9,000
Cost of sales	20,000	15,000

The finance manager has also provided the following balances from Legacy's statement of financial position as at 31 December 20X7 and 31 December 20X6:

	20X7 €/£000	20X6 €/£000
Inventory	4,500	2,400
Trade receivables	5,250	2,750
Trade payables	1,750	1,000

The average 20X7 working capital ratios for the manufacturing industry in which Legacy operates are as follows:

	20X7
Inventory conversion period	65 days
Trade receivables conversion period	55 days
Trade payables conversion period	45 days

Requirement

(a) Calculate the following ratios for Legacy for both 20X7 and 20X6:
   (i) Inventory conversion period;
   (ii) Trade receivables conversion period;
   (iii) Trade payables conversion period.

   Assume a 365-day year in all calculations.

6 Marks

(b) Explain the working capital cycle (cash conversion cycle) and briefly outline why it is important to the management of Legacy.

4 Marks

(c) Calculate Legacy's working capital cycle for BOTH 20X7 **and** 20X6.

4 Marks

(d) Based on your calculations above, write a report to management which analyses Legacy's performance in respect of its working capital, including any recommendations which you feel are appropriate.

6 Marks
Total 20 Marks

(Based on Chartered Accountants Ireland, CAP 1, Finance, Autumn 2018, Q2)

Question 6.6 Cello Plc, Flute Plc and Trumpet Plc (Level 2)

Three companies, Cello Plc, Flute Plc and Trumpet Plc, have implemented different working capital management policies. Summary statements of financial position for the three companies are as follows:

	Cello Plc	**Flute Plc**	**Trumpet Plc**
	€/£	**€/£**	**€/£**
Non-current assets	200,000	200,000	200,000
Current assets	150,000	200,000	300,000
Total assets	350,000	400,000	500,000
Equity and reserves	150,000	200,000	250,000
Long-term debt (10%)	–	100,000	200,000
Short-term debt (12%)	100,000	50,000	25,000
Trade payables	100,000	50,000	25,000
Total equity and liabilities	350,000	400,000	500,000
Current ratio	0.75 : 1	2 : 1	6 : 1

The costs of goods sold functions are as follows:

Cello Plc	Cost of goods sold = €/£200,000 + 0.70 (Sales)
Flute Plc	Cost of goods sold = €/£270,000 + 0.65 (Sales)
Trumpet Plc	Cost of goods sold = €/£385,000 + 0.60 (Sales)

As a consequence of the differences in working capital, expected sales for the three companies will vary under different economic conditions as follows:

	Cello Plc €/£	**Flute Plc** €/£	**Trumpet Plc** €/£
Expanding economy	1,200,000	1,200,000	1,200,000
Stagnant economy	900,000	1,000,000	1,150,000
Declining economy	700,000	800,000	1,050,000

Requirement

(a) Discuss the different working capital management policies utilised by the three companies.

6 Marks

(b) For each company, construct a statement of profit or loss under each set of economic conditions. Assume that the corporation tax rate is 30%.

9 Marks

(c) Examine the implications for working capital management that arise from your results in part (b).

7 Marks

Total 22 Marks

(Based on Chartered Accountants Ireland, MABF II, Autumn 1996, Q5)

Question 6.7 Icon Plc (Level 1)

Icon Plc operates a large chain of supermarkets. The most recent annual report of the company includes the following:

STATEMENT OF PROFIT OR LOSS
for the year ended 30 June

	Current year €/£ million	**Comparative year** €/£ million
Turnover	6,000	5,900
Cost of sales	(5,000)	(4,870)
Gross profit	1,000	1,030
Administration and distribution expenses	(584)	(660)
Profit before tax	416	370

STATEMENT OF FINANCIAL POSITION (EXTRACT)
as at 30 June

	Current year €/£ million	Comparative year €/£ million
Current assets		
Inventories	292	280
Trade receivables	67	64
Short-term investments	98	90
Cash at bank and in hand	15	10
	472	444
Current liabilities	(1,356)	(1,200)
Net current liabilities	(884)	(756)
Current ratio	0.34 : 1	0.37 : 1
Acid test ratio	0.13 : 1	0.14 : 1
Cash to current liabilities	0.01 : 1	0.008 : 1

An equity holder of Icon Plc has expressed concern about the liquidity of the company. He is particularly concerned that the current and acid test ratios are significantly poorer than the theoretical average of 2 : 1 and 1 : 1, respectively.

Requirement

(a) Explain the term 'working capital cycle' and state why this concept is important in the financial management of a business.

5 Marks

(b) (i) Calculate the working capital cycle for Icon Plc for both the current and the comparative year, based on the information supplied.
(ii) Comment on the results in (i). Include in your comments your opinion as to whether or not the concerns of the equity holder are justified.

9 Marks

(c) List three ways in which information technology can assist a company in the management of its working capital.

4 Marks
Total 18 Marks

(Based on Chartered Accountants Ireland, MABF II, Summer 2002, Q7)

Question 6.8 Bidor Ltd (Level 1)

You work for a commercial bank and you have been asked to examine the draft financial statements of Bidor Ltd whose principal activities are road transport, warehousing services and the repair of commercial vehicles.

You have been provided with the draft financial statements for the year ended 31 October 20X5.

Summary Statement of Profit or Loss

	Draft 20X5 €/£000	Comparative Year €/£000
Turnover	10,971	11,560
Cost of sales	(10,203)	(10,474)
Gross profit	768	1,086
Administrative expenses	(782)	(779)
Interest payable and similar charges	(235)	(185)
Net (loss)/profit	(249)	122

Summary Statement of Financial Position
as at 31 October

	20X5 €/£000	20X4 €/£000
ASSETS		
Non-current assets	5,178	4,670
Current assets		
Inventory (parts and consumables)	95	61
Trade receivables	2,975	2,369
	3,070	2,430
Total assets	8,248	7,100
EQUITY AND LIABILITIES		
Equity and reserves		
Ordinary share capital	3,000	3,000
Reserves	534	793
	3,534	3,793
Long-term liabilities		
Bank loan	750	1000
Lease obligations	473	–
	1,223	1,000
Current liabilities		
Bank loan	250	–
Overdraft	1,245	913
Trade payables	1,513	1,245
Lease Obligations	280	-
Other Payables	203	149
	3,491	2,307
Total equity and reserves	8,248	7,100

You are also aware of the following facts:

1. The decline in turnover is attributable to:
   - the loss, in July 20X5, of a long-standing customer to a competitor; and
   - a decline in trade in the repair of commercial vehicles.
2. Due to the reduction in the repairs business, the company has decided to close the workshop and sell the equipment and spares inventory. No entries resulting from this decision are reflected in the draft financial statements.
3. The draft financial statements show a loss of 2.3%, but forecasts indicate a return to profitability in 20X6 as the directors are optimistic about generating additional revenue from new contracts.
4. During the year, the company replaced a number of vehicles, funding them by a combination of leasing and an increased overdraft facility. Your examination forms part of the annual review of Bidor's facilities.

Requirement Prepare a report on the company's application to extend its financing facilities, including the renewal of its overdraft, the limit of which currently stands at €/£1.2 million.

In particular, the report should:

(a) Analyse Bidor's working capital policies for the two years ended 31 October 20X5.

8 Marks

(b) State the circumstances particular to Bidor, which may indicate that the company is not a going concern; explain why these circumstances give cause for disquiet.

6 Marks

(c) State what further information you would require before making a final decision on the extension of the overdraft facility.

2 Marks

(d) Suggest some conditions that could be imposed if the facility were to be continued.

2 Marks

Total 18 Marks

(Based on Chartered Accountants Ireland, MABF II, Autumn 2006, Q6)

Question 6.9 Wesley Ltd (Level 2)

Wesley Ltd is a small company involved in the wholesale supply of office stationery. The company was established 10 years ago. Below is an extract from the company's financial statements for the year ended 31 December 20X4:

STATEMENT OF PROFIT OR LOSS
for the year ended 31 December 20X4

	€/£	€/£	
Revenue		320,000	
Cost of sales			
Opening inventory	(18,000)		
Purchases	(240,000)		
	(258,000)		
Closing inventory	20,000	(238,000)	
Gross profit		82,000	(25.6%)
Overheads		(64,000)	
Net Income		18,000	(5.6%)

STATEMENT OF FINANCIAL POSITION (WORKING CAPITAL EXTRACT)
as at 31 December 20X4

	€/£
Current assets	
Trade receivables	49,000
Inventories	20,000
	69,000
Current liabilities	
Trade payables	18,000
Bank overdraft	5,000
	23,000
Net current assets	46,000

The average trade receivables conversion period and trade payables conversion period for the year 20X4 were 56 and 27 days, respectively. During 20X4, inventories were held for 29 days on average.

The company has forecast the following for the year ended 31 December 20X5:

- Revenue will increase by 8% each year for the next two years.
- A discount scheme will be introduced whereby customers will receive a 2% discount if payment is made within 30 days. It is expected that 60% of customers will accept this offer. The remaining customers will take five days more than they currently do.
- The company estimates that, as a result of the changes to the debt-collection policies, administration costs will rise by €/£8,000 in 20X5.
- Gross profit margin will increase to 26.4% in 20X5, but will remain static after that.
- Closing inventories in 20X5 are estimated to be €/£1,000 plus 1/8 of the next period's sales (at cost).
- Suppliers will increase the period of credit by 10 days.
- The bank overdraft should be cleared and there is a credit balance expected by 31 December 20X5 of €/£2,800.

Requirement

(a) Describe briefly the potential consequences of each of the following working capital strategies on the profits of a business:
   (i) Aggressive policy.
   (ii) Relaxed policy.

5 Marks

(b) (i) Draft each of the following:
   - The budgeted statement of profit or loss of Wesley Ltd for the year ended 31 December 20X5.
   - The working capital investment as at 31 December 20X5.

9 Marks

(ii) Comment on the business implications of these figures.

4 Marks

(***Note:*** assume there are 360 days in the year.)

Total 18 Marks

(Based on Chartered Accountants Ireland, MABF II, Autumn 2001, Q6)

Question 6.10 Pulse (Level 2)

Background Pulse Plc produces and sells a range of electrical components to both multinational and independent retailers on a global basis. Pulse is organised on a divisional product basis, with each division classified as an investment centre and allowed to sell their 'distinctive' output both nationally and internationally. The performance of each division is evaluated by the senior management team of Pulse on an annual basis, using a combination of both financial and non-financial performance metrics.

Working Capital Management Joe Smith, the Financial Controller of Watt Ltd, recently saw some data on the inventory levels held by Power. He noted that these inventory levels were much lower than those Watt holds in its warehouses. While the two divisions were involved in different manufacturing activities, Joe was surprised at the scale of the difference in inventory levels. He had been extremely busy on several projects over the past 18 months and wonders if he may have paid less attention than he should have to the management of working capital in Watt (see Appendix I, which includes information relevant to working capital).

Requirement

(a) Using the information in Appendices I and II, prepare a comprehensive analysis of the working capital position in Watt and compare this to Power. (***Note:*** you are not required to calculate any additional ratios for Watt.)

10 Marks

(b) Suggest proposals to correct any deficiencies in Watt's working capital position identified in (a) above.

8 Marks

Total 18 Marks

(Based on Chartered Accountants Ireland, CAP 2, MABF, Autumn 2012, extract from Q1)

APPENDIX I

Watt Ltd

EXTRACT FROM STATEMENT OF PROFIT OR LOSS

for year ended 31 December

	20X4	**20X3**	**20X2**
	€/£000	**€/£000**	**€/£000**
Turnover	2,900	2,320	1,450
Cost of sales (Note 1)	(1,852)	(1,299)	(812)
Gross profit	1,048	1,021	638
Operating expenses	(610)	(520)	(395)
Operating profit	438	501	243
Interest	(79)	(70)	(52)
Profit before tax	359	431	191
Tax	(45)	(54)	(24)
Net profit	314	377	167

Note 1: Analysis of Inventories	**20X4**	**20X3**	**20X2**
	€/£000	**€/£000**	**€/£000**
Total raw materials used during year	1,296	909	568

Watt Ltd
Extract from Statement of Financial Position
for year ended 31 December

	20X4 €/£000	20X3 €/£000	20X2 €/£000
Non-current assets	1,400	1,400	1,200
Raw materials	475	320	114
Work in progress	396	266	95
Finished goods	713	479	171
Total inventories	1,584	1,065	380
Trade receivables	600	550	310
Cash and cash equivalents	330	240	180
Current assets	2,514	1,855	870
Total assets	3,914	3,255	2,070
Trade payables	410	195	160
Bank (overdraft)	332	164	77
Current liabilities	742	359	237
Share Capital	1,003	1,023	550
Retained Earnings	1,184	870	493
Total equity	2,187	1,893	1,043
Non-current liabilities	985	1,003	790
Total equity and liabilities	3,914	3,255	2,070

Appendix II
Working Capital Position

	Power Inc 20X4	Watt Ltd 20X3	20X2
Net working capital		1,772	1,496
Net working capital/sales revenue	0.4	0.61	0.64
Net operating working capital		2,104	1,660
Current ratio	1.3	3.39	5.17
Quick ratio	1	1.25	2.20
Raw materials inventory period (days)		133.78	128.49
Work in progress period (days)		78.05	74.74
Finished goods inventory period (days)		140.52	133.19
Inventory conversion period	125	352.35	336.42
Cash conversion cycle	125	347.07	368.16
Inventory turnover	5	1.83	2.18
Trade receivables days	30	75.52	86.53
Trade payables days	30	80.80	54.79

(***Note:*** you may assume all ratios are calculated correctly.)

Question 6.11 Bourne (Level 2)

Background Bourne Plc is an Irish-based company operating in the pharmaceutical sector and was established by Ms Olive Barry over 20 years ago. Olive currently occupies the position of chair of Bourne's board of directors. Bourne specialises in the research, development, production and sale (on a global basis) of a range of medications targeting certain neurological conditions.

As a result of the expensive nature of the industry in which Bourne competes, coupled with continual downward price pressures (e.g. repeated Government demands for cheaper medicines), cost control is of critical importance for Bourne in achieving the company's annual financial targets. Consequently, Bourne's newly appointed managing director, Mr Ken Walsh, has been heavily incentivised by Bourne's board of directors to ensure that Bourne achieves its 20X7 profit target of €/£3,500,000.

Financial Analysis Ken has met with Bourne's finance director, Mr Ted Moles, to discuss a proposal to acquire Dexcon Limited, a rival company in the pharmaceutical industry. Dexcon is attractive because its products would complement those manufactured by Bourne. Following preliminary discussions with Dexcon's board of directors, Bourne has been provided with financial information on Dexcon (see Appendix I). Ted has informed Ken that he has some concerns about the financial performance and the management of working capital in Dexcon and wants to investigate these issues further before making any recommendation, regarding the potential acquisition of the company. In order to assist Ted with his recommendations, he has collected financial performance data for Bourne's 'Charlie' division (see Appendix I). The financial performance of the 'Charlie' division is very similar to the other divisions in Bourne and Ted feels this information would prove useful in analysing Dexcon's financial performance.

Requirement

(a) Calculate the 20X5 cash conversion cycle for Dexcon (using the data provided in Appendix I) and briefly explain the significance of this number.

5 Marks

(b) Using the data provided in Appendix I, analyse the financial performance of Dexcon.

10 Marks

(c) Based on your analysis in part (b), suggest and describe four actions which Bourne should take to remedy any areas of underperformance evident in Dexcon should Bourne proceed with the acquisition.

8 Marks

Total 23 Marks

(Based on Chartered Accountants Ireland, CAP 2, MABF, Summer 2013, extract from Q1)

APPENDIX I

Extracts from Financial Statements for Dexcon Limited

STATEMENT OF PROFIT OR LOSS

	20X3	**20X4**	**20X5**
	€/£000	**€/£000**	**€/£000**
Sales	8,900	8,000	7,500
Cost of sales	(5,340)	(5,360)	(5,025)
Gross profit	3,560	2,640	2,475
Expenses	(1,850)	(1,260)	(1,250)
Earnings before interest & tax (EBIT)	1,710	1,380	1,225
Interest	(155)	(152)	(148)
Tax	(194)	(154)	(135)
Profit for the year	1,361	1,074	942

Dexcon Limited

STATEMENT OF FINANCIAL POSITION

ASSETS	20X3 €/£000	20X4 €/£000	20X5 €/£000
Non-current assets	2,390	2,600	2,600
Current assets			
Cash	450	675	1,000
Inventories	3,200	4,150	4,200
Trade receivables	650	890	1,750
	4,300	5,715	6,950
Total assets	6,890	8,315	9,550
EQUITY AND LIABILITIES			
Equity and reserves			
Shareholder funds	4,040	5,760	6,935
Non-current liabilities			
Long-term debt	1,940	1,900	1,850
Current liabilities			
Trade payables	565	435	380
Overdraft	145	220	385
	710	655	765
Total equity and liabilities	6,690	8,315	9,550

FINANCIAL ANALYSIS

Bourne Division 'Charlie'

Leverage	
Debt / (debt and equity)	40%
Interest cover	5
Efficiency	
Inventory turnover	3
Asset turnover	1.95
Liquidity	
Acid test	1.2
Current ratio	2.3
Profitability	
Gross profit margin	50%
Net profit margin	18%
Sales growth rate	8%

7

Inventory Management

Learning Objectives

Upon completing this chapter, readers should be able to:

- list the different types of inventory in different industries;
- explain the objective of inventory management;
- discuss influences on inventory levels;
- calculate the optimum inventory reorder level and the inventory costs at this level;
- evaluate the costs and benefits of deviating from the optimum reorder level where a discount is offered for bulk purchasing;
- determine reorder levels under conditions of uncertainty in usage and/or lead times;
- calculate the optimum batch size to produce in manufacturing companies, to minimise holding and set-up costs;
- discuss the JIT inventory classification and perpetual inventory system; and
- discuss other influences on inventory management.

INTRODUCTION

Managing **inventory** appropriately is important as losses in inventory value or incorrect recording of inventory value have a direct impact on profitability, as highlighted in **Real World Example** 7.1.

Real World Example 7.1: Aer Lingus

In December 2018, Aer Lingus Chief Operating Officer, Mike Rutter, issued a memorandum to staff telling them that CCTV cameras were going to be installed in airport terminals to monitor staff due to the millions of euro of theft that had been occurring each year. It was noted that a small proportion of staff were stealing from other staff, from customers and from the company itself – in particular, its duty-free products.

The business finance manager does not typically have direct control over levels of inventory. This is usually agreed upon as a result of negotiations between the stores/purchasing manager, the production manager and the sales/marketing manager as these individuals can provide information on expected sales and production needs. However, the business finance manager can shed light on the financial costs and benefits of various scenarios, such as whether to buy in bulk to achieve a discount.

As mentioned in the previous chapter, a simple means of assessing the efficiency of inventory management is to consider the number of days that each type of inventory item (i.e. finished goods, work in progress, raw materials) remain in inventory. However, if comparing different companies/competitors, this detail may not be available, though an overall average inventory day's value can be calculated and is a useful starting point.

$$\textbf{Average number of days' inventory} = \frac{\textbf{Inventory value} \times \textbf{365}}{\textbf{Cost of sales}}$$

Industry averages for this ratio are usually available and these can also be used as a guide to assessing the efficiency of a company's inventory management.

This chapter focuses on explaining the importance of inventory management. It also discusses influences on inventory levels, the costs associated with holding inventory and the most common types of inventory management techniques in use.

TYPES OF INVENTORY: INDUSTRY-SPECIFIC

Manufacturing Companies

In manufacturing industries, inventory levels can account for about 15% of a company's assets. They are regarded as material assets that require careful management. There are four types of inventory, as highlighted in **Figure 7.1**.

Any company that manufactures goods will have varying amounts of each type of inventory.

Retail Entities

Retail entities typically have two types of inventory: purchased finished goods that are ready for resale and consumables. Consumables in this sector will include items such as price tags, hangers, bags, etc. The liquidity of purchased inventory depends on demand for the products. Retail entities normally have high levels of inventory relative to other industries.

Entities with Intangible Inventories

Other industries, such as service-type sectors, have intangible inventory and consumables. **Intangible inventory** is normally work in progress. For example, in an accountancy or law firm, at any point in time there will be a certain level of unbilled work in progress. This amount can be obtained from timesheets. Timesheets detail time charged each week to clients for ongoing work or advice provided in the week. This is work in progress that will be billed at a later stage.

FIGURE 7.1: INVENTORY TYPES IN A MANUFACTURING ENTITY

Raw materials	• Can be resold and are considered less risky to hold relative to other types of inventory. • For example, the rolls of denim that are purchased from a cloth manufacturer in a company that makes jeans.
Work in progress	• Captures the value of partially complete inventory items at any one point in time. • Includes raw materials used, labour and overhead costs attributed to the inventory at its stage of completion. • Considered to be the most risky type of inventory in terms of liquidity as it cannot be readily sold. It is most likely that a scrap value amount is all that is recoverable, were the work in progress to be sold.
Finished goods	• Fully complete items that are ready for sale. The liquidity of this type of inventory is dependent on demand for the good. The greater the demand, the lower the risks associated with holding it.
Consumables	• Captures all other, usually immaterial, resources that are required for the production process. An example might be thread or buttons for use in the production of jeans.

INFLUENCES ON INVENTORY LEVELS

The type of industry, as discussed in the previous section, influences the type of inventory that a company holds. Other factors that influence the *level* of inventory held are now examined.

Potential Consequences of Stock-outs

The economic impact on the company of a stock-out will influence the level of inventory that a company holds. When a company runs out of inventory (i.e. experiences a **stock-out**), this may result in a lost sale, directly costing the company the contribution that could have been earned from the sale. Where a company's products are specialised, this is less likely to happen, as a customer is more likely to order the product and wait for it. However, if the product is homogenous and the customer can obtain it elsewhere with ease, then the sale is likely to be lost. The state of the economy also influences the economic impact of a company experiencing a stock-out. When an economy is in boom, a lost sale is more easily replaced by another sale as demand is usually high. However, when an economy is in recession, a lost sale is not easily replaced by another, and hence has greater economic impact for a company.

Where a company is a manufacturing entity, a stock-out of raw materials will affect production. For example, if a jeans factory ran out of denim material, this would result in idle time and overheads not being absorbed into products. This will result in an under-absorption cost adjustment for overheads at the period end.

Finance Cost

Holding inventory is a necessity for most companies and deemed to be a good investment. However, as explained in the previous chapter, tying up funds unnecessarily in working capital has a cost. This cost is either the interest saving that could be achieved were the monies in the bank (if in an overdraft situation) or the opportunity return that could be achieved if the funds were used for another income-generating investment. Therefore, the quality of investment that is available to the company and the company's ability to finance the additional investment will influence the cost associated with tying up funds in inventory. Where a company is experiencing capital rationing (see **Chapter 3**), these costs will be accentuated.

Value of Inventory

Related to the previous paragraph, the value of individual items of inventory will influence the level held. The opportunity cost of holding expensive items is greater (due to higher finance cost), hence companies are more likely to hold lower levels of these items and to spend more time managing them, relative to low cost items that tie up less resources.

Sales Forecasting/Demand Management

Where demand for a company's products is known with reasonable certainty or according to a predictable pattern, then inventory levels can be anticipated in light of the demand information and lower levels held. The quality of inventory management is reliant on having accurate forecasts of demand for inventory. This means that sales forecasting or production requirements scheduling must be accurately determined. Accuracy is influenced by the sales team's industry awareness (i.e. its ability to recognise new trends and changes in preferences) and the reliability of information received from research teams developing new products. Recognising declines in product demand and demand for new products is vital in achieving successful inventory management.

Relationship with Suppliers

The relationship with suppliers can also influence the required inventory holding. Where suppliers have established quick, effective distribution channels and the company has built a strong relationship with its suppliers, then lower levels of inventory can be held, as new supplies will be received quickly.

Nature of Inventory

The nature of the item being stored also affects the stock level and length of time an item can remain in stores. For example, highly perishable inventory, such as fresh fruit and vegetables, might remain in the stores of a fruit and vegetable distributor for a couple of hours each morning before being distributed to shops. On the other hand, a jeweller's inventory may be held, with its value unscathed, for periods extending beyond one year. Other product-specific influences can alter the liquidity and value of inventory.

For example, fashion changes can influence demand. If these changes are not anticipated, then the liquidity/saleability of inventory reduces as demand for it slows down. Technological change can also cause a shift in the liquidity/saleability of inventory. This is most evident in the computer hardware industry. New software, which runs on hardware, usually requires larger memory space. As a result, the hardware industry continually has to develop its products to cater for new higher memory-utilising software packages; the result is that hardware becomes obsolete relatively quickly and a computer retailer needs to ensure that it does not hold large quantities of these relatively risky items, as they can date quickly.

Systems and Procedures in Place

When a company has good systems and procedures in place to keep track of inventory, to highlight potential stock-outs and action the replenishment of inventory quickly, then less inventory needs to be held. Computers save costs by reducing staff time, they usually require a large initial capital investment, staff training and ongoing maintenance. Most systems are integrated with the sales and purchases processes, with bar codes being used as a tracking device. The use of bar codes removes the requirement to manually have to record inventory details as items enter stores, when items are removed from stores and when items are sold by the company. Having one data entry point reduces the potential for recording error and also reduces input time. Most systems also have the facility to produce invoices, statements and receipts. In addition, an integrated system can be used for inventory management as it can be linked to sales forecasts, which can be used to predict inventory demand, calculate reorder levels, rolling economic order quantities (EOQs) and prepare exception reports – highlighting those items of inventory that need replenishment. Indeed, some systems can automatically email reorder requirements directly to suppliers.

COSTS ASSOCIATED WITH HOLDING INVENTORY AND ITS MANAGEMENT

Some of the costs associated with holding inventory have been discussed in the previous section: finance costs, obsolescence, deterioration and stock-out costs. These costs influence the **level** of inventory that a company chooses to maintain. The costs associated with inventory are usually sub-divided into four categories, as shown in **Figure 7.2**.

Inventory Management

Inventory management involves determining the **optimum inventory level**. The optimum inventory level is the level of inventory to keep that optimises the return achievable from the sale of inventory, whilst at the same time minimising the costs associated with holding inventory. There is conflict between these objectives. Holding high levels of inventory will ensure that no stock-outs occur. In addition, the company may benefit from bulk discounts and reduced ordering costs. However, high inventory levels will tie up funds, resulting in high holding costs.

FIGURE 7.2: INVENTORY COST CATEGORIES

Purchase price	• Dependent on competition between suppliers, a company's relationship with the suppliers and the potential to avail of bulk discounts.
Stock-out costs	• Lost sales. • Stalled production.
Holding costs	• Finance costs. • Obsolescence (trend changes) and deterioration (perishable products). • Other incidental costs, such as: store's heat and light, store's rent and rates, store's insurance (buildings and inventory), damage, pilferage and the salaries of storemen.
Ordering costs	• Costs incidental to the ordering of inventory, such as the salaries of purchase staff, telephone and stationery. • In manufacturing companies, the ordering costs associated with raw materials are overshadowed by manufacturing set-up costs that are incurred when there is a change in the product being manufactured. In manufacturing companies, set-up costs include idle time, engineer time, etc.

TOOLS TO CALCULATE INVENTORY ORDER QUANTITIES AND REORDER LEVELS

The Economic Order Quantity Model

The **economic order quantity model** analyses two of the costs associated with the management of inventory (i.e. holding costs and ordering costs) at various order quantity amounts.

The objective of the model is to find the **economic order quantity (EOQ)**, which is the order quantity that minimises total holding and ordering costs. The relationship between the two costs and reorder quantities is presented in graphical form in **Figure 7.3**.

This graph shows that the EOQ is the order size at which ordering costs equal holding costs. This order size can be calculated using the following formula:

$$\text{EOQ} = \sqrt{\frac{2FU}{CP}}$$

where EOQ is the quantity that should be ordered, F is the fixed cost per order, U is the total usage (i.e. demand/sales) in units for the period and CP is the holding cost per unit.

FIGURE 7.3: THE RELATIONSHIP BETWEEN INVENTORY COSTS AND REORDER LEVELS

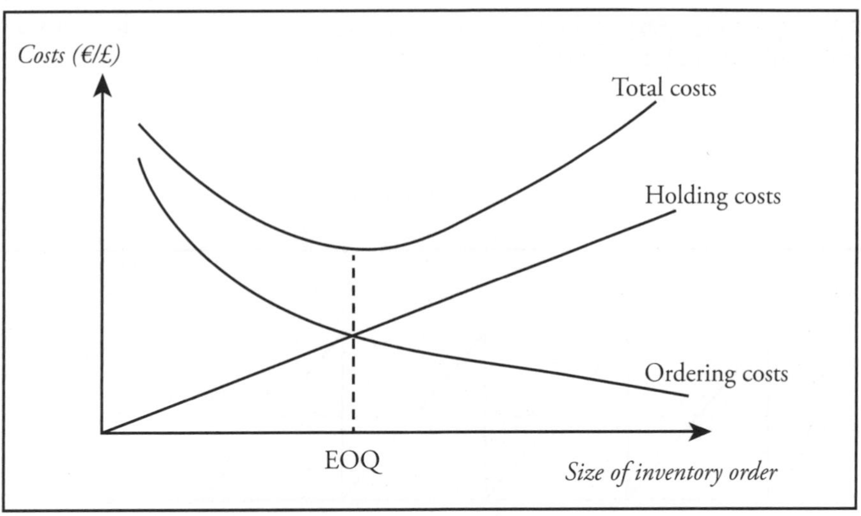

WORKED EXAMPLE 7.1: CALCULATING THE EOQ

Lunes Ltd sells 2,000 items during a 150-day period. Ordering costs are €/£100 per order and holding costs are €/£10 per unit per 150 days.

Requirement

(a) Calculate Lunes Ltd's EOQ.
(b) Using the EOQ calculated in part (a), calculate how often Lunes Ltd has to order the product in each 150-day period (provide the number of times and interval of time between orders being made).

Solution

(a) *U* for this period is 2,000, *F* is €/£100 per unit and *CP* is €/£10.

(b) The EOQ is therefore: $\sqrt{\frac{2 \times 2,000 \times 100}{10}}$ = 200 units

(c) The order needs to be made 10 times in each 150-day period [2,000/200 = 10 times].

This means that the inventory manager needs to place an order every 15 days [150/10 = 15 days].

Under the basic form of this model it is assumed that demand is known with certainty and is constant in the period. Demand can be ascertained from sales forecasts. Costs are also known with certainty and have a predictable relationship to quantities held and number of orders made in a period. Moreover, holding costs have a variable linear relationship with reorder quantities, wherein the higher the reorder quantities (resulting in higher inventory levels being held), the higher the holding costs. Ordering costs are assumed fixed per order, and hence are variable with the number of orders made. Therefore, total ordering costs per period fall as the size of the inventory order increases. The simple form of the model also assumes that inventory can be delivered immediately when the level in storage reaches zero. The graph in **Figure 7.4** depicts the pattern of inventory usage and replenishment assumed under the simple EOQ model. This assumes constant demand, for example per day, for inventory in each time period.

FIGURE 7.4: THE PATTERN OF INVENTORY LEVELS HELD OVER TIME ASSUMED BY THE BASIC EOQ MODEL

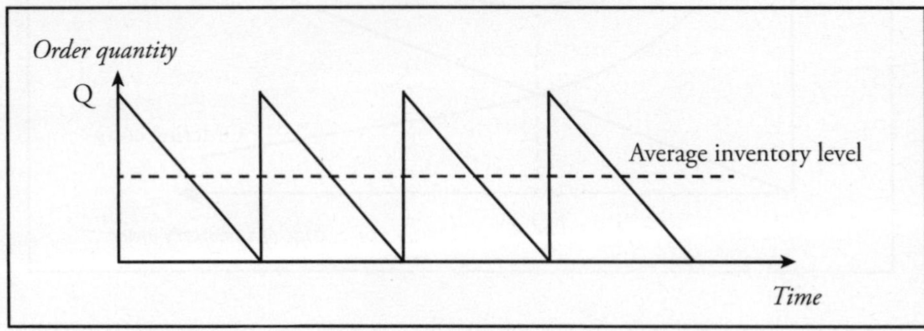

Therefore, the average inventory held by a company will be Q/2 and the total holding costs for a period will be:

Total holding costs = Average inventory × Holding cost per unit

$$= \frac{Q}{2} \times CP$$

where Q is the quantity ordered and CP is the holding cost per unit. The total ordering costs for a period will be directly related to the number of orders and can be calculated using the following equation:

Total ordering costs = Number of orders × Fixed cost per order

$$= \frac{U}{Q} \times F$$

where U is the usage or demand level for the period being considered, Q is the reorder number of units and F is the fixed cost per order.

Finally, the total inventory management costs will be:

Total inventory management costs = Holding costs + Ordering costs

These costs are minimised when the quantity reordered (Q) each time is at the EOQ level.

Worked Example 7.2: Calculating Inventory Costs

Lunes Ltd sells 2,000 items during a 150-day period. Ordering costs are €/£100 per order and holding costs are €/£10 per unit per 150 days.

Requirement

(a) Calculate Lunes Ltd's holding costs, ordering costs and total inventory management costs, if it orders at the EOQ level of inventory each time.

(b) Calculate the same information assuming Lunes Ltd orders 1,000 units each time it makes an order and explain the reason for the difference from the result found in (a).

Solution

(a) Total holding costs for the period is as follows: (see **Worked Example 7.1**, the EOQ is calculated as being 200 units and *CP* is €/£10 per unit)

$$= \frac{EOQ}{2} \times CP \qquad = \qquad \frac{200}{2} \times €/£10 = €/£1,000$$

Total ordering costs for the period are as follows:

(*U* for the period is 2,000 and F is €/£100 per order)

$$= \frac{U}{\text{EOQ}} \times F \qquad = \qquad \frac{2,000}{200} \times €/£100 = €/£1,000$$

Total costs are therefore: €/£2,000 [€/£1,000 + €/£1,000].

(b) The quantity ordered (*Q*) is 1,000 units, therefore the costs will change to:

$$\text{Holding costs} = \frac{1,000}{2} \times €/£10 = €/£5,000$$

$$\text{Ordering costs} = \frac{2,000}{1,000} \times €/£100 = €/£200$$

Total costs = €/£5,200 [€/£5,000 + €/£200]

The company is worse off by €/£3,200 [€/£5,200 − €/£2,000] if it orders 1,000 units each time, as opposed to ordering the EOQ amount of 200 units, as the inventory holding costs outweigh the benefits obtained from a reduction in ordering costs.

This example uses an extreme variation from the EOQ to highlight the potential additional costs that may be incurred by not ordering at the EOQ level. However, it should be noted that small variations from the EOQ do not really change costs to a great extent. For example, using the metrics of **Worked Example 7.1**, if 250 units are ordered each time instead of the EOQ of 200 units, then the total costs will increase by €/£50. The range within which total costs do not vary by material amounts is called the **economic order range (EOR)**. The implication of this range is that the EOQ model can be successfully used in situations where demand is not completely certain.

Discounts and the EOQ Model

One disadvantage of the EOQ model is that it does not incorporate the cost of the unit, and how this may be impacted on by order size, in its formula. The only time it will become relevant is when the EOQ lies above a particular minimum quantity that has to be ordered to obtain a discount, as the EOQ can pinpoint the exact quantity to order to minimise costs whilst obtaining the discount. If the EOQ is less than the minimum quantity required to qualify for a discount, then the total costs need to be calculated at the minimum order level allowed and compared to the costs at the EOQ level to determine if the discount is worthwhile. In this instance, product cost becomes a relevant cost. If the total costs with the discount are lower, then bulk ordering should take place.

Worked Example 7.3: EOQ and Discounts

Lunes Ltd has an annual demand for 2,000 units. The unit cost price is €/£60 and the cost per order is €/£100. The inventory holding cost per unit is €/£10, of which €/£8 relates to the financing of the purchase price of each unit.

Requirement

(a) Calculate the EOQ level and total costs at this level, including the cost of the units.
(b) Recalculate the EOQ level where a 4% discount is available for orders of between 300 and 599 units.
(c) Recalculate the EOQ level where a 10% discount is available for orders of 600 units and above.
(d) Recommend the optimal ordering policy for Lunes Ltd based on the information calculated for requirements (a) to (c).

Solution

(a) U for this period is 2,000 units, F is €/£100 per unit and CP is €/£10. The EOQ is therefore:

$$\sqrt{\frac{2 \times 2{,}000 \times 100}{10}} = 200 \text{ units}$$

(b) The EOQ changes when a discount of 4% is offered as this impacts on holding costs. As 80% of the holding cost is related to the financing of purchases, the discount will reduce the finance requirements and hence the finance cost by 4%. Therefore, holding costs will now be: €/£9.68 per unit [€/£2 + (€/£8 × 96%)]. The new EOQ is therefore:

$$\sqrt{\frac{2 \times 2{,}000 \times 100}{9.68}} = 203 \text{ units}$$

(c) The EOQ changes again when the discount of 10% is offered as the holding cost reduces further. The holding costs will now be: €/£9.20 per unit [€/£2 + (€/£8 × 90%)]. The new EOQ is therefore:

$$\sqrt{\frac{2 \times 2{,}000 \times 100}{9.20}} = 208 \text{ units}$$

To determine the optimal ordering policy, the total costs with ordering at: the EOQ level of 200 units; the minimum order (i.e. 300 units) at the 4% discount rate (because this is closest to the EOQ calculated in (b)); and the minimum order (i.e. 600 units) at the 10% discount rate (as this is closest to the EOQ calculated in (c)) should be compared to ascertain the least costly scenario.

Order quantity units	Purchase cost €/£	Order costs €/£	Holding cost €/£	Total cost €/£
200 **(W1)**	120,000	1,000	1,000	**122,000**
300 **(W2)**	115,200	667	1,452	**117,319**
600 **(W3)**	108,000	333	2,760	**111,093**

The optimal order quantity is 600 units. The cost saving in the purchase price (€/£12,000) more than outweighs the increase in the total of the ordering and holding costs of €/£1,093 [€/£333 + €/£2,760 − €/£2,000]. Therefore, Lunes Ltd will be better off by €/£10,907.

W1: Calculation of costs at the EOQ: order quantity 200

Purchase cost:	2,000 × €/£60	€/£120,000
Order cost:	See Example 7.2	€/£1,000
Holding cost:	See Example 7.2	€/£1,000

W2: Calculation of costs at discount one: order quantity 300

Purchase cost: 2,000 × (€/£60 × 96%) €/£115,200

Ordering cost: $\frac{2{,}000}{300} \times$ €/£100 €/£667

Holding cost: $\frac{300}{2} \times$ €/£9.68 €/£1,452

W3: Calculation of costs at discount two: order quantity 600

Purchase cost: 2,000 × (€/£60 × 90%) €/£108,000

Order cost:	$\frac{2,000}{600} \times$ €/£100	€/£333
Holding cost:	$\frac{600}{2} \times$ €/£9.20	€/£2,760

Lead Times, Uncertainty and the EOQ Model

The EOQ model can still be used even where some of the assumptions underpinning the basic model are relaxed. It can be used where there is uncertainty in respect of demand for the goods and immediate delivery of the goods is not possible. These issues are now considered.

Delivery delay for units: under certainty In practice, it is unlikely that a supplier will be able to replenish inventories the minute they run out. Suppliers usually require time to prepare an order and to deliver it. The time taken between placing an order for inventory and receiving the units is called **lead time**. If an inventory manager knows the lead time of a supplier, then a reorder level of inventory can be set. The **reorder level** is the point at which a new order has to be made to ensure that inventories do not run out. When demand for inventory is known with certainty for a period, the reorder level is:

Reorder level = Lead time in days/weeks × Usage in days/weeks

The average inventory level will not change, the assumption being that if the next order is made at the reorder level, this assures that delivery happens when inventory reaches zero.

Worked Example 7.4: Lead Times

Miercoles Ltd has an EOQ of 500 units and reorders every 10 days. Its usage is constant per day. The supplier takes three days to deliver the goods.

Requirement Under conditions of certainty, calculate the reorder level of inventory to be set to ensure there are no stock-outs.

Solution

The reorder level is: Usage per day × Lead time per day [(500 ÷ 10) × 3 = 150 units].

Delivery delay for units: under uncertainty Where suppliers are located far away, or are unable to guarantee delivery in a set lead time, then a company will have to hold safety stock. **Safety stock** is the minimum level of inventory a company needs to maintain to ensure there are no stock-outs. The level held depends on the uncertainty surrounding lead times and demand. Where there is uncertainty, the average inventory held will be:

$$\textbf{Average inventory} = \frac{\textbf{EOQ}}{\textbf{2}} + \textbf{Safety stock}$$

The reorder level will be:

Reorder level = (Average usage × Average lead time) + Safety stock

WORKED EXAMPLE 7.5: REORDER LEVELS AND UNCERTAINTY

Miercoles Ltd has an EOQ of 500 units and reorders every 10 days. Its usage is constant per day. The supplier takes three days to deliver the goods.

Requirement

(a) You are informed that the delivery delay on purchases may vary between three and six days. Calculate the new reorder level which should ensure no stock-outs (assume demand is a steady rate per day).

(b) You are informed that sales demand for inventory can range from 400 to 600 units every 10 days. Calculate the new reorder level, which should ensure no stock-outs (assume the lead time is known with certainty).

(c) Assume that both uncertainties outlined in (a) and (b) exist. Calculate the new reorder level, which should ensure no stock-outs.

Solution

(a) As the lead time may vary between three and six days and it is company policy not to run out of inventory, then the worst case scenario (i.e. six-day lead time) is assumed. Therefore, Miercoles Ltd needs to hold six days of inventory. The daily usage of inventory is 50 [500 ÷ 10] units per day. Therefore, the reorder level should be set at 300 units [50 × 6]. This means that the company should hold a safety stock of 150 units [300 – (50 × 3)].

(b) Usage of inventory can range from 400 to 600 units in the 10-day period. The policy is not to run out of inventory, therefore it will be assumed that the worst case scenario exists over the lead time period, i.e. demand is at its highest per day. The maximum demand is 600 ÷ 10 = 60 units per day. Assuming three days' lead time, a reorder level of 180 units [60 × 3] is required. Therefore, the safety stock level is 30 units [180 – (50 × 3)].

(c) Where the lead time is variable, demand is variable and the company still maintains a policy of ensuring no stock-outs, then the reorder point will be the longest lead time multiplied by the highest usage, which is 360 units [6 × 60]. Therefore, a safety stock of 210 units will have to be held [360 – (50 × 3)].

INVENTORY MANAGEMENT SYSTEMS

Just-in-time Inventory Management

Just-in-time inventory management (JIT) is a demand-driven inventory management technique that evolved in Japan in the early 1980s. When it works efficiently, no inventory is held by a company in stores as inventory is delivered by suppliers straight to where it is required. The amount delivered should equate to the demand requirements of a company. This management technique is used by many companies throughout the world. Evidence of it can be seen in local retail grocery shops, wherein local bakery distributors and fruit and vegetable distributors bring their products straight to the shelves. The benefits of this system are reduced inventory levels (resulting in reduced storage and finance costs), reduced damage, reduced defects and reduced deterioration, as inventory is being managed, to an extent, by suppliers. The supplier takes some responsibility for monitoring and ensuring there are no stock-outs. This should lead to greater productivity.

There are risks associated with this type of inventory management, as the responsibility for stock-outs is moved away from the company to a certain extent. Though it is a straightforward idea, it usually has hidden costs in that a company's quality procedures need to be strong and this involves a lot of management time. The company should have strong links, both on a personal basis and an information basis, with its suppliers. This means that suppliers should have access to the inventory monitoring system. Therefore, a computerised system is usually required with real-time information that is accessible by suppliers. To work efficiently, suppliers are more likely to be local and have quick, efficient distribution channels in place. Deliveries are frequent and cannot be incorrect. JIT is most suited to a manufacturing company that has high volume and steady, homogenous products and processes.

INVENTORY MONITORING SYSTEMS

The most common type of physical inventory monitoring systems is the perpetual inventory control system. The latter is sometimes referred to as the **continuous inventory control system**.

Perpetual Inventory Control Systems

This system ensures that production or sales are not affected. A **perpetual inventory control system** involves constantly monitoring inventory and reordering items at any time when reorder levels are reached. These systems are usually computerised and use EOQ, minimum reorder levels and safety stocks. Inventory counts are continuous and organised. It is normal to also undertake a physical count of total inventory once a year for the purpose of preparing the year-end accounts/audit. The margin of error between inventory records and physical inventory is expected to be low. This is because errors/differences are noted quickly and fixed throughout the year. This system is time-consuming and expensive to administer; however, low levels of inventory can be held. Before implementing this type of system, a company needs to weigh up the additional costs to be incurred against the benefits to be gained. These systems usually involve tracking inventory from its arrival in the store, to its sale or use in production. Large retail companies use this form of inventory management system, wherein each item has its own barcode, which is scanned when the item is sold or enters the store.

OTHER INVENTORY MANAGEMENT CONSIDERATIONS

Choosing an inventory management technique or strategy is only a starting point in inventory management. Other practical issues that need to be considered are outlined in brief in **Figure 7.5**.

Figure 7.5: Other Inventory Issues

Obsolescence management	Actual sales may differ from forecast sales figures. Therefore, it is important that an **obsolescence inventory management policy** is in place to deal with excess inventories that may be obsolete or going out of date. Regular reviews should assess the potential for inventory becoming obsolete. Computerised systems could be programmed to identify slow-moving inventory. If the inventory is still in date and part of the sales plan, then discussions with the sales team should ensue. Perhaps a more aggressive approach could be taken to the sale of items. Techniques used include: placing items in prime sale locations; putting the items on promotion; offering a discount if purchased in bulk (for example **Buy One Get One Free (BOGOF)**). Obsolete inventories do not move fast. Obsolete inventories take up store space, which increases holding costs, uses space that could be used for other products and may result in wastage costs.
Waste management	When an obsolete item is no longer part of a company's sales plan, that item is regarded as waste. A company should have a **waste management policy**. This may involve: selling the items at a price below cost; reworking the product (for example, where a new model of an item comes out, the parts of the old model may be saleable) or even removing the product from stores by the most environmentally friendly and low-cost method. Dumping waste has a cost per tonne, therefore, if a company can recycle its inventory, this would be more economical and would give the company better publicity.
Quality maintenance	In today's competitive market, a concern for all management within a company is quality. Poor quality services or products can result in lost sales. Therefore, inventory management should also consider the quality of products and how customers are treated. When sourcing a supply, an inventory manager should not just be attracted to the cheapest product, but should consider durability, taste, etc. When dealing with customers there should be a **target delivery time set** (if not immediate), a **returns policy** and a **customer complaints policy**.

CONCLUSION

Managers should try to balance the cost of holding and ordering inventory with the opportunity cost of losing sales when an item is not available in inventory to sell. The objective is to reduce the overall cost to a company and its equity holders. This management process not only involves an acute awareness of the separate inventory costs, but is also reliant on there being sound information in respect of expected demand for inventory items. This can be achieved where there are strong communication channels between the stores manager and the sales and marketing department, the quality control department and the research and development department. Inventory management should also have operational procedures in place to identify and manage obsolete and waste inventories. There are many inventory management systems available and an appropriate system should be selected to suit the type of industry a company is in and the type of product a company makes and/or sells. The choice of system should balance initial costs (i.e. capital and training) of a system and its ongoing maintenance, with the benefits to be received from the system (i.e. reduction in inventory holding costs, wastage, obsolescence, less stock-outs, etc.). **Figure 7.6** summarises, in brief, the main influences on inventory levels.

Figure 7.6: General Influences On Inventory Levels Held

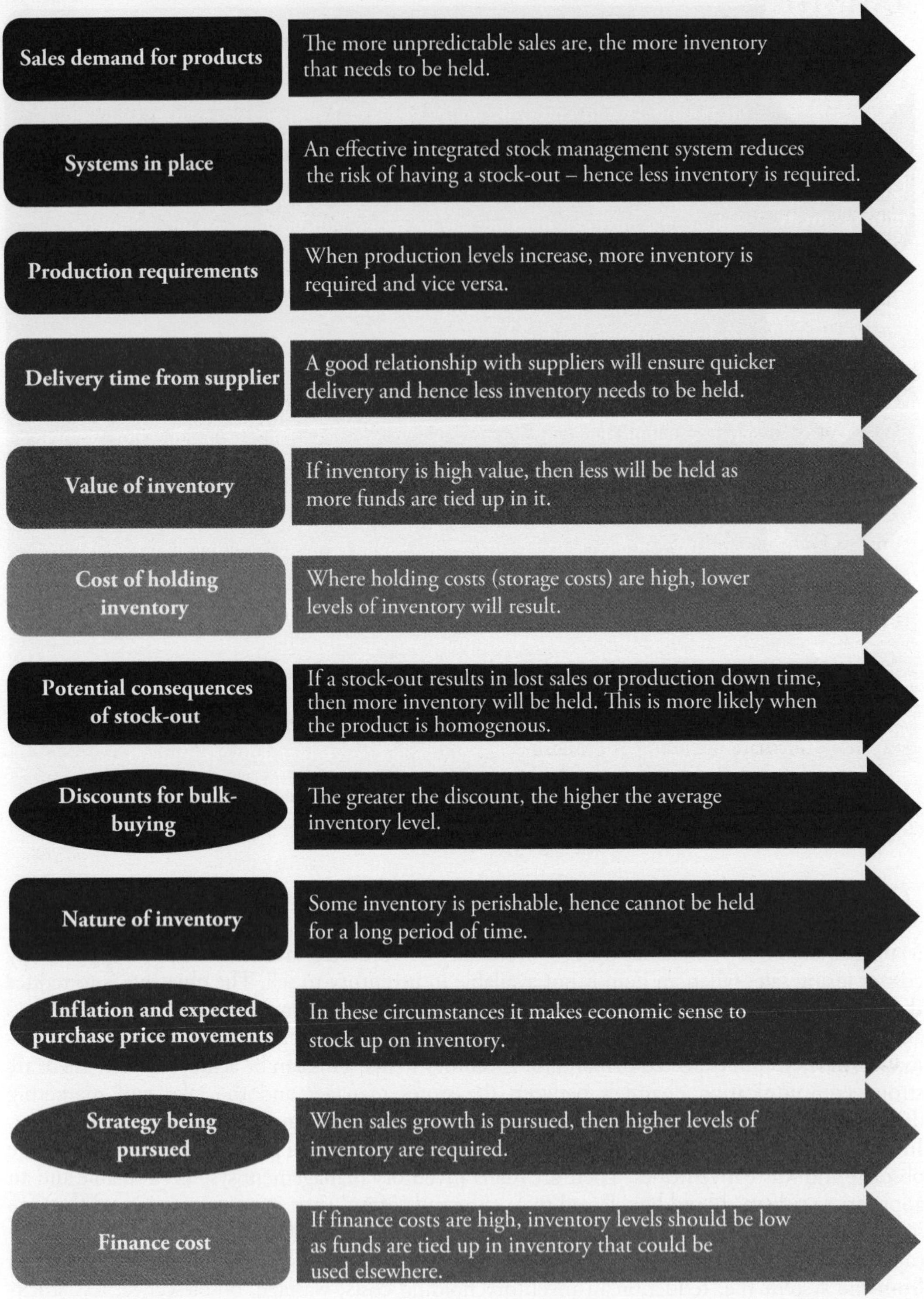

Sales demand for products	The more unpredictable sales are, the more inventory that needs to be held.
Systems in place	An effective integrated stock management system reduces the risk of having a stock-out – hence less inventory is required.
Production requirements	When production levels increase, more inventory is required and vice versa.
Delivery time from supplier	A good relationship with suppliers will ensure quicker delivery and hence less inventory needs to be held.
Value of inventory	If inventory is high value, then less will be held as more funds are tied up in it.
Cost of holding inventory	Where holding costs (storage costs) are high, lower levels of inventory will result.
Potential consequences of stock-out	If a stock-out results in lost sales or production down time, then more inventory will be held. This is more likely when the product is homogenous.
Discounts for bulk-buying	The greater the discount, the higher the average inventory level.
Nature of inventory	Some inventory is perishable, hence cannot be held for a long period of time.
Inflation and expected purchase price movements	In these circumstances it makes economic sense to stock up on inventory.
Strategy being pursued	When sales growth is pursued, then higher levels of inventory are required.
Finance cost	If finance costs are high, inventory levels should be low as funds are tied up in inventory that could be used elsewhere.

EXAMINATION STANDARD QUESTION: OPTIMAL ORDER QUANTITIES

Pageant Ltd uses the EOQ to determine the optimal quantity of inventory that should be purchased at a time.

The company's product, 'Gamma', which is ordered in by Pageant as a finished product, is normally consumed at a steady, known rate over the company's planning horizon of one year. However, in recent times, demand has fluctuated throughout the year and in order to protect itself against possible deviations, the company keeps a buffer inventory of 100 units. Further supplies are ordered whenever the inventory falls to this minimum level. The time lag between ordering and delivering is so small, it can be ignored.

The costs of ordering Gamma include fixed costs of €/£40 per order plus a variable cost of €/£0.10 per unit ordered. Pageant stores its inventories in a warehouse that it rents on a long lease for €/£6 per square foot per annum. Warehouse space available exceeds current requirements and, as the lease cannot be cancelled, spare capacity is sub-let on annual contracts at €/£8 per square foot per annum. Each unit of product Gamma stores requires 1.5 square feet of space. The company estimates that other holding costs amount to €/£4 per unit of Gamma per annum.

The purchase price of each unit of Gamma is €/£15 and Pageant's selling price is €/£25 per unit.

Annual demand for product 'Gamma' is currently 8,000 units.

Requirement

(a) (i) Calculate the EOQ for Gamma.

4 Marks

(ii) Calculate the annual expected profit on the sale of Gamma.

6 Marks

(b) Discuss the principal issues to be considered in managing inventories. Include in your answer how information technology can assist in dealing with these issues.

8 Marks

Total 18 Marks

(Based on Chartered Accountants Ireland, MABF II, Autumn 2002, Q6)

Solution

(a) (i) *EOQ*

Annual demand	8,000 units
Fixed cost per order	€/£40
Holding opportunity cost	€/£12 [€/£8 × 1.5]
Other holding cost per unit	€/£4

$$\text{EOQ} = \sqrt{\frac{2(40)(8{,}000)}{(12+4)}} = 200 \text{ units per order}$$

(ii) *Calculation of annual profit of Gamma*

		€/£	
Sales	[8,000 × €/£25]	200,000	
Cost of sales (W1)		125,600	
Profit		74,400	(37.2% of sales)

W1: Annual costs at the EOQ

		€/£	€/£
Ordering costs:			
Fixed cost	[€/£40 × (8,000 ÷ 200)]	1,600	
Variable cost	[€/£0.10 × 8,000]	800	2,400
Holding costs	[€/£16 × (200 ÷ 2)]	1,600	
(buffer inventory)	[€/£16 × 100]	1,600	3,200
Purchase cost	[8,000 × €/£15]		120,000
Total costs			125,600

(b) Issues to consider when managing inventory should include the following points:

- Type of inventory: raw materials; work in progress; finished goods; consumables.
- Variability of demand: the higher the level of uncertainty, the higher the level of finished goods inventory.
- Lead time, cost and reliability of supplies: EOQ assumes lead time is constant, and when it is not, additional inventory must be held as a supplier may not deliver when required.
- Length (or complexity) of the production process.
- Relationship with suppliers: a JIT system requires an excellent relationship with suppliers as responsibility for stock-outs is passed to them. If the relationship is poor, then safety stock must be held.
- Proximity to customers.
- Physical condition of inventory.
- Special requirements for storage.
- Discounts available for bulk-buying of inventories.
- Quantity of inventory.
- Information technology developments in inventory control.

- Value of inventory.
- Costs of holding inventories versus the cost of a stock-out.
- Financing inventories.
- Obsolete inventory review.
- Quality issues.
- Waste management.

(***Note:*** the solution should incorporate the use of information technology in dealing with inventory management (for example, EOQ and JIT systems). Some areas where these systems could be incorporated are mentioned briefly above. A full solution would expand on these explanations.)

Key Terms

Buy One Get One Free (BOGOF)
Consumables
Continuous inventory control system
Customer complaints policy
Economic order quantity (EOQ)
Economic order range (EOR)
Finished goods
Holding costs
Intangible inventory
Inventory
Just-in-time inventory management
Lead times
Obsolescence inventory management policy
Optimum inventory level
Ordering costs
Perpetual inventory control system
Raw materials
Reorder level
Returns policy
Safety stock
Stock-outs
Stock-out costs
Target delivery time
Waste management policy
Work in progress

REVIEW QUESTIONS

Question 7.1

What are the different types of inventory?

Question 7.2

What is the purpose of inventory management?

Question 7.3

What are the possible consequences of having a poor inventory control system in a manufacturing company?

Question 7.4

Why does a company use the EOQ model?

Question 7.5

What is JIT inventory management?

Question 7.6 Greenside

Greenside Plc has expanded the production of its microcomputer range and now requires 200,000 hard drives each year, which it obtains from an outside supplier. The cost of placing an order for the drives is €/£32 and it has been estimated that the holding cost per drive is 10% of its cost. The hard drives cost €/£8 each. Demand for the hard drives occurs evenly over the year.

Requirement

(a) Estimate the optimal order size and calculate how many orders will be required each year. Calculate the ordering costs and holding costs per annum.

4 Marks

(b) If actual demand for the drives is 242,000 drives per annum, what is the impact on the cost of retaining the order size estimated in (a) above, instead of using a new order quantity? Comment on your results.

6 Marks

(c) Are there any situations where the use of the EOQ is not appropriate?

2 Marks

Total 12 Marks

(Based on Chartered Accountants Ireland, MABF II, Autumn 1999, Q6)

CHALLENGING QUESTIONS

(Suggested Solutions to Challenging Questions are available through your lecturer.)

Question 7.1 JIT systems (Level 1)

It has been stated that the target objectives of just-in-time (JIT) are as follows:

1. Zero inventories.
2. Zero defects.
3. Zero breakdowns.
4. Batch sizes of one.
5. Elimination of non-value-added activities.

Requirement Discuss the managerial action that must be taken to try to achieve the target objectives of:

(i) Zero defects.
(ii) Batch sizes of one.

10 Marks

(Based on Chartered Accountants Ireland, MABF I, Summer 1999, Q3)

Question 7.2 Stockit Ltd (Level 1)

Stockit Ltd produces 20,000 units of Product X every month. Each unit of Product X requires an input of 2 kilograms of Product Y, which the company purchases from a supplier at a price of €/£7.50 per kilogram. It is estimated that the cost of keeping one kilogram of Product Y in stock for one year is €/£2.50. The cost incurred in generating one order for Product Y is €/£1.60.

Requirement Calculate the economic order quantity (EOQ) for Product Y and estimate the annual cost of this policy.

9 Marks

(Based on Chartered Accountants Ireland, CAP 1, Summer 2011, Q6(b))

Question 7.3 Celtic Candles (Level 1)

Jane and her partner operate a small candle manufacturing business trading as Celtic Candles. Their main raw material is beeswax, of which they use about 8,000 kilos a year. The cost of each delivery is €/£40 and they estimate that annualised storage costs per unit are 50c/p. Jane and her partner are not sure how much stock they should purchase each time they order.

Requirement Calculate the economic order quantity (EOQ) and show the consequent total ordering and holding costs for one year.

5 Marks

(Based on Chartered Accountants Ireland, CAP 1, Autumn 2008, Q6(a))

Question 7.4 Magnum (Level 1)

Magnum Ltd sells DVDs at a standard price of €/£12 each. The purchase cost of the DVDs from the wholesale distributor is €/£5 each. The total cost of placing an order with the wholesaler is estimated as €/£7.50 per order, and the annual cost of carrying inventory is estimated at 25% of the cost of the inventory. Magnum's shop is open 312 days per year, and an average of 150 DVDs are sold per day. Demand is relatively stable from day to day.

Requirement Calculate the economic order quantity (EOQ) for the purchase of DVDs from the wholesale distributor, and estimate the annual cost of this EOQ policy.

8 Marks

(Based on Chartered Accountants Ireland, CAP 1, Autumn 2011, Q1(b))

Question 7.5 Justin Casey (Level 1)

(a) Justin Casey uses an estimated 44,000 units of a component each year. The cost of holding one component for a year is €/£3.00 and it is estimated that it costs €/£100 to process each order for the component. The delivery from the supplier usually takes place within one week of the order being placed.

Requirement

(i) Calculate the economic order quantity (EOQ) for the component and determine the total holding and ordering costs for that EOQ.

4 Marks

(ii) At what level of inventory should Justin place an order, so as to avoid a stock-out?

2 Marks

(b) Justin has obtained some industry average figures and is concerned that he holds, on average, almost twice the level of inventory in relation to sales as his competitors.

Requirement List the advantages and disadvantages of holding inventory.

4 Marks

Total 10 Marks

(Based on Chartered Accountants Ireland, CAP 1, Summer 2012, Q5(a),(b))

Question 7.6 Samson (Level 1)

Samson Limited sells a top brand of high-quality suitcases. On average, Samson sells 200 suitcases a day and the business is open 360 days a year. The purchase price of each suitcase from the manufacturer is €/£45. The manufacturer requires Samson to buy in bulk and a minimum of 6,000 suitcases must be purchased at any one time. The order processing charge is €/£250 per order and the average cost of holding each suitcase per annum is 6% of its purchase price.

A new manufacturer has approached Samson with an offer to sell Samson the suitcases for the same price of €/£45, but with no minimum order requirement. This would allow Samson to order as many suitcases as it wishes when placing an order.

Requirement

(a) Calculate the total annual cost of stocking the suitcases under Samson's existing inventory management system.

4 Marks

(b) Calculate the total annual cost of stocking the suitcases, to the nearest €/£, if Samson were to change to the new manufacturer.

(***Note:*** assume that Samson will order the economic order quantity (EOQ) when placing an order.)

5 Marks

(c) Discuss what is meant by the just-in-time (JIT) approach to inventory management and briefly describe FOUR of its main features.

6 Marks

Total 15 Marks

(Based on Chartered Accountants Ireland, CAP 1, Summer 2013, Q4)

Question 7.7 Caveat (Level 1)

Caveat is finalising its annual review of suppliers for product K. Caveat sells 300 cartons of K per week, and estimates that the storage costs for a carton of K are €/£2.50 per annum per carton. Caveat estimates that its administration costs incurred each time it places an order are €/£50, regardless of the order size.

The existing supplier sells to Caveat at a price of €/£30 per carton, taking two weeks to deliver, and charges a fixed charge of €/£32 per order, regardless of the order size.

A new supplier has offered to supply Caveat at a price of €/£26 per carton, with delivery in one week, but has a fixed order processing charge of €/£240 regardless of order size.

Requirement:

(a) Calculate for both suppliers:

(i) The economic order quantity.

(ii) The reorder level/quantity.

(iii) The total cost of stocking K for one year.

8 Marks

(b) Advise Caveat, based on relevant cost considerations, whether it should continue to use its current supplier or change to the new supplier.

4 Marks

(c) Indicate, briefly, THREE other non-financial factors which should be considered before a final decision is made.

3 Marks

Total 15 Marks

(Based on Chartered Accountants Ireland, CAP 1, Finance, Summer 2010, Q4)

Question 7.8 Octagon (Level 1)

(a) Discuss and give examples of each of the following inventory management costs:

(i) Ordering costs.

(ii) Holding costs.

(iii) Stock-out costs.

6 Marks

(b) Octagon Plc utilises an EOQ model to determine optimal levels of raw materials. The following information is available for Material XY:

Current usage: 4,000 units per annum
Holding costs: €/£15 per unit per annum
Ordering cost: €/£30 per order.

Requirement

(i) Estimate the optimal order level of material XY. Ignore the discount referred to below.

4 Marks

(ii) Recently another supplier has offered Octagon Plc a 2% discount on the current price of €/£24 per unit, if the company orders in excess of 300 units each time.

Assuming that all other costs remain constant, advise Octagon Plc as to whether it should accept the discount offered by the alternative supplier.

8 Marks
Total 18 Marks

(Based on Chartered Accountants Ireland, MABF II, Autumn 1997, Q6)

Question 7.9 Crystal Plc (Level 1)

(a) Outline the main features of a perpetual inventory control system.

2 Marks

(b) Crystal Plc is inviting tenders for the supply of a raw material to be included in a new product. The annual demand for the raw material is expected to be 4,000 units and the purchase price €/£90 per unit. The incremental cost of processing an order is €/£135 and the cost of storage is estimated to be €/£12 per unit.

Requirement

(i) Estimate the EOQ and the total relevant cost of that order quantity.

4 Marks

(ii) Assume that the €/£135 estimate of the incremental cost of processing an order proves to be incorrect and that it should have been €/£80, but that all other estimates are correct.

What is the cost of this prediction error, if the solution to part (a) is implemented for one year before the error is discovered?

3 Marks

(iii) One potential supplier has offered to supply all 4,000 units at a price of €/£86 each, if Crystal Plc agrees to accept delivery of the entire amount immediately. Assume that the incremental cost of processing this order is zero and that the original estimate of €/£135 for placing an order is correct.

Calculate the relevant cost considerations and, on the basis of your findings, indicate whether the company should accept the offer.

3 Marks
Total 12 Marks

(Based on Chartered Accountants Ireland, MABF II, Summer 1995, Q6)

Question 7.10 Parmeneon (Level 1)

(a) Parmeneon Ltd uses 200,000 units of a particular good per year on a continuous basis (assume 50 weeks in the year). The store manager estimates that it costs €/£0.25 to hold a unit of inventory in stores for one year. The purchasing department estimates that it costs €/£90 per order to place and process each order. The current supplier is located one mile down the road and can deliver the goods immediately.

Requirement As finance manager of Parmeneon Ltd you have been approached by the managing director to evaluate the cost effectiveness of the current ordering strategy, wherein 10 orders are made each year. Outline any changes you would suggest.

9 Marks

(b) The local supplier has retired and the goods are no longer available locally. A new supplier has been located in Britain. You are informed that the new supplier of the goods will take three weeks to deliver the products.

Requirement Given this information, advise the manager of Parmeneon on an appropriate reorder level to ensure no stock-out occurs (assuming certainty).

2 Marks

(c) The new supplier telephones to let you know that they are having problems sourcing the goods and transporting them from overseas as their local source is no longer available. In light of the uncertainty due to the involvement of an additional third party, the supplier estimates that the earliest delivery time will be two weeks and the worst case scenario will be delivery within five weeks.

Requirement Advise management as to the new reorder level and identify the number of goods to be held as a safety stock to ensure no stock-out occurs.

3 Marks

(d) At present, sales of the good occurs evenly over the 50 weeks of the year and do not vary from week to week. However, the marketing manager has suggested that this pattern will definitely change and demand is expected to vary between half to double the current estimated weekly production.

Requirement Assume the lead time is three weeks. Given the uncertainty in demand for the good, advise management as to the new reorder level and identify the number of goods to be held as a safety stock to ensure no stock-out occurs.

3 Marks

(e) Assume that sales can vary as highlighted in part (d) and that the lead time can vary between two and five weeks as in part (c).

Requirement Calculate the new reorder level and safety inventory that Parmeneon must maintain to ensure no stock-outs.

3 Marks

Total 20 Marks

Question 7.11 Warden (Level 1)

Warden Limited has an Economic Order Quantity (EOQ) of 756 units and reorders every 12 days. Its usage is constant per day. The supplier typically takes four days to deliver the goods.

Requirement

(a) You are informed that the lead time on purchases may now vary between four and six days. Calculate the reorder level which should ensure that there are no stock-outs.

2 Marks

(b) You are informed that sales demand for the inventory can range from 538 to 852 units every 12 days. Calculate the reorder level which should ensure that there are no stock-outs.

2 Marks

(c) Assume that both uncertainties outlined in (a) and (b) exist. Calculate the reorder level which should ensure that there are no stock-outs.

2 Marks

Total 6 Marks

(Based on Chartered Accountants Ireland, CAP 1, Finance, Autumn 2017, extract from Q6)

8

Management of Trade Receivables and Trade Payables

Learning Objectives

Upon completing this chapter, readers should be able to:
- explain the importance of trade credit to a company;
- explain the objective of trade receivables/payables management;
- discuss influences on credit limits and credit periods;
- discuss the costs and benefits associated with allowing credit sales and receiving credit purchases;
- list and explain the three stages of credit management;
- evaluate the costs and benefits of reducing/increasing a credit period;
- determine the annual equivalent cost of a cash discount (sales and purchases);
- discuss the role of information technology in the management of trade receivables and trade payables; and
- discuss ethics in relation to the management of trade receivables and trade payables.

INTRODUCTION

When a company supplies goods or services to another entity in advance of being paid for the goods or services, they have the option of allowing **trade credit** to their customers. Sales provided on credit are called credit sales, as opposed to cash sales. **Trade receivables** are the total outstanding balances on credit sales, due from customers to a company, at a point in time. Trade receivables are current assets. **Trade debtors** is another term to describe the balance of credit sales outstanding; however, the term trade receivables is used internationally. As highlighted in **Chapter 6**, a simple means of evaluating efficiency in the management of trade receivables is by measuring the **trade receivables cash conversion period**.

$$\textbf{Average trade receivables cash conversion period} = \frac{\textbf{Trade receivables} \times \textbf{365}}{\textbf{Credit sales}}$$

Industry averages for this ratio are usually available and these can be used as a benchmark when assessing the efficiency of a company's **credit management** policies.

When a company receives goods from another entity in advance of paying for the goods or services, they may receive trade credit. Purchases obtained on credit are called credit purchases, as opposed to cash purchases. The balance of credit purchases owed by a company at any point in time is called its **trade payables**. Trade payables are current liabilities. **Trade creditors** is another term to describe the balance of credit purchases owing; however, the term trade payables is used internationally. International phraseology is used in this textbook.

This chapter evaluates the management of trade receivables, otherwise known as credit management, and trade payables. The two areas are included in one chapter because they are inherently linked; trade receivables in one company are trade payables in other companies. Therefore, the management policies in relation to both should be similar. There are greater risks associated with a company having trade receivables; therefore, this area receives more attention in companies and, hence, is given prominence in this chapter also. The management of trade payables is considered at the end of the chapter.

TRADE CREDIT

Cost Implications of Trade Credit

When a company allows trade credit, it is foregoing a cash inflow. This results in an immediate finance cost to the company. The average amount of trade receivables due to the company is a long-term investment, which has an opportunity cost. The funds, if received as cash, could be used to reduce an overdraft, thus reducing interest. They could also be invested in a deposit account, earning interest, or could be used to finance a new project, which could yield a return. In addition, allowing credit creates other costs that would not otherwise occur. First, granting credit creates exposure to payment default **(bad debts)**. Secondly, funds are tied up, resulting in a reduction in liquidity. This may have cost implications in other areas; it might hinder a company's ability, for example, to pay suppliers within a specified timeframe that would enable the company to avail of a discount. Thirdly, credit management and control practices, policies and procedures need to be established and maintained, which will result in incremental administrative costs. The next two examples present methods that are used to estimate the finance requirements associated with granting credit. The first assumes that a constant trade credit policy is adopted for all credit customers; the second incorporates uncertainty into the scenario.

Worked Example 8.1: Finance Requirement under Certainty

Cuatro Ltd has €/£10 million in sales; 20% of these are cash sales. A credit period of 30 days is allowed, although 50% of credit customers take 50 days. Assume there are 360 days in a year.

Requirement

(a) Calculate the overdraft facility that Cuatro Ltd has to arrange to ensure that trade receivables are adequately financed.

(b) What is the cost of the current credit policy, given that the bank overdraft rate is 12%?

Solution

The company will need to finance the funds that are tied up in average trade receivables.

(a) Credit sales are: €/£8,000,000 [€/£10,000,000 × 80%]

Average trade receivables are:	**€/£**
[€/£8,000,000 × 50% × 30/360]	333,333
[€/£8,000,000 × 50% × 50/360]	555,555
Total trade receivables (finance requirement)	888,888

Cuatro Ltd will need to arrange a €/£888,888 overdraft facility to finance its trade receivables.

(b) The finance cost of this credit policy is therefore:

€/£888,888 × 12% = €/£106,667

In **Worked Example 8.1**, 30 days' credit are allowed; however, customers take, on average, 40 days to pay for credit sales [(50% × 30) + (50% × 50)]. Therefore, the finance requirement could also be calculated using the weighted average trade receivables cash conversion period [i.e. €/£8,000,000 × 40/360 = €/£888,888]. **Worked Example 8.2** uses this approach and extends it to incorporate risk (the probability that a variety of given outcomes will occur).

Worked Example 8.2: Finance Requirement under Uncertainty

Cuatro Ltd has €/£10 million in sales; 20% of these are cash sales. A credit period of 30 days is allowed. Cuatro Ltd has analysed the payment pattern of its credit customers and considers that there is a 10% chance that credit customers will take 25 days, a 50% chance that they will take 30 days, a 30% chance that they will take 50 days and a 10% chance of them not paying at all. Assume there are 360 days in a year.

Requirement

(a) Calculate the overdraft facility that Cuatro Ltd has to arrange to ensure that its trade receivables are adequately financed.

(b) What is the cost of the current credit policy, given that the bank overdraft rate is 12%?

Solution

(a) Credit sales are: €/£8,000,000 [€/£10,000,000 × 80%]

Average no. of days' credit sales are outstanding	Expected cash conversion period
$\frac{10}{90} \times 25$	2.78
$\frac{50}{90} \times 30$	16.67
$\frac{30}{90} \times 50$	16.67
	36.12

The trade receivables that need financing are: credit sales less bad debts, multiplied by the expected trade receivables cash conversion period:

€/£722,400 [(€/£8,000,000 × 90%) × 36.12/360].

(b) The finance cost of this credit policy is:

€/£722,400 × 12% = €/£86,688

The company also expects to incur €/£800,000 in bad debts [€/£8,000,000 × 10%]. Therefore, the total cost of the current credit policy is €/£886,688.

Trade Credit: The Benefits

Trade credit is used by many companies to attract sales. Indeed, it has become so enshrined in marketing strategies that, in some industries, a normal credit period is expected and if a company chooses not to provide trade credit, this would seriously damage demand for the company's goods or services as customers would go to a competitor for the good or service.

THE OBJECTIVE OF TRADE CREDIT MANAGEMENT

The provision of credit is not a productive use of company funds unless the granting of credit results in either a profitable sale that would not otherwise have taken place or in keeping a sale that would otherwise transfer to a competitor. Just as tying funds up in inventory is considered a necessary investment, allowing trade credit should also be regarded as a necessary investment (in most industries). The objective of trade receivables management is to balance the costs of not allowing credit (i.e. lost contribution from sales as customers turn to competitors who provide credit) with the costs of providing credit (e.g. holding costs, such as bad debts, the opportunity cost of funds tied up or increased administration costs) to provide the maximum net benefit to equity shareholders.

WORKED EXAMPLE 8.3: SPECIAL CONTRACT/ORDER

Cero Ltd is currently evaluating a new contract that will result in annual sales of €/£3 million. The company has a contribution margin of 20%. The average credit period allowed to customers is 80 days; 80 days' credit is also received from suppliers. Annual marketing costs amount to €/£170,000, payable on the first day of each year. Cero Ltd expects 10% of the sales to be uncollectable. Cero Ltd has a cost of funds of 12%.

Requirement Evaluate whether Cero Ltd should accept this new contract or not.

Solution

		€/£
Benefit		
	Additional contribution: [€/£3,000,000 × 20%]	600,000
Costs		
	Marketing	(170,000)
	Bad debts: [€/£3,000,000 × 10%]	(300,000)
	Financing (W1)	(7,890)
	Net annual gain	122,110

		€/£
W1: Financing		
	Trade receivables	
	$[(€/£3,000,000 - €/£300,000) \times \frac{80}{365}]$	591,781
	Trade payables	
	$[(€/£3,000,000 \times 80\%) \times \frac{80}{365}]$	(526,028)
	Net finance required	65,753
	Expected additional finance cost: [€/£65,754 × 12%]	€/£7,890

Based on the above cost–benefit calculations, it is expected that the company will benefit, to the tune of €/£122,110 each year from the new contract. Therefore, the company should accept the contract.

Most companies have trade receivables. There are some exceptions, such as food stores, hairdressers or off-licences. In the UK and Ireland, trade receivables, on average, account for 25–35% of total business assets. In most companies, the trade receivables balance is regarded as material. Hence, effective management can impact significantly on company performance. In the last paragraph, the objective of credit management was explained, however, a cost–benefit analysis is not the only factor influencing trade credit policy – other influences are now considered.

TRADE CREDIT: INFLUENCES ON POLICY

Marketing Strategy and Strategic Growth

Every company has to market its products to gain sales. Where a company's products are specialised and there is high demand for its items, then the marketing strategy can focus on these features. However, in a market where products are more or less homogenous, terms of sale become very important and discounts and credit periods are regarded as important marketing tools.

These are used very effectively by, for example, furniture stores that market their credit period with 'buy now, pay nothing until 2030'. In these circumstances, the cost of financing the item is usually factored into the price of each item. When a company offers an unusually long credit period, it is likely to be pursuing more than one agenda. It recognises that trade credit costs and risks increase when long credit periods are offered; however, it will balance this with the benefits to be achieved from, for example, breaking into a market or expanding a market (which will lead to future, more profitable sales). Other situations that increase the attractiveness of allowing long credit periods include allowing credit to get rid of slow-moving inventory or inventory that is subject to obsolescence. The alternative may be to scrap these items.

Industry Influence

In most industries, companies try to conform to an industry norm. Therefore, where a company allows a credit period of 40 days and the industry norm is a credit period of 30 days then, theoretically, this company can reduce its credit period to 30 days without losing sales, as the competing companies do not offer better terms. A company that allows longer credit terms than the industry norm can usually charge slightly higher prices, resulting in a return on the additional investment.

If a company were to reduce its credit period below the industry average, then it is likely that it would lose sales, unless its sales price was lower or it offered discounts. In these instances, the additional costs (e.g. discounts or loss in sales price) and benefits (e.g. reduction in bad debts, reduced finance costs) would need to be evaluated to determine whether reducing price is worthwhile.

Quality Control Mechanism

The **trade credit period** is sometimes used by a customer to assess the quality and effectiveness of a good that has been purchased. If the good is not of the same quality as was advertised, is faulty or not fit for purpose, then the customer is in a much stronger position to reverse the transaction and send the good back, compared with a situation where the good has been paid for upfront.

EFFECTIVE TRADE CREDIT MANAGEMENT

A company should have a **credit systems and procedures manual** to formally record its policies and practices in respect of the management of its trade receivables. This is extremely important as failure to have such a manual can lead to the demise of companies, as outlined in **Real World Example 8.1**.

Real World Example 8.1: Construction Companies

The Creditsafe Watchdog report, which tracks the quarterly economic development of a number of sectors in the UK, highlighted the severe impact of the failure of companies such as Carillion and Lagan Construction Group in 2018. Many suppliers of these companies faced financial difficulties due to outstanding balances from these companies turning bad. Approximately £17 million of bad debts were written off by the sector. Not only were bad debt levels high, the watchdog noted that the average credit period taken by construction company customers was 16 days beyond what was agreed and the construction companies in turn took 11 days longer to pay their suppliers.

There are three main stages associated with managing trade receivables, as portrayed in **Figure 8.1**.

FIGURE 8.1: THE STAGES OF TRADE RECEIVABLES MANAGEMENT

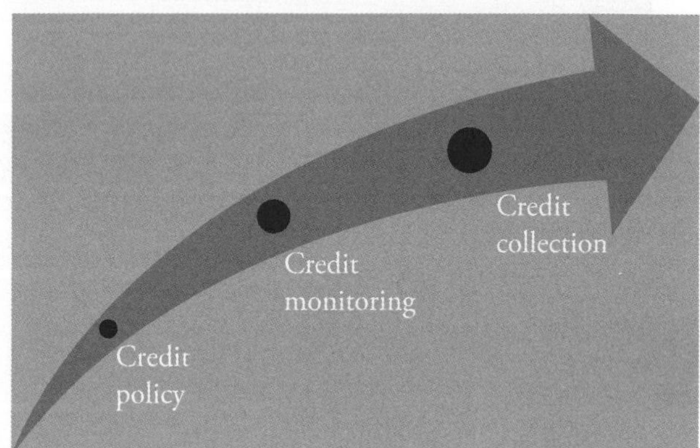

Credit Policy

A company's **credit policy** outlines the conditions underlying the provision of goods or services for credit. This is different from a company's **terms of sale**, which are the conditions underlying the sale of goods or services for cash or on credit.

Getting the credit policy correct is very important. Allowing longer credit periods usually stimulates more sales, resulting in larger trade receivables balances, with higher holding costs. As long as the contribution from the additional sales exceeds the costs associated with holding larger trade receivables, and liquidity is not jeopardised, this will be beneficial for a company. A company's credit policy should be flexible, though within boundaries. It should be clear and should answer several questions, as highlighted in **Figure 8.2**.

Some of these questions are now considered in more depth.

FIGURE 8.2: QUESTIONS TO ASK WHEN DETERMINING CREDIT POLICY

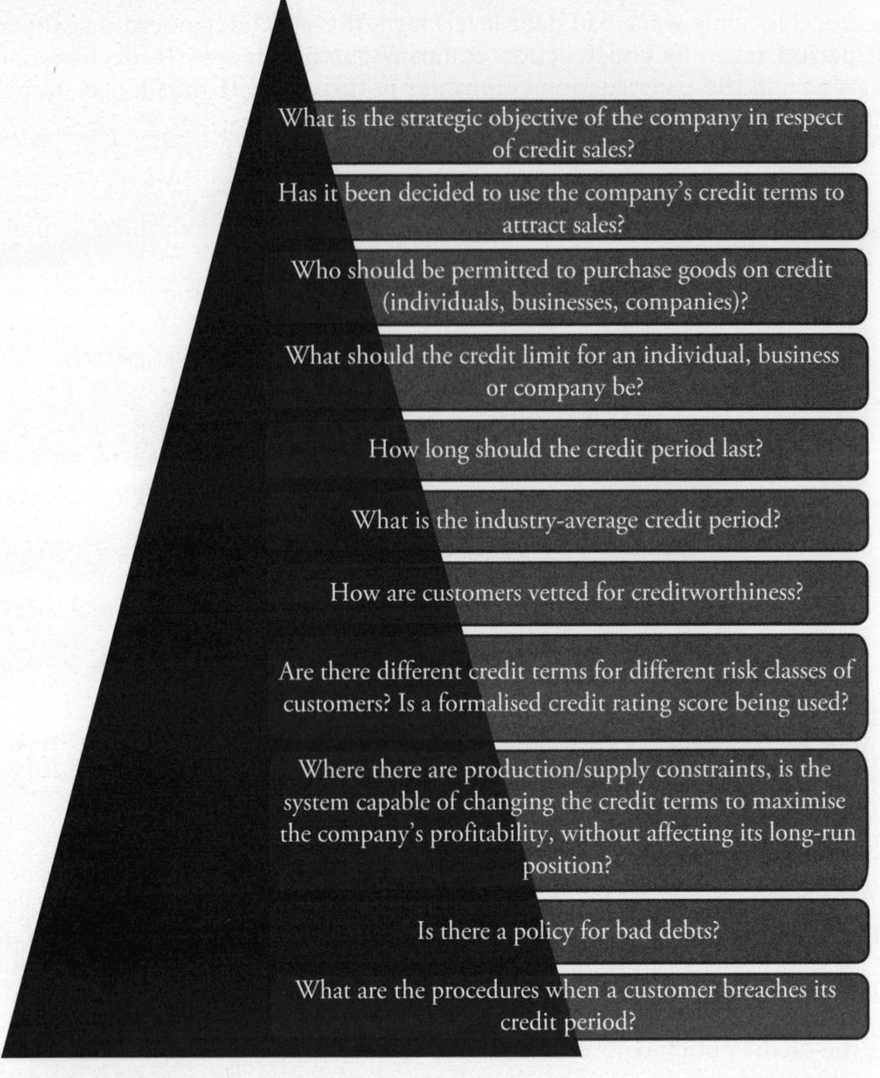

What is the strategic objective of the company in respect of credit sales?
Has it been decided to use the company's credit terms to attract sales?
Who should be permitted to purchase goods on credit (individuals, businesses, companies)?
What should the credit limit for an individual, business or company be?
How long should the credit period last?
What is the industry-average credit period?
How are customers vetted for creditworthiness?
Are there different credit terms for different risk classes of customers? Is a formalised credit rating score being used?
Where there are production/supply constraints, is the system capable of changing the credit terms to maximise the company's profitability, without affecting its long-run position?
Is there a policy for bad debts?
What are the procedures when a customer breaches its credit period?

Credit Assessment

The decision to allow trade credit to a customer is exactly the same decision a bank has to make when granting a loan. Therefore, each company should have a credit policy, with set credit assessment procedures in place, to assess the probability of a credit customer being a slow or bad payer. Steps are included in **Figure 8.3**.

Each of the actions outlined in this figure involves time and money; therefore, the extent of investigation required should depend on the size of the credit account requested and the potential profits to be made.

FIGURE 8.3: CREDIT ASSESSMENT STEPS

CREDIT RATING

- Obtain from a credit rating company, for example Dun & Bradstreet or Experian. The credit rating awarded is influenced by feedback from a company's suppliers.
- Other companies, such as Equifax, can also provide credit information for individuals.

TRADE REFERENCES

- Obtain from companies that a customer has traded with in the past.
- The quality of this source of information is influenced by the reputation of the company providing the reference.
- The companies to be approached for a trade reference should be selected by the credit manager, not those recommended by a customer requesting credit.
- A pro forma request form that is quick and easy to complete will improve the chance of another company providing a reference, as will an offer to reciprocate the task in future.

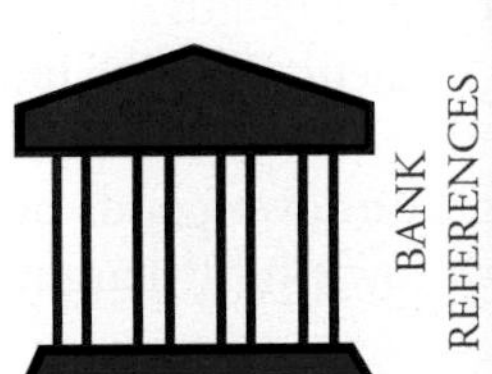

BANK REFERENCES

- Customers have to give the bank consent to release the information.
- The bank charges the customer a fee for providing this service.
- Banks in debt to a credit customer may be more interested in the customer obtaining funding using trade credit, than from an extension to an existing overdraft. A bank's loyalty will always be to its customer, not to an external company making a credit enquiry.
- Bank references are usually carefully worded pro forma letters; they should be used in conjunction with other evidence on creditworthiness.
- A company can also request information on whether inventories or trade receivables are secured against debt.

OTHER DEPARTMENTS

- Enquire of individuals within your own company who have a history or knowledge of the customer applying for credits.
- Where the potential credit account is sufficiently large, a visit to their premises can provide valuable information.

PUBLISHED REPORTS

- Use copies of financial statements for the past three years to analyse the company's liquidity and financial position.
- Financial statements can be obtained from the Companies Registration Office (in Ireland) or Companies House (in the UK) for a small fee, alternatively the customer could be asked to supply copies.

Credit Limit

A **credit limit** is the maximum amount of sales that a company will allow on credit to a customer. This is influenced by the credit assessment outcome. There are usually two approaches to setting a credit limit. The first links the credit limit to the sales requirements of a customer. This policy allows the credit limit to grow, and shrink, in line with customer needs. It needs constant review and is best suited to customers who are regarded as having low credit risk. The second method is to set a maximum amount that the company is prepared to be owed by customers as a whole. A common benchmark is the lower of 10% of net worth or 20% of working capital. This approach is easier to implement and needs less revision, though may not be as popular with customers.

Credit Period

The **credit period** is the length of time customers are permitted to pay for credit sales. A company's allowable credit period is sometimes detailed on invoices or credit agreements and may be shortened to, for example, 5/7, net 40. The first part of this (5/7) means that a discount of 5% is permitted if payment is received within seven days; the second part (net 40) means if payment is not made within seven days, the full amount is due within 40 days. Where a customer is a company, a review of its trade receivables period should provide guidance on the maximum period of credit to allow. The customer's trade receivables days should be used to guide the credit period allowed to them. If the trade credit period allowed to them (i.e. their trade payables) is longer than the credit period that they allow (i.e. their trade receivables), then the credit period allowed to them is too long and the customer is using the additional credit period to finance other activities. A company's policy in respect of the length of credit period given does not necessarily have to be homogenous, and may be influenced by the individual credit rating of a customer. In addition, the type of industry and normal credit period awarded will influence this decision, as will the type of good (e.g. high-turnover goods normally have short credit periods, as do perishable goods or goods with low profit margins), competition for sales and customer type.

REAL WORLD EXAMPLE 8.2: INDUSTRY CREDIT PERIODS

Having a long credit period does not necessarily infer that a company has poor credit control procedures. Indeed, accountants and auditors allow the longest credit period out of several sectors examined. The average durations of some sectors that allow long credit periods are as follows:

Accountants and auditors	About 120 days
Oil and gas companies	About 110 days
Car rental companies	About 100 days
Architectural and engineers	About 75 days
Scientific research companies	About 70 days
Civil engineer contractors	About 65 days

Source: adapted from https://www.inc.com/sageworks/10-industries-that-take-the-longest-to-get-paid.html

Credit Agreement

When an initial risk assessment has been completed, a credit agreement should be prepared and signed by all parties involved. The customer should be made fully aware of the rewards for paying within a discount period and the consequences of failing to pay within the credit period permitted.

The **credit agreement** should outline all the terms and conditions pertaining to the credit allowed, including discounts, interest penalties and formalised processes adopted by the company to recover overdue debts. Areas to be considered in a credit agreement are outlined in **Figure 8.4**.

FIGURE 8.4: AREAS TO COVER IN A CREDIT AGREEMENT (TRADE RECEIVABLES AND PAYABLES)

Credit Agreement

- Definitions (e.g. buyer, seller)
- Quality
- Price
- Quotations
- Delivery/date/arrangements
- Risk and property/retention of title
- Terms of payment
- Time limit for raising disputes
- Right to interest and compensation for debt-recovery costs
- Loss or damage in transit
- Acceptance of goods
- Variations to contract
- Patent rights/indemnity
- *Force majeure**
- Jurisdiction/applicable law
- Assignment and sub-letting contracts
- Right to inspect goods
- Warranties and liability
- Severability
- Insolvency and bankruptcy

* *Force majeure:* legal term to describe a clause in contracts that covers what happens when an uncontrollable event causes a breach of contract.

All companies should prepare a standard credit agreement that considers all these areas, where relevant. This agreement should be tailored for each customer. When agreed, a letter should be sent to the customer confirming key terms. This introduces the person who is managing the account to the customer and reiterates key conditions.

Document Processes

A company should also have a **prompt action code of practice**. This involves issuing invoices when goods are delivered, highlighting the credit period agreed and generating statements automatically for each outstanding customer account and sending them either by email or by post to each customer a few days before the credit period is breached. Statements should detail the total outstanding balance and should break it down into the periods of time outstanding. This may be split into amounts due in more than one month, within one month, immediately and overdue – with the last named highlighted as urgent. Statements may include interest on overdue amounts, if this has been agreed in the credit agreement.

Credit Monitoring

This is the second phase in credit management. **Credit monitoring** involves analysing customers' payment patterns, with the aim of classifying customers according to their credit record. This involves assessing the associated risks based on changes in payment behaviour and determining the likelihood of a debt becoming bad. It may also lead to a renegotiation of the credit limit where it is deemed to impede potential additional sales from a growing customer. The whole process weighs up the cost of monitoring and chasing up a debt, with the benefit to be derived by receiving the debt at all or receiving it earlier than expected.

The BPPG suggested using an 80/20 rule for the management of trade receivables, wherein the few customers (20%) making up the majority of the sales (80%) receive most attention and are prioritised in terms of service and when queries arise.

Reporting

Good credit monitoring can be simplified with the use of an appropriate bookkeeping software package that allows exception reporting. For example, Sage allows a user to set up default credit limits and periods. When a customer breaches a limit, their account is flagged (the font automatically appears in red). Aged analysis can also be viewed at the touch of a button. This breaks a customer's outstanding balance into amounts that are due in the current period, within one month, within two months and so on. The use of an aged receivables analysis is vital for highlighting customers who are starting to slow their normal payment pattern, stimulating further investigation. It can also highlight growth and spark renegotiations about a new limit.

Risk Rating

On an ongoing basis, credit monitoring should continually classify and code customers according to their perceived credit risk. This will involve, in part, the reports explained in the last paragraph. These should allow a credit manager to quickly assess a customer's payment record and to identify early signs of financial problems. These may include breaches in the agreed credit period or paying round sums that are below the balance that is in the statement as being due.

If a customer is considered to be becoming higher risk, then this should spark other credit assessment procedures, such as meeting with the client to discuss the situation or obtaining fresh credit reports, bank references, trade references or copies of the latest financial statements. These procedures might also include talking to sales people who visit the client and visiting the client. A benchmark risk coding structure is suggested in **Figure 8.5**.

FIGURE 8.5: BENCHMARK RISK CODING PROFILE

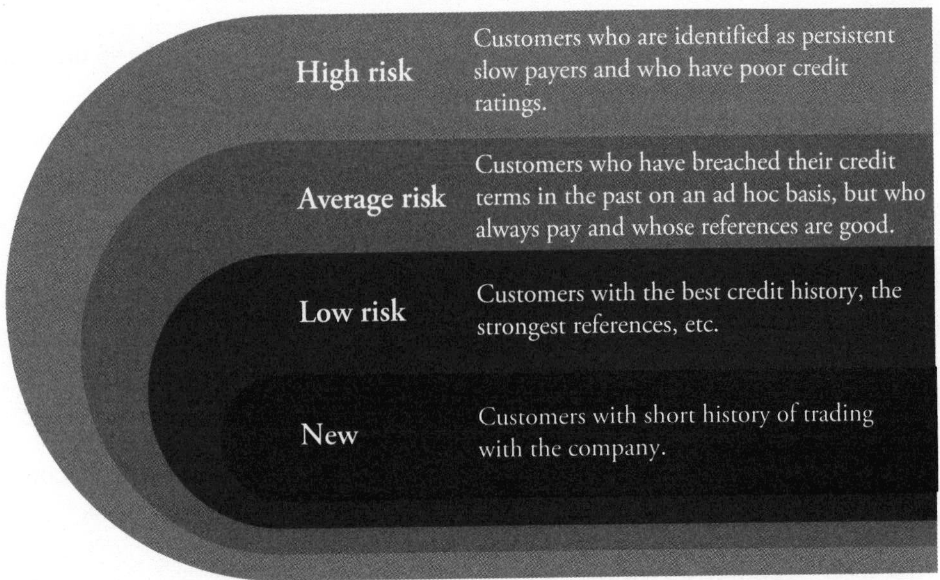

High risk
Customers who are identified as persistent slow payers and who have poor credit ratings.
Average risk
Customers who have breached their credit terms in the past on an ad hoc basis, but who always pay and whose references are good.
Low risk
Customers with the best credit history, the strongest references, etc.
New
Customers with short history of trading with the company.

A company should focus its attention on selling goods or services to those customers coded as 'low' and 'average' risk; however, it should not rule out selling to customers coded as 'high' risk when enough business cannot be generated from the safer categories. Where this happens, the proportion of sales to these customers should not deviate from a set level, the agreed price should reflect the increased risk and the accounts should be monitored closely.

Credit Collection

There are many techniques that can be used to assist with credit collection. These range from document design, offering cash discounts for early payment and having clearly agreed overdue account procedures.

Document Design

Invoices may be designed to include a detachable bank paying in slip or direct debit slip, to allow customers to process their payment with ease. A direct debit mandate may be agreed at the outset, and the invoice amount automatically transferred from the customer's bank account to the company's bank account within the specified credit period. Each statement should have a detachable part, which should be returned with payment. This will quicken the processing of payments by the credit department. Statements should detail payment address, details for the bank account to which the funds should be transferred, a contact name and a contact number for the customer to use, if there is a query. Queries should be appropriately recorded in a queries book or database and there should be a policy of dealing with queries within a pre-determined time frame.

Cash Discounts

Cash discounts are used as incentives to encourage customers to pay their accounts within a short period, which is usually shorter than the agreed credit period. Cash discounts are a reduction in the outstanding balance, usually by a set percentage and only apply until a set date.

Worked Example 8.4: Cash Discounts

Pero Plc offers its customers 30 days' credit; although customers normally take 45 days' credit. It is considering whether to offer a 2% discount for payment within 10 days.

Requirement Calculate the effective annual cost for Pero Plc of offering a 2% discount for payment within 10 days.

Solution

The cost of the discount is: 2 ÷ (100 − 2) = 0.0204% for a 35-day [i.e. 45 − 10] period.

Number of 35-day periods in a year is: 365 ÷ 35 = 10.43 periods.

Effective annual interest rate is: $(1.0204)^{10.43} - 1 = 23.44\%$

As is highlighted in **Worked Example 8.4**, cash discounts are expensive, therefore companies should only allow discounts in certain circumstances, as outlined in **Figure 8.6**.

Figure 8.6: When a Discount should be Offered

Discount Allowed

When there are liquidity problems and no cheaper source of finance is readily available.

When competitors provide discounts and failure to join the trend will result in lost sales.

When the discount will significantly reduce bad debts.

When the discount will attract new customers.

As discounts are not recoverable, they do not have an opportunity cost of finance; therefore, discounts are deducted from credit sales when determining the finance cost.

Worked Example 8.5: Cost of Finance – Net of Discounts

Gato Plc currently offers 60 days' credit to its customers (i.e. credit terms are net 60). Annual sales amount to €/£500,000 and are spread evenly over the year. The company's cost of funds is 16% per annum. A cash discount of 3% for payment by customers within 30 days is currently being considered (i.e. the revised credit terms would be 3/30, net 60). It is expected that 40% of customers would avail of the discount.

Requirement Determine whether the discount should be offered. Assume that all sales are on credit.

Solution

This can be assessed by calculating the cost of the current credit policy, relative to the alternative policy of offering the discount.

Current costs	**€/£**	**€/£**
Finance costs		
Customer balances requiring financing: [€/£500,000 × $\frac{60}{365}$]	82,192	
Cost of finance: [€/£82,192 × 16%]		13,151
Proposed costs		
Discount (40% of customers): [€/£500,000 × 40% × 3%]		6,000
Finance costs		
Customers with no change (60%): [€/£300,000 × $\frac{60}{365}$]	49,315	
Customers taking discount: [(€/£200,000 − €/£6,000) × $\frac{30}{365}$]	15,945	
Trade receivables balance requiring financing	65,260	
Cost of finance: [€/£65,260 × 16%]		10,442
Total proposed costs		16,442
Incremental cost of new scheme: [€/£16,442 − €/£13,151]		3,291

Therefore, the discount should not be implemented as this will increase credit costs by €/£3,291.

Late Payment Procedures

At the outset, customers should be categorised according to a risk assessment of their creditworthiness. This allows the more risky customers to be monitored closely. However, even with close monitoring, customer accounts may become overdue. Therefore, when accounts become overdue, a series of payment-collection steps should be followed, in order of severity, as outlined in **Figure 8.7**. In cases where, at the outset, a customer is categorised as having a high level of credit risk, then the credit policy should be strict in respect of breaches in the credit limit. Where breaches do occur, goods should not be supplied to the customer until earlier supplies are paid for. This will limit the exposure to even greater losses.

FIGURE 8.7: A POSSIBLE LATE PAYMENT PROCEDURE POLICY

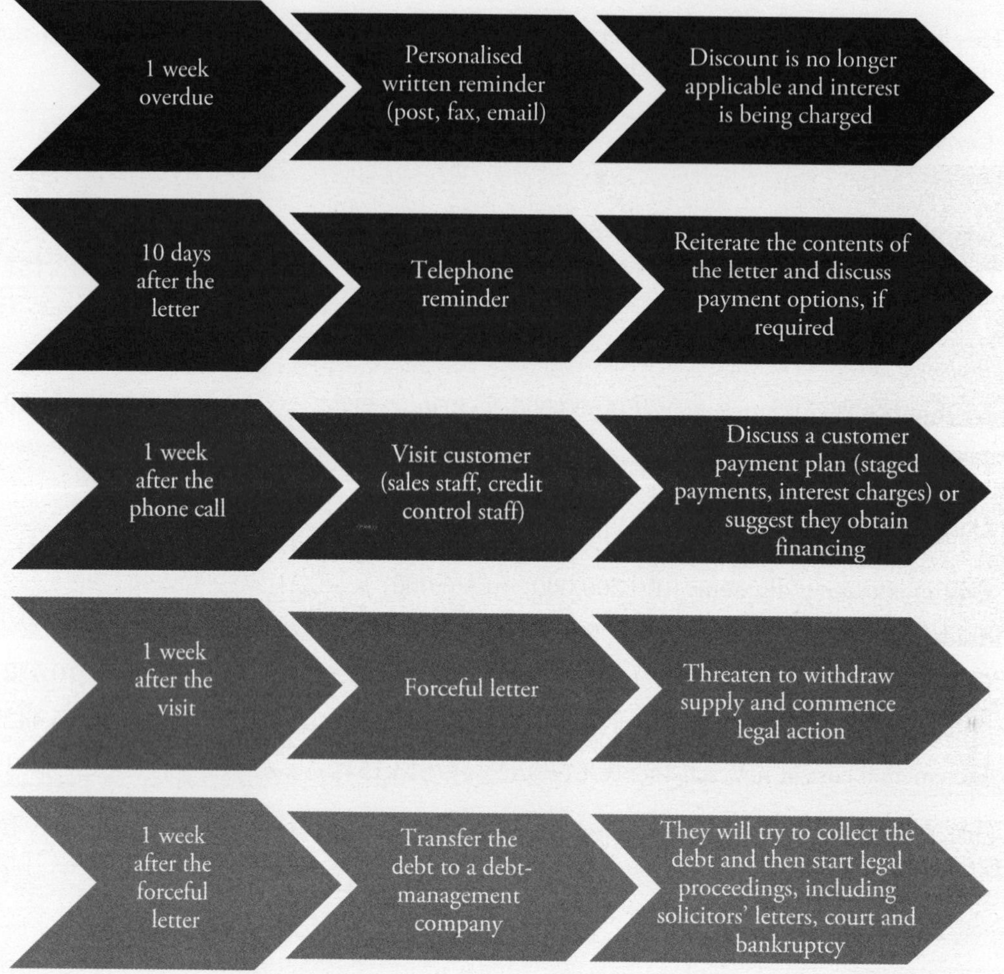

PROTECTION AGAINST BAD DEBTS

Industry bodies, such as the Confederation of British Industries, promote an overall prompt payment ethos in the business world. Support for companies on credit management policies and practices can be sourced easily on the internet. For example, several websites provide advice and guidance on how to establish and maintain a robust credit-management system, supplies information leaflets and provides information on legislation in respect of late payment. The authoritative legislation on late payment is the EU Directive on Late Payment. The aim of this legislation is to combat late payment in commercial transactions in EU companies. The existence of similar legislation across different countries should provide companies that trade in other EU countries with greater payment certainty. This legislation allows companies to charge interest when there is late payment of commercial debt, to claim reasonable compensation for debt-recovery costs incurred as a result of chasing late payments and to challenge grossly unfair terms and conditions where these undermine the legislation. It is worth noting that legislation in the UK may alter over the coming years as a result of Brexit.

REDUCING CREDIT RISK EXPOSURE

Steps that can be taken to reduce the risk of bad debts are outlined in **Figure 8.8**.

FIGURE 8.8: STEPS TO REDUCE THE RISK OF BAD DEBTS

Discounts: discounts for early settlement, as discussed earlier.

Percentage rebates for prompt payment: these are similar to discounts, though are usually linked to volume also. Like discounts, percentage rebates are expensive and should only be awarded when a customer pays on time.

Special payment terms: these may be started where a customer has been categorised as high risk and can include stopping supply and renegotiating the current debt or allowing a limited supply of goods for cash, or a shorter credit period while an agreement about the existing debt is made. When the existing credit balance is recovered, a short special credit period should be maintained, until confidence in the customer's financial position improves.

Part payment: this is typically used where a customer is regarded as being risky. A payment is required upfront and then in stages. The balance is usually payable within the normal credit period.

Payment protection insurance: where the sums involved are high and a customer is risky, it may be worthwhile having an arrangement with a finance house with a link to an insurance company to provide finance to the customer and to allow them to purchase payment protection insurance.

Legal expenses insurance: this may be purchased through a broker. Its aim is to cover the legal costs associated with bringing a customer to court to recover a debt. This can be a deterrent to some customers who might chance not paying their bill on the premise that it will cost too much to recover the debt.

Stakeholder accounts/secure deposits: the customer lodges funds for the goods or services with an independent intermediary. This type of arrangement is normally used where the customer has requested or purchased an item that has a long-term impact on the company providing credit; for example, a contract to construct a building. The sums involved are usually large and intermediaries are normally used as risk-reducing half-way houses to ensure that the company supplying the good knows that funds are available in an account for the sole purpose of paying for the project, and the customer has assurance that the funds will not be released until quality targets and set stages of the build are complete.

THE USE OF TECHNOLOGY IN CREDIT MANAGEMENT

Small, owner-managed companies can sometimes, if an owner is well organised and devotes sufficient time to credit management, operate without a formalised, effective credit-management system. However, the majority of companies need a formal system in place to keep track of transactions. A good customer management system will allow the collection, compilation, storage, analysis and retrieval of information. The main benefits are summarised in **Figure 8.9**.

Figure 8.9: Advantages of Information Technology for Credit Management

Saves time	Information technology usually saves credit control staff time as invoices are entered once by the sales department. In addition, a customer's credit agreement terms can be viewed at the touch of a button.
Monitoring tool	The accounting package can be programmed to monitor overdue accounts by highlighting those that are close to, or in breach of, their predetermined credit limits.
Decision-making	The system can be programmed to accept or reject a sale depending on the credit limit. This may be beneficial for front-line sales staff who can blame the system for a refused sale and not have to bear the brunt of customer dissatisfaction directed at them.
Documentation	The system can be programmed to produce standard invoices, statements, emails and reminder letters and to produce labels for envelopes.
Management by exception	This should improve credit managers' decision-making as they can focus on more risky customers. This is made possible by the use of exception reporting, wherein the system can produce aged analysis reports, payment pattern reports and forecast payment cycles. In addition, the system may generate a report that analyses the payment patterns by, for example, comparing a company's payment patterns with industry averages, analysing payment patterns by region or analysing payment patterns by product type.

In all instances, a cost–benefit analysis should be undertaken to determine whether a technological system should be used. The costs associated with a computerised credit management system include:

- the substantial capital investment required at the outset;
- training of credit control and sales staff at the outset and when there are upgrades; and
- software upgrades and computer maintenance costs.

OVERSEAS TRADING

Although it is a source of growth, overseas trading brings with it increased risks, in particular, currency exposure and credit risks. Managing these risks is costly and requires specialist knowledge about the foreign country. There may be different payment cultures, attitudes to credit limits and cash discounts that are country specific. Some guidance on the practices and economic climate in different countries can be sourced within the UK from the Department for International Trade (https://www.gov.uk/government/organisations/department-for-international-trade) and international insurance provider COFACE's website (www.coface.com). The latter site provides ratings, insolvency trends, collection methods, a payment incidents index and risk assessment, for different countries. Another useful website is the Credit Services Association website (www.csa-uk.com). It provides information on how to select an overseas collection agent and has a list of registered collection agent members.

Trade Receivables and Financing

A company's trade receivables are an asset. They represent monies that are due to a company in the short term. As such, they can be used by a company to raise funds. The two most common forms of security on trade receivables are the assignment of debt to specific invoices (such as invoice discounting or acceptance credits) or the sale of all customer accounts or a proportion of the total customer accounts or a collection of specific customer accounts, to a factor for an upfront amount. These sources of finance are discussed in detail in **Chapter 11**.

TRADE PAYABLES MANAGEMENT

Credit suppliers or creditors supply goods and services to a company in advance of receiving payment from the company. Therefore, they can be considered a source of finance to a company. In most instances, companies would not be able to trade if they did not receive trade credit from suppliers. Like the other working capital areas (inventory, trade receivables, cash), the aim of sound trade payables management is to maximise equity holder wealth. This involves minimising the costs of administering the trade payables function and maximising the opportunity gain from this low cost form of finance (by maximising the trade payables cash conversion period), while ensuring that supplies are not disrupted and discounts are taken when it is cost beneficial to do so. The policy to be followed by a company in respect of the payment of supplies should not be decided in isolation. The policy has to be viewed in terms of its impact on production, stores, costs and sales.

MEASURING THE TRADE PAYABLES PERIOD

As highlighted in **Chapter 6**, a simple means of determining a company's policy in respect of trade payables is to measure the length of the trade payables cash conversion period ratio. This ratio calculates the number of days that credit purchases are outstanding on average.

$$\textbf{Average trade payables cash conversion period} = \frac{\textbf{Trade payables} \times \textbf{365}}{\textbf{Credit purchases}}$$

Industry averages for this ratio are usually available and these can be used as a benchmark when assessing the efficiency of a company's trade payables management policies.

TRADE PAYABLES MANAGEMENT: A COST–BENEFIT ANALYSIS

Costs

Every company that operates on a credit basis has a higher administrative burden than a company that operates on a cash-only basis. Purchase ledger clerks need to be employed to manage suppliers' accounts. Most companies also require an appropriate computer software package to record and keep suppliers' account information up to date. The benefits of information technology are similar to those outlined above for trade receivables.

If a supplier feels that a company is abusing an agreed credit limit, then this will diminish supplier goodwill. The result is that the supplier may withdraw agreed cash discounts, remove trade discounts (pushing up purchase price), charge interest on overdue accounts and place *less* emphasis on getting supplies to a company promptly. The latter will increase the uncertainty of inventory lead time, causing stock-outs initially and subsequently causing the inventory manager to hold a higher level of safety inventories, which will result in higher inventory holding costs.

An additional cost is managerial time. An important aspect of trade payables management is the maintenance of good relations. Time should be scheduled for improving relations with the main suppliers, as this will increase the likelihood of negotiating a better price and will help to smooth over instances where a problem occurs (so long as this is not a frequent occurrence) – for example, where payment is not issued within the appropriate agreed timescale.

Benefits

As mentioned in the introduction to the section on the management of trade payables, receiving credit from suppliers is a source of finance. It is the same as receiving a free loan.

The benefit can be quantified as it equates to an opportunity saving in finance costs, which equals the amount of credit received multiplied by the relevant finance rate. Therefore, the longer the trade payables cash conversion period, the greater the benefit to a company. Availing of discounts receivable is also beneficial. As highlighted earlier in the trade receivables section, discounts allowed are costly to a company; therefore, in a similar vein, availing of cash discounts receivable is an attractive option, as highlighted in the next example.

Worked Example 8.6: Trade Payables – Discounts Received

Late Ltd normally pays its main supplier after 60 days. The supplier is offering a discount of 3% for payment in 10 days. Late Ltd has a cost of funds of 16%.

Requirement Advise whether Late Ltd should avail of the discount on offer.

Solution

The return on the discount is 3 ÷ (100 − 3) = 0.03092% for a 50-day [60 – 10] period

Number of 50-day periods in a year = 365 ÷ 50 = 7.3 times

Effective annual interest rate = $(1.03092)^{7.3} - 1 = 24.9\%$

This return is higher than the reported cost of funds (16%); therefore, Late Ltd should avail of the discount and pay its main supplier within the 10-day limit.

TRADE PAYABLES MANAGEMENT: POLICY AND PROCEDURES

Fostering a Strong Credit Reputation and Ethical Approach

In all instances, a company should negotiate a suitable credit policy with its suppliers, as discussed earlier in this chapter under 'Credit Policy'. Therefore, a starting point is to make the credit reputation of the company strong, as this will be used by a supplier to assess the level and length of period to allow credit. Some steps to improve, or create, a good credit reputation include:

- always paying bills on time;
- fostering good relationships with suppliers, who will then report positively on their experiences of trading with the company;
- getting listed with a credit-rating agency;
- filing financial statements and the annual return with the Companies Registration Office (in Ireland) or Companies House (in the UK) on time (if a limited company); and
- encouraging key personnel in the company to have good personal credit practices.

The latter is particularly important where a company is very small, as a supplier may request credit references for an owner or for directors.

Where the sums involved are material, the terms of the negotiations can be formalised into a written credit agreement. At this stage, it is up to managers to negotiate the best deal, in terms of purchase price, discounts, credit period and credit limit, with the supplier. This may be achieved by agreeing to direct a significant portion of the company's purchase requirements to the supplier.

Procedural Issues

When a credit agreement is finalised, the trade payables function should ensure that the maximum period of credit is taken, but not breached. This will involve checking that invoices are not received or dated until the date the goods or services are received. The credit period should start when goods arrive, not when an order is made. Where invoices have an earlier date, the supplier should be informed immediately and asked to reissue a correctly dated invoice. At this stage, the accuracy of the invoice should also be verified, by ensuring that stores have checked the goods received to the purchase order and the invoice. Problems should be immediately brought to the attention of the supplier. It is unethical to use a minor error as an excuse to delay payment where there is no issue with the quality of the product or service. If the error is material or if the quality of the product is an issue, then this is a different matter.

Where an invoice has been authorised by a purchases/stores manager for payment and the dates agreed, it should be inputted promptly into the system. This will ensure that management are fully aware of their company's financial commitments at all times, that cash flow forecasting is more accurate and that disputes can be settled more efficiently.

When statements arrive from suppliers, only the balance that is due for payment within the agreed credit period should be paid. Statements normally include **all** outstanding amounts. Where a discount is offered by a supplier for payment earlier than that negotiated in the original agreement, this should be referred to the payables manager immediately. The payables manager will undertake a cost–benefit analysis to compare the equivalent annual rate of the discount to the company's weighted average cost of capital. The manager should also consider the company's liquidity position, arrange additional financing through the treasury department if necessary, and inform creditor ledger staff of the decision in sufficient time to allow them to process the relevant payment earlier.

PAYMENT CULTURE/ETHICS

In the Republic of Ireland, the Prompt Payment of Accounts Act 1997, as amended by the European Communities (Late Payment in Commercial Transactions) (S.I. No. 580 of 2012), places a legal obligation on Plcs and private sector companies to pay their accounts within agreed time limits or face interest penalties. This interest is limited to the European Central Bank (ECB) rate plus 7%. In addition, the Regulations allow suppliers to claim compensation for debt-recovery costs, where applicable. The Act also placed a legal obligation on public bodies to publish a yearly report in respect of their payment policies.

In Great Britain and Northern Ireland, the Late Payment of Commercial Debts (Interest) Act 1998 allows businesses to claim statutory interest (set at the Bank of England Base Rate plus 8%) for late payments and gives them the right to claim reasonable debt-recovery costs. Small- and medium-sized companies also have a right to ask a representative body to challenge grossly unfair credit-contract terms used by customers.

To change the culture of taking long credit periods, the Confederation of British Industry (CBI) issued a *Prompt Payment Code,* which suggests that a responsible company should: have a clear, consistent policy that it pays its bills in accordance with; not extend or alter payment terms without prior agreement from a supplier; provide clear guidance on payment terms to suppliers; and ensure that an appropriate system is implemented for dealing with supplier disputes and complaints quickly. Detailed guidance on good management practices for dealing with suppliers and customers can be found by accessing its support website (http://payontime.co.uk).

In addition, the Chartered Institute of Credit Management administers the *Prompt Payment Code* for the Department for Business, Energy and Industrial Strategy (BEIS). The BEIS has also issued a report on large companies: *'Duty to Report on Payments Practices and Performance'*. This requirement, to report every six months on a government online site that is accessible to the public, has been compulsory for accounting periods beginning after 6 April 2017.

CONCLUSION

Credit managers should try to balance the cost of allowing credit with the benefits to be derived from the additional contribution earned because of allowing credit. Purchase managers should try to balance the benefits to be derived from paying for items quickly with the opportunity finance cost of allowing funds to leave the company before necessary.

Best practice includes having an ethical collection and payment policy, which is clearly defined in a written credit agreement. Each function should have clearly defined procedures and controls to ensure that personnel adopt an appropriate approach to dealing with customers/suppliers. Quality in these processes is vital for the smooth management of collection and payment functions. Information technology can greatly assist the management process within each function, by keeping an up-to-date database of the individual details of customer and supplier companies, providing exception reports, graphical patterns of customer and supplier behaviour, timely documents and letters and up-to-date information on balances. ePurchases and eSales can also save time and improve company profitability. However, the importance of human interaction with suppliers and customers cannot be overstated. In addition, the efficiency and accuracy of information that is input to computer systems influences the quality of reporting from the system.

EXAMINATION STANDARD QUESTION: CREDIT POLICY

(a) Outline the factors that a company should consider before giving credit to a new customer.

7 Marks

(b) Sedley Plc is a wholesale supplier of office stationery with an annual turnover of €/£1 million. It gives its customers 30 days' credit. Credit control has been very relaxed, but management has become concerned because customers are now taking an average of 60 days' credit and bad debts average 2% of total annual turnover.

Two options to improve the situation have been proposed.

(i) A discount of 2.5% could be offered to all customers who pay their debts within 20 days. It is expected that 60% of customers would pay within the discount period. The costs of administering this scheme are estimated at €/£3,000 per annum, but it is expected that bad debts would be reduced by 50%.

(ii) Sedley could use the services of a local credit control company to collect the debts on its behalf. Sedley would still be responsible for the debts. However, it is likely that the credit control company would take an aggressive approach to collection and that 70% of the debts would be collected within the official collection period of 30 days. The remaining 30% would continue to take the 60 days.

The fee for this service is 1.5% of annual turnover. However, bad debts are expected to fall to 30% of their original level and there would be administration savings of €/£7,000 per annum.

Annual turnover is expected to fall by €/£30,000 as a result of the aggressive approach of the credit control company.

The gross profit margin of Sedley is 20% and the cost of capital is 10%.

Requirement Recommend which option would be more profitable for Sedley, setting out clearly your reasoning and showing the calculations necessary to support your recommendation.

11 Marks

Total 18 Marks

(Based on Chartered Accountants Ireland, MABF II, Summer 2003, Q7)

Solution

(a) The main factors to be considered before giving credit to a new customer can generally be discussed using five Cs from the seven Cs of lending model (White 1990).

1. **Capacity:** refers to a customer's ability to repay. A credit check with a reputable credit agency, such as Experian, should be performed.
2. **Capital:** refers to the financial soundness of a potential creditor. The overall financial standing can be checked by analysing recent financial statements using ratio analysis.
3. **Conditions:** refers to the agreed terms of sale and 'normal' industry conditions.
4. **Character:** sources of character references include bank references, trade references, published financial statements, credit-rating agencies, etc. Generally, as a matter of course, references should be sought from a bank and at least two trading customers.
5. **Collateral:** refers to the value of security that a customer can offer, if any.

As well as the above, two other major considerations are the length of the credit period requested and the maximum value of credit allowed at any one time. These depend on the following:

- credit terms operating in the industry;
- degree of competition in the industry;
- bargaining power of particular customers (average purchase size);
- risk of non-payment; and
- marketing strategy.

(b) *Option 1: Discount scheme*

	€/£
Benefits:	
Bad debts reduction: [€/£1m × 2% × 50%]	10,000
Release of cash (W1)	6,493
Costs:	
Administration	(3,000)
Discount: [€/£1m × 2.5% × 60%]	(15,000)
Net Cost	(1,507)

W1: Finance saving from cash being made available	**€/£**	**€/£**
Existing investment in trade receivables:		
$[\text{€/£}1\text{m} \times 98\% \times \frac{60}{365}]$		161,096
New investment in trade receivables:		
$[\text{€/£}1\text{m} \times 60\% \times 97.5 \times \frac{20}{365}]$	(32,055)	
Plus: $[((\text{€/£}1\text{m} \times 40\%) - \text{€/£}10{,}000) \times \frac{60}{365}]$	(64,110)	(96,165)
Release of cash		64,931
Saving of 10% cost of capital: [€/£64,931 × 10%]		6,493

Option 2: Credit controller

Benefits:		**€/£**
Bad debts reduction		14,000
Administration		7,000
Release of cash (W1)		5,844
Costs:		
Release of cash (€/£970,000 × 1.5%)		(14,550)
Loss of turnover (€/£30,000 × 20% margin)		(6,000)
Net benefits		6,294
W1: Finance saving from cash being made available	**€/£**	**€/£**
Existing investment in trade receivables: [€/£1m × 98% × $\frac{60}{365}$]		161,096
New investment in trade receivables: [€/£970,000 × 70% × $\frac{30}{365}$]	(55,808)	
Plus: [((€/£970,000 × 30%) – €/£6,000) × $\frac{60}{365}$]	(46,849)	(102,657)
Release of cash		58,439
Saving of 10% cost of capital: [€/£58,439 × 10%]		5,844

Key Terms

Bad debts
Bank reference
Cash discounts
Credit agreement
Credit limit
Credit management
Credit monitoring
Credit period
Credit policy
Credit rating
Credit systems and procedures manual
Legal expenses insurance
Part payment
Payment protection insurance
Percentage rebates
Prompt action code of practice
Special payment terms
Stakeholder accounts/ secure deposits
Terms of sale
Trade credit
Trade creditors
Trade credit period
Trade debtors
Trade payables
Trade receivables
Trade reference

REVIEW QUESTIONS

(See Suggested Solutions to Review Questions in **Appendix B**.)

Question 8.1

What is the 80/20 rule?

Question 8.2

What steps should be taken when a customer starts to exceed their credit limit?

Question 8.3

Explain the term 'credit period'.

Question 8.4

Explain the term 'credit quality'.

Question 8.5

What are the costs and benefits associated with granting credit?

Question 8.6

Ocho Ltd has been offered an order for 10,000 computers at €/£500 per computer. The following table outlines the probability estimates of repayment terms:

Probability of repayment	Payment terms
10%	36 days
60%	45 days
20%	72 days
10%	Bad debt

Requirement Calculate the average level of trade receivables which must be financed were this order to be accepted.

Question 8.7

Insight Ltd is currently considering whether to expand into a new market. Revenue costs are projected as follows:

- It is estimated that sales in the new market will be €/£10 million per annum.
- 60 days' credit would be allowed.
- Insight Ltd earns a contribution margin of 20% on sales.
- Insight Ltd's suppliers give 30 days' credit.
- Collection costs are expected to amount to €/£100,000.
- The bad debt risk is estimated at 5% of sales.
- Inventories held by the company will increase by €/£1 million.
- Insight Ltd has an annual cost of funds of 12%.

Requirement Evaluate Insight Ltd's proposal to expand into the new market.

10 Marks

(Based on Chartered Accountants Ireland, CAP 1, Pilot paper, 2007, Q3)

Question 8.8

The directors of Weston Plc are concerned about the level of the company's interest payments. Financial information for two six-month periods is given below:

	January to June 20X5 €/£000	**January to June 20X7 €/£000**
Revenue	3,300	3,600
Credit sales as % of total revenue	85%	95%
Average trade receivables	700	1,350
Average inventories		
Raw materials	95	120
Work in progress	210	220
Finished goods	115	80
Average overdraft interest rate (% per year)	8.5%	17%

Requirement

(a) The directors have estimated that the interest cost of financing inventories and trade receivables has more than trebled in the period under investigation.
Evaluate Weston Plc's policy in relation to inventories and trade receivables over the period.
6 Marks

(b) Discuss strategies that the company could implement to reduce the interest cost of trade receivables and inventories.
6 Marks
Total 18 Marks

(Based on Chartered Accountants Ireland, MABF II, Autumn 1998, Q7)

Question 8.9

Design a risk-assessment checklist to be used in the monitoring of customer balances.

Question 8.10

What is the key aim in the management of payables and how can a company achieve this?

CHALLENGING QUESTIONS

(Suggested Solutions to Challenging Questions are available through your lecturer.)

Question 8.1 Murrell (Level 1)

You are a Chartered Accountant in Murrell Limited and you have been asked to advise the credit controller on how the company can reduce the rising cost of financing its receivables.

Murrell generated sales of €/£3,250,000 in 20X4. Variable costs are 83% of sales. 60% of the sales are on credit and this is expected to remain unchanged for the foreseeable future. 70% of the receivables take 30 days to pay and the remainder will take 60 days to pay. The bad debt provision is expected to be 1.5% of total sales (i.e. €/£3,250,000). Mary Lee, the credit controller of Murrell, is concerned with the rising cost of financing the receivables and forwarded the following options.

Option one Mary calculates that if the credit terms are relaxed and all receivables are given 60 days to pay, this would increase total sales by 15%. However, bad debts would increase to 3% of total sales.

Option two Offer customers who pay on credit a 1.5% discount for payment within 15 days. Mary expects that 80% of the customers who pay on credit would avail of the discount and the remainder would pay within 60 days. There will be no increase in sales; however, bad debts will be reduced to 1% of total sales.

Murrell pays interest at 11% per annum on its bank overdraft.

(***Note:*** assume 365 days in a year.)

Requirement

(a) Advise Mary Lee which option (if any) she should proceed with in order to reduce the rising cost of financing the receivables.

10 Marks

(b) Discuss any THREE advantages of information technology in credit management.

5 Marks

(c) An important aspect of working capital management is the management of trade payables. Trade credit is often mistakenly believed to be cost-free. You are required to briefly discuss this statement.

5 Marks

Total 20 Marks

(Based on Chartered Accountants Ireland, CAP 1, Autumn 2013, Q2)

Question 8.2 Mulligan (Level 1)

The financial controller of Mulligan Ltd is considering changing its existing prompt payment discount policy credit terms for trade receivables. The proposal is to increase the discount, from the present level of 2%, to 3%, when invoices are paid within 15 days. Annual credit sales are €/£1,600,000 and the revised policy is expected to increase sales by 5%. The average contribution margin is 25% of sales and the relevant cost of capital is 8% per year.

If the new policy is implemented, the following effects are expected (in addition to the impact on the level of sales):

	Present policy	**Proposed policy**
% value of customers taking discount	10%	25%
Average collection period	55 days	35 days
Bad debts as % of sales	4%	3%

Requirement

(a) Analyse the discount proposal and recommend whether or not it should be implemented. (***Note:*** assume a **360-day year** in all calculations.)

8 Marks

(b) Discuss how a company should evaluate trade credit applicants, to determine the amount and duration of any credit offered.

4 Marks

(Based on Chartered Accountants Ireland, CAP 1, Autumn 2011, Q1(a))

Question 8.3 Crunch (Level 1)

Crunch Confectionery Ltd is suffering a fall in sales of many of its product lines. Prior to a strategy meeting, all department managers have been asked by the managing director to review their activities. The accounts department has been asked to review specifically the company's credit control policy. At present the company offers 30 days' credit to customers subject to satisfactory trade references. It does not offer a discount for prompt payment, but does threaten to charge interest at 3% per month for late payments. In most cases the interest charged after 30 days is cancelled on receipt of payment. The marketing manager is critical of this policy as she regards it as pointlessly antagonising customers, and possibly a cause of lost sales. She points out that most customers take an average 45 days' credit and any tightening of this period would further jeopardise sales in today's difficult trading conditions.

Requirement

(a) Outline the advantages and disadvantages of introducing discounts for prompt payment by customers.

7 Marks

(b) Evaluate the approximate cost of offering 1.5% discount for payment within 10 days, if the normal credit period taken continues to be 45 days.

4 Marks

(c) Indicate FOUR important factors that should be considered when assessing the creditworthiness of new customers.

4 Marks

Total 15 Marks

(Chartered Accountants Ireland, CAP 1, Autumn 2009, Q4)

Question 8.4 Nash (Level 1)

Nash Ltd is a bulk manufacturer of leather footballs. Nash has recently been in discussions with its bank, which has decided to reduce the level of overdraft available to the company. Consequently, the management team of Nash has been reviewing the cash position of the company and is considering the credit period it is currently offering to its customers. Following this review, current details relevant to Nash can be summarised as follows:

- Nash allows credit on sales of 30 days. However, due to the loss of skilled credit control staff in recent times, customers are now taking an average of 50 days to pay;
- Bad debts amount to 1.75% of sales value;
- Sales for the forthcoming year are forecast at 1.2 million units at a selling price of €/£10 per unit;
- Nash uses an overdraft on which the bank charges interest at 10% per annum.

In order to improve its liquidity position, Nash is proposing to make the following changes:

1. The credit period should be relaxed from 30 days to 45 days. This new credit period will be strictly enforced.
2. Sales are expected to increase by 5% over the next year as a consequence of the increased credit period.
3. New credit control staff will be hired at an additional cost of €/£65,000 per annum. As a consequence, bad debts are expected to fall to 1.50% of total sales value.
4. It is estimated that additional administration costs of €/£25,000 per annum will be incurred to handle the increased sales volume.
5. There will be no change to the variable cost element of sales, which is currently 75%.

Requirement

(a) Calculate the impact the proposed changes will have on Nash's cash position and advise Nash whether it should proceed with the introduction.

6 Marks

(b) Outline FOUR sources which may be used by Nash in evaluating the creditworthiness of a potential new customer.

4 Marks

(c) Explain the content of an 'aged analysis of receivables' and list TWO benefits which it may provide for the management of Nash.

3 Mark

Total 13 Marks

(Based on Chartered Accountants Ireland, CAP 1, Finance, Summer 2018, Extract from Q2)

Question 8.5 Packard (Level 2)

(a) Define 'working capital' and discuss the main factors that determine the amount of investment in working capital.

6 Marks

(b) Packard Plc wishes to improve the collection of payments from its customers and is considering the introduction of a cash discount scheme to encourage early payment. In the financial year 20X3/X4, the company's sales (which are all on credit) were €/£2 million and its trade receivables at the year-end were €/£500,000.

The proposed discount scheme would offer a 4% discount for payment within 10 days and a 2.5% discount for payment within 30 days. It has been estimated that customers representing 30% of the sales will take advantage of payment within 10 days, and a further 20% will pay within 30 days. The remaining customers will not change their payment policy. The cost of finance for Packard is 12% per annum. It can be assumed that sales and payments are spread evenly over the year.

Requirement

(i) Calculate the current trade receivables cash conversion period and the trade receivables cash conversion period were the proposed discount scheme implemented.

4 Marks

(ii) Estimate the benefits and costs which would result from the proposed discount scheme and advise whether, on these criteria, the scheme should be implemented.

6 Marks

(iii) Comment on any qualitative factors which should be considered prior to implementation of a discount scheme.

2 Marks

Total 18 Marks

(Based on Chartered Accountants Ireland, MABF II, Summer 1999, Q6)

Question 8.6 Trade Receivables (Level 2)

(a) Outline briefly SIX procedures that a company could implement if it wished to keep good control over its trade receivables. State briefly the disadvantages associated with these procedures.

6 Marks

(b) A company currently has annual sales of €/£500,000 and an average collection period of 30 days. The company is considering a more liberal credit policy. If the collection period is extended, sales are expected to increase, but so too are the chances of bad debts arising. The following table summarises the current predictions:

Credit policy	Increase in collection period	Increase in sales (over current level) €/£	% Default (of total receivables)
A	10 days	25,000	2%
B	15 days	35,000	4%
C	30 days	38,000	6%
D	45 days	40,000	7%

The selling price is €/£2 per unit. Average total cost per unit at the current level of sales is €/£1.50 and variable cost per unit is €/£1.20. The current rate of bad debt losses is 1% of turnover. The cost of capital is 8%. Assume a 360-day year.

Requirement Decide which (if any) of the four proposals above should be adopted. Show clear workings in support of your answer.

8 Marks

(c) Describe briefly factoring and invoice discounting and describe one situation in which each might be useful to an entity attempting to raise funds (research the relevant information in **Chapter 11** before answering this part of the question).

4 Marks
Total 18 Marks

(Based on Chartered Accountants Ireland, MABF II, Summer 2008, Q6)

Question 8.7 Gula (Level 2)

Gula Ltd is a recently established company, purchasing electrical equipment for resale to building contractors and retail traders within Ulster and North Leinster. The terms of sale require payment within a month of invoicing. Customers do not adhere strictly to this and, being new in the marketplace, the company is not in a position to enforce very rigorous credit controls. However, it is anticipated that the company will have no difficulty in maintaining its current monthly sales at a constant value of about €/£150,000.

At present the average pattern of payment by customers is as follows:

Month 1	15%
Month 2	35%
Month 3	30%
Month 4	15%
Month 5	5%

The company relies heavily on bank finance at an existing interest rate of 2% per month. The managing director is anxious to reduce the cost of finance, and has suggested a possible alternative scheme.

Alternative scheme To give cash discount of 2.5% for payment within one month. It is believed that this will give a revised payment pattern as follows:

Month 1	40%
Month 2	30%
Month 3	10%
Month 4	15%
Month 5	5%

The additional cost of implementing improved credit control procedures would be €/£500 per month.

Requirement

(a) Detail at least FOUR steps that a company should undertake (either before or after the granting of credit) if it wishes to pursue a rigorous policy in relation to the collection of debts. Expand briefly upon the consequences of these steps.

6 Marks

(b) State the circumstances under which a customer might decide to take advantage of cash discount terms.

4 Marks

(c) Calculate the net present value of the cash flows arising from the sales in perpetuity under each of the following assumptions:

(i) That all customers always pay in full on the last day of the month in which a sale is made.

2 Marks

(ii) That the cash flows are in line with the existing credit terms being taken by customers.

3 Marks

(iii) That the cash flows followed the pattern described in the alternative scheme as proposed above.

(***Note:*** the discount factors for periods in years at annual rates are equally applicable to periods in months at monthly rates.)

3 Marks

Total 18 Marks

(Based on Chartered Accountants Ireland, MABF II, Autumn 2005, Q7)

9

Cash Management

Learning Objectives

Upon completing this chapter, readers should be able to:

- explain the objective of cash/float management;
- list the main sources and uses of cash in a company;
- discuss the motives and influences on the amount of cash to hold;
- outline the costs and benefits associated with holding cash;
- discuss ways to manage a cash float;
- calculate the costs to a company of implementing different float-management decisions;
- calculate the optimal lodgement policy for a company;
- recommend sources of short-term investment for surplus cash balances;
- recommend actions to be taken by a company when a deficit of cash is predicted;
- prepare cash budgets; and
- outline the benefits of cash budgeting.

INTRODUCTION

Sound cash management is vital for the survival of a company. A profitable company can fail if it does not maintain liquidity. Though 'cash is king', holding large cash balances may be detrimental to a company; funds held in cash have an opportunity cost as these funds could be invested elsewhere to earn a return. Therefore, cash management is concerned with maintaining a balance between servicing operating needs (liquidity) and earning maximum returns (profitability).

The introductory part of this chapter discusses uses of cash in a company, influences on the level of cash held by a company, underlying motives for holding cash, approaches to cash management and techniques used to manage cash. Then the practical aspects of cash management are discussed in two separate sections. The first considers float management and the second considers cash budgeting as a management and control tool.

The Importance of Good Cash Management

The importance of good cash management and how liquidity issues impact on the value of a company is emphasised in **Real World Example 9.1**.

Real World Example 9.1: Thomas Cook

Despite obtaining an emergency £300 million short-term credit line in May 2019, the tour operator and airline, Thomas Cook, ran out of cash and went into compulsory liquidation on 23 September 2019. The immediate result was that 21,000 employees lost their jobs and 600,000 customers were left stranded abroad. This included 150,000 UK citizens and triggered the UK's largest peacetime repatriation.

This example shows the cost of not having sufficient liquidity.

Cash Flows

The cash flows of a company are analysed separately for different stakeholders in a company's annual report and financial statements. The information is contained in a primary statement – the **statement of cash flows.** This statement shows the sources and uses of cash by a company in its financial year. It breaks cash flow activity into three main categories, as depicted in **Figure 9.1**.

Figure 9.1: Cash Flow Analysis in the Statement of Cash Flows

Cash flows from operating activities

This shows the cash that is generated from the continual operating activities of the company, including the tax effect and interest paid on finance used to service the operating activities.

Cash flows from investing activities

This details cash flows from the disposal or purchase of non-current assets and income or expenses resulting from investing activities that are not in direct support of operating activities, such as interest received or dividends received on investments.

Cash flows from financing activities

This includes cash flows relating to the financing of the entity, for example, proceeds received on an issue of shares or loan stock and related expenses, movements in interest-bearing loans and borrowings, and movements in finance lease liabilities. Equity dividends paid are also typically included under this heading.

THE OBJECTIVE OF CASH MANAGEMENT

Like the other working capital areas, cash management should focus on maximising equity holder return. This can be achieved by maximising the return that can be obtained from investing cash after having taken into account the costs associated with not maintaining an appropriate level of liquidity. The level of cash held by a company is also influenced by many internal and external factors.

INFLUENCES ON CASH BALANCES HELD

Cash is central to the operational activities of a company. This was highlighted in respect of working capital in **Chapter 6**. However, a standard approach to cash management is not suitable for all companies. Different companies pursue different working capital policies, operate in different markets with different products and may have branches in different countries. Some influences on cash management are now discussed. These have been categorised as internal or external.

Internal Influences

Type of Business

Though some companies have constant demand for their products throughout a year, other companies have varying levels of demand. Many companies have seasonal or cyclical sales. Polar examples of this pattern of seasonal business are the ice cream/swimwear/sunglasses industries and the umbrella/boots/scarf industries. Companies with **cyclical/seasonal cash flows** require strong cash management; they may have a cash demand for most of the year, with immaterial cash inflows, and huge cash surpluses in the remaining months.

Profitability

A company that generates profits each year should have a pattern of increasing cash. The objective of cash management in these circumstances should be to focus on maximising the return that can be generated from this cash (taking all other influences into consideration). In a loss-making company, the focus of cash management changes. It becomes more important to balance liquidity, as the survival of the company might be at risk. A loss-making company does not necessarily have liquidity issues, so long as cash flows are positive. In these circumstances the reported losses would be as a result of accounting adjustments for non-cash items, such as depreciation or movements in provisions. Liquidity difficulties will arise if losses are prolonged, as extra cash above and beyond the cash needed to cover running costs will be required to purchase capital and repay debt.

Strategy for Growth/Overtrading

The strategic goals of a company should be assisted by ensuring a company holds an appropriate level of cash. If a company is pursuing a growth strategy, then higher levels of cash need to be available to meet the increased working capital demands. In addition, a growing company usually requires capital investment. Capital investment requires funding, which is likely to have to be redeemed, hence has cash flow implications. Therefore, cash management needs to encompass the whole picture, which requires careful prediction and monitoring. When growth is not financed appropriately and liquidity problems are a real risk, then the company is regarded as overtrading.

Strategy for Capital Investment

Management may pursue a strategic policy of replacing capital items in a cyclical pattern (e.g it may be company policy to replace all sales representatives' cars every three years) or on a one-off basis (for example, when a production machine is starting to break down quite regularly). These decisions have cash implications and will influence the level of cash flow to be maintained by a company.

Strategy for Capital Structure

A company may have chosen a specific type of capital structure to minimise its cost of capital and subsequently optimise the value of the company (dealt with in **Chapter 16**). This will have cash flow implications. Debt usually has yearly cash outflows in respect of interest payable and capital redemption payments. The pattern of capital repayments depends on the type of debt used. Bank loans normally require periodic cash outflows, whereas loan stock may be converted to shares or redeemed using the proceeds of another debt issue. Equity share capital does not require repayment. However, equity usually has cash outflows – the majority of companies pay dividends. Dividends can result in one to four cash outflows in a year, depending on a company's dividend policy. How capital structure and dividend policy contributed to Thomas Cook's demise is outlined in **Real World Example 9.2.**

REAL WORLD EXAMPLE 9.2: THOMAS COOK

Thomas Cook's capital structure and dividend policy contributed to its demise. By 2019, the company had amassed £1.6 billion of debt and repayments had an adverse impact on its liquidity. To compound the financial distress, the company directors made the mistake of starting to pay a dividend in 2017. This decision undoubtedly amplified its liquidity problem.

External Influences

The Economy

The state of an economy will indirectly influence the level of cash a company should hold. This decision is risk-based and the risk of having a 'cash-out' is more costly when an economy is not strong, as short-term funding is not as easily obtained (for example, suppliers will not be happy if the credit payment period is lengthened). In these circumstances a company will have to hold a higher buffer level of cash. When an economy is in boom and the company is mirroring the success of the economy, then it is not as risky to have cash-outs (suppliers will not be too upset at not having been paid and bank credit lines are easily obtained) and lower levels of buffer cash can be held.

Inflation

When there is high inflation, the effect is similar to that of growth or overtrading. There is an increased working capital requirement that needs financing from a source beyond normal operating activities. This is even when a company is profitable, as the replacement cost of working capital, expenses and assets may outstrip the income that is profitably obtained from the sale of older items. In these circumstances, cash management is very important as the opportunity cost of getting it incorrect is quite high. This also applies to surplus cash in a high-inflation economy, wherein bulk-buying of supplies that are increasing quickly in price is a lucrative investment.

MOTIVES FOR HOLDING CASH

There are three motives for holding cash: transaction motive, precautionary motive and speculative motive, as explained in **Figure 9.2**. The extent to which these motives influence management will depend on management's attitude to risk, the economy and the strategic aim of a company.

FIGURE 9.2: MOTIVES FOR HOLDING CASH

Transaction motive	Holding sufficient levels of cash to ensure that the operating activities of a company are not disrupted by the non-payment of transactions. Ensuring cash is available to pay wages, heat and light, materials, stationery, consumables; for the replacement of capital, such as production machinery, cash tills, shelving; tax and payments required by financiers (interest, capital and dividends).
Precautionary motive	This is where there is a risk that actual cash outflows will exceed expected cash outflows, or actual cash inflows are less than expected cash inflows. The level of risk attributed to cash flows will influence the buffer level of cash a company holds. Companies with unpredictable sales demand or that are prone to strike action should, as a precaution, hold higher levels of cash than companies who do not deviate materially from their predicted cash flow projections.
Speculative motive	This is an investment strategy whereby excess cash is held so management can act quickly when profitable opportunities arise. These profitable opportunities are unexpected, hence cannot be planned for. The speed of access to cash gives management a comparative advantage over other companies. For example, a small supplier in financial difficulty may be open to a takeover bid or may allow a large discount for cash payment for its goods.

CASH MANAGEMENT: THE COST IMPLICATIONS

There are several costs associated with holding cash.

Costs Associated with Holding Too Much Cash

There are costs associated with holding cash, such as loss of interest were the funds to be invested (for example, in a deposit account or in short-term securities) and devaluation of the cash as inflation reduces its buying potential

Costs Associated with Holding Insufficient Cash

The costs associated with holding insufficient cash include higher bank interest and fees, where a company has to obtain an overdraft or breach an overdraft limit. Where a company has funds that are invested in short-term securities, penalties associated with having to draw down time-related investments before their maturity date may be incurred. When there is insufficient cash many companies delay the payment of suppliers, which may result in ineligibility for a cash discount. Indeed, if a company does not pay within an agreed credit period, this may negatively affect the relationship with the supplier, resulting in a reduction or loss of trade discount in the future, and may even threaten the supply of goods. The overall cost to a company will vary depending on the substitutability of suppliers. An indirect consequence of extending the credit period taken without permission from suppliers may be a reduction in the credit rating and reputation of a company, which will have future ramifications for the company when it tries to obtain credit or finance. When too little cash is held, a company could end up in liquidation if something unexpected happens, such as a fire in a store, a strike by the workforce or a legal claim against the company. Finally, a company will incur opportunity costs by not holding cash for speculative purposes, as profitable opportunities will be foregone.

CASH MANAGEMENT TECHNIQUES

Cash management is all about managing cash so as to minimise the overall cost to a company. There are three main areas in relation to cash that require management: cash float management, cash investment management and cash budgeting.

Cash Float Management

The term **cash float period** is used to describe the period of time between the point at which payment is initiated (for example, when a customer decides to pay their balance) and when the cash is cleared for use in the company's bank account. This can be substantial when a customer pays by cheque, as shown in **Figure 9.3**.

FIGURE 9.3: POTENTIAL FLOAT PERIOD

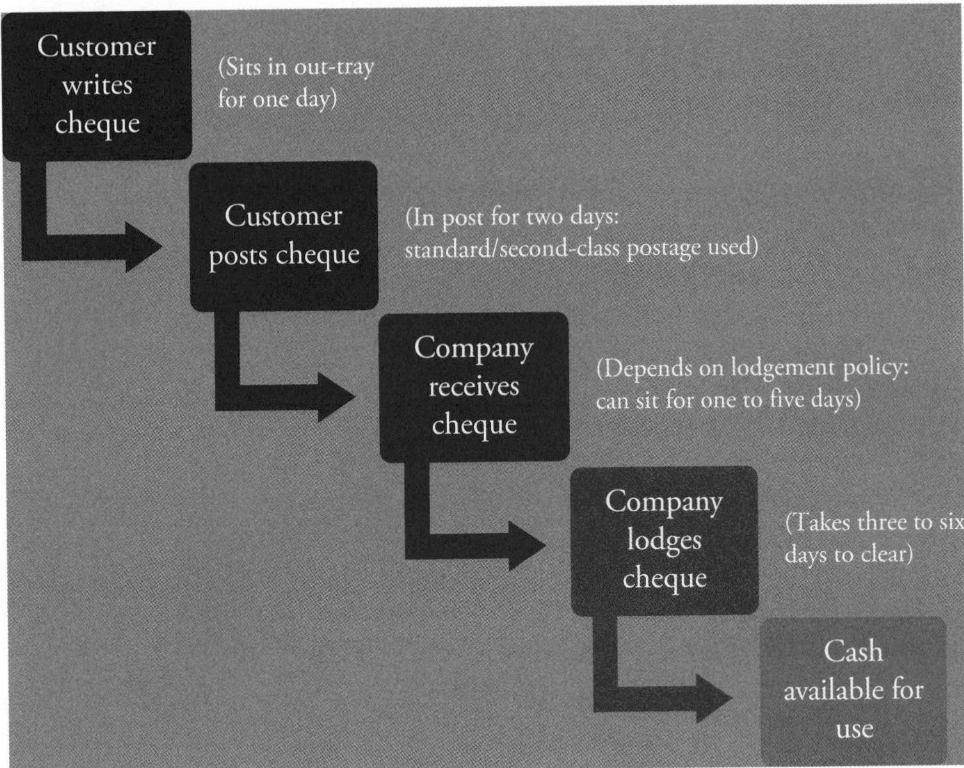

Inefficient Credit Procedures

If the inventory, sales and credit-control departments do not have in place a system that allows prompt communication between departments, then the period of time before cash is usable is lengthened. Stores need to inform the sales department when goods leave. The sales department should issue an invoice immediately and inform the credit control department, which will start the debt-collection process. This is dealt with in depth in **Chapter 8**.

Transmission Delay

Transmission delay refers to the period of time that a payment spends travelling between a customer and a supplier. Most companies make payments using electronic transfers, which take a day or two to clear. However, it is possible to pay the bank to process immediate clearance.

WORKED EXAMPLE 9.1: TRANSMISSION DELAY

Overdrawn Ltd seems to be in a permanent overdraft situation, on which it pays interest at a rate of 10%. Overdrawn Ltd's new financial accountant has suggested that, if the bank was paid to process the electronic transfer immediately, then considerable savings on overdraft interest would result. Assume banks charge €/£10 for immediate clearance.

Requirement Calculate the minimum value at which immediate clearance should be arranged assuming:
(a) a one-day delay in normal electronic transfer clearance;
(b) a two-day delay in normal electronic transfer clearance.

Solution

When the company saves €/£10 in interest, then this will cover the cost of the immediate clearance and result in a net benefit to the company. Therefore, the amount should be of sufficient size to earn 10% interest in one day. The amount is represented by y.
(a)

$$y = \frac{\text{€/£}10}{10\% \div 365} = \text{€/£}36{,}500$$

Only amounts of €/£36,500 or over should be collected by immediate clearance.
(b)

$$y = \frac{\text{€/£}10}{10\% \div (365/2)} = \text{€/£}18{,}250$$

Only amounts of €/£18,250 or over should be collected by immediate clearance.

The fee that banks charge for this service varies and should be negotiated with the bank on a regular basis.

Lodgement Delay

Lodgement delay is the delay in banking payments that have already been physically received by a company. Companies may have a policy in place of banking monies received every day, or every two days, or every week. This delay has a cost as the cash could be used to reduce an overdraft, hence save interest costs, or could be invested in a new project, which could earn a good return. When assessing a company's lodgement pattern, a cost–benefit analysis is required. This will balance the cost of lodging daily (e.g. transaction fee, opportunity loss from revenue that could be earned in the time taken to visit the bank, and possibly travel expenses).

Worked Example 9.2: Lodgement Delay

Weekly Ltd has €/£25 million of sales in the year. Most of these are paid by debit/credit card, however €/£2,880,000 is received in cash. These cash payments are received evenly over 360 working days. Weekly Ltd goes to the bank every five days to lodge all the cash receipts for the week. Weekly is always in overdraft and pays an interest rate of 12% per annum. The company estimates that cash lodgements incur administration costs of €/£10 per lodgement. There are only 360 working days in the year. Assume the bank is open every working day.

Requirement Calculate the optimal lodgement schedule.

Solution

The way to work out the optimal lodgement schedule is to calculate the costs associated with every possible scenario: lodge daily or lodge every two, three, four, or five days. The objective of this exercise is to find the policy that minimises total costs (administration costs and interest foregone).

$$\text{Daily sales are: } \frac{\text{€/£}2{,}880{,}000}{360} = \text{€/£}8{,}000$$

Interest paid on each day's takings not lodged is:

$$\text{€/£}8{,}000 \times \frac{12\%}{360} = \text{€/£}2.67 \text{ per day}$$

Scenario 1: Lodge daily (total costs)

	€/£
Administration fee:* [360 × €/£10]	3,600.00
Interest lost	–
Total cost	3,600.00

*The administration fee is: number of lodgements × cost per lodgement.

Scenario 2: Lodge every two days (total costs)

	€/£
Administration fee: [(360 ÷ 2) × €/£10]	1,800.00
Interest lost: [(360 ÷ 2) × €/£2.67]	480.60
	2,280.60

Scenario 3: Lodge every three days (total costs)

	€/£
Administration fee: [(360 ÷ 3) × €/£10]	1,200.00
Interest lost: [(360 ÷ 3) × €/£2.67 × 3]**	961.20
	2,161.20

**By lodging every three days, interest will be lost on the first day's takings for two days and on the second day's takings for one day (total 3 days).

Scenario 4: Lodge every four days (total costs)

	€/£
Administration fee: [(360 ÷ 4) × €/£10]	900.00
Interest lost: [(360 ÷ 4) × €/£2.67 × 6]***	1,441.80
	2,341.80

***By lodging every four days, interest will be lost on the first day's takings for three days, on the second day's takings for two days, and on the third day for one day (total six days).

Scenario 5: Lodge every five days (total costs)

	€/£
Administration fee: [(360 ÷ 5) × €/£10]	720.00
Interest lost: [(360 ÷ 5) × €/£2.67 × 10]	1,922.40
	2,642.40

The optimum policy is to lodge the takings every three days. At present the lodgement policy costs the company €/£2,642.40. This will fall by €/£481.20 to €/£2,161.20 if the company starts to lodge every three days instead.

Clearance Delay

Clearance delay refers to the time it takes for a bank to clear a cheque. If a customer writes a cheque from the same branch to which the cheque is lodged, then clearance might only take one day. If the lodgement is to the same bank but the account is in a different branch, then clearance normally takes three days. If the lodgement is to a different bank in the same country, clearance can take five or six days. If the lodgement is to a bank in a different country, then clearance can take a minimum of six days. This process can be expedited by commissioning the bank that receives the cheque to apply through the **Clearing House Automated Payments System (CHAPS)** for immediate clearance. This service normally attracts a fee and therefore should only be pursued if the interest to be saved or earned by having the cash cleared more quickly exceeds the fee for the facility. A similar calculation to **Example 9.1** is required. As a result of this, the majority of companies insist on electronic payment from customers.

Reducing the Float Time Delay

Some management techniques used to reduce transmission and lodgement delay are outlined in **Figure 9.4**.

Figure 9.4: Steps to Take to Reduce Transmission and Lodgement Delay

Bank giro credit slips	Encouraging customers to initiate payments themselves by supplying a bank giro credit slip at the bottom of invoices and/or statements.
Bankers' Automated Clearing Services (BACS)	Set up a BACS payment system. Payments are usually cleared within two days of being initiated by a company.
Direct debit or standing orders	Direct electronic transfers from a customer account to the company account. **Standing orders** are set amounts that are paid at set times. To encourage this form of payment a discount is usually offered. **Direct debits** are variable amounts and can be paid out on variable dates.

CASH INVESTMENT MANAGEMENT

Cash balances held in a bank's current account earn marginal returns. It makes good cash management sense to invest surplus funds to earn a higher return, whilst maintaining liquidity. Funds that are identified as being long-term surpluses can be invested in long-term projects or investments, which usually earn the highest returns. However, to maintain liquidity, a set amount should be readily available to meet cash demands. There are several short-term options available to management for this purpose. Some of these are now described.

Bank Deposit Accounts

The main types of bank deposit account are outlined briefly in **Figure 9.5**.

FIGURE 9.5: KEY TYPES OF BANK DEPOSIT ACCOUNT

Normal deposit account	Attracts a slightly higher interest rate than a current account. Funds can typically be withdrawn and deposited without incurring bank fees. These accounts sometimes have bonuses at the end of each year, where funds have remained intact for the year.
Term deposit account	Attracts a higher interest rate than a normal deposit account. Funds are lodged for a fixed period, ranging from one month to several years. The interest rate allowed by a bank is usually related to the length of time funds are locked in and the bank's base rate. Fixed interest rates can be negotiated for long-term fixed deposits. When funds are withdrawn before term, there is usually a penalty.
Certificates of deposit	Deposits at a fixed interest rate for a fixed period. These usually cover periods ranging up to 13 months. These can be sold in the money markets.

Treasury Bills

Treasury bills are short-term government bonds that have a term of 1 to 364 days. They are sold at an auction and the most common durations are 1 month, 3 months and 6 months. They do not attract an interest rate but are issued at a discount, and hence have an implied rate of interest. They can be re-sold in the money markets at any time: this will incur a broker's fee and the price obtained may not be as good as the return that could be earned were the bill held to maturity. A company with surplus funds can purchase a discounted treasury bill at the auction and receive the full amount back at the end of the bill's life.

Money Market Funds

Money market funds are low-risk investments that are offered by finance houses. The funds are made up of short-term commercial bonds, commercial paper and overnight bank deposit products. The return on the underlying products is typically interest. The aim is not growth, but maintenance of value and a small return. Though low-risk, it is still an investment account and as such its value can go down. The rate negotiated usually depends on the size of a deposit and the term required. The advantages and disadvantages of money market accounts are outlined in **Figure 9.6**.

FIGURE 9.6: MONEY MARKET ACCOUNT ADVANTAGES AND DISADVANTAGES

ADVANTAGES	DISADVANTAGES
Responsive: variable rates, which are beneficial if rates increase.	**Minima:** usually requires deposits of at least €/£25,000.
Flexible: durations can vary from one day to one year.	**Commission:** varies between banks.
Convenient: easy to set up, change and cancel.	**Competitiveness:** so much competition in the deposit account market means the money market accounts are less attractive.
Renewal: can be automatically renewed, including interest accrued.	**Availability:** fewer banks are offering money market accounts.

Stock Market

Stocks can be purchased or sold within the same day. However, this is a risky strategy as the value of the amount deposited (used to purchase shares) can fall as well as rise and there are transaction costs.

CASH BUDGETS

A **cash budget** is a monthly/weekly running account of the expected cash income and expenditure of a business. It projects expected cash inflows and outflows into the future. It is seen as a key planning tool, not only for cash management but also for dividend, investment and finance decisions, as it can help predict future liquidity. It is also used as a control tool: the actual cash flows can be compared to budgeted cash flows and questions can be asked or investigations sparked into areas where there are deviations from the plan. This can be used for **management by exception**, wherein management's attention is directed at problem areas and not wasted on managing areas that are performing according to plan.

In terms of cash management, the cash budget can identify whether a deficit/surplus is expected. It can also estimate whether this deficit/surplus is long-term or short-term. This assists a business finance manager in their decision on the best course of action to deal with the deficit/surplus. Some suggestions are included in **Figure 9.7**.

Figure 9.7: Possible Uses for Short-term Cash Surpluses

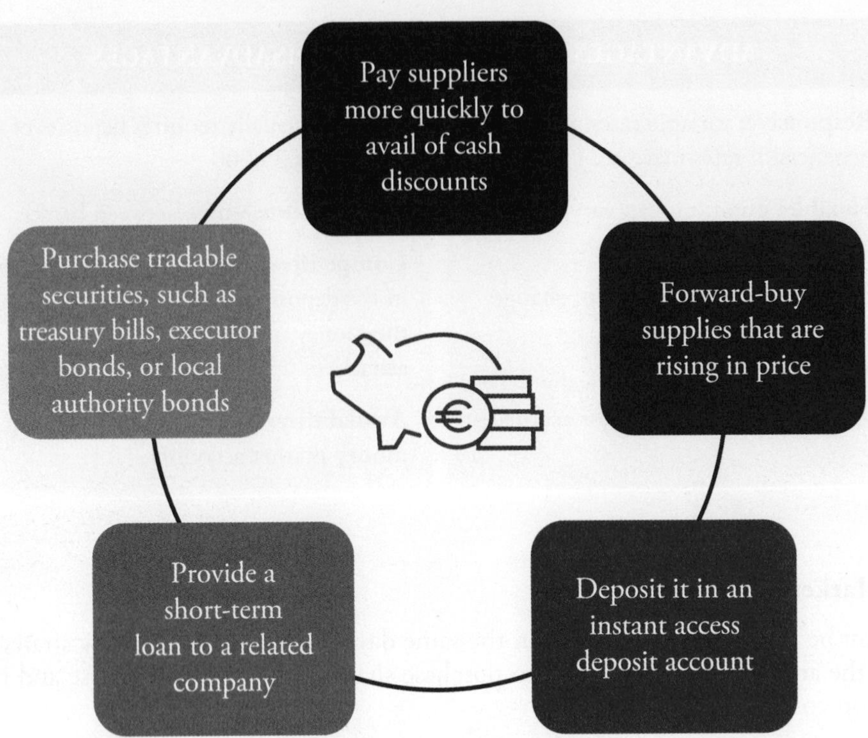

Where a surplus is regarded as long-term, a business finance manager might consider investing in long-term securities, buying additional non-current assets, paying back debt, repurchasing equity, or investing in another business. This puts the business finance manager in a position to suggest changes in the strategic decisions of a company. Decisions might include, for example, changing the dividend policy, changing the capital structure of the company or undertaking a new investment.

If a cash budget predicts a short-term cash deficit, then a business finance manager would put in place actions to alleviate the liquidity problem. Readily available cash is vital for the operational survival of an entity. Some expenses cannot be stalled, such as wages or utility bills. Actions taken by a business finance manager when short-term deficits are predicted are outlined in **Figure 9.8**.

Figure 9.8: Action to Alleviate Short-term Deficits

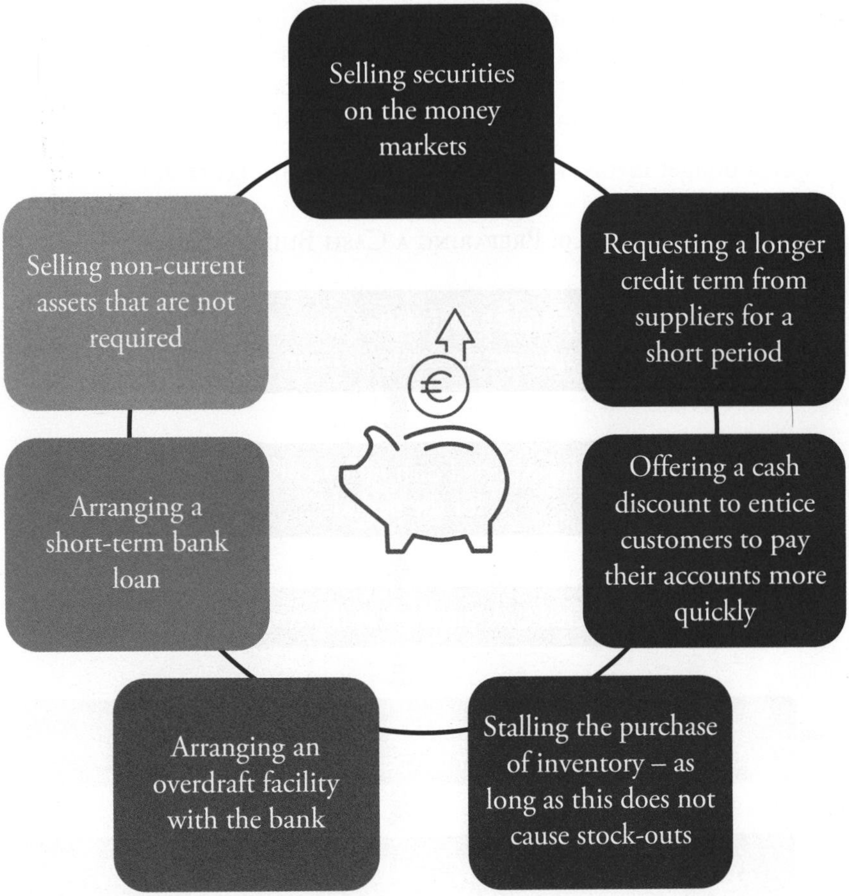

Selling securities on the money markets

Requesting a longer credit term from suppliers for a short period

Offering a cash discount to entice customers to pay their accounts more quickly

Stalling the purchase of inventory – as long as this does not cause stock-outs

Arranging an overdraft facility with the bank

Arranging a short-term bank loan

Selling non-current assets that are not required

Where the deficit is regarded as being long-term, then a business finance manager should start negotiations to, for example:

- raise a long-term loan;
- sell unwanted non-current assets;
- sell long-term investments that are not required for operational duties;
- issue debt securities; or
- issue equity share capital.

Ethical Issues

The actions outlined in **Figures 9.7** and **9.8** assume that a company is profitable or is loss-making in the short term, but will be profitable in the future. Where a company is loss-making and the cash flows are decreasing, a business finance manager should discuss this with the board of directors and possibly suggest that the company apply for voluntary liquidation.

Preparing a Cash Budget

The cash budget deals only with expected cash flows. It does not deal with non-cash transactions, such as depreciation, bad debts, discounts or movements on provisions.

These items are included in the statement of profit and loss. To provide a check on the accuracy of the master cash budget it should be integrated with the budgeted statement of profit and loss and budgeted statement of financial position. The opening cash balance on the opening statement of financial position should form the opening balance of the cash budget, and the closing balance on the cash budget should equate to the closing cash balance on the expected closing statement of financial position.

Preparing a cash budget involves five steps, as outlined in **Figure 9.9**.

Figure 9.9: Preparing a Cash Budget (Steps)

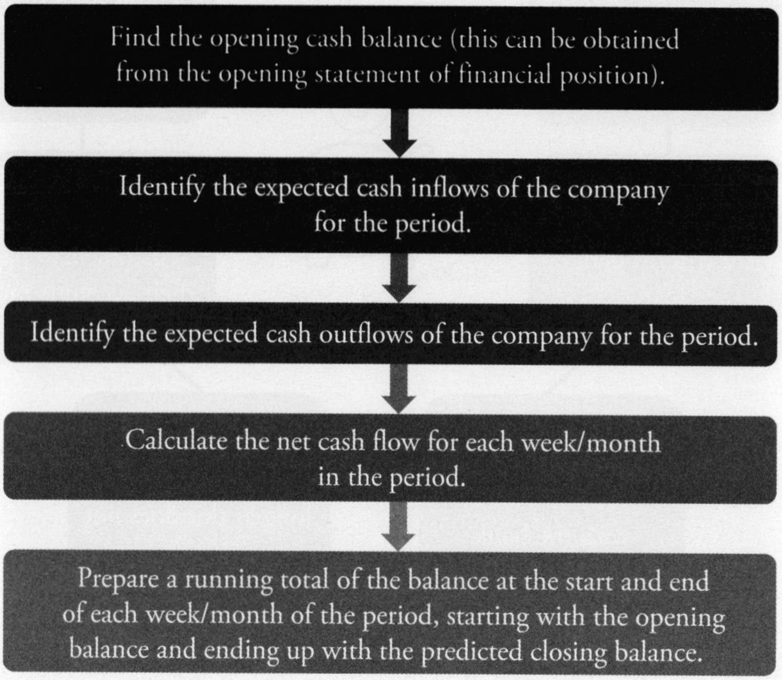

Find the opening cash balance (this can be obtained from the opening statement of financial position).

↓

Identify the expected cash inflows of the company for the period.

↓

Identify the expected cash outflows of the company for the period.

↓

Calculate the net cash flow for each week/month in the period.

↓

Prepare a running total of the balance at the start and end of each week/month of the period, starting with the opening balance and ending up with the predicted closing balance.

Worked Example 9.3: Cash Flows from Sales

Pajaro Ltd estimates the percentage of its customers that pay within certain timescales as follows:

1 month	30%
2 months	60%
3 months	5%
Bad debts	5%

The expected sales activity for Pajaro Ltd for the four months from November to February is:

November	€/£90,000
December	€/£120,000
January	€/£150,000
February	€/£100,000

Requirement

(a) Show the expected cash flows for January and February.

(b) What are the statement of profit or loss sales entries for these two months? Will there be any other entries in the statement of profit or loss in respect of the above information?

(c) What is the statement of financial position entry for trade receivables at the end of February?

Solution

(a) The cash flows for each month's sales span a three-month period. January's total cash flow will include cash received from sales made in November, December and January. Therefore, a spreadsheet showing accounting sales and resultant cash flows should be prepared for the period November–May.

Schedule of sales and resultant cash flows for the period November to May

	Nov	**Dec**	**Jan**	**Feb**	**Mar**	**Apr**	**May**
	€/£	**€/£**	**€/£**	**€/£**	**€/£**	**€/£**	**€/£**
Sales	90,000	120,000	**150,000**	**100,000**	–	–	–
Cash flows							
Within 1 month (30%)	–	27,000	36,000	45,000	30,000	–	–
Within 2 months (60%)	–	–	54,000	72,000	90,000	60,000	–
Within 3 months (5%)	–	–	–	4,500	6,000	7,500	5,000
Total expected cash	–	27,000	**90,000**	**121,500**	126,000	67,500	5,000

The pattern of expected cash from November's sales is highlighted by shading in the above schedule.

The expected cash inflow from sales in January is €/£90,000, with €/£121,500 expected in February.

(b) The budgeted statement of profit or loss will disclose sales of €/£150,000 for January and €/£100,000 for February. In addition, it will also include the expected bad debts for this period that relate to the sales in the period.
These will amount to €/£12,500 [(€/£150,000 + €/£100,000) × 5%].

(c) Trade receivables will amount to the cash outstanding at the end of February.
This is €/£198,500 [€/£126,000 + €/£67,500 + €/£5,000].

Advantages of Cash Budgets

Cash budgets increase the quality of planning within an organisation as they can provide a clear picture of the timing of cash flows. This allows a business finance manager to manipulate cash flows to attain cash flow synchronisation. **Cash flow synchronisation** refers to the matching of cash inflows to cash outflows. A good example of this is the policy of paying suppliers at the end of each month, and insisting on payment from customers by the end of the month.

Cash budgets can also be used to maximise the return receivable from surplus cash by providing information on the amount of cash and period of time that cash is available. Where deficits are predicted, the most cost-effective and appropriate finance can be obtained in time ensuring that the operational activities of a company are not disrupted. One-off cash outflows can be planned for, such as taxation liabilities, dividend payments, repayments of bank loans or capital expenditure. Moreover, cash budgets can help inform the term and pattern of repayments that a company should agree to pay to their financers.

ETHICS AND MONEY LAUNDERING

Ethics: The Management of Cheques

Many payments in the business world are conducted electronically – direct debits, standing orders, BACS or CHAPS. However, cheques are still regarded as an important payment method, particularly for small companies. Where cheques are written manually, care should be taken to ensure that the cheque is legible and for the correct amount. All parts of a cheque should be completed and if changes are made, these changes should be signed. The written amount of a cheque should equate to the numbers and any blank spaces on a cheque ruled out with a pen. Cheques should be crossed 'account payee only' and dated with the day the cheque is written.

It is bad practice to post-date cheques, as this will only cause problems in the banking system. Indeed, the cheque may get processed anyway irrespective of the date, causing a company liquidity problems or even causing the bank to dishonour ('bounce') the cheque. It is bad etiquette to knowingly complete a cheque incorrectly. Though this would allow a company to state that it had written and posted a cheque, it will cause a serious delay for the company waiting for the payment, as the cheque could be returned from their bank and a duplicate cheque would have to be requested.

Ethics: Money Laundering

Businesses that deal mostly in cash are sometimes the target of criminals who wish to legitimise illegal cash. Businesses should not engage in money laundering and finance managers are liable to prosecution if they are involved in this activity. Indeed, finance managers will still be liable even if they are not actually involved in money laundering, but know that it is going on. This is commonly known as **wilful blindness** and is an offence. Tipping off a money launderer or giving advice to them is also a criminal offence. **Money laundering** involves exchanging money or assets that were obtained criminally for money or other assets that are 'clean'. It typically involves engaging in financial transactions to hide the identity, source and destination of money or money value. Any financial transaction that generates an asset (tangible or intangible), reduces a liability from an illegal act, constitutes tax evasion or false accounting is considered to be money laundering. Money laundering typically has three stages:

- The first is called either 'placement' or 'hide' and refers to the point of entry of illegal cash to the economy.
- The second is called 'layering' or 'moving' and refers to the actions taken by a money launderer to obscure the link between the criminal and the money. This can involve the money launderer setting up captive businesses, which mostly deal in cash, and introducing some of the funds through this, or setting up a network of shell companies, holding companies and offshore accounts to process the cash through.
- The third and final stage is called 'integration' or 'investing' and refers to the return of the funds through the legitimate economy to the criminal for investment.

An individual can be imprisoned for up to 14 years for participating in a money laundering offence.

Money Laundering: The United Kingdom

In the UK, money laundering is regulated under the Money Laundering Regulations 2019. The regulations are designed to protect the UK financial system. The regulations apply to a number of different business sectors, including financial and credit businesses, accountants, solicitors and estate agents. These businesses must be supervised by a supervisory authority, such as the ICAEW Regulatory Board (IRB) or the Financial Conduct Authority, or must register directly with HMRC. Businesses must put in place controls, including assessing the risk of money laundering, checking the identity of 'beneficial owners' of corporate bodies, appointing a 'money laundering reporting officer', training staff about money laundering, checking the identity of customers and keeping relevant documentation, to prevent the business from being used for money laundering by criminals or terrorists (HMRC website, 2019).

The regulations cover typical money laundering activity but go further to include other transactions that may not involve any laundering activity – the legislation is relevant when a criminal has possession of stolen assets. These assets would not have been typically 'laundered', however they are considered to be 'money laundering'. All individuals in the UK are required to report suspicious activities in relation to any asset to the National Crime Agency. An individual can be imprisoned for a period of up to five years for failing to report a suspected money laundering offence. There is no lower limit on the amount to be reported. Any involvement with suspected 'dirty money' or 'dirty assets' is an offence. In a business, employees must report their suspicions to the money laundering reporting officer, who then deals with SOCA.

Money Laundering: The Republic of Ireland

In Ireland, money laundering is regulated under the Criminal Justice (Money Laundering and Terrorist Financing)(Amendment) Act 2018. This Act reflects the requirements of the fourth EU Anti-Money Laundering Directive (2015/849/EU). The Central Bank of Ireland monitors credit institutions and financial institutions. Some professions have competent authorities, such as the Law Society of Ireland for solicitors and the Chartered Accountants Ireland Professional Standards Board (PSB). The Anti-Money Laundering Compliance Unit (AMLCU), under the Minister for Justice and Equality, is the competent authority for any other designated person, including auditors, tax advisors, bookmakers, private members clubs, trust and company service providers and businesses that trade in goods where cash payments may exceed €10,000.

The law is as wide as that in force in the UK. It also goes further than dealing with the conversion and concealment of money to include other transactions that may not involve any laundering activity. Possession, acquisition or use of illegal assets are considered to be categories of the crime of money laundering. Tax evasion is also considered to be a form of money laundering. All individuals in the Republic of Ireland are required to report suspicious activities in relation to any asset to the Garda Síochána and the Revenue Commissioners. An individual can be imprisoned for a period of up to five years for failing to report a suspected money laundering offence. There is no lower limit on the amount to be reported. Any involvement with suspected 'dirty money' or 'dirty assets' is an offence. A conviction of money laundering may result in a fine of up to €5,000 and/or a jail sentence of up to 14 years (AMLCU, 2019).

CASH MANAGEMENT: GROUP ENTITIES AND FOREIGN TRANSACTIONS

Where a company has subsidiaries or branches, it makes sense to centralise the cash function. This is possible with relative ease due to the growth in internet banking. A group can have many bank accounts and can undertake transfers between accounts when surpluses and deficits arise. This will reduce the overall banking fees and interest costs. Many banking internet sites provide information on exchange rates, interest rates and short-term deposit rates, making the management of cash easier. A company can make better use of surplus cash, which overall might be a substantial sum, but across individual accounts are of insufficient size to manage on their own.

CONCLUSION

Cash is the lifeblood of any company and its management is crucial to the operational success of a company. Cash management should aim to maximise profitability whilst maintaining adequate liquidity. This can be achieved by good planning and control of cash. A company should have a strong policy for the collection of debt, the minimisation of the float period and an appropriate investment policy for surplus cash. Cash budgets should be prepared on an ongoing basis. These are particularly important to a company that has seasonal activities and one-off flows, such as the purchase or sale of non-current assets, dividend payments or loan repayments. However, cash budgets can also integrate the impact of growth and inflation on cash flows and can visibly portray the impact of this.

EXAMINATION STANDARD QUESTION: CASH BUDGET

Satu Plc plans to establish a subsidiary to manufacture and sell a new product. The following estimates of sales and production have been made for the first six months of the life of the new company, this being regarded as the critical setting-up period.

Month	Sales units 000	Production units 000
1	Nil	15
2	Nil	20
3	10	20
4	20	20
5	30	30
6	30	30

1. After this time, production will be steady at 30,000 units per month. The sale price will be €/£10 per unit. Half of all sales will be for cash and the other half on one month's credit.
2. Variable costs of production are expected to be as follows:

	€/£	
Material	1	
Labour	2	
Overhead	3	
	6	per unit

3. All materials will be purchased on credit, with one month being taken for payment.
4. Labour will be paid one week (one quarter month) in arrears and variable overheads will be paid one month after the expense is incurred.
5. Fixed overheads will amount to €/£300,000 per annum and will be paid quarterly in advance.
6. In the first month, machinery costing €/£450,000 (payable immediately) will be bought and this is expected to last for five years (ignore depreciation).
7. Inventories of raw material equal to three months' usage will also be bought in the first month and this level of inventory will be maintained by purchases in subsequent months.
8. Satu is able to provide €/£500,000 of permanent finance from a subscription of shares in the new subsidiary. It will also source a loan of a further €/£288,240, to be repaid over three years by the subsidiary (capital and interest) in equal monthly instalments, starting at the end of Month 1. Interest is fixed at 12% per annum.

Requirement

(a) Prepare each of the following:

(i) A cash budget for the subsidiary for the first six months of its life.

9 Marks

(ii) A forecast of the statement of financial position of the subsidiary at the end of month six.

5 Marks

(b) List two factors likely to influence the level of cash held by a company at any given time.

4 Marks

Total 18 Marks

(Based on Chartered Accountants Ireland, MABF II, Summer 2004, Q7)

Solution

(a) (i) Satu Plc's subsidiary: cash budget for first six months of its life.

	Month 1 €/£000	**Month 2 €/£000**	**Month 3 €/£000**	**Month 4 €/£000**	**Month 5 €/£000**	**Month 6 €/£000**
Total cash receipts from sales (W1)	–	–	50.00	150.00	250.00	300.00
Other cash inflows						
Share issue	500.00	–	–	–	–	–
Loan	288.24	–	–	–	–	–
Total cash inflows	788.24	–	50.00	150.00	250.00	300.00
Costs:						
Materials	–	(55.00)	(20.00)	(20.00)	(30.00)	(30.00)
Labour (W2)	(22.50)	(37.50)	(40.00)	(40.00)	(40.00)	(55.00)
Variable overhead	–	(45.00)	(60.00)	(60.00)	(60.00)	(60.00)
Total variable cost	(22.50)	(137.50)	(120.00)	(120.00)	(130.00)	(145.00)

	Month 1 €/£000	Month 2 €/£000	Month 3 €/£000	Month 4 €/£000	Month 5 €/£000	Month 6 €/£000
Fixed overhead	(75.00)	–	–	(75.00)	–	–
Loan repayments (W3)	(10.00)	(10.00)	(10.00)	(10.00)	(10.00)	(10.00)
Machinery	(450.00)	–	–	–	–	–
Total cash outgoings	(557.50)	(147.50)	(130.00)	(205.00)	(140.00)	(155.00)
Opening cash position	–	230.74	83.24	3.24	(51.76)	58.24
Monthly cash surplus/ (deficit)	230.74	(147.50)	(80.00)	(55.00)	110.00	145.00
Cumulative cash position	230.74	83.24	3.24	(51.76)	58.24	203.24

W1: Sales cash receipts

	Month 1	Month 2	Month 3	Month 4	Month 5	Month 6
Sales (in units)	–	–	10	20	30	30
	€/£000	€/£000	€/£000	€/£000	€/£000	€/£000
Sales in money	–	–	100	200	300	300
Cash receipts: cash	–	–	50	100	150	150
Cash receipts from credit sales	–	–	–	50	100	150
Total cash receipts from sales	–	–	50	150	250	300

W2: Labour cash payments

	Month 1	Month 2	Month 3	Month 4	Month 5	Month 6
Production (in units)	15	20	20	20	20	30
	€/£000	€/£000	€/£000	€/£000	€/£000	€/£000
Labour variable costs per unit	2	2	2	2	2	2
Total labour variable costs	30	40	40	40	40	60
Payable in month incurred (3/4)	22.5	30	30	30	30	45
Payable one month in arrears (1/4)	–	7.5	10	10	10	10
Total payable in month	22.5	37.5	40	40	40	55

W3: Loan repayments

PV = Periodic cash flow × 3-year annuity factor @ 12%

€/£288,240 = x + 2.402

x = €/£120,000

Monthly repayment = €/£10,000 [€/£120,000 ÷ 12]

W4: Balance on long-term loan

Interest portion of repayments in Year 1:	€/£288,240 × 12%
Present value of interest repayments:	€/£34,588 × 0.892
Monthly interest portion:	€/£30,852/12
	= €/£2,571
Total capital repayment is therefore:	€/£10,000 − €/£2,571
Capital repayment for six months:	€/£7,429 × 6
	= €/£44,574
Closing balance:	€/£288,240 − €/£44,574
	= €/£243,666

(ii) Forecast statement of financial position of subsidiary at the end of month six.

	€/£000
ASSETS	
Non-current assets	
Property, plant and machinery	450.00
Current assets	
Trade receivables: [€/£900,000 − €/£750,000]	150.00
Inventory of materials: [€/£30,000 × 2]	60.00
Finished goods inventory: [125 – 90 = 35 units × €/£6]	210.00
Cash	203.24
	623.24
Total assets	1,073.24
EQUITY AND LIABILITIES	
Equity and reserves:	
Equity share capital	500.00
Revenue reserves (balancing figure)	194.57
	694.57
Non-current liabilities	
Long-term loan *(W4)*	243.67
Current liabilities	
Trade payables: materials: [€/£30,000 × 1]	30.00
Labour: [€/£250,000 − €/£235,000]	15.00
Overheads: [€/£30,000 × 3]	90.00
	135.00
Total liabilities	378.67
Total equity and liabilities	1,073.24

(b) Two factors likely to influence the level of the cash balance held by a company at any given time (any two of the following would be appropriate):
- the predictability of future cash flows;
- the existence of readily realisable securities;
- the availability of short-term finance;
- the period of credit given by suppliers;
- the variation in demand for cash from regular trading transactions; and
- the assessment of the company's need for precautionary or speculative cash.

Key Terms

Bank Giro credit slips
Bankers' Automated Clearing Service (BACS)
Cash budget
Cash float period
Cash flows from financing activities
Cash flows from investing activities
Cash flows from operating activities
Cash flow synchronisation
Certificate of deposit
Clearing House Automated Payments System (CHAPS)
Clearance delay
Cyclical cash flow
Direct debits
Local authority bonds
Lodgement delay
Management by exception
Money laundering
Normal deposit account
Precautionary motive
Seasonal cash flow
Speculative motive
Standing orders
Statement of cash flows
Stochastic cash flows
Term deposit account
Transmission delay
Transaction motive
Treasury bills
Wilful blindness

REVIEW QUESTIONS

(See Suggested Solutions to Review Questions in **Appendix B**.)

Question 9.1

What are the main motives for holding cash?

Question 9.2

List the three main areas of float management.

Question 9.3

List five factors that can result in cash shortages.

Question 9.4

Thomas McKee owns three shops in Belfast. Takings from each shop are brought once a week, on a Saturday night, to the main central shop. There they are collated with the shop's own week's takings and banked on the Monday morning. The accountant has suggested that Thomas could save money by lodging more regularly.

Overall sales are €/£3,900,000. These occur evenly over the year. The overdraft rate is 12%. The accountant suggests that Thomas would save interest if lodgements were made at the end of each day.

He suggests that Saturday's takings be lodged on the Monday. Assume there are no costs associated with making lodgements and that the shop is open from Monday to Saturday each week of the year.

Requirement Calculate the cost of the current policy and compare this to the cost of the suggested lodgement policy. Advise Thomas on the appropriate course of action.

CHALLENGING QUESTIONS

(Suggested Solutions to Challenging Questions are available through your lecturer.)

Question 9.1 Hawthorn (Level 1)

(a) Hawthorn Plc is currently attempting to improve the management of its cash and is investigating alternative methods for banking its cash receipts. The annual cash receipts of €/£21 million are spread evenly over each of the 50 weeks of the working year. However, during each week the daily rate of cash received on Mondays and Tuesdays is expected to be twice that for Wednesdays, Thursdays and Fridays. There are no receipts on Saturdays or Sundays.

Current practice is to bank cash receipts only on Friday, but two alternatives are being considered:

(i) bank cash receipts every day; or
(ii) bank cash receipts on Tuesday and Friday.

The company always operates with a bank overdraft and the current rate charged on its overdraft is 15%. The incremental cost of each banking lodgement is €/£50.

(To simplify calculations, use a 360-day year.)

Requirement Advise Hawthorn Plc as to whether the company should change from its current practice and, if so, which alternative it should choose.

10 Marks

(b) "The cash flow forecast, or cash budget, is the primary tool in short-term financial planning." (Pike and Neale, 2003)

Requirement Discuss the above statement.

8 Marks
Total 18 Marks

(Based on Chartered Accountants Ireland, MABF II, Summer 1998, Q6)

Question 9.2 Caveat Ltd (Level 1)

Caveat Ltd runs a chain of garden equipment stores. The business is seasonal in nature regarding the garden tools and equipment. The forecast sales for 20X4 are as follows:

	€/£000		€/£000
January	18	July	120
February	18	August	75
March	30	September	75
April	150	October	20
May	240	November	15
June	210	December	90

1. You should assume that the sales in the last few months of 20X3 were similar to the corresponding month's forecast for 20X4.

2. 60% of Caveat sales are on cash terms, and 40% are on credit terms. Approximately half the credit sales pay one month after sale, and the balance pay during the second month after sale.
3. Caveat purchases goods for resale three months prior to sale and pays for them one month after purchase. Typically the goods are sold at a profit mark-up on cost of 50%.
4. Wages and administration costs amount to €/£35,000 per month, including depreciation costs of €/£8,000 per month.
5. A tax payment of €/£30,000 needs to be made in February 20X4.

Requirement

(a) Prepare a monthly cash budget for the six months from January to June 20X4. Assume an opening cash balance of €/£27,000 on 1 January 20X4.

8 Marks

(b) If sales in the early months of 20X4 turn out to be lower than forecast, what action might Caveat take in order to prevent a deterioration of its liquidity position?

4 Marks

(c) Discuss briefly whether, in general, the assumptions on which a cash budget is based should be realistically attainable or more challenging in order to encourage improved performance.

3 Marks

Total 15 Marks

(Based on Chartered Accountants Ireland, CAP 1, Finance, Autumn 2008, Q3)

Question 9.3 Venus (Level 1)

Venus Limited is currently suffering cashflow problems and the finance director wants you to prepare the cash budget on the basis of the following information for the next quarter to 30 September 20X2.

Venus Limited
STATEMENT OF FINANCIAL POSITION (UNAUDITED)
as at 30 June 20X2

	€/£000	€/£000
ASSETS		
Non-current assets		1,000
Current assets		
Inventory	500	
Trade receivables	750	
Other	100	1,350
Total assets		2,350
EQUITY AND LIABILITIES		
Equity and reserves		
Ordinary share capital (nominal value €/£1)		100
Retained earnings		1,200
		1,300
Current liabilities		
Bank overdraft	250	
Trade payables	500	
Tax	300	1,050
Total equity and liabilities		2,350

QUESTIONS – CHAPTER 9

Additional information:

1. Sales for the next three months are forecast as follows:

July €/£000	August €/£000	September €/£000
1,100	1,200	1,250

   10% of the sales are cash sales. The remainder of the sales are on credit and are paid one month after the sale. 5% of the credit sales are usually irrecoverable.

2. Purchases for the next three months are forecast as follows:

July €/£000	August €/£000	September €/£000
550	575	580

   All of the purchases are on credit, with suppliers allowing one month's credit.

3. Salaries of €/£250,000 will be paid each month. The directors will receive a bonus of €/£50,000 in July.
4. Venus will undertake an extensive television and radio marketing campaign costing €/£20,000, which is payable in August.
5. Venus will make a legal settlement for an ongoing court case in respect of an unfair dismissal claim for €/£35,000 in July.
6. The tax liability is due for payment to the tax authorities in September.
7. Venus has purchased a non-current asset in July for €/£500,000. This will be paid for in September. This asset will be depreciated straight-line on a monthly basis from the month of purchase.
8. An additional 100,000 ordinary shares will be issued in July for a premium of €/£0.50 per share.
9. Venus will pay a dividend of €/£0.30 per share in issue in September.

Requirement You are required to prepare a cash budget for each of the three months July–September 20X2, showing the net cash position at the end of each month.

(***Note:*** figures should be rounded to the nearest €/£000. Your answer should consider appropriate actions to deal with any surpluses or deficits arising.)

Total 15 Marks

(Based on Chartered Accountants Ireland, CAP 1, Finance, Autumn 2012, Q5)

Question 9.4 The Pine Loft Company (Level 1)

The Pine Loft Company manufactures a range of pine furniture, which it sells to a number of retail outlets around the country. The company's accounting year-end date is 31 December. The financial accountant has recently prepared estimates of income and expenditure for the first five months of the next accounting period. These include the following:

1. Sales (units):

Nov (actual)	Dec (actual)	Jan	Feb	Mar	Apr	May
220	220	260	240	290	320	350

2. The average unit sales price for the period is expected to be €/£350. This is an increase of €/£20 on current-year prices. It is estimated that 70% of income will be received in the month of sale, and the remainder one month after sale. However, it is expected that 20% of all debts outstanding at the end of the month of sale will be uncollectable.
3. The company purchases pine wood from one supplier who gives 30 days' credit. The wood is purchased in a treated state and is immediately available for use. The company purchases enough wood each month to meet the current month's sales and to maintain a closing inventory level equal to 10% of the next month's sales. The opening inventory in hand on 1 January is 26 units. The material cost per unit is forecast at €/£150.
4. The company employs 10 carpenters and two administrative staff. Carpenters work 170 hours per month and will be paid €/£20 per hour, rising to €/£24 in April. Administration and management salaries amount to €/£4,000 per month. All wages and salaries are paid one month in arrears. The wages and salaries bill for December of the current year is €/£30,000.
5. The company's insurance premium for the forthcoming year is €/£10,000. This will be paid in January.
6. Other overheads amount to €/£5,900 per month. These include depreciation of €/£1,500 and increases in provisions for bad debts and potential legal costs of €/£600 per month. Overheads are paid in the month in which they are incurred.
7. Expenditure on non-current assets for the forthcoming period includes the following:

March	Replacement of a delivery van	€/£20,000
April	Computer system upgrade	€/£5,000

8. A dividend of €/£10,000 will be paid in March.
9. The company upgraded some of its machinery last year. It took out a commercial loan of €/£200,000 to finance this upgrade. The company is repaying the loan (capital and interest) in equal monthly payments over a three-year period. Interest is fixed at 10% per annum.
10. Overdraft interest is charged on any debit balance on the company's current account at the end of each month at a rate of 14% per annum.
11. The balance on the company's current account at the start of the forecast period is estimated to be €/£15,000.

Requirement

(a) Prepare a cash budget, on a monthly basis, for the months of January, February, March and April.

12 Marks

(b) Comment on the cash budget and advise management on how it might improve its forecast liquidity position.

6 Marks

(c) Discuss briefly how information technology can assist a company in the management of its cash flows.

4 Marks

Total 22 Marks

(Based on Chartered Accountants Ireland, MABF II, Summer 2001, Q5)

Question 9.5 A Ltd (Level 2)

A Ltd has produced a plan for its activities for the forthcoming financial period of six months. This is summarised in the form of a budgeted statement of profit or loss for the period, as follows.

Budgeted Statement of Profit or Loss
for the forthcoming six months

	€/£	€/£
Sales (50,000 @ €/£10 each)		500,000
Cost of sales		
Material	(100,000)	
Labour	(75,000)	
Variable overhead	(100,000)	(275,000)
Operating profit		225,000
Less: Fixed overheads	(125,000)	
Depreciation	(20,000)	(145,000)
Net income		80,000

A Ltd's (Summarised) Statement of Financial Position Immediately Prior to the Commencement of the Six Months

	€/£	€/£
ASSETS		
Non-current assets		99,000
Current assets		
Inventory of raw materials @ €/£2 each	20,000	
Inventory of finished goods @ €/£5.50 each	44,000	
Receivables (80% of previous month's sales)	32,000	
Cash	50,000	146,000
Total assets		245,000
EQUITY AND LIABILITIES		
Equity and reserves		200,000
Payables (previous month's supplies)	20,000	
Payables (previous month but one supplies)	25,000	45,000
Total equity and liabilities		245,000

Additional information in respect of A Ltd's cash flows is as follows:

1. A Ltd's trade is seasonal and its forecast sales for the next full year (of which the current budget is Months 1–6) are:

Month	Sales €/£	Month	Sales €/£
1	40,000	7	140,000
2	40,000	8	80,000
3	60,000	9	60,000
4	80,000	10	60,000
5	120,000	11	50,000
6	160,000	12	40,000

2. It is A Ltd's policy to hold an inventory of finished goods equal to the requirements of the next two months' sales and inventories of raw materials equal to the next one-and-a-half months' production requirements. It pays its suppliers, on average, two months after the goods are delivered.
3. A Ltd pays for its labour and variable overheads in the month in which they are incurred.
4. Fixed overheads are paid quarterly in advance.
5. 80% of the company's sales are to credit customers (the rest being for cash) and credit customers are allowed one month's credit.
6. Depreciation is a composite figure made up of the appropriate amounts for each of the non-current assets in use.
7. No cash receipts or payments are expected during the six months of the budget period except those referred to above.

Requirement Prepare the cash budget for the six-month period.

15 Marks

(Based on Chartered Accountants Ireland, CAP 1, Mock 2008, Q4)

Question 9.6 Garner (Level 2)

Garner Ltd is a company involved in the construction industry. It has a central depot located in the midlands, into which inventories are received and from which they are distributed to sites throughout the country. However, local site managers are also empowered to order materials directly from suppliers to be delivered straight to the individual sites. These are referred to as 'direct purchases to contract'. In such cases the materials are usually consumed almost immediately after receipt on site.

In order to determine the company's ongoing need for working capital, budgets are being prepared as part of the cash management process. You are given the following information:

MONTHLY PROFIT FORECAST

	June €/£000	July €/£000	Aug. €/£000	Sept. €/£000	Oct. €/£000	Nov. €/£000	Dec. €/£000	Jan./Mar. €/£000 (Note 1)
Contracts invoiced (Note 2)	688	560	1,600	2,000	320	600	720	800
Material from inventory		190	190	180	180	160	210	
Direct purchases to contract		550	626	511	400	330	400	
Direct wages		50	60	60	75	60	72	
Direct input to WIP		790	876	751	655	550	682	
Decrease/(increase) in WIP		(400)	300	610	(395)	(75)	(102)	
Direct cost of sales		390	1,176	1,361	260	475	580	
Factory overhead		60	70	80	75	60	80	
Selling and administration costs		72	72	92	102	82	72	
Royalties		27	80	100	15	30	35	

Premises charges rent and rates		8	8	8	8	8	8
Depreciation		5	5	5	5	5	5
		562	1,411	1,646	465	660	780
Net profit before tax, subject to commissions (Note 3)		(2)	189	354	(145)	(60)	(60)
Materials in inventory at month end	196	176	200	229	250	240	250

1. The contracts invoiced are €/£800,000 for each of January, February and March.
2. There is frequently a large resource commitment from Garner in making a sale. Accordingly, customers are often required to pay part of the final price in stages. Research into the pattern of sales shows that, of the total sales invoiced, the amounts are paid in equal instalments as follows:
   25% on signing of sales agreement, three months before invoicing;
   25% on delivery, on average one month before final invoicing;
   25% on the day of final invoicing;
   25% on one month's credit after invoicing.
   The scheduled invoiced amounts represent the 'final' invoiced amounts for each month.
3. Commissions are payable to staff to the nearest €/£1,000 at the rate of 2% on receipts from contracts invoiced, and will be paid one month in arrears. You are provided with the following additional information:
   (i) Of the total purchases for inventory and contract, about one-third will attract 2% cash discount, and will be paid for in the month following delivery. The remaining 2/3rds will be paid for, on average, two months after delivery.
   (ii) Direct wages, factory, selling and administration overheads are paid in the month in which they are incurred.
   (iii) Royalties are paid quarterly at the end of February, May, August and November in respect of the quarters ending on 31 January, 30 April, 31 July and 31 October respectively.
   (iv) Rent and rates are paid in arrears at the end of March, June, September and December.
   (v) Outlays on capital purchases during the period are expected to be as follows:
   August……€/£80,000 October…..€/£40,000 December…€/£100,000
   No investment grants are expected during the period under review.
   (vi) The cash balance at 30 September is €/£120,000.

Requirement

(a) Prepare a cash budget for each of the three months: October, November and December.

18 Marks

(b) Comment briefly on the cash position of the company at the end of each of the three months.

4 Marks

Total 22 Marks

(Based on Chartered Accountants Ireland, MABF II, Autumn 2007, Q5)

Question 9.7 Alcobex (Level 2)

Alcobex Metal Corporation Plc (AMC) sells three products: P1, P2 and P3. Products P1 and P2 are manufactured by the company, while P3 is procured from outside and resold as a combination with either Product P1 or P2. The sales volume budgeted for the three products for the period from December 20X4 to March 20X6 is as follows:

Product P1	€/£10 million per month each month	
Product P2	€/£4.167 million per month each month	
Product P3	Dec. 20X4 to March 20X5 inclusive	€/£2 million per month
	April 20X4 to July 20X5 inclusive	€/£2.5 million per month
	Aug. 20X4 to Nov. 20X5 inclusive	€/£3.0 million per month
	Dec. 20X4 to March 20X6 inclusive	€/£4.5 million per month

Based on the budgeted sales value, and the following assumptions, the cash flow forecast for the company is prepared:

1. It is anticipated that cash will be received from sales as follows:
   50% in the current month;
   25% in the second month;
   25% in the third month.
2. The production programme for each month is based on the sales value of the next month.
3. Raw material consumption of AMC is kept at 60% of each month's production.
4. 80% of the raw materials consumed are components.
5. Components are procured in the month of consumption.
6. The company avails of the following credit terms from suppliers:
   (i) company gets one month's credit for its components;
   (ii) other raw materials are paid for one month prior to the dates of purchase. They are received on a just-in-time basis.
7. Currently AMC has an overdraft facility of €/£14.088 million. At the beginning of the period under review this facility is being fully utilised.
8. Expenses are given below and are expected to be constant throughout the year:

	€/£ million
Wages and salaries	31.2
Administrative expenses	32.2
Selling and distribution expenses	5.3

9. The term loan of €/£23.732 million is repayable in two equal instalments half-yearly, i.e. June and December 20X5.
10. Capital expenditure of €/£29.244 million for the year 20X5 is expected to be spread equally over the 12-month period.
11. A dividend of €/£5.803 million is to be paid in October.
12. Tax of €/£2.392 million will be paid in equal instalments half-yearly, i.e. June and December 20X5.

Requirement

(a) Prepare statements showing the following:
   (i) The cash to be collected from accounts receivable in each month from June to October 20X5 inclusive.

4 Marks

   (ii) The payments to be made to suppliers in the same period.

6 Marks

   (iii) An overall cash budget for this period.

4 Marks

(b) Discuss briefly TWO disadvantages of using spreadsheets in the preparation of cash budgets such as the one above.

4 Marks

Total 18 Marks

(Based on Chartered Accountants Ireland, MABF II, Autumn 2008, Q6)

Question 9.8 Hogwash Harry (Level 2)

You have recently been recruited to the finance function of a privately owned manufacturing company. The managing director of Hogwash Harry is concerned about the budgeted cash flows that have been forecast for the next six months and is looking for your advice on how to alleviate the potential liquidity problems. He asks you to create a one- or two-page memo detailing some action points to put to the board of directors.

You are supplied with the following information in respect of expected cash flows:

	Jan €/£000	Feb €/£000	Mar €/£000	Apr €/£000	May €/£000	June €/£000
Change in month	(685)	(80)	(180)	(825)	90	780
Opening balance	500	(185)	(265)	(445)	(1,270)	(1,180)
Closing balance	(185)	(265)	(445)	(1,270)	(1,180)	(400)

In addition you are told (after enquiry) that:

1. The company's trade is seasonal: it manufactures Sombreros and children's play floats. There has been strong demand for the company's products and this is expected to continue for the next five years. There is some uncertainty about demand after this time.
2. The company plans to purchase new machinery, costing €/£700,000, in January. Installation costs amounting to €/£50,000 will be incurred in February.
3. The company replaces the four directors' motor vehicles each March. The new cars will cost €/£60,000 each, the old cars are expected to be traded in for €/£35,000 each, against the cost of the new vehicles.
4. The shipping company, which has agreed to ship all the company's products to the company's customers, has agreed to give the company a 1% discount if they pay in full for the shipping in March. The net amount budgeted to be paid to the shipping company in March is €/£250,000. The directors currently earn 4% on their current accounts. One of the directors has argued that a 1% interest rate for payment in a month (March) is equal to about 12% per year. This account is normally settled in September.
5. The company is a private limited company. In April of each year it distributes a dividend of €/£300,000.
6. The company has a €/£1 million loan. It pays the interest and capital repayment on the loan in April. The yearly fixed repayment is €/£300,000 (interest and capital). Interest is charged on the yearly opening balance of the loan (the €/£1 million). The interest is charged at 15%.
7. The company's tax is due in April. The corporation tax liability is €/£350,000. This has been included in the above projections.

Requirement Prepare a memo to the Board of Directors. This memo should evaluate the position of the company's finances and should (taking into account the points mentioned above) suggest steps that the company can take to ease the company's short-term financial problem.

Total 20 Marks

Part III

THE FINANCIAL ENVIRONMENT AND SOURCES OF FINANCE

Chapters

10. The Financial Environment and Asset- and Finance-Mix Decisions
11. Short-term Sources of Finance
12. Medium-term Sources of Finance and the Finance Gap
13. Long-term Sources of Finance: Debt and Mezzanine Finance
14. Long-term Sources of Finance: Equity Capital and Preference Shares

10

The Financial Environment and Asset- and Finance-Mix Decisions

Learning Objectives

Upon completing this chapter, readers should be able to:

- describe the financial and economic environment and its impact on the organisation;
- discuss the market efficiency theory;
- explain the importance of achieving an optimal asset mix;
- explain the difference between permanent and temporary current assets;
- discuss various approaches to asset mix (neutral, conservative, aggressive);
- explain the finance mix choices available and discuss various approaches (matching, flexible, restrictive); and
- discuss general influences on the cost of finance.

INTRODUCTION

As well as having a knowledge of the economic environment within which an entity operates, (covered in **Chapter 1**), the business finance manager requires knowledge of the financial environment, including the economic environment, financial institutions and financial markets. There are two main approaches to obtaining finance. The first is **intermediation**, whereby finance is arranged through **financial institutions**, such as commercial banks or merchant banks. The type of finance obtained can range from an uncomplicated overdraft, which is provided internally by the financial intermediary, to a piece of paper (a bill), which can be traded for cash in the markets, to shares or bonds being sold on capital markets. The second approach, **disintermediation**, is where the financial intermediary's role is bypassed, with companies going direct to the investors or stock exchanges to obtain finance. The latter is restricted to large, reputable companies seeking large amounts of finance.

This chapter begins by providing some background information on the financial environment in Ireland and the UK, including a brief summary of the financial crisis. The other chapters in Part III provide more information on the specific financial markets that are relevant to the particular form of finance being sourced by the company. This chapter then considers influences on the type of finance to obtain, including an evaluation of asset type and finance characteristics, such as its term and typical costs associated with finance.

THE FINANCIAL ENVIRONMENT

Business finance managers and strategic decision-makers have to be aware of the financial environment and how external factors can impact on financial decision-making. The **financial environment** encapsulates the **economic environment** within which a company operates and the financial markets in which a company's long-term funds are sourced and traded. These are now discussed in turn.

Economic Influences

Business finance managers need to be aware of their microeconomic and macroeconomic environment. The **microeconomic** environment includes factors that affect an individual company's resources, for example, labour supply and cost, product pricing, suppliers, customers and shareholders. **Macroeconomics** describes the effect of factors in the economy, national and global, that impact on the company. These include interest rates and exchange rates.

Inflation has been earmarked by governments as a major influence on a country's economic growth. When demand for a good outstrips supply, **inflation** results. In these circumstances, the supplier can increase the price of the good without losing sales. The consequence is that the good becomes more expensive to purchasers who, as a result, experience a fall in the real value of their wages and capital. Purchasers will subsequently put pressure on their employers to increase their wages so that they can maintain their current spending power. Due to the fall in the purchasing value of individuals' incomes, demand for products will fall. Individuals may become conservative and reduce overall spending, which will result in an economic downturn in the economy. When the purchaser is a company, pressure grows to increase the price of the end product, due to the increased production/supply costs. This may result in a loss of sales for the company and, consequently, financial difficulties. When there are financial difficulties, companies will try to cut costs, which can mean job losses.

Interest rate changes are used as a means of controlling demand for goods. The assumption is that interest rate increases will reduce the overall spending power of consumers (who usually have a reasonable amount of debt), bringing demand for goods down to a level that discourages companies with excess demand from increasing prices. Therefore, the price of goods does not increase, just the price of debt.

Foreign exchange rates also exert great influence on a company that imports supplies, exports goods, borrows or invests in countries that use a different currency. When the value of a currency in one monetary area rises, the subsequent cost of goods exported from that monetary area increases, resulting in a loss of demand for the monetary area's goods (assuming that demand is related to price) and vice versa.

Economic Influences and Business Finance

Inflation and foreign exchange rate changes affect asset values, costs and revenues, making it difficult to accurately predict future cash flows (and so the outcomes from any financial decision-making). Where inflation causes the value of assets to rise, an additional financing requirement will result, as replacement assets (such as inventories, trade receivables or machinery) will be more expensive to purchase. Business finance managers should be aware of the financing implications of inflation and should ensure that sufficient financing is in place to meet future increased cash demands. Where inflation causes the costs of production to rise, an analysis of the impact on profitability should be undertaken. A strong knowledge of the market for the good being sold by the company is vital, as the business finance manager would need to be able to estimate the reaction of customers and competitors to price changes. If this reaction is wrongly anticipated, the company could lose market share and profitability.

When interest rates increase, the required return by company financiers will also increase. This is because the risk-free rate of interest (i.e. the guaranteed return on a risk-free investment such as a bank deposit account) has increased, therefore the premium required by financiers (i.e. equity holders and debt holders) will increase the overall return expected. When the return expected by a company's financiers increases, the number of potential investments that can be undertaken by a company falls, as only those investments that cover the new, higher required return by financiers will be accepted. All existing investment and assets will need to be reviewed and any that are not meeting the new, higher required rate of return should be liquidated and utilised to reduce current debt levels. The cash outflow on debt finance cannot be waived; hence debt finance increases financial risk.

Company managers should also have hedging policies in place to reduce the exposure to loss in company value caused by changes in exchange rates. One simple, commonly used technique is to have a bank account located in the foreign country. Exchange rates can be fixed using derivative financial instruments, such as forward rate contracts, futures contracts or swap contracts (which are discussed in detail in **Chapters 19–21**).

The Financial Markets

The financial environment also encompasses the markets in which a company's long-term funds are sourced and traded (the financial system). The **financial system** encompasses the **financial markets**, which include the **capital markets**, the money markets and financial institutions. Equity and long-term debt are typically obtained through the capital markets (e.g. stock exchanges and over-the-counter markets), though financial institutions are also a source. Short-term finance is typically sourced through financial institutions, which are reliant on the money markets for liquidity.

The Money Markets

A business finance manager requires knowledge of the money markets so that he or she can assess the vulnerability of the financial system in the future. The **money markets** are markets that specialise in lending and borrowing for short periods of time, typically less than 13 months. Indeed, funds can be loaned for a matter of hours. There are many participants in the money markets, including discount houses, large entities and the government, but the majority of transactions within the money markets are undertaken by banks and other financial institutions. The products traded on money markets include certificates of deposit, commercial paper, acceptance credits, asset-backed securities, bills of exchange and treasury bills. The money markets provide liquidity for the global financial system, in particular, liquidity for banks. For example, a bank in the US may lend funds to a UK bank at the close of business each night so that the UK bank has the funds available when it opens in the morning. Due to the time difference, the US bank is closed, yet using the money markets can earn interest overnight from the UK bank. When the UK bank closes, it pays the funds back to the US bank with interest for the overnight loan.

Many financial institutions are involved, and liquidity is maintained in the financial system without financial institutions having to hold high levels of cash to ensure liquidity. However, in late 2007 the unthinkable occurred: the money markets started to grind to a halt, destabilising the financial system worldwide. The consequences for the financial system worldwide were catastrophic: public confidence eroded and a global downturn resulted. A summary of some of the main events resulting from the financial crisis are included in **Real World Example 10.1**.

Real World Example 10.1: The Financial Crisis (in brief)

The start of the crisis can be tracked back to the US and the property crash that occurred there due to sub-prime lending, securitisation and the realisation within the financial system that many of the financial institutions' assets were 'toxic'. As a result of the drop in market confidence, fewer institutions (both financial and otherwise) made their cash available for others to use, worried that repayment might not be forthcoming. This lack of liquidity forced many of the financial institutions into distress.

The first big players to be affected were Bear Stearns, which was taken over by J.P. Morgan in March 2008. In September 2008, 'Fannie Mae' and 'Freddie Mac', the world's largest mortgage providers, were placed into a conservatorship run by a US government agency. Then, in October 2008, Lehman Brothers collapsed with the loss of 26,200 jobs worldwide (Osborne, Aldrick and Quinn, 2009). This was the world's largest bankruptcy, 10 times the scale of Enron. The consequence was catastrophic.

To this point in time, the financial system (i.e. markets, investors, business, etc.) believed that no government would let a bank go bankrupt. The UK had bailed out Northern Rock and the US government had intervened to ensure that Bear Stearns and 'Fannie Mae' and 'Freddie Mac' takeovers went smoothly. A consequence was that market confidence plummeted, investors started to withdraw their deposits and to sell their investments. A potential worldwide run on the banks was possible. The US government had to make a lot of assurances that it would not allow the financial system to collapse. It put pressure on the Bank of America to take over Merrill Lynch and it had to bailout the world's largest insurer, AIG.

During the period following the collapse in 2008, the US, UK and Irish governments, as well as those of many other countries, injected funds into the financial system to ensure that it did not collapse. Propublica (2013) records the flows from and to the US Treasury as a result of the bailout. It reported that by 2013 the US Treasury had injected $608 billion into the financial system to ease the burden of the financial crisis (i.e. $245 billion into the banks, $187 billion into 'Fannie Mae' and 'Freddie Mac',

$79.7 billion into auto companies, $67.8 billion into AIG, purchased $18.6 billion of toxic assets and input a further $9.1 billion to other institutions). By October 2013, $554 billion had been returned, made up of $371 billion in capital repayments and $183 billion in fees and revenue due on loans. Many of the banks had returned the liquidity loans within one year of the loan being granted.

At the peak of the crisis, the UK government had pledged to spend £1.2 trillion to support the financial system; however, the government's net exposure peaked at £955 billion made up of cash injections, guarantees made and fees paid. By March 2013 the exposure had fallen to £141 billion, made up of £115 billion in cash and £26 billion in contingent liabilities (NAO, 2013). As part of the bailout, the government purchased shares in a number of financial institutions including £45.5 billion in RBS (the UK government is currently a 62.4% shareholder, down from 84.4% in 2009), £20 billion in Lloyds, £22.99 billion in Northern Rock, £8.55 billion in Bradford and Bingley (*Guardian*, 2012). In addition the government, in conjunction with the Bank of England, made several cash loans to banks including £163 billion to RBA and a further £26.05 billion in loans to protect deposits. Efforts have been made at restructuring the banking sector and in recouping funds invested in the financial system. In addition, the UK government does not have any intention of being bankers and is keen to get the banking institutions that they own back into private hands. To this end, Northern Rock's mortgage book and Bradford and Bingley were merged to form the UK Asset Resolution Bank (this bank borrowed £48.7 billion from the government, but repaid it in full by 2019) and the rest of Northern Rock was sold to Virgin for £820 million. In 2013 the government sold some of its Lloyds shares for £3.2 billion, generating a paper profit of £61 million. By 2012 RBS had paid back the £163 billion bailout received from the Treasury, the Bank of England and the US Treasury (*The Telegraph*, 2012). Over the years, the UK government made two share placings and by 2019 these sales had realised a loss of £2 billion for the UK government.

In Ireland, it is estimated that by July 2012 the Irish government had injected €63 billion of capital into the banking system, the bulk of the funding going to Anglo Irish Bank. In the shake-up that followed the financial crisis, the National Asset Management Agency (NAMA) was formed in December 2009 to take over toxic land and development loans, with a nominal value of €74 billion, from participating financial institutions. NAMA's objective was to obtain the best possible financial return for the State over an expected lifetime of 10 years. In addition, Anglo Irish Bank was nationalised in 2009 and merged in 2011 with the Irish Nationwide Building Society (which had been nationalised in December 2008) to form a new bank, the Irish Bank Resolution Corporation. This bank was then controversially dissolved in February 2013 and the assets transferred to NAMA. The Irish banking system has also received indirect funding from UK banks, with RBS transferring over £10 billion to cover bad debts at Ulster bank, which is one of its subsidiaries. Indeed, losses on Ulster Bank's loan book of £12.7 billion equate to one-quarter of RBS's total bad debts write-offs (£44.3 billion) to date. In addition, the UK bank, Lloyds, transferred €8 billion (£6.81 billion) into its Irish subsidiary before absorbing it back into its own books in 2010.

The consequence of the financial crisis was deep recession in the US, the UK and in Ireland. All three countries experienced the highest debt levels ever recorded and implemented severe austerity measures. Even so, Ireland had to seek assistance (in the form of a bailout) from the European Union in November 2010. This bailout was for €85 billion: €17.5 billion from the National Pensions Reserve Fund, €22.5 billion from the International Monetary Fund (IMF), €22.5 billion from the European Financial Stabilisation Mechanism, €22.5 billion from the European Financial Stabilisation Facility and €4.8 billion in bilateral loans from the UK, Sweden and Denmark. The cost of funding was initially at 6% but was adjusted to 3% shortly afterwards. Ireland has been steadily repaying its debt. By 2019, it still owed €44.5 billion. It has paid off the IMF loan facility completely and the debt owed to both Sweden and Denmark (Taylor, 2017) and has built up cash reserves in the National Treasury Management Agency.

Sources: Simon Carswell, The *Irish Times*, 30 January 2012.

RBS (2019), Equity Ownership Statistics, https://investors.rbs.com/share-data/equity-ownership-statistics.aspx; accessed November 2019.

Taylor, C. (2017), "Ireland still owes €44.5bn in bailout loans after paying off IMF early", *The Irish Times*, 21 December 2017, https://www.irishtimes.com/business/economy/ireland-still-owes-44-5bn-in-bailout-loans-after-paying-off-imf-early-1.3334972; accessed November 2019.

UK Asset Resolution, "Report and Accounts 2019", https://www.ukar.co.uk/media-centre/press-releases/2019/05-06-2019; accessed November 2019.

The main concerns facing UK and Irish companies at the time of writing are Covid-19, Brexit and domestic and international politics, particularly the potential consequence of a trade war between China and America. At this time there is much global uncertainty, which is always a cause for concern for financial managers in companies that trade in a global market. It is difficult to predict how these issues will influence the financial markets.

The Financial Markets and Business Finance

A business finance manager needs to be able to predict the reaction of the market to, for example, the company dividend policy and any changes proposed to it (discussed in depth in **Chapter 22**). Changes in capital structure will also be judged by the market (discussed in depth in **Chapter 16**). A business finance manager needs to know how to raise equity and debt in the financial markets. To do this efficiently, a good knowledge of the equity markets and bond markets is required (discussed in depth in **Chapters 13** and **14**). Knowledge of the sources of private equity and debt finance also supports business finance decision-making (venture capital finance is discussed in **Chapter 12**).

EFFICIENT MARKETS AND MARKET THEORIES

There are several theories that try to explain the behaviour of capital markets, including the efficient market hypothesis, behavioural finance and chaos theory.

The Efficient Market Hypothesis (EMH)

In an **efficient market**, share price encapsulates all the information that is currently available about a company and the economy. In this situation speculative trading would not reap gains above average market gains. The EMH suggests that in an efficient market, competition between market participants wipes out excess profits that can be made from owning shares. Where market shares are mispriced, market participants will react quickly and buy or sell shares, driving share price up or down depending on whether the shares are under- or over-priced. Therefore, shares are priced in accordance with their worth and no speculative gains or losses can be made by equity holders above and beyond the gains on the market overall, which responds to economic influences. It is assumed that share price includes all price-sensitive information there is about the company and reflects the impact of changes in the economy on the value of equity. In a nutshell, there is no information asymmetry. **Information asymmetry** is a term used to describe an information gap, or misinterpretation of information provided. In the context of the market price of shares, it usually refers to the misinterpretation of price-sensitive information or the failure to provide this information by a company to the market.

In 1970, the American economist, Eugene Fama, suggested that market efficiency be analysed using three levels of efficiency: weak-form efficiency, semi-strong-form efficiency and strong-form efficiency.

Weak-form Efficiency

When markets are considered to be **weak-form efficient**, it means that the share price reflects all historical information in respect of a company. This form of market efficiency suggests that chartists (who chart the past pattern of performance of a company in an attempt to predict the future pattern of price movement to make gains) will not be successful, as market participants will be fully aware of all historical information and will know that selling shares when the price falls would be irresponsible, given that they know the share price will rise after a short period of time to a level beyond its initial position – hence there will not be a market for the shares and no excess gains can be made from speculative trading. According to this theory, investors who can anticipate the future performance and investors with inside information can make excess returns.

Semi-strong-form Efficiency

This goes further than weak-form efficiency. **Semi-strong-form efficiency** assumes that equity share price reflects all historical information in respect of a company and all publicly available information. If one equity holder reads a price-sensitive publication by the company, then all equity holders will read the information and interpret it in the same way, instantaneously. Therefore, there will not be a surge in trade for shares if, for example, a company issues a profit statement above what was initially publicised as expected, as the equity holders will require a premium to sell the shares, effectively cancelling the potential gain that could be made were the equity shares to be purchased at the price quoted before the announcement went public. According to this theory, only investors with insider knowledge will consistently make excess returns.

Strong-form Efficiency

When a market is assumed to be **strong-form efficient**, equity share price is deemed to reflect all historical, publicly available and private information in respect of a company. Therefore, no market participant can make excessive gains above average market gains. This form of market has no information asymmetry and market participants with insider information cannot make returns in excess of the market.

Empirical Research

Empirical research has indicated that markets are generally weak-form or semi-strong-form efficient, not strong-form efficient. In practice, it is difficult to determine the extent of efficiency in markets or to pigeonhole markets into one of the aforementioned efficiency levels. Investors do make gains (and losses), suggesting that markets are not fully efficient. Therefore, a certain level of inefficiency must exist, otherwise there would be no need for investors at all, as anyone (without any expert knowledge) would be able to purchase a portfolio of well-balanced shares and perform as well as the overall market. In reality, expert investors analyse financial statements and make adjustments for creative accounting, economic influences and the expected outcome of new investments, and then use the resultant figures to assist them in their decision on whether to buy, sell or hold a block of shares. There are many critiques of EMH and its narrow view that share price is associated with the 'information content of shares' and the interpretation of information that is available in respect of a company. Two opposing views are now considered in brief.

Behavioural Finance

Behavioural finance suggests that other factors also influence share price. Behavioural finance advances that psychology- and sociology-based theories can explain stock market anomalies and investment decisions. For example, paying more for shares in a company now than they are worth in the expectation that the company will generate more funds in the future when available information does not back up that assumption. 'Herding' is also an example of the behavioural nature of the stock markets. When herding occurs, market participants buy and sell certain shares because it is topical to do so, not because of any information that has come to light. A prime example of this herd mentality was the dotcom boom and bust wave that ended in 2000 (Shiller, 2003). When behavioural finance is accepted as a plausible theoretical explanation for some stock market behaviour, this suggests that the EMH does not explain market prices fully and that there are other 'behavioural' influences.

Chaos Theory

It has also been suggested that stock markets are chaotic. This means that small changes can have major impacts in the future, that even though there seems to be an apparent lack of order in the stock market, prices nevertheless follow set rules – they are deterministic; however, the outcome cannot be predicted. Under **chaos theory**, stock price is affected by a trader's own personal motives, volume changes, acceleration of these changes and the momentum behind the changes.

COMPANY FINANCE

Company finance is categorised into three classifications according to the term of the finance instrument. A finance instrument's **term** is the length of time the finance is arranged for. The three finance classifications are: short term, medium term and long term.

FIGURE 10.1: FINANCE DURATION

Short-term finance	Finance with a term of up to one year.
Medium-term finance	Finance with a term of between one and seven years.
Long-term finance	Finance with a term of over seven years.

Details of the most common types of finance by term are considered in **Chapters 11–14**, though it should be noted that sources of finance cannot be neatly pigeonholed according to their duration; in reality, there are overlaps. For example, leases are commonly regarded as being medium-term sources of finance, yet a computer can be leased for a week and a building may be leased for 20 years.

ASSET MIX

All assets have to be financed. A company's finance needs will be influenced by the make-up of its assets – the **asset mix**. A company's assets are split into two categories: non-current (fixed assets) and current assets. **Non-current assets** are assets that are deemed to have a life of more than one year, whereas **current assets** are expected to be realised as cash within one year.

Characteristics of Non-current Assets

Non-current assets are usually the result of a conscious strategic management decision to invest funds in capital items for operating activities (for example, buildings, machinery, motor vehicles or fixtures and fittings) or for investment purposes (for example, obtaining a portfolio of shares, investment properties or business ventures). In all instances, the expected return should exceed the average cost of the company's funds and the return that could be obtained from other opportunities. Due to their nature, non-current assets are generally not very liquid relative to current assets. For example, it may take considerable time to construct/modify a building for sale, particularly where it has been purpose-built for the company's needs.

Lack of liquidity also increases the risk associated with investing in non-current assets, as the return from most non-current asset investments is susceptible to changes in the financial environment. For example, if a company manufactures luxury goods and a recession begins, production will slow down and the resale value of its machines will fall. Each machine might have been costly to purchase, hence the relative impact of the recession on the company is high. A change in technology will have the same impact, as will changes in trends or fashions. Obtaining a portfolio of non-current assets across various complementary and negatively correlated business projects might spread and reduce the risk to a company's future, were one long-term project to fail.

Characteristics of Current Assets

Current assets encompass a company's investment in inventories, trade receivables, short-term financial securities and cash. Current assets have a lower return when compared with non-current assets. For example, monies held in a bank account will provide a marginal return as will monies in short-term monetary securities. However, investment in working capital can range from being a cost – for example, when there are inventory shortages (i.e. stock-outs) – to being a return – when additional sales result from the policy being pursued, i.e. providing longer credit terms relative to competitors. Current assets, if managed appropriately (see **Chapter 6** for more detail), are not as risky as non-current assets because they are not as prone to losses resulting from changes in the environment or to a downturn in a particular company or product. For example, when there is a downturn or reduction in demand, inventories can be reduced, minimising the overall loss if, for example, a product line were to be dropped.

OPTIMAL ASSET MIX

A business finance manager should aim to hold the correct mix of assets by balancing the carrying costs associated with holding current assets with the shortage costs that may occur when investment in current assets falls. The **carrying cost** associated with investing in current assets includes an **opportunity cost**, in that it reflects the revenue lost had the funds been invested in non-current assets. **Shortage costs** include all those costs that result from current asset levels being kept too low. These include: lost sales when there are stock-outs; disruption in production caused by stock-outs; lost sales caused by the credit period on offer being too tight; default payments being required when money securities have to be encashed before their maturity; overdraft interest when the cash account runs out; defaulting on loan repayments; and, the most severe cost of all, the company being put into liquidation by its creditors because of lack of liquidity.

The following inventory economic order quantity cost graph portrays the relationship between the two types of costs and highlights the optimal level of current assets to hold.

FIGURE 10.2: THE RELATIONSHIP BETWEEN THE COSTS ASSOCIATED WITH HOLDING CURRENT ASSETS AND THE LEVEL OF INVESTMENT IN CURRENT ASSETS (NEUTRAL POLICY)

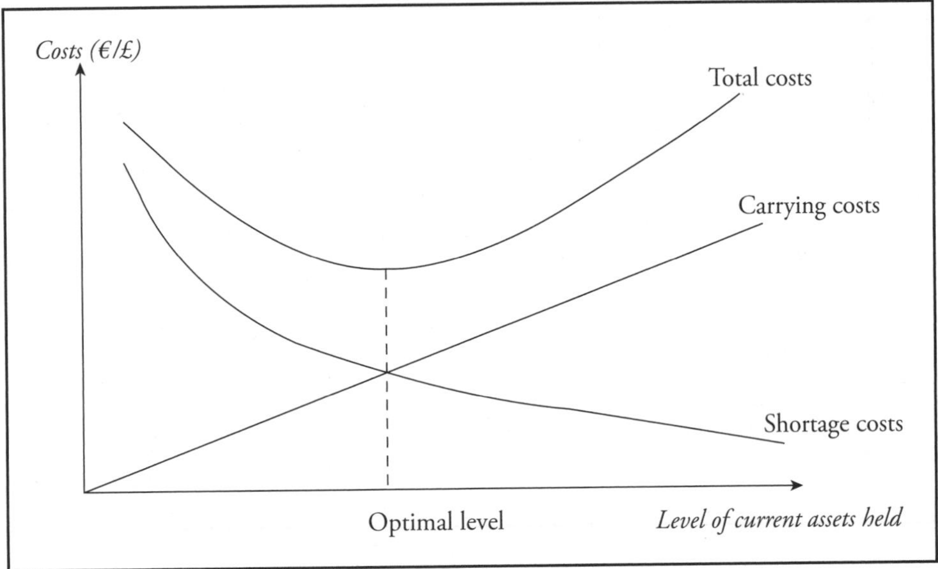

In this example, the optimal level of current assets to hold is the amount at which the total cost of holding current assets is minimised. The differences in these costs and how they change relative to the change in the investment in current assets will influence the asset mix investment policy.

Current Assets: Investment Policies

There are typically three polarised policies in relation to the investment of a company in its current assets. They are referred to as the aggressive, neutral and conservative policies. These terms are also used in relation to a company's working capital policy, which underlies the investment in current assets (see **Chapter 6** for more detail) and, furthermore, are used in relation to the finance policy adopted by a company. The **neutral policy** is sometimes referred to as the **traditional policy**. The typical pattern of costs of a company pursuing this policy would be similar to those reflected in the above graph.

When the carrying costs of current assets are low relative to shortage costs, a **conservative policy** should be adopted. The conservative policy is sometimes referred to as a

flexible policy. This involves holding higher levels of current assets (i.e. inventories, trade receivables, marketable securities and cash). The patterns of costs that may stimulate a business finance manager to pursue a conservative policy are portrayed in the following graph.

FIGURE 10.3: THE RELATIONSHIP BETWEEN THE COSTS ASSOCIATED WITH HOLDING CURRENT ASSETS AND THE LEVEL OF INVESTMENT IN CURRENT ASSETS (CONSERVATIVE POLICY)

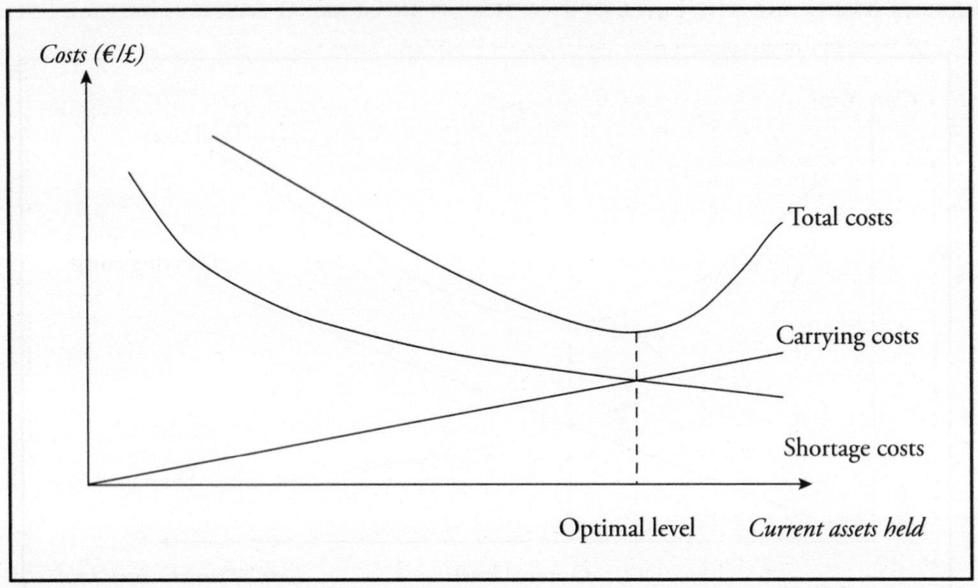

This policy is appropriate where the carrying cost of current assets is not high. This may be the case when there are not many profitable investment opportunities and the return to be earned from long-term equity or money market investments is not high. This is most likely the case when the economy is in recession. Shortage costs will also be lower, as the risk of stock-outs is lower due to higher inventory levels. In addition, a company is more likely to obtain high sales levels, because of higher inventory levels and long credit periods. Companies pursing this policy may be able to charge a higher sales price. On the downside, there may be increased bad debts. The conservative policy is characterised by a high ratio of current assets to total assets. Another indicator is where there is a high ratio of current assets to sales.

The third policy that might be adopted is the **aggressive** or **restrictive policy**. This is where a company holds low levels of current assets, if any at all. It is characterised by a company having a low ratio of current assets to total assets, and a low ratio of current assets to sales. This policy should be pursued when the carrying cost of current assets is high relative to the shortage costs. This is likely to happen when an economy is in boom and the carrying costs – or opportunity cost – of investing in current assets is high as there are many alternative high-return investment opportunities available. In addition, shortage costs are not as high as they would be under the neutral or conservative situations. Again, this would be the case when the economy is in boom as a lost sale from having a stock-out is easily substituted by another sale. In these circumstances demand is high, outstripping supply. The patterns of costs that would support a finance manager pursuing this type of policy are portrayed in **Figure 10.4**.

FIGURE 10.4: THE RELATIONSHIP BETWEEN THE COSTS ASSOCIATED WITH HOLDING CURRENT ASSETS AND THE LEVEL OF INVESTMENT IN CURRENT ASSETS (AGGRESSIVE POLICY)

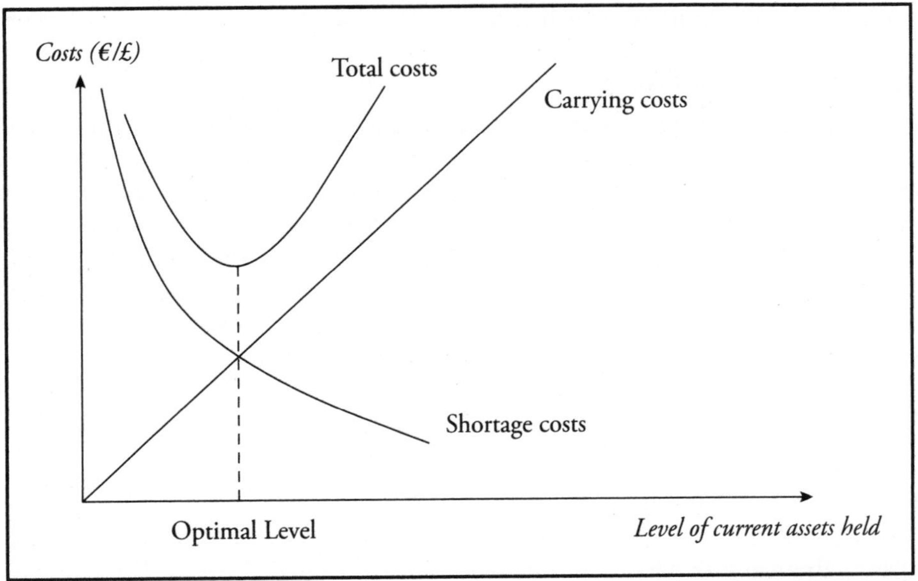

Other Influences on Asset Mix

The Nature of the Business

Some industries have to carry higher proportions of non-current assets to service their core operational activities. For example, manufacturers are likely to operate from bespoke premises, which normally have to be built by the company, as the cost of getting a landlord to provide a bespoke building is high. The production process usually requires a substantial investment in plant and equipment. These non-current assets are likely to be a permanent feature of a manufacturing company's statement of financial position. The investment in inventories will also form a significant proportion of the current-asset investment, as the costs associated with having a stock-out are high.

On the other hand, software development companies can operate with relatively low levels of operational non-current assets and can invest surplus funds into new projects, achieving faster growth. Due to the nature of their business, software companies can rent premises, as only standard office space is required, and lease their hardware requirements. The main non-current asset likely to be found in the statement of financial position of a software development company is development expenditure – an intangible asset, and a riskier type of non-current asset when compared with tangible assets. The life of capitalised development expenditure may be volatile as it is linked to the potential economic benefits that are expected from the project. Where earnings expectations fall or viability is called into question, an immediate write-down will result.

Seasonal Nature of Revenue

Where a company has a constant pattern of revenue throughout the year, its investment in current assets can remain constant. However, where the company has seasonal fluctuations in its trade, levels of current assets will vary.

Managerial Attitude to Risk

Holding low levels of current assets is regarded as a risky strategy, as a company is more likely to have liquidity issues. This may not be an attractive policy to management, even in a boom economy where this policy works best, as there may be long-term repercussions. Such repercussions include loss of supplier goodwill resulting from taking too long a credit period, loss of goodwill with the bank as a result of breaching the overdraft too often and loss of customer goodwill because of inconsistent supply of the product due to stock-outs. Therefore, though the most profitable strategy in the short term might be to pursue an aggressive policy, management could opt for a long-term strategy and hold higher levels of current assets.

THE FINANCE MIX

A company's **finance mix** refers to the proportion of a company's assets that are financed by short-term, medium-term and long-term finance.

The Structure of Assets from a Finance Perspective

Investment in non-current assets is a long-term financial commitment. Investment in current assets is a commitment for a short period of time, usually less than one year. However, a portion of the investment in current assets is permanent (though constantly turning over) as a company always requires inventories to sell, must provide credit and must have sufficient liquidity to pay operational costs, such as wages. Therefore, a long-term investment in **permanent current assets** is required. Few companies have constant demand and constant costs. There is usually some seasonal variation or surge in costs. For example, in winter utility costs might be higher due to poor weather conditions, or revenue may increase because of Christmas. This results in a company having a requirement to build up **temporary current assets** to service increased demand or increased costs. For example, before Christmas there may be a build-up of inventory, which will be run down over the Christmas and January sales period.

Figure 10.5 depicts the possible pattern of investment in a company's assets, where the company is not experiencing any growth.

FIGURE 10.5: THE STRUCTURE OF A COMPANY'S ASSETS (NO GROWTH)

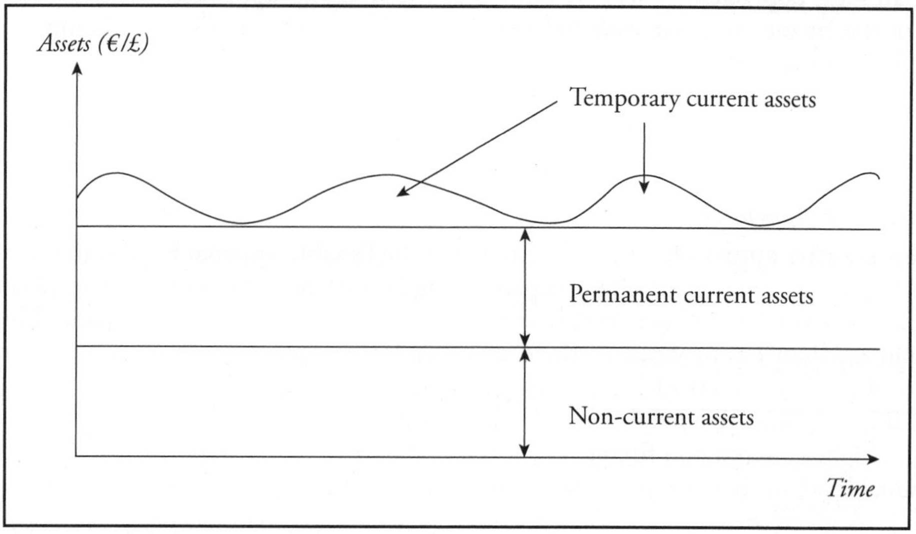

Assets (€/£)
Temporary current assets
Permanent current assets
Non-current assets
Time

Where a company experiences growth, the structure of its assets will change in line with the pattern portrayed in **Figure 10.6**. Additional finance will be required for the increased investment in total assets.

FIGURE 10.6: THE STRUCTURE OF A COMPANY'S ASSETS (GROWTH)

Assets (€/£)
Temporary current assets
Permanent current assets
Non-current assets
Time

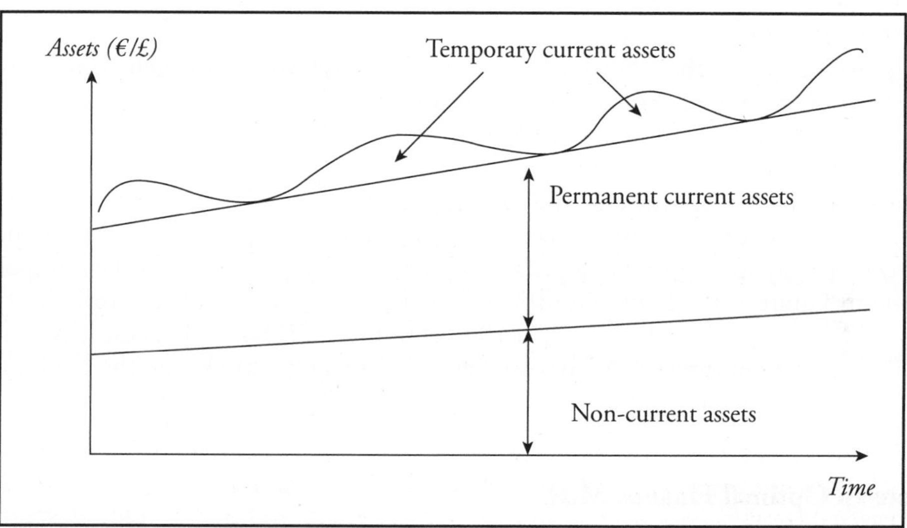

Finance Mix: Three Policies

There are three approaches to the financing of a company's assets: matching approach; conservative approach; and aggressive approach. These are discussed in turn.

Matching Approach

The **matching approach**, otherwise known as the **hedging approach**, aims to match the terms of the finance sourced with the maturities of the investments/assets being financed. Therefore, non-current assets and permanent current assets will be financed using mostly long-term, and possibly some medium-term, sources of finance. Temporary current assets will be financed using short-term sources of finance, such as a bank overdraft. This approach is best suited to a steady economy.

Conservative Approach

The **conservative approach**, otherwise known as the **flexible approach**, aims to fully match the peak finance requirement of a company using long-term sources of finance. This means that non-current assets and permanent and temporary current assets are all financed by long-term and medium-term sources of finance. When the temporary current asset requirement reduces, there is an excess of funds available. These excess funds are invested in temporary marketable securities. Under this policy, the company never has liquidity issues, though it will have higher interest and finance costs and higher debt capital repayments. This policy is most suitable when there is a recession, as it will be more difficult to obtain short-term funds quickly and, given the increased risk, these funds are likely to be more costly than they would be if the economy were in boom. In a recession, customers may take longer to pay and more might default, hence the company cannot be fully reliant on trade receivables as a reliable source of finance. In addition, suppliers will give premium discounts for quick payment, so having surplus funds available will increase profitability. Finally, the company will have a comparative advantage over others that do not have readily available funds, when speculative opportunities arise.

Aggressive Approach

The **aggressive approach**, otherwise known as the **restrictive approach**, aims to maximise the level of short-term finance and to minimise the level of long-term finance that a company uses. Short-term sources are used to finance all temporary current asset requirements, a portion of the permanent current asset requirements and, in extreme cases, some of the non-current asset requirements. This approach will result in a company having little or no cash. Such a company usually conducts its business using a large overdraft and takes a long time to pay its suppliers. Liquidity is likely to be a problem and the company will be prone to failure if the bank withdraws its support, regardless of its profitability. This approach will only be successful when the economy is in boom because customers are more likely to pay on time, bad debts are lower, interest rates are lower, the bank manager is more likely to have an optimistic view and creditors will not be too annoyed at late payments.

Is There an Optimal Finance Mix?

When managing the finance mix, the objective should be to determine the optimal investment level in short-term, medium-term and long-term sources of finance. This will require an investigation into the costs and benefits to be obtained from the various alternative approaches. This process will involve investigating the trade-off between an aggressive and a conservative approach and coming up with the option that minimises costs, hence maximising equity holder wealth. However, there are various factors that may restrict or influence the approach that is pursued. These are now discussed.

ATTRIBUTES OF FINANCE WITH DIFFERENT TERMS

Several factors influence the decision on whether to raise short-term or long-term finance. Each different type of finance, regardless of its term, has differing costs and benefits and these are outlined under the specific finance type in the chapters in **Part III**. Some of the generic factors that influence the decision to opt for long-term or short-term finance are now outlined. This should aid understanding of the motivation for business finance managers to pursue either the aggressive, matching or conservative approach.

Set-up Costs

Set-up costs are the initial costs that are incurred in obtaining finance. These include costs such as bank commission, broker fees and administration fees. Short-term finance has lower set-up costs relative to long-term finance, due to having lower credit risk – as the term of finance is shorter, the risk of default is lower.

Interest Costs (and Liquidity)

Short-term sources of finance normally have lower interest costs relative to long-term sources. The relationship may be similar to that represented in **Figure 10.7**.

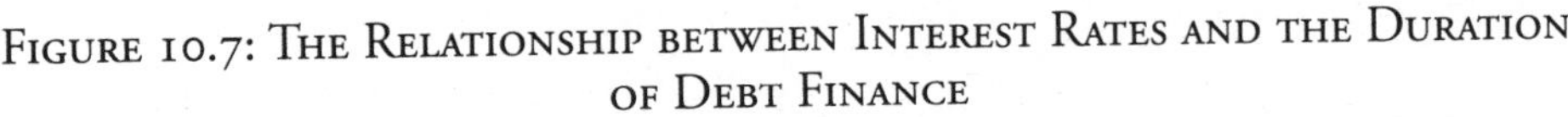

FIGURE 10.7: THE RELATIONSHIP BETWEEN INTEREST RATES AND THE DURATION OF DEBT FINANCE

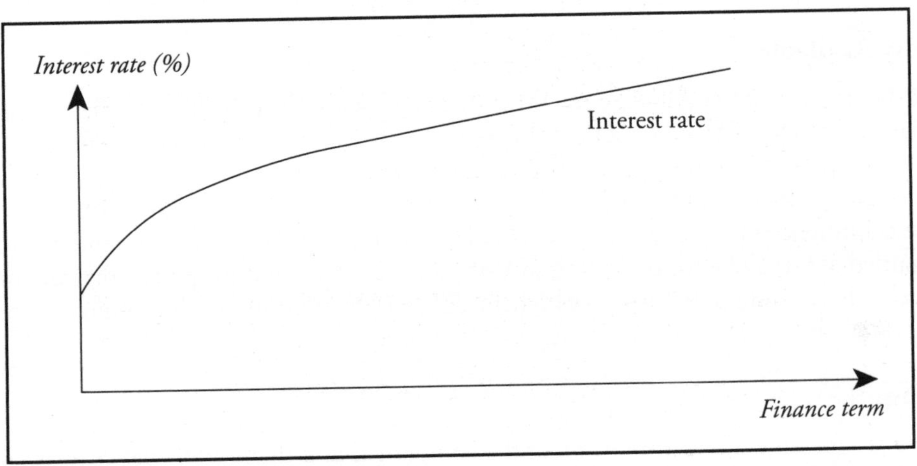

As there is more risk associated with providing finance for longer periods of time, the premium or interest rate charged is higher. The interest differential between short-term and long-term sources of finance is said to be explained by the **liquidity preference theory**. This theory suggests that borrowers prefer to obtain long-term finance as this is less risky for them; however, lenders prefer to provide short-term finance as this is less risky for them. Therefore, to encourage lenders to provide long-term finance, a premium has to be given in the form of increased interest rates. Another theory suggests that long-term finance attracts a higher interest rate due to the influence of inflation. Long-term rates are adjusted upwards to take account of expected inflation – the higher rate equates to a real rate, which is similar to that charged on short-term finance. This is known as the **pure expectations theory**.

Type of Finance

This is discussed in detail in **Chapters 11–14**. Some sources of finance are more costly to set up than others. Tradable market sources, such as equity and tradable debt, are more costly to arrange than non-marketable sources, such as bank debt. For example, issuing equity may involve holding meetings with current equity holders, preparing and publicising a prospectus, paying broker fees and commission and substantial managerial time. Over the past decade there has been an increase in the use of sustainable finance. **Sustainable finance** involves the integration of ESG (environmental, societal and governance) motivations into mainstream investment and lending decisions and products with specific environmental or social aims. Lenders who buy sustainable finance products from companies, such as Green bonds, typically require lower coupon rates when compared to normal bonds.

Size of Company

Small companies find it more difficult to raise long-term finance. They may not be quoted on the stock exchange. Even if they are, it may not be economical to issue shares or tradable debt securities. Large companies are also restricted, to an extent, as they have to be careful not to deviate from their optimal capital structure (see **Chapter 16**). Small companies are more likely to opt for a mixture of medium-term and short-term finance to service their investment needs and are more likely to source their needs from suppliers, banks and finance houses.

Security Available

Where a company has tangible assets, these can be provided as security to a finance provider for finance received. The assets act as a form of guarantee, in that the finance provided has a charge, or first claim, to the proceeds when an asset is sold. This reduces the risks associated with providing finance and usually brings down the cost of finance. Therefore, the cost of finance is influenced by the type of assets held by a company. Assets, such as land or property, are regarded as attractive for providing security (because land and property normally increase in value), whereas intangible assets (which are subject to variation in value and are susceptible to economic changes) are not as attractive.

Gearing

Gearing is a measure of the proportion of the company that is financed by debt sources relative to equity sources (see **Chapter 16** for further information on gearing). A high level of gearing is indicative of high **financial risk**. Debt sources of finance are regarded as more risky than equity sources of finance because debt capital is repayable and has an interest cost. Therefore, debt levels will impact on the liquidity and profitability of a company. The current level of financial risk influences the costs (i.e. set-up and interest costs) of new sources of finance.

Business Risk

Different companies have different cost structures. Some have higher proportions of fixed costs, hence they have higher business risk, whereas other companies have predominantly variable costs and hence lower business risk. The sensitivity of a company's cost structure can be measured using the operating leverage ratio. Business risk also encapsulates the sensitivity of a company's activities to changes in the financial environment (for example, inflationary increases or changes in exchange rates). The elasticity of demand for a company's products will also influence business risk. The higher the level of business risk associated with a company, the higher the cost of finance.

Credit Rating

A company's credit rating is also important (see **Chapter 8** for a fuller discussion of this). A company that is well established, with a history of strong performance and financial management, can negotiate lower set-up costs and interest costs relative to a company that is just starting out and has no credit history, or a company that has a poor credit history. Companies without a track record will incur hidden costs, in addition to set-up and interest fees. These costs may include providing quarterly accounts, regular review meetings and having their decision-making curbed by restrictive covenants (see **Chapter 13** for a discussion of restrictive covenants).

CONCLUSION

The financial environment encompasses the economic environment and the financial markets. Business finance managers need knowledge of the potential influence of shifts in macro-economic variables on a company's operating activities and finances. They also need to know where to source finance, how the financial system operates and influences on the financial system, including theories on the behaviour of share price within capital markets.

When selecting finance, a company should first look to its own assets to determine the correct type and duration of finance to obtain. The asset-mix decision will influence the finance-mix decision. Potential influences on the asset mix (type and level of asset to hold, i.e. non-current and current) include industry norms, nature of the products being sold, seasonality of sales, the state of the economy and managerial attitude. The finance mix refers to the portion of short-, medium- and long-term finance a company should source. Theoretically, a matching approach is deemed to be most appropriate, wherein the term of the finance should match the term of the investment.

EXAMINATION STANDARD QUESTION: EMH

Enero Plc announces a breakthrough in computer memory storage devices that are so small they can be fitted to mobile phones. Knowledge of this information was secret up to the point of the announcement. The price of the share before the announcement was €/£5.00. Consider the following outcomes:

(a) Following the announcement, the price of each equity share jumps to €/£6.50 and then over the subsequent week falls to €/£5.75.
(b) Following the announcement, the price of each equity share jumps to €/£5.75 and stays there.

(c) Following the announcement the price of each equity share slowly climbs to €/£5.75.

Requirement Which outcome indicates market efficiency? Which outcomes do not, and why?

Solution

(a) Inefficient market: the market initially overreacts to the good news about the breakthrough, causing share price to increase to €/£6.50. After a period of time, the share price returns to its 'true value' of €/£5.75.
(b) Efficient market: this is evidence of a 'semi-strong-form efficient market', wherein the good news is reflected immediately, with the share price rising to €/£5.75 when the information is made public. The share price before the announcement was €/£5.00, reflecting the situation before the announcement.
(c) Inefficient market: this is evidence of an inefficient market as the market is slow to react to the announcement.

Key Terms

Aggressive approach/policy
Asset mix
Behavioural finance
Capital markets
Carrying cost
Chaos theory
Conservative approach/policy
Current assets
Disintermediation
Economic environment
Efficient market
Finance mix
Financial environment
Financial institutions
Financial markets
Neutral policy
Financial risk
Financial system
Flexible approach/policy
Gearing
Hedging approach
Inflation
Information asymmetry
Intermediation
Liquidity preference theory
Long-term finance
Macrofinance
Matching approach
Medium-term finance
Microfinance
Money markets
Non-current assets
Opportunity cost
Optimal asset mix
Permanent current assets
Pure expectations theory
Restrictive policy
Semi-strong-form efficiency
Set-up costs
Strong-form efficiency
Short-term finance
Shortage costs
Temporary current assets
Term
Traditional policy
Weak-form efficiency

REVIEW QUESTIONS

(See Suggested Solutions to Review Questions in **Appendix B**.)

Question 10.1

Explain the term 'disintermediation'.

Question 10.2

Explain the difference between current assets and non-current assets.

Question 10.3
Explain the difference between permanent current assets and temporary current assets.

Question 10.4
What are the costs that have to be balanced when deciding on the most appropriate asset mix?

Question 10.5
Outline the main characteristics of neutral, flexible and restrictive policies in relation to asset-mix choice.

Question 10.6
Outline the main characteristics of matching, flexible and restrictive policies in relation to finance-mix choice.

Question 10.7
Explain the three forms of market efficiency as suggested by Fama in 1970.

CHALLENGING QUESTIONS

(Suggested Solutions to Challenging Questions are available through your lecturer.)

Question 10.1 Alexander (Levels 1 and 2)
Write an essay for the board of directors of Alexander Ltd about the impact that changes in the economy may have on its business. The essay should cover three issues. The first two are:

(a) how changes in the economic environment might impact on the demand for the company's products and on the performance of the company; and

(b) how changes in the economic environment would impact on business finance decision-making.

The third issue is to respond to a suggestion made by one of the directors to you (the finance director) over tea: Ian Smart informed you that a way to alleviate the impact of the expected downturn in the economy would be to open a factory in Tioeti (a fictional country). He suggests that with a couple of small bribes to the right people, a suitable factory can be obtained and that the local indigenous population (from the age of five upwards) would be delighted to work for a mere fraction of the wages being paid in this country. This would reduce costs and increase profit margins, which would more than outweigh the expected reduction in sales units.

(c) Advise the board as to the appropriateness of this proposal.

Total 15 Marks

Question 10.2 Stock Market Efficiency (Levels 1 and 2)
(a) Why are new equity issues more common when the stock market index is high, relative to when it is low?

10 Marks

(b) Are the reasons provided in (a) inconsistent with the efficient market hypothesis?

10 Marks

Total 20 Marks

Question 10.3 Efficient Markets (Levels 1 and 2)

(a) Describe the efficient market hypothesis and explain its three forms.

15 Marks

(b) Discuss the relevance of the hypothesis outlined in (a) for the internal business financial management of public quoted companies.

10 Marks

Total 25 Marks

Question 10.4 Flash (Level 1)

The country's economy is contracting. You are the financial controller of Flash Ltd, a medium-sized company. You have noted a recent disimprovement in the credit control average collection period for sales. Also, in the course of a recent routine meeting with the company's bank manager, you were mildly irritated by the bank's comment that all companies need to avoid overtrading in the current international 'credit-crunch' climate, as lending criteria would be applied more strictly to future loan applications.

Your managing director reminds you that two aspects of working capital policy that require managerial decisions are:

1. the level of net current assets; and
2. the manner in which they are financed, i.e. the mix of short-, medium- and long-term finance.

Requirement Discuss aggressive, moderate and prudent (conservative) policies in these two areas, indicating the relative advantages and disadvantages of each of the three policies for Flash Ltd.

15 Marks

(Based on Chartered Accountants Ireland, CAP 1, Finance, Autumn 2008, Q5)

Question 10.5 EMH/Hearts (Level 1)

(a) Describe the Efficient Market Hypothesis (EMH) and outline the differences between the three levels of efficiency in the EMH.

4 Marks

(b) Hearts Plc agreed to purchase the shares of Queen Plc. The share price of Queen Plc increased substantially **before** the official announcement of the takeover. Explain this movement in Queen's share price in the context of the Efficient Market Hypothesis (EMH).

3 Marks

(Based on Chartered Accountants Ireland, CAP 1, Finance, Summer 2008, Q6(b))

Question 10.6 Economic Environment (Level 1)

Explain the difference between microeconomics and macroeconomics and provide ONE example of each.

4 Marks

(Based on Chartered Accountants Ireland, CAP 1, Finance, Autumn 2019, Q1)

Question 10.7 Asset Mix (Level 1)

Establishing an appropriate asset-mix policy is a dynamic process and it plays a key role in determining a company's overall risk and return. Discuss THREE asset-mix policies a company could adopt.

6 Marks

(Based on Chartered Accountants Ireland, CAP 1, Finance, Autumn 2017, Q2)

11

Short-term Sources of Finance

Learning Objectives

Upon completing this chapter, readers should be able to:

- list and explain internal short-term sources of finance;
- list and discuss short-term sources of finance from banks, other providers and the money markets; and
- outline short-term sources of finance for the sale of goods on credit to foreign customers.

INTRODUCTION

Short-term sources of finance are loosely considered to be sources that meet requirements that do not extend beyond one year or are repayable on demand. Short-term sources are the most commonly used type of finance. The majority of companies, regardless of size, use some form of short-term finance. There are several sources of short-term finance, including suppliers, financial intermediaries, the public and owners. Over the past decade, new regulation and advances in technology have encouraged a range of innovative sources of finance, as detailed in **Real World Example 11.1**.

Real World Example 11.1: Growth of Fintech

The Competition and Markets Authority introduced regulation in support of open banking which came into force in the UK in 2018. This regulation is designed to promote competition and innovation in the financial services markets. As a safeguard, all providers who use open banking to offer products and services must be regulated by the Financial Conduct Authority (FCA) or European equivalent. The regulation has provided opportunities for 'fintech' (financial technology) companies that work with banks and other financial services providers to provide data that should improve credit decision-making and management. The reach of fintech companies is extending and is resulting in innovative technologies that are disrupting traditional financial services. It is advancing technologies in the area of mobile phone payments, money transfers, loans, fundraising and asset management.

Money market finance can be obtained for short periods: this involves channelling funds from lenders to borrowers. The main participants in the money markets are financial intermediaries. Financial intermediaries include banks, discount houses and factor companies, to name a few. Though innovative sources of short-term funds are increasing, the bank is probably the most important source as it fosters long-term relationships with clients that focus on providing banking services, including servicing their finance needs. Therefore, this chapter provides more detail on finance provided by banks and what this entails relative to the other sources. Types of short-term finance include extending trade credit received, overdrafts, short-term loans, factoring, invoice discounting, inventory financing and bill finance. Factoring can be entered into as a long-term source of finance; however, the agreement can be stopped by the factor company with short notice, hence is considered in this chapter.

This chapter starts by briefly discussing the providers of short-term finance, then the most common forms of short-term finance are described; in particular, bank-sourced, short-term finance. Finally, finance for international trade is considered in brief.

PROVIDERS OF SHORT-TERM FINANCE

Most short-term finance is obtained through **intermediation** (i.e. from the national clearing banks, foreign-owned clearing banks, consortium banks or other financial institutions). Financial intermediaries will arrange finance internally or may use acceptance houses, discount houses and the money markets.

Acceptance Houses

Acceptance houses are mostly merchant banks that take in short-term deposits and issue longer-term loans. They may not even have to pay out funds, but may provide a guarantee to pay a set amount on a set date. This guarantee can then be sold by a customer, who pays the acceptance house a commission for providing the guarantee. At the end of the period, either the company pays the agreed sum, or the acceptance house does. If it is the latter, then the company will have to pay the acceptance house back according to the agreement. This may be by installment and typically includes interest. Acceptance houses mostly deal with financial intermediaries on behalf of themselves and their customers, though they also have a strong relationship with large corporate companies. In terms of short-term sources of finance, acceptance houses trade in term loans, bills of exchange, acceptance credits, commercial paper and certificates of deposits (in various currencies). The role of acceptance houses is vital in ensuring that a liquid market for short-term paper finance (i.e. bill finance) exists.

Discount Houses

Like acceptance houses, discount houses also create liquid markets for short-term financial products. **Discount houses** buy and sell short-term financial instruments, such as government securities (e.g. treasury bills and local authority bills), commercial paper, certificates of deposit, bills of exchange and acceptance credits. They operate in a similar manner to a stock exchange or bond market and quote prices at which they are willing to trade. The dealers are usually other discount houses, merchant banks and major banks – most major banks have a discount house department. The dealers purchase and sell these bills on behalf of their own organisation, large companies, pension companies and insurance companies.

SHORT-TERM SOURCES OF FINANCE

The rest of this chapter explains the main sources of short-term finance that are available either internally through intermediation or independently (i.e. disintermediation).

Internally Generated Sources of Short-term Finance

Internally generated finance is the easiest and most commonly used source of short-term finance. There are two potential sources of funds: expense accruals and working capital. These are now discussed in turn.

Expense Accruals

Accruals are a source of finance as the service or good is consumed in advance of payment being required. For example, VAT is collected from customers on sales made, but is not paid to the government until a set period has elapsed. In addition to internal sources, companies can arrange credit deals with financial intermediaries to fund the payment of major accruals, such as taxes, including VAT, accounting and audit fees or insurance fees. A financial intermediary might agree to pay the debt, after which the company pays the financial intermediary the amount outstanding, plus interest, over a short period, ranging from one month to 12 months. This is usually a costly source of finance, with the financial intermediary charging a high rate of interest relative to the base rate.

Working Capital

The company can manage its working capital to release funds in the short term. When a company makes a sale on credit, it is effectively providing a loan to the customer for an agreed period. If the credit terms have not been strictly administered in the past and the customers have become slack in paying on time, then emphasis could be put on making the credit-collection system more efficient (see **Chapter 8**). This will get funds in quicker. Another option is to put incentives in place to encourage customers to pay their accounts quicker than the agreed credit terms. Such an incentive could involve offering a discount. Discounts are a costly form of finance, as the effective yearly interest rate of even a small discount is quite high, usually more than an overdraft rate, and the decision should only be taken if it is beneficial for the company. Providing credit is a complicated decision that takes many factors into account (see **Chapter 8**). The crux of the decision is to weigh up the loss of sales that would result from reducing the credit period with the finance, administration and bad debt costs that would be saved. In addition, liquidity and the ease of sourcing finance are major influences.

Trade payables are another internal source of finance for a company. Trade credit can be used as a further source of credit where a company takes longer than the initial agreed period to pay the amount owing. This is best done with agreement from the supplier, as goodwill might be reduced otherwise. This is a simple, convenient and cheap source of finance, so long as discounts are not lost. It is flexible and is available to all companies regardless of size. The potential cost of not paying a supplier within the agreed timeframe is portrayed in **Worked Example 11.1**.

Worked Example 11.1: Discounts

Gate Plc has an overdraft facility of up to €/£1 million. The bank charges 10% on the outstanding balance. Gate Plc is not near its limit. Verano Plc (a supplier) offers Gate Plc a 2% discount if it pays its account within 10 days. Gate Plc currently takes 50 days' credit.

Requirement

(a) Calculate whether it would be more beneficial for Gate Plc to pay Verano Plc in sufficient time to avail of the discount, or to take the full 50 days' credit.

(b) Assume the information relates to an invoice for €/£100,000. Show the benefit to the company of both options.

Solution

(a) This question involves working out the effective yearly cost of each option to Gate Plc.

Discount The cost of the discount is: 2%/(100% − 2%) = 0.0204 for a 40-day (i.e. 50 − 10) period.

Number of 40-day periods in a year is: 365 ÷ 40 = 9.125

Therefore the effective annual interest rate is: $(1.0204)^{9.125} - 1 = 20.23\%$

Overdraft The effective annual interest rate on the overdraft is 10%. Therefore the company will be better off extending its overdraft and paying Verano Plc within 10 days to avail of the discount.

(b) *Discount* Taking the discount option will result in a reduction in the amount to be paid by the company of €/£100,000 × 2% = €/£2,000.

Overdraft If the company does not take the discount, but elects not to have to pay the funds until day 50, then the company will save interest on the additional 40 days that the €/£100,000 can remain in the bank. The daily rate of interest (i) is:

$$(1 + i)^{365} = 1.1$$

$$i = \sqrt[365]{1.1} - 1$$

$$i = 0.00026$$

Therefore the total interest saving for 40 days is 0.00026 × 40 = 0.0104 = 1.04%.

The total saving in interest to the company will be €/£100,000 × 1.04% = €/£1,040.

Therefore, the company will be €/£960 [€/£ 2,000 − €/£1,040] better off by taking the discount and incurring the additional interest cost.

SOURCING FINANCE FROM FINANCIAL INTERMEDIARIES

Traditional Bank Sources

The most common types of finance provided by banking institutions are bank overdrafts and loans. Bank overdrafts are granted for short periods of time, though are commonly rolled over on review dates and are used by some companies as permanent sources of finance. Term loans can range from short-term loans to long-term mortgages. Banks also provide finance secured on a company's trade receivables and inventory, though this is less common. In all instances, banks assess the credit risk associated with providing finance and vary the terms according to this risk assessment. This section starts by considering the lending decision from a bank manager's perspective, then information required to inform this decision is outlined. Finally, various forms of finance provided by banks are explained.

Lending Decision

Banks normally consider two aspects of each lending decision. The first involves determining whether the borrowing company can afford to make repayments. This is a **going concern issue.** Most banks try to ensure that they are not the cause of their client going out of business – this would be counterproductive for both parties. The second involves the recoverability of capital in the event of the company going into liquidation (i.e. a **liquidation issue**). Banks have been criticised in the past for focusing on ensuring that there has been sufficient security for their loans. This meant that many small companies with low levels of tangible assets found it difficult to obtain debt at reasonable rates. Banks have been urged to give precedence to affordability and to support their clients, rather than ensuring that loans are secured on property. In most instances, banks write into the finance agreement a right to appoint a receiver if the payments go into arrears. In practice, banks will try to reschedule the finance to suit the company and still ensure that the debt does not end up bad.

A helpful shorthand used to summarise the key information sought by lenders when assessing credit risk in respect of consumer lending is the '7Cs of credit'. The 7Cs are explained in **Real World Example 11.2.**

REAL WORLD EXAMPLE 11.2: THE 7CS OF CREDIT

Credit providers regularly consider the '7Cs of credit' when assessing whether to provide credit or not. The 7Cs of credit are:

1. Character
2. Capacity
3. Capital
4. Collateral
5. Conditions
6. Credit history
7. Common sense

Character refers to the willingness of the customer to pay as per the credit agreement. It involves assessing how often the consumer pays retail accounts, credit cards and other obligations.

Capacity reflects the consumer's ability to repay credit. This involves assessing the customer's earnings and outgoings and seeing if there is sufficient surplus funds left to repay any credit given.

Capital is the net worth of the customer. In particular, the availability of assets as these can be regarded as a wealth cushion that can be tapped if the customer's earnings were to decrease. The view is, if the credit provider is putting a certain amount into the investment, what is being invested in hard cash by the company? The credit provider does not want to accept all the risks associated with the venture.

Collateral refers to the security offered by the consumer. Tangible, appreciating assets, such as buildings, are considered the most attractive for credit providers, though motor vehicles are commonly used as collateral by lease companies who provide finance on the vehicle. Inventory and trade receivables can also be used as collateral.

Conditions includes both microfinance and macrofinance factors and their current and expected impact on the customer's ability to make credit repayments in the future.

Credit history involves assessing the customer's prior credit record. This allows the credit provider to assess the customer's credit management in the past.

Common sense is an intangible feature. It involves intuition and an overall assessment of what the credit is required for, how likely it is to succeed, how good the management team are and whether they are likely to default if times get tough.

The following information may be requested from a company by a bank to assist it in making its lending decision. The quantity of information required depends on the size of the loan requested. The information is normally presented as part of a **business plan**.

Business Plan Contents

Requirements

The introduction to a business plan should set out the *finance requirement* being requested. This will identify the *amount*, *interest structure* (e.g. overdrafts are normally variable rate; term loans can be variable or fixed rate), *term*, *purpose* of the funds and *source of repayment*. The main body of the business plan should refer to projections in the appendices that provide details of the repayment structure. This allows the bank to assess the company's ability to meet the repayment commitment.

Purpose of the Finance

The company should highlight the investment it plans to undertake. Examples include: purchasing machines, a factory, land or a business; increasing working capital for growth; or undertaking a long-term contract, such as a construction job. Banks generally prefer **self-liquidating** loans. These loans stand alone in that they are not dependent on cash flows from current operating activities and assets for repayment, but can be repaid from the proceeds of the investment.

Background Information on the Company

The plan should document the *ownership structure* of a company, detailing whether it is a single company or part of a group. Share ownership details should be provided. In addition, the internal management structure could be provided.

Creditworthiness

To assess the creditworthiness of a company, a bank manager will need to get a 'feel' for the company. Therefore the business plan might include a *brief history* of the company, including what it trades in, the main products, when it started, location(s), growth/restructuring, key customers, key suppliers, profitability (this section would refer to financial statements that would be included in an appendix to the business plan, as would key accounting ratios), markets and employment statistics. This list is not exhaustive. People are also important and *managerial talent* is an intangible asset that has value. Therefore, banks should be made aware of the strengths of the management team. The business plan could include the curriculum vitae of key personnel.

Business Stake

The plan should outline the company's financial commitment to the investment. The larger the portion of the investment being committed by the company, the less risk attached to the lending decision for the bank. This is regarded as a positive signal by a bank.

Security

The business plan should highlight whether the company has assets that can be used for security. Loans can either be **secured** (otherwise known as a **committed line of credit**) or **unsecured** (otherwise known as an **uncommitted line of credit**). Unsecured loans are more risky to the bank, hence they are more costly for the borrower than secured loans. Security is usually of three types: fixed security, floating security and third-party guarantees, as highlighted in **Figure 11.1**.

FIGURE 11.1: SECURITY TYPES

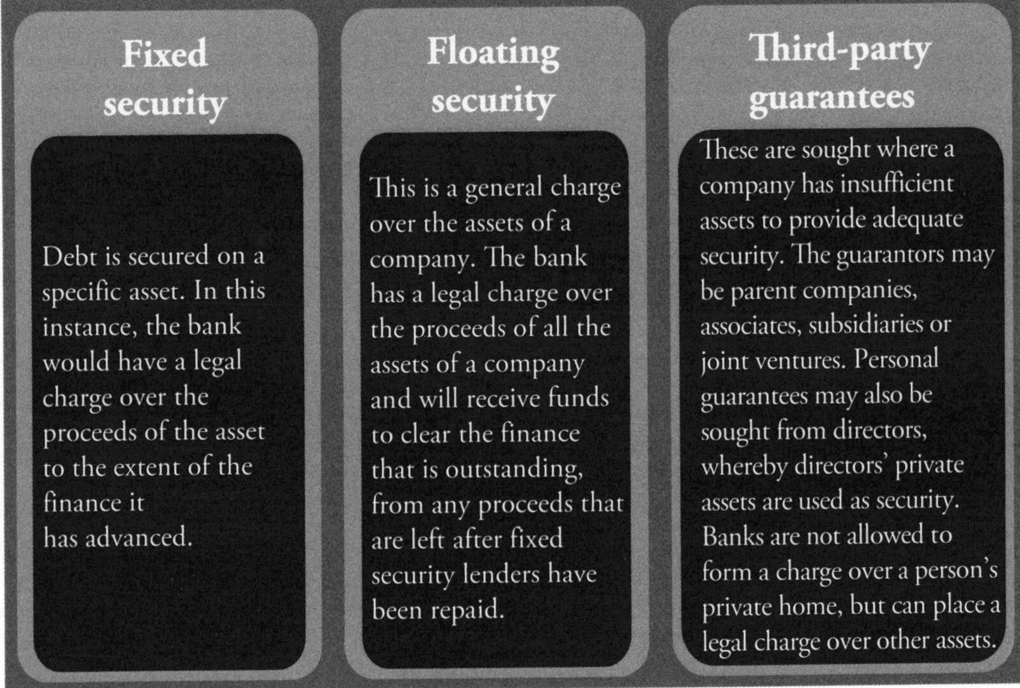

Fixed security
Debt is secured on a specific asset. In this instance, the bank would have a legal charge over the proceeds of the asset to the extent of the finance it has advanced.
Floating security
This is a general charge over the assets of a company. The bank has a legal charge over the proceeds of all the assets of a company and will receive funds to clear the finance that is outstanding, from any proceeds that are left after fixed security lenders have been repaid.
Third-party guarantees
These are sought where a company has insufficient assets to provide adequate security. The guarantors may be parent companies, associates, subsidiaries or joint ventures. Personal guarantees may also be sought from directors, whereby directors' private assets are used as security. Banks are not allowed to form a charge over a person's private home, but can place a legal charge over other assets.

The *type of asset* being used for security also impacts on the lending decision. Assets that do not have a volatile market value, and that generally appreciate in value, are viewed in a more positive light by banks. Where a company has assets that could be used for security, then a schedule of these can be included in the appendix to the business plan, with up-to-date valuations, where appropriate.

Projections

Most business plans include cash flow projections in an appendix. *Cash flow projections* help banks assess the *affordability* of the bank overdraft or loan. They should show that the company will be generating sufficient liquid funds from operating activities to cover operating expenses, other expected outflows and capital and interest repayments. They are normally quite detailed and show monthly (or quarterly) cash inflows, outflows and the resultant expected cash balance. They should be for either the period of the debt being requested (if short term) or for a period of up to five years, whichever is the shorter. The projections could include **scenario analysis**, showing the worst-case, most likely and best-case scenarios, and **sensitivity analysis** – an analysis of the impact of changes to variables used in the cash flow, such as sales price. Any assumptions made when preparing the projections should be included and explained.

Financial Statements

Budgeted financial statements should also be prepared, showing the expected net income for each quarter/year and the expected statement of financial position on the dates chosen. These statements should tie in with the cash flow projections. In addition (to help the bank manager assess the reasonableness of the budgeted statements of profit or loss, statements of financial position and cash flows), copies of the last three years' audited financial statements could be included as an appendix.

ESG Issues

Over the past decade, debt providers have become increasingly interested in the issue of sustainability and how the company impacts on society and the environment. Indeed, a company that is seen as acting responsibly is likely to obtain better finance terms. Devoting a section of the business plan to environmental, social and governance (ESG) issues allows the debt provider to better assess the risk of providing the finance.

TYPES OF FINANCE AVAILABLE FROM BANKING INSTITUTIONS AND OTHER FINANCIAL INTERMEDIARIES

The various types of finance available from banking institutions and other financial intermediaries are now explained.

Overdrafts

Normally banks provide customers with a bank account, which is a secure way of pooling and managing money. Bank customers deposit funds and withdraw them at a later date. Normally, the amounts that can be withdrawn are limited to the sum of the prior deposits made. An **overdraft** is where the bank allows its customer to withdraw more than was deposited, up to an agreed limit. The bank will start to charge interest on the account when the balance becomes negative, and will do so for every day that the account is overdrawn. Overdrafts are normally unsecured and are legally **repayable on demand**. This means that a company has to be able to clear the overdraft immediately if requested to do so by the bank. In practice, this is rarely the case. Banks normally provide assurances that the facility will be in place for periods of up to a year, when the situation is reviewed and another agreement is reached. It is not in any bank's interest to demand repayment without notice, as it would put the customer under financial pressure, which may put the customer out of business – this would have a negative impact on the bank's reputation. As overdrafts are arranged for short periods, it is recommended that they are **self-liquidating**, in that they are only used to finance short-term requirements that will repay the finance obtained. An overdraft is a flexible form of finance, with an overall low interest rate cost. This is due to the fact that interest is only charged on the amount outstanding, not the full amount of the facility, and is calculated on a daily basis.

Arranged Overdraft

When arranging an overdraft, three types of cost can result. First, interest is charged. The interest rate is variable and normally ranges between 1.5% and 5% above the bank's base rate, depending on the bank's credit assessment (where pre-agreed). Debt interest is tax deductible. There are other costs associated with an overdraft, such as an arrangement fee. This is usually about 1% of the facility being requested. In addition, the facility is reviewed periodically and the review usually incurs a fixed fee.

Overdraft Breaches

If a company goes into overdraft without prior agreement or if the agreed overdraft limit is breached, the consequences are punitive. The bank can refuse to honour cheques or payments made by a company. This may sour the relationship between a company and a supplier, who received a cheque in good faith – the supplier will be charged by its bank for dealing with the unpaid cheque. In addition, the supplier may lose interest or even breach its overdraft limit, incurring penalties. Breaching an overdraft limit also sends a negative message to the bank manager, as it is a sign of a deteriorating financial position and/or poor cash management. This will impact on a bank's willingness to provide future credit. It may also impact on a company's credit rating, causing it problems when negotiating credit from suppliers in the future. When an overdraft limit is breached, the bank immediately charges a referral fee for each payment made whilst the limit is breached. In addition, the rate of interest on the whole overdraft increases to rates of up to 18% or more above the bank's base rate. In the worst-case scenario, the bank may withdraw the facility.

Short-term Loans

Over the past two decades, companies in the UK and Ireland have changed their short-term lending habits, from predominant use of overdrafts to a greater use of short-term loans. Short-term loans are usually provided for periods of up to one year and are earmarked for a specific purpose. They are usually secured and provide a lender with confidence that repayment will not be demanded by the bank, unless the payments go into default. The interest rate charged is usually lower than the rate charged on an overdraft, typically ranging from 1.5% to 4% above the bank's base rate. However, it is charged on the full amount of the loan, even if not in use, unless a predetermined draw-down timetable has been agreed. There is usually an arrangement fee, which can be up to 3% of the amount borrowed. The fees depend on the bargaining power of each of the parties. Getting the terms right at the outset is very important, as deviations from the agreement can be costly. Early repayment will incur a penalty.

Figure 11.2: Common Agreed Loan Repayment Patterns

Annuity basis	Fixed periodic repayments, including a variable interest portion, are made periodically (typically monthly) over the duration of the loan with the capital portion of the repayment starting off as a small portion of the total repayment amount but increasing with each repayment and the interest portion decreasing. The interest is charged on the balance after each capital repayment has been made.
Tailored annuity basis	Loans are tailored, with the possibility of arranging interest-only payments for the first few months; payment breaks or repayments timetabled to match the cash flows of the company.
Balloon payment terms	An agreement to repay the interest and only a small portion of the capital during the term of a loan. The majority of capital is repaid at the end.
Bullet payment terms	The interest is paid throughout the term of the loan and all the capital is paid at the end.
Pure discount only payment terms	Only one repayment is made at the end of the agreed term that encapsulates all the accumulated interest and capital that is outstanding. This is usually used for large projects that do not have recurring revenue, but periodic lump sum payments. The loan advance is determined by the bank based on the present value of the future lump sum to be received, discounted at the required rate of return (interest rate) by the bank.

If properly predicted, short-term loans can be reasonably flexible. There may be a facility to repay in such a manner as to match predicted cash flows. There are various off-the-shelf, short-term loan products with predefined repayment terms that may suit certain types of company. These are outlined briefly in **Figure 11.2**.

Interest can either be fixed or variable. **Fixed interest rate** loans are usually more expensive than variable rate loans, though have the advantage of reducing uncertainty in respect of cash outflows, as the interest charge does not change when base rates change. When interest rates rise, they benefit the borrower; when interest rates fall, they benefit the bank. The initial fixed rate offered by the bank will take future expectations about interest rates into account. In **variable interest rate** loans, the interest rate is usually pegged to the bank's base rate, which usually moves in line with the EURIBOR (Euro Inter-Bank Offered Rate) (RoI), or LIBOR (London Inter-Bank Offer Rate) (UK). The repayments on variable interest rate loans will increase when base rates increase and fall when base rates fall.

The bank will usually require more information from a company when deciding on whether to grant a term loan, relative to an overdraft, as the risk is higher. To reduce the risk, some banks write restrictive covenants into loan agreements. These may limit the company's ability to raise more debt or to pay dividends beyond a certain level, if at all. Overdrafts are legally repayable on demand, whereas loans are not – unless repayments fall into arrears.

Funding for SMEs

Since the financial crisis, regulatory changes and advances in technology have led to an increase in innovative sources of funds for SMEs. Three common types are outlined in **Real World Example 11.3**.

Real World Example 11.3: Funding for SMEs

Peer-to-Peer Lenders

Another source of funding for SMEs that have achieved growth over the period since the financial crisis. Examples from the UK include Funding Circle, RateSetter and Zopa. See Brismo[1] for details of a range of peer-to-peer lenders, their lending volumes for the last month, the last 12 months and cumulative to date. In Ireland the main players are Linked Finance, Grid Finance and Spark Crowdfunding. These companies were originally established to enable individuals to loan funds to other individuals, however the model was quickly adapted to enable individuals to lend to SMEs.

eCommerce Lenders

Growth in eCommerce lenders, such as PayPal or Alipay, have provided flexible finance for many companies who operate using their platforms. For example, PayPal Working Capital provided over £1 billion in short-term loans to SMEs in the UK in 2018. These loans were typically to merchants who sell their products on eBay, which was PayPal's parent company until July 2015. PayPal uses historic data on the Merchants PayPal account to assess their creditworthiness and it can collect debt from future sales receipts through PayPal.

Other Non-bank Direct Lenders

Specialist SME lenders, such as Spotcap, Liberis and iwoca, have raised debt capital, which they then lend to SMEs that banks are reluctant to lend to. These companies make profits from the spread between the amount they charge to the SMEs and the amount they can borrow for. This is used to pay their costs and generate a profit. The difference between this facility and peer-to-peer lending companies is that these companies absorb the credit risk.

[1] https://brismo.com/market-data/

Factoring

Factoring is where an outside company, usually a financial institution, provides finance to a company on the strength of its trade receivables. The factor obtains legal right to the proceeds of the trade receivables. In effect, a company is selling its future trade receivables in exchange for up-front finance. Up to 80% of the book value of trade receivables can be obtained under a factor agreement. The factor interest rate is usually higher than an overdraft rate, ranging from 2% to 5% plus above the bank's base rate. The margin charged by a factor company is influenced by its credit assessment of the lender. There are three main forms of factoring: non-recourse factoring; factoring with recourse; and confidential factoring.

Non-recourse Factoring

Non-recourse factoring (also known as **without recourse**) is the 'all-singing, all-dancing service', whereby a factor provides upfront finance on credit sales made, takes over the whole administration of the sales ledger and provides credit protection. This type of factoring is the most expensive, with the factor charging a service fee of typically 0.5% to 3% of total credit sales value. They may also charge a standard annual administration fee. The fee will be influenced by the expected number of transactions, level of late payers and bad debts. The service provided by a factor includes assessing the creditworthiness of potential credit customers, reviewing the creditworthiness of current customers, preparing invoices, preparing statements and chasing late payments. Factor companies specialise in this type of activity, and hence are likely to be more efficient and successful at chasing late payments, compared with many companies' in-house credit departments. This may reduce the costs of the company whose trade receivable has been factored and also free-up management time, which can be devoted to other issues.

The most identifiable feature of non-recourse factoring is the fact that the risk of bad debts is taken over by the factor company. This removes uncertainty for the company. However, the factor company decides whether a credit sale should be made or not. Given this, a factor company is more likely to turn away potentially profitable sales, so as to restrict its own exposure to bad debts. This may cause conflict between a company and a factor company. The usual procedure when a credit sale is made under a factor agreement is set out in **Figure 11.3**.

Figure 11.3: Non-recourse Factoring (Steps)

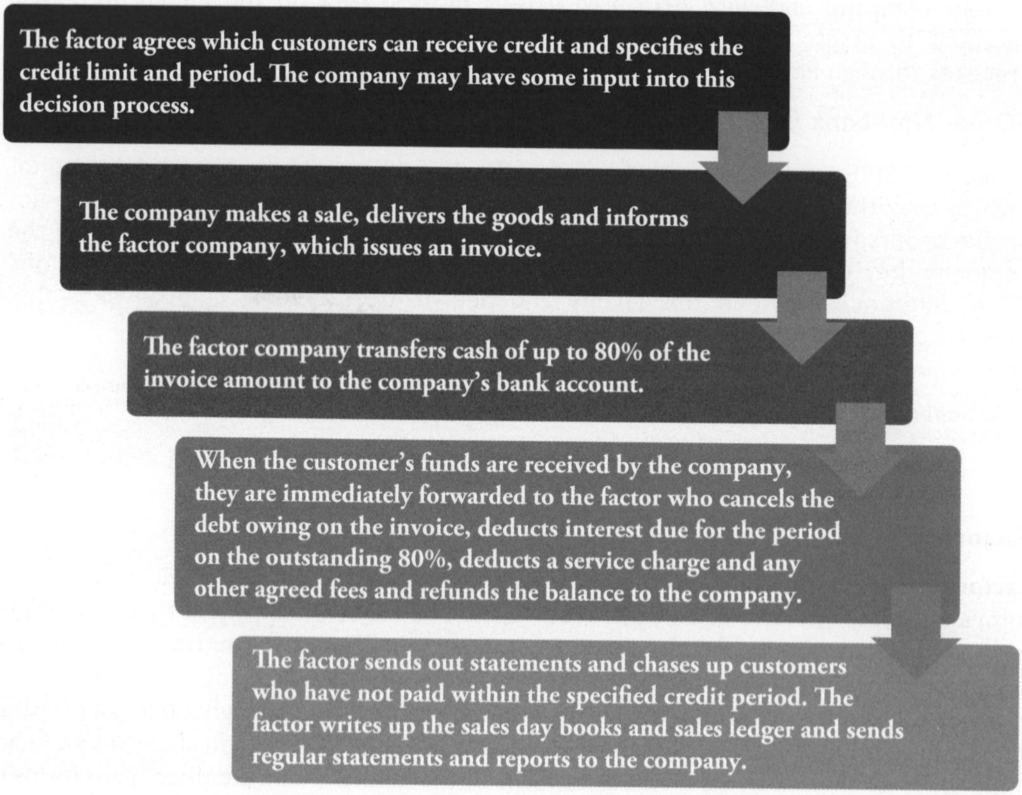

The factor agrees which customers can receive credit and specifies the credit limit and period. The company may have some input into this decision process.

The company makes a sale, delivers the goods and informs the factor company, which issues an invoice.

The factor company transfers cash of up to 80% of the invoice amount to the company's bank account.

When the customer's funds are received by the company, they are immediately forwarded to the factor who cancels the debt owing on the invoice, deducts interest due for the period on the outstanding 80%, deducts a service charge and any other agreed fees and refunds the balance to the company.

The factor sends out statements and chases up customers who have not paid within the specified credit period. The factor writes up the sales day books and sales ledger and sends regular statements and reports to the company.

With-recourse Factoring

With-recourse factoring is similar to non-recourse factoring – the only difference is that the company retains the right to provide credit and to chase up overdue debts that have breached their credit limit and retains responsibility for bad debts. This overcomes the conflict that may arise between a factor company and the lending company under a strict non-recourse factoring arrangement, as the factor is likely to restrict credit to poor payers, whereas the company may recognise that the customers are slow payers, but are still profitable sales. In addition, it overcomes problems that may arise when a factor is used to chase up overdue trade receivable accounts – the use of an outside third party may upset customers and damage the relationship between the customer and the company. In this circumstance the factor may only take on management of part of the trade receivables ledger.

FIGURE 11.4: WITH-RECOURSE FACTORING (STEPS)

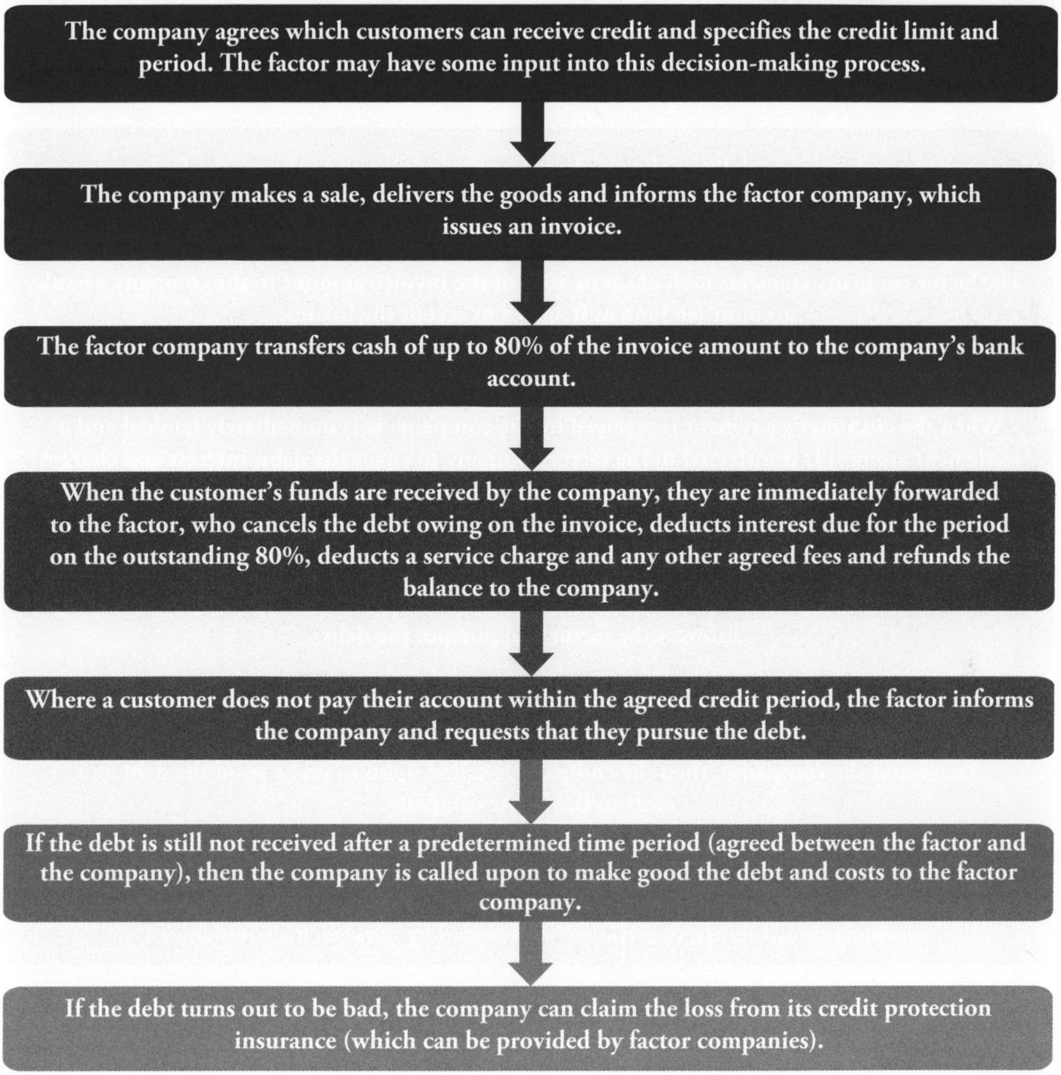

The company agrees which customers can receive credit and specifies the credit limit and period. The factor may have some input into this decision-making process.

↓

The company makes a sale, delivers the goods and informs the factor company, which issues an invoice.

↓

The factor company transfers cash of up to 80% of the invoice amount to the company's bank account.

↓

When the customer's funds are received by the company, they are immediately forwarded to the factor, who cancels the debt owing on the invoice, deducts interest due for the period on the outstanding 80%, deducts a service charge and any other agreed fees and refunds the balance to the company.

↓

Where a customer does not pay their account within the agreed credit period, the factor informs the company and requests that they pursue the debt.

↓

If the debt is still not received after a predetermined time period (agreed between the factor and the company), then the company is called upon to make good the debt and costs to the factor company.

↓

If the debt turns out to be bad, the company can claim the loss from its credit protection insurance (which can be provided by factor companies).

Confidential Factoring

Using factor companies as a source of finance is expensive and is usually only used when a company has exhausted its overdraft facility and still requires additional short-term funds. As this is the case, the use of a factor company can be interpreted as a sign of liquidity problems. This makes the company riskier to grant credit to, and so may affect the company's ability to obtain credit. To counteract this problem, a company can enter into a confidential factoring agreement. Under a confidential factoring agreement, the factor's involvement is not visible; the company remains responsible for the administration of the trade receivables ledger and issues invoices, statements and letters, using its own stationery. The company still sells the trade receivables to the factor; however, it acts as an agent for the factor company in the collection of the debts. This agreement will have lower service and administration fees relative to the first two types of factoring.

FIGURE 11.5: CONFIDENTIAL FACTORING (STEPS)

The company agrees which customers can receive credit and specifies the credit limit and period. The factor may have some input into this decision process.

↓

The company makes a sale, delivers the goods, issues the invoice and informs the factor company.

↓

The factor company transfers cash of up to 80% of the invoice amount to the company's bank account (so long as it agrees to accept the invoice).

↓

When the customer's payment is received by the company, it is immediately banked and a settlement amount is transferred to the factor company to cover the debt, interest and charges that are outstanding on the invoice.

↓

Where a customer does not pay their account within the agreed credit period, the company informs the factor and pursues the debt.

↓

If the debt is still not received after a predetermined period of time (agreed between the factor and the company), then the company is called upon to make good the debt and costs to the factor company.

↓

If the debt turns out to be bad, the company can claim the loss from its credit protection insurance (which can be provided by most factor companies).

Factoring: Summary of Advantages and Disadvantages

The key advantage of factoring is that it is a quick source of short-term funds, which fluctuates in line with credit sales. In addition: set-up costs are low relative to other forms of finance; the only sources of security required are trade receivables; the finance can be obtained without the factor company placing restrictive covenants on the company's other decisions; the finance is not repayable on demand; and, where the factor takes over the administration of trade receivables, savings can be made within the company and managerial time can be devoted elsewhere.

On the downside, factoring is costly. The interest rates charged are usually in excess of overdraft rates and the service fees can be high. Profitable sales can be lost due to strict credit control, or the factor will not provide finance against certain credit invoices as the factor will only be interested in taking over clean accounts. In addition, trade receivables cannot be encumbered by any other debt. Factor companies are usually only interested in large value invoices and the use of a factor may cause suppliers to reassess the credit period they allow to the company, due to perceived increased liquidity risk. **Worked Example 11.2** shows the typical cash flows associated with a factor arrangement and **Worked Example 11.3** outlines the typical services provided by a factor.

Worked Example 11.2: Factoring

Enero Plc has been set up for the purpose of importing commodities that will be sold to a small number of reliable customers. Sales invoicing is forecast at €/£300,000 per month. The average credit period for this type of business is 2.5 months.

The company is considering factoring its accounts receivable under a full factoring agreement without recourse (i.e. non-recourse factoring). Under this agreement, the factor will charge a fee of 2.5% on total invoicing. He will give an advance of 85% of invoiced amounts, at an interest rate of 13% per annum.

The agreement should enable Enero Plc to avoid spending €/£95,000 per annum on administration costs.

Requirement As the company finance director, you are responsible for strategic financial management. For the next board meeting you need to:

(a) calculate the annual net cost of factoring; and
(b) discuss the financial benefits of such an agreement, having regard to a current interest rate on bank overdrafts of 12.5%.

Solution

(a) (***Note:*** an incremental approach has been adopted in this solution.)

		€/£
Annual sales	€/£300,000 × 12	3,600,000
Fee	€/£3,600,000 × 2.5%	(90,000)
Interest:		
Amount advanced		
€/£3,600,000 × 85% = €/£3,060,000		
Charges		
€/£3,060,000 × 13% × 2.5/12		(82,875)
Administrative costs saved		95,000
Net cost per annum		(77,875)

An alternative source of finance is a bank overdraft. Assume 85% of the invoiced amount is the amount of finance required (so that like is being compared with like).

	€/£
Cost of finance (bank)	
€/£3,060,000 × 12.5% × 2.5/12	(79,688)
Annual net cost of factoring	(77,875)
Annual benefit of factoring	1,813

(b) Factoring: other financial benefits.
(i) Factoring offers flexibility as sales volumes fluctuate. If sales increase, additional finance is automatically received.
(ii) Bad debts are not lost money to Enero Plc, as the factoring agreement in this instance is without recourse.
(iii) A semi-fixed cost of administration is removed from Enero Plc's costs and fluctuations in sales volumes can easily be accommodated.

Worked Example 11.3: Factoring

Requirement Summarise the services that can be obtained from a factor.

5 Marks

(Chartered Accountants Ireland, MABF, *Questions and Solutions Manual 2000/2001*)

Solution

Factors collect trade debts on behalf of client companies.

The various services provided by a factor include:
- relieving a trading company of an administrative function for invoicing and debt collection;
- providing finance on the face value of invoices;
- covering bad debts (if the arrangement is 'without recourse'); and being confidential, so the customer is not aware of the arrangement.

Invoice Discounting

Similar to factoring, **invoice discounting** is the sale of selected credit sales invoices to a financial intermediary, usually a bank. The bank normally provides finance secured on the invoice of about 75–80% of the invoice value. The credit period allowed can range up to periods of 90 days. The borrowing company collects the amounts owing on the invoice and forwards the full amount to the invoice discounter, who takes out the capital sum advanced to the company, the interest due and any set-up fee or administration fee, and returns the balance to the company. This form of finance is more expensive than a conventional overdraft. The interest rates typically range from 3% to 6% above the bank's base rate and the administration fee is typically 0.5% of the finance allowed. The company retains more control over this method of finance relative to a factoring agreement, as the company selects the invoices to discount, decides on the frequency of undertaking each transaction, administers the debt collection and is responsible for any bad debt that might occur on the invoice. Customers are usually unaware that an invoice discounter is involved, whereas under a standard factoring arrangement (i.e. not confidential factoring), customers know a factor is administering the debt. The cash flows involved in invoice discounting are portrayed in **Worked Example 11.4**.

Worked Example 11.4: Invoice Discounting

Top Parts has just breached its €/£3,000,000 overdraft limit and the finance manager met the local bank manager to seek additional urgent short-term finance. The bank manager agreed that the fundamentals of the business were sound and offered an invoice discounting service on Irish customers, representing 100% of the total of 30 June 20X4 receivables (€/£2,704,000). The bank was prepared to offer non-recourse finance on 75% of the Irish customer's June receivables at an interest rate of 12% plus an administration fee of 1% of the funds advanced. Existing borrowing facilities are priced at 8%. The bank refused to consider any other financing options and Top Parts expects to collect the Irish customer debts in 45 days.

Requirement Evaluate the invoice discounting proposal offered by the local bank and recommend whether Top Parts should avail of this service. (***Note:*** assume there are 360 days in the year.)

4 Marks

(Based on Chartered Accountants Ireland, CAP 2, MABF, Summer 2011, Q1(e))

Solution

	€/£000
Invoice discounting option:	
Receivables at 30 June	2,704
% finance offered 75%	2,028
Administration fee 1%	20.28
Finance charge [€/£2,028 × (45 ÷ 360)] × 12%	30.42
	50.70
If Top Parts could finance the receivables itself, the cost would be:	
[€/£2,704 × (45 ÷ 360)] × 8%	27.04

Recommendation The option is costly, but the finance manager may not have another option at this point as the company has breached the €/£3,000,000 overdraft limit.

There are benefits. First, a non-recourse finance arrangement eliminates bad debt exposure and hence the credit risk associated with the current receivables ledger. Secondly, the bank is taking over the whole receivables ledger, which is unusual for an invoice discounting arrangement, and the receivables are likely to contain some old balances that the bank is now more or less guaranteeing.

The €/£2,028,000 advance will bring the company comfortably within its overdraft limit and provides a short period of time for the finance manager to get the company's financing in order.

In recent years, innovative peer-to-peer lending companies have entered the invoice discount market, as identified in **Real World Example 11.4.**

REAL WORLD EXAMPLE 11.4: PEER-TO-PEER LENDING

Variation on Invoice Discounting

A further variation of peer-to-peer lending was established by the company, Market Finance. This peer-to-peer company hosts a platform that enables high-worth individuals to purchase a portion of a SME's outstanding invoices at a discount. This helps to free-up funds that the SME can use to finance its working capital needs.

INVENTORY FINANCING

Inventory financing is where banks and/or other financial institutions provide finance using a company's inventory as security. Five types of arrangement exist: blanket lien, trust receipt, warehouse receipt, terminal warehousing and field warehousing. These are explained in brief in **Figure 11.6**.

FIGURE 11.6: INVENTORY FINANCING TYPES

Blanket lien	Where the lender holds a charge against a company's total inventory balance. The company is free to sell the inventory, reducing the benefit of this lien as a form of security.
Trust receipt	The company signs a trust receipt promising to hold inventory in trust for the benefit of the lender. The lender may physically inspect the inventory from time to time. When the inventory is sold, the revenue goes to the lender to settle the debt. The difference between the sums received for the inventory and the amount advanced on the strength of the value of the inventory is the cost of finance.
Warehousing receipt	The lender takes physical and legal possession of the inventory and receives revenue from the sale of the specific inventory to settle the debt. The finance cost to a company (and the return to a lender) is the difference between the sale value of the inventory and the amount advanced to the company.
Terminal warehousing	Like a warehouse receipt arrangement, the inventory is physically moved to a lender's warehouse. However, it is more expensive, as the borrowing company agrees to pay a third party to manage and monitor the inventory. The inventory is released when the lending company receives payment for the goods.
Field warehousing	A mixture of a trust receipt and terminal warehousing. The inventory remains in the possession of the borrowing company; however, it is monitored by a third party at the borrowing company's expense. The inventory is only released from stores when the lender authorises the third party to do so.

Banks are also players in the money markets and can offer most of the products discussed. In addition, banks, though not providing specific products, have a role to play in reducing the risk of products, by acting as guarantor for companies.

RAISING FINANCE USING BILL FINANCE

Bill finance refers to paper documents (i.e. **negotiable instruments**) that are similar to IOUs. The bill usually sets out the terms of the IOU; for example, usually a bill states that the issuer will pay the holder of the bill a set amount of money on a set date in the future. This bill is then traded in the money markets (e.g. between the commercial banks, discount houses and acceptance houses, depending on the particular bill). There are three main types of bill finance: bills of exchange, acceptance credits and commercial paper. These are now discussed in turn.

Bills of Exchange

A **bill of exchange** is defined in the Bills of Exchange Act 1882 as:

> "an unconditional order in writing, addressed by one person to another, signed by the person giving it, requiring the person to whom it is addressed to pay on demand, or at a fixed or determinable future time, a sum certain in money to or to the order of a specified person, or to bearer."

FIGURE 11.7: BILLS OF EXCHANGE (STEPS)

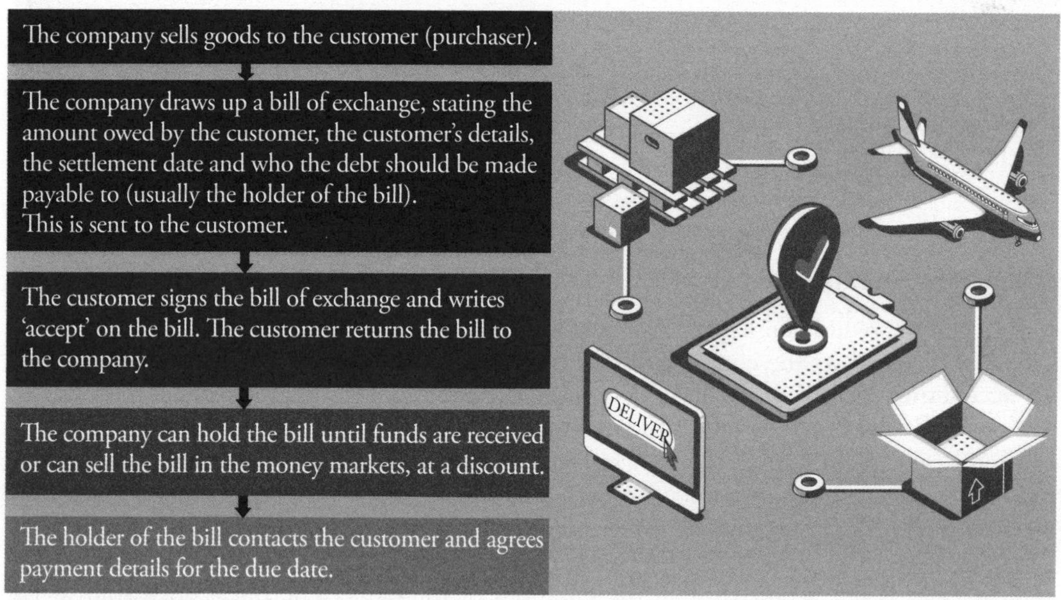

Historically, bills of exchange were used when goods were sold overseas and were in transit for long periods of time. The seller prepares a bill, which is signed by a purchaser as being agreed. This is a legal contract in which the purchaser has to pay the seller or holder a sum agreed for the goods (stipulated on the bill of exchange) at a future date (usually when the goods are expected to be received by the purchaser). This means that no funds change hands while the goods are in transit. The seller can then sell the bill to obtain finance and usually receives a discounted amount for the bill. The discount given is the interest cost of the finance.

Bills of exchange can be arranged for domestic supplies and can cover periods of up to 180 days. The most frequent duration is 90 days and bills are usually for amounts of over €100,000/£75,000. The discount usually reflects a margin over the EURIBOR or LIBOR of between 1.5% and 4%. When credit difficulties arise, the holder of the bill usually has recourse to both the seller of the goods and the purchaser. It is not uncommon for the seller of the bill to take out credit insurance on the debt; where this is the case, the discount is usually less, reflecting the reduced risk.

WORKED EXAMPLE 11.5: BILLS OF EXCHANGE

A €/£100,000 bill, dated three months from now, is sold by Egg Plc to a commercial bank at 2% discount.

Requirement Calculate the effective yearly cost of the bill to Egg Plc.

Solution

The cost of the finance to Egg Plc is a loss of 2% out of 100% for a three-month period. This represents a cost of 2% ÷ 98% = 2.04% for three months.

Yearly, then, this equates to an effective annual interest cost of:

$$(1.0204)^4 - 1 = 8.4\%$$

This represents the cost to Egg Plc and the return received by the commercial bank.

Acceptance Credits

An acceptance credit is similar to a bill of exchange, except it is not attached to an underlying sale. It is prepared by the company wishing to raise finance and is guaranteed by its bank. An **acceptance credit** bill is a legal document prepared by a company, which states that its bank will pay a set amount on a specified date in the future to the holder of the document. After it is prepared, the bank signs or stamps the agreement. At this juncture, the company pays the bank a commission for using its name as guarantor. This commission is typically between 0.5% and 1% of the face value of the bill. The fee for the guarantee is quite low. The guarantee is an off-balance-sheet commitment by the bank. It is a contingent liability and, as such, is not accrued for in the liabilities of the bank. The bill is then sold in the money markets by the company.

The bank pays the holder of the bill on the specified day and collects the debt due to it from the company by the agreed terms (e.g. the company may pay the bank the full amount on a specified date or the balance can be paid to them in instalments). This is a separate arrangement and will include interest and commission for the additional source of finance. Alternatively, the balance may be rolled over into a new acceptance credit bill. Acceptance credits usually attract a lower discount rate than bills of exchange because of the lower risk resulting from having a bank guarantee. Acceptance credit arrangements are not repayable on demand. Once sold, the borrowing company (i.e. the seller of the bill) is hedged against interest rate movements and the discount cannot change. Acceptance credits are usually prepared for a minimum amount of €400,000/£250,000 and can range in duration from 30 to 180 days.

Government-backed notes that are issued by local authorities are examples of acceptance credits. In these instances, the government acts as guarantor.

FIGURE 11.8: ACCEPTANCE CREDIT (STEPS)

Acceptance credit

- The company prepares an acceptance credit, declaring that its bank will pay a specified sum on a set date in the future. This is sent to the bank.
- The bank signs the acceptance credit, confirming that it will guarantee payment of the sum on the specified date. The bank returns the bill to the company.
- The company pays the bank a commission for the guarantee.
- The company sells the acceptance credit bill in the money markets, at a discount.
- On the due date, the bank pays the holder of the acceptance credit the full amount on the bill.
- The company pays the bank on the same day or prepares another acceptance credit (the proceeds of which are used to repay the bank), or makes an arrangement to repay the bank in instalments (this part can be quite flexible).

Worked Example 11.6: Acceptance Credits

A Plc wishes to raise some finance using the money markets. It approaches its bank, which agrees to guarantee an amount, limited to €/£500,000. A commission of 0.5% is payable for this service on the amounts of the facility used. A Plc prepares an acceptance credit agreement, the terms of which are that the bank agrees to pay €/£400,000 in three months' time to the holder of the bill. A Plc has agreed to repay €/£425,000 to the bank in one year's time in respect of the bill. A Plc sells the bill on the money markets at 8% discount.

Requirement Calculate:
(a) the effective yearly cost of the discount rate given by the money markets to A Plc;
(b) the return earned by the bank by agreeing to accept repayment from A Plc in one year's time (this will represent the cost to A Plc also); and
(c) the overall cost of the arrangement to the company.

Solution

(a) The company will receive €/£368,000 now in respect of the acceptance credit.
The return on the discount is: 8% ÷ (100% – 8%) = 8.7% for three months.
The number of three-month periods in a year is: 12 ÷ 3 = 4.
Therefore, the effective annual interest rate is: $(1.087)^4 - 1 = 39.6\%$.

(b) The return received by the bank (and the cost to the company) of providing nine months' credit is as follows:
€/£25,000/€/£400,000 = 6.25% for a period of nine months.
The number of nine-month periods in the year is: 12 ÷ 9 = 1.33. Therefore, the effective annual interest rate is: $(1.0625)^{1.33} - 1 = 8.4\%$.

(c) The overall cost of the finance to the company is:
€/£425,000 – €/£368,000 = €/£57,000
€/£57,000 + €/£2,500 [€/£500,000 × 0.5%] = €/£59,500
€/£59,500 ÷ €/£368,000 = 16.168% for a 12-month period.

Commercial Paper

A **commercial paper** bill is a legal commitment by a company to pay a set amount on a specified date. The paper is traded directly in the money markets by the company and is a perfect example of disintermediation, as the company can cut out the role of the bank or financial intermediary. The company issuing the commercial paper should have sufficient in-house expertise to set up the documentation and does not necessarily require the debt to be guaranteed, making this a cheap form of short-term finance. The cost of commercial paper is typically the EURIBOR or LIBOR rate, plus 0.15% to 1% (depending on the company's reputation). Most commercial paper transactions are in multiples of over €750,000/£500,000 and their terms can range from 7 to 270 days. Only large, reputable companies that are quoted on the stock exchange can raise finance in this manner.

A company with a strong reputation has a reduced need for a bank guarantee; however, in many instances the commercial paper being issued is guaranteed by a bank. Banks will normally agree a **revolving underwriting facility**, wherein the bank guarantees the issuing of commercial paper at a specified rate in the commercial paper market, for an agreed period of time. The company can then issue several short-dated bills up to the limit of the agreed facility. The bank usually is more involved in this arrangement and sells the bills on behalf of the company at the specified rate in the money market. The bank purchases any bills not taken up by the money market. The company pays the bank a fee for the guarantee and commission on the sale of the bills.

A downside to bill finance is that it is not flexible. If an issuer runs into liquidity problems, repayment terms will not be changed – the market will require repayment of the bill, whereas finance obtained directly from a bank can be renegotiated.

INTERNATIONAL TRADE

Low-risk Transactions: Background

Most large companies export goods and import supplies from other countries. Exporting is riskier than domestic trading due to greater uncertainty when dealing with overseas companies, as it is more difficult to assess their credit standing. In addition, there are country-specific risks (such as the risk of war or recession) and currency risks. Where an importer's reputation is strong and the country in which it is located is regarded as being low risk, then transactions can be open account. An **open account** arrangement is not too different from the type of agreement found in domestic credit sales. A written credit agreement between two parties to a trade, about the settlement amount and date, is prepared. This is usually the only documentation that is required and cuts costs, as shipping documentation or bills conferring conditions as to transfer of legal title to the goods are not required. This is termed **clean bill collection**. If the importer defaults on the agreement, the exporter can pursue the debt through the legal system. Most internal European trade is undertaken by open account arrangement. The invoices that are issued can be used to obtain finance in the same manner as in domestic transactions, though this may be more costly, as there are additional risks. In particular, export invoice discounting and export factoring are common sources of finance. The latter is now discussed.

Export Factoring

Export factoring is virtually the same as domestic factoring. It can be set up with recourse or as non-recourse; the only exception is that the factor takes over foreign currency exchange risk. The factor purchases the credit invoices, which might be denominated in a foreign currency, and pays the exporter a set portion of this upfront, in the domestic currency. This hedges a portion of the credit transaction against future exchange rate movements. This additional feature increases the cost of factoring, making the service fees more expensive than domestic factor service fees. Another influence on fees is the additional time that is required to assess the creditworthiness of importers. Many factors have branches in other countries and this helps with the assessment. Those that do not, and who still provide export factoring, are usually members of an international factoring organisation, such as Factors Chain International (FCI). This organisation will provide information to help a domestic factor company assess the credit risk of an importer.

High-risk Transactions: Role of Bills in International Finance

Where there is doubt as to the reputation of an importer or there are concerns regarding currency risk or country risk, then a credit sale is normally processed by an intermediary (usually a bank), using carefully predetermined document flows or bills that are agreed by both parties to the transaction. As goods can be in transit for a long period of time, shipping documentation, which includes information affecting the timing of transfer of legal title to the goods, is also written into each sale arrangement. A **bill of lading** is usually prepared; this is a shipping document that transfers title of the goods. There will be periods when neither the exporter nor importer has physical possession of the goods – therefore having adequate transit insurance is important. Three main types of bill or arrangement are commonly used in exporting arrangements: bills of exchange, letters of credit or forfaiting.

Export Bills of Exchange

An **export bill of exchange** is the same as a bill of exchange used for domestic transactions (discussed earlier). The exporter prepares the bill, which is addressed to the importer, specifying the amount and date the bill should be settled. This bill is then sent to the importer (usually through banking channels), who accepts the bill by signing it and writing that it is accepted. Only when the bill is accepted will the exporter start to transport the goods. The exporter retains legal title (evidenced by possession of the bill of lading). When the goods arrive in the importer's country, the bill of exchange is presented to the importer before legal title to the goods passes – the bill of lading is held until the conditions of the bill of exchange are fulfilled. If it is a sight draft, the importer has to pay immediately; if it is a term draft, the importer has the specified term to pay the bill. The exporter can sell the bill of exchange to its bank at a discount when it needs to raise short-term finance. A sight draft is used when the reputation of the importer is uncertain. Export bills of exchange are not as costly as documentary letters of credit.

Documentary Letters of Credit

A **documentary letter of credit** is a bank guarantee (provided by the importer's bank) to pay the amount on the **letter of credit** at a set time to the exporter, providing certain conditions are met in respect of the delivery of the goods (e.g. their type, quantity, quality, price and timing of shipment and delivery). The letter of credit is prepared by the importer, accepted by its bank and delivered to the exporter, who can then sell it to its bank at a discounted rate to raise finance. Payment on documentary letters of credit can be immediate (i.e. **sight drafts**) or follow an agreed credit term (i.e. **term drafts**).

There are two types of documentary letter of credit: an irrevocable documentary letter of credit and a revocable letter of credit. An **irrevocable documentary letter of credit** provides an exporter with the most protection. It is prepared by the importer, guaranteed by its bank and sent to the exporter's bank, which signs as having accepted it. An accepted irrevocable documentary letter of credit is known as a **confirmed documentary letter of credit**. This is a legally binding arrangement detailing the payment to be made, the documents to be delivered and the range of dates by which the documents should be received. This contract cannot be altered or cancelled without the consent of all parties. An irrevocable documentary letter of credit is usually requested by an exporter where the uncertainties are greatest. It is expensive for the importer to set it up and importers normally bargain for a lower product price to compensate for the additional costs. The document flows are very important to banks – more important than the goods. If the relevant documents are not received within the time frames specified in the letter of credit, then the exporter's bank may not accept payment. The legal title of the goods, as conferred by the bill of lading, normally goes to the importer's bank. It usually does not release title until it is paid by the importing company.

FIGURE 11.9: LETTER OF CREDIT (STEPS)

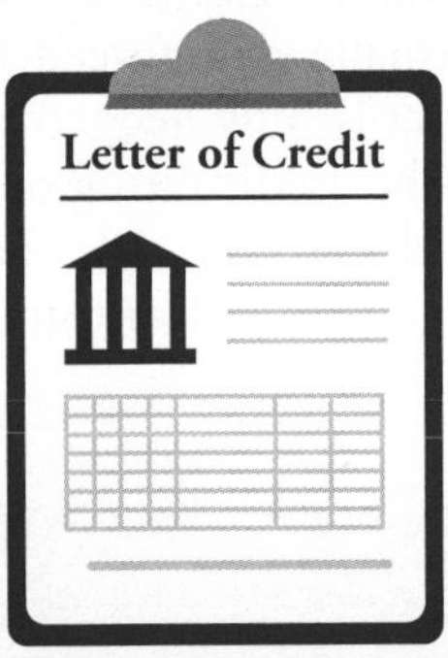

Letter of credit

- A sale is agreed between an exporter and an importer.
- The importer prepares a letter of credit, stating the amount and date to pay the exporter. This is guaranteed by the importer's bank. The legal title to the goods will pass to the importer's bank (which will hold the bill of lading).
- If irrevocable, the importer's bank forwards the letter of credit to the exporter's bank for acceptance. If revocable, the importer's bank forwards the letter of credit to the exporter for acceptance.
- The exporter delivers the products and presents the sight draft/term draft of the letter of credit (or its bank does so on its behalf) at the importer's bank, which pays the specified amount.
- The importer's bank then passes title of the goods to the importer.
- The importer pays the bank the capital outlay plus any commission and interest (if there is a timing difference).

A less expensive but more risky option for an exporter is to require a **revocable documentary letter of credit**. This type of letter of credit is not legally binding, cannot be confirmed by the exporter's bank and can be altered or cancelled at any time by the importer, without having to give any notice to the exporter. A deterrent to this type of letter of credit turning bad is the involvement of the importer's bank, which (if reputable) will not wish to be associated with transactions that are cancelled.

Forfaiting

Forfaiting is a medium-term source of export finance. It is used where an importer has a long-running trading arrangement with an exporter. The importer prepares a series of bills, detailing amounts owed for goods ordered from the exporter. Individual bills are for periods of up to six months; however, the arrangement is usually established for periods of up to five years. The exporter takes the bills to a forfaiter (i.e. a bank), which buys the bills at a discount. The bills are usually guaranteed by the importer's bank and are without recourse. Therefore, the exporter is fully hedged against credit risk. The discount taken by the bank varies depending on the credit rating of the importer, the reputation of its bank, currency exposure, if any, and country risk. Forfaiting can be expensive, though the exporter is usually aware of the cost upfront and can increase the product price to take account of the increased cost.

CONCLUSION

Short-term finance is finance that has a term of up to one year. A variety of short-term finance products are available and the products on offer in the market range from simple to quite complicated. Financing institutions typically require security when providing finance and a number of bespoke products have been developed to cater for the type of security desired. For example, a blanket lien, trust receipt, warehousing receipt, terminal warehousing or field warehousing can be used when the security is inventory. Factoring, invoice discounting and bill finance are sources of finance that typically used trade receivables as security.

EXAMINATION STANDARD QUESTION: FACTORING

Poppet Ltd is a manufacturing company. It sells goods for a total value of €/£500,000 per annum to regular customers. In order to secure this business, the company is flexible on debt collection and, on average, customers take 60 days to pay.

The company needs to improve its cash flow situation and does not want to wait a full 60 days to collect its debts. Invoice discounting has been put forward as an option to secure early payment. An invoice discounter has agreed to purchase the debts. The invoice discounting agreement involves the immediate cash payment of 70% of the face value of each invoice. The balance will be paid after 60 days less:

- an administration charge of 0.6% of turnover accepted by the discounter; and
- interest of 12% per annum on outstanding debts.

Requirement

(a) Explain THREE principal differences between factoring and invoice discounting.

4 Marks

(b) Calculate the annual percentage cost of Poppet's proposed invoice discounting.

8 Marks

(c) If Poppet could secure alternative short-term finance at an annual rate of 15%, should it proceed with invoice discounting or accept the alternative?

2 Marks

(d) Outline briefly TWO other ways in which Poppet might use its trade receivables to improve cash flow.

4 Marks

Total 18 Marks

(Based on Chartered Accountants Ireland, MABF II, Autumn 2000, Q6)

Solution

(a) Factoring and invoice discounting are ways in which a company can obtain cash from its trade receivables, without waiting for the period of credit to expire. The principal differences between the two are as follows:
- Invoice discounting involves the discounter purchasing only selected invoices, perhaps just one. With factoring, the entire trade receivables ledger is sold to the factoring company.
- Invoice discounting is only concerned with providing finance on customer accounts. It is not involved in sales administration. Invoice discounting involves the purchase of invoices by the discounter. The discounter will immediately advance cash, up to 80% of the face value of the invoices. Unlike factoring, which involves the purchase of the trade receivables ledger, it assumes no responsibility for the administration of the accounts receivable or the collection of debts.
- The selling company retains responsibility for bad debts with invoice discounting. As mentioned above, invoice discounting is simply the advance of finance on certain invoices. The discounting company does not take responsibility for the collection or non-collection of debts. With factoring, the selling company can retain responsibility for non-collection of bad debts, but the possibility of the discount company taking that responsibility exists if a non-recourse arrangement is put in place.

(b) The calculation of the cost to Poppet Ltd of invoice discounting:
- Administration charge of 0.6% of turnover accepted by the discounter. If the discounter has agreed to accept all invoices of Poppet Ltd in the year, then the accepted turnover is €/£500,000.
  Therefore the administration charge will be €/£500,000 × 0.6% = €/£3,000.
- Interest of 12% per annum on outstanding debts.
  Total interest will be the amount advanced by the interest rate.
  The amount advanced is: €/£500,000 × 70% × 60 ÷ 365 = €/£57,534.
  Therefore, the interest charge will be €/£57,534 × 12% = €/£6,904.
  The total cost is €/£9,904 [€/£3,000 + €/£6,904].
  Total cost as a percentage of sales = €/£9,904 ÷ €/£500,000 = 1.98%.
  Total cost as a percentage of funds advanced = €/£9,904 ÷ €/£57,534 = 17.21%.

(c) The cost of invoice discounting at 17.21% per annum is higher than the cost of the alternative short-term finance (i.e. 15%). Poppet Ltd should, from a financial perspective, choose the short-term finance option. Non-financial factors should also be considered, such as the reputation and trading history of the finance provider.

(d) Ways (other than invoice discounting) that the company might use its trade receivables to improve cash flow (**two** suggestions are required):
- **Factoring** Factoring effectively involves the selling of a company's trade receivables. Typically, a factoring company will advance the selling company a percentage of the value of trade receivables on making the arrangement and will then advance more cash to the seller as the debts are recovered. The advantage to the seller of this form of finance is that they can acquire cash immediately; however, it is an expensive form of finance as the fees, etc., of the factoring company can be high. In addition, factoring arrangements are often 'with recourse', in that if the debts cannot be recovered, the factoring company has recourse to the selling company, that is, the selling company bears the cost of bad debts.
- **Bill of Exchange** A bill of exchange is a form of IOU. It is a document drawn up by the seller of goods detailing the date and the amount of payment. The bill of exchange is sent to the purchaser of the goods, who signs it and returns it to the seller. The seller

can then either hold the bill until maturity and claim payment from the purchaser or sell the bill at a discount in the market and get cash immediately.
- **Short-term Bank Finance** The company could use its trade receivables as security for acquiring a short-term loan or the extension of an overdraft facility with a bank.
- **Offer Settlement Discounts to Customers** The company may offer early settlement discounts to customers to encourage early payment of debts. This would enhance the cash flow of the company.

With regard to each option for cash flow improvement listed above, the cost of the approach versus the benefits should be evaluated.

Key Terms

Acceptance credit
Acceptance house
Annuity basis
Balloon payment
Bill finance
Bill of exchange
Bill of lading
Blanket lien
Bullet payments
Business plan
Clean bill collection
Commercial paper
Committed line of credit
Confidential factoring
Confirmed documentary letter of credit
Discount houses
Disintermediation
Documentary letter of credit
Export bill of exchange
Export factoring
Factoring
Field warehousing
FinTech
Fixed interest rate
Fixed security
Floating security
Forfaiting
Going-concern issue
Intermediation
Inventory financing
Invoice discounting
Irrevocable documentary letter of credit
Letter of credit
Liquidation issue
Negotiable instruments
Non-recourse factoring
Open account
Overdraft
Peer-to-peer
Pure discount only payments
Repayable on demand
Revocable documentary letter of credit
Revolving underwriting facility
Scenario analysis
Secured
Self-liquidating loans
Sensitivity analysis
Short-term finance
Sight draft
Tailored annuity basis
Term draft
Terminal warehousing
Trust receipt
Third-party guarantees
Uncommitted line of credit
Unsecured
Variable interest rate
Warehouse receipt
With-recourse factoring
Without-recourse factoring

REVIEW QUESTIONS

(See Suggested Solutions to Review Questions in **Appendix B**.)

Question 11.1

List two types of institution that provide short-term finance.

Question 11.2

List four forms of short-term finance that can be provided by banks.

Question 11.3

What is the difference between factoring and confidential factoring?

Question 11.4

Newman Plc has been experiencing continuing difficulties with the collection of debts from its customers. The managing director has requested a report detailing the main debt-collection techniques available in the domestic market.

Requirement Critically evaluate the costs and benefits associated with each of the following:

(a) Factoring.
(b) Invoice discounting.

8 Marks

(Based on Chartered Accountants Ireland, MABF II, Summer 1997, Q7)

Question 11.5

What type of credit arrangement would you recommend to an exporter who is concerned about the reputation of a potential foreign customer?

CHALLENGING QUESTIONS

(Suggested Solutions to Challenging Questions are available through your lecturer.)

Question 11.1 Lending (Level 1)

(a) Lending bankers generally apply a number of credit principles when evaluating loan applications – whether from companies or individuals.

Requirement Explain FOUR principles/criteria and outline their implications for a company or an individual that is seeking bank finance.

10 Marks

(b) Explain THREE significant differences between factoring and invoice discounting.

5 Marks
Total 15 Marks

(Based on Chartered Accountants Ireland, CAP 1, Finance, Summer 2010, Q5)

Question 11.2 Nada (Level 1)

Nada Ltd is a small decorating business whose customer base mainly comprises domestic customers who pay Nada at the time the work is done. Recently, the company has been offered a number of commercial contracts instead of the domestic work, which, if accepted, would replace the domestic work; commercial customers offer profit margins that are much higher. However, these commercial customers typically demand 30-day credit terms.

If Nada changes to commercial contracts, it expects sales for next year to be €/£360,000, with an average credit period taken of 45 days, even though only 30 days are offered. Employing additional part-time administrative staff to contact and collect receivables (debtors) would cost €/£12,000 per annum.

Alternatively, Nada's local bank, which currently charges 10% per annum on Nada's overdrawn bank account, has offered to provide a factoring service to Nada. The factor will advance 75% of the sales invoices, based on a 30-day payment period by customers. The credit control by the factor would save €/£6,000 of Nada's administration costs. However, the factor will charge 2% of sales turnover for this service, in addition to charging interest of 8.5% per annum on advances.

Nada is also considering a change in policy concerning payment of its suppliers. Nada is typically offered 40 days' credit, with a 1.5% discount for prompt payment if the amount is paid within 12 days. Nada usually takes a 50-day payment period. The company is now considering taking advantage of the discount opportunity by paying its suppliers on day 12 of the credit period.

Requirement

(a) Calculate the net cost of the factor agreement.

8 Marks

(b) Based on your calculation in (a), recommend whether or not Nada should factor its receivables (debtors).

2 Marks

(c) Calculate the approximate annual percentage cost of foregoing prompt payment discounts offered by suppliers and recommend whether or not Nada should change its policy in favour of taking the discounts offered.

5 Marks

Total 15 Marks

(Based on Chartered Accountants Ireland, CAP 1, Finance, Summer 2008, Q5)

Question 11.3 Tiga Sales (Level 2)

Tiga Sales Ltd sells to the general public by way of catalogue, telephone and internet sales. The credit controller of Tiga has been reviewing the sales ledger and credit balances as well as the procedures in the credit control section.

The results of the credit controller's review are summarised in Table A. Tiga divides its sales into three separate geographic regions (Area 1, Area 2 and Overseas Area) and the sales for each region in €/£ millions are given in Table A.

The average outstanding balances over the year for customers in the various areas are also shown in Table A, e.g. in Area 1 the average balance is €/£500 and there are 10,000 customers in that area. The cost of collecting, or attempting to collect, outstanding amounts varies from area to area, with overseas customers costing the greatest amount. In spite of the efforts of the credit department, 22% of the total sales to the overseas area turn out as bad debts during the course of the year (as can be seen from Table A).

All products sold by Tiga produce a contribution of 25% of selling price from which collection costs, bad debts and selling costs have to be deducted. These vary by area also – from the table below it can be seen that the overseas area requires 8% of revenue to be spent on selling costs in order to achieve a sale.

TABLE A

Area	Sales	Average balance outstanding per customer	Number of customers	Collection costs (% of average balance)	Bad debts (% of area sales)	Selling costs (% of area sales)
	€/£m	€/£		%	%	%
Area 1	80	500	10,000	0	0	2
Area 2	70	300	30,000	8	18	6
Overseas Area	60	600	17,000	10	22	8

The credit controller has had discussions with Domba Ltd, a factoring company that believes it can improve the overall profitability of Tiga by introducing better credit control procedures and incorporating new and strict guidelines for sales personnel to follow, which will speed up debt collection and reduce the bad debt problem. It will charge an annual sum of €/£3,500,000 for its administration, thereby cutting out all the existing collection costs.

Domba has offered to take over the administration of the sales ledger, debt collection and general management of trade receivables. It will not take over any losses arising from bad debts. It will lend funds to Tiga at 8% p.a. for the amount and period of the outstanding trade receivables balances, e.g. for every Area 1 customer it will lend €/£500 at 8% per annum. It predicts that its operating efficiency and credit guidelines for sales personnel will cut the bad debts percentages in respect of Area 2 and Overseas Area customers to 8% and 10%, respectively. It will also mean that total overseas sales will decline by €/£20 million, with a proportionate effect on balances outstanding.

The existing interest rate on Tiga's overdraft is 7% per annum.

Requirement

(a) Prepare a table of results to show the various revenues and costs for each area under both the existing approach and the suggested Domba plan for Tiga.

13 Marks

(b) Write a brief report, including your recommendation, on your findings in (a) above for the credit controller of Tiga.

5 Marks

(c) Outline the advantages and disadvantages of using short-term debt, as opposed to long-term debt, in the financing of working capital.

4 Marks

Total 22 Marks

(Based on Chartered Accountants Ireland, MABF II, Summer 2006, Q5)

Question 11.4 ABC (Level 1)

ABC Ltd offers its goods to customers on 30 days' credit – subject to satisfactory trade references. It also offers a 2% discount if payment is made within 10 days of the date of invoice.

Requirement

(a) Calculate the cost to the company of offering the discount, assuming a 365-day year.
(b) Compare offering discounts to customers, to encourage early settlement of bills, with using debt factors.
(c) Describe TWO methods, other than debt factoring, that a company might use to obtain finance using trade receivables as security.

15 Marks

Question 11.5 Raphael (Level 1)

Raphael Ltd is a small engineering company which has annual credit sales of €/£2.4 million. In recent years, the company has experienced credit control problems. The average collection period for sales has risen to 50 days, even though the stated policy of the company is for payment to be made within 30 days. In addition, 1.5% of total sales are written off as bad debts each year.

The company has recently been in talks with a factor company. The factor is prepared to make an advance to the company equivalent to 80% of trade receivables, based on the assumption that all customers will, in future, adhere to a 30-day payment period. The interest rate for the advance will be 11% per annum. The trade receivables are currently financed using a bank overdraft, which has an interest rate of 12% per annum. The factor will take over the credit control procedures of the company and this will result in a saving to the company of €/£18,000 per annum. However, the factor will make a charge of 2% of sales for this service. The use of the factoring service is expected to eliminate the bad debts incurred by the company.

Raphael Ltd is also considering a change in policy towards payment of its suppliers. The company is given credit terms that allow a 2.5% discount providing the amount due is paid within 15 days. However, Raphael Ltd has not taken advantage of the discount opportunity to date and has, instead, taken a 50-day payment period, even though suppliers require payment within 40 days. The company is now considering the payment of suppliers on the 15th day of the credit period in order to take advantage of the discount opportunity.

Requirement

(a) Calculate the net cost of the factor agreement to the company and state whether or not the company should take advantage of the opportunity to factor its trade debts.

10 Marks

(b) Explain ways in which factoring differs from invoice discounting.

6 Marks

(c) Calculate the approximate annual percentage cost of foregoing trade discounts to suppliers and state what additional financial information the company would need in order to decide whether or not it should change its policy in favour of taking the discounts offered.

5 Marks

(d) Discuss any other factors that may be important when deciding whether or not to change the existing policy towards payment of trade payables.

4 Marks

Total 25 Marks

(Based on Chartered Accountants Ireland, MABF, *Questions and Solutions Manual 2000/2001*)

Question 11.6 Puppet (Level 1)

(a) Outline the advantages and disadvantages of delaying payment to suppliers as a source of finance.

5 Marks

(b) Indicate TWO significant differences between factoring and invoice discounting.

2 Marks

(c) Puppet Manufacturing Plc is a manufacturing company with annual sales of €/£1 million to regular (repeat) customers. Due to difficult economic conditions, debt collection is deteriorating and now customers take on average 50 days to pay. The official credit policy is to offer 30 days' credit.

Puppet's bank is reluctant to increase existing overdraft facilities costing 11% per annum.

A factor has offered to provide finance against the trade receivables as follows:

1. The factor will assume responsibility for the management of the receivables ledger. Due to its superior skills, it expects to be able to reduce the credit period to 30 days. The charge for providing this service is 1% of turnover. However, the arrangement is expected to generate administrative savings of €/£5,000 per annum for Puppet.
2. The factor has offered to provide finance equivalent to 75% of the trade receivables balance when a sale is made, at a cost of 12.5%. This factor finance is optional.

Bad debts may be ignored.

Requirement

(i) Evaluate the offer of factor finance.

(ii) Based on your calculations, advise, including the option of factor finance, whether this offer should be accepted.

8 Marks

Total 15 Marks

(Based on Chartered Accountants Ireland, CAP 1, Finance, Summer 2009, Q4)

Question 11.7 Types of loan (Level 1)

Briefly discuss what is meant by a balloon payment loan, bullet loan and a pure discount loan.

4 Marks

(Based on Chartered Accountants Ireland, CAP 1, Finance, Summer 2017, Q6)

Question 11.8 Overdraft (Level 1)

A newly incorporated client, Start-up Ltd, is considering availing of a bank overdraft facility as a means of financing some of its working capital requirements. Additionally, the owners of Start-up are looking to source some long-term company finance and are considering approaching a venture capitalist to discuss this.

Requirement Explain the features of a bank overdraft **and** outline TWO advantages and TWO disadvantages to Start-up of using a bank overdraft.

3 Marks

(Based on Chartered Accountants Ireland, CAP 1, Finance, Autumn 2018, Q6)

Question 11.9 Factoring (Level 1)

Jack Ltd is a leading producer and installer of windows for both residential and commercial customers. You are a newly recruited finance manager and are keen to provide assistance to Jack.

Jack's managing director has asked you to investigate the possibility of improving the company's management of trade receivables. Jack earns revenue of €/£500,000 per month. Cash sales comprise 10% of total sales. On average, credit customers are offered terms of 60 days; this term is fully utilised. Jack's bank overdraft interest rate is 7.5%.

After much research, you have established two factoring possibilities:

1. A factoring agency, Cello Ltd, will advance 80% of receivables to Jack in exchange for a fee of 1% of total revenue. In addition, Cello will charge an interest rate of 14% for this cash advance. All receivables will continue to be collected after an average period of 60 days.
2. Violin Ltd, a separate factoring agency, will advance 75% of Jack's receivables. The collection period for this level of receivables will fall to 30 days. The remaining receivables will continue to be collected after 60 days. Violin will charge an interest rate of 15% for this cash advance service. In exchange, Violin will charge a fee of 0.95% of total revenue.

In each case, Jack expects to make an administrative saving of €/£120,000 per annum. A 365-day year should be assumed in any calculation.

Requirement

(a) Calculate the cost of Jack's current trade receivables policy.

2 Marks

(b) Calculate the revised cost of Jack's trade receivables policy if the company engages with:
  (i) Cello;
  (ii) Violin.

7 Marks

(c) Determine, based on your calculations, which factoring agency (if any) should be used.

1 Mark

10 Marks

(Based on Chartered Accountants Ireland, CAP 1, Finance, Autumn 2019, Q5)

Question 11.10 Shock (Level 2)

(The full question is included in Chapter 5 (Challenging Question 5.3).)

The relevant information for this part of the question is that current credit customers take 85 days to pay and the current trade receivables balance is £/€11,390,000.

Invoice collection service

A financial institution provides an invoice collection service. The terms of the service are as follows:

- Flat fee 0.3% of receivables taken over;
- Percentage of receivables which the institution invoice collector is prepared to take over is 80%;
- Overdraft interest rate is 12%;
- Collection period using invoice collection service is 30 days; and
- Collection period for all other customers is expected to be 80 days.

Requirement Assess the invoice collection proposal and make a recommendation as to whether Shock should avail of this service.

5 Marks

(Based on Chartered Accountants Ireland, CAP 2, SFMA, Autumn 2009, Q1)

Question 11.11 Beltway (Level 2)

Beltway Toys Ltd design and manufacture children's toys. Beltway was founded by Jane Moloney, who owns the business but has retired from her management role. The current managing director, Billy O'Meara, has announced that he is leaving next month after a decade in the position to join a rival firm. Beltway has grown significantly in the past decade, but some aspects of the management systems have not kept pace with this growth. Beltway has always sourced materials from EU suppliers, but is in the process of negotiating a major contract with a relatively new manufacturer of toy components in China. At today's €/£: Chinese Yuan exchange rate, the €/£ cost of these Yuan denominated inputs will be 35% less than the current cost from the EU suppliers. Despite some concerns about quality standards at the Chinese manufacturer, the low price enticed Beltway to consider the supplier.

The management of working capital is of particular concern to Jane:

Inventory management and creditors Beltway is examining two proposals to improve its working capital situation:

(i) Invest in an upgraded inventory management system and additional staff, costing €/£195,000 per year. This is expected to reduce days in inventory to 37 days. This change would be expected to reduce warehousing costs by €/£45,000 per year and increase sales by 3.5%;
(ii) One of the main suppliers to Beltway, Fusion Mouldings Ltd, offers a 2% discount for payment within 30 days. Currently, Beltway does not avail of this, opting to settle invoices in 75 days. Fusion accounts for 10% of Beltway's purchases and payables. Beltway is now considering availing of this discount.

Invoice factoring Beltway is also considering availing of an invoice factoring service. The factoring company would take on 75% of receivables on a non-recourse basis, charging a fee of 4.5% of receivables taken on. The factor will pay Beltway 100% of the invoice amount five days following a sale. For receivables not taken on, the collection period would be expected to remain at the current level. Bad debts for the non-factored receivables are expected to be 2.5%, which is the current bad debt percentage for all receivables.

FINANCIAL INFORMATION

DATA EXTRACTED FROM 20X5 FINANCIAL REPORTS

	€/£000
Turnover	18,320
Cost of goods sold	11,725
Accounts payable	2,400
Accounts receivable	3,560
Inventory	2,088

- Beltway's weighted average cost of capital is 12%.
- Beltway earns a contribution on sales of 36%.
- All purchases and sales are on credit.

Requirement

(a) Advise Beltway on whether it should implement the inventory management and creditors proposals. You should provide a financial analysis and ONE non-financial consideration for each proposal.

10 Marks

(b) Advise Beltway on whether the invoice factoring service should be availed of, based solely on financial criteria.

5 Marks

(c) Identify THREE key risks facing Beltway and suggest how these should be managed.

6 Marks

Total 21 Marks

(Based on Chartered Accountants Ireland, CAP 2, SFMA, Autumn 2016, Q4)

12

Medium-term Sources of Finance and the Finance Gap

Learning Objectives

Upon completing this chapter, readers should be able to:

- describe and evaluate various forms of medium-term finance;
- list the advantages and disadvantages of hire-purchase finance;
- outline the difference between hire-purchase finance and lease finance;
- list the advantages and disadvantages of lease finance;
- explain the purpose of the 'government-backed finance scheme'; and
- discuss the role of venture capitalists and business angels in closing the finance gap.

INTRODUCTION

Finance that is repayable within one year is regarded as short-term. Finance repayable between one and seven years is considered to be medium-term financing. Finance repayable for periods extending beyond seven years is considered to be long-term. The lines between what is classified as short, medium- and long-term are blurred. Some of the sources of finance discussed in **Chapter 11** can extend for periods beyond one year (for example, factoring); whereas some of the sources discussed in this chapter may be organised for periods of beyond seven years. Conversely, some sources that are typically categorised as long-term are structured for periods of less than seven years. For example, some large organisations (i.e. companies, governments or financial institutions) issue **medium-term bond debt** for periods of between two and 10 years. However, in this textbook bond issues are considered in **Chapter 13**, with the information not repeated in this chapter. Nonetheless, readers should be aware of the option that some companies have in respect of issuing bond debt for medium-term finance needs.

Medium-term sources of finance can be utilised by all sizes and types of company. However, medium-term sources are regarded as a more important source of finance for small- and medium-sized (SME) companies, as they have restricted access to long-term sources. This is due to barriers to entry that exist in relation to some long-term sources. For example, the costs associated with raising equity on a stock exchange are prohibitive for small and medium-sized companies (SMEs) that wish to raise a limited amount of capital.

This chapter considers the main sources of medium-term finance: term loans (these were explained in detail in **Chapter 11** so are revisited in brief), hire-purchase and leasing agreements.

TERM LOANS/REVOLVING CREDIT FACILITIES

As mentioned in **Chapter 11**, term loans can be arranged for periods of over one year. The interest charged can be either fixed or variable and there usually is an arrangement fee. The interest rate and arrangement fee is influenced by the creditworthiness of a company, the base rate and whether there is security for the loan, or not – the quality of the assets being used as security will also influence the rate. Loan repayments can be tailored to match the cash inflows received from the asset or investment for which the funds were used. It is not uncommon for term loans to have a **grace period** (i.e. an initial period with no repayments), repayment breaks (known as repayment holidays) or increasing repayment amounts. Most bank debt packages are bespoke but, in the main, when a company organises a standard term loan, a repayment profile is arranged and capital, once repaid, cannot be accessed again.

Banks can also provide revolving credit facilities. A **revolving credit facility** is a hybrid of a term loan and an overdraft facility. It is normally secured on the working capital of a company, though this is not a requirement – many large companies have a revolving facility that is unsecured. Repayments are made to reduce the capital element of the debt; however, the capital that has been repaid can be accessed again over the agreed life of the facility up to the original agreed sum. A company needs to give the bank notice of its intention to draw down an additional sum up to the limit of the committed total. As banks have to keep sufficient funds in reserve to service this type of finance, it is more costly than a straightforward term loan. The additional cost comes in the form of a commitment fee. This is usually a percentage of the undrawn balance. In all other respects, the costs are the same as those for a term loan.

HIRE PURCHASE

A **hire-purchase agreement** is a form of finance whereby the ownership of an asset being purchased on credit passes from a supplier (the company selling the asset) to a finance house. The finance house then rents the asset to the purchaser. Ownership passes from the finance house to the purchaser when the final instalment is paid. The finance company, which legally owns the asset and provides the finance, is called the **hirer**. The company possessing and using the asset for the period of the agreement (the purchaser) is called the **hiree**. The arrangement is shown in **Figure 12.1**.

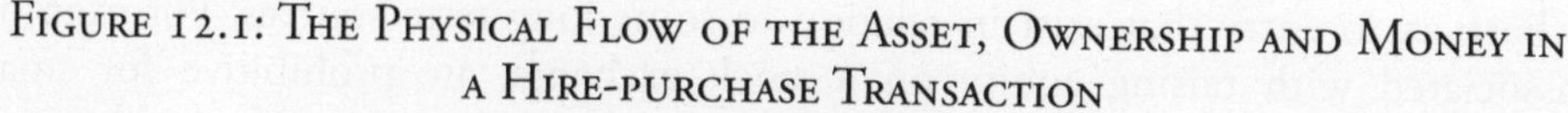
FIGURE 12.1: THE PHYSICAL FLOW OF THE ASSET, OWNERSHIP AND MONEY IN A HIRE-PURCHASE TRANSACTION

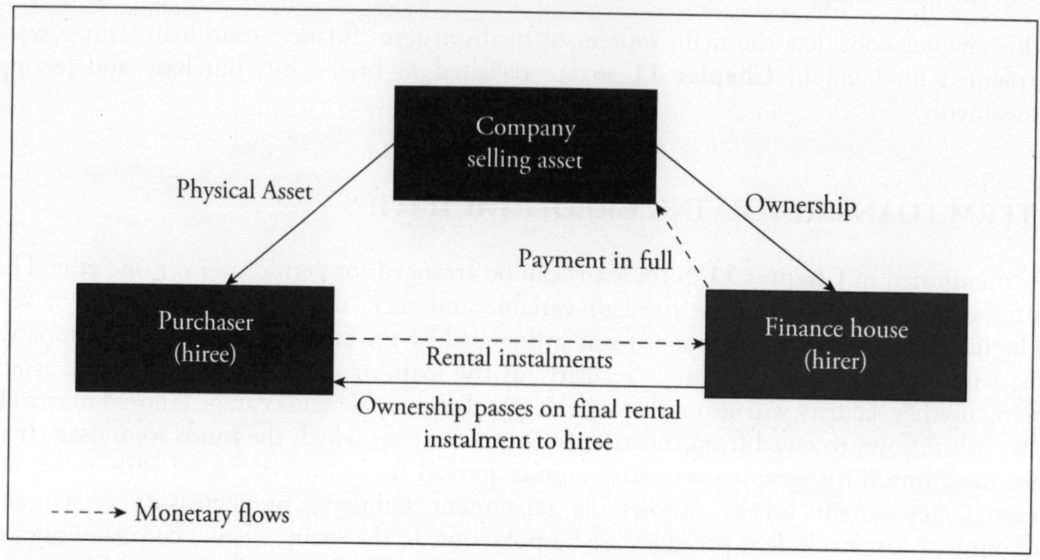

Hirer companies usually specialise in hire-purchase and leasing transactions. In the UK they are normally affiliated to the Finance and Leasing Association (FLA), a body that lobbies government, accounting standards setters and others. Most commercial banks have a subsidiary that deals solely with this type of financing transaction, although many large companies also have their own financial subsidiary to cater for their hire-purchase and leasing business.

Hire-purchase agreements are usually for periods of between one and five years, though this depends on the useful economic life of the asset being financed. Assets financed in this manner typically have a useful economic life of less than 10 years. Examples include: motor vehicles, equipment (e.g. factory plant and machinery and agriculture equipment), fixtures and household goods. A hire-purchase agreement usually involves the hiree having to pay a down-payment and sign a legal contract committing the hiree to the payment of a predetermined number of periodic set payments to the hirer. This agreement is legally binding and usually provides for the transfer of legal title to the asset (from the hirer to the hiree) on the last payment.

The rental instalments are sufficient to pay off the whole capital that the hirer has spent on the asset, and provide a profitable return. The hirer has the right to repossess the asset if the hiree defaults on payment. If default occurs, the hiree loses all rights to the asset and has no claim on the payments made to date. The right of repossession may not protect the hirer in certain circumstances. For example, where the hire agreement is for a long period of time, but the asset becomes obsolete, then the hirer runs the risk of the hiree defaulting on the agreement on purpose, as the asset is no longer of use. To reduce exposure to this type of risk, the terms of hire-purchase agreements are usually arranged for periods that are much less than the useful economic life of the asset. For example, motor car agreements are usually for three to four years, yet most motor vehicles will still have a useful economic life left after four years. This reduces the risk of the hiree defaulting on the agreement, as the asset is of higher value than the payments outstanding at any time during the agreement period.

Another potential risk to the hirer is the condition of the asset on hire; the hiree assumes all the risks of maintaining and insuring the asset. If this is not adequate and the asset becomes damaged, then the hiree is more likely to default on the agreement. In this instance, the asset that can be repossessed may not be in a fit state for resale or rehire. Therefore, hire purchase is an expensive form of finance, as some of the risks associated with ownership stay with the hirer (e.g. deterioration in the asset value and condition) and a premium for these additional risks is factored into the rental payments. In addition, it is costly to terminate the agreement as penalty payments may be built into the hire-purchase agreement.

The companies selling the assets (who recommend the hire-purchase companies), usually do not fully explain the true cost of this form of finance to potential customers. The marketing approach adopted focuses on affordability (for example, this fridge will only cost you €10/£7 per week). The annual percentage rates (APR) can be high, over twice the flat rate of interest, as the flat rate does not take into consideration any of the capital repayments that have been made when working out the interest, whereas the APR calculates interest based on the reducing balance of capital after each repayment. The difference between flat rates of interest and APR is highlighted in the following example.

Worked Example 12.1: Hire Purchase

Amarillo Plc is in negotiations to purchase a machine for €/£500,000 on 1 January 20X4 from Exit Plc. The sales representative at Exit Plc informs Amarillo Plc that he can get finance for the sale from Exit Hire Finance Ltd at the rate of 8%, to be repaid over the next three years in three equal yearly instalments.

Requirement

(a) Calculate the yearly payments to be made by Amarillo Plc to the hire-purchase company, assuming a flat rate of 8%.

(b) Using these repayment amounts, calculate the effective APR being charged by Exit Hire Finance Ltd.

(c) Assume that Amarillo Plc can get a term loan with an APR of 10%. This term loan will also have three repayments, one at the end of each year. What will the yearly cash outflow be if the term loan is selected instead of the hire-purchase finance? What will the cash flow implication of this option be to Amarillo Plc?

Solution

	€/£
(a) Interest repayment each year will be: [€/£500,000 × 8%]	40,000
Capital repayment each year will be: [€/£500,000 ÷ 3]	166,667
Total yearly repayment:	206,667

(b) The annuity, i.e. the three-yearly repayment amount, discounted using a determinable annuity factor (representing three years at an unknown rate) will equate to the present value of the loan advanced, as expressed in the following formula:

Present value = annuity × annuity factor

where the present value is €/£500,000 and the annuity is €/£206,667 over three years.

€/£500,000 = €/£206,667 × annuity factor
Annuity factor = €/£500,000 ÷ €/£206,667
Annuity factor = 2.419

Using the annuity tables, look along the three-year annuity row. 2.419 lies between 11% (2.4437 is the factor corresponding to 11%) and 12% (2.4018 is the factor corresponding to 12%). Therefore, the effective interest rate being used is: 11% + [(2.4437 − 2.419)/(2.4437 − 2.4018)] = 11.59%.

(c) In this instance, the yearly interest rate is given (therefore, using the tables, you can get the annuity factor: three years at 10%). The present value of the capital being advanced is also given. The requirement asks you to calculate the annuity payment.

Present value = annuity × annuity factor

€/£500,000 = annuity × 2.487
Annuity = €/£500,000 ÷ 2.487
Yearly repayment is: €/£201,045

The cash benefit of using the term loan over the hire-purchase option is €/£5,622 per year [€/£206,667 − €/£201,045].

Although hire purchase is usually an expensive option, it is commonly used by companies because it has a number of advantages, as listed in **Figure 12.2**.

FIGURE 12.2: ADVANTAGES TO A HIREE OF USING HIRE-PURCHASE FINANCE

Easy to arrange	The vendor has a pre-arranged agreement with a finance house and is trained in the documentation.
Quick source of finance	Hire purchase is usually arranged at the point of sale and is in place by the time the asset is delivered.
Availability	Hire-purchase finance is usually available when other sources are not. As ownership does not pass until the end of the agreement, the asset itself forms the security for the finance arrangement.
Cash flow certainty/ budgeting is easier	Unlike variable rate finance, hire-purchase finance is fixed rate, hence repayment amounts will not fluctuate when interest rates change.
Not repayable on demand	Unlike an overdraft, hire-purchase finance is not repayable on demand. Therefore it does not increase the liquidity risk of the hiree. The only time the agreement becomes repayable on demand is when the hiree defaults on payments.
Cash flow advantages	The hiree gets use of the asset immediately, without having to make a major cash outlay to acquire it.
Tax relief	The hiree qualifies for tax relief on the interest element of the rental and for capital allowances on the capital value of the asset being financed.
Ownership	The hiree automatically gains legal ownership of the asset at the end of the hire-purchase agreement. The asset can then be utilised further in the company to generate income or can be sold.

The disadvantages of using hire purchase to a hiree are listed in **Figure 12.3**.

FIGURE 12.3: DISADVANTAGES TO A HIREE COMPANY OF USING HIRE-PURCHASE FINANCE

Cost	Hire-purchase agreements are usually quite expensive relative to other forms of finance, such as term loans.
Lack of flexibility	Hire-purchase agreements are not flexible and the hirer has the right to repossess an asset, if a payment is missed.
Cancellation is costly	The hire-purchase agreement usually includes costly fixed penalties, were the agreement to terminate, and may include surcharges in the eventuality of contractual payments being missed.
Maintenance/insurance	The hiree assumes responsibility for the maintenance, upkeep and insurance costs associated with the asset.
Risks of ownership	The risks associated with the ownership of the asset transfer to the hiree. If the asset were to be destroyed, the rental agreement payments would still have to be met. If the agreement were to be terminated, default charges would result.
Underutilisation	Rental payments have to be met even when the asset is not in use.

Accounting and Tax Treatment of Assets Purchased using Hire Purchase

The substance of a hire-purchase transaction is that it is a form of financing. Most of the risks and rewards associated with asset ownership pass to the hiree at the outset of the agreement, as the hiree has full control over the asset. If the asset generates more revenue than anticipated, it falls to the hiree; likewise where the asset is not being used, the hiree bears the opportunity cost. The hiree will also treat the asset like any other fully owned asset, having to maintain it, insure it and service it. Therefore, from the outset it is considered, both for accounting and tax purposes, that the hiree owns the asset and it is accounted for in exactly the same way as any other asset that is purchased outright.

Therefore, the hiree is not able to claim a tax-deductible expense for the full amount of the rental payment; however, the hiree can claim an allowance on the capital value of the asset and also gets a tax deduction for the interest paid. The tax allowance on assets is called a capital allowance. This is the tax authority's equivalent of depreciation. Depreciation is not an allowable expense for taxation purposes; however, a capital allowance is. The tax deduction allowed by the tax authorities will result in a saving for the hiree. The extent of this saving is dependent on the tax rate applying at the time. The higher the tax rate, the higher the saving from the tax deduction. It should also be noted that a tax deduction in a particular year is only possible if the company is profitable. The next example considers the tax saving that is available to a company from undertaking a hire-purchase agreement.

Worked Example 12.2: Tax Implications of Hire-purchase Assets: Hiree

Corter Plc has taken delivery of a machine worth €/£50,000. This is being financed using hire purchase. The repayments are four equal instalments of €/£17,500 over the next four years (starting at the end of this year). This equates to an APR of 15%. Assume that the corporation tax rate for this type of company is 30% per annum and that capital allowances are 25%. Ignore deferred taxation.

Requirement

(a) Calculate the tax deduction (for the first year) that the company would receive if it were to purchase the asset using cash reserves.
(b) Calculate the tax deduction (for the first year) that the company would receive if it were to purchase the asset using hire purchase.
(c) Calculate the after-tax interest rate implicit in this agreement.

Solution

(a) The tax-deductible capital allowance on this asset will be €/£50,000 × 25% = €/£12,500. Assuming that Corter Plc is profitable, this will result in a tax saving in the first year of €/£3,750 [€/£12,500 × 30%].
(b) The capital allowance will remain the same (€/£12,500). However, the finance interest paid is also tax deductible.
The interest will be for a full year at 15% = €/£50,000 × 15% = €/£7,500.
Therefore, the new tax deduction is €/£6,000 [(€/£12,500 + €/£7,500) × 30%]. This increased tax deduction means that the finance element of the hire-purchase contract is not as expensive as it might first seem.
(c) The fact that interest is tax deductible reduces its overall cost to $i(1 - t)$, where i is the interest rate and t is the corporation tax rate. Therefore, the net cost of the hire-purchase interest in this instance is 15%(1 – 30%) = 10.5%.

Finally, the hirer will be taxed on the hire-purchase interest income receivable in each year.

LEASING

International Financial Reporting Standard 16 *Leases* (IFRS 16) defines a **lease** as:

> "a contract, or part of a contract, that conveys the right to use an asset (the underlying asset) for a period of time in exchange for consideration".

Leasing is an increasingly popular form of finance, as highlighted in **Real World Example 12.1**.

Real World Example 12.1: Finance and Leasing Association (FLA)

According to the Finance and Leasing Association (FLA)'s annual report (2019), FLA members provided £137 billion of new lending in the calendar year 2018. £32.6 billion of this was on asset finance, with £18.8 billion to SMEs. FLA members funded 34.1% of UK investment in machinery, equipment and purchased software. The remaining £104.3 billion was consumer finance, of which £41.1 billion was for motor vehicle purchases, £9.6 billion was for retail store credit purchases, £52.5 billion was for personal loans and credit card finance and £1.1 billion was loaned through the second change mortgage market.

The FLA's annual report is available at: https://www.fla.org.uk/business-information/documents/2019-annual-review/, accessed November 2019.

The leasing industry in Ireland is also bouyant and as a result a dedicated trade association has been established, as highlighted in **Real World Example 12.2.**

Real World Example 12.2: Aircraft Leasing in Ireland

Ireland is the world's leading centre for aircraft. It currently finances 60% of the world's fleet of leased aircraft, with an estimated value of $100 billion. As a result of success in this niche, the leasing companies have joined forces to form Aircraft Leasing Ireland (ALI), a group that forms part of the Irish financial services trade association, Financial Services Ireland (IBEC). The aircraft leasing sector provides highly skilled jobs in both Dublin and the Shannon region, with growth predicted in the coming years.

Updated information on ALI can be obtained at: https://www.aircraftleasingireland.ie, accessed November 2019.

A **leasing agreement** is similar to a hire-purchase agreement; a company wishing to acquire an asset approaches the selling company, which sells the asset immediately to a third party (e.g. a finance house). The finance house then leases the asset to the purchasing company. The finance house is usually a member of the FLA in the UK or the IBEC in Ireland and may be a subsidiary of a commercial or merchant bank, or a subsidiary of the corporation selling the asset. The company taking possession of the asset is called the **lessee** and the finance house that takes ownership of the asset (but not possession) is called the **lessor**. The selling company is no longer involved in the transaction (unless there is a warranty agreement or a fault with the asset) after the initial sale is made, as the lessor pays them for the asset at the outset. The selling company records the profit made on the sale in the same manner as for any other sale. The process is portrayed in **Figure 12.4**.

When a lease is obtained, the asset is capitalised in the books of the lessee and the lessee pays the full price for the asset, more or less, over the term of the lease period. The purchase price of the asset plus finance cost is usually recovered from the payments made during the lease period.

Figure 12.4: The Physical Flow of Asset, Ownership and Money in a Lease Transaction

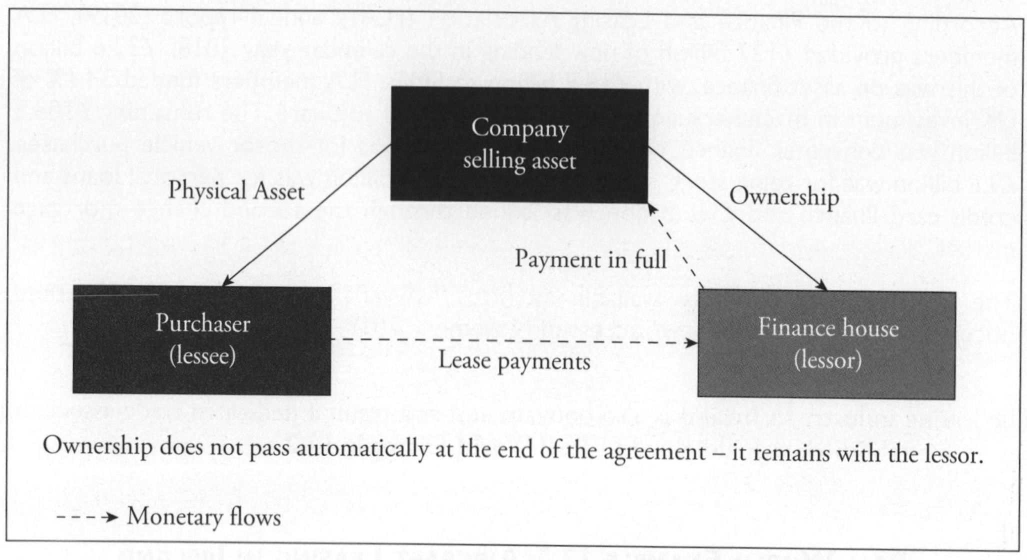

An example of the typical cash flows and cost of a lease is included in **Worked Example 12.3**.

Worked Example 12.3: Lease Agreements

Ruby Ltd wants to lease a machine which is manufactured by Wax Ltd. The fair value of the machine is €/£500,000. Finance House Ltd agrees to purchase the machine from Wax Ltd, and lease it to Ruby Ltd on the following terms: 12 payments of €/£50,000, payable quarterly in advance, after which, six further annual payments of €/£5 per year in arrears are required.

Requirement

(a) Describe the pattern of these lease payments.
(b) Calculate the interest rate that is implicit in this agreement.

Solution

(a) The period during which the 12 lease payments of €/£50,000 are paid is called the primary lease period. In subsequent years, only a nominal rental is charged for the use of the asset; this is called the secondary lease period.
(b) **Present value = annuity amount × annuity factor**
(The secondary lease rentals are ignored in this instance as they are immaterial.)
€/£500,000 = €/£50,000 × annuity factor (***Note:*** assume 12 periods, then multiply the rate by four to get a more reflective yearly rate.)
Annuity factor for 12 periods is 12. The annuity factor tables disclose that the annuity rate for 12 periods with an annuity factor of 10 is 3% (rounded). This is for a three-month period. This equates to a yearly rate of 12% [3% × 4]. A more precise rate is 12.55% [$(1.03)^4 - 1$].

Sometimes companies can obtain the use of an asset by hiring an asset. When the asset is not considered to be an identified asset, and the company does not have the right to obtain substantially all of the economic benefit from use of the identified asset throughout the period of use and the company does not have the right to direct the use of the identified asset, then the arrangement is considered to be a hire arrangement and not a lease. An asset is not classed as identified if it is not separately identified in the agreement and can be easily substituted by the supplier. The disadvantages of using hire assets is listed in **Figure 12.5**; the advantages are listed in **Figure 12.6**.

FIGURE 12.5: DISADVANTAGES OF HIRING ASSETS OVER LEASING ASSETS

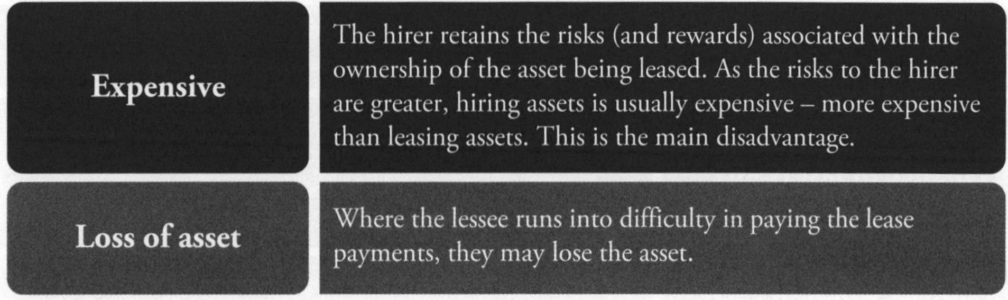

Expensive
The hirer retains the risks (and rewards) associated with the ownership of the asset being leased. As the risks to the hirer are greater, hiring assets is usually expensive – more expensive than leasing assets. This is the main disadvantage.
Loss of asset
Where the lessee runs into difficulty in paying the lease payments, they may lose the asset.

Taxation Treatment for Leases

The taxation treatment for lessee companies is exactly the same as that outlined for the hiree company that purchases an asset using a hire-purchase agreement – see **Worked Example 12.2**. The taxation treatment for lessors is exactly the same as that outlined for a hirer company (see the hire-purchase section above). The lessor company is taxable on lease interest income receivable in the year.

Sale and Leaseback Agreements

Another common source of medium-term finance is where a company sells an asset and then leases that asset back again. The sale may be made to a newly established subsidiary company that has been formed to raise equity capital. The parent company sells the asset to the subsidiary and enters a lease agreement, committing to pay lease rentals in return for the use of the asset. This sort of arrangement is regarded as a lease and is accounted for as such.

REAL WORLD EXAMPLE 12.3: SUPERMARKET LEASE AND SALE BACK ACTIVITY

In the early 2000s, the big UK supermarket operators – Tesco, Sainsbury's, Morrisons and ASDA – used sale and leaseback deals to finance growth. Tesco, for example, sourced £2.7 billion in this way and used the funds to pay back debt and finance growth. However, the trend is changing. In an 18-month period straddling 2016, roughly £1.1 billion of supermarket assets were traded, but there were no sale and leaseback deals as the big supermarkets sought to get their costs down and to reduce their exposure to inflationary building costs. Indeed, Tesco is reversing the early trend of releasing its property to source cash. It has been exercising 'buy back' options and repurchased about £450 million worth of property over the period 2016–2017.

For more information, see: https://property-investor-news.com/news/uk_news/2017/05/05/supermarket_properties_rising_in_popularity_with_investors.html#.XdLcjlX7SUk, accessed 18 November 2019.

FIGURE 12.6: ADVANTAGES OF HIRING ASSETS INSTEAD OF LEASING THEM

Advantage	Description
Cancellation	They are easier and less costly to cancel relative to a lease.
Quick and easy to obtain	They are usually arranged at the point of sale of the asset or when ordering the asset.
Possession of asset	The company can obtain immediate possession of the asset, without any major initial cash outlay.
No security required	The asset acts as security; therefore, the supplier can take possession of the asset if the payments are in default.
Finance of last resort	Assets can be hired when the company cannot get finance elsewhere. This is more important for small emerging companies that do not have a strong track record or have insufficient security or cash.
Reduced running costs	Maintenance and insurance costs usually remain with the supplier.
No obsolescence risk	The risk of obsolescence remains with the supplier. If the asset becomes obsolete, then the agreement can be cancelled or not renewed.
Tax relief	The full rental payment is tax deductible.
Cash flow planning and budgeting	Some hire agreements are arranged on a set rental basis, making the budgeting process easier.
Cash management	Some rentals are arranged and have a fixed and variable element: a fixed standing rental and a charge per unit used. This means that the rental will move in line with income, assuming more activity from the asset results in more revenue.
No restrictive covenants	There are not usually any restrictive covenants written into hire agreements.
Off-balance-sheet finance	Hiring an asset ties the company into paying a future stream of payments; however, the present value of this liability is not accrued in the financial statements (it is disclosed).
Cheaper	Where the company is loss-making, hiring an asset may be cheaper for them, relative to leasing the asset, as the supplier can pass on the tax benefits that are available for purchasing capital items.This results in lower rentals.

As a means of obtaining finance, a sale and leaseback is a way to source cash without upsetting the equity equilibrium in the parent company, whilst retaining control over the asset. In other instances, an asset might be sold to an external company and leased back. The risk with this agreement is that the lease payments in the period beyond the lease term may increase by more than is anticipated.

Factors Influencing the Decision to use Leasing as a Source of Finance

Leasing should be used as a source of finance when it is cheaper than other sources. The cost of a lease will depend on the tax situation of the lessee and the lessor. Another influence on the cost of a lease will be competition amongst finance houses and interest rates. When interest rates are low, lessors are likely to reduce the required rate of return on a lease agreement.

GOVERNMENT-BACKED FINANCE SCHEMES

In both the UK and Ireland, the governments have formed joint initiatives with banks to provide funding for entrepreneurial activity to companies and start-ups. The main initiatives are now discussed for each jurisdiction.

United Kingdom

A direct initiative established by the government in the UK, through the British Business Bank, to provide medium-term debt finance to small and medium-sized companies with a turnover of under £41 million is the government-backed **Enterprise Finance Guarantee Scheme**. Under this scheme, the government guarantees up to 75% of loans to small- or medium-sized companies that are less than five years old. Loans range in size from £1,000 to £1 million and are provided for terms of between three months and 10 years. The company sourcing the loan pays a 2% premium on the outstanding loan balance. The guarantees provided under the scheme are for certain products, as outlined in **Figure 12.7**.

Regional funding is available in Northern Ireland, the **NI Small Business Loan Fund** provides access to up to £100,000 finance for small businesses, sole traders and partnerships which are keen to develop their business, but find it difficult to access funding through traditional sources. In addition, Enterprise Northern Ireland may provide a start-up loan to SMEs of up to £25,000 over 1–5 years. These businesses may also access up to 15 hours of mentoring support.

FIGURE 12.7: ENTERPRISE FINANCE GUARANTEE SCHEME (PRODUCTS GUARANTEED)

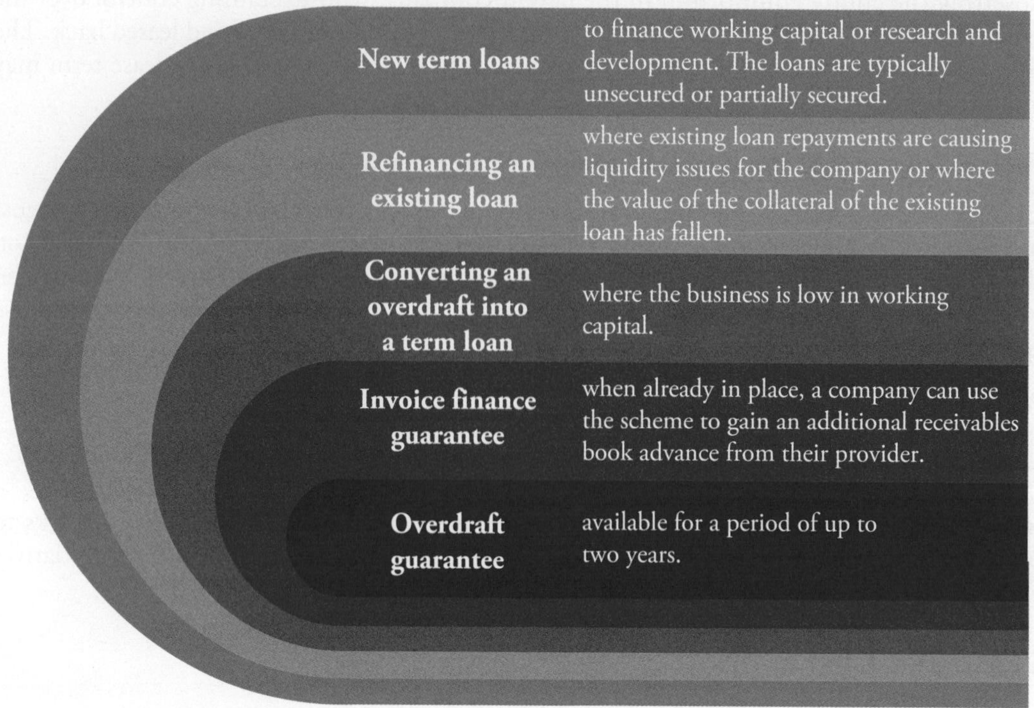

New term loans
to finance working capital or research and development. The loans are typically unsecured or partially secured.
Refinancing an existing loan
where existing loan repayments are causing liquidity issues for the company or where the value of the collateral of the existing loan has fallen.
Converting an overdraft into a term loan
where the business is low in working capital.
Invoice finance guarantee
when already in place, a company can use the scheme to gain an additional receivables book advance from their provider.
Overdraft guarantee
available for a period of up to two years.

Republic of Ireland

Two main government-backed schemes are available in the Republic of Ireland: the Microenterprise Loan Fund Scheme and the Credit Guarantee Scheme.

The **Microenterprise Loan Fund Scheme** is administered by Microfinance Ireland on behalf of the Minister for Business, Enterprise and Innovation. It provides loans of up to €25,000 for start-up or growing businesses with less than 10 employees that have commercially viable proposals but do not meet the conventional risk criteria applied by banks. The business must show that it has been refused finance by the bank and show capacity to repay the funds in the future (a business plan is required).

The **Credit Guarantee Scheme** was set up by the Department of Business, Enterprise and Innovation to encourage additional lending to SMEs, not to substitute for conventional lending that would otherwise have taken place. The scheme targets companies that are unable to access credit because: they have inadequate collateral; they operate in a novel business market or in a sector or technology that is perceived by lenders as higher risk under current credit risk evaluation practices; or their need for refinancing resulted from the exit of a SME lender from the Irish market.

FINANCE GAP

The finance needs of most small companies can be met from capital introduced by the private equity holders who own the company, retained earnings or bank-sourced debt. A **finance gap** emerges when new companies reach a certain size or small companies start to grow. In these instances, the bank usually does not wish to provide all the finance – the risks are too great. There are usually insufficient retained earnings and the private equity holders do not have the wealth to support a large-scale venture; yet the finance requirement is not large enough to substantiate flotation. This finance gap is also referred to as the **equity gap**. In the UK and Ireland the finance gap is, to some extent, met by venture capitalists.

Venture Capital

Venture capital is provided by venture capitalists to finance high-risk, high-return projects, with high-growth potential. It is also known as **private equity (PE) finance**. The expectation is that a successful investment will yield a 30% annual return, though this depends on the risk of the investment and the type of funding provided. Venture capital is a major source of finance for companies in the UK and Ireland, as highlighted in **Real World Example 12.4** and **12.5**.

Real World Example 12.4: Private Equity UK

KPMG's study of UK transactions involving private equity investors over 2019 indicates that both deal volumes and value have fallen to below levels last seen in 2014, with 384 deals completing between January and June 2019 with a combined value of £28.5bn. This compares to 483 deals totalling £31.5bn which completed during the first half of 2014. The latest figures also represent a 35% fall in volumes and 40% decline in values when compared to the same period last year – 2018 saw 594 deals with a combined value of £47bn ... Jonathan Boyers, head of KPMG's M&A practice, said: "The slowdown in transaction activity witnessed during the first half of the year certainly doesn't appear to be a result of investors pulling down the shutters while they wait for the economic and geopolitical headwinds to blow over. Rather, it is being driven by a reticence amongst vendors to bring assets to market."

Source: KPMG website (2019), https://home.kpmg/uk/en/home/media/press-releases/2019/08/uk-private-equity-activity-at-lowest-levels-for-five-years.html, accessed 18 November 2019.

Real World Example 12.5: Private Equity ROI

Private-equity buyouts have accounted for 19.8% of all M&A [mergers and acquisitions] deals in Ireland so far [in 2019], the highest percentage recorded since the financial crisis.

According to new data compiled by Mergermarket the volume of buyouts is at its second highest to date, with 21 deals worth €1.9 billion.

Technology continues to be the most active M&A sector with 21 deals so far in 2019, just one short of last year's total count. The largest tech deal of the year so far is the €447 million investment by Insight Venture Partners and TPG Capital into Dublin-headquartered management software company Kaseya in May.

In addition, M&A activity in the financial services sector has also been strong with 17 deals to date, one more than for the whole of 2018. The biggest deal in the sector so far this year has been the €250 million investment in Castlehaven Finance by Avenue Capital Group.

Last year saw a record 163 M&A transactions taking place locally worth a combined €76 billion. Last year's deal values were skewed by the $62 billion deal by Japan's Takeda Pharmaceutical for Dublin-headquartered Shire.

Ion Investment Group, a Dublin-based company, took a majority stake in Mergermarket's parent Acuris earlier this year in a deal valued at more than £1 billion.

Source: Taylor, C. (2019), Private-equity buyouts soar as tech sector dominates M&A deals, *The Irish Times*, 26 September 2019, https://www.irishtimes.com/business/technology/private-equity-buyouts-soar-as-tech-sector-dominates-m-a-deals-1.4029889, accessed November 2019

Two out of 10 venture capital deals usually have excellent results, six are regarded as being good to poor and two usually fail. In general, venture capitalists will consider offering loans of €/£250,000 or more, though deals ranging from €/£1 million to over €/£1 billion are more common for private equity purchases. Venture capitalists may purchase the whole company or require an equity stake in the company in return for their investment, though they may also keep part of their stake as debt, as this is less risky than equity and is more likely to provide a return. Interest has to be paid, whereas dividends can be waived. In addition, debt has to be repaid, whereas equity does not and, finally, equity shares are not marketable.

Venture capital is normally only provided for companies that have a track record, though in some instances capital will be provided based on the strength of the project or idea, the quality of the managerial team (entrepreneurial skills) and the expectation of the project becoming a success. The various types of project that venture capitalists are approached with are outlined in **Figure 12.8**.

FIGURE 12.8: CLASSIFICATION OF TYPES OF PROJECT SEEKING VENTURE CAPITAL

Seed-corn venture capital

Is difficult to obtain and generally involves funding an idea or the creation of a prototype. Corporate venture capitalists trading in intellectual capital industries are the best source of this type of capital. It is an inexpensive way for them to invest in research and development. The government is also supportive of this type of venture and provides incentives to venture capitalists to invest in them.

Start-up venture capital

Involves developing an idea further and starting to produce the product. It naturally follows on from a successful seed-corn venture capital and the same venture capitalists will usually support the next stage. There are usually no sales and the risk of not receiving a return is high.

Early-stage venture capital

Is provided for successful start-ups that are starting to trade. The company is usually not yet profitable and is likely to be sourcing markets for its products.

Growth venture capital

Is less risky relative to the types listed above. The company is usually successful, but does not have the capitalisation to fund growth. The funds are usually used to increase working capital in support of growth.

Management buy-out (MBO)

Usually occurs where a parent company no longer sees a section of its business as being part of its strategic plan. In these instances, the management buy the section, backed by large personal investments (usually placing themselves in debt), large amounts of debt finance and venture capital finance (usually 15–20%). Venture capitalists are interested in this type of venture, as they consider that management are more aware of the future prospects of the company than the parent company (i.e. there is information asymmetry).

Management buy-in (MBI)

Occurs where the management team of one company purchases the shares of a similar company and assumes responsibility for the running of the company. The arguments for financing these ventures are similar to those for an MBO. The value placed on this type of project by venture capitalists depends on the reputation and experience of the management team.

Combination of a management buy-in and buy-out (BIMBO)

Occurs where the management of a company gets together with the management of a similar type of company to buy a company and run it together.

Venture capitalists usually aim to get a 30–40% share of the company in return for their investment. Private-equity venture capital typically involves the purchase of whole companies and can include MBIs, MBOs and BIMBOs or outright purchases by private equity firms. Regardless of the level of ownership, venture capitalists typically like to have a veto on some decisions, such as the raising of additional finance, the distribution of dividends and the sale of the company. In addition, venture capitalists like the company to have a clear exit plan for liquidating the venture capitalists' investment – usually in a five- to seven-year timescale. The most common **exit strategies** are outlined in **Figure 12.9**.

FIGURE 12.9: VENTURE CAPITAL EXIT STRATEGIES

Flotation

This is the most attractive option to venture capitalists, but it will only happen if the company is very successful.

Management buy-back

The current management team agrees terms at the outset at which to buy back the shares from the venture capitalists at a specified date in the future.

Sale to an institutional investor

If successful, the venture capitalists may approach an institutional investor to buy out their holding. The institutional investor will usually **only** be interested if it is likely that the company will eventually float or be taken over by another company.

Sale of the whole company

To another company. This **usually** happens when smaller research companies strike gold; larger, more established companies will pay a premium to access the new intellectual capital.

The company usually benefits from the relationship with the venture capitalist in more ways than just receiving much needed cash at a low issue price. If the investment is all equity, then dividends can be waived. In addition, the venture capitalist may provide business expertise (e.g. financial planning, marketing advice) and trade contacts. Venture capitalists ultimately have the same objective as management – to foster a successful, growing company. They may be prepared to provide future capital injections. On the down side, the current equity holders will experience a loss of absolute control, a loss in earnings and will have to justify their decision-making and be accountable to the venture capitalist.

Venture Capital Providers

There are five main providers of venture capital: venture capital companies; captive firms; financial institutions providing venture capital trusts; corporate venturing; and 'business angels'. These are now explained in turn.

Venture Capital Companies Venture capital companies are independent companies that are set up initially by private venture capital individuals to raise funds and invest in venture capital projects (also called **private equity firms**). The aim is to invest in projects that are likely to achieve a flotation and to sell the shares in the company when this is achieved. The largest and best-known venture capital company in the UK is *3i*. It is listed on the main market of the London Stock Exchange. According to the company's website, *3i* considers itself to be a world leader in private equity and venture capital. It focuses on: buyouts; growth capital; venture capital; and invests in companies across Europe, the US and in Asia-Pacific.

Captive Firms Captive firms are usually subsidiaries of large intermediaries, such as banks, insurance companies and pension companies. They are created as specialist companies to invest a portion of their parent company's portfolio in riskier ventures, which have the potential to make large returns.

Financial Institutions providing Venture Capital Trusts (VCT) These are similar in nature to captive firms except the financial intermediary offers a VCT direct to their clients, for their investment. To promote investment into entrepreneurial ventures, the UK government introduced a tax break in 1995 for all investors who invest in VCTs (see below for information on the tax relief available to investors). A VCT invests in a range of high-risk, venture capital deals, with several companies. The VCT is limited to investing a maximum of 15% of its capital in each company. This ensures that there is some diversification of risks. Investors can buy units in this trust, similar to any other investment trust.

Corporate Venturing Corporate venturing occurs when a large company supports a small company in the early stages of its development, or when it undertakes a new venture. The large company usually takes a small equity stake in the company, in return for finance. It is usually a symbiotic relationship with the large company: getting tax relief from the government on the sums invested and on the capital gain made if shares are held for more than three years; gaining access to the small company's intellectual capital; selling products to it; or getting access to a new market. The small company gains finance, technical resources, help with strategic and financial management, and access to a wider market.

Business Angels 'Business angels' are private equity investors who invest in high-risk, high-return companies. They typically require an equity investment, though may hold both debt and equity in a company. They are usually wealthy individuals who have surplus cash and wish to use it in an entrepreneurial manner. There is an element of altruism in respect of the motives behind many business angels. They usually invest in local ventures and are keen to see them succeed for the benefit of the community, as well as for their own benefit. Business angels do not push for as early an exit route as other venture capital providers. They usually require that a company has a trading history, though are more likely to invest in seed-corn, or start-up ventures, than other venture capital providers. Many like a hands-on approach and often require the terms of the finance agreement to allow them to sit on the board of directors and have a veto on some decisions. They are usually successful business persons who can contribute to the strategy and financial management of a company. Companies that are looking for business angels are usually put into contact with them by their bank, accountants, solicitors, corporate acquaintances or by searching the internet. There are dedicated sites set up to assist in this introduction process. For example, as highlighted in **Real World Example 12.6**, the Halo Business Angel Network (HBAN) provides a forum for the establishment of angel networks in Ireland to bring together high-risk, high-return start-up companies and business angels. Many partnerships have been supported since its inception.

Real World Example 12.6: Halo Business Angel Network (HBAN)

The Halo Business Angel Network (HBAN) is an all-island umbrella group responsible for the development of business angel syndicates. HBAN actively works to increase the number of angel investors involved in investing in early stage companies and supports the formation of new and existing angel networks, both regionally and internationally, and within industry sectors.

In 2018, HBAN business angels across the island invested €9.3 million into 44 companies. This direct investment leveraged a further €27.5 million of additional public and private funds into these companies from organisations such as Enterprise Ireland, venture capital companies and founders. These numbers have risen steadily from 2011 when HBAN helped 29 companies raise €12 million of which €6 million came from angel investors.

Business angel investors are high net worth individuals who provide smaller amounts of finance (typically in the range of €50,000/£40,000 to €250,000/£200,000) at an earlier stage than many venture capital funds are able to invest. They are increasingly investing alongside both seed venture capital funds and government agency funding on the island.

Source: HBAN website (2019), https://www.hban.org/about, accessed November 2019.

THE GOVERNMENT'S INVISIBLE HAND: SOLVING THE FINANCING GAP PROBLEM

United Kingdom

The British government has four venture capital products on offer, including: the Enterprise Investment Scheme; Venture Capital Trusts; the Seed Enterprise Investment Scheme and the Social Investment Tax Relief scheme. Each is now explained in brief.

The **Enterprise Investment Scheme** (EIS) was introduced by the UK government in January 1994. Under this scheme, investors can invest up to £1,000,000 per annum in a qualifying company (i.e. not quoted on the main market and undertaking a qualifying activity – not property investment or financial investment activities). This initial investment can benefit from 30% income tax relief and qualifies for capital gains tax relief, if the shares are held for a minimum period. If capital losses are made, these can be set off against other income, for the purpose of calculating the income tax liability, in the year the shares are sold. Any dividends received on the equity investment are also tax-free. Companies that have no more that £15 million in gross assets, fewer than 250 employees and that are within seven years of their first commercial sale can raise £5 million per year to a maximum of £12 million overall from the four schemes identified in this section.

The **venture capital trusts** (VCT) scheme was introduced in 1995. Investors to this type of company will receive the same tax benefits as are available to investors in EIS companies. The only difference is that the investor must retain the shares for five years to qualify for the tax relief. Companies that have no more than £15 million in gross assets, fewer than 250 employees and that are within seven years of their first commercial sale can raise £5 million per year to a maximum of £12 million overall from the four schemes in this section.

The **Seed Enterprise Investment Scheme** (SEIS) provides tax breaks on funding of up to £150,000 for companies with less than £200,000 in gross assets, fewer than 25 employees and that are less then two years old. Finally, **Social Investment Tax Relief** (SITR) is available to social enterprises on finance of up to £1.5 million. To qualify they must be a registered charity, a community interest company or a community benefit society. The social enterprise must have gross assets of less than £15 million and have fewer than 250 employees.

Republic of Ireland

The Department of Business, Enterprise and Innovation develops, promotes and co-ordinates innovation, research and development policy. It funds Enterprise Ireland, Science Foundation Ireland (SFI) and the Programme for Research in Third Level Institutions. Recent funding initiatives, through Enterprise Ireland, include the establishment of a **Disruptive Technologies Innovation Fund**. This is a €500 million fund established under Project Ireland 2040. In addition, again through Enterprise Ireland, the Department has made €175 million available as part of the **Seed & Venture Capital Scheme** (2019–2024). The aim of this finance is to stimulate job creation and support the funding requirements of young innovative Irish companies. The scheme makes funds available to commercially focused venture capital funds.

CONCLUSION

The most common medium-term finance used by companies is debt finance. Term loans, hire-purchase agreements and leasing agreements are commonly used by all sizes of companies, though larger companies can also source medium-term debt by selling bonds with maturities of less than seven years. The cost associated with each type of finance varies, depending on the individual agreement, and will usually be reflective of the risks that are inherent within the agreement, the credit standing of the company seeking credit and its ability to obtain finance from a range of sources.

Venture capital has become an increasingly important source of finance in the UK and Ireland. Though raising venture capital is cheaper initially, the returns required by venture capitalists over the five- to seven-year period are high. If a project is successful, then venture capitalists stand to gain much financially, for what seems like little effort relative to the entrepreneurs' input. This may cause conflict. A strong personal relationship between a company's management and the venture capitalists needs to be maintained for the full duration of an investment. Companies raising finance in this manner should see the venture capitalists not only as providers of funds but as business partners who can provide valuable strategic and business advice and contacts.

EXAMINATION STANDARD QUESTION: LEASE OR BUY

Albany Ltd manufactures sports equipment. It has developed a new product and will commence manufacturing this product in the next few months. This requires the purchase of machinery costing €/£750,000. The purchase is to be entirely funded by debt. In line with Albany's investment appraisal policy, the project was approved after calculating an internal rate of return for the project that exceeded Albany's cost of debt.

Alternatively, the machinery could be leased for five years with five annual payments of €/£170,000 payable at the beginning of each year. Capital allowances can be claimed on a straight-line basis at 20% per annum for five years. Corporation tax is payable one year in arrears at a rate of 25%. Albany's weighted average cost of capital is 12% and its cost of debt is 8%. The machinery would have a residual value of zero after five years.

Requirement Advise Albany on whether it should buy or lease the machinery.

7 Marks

(Based on Chartered Accountants Ireland, CAP 1, SFMA, Autumn 2018, Q3)

Solution

To determine whether Albany should buy or lease the equipment, the present value of each alternative should be computed, using the after-tax cost of debt as a discount rate. This analysis should account for the direct costs of purchase/lease as well as the tax impact of each alternative. The alternative with the lower present value should be selected.

Cost of machine	(€/£750,000)	
Capital allowances	20%	5 years
Cost of debt	8%	
Tax rate	25%	
After-tax cost of debt	6%	

Purchase	€/£
Cost of machine at t=0	(750,000)
Annual capital allowance [€/£750,000 × 20% = €/£150,000]	
Capital allowance tax saving [€/£150,000 × 25% = €/£37,500]	
5-year annuity of 37,500 @ 6%	
PV of capital allowance tax saving [€/£37,500 × 4.212]	157,950
Present value of purchase	**(592,050)**
Lease	
Lease payment (first year, at t=0)	(170,000)
PV of lease payments 2–5	
4-year annuity @ 6%	
PV of lease payment [€/£170,000 × 3.465]	(589,050)
PV of tax savings on lease payments	
5-year annuity of [€/£170,000 × 25%] @ 6%	
PV of tax savings on lease payments [€/£170,000 × 25% × 4.212]	179,010
Present value of lease	**(580,040)**

Since the present value of leasing the equipment is lower, Albany should **lease the equipment.**

Key Terms

BIMBO
Business angels
Capital lease
Captive firms
Corporate venturing
Credit Guarantee Scheme
Development Capital Scheme
Disruptive Technologies Innovation Fund
Early-stage venture capital
Enterprise Finance Guaranteed Scheme
Enterprise Investment Scheme
Equity gap
Exit strategies
Finance lease
Finance gap
Full payout lease
Government-backed business bank
Grace period
Growth venture capital
Hire-purchase agreement
Hiree
Hirer
Innovation Fund Ireland
Lease
Leasing agreement
Lessee
Lessor
Management buy-in (MBI)
Management buy-out (MBO)
Medium-term bond debt
Microenterprise Loan Fund Scheme
Primary lease period
Private equity firms

Revolving credit facility
Sale and leaseback agreements
Secondary lease period
Seed & Venture Capital Scheme
Seed-corn venture capital
Seed Enterprise Investment Scheme (SEIS)
Social Investment Tax Relief (SITR)
Start-up venture capital
Venture capital
Venture capital companies
Venture capital trusts (VCT)

REVIEW QUESTIONS

(See Suggested Solutions to Review Questions in **Appendix B**.)

Question 12.1

Explain the term 'revolving credit facility'.

Question 12.2

List briefly the advantages and disadvantages of hire-purchase agreements from a hiree's perspective.

Question 12.3

List the main motives for using lease finance.

Question 12.4

Bargain Ltd wishes to obtain a delivery lorry using hire purchase. The lorry has a useful economic life of four years. They approach a manufacturer, who arranges a hire-purchase contract with a finance house. The finance house purchases the lorry for €/£60,000. The hire-purchase agreement requires that Bargain Ltd pay a down-payment of €/£10,000. The agreement states that interest at the rate of 10% per annum on the remaining €/£50,000 will be charged and the capital should be repaid in three equal annual instalments.

Requirement Given that the 10% is the flat interest rate, what will Bargain Ltd's yearly repayments be?

Question 12.5

You have been approached by a client, Kaits Ltd, which is considering the purchase of a new machine with a market value of €/£15,000. The machine can be acquired by way of hire purchase. Under the terms of the hire purchase agreement, Kaits is required to pay an upfront deposit of 10% of the machine's market value. An annual interest rate of 7.5% would be applied to the balancing capital amount of €/£13,500 each year for four years. The capital is to be repaid in four equal instalments over the four-year term.

Requirement

(a) Calculate the annual repayment that will be made by Kaits under the terms of the hire purchase agreement.

3 Marks

(b) Calculate the annual percentage rate (APR) of the hire purchase agreement.

3 Marks

(Based on Chartered Accountants Ireland, CAP 1, Finance, Autumn 2019, Q6)

Question 12.6

You work as a self-employed financial consultant. One of your clients has approached you for advice regarding short-term and medium-term sources of finance.

Requirement Prepare a report for your client covering the following:

(a) Discuss any THREE factors which should be considered when selecting an appropriate source of finance.

6 Marks

(b) Outline the main features of each of the following sources of finance:

(i) Bank overdraft.

3 Marks

(ii) Medium-term bank loan.

3 Marks

(iii) Hire purchase.

4 Marks

(iv) Leasing.

3 Marks
Presentation 1 Mark
Total 20 Marks

(Based on Chartered Accountants Ireland, MABF I, Summer 2002, Q6)

Question 12.7

What are the key factors a venture capitalist considers when evaluating whether or not to invest in a company?

CHALLENGING QUESTIONS

(Suggested Solutions to Challenging Questions are available through your lecturer.)

Question 12.1 Davidon (Level 1)

Davidon Ltd is currently reviewing a capital expansion project for next year. The project has an estimated cost of €/£50 million and Davidon is considering how much additional finance it will need if the project goes ahead. The projected profit for next year after interest and taxes is €/£22 million. The company paid a dividend of €/£5 million in the current year and it is planning to increase this by €/£2 million next year. The working capital requirements of the company are expected to increase by €/£8 million if the project is accepted. Depreciation is expected to be €/£13 million in the coming year and there are no planned disposals of property, plant and equipment.

Requirement

(a) Calculate the additional finance required and recommend, using the matching principle, the most appropriate finance for the project, including working capital.

9 Marks

(b) Describe any two different types of security that may be required by a bank when providing finance over the medium to long term.

6 Marks
Total 15 Marks

(Based on Chartered Accountants Ireland, CAP 1, Finance, Summer 2011, Q4)

Question 12.2 Hardup (Level 1)

List the main advantages of using lease finance.

4 Marks

Hardup Transport Ltd has emerged from a loss-making period and is expecting to earn profits next year. However, due to accumulated loss relief, it expects it will not be liable to 20% corporation tax for at least another five years.

Hardup needs new equipment, which it can either:

- purchase for €/£52,000 using loan finance costing 18% (due to failure to meet previous loan obligations, Hardup is charged penalty rates); *or*
- lease by making five annual payments, in advance, of €/£13,000.

Requirement Prepare calculations showing whether the equipment should be purchased or leased.

6 Marks

(Based on Chartered Accountants Ireland, CAP 1, Finance, Summer 2009, Q5)

Question 12.3 Bulldog (Level 1)

Bulldog Systems Ltd has experienced a series of operating losses in recent years and has accumulated large amounts of loss relief so that it will not be liable to 25% corporation tax for more than five years. Bulldog now has good prospects of returning to profitability and wishes to acquire new equipment. Bulldog's management are considering either:

- leasing the equipment by making *five* annual payments of €/£25,000 at the start of each year; *or*
- purchasing the equipment for €/£98,000 using loan finance costing 17% interest.

Requirement Assuming the acquisition of the equipment is worthwhile, prepare calculations showing whether the equipment should be purchased or leased.

8 Marks

(Based on Chartered Accountants Ireland, CAP 1, Finance, Summer 2012, Q3b)

Question 12.4 Alright & Bilson (Level 2)

Alright & Bilson Plc is a chemical company that has recently had legal difficulties over its pollution record. The company is assessing a proposal to acquire new equipment to improve waste disposal. The equipment would cost €/£500,000, have an economic life of four years and, at the end of Year 4, is expected to have a disposal value of €/£50,000. The equipment will dispose of waste more efficiently and is expected to generate cost savings of €/£200,000 in each of the four years.

The company is currently entirely equity financed and its equity holders require a return of 10% after allowing for all taxes. The company is subject to a corporation tax rate of 30% and, if the equipment is purchased, a 25% straight-line writing down allowance is available. Assume that corporation tax is payable one year after the financial year-end.

Requirement

(a) Evaluate the financial returns from the acquisition of the equipment and state whether the acquisition should be made.

8 Marks

For the purpose of answering part (b) (see below), assume that the equipment should be acquired. The equipment can be acquired in two ways:

(i) The equipment can be purchased using a four-year bank loan at a pre-tax interest cost of 7% per annum.

(ii) The equipment can be leased with a rental payment of €/£70,000 at the end of each of the four years.

(b) Calculate which of the two methods presented is the most cost effective for the company.

8 Marks

(c) Set out and critically assess the arguments put forward in favour of using operating leases for obtaining equipment.

6 Marks

Total 22 Marks

(Based on Chartered Accountants Ireland, MABF II, Summer 1999, Q5)

Question 12.5 Ahoghill (Level 2)

Ahoghill Ltd is a finance house. It is approached by Randalstown Ltd, an equity-financed company operating in the private education industry, with a request to arrange a lease for the purchase of a new internet system for computer-based learning (including the equipment). The outlay will be €/£10 million. The equipment and software are expected to become obsolete in four years' time and will have no scrap value. The investment has a positive net present value when operating cash flows are discounted at the company's current cost of capital (which is the equity holders' required rate of return).

Ahoghill Ltd would finance the purchase by borrowing the €/£10 million at an interest rate of 10% (gross rate before tax). The transaction would take effect on the last day of the accounting year. The first lease payment will also be received on that day.

Under the terms of the lease agreement, Ahoghill Ltd would also provide maintenance services, valued by Randalstown Ltd at €/£600,000 per year. These services have no cost to Ahoghill Ltd as they currently have several technicians who are not working at full capacity, and are not expected to do so for the four-year period.

Requirement

(a) Briefly explain the main features of a sale and leaseback transaction.

5 Marks

(b) Calculate the minimum rental Ahoghill Ltd should charge Randalstown Ltd to break even. (***Note:*** Randalstown Ltd and Ahoghill Ltd pay tax at 30%. The tax authorities allow a writing down allowance on this type of system of 25%, calculated using the reducing balance method.)

6 Marks

Assume the rental proceeds, and Ahoghill Ltd charges an annual rental of €/£3.5 million.

(c) Calculate whether, using purely financial criteria, Randalstown Ltd should lease the asset or borrow in order to purchase it outright (assume that Randalstown Ltd can obtain bank finance at 12.85% gross):

(i) Ignoring the benefit of the maintenance savings.

6 Marks

(ii) Allowing for the maintenance savings.

3 Marks

Total 20 Marks

Question 12.6 Rapids Ltd (Level 1)

Rapids Ltd is a small, family-owned manufacturing company that was established over 20 years ago by its main shareholder, Mr Taggart, who is also the managing director of the company.

The company has recently won a substantial four-year contract to supply a nationwide chain of stores. The contract may be renewed after four years. The contract involves a lengthy credit period. Rapids is obliged to supply the stores within three days of an order being placed.

This will require additional inventory and receivables as well as extra production plant and equipment.

The company is already quite highly geared and Mr Taggart is concerned that the bank will not lend it any more money although he is willing to offer the bank a personal guarantee, if necessary.

Requirement

(a) Write a memo to Mr Taggart, listing and explaining the general factors a bank is likely to consider when evaluating a loan application from a small firm.

14 Marks

(b) Discuss the factors that a venture capital investor would take into account when deciding whether to invest in Rapids.

6 Marks

Total 20 Marks

(Based on Chartered Accountants Ireland, CAP 1, Summer 2008, Q1)

Question 12.7 Gameathon (Level 1)

Gameathon Limited, which was established by Martin and Paul McGovern nine months ago, designs and supplies software for the computer games market. Martin and Paul are both computer science graduates and are the only directors and shareholders in Gameathon. Both Martin and Paul made an initial investment of €/£20,000 each into the company and received an additional loan of €/£30,000 from the bank.

Gameathon has grown significantly in the nine months since its establishment and has been invited to supply a new form of specialised gaming software. Both Martin and Paul are extremely excited about this new project and feel that they have the skills to develop this software.

Martin and Paul estimate that they will require a further €/£90,000 to finance the new project. The banks have refused to lend Gameathon any additional funds. Martin and Paul have heard that venture capital financing might be a good option to raise the additional €/£90,000.

Requirement

(a) Outline any THREE key factors a venture capitalist would have to consider before making an investment in Gameathon.

7 Marks

(b) What are the common exit strategies used by venture capitalists to liquidate their investment?

4 Marks

(c) Discuss any TWO key differences between equity and preference share capital.

4 Marks

Total 15 Marks

(Based on Chartered Accountants Ireland, CAP 1, Autumn 2013, Q4)

Question 12.8 Bluerock (Level 1)

Bluerock Ltd is an Irish subsidiary with an Indian parent company. Bluerock has recorded growing losses since the 2008 international recession. Local management of Bluerock have been instructed to prepare a cost-cutting plan involving substantial redundancies for the Irish workforce, but no funding for capital investment, which local management regards as vital for Bluerock to remain viable.

While the redundancies would involve sizeable redundancy payments being given to the majority of (long service) employees, local management is considering a management buy-out of Bluerock from the Indian parent company.

Requirement

(a) Explain what a management buy-out is.

2 Marks

(b) Indicate briefly the advantages of a management buy-out to local management and to the parent company of Bluerock.

4 Marks

(c) Outline FOUR significant problems that may be faced by either the local managers (buyers) or the selling Indian parent company in achieving a buy-out and helping the company to succeed under its new ownership.

5 Marks

(d) Indicate FOUR possible sources of finance that may be appropriate in a management buy-out situation.

4 Marks
Total 15 Marks

(Based on Chartered Accountants Ireland, CAP 1, Finance, Autumn 2010, Q4)

Question 12.9 Venture Capital

Describe any four types of business project/investment that may be suitable for venture capital investment and outline the risk(s) involved with each.

8 Marks

(Based on Chartered Accountants Ireland, CAP 1, Finance, Summer 2011, Q5(b))

Question 12.10 Pulse (Level 2)

Management Buyout Proposal The board of directors of Pulse has been conducting a strategic review of its global divisions. One of these divisions, Wave Limited, which is based in the UK, manufactures electrical components for the automotive industry. Several of the directors of Pulse argued strongly that the synergies between Wave and the other two divisions were minimal and that Wave should be disposed of to raise cash, which could be used to finance expansion. While there was not unanimous agreement by the Board on the disposal of Wave, it was agreed that the option should be explored further.

Four directors of Pulse, who were closely involved in the operational management of Wave, have brought a proposal to the board that they would acquire Wave in a management buyout. The four directors have made an offer of €/£3,768,000, a multiple of 12 times net profit. This is a similar multiple to that paid recently for other companies in that sector. Of this sum, €/£1,000,000 would be in the form of an earn-out payment, which would only be payable if Wave achieved a net profit margin of 13% within three years. The profit margin in the year just passed was 10.8%. The four directors are keen to move quickly; they have resigned their positions as directors and have given Pulse one month to consider the offer, after which it will be withdrawn. The directors of Pulse have begun collecting data to assess the offer.

Requirement Advise Pulse on the offer made by the directors to acquire Wave in a management buyout. Highlight any concerns Pulse should have about the offer. Your answer should focus on issues other than the total price offered.

5 Marks

(Based on Chartered Accountants Ireland, CAP 2, MABF, Autumn 2012, Q1)

Question 12.11 Advance (Level 2)

Advance Analytic Systems Ltd is a software company. It was founded by Jim Mack (CEO), Kevin Lynch (Chair of the Board) and Andrea Kidney (Chief Operating Officer), each of whom is a director and owns one-third of the equity of the company. There are no other directors. Advance has been successful since its foundation 20 years ago and the book value of its equity in its most recent financial statements was €/£15,000,000. Advance has predominantly reported annual profits, although losses have been reported in some years. The shareholders are very confident that the company is going to maintain strong profitability and growth into the future. Advance has long-term debt of €/£3,000,000 and its gearing ratio is in line with other companies in its sector. Advance is planning a major expansion that requires funding of €/£10,000,000, which cannot be financed with internal funds. Advance forecasts that this expansion will have a net present value in excess of €/£5,000,000. In conjunction with its financial advisors, three alternative sources of finance are being considered, as follows.

1. A commercial bank is willing to lend Advance €/£10,000,000 for 10 years at an annual interest rate of 9%. This is 3% more than the annual interest rate Advance's existing debt was refinanced at earlier this year.
2. A private equity fund that specialises in the software sector is willing to invest €/£10,000,000 for a 45% share in Advance. The fund will require a shareholders' agreement to be signed, the key terms of which give the fund the right:

   (i) to appoint half of the board of directors;
   (ii) of first refusal on any new shares subsequently issued by Advance or any existing shares being sold.
3. A listing on the Euronext Access/Alternative Investment Market of the stock exchange and a private placement to raise €/£10,000,000 of new equity capital. Professional advice suggests that 40% of the equity in Advance would have to be offered to raise this sum from investors.

Requirement

(a) Critically assess both the loan and the private equity fund proposal as alternative ways of funding the expansion.

12 Marks

(b) Advise Advance on the advantages and disadvantages of seeking a stock market listing as outlined.

6 Marks

(c) Based on your analysis of the funding alternatives, advise Advance on how to proceed, giving reasons for your recommendation.

3 Marks

Total 21 Marks

(Based on Chartered Accountants Ireland, CAP 2, SFMA, Summer 2018, Q3)

13

Long-term Sources of Finance: Debt and Mezzanine Finance

Learning Objectives

Upon completing this chapter, readers should be able to:

- explain the benefits of term loans;
- outline the key characteristics of bond debt;
- list the advantages and disadvantages of bond debt;
- list factors that will influence the level of debt to source;
- discuss factors that influence the market value of bonds;
- describe methods that can be used by a company to finance the redemption of debt;
- explain the difference between debentures and loan stock;
- calculate the value of redeemable and irredeemable bonds;
- calculate the cost of redeemable and irredeemable bonds; and
- explain the terms securitisation, mezzanine finance and Eurobonds.

INTRODUCTION

There are two main sources of finance: equity and debt. Equity is considered in the next chapter, whereas this chapter focuses on long-term debt sources. Debt finance is cheaper to obtain than equity finance and, therefore, is more popular. In particular, the costs associated with obtaining bank finance are low. The costs of issuing tradable bonds are higher; however, they are not as high as the costs associated with an equity issue. Debt is less risky for an investor, but is more risky from a company's perspective. This financial risk is attributable to the fact that interest on debt is a fixed cost, which affects a company's earnings per share and its liquidity. In addition, debt has to be repaid, whereas equity does not.

This chapter starts by explaining the common characteristics of long-term debt finance, before discussing the various options that are available to a company. The most popular option, the term loan, is discussed first. As bank finance is discussed in depth in the previous two chapters, its treatment in this chapter is brief. The bulk of this chapter deals with bond finance. Bonds are introduced, common characteristics are identified and different types are outlined. The methods companies put in place to ensure that they can afford to redeem bonds are described, as are the roles of trust deeds, covenants and credit-rating companies. The differences between debentures and loan stock are highlighted and the calculation of the value and cost/return of redeemable and irredeemable bonds is outlined. This enables the reader to work out whether or not it is worthwhile investing in a bond. The latter part of this chapter explains securitisation (i.e. how companies can package assets into tradable securities and sell them to obtain cash), mezzanine finance (i.e. hybrid finance) and project finance (i.e. finance raised for a specific project) and outlines international sources of long-term debt.

DEBT

The two main sources of long-term debt are bank loans and bonds. There are other less common sources of finance that are **hybrid** in nature. Hybrid sources usually start off as debt instruments and then convert into equity instruments when certain conditions are fulfilled. The principles of financing, outlined in **Chapter 10**, also apply to long-term debt. For example, the term of the debt and repayment schedule should be planned to match the cash flows that are generated from the investment that was purchased by the debt. The cost of debt will be influenced by the perceived risk of default and any factors that may cushion this risk, such as the availability of tangible assets as security or credit insurance.

To protect investors and companies seeking to purchase assets that may have a legal encumbrance, company law requires that a central record is kept of all charges held on company assets. When debt is secured, this is registered with the Registrar of Companies, which maintains a *Register of Mortgages and Charges*. This register is open to public inspection and solicitors normally request searches for charges on particular assets, when they are being purchased by their clients, to ensure they are free of any encumbrance.

TERM LOANS

Term loans are advances made by a lender to a borrower for a predetermined period. They can be provided by one lender (usually a bank, insurance company or pension company) or syndicated. **Syndicated loans** are usually large in size and are provided by several lenders (through one main lead bank that administers the loan) to a company. The reason for getting several parties involved in one transaction is to spread the credit risk across several lenders. An example of a syndicated loan is provided in **Real World Example 13.1**.

Real World Example 13.1: First Derivatives

In 2019, Newry-headquartered First Derivatives secured a five-year funding package of £130 million with a consortium of four banks. The lead bank is the Bank of Ireland, with Barclays, First Trust and Silicon Valley all involved. The facility is a term loan that has built-in flexibility in the form of a revolving loan facility of £65 million. The investment is to fund growth and acquisition activity over the next five years.

Long-term 'term loans' are normally secured on assets and are referred to as **mortgage loans.** Companies usually prefer this type of debt to bond debt as it is: quick to obtain; flexible in its terms (both at the outset and for the duration of the loan agreement); less costly; not repayable on demand and available to all sizes of company. Another attraction is that any asset used as security for a term loan remains under the legal ownership of the company; therefore, the rewards associated with owning it, such as capital appreciation, accrue to the company. On the downside, the asset cannot be sold and permission is usually required from the lender to change the use of the asset – for example, if the company wishes to rent out a building it owns that is encumbered by a term loan.

The costs of a long-term loan are similar to those discussed for shorter term loans. The costs include an arrangement fee and a yearly interest charge, which can be either fixed rate or variable rate. Interest is tax deductible, that is, it reduces the tax bill each year, provided the company is making a profit. The interest rate is influenced by the risks associated with the debt. Risk is affected by: the reputation of the borrower; the availability of security and guarantees; the quality of management and the risk of the project. A more detailed business plan is required, relative to a business plan used to obtain shorter-term debt, as there is more information asymmetry in long-term loan decisions. The bank has less information about the future of the company and the business plan can be used to provide this information to the bank. Lenders can write restrictive covenants into the loan agreement (discussed later in this chapter) to protect the liquidity of the company until the loan is repaid. As mentioned in **Chapter 12**, a variety of repayment schedules can be arranged, including repayment breaks, bullet payments and balloon payments, depending on the needs of the borrower.

Small and medium-sized enterprises (SMEs) in Ireland have traditionally sourced the majority of their finance from banks and the amount involved can be substantial. However, the financial crisis caused capital rationing, which resulted in a shift in reliance on bank debt, as noted in **Real World Example 13.2**.

REAL WORLD EXAMPLE 13.2: SME FINANCE IN IRELAND

According to the Central Bank of Ireland's SME market report (2019), at the end of 2018 about €15.5 billion of credit was outstanding from non-financial and non-real estate SMEs in Ireland. The report noted that credit demand from banks is lower in Ireland relative to the rest of Europe, with many SMEs opting to fund from internal funds. Indeed, Irish companies are more reliant on leasing and hire purchase to fund investment than relying on bank loans and other credit. In terms of bank loans, working capital is the most common reason for sourcing funds by small companies, with growth and expansion cited by medium-sized companies. Default rates are about 17.5%.

For more details, see: https://centralbank.ie/docs/default-source/publications/sme-market-reports/sme-market-report-2019.pdf, accessed November 2019.

BONDS

Bonds are simply tradable loans arranged by a borrower (the issuer) and bought by investors (the bondholders). They can be redeemable or irredeemable. **Redeemable bonds** normally have a maturity of between seven and 30 years, although the period can be either shorter or longer. **Irredeemable debts** do not have a maturity date, though they commonly are redeemed at the borrower's request. Bonds can be sold by way of a public issue, in which the company has to undertake similar steps to those followed when issuing equity (i.e. the company will have to prepare a prospectus, apply to the stock exchange and provide financial statements to the lenders, at least annually). Bonds can be traded on the London Stock Exchange (UK) and on Euronext Dublin (Ireland). The LSE has three platforms: the Main Market, the Professional Securities Market and the Electronic Order Book for Retail Bonds. The bulk of corporate bond issues in Ireland are to the Euronext Dublin Market. Another option is a private issue through a financial intermediary to a limited number of lenders. These bonds are not tradable on stock exchanges, but can be traded in private deals between bond brokers.

The issue price of a corporate bond is predominantly influenced by bank base rates, the price of government bonds, the price of similar risk bonds, the volatility of interest rates, the type of bond being issued (e.g. secured, unsecured, coupon, redeemable or convertible) and the extent of covenants within the trust deed. Bonds on the London Stock Exchange are issued in Sterling and sometimes UK companies provide bonds in foreign markets, which are termed **bulldog bonds**. They are also traded in Sterling.

Another underlying feature of bonds is how they are administered by a company. Bonds can either be 'registered' or 'bearer'. The details of the owners of **registered bonds** are included in a register within the issuing company. The register is a formal record of who has claims against the company and is also used to distribute coupon payments. Details of the owners of **bearer bonds**, on the other hand, are not kept by the company. These bonds are issued with coupons attached and the bearer (i.e. the holder) has to present these coupons to the company, or their bank, to receive payment. The anonymity of these bonds makes them more attractive to investors, who are willing to accept a lower coupon. On the downside, were the bearer to lose a bond, or have it stolen, it is difficult to prove ownership, whereas a registered bond can be reissued. Though there are a variety of different kinds of bonds, most have common characteristics, as outlined in **Figure 13.1**.

Where a company issues €/£10 million of debentures with a 5.5% annual coupon rate that are redeemable on 30 June 2030, then they would have to budget and manage their liquidity so as to be able to pay €/£550,000 each year when the coupon is due and to pay €/£10 million to the bondholders on 30 June 2030.

Variations of the most common characteristics are possible. The coupon can be a fixed percentage or can be pegged to the base rate or inflation. In some instances, the coupon rate may be pegged to the price of a commodity such as oil or gold. Therefore, the company's fortunes help determine the coupon it has to pay. For example, if a major expense of the company is oil, then the bond coupon may be set to vary with oil price such that when the

FIGURE 13.1: TYPICAL BOND CHARACTERISTICS

Nominal value

Bonds all have a predetermined **nominal value**. This is also known as the **par value** and is the set amount that will be paid by a company on the redemption of the bond. In the UK and Ireland, the nominal value is normally €100/£100.

Coupon rate

Each bond will have a **coupon rate** attached to it. This is the interest that is payable on the bond. It is usually annual or semi-annual, though variations exist. The amount paid by the borrower is the coupon rate multiplied by the nominal value. The coupon rate does not change when the market value of the bond changes.

Redemption value

Redeemable bonds have a predetermined **redemption value**. This is usually set at the nominal amount (€100/£100). However, it can include a premium or be at a discount.

Redemption date

Redeemable bonds have a predetermined redemption date, or range of dates, within which redemption can take place.

commodity price goes down, the coupon rate goes up and vice versa. This means that when the price of oil goes down, the company's costs fall, leaving more cash to pay the higher coupon.

Bond Repayment

A number of approaches a company can take to ensure that it has sufficient liquidity to redeem bonds when they fall due are now outlined.

Sinking Fund

Many companies set up a **sinking fund**. This is where a company puts a certain amount of cash into a separate investment fund each year, which earns a return. The theory is that the capital being input each year (an annuity), plus the return earned on the fund being built up over the period of the bond, will be sufficient to repay the bond issue on its redemption date. The calculation of the annuity is provided in the next example.

Worked Example 13.1: Sinking Fund

A company has decided to set up a sinking fund to provide sufficient funds to redeem a bond issue. The trust deed states that a total of €/£1,000,000 should be paid to the bondholders, on redemption of the bonds in five years' time. The trustees of the sinking fund have informed the company that they can guarantee an annual return of 12% on the sums invested over the next five years. Assume the return equates to 6% in each six-month period.

Requirement Calculate the amount that should be input by the company to the sinking fund, every six months, to ensure that the €/£1,000,000 is repaid in full from the proceeds of the sinking fund.

Solution

There will be 10 repayments, earning a return of 6% [12% ÷ 2] every six months. The terminal value of an annuity for 10 payments at 6% is 13.181 (see **Appendix F** for future value annuity factors).

Therefore, the amount required to be input every six months (X) is:

$$X \times 13.181 = €/£1{,}000{,}000$$

$$X = €/£75{,}867$$

As long as the sinking fund earns the target return (i.e. 12%), then a transfer of €/£75,867 every six months for 10 years will result in the sinking fund having a terminal value of €/£1,000,000.

Stagger Repayments

A company may set a redemption period, not a specific date. For example, instead of redeeming bonds in 2030, a bond may have redemption dates ranging from 2030 to 2035. Within this period, the company can decide which bonds to redeem and the dates of redemption – the bondholder has to agree.

Purchase the Bonds

Another approach that can be used by companies is to repurchase the bonds in the markets when they have the funds available to do so. This reduces the coupon payable and the capital sum required on the redemption date. Where a company wishes to purchase more bonds than are for sale in the markets, they can make an offer to the existing bondholders. The amount offered is usually the market price of the bond – though it may be at the nominal value (if higher) or may include a premium.

Issue of Irredeemable Bonds

A company may set a policy of issuing only irredeemable bonds and redeeming the bonds when it has the funds to do so. If a company has a history of redeeming irredeemable bonds, the market will value the bonds as though they were redeemable – though the value is reduced due to the uncertainty of not having a set redemption date.

Issue of Capital

Strong companies can redeem one issue of bonds using the finance raised by a new issue of bonds, on current terms. Alternatively, they may redeem the bonds using the proceeds of a stock issue. In these instances, the bondholders may be offered the right to exchange the bonds for equity stock. An exchange is not permitted where bonds were issued at a discount, unless the shares issued are reduced in number to take account of the discount (in this instance, there will be no premium to the new equity holders). This is to ensure that the new equity holders are not given benefit to the detriment of existing equity holders.

Typical reasons for redeeming bonds before redemption date are outlined in **Figure 13.2**.

FIGURE 13.2: REASONS FOR REDEEMING BONDS BEFORE MATURITY

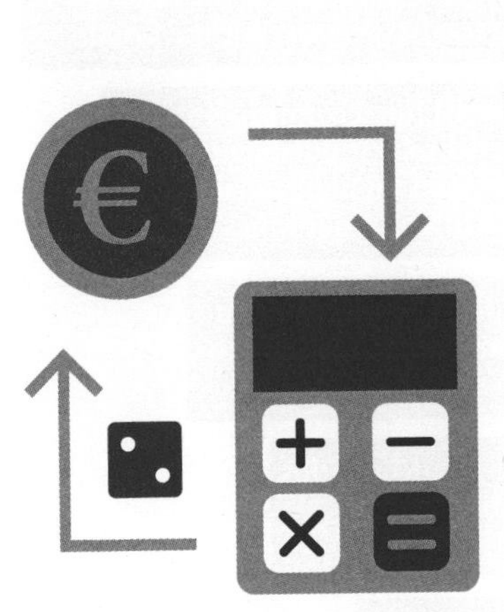

- When market interest rates fall, the bond becomes an expensive source of finance.
- When the company's net cash inflows are better than anticipated when they were planning the redemption schedule for the bond issue.
- Changes in tax laws may increase the cost of the bond finance, making it attractive to redeem the bonds.
- The company directors may make a strategic decision to change the captial structure of the company to one that is less general.
- The company may be in default of the restrictive covenants written into the trust deeds (see below) and may be forced to redeem the bonds early.
- The directors may see the covenants attached to a bond as hindering the future development of the company and so redeem the bond to allow them to widen the investment portfolio of the company.

Investors may not be happy to go along with the redemption plans of a company as they may have their cash requirements timed around the steady coupon receipts and there may not be suitable alternative investments available. Regardless, when a company decides to redeem its bonds, bondholders have to co-operate.

Trust Deeds

When a company issues bonds, a **trust deed** is established, which sets out the terms of the contract between the company and the bondholder and establishes the identity of the trustee and their powers. The trustee of a bond is normally the issuing broker house or financial institution. The trustee usually monitors the company's behaviour throughout the term of the bond and ensures that it complies with the terms of the trust deed. In the event of default, the trustee will try to resolve the issue. The trustee may try to broker an agreement between the bondholders and the company, which usually involves rescheduling the coupon and redemption payments to suit the company. Where this is not possible, the trust deed normally gives the trustee the power to appoint a receiver.

The trust deed is also used as a means of reducing the risk of a bond, in that it can contain conditions or benchmarks that the company must achieve, or otherwise be considered to be in default. These conditions are known as **restrictive covenants** and can either be **negative covenants** or **positive covenants**. The main aim of restrictive covenants is to curb the financial activities of a company to ensure that sufficient liquidity and reserves are maintained to protect bondholders. The most common forms of restrictive covenants are listed in **Figure 13.3**.

Figure 13.3: Examples of Negative Restrictive Covenants Written in Trust Deeds

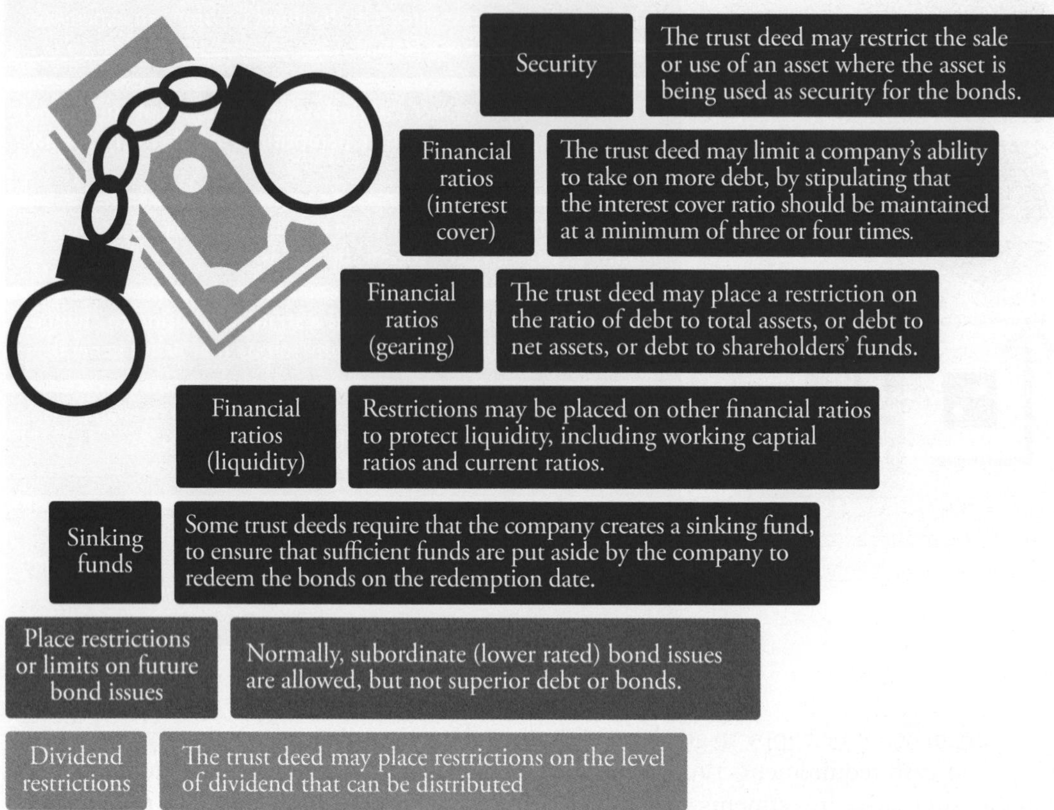

Security
The trust deed may restrict the sale or use of an asset where the asset is being used as security for the bonds.
Financial ratios (interest cover)
The trust deed may limit a company's ability to take on more debt, by stipulating that the interest cover ratio should be maintained at a minimum of three or four times.
Financial ratios (gearing)
The trust deed may place a restriction on the ratio of debt to total assets, or debt to net assets, or debt to shareholders' funds.
Financial ratios (liquidity)
Restrictions may be placed on other financial ratios to protect liquidity, including working captial ratios and current ratios.
Sinking funds
Some trust deeds require that the company creates a sinking fund, to ensure that sufficient funds are put aside by the company to redeem the bonds on the redemption date.
Place restrictions or limits on future bond issues
Normally, subordinate (lower rated) bond issues are allowed, but not superior debt or bonds.
Dividend restrictions
The trust deed may place restrictions on the level of dividend that can be distributed

There is a wealth of literature that suggests that management alter their behaviour, or their accounting practices, in response to restrictive covenants. Restrictive covenants usually restrict a company's ability to raise more finance by not allowing them to become more geared. This usually restricts management's ability to invest, especially if they do not have sufficient cash generated from current activities. This restriction might be detrimental to the value of the company. Research on companies subject to restrictive covenants has shown that management will use a variety of means to relax restrictive covenants, including changing accounting policies. Companies with restrictive covenants are more likely to revalue their tangible assets and capitalise development expenditure (Whittred and Zimmer, 1986). However, most bondholders are aware of the loosening impact of these accounting adjustments and place restrictions on them within the trust deeds (Whittred and Zimmer, 1986). For example, revaluations are usually only allowed on land and buildings and the valuation must be performed by an independent valuer before the financial statements are finalised. Some trust deeds state that only tangible assets can be included in the assets part of ratios being used as restrictive covenants. See also: Whittred and Chan (1992); Brown, Izan and Loh (1992); and Henderson and Goodwin (1992). Examples of positive restrictive covenants are set out in **Figure 13.4**.

Figure 13.4: Examples of Positive Restrictive Covenants Written in Trust Deeds

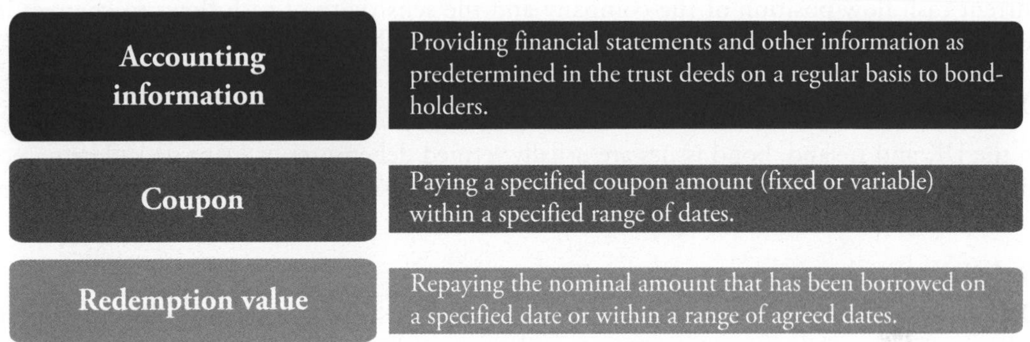

Accounting information
Providing financial statements and other information as predetermined in the trust deeds on a regular basis to bondholders.
Coupon
Paying a specified coupon amount (fixed or variable) within a specified range of dates.
Redemption value
Repaying the nominal amount that has been borrowed on a specified date or within a range of agreed dates.

The more restrictive covenants a trust deed contains, the less risk to the bondholder – therefore these bonds will be more highly valued by the market. Other risk-reducing features might include a requirement to obtain credit insurance, security, a guarantee from a parent company or personal guarantees from directors. In these instances, the bonds are usually referred to as **guaranteed loan stock**. In addition to market restrictions, the level of debt that a company can raise is usually limited by its articles of association.

Bond Ranking and Credit Rating

When a company undertakes a large public bond issue, it may consider it worthwhile to pay to have the issue rated by one of the specialist credit-rating companies, such as Moody's Investors Service, Standard & Poor's, Fitch Ratings, Kroll's Subscription Rating Service or DBRS Limited. These companies rate bonds from a triple A score (strongest) to a D, which stands for default (some only rate as far as Bbb). There are varying ratings between these scores, including AAA (Aaaa), AA+ (Aa1), AA (Aa2), AA- (Aa3), A+ (A1), A(A2), A-(A3), BBB (Baa1), … and so on. Anything graded BBB- (Baa3) or above is considered to have hit the investment grade and any bond rated below BBB- (Baa3) is regarded as being a junk bond (discussed later in this chapter). When an investment grade bond is re-rated from investment grade to a junk bond, it is referred to as a **'fallen angel'**. An example is provided in **Real World Example 13.3**.

Real World Example 13.3: Downgrading to Junk Bond Status

In September 2019, Moody's Investor Service downgraded the iconic car manufacturer Ford's credit rating from Baa3 to Ba1. The bonds are now regarded as junk bonds. Moody's are concerned about Ford's statement of financial position: at the time of writing, the company is undergoing a costly restructuring, amounting to about $11 billion and has reported weak earnings and cash generation. This has led Moody's to question the company's ability to service its future bond repayment commitments.

Having a strong rating helps the marketability of a bond issue and reduces the costs associated with an issue. The rating depends on the interest and redemption default risks associated with the bond issue. Therefore, in terms of corporate debt, factors such as the type of industry, whether the bond is secured or unsecured, gearing levels within the company, the current cash flow position of the company and the sensitivity of cash flows to changes in economic variables, such as interest or inflation, will influence the credit score awarded.

Debentures and Loan Stock

In the UK and Ireland, bond issues are usually termed debentures or loan stock. The names highlight the difference between the two types of bond issue, in terms of the lien that they have over the assets of an issuing company.

Debentures

Debentures are bonds that are secured on the assets of the issuing company. The security can either be fixed to a specific asset or assets, or 'float' over all assets in general (in the US debentures are usually unsecured bonds, with only those bonds referred to as **mortgage debentures** or **mortgage bonds** being secured). Where the security is floating in nature, the bond is usually referred to as a **loan note**. With such security, management have more freedom over their use of company assets. They can sell assets or use them for different purposes so long as the overall monetary level is maintained. When the company breaches or defaults on any of the covenants within the trust deed, the floating charge crystallises into a fixed charge and the assets cannot be sold, or have their use changed, without the permission of the trustee or the receiver appointed by the trustee. Moreover, the receiver may sell the assets to redeem the bonds.

Loan Stock

In the UK and Ireland, **loan stock** usually refers to unsecured long-term bonds with coupons payable at intervals over the life of the bond. In the US, these are called loan notes. Because they are not secured, they are regarded as higher risk when compared to debentures and hence are more expensive for a company to service – they usually have a higher coupon rate.

Bond Ranking on Liquidation

When a company goes into liquidation, bonds do not have equal claim to its assets. The different types are ranked, with the highest ranking bonds having their claims met first. The general rule is that debentures, which are secured, qualify first and debentures with a fixed lien over a specific asset rank in front of debentures that have a floating lien over the general assets of a company. In addition, where there are several debenture issues, the earliest ranks first, unless the trust deeds of subsequent issues rank those issues in front of the earlier issues (covenants written into the trust deeds of the earliest debenture issues usually ensure that no subsequent bond issues are allowed, unless they are subordinate). Loan stock ranks below debentures and is also ranked in order of age; the earliest issues are considered superior to later issues. The ranking is not only important when a company is in liquidation, but also applies to coupon payments. The oldest debentures have their coupon paid first, the youngest loan stock coupons are paid last. When debentures or loan stock are ranked below other bonds, they are referred to as either **junior bonds** or **subordinated bonds**. An example is provided in **Real World Example 13.4**.

REAL WORLD EXAMPLE 13.4: BOND FINANCE

In October 2019, two of the large banks in Ireland, Allied Irish Banks (AIB) and Bank of Ireland (BOI), secured €800 million in funding from junior bond issues. Junior bond issues rank behind other bonds when the issuer goes into liquidation, therefore their coupon rate is usually higher to reflect this. The AIB bond issue was for €500 million and the coupon was 5.25%. The BOI 10-year bond issue was for €300 million and had a coupon rate of 2.375%. The difference in coupon rates reflects differences in the risks involved.

Plain Vanilla Bond

The most straightforward bond is the **plain vanilla bond**. This can also be called the **straight bond** or the **bullet bond**. These bonds are either redeemable or irredeemable. **Redeemable bonds** usually have an annual or semi-annual fixed coupon rate and a predetermined redemption value and date. In these instances, the company sells the bonds to an investor, receives money immediately and, in return, pays a stream of coupon payments and a final lump sum (usually the nominal value) on the redemption date. **Irredeemable bonds** do not have a redemption date and the company only commits itself to paying the coupon rate either annually or semi-annually, depending on the initial terms of the bond. In practice, most companies redeem these bonds when it suits them. An example of the different types of long-term debt finance used by a large company, Ryanair, is included in **Real World Example 13.5**.

REAL WORLD EXAMPLE 13.5: RYANAIR HOLDINGS PLC

Ryanair Holdings Plc *Annual Report and Financial Statements 2019 (Extract)*

11. Financial instruments and financial risk management (extract)

(c) Maturity and interest rate risk profile of financial assets and financial liabilities

At March 31, 2019, the Company had total borrowings of €3,644.4m (2018: €3,963.0m; 2017: €4,384.5m) from various financial institutions and the debt capital markets. Financing for the acquisition of 144 Boeing 737-800 "next generation" aircraft (2018: 153; 2017: 174) was provided on the basis of guarantees granted by the Export-Import Bank of the United States. The guarantees are secured with a first fixed mortgage on the delivered aircraft. The remaining long-term debt relates to three unsecured Eurobonds, two for €850m and one for €750m, 42 aircraft held under finance leases (2018: 16; 2017: 22) and 3 aircraft financed by way of other commercial debt (2018: 6; 2017: 6).

The maturity profile of the Company's financial liabilities (aircraft provisions, trade payables and accrued expenses) at March 31, 2019 was as follows:

	Weighted average rate (%)	2020 €M	2021 €M	2022 €M	2023 €M	Thereafter €M	Total €M
Fixed rate							
Secured long-term debt	2.52	75.8	63.3	64.9	62.5	63.8	330.3
Unsecured long-term debt	1.30	34.0	34.0	876.9	877.5	819.7	2,642.1
Long-term debt	1.44	109.8	97.3	947.8	940.0	883.5	2,972.4
Finance leases	2.54	(2.8)	116.0	–	–	–	113.2
Total fixed rate debt		107.0	213.3	941.8	940.0	883.5	3,085.6
Floating rate							
Secured long-term debt	0.75	181.1	161.9	105.8	26.0	–	474.8
Finance leases	1.27	21.4	62.6	–	–	–	84.0
Total floating rate debt	0.83	202.5	224.5	105.8	26.0	–	558.8
Total financial liabilities		309.5	437.8	1,047.6	966.0	883.5	3,644.4

All of the above debt maturing after 2023 will mature between fiscal year 2023 and fiscal year 2026.

Source: https://investor.ryanair.com/wp-content/uploads/2019/07/Ryanair-2019-Annual-Report.pdf, accessed November 2019.

Green Bonds

'Green bonds' are a form of sustainable finance, wherein the proceeds of the bond issue are used for environmental or social projects. Examples of companies who have issued green bonds include the energy company SSE plc and Anglian Water.

BOND VALUATION

Valuing Redeemable Bonds

Redeemable bonds are valued at the present value of future stream of periodic coupon payments for a set period (this is an annuity), plus a final redemption payment discounted at the bondholder's required rate of return. This return will be the same as the return on bonds in comparable companies. The following formula can be used to determine the market value of the bond (or what it should be):

$$P_0 = \frac{I_1}{(1+r)} + \frac{I_2}{(1+r)^2} + \ldots + \frac{R_n}{(1+r)^n}$$

where P_0 is the market value of the bond in year 0, r is the discount rate or return on the bond, I is the annual coupon paid by a company (i.e. the coupon rate multiplied by the nominal value), R is the redemption value of the bond and n is the number of years to maturity. The net present value (NPV) approach can also be used to determine the price of the bond. The initial stream of interest payments is typically an annuity and the redemption value is a single expected cash flow, as highlighted in **Worked Example 13.2**.

Worked Example 13.2: Valuing Redeemable Bonds

ABC Plc has €/£2,000,000 of 8% bonds that are due for redemption in three years' time. The expected return by bondholders is 5% (before taxation).

Requirement Calculate the equilibrium market value for a single bond.

Solution

The bondholder will pay a market price that equates to a return of 5% on an annuity of €/£8 [€/£100 × 8%] for three years, plus a final payment of €/£100 in three years' time.

$$P_0 = \left(€/£8 \times 2.723^{*}\right) + \frac{€/£100}{(1.05)^3}$$

* This is the annuity factor for three years at 5%.

$$P_0 = €/£108.17 \text{ per bond}$$

The market value of a bond will vary over the life of the bond and is impacted on by many factors, some of which are outlined in **Figure 13.5**.

Figure 13.5: Influences on the Market Value of Bonds

- Whether the bond is secured or not.
- Whether the coupon is fixed or variable rate.
- The extent of restrictive covenants.
- The nature and return being allowed by bonds issued from similar companies with similar risks.
- Coupon rates on offer in government-issued bonds (the risk-free rate)
- Market interest rates.
- The redemption value (nominal or with a premium/discount).
- On issue, demand for a bond will be influenced by the issue price, which may be at a premium or discount.

Return on Redeemable Bonds/Cost of Redeemable Bonds

When investors are considering whether to purchase particular bonds or not, they will calculate the return the bond is currently providing, given the term to redemption, the market price the bond is currently trading at and the coupon receivable. In the case of redeemable bonds, the return has two elements, the yearly return and the capital gain (or loss) that will be made on the price of the bond. A quick way to work out the return is to use the following formula:

$$r = \frac{I_1}{P_0} + \frac{(R - P_0)/n}{P_0}$$

where r is the return on the bond, I is the coupon received, P_0 is the current market price, n is the number of years to maturity and R is the redemption price of the bond.

Worked Example 13.3: Approximate Cost of Redeemable Bonds

ABC Plc has €/£2,000,000 of 8% bonds that are due for redemption in five years' time. The bonds are currently trading at €/£80.

Requirement Calculate the approximate yield received by bondholders, given an income tax rate of 40%.

Solution

The bondholder will receive €/£8 per year after investing €/£80. A quick guide to the yearly return is:

$$r = \frac{\text{€/£}8(1-0.40)}{\text{€/£}80} = 6\%$$

The bond will be held for five years, at which point the company will redeem the bond at its nominal value of €/£100. The capital return per year is estimated at:

$$\text{Capital return (estimate)} = \frac{\text{€/£}100 - \text{€/£}80}{5} = \text{€/£}4 \text{ per year}$$

This represents a capital gain of approximately $\frac{\text{€/£}4}{\text{€/£}80} = 5\%$ each year

Therefore, the overall approximate return is about 11% [6% + 5%], assuming the investor can avail of an exemption from capital gains tax.

The method used in the last example is quick and simple. It does not take into account the time value of money. To determine accurately the return of a redeemable debt instrument, the interpolation technique (covered in depth in **Chapter 2**) should be used.

Worked Example 13.4: Cost of Redeemable Bonds

ABC Plc has €/£2,000,000 of 8% bonds that are due for redemption in five years' time. The bonds are currently trading at €/£80.

Requirement Calculate the approximate yield being received by bondholders, given an income tax rate of 40%.

Solution

The bondholder will receive €/£8 per year after investing €/£80 and will also receive €/£100 from the company in five years' time. The aim is to work out the discount rate that equates the present value of this stream of payments to zero. The first rate selected is 10%.

(***Note:*** as this results in a negative net present value, a higher discount factor is chosen for the second rate to try. As the first guess has resulted in a net present value that is close to zero, the second guess is marginally higher, at 11%.)

Year	Cash flow €/£	Discount factor Try 10%	Present value €/£	Discount factor Try 11%	Present value €/£
0	80	1.000	80.00	1.000	80.00
1 – 5	(8 (1 – 0.40))	3.791	(18.20)	3.696	(17.74)
5	(100)	0.621	(62.10)	0.593	(59.30)
			(0.30)		2.96

Using interpolation, the approximate rate is obtained:

$$10\% + \frac{-0.30(11-10)}{-0.30-2.96} = 10.09\%$$

Valuing Irredeemable Bonds

Irredeemable bonds are valued by treating the coupon as being receivable in perpetuity. The value is obtained using the following formula:

$$P_0 = \frac{I}{r}$$

where P_0 is the market value of the irredeemable bond at time 0, I is the annual coupon and r is the discount rate, or yearly return/yield required by bondholders. The market value of irredeemable bonds will be affected by the same factors that influence the market value of redeemable bonds (listed in **Figure 13.5**).

Worked Example 13.5: Valuing Irredeemable Bonds

ABC Plc has €/£2,000,000 of 8% irredeemable bonds. The expected return by bondholders is 5%.

Requirement Calculate the equilibrium market value for a single bond.

Solution

The bondholder will pay a market price that equates to a return of 5% on a payment of €/£8 [€/£100 × 8%] in perpetuity:

$$P_0 = \frac{8}{0.05}$$

$$P_0 = \text{€/£}160 \text{ per bond}$$

A value greater than the nominal value is expected, as the yearly return of 8% greatly exceeds the bondholders' required return of 5%, hence they will pay more for the bond.

When a company decides to issue bonds, it needs to get the issue price correct, otherwise the bond will not sell. The company has to work out what the bondholders' return is for the type of bond being issued. To do this, it is common to look at the return bondholders are willing to pay for a similar bond, in a similar risk company. This next example highlights how to do this.

Worked Example 13.6: Calculating the Issue Price

ABC Plc wants to issue €/£2,000,000 of 8% irredeemable bonds. It is unsure of the issue price to market the bonds at. A similar company, XYZ Plc, has already in issue 6% irredeemable bonds. These are currently trading at €/£80.

Requirement Calculate the issue price ABC Plc should include in its prospectus in respect of its bonds to achieve a full sell-out of the bonds in a public issue (ignore tax).

Solution

The return being earned by the bondholders of XYZ Plc is:

$$r = \frac{\text{€/£}6}{\text{€/£}80} = 7.5\%$$

Therefore, ABC Plc should set its issue price at an amount that, at a minimum, provides a return of 7.5%. The price is:

$$P_0 = \frac{\text{€/£}8}{0.075} = \text{€/£}106.67$$

The existing market will pay €/£106.67 for this future stream of interest payments. It is up to ABC Plc to determine whether to issue the bonds at a value lower than this to make the bonds attractive to bondholders, ensuring a complete sell-out quickly.

Return on Irredeemable Bonds/Cost of Irredeemable Bonds

The cost of servicing coupons on bonds is reduced by the tax saving as the coupon is tax deductible (so long as a company is profit-making and has sufficient profits to obtain a full tax benefit). In these instances, the cost of a bond to a company is reflected by the following formula:

$$r = \frac{I(1-t)}{P_0}$$

where r is the cost of the bond (after tax) to the company, I is the annual interest payment, t is the tax rate and P_0 is the market value of the bond. This formula can also be used to find the actual return being sought by bondholders, who have different marginal rates of tax.

WORKED EXAMPLE 13.7: IRREDEEMABLE DEBT: AFTER-TAX COST TO THE COMPANY

ABC Plc has €/£2,000,000 of 8% irredeemable bonds in issue. These are currently trading at €/£80. ABC Plc pays tax at 30%.

Requirement Calculate the cost of this debt to ABC Plc.

Solution

The cost of the bond to ABC Plc is:

$$r = \frac{€/£8(1-0.30)}{€/£80} = 7\%$$

Bondholders who purchase irredeemable bonds will be subject to income tax on the coupon earned. As the bond is not redeemed, they will only have to pay capital gains tax if they sell the bond at a premium above the rate they paid for the bond, on the difference between the selling price and the buying price. This will also only be payable if the bondholder does not have, or has exhausted, the yearly capital gains tax allowance.

Zero Coupon Bonds

Some bonds pay no coupon at all. The latter are termed **zero coupon bonds** or **deep discount bonds**. Zero coupon bonds are sold at a large discount to their par value and do not pay any coupon to the holder. This means that the income to the investor is only in the form of a capital gain, either on the sale or redemption of the bond. Therefore, the demand and marketability of this type of bond will be affected by the tax differential between capital gains tax and income tax. It will be more attractive to investors who are higher rate taxpayers, as they are better able to manipulate capital gains and have a tax-free capital gains allowance, which can be used each year. It is attractive to companies who have liquidity issues in the short term as no coupon needs to be paid yearly. The next example shows how to calculate the return being offered by a zero coupon bond.

Worked Example 13.8: Zero Coupon Bonds

Marta Plc issues 100,000 bonds at a price of €/£60 to be repaid at their nominal value of €/£100 in six years' time.

Requirement Calculate the annualised rate of return from the capital gain if the bond is held to maturity for the full six years.

Solution

The approach is to find the discount (compound interest rate) 'r' which would be achieved if €/£60 were to be invested now to achieve a terminal value payment of €/£100 in six years' time.

This is represented by the following equation:

$$€/£60(1+r)^6 = €/£100$$

This can be rearranged to:

$$r = \sqrt[6]{100 \div 60} - 1$$

$$r = 0.089 = 8.9\%$$

Alternatively, it can be rearranged as:

$$\frac{€/£60}{€/£100} = \frac{1}{(1+r)^6}$$

$$0.6 = ?$$

By reading the discount tables, it can be seen that the present value discount factor of 0.6, given the term is six years, lies between 8% and 9%. Interpolation can then be used to determine the exact rate.

- The discount factor for six years at 8% is 0.630.
- The discount factor for six years at 9% is 0.596.

Therefore, the rate of return before tax is:

$$= \frac{0.630 - 0.6}{0.630 - 0.596}$$

= 0.88% more return over and above the 8%, resulting in an overall return of 8.88% (before taxation).

The following formula can be used to calculate the annualised return from an investment in zero coupon bonds:

$$r = \sqrt[n]{\frac{R}{IP}} - 1$$

where r is the annualised return, R is the redemption value, IP is the issue price and n is the number of years to maturity.

SECURITISATION

Securitisation is a term used to describe the packaging of a company's claim to future income streams into tradable securities (typically bonds) and the selling of that claim to third parties, in the markets, for a price. Securitisation is widely used by banks to gain finance, which is secured on their claim to interest and repayment cash flows from mortgage holders. The right to income from mortgages is sold as securities in the markets for an upfront cash payment. This process ensures that a bank's liquidity remains intact. The following diagram encapsulates the steps involved in the securitisation of a bank's assets (i.e. their claim to future income). These securities are sometimes referred to as **asset-backed securities**.

FIGURE 13.6: SECURITISATION OF CLAIMS (STEPS)

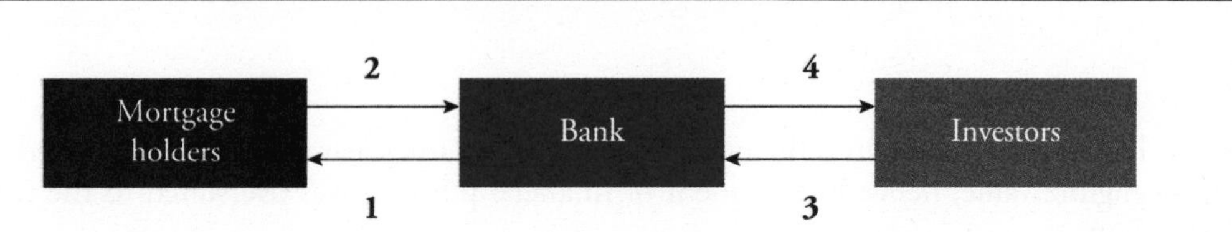

1. The bank provides the mortgage holders with the capital to buy their properties (say, €/£10 million). The debt is secured on the mortgage holders' properties.
2. The mortgage holders pay the bank set-up fees, interest and capital (interest at, say, 6%).
3. The bank sells the right to the future stream of income (interest and capital) in the markets as bonds with a coupon of 5% (issue price is typically below par, whereas redemption is at par) for, say, €/£9 million. The bank now has an additional €/£9 million capital and can keep awarding mortgages.
4. The bank pays the bondholders 5% each year and the nominal value of the issue (€/£10 million) on redemption.

The bank has the potential to make profits where the mortgage set-up fees exceed the issue costs, where the coupon paid to the bondholders is less than the interest being paid by the mortgage holders (in this example, 1%) and where the capital repayments made throughout the life of the mortgage are invested and the sum of the capital and its return exceed the redemption value of the initial issue on maturity (€/£10 million). This system works well as long as the income stream does not default!

The legal right to the stream of mortgage payments passes to the bondholders, though the bank administers the whole process. The bank may also guarantee the payments, so that the process is not affected by bad debts. These are called without-recourse asset-backed securities. In some instances, the bank provides partial guarantees and this issue is termed limited-recourse asset-backed securities. The assets (i.e. the claim to future payments from mortgage holders) are usually removed from the bank's statement of financial position and placed in a new fund, or an entity is set up specifically to administer the whole process (the entity is called a **special purpose entity**). Mortgages claims are the dominant type of securitisation. Securitisation is also used to package and sell commercial paper claims, car loan claims, credit card claims and export credit claims.

Securitisation can 'muddy' the waters when it comes to repackaging debt for sale to investors and this form of finance contributed to the global financial crises that started in the US in 2007, as highlighted in **Real World Example 13.6**.

Real World Example 13.6: Lehman Bros

"Lehman Bros has $80 billion of liabilities based on fantasy real estate projects and lending to a class of borrower which are popularly known as NINJAS (No Income, No Job, No Assets). Lehman had built a business from originating these loans, packaging them up and selling them into the market as securitisations."

Source: Osborne, A. Aldrick, P. and Quinn, J., "Lehman collapse: the drama of a mad 48 hours that will never fade", *The Telegraph*, 13 September 2009, https://www.telegraph.co.uk/finance/financialcrisis/6179138/Lehman-collapse-the-drama-of-a-mad-48-hours-that-will-never-fade.html

When Lehman Bros went into financial difficulty, it became clear that these securitised assets had negligible value; hence its statement of financial position was overstated to the tune of $80 billion.

MEZZANINE FINANCE

Mezzanine finance is the term used to encapsulate long-term, high-risk, high-return financing. This type of finance is usually sought after all other debt sources have been exhausted and a company does not wish to issue equity (an equity issue is usually more expensive and may upset the control equilibrium within a company). The finance can be hybrid in nature, usually starting as debt, but having the option to convert to equity at some point in the future if the project or company succeeds. The finance is unsecured. As the finance is riskier, the premium or coupon rate is high. In the initial years, this type of finance is regarded as debt, hence it ranks in front of equity when it comes to yearly distributions of surpluses (interest is paid before dividends) and, if the company goes into liquidation, the debt holders are paid after other creditors, but before the equity holders. This means that, though the finance is risky, it is not as risky, from an investor's viewpoint, as equity. When a company does well, the investors can convert their holding into equity and thereafter enjoy high dividends and/or capital gains in share price. The main types of mezzanine finance are junk bonds, convertible bonds and preference shares. Mezzanine finance is most commonly sought when there is a management buyout, a takeover, a merger, recapitalisation within a company to finance growth, when Plcs go private or when a project requiring finance is capital intensive. Generally, about 20–30% of the financing provided for these types of projects is mezzanine finance. The bulk of the finance requirement is usually provided by banks (50–60%) or by another source of debt, with only 10–20% being invested as equity. The most common types of mezzanine finance are now explained in brief.

Junk Bonds

Junk bonds are low-grade, risky bonds that carry a high coupon (about 5% higher than AAA-rated bonds) and have the potential to make a strong capital gain on issue price. These bonds normally have a rating of below BBB. Investors find them attractive as there is the potential to make large returns. Indeed, a proportion of investors' investment pots are usually targeted at speculative investment opportunities, such as junk bonds. Junk bonds may be plain vanilla (see earlier in this chapter), convertible or have warrants attached (explained below).

Convertible Bonds

A **convertible bond** is a type of hybrid finance. It starts off as a plain vanilla bond and, rather than being redeemed, can be converted into equity (usually at a premium, e.g. the premium might be that the shares are converted at a predetermined share price or at a rate of 10–30% above the prevailing share price). There is much terminology surrounding convertible bonds, which is outlined in brief in **Figure 13.7**.

FIGURE 13.7: CONVERTIBLE BONDS TERMINOLOGY

Term	Description
Conversion date	The date bonds can be converted to equity.
Conversion price	This is calculated as the par value of the bond divided by the number of shares the bond can be converted into.
Conversion ratio	The number of shares that will be obtained from one bond on conversion, e.g. 13 for 1.
Conversion value	The market value of shares that the bond can be converted into. It is calculated as the conversion ratio × market value per share.
Conversion premium	This represents the premium over and above the market price of the shares that bondholders have to accept, to obtain the shares. It is calculated as: $\frac{\text{Conversion price per share} - \text{market price per share}}{\text{Market price per share}}$

When share prices rise, the value of a convertible bond increases and it is more likely that the bondholder will convert on maturity. In these circumstances, the conversion premium is likely to be small.

Worked Example 13.9: Convertible Debt

Oslo Plc's equity shares are currently trading at €/£2.50. It issues 15-year convertible 7% bonds, with a fixed conversion price of €/£4.00.

Requirement

(a) Calculate the conversion ratio.
(b) Calculate the conversion premium at the time of issue.
(c) In 10 years' time the share price has increased to €/£3.50. Calculate the new conversion premium.
(d) Under what circumstances are the bondholders likely to convert their bonds into equity share capital?
(e) If the shares were to rise in value to €/£5.00, what would the conversion value be?

Solution

(a) The conversion ratio is €/£100 ÷ €/£4.00 = 25 shares for each bond.

(b) The conversion premium at the time of issue is:

$$\frac{€/£4.00 - €/£2.50}{€/£2.50} = 60\%$$

(c) The new conversion premium will fall to:

$$\frac{€/£4.00 - €/£3.50}{€/£3.50} = 14.28\%$$

(d) The bondholders are likely to convert their bonds to equity share capital if the share price keeps rising and the conversion premium falls. A good scenario for the bondholder would be where the conversion premium is zero, in that the conversion price is the same as the market price at the date of conversion. It is even better for the bondholder if the share price increases to a value above the fixed conversion price. The current equity holders would not be happy with this result.

(e) The conversion value of one bond in this instance will be: €/£5.00 × 25 = €/£125. In this scenario, the bondholder will have made a capital gain on his investment in the convertible bonds.

Current equity holders do not normally like it when their company issues convertible debt, due to the fact that at some stage in the future their earnings per share will be diluted, as will their holding due to the increased number of shares in existence after the conversion. In addition, as highlighted in the above example, the market value of shares may rise above the anticipated conversion price. To overcome this problem, some companies issue the convertible debt like a rights issue, allowing existing equity holders the first chance to purchase the bonds.

Convertible bonds are attractive to companies as they are generally more marketable than plain vanilla bonds. This is because the coupon is usually lower than a normal bond (the conversion right is considered to have value) and the interest is tax deductible. Convertible bonds also have cash flow benefits as conversion does not result in a cash outflow. In addition, when the bonds are converted, gearing is reduced. Companies use this option when they wish to raise equity finance, but consider that the current share price is undervaluing the company; the hope is that the share price will be more reflective of management's view of company value by the time conversion is due. However, if the company does not perform as management expect, it is left with a source of finance that has fixed yearly outflows (the coupon) and a large cash outflow on the conversion date if the bondholders elect to redeem the bonds, rather than convert them.

Investors generally like convertible shares; they are able to invest in a risky venture and be ranked higher than the equity holders when it comes to yearly distributions and liquidation payments. They have the option to redeem the bonds if the company does not perform as expected, yet can convert them to equity share capital if the company does perform. In addition, they can sell the bonds in the markets at any time.

Over the past decade **contingent convertibles** (known as **CoCo bonds**) have become more common. In contrast to convertible bonds, the conversion of CoCo bonds to equity is contingent on a specified event, such as the stock price of the company exceeding a certain level for a set period of time or liquidity levels falling to specified levels. The value of the CoCo bond will depend on the nature of the contingency.

Warrants

Warrants give the holder the right to subscribe for a specified number of equity shares in the company for a specified price at a specified time in the future or when the company meets set performance targets. They have their own value and can be bought and sold separately from the security to which they are attached. Their value is quite low and investors usually find it worthwhile keeping them, as the reward is high if the company performs well. For example, an investor who purchases junk bonds may have five warrants attached to each, giving him the right to purchase five shares in three years' time at a cost of €/£3.00 per share. The market value of each share is currently €/£2.00. Each warrant could be sold today for 10c/p. If, in three years' time, the share price rises to €/£4.00, the investor will make a large gain. The investor can purchase the shares for €/£3.00 each and sell them immediately for €/£4.00 each. This is a way of rewarding those investors who invest in the company when it is risky to do so. The main difference between a warrant and an option is that warrants are issued directly by companies.

PROJECT FINANCE

When a large company (or a consortium of companies) undertakes a new major project, it is common for it to set up a separate legal entity to deal solely with that particular project. The separate legal entity, usually backed by the parent company, seeks project finance. **Project finance** is finance obtained to fund a specific project. The project is usually large – for example, the building of a bridge, a motorway, an oil rig or a dam – with easily separable cash inflows and outflows. The parent company usually issues equity to help fund the project and the remainder of the finance is sourced from a bank (usually by a syndicated loan) or the bond markets. The bonds are issued by the new separate legal entity, but may be guaranteed by the parent company (this is an example of **with-recourse financing**). If the parent company does not provide a guarantee, this is called **non-recourse financing**. The terms of the bonds or bank debt are usually designed to be self-liquidating or self-servicing (wherein the cash inflows from the project repay the interest or coupon and capital repayments or redemption payments). The project is the determining influence on the ability to obtain finance, with the guarantee from the parent company usually only regarded as security (this helps the project obtain cheaper funding). The reputation of the parent will also impact on the credit risk assessment.

Project finance is usually more expensive than conventional loans from a lender. However, the advantages to companies of raising project finance usually outweigh the costs. The advantages include:

- the risk associated with taking on a major project is transferred to a new legal entity;
- high levels of debt can be obtained to finance the project, yet not be included in the parent company's statement of financial position;
- when the project is located in a foreign country, local banks and markets can be used to source finance, which may promote greater acceptance in that country; and
- having a separate legal entity, with its own agreement with the financiers, does not complicate the company's own finances. This is particularly relevant when more than one company has an interest in a project.

INTERNATIONAL SOURCES OF FINANCE

Many large companies make strategic decisions to issue bonds on foreign markets. They do this where there is high demand for bonds in these markets and the coupon rate is competitive. However, a low coupon rate is usually a false economy, as there is a greater risk of a capital loss when it comes to the repayment of the bond, because of exchange rate movements. The bonds are usually issued in the currency of the country of the market that they are being issued in and are termed **Eurobonds**. The name has nothing to do with Europe – it denotes any bond issued in a different currency than the country of the issuer. Being issued in another currency means that the company is open to foreign exchange risk (in most instances, companies will have a business interest in the country the bond is issued in. Selling bonds in the currency of this country will reduce exposure to currency risk, to some extent). The interest on Eurobonds is usually fixed, is paid annually and is paid gross. Where the interest rate is variable, bonds are referred to as **Floating Rate Notes** (FRNs). Eurobonds and FRNs are tradable and usually have fewer restrictive covenants and less disclosure demands, relative to UK or Irish debt issues.

CONCLUSION

One of the key decisions a finance manager has to face is how to finance investments. Research has shown that there is a preference for using internal sources (see **Chapter 14**) and that debt is the next preferred option, with bank loans being more attractive than bonds. The driving influence in the decision is cost. However, there are hidden costs with debt. Companies with high levels of debt have greater financial risk and operating risk or leverage risk. This may influence operational activities and cause equity holders to demand a higher return. High levels of debt may even tie the hands of managers when they wish to invest in further projects (due to restrictive covenants having been entered into). The decisions regarding the amount and source of debt to obtain are more complicated than they might seem initially. Finance managers have to weigh up the pros and cons of each potential source in light of current gearing levels, ownership structure and stability of future cash flows from operating activities.

EXAMINATION STANDARD QUESTION: LONG-TERM FINANCE

'In recent years it has been rare for medium or long-term debt to be issued at a fixed interest rate; a floating (or variable) rate of interest, usually a few percentage points different from some variable base interest rate, has become much more common.'

Requirement

(a) Outline briefly, from the viewpoint of corporate financial management, the main advantages and disadvantages of floating rate debt.

6 Marks

An engineering company with €/£60 million of assets believes that it is at the beginning of a three-year growth cycle. It has a total debt to assets ratio of 16%, and expects revenues and net earnings to grow at a rate of 10% per annum and its share price to rise at 30% per annum over the three-year period. The company will require additional financing amounting to €/£6 million at the start of the period and another €/£3 million by the middle of the third year. The economy is at the beginning of a general upturn and, by the middle of the third year, money and capital costs will show their characteristic pattern near the peak of an upturn in the economy.

Requirement

(b) Advise the company how the two amounts of additional financing should be raised.

6 Marks

A chemical company has been growing steadily. Currently, it requires €/£2 million of new capital equipment to increase sales from €/£40 million to €/£50 million over the next two years. When additional working capital requirements are taken into account, the total additional financing required during the first of these two years will be €/£5 million. Profits will remain unchanged in Year 1, but will rise by 50% in Year 2. The shares are currently selling on a price earnings ratio of 20. The company can either borrow straight debt at 7.5% per annum or convertible debt at 6.75%. The present debt to total assets ratio is 25%.

Requirement

(c) Advise the company as to which form of finance it should employ.

6 Marks

Total 18 Marks

(Based on Chartered Accountants Ireland, MABF II, Autumn 1996, Q6)

Solution

(a) The advantages of using floating rate debt are:

- Interest rates will reduce if economic conditions improve.
- The rate of interest will reflect the actual economic climate.

The disadvantages of using floating rate debt are:

- Interest rates may increase.
- Uncertainty surrounds the amounts of the repayments.
- The cash budget will be difficult to complete, due to the uncertainty surrounding the interest rate outflows.

(b) The engineering company is in good shape financially and seems to have low gearing (16%), when expressed as the debt to total assets ratio. As the economy begins a three-year growth cycle, interest rates may be currently low, but will rise as the first year elapses. Therefore, the company should raise the €/£6 million using fixed rate debentures. To avoid any increase in gearing, the company might consider issuing them as convertible debentures (so long as the agreement reached with the convertible debenture holders does not damage current equity holder value). From the company's viewpoint, the use of debt is cheaper than equity, because of the tax deductibility of interest.
The company's share price is beginning to rise and is expected to peak at the end of the three-year period. Therefore, the company should wait until it is at its peak and then issue new equity shares to raise the €/£3 million required by the middle of the third year. The higher the share price, the fewer new shares will have to be issued and the less the dilution of control. Very often after a period of growth, a company may be slightly under capitalised, so the addition to the permanent capital base of the company provided by the new equity should be welcomed as good financial management.

(c) The current gearing of the company, measured as the debt to total assets ratio, is low, so the company can take on more debt without increasing the risk to either debt or equity holders. The convertible debenture is the cheapest option, at 6.75%, a full 0.75% cheaper than straight debt. The expected growth in profits over the two-year period should ensure that sufficient funds will be available to repay the debt. The option to convert will eliminate the interest payments and the gearing ratio will also fall after conversion has taken place. The industry is very volatile and forecasting profits can be hazardous. Therefore, the share price might fall, should profits take a downturn. The price earnings ratio of 20 is very high and indicates market confidence. However, it can also indicate susceptibility to an attractive takeover offer. The issue of shares now would also be a possible option, if the share price was expected to fall. However, if the share price is only beginning to rise, it would be expensive for the company to issue the shares now, as more shares than necessary would have to be issued. On balance, convertible debt should be used, as it also offers the flexibility of being easy to adjust should the company have made errors in computing the amount of finance required for the equipment.

Key Terms

Asset-backed securities
Bearer bonds
Bonds
Bond credit rating
Bulldog bonds
Bullet bond
CoCo bonds
Contingent convertibles
Conversion date
Conversion premium
Conversion price
Conversion ratio
Conversion value
Convertible bond
Coupon rate
Debentures
Deep discount bonds
Eurobonds
Fallen angel
Floating Rate Notes
Green bonds
Guaranteed loan stock
Hybrid finance
Irredeemable bonds
Junior bonds
Junk bonds
Loan notes
Loan stock
Mezzanine finance
Mortgage bond
Mortgage debentures
Mortgage loans
Negative covenants

Nominal value
Non-recourse financing
Plain vanilla bonds
Positive covenants
Project finance
Redeemable bonds
Redemption value
Registered bonds
Restrictive covenants
Securitisation
Sinking fund
Special purpose entity
Straight bond
Subordinated bonds
Syndicated loans
Term loans
Trust deed
Warrants
With-recourse factoring
Zero coupon bonds

REVIEW QUESTIONS

(See Suggested Solutions to Review Questions in **Appendix B**.)

Question 13.1

What are the purposes of restrictive covenants?

Question 13.2

What is a trust deed?

Question 13.3

List five methods a company can use to repay €/£1 billion of bonds on their redemption.

Question 13.4

What do you call a bond that was once rated as an AAA, but is subsequently rated as a Caa by a bond credit-rating agency?

Question 13.5

Calculate the annual amount that should be input by a company to a sinking fund that earns 15% per annum, to ensure that it can repay bonds with a nominal value of €/£2,500,000 in 15 years' time. The bonds are to be redeemed at a premium of 5%.

Question 13.6

An investor is currently viewing the irredeemable bonds of Jock Plc to determine whether or not to invest in the bonds. The bondholders' required rate of return (gross) is 8%. Jock Plc's 9% redeemable bonds are currently trading at €/£90. The coupon is paid annually and is due in one year's time.

Requirement Determine whether the investor should invest in Jock Plc.

Question 13.7

Jock Plc currently has a 10% bond outstanding that will be redeemed in two years at €/£100. The current market value of this bond is €/£95 and interest is paid semi-annually.

Requirement Calculate the return on this bond.

Question 13.8

Hola Plc issues 1,000,000 bonds at a price of €/£50 each to be repaid at their nominal value of €/£100 in 10 years' time.

Requirement Calculate the annualised rate of return from the capital gain if the bond is held to maturity for the full 10 years.

CHALLENGING QUESTIONS

(Suggested Solutions to Challenging Questions are available through your lecturer.)

Question 13.1 Bond price (Level 1)

Your company invests €/£50,000 now in a 5% corporate bond that can be redeemed at a premium of €/£3 over par (par is €/£100) in 10 years' time. The current gross redemption yield (cost of debt) is 4%.

Requirement Calculate the current market value of the 5% corporate bond. (Ignore taxation.)

2 marks

(Based on Chartered Accountants Ireland, CAP 1, Finance, Summer 2017, Extract from Q5)

Question 13.2 Convertible loan notes (Level 1)

A client, Brook Ltd, has undertaken extensive research and investment appraisal, and consequently has decided to diversify into a new business sector. External finance of €/£20 million is required by Brook for this project. Brook's finance director is considering raising the finance by issuing 6.5% convertible loan notes.

Requirement

(a) Explain the meaning of 'issuing 6.5% convertible loan notes'.

2 Marks

(b) Outline THREE benefits to Brook of using convertible loan notes to raise long-term finance.

3 Marks

(Based on Chartered Accountants Ireland, CAP 1, Finance, Summer 2019, Extract from Q4)

Question 13.3 Mezenar (Level 1)

You are a trainee accountant in Mezenar Limited and have been asked to prepare a memo for the board of directors regarding raising finance for a proposed new investment in equipment. The following is an extract from the forecasted financial statements of Mezenar, a manufacturing company, for the year ended 31 December 20X3.

EXTRACT FROM THE FORECASTED STATEMENT OF FINANCIAL POSITION FOR YEAR ENDED 31 DECEMBER 20X3

	€/£000
ASSETS	16,500
EQUITY AND LIABILITIES	
Equity share capital (€/£2 each)	8,000
Share premium	3,600
10% debentures	4,900
	16,500

The debenture agreement states that the debt/equity ratio cannot exceed 75%.

Potential New Investment

- Mezenar is considering making a substantial investment of €/£3,500,000 in equipment to enhance their manufacturing facilities. The finance manager has done preliminary research and has found that this investment would increase Mezenar's current profit of €/£4,200,000 (before interest and tax) by 15%.
- The board of directors are looking to raise either debt or equity to finance the purchase of the equipment.

- The bank has informed Mezenar that they would charge an interest rate of 7% per annum for the loan of €/£3,500,000 over 15 years. The board of directors are curious as to what factors the bank considers when they are setting the interest rate.
- If Mezenar decide to raise equity finance, it would be by way of a share issue. The share price is currently trading at €/£2.80.
- Mezenar has a current policy of paying a dividend of 40 cents/pence per share.
- The rate of taxation is 20%.

Requirement Prepare a memo to the board of directors which:

(a) Outlines the factors that affect the rate of interest a customer will be charged on a loan.

4 Marks

(b) Explains the term 'restrictive covenant' and gives TWO examples of the types of covenants that could be included in a loan agreement.

4 Marks

(c) Demonstrates the effect the potential investment in equipment could have on the following ratios that Mezenar use as key performance indicators:
   (i) debt to equity;
   (ii) interest cover;
   (iii) earnings per share.

8 Marks

(d) Recommends (with a reason) whether Mezenar should choose debt or equity to finance the investment in equipment to enhance its manufacturing facilities.

2 Marks
Presentation 2 Marks
Total 20 Marks

(Based on Chartered Accountants Ireland, CAP 1, Finance, Summer 2013, Q2)

Question 13.4 Doodle (Level 1)

Doodle Limited, a company in the technology sector, has made substantial investments in three projects: Project Alpha, Project Beta and Project Gamma. Doodle has financed these projects using debt finance.

Project Alpha is financed by €/£1,500,000 7% debentures, which are currently trading at €/£98. The debenture is due for redemption at par (€/£100) on 31 December 20X7. Interest has just been paid on the debenture.

Project Beta is financed by €/£700,000 6% irredeemable bonds that are currently trading at €/£95. Interest has just been paid on this bond.

Project Gamma is financed by €/£2,000,000 9% redeemable bonds, which are due for redemption at premium of 10% over par (€/£100) on 31 December 20X8. The expected return to the bondholder is 7% (after tax at 20%).

(***Note:*** assume today is 31 December 20X4.)
The current tax rate is 20% and the payment of tax occurs in the same year interest is paid.
Assume interest is paid at the end of the year.

Requirement

(a) Calculate the after-tax cost of debt of the 7% debentures used to finance Project Alpha.

4 Marks

(b) Calculate the after-tax cost of debt of the 6% irredeemable bonds used to finance Project Beta.

2 Marks

(c) Calculate the current market value of one unit of the 9% redeemable bonds used to finance Project Gamma.

3 Marks

(d) Identify any SIX factors that influence finance managers when choosing between sources of finance.

6 Marks

Total 15 Marks

(Based on Chartered Accountants Ireland, CAP 1, Finance, Autumn 2013, Q7)

Question 13.5 Endrun (Level 1)

Joan Ensider is a junior manager working for Endrun Plc. Joan owns some equity shares in Endrun, but they have declined in value recently to only €/£1.05 each. Joan asked Maria Smart, the financial controller, what the prospects for the share price were like, but was told she could not divulge such information. However, while Maria Smart was temporarily absent from her office, Joan noted that the financial controller had calculated the cost of a proposed issue of convertible loan stock by Endrun at 15% p.a. before tax. Joan is aware that the existing convertible loan stock has a current market value of €/£109 per €/£100 ex interest. The firm will pay interest at a coupon rate of 12% at the end of each of the next four years. In four years' time it is expected that the loan stock will be converted into equity shares at the rate of 20 equity shares per €/£100 nominal value loan stock.

Requirement What value per share does the financial controller believe that the equity shares will have in four years' time?

11 Marks

(Based on Chartered Accountants Ireland, CAP 1, Finance, Summer 2009, extract from Q5)

Question 13.6 Greenwood (Level 2)

Greenwood Ltd is hoping to expand its business. The company runs a very successful job recruitment agency. Extracts from the company's financial statements for the last two years are as follows.

Greenwood Ltd

Statement of Profit or Loss (Extract)

	20X4 €/£000	20X3 €/£000
Revenue	2,250	1,350
Profit after tax	763	485
Dividends	538	440

Statement of Financial Position (Extract)

	Note	20X4 €/£000	20X3 €/£000
Non-current assets	(1)	350	250
Net current assets		390	315
		740	565
Issued share capital (€/£1 equity shares)		250	250
Reserves		340	165
Long-term bank loan		150	150
		740	565

Note (1): non-current assets comprise motor vehicles, furniture and fittings and computers. The company does not own its premises.

The directors are hoping to raise €/£2 million in long-term finance to implement the proposed expansion of the company. They are looking at a number of financing options, including the following:
1. Bank term loan.
2. Retained earnings.
3. Venture capital.
4. Redeemable debentures.

Requirement

(a) Outline the characteristics of *any three* of the sources of finance listed above.

10 Marks

(b) Prepare a report for the directors of Greenwood Ltd outlining the more appropriate method, or methods, of financing from the list above, having regard to the particular circumstances of the company. Your report should contain reasoned arguments for the method or methods selected.

8 Marks
Total 18 Marks

(Based on Chartered Accountants Ireland, MABF II, Autumn 2002, Q7)

Question 13.7 Bintulu Plc (Levels 1 and 2)

(a) Explain what you understand by the terms 'operational gearing' and 'financial gearing'.

4 Marks

(b) Why do different levels of gearing exist in different industries? Briefly explain your answer and your understanding of why these differences arise.

6 Marks

Bintulu Plc is a middle-sized quoted company which manufactures plastics. The last two years have been very successful for the company following on from a period of static profits. The company now has surplus cash of €/£100 million. Its factories are not operating at 100% capacity. It has no immediate plans for major investment projects.

The following table shows a comparison between various ratios for the company and for the plastics industry as a whole.

	Bintulu	**Industry**
Debt ratio	28%	32%
Debt interest coverage	3.6 times	2.9 times
Dividend yield	4.4%	4.6%
Dividend cover	3.4 times	3.2 times
Market capitalisation	€/£1,000 million	

Requirement

(c) Write a report to the Finance Director of Bintulu Plc advising him on alternative courses of action in respect of the surplus cash; set out clearly your recommendation as to the best course of action to follow. Describe the factors you have taken into account in your analysis.

7 Marks
Presentation 1 Mark
Total 18 Marks

(Based on Chartered Accountants Ireland, MABF II, Summer 2003, Q6)

Question 13.8 Sesco (Level 2)

Sesco Plc operates 37 supermarket stores selling food and other household supplies in the domestic market. The management of Sesco is planning to borrow €/£20,000,000 to fund an overseas expansion programme commencing in May 20X6. It will take more than 18 months before significant cash flows are generated from this investment. The management is worried about servicing the interest on the borrowed funds for an 18-month period (May 20X6 to October 20X7), as interest rates are volatile.

The company's advisors believe that interest rates will remain stable for the first six months of the period. During the second six months of the period there is an equal chance of interest rates rising or falling by 2%. In the final six months of the period there is a 60% chance of rates continuing to move by a further 2% in the same direction as in the previous six-month period and a 40% chance of a 2% move in the opposite direction. Interest is payable at the end of each six months.

The management are undecided whether to borrow the €/£20,000,000 in either:

1. A €/£15,000,000 short-term floating rate loan at an initial interest rate of 10% per year and renewable every six months, and a €/£5,000,000 five-year fixed rate loan at 12% per year; or
2. A €/£5,000,000 short-term loan, and a €/£15,000,000 five-year loan, both on the same terms as (1.) above.

All loans are secured. Interest rate reviews for floating rate loans take place every six months.

Issue costs are 1% of the loan size for each short-term loan (payable on initial issue only), and €/£80,000 for the five-year loan. Tax relief is available on the interest payments. No tax relief is available on issue costs. Corporate Tax is at the rate of 25%.

Summary financial data and selected data for Stores A, B and C (gathered by internal audit for Sesco) are set out in Appendix I in respect of the year ended 30 April 20X6 and in Appendix II in respect of the year ended 30 April 20X5.

APPENDIX I
SUMMARY DATA FOR SESCO FOR YEAR ENDED 30 APRIL 20X6

	Store A	**Store B**	**Store C**	**Group Total (37 stores)**
Floor area (m²)	1,200	1,000	1,100	31,500
Number of employees	72	70	67	1,785
Number of competitors in catchment area	8	4	5	
Average number of customer complaints	115	106	98	
Number of coding errors per 1,000 transactions	12	9	4	
	€/£000	**€/£000**	**€/£000**	**€/£000**
Revenue	7,680	7,200	7,370	192,450
Gross profit	1,698	1,744	1,738	43,100
Labour	(917)	(907)	(886)	(21,700)
Other costs	(731)	(647)	(692)	(16,400)
Total costs	(1,648)	(1,554)	(1,578)	(38,100)
Profit from operations	50	190	160	5,000

(***Note:*** gross profit is calculated after wastage.)

	%	%	%	%
Gross profit pre-wastage	24.4	25.6	25.5	24.2
Wastage	(2.3)	(1.4)	(1.9)	(1.8)
Gross profit	22.1	24.2	23.6	22.4

Simplified Capital Employed in Sesco Supermarkets at 30 April 20X6 is as follows:

	€/£000	**€/£000**	**€/£000**	**€/£000**
Inventory	324	329	343	8,500
Less: Payables	(1,241)	(1,164)	(1,191)	(31,100)
Other assets	720	940	1,122	27,400
Net assets	(197)	105	274	4,800

There are no significant receivables.

Appendix II

Summary Data for Sesco for Year Ended 30 April 20X5

	Store A	**Store B**	**Store C**	**Group Total (37 stores)**
	€/£000	**€/£000**	**€/£000**	**€/£000**
Revenue	8,320	6,963	7,038	186,950
Gross profit	1,947	1,693	1,655	42,050
Profit from operations	317	232	152	5,700
Number of competitors in catchment area	6	4	5	
Average number of customer complaints	99	107	101	
Number of coding errors per 1,000 transactions	8	8	3	

Requirement

(a) Set out briefly the strategic risks associated with a 'domestic company', such as Sesco, expanding its operations into a foreign country (see **Chapter 19** to answer this part of the question).

6 Marks

(b) Discuss briefly the main considerations for Sesco in deciding on an appropriate form of debt finance for this expansion.

6 Marks

(c) Explain briefly what 'mezzanine finance' is and how might it be useful to Sesco.

4 Marks

(d) Estimate the cost to Sesco, in terms of interest and fees, of each of the TWO proposed forms of financing during the 18-month period.

8 Marks

(e) Discuss the role of management accountants in risk management (see **Chapters 19, 20** and **21**).

10 Marks

Professional & presentation 4 Marks

Total 38 Marks

(Based on Chartered Accountants Ireland, CAP 2, SFMA, Summer 2009, Q1)

14

Long-term Sources of Finance: Equity Capital and Preference Shares

Learning Objectives

Upon completing this chapter, readers should be able to:

- explain the risk of investing in equity to an investor, relative to other sources of finance;
- outline the risk of issuing equity from a company's perspective;
- understand the difference between the book value, nominal value and market value of equity;
- list and describe various types of equity;
- describe the main equity markets in the UK and Ireland;
- list the advantages and disadvantages of flotation;
- describe the main approaches used to raise equity in the markets (on initial joining and subsequent to this); and
- explain the characteristics, advantages and disadvantages of preference shares from a company's and a shareholder's perspective.

INTRODUCTION

Equity finance is one of the most important long-term sources of finance to companies. It is the least risky source of finance, from a company's perspective, yet the most risky investment to make, from an investor's viewpoint. This chapter is written from the viewpoint of a company and considers equity in terms of a source of finance, not as an investment. Sourcing equity is not straightforward for a company; there are different types of equity finance and different methods of obtaining equity. Some avenues (such as public issues) are closed to some companies (for example, small companies). The decision on whether to grow and raise equity is strategic and needs to take the following into account:

- the risks involved (including market risk, business risk and finance risk);
- the ownership structure of the company (control);
- the period of time the finance is required for;
- whether the funding from equity finance matches the finance requirements; and
- the current gearing of the company.

This chapter tries to shed some light on the equity finance options available to different types of companies. Public equity is mainly sourced from the equity markets; therefore, the UK and Irish markets are explained and the process involved in obtaining a public listing is outlined. The advantages and disadvantages to a company that result from becoming listed are also discussed. The various approaches available on an initial public offering are detailed, with diagrams being used to show the role of issuing houses in the process. A myriad of stakeholders and advisors, along with the issuing house, are involved in the process of raising equity and these roles are outlined in brief. Then the options available to an already listed company, to raise additional equity finance, are discussed. In the latter part of the chapter preference shares are explained. These shares are hybrid in nature; they are not strictly equity, nor are they strictly debt.

In practice companies fund their projects using internally generated equity (i.e. retained earnings), after which bank debt is the preferred source of finance, followed by tradable debt – with equity being the least preferred source of finance. This ranking is mostly down to the cost of each source and is known as **pecking order theory** (see **Chapter 16**.)

EQUITY AS A SOURCE OF FINANCE

Different Types of Companies

Equity is the term used to describe an owner's investment in a company. There are many forms of business, with differing types of equity, as detailed in **Figure 14.1**.

FIGURE 14.1: EQUITY IN DIFFERENT ORGANISATIONS

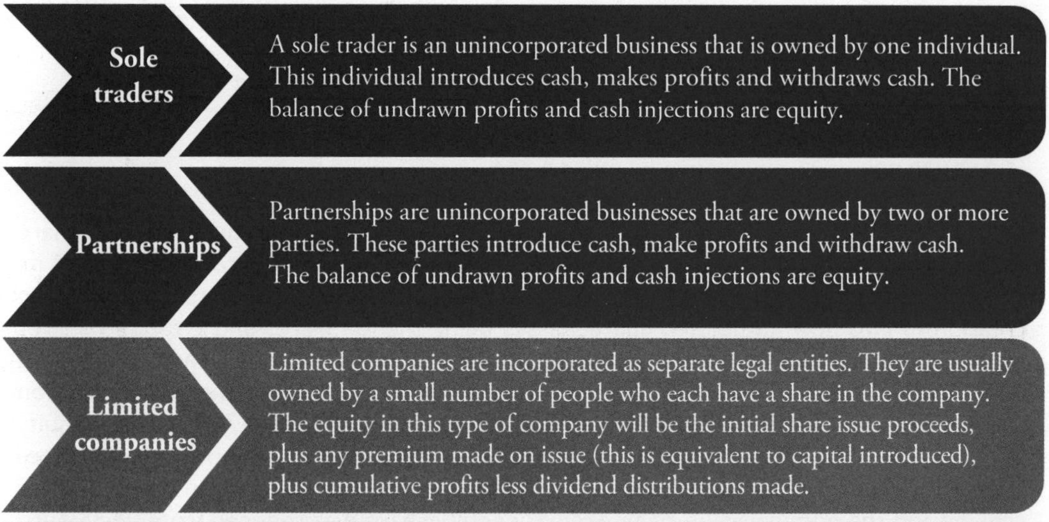

Sole traders	A sole trader is an unincorporated business that is owned by one individual. This individual introduces cash, makes profits and withdraws cash. The balance of undrawn profits and cash injections are equity.
Partnerships	Partnerships are unincorporated businesses that are owned by two or more parties. These parties introduce cash, make profits and withdraw cash. The balance of undrawn profits and cash injections are equity.
Limited companies	Limited companies are incorporated as separate legal entities. They are usually owned by a small number of people who each have a share in the company. The equity in this type of company will be the initial share issue proceeds, plus any premium made on issue (this is equivalent to capital introduced), plus cumulative profits less dividend distributions made.
Public limited companies (Plcs)	Plcs are incorporated separate legal entities. Plc equity is obtained from the issues of shares on the financial markets and/or cumulative profits less dividend distributions made.

Equity in Financial Statements

The main equity account in the statement of financial position is equity share capital – otherwise known as **ordinary share capital**. This is a monetary value that represents the number of shares a company has issued, multiplied by the nominal value of one share. The nominal value is sometimes referred to as **par** or **face value**. The **nominal value** is established by the directors of a company when a company is being incorporated. The issued share capital divides the overall value of a company after debt claims into portions (shares), which are then traded. An example of the disclosures required for equity shares is provided in **Real World Example 14.1**.

Real World Example 14.1: Ryanair Holdings Plc

Ryanair Holdings Plc *Annual Report and Financial Statements 2019* (Extract)

15. Issued share capital, share premium account and share options (extract)

Share capital

	At March 31		
	2019 €M	**2018 €M**	**2017 €M**
Authorised/share capital reorganisation			
1,550,000,000 ordinary equity shares of 0.600 euro cent each	9.3	9.3	9.3
1,368,000,000 'B' Shares of 0.050 euro cent each	0.7	0.7	0.7
1,368,000,000 deferred shares of 0.050 euro cent each	0.7	0.7	0.7
	10.7	10.7	10.7
Allotted, called-up and fully paid:			
1,133,395,322 ordinary equity shares of 0.600 euro cent each	6.8	—	—
1,171,142,985 ordinary equity shares of 0.600 euro cent each	—	7.0	—
1,217,870,999 ordinary equity shares of 0.600 euro cent each	—	—	7.3

During fiscal year 2016, the Group returned €398m to shareholders via a B share scheme and completed a capital reorganisation which involved the consolidation of its ordinary share capital on a 39 for 40 basis. The Group's shareholders approved the creation of two new authorised share classes being the 'B' Shares and Deferred Shares classes to effect this B share scheme and 1,353,149,541 'B' Shares and 663,060,175 Deferred Shares were subsequently issued.Arising out of the ordinary share consolidation the number of ordinary equity shares in issue was reduced by 33,828,739 ordinary equity shares from 1,353,149,541 immediately prior to the implementation of the B Share scheme to 1,319,320,802 ordinary equity shares in issue upon completion of the B Share scheme and the nominal value of an ordinary equity share was reduced from 0.635 euro cent each to 0.6 euro cent each.All 'B' Shares and Deferred Shares issued in connection with the B Share scheme were either redeemed or cancelled during the year ended March 31, 2017 such that there were no 'B' Shares or Deferred Shares remaining in issue as at March 31, 2017.

For full details, see: https://investor.ryanair.com/wp-content/uploads/2019/07/Ryanair-2019-Annual-Report.pdf; accessed November 2019.

The nominal value bears no relation to **market value**, which is the price the market places on the equity of a company. The holder of an equity share is a part owner of a company. The holder has a right to vote at equity shareholders' meetings. Decisions that can be influenced by equity shareholders include: the employment of directors, non-executive directors and auditors; the dividend level (equity holders can elect to reduce a dividend, but not increase it); and major strategic decisions.

When a company is initially incorporated and shares are issued, directors usually try to select a nominal value that they feel represents the market value of the company (they discount it initially to ensure that all shares are taken up by the market).

Shares may be issued at a higher price than the nominal value; in this instance, the surplus is regarded as a premium on issue and is accounted for in the **share premium** account. Therefore, the equity share capital and share premium account together represent the net investment by equity holders in a company.

Equity holders also make other contributions (indirectly) to the financing of a company. Each year the profits remaining after bond interest, taxation and preference dividends are attributable to equity holders and can be distributed as a dividend. However, to do so would undermine the liquidity of a company and limit the funds available for directors to invest in new projects. Therefore, a portion, if not all, of the yearly **realised earnings** available for distribution may be retained in the company. This is an opportunity cost to the equity holders in terms of it being a dividend foregone. Therefore, it represents an additional supply of finance by equity holders. Each year the amount not distributed is transferred to the **revenue reserves** account (otherwise known as **retained earnings**). This also forms part of the equity of the company. It is a record of the past dividends foregone by the equity holders. Retained earnings do not equate to cash reserves.

In addition to the realised earnings, a company normally makes other gains each year. These are usually capital gains, which are not realised. Depending on the accounting policies adopted, the financial statements of a company might incorporate these unrealised gains on some assets, for example, property. Property values usually increase each year. The increase in value is attributable to the equity holders (debt holders' claims on a company are fixed as interest payable on debt is not related to profitability and, so long as the interest expense is covered, all other gains accrue to the equity holders) and is posted to a revaluation reserve. The **revaluation reserve** represents the difference between the market value of the property and the historical cost (i.e. the price the company paid) of the property. Other types of equity share are outlined in **Figure 14.2**.

FIGURE 14.2: OTHER TYPES OF EQUITY SHARE

Non-voting equity shares

These have the same rights as ordinary equity shares, except they do not carry a vote. They are not allowed to be issued by companies listed on the **LSE**, but are common in family-run limited companies. This allows a family to retain full control.

Golden shares

These have the same rights as ordinary equity shares, though they also have special decision-making powers. They are issued to key equity holders (usually founding equity holders/board members) when the company is first incorporated. Their aim is to preserve certain characteristics of a company. For example, a football club may restrict decisions about the colour of the strip, the logo, the football grounds or the sale of players to meet debts to holders of golden shares.

Preferred ordinary shares

The claims of holders of **preferred ordinary shares** are met before the claims of other equity holders (i.e. the holders of **deferred ordinary shares**). On the down side, their claim to surplus returns is limited when a company performs well.

The liquidity associated with investing in shares of Plcs is a key attraction to many equity holders as they can sell their shares at short notice (this advantage only applies to equity holdings that are listed on an exchange – if the equity holding is in an unlisted company, the shares are difficult to liquidate).

Equity: Investors' Perspective

As investors, equity holders carry the greatest risks: they are last in line (of the financiers) to get yearly distributions and are last when it comes to capital repayment, were a company to go into liquidation. However, they can also reap the highest rewards when a company performs well, benefiting from increases in share price and large dividends. They demand the highest return of all the financiers of a company. If a successful company were to go into voluntary liquidation, the equity holders would get any residual surplus after all proven creditors' and debt holders' claims had been settled. They have a right to receive the annual report of the company each year and to be invited to and attend the annual general meeting. At this meeting, they can exercise control by voting on pre-informed decisions that the company directors are proposing. This control is limited, particularly where an equity holder has a minority interest in a company. However, equity holders have the right to sell their shares at any time and can easily do so where the shares are quoted on a securities exchange. If sufficient numbers do so, this will drive down the share price and directors will have to alter their decisions accordingly, or the company will be taken over and the directors removed.

Equity: Company's Perspective

Raising equity is the least risky form of external finance a company can obtain; dividends can be waived and the issued share capital does not have to be redeemed. (A company is permitted to buy back its shares and companies usually do this if they feel that their shares are currently underpriced.) The ability to waive dividend payments is attractive to directors, particularly where there is a possibility of the company experiencing liquidity problems. However, it must be stressed that companies usually do pay a dividend and having a stable dividend policy is considered to influence the value of a company – dividends are interpreted as a means of signalling the future performance of a company to the market (see **Chapter 22**). Companies rarely distribute all the available earnings and usually build up retained earnings, which can be used to finance future investments. This is a quick and cheap source of finance, the most popular source of finance from the perspective of directors.

The main disadvantage of equity finance is the cost of issuing equity shares. Issue costs can exceed 10% of the funds raised. Indeed, there is usually a minimum fixed level of fees, making this a source of finance that is only appropriate for large companies. Expenses that need to be covered include:

- accountants' fees (additional work may include preparing projections, reports on financing, tax planning, working capital requirements);
- solicitors' fees (tasks may include updating directors' contracts, registering the company as a Plc, underwriting agreements, share options);
- broker fees (usually 0.5% of the amount being raised), sponsor/issuing house fees (this includes the cost of underwriting and sub-underwriting the issue – up to 2% of the amount being raised);
- Company Registrar fees (maintaining a record of the equity holders and issuing certificates); and
- the costs of preparing a prospectus and advertising the imminent issue.

The cost estimate does not include the indirect costs that are incurred, such as administrative costs, transaction costs, managerial time and the burden of having to service this finance in the future. Equity holders will not retain their investment in the company if the company does not provide an annual return, either in the form of a dividend or an increase in share price (or a combination of the two). By increasing the equity of a company, the weighted average cost of capital (WACC) may also increase, resulting in a loss of equity value (see **Chapter 16** for a discussion of the impact of shifts in a company's WACC on the value of its equity). Another factor that usually influences the decision on whether to raise equity finance is the relationship the directors have with existing dominant equity holders. If the dominant equity holders are supportive of the strategic decisions made by directors, then the directors are less likely to risk a change in the control status of the company. However, if the relationship is poor, the directors are more likely to opt for a new share issue. Finally, dividends are not tax deductible, making them expensive relative to interest on debt finance.

RAISING EQUITY FINANCE

Quoted Equity: The Exchanges

In the UK the main exchange is the **London Stock Exchange**. It has three key markets for equity shares: the **Main Market**, which is typically made up of shares in large companies, the

Alternative Investment Market (AIM), which caters for smaller companies, and the **Professional Securities Market (PSM)**, which specialises in debt issues. The LSE also has the **Specialist Fund Market (SFM)**, a market for sophisticated fund vehicles, in which only knowledgeable investors should trade.

In Ireland there is one exchange, **Euronext Dublin**. It has three markets: Euronext Dublin (for large companies and government bonds); Euronext Access & Access+ (for small to medium-sized companies); and Euronext Growth (a market for high-growth companies).

The costs of flotation on a stock exchange are high; however, many benefits are argued to arise for a company as a result of flotation, as outlined in **Figure 14.3**.

Figure 14.3: Benefits to a Company of Flotation

Access to capital both straightaway and through further capital issues in the future.	Creating an easily accessed market for the company's shares, this broadens the shareholder base and increases the marketability of the shares.	Increases the credibility and reputation of the company as stock exchanges typically have rigorous rules that extend beyond company law.
Provides a quick exit route for equity investors.	Increased public profile because Plcs get more media attention.	Enables the market to place an objective value on the company's business.
Plcs can easily set up employee share schemes, which can motivate and encourage employees' commitment to the company.	Provides a platform for the purchase and sale of whole companies.	Companies can issue shares and use these to purchase other companies.

Current company investors also benefit as the management of a Plc has to be more accountable to its equity holders for decisions made, relative to non-public companies. Indeed, it is against stock exchange rules to fail to disclose information that may influence share price, whether good or bad. Information that would influence share price is termed **price-sensitive information**. This disclosure of information need not be financial. For example, Tesco announced in 2019 that its chief executive, Dave Lewis, was stepping down after overseeing a five-year turnaround from a financial crisis and accounting scandal. Finally, a company must have in place a board of non-executive directors to police the activities of the board of directors (see **Chapter 1**).

There are several disadvantages associated with flotation, as highlighted in **Figure 14.4**.

FIGURE 14.4: DISADVANTAGES OF FLOTATION[1]

Market risk

The company may become vulnerable to market fluctuations that are beyond its control.

Costs

Issue costs are high and yearly compliance costs are substantial.

Agency theory

When a company is floated, the directors have to consider the interests of the equity holders, not just their own. This may lead to conflict.

Loss of control

There will be a certain amount of loss of control of the company and ultimately the company may be taken over by another company.

Regulatory burden

Increased responsibility on directors to ensure that appropriate regulatory requirements are adhered to.

Managerial time tied up

The amount of managerial time required when a company floats is quite high; this means that other areas of the business are deprived of managerial attention.

Employee demotivation

If the company offers share options to some employees, this may cause others to become disgruntled.

Which Securities Exchange?

There are several strategic decisions that will influence the decision on which securities exchange to issue shares. When a company goes public for the first time, the issue is referred to as an **Initial Public Offering (IPO)**. Floating shares is a costly exercise and this effectively prohibits many companies, particularly small or medium-sized companies, from seeking this as a source of finance. A brief summary of the key exchanges is now provided. The main exchanges in the UK and in Ireland are now discussed.

[1] Source: summarised from the guide, "Floating on the stock market", https://www.nibusinessinfo.co.uk/content/floating-stock-market; accessed April 2020.

London Stock Exchange: Main Market

Only very large companies that are seeking to raise large sums of capital will find that the benefits of a full official listing on the main market outweigh the costs. The LSE charges a one-off fee for an initial listing. The size of this fee depends on the size of the funds raised. In addition, it charges an annual fee thereafter depending on the size of the company's market capitalisation.

There are three routes to listing on the Main Market, as shown in **Figure 14.5**.

Figure 14.5: Routes to Listing on the LSE Main Market

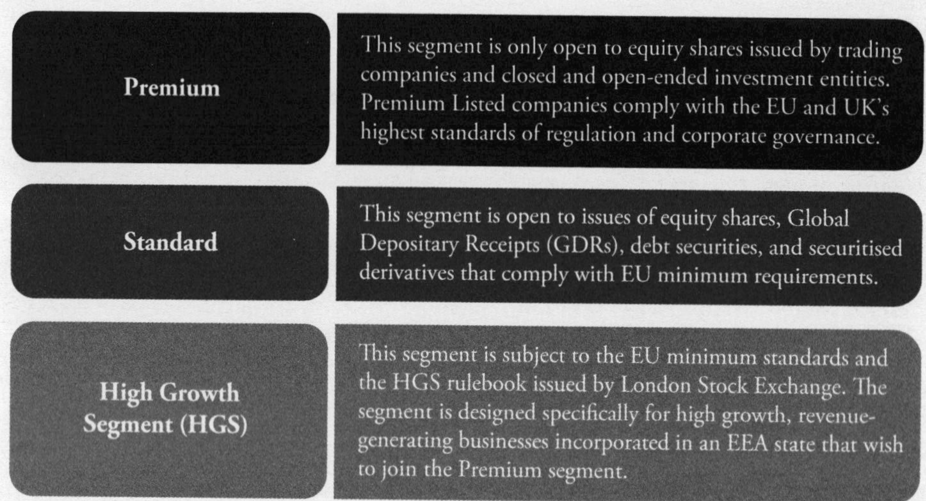

Premium
This segment is only open to equity shares issued by trading companies and closed and open-ended investment entities. Premium Listed companies comply with the EU and UK's highest standards of regulation and corporate governance.
Standard
This segment is open to issues of equity shares, Global Depositary Receipts (GDRs), debt securities, and securitised derivatives that comply with EU minimum requirements.
High Growth Segment (HGS)
This segment is subject to the EU minimum standards and the HGS rulebook issued by London Stock Exchange. The segment is designed specifically for high growth, revenue-generating businesses incorporated in an EEA state that wish to join the Premium segment.

The company also has to be suitable from the stock exchange's perspective. To operate effectively, the exchanges need to ensure that companies trading are as their financial statements portray them to be. Indeed, to gain access to the Premium segment of the Main Market of the London Stock Exchange, there are additional stringent regulatory requirements (many of which centre around policing the corporate governance of a company) and the initial flotation documents need to be approved by the UK Listing Authority (part of the Financial Conduct Authority (FCA)). When a company is listed, it has to continue to adhere to high standards. It runs the risk of having trading in its shares suspended, followed by disciplinary action, if it breaches the rules. In addition, to protect potential investors, the stock exchange has put in place steps to ensure that funds are not taken from the public without the public having a voice in the control of a company. To this end, companies floated on the main market cannot issue non-voting shares, no one can have control of more than 30% of the shares (there is no dominant controlling shareholder) and at least 25% of the total issued equity shares have to be held by the public.

The main information required on flotation is contained in a company's **prospectus**. The aim of this glossy publication is to inform potential investors about a company. It is a key marketing tool, which will influence the success of a flotation and, therefore, runs the risk of being overly optimistic. It is the responsibility of the directors to ensure that the prospectus is not misleading; the UK Listing Authority vets the documentation to provide an independent check on the accuracy of the information being provided. The prospectus must cover the information set out in **Figure 14.6**.

Figure 14.6: Summary of Information Required in a Prospectus (Premium Listing)[2]

Summary	This section must briefly (limited to 2,500 words) convey in non-technical language the essential characteristics of, and the risks associated with, the company and its securities. This will usually include a summary of the company, its business, strategy and prospects along with a summary of its financial information and the risk factors.
Risk factors	This section must describe the principal risks of relevance to the company and an acquisition of its shares. The former should be specific to the company and its industry – often a prospectus will classify the risk factors so as to address these types of risk separately.
Business description	This section describes and discusses the company's business and operations. It will generally start with an overview, followed by a summary of the company's strengths and strategies. Following this, there will be a description of the principal products or services sold by the company, together with details of where and how these are produced and sold, including information on the company's customers and suppliers. An overview of the industry in which the company operates will also be included in this section, or included as a standalone section. The business description section will also typically include information on the company's employees, research and development, the company's competitors and the legal and regulatory framework in which the company operates.
Operating and financial review	This section should enable investors to assess the key drivers of the company's business (for both past and future performance) and to understand management's perception of these matters. It will also include a description and explanation of the trends in the financial information included in the prospectus and a description of the company's sources and uses of liquidity and capital resources.
Financial information	This section includes information about the company's assets and liabilities, financial position and profits and losses for the three most recent financial years, including interim results published. The financial information needs to be audited (subject to certain exceptions) and prepared in accordance with IFRS or an 'equivalent' GAAP. As well as the historical financial information, the prospectus must include a 'pro forma' table, illustrating the effect of the IPO on the statement of financial position and income statement. If a profit forecast or estimate is included in its prospectus, it must be reported on by an auditor and that report must be included.
Working capital and no significant change	The directors must make a working capital statement stating that the company has sufficient working capital for the 12 months following publication of the prospectus. In addition, it must include a statement confirming that there has been no significant change in the financial or trading position of the company since the end of the last annual or interim financial period (or, if there have been changes, include details).
Other information about the company	• Dividend policy • Material litigation • Directors and senior management • Related-party transactions • Major shareholders • Terms of the share offering and share capital

[2] Source: London Stock Exchange, "The legal framework for an IPO" in *A guide to listing on the London Stock Exchange* (London Stock Exchange, November 2010), p. 37.

After a company is listed on the Main Market, the directors have increased responsibilities towards the equity holders to supply them with any price-sensitive information when it comes to light. This normally means that public statements will have to be made in respect of any major developments affecting the company. Major developments typically include the sale or purchase of any material asset, profit announcements, dividend payout announcements, interim reports, final financial statements (within six months of the year-end), changes in directors, share dealings/issues that are planned and directors' dealings with the company (including the purchase and sale of shares). The last named activity is severely restricted by law, so that insider trading cannot take place to benefit directors, who have more information about the company, to the detriment of equity holders.

The LSE prepares an index of the weighted average price of its largest 100 companies (called the FTSE 100). It also prepares an index of the top 250 and top 350 companies (called the FTSE 250 and the FTSE 350) and the FTSE All-Share Index. The latter is used by investors to gauge the performance of the equity market overall and to determine how the market responds to changes in government policy and interest rate changes.

The Over-the-counter Markets

Several transactions in shares do not go through any exchange; they are conducted between dealers who buy and sell to each other electronically. This keeps transaction costs low (though the dealers still have to be paid). Brokers who undertake such activities are termed **market makers** and the market for these types of transactions is referred to as the **over-the-counter** (OTC) market. The LSE's Alternative Investment Market (AIM) and PLUS Markets are examples of OTC markets.

London Stock Exchange: AIM The AIM provides a trading exchange for companies that are either too young or too small to make flotation on the main market a possibility. It is suited to early stage, venture capital-backed and established companies. The cost of an IPO is usually about 10–12% of the total funds being raised. To be accepted on to the exchange, a company must appoint a **nominated advisor**, whose role is to ensure that the company complies with the rules and regulations of the AIM, and a **nominated broker** to assist with share transactions. The nominated advisor has to be retained for the whole period of listing. The regulatory requirements are not as stringent as those required on the main market. Unlike the main market, there is no minimum market capitalisation, no minimum level of shares that need to be made available to the public and the company does not have to have been in existence for over three years. However, where the company is less than two years old, the existing equity holders must retain their holding for a period of one year after flotation before they start trading.

Professional Securities Market (PSM) The PSM is a specialised market designed to suit the specific needs of issuers that wish to raise funds without detailed expensive requirements that are necessary for equity listings. The products issued by companies are specialist debt securities or **depositary receipts** (DRs) and the traders are restricted to professional investors. It is a recognised investment exchange and issuers must get approval from the UK Listing Authority before securities are admitted, after which the LSE vets the issuer before trading is permitted. DRs are negotiable certificates that represent ownership of a given number of a company's shares (typically a foreign company) and are traded separately from the shares. For example, a US bank might purchase a local company's shares, package them together into a DR and then apply to the LSE to sell the DR. They will be priced in US$ and the dividends paid will be in US$. The physical shares do not leave the US. These are known as American Deposit Receipts (ADRs). In terms of specialist debt securities, the PSM lists a variety of different types of debt instrument ranging from Eurobonds, credit-linked notes, high-yield bonds, asset-backed issues and convertible or exchangeable bonds. Bonds of any denomination can be issued.

Specialist Fund Market (SFM) The SFM is not open to trading companies or companies that are intending to make a retail equity offering in the UK. It is the LSE's regulated market for highly specialised investment entities that wish to target institutional, professional and highly knowledgeable investors only, including those managing large hedge funds, private equity funds, and certain emerging market and specialist property funds, seeking admission to a public market in London.

Euronext Dublin

The Euronext Federal Model Group took over the Irish Stock Exchange in 2018 and all securities on Euronext Dublin trade on the Euronext pan-European trading platform. The exchange has three markets: Euronext; Euronext Access & Access+ and Euronext Growth. Euronext Dublin prepares an index (the **Irish Stock Exchange Quotation (ISEQ)**) of the weighted average price of many of the shares listed on its exchange.

Euronext is similar to the main market of the LSE. This market is EU-regulated and suits highly structured companies that have the resources to meet the requirements of the most demanding and largest investors from across the globe. The average trade on this market is over €22 million (2020).

Euronext Access & Access+ is tailored for small to medium-sized companies. As such, the entrance requirements are much less stringent than for the main market.

The third exchange, **Euronext Growth**, is tailored to cater for fast-growing SME companies.

METHODS OF OBTAINING A LISTING

There are three methods of going public: an Initial Public Offering (IPO), a placing and an introduction.

Initial Public Offering (IPO)

An IPO is the most expensive method and is used by large companies or companies seeking large capital sums. There are several approaches to obtaining an IPO, including an offer for sale by prospectus, an offer for sale by subscription and an issue by tender. These processes all involve a financial advisor/issuing house/sponsor company. The sponsor company not only administers the actual purchase and sale of the shares, but also advises the company making the IPO on: the price to charge for each share; the contents of the prospectus; how to market, prepare and timetable the issue; and how to identify the correct type of issue to pursue. This decision will take into account the reputation of the company, stability and growth in its profits, its liquidity, the motives for flotation and, finally, the cost of each option available to the company. Indeed, a variety of advisors are usually involved, as highlighted in **Figure 14.7**.

FIGURE 14.7: ADVISORS' ROLES AND RESPONSIBILITIES[3]

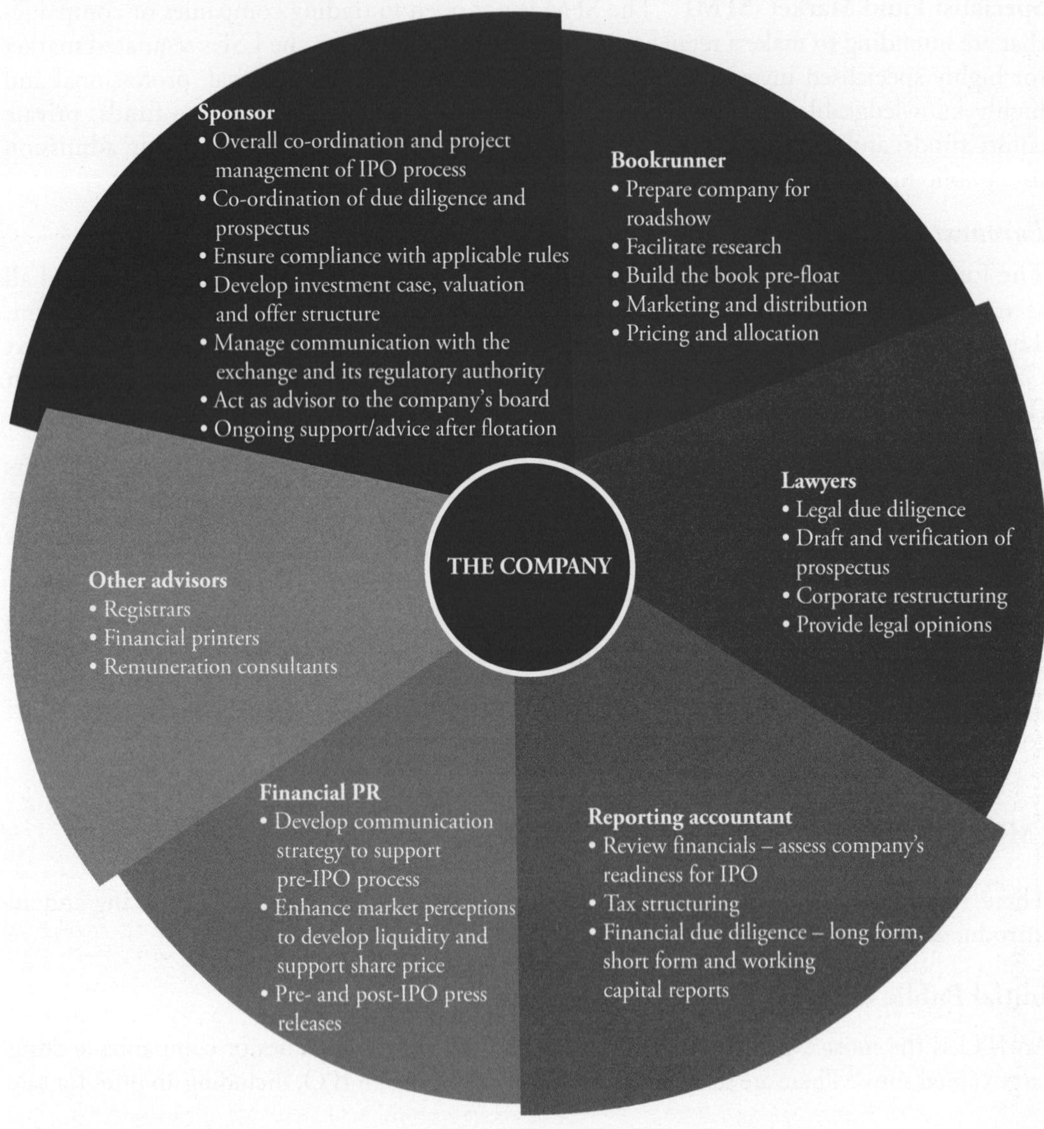
Sponsor
• Overall co-ordination and project management of IPO process
• Co-ordination of due diligence and prospectus
• Ensure compliance with applicable rules
• Develop investment case, valuation and offer structure
• Manage communication with the exchange and its regulatory authority
• Act as advisor to the company's board
• Ongoing support/advice after flotation
Bookrunner
• Prepare company for roadshow
• Facilitate research
• Build the book pre-float
• Marketing and distribution
• Pricing and allocation
Lawyers
• Legal due diligence
• Draft and verification of prospectus
• Corporate restructuring
• Provide legal opinions
THE COMPANY
Other advisors
• Registrars
• Financial printers
• Remuneration consultants
Financial PR
• Develop communication strategy to support pre-IPO process
• Enhance market perceptions to develop liquidity and support share price
• Pre- and post-IPO press releases
Reporting accountant
• Review financials – assess company's readiness for IPO
• Tax structuring
• Financial due diligence – long form, short form and working capital reports

[3] Source: London Stock Exchange, *A Guide to Listing on the London Stock Exchange* (November 2010), p. 10.

Offer for Sale by Prospectus

An **offer for sale by prospectus** is the most expensive method of issuing shares to the public and is obligatory if the sums being sought publicly exceed £30 million. There are three main steps to the process, as highlighted in **Figure 14.8**.

FIGURE 14.8: THE OFFER FOR SALE BY PROSPECTUS PROCESS

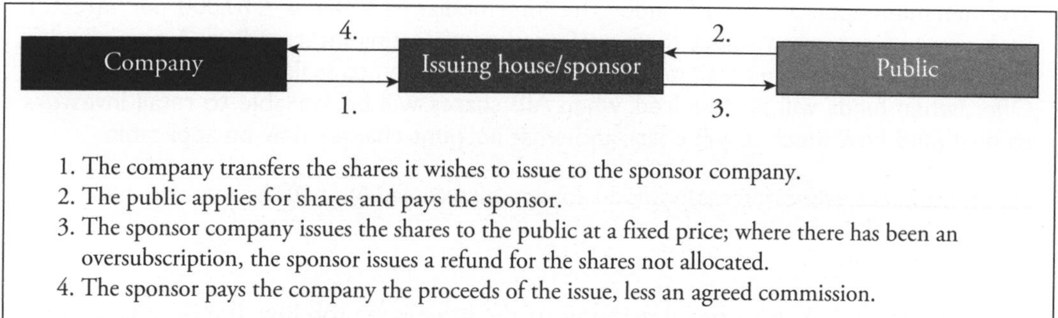

1. The company transfers the shares it wishes to issue to the sponsor company.
2. The public applies for shares and pays the sponsor.
3. The sponsor company issues the shares to the public at a fixed price; where there has been an oversubscription, the sponsor issues a refund for the shares not allocated.
4. The sponsor pays the company the proceeds of the issue, less an agreed commission.

There are many other parties involved in preparing and guiding the process. A full prospectus and application form will have to be prepared and advertised in the national press. Therefore, the company will require the services of accountants, solicitors, advertisers, graphic designers and a broker, as well as the sponsor company. Some of these parties will help the company to come up with a suitable price at which to offer the shares to the public. Brokers/bookrunners provide specialist advice on the timing of the issue, given that the market, hence market price, can be impacted by many factors that are outside the control of the company. When the issue is large, more than one bookrunner may be involved. A high-profile offer for sale by prospectus was the IPO of Allied Irish Bank (AIB), as highlighted in **Real World Example 14.2**.

REAL WORLD EXAMPLE 14.2: ALLIED IRISH BANK IPO

Extract from the Information on the Sale of AIB Shares by the Minister for Finance

Information on the Sale

On 30 May 2017, the Minister for Finance announced his intention to proceed with an initial public offering (the "IPO" or the "Offer") of Allied Irish Banks, p.l.c. ("AIB") by selling AIB shares to institutional and retail investors … The Offer involves the offer by the Minister for Finance alone of existing ordinary shares in AIB. AIB will not issue any new ordinary shares in connection with the Offer. Accordingly, existing AIB shareholders will not suffer dilution as a result of the Offer. The Offer will be open to eligible institutional and retail investors.

Retail Investors

A retail investor is a private investor who is not an institutional investor. Retail investors resident or incorporated in Ireland or the United Kingdom who wish to participate in the Offer are required to apply for AIB shares being offered by the Minister for Finance through the participating intermediaries appointed by the Minister for Finance (the "Intermediaries Offer").

The minimum application size under the Intermediaries Offer is €10,000 per investor. Each retail investor can select their preferred participating intermediary. A participating intermediary can inform retail investors of how and when to make an application for the Offer; when funds will be required; when AIB shares will be available to retail investors to deal (and how much it will cost); and what account charges may be applicable.

Source: https://aib.ie/investorrelations/ipo-information; accessed April 2020.

Getting the price right is a crucial decision. If the price is set too low, the issue will damage the wealth of existing equity holders; if it is set too high, the company runs the risk of the full issue not being taken up. The latter is hedged against because the sponsor company usually **underwrites** the issue. This is a form of insurance, which guarantees the company the full amount of the capital it wishes to raise by contracting with the sponsor company to purchase all the shares that have not been taken up by the public. To reduce its exposure, the sponsor company usually **sub-underwrites** the issue by contracting with several other intermediaries to take up a portion of the issue where a residual of shares remain after the issue. This rarely happens in practice. If it were to happen to a company, it would severely damage the company's ability to raise funds by an equity issue in the future. However, some sponsor companies use stabilising methods to effectively underwrite an IPO. **Stabilising** happens when the sponsor company, or its sub-underwriters, purchase large quantities of the new issue on the market at a price not exceeding the issue price. It is allowed by law, though it is seen as a form of price manipulation and reduces the transparency of the market, as the purchaser is not made known.

Offer for Sale by Subscription

An **offer for sale by subscription** is similar to an offer for sale by prospectus, except that it is partially underwritten. This method is usually used by new companies that have problems getting a full underwritten agreement from their sponsor. If insufficient public demand materialises, the company has the option to abort the issue.

Issue by Tender

This method is popular in the US. It has been used in the UK where there are no comparable companies listed on the stock exchange to use as a guide when pricing the shares. The process for an **issue by tender** is exactly the same as that outlined above for an offer for sale by subscription, except that the price of the issue is not fixed. The same parties are involved and, as a result, the costs are also high; however, they are not as high as the costs of an offer for sale by prospectus. In this scenario, members of the public are invited to tender for the shares.

They get one shot at it. When the tenders are received by the sponsor company, a strike price is determined. This takes into account the weight of applications at the prices bid. The **strike price** is the price at which the shares will be sold. It is determined by supply and demand and therefore there is less chance of the shares being underpriced (as long as management has produced sufficient information in the prospectus and application to reduce any information asymmetry about the future earnings of a company). Any bidders who offered the strike price or above will be awarded shares; any bidders who offered an amount below the strike price do not qualify for any shares on issue and they will have to wait until the shares start trading on the exchange before they can purchase them. Any bidders who offered sums above the strike price will be allocated the number of shares requested at the strike price and given a refund for the surplus.

Placing

Becoming public can also be achieved by a **private issue**. This avenue is open to well established, large companies with strong reputations. In these instances, the companies can forego the large costs of a public issue and go for a **private placing**. There are three main types of placing: a sponsor offer, an intermediaries placing and vendor placing.

Sponsor Offer

A private placing is usually organised by an intermediary (a broker firm or an issuing house/sponsor). In these circumstances, an intermediary buys all the shares from the company at a fixed price and places them with selected clients. This is a less expensive method of getting shares quoted on a stock exchange. It usually costs about 5% of the total funds raised. It is commonly used by smaller companies seeking a listing on the AIM. The process is outlined in **Figure 14.9**.

FIGURE 14.9: PLACING PROCESS

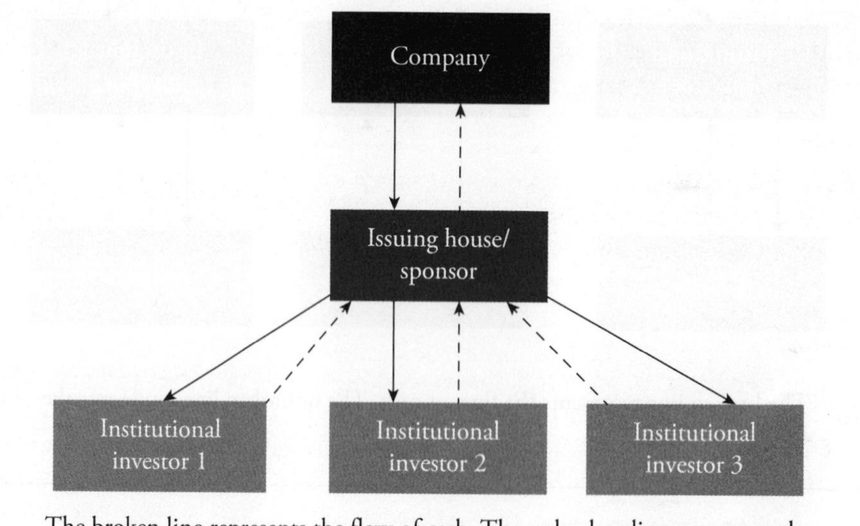

The broken line represents the flow of cash. The unbroken line represents the transfer of shares.

The public has to wait until official share trading begins on the stock exchange before it can purchase shares in the company. To ensure marketability of the shares, the stock exchange usually requires that several institutional investors are involved in the initial placing. These large investors are usually pension companies, insurance companies, stockbroker companies, merchant banks and commercial banks. The sponsor invites them to take up the shares on issue. There is a risk that there will be fewer trades in shares when the company is admitted to market due to the small number of initial investors.

Intermediaries Offer

Another variant of the placing method is the **intermediaries offer**. This approach effectively cuts out the role of the sponsor company and the broker. It is only an option for large, very reputable companies. The issue is not underwritten and hence is less costly. In this instance, the company approaches several large institutional investors and brokers and asks them to tender for shares. The brokers and institutions subsequently sell the shares to their clients. When using this approach, the resultant number of equity holders can be quite low – hence fewer trades are likely when the company is admitted to the securities market. To counteract this, the stock exchange usually insists that a large number of final equity holders should result. The process is shown in **Figure 14.10**.

FIGURE 14.10: INTERMEDIARIES OFFER PROCESS

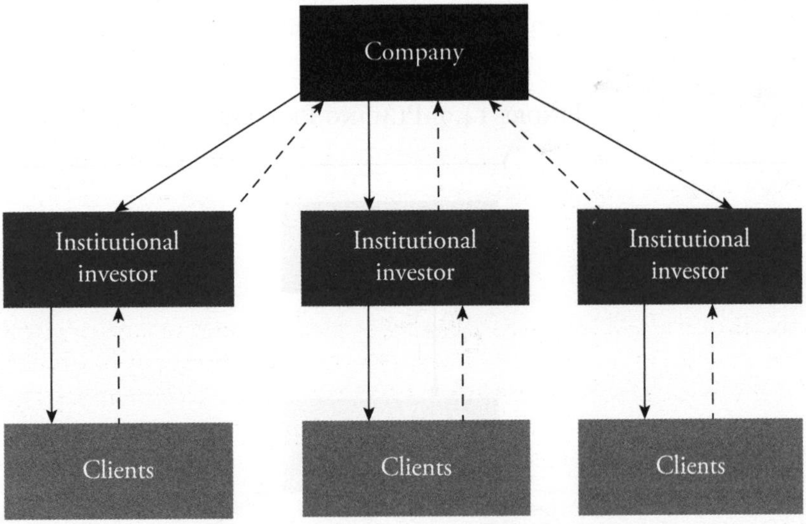

Company

Institutional investor | Institutional investor | Institutional investor

Clients | Clients | Clients

The broken line represents the flow of cash. The unbroken line represents the transfer of shares.

Vendor Placing

A **vendor placing** occurs when a company wishes to purchase another company using a share issue, but the other company wants to receive cash for its shares (it does not want to hold the purchasing company's shares on its books). The process is achieved by the following steps. The purchasing company issues shares to the company being purchased, in return for all its shares. The company being purchased then sells the shares to an institutional investor, for cash. Therefore, the purchasing company gains a new subsidiary in return for shares and the subsidiary's equity holders get cash from selling the shares on to an institutional investor. The agreement with the institutional investor is usually pre-arranged.

Stock Exchange Introduction

A **stock exchange introduction** is usually only available to companies that are already listed, or have over 25% of their shares already held by the public and these equity holders do not wish to sell their holdings. In these instances, the remaining shares are introduced to the market. Investors in the new market will purchase the shares from the existing equity holders. The price will be determined by demand for the shares relative to the willingness of the current equity holders to sell at the price offered. This method is the cheapest as no money changes hands, there are no underwriting fees, there is no need to prepare a prospectus and limited advertising is required. It normally occurs when companies that are quoted on the AIM wish to transfer their holding to the main market to gain access to a wider investor pool. Indeed, some companies make the strategic decision to join the AIM, with the objective of getting an introduction to the main market in the future.

EQUITY ISSUES AFTER INITIAL LISTING

After a company is listed on an official exchange, it is easier, and not as costly, to obtain finance from further share issues. The most common method used to issue further equity shares is a rights issue.

Rights Issue

A **rights issue** invites the existing equity holders to subscribe for new shares in the same proportions as their existing equity holdings. Therefore, if a company has 2,000,000 issued equity shares and decides to issue a further 1,000,000 equity shares, an equity holder will be entitled to purchase one additional share in the company for every two shares currently held. This would be called a 'one for two' rights issue. Companies that are already listed time the issue carefully to ensure that the market is high when the issue is made, hence maximising the cash the company receives from the issue. To encourage equity holders to take up a new issue, the company normally issues the shares at a discount of 15–20% of the current market price.

Companies typically have to issue shares using a rights issue because equity holders legally have **pre-emptive rights** to new shares (exceptions can apply; for example, pre-emptive rights do not apply when there is an allotment of bonus shares, or if the allotment of shares is part of an employee's share scheme). Pre-emptive rights allow existing equity holders to retain their relative ownership portion of a company. Pre-emptive rights can be waived by a special resolution, supported by greater than 75% of the equity holders in attendance at an Annual General Meeting (AGM). Where this agreement is sought, the new shares cannot be issued at a discount of greater than 10% of market price, so that current equity holder wealth is protected to some extent.

Valuing Rights/Equity Holdings

When a company makes a rights issue, the process is intended to ensure that no equity holder is disadvantaged, even where they do not take up a rights issue. To make this work, a value is placed on the right to purchase the new shares. The existing equity holders have three options: they can purchase the new shares at a discount; sell the right to purchase the shares at a discount; or do nothing, in which case the company sells the right to purchase the shares on behalf of the equity holder, forwarding the proceeds less any costs of sale. The following example is provided to show how the process works and how equity holder value is affected. The market price at which shares are expected to trade after a rights issue is called the **theoretical ex-rights price**.

Worked Example 14.1: Rights Issue

Rojo Plc has recently announced a 'one-for-four' rights issue. The price of a share before the announcement was €/£3.00 and the current equity holders will be given pre-emptive rights to purchase new shares at €/£2.00 each.

Requirement

(a) Calculate the theoretical ex-rights price.
(b) Calculate the value of each right (assuming it is attached to an existing share).
(c) Calculate the price at which each equity holder can sell their right (i.e. the value of the right, assuming it is attached to a new share).
(d) An equity holder owns 1,000 shares. Calculate the value and number of shares in their possession before and after the rights issue, assuming that the equity holder purchases the new shares.
(e) An equity holder owns 1,000 shares. Calculate the value of their holding after the rights issue, assuming that the equity holder sells the rights.
(f) Assume the equity holder is short of cash. Calculate the number of rights the equity holder has to sell to provide cash to purchase the balance available to them. Show the value and number of shares in their possession after the rights issue.
(g) Assume the equity holder does nothing. Calculate the value and number of shares in their possession before and after the rights issue and the monies given to them by the company.

Solution

(a) Each lot of four shares is currently worth: 4 × €/£3.00	€/£12.00
One new issue will be priced at: 1 × €/£2.00	€/£2.00
The total holding is worth	€/£14.00

Therefore, after the issue the theoretical ex-rights share price expected will be: €/£14.00÷5 | €/£2.80

(b) The value of the right attached to each existing share will be:

€/£3.00 – €/£2.80 = €/0.20 per existing share.

(c) The value of the right were it assumed to be attached to the new share is:

= €/£2.80 – €/£2.00 = €/£0.80 per new share.

This can also be found by multiplying the existing shares required to qualify for a new share by the value of the rights per current share: €/£0.20 × 4 = €/£0.80

(d) *Before:* the equity holder owned 1,000 shares valued at €/£3.00 per share:

1,000 × €/£3.00	€/£3,000

To have received the 250 new shares, the equity holder will have to pay the company:

250 × €/£2.00	€/£500

After: the equity holder will own: 1,250 [1,000 + (1,000 ÷ 4)] shares valued at €/£2.80. The total holding will be worth:

1,250 × €/£2.80	€/£3,500

Therefore, the equity holder's wealth has not increased, but the company will have €/£500 additional cash to invest in projects.

(e) *Before:* the equity holder owned 1,000 shares valued at €/£3.00 per share:

1,000 × €/£3,000	€/£3,000

After: the equity holder decides to sell his rights. He is issued with 250 rights, which he can sell for €/£0.80 each, so he gets cash worth:

250 × €/£0.80	€/£200

He still has his 1,000 shares, though they are worth €/£2.80 each after the issue:

1,000 × €/£2.80	€/£2,800
Total equity holder value:	€/£3,000

(f) The number of shares the equity holder can purchase can be calculated using the following formula:

$$\frac{\textbf{Rights price} \times \textbf{Number of shares allotted}}{\textbf{Theoretical ex-rights price}}$$

(€/£0.80 × 250) ÷ €/£2.80 = 71 shares

Therefore, the equity holder will have to sell (250 – 71), i.e. 179 rights, providing him with cash of:

179 × €/£0.80	€/£143.20

He will use this to purchase 71 shares at €/£2.00 each:

71 × €/£2.00	€/£142.00

(The difference is due to rounding.)

After the sale, the equity holder will have:

1,071 shares valued at €/£2.80	€/£2,998.80

(Equivalent to his original investment of €/£3,000 – there is a small rounding difference.)

(g) The company will sell the rights at an auction and reimburse the equity holder the proceeds, net of costs incurred in selling the rights: €/£0.80 × 250 = €/£200

A payment of €/£200, less any auction fees, will be issued to the equity holder by the company.

Scrip Issues

A **scrip issue** involves issuing shares to existing equity holders, in proportion to their existing holding. A scrip issue does not involve the transfer of any cash; it splits the value of equity into smaller portions.

A scrip issue is otherwise known as a **bonus issue** or a **capitalisation issue**. When accounting for a scrip issue, funds from a company's reserves are converted into shares, which are then issued to equity holders. The company is converting past profits not paid out as dividends into equity share capital. This is an accounting adjustment.

Worked Example 14.2: Scrip Issue

Rojo Plc has recently announced a 'one-for-four' bonus issue. The price of shares before the announcement was €/£3.00.

Requirement An equity holder owns 1,000 shares. Calculate the total value, value per share and number of shares in his possession before and after the bonus issue.

Solution

Before: 1,000 × €/£3.00	€/£3,000
The equity holder is issued with (1,000 ÷ 4) 250 shares	
After: the equity holder will have 1,250 shares worth:	€/£3,000
The value per share will fall to: €/£3,000÷1,250	€/£2.40

The main reason for this type of transaction is to reduce the market price of individual shares in order to make them more marketable.

Share Splits

This is similar to a scrip issue, except that the nominal value of all the shares in the company is reduced or split. The aim of a **share split** is to reduce the market price of the share, which should make the shares more marketable and improve the volume of trading in shares.

WORKED EXAMPLE 14.3: SHARE SPLIT

Rojo Plc has recently announced a 'two-for-one' share split. The price of shares before the announcement was €/£3.00. The nominal value of each share before the split was €/£1.00.

Requirement An equity holder owns 1,000 shares. Calculate the total market value, market value per share, nominal value per share and number of shares in his possession before and after the bonus issue.

Solution

Before: the equity holder has 1,000 €/£1.00 equity shares valued at €/£3.00:

1,000 × €/£3.00	€/£3,000

The equity holder is issued with (1,000 × 2) 2,000 new shares and the old shares are cancelled.

After: the equity holder will now have 2,000 50c/p equity shares valued at:	€/£3,000
The market value per share will be: €/£3,000 ÷ 2,000	€/£1.50

PREFERENCE SHARES

Preference shares are part of a company's share capital; however, they are not usually regarded as equity. They have similar characteristics. They may be issued at a premium above their nominal value, the dividend can be waived and they can be traded in the markets. However, they usually carry a fixed dividend (a percentage of the nominal value), do not confer voting rights to their holders (unless the dividend goes into arrears, or the company goes into liquidation, whereupon they have the same voting rights as creditors), may be redeemable or may be convertible. Like any public share issue, raising finance by issuing preference shares is costly and the return required by preference shareholders is quite high (higher than the return required by bond holders, though not as high as the return required by equity holders). This is connected to the risks faced by each type of security holder. Preference shareholders rank after debt and bondholders, but in front of equity holders, when it comes to the payment of interest and dividends and also on the liquidation of a company. Therefore, the risk preference shareholders face is not as great as the risk faced by equity holders – hence the return required is less. Several types of preference shares can be issued, as highlighted in **Figure 14.11**.

Figure 14.11: Types of Preference Shares

Irredeemable preference shares

Carry a fixed dividend and are not intended to be redeemed or converted into shares by the company. The shareholders can sell the shares in the markets to liquidate their capital.

Redeemable preference shares

Are issued for a set period of time. When the redemption date arrives, the company pays the holder of the preference shares the nominal value of the shares.

Cumulative preference shares

Provide protection to the shareholder over their yearly claim on the dividend distribution. The dividend becomes a liability when it is waived. Dividends cannot be paid to equity holders until the total of the cumulative preference dividends outstanding are honoured.

Non-cumulative preference shares

When dividends on non-cumulative preference shares are waived, the shareholders lose their right to the dividend for that year.

Participating preference shares

The holders can 'participate' in the gains of a company, when it performs well. This makes these shares more attractive to potential investors.

Convertible preference shares

May be converted to equity share capital at some specified date in the future or if the company achieves pre-determined performance targets. They are usually converted at a premium so that current equity holders are not disadvantaged.

Classifying Preference Shares

When it comes to accounting for preference shares, difficulties arise. Under international accounting standards, preference shares have to be categorised as either debt or equity and included in the appropriate section of a company's statement of financial position. However, preference shares cannot be categorically classified as either element. In practice, the terms of each preference share issue have to be reviewed and aligned as either more like debt or more like equity. **Figure 14.12** highlights characteristics that can be used to class preference shares as either debt or equity.

Preference Shares: Investor's Perspective

Preference shares are attractive to investors because they provide a fixed yearly return that is in excess of the return earned on bonds. They rank in front of equity when it comes to having their claims met. When preference shares are issued by public issue, a readily

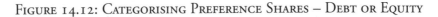

FIGURE 14.12: CATEGORISING PREFERENCE SHARES – DEBT OR EQUITY

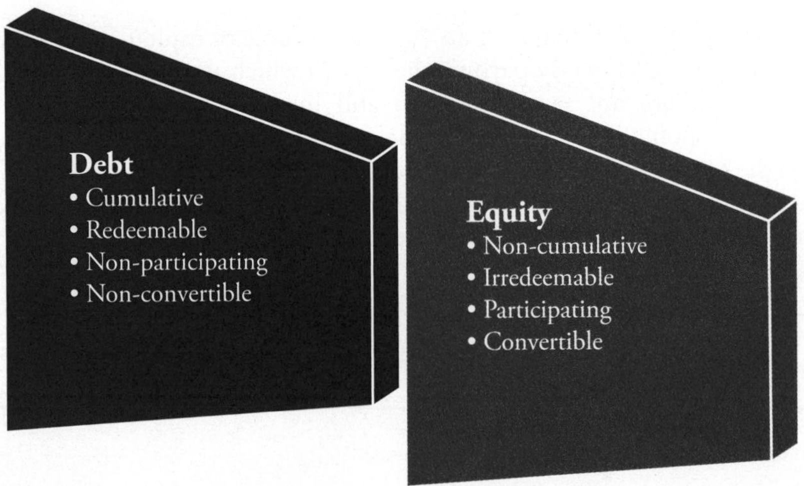

available market exists; therefore, investors have an exit avenue at all times. The liquidity makes them attractive. When preference shares are convertible, there is an added attraction: they may be converted into equity share capital if the company performs well. Thereafter, the investor will be able to share in the fortunes of the successful company. Where the shares are redeemable, the investors are certain of getting a set cash flow on a specified date. So long as the company is not in financial difficulties, this allows investors to plan and manage their cash flows.

On the down side, preference shares are more risky than bond investments. They rank behind bond investments, both in terms of yearly distributions and on liquidation. In addition, preference shareholders do not usually benefit when a company performs well (unless they are participating), as their dividend is fixed.

Preference Shares: Company's Perspective

Companies also find preference shares attractive because dividends can be waived. Even where dividends are cumulative and have to be paid at some point in the future, the fact that they can be waived provides the company with assurance that cash can be retained in the business for operating activity purposes when there are liquidity problems – dividends can be paid at a later stage when the liquidity issues are resolved. In addition, preference shares do not confer ownership rights on the holder; therefore, issuing them does not upset the ownership structure of a company. This is particularly important where the current dominant equity holders support management decision-making. When the company does well, unlike equity holders, preference shareholders cannot make a claim for a larger return; their dividend is set (unless they hold participating shares). This allows management to retain more funds for investment, resulting in more capital growth and a rise in the share price of equity shares, or allows an even greater dividend to be distributed to equity holders. Where preference shares are convertible, gearing will be improved after the conversion date. This may relax restrictive covenants and allow management the option of raising additional finance, which they can use to take on more investments, resulting in growth. Finally, preference shares are another possible source of finance when the company is highly geared and has problems raising debt finance.

On the downside, preference shares are an expensive source of capital. They cost more than debt to issue, have a higher yearly payout (the cost of which is accentuated by the fact that preference dividends are not tax deductible) and in many cases have to be repaid, or converted, at some point in the future. If they are redeemable, this may cause cash flow problems for the company. If they are convertible, the ownership structure of the company may change, resulting in a change in the control of the company. The next example highlights the difference in cost between preference shares and bonds to a company.

WORKED EXAMPLE 14.4: PREFERENCE SHARES

A Plc has the following capital structure:	**€/£000**
Equity shares of 50c/p each	5,200
Reserves	4,850
9% preference shares	4,500
14% debentures	5,000
	19,550

The preference shares are trading at 63c/p and the debentures (irredeemable) at par. Corporation tax is 33%.

Requirement

(a) Calculate the cost of the preference shares and the debentures to the company.

(b) Assume that, instead of the 14% debentures, the company raised the €/£5 million by way of preference shares giving the same yield as the existing preference shares. What is the effect on earnings available to the equity holders?

(Based on Chartered Accountants Ireland, MABF II, Autumn 1997, Extract from Question 5(b))

Solution

(a) Cost of preference shares. This is calculated as the yearly dividend divided by the market price per share (see **Chapter 15**). In this instance, this is 9c/p ÷ 63c/p = 14.29%. The cost of the debentures to the company is the interest (less tax) divided by the market price per debenture (see **Chapter 13**). In this instance, this is €/£14(1 − 0.33)/€/£100 = 9.38%. This shows that the cost of debt (9.38%) is lower than the cost of the preference shares (14.29%) to the company.

(b) The current situation means that the equity holders have to forego the following amount of earnings to service the debentures:

	€/£
Yearly interest charge: €/£5,000,000 × 14%	700,000
Less reduction in tax in the year: €/£700,000 × 33%	231,000

Net earnings cost of the debenture to the company	469,000
To raise €/£5,000,000 the company would need to issue:	

€/£5,000,000 ÷ €/£0.63 = 7,936,508 preference shares. The yearly cost then would be the dividend payable on these new shares. The dividend is 9c/p per year.

Yearly dividend charge: 7,936,508 × €/£0.09	€/£714,286
Therefore, the earnings available for distribution to the equity holders will fall by: €/£714,286 − €/£469,000	€/£245,286

CONCLUSION

Raising equity capital is time-consuming and can be expensive. There are different approaches to obtaining equity funding and the appropriate method depends on the characteristics of the company (for example, its age, size, financial strength and reputation) and the funding being sought (for example, the cost of an offer for sale by prospectus is great and it would only make economic sense to use this option when the finance requirement is extensive). It is a complicated decision which requires expert help (particularly where an IPO is being considered). Raising equity finance can take anything from three months to over a year to complete. As it is costly, it is important that a company is ready for it in advance; indeed, as a prospectus requires three years' financial information, the company should be gearing up for an issue for this period of time. Steps taken can include: preparing financial statements in accordance with international financial reporting standards and setting up the structures within the company to enable it to comply with the stock exchange regulations; giving a suitably qualified person responsibility for preparing the company for flotation; getting advice from market advisors, including the stock exchange's own advisors; and deciding on the best approach to achieving the most beneficial IPO for the company.

EXAMINATION STANDARD QUESTION: PREFERENCE SHARES

Requirement Outline briefly the major functions performed by the capital market and explain the importance of each function in assisting corporate financial management.

7 Marks

(Based on Chartered Accountants Ireland, MABF II, Autumn 2007, Q6(a))

Solution

The capital market performs the following functions:

- It enables new capital (debt and equity) to be raised through the issue of securities. This provides the financial manager with funds as required.
- It is a complex web of intermediaries that act as middlemen between those requiring funds (the companies/finance managers) and those with funds to invest (investors). Consequently, the finance manager does not need to know each of the investors personally, so raising funds can be done much more efficiently.

- It acts as a means of allocating/transferring risk efficiently. Investors who require a safe return (for example, short-term deposits) can invest their funds in banks, which then can lend the funds through the capital markets to risky companies over longer periods. The banks assume any risk of non-payment, which they can manage by insisting on collateral, restrictive covenants, etc. Thus finance managers of risky businesses can obtain funds.
- It provides an outlet where excess cash can be invested, thereby earning a return for the company while a decision is taken on what to do with the excess cash.
- Since many of the securities are traded, an efficient price for the security is obtained. This will help the finance manager of an acquisitive company if it is intending to purchase another company.
- In the case of the equity markets, it provides a mechanism whereby one company can purchase another company without necessarily paying cash – it can instead satisfy the shareholders of the target company with shares in its company. This provides the finance manager of an acquisitive company with greater options when trying to finance expansion.
- In cases where securities are traded, the capital markets will allow the finance manager to calculate and monitor the cost of capital. This will provide the finance manager with a yardstick when evaluating the investment opportunities available to the firm. In addition, it provides discipline on the activities of the finance manager and the company as all actions will be judged by the market.

Key Terms

Alternative Investment Market
Bonus issue
Bookrunner
Capitalisation issue
Convertible preference shares
Cumulative preference shares
Equity
Euronext Access & Access+
Euronext Dublin
Euronext Growth
Face value
Golden shares
Initial public offering (IPO)
Intermediaries offer
Irish Stock Exchange Quotation (ISEQ)
Irredeemable preference shares
Issue by tender
London Stock Exchange
Main Market
Market makers
Market value
Nominal value
Nominated advisor
Nominated broker
Non-convertible preference
Non-cumulative preference shares
Non-voting equity shares
Offer for sale by prospectus
Offer for sale by subscription
Ordinary share capital
Over-the-counter market
Par value
Participating preference shares
Pecking order theory
Placing
Pre-emptive rights
Preference shares
Preferred ordinary shares
Price sensitive information
Private issue
Private placing
Professional Securities Market
Prospectus
Realised earnings
Redeemable preference shares
Retained earnings
Revaluation reserve
Revenue reserves

Rights issue
Scrip issue
Share split
Specialist Fund Market
Sponsor
Stabilising
Stock exchange introduction
Strike price
Sub-underwriters
Theoretical ex-rights price
Underwrite
Vendor placing

REVIEW QUESTIONS

(See Suggested Solutions to Review Questions in **Appendix B**.)

Question 14.1

Explain the difference between the book value, nominal value and market value of equity.

Question 14.2

Describe, in brief, the main stock exchanges in the UK and Ireland.

Question 14.3

List the advantages and disadvantages of flotation.

Question 14.4

Explain the term 'pre-emptive rights'.

Question 14.5

A company has made yearly profits of €/£2,000,000. It pays corporation tax at 40%.

The company is considering raising €/£2,000,000 redeemable preference shares or redeemable debentures to finance its long-term growth needs. To obtain an issue price worth par, the company has to offer a fixed dividend on the preference shares of 9c/p per €/£1 share, or a fixed coupon of 14% on each debenture.

Requirement Calculate which alternative is cheaper to the company in terms of the yearly impact on earnings available for distribution to the equity holders.

Question 14.6

Amarillo Plc has recently announced a 'one-for-two' rights issue. The price of the shares before the announcement was €/£5.00 and the current equity holders will be given pre-emptive rights to purchase new shares at €/£4.00.

Requirement

(a) Calculate the theoretical ex-rights price.
(b) Calculate the value of each right (assuming it is attached to each existing share).
(c) Calculate the price at which each equity holder can sell their right (value the right assuming it is attached to the new share).
(d) An equity holder owns 2,000 shares. Calculate the value and number of shares in their possession before and after the rights issue, assuming that they purchase the new shares.
(e) Calculate the value of the holding after the rights issue, assuming that the equity holder sells the rights.
(f) Assume the equity holder is short of cash. Calculate the number of rights the equity holder has to sell to provide cash to purchase the balance available. Show the value and number of shares in their possession after the rights issue.
(g) Assume the equity holder does nothing. Calculate the value and number of shares in their possession before and after the rights issue and the monies given to them by the company.

CHALLENGING QUESTIONS

(Suggested Solutions to Challenging Questions are available through your lecturer.)

Question 14.1 Tom Higgins (Level 1)

Tom Higgins has been running a successful business for the last five years and has just decided to incorporate. He is not sure about the different methods available to raise long-term and medium-term finance or how best to proceed and he has asked your advice on the following matters.

Requirement

(a) Describe the features of ordinary share capital as a long-term source of finance for a company.

4 Marks

(b) Compare the features of ordinary share capital with preference share capital as a source of long-term finance.

6 Marks

(c) A company can raise various other types of finance. Explain your understanding of the following terms (you will have to review **Chapter 11** to answer this part):
(i) Bills of exchange.
(ii) Factoring of receivables.
(iii) Hire purchase.

5 Marks
Total 15 Marks

(Based on Chartered Accountants Ireland, CAP 1, Finance, Autumn 2011, Q4)

Question 14.2 Tideflow (Level 1)

A small company, Tideflow Ltd, has developed a new generator of renewable energy. The equipment has been developed using the company's own resources. The results of initial testing have exceeded expectations and market research indicates the probability of high sales volumes. A significant amount of additional capital is now needed to finance production over the next 10 years.

Tideflow's current shareholders are senior managers of the company and have limited personal financial resources, with one exception, the human resource manager, J. Duddy, who is very wealthy.

Requirement

(a) State TWO advantages and TWO disadvantages of equity funding from the company's point of view.

6 Marks

(b) Outline FOUR types of finance likely to be available to Tideflow and indicate the sources from which they might be obtained.

7 Marks

(c) Identify FIVE issues that should be considered when selecting long-term finance in circumstances such as this.

5 Marks

(d) Of the four types of finance identified in (b) above, state with reasons which source is likely to be most suitable to Tideflow in its particular circumstances.

2 Marks
Total 20 Marks

(Based on Chartered Accountants Ireland, CAP 1, Summer 2009, Q1)

Question 14.3 Drainco (Level 2)

The current equity holders of Drainco have suggested that in three years' time they would like to sell their equity holdings and dispose of the company. This would likely occur by either a trade sale (i.e. sale to a competitor), or a flotation of the company on a recognised stock exchange. They have asked you for your advice on the merits of each type of disposal.

Requirement Prepare an Internal Memorandum to the Board advising on the relative merits of both a trade sale and a flotation of the business, as a means of disposing of the equity holders' ownership of Drainco.

14 Marks

(Based on Chartered Accountants Ireland, MABF, FAE, Extract from Autumn 2006)

Question 14.4 Bourne (Level 2)

Bourne intends to raise additional capital to fund investment in several projects over the next year. Part of this financing plan involves a rights issue, to raise a total of €/£1,500,000. The issue will be announced next week on the following terms: one new share for six existing shares at a discount of 30% of Bourne's current share price. Bourne's shares are currently trading at €/£3.45. Ken has held preliminary discussions with Bourne's larger shareholders over the last few weeks about Bourne's plan to raise additional equity capital. Terry Neil, Bourne's largest shareholder, with a 9% interest in Bourne, has told Ken he would not be in a position to subscribe to a rights issue.

Requirement Calculate the theoretical ex-rights share price and outline the options open to Terry Neil if Bourne proceeds with the rights issue.

6 Marks

(Based on Chartered Accountants Ireland, MABF, CAP 2, Summer 2013, Q1(h))

Question 14.5 Hexagon (Level 2)

The board of directors of Hexagon Limited has just had a stormy meeting where the future direction of Hexagon was discussed at length. No agreement was reached. The board comprises three directors: Bill O'Brien and Michaela Melvin, the founders of Hexagon, each of whom owns 33% of the equity in Hexagon. The remaining 34% of the equity is owned by Tony Long, an investor who bought shares in Hexagon when it was expanding several years ago.

Tony was pushing for a stock market flotation as he has always considered his investment in Hexagon to be a medium-term one. Hexagon has grown strongly since Tony's investment and Tony saw the current buoyancy of the stock market as an opportunity to cash-out. Tony also argued that the three directors had all of their wealth tied up in Hexagon and that this was not sensible. Bill, however, strongly believed that Hexagon was going to grow rapidly over the next few years and couldn't see the sense in sharing that growth with new investors who would buy shares at an initial public offering (IPO). Hexagon wouldn't need any funding for the foreseeable future, in fact it was generating significant profits every year, more than enough to finance any investments required. Bill saw a stock market listing as an unnecessary expense and argued that, after the listing, the three directors would no longer be able to pursue their chosen strategy for Hexagon – they would have to satisfy the market, which was obsessed with the next year's earnings.

Michaela could see merits in the proposal to float Hexagon, but had some concerns. She was not convinced the directors could get a fair price for any shares sold to new investors in an IPO and was also concerned about losing control of Hexagon and any conflict with new shareholders.

Requirement Critically assess the arguments each of the shareholders has made for and against Hexagon seeking a listing on the stock market.

6 Marks

(Based on Chartered Accountants Ireland, MABF, CAP 2, Summer 2013, Q4(c))

Question 14.6 Endorphin Ltd (Level 2)

A small company, Endorphin Ltd, has developed a new piece of medical equipment that will considerably reduce the trauma suffered by patients undergoing certain medical procedures. So far, the equipment has been developed using the company's own resources.

Market research indicates the possibility of a large volume of demand and a significant amount of additional capital being needed to finance production.

Requirement Advise the finance manager of Endorphin as follows:

(a) State the advantages and disadvantages of equity funding from the company's own point of view.

6 Marks

(b) Outline FOUR types of finance likely to be available and the sources from which they might be obtained.

6 Marks

(c) Of the sources outlined above, state which are likely to be most suitable to Endorphin in the particular circumstances of this company. Give reasons for your answer.

6 Marks

Total 18 Marks

(Based on Chartered Accountants Ireland, MABF II, Summer 2004, Q6)

Question 14.7 Bandaraya (Level 2)

Bandaraya Plc is a stock exchange listed business that owns a chain of retailers situated throughout the island of Ireland. It is currently financed principally by equity and has grown organically since its inception.

An opportunity has arisen for Bandaraya to purchase all of the shares of an unlisted business, Segar Ltd, which is in a similar line of business and has many branches in Great Britain, an area into which Bandaraya is keen to expand. The price being asked by the shareholders of Segar equals about 30% of the total market capitalisation of Bandaraya. Given the price, the perceived strategic fit, and the prospects, the directors of Bandaraya are anxious to acquire the shares.

The scale of the investment is such that Bandaraya could not raise the cash from internal sources and will have to either make a rights issue of equity shares, an issue of preference shares, or an issue of loan stock. A decision now needs to be made on the method of funding.

The minutes of a recent meeting of the board of directors, called to discuss the issue, record that the following were among the views put forward:

- Director, Ms Banda: 'Im not keen on loan finance because the interest will inevitably reduce our earnings per share and, therefore, our share price.'
- Director, Ms Raya: 'I don't want a rights issue because inevitably many of our shareholders do not want to increase their investment and will lose out as a result. Irrespective of the direct effects of a rights issue on our share price, this will have an adverse effect on the total market value of our company. An issue of loan stock seems the best idea.'
- Director, Mr Dar: 'I favour a preference share issue because it would be neutral as far as the capital gearing question is concerned; it will neither increase nor reduce it.'

The matter is listed for decision at the next board meeting.

Requirement As finance director, you are asked to provide a briefing note for the directors to read in preparation for the meeting. Your briefing note should raise all the relevant issues about the raising of finance and the points expressed by the directors at the recent meeting. This briefing note should be in simple, non-technical language. All relevant factors must be clearly explained and placed in the appropriate context.

18 Marks

(Based on Chartered Accountants Ireland, MABF II, Autumn 2006, Q7)

Question 14.8 Medicon/Schoolweb (Level 2 – case study – see also Chapter 1)

Background You are a partner in a 'Big 4' firm of Chartered Accountants that specialises in offering advice to high-growth companies, mainly in the pharmaceutical and technology sectors.

Schoolweb Ltd Michael Jones owns Schoolweb Ltd, an e-commerce company that sells a wide selection of children's schoolbooks via the internet. Schoolweb's turnover has grown rapidly since its formation in early 20X3, and Jones is keen to raise additional finance to fund a marketing campaign aimed at further increasing the awareness of its website which, in turn, should yield additional turnover.

Schoolweb is considered to operate in a higher risk industry than the pharmaceutical sector and, like many similar e-commerce companies, is currently making losses. However, revenues are projected to continue to grow significantly over the next three years, with profitability likely to be achieved within that period. Jones has undertaken to provide a business plan showing projected earnings and cash flow over the next three years, which can be used by Smith to determine if Medicon should consider investing in Schoolweb.

Flotation Michael Jones has indicated that he is keen to float Schoolweb at some point within the next couple of years. This would provide the long-term finance necessary to fund the increased size of operations that are projected over the coming years. However, given that the company is currently making losses and has only been incorporated for two years, Jones considers that Schoolweb currently does not have the necessary track record to contemplate undertaking a flotation. Given your experience of the technology sector in general, Smith has asked you to prepare a brief report on the feasibility of floating Schoolweb.

Requirement Given Michael Jones' decision to float Schoolweb within the next couple of years, advise on whether you consider flotation feasible, outlining the specific reasons for your answer.

10 Marks

(Based on Chartered Accountants Ireland, MABF, FAE, Autumn 2001, Q1)

Question 14.9 Hawk (Level 2)

Hawk has 100,000,000 shares in issue, which currently trade at €/£2.22.

Hawk is proposing a rights issue on the following terms:

- Issue price of €/£1.50;
- Total sum to be raised €/£19,000,000;
- The €/£19,000,000 will be invested in a project that is expected to add €/£1,000,000 to net profit in the first year (20X8). The returns on this project will be equal to the average return on Hawk's existing projects.

The following information is made available from Hawk's forecast financial statements for 20X8:

EXTRACTS FROM HAWK'S FORECAST FINANCIAL STATEMENTS

	Forecast 20X8
	€/£000
Turnover	195,220
Cost of sales	(126,893)
Gross profit	68,327
Expenses (excluding interest)	(38,552)
Interest	(1,502)
Profit before tax	28,273
Tax	3,534
Net profit	24,739
Dividend to be paid in 20X8	12,369

Requirement Based on the proposed rights issue details:

(a) Calculate the theoretical ex-rights share price.

(b) Calculate the percentage dilution in earnings per share.

(c) Identify an alternative approach that Hawk could use to raise equity **and** highlight TWO key differences when compared to a rights issue.

8 Marks

(Based on Chartered Accountants Ireland, CAP 2, SFMA, Autumn 2018, extract from Q1)

Part IV

COMPANY VALUE, MERGERS AND ACQUISITIONS

Chapters

15

Cost of Capital

Learning Objectives

Upon completing this chapter, readers should be able to:

- explain the cost of capital from a company's perspective and, separately, an investor's perspective;
- describe the link between a company's cost of capital and its value;
- calculate the value and cost of equity capital (using the: dividend valuation model; capital asset pricing model; book value; price earnings ratio);
- calculate the value and cost of untraded debt, redeemable traded debt and irredeemable traded debt;
- calculate the value and cost of preference shares;
- calculate the weighted average cost of capital;
- discuss the assumptions and limitations of the weighted average cost of capital; and
- explain the weighted average cost of capital's suitability for project appraisal.

INTRODUCTION

Determining a discount rate to use in the evaluation of projects is both a scientific process and an art. This chapter is mostly concerned with the scientific processes used to calculate a discount rate based on the company's weighted average cost of capital (WACC). The WACC provides an estimate of the required return that must be achieved by a company to entice its investors to retain their investment and to provide more finance to the company when it needs it. The various sources of finance have different required returns; however, if a company consistently achieves the weighted average return required by all its financiers from its investments, then the financiers will be satisfied. Where a company can obtain a return in excess of this minimum threshold, the additional return will add value to the company, which will benefit equity holders. The art (i.e. the subjective process) of determining an appropriate discount rate for evaluating a specific project/investment starts after the WACC has been determined: for example, a project being evaluated by a company may not have the same business risk as the company; therefore, a premium return above the WACC hurdle rate is required to compensate for this additional risk.

THE COST OF CAPITAL

Every investment undertaken by a company requires financing. This is normally sourced as either debt or equity capital. Each source of finance has a cost.

The **cost of capital** can be considered from two perspectives: an investor's viewpoint and a company's viewpoint. Investors regard the cost of capital as the opportunity cost of capital invested in a company. The opportunity cost is the return that can be gained by investors from reinvesting their funds in the next-best alternative. In considering the opportunity cost, investors will assess whether they are getting an appropriate return from the company, relative to the risks taken, when compared to other investments.

A company regards the cost of capital as the minimum return it has to provide to investors to induce them to retain their investment, or to supply more finance to the company when additional sources are required. Therefore, when considering whether to invest in a particular project, the returns from that project should, at a minimum, cover a company's current cost of finance. Getting the cost of capital right is vital for appropriate project appraisal. If the discount rate applied is too high, a company is likely to turn down worthy investments, resulting in damage to company profitability. If it is too low, it will result in projects being accepted with returns that are not appropriate to investors' expectations, which may cause investors to withdraw their investment.

Therefore, when calculating an appropriate discount rate to apply in investment decision-making, the business finance manager has to determine the minimum return required on investments to satisfy all investors. This is usually approximated as the weighted average cost of all the capital invested in the company.

THE WEIGHTED AVERAGE COST OF CAPITAL (WACC)

The **weighted average cost of capital (WACC)** is the overall cost of long-term funds invested in a company. When calculating the WACC, the business finance manager has to use up-to-date information, as debt and equity security holders have a freely available market in which they can trade their shares. The required return on investment should reflect the current risk and return payoff prevalent in the marketplace. Therefore, the WACC is the cost of raising new capital that would be incurred, assuming it is raised in the same proportion as the existing capital structure of a company.

A simple weighting formula may be used to calculate the WACC:

$$\text{WACC} = \frac{E(K_e)}{(D+E)} + \frac{D(K_d(1-t))}{(D+E)}$$

where E is the market value of equity, D is the market value of debt, K_e is the cost of equity, K_d is the cost of debt and t is the current tax rate.

WORKED EXAMPLE 15.1: CALCULATING THE WACC

Primavero Plc has recently had its capital valued at market rates. Its equity amounted to €/£2 million, as did its debt capital. The cost of equity is 16% and the cost of debt is 12.5%. The current tax rate is 20%.

Requirement What is the market value of Primavero Plc? What is Primavero Plc's WACC?

Solution

The market value of Primavero Plc's debt capital (*D*) is €/£2 million and the market value of its equity (*E*) is €/£2 million. A company's market value is the combined value of its long-term equity and long-term debt. In this instance, that is €/£4 million [€/£2 million + €/£2 million].

Its cost of equity (K_e) is 16% and its cost of debt (K_d) is 12.5%. The tax rate (*ct*) is 20%. Therefore, Primavero Plc's WACC is:

$$\frac{\text{€/£2m (16\%)}}{(\text{€/£2m} + \text{€/£2m})} + \frac{\text{€/£2m (12.5\%(1–20\%))}}{(\text{€/£2m} + \text{€/£2m})} = 13\%$$

THE RELATIONSHIP BETWEEN THE WACC, EARNINGS AND MARKET VALUE OF A COMPANY

From scrutiny of the WACC formula, it is clear that, theoretically, there is a direct link between the market value of a company, its earnings and the WACC. To remain attractive to its investors, a company will have to have a return equal to or in excess of its current market value multiplied by the required rate of return. So in Primavero Plc's case, a return of €/£520,000 [€/£4,000,000 × 13%] is required to keep its current investors happy.

Therefore, the WACC is a fundamental determinant of a company's market value. If the earnings and the WACC of a company are known, then the theoretical market value of the company can be calculated.

$$\textbf{Market value of a company} = \frac{\textbf{Earnings}}{\textbf{WACC}}$$

The following example is provided to emphasise the importance of managing the WACC in light of the impact of movements in it on the market value of a company.

WORKED EXAMPLE 15.2: MARKET VALUE AND THE WACC

Verano Plc has earnings of €/£1 million for the year. Its WACC is 20%. A similar company, Aotono Plc, has similar earnings and a WACC of 10%.

Requirement
(a) Calculate the market value of Verano Plc.
(b) Calculate the market value of Aotono Plc.

Solution

$$\text{(a) Verano Plc market value} = \frac{\text{€/£1,000,000}}{20\%} = \text{€/£5,000,000}$$

$$\text{(b) Aotono Plc market value} = \frac{\text{€/£1,000,000}}{10\%} = \text{€/£10,000,000}$$

As is highlighted in **Worked Example 15.2**, the lower the WACC, the higher the market value of a company, and vice versa. Therefore, a business finance manager will strive to minimise the WACC – hence maximise the market value of a company. However, it is not just a simple case of obtaining the cheapest form of finance each time a company requires finance for an investment. There are differing views as to how changes in the capital structure impact on the cost of each source of finance and the resultant WACC. This is considered in **Chapter 16**.

INVESTORS AND THE RISK–RETURN RELATIONSHIP

There is a general risk–return trade-off. The more risk associated with an investment, the higher the expected return and vice versa. Different investors will be attracted to differing risk levels. Risk-averse investors will wish to invest in more or less risk-free investments, such as government bonds. Speculative investors will be attracted to junk bonds that are very risky, but will yield high returns if they reach maturity. It is assumed, for the purpose of this chapter, that investors hold well-diversified portfolios of investments with a variety of complementary investments of differing risk levels. Hence, they will be happy to take on more risk, so long as sufficient return is offered.

EQUITY

Equity is the owners' investment in a company. On a company's statement of financial position, it is reflected in the equity (ordinary) share capital and equity reserve accounts. One of these reserve accounts is retained earnings. As discussed in **Chapter 14**, a misconception held by some managers is that retained earnings are a free source of finance. This is not the case. Retained earnings are the opportunity cost of dividends foregone by current equity holders. If equity holders had these funds, they could invest them elsewhere, hence they have an opportunity cost. Therefore, the cost of retained earnings is the same as the cost of externally held equity, except there are no issue costs. The market value of a company's equity share capital reflects the value placed on retained earnings by equity holders.

Value of Equity

As mentioned previously, a company's equity should be valued as though it were being sourced from the market at current prices. This means that the market value should not include any premium to reflect a declared dividend payment and should be reduced to reflect costs associated with issuing the shares. The market value of equity (E or P_0) is calculated as follows:

$$\boldsymbol{E \text{ or } P_0 = \textbf{Share issue price} \times \textbf{Number of shares currently in use}}$$

The **share issue price** is the current long-run market price for each equity share (ex-dividend) less issue costs. Companies usually distribute dividends twice a year. A dividend payout transfers value from a company to its equity holders. This value cannot be recouped from equity holders. Therefore, the long-run equilibrium share price will exclude a declared dividend that is about to be paid. The market value of equity shares in the period up to payment of the dividend is inflated by the amount of the dividend and is called trading **cum-dividend** (with the dividend right attached to it). When the dividend is paid, the share price falls to its perceived equilibrium level again. This is known as trading **ex-dividend** (without the dividend right attached to it).

WORKED EXAMPLE 15.3: CALCULATING THE MARKET VALUE OF EQUITY

Invierno Plc has two million issued equity shares. The current market price (cum-dividend) is 240c/p per share. The accrued dividend is 22c/p per share. A discount of 10% would be allowed on a new issue of equity shares.

Requirement Calculate the market value of Invierno Plc's shares that should be used in the calculation of its WACC.

Solution

The market value of Invierno Plc's equity shares (P_0) is:

€/£3,924,000 [((€/£2.40 − €/£0.22) × 90%) × 2,000,000].

Cost of Equity

There are various methods of valuing a company's cost of equity. It could be considered in terms of returns currently received by equity holders or returns required to compensate for risks associated with investing in a company relative to other investments. These two approaches are now considered.

Dividend Valuation Model

The return made to equity holders should maximise their wealth. Returns can either be a cash distribution (i.e. a dividend) or capital growth (i.e. retention of profits in equity reserves). The **dividend valuation model** uses the pattern of dividends paid historically to work out the return on (i.e. the cost of) a company's equity, when the market value of the company's equity shares is known. A key assumption of the dividend valuation model is that the market value placed on an equity share by equity holders is the present value of the expected future stream of dividends (to infinity) paid by a company. Therefore, the dividend valuation model is the value of a company's dividends in perpetuity. When a company distributes all its earnings each year, its dividends are constant (assuming there is no growth in earnings or dividends, hence there will be no increase in share price). The equity market will value the future stream of dividends as:

$$P_0 = \frac{D_1}{K_e}$$

where P_0 is the market value of equity, D_1 is the annual dividend and K_e is the equity holders' required return (i.e. the company's cost of equity). This formula can be rearranged to work out the return provided by a company on its equity shares (so long as the market price of the equity shares and the constant dividend amount is known).

$$K_e = \frac{D_1}{P_0}$$

Investors can use this model to decide whether or not to invest in equity shares, which provide a set dividend. By working out the return on offer, they can compare it to the expected return (given the level of risk associated with investing in the particular company). Companies can use this model to work out the current cost of their equity capital (given the dividend policy and share price are known).

Worked Example 15.4: Cost of Equity Capital: Dividend Valuation Model

Febrero Plc pays an annual dividend of 16c/p per share. The shares are currently trading at 188c/p. An interim dividend of 8c/p is about to be paid. The flotation cost of issuing new shares is 5%.

Requirement Calculate the cost of equity capital for Febrero Plc.

Solution

The first step is to calculate the market price that Febrero Plc would expect to receive on a new share issue.

$$P_0 = [(188\text{c/p} - 8\text{c/p}) \times 95\%] = 171\text{c/p}$$

The question states at Febrero Plc pays an annual dividend of 16c/p. Therefore, dividends are constant. Therefore the cost of equity (K_e) is:

$$\frac{16\text{c/p}}{171\text{c/p}} = 9.36\%$$

Growth The majority of companies retain some of their earnings, which they invest for future growth. Two different methods are used to calculate the expected growth of dividends in a company. The first assumes there is a linear relationship between retentions and growth: the more a company retains, the higher the growth levels. Higher growth leads to larger future earnings; hence higher future dividends. This relationship is expressed as follows:

$$g = br$$

where g is growth in dividends, b is the percentage of earnings that are retained for investment and r is the return on the company's investments, i.e. the ROCE.

The second method estimates growth based on the historical pattern of dividends paid. The assumption is that growth in dividends is more or less constant from one year to the next.

There will be slight variation from the mean growth rate each year depending on the performance of a company; however, over time a constant pattern emerges. This assumption is not too unrealistic, as managers manage dividends so that they grow in line with equity holders' expectations of how they should grow. These expectations are formulated by equity holders based on projected earnings forecasts made by managers. Many companies distribute dividends that are slightly higher than those distributed in the previous year, irrespective of fluctuations in performance. For example, when a company is very profitable, a small increase in dividends usually results. When a company makes losses, the dividend level is usually maintained (see **Chapter 22** for more detail on dividend policies and their impact on equity holder wealth). The formula for calculating growth using this method is as follows:

$$g = \sqrt[y]{\frac{D_{t0}}{D_{t0-y}}} - 1$$

where g is the growth rate, D_{t0} is the dividend that has just been paid and D_{t0-y} is the dividend that was paid y years ago.

These models provide an estimate for growth. However, other factors should be considered. For example, a full evaluation of a company's performance using ratio analysis would provide insight into the operational performance, efficiency, liquidity and risk of a company relative to other companies in the industry. An evaluation of the management team would provide some evidence to substantiate the appropriateness of the growth rate calculated using the above formulae.

When a growth rate is estimated, this is then factored into the dividend valuation model to provide a cost of equity that takes future increases in dividends into consideration. Therefore, the dividend valuation model takes the capital appreciation of equity shares into consideration. The adjusted model is as follows:

$$K_e = \frac{D_0 (1+g)}{P_0} + g$$

In this formula D_0 is the last dividend paid, P_0 is the market value of equity on issue, g is the constant growth rate and K_e is the cost of equity capital.

Worked Example 15.5: Calculating Growth

Junio Plc has made the following earnings and dividends over the past five years:

Year	Earnings €/£	Dividends €/£
20X2	520,000	195,000
20X3	663,000	249,600
20X4	715,000	267,800
20X5	845,000	318,500
20X6	910,000	341,055

Junio Plc has an authorised equity share capital of 2,000,000 shares, of which 50% are allotted and fully paid up. The statement of financial position of Junio Plc shows €/£3.8 million in equity capital and reserves and no long-term debt. The shares are currently trading at €/£5.00. Issue costs associated with a new allotment of shares amount to 64.5c/p per share.

Requirement

(a) Calculate the growth in Junio Plc's dividends using two different methods.
(b) Calculate the resultant cost of equity capital for Junio Plc using both growth rates.

Solution

(a) The first method adopted is to calculate growth using the retentions return formula ($g = br$). There is sufficient information provided in the question to allow the calculation of b (retentions) and r (return on capital invested).

The retentions percentage b is now calculated:

Year	Earnings €/£	Dividends €/£	Ratio €/£	Retentions %
20X2	520,000	195,000	325,000* ÷ 520,000	62.5
20X3	663,000	249,600	413,400 ÷ 663,000	62.4
20X4	715,000	267,800	447,200 ÷ 715,000	62.5
20X5	845,000	318,500	526,500 ÷ 845,000	62.3
20X6	910,000	341,055	568,945 ÷ 910,000	62.5

*Retentions are earnings less dividends paid in the year, i.e. €/£520,000 – €/£195,000

The return earned by a company is the earnings divided by the capital employed in the company r.

$$r = €/£910,000 \div €/£3,800,000$$

$$r = 23.95\%$$

Therefore growth is 62.5% × 23.95% = 14.97%

The second method of calculating growth uses the pattern of historical growth as an indicator of future growth:

$$\sqrt[4]{\frac{€/£341,055}{€/£195,000}} - 1 = 15\%$$

In this example, growth is similar using both methods.

(b) The market value of the shares to be used in the dividend valuation model has to be net of issue costs. Therefore, in Junio Plc's case, the market value is:

€/£4,355,000 [(€/£5.00 − €/£0.645) × 1,000,000]. The cost of equity is:

$$K_e = \frac{€/£341{,}055\,(1+0.147)}{€/£4{,}355{,}000} + 0.147 = 0.2368\,(23.68\%)$$

$$K_e = \frac{€/£341{,}055\,(1+0.15)}{€/£4{,}355{,}000} + 0.15 = 0.24\,(24.00\%)$$

As expected, equity holders who invest in a company that achieves a return of 24% will pay an amount that ensures they receive that return. Therefore, the market price of the shares, hence the value of the company, in this instance depends on the returns achieved and the resultant growth.

Limitations with Using the Dividend Valuation Model As with most models, the limitations with using the dividend valuation model are the assumptions that underlie the model. In particular, the proxies for growth and return are open to much variation. It could be argued that dividends do not grow smoothly and that the growth calculations are only possible when a company's dividend payout increases over time. Indeed, some companies pay zero dividends, arguing that they are better-placed to invest the earnings than equity holders are. The return they provide to equity holders is solely by capital appreciation. Dividend valuation models cannot be used to calculate the cost of equity in these circumstances.

The return variable is also open to debate. The financial statements of an enterprise disclose one return. Yet, when assessing projects, discounted cash flows are taken as the ultimate performance measure and it is argued that cash flows are a better proxy for return (Rappaport, 1986). Another view taken is that a charge for the opportunity cost of capital employed should be deduced from operating profit; this return is known as the **economic profit** (Solomons, 1965). Some financial consultants have been calculating return using a technique called **economic value added (EVA)**, wherein the earnings reported by a company are adjusted (there can be over 150 different adjustments) and a 'true' return calculated.

Capital Asset Pricing Model

A second method of determining the cost of equity capital expected on a company's shares is to evaluate the risks associated with investing in a company relative to other capital market investments. The risk associated with investing in a particular share is that the return received will be different from the return expected. There are two types of influence that lead to variations from expected return. These influences are categorised as being either specific to a company or industry (**unsystematic risk**), or affecting the whole market (**systematic risk**), as highlighted in **Figure 15.1**.

Figure 15.1: Two Risk Categories

Unsystematic risk

- Captures the exposure of a company's returns to all events that are unique or company-specific (these events are likely to result in a variation of the actual returns from expected returns).
- Examples of events that affect an industry or company include strike action by employees or a merger with another company. These events will impact on a particular company's expected return, but will not affect the whole market.
- Unsystematic risk is sometimes referred to as **business risk**.

Systematic risk

- Captures events that impact on a large number of companies' expected returns.
- For this reason, systematic risk is sometimes referred to as **market risk**.
- Macroeconomic influences, such as inflation, interest base rate changes or GDP, are considered to be examples of systematic risk. On average, all market-share returns will vary from expected returns, with the whole market either performing better or worse.

Portfolio theory suggests that an investor can diversify away unsystematic risk by holding a **well-diversified portfolio** of shares as not all the eggs will be in one basket. The larger the number of differing types of shares held, the more likely that unsystematic risk will be reduced. It is thought that holding shares in eight to 10 carefully chosen different companies is sufficient to diversify away unsystematic risk. The relationship between the number of different shares held and risk is shown in **Figure 15.2**.

Figure 15.2: Relationship between Portfolio Risk and the Number of Shares Held in a Portfolio

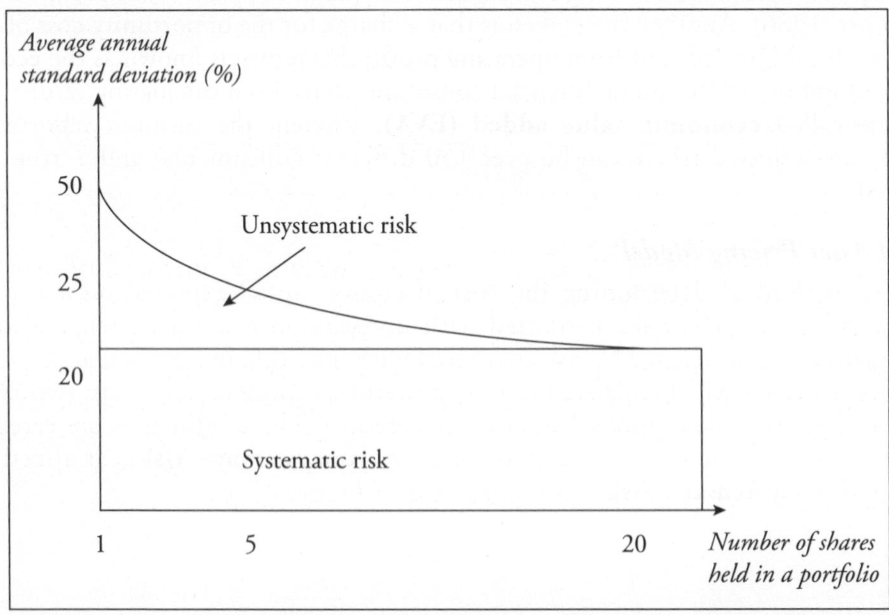

An investor who holds a portfolio with a small number of shares will be exposed to systematic risk and some unsystematic risk. Risk is measured as the average standard deviation (i.e. the average fluctuation) of actual returns from the expected mean return. Investors who hold a balanced portfolio of shares that reflect the market will only be exposed to systematic risk. Systematic risk cannot be diversified away, as shown in the above graph. It remains constant, regardless of the number of differing types of share held. As unsystematic risk can be diversified away, it is not taken into account when determining the required return on a share. Therefore, the only risk assumed to impact on the expected return from a share is systematic risk.

Though an average level of systematic risk is used to reflect overall market risk, each individual company has a different sensitivity to systematic risk. Some are more sensitive than others. Therefore, systematic risk is a key influence on the expected return from an equity share. Systematic risk is commonly measured by a beta coefficient.

Beta (β) Beta is a measure of the systematic risk of an individual equity share relative to the systematic risk experienced by the market. It is obtained by plotting the returns of a company against the returns of the market over time and estimating a line of best fit from the pattern that emerges. Beta represents the gradient of this line (see **Figure 15.3**).

FIGURE 15.3: GRAPH TO SHOW THE RELATIONSHIP BETWEEN THE RETURN OF THE MARKET AND SYSTEMATIC RISK

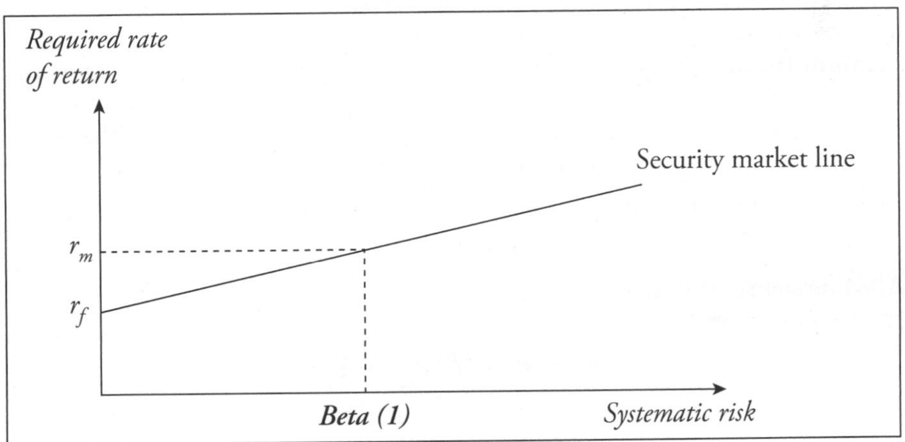

A key assumption of this measurement is that the volatility in an individual share's returns over time will consistently be more or less risky than market volatility to the same external influence, hence the volatility or expected movement in a share's return is predictable as it can be determined by observing historical behaviour. The market beta is always pegged at 1.0 (regardless of the influence of systematic risk on the expected market return). The assumed linear relationship between the expected rate of return of the market (r_m) and systematic risk (beta) is called the **security market line**. The **beta factor/coefficient** of a share represents the sensitivity of the share's return to systematic risk, relative to the market.

A company with a beta factor of 1.0 experiences the same movement in its returns as the market when factors that affect systematic risk come into play. For example, if market returns increase by 5%, then it is expected that the increase in the return on that company's shares will also increase by 5%. This company's expected return will lie on the security market line. A company with a beta factor greater than 1.0 is more sensitive to factors that affect the market. Hence, when an external stimulus causes the expected market return to increase, the returns experienced by this type of company will increase by a greater amount, and vice versa. This company's equivalent security market line will be steeper than that presented in the graph in **Figure 15.3**.

A company with a beta factor of less than 1.0 is not as sensitive as the market to factors that influence systematic risk. It will not benefit from the same level of return as the market when there is a market-wide influence that increases the expected market return, nor will it experience the same reduction in return when a market-wide influence reduces the expected market return. This company's equivalent security market line will have a smaller gradient than the security market line in **Figure 15.3**. This type of company may have its systematic risk diversified by spreading its operations across countries.

The securities market line is the graphical representation of the capital asset pricing model (CAPM). It shows the expected rate of return for an overall market as a function of systematic risk. The expected return on a share (r_j) is dependent on three factors.

1. The **risk-free rate** (r_f): it can be observed from the previous graph that for zero systematic risk, a guaranteed return is available. This is known as the risk-free rate. Investors do have the option of putting their funds into investments that have guaranteed returns, such as government bonds.
2. A **premium for accepting systematic risk** ($r_m - r_f$): investors require a return in excess of the risk-free rate to compensate them for accepting systematic risk. This is expressed as the difference between the average expected market return (r_m) and the risk-free rate (r_f), and is referred to as the **market-risk premium**.
3. The **level of systematic risk** (β): this represents the sensitivity of a particular company's returns to systematic risk, relative to the market.

The CAPM model is expressed as:

$$\boldsymbol{r_j = r_f + \beta(r_m - r_f)}$$

where r_j is the return expected from company j, r_f is the risk-free rate of return, β is the level of systematic risk and $(r_m - r_f)$ is the market-risk premium.

WORKED EXAMPLE 15.6: CAPM

Julio Plc has a beta factor of 1.2. The yield on government bonds is 6% and the market-risk premium is 5%.

Requirement Calculate Julio Plc's equity cost of capital.

Solution

$$r_j = 6\% + 1.2(5\%)$$

$$r_j = 12\%$$

In this example you are given the market-risk premium, which is $(r_m - r_f)$. The return on the market is different. In this instance r_m is: 11% [5% + 6%].

VALUING THE EQUITY OF UNQUOTED COMPANIES

Unquoted companies do not have a market value for their equity. Three methods can be used to obtain an equity value. First, the accounting-equity book value can be ascertained from the statement of financial position. However, this may not represent the true value of a company as assets may be recorded at historical cost, which may be less than their market value or not recorded at all, e.g. goodwill. Consequently, equity will be undervalued whereas debt will reflect the actual balance owed. Equity usually costs more than debt; hence underestimating the proportion of the company financed by equity will understate the WACC, which may lead to a company accepting projects it shouldn't.

WORKED EXAMPLE 15.7: UNQUOTED COMPANIES: BOOK VALUE OF EQUITY

Agosto Ltd has the following entries in its statement of financial position.

	€/£m
Equity share capital	50
Share premium account	40
Preference shares	100
Loan stock	50
Irredeemable loan stock	50
Long-term bank loan	10
Retained earnings	100
	400

Requirement Calculate the book value of Agosto Ltd's equity capital.

Solution

The equity share capital, share premium and retained earnings are equity accounts; all the others are debt. The book value of equity is, therefore, €/£190 million.

The second method is to use the **earnings per share** of an unquoted company and apply the **price earnings ratio** of a similar quoted company (adjusted to reflect the lack of marketability) to estimate the equity value.

Worked Example 15.8: Unquoted Companies: Valuing Equity Using the Price Earnings Ratio

Septiembre Ltd has 2,000,000 issued equity shares. Its earnings per share are 28c/p. The price earnings ratio of Enero Plc, a similar quoted company, is 10. It is estimated that this should be reduced by 20% to allow for the fact that Septiembre Ltd's shares are not readily marketable.

Requirement Estimate the value of Septiembre Ltd's equity for inclusion in the WACC.

Solution

$$P_0 = 2{,}000{,}000 \times (€/£0.28 \times (10 \times 80\%))$$

$$P_0 = €/£4{,}480{,}000$$

Finally, as long as the cost of equity is known, the dividend valuation model can be used to determine the expected share price, hence the value of equity of an unquoted company. The dividend valuation model is rearranged to:

$$P_0 = \frac{D_0(1+g)}{K_e - g}$$

Worked Example 15.9: Unquoted Companies: Valuing Equity Using the Dividend Valuation Model

Noviembre Ltd has one million authorised equity shares, of which 50% are issued. The dividend to be paid in the next period is 18c/p. The equity holders' required return is 15% and growth is estimated at 5%.

Requirement Calculate the value of equity capital for Noviembre Ltd.

Solution

The dividend of the next period (in this case 18c/p) is D_1, which is the equivalent of $D_0(1 + g)$. The equity holders' cost of equity is 15%. Therefore, the current market price (P_0) of the shares is:

$$= \frac{18\text{c/p}}{0.15 - 0.05} = €/£1.80$$

The expected market value of equity is: €/£900,000 [500,000 × €/£1.80].

DEBT

Debt capital is part of the long-term funding of a company, which can be traded or untraded. The same principles are used to value debt as are used to value equity, i.e. the current market value and opportunity cost should be sought for input to the WACC model. The main difference is that the yearly distribution (interest) on debt capital is usually pre-arranged, non-negotiable and tax deductible. In addition, debt capital is usually repayable in either cash or equity.

Untraded Debt Capital

When long-term debt is untraded, such as a bank loan, the market value equates to the book value and the cost is the after-tax market interest rate charged. This is usually the current market rate, which is the opportunity cost to a lender. If lenders do not get the current market rate, they may either not issue funds or withdraw their funds for investment elsewhere. The after-tax rate is:

$$K_{dt} = i(1-t)$$

where K_{dt} is the cost of debt after taxation, i is the interest rate and t is the taxation rate.

Traded Debt Capital

There are two main types of traded debt capital: irredeemable and redeemable. When a company opts for raising traded debt capital, it issues bonds that are traded in the stock markets. In the UK these 'bonds' have a nominal value of £100; in the RoI the equivalent is €100. The most common type of bond is the plain vanilla bond, which carries an annual fixed interest rate. Traders will value the bond based on the coupon (i.e. the interest) on offer, compared to the returns offered by other similar types of investment.

Irredeemable Debt

When a bond is irredeemable, its interest is paid for into infinity and the bond nominal amount will not be redeemed by a company. Therefore, this is valued as the present value of a future stream of coupon cash inflows into infinity, i.e. in perpetuity:

$$D = \frac{i(1-t)}{K_d}$$

where D is the market value of the bond, i is the yearly coupon rate, t is the current tax rate and K_d is the bondholders' required return, or the cost of debt.

This calculation is usually required when bonds are first issued – when bonds are already in issue the market will dictate the bonds' market value. When this is the case, the formula can be rearranged to determine the current return expected by debt holders based on the price they are willing to pay for the future stream of income. This is the cost of debt. It is calculated by rearranging the above formula, as follows:

$$K_d = \frac{i(1-t)}{D}$$

WORKED EXAMPLE 15.10: IRREDEEMABLE DEBT CAPITAL

Octubre Plc has €/£500,000 10% debentures issued that are currently trading at €/£90.00. The half-yearly interest has just been paid. The company is profitable and is paying tax at 40%.

Requirement Calculate the value and cost of debt capital for Octubre Plc for inclusion in its WACC.

Solution

There are €/£500,000÷€/£100 = 5,000 bonds in issue, which are currently valued at €/£90 each.

Therefore the total market value of the company's debt capital is €/£450,000 [5,000 × €/£90].

Octubre Plc's cost of debt (K_d) is:

$$\frac{€/£10(1-0.40)}{€€/£90} = 6.67\%$$

When valuing debt for inclusion in the WACC model, market value should be adjusted to reflect cash inflows that would be receivable by a company were it to issue new debt. Therefore, it should be valued ex-interest and less issue costs. The market price of traded debt leading up to a coupon payment date reacts in a similar manner to the market price of equity in the lead-up to a dividend distribution. The price of debt will include the value of the coupon that is about to be received by the holder; this is called the cum-interest price. This is not the equilibrium long-term value of the debt. To find a better representation of the long-term value of debt, the coupon that is about to be paid should be deducted from current price; this will give the ex-interest price. In the market, prices are quoted as being either cum-interest or ex-interest.

WORKED EXAMPLE 15.11: DEBT – CALCULATING MARKET VALUE FOR USE IN THE WACC

Noviembre Plc has €/£200,000 10% irredeemable loan stock in issue. The loan stock is currently trading at par. This includes six months' accrued interest. The company pays tax at 40%. Issue costs for loan stock are €/£5.

Requirement Calculate the value and cost of debt capital for Noviembre Plc for inclusion in its WACC.

Solution

There are €/£200,000 ÷ €/£100 = 2,000 bonds in issue, which are currently valued at €/£100 each. However, this value includes six months' interest, which is €/£5 [€/£100 × 10% × 6/12] per bond. Therefore, the equilibrium market value of the bonds is €/£95 and Noviembre Plc would expect to get €/£95 less the €/£5 issue costs if it were to raise new debt.

Therefore, the total market value of the company's debt capital is €/£180,000 [2,000 × €/£90].

Noviembre Plc's cost of debt (K_d) is as follows:

$$= \frac{€/£10(1-0.40)}{€/£90} = 6.67\%$$

A more accurate valuation would be to find the current cost for the six months' interest payment and to annualise it.

$$= \frac{€/£5(1-0.40)}{€/£90} = 3.33\%$$

Annualise the answer:

$$(1 + 0.0333)^2 - 1 = 6.77\%$$

Redeemable Debt

A similar approach is used to ascertain the cost of redeemable debt except the coupon is an annuity for a set number of years. At the end of the annuity period the nominal value (typically €/£100) is redeemed (sometimes at a premium or at a discount). The coupon is tax deductible by the company, but the debt capital repayment is not. The calculation of the cost of redeemable debt can be split into three steps, as outlined in **Figure 15.4**.

Figure 15.4: Steps to Calculate the Cost of Redeemable Debt

1. Calculate the current market value to be received by a company were it to issue the debt now.

2. Calculate the cash outflows, net of tax, expected by a company.

3. Use interpolation to find the rate that bondholders are willing to pay for this stream of cash payments.

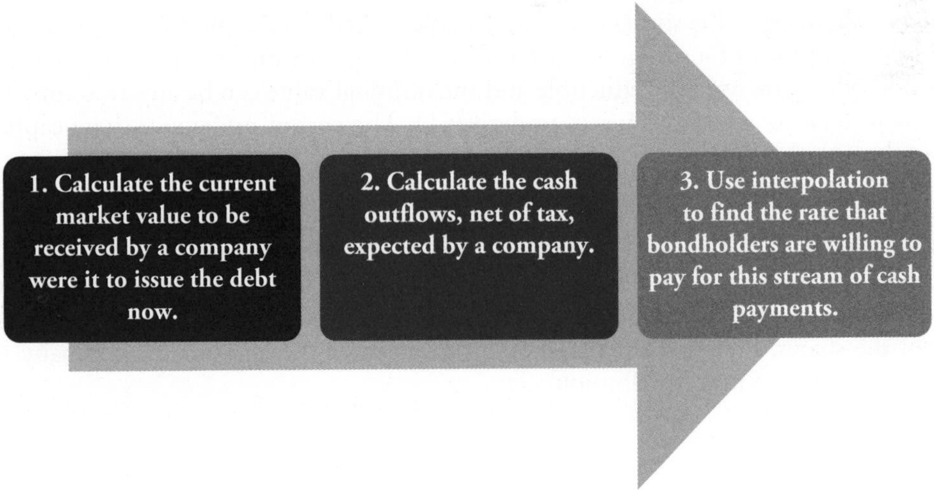

Worked Example 15.12: Calculating the Cost of Redeemable Debt

Diciembre Plc has €/£5,000,000 8% debentures (20X9) that are trading at €/£90. The interest payment for 20X4 has just been made. The company is profitable and is paying tax at 50%.

Requirement Calculate the value and cost of Diciembre Plc's debentures. Assume it is 31 December 20X4 and the tax cash outflow occurs in the same year as the interest cash outflow.

Solution

The market value of the debentures is €/£90.00 for each €/£100.00 block. There is no mention of issue costs and the debentures are trading ex-interest. Therefore, the market value of the debt to be included in the WACC is €/£4,500,000 [€/£5,000,000 ÷ €/£100 × €/£90].

The cost of the debentures is as follows:

Year	Cash flows	Discount Try 5%	PV	Discount Try 7%	PV
	€/£		€/£		€/£
0	90	1.000	90.00	1.000	90.00
1–5	(8(1 – 0.5))	4.329	(17.32)	4.100	(16.40)
5	(100)	0.784	(78.40)	0.713	(71.30)
			(5.72)		2.30

$$K_d = 5\% + \frac{-€/£5.72(2\%)}{-€/£5.72 - €/£2.30} = 6.43\%$$

PREFERENCE SHARE CAPITAL

Preference share capital is similar to irredeemable traded debt capital in that both require a yearly distribution of a set amount. However, the payout on preference share capital is dividends, which are not tax deductible and the nominal value can be any amount (though typically is denominated in values of under €/£1). The cost of preference share capital can be found using the formula:

$$K_p = \frac{D_1}{P_p}$$

where K_p is the cost of the preference shares, D_1 is the annual dividend and P_p is the market value of the shares. Preference shares should be valued at the amount the company would expect to receive in a new distribution.

Worked Example 15.13: Calculating the Value and Cost of Preference Shares

Sol Plc has issued 11% irredeemable preference shares. Their nominal value is €/£300,000 and they were issued at €/£1 each. They are currently trading at €/£1.04 and the dividend has recently been paid.

Requirement Calculate the value and cost of the preference share capital for Sol Plc.

Solution

There are €/£300,000 ÷ €/£1 = 300,000 shares in issue, which are currently valued at €/£1.04 each. Therefore, the total market value of Sol Plc's preference share capital is €/£312,000 [300,000 × €/£1.04].

Sol Plc's cost of preference shares (K_p) is as follows: $\frac{11c/p}{104c/p} = 10.57\%$

WEIGHTED AVERAGE COST OF CAPITAL

The WACC model provided at the start of the chapter can be adapted to include various different types of debt:

$$\text{WACC} = \frac{E(K_e)}{(E+D_1+D_2\ ...)} + \frac{D_1\ (K_d(1-t))}{(E+D_1+D_2\ ...)} + \frac{D_2\ (K_d(1-t))}{(E+D_1+D_2 ...)}$$

When the tax benefit is adjusted for in the workings to find the cost of debt, do not include the '(*1 – t*)' again in the WACC model. This would result in a double deduction for tax.

Limitations of Using the WACC for Investment Appraisal

The limitations of the WACC for investment appraisal are its assumptions as detailed in **Figure 15.5**.

Any theory based on assumptions is limited by those assumptions. Other limitations of using the WACC are that sometimes companies raise floating-rate debt capital, the cost of which fluctuates, impacting on the WACC, and sometimes the variables used are not so easily determined. For example, some forms of debt capital are quite complicated and at some stage in the future may even convert to equity.

However, regardless of its limitations, the WACC is a good approximation for a discount rate to use in the evaluation of projects. An appreciation of its limitations will allow a business finance manager to adjust the WACC rate in light of knowledge about the current capital structure of the company and the riskiness of any project being evaluated. Higher-risk projects should require a higher return to compensate a company for the increased risk, hence they should be discounted using the WACC plus a premium for additional risk. The premium to be added is a matter of judgement.

FIGURE 15.5: ASSUMPTIONS IF USING WACC FOR CAPITAL INVESTMENT APPRAISAL

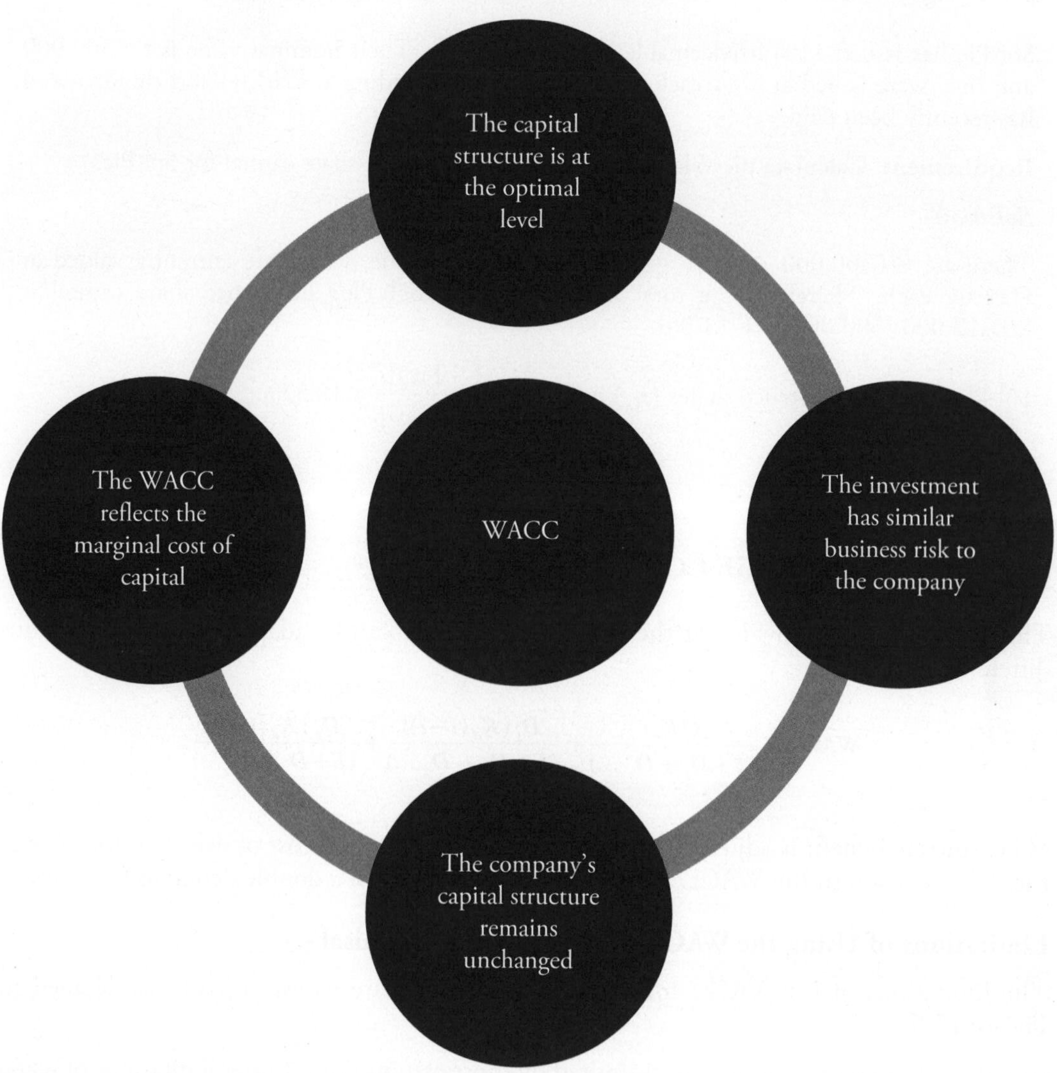

CONCLUSION

Finding an appropriate discount rate for evaluating investments for a company is more difficult than just calculating the WACC. This rigorous process does provide a framework upon which a business finance manager can estimate an appropriate discount rate for project evaluation. However, it should be regarded as a starting point. Calculating the WACC has another advantage in that it keeps business finance managers ever-conscious of the return required by financiers in current terms. However, business finance managers have to be careful: if the discount rate estimate is too high, projects will be turned down that would satisfy equity holders and provide wealth for them; if too low, the resources of a company will be depleted and equity holders will lose wealth.

EXAMINATION STANDARD QUESTION: WACC

Llueva Plc
Statement of Financial Position
at 31 December 20X4

	€/£000
ASSETS	
Non-current assets	
Tangible assets	2,100
	2,100
Current assets	
Inventories	1,200
Trade receivables	1,500
Bank and cash	500
	3,200
Total assets	5,300
EQUITY AND LIABILITIES	
Equity and reserves	
Equity share capital	900
Share premium	500
Revenue reserves	1,100
	2,500
Non-current liabilities	
Loan stock (8%)	1,000
	1,000
Current liabilities	
Trade payables	1,350
Taxation	450
	1,800
Total equity and liabilities	5,300

Additional information:
The equity share capital has a nominal value of 25c/p per share and is currently trading at €/£1.40. A dividend of 5c/p per share will be paid shortly (it is out of profits made in the year to 31 December 20X4). It is expected that this dividend will increase by 7% each year.

The current market value of the loan stock is 98%. The half-yearly interest coupon has just been paid.

The current corporation tax rate is 40%.

Requirement Calculate the WACC for Llueva Plc.

Solution

Llueva Plc has two sources of finance: equity and traded debt. To work out the WACC, five steps are required:

1. Work out the total market value of the equity share capital.
2. Work out the cost of equity.
3. Work out the total market value of the debt capital.
4. Work out the cost of the debt capital.
5. Use the data obtained from steps 1. to 4. to calculate the WACC.

1. The equity is currently trading at €/£1.40 (cum-dividend). Therefore, the value to be used in the WACC is €/£1.35 [€/£1.40 − €/£0.05]. Multiply this by the number of shares in issue: 3,600,000 shares [€/£900,000 × €/£1.00 ÷ €/£0.25] to give the market value of equity of €/£4,860,000 [3,600,000 × €/£1.35].
2. In this question, the information is directing the reader to use the dividend valuation model. You are told that g is 7%, D_0 is 5c/p and the market value (P_0) is €/£1.35. Therefore, the cost of equity (K_e) is:

$$\frac{5c/p(1+0.07)}{135c/p} + 0.07 = 0.1096\ (10.96\%)$$

3. The market value of the loan stock is €/£980,000 [(€/£1,000,000 ÷ €/£100) × (€/£100 × 98%)].
4. The loan stock is assumed to be irredeemable as there is no information to indicate that it is redeemable. The yearly interest is €/£100 × 8% = €/£8, taxation is 40% and the loan stock is trading at €/£98. Therefore, the cost of debt (K_d) is:

$$\frac{€/£8(1-0.4)}{€/£98} = 0.0489\ (4.89\%)$$

5. The WACC for Llueva Plc is (in 000s):

$$\text{WACC} = \frac{€/£4{,}860\ (10.96\%)}{€/£980 + €/£4{,}860} + \frac{€/£980\ (4.89\%)}{€/£4{,}860 + €/£980} = 9.94\%$$

KEY TERMS

Beta
Beta factor/coefficient
Business risk
Capital asset pricing model (CAPM)
Cost of capital
Cum-dividend
Diversified portfolio
Dividend valuation model
Economic profit
Economic value added
Equity
Ex-dividend
Market return
Market-risk premium
Portfolio theory
Risk-free rate
Security market line
Share issue price
Systematic risk
Unsystematic risk
Weighted average cost of capital (WACC)

REVIEW QUESTIONS

(See Suggested Solutions to Review Questions in **Appendix B**.)

Question 15.1

Enero Plc has one million authorised equity shares, of which 50% are issued. Issue costs amount to 10c/p per share. Its shares are currently trading at €/£2.05. A dividend of 15c/p will be paid shortly.

Requirement Calculate the value of Enero Plc's equity shares, which should be used in the calculation of its WACC.

Question 15.2

The equity share capital of Marzo Plc is currently trading at €/£2.50 (ex-dividend). Issue costs are 20c/p per share. The company pays a fixed dividend each year of 46c/p.

Requirement Calculate the cost of equity for Marzo Plc.

Question 15.3

The equity share capital of Abril Plc is currently trading at 90c/p. A dividend of 8c/p has recently been paid. Dividends grow at 6% per year.

Requirement Calculate the cost of equity for Abril Plc.

Question 15.4

Mayo Plc has an ROCE of 20%. Each year it retains 50% of its earnings to invest in projects.

Requirement Calculate the expected growth in Mayo Plc's dividends.

Question 15.5

Octubre Ltd has one million authorised equity shares, of which 50% are issued.

Its earnings per share are 20c/p. A similar quoted company, Febrero Plc, has a price earnings ratio of 10.

Requirement Estimate the market value of Octubre Ltd to be used in the calculation of its WACC. Assume a reduction of 10% for lack of marketability.

Question 15.6

Frio Plc has €/£1 million of 10% debentures, which are redeemable after eight years. The debentures are currently trading at €/£112 and a full year's interest is about to be paid by the company. The tax rate is currently 30%.

Requirement
(a) Calculate the value and cost of Frio Plc's debentures.
(b) When can the WACC be used as an appropriate discount rate for capital investment appraisal?

Question 15.7 Crystal Plc (Level 2)

The following figures have been extracted from the most recent financial statements of Crystal Plc.

Crystal Plc
STATEMENT OF FINANCIAL POSITION
as at 30 June 20X5

	€/£000
ASSETS	
Non-current assets	
Tangible assets	10,115
Financial assets	821
	10,936
Current assets	3,658
Total assets	14,594
EQUITY AND LIABILITIES	
Equity and reserves	
Equity share capital	
Authorised: 4,000,000 shares of €/£1	
Issued: 3,000,000 shares of €/£1	3,000
Reserves	6,542
Total equity and reserves	9,542
Non-current liabilities	
7% debentures	1,300
Deferred taxation	583
	1,883
Current liabilities	
Trade and other payables	1,735
Corporation tax	1,434
	3,169
Total equity and liabilities	14,594

SUMMARY OF PROFITS AND DIVIDENDS
Year ended 30 June

	20X1 €/£000	20X2 €/£000	20X3 €/£000	20X4 €/£000	20X5 €/£000
Profit after interest and before tax	1,737	2,090	1,940	1,866	2,179
Less tax	573	690	640	616	719
Profit after interest and tax	1,164	1,400	1,300	1,250	1,460
Less dividends	620	680	740	740	810
Added to reserves	544	720	560	510	650

The current (1 July 20X5) market value of Crystal Plc's equity shares is €/£3.27 per share cum-dividend. An annual dividend of €/£810,000 is due for payment shortly. The debentures are redeemable at par in 10 years' time. Their current market value is €/£77.10. Annual interest has just been paid on the debentures. There have been no issues or redemptions of equity shares or debentures during the past five years. The current rate of corporation tax is 33%, and the current basic rate of income tax is 25%. Assume that there have been no changes in the system, or rates of taxation, during the last five years.

Requirement

(a) Estimate the cost of capital Crystal Plc should use as a discount rate when appraising new investment opportunities.

17 Marks

(b) Discuss any difficulties and uncertainties in your estimates.

8 Marks
Total 25 Marks

(Based on Chartered Accountants Ireland, MABF, *Questions and Solutions Manual 2000/2001*)

CHALLENGING QUESTIONS

(Suggested Solutions to Challenging Questions are available through your lecturer.)

Question 15.1 Marco and Polo Ltd (Level 1)

You are given the following information about two companies, which are both financed entirely by equity capital:

	Marco Ltd	**Polo Ltd**
Number of equity shares of €/£1 (000)	150,000	500,000
Market value per share, ex-dividend (€/£)	3.42	0.65
Current earnings (total) (€/£000)	62,858	63,952
Current dividend (total) (€/£000)	6,158	48,130
Statement of financial position value of capital employed (€/£000)	315,000	293,000
Dividend five years ago (total) (€/£000)	2,473	37,600

Both companies are in the same line of business and sell similar products.

Requirement

(a) Estimate the cost of capital for both companies, using two growth models.

10 Marks

(b) Describe, giving your reasons, any additional evidence you would refer to in order to increase your confidence in the estimates of the cost of capital in practice.

5 Marks
Total 15 Marks

(Based on Chartered Accountants Ireland, MABF, Questions and Solutions Manual 2000/2001)

Question 15.2 Supreme (Level 1)

Detailed below is an extract of the financial information of four separate unrelated companies.

Supreme Holdings has 1,000,000 €/£1 ordinary shares in issue. Supreme has just paid an interim ordinary dividend of €/£70,000 and intends to pay a final dividend of €/£30,000. The dividend payout is expected to remain constant for the foreseeable future. Supreme has a current share price of €/£1.75.

Excellence Plc paid a dividend of 75 cents/pence per share on 31 December 20X4. The shareholders are particularly pleased considering the fact the dividend was 25 cents/pence per share on 31 December 20X0. This rate of dividend growth is expected to continue for the foreseeable future. Excellence's share price is currently trading at €/£7.55 ex-dividend.

Prime Plc has a beta of 0.96. The finance director expects this to increase by 25% as a result of Prime taking on a number of projects that will increase the overall business and financial risk of the company. The current risk-free rate is 3% and the return on the market is 6%.

Best Limited has the following items in its statement of financial position at 31 December 20X4:

	€/£000
Equity share capital	1,000
Share premium	2,500
Preference share capital	5,250
10% loan note	7,000
5% irredeemable debentures	1,250
Revaluation reserve	3,000
Retained earnings	13,000
	33,000

Requirement

(a) Calculate the cost of equity for the following companies:
  (i) Supreme Holdings.
  (ii) Excellence Plc.
  (iii) Prime Plc.

6 Marks

(b) Calculate the book value of equity for Best Limited.

2 Marks

(c) List THREE limitations of the dividend valuation model.

3 Marks

(d) Explain the difference between systematic and unsystematic risk, giving ONE example of each type of risk.

4 Marks
Total 15 Marks

(Based on Chartered Accountants Ireland, CAP 1, Finance, Summer 2013, Q3)

Question 15.3 Neuron (Level 1)

You have been asked to calculate the Weighted Average Cost of Capital (WACC) of Neuron Plc based on the following information:

1. Neuron has in issue 2 million ordinary shares of 50c/p each. The ordinary share value is estimated to be €/£1.80 ex-dividend. Neuron's equity beta is 1.2, the risk-free rate is 4% and the estimated market return is 14%.
2. Neuron has 1 million 7.5% cumulative preference shares of €/£1 each in issue; these have an estimated market value of €/£0.92 cum div. and the annual preference dividend has been declared and is due to be paid soon.
3. Neuron has in issue €/£750,000 of 6% debenture loan stock redeemable at par in five years' time. The current market price of these debentures is €/£82.50, including interest. The yearly payment of interest is due to be made soon.

Neuron is liable to corporation tax at 25%.

Requirement

(a) Calculate the weighted average cost of capital (WACC) for Neuron.

13 Marks

(b) Identify THREE major assumptions needed for WACC to be an appropriate discount rate.

3 Marks

(c) Comment briefly on TWO significant practical factors that a company would be likely to take into account when determining the relative mix of debt and equity in its capital structure.

4 Marks
Total 20 Marks

(Based on Chartered Accountants Ireland, CAP 1, Finance, Summer 2012, Q2)

Question 15.4 Tango (Level 1)

(a) When calculating the weighted average cost of capital (WACC) indicate, with reasons, whether it is appropriate to use market values or nominal/balance sheet values as the weighting of debt and equity.

4 Marks

(b) The capital structure of Tango Plc, based on its most recent balance sheet, is as follows:

	€/£m
Ordinary shares of 50 cents/pence each	4.0
10% cumulative preference shares of €/£1 each	2.5
Retained profits	3.0
12% irredeemable debentures	5.0

Tango pays corporation tax at the rate of 25% and is expected to achieve a consistent annual profit, before interest and tax, of €/£4.5 million.

You may assume that any annual profits available to ordinary shareholders will, in future, be fully distributed as dividends.

The current market price of Tango's shares (ex-div.) are:

Ordinary share	€/£1.80
Preference share	€/£0.68

The irredeemable debentures have a market value (ex-interest) of €/£104 per €/£100 nominal value.

Requirement Calculate the weighted average cost of capital of Tango.

12 Marks
Total 16 Marks

(Based on Chartered Accountants Ireland, CAP 1, Finance, Autumn 2009, Q2)

Question 15.5 Marilla Plc (Level 1)

The following information is available on the long-term capital structure of Marilla Plc:

	€/£
Ordinary share capital	
(2,000,000 shares of €/£2 nominal value)	4,000,000
Share premium	1,500,000
Revenue reserves	2,500,000
Shareholders' funds	8,000,000
14% Debentures	2,000,000
Capital employed	10,000,000

The company has recently paid a dividend of 40 cents/pence per share. This represents a growth rate of 10% over the previous annual dividend and this growth rate is expected to continue for the foreseeable future. The shares are now quoted in the market at €/£2.35 each. A study of past share price behaviour relative to the market index suggests a beta value of 1.5 for the company's shares.

The expected rate of return on the market portfolio is 15% per annum for the foreseeable future. The rate of corporation tax is 25%. The current yield on government debt is 9% per annum.

The debt of Marilla is currently quoted at €/£110 per €/£100 (nominal) of debt issued. The debt currently in issue is due for redemption at par value in 10 years' time.

Requirement

(a) Estimate the weighted average cost of capital for Marilla. Use an **average** cost of equity, the dividend valuation model and the capital asset pricing model.

10 Marks

(b) Discuss briefly the arguments for and against the use of weighted average cost of capital as an appropriate rate for investment appraisal.

5 Marks
Total 15 Marks

(Based on Chartered Accountants Ireland, CAP 1, Finance, Summer 2011, Q3)

Question 15.6 Menlo (Level 1)

Menlo Magic Plc operates in the pharmaceutical industry. The Board of Directors is disappointed that "the financial markets are applying a bearish view to their share price as if it were in the construction or banking industry", which they feel is not appropriate. Although many companies have cut dividends, Menlo is confident that it will not do so, but the chief executive feels her reassurances are not believed.

Menlo's current share price is only €/£1.30 cum-dividend, and a proposed dividend of 10 cent/pence is due to be paid shortly. The dividends have increased from 7.4c/p to 10c/p from 20X1 to 20X5.

The beta factor/coefficient of Menlo's shares is estimated to be 0.6, while the expected return on risk-free securities is 5% and the expected market return is 9%.

Menlo finances its net assets with 18 million ordinary shares and with €/£9,350,000 of 5% debentures redeemable at par in 10 years' time. The debentures have an estimated market value ex-interest €/£82 per €/£100 nominal. Menlo pays corporation tax at a rate of 20%.

Requirement Calculate the current weighted average cost of capital (WACC) for Menlo using the CAPM to determine the cost of equity.

Total 15 Marks

(Based on Chartered Accountants Ireland, CAP 1, Finance, Summer 2010, Q6(b))

Question 15.7 Morgan (Level 1)

Morgan Sports Plc is a company that specialises in developing technology and education products for a wide range of sports and activities to enhance the performance of elite athletes. Morgan has made substantial investments in the past in research and development using various different sources of finance to fund these investments. You have been asked to calculate Morgan's cost of capital. To do this you have compiled the following information:

Morgan currently has 739,000 €/£1 ordinary shares in issue. The shares currently have a market value of €/£2.45 per share. The company has just paid a dividend of €/£0.09 per share. Morgan's shareholders are satisfied with the dividend policy as dividends have been growing steadily over the past few years as follows:

Year	Dividends (€/£)
20X1	48,000
20X2	50,000
20X3	52,500
20X4	59,500
20X5	66,510

Morgan has also issued 500,000 €/£1 9% irredeemable preference shares. They are currently trading at €/£1.45 and the dividend is due to be paid in two weeks.

Morgan also has €/£900,000 7.5% redeemable debentures in issue. The debentures are due for redemption at par in four years' time. The current market price of the debentures is €/£97. Assume a 25% tax rate.

Requirement

(a) You are required to calculate:

(i) The cost of equity.

3 Marks

(ii) The cost of preference share capital.

3 Marks

(iii) The cost of the redeemable debentures.

4 Marks

(iv) The weighted average cost of capital (WACC).

4 Marks

Morgan's Board is considering making a substantial capital investment in a state-of-the-art laboratory for testing professional athletes for banned substances. The Board is unsure whether to finance this project with internally generated funds or externally sourced debt or equity finance.

The finance manager has decided to appraise this investment using the net present value (NPV) method using the weighted average cost of capital (WACC) calculated in part (a) as the discount factor. He is concerned, however, that this might not be an appropriate discount factor to appraise the project and has sought your advice.

Requirement

(b) (i) Discuss whether or not you believe that the WACC calculated in part (a) is an appropriate discount factor in appraising this new project.

3 Marks

(ii) Discuss the issues that the finance manager should consider when choosing between debt and equity finance.

3 Marks

Total 20 Marks

(Based on Chartered Accountants Ireland, CAP 1, Finance, Autumn 2012, Q2)

Question 15.8 Bindaroo Plc (Level 2)

Bindaroo Plc had the following statement of financial position at 31 March 20X5:

	€/£000
Equity share capital (€/£1 nominal value)	
Authorised	1,000
Issued and fully paid	500
8% cumulative irredeemable preference share capital	100
9% non-cumulative irredeemable preference share capital	80
Capital redemption reserve fund	90
Revaluation reserve	150
Revenue reserves	448
Equity holders' funds	1,368
6% irredeemable loan stock	156
4% debentures (redeemable on 31 March 20X9 at €/£115)	300
Total capital employed	1,824
Represented by	
Sundry net assets	1,824

Additional information:

1. The equity shares are trading at €/£3.60 ex-dividend.
2. The 8% preference shares are quoted at €/£1.09.
3. The 9% preference shares are quoted at €/£1.14.
4. The current price of the 6% loan stock is €/£105.
5. The current price of the 4% debentures is €/£104.
6. In the year to 31 March 20X5, a dividend of €/£0.06 was paid on the equity share capital of the company. Recent trends indicate that Bindaroo increases its dividend payment on average by 3% per annum.
7. The risk-free rate of interest is 2.5%. The market rate of return is 6%.
8. The beta factor applicable to the equity of Bindaroo is 1.04.
9. Profit before interest and tax for the year ended 31 March 20X5 was €/£650,000.
10. Assume that the taxable profit is identical to the accounting profit. Ignore deferred tax.
11. The corporation tax rate applicable to Bindaroo is 12.5%.

Requirement

(a) Calculate, in respect of Bindaroo, as at 31 March 20X5, each of the following:

(i) The profit retained for the year ended 31 March 20X5.

4 Marks

(ii) The capital gearing ratio and the income gearing ratio (i.e. times interest earned).

3 Marks

(iii) The cost of equity using both the CAPM and the dividend valuation model (i.e. Gordon's growth model).

3 Marks

(iv) The cost of redeemable debentures. The cost of irredeemable debentures.

4 Marks

(v) The WACC, using either of the figures for cost of equity in part (iii) above.

5 Marks

(b) Explain why the two different methods of calculating the cost of equity noted above give different results. State which method is superior in your opinion, and why.

3 Marks

Total 22 Marks

(Based on Chartered Accountants Ireland, MABF II, Summer 2004, Q5)

Question 15.9 Lubok Plc (Level 2)

(a) It is commonly accepted that a crucial factor in the financial decisions of a company, including the evaluation of capital investment proposals, is the cost of capital. Explain, in simple terms, what is meant by the 'cost of equity capital' for a particular company. Specifically, what is the difference between the cost of equity capital and the weighted average cost of capital?

5 Marks

(b) Calculate the cost of equity capital for Lubok Plc, as at the beginning of 20X6, from the data given below, using the following methods:

(i) The dividend growth model.

4 Marks

(ii) The capital asset pricing model.

3 Marks

Lubok Plc data:

1. Price per share on the stock exchange at 1 January 20X6 is €/£1.20, ex-div.
2. Annual dividend per share:

	20X1	20X2	20X3	20X4	20X5
c/p per share	7.63	8.31	8.88	9.35	10.00

3. The beta coefficient for Lubok shares is 0.7.
4. Expected rate of return on risk-free securities is 8%.
5. Expected return on the market portfolio is 12%.

(c) State, for each model separately, the main simplifying assumptions made. In view of these assumptions, what is your opinion as to whether or not the models yield results that can be safely used in practice.

6 Marks
Total 18 Marks

(Based on Chartered Accountants Ireland, MABF II, Summer 2006, Q6)

Question 15.10 Milo (Level 2)

(a) Define the 'cost of capital' and explain its significance in financial decision-making.

6 Marks

The information on Milo Plc below is available to you.
The capital structure (book value) of Milo Plc is:

	€/£
Redeemable debentures (€/£100 per debenture)	800,000
Redeemable preference shares (€/£100 per share)	200,000
Equity shares (€/£10 per share)	1,000,000
Retained reserves	800,000
	2,800,000

All these securities are traded in the capital markets. Recent prices are as follows:

- debentures at €/£110 per debenture;
- preference shares at €/£120 per share;
- equity shares at €/£22 per share.

Anticipated external financing opportunities are as follows:

1. €/£100 per debenture redeemable at par; 14-year maturity, 8% coupon rate, 4% issue costs, sale price €/£100.
2. €/£100 preference share redeemable at par; 15-year maturity, 10% dividend rate, 5% flotation costs, sale price €/£100.
3. Equity shares: €/£2 share flotation costs, issue price €/£22.

In addition, the dividend expected on the equity share at the end of the current year is €/£2 per share; the anticipated growth rate in dividends is 5% per annum. The corporation tax rate is 12.5%.

Requirement

(b) Determine the weighted average cost of capital of Milo Plc using:
  (i) book value weightings; and
  (ii) market value weightings.

12 Marks
Total 18 Marks

(Based on Chartered Accountants Ireland, MABF II, Autumn 2007, Q7)

Question 15.11 Equinox (Level 2)

Equinox Plc is attempting to evaluate its cost of capital. You are provided with the following information:

1. The rate of return on a one-month government bond is 6% per annum.
2. The long-term equity risk premium in the market is 3.5%.
3. The firm is 14% riskier than the market.
4. The market price of a riskless government bond of the same type and average duration as the company's fixed interest loan stock is €/£90 per €/£100 nominal. The company's debt has a duration of four years before redemption at par. The company pays 7% per annum on its loan stock and its credit rating suggests that it should carry a 1% risk premium over and above an equivalent risk-free government bond.
5. Fixed interest is tax deductible at the corporation tax rate of 30% per annum.
6. The company's market gearing is 0.65.

Requirement

(a) Calculate the following for Equinox:

(i) Cost of equity capital.

4 Marks

(ii) Cost of debt capital.

4 Marks

(iii) Weighted average cost of capital (WACC).

4 Marks

(b) The WACC is normally used to derive the discount rate to be applied when a firm is appraising capital expenditure proposals. List TWO circumstances when this should **not** be done without further modifying the WACC.

6 Marks

Total 18 Marks

(Based on Chartered Accountants Ireland, MABF II, Autumn 2008, Q6)

Question 15.12 GTL (Level 1)

Green Tees Limited (GTL), an Irish company, is considering whether or not to make a substantial investment in developing a golf course, clubhouse and spa in the northwest of Ireland.

GTL has used the services of Robert McLeavy, a high-profile Irish golfer, to design the course. Robert has been paid €/£500,000 for his design.

The development of the golf course will take place during 20X4, with an expected completion of the course by the end of the year. GTL will pay €/£1,500,000 to a company called Gravel to Golf Limited to develop the course. A further €/£2,500,000 will be paid to a contractor to build a state-of-the-art clubhouse with spa. Both these payments will be made in full by the end of 20X4.

GTL expects to have 150 members by the end of 20X5 and it is expected that this will grow by 25 members each year until 20Y0. GTL will charge each new member an upfront once-off joining fee of €/£11,000. Green fees of €/£1,200 will be payable by each member each year thereafter. A full year's annual green fee is also payable in full in the year the member joins the club. You can assume that all cash flows occur at the end of the year and that today is 1 January 20X4.

The clubhouse will generate an average contribution of €/£400 per member per annum. These earnings arise primarily from the sale of golf clubs and accessories in the golf shop.

It is estimated that the spa will earn a contribution of €/£800,000 in 20X5 and it is expected that this will increase by 10% each year thereafter.

GTL will incur fixed costs of €/£500,000 in 20X5 and it is expected that these costs will increase by 6% each year thereafter.

GTL will also have to pay a licence fee of €/£100 per member per annum to the Irish Golf Association.

At the end of 20X9, GTL expects to sell the golf course and clubhouse with spa to an American company for €/£8,100,000.

GTL is an all equity financed company and has 1,000,000 €/£1 ordinary shares in issue, which are currently trading at €/£7.50 each. The risk-free rate is 3%, the return on the market is 7% and GTL's beta is currently 1.50. The beta will rise to 1.75 given the change in capital structure.

GTL wishes to raise debt in order to finance the initial investment of €/£4,000,000. The debt will be issued at par and the after-tax cost of debt is 7.2%.

The effects of taxation may be ignored.

Requirement

(a) Calculate the net relevant cash flows arising from the investment in the golf course, clubhouse and spa between 20X4 and 20X9.

9 Marks

(b) Calculate the weighted average cost of capital (WACC), rounded to the nearest whole number, to be used by GTL for this project.

5 Marks

(c) Calculate the net present value (NPV) of the project using the WACC calculated in part (b) above.

2 Marks

(d) Discuss the appropriateness of using the WACC as a discount factor in investment appraisal.

4 Marks

Total 20 Marks

(Based on Chartered Accountants Ireland, CAP 1, Finance, Autumn 2013, Q1)

Question 15.13 Skarok (Level 2)

Skarok Plc plans to raise finance some time within the next few months. Skarok's managing director is acutely aware of the recent stock market downturn and is worried about the possible effects on the company's cost of capital.

The managing director has asked for your advice and has provided you with the following information:

Skarok Plc
SUMMARISED STATEMENT OF FINANCIAL POSITION
as at 31 March 20X5

ASSETS	**€/£m**
Non-current assets at net book value	619.51
Current assets	
Inventories	163.03
Trade receivables	195.63
Bank	65.21
	423.87
Total assets	1,043.38

EQUITY AND LIABILITIES	
Equity and reserves	
Equity shares (€/£1 par value)	163.03
Reserves	293.46
	456.49
Non-current liabilities	
11% debentures, redeemable in 20Z0* at par	326.05
Current liabilities	
Trade payables	199.17
Taxation	61.67
	260.84
Total liabilities	586.89
Total equity and liabilities	1,043.38

* Each decade is reflected by a letter that runs consecutively in line with the alphabet, for example, X, Y, Z.

FIVE-YEAR SUMMARISED STATEMENT OF PROFIT AND LOSS

Year ended 31 March	**Turnover**	**Profit before tax**	**Tax**	**Profit after tax**	**Dividend**
	€/£m	**€/£m**	**€/£m**	**€/£m**	**€/£m**
20X1	1,379.10	117.26	46.90	70.36	23.30
20X2	1,522.98	138.03	48.32	89.71	25.85
20X3	1,610.94	140.84	49.29	91.55	28.75
20X4	1,753.83	147.50	51.62	95.88	31.85
20X5	1,915.20	176.19	61.67	114.52	35.39

The company's current share price is €/£12.90 ex-dividend, and the debenture price is €/£93. No new share or debenture capital has been issued since 20W8. Corporation tax is at the rate of 35%.

Requirement

(a) Calculate the existing cost of equity for Skarok.

4 Marks

(b) Calculate the existing cost of debt for Skarok.

4 Marks

(c) Calculate the existing WACC for Skarok.

4 Marks

Academic papers concerning cost of capital and capital structure often appear highly theoretical and seem to have little practical relevance. Discuss the significance of the theories of capital structure, especially those of Modigliani and Miller (M&M) (see **Chapter 16**).

4 Marks

(d) Describe briefly two weaknesses of sensitivity analysis in capital budgeting.

5 Marks
Presentation 1 Mark
Total 22 Marks

(Based on Chartered Accountants Ireland, MABF II, Summer 2003, Q5)

16

Capital Structure

Learning Objectives

Upon completing this chapter, readers should be able to:

- discuss the link between a company's capital structure, its WACC and company value;
- discuss the link between gearing, financial risk and bankruptcy;
- analyse the impact of capital structure changes on distributable profits and key ratios;
- evaluate the traditional theory of capital structure;
- discuss Modigliani and Miller's theory of capital structure, with and without taxation;
- discuss the assumptions and limitations of each theory; and
- discuss other issues deemed to impact on the level of gearing in a company's capital structure.

INTRODUCTION

One of the key financial decisions that a business finance manager has to be concerned with is how a company should finance its long-term investments. A company's **capital structure** is the mixture of long-term debt and equity the company has used to finance its projects and operations. The value of a company is regarded as the market value of its capital, i.e. its debt and equity.

$$\mathbf{MV} = D + E$$

where MV is the total value of a company, D is the market value of its debt and E is the market value of its equity.

Debt is regarded as a cheaper form of finance than equity, hence debt would appear to be the best alternative; however, the level of gearing in a company's capital structure is argued to impact on the required return by existing equity and debt holders due to increased levels of financial risk. A financial manager has to strive to obtain the level of debt and equity that minimises a company's WACC, as this will maximise company value. The capital structure that minimises the WACC is called the **optimum capital structure**.

DEBT, EARNINGS AND FINANCIAL RISK

From a company's perspective the costs of issuing debt are usually less than the costs associated with issuing equity; moreover, the annual cost to a company is cheaper than debt's observed coupon/interest rate, as the interest is tax deductible. Therefore, so long as a company is profitable, the cost of debt is reduced by the rate of tax payable. Debt holders require a lower rate of return than equity holders because they face less risk. Debt holders have claim to a company's profits in front of equity holders and, in the event of a company winding up, their claims have to be settled before those of equity holders. Indeed, many trading debt instruments are secured on the assets of a company and may impose covenants on the actions of management.

Though there are benefits to having debt in a company's capital structure, there are practical limitations that can restrict the level of debt used, as highlighted in **Figure 16.1**.

FIGURE 16.1: PRACTICAL LIMITATIONS ON THE LEVEL OF A COMPANY'S DEBT

Management preferences	Management may prefer not to gear a company to high levels, due to the increased risk attached to borrowing. In addition, management like to keep a borrowing facility in reserve so that when they do require finance, they do not have to justify their requirement to equity holders.
Industry norms	The market usually reacts negatively to companies that veer away from industry norms.
Constitution	A company's articles of association may contain borrowing restrictions.
Covenants	Prior debt trust deeds/loan agreements may have covenants that restrict further borrowing.
Security	Security for long-term debt may run out.
Financial risk	Lenders may feel a company has saturated its debt levels and are unwilling to provide more debt. Alternatively, to compensate for the increased risk of default, they may increase the cost of borrowing to the extent that it is no longer a viable alternative.
Liquidity	Most debt finance has a compulsory fixed interest coupon that has to be paid yearly; in addition, the nominal value of debt capital has to be repaid on its maturity (sometimes with a premium). Floating-rate debt is sensitive to market interest rates and the capital element is usually repaid over the term of the debt.

When the proportion of long-term debt to equity capital reaches a certain level, the benefits (i.e. debt being cheaper and easier to obtain) are outweighed by the financial risk associated with holding debt. **Gearing** is the proportion of a company's capital financed by long-term debt and is calculated as follows:

$$\frac{D}{D+E}$$

where D is the market value of debt (including preference shares) and E is the market value of equity. Book values or market values can be used to calculate the gearing ratio. An example using market values is provided in **Worked Example 16.1.**

WORKED EXAMPLE 16.1: GEARING

Bastante Plc has 40,000 equity shares in issue. They are currently trading at €/£3.00 each. Bastante Plc also has 400 debentures, trading at par.

Requirement

(a) Calculate the gearing ratio for Bastante Plc.
(b) Explain the outcome.

Solution

(a) The market value of Bastante Plc's equity is €/£120,000 [40,000 × €/£3.00]. The market value of its debt is €/£40,000 [400 × €/£100]. Therefore, the gearing level is 25% [€/£40,000 ÷ (€/£40,000 + €/£120,000)].
(b) 25% of Bastante Plc is financed by debt; the remaining 75% is financed by equity. This is a low level of gearing for a Plc.

The level of gearing provides an indication of the financial risks associated with investing in a company. Financial risk occurs because debt has a fixed yearly return that has to be paid, whereas the distribution to equity holders (i.e. dividends) can be waived when cash flows are insufficient. From equity holders' perspectives, debt has a fixed cost element: this is a constant drain on a company's liquidity and, beyond a certain point, may even lead to bankruptcy risks. Equity holders will regard companies with higher levels of gearing as being riskier as interest is a fixed cost that must be paid before equity holders can receive a return. The additional fixed cost makes net income more sensitive (i.e. more likely to fluctuate) when there are changes in operating profit. This risk is termed financial risk. **Financial risk** is the additional sensitivity in returns to equity holders that arise due to the level of debt in a company's financial structure. The impact of gearing on equity holders is highlighted in the following example.

WORKED EXAMPLE 16.2: FINANCIAL RISK

The directors of Atono Plc were informed at a golf outing by fellow directors that it is more valuable to have debt in a company's capital structure than equity, as debt is cheaper than equity. Atono Plc currently has no debt in its capital structure, though it is considering borrowing funds, which it will use to buy back the more expensive equity capital. The capital structure of Atono Plc is as follows:

	Current €/£000	Suggested €/£000
ASSETS	10,000	10,000
Equity and reserves	10,000	5,000
Long-term debt		5,000
TOTAL EQUITY AND LIABILITIES	10,000	10,000
Shares outstanding	500,000	250,000

Additional information:

- The company's equity shares are currently trading at €/£20 each and it is assumed that this value does not change when the suggested capital structure change takes place.
- The long-term debt attracts an interest rate of 8%.
- Taxation is 30%.

Requirement

(a) Calculate the gearing ratio for Atono Plc under both scenarios.

(b) Assume the company faces three differing external environment scenarios: boom, steady state and recession. Each scenario has different income potentials: if there is a boom economy, earnings before interest and taxation (EBIT) of €/£1 million are expected; if the economy stays steady, EBIT are expected to remain at €/£660,000; whereas if the economy goes into recession, EBIT are expected to fall to €/£450,000. Calculate the impact of the change in gearing on the *return on equity* and the *earnings per share* for each scenario.

Solution

(a) At the present time Atono Plc has no debt, therefore its gearing ratio is zero. When Atono Plc raises €/£5 million in debt capital to purchase back 50,000 shares at €/£20 each, the gearing ratio becomes €/£5m ÷ (€/£5m + €/£5m) = 50%.

(b) The impact of the economy on the return on equity and the earnings per share is evaluated, assuming capital structure does not change:

Current

	Recession €/£000	Steady €/£000	Boom €/£000
EBIT	450	660	1,000
Interest	0	0	0
Taxation	(135)	(198)	(300)
Net income	315	462	700
Return on equity ratio	€/£315,000 / €/£10,000,000	€/£462,000 / €/£10,000,000	€/£700,000 / €/£10,000,000
Return on equity	3.15%	4.62%	7%

Earnings per share ratio	€/£315,000 / 500,000	€/£462,000 / 500,000	€/£700,000 / 500,000
Earnings per share	63c/p	92.4c/p	140c/p

Suggested

	Recession €/£000	**Steady €/£000**	**Boom €/£000**
EBIT	450	660	1,000
Interest	(400)	(400)	(400)
EBT	50	260	600
Taxation	(15)	(78)	(180)
Net income	35	182	420

Return on equity ratio	€/£35,000 / €/£5,000,000	€/£182,000 / €/£5,000,000	€/£420,000 / €/£5,000,000
Return on equity	0.7%	3.6%	8.4%
Earnings per share ratio	€/£35,000 / 250,000	€/£182,000 / 250,000	€/£420,000 / 250,000
Earnings per share	14c/p	72.8c/p	168c/p

The increased gearing has exposed equity holders to higher risk, as captured by the higher spread in the potential return on equity and the earnings per share.

The impact of gearing on equity holder return can be better assessed in light of the evidence from **Worked Example 16.2**. Under the three different scenarios, the return on equity and the earnings per share are more variable when there is debt in the capital structure. When a geared company makes lower EBIT, the return to equity holders is markedly lower compared to a similar ungeared company. Similarly, the return to equity holders is increased when a company performs well.

The Impact of Capital Structure Changes on Earnings

When a company decides to raise additional finance by way of equity, preference shares or debt, there will be different consequences on the reported performance, financial position and value of the entity. The consequential change in capital structure may not be what the market expected, the resultant reaction (e.g. a sale of shares) may cause the share price to fall and the price earnings ratio to fall. Gearing will also change. In addition, there will be different consequences on reported profits as interest is fixed and is tax deductible, whereas the dividend on preference shares is not. Finally, the dividends on equity shares do not even enter the statement of profit and loss. See **Worked Example 16.2** and the **Examination Standard Question** at the end of this chapter for examples.

The Impact of Gearing on the Cost of Equity

The most debated topic in capital structure theory is the likely behaviour of equity holders in response to increased levels of gearing. Four outcomes are outlined in **Figure 16.2**.

FIGURE 16.2: INCREASED GEARING AND THE REACTIONS OF EQUITY HOLDERS

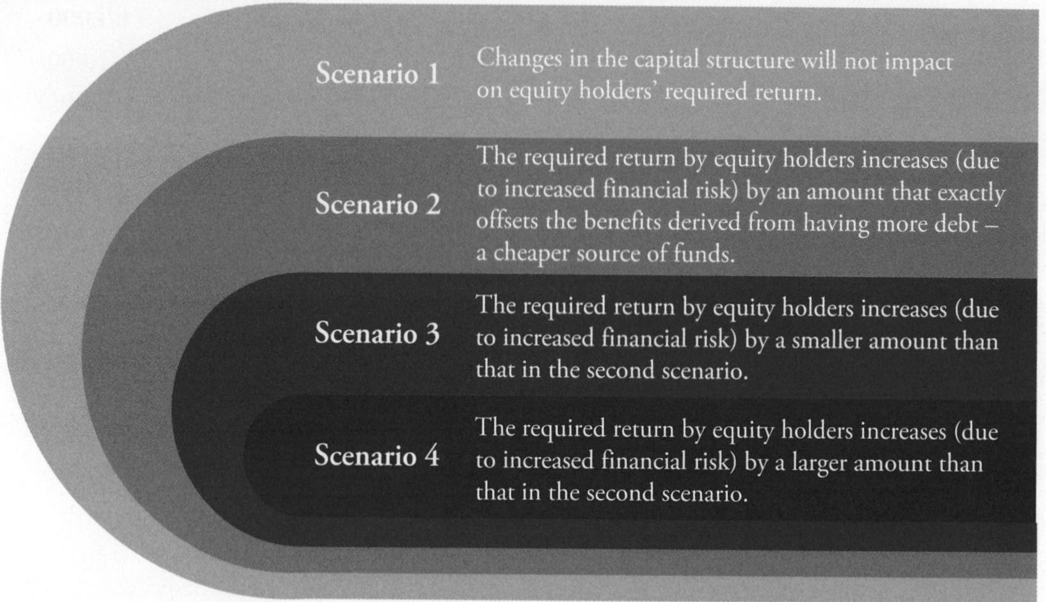

Scenario 1
Changes in the capital structure will not impact on equity holders' required return.
Scenario 2
The required return by equity holders increases (due to increased financial risk) by an amount that exactly offsets the benefits derived from having more debt – a cheaper source of funds.
Scenario 3
The required return by equity holders increases (due to increased financial risk) by a smaller amount than that in the second scenario.
Scenario 4
The required return by equity holders increases (due to increased financial risk) by a larger amount than that in the second scenario.

Capital Structure and the Value of a Company

The relationship between the cost of capital and the value of a company was explained in **Chapter 15**. In brief, the lower a company's cost of capital, the higher the value of a company (assuming earnings and cash flows remain constant).

$$\textbf{Market value of a company} = \frac{\textbf{Earnings}}{\textbf{WACC}}$$

Given this relationship, the impact of the four scenarios outlined in **Figure 16.2** can be interpreted in light of the expected shift in company value. As explained previously, debt is a cheaper source of funds than equity. Therefore, in the first scenario (wherein the cost of equity does not change), when debt is introduced, the overall WACC falls, resulting in an increase in company value. However, this first possibility is not considered realistic, as debt exposes equity holders to financial risk; in consequence, they require a higher return to compensate for it.

In the second scenario (wherein the cost of equity increases by an amount to exactly offset the reduction in the WACC, caused by having a greater proportion of cheaper debt), when debt is introduced, the overall WACC remains unchanged, as does the market value of a company. In the third scenario (wherein the cost of equity increases by a smaller amount), when debt levels increase, the overall WACC falls, resulting in an increase in company value. In the fourth scenario (wherein the cost of equity increases by a larger amount), when debt levels increase, the overall WACC increases, resulting in a fall in company value.

CAPITAL STRUCTURE THEORIES

The last three scenarios outlined in **Figure 16.2** form the basis of two schools of thought on how changes in capital structure impact on both the WACC and the resulting market value of a company. The two schools of thought can be categorised as the **relevancy theory (traditional theory)** and the **Modigliani and Miller irrelevancy theory** on capital structure.

Relevancy Theory (Traditional Theory)

The traditionalists consider that equity holders' behaviour changes from the third scenario outlined in **Figure 16.2** above, through the second scenario to the fourth scenario as the level of gearing increases. Indeed, they also argue that the premium required by debt holders also increases when financial risks exceed a certain point. The exact point differs between companies depending on their business risk and operating risks. Therefore, to a certain level of gearing, additional debt is actually beneficial to a company and increases company value. The relationship is illustrated in **Figure 16.3**.

FIGURE 16.3: THE COST OF EQUITY, DEBT AND THE WACC UNDER THE TRADITIONAL THEORY

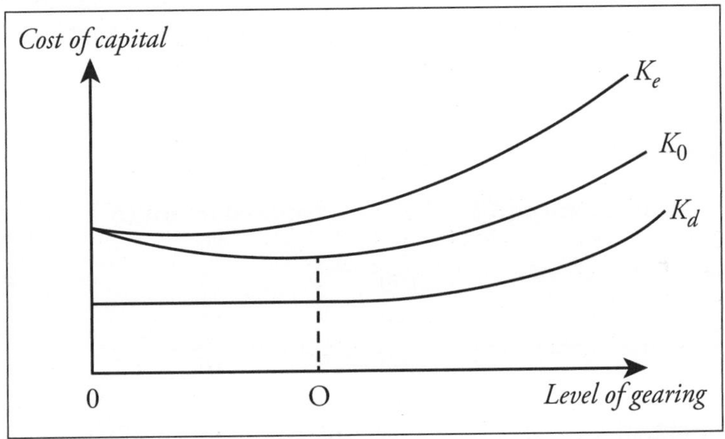

Where K_e is the cost of equity capital, K_d is the cost of debt capital and K_0 is the WACC. At a certain level of gearing, point O, the WACC is minimised. Point O represents the **optimum capital structure**. At this level of gearing the value of a company is maximised. As is illustrated in the above graph, the traditionalists assume that the cost of debt (K_d) remains constant up to a certain level of gearing, beyond this, the financial risks associated with having more debt cause new debt holders to require a premium for increased financial risk. When there are low levels of gearing, equity holders will require a small increase in their return; however, when gearing levels increase beyond a certain threshold, equity holders will command a much higher return to compensate them for increased financial risk. The impact of the behaviour of debt and equity holders on the WACC is to cause it to fall when there are low levels of gearing. However, beyond a certain threshold (O), the premium required by equity holders, is greater than the benefit to be derived from obtaining cheaper debt capital. Moreover, at certain levels of gearing, this increase in the WACC will be accentuated by an increase in debt holders' required return. The expected return investors require and the resultant impact on the WACC at increasing levels of gearing might be similar to that presented in **Worked Example 16.3**.

Worked Example 16.3: Traditional Theory: Changes in Gearing

The required return of debt and equity holders was recorded for a company as it increased its gearing levels.

Debt %	**Required return (K_d)** %	**Equity** %	**Required return (K_e)** %	**WACC (K_0)** %
0	5	100	15	15*
20	5	80	16	?
40	5	60	18	?
60	10	40	23	?
80	15	20	35	?

*0%(5%) + 100%(15%) = 15%

Requirement Assume the traditional theory on capital structure is relevant. Complete the table and identify which capital structure is most beneficial for this company.

Solution

As the traditional theory on capital structure is relevant, it is assumed that the cost of equity is at its equilibrium level for each gearing level.

Debt %	**Required return (K_d)** %	**Equity** %	**Required return (K_e)** %	**WACC (K_0)** %
0	5	100	15	15
20	5	80	16	13.8[1]
40	5	60	18	12.8[2]
60	10	40	23	15.2[3]
80	15	20	35	19[4]

[1] 20%(5%) + 80%(16%)

[2] 40%(5%) + 60%(18%)

[3] 60%(10%) + 40%(23%)

[4] 80%(15%) + 20%(35%)

The optimum gearing level is to hold 40% debt and 60% equity, as this results in the lowest WACC value (12.8%).

In **Worked Example 16.3**, debt holders require a constant return (5%) until debt reaches a certain level of gearing (60% in this instance); at this stage, their required return has increased to 10% and increases further as the company becomes more geared. Equity has a higher cost than debt at all levels of gearing, though the increases in the required return are marginal until gearing reaches 60%, when the required return increases by large amounts due to financial risk.

The result of the behaviour of both debt and equity holders in response to increases in financial risk is that, to a certain level of gearing (in this case 40%), more debt is actually beneficial to the company. The cost savings from obtaining a cheaper source of capital (debt at 5%), outweighs the increased return required by equity holders (increases from 15% to 18% – for a shift in gearing from 0% to 40%); the consequence of this is a fall in the WACC from 15% to 12.8%. This will increase company value. Any increases in gearing beyond this level are damaging to company value.

Worked Example 16.4: Traditional Theory: Impact on the Value of Equity

Calor Plc is partly financed by equity (cost 19%) and partly financed by debt (cost 12%). Its current WACC is 16.5%. The company pays all its profits as dividends. These amount to €/£3.8 million each year. The company wishes to invest in a new project, which would return €/£1.12 million each year before interest charges. This project would cost €/£6 million and will be financed using debt capital, which can be obtained at 12%. As a result of the increased financial risks the cost of equity is expected to increase to 20%. (Taxation is to be ignored.)

Requirement Assuming a traditional perspective:

(a) Show the impact on the value of equity of Calor Plc undertaking the project.

(b) Analyse the change in the value of Calor Plc's equity into returns expected from the new project (i.e. its NPV) and the resultant change in capital structure.

Solution

(a) The current market value of equity can be calculated using the dividend valuation model. As all earnings are paid out in dividends, there is no growth. The current dividend is €/£3.8 million and the required return by the equity holders is 19%. Therefore, the current market value of equity is:

$$P_0 = \frac{D_1}{K_e} = \frac{€/£3{,}800{,}000}{0.19} = €/£20{,}000{,}000$$

The new market value can be ascertained in the same manner. The first step is to calculate the new dividend.

	€/£000
Current dividend	3,800
Additional dividend: €/£1,120,000 – [€/£6,000,000 × 12%]	400
New dividend	4,200

The market value of equity is expected to increase from €/£20,000,000 to:

$$\frac{€/£4,200,000}{0.20} = €/£21,000,000$$

(b) The project is evaluated at the original WACC to determine what the NPV would have been had the capital structure not changed. The difference between the project's NPV and the €/£1,000,000 gain is the change in the value of equity that is attributable to the change in capital structure.

The NPV of the project is:

$$\frac{€/£1,120,000}{0.165} = €/£6,787,878$$

$$€/£6,787,878 - €/£6,000,000 = €/£787,878$$

Therefore, the remaining increase in equity value, €/£212,122 [€/£1,000,000 – €/£787,878], is due to the inclusion of additional debt. It must reduce the WACC and, hence, increase company value.

Modigliani and Miller Theory (M&M Theory)

Franco Modigliani and Merton Miller, two Nobel Laureates, formulated their capital structure theory in 1958. They argued that in a simplified world where certain assumptions hold true (listed in **Figure 16.6**), the value of a company will not be influenced by its capital structure. The reasoning for this is that equity holders will require a premium on their return equating to the amount that keeps the WACC constant. Therefore, a company's capital structure is irrelevant as changes to it do not impact on its WACC, which remains constant. As the WACC remains constant, capital structure does not influence company value. It is for this reason that M&M theory is sometimes referred to as the **irrelevancy theory**. M&M argue that market value is solely determined by the quality of a company's past investment record, which is evidenced by its operating profits/cash flows, before distributions to stakeholders. Due to this view, it is also sometimes referred to as the **net operating income theory**. The assumed behaviour of debt and equity holders is illustrated in **Figure 16.4**.

FIGURE 16.4: GRAPH SHOWING THE COST OF EQUITY, DEBT AND THE WACC UNDER M&M THEORY (NO TAXES)

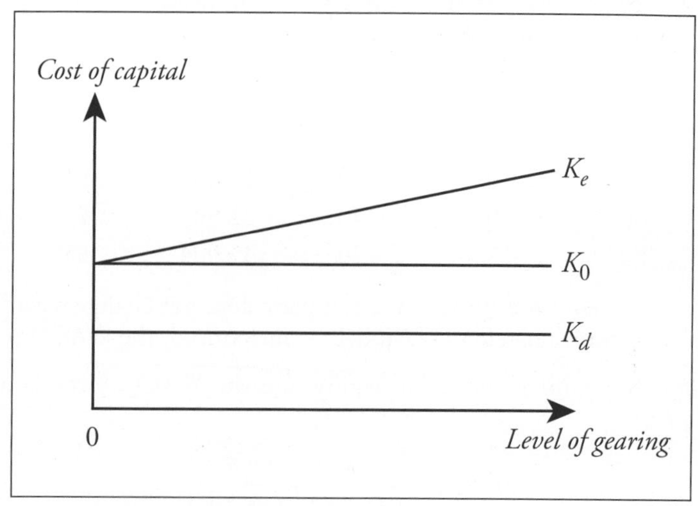

The cost of debt (K_d) remains constant regardless of the level of gearing. The cost of equity (K_e) rises in such a manner as to keep the WACC (K_0) constant. (See **Worked Example 16.5** for changes in the required returns of debt and equity holders as gearing increases.)

WORKED EXAMPLE 16.5: M&M THEORY – APPLICATION

A company is ungeared and has a cost of equity of 15%. The following table highlights the expected return required by debt holders (under M&M theory) were the company to alter its capital structure and become more geared.

Debt value %	**Required return (K_d)** %	**Equity value** %	**Required return (K_e)** %	**WACC (K_0)** %
0	10	100	15	15
20	10	80	?	?
40	10	60	?	?
60	10	40	?	?
80	10	20	?	?

Requirement

(a) Complete the table and identify which capital structure is most beneficial for the company (assuming M&M theory, without taxation).

(b) Explain the behaviour of the equity holders (assuming M&M theory, without taxation).

Solution

(a)

Debt value %	Required return (K_d) %	Equity value %	Required return (K_e) %	WACC (K_0) %
0	10	100	15.00	15
20	10	80	16.251	15*
40	10	60	18.332	15*
60	10	40	22.503	15*
80	10	20	35.004	15*

* Under M&M theory the WACC of a company does not change regardless of changes in capital structure. Therefore, when debt is introduced, the WACC remains at 15%.

To work out the required return on equity, use the WACC formula and work back (assume no tax).

$$WACC = \frac{E(K_e)}{(D+E)} + \frac{D(K_d)}{(D+E)}$$

$$15\% = \frac{80\%(K_e)}{100\%} + \frac{20\%(10\%)}{100\%}$$

$$15\% - 2\% = 0.8\ (K_e)$$

$$16.25\% = K_e$$

Only one calculation is shown here.

(b) Equity holders require an additional return to compensate them for additional financial risk, which is sufficient to keep the overall WACC constant. Therefore, at very high levels of gearing, say 80%, their required return has increased from 15%, when the company was ungeared, to 35%.

M&M's Propositions

As the relationships between the cost of debt, the cost of equity, the WACC and their required return is linear, M&M theory has been formulated into three propositions. The first proposition considers the relationship between company value and gearing levels; the second captures the change in return required by equity holders as a company becomes more geared; and the third considers the change in the investment appraisal discount rate to use for investment appraisal (i.e. the WACC), as a company becomes more geared. These propositions are outlined in **Figure 16.5**.

Assumptions

To examine the impact of changes in capital structure, M&M theory assumes certain restrictions to the operating and business environment of a company. These are summarised in **Figure 16.6**.

Critical Appraisal of these Assumptions Individuals cannot borrow at the same rate as companies; banks issue loans using the base rate as a benchmark and add premiums to it for

FIGURE 16.5: M&M PROPOSITIONS (NO TAXATION)

Proposition I (Company value)

M&M Proposition I states that capital structure is irrelevant to the value of a company; therefore, the value of a geared company (V_g) is the same as the value of a similar ungeared company (V_u).

$$V_g = V_u$$

The value of a geared company is the market value of its equity and debt ($V_g = D + E$). The value of an ungeared company will be the market value of its equity.

Proposition II (Cost of equity)

M&M Proposition II describes the behaviour of equity holders when the capital structure of a company changes. M&M Proposition II assumes that a company's cost of equity has a positive linear relationship to gearing levels and that equity holders will require a premium to compensate them for any additional financial risk faced.

Therefore, the expected cost of equity in a geared company (K_{eg}) is equal to the expected cost of equity in a similar but ungeared company (K_{eu}) plus a premium for financial risk. In all eventualities:

$$K_{eg} > K_{eu}$$

Proposition III (WACC)

M&M Proposition III suggests that the WACC of a geared company is the same as the WACC of an ungeared company.

$$WACC_g = WACC_u$$

Therefore, the cost of equity in an ungeared company can be used to discount capital appraisal projects in a similar geared company. All investments, or projects undertaken by a company, should have a return equal to or exceeding its WACC.

different classes of borrowers. Individuals do not have unlimited liability. Therefore, individuals have higher borrowing costs than companies. In addition, individuals are not happy to take on personal debt to the same levels as is held by companies they invest in. Personal debt has greater financial risk implications for an investor. Arbitrage may not work due to taxation and market imperfections, including information asymmetry and transaction costs. These imperfections limit the arbitrage process; however, this does not destroy the essential message of the M&M argument – an arbitrage mechanism can exist. Whether it works fully depends on the degree of market imperfection.

FIGURE 16.6: ASSUMPTIONS UNDERLYING M&M CAPITAL STRUCTURE THEORY

Assumption	Description
Growth	There is no growth, as companies pay out all their earnings in dividends. Therefore, earnings are constant and equity holders' expectations regarding future earnings are constant.
Business risk	Business risk is constant. Where a company raises capital for investment, it is assumed that the investment is into similar projects that do not alter the company's risk profile. When comparing two similar companies, it can be assumed that they have identical business risks.
No transaction costs/or delay	The capital structure of a company can be changed quickly, i.e. debt securities can be redeemed by the proceeds of an equity issue and vice versa. This process does not involve any costs, i.e. no issue costs.
Perfect capital markets	The capital markets are perfect. There is no information asymmetry or insider trading and market participants act rationally.
Arbitrage	The arbitrage process is the cumulative action of equity investors selling and purchasing shares in mispriced, similar companies across markets, until equilibrium prices are reached. Differences in the value of two similar companies that have different capital structures will be temporary as arbitrage will occur until the equilibrium price is achieved.
Individuals are similar to companies	Individuals can borrow funds at the same rate as companies and are happy with similar levels of gearing.
Taxation and bankruptcy	At the earlier phase of the theoretical debate on capital structure, taxation and bankruptcy risks were ignored.

Limitations of the M&M Theory

As with all theories, the underlying assumptions (detailed in **Figure 16.6** above) are its main weakness. In the case of the M&M irrelevancy theory, the assumptions are considered to be unrealistic. For instance: capital markets are not perfect (for example, there are issue costs with every transaction); individuals do face different financial risks compared to companies and their costs of borrowing are usually higher; it is almost impossible to find two companies that are exactly the same, except for their capital structures; most companies retain earnings each year for investment; and investors do not act rationally. The two most-criticised assumptions of M&M's earliest theory were that tax should not be ignored, as the effect of taxation makes debt cheaper, which directly impacts on a company's WACC and market value. The second is that gearing levels beyond a certain point do impact on returns required by new debt holders as they rank behind current debt holders when it comes to interest payments and capital repayments. The cost of debt increases greatly when a company reaches bankruptcy levels. In later published papers, M&M adjusted their theory to take account of tax and bankruptcy risk. These amended views are now presented.

M&M Theory (with Taxation)

Interest on debt is tax deductible, whereas dividend distributions are not. This makes the cost of debt to a company cheaper than the coupon rate or cash flow that is paid, so long as a company is profitable. For example, in a profitable company that pays interest at 8% and tax at 50% (assuming the debt is trading at par), the net cost of debt to the company will actually be 4% [8%(1 − 0.50)]. M&M argue that the behaviour of equity and debt holders will be as in the model without tax, except the cost of debt is lower. The impact of this is that as gearing increases, the premium required by equity holders reduces, and the WACC reduces by the impact of the tax benefit gained. The relationship between the cost of equity, debt and the WACC is illustrated in **Figure 16.7**.

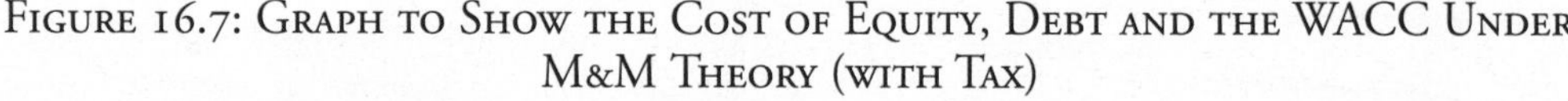

Figure 16.7: Graph to Show the Cost of Equity, Debt and the WACC Under M&M Theory (with Tax)

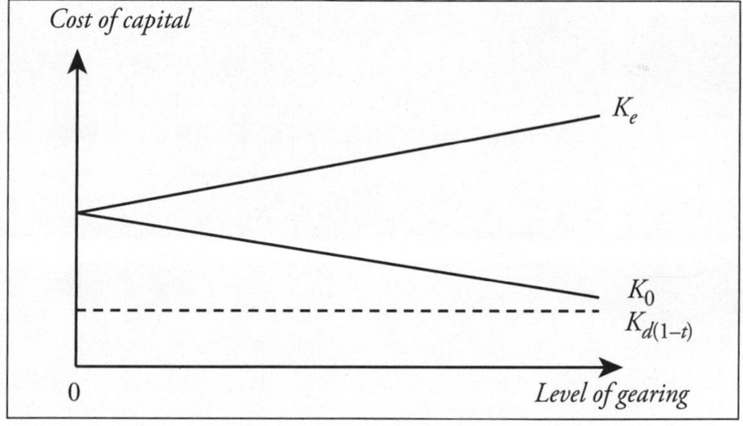

When taxation is factored in, M&M theory would suggest that companies should aim to increase their gearing levels and that the optimum capital structure is now 100% debt, because the WACC falls when debt levels increase. However, in the real world this would not be recommended. Debt has another consequence, in that failure to meet debt obligations as they fall due will eventually result in bankruptcy. This is likely to occur when gearing levels are very high. **Figure 16.8** considers the impact of taxation on M&M's three propositions. It is considered that the propositions have merit to a certain level of gearing, beyond this, the risk of bankruptcy becomes so great as to make the assumptions totally unrealistic.

FIGURE 16.8: M&M PROPOSITIONS (WITH TAXATION)

Proposition I (Company value)

As interest is tax deductible, it has a lower cost to the company than that assumed by M&M's initial theory. Therefore, when it is factored in, the difference between an ungeared company (V_u) and a similar geared company (V_g) is the present value of the tax saving on the interest differential. This is known as the **interest tax shield** and is calculated as D_t, where D is the market value of debt and t is the tax rate. Proposition I (with taxes) becomes:

$$V_g = V_u + D_t$$

Therefore, a geared company will always be valued higher than a similar ungeared company.

Proposition II (Cost of equity)

M&M argue that when tax is considered, equity holders behave in a similar manner as when it was assumed there was no tax. Hence:

$$K_{eg} > K_{eu}$$

However, they recognise the benefit of having debt in the capital structure. The tax deduction reduces the risk associated with having debt. Therefore, the risk premium required is smaller. It is reduced by the tax benefit $(1 - t)$.

Proposition III (WACC)

The market value of a geared company is always larger than the market value of a similar ungeared company. As such, the WACC of a geared company is always smaller than the WACC of an ungeared company.

$$\text{WACC}_g < \text{WACC}_u$$

M&M THEORY: OTHER ISSUES?

Financial Distress and Bankruptcy

M&M's theory with taxation suggests that the value of a company increases by the present value of the tax shield. This suggests that there are benefits to having very high levels of debt; however, there comes a point when the company starts to incur costs associated with financial distress. At a certain level of gearing it will no longer be advantageous for a company to seek more debt finance as the benefit of the tax shield becomes outweighed by the additional costs associated with financial distress. **Financial distress** increases in line with gearing and is related to the probability of a company not being able to pay its debt holders. Assets are used to pay a company's debts; therefore, theoretically, when a company's assets equal its debts, equity has no value. When this happens, ownership of a company's assets becomes the debt holders', as they have first claim to the assets in the event of bankruptcy. In addition, there are liquidity risks associated with debt capital. It has a guaranteed yearly interest cash outflow, whereas dividends can be waived.

Financial distress costs are also known as bankruptcy costs and can be categorised into indirect and direct costs. **Indirect costs** are difficult to measure. When a company is experiencing financial distress, management may direct their attention to trying to avoid bankruptcy, instead of properly running the business. It is in this climate that indirect costs are more likely to occur. They encompass: lost sales to customers who are concerned about the security of supply; the inability to source supplies at competitive rates, as suppliers become aware of the additional default risk associated with trading with the company; the loss of valuable employees, who become aware of the situation; and sub-optimal decision-making, resulting in lost profits. **Direct costs** are the actual costs incurred when a company goes bankrupt. At this stage, the assets of a company are legally distributed to its debt holders. The process includes direct costs such as solicitor's fees, insolvency practitioner's fees and general administrative costs associated with the bankruptcy, including managerial time.

In reality, no two companies are alike. They have different business risks and cost structures. This will impact on the capital structure their financial managers choose to pursue. Companies with high levels of tangible assets, strong operating income and cash flows that are not sensitive to changes in the economic environment are better placed to adopt higher geared capital structures, as they can benefit from the tax shield. Companies with intangible assets and fluctuating income that are affected by changes in the economic environment are more likely to pursue more equity funding in their capital structures. In addition, there are the actions of management. Under M&M, it is assumed that business finance managers act in a manner to maximise company value, even if this means pursuing a capital structure with 100% debt or awarding a 100% dividend payout policy. Several research studies suggest that this does not take place, that management have a preference for particular sources of finance (pecking order theory) or that management will finance the company to benefit themselves personally (agency theory). These two theories are now discussed in brief.

Pecking Order Theory

Pecking order theory suggests that when managers source finance, they do not seek an optimal capital structure, instead they have a preference for using retained earnings over external funds, and a preference for sourcing debt capital in front of equity capital (Donaldson, 1961). An explanation for this behaviour is effort and cost. Internally generated funds can be sourced with no effort and have no issue costs. At the other extreme, it takes a considerable amount of management effort to raise equity, and equity issues are costly. Another reason for this ranking is provided by Myers and Majluf (1984), who suggest that asymmetric information provides an explanation: an issue of equity is perceived by stock markets to indicate that shares are overvalued, and the internal management is cashing in on the potential gains to be made. This means it is unattractive to issue shares as it may signal that current shares are overpriced, resulting in the current equity holders selling their shares to cash in on the mis-pricing, hence driving share price downwards.

Agency Costs

In conflict with M&M theory, it is argued that the level of debt capital raised by a company is influenced by agency costs built into, for example, debt capital trust deeds. **Agency costs** are direct or indirect costs that strive to ensure that agents (i.e. company managers) act in the interest of the principals (i.e. equity and debt holders) (Jensen and Meckling, 1976; see also **Chapter 1**). When a company is geared, debt holders usually introduce agency costs to ensure that their interests are protected. The most obvious agency cost is **covenants**. These can be written into debt contracts and usually restrict management decision-making in a manner that protects debt holders' positions. Examples of typical covenants include: restrictions on dividend payouts, restrictions on asset disposals, restrictions on the type of projects invested in or restrictions on further gearing.

OTHER PRACTICAL ISSUES CONSIDERED TO INFLUENCE A COMPANY'S CAPITAL STRUCTURE

Level of Tangible Assets

Most lenders require security for loans provided. This can restrict gearing levels, as only some types of asset are considered appropriate as security; for example, property is more attractive to lenders than other tangible assets. The reason for this is that other tangible assets, such as plant and machinery, may have restricted external sale markets. This results in uncertainty in respect of the recoverability of capital for lenders, making these tangible assets less attractive as security than property, which is likely to increase in value. Hence the level of gearing in a company's capital structure may actually be determined by lenders and not be the result of managerial policy.

Managerial Conservatism

All investors (in both equity and debt) lose when a company goes into liquidation. The parties to suffer the greatest loss are management and employees. Investors usually have portfolios made up of several investments. If one fails, then the loss to the investor is restricted, as there will be income from other parts of their portfolio. However, a manager or employee will lose their main source of income. This may cause managers to restrict gearing, as higher levels of gearing increase the likelihood of liquidation. Ross (1977) argues that the decision to increase gearing levels is, in fact, an indication of managerial confidence in the future of a company. The reason for this is that, as management are naturally conservative, they are more likely to raise debt if they are confident about a company's ability to repay the cash flows; therefore, this can be interpreted as a signal to the market about the strength of expected cash flows and should lead to an increase in share price.

Investment Opportunities

When there are many profitable investment opportunities, it is more likely for a company to change its capital structure and increase the level of gearing, particularly if there is a shortage of available funds. Indeed, it can be argued that management prefer to hold on to a certain level of liquid funds than to invest them, as this provides flexibility for future decision-making. When possible investment opportunities are not as profitable, management are more likely to build up reserves and increase the equity proportion of capital.

Control

When there are dominant equity holders, they are more likely to oppose raising equity finance, particularly if the balance of control might be shifted. In these circumstances, the current equity holders are more likely to support raising debt finance.

CONCLUSION

This chapter explains the relationship between capital structure, distributable profits, key accounting ratios, the WACC and company value. The chapter discusses financial risk and outlines the assumptions regarding the behaviour of equity holders under each of the capital structure theories. The latter part of the chapter explains the theoretical views regarding whether an optimum capital structure exists. The traditional argument, M&M theory, and its amended version, M&M theory with tax, are outlined. The latter theory suggests that an optimum capital structure has very high levels of debt. High levels of debt result in financial risk, which has many repercussions on a company, the most severe of which is bankruptcy.

Finally, practical considerations that affect a company's capital structure are presented. For example, as a company gears, it starts to incur financial distress costs; at some stage these costs outweigh the benefit of having lower cost debt. Also, some types of company are more suited to having debt in their capital structures. These companies are likely to have: higher levels of tangible assets, such as property; steady operating cash flows; and low levels of fixed costs. Then there are the influences of the decision-makers: the managers and equity holders. Managers' salaries usually provide the bulk of their personal income; therefore, their actions are likely to be risk-averse. Indeed, it is considered that managers use a pecking order when selecting the type of finance they source, having a preference for retained earnings, followed by debt, and lastly equity capital. This is because of cost issues and the fact that equity holders have to approve any approaches to the market for more finance. Dominant equity holders are unlikely to support any action that reduces their control within a company.

EXAMINATION STANDARD QUESTION: IMPACT OF CAPITAL STRUCTURE CHANGES ON DISTRIBUTABLE PROFIT AND KEY ACCOUNTING RATIOS

You are a trainee accountant in Mezenar Limited and have been asked to prepare a memo for the board of directors regarding raising finance for a proposed new investment in equipment.

The following is an extract from the forecasted financial statements of Mezenar, a manufacturing company, for the year ended 31 December 20X4.

Extract from the Forecasted Statement of Financial Position
for Year Ended 31 December 20X4

	€/£000
ASSETS	16,500
EQUITY AND LIABILITIES	
Ordinary share capital (€/£2 each)	8,000
Share premium	3,600
10% debentures	4,900
	16,500

The debenture agreement states that the debt/equity ratio cannot exceed 75%.

Potential New Investment:

- Mezenar is considering making a substantial investment of €/£3,500,000 in equipment to enhance its manufacturing facilities. The finance manager has done preliminary research and has found that this investment would increase Mezenar's current profit of €/£4,200,000 (before interest and tax) by 15%.
- The board of directors is looking to raise either debt or equity to finance the purchase of the equipment.
- The bank has informed Mezenar that it would charge an interest rate of 7% per annum for the loan of €/£3,500,000 over 15 years. The board of directors is curious as to what factors the bank considers when it is setting the interest rate.
- If Mezenar decides to raise equity finance, it would be by way of a share issue. The share price is currently trading at €/£2.80.
- Mezenar has a current policy of paying a dividend of 40 cents/pence per share.
- The rate of taxation is 20%.

Requirement Prepare a memo to the board of directors which:

(a) Demonstrates the effect the potential investment in equipment could have on the following ratios that Mezenar uses as key performance indicators:
  (i) Debt to equity.
  (ii) Interest cover.
  (iii) Earnings per share.

8 Marks

(b) Recommend (with a reason) whether Mezenar should choose debt or equity to finance the investment in equipment to enhance its manufacturing facilities.

2 Marks
Presentation 2 Marks
Total 12 Marks

(Based on Chartered Accountants Ireland, CAP 1, Summer 2013)

Solution

Memo

To: Board of Directors
From: Trainee Accountant
Re: Investment in Equipment
Date: June 20X4

Mezenar Limited is considering making a substantial investment of €/£3,500,000 in equipment to enhance its manufacturing facilities. This memo considers:

(a) the impact the investment and change in capital structure will have on the key performance indicators; and
(b) whether debt or equity should be chosen to finance the investment in equipment.

(a) **Impact the investment and the loan will have on the forecasted financial information**
I have summarised the ratios used in my analysis below. You will find a breakdown of these ratios in the Appendix to this memo.

	20X4 (current)	**20X4 (increased debt)**	**20X4 (increased equity)**
Debt to equity	42%	72%	32.4%
Interest cover	8.6 times	6.6 times	9.8 times
EPS	€/£0.742	€/£0.819	€/£0.66

- It is clear to see that if the company were to increase its debt levels, it would be highly geared and the 75% debt covenant would be close to being breached. In saying this, the company could cover its interest payments nearly seven times out of its profits. We also need to consider the fact that interest on debt is tax deductible and the more debt Mezenar Limited takes on, the less tax it will have to pay. The obligatory payments of interest and capital will, however, also put a strain on the company's liquidity.
- If Mezenar Limited were to raise finance through a share issue, the debt to equity ratio would be reduced and be well below the 75% restriction imposed by the bank. The EPS has fallen to 11% from current levels even though the profits after tax have increased. The reason for this fall is as a result of the increase in the number of shares in issue. A falling EPS may send out a negative signal to the existing shareholders.

The dividend policy of Mezenar Limited is to distribute a dividend of 40 cents/pence per share. Thus the company will be required to make a further payout of €/£500,000 as a result of the increase in the number of shares in issue. If the company is reluctant to change its current dividend policy, this further payout in dividends may result in the company being unable to plough back profits into the company to invest in projects that yield a positive net present value. In saying this, it is up to Mezenar Limited whether or not it wants to continue paying dividends. Interest on loans, on the other hand, does have to be paid.

(b) **Recommendation**
As outlined above, both sources of finance have their merits and pitfalls. It may be worth investigating further whether a combination of both of these sources may be better as opposed to just using debt or equity.

APPENDIX

	20X4 (current)	**20X4 (increased debt)**	**20X4 (increased equity)**
	€/£000	**€/£000**	**€/£000**
Debt to equity	4,900 ÷ 11,600	8,400 ÷ 11,600	4,900 ÷ 15,100
	42%	72%	32.4%
Earnings per share			
PBIT	4,200	4,830	4,830
Interest:			
10% debentures	(490)	(490)	(490)
7% loan	—	(245)	—
	3,710	4,095	4,340
Tax @ 20%	(742)	(819)	(868)
Profit after tax	2,968	3,276	3,472

$$\frac{\text{PAT}}{\text{Shares in issue}} \quad \frac{2{,}968}{4{,}000} = \text{€/£}0.742 \quad \frac{3{,}276}{4{,}000} = \text{€/£}0.819 \quad \frac{3{,}472}{5{,}250} = \text{€/£}0.66$$

Interest Cover

$$\frac{\text{PBIT}}{\text{Interest}} \quad \frac{4{,}200}{490} = 8.6 \text{ times} \quad \frac{4{,}830}{735} = 6.6 \text{ times} \quad \frac{4{,}830}{490} = 9.9 \text{ times}$$

Key Terms

Agency costs
Arbitrage process
Capital structure
Covenants
Direct costs of bankruptcy
Financial distress
Financial risk
Gearing
Indirect costs of bankruptcy
Interest tax shield
Irrelevancy theory
Modigliani and Miller (M&M) theory
Net operating income theory
Optimum capital structure
Relevancy theory
Traditional theory
Pecking order theory

REVIEW QUESTIONS

(See Suggested Solutions to Review Questions in **Appendix B**.)

Question 16.1

What is a company's capital structure?

Question 16.2

Explain the relationship between a company's capital structure and its WACC.

Question 16.3

What is financial risk?

Question 16.4

Pero Plc and Gato Plc are two identical companies. They have similar business risks, similar operating risks and identical operating profits (€/£300,000), which are distributed in full every year, after interest is deducted.

Pero Plc is financed entirely by equity, having 1,600,000 50c/p equity shares that are currently trading at €/£1.40. Pero Plc has just paid a dividend.

Gato Plc has 800,000 50c/p equity shares that are currently trading at €/£1.60. They have also just paid a dividend. In addition to equity shares, Gato Plc has €/£1.2 million (10%) irredeemable loan stock that is currently trading at par value. Assume traditional capital structure theory applies.

Requirement

(a) Calculate the cost of equity for each company (ignore taxation).
(b) Calculate the WACC for each company (ignore taxation).
(c) Provide explanations for any differences between the rates reported for both companies, arising from your calculations in (a) and (b).
(d) What would M&M say about the results in (a) and (b)?

Question 16.5

Discuss M&M's propositions concerning the cost of capital and the value of a company under different levels of gearing (assume a world of no taxation).

7 Marks

(Based on Chartered Accountants Ireland, MABF II, Summer 1996, Q5(a))

Question 16.6

Jack has 200,000 ordinary shares in issue. Each share has a nominal value of €/£0.50. To date, Jack has accumulated retained earnings of €/£4,200,000. The company also has long-term bank borrowings of €/£5,500,000.

Requirement

(a) Calculate the gearing ratio of Jack.

2 Marks

(b) Explain TWO ways in which your answer, calculated in part (a) above, can have significance for Jack.

2 Marks

(c) Outline THREE practical factors that may influence a company's choice of capital structure.

3 Marks

(Based on Chartered Accountants Ireland, CAP 1, Finance, Autumn 2019, extract from Q5)

Question 16.7

An increase in debt financing can increase the likelihood of a company going bankrupt. The direct costs associated with financial distress are legal and administrative costs associated with bankruptcy.

Requirement Identify TWO indirect financial distress costs.

3 Marks

(Based on Chartered Accountants Ireland, CAP 1, Summer 2016, extract from Q2)

Question 16.8

Requirement Briefly identify FOUR factors (other than cost and duration) that should be considered when selecting sources of finance.

4 Marks

(Based on Chartered Accountants Ireland, CAP 1, Summer 2016, extract from Q2)

CHALLENGING QUESTIONS

(Suggested Solutions to Challenging Questions are available through your lecturer.)

Question 16.1 Yuki (Level 2)

You have just been employed as assistant financial controller in Yuki Plc. The capital structure of the company is set out below.

	€/£ million
Equity shares of €/£100 each	20
Retained earnings	10
9% preference shares of €/£100 each	12
7% debentures	8
Total	50

The company earns a pre-interest and tax return on capital of 12%. The corporation tax rate is 25%. The company requires a sum of €/£2,500,000 to finance an expansion programme, which will also be required to earn a pre-tax return of 12%.

The following funding alternatives are available to the company:

1. Issue 20,000 equity shares at a premium of €/£25 per share.
2. Issue 10% preference shares at par.
3. Issue 8% debentures at par.

It is estimated that the following price earnings ratios will apply in respect of each of the financing options:

Equity	17.25
Preference	17.00
Debentures	15.07

Requirement

(a) Calculate the expected earnings per share and market price per share under each of the three alternatives.

9 Marks

(b) Write a memorandum to the financial controller explaining the impact of each funding alternative on this company's share price, gearing and level of financial risk.

9 Marks
Total 18 Marks

(Based on Chartered Accountants Ireland, MABF II, Summer 2007, Q6)

Question 16.2 Supuro (Level 2)

Supuro Plc
STATEMENT OF FINANCIAL POSITION
as at 31 March 20X5

	€/£	€/£
Share capital:		
10,000 equity shares of €/£100 each fully paid-up	1,000,000	
25,000 11% cumulative preference shares of €/£10 each fully paid-up	250,000	1,250,000
Revenue reserves		2,500,000
Secured loans		2,000,000
Unsecured loans		1,200,000
Trade payables		1,800,000
Outstanding expenses		750,000
		9,500,00
Represented by:		
Non-current assets	5,500,000	
Current assets	3,700,000	
Advances and deposits	300,000	9,500,000

The company plans to manufacture a new product in line with its current production. The capital cost is estimated to be €/£2,500,000. The company desires to finance the new project by either of the following methods:

- *Scenario (i)* Raising €/£1,600,000 by the issue of equity shares at a premium of €/£100 per share (on the nominal value of the shares) and the balance to be derived from internal sources.
- *Scenario (ii)* Raising €/£1,600,000 by the issue of 15% irredeemable debentures at par and the balance from internal sources as above.

Additional information:

1. Rate of dividends declared in the past five years were as follows:

	%
31 March 20X5	24
31 March 20X4	24
31 March 20X3	20
31 March 20X2	20
31 March 20X1	18

   Dividend percentages refer to the nominal value of shares.
2. Net profit before tax (but after interest on existing loans) in the business is normally 10% of turnover. It is anticipated that this will rise to 12% of all sales after the introduction of the new product.
3. Turnover in the last three years was as follows:

	€/£
31 March 20X5	8,000,000
31 March 20X4	6,000,000
31 March 20X3	5,000,000

4. Anticipated additional sales from the new project is €/£3,000,000 annually.
5. The tax rate is 35%.
6. The trend of market price of the equity share of the company, quoted on the Stock Exchange, has been as follows:

Year	**High €/£**	**Low €/£**
20X4–X5	300	190
20X3–X4	250	180
20X2–X3	240	180

Requirement

(a) Explain briefly the significance of the 11% preference shares in Supuro's capital structure being 'cumulative'.

3 Marks

(b) Calculate Supuro's earnings per share (EPS) and price earnings (P/E) ratio for the year ended 31 March 20X5. Use the average market price per share in the latter calculation.

5 Marks

(c) Calculate Supuro's anticipated EPS and the anticipated market price per share following the introduction of the new product financed in the manner described in Scenario (i).

4 Marks

(d) Calculate Supuro's existing debt–equity ratio on the basis of book values.

2 Marks

(e) Calculate Supuro's anticipated EPS and the anticipated market price per share following the introduction of the new product financed in the manner described in Scenario (ii).

4 Marks

(f) On the basis of your calculations in parts (b) to (e) above, conclude on whether the new product proposal is worthwhile and, if so, how it should be financed.

4 Marks
Total 22 Marks

(Based on Chartered Accountants Ireland, MABF II, Autumn 2008, Q5)

Question 16.3 Komtar (Level 2)

The following figures of Komtar Ltd are presented to you:

	€/£	€/£
Earnings before interest and tax		2,300,000
Less: Debenture interest @ 8%	80,000	
Long-term loan interest @ 11%	220,000	300,000
		2,000,000
Less: Corporation tax (12.5%)		250,000
Earnings after tax		1,750,000
Number of shares of €/£10 each (nominal value)		500,000
Earnings per share (EPS)		€/£3.50
Market price of shares		€/£20
Price earnings ratio (P/E ratio)		5.7143 times

The company has undistributed reserves of €/£2 million. It is in need of €/£3 million to pay off the debentures and modernise its plant. It seeks your advice on the following alternative methods of raising long-term finance.

- Alternative 1: raise the entire amount as a term loan from the banks @ 12% interest per annum.
- Alternative 2: raise part of the funds by the issue of 100,000 shares (nominal value €/£10 each) at a market price of €/£20 each and the rest by term loan @ 12% interest per annum.

The company expects to improve its rate of return on capital employed by 2% as a result of the modernisation, but the P/E ratio is likely to go down to 5.0 if the entire amount is raised by term loan.

Requirement

(a) (i) Calculate the current total capital employed. *(Use book values in your calculations.)*
(ii) Calculate the rate of return on total capital employed.
(iii) Calculate the expected improved rate following the proposed modernisation.
(iv) Calculate the capital employed after the raising of the funds referred to above.

6 Marks

(b) Which of the two methods of raising funds referred to above would you recommend? Use calculations to support your answer.

10 Marks

(c) If it is assumed that there will be no change in the P/E ratio if either of the two alternatives are adopted, would your recommendation in (b) still hold good?

2 Marks
Total 18 Marks

(Based on Chartered Accountants Ireland, MABF II, Summer 2008, Q7)

Question 16.4 Cadence (Level 2)

You are a financial consultant for Cadence Ltd, a registered financial advisory company that provides a range of financial services to companies and individuals. Recently, the firm has been approached by three client companies, each requiring €/£10 million of new funds to expand their business. The firms are considering the following financing options, but would like the advice of Cadence before proceeding:

1. Ordinary shares.
2. Secured debenture.
3. Convertible loan stock.
4. Bank term loan.

The following summary financial information has been prepared by Cadence on each of the three companies based on the most recent financial statements for the year ended 31 December 20X5, all publicly available information, and on the basis of individual meetings with each company managing director. None of the companies has issued preference shares.

	Company A	**Company B**	**Company C**
Type of company	Medical devices	Property investment	Online betting
Market capitalisation	€/£36m	€/£50m	€/£48m
Shares issued	10m	5m	10m
Current share price	€/£3.60	€/£10	€/£4.8
Min.-max. share price	€/£3.00–€/£5.50	€/£5.00–€/£11.50	€/£4.50–€/£8
P/E ratio	12	N/A (loss-making)	10
Earnings after tax	€/£3.0m	N/A (loss-making)	€/£4.8m
Dividend cover	High	Nil	Medium
Interest cover	Medium	Nil	High
Debt	€/£15m long-term	€/£37.5m (80% short-term)	€/£5m long-term
Net asset value per share	€/£3	€/£12	€/£4
Use of funds	Develop new high-tech medical device, sales commence 20X8	Buy land overseas considered by B to be undervalued	Expand portfolio offering and increase back office to support the expansion

John Bauer, a private individual not connected with any of the above companies, is considering an investment of €/£1 million in Company A. John has never invested in the stock exchange before.

Requirement

(a) Prepare a briefing memorandum for Cadence outlining the method or methods of financing you would consider most appropriate for each of the respective companies above and why.

14 Marks

(b) Identify and *briefly* explain FOUR factors that John should consider prior to making any investment in Company A.

4 Marks

(c) Briefly describe any ethical considerations for Cadence in providing investment advice to John Bauer on Company A and how these *could* be resolved.

3 Marks
Total 21 Marks

(Based on Chartered Accountants Ireland, CAP 2, MABF, Summer 2010, Q2)

Question 16.5 Enam (Level 2)

The board of directors of Enam Plc is considering an expansion programme that will require raising €/£79.25 million. The expansion should increase operating profits by €/£15.24 million per annum in the foreseeable future. The expansion apart, operating profit in 20X5 is expected to be 3% higher than in 20X4. The board has been presented with three possible options for raising the necessary finance.

Option 1 The company would issue equity shares at a price of 317c/p each.
Option 2 The company would issue 12% debentures dated 20Y4.
Option 3 The company would raise a 10-year (9%) loan from a financial institution. If this option is chosen, the institution would require that an interest cover of at least three times is maintained and that the dividend cover is at least 2.5 times.

The board has also been presented with extracts from the published financial statements of the past three years.

STATEMENT OF PROFIT OR LOSS (EXTRACT)
for the Year Ended 30 June

	20X2 **€/£ million**	**20X3** **€/£ million**	**20X4** **€/£ million**
Operating profit	27.81	54.85	41.77
Interest	(9.40)	(11.94)	(13.49)
Profit before tax	18.41	42.91	28.28
Tax at 30%	(5.52)	(12.87)	(8.48)
Profit after tax	12.89	30.04	19.80
Dividends	(8.79)	(9.23)	(9.69)
Retained earnings	4.10	20.81	10.11
Share price (cents/pence) as at 30 June	305c/p	495c/p	413c/p

STATEMENT OF FINANCIAL POSITION (EXTRACT)
as at 30 June

	20X2 **€/£ million**	**20X3** **€/£ million**	**20X4** **€/£ million**
Long-term loans	89	114	127
Issued equity share capital (nominal 50c/p each)	63	63	63
Share premium account	32	32	32
Revenue reserve	48.54	69.35	79.49

The chair of the board, Jemima Oswald, is concerned about the implications of the various financing options. She and her family hold 48.25 million of the issued shares at the moment. It has been company policy to increase dividends at a rate of 5% per annum and it is intended to continue this policy in the future. Corporation tax is expected to remain at 30%.

Requirement

(a) Calculate the current (year ended 30 June 20X4) dividend per share in cents/pence.

2 Marks

(b) Calculate the number of shares that would need to be issued under Option 1.

1 Mark

(c) Draft the projected statement of profit or loss (in the same format as in the question) for each of the three options outlined for the year ended 30 June 20X5. (Assume that taxable profits are the same as accounting profits and ignore deferred tax.)

9 Marks

(d) Produce projected statement of financial position extracts as at 30 June 20X5 under each of the options in the question, showing the following balances only:

- Long-term loans.
- Issued equity share capital.
- Share premium account.
- Retained earnings.

3 Marks

(e) Prepare a brief report to the chair of the board outlining which of the financing options you prefer, giving reasons for your decision.

6 Marks
Presentation Mark 1 Mark
Total 22 Marks

(Based on Chartered Accountants Ireland, MABF II, Autumn 2005, Q5)

Question 16.6 Equitas (Level 1)

(a) Define financial gearing and explain its significance for corporate financial management.

4 Marks

(b) Discuss the factors that can limit the amount of debt finance a company might utilise.

6 Marks
Total 10 Marks

(Based on Chartered Accountants Ireland, MABF II, Autumn 1996, Extract from Q7)

Question 16.7 M&M (Level 1)

"Capital structure can have no influence on the value of the firm." (Modigliani and Miller.)

Requirement Discuss this statement and comment briefly on the main factors a company should consider when determining capital structure.

8 Marks

(Based on Chartered Accountants Ireland, MABF II, Autumn 1997, Extract from Q5)

Question 16.8 A (Level 2)

A Plc has an annual operating income of €/£1 million in perpetuity, and a market value of €/£15 million. The market value of A Plc's debt is €/£5m, at a cost of 3% (ignore taxes).

Requirement

(a) Estimate the company's WACC.

3 Marks

(b) Calculate the market value using the traditional method – assuming the gearing ratio increases to 0.5. (You are informed that the equity holders do not consider that the change in gearing impacts on the overall risks of investing in the company.)

4 Marks

(c) Calculate the market value and the WACC using M&M theory, assuming the gearing ratio increases to 0.5 (ignore taxation). What implications does this have for the cost of equity?

5 Marks

(d) Compare and contrast the traditional and M&M theories of the cost of capital and discuss how useful they may be in the determination of an appropriate capital structure for a company.

10 Marks
Total 22 Marks

(Based on Chartered Accountants Ireland, MABF II, Summer 1998, Q5)

Question 16.9 Nadel (Level 1)

Nadel Ltd is a successful Irish company which has been in existence for several years. The most recent profit before interest and tax was €/£12 million. Nadel expects to achieve the same result for the forthcoming financial year.

Nadel has recently appraised an investment opportunity and determined that the project is financially very attractive. The project requires an investment of €/£25 million. Nadel estimates that if this investment is undertaken, then existing profit before interest and tax will increase by 20% next year. The directors of Nadel have decided to proceed with the investment and they are now considering the best method of financing it. Two options are currently being considered:

(i) issue €/£25 million of 7% loan notes; or
(ii) issue ordinary shares at a price of €/£5 per share.

Nadel's current capital structure is as follows:

	€/£000
Equity shares (€/£1 per share)	20,000
Reserves	15,000
10% loan notes	6,000
5% preference shares	4,000
	45,000

Nadel pays corporation tax at the rate of 20% and has a policy of distributing all earnings as dividends to its ordinary shareholders.

Requirement

(a) Calculate the current earnings per share (EPS) **and** current gearing (calculated as debt/equity) of Nadel.

5 Marks

(b) Calculate the revised EPS **and** revised gearing of Nadel for the next year, assuming it proceeds with the above investment and finances it by means of:
   (i) The issue of 7% loan notes;
   (ii) The issue of ordinary shares at a price of €/£5 per share.

6 Marks

(c) Discuss, based on your calculations in part (b) above, which financing option would be preferable to the shareholders of Nadel.

3 Marks

(d) Outline FOUR factors which impact the rate of interest Nadel must pay on its loan notes.

4 Marks

(e) Discuss TWO key differences between ordinary share capital and preference share capital.

2 Marks

Total 20 Marks

(Based on Chartered Accountants Ireland, CAP 1, Finance, Summer 2018, Q3)

Question 16.10 Mitcon (Level 1)

Mitcon Solutions Limited, a company engaged in data analytics, has identified new software in which it wants to invest €/£225,000. The financial manager of Mitcon has performed an investment appraisal and concluded that the investment is worthwhile, but is interested in how financing the investment will affect the company's debt:equity (D:E) ratio and its weighted average cost of capital (WACC). Mitcon is considering either raising debt or equity to finance the acquisition of this software.

Mitcon has had preliminary discussions with its bank and a third-party equity investor to raise the €/£225,000. The conditions are set out below:

Bank: Issue €/£225,000 6% loan redeemable at par in 10 years' time and secured on Mitcon's non-current assets.

Equity Investor: Mitcon will issue 45,000 ordinary shares at a premium of €/£4.50 per share.

You have been provided with extracts of Mitcon's most recent statement of financial position (before the investment) as follows:

Equity	**€/£000**
Ordinary shares (€/£0.50 nominal value)	120
Reserves	1,224
	1,344
Non-current liabilities	
5% irredeemable loan notes	80
7% redeemable loan notes	96
	176
Current liabilities	
Trade payables	22
Bank overdraft	15
	37
Total equity and liabilities	**1,557**

The ordinary shares of Mitcon are currently trading at a premium of €/£4.50 per share over the nominal value. A dividend of €/£12,000 is due to be paid in the next few days. The 5% irredeemable loan notes are currently trading at €/£98 per €/£100. The 7% loan notes will be redeemed at a discount of 3% below par (par is €/£100) in five years' time.

You can assume the following:

- All debt finance (current and proposed) will have a cost of debt (or gross redemption yield) of 6%;
- The market value of the existing debt finance will remain unchanged after the acquisition of the software;
- The growth rate in dividends is 8% year on year. The cost of debt will remain unchanged at 6% regardless of whether debt or equity finance is chosen;
- Taxation can be ignored.

Requirement

(a) Calculate Mitcon's debt:equity (D:E) ratio **before** the investment in the new software on the basis of:

(i) Book value of debt and equity; and

(ii) Market value of debt and equity.

6 Marks

(b) Calculate the weighted average cost of capital (WACC) of Mitcon **after** the acquisition of the software based on:

(i) Choosing debt to finance the acquisition of the software; and

(ii) Choosing equity to finance the acquisition of the software.

7 Marks

(c) Briefly discuss what is meant by the 'pecking order theory'.

3 Marks

(d) Identify FOUR practical limitations of using long term-debt as a source of finance.

4 Marks

Total 20 Marks

(Based on Chartered Accountants Ireland, CAP 1, Finance, Autumn 2017, Q1)

17

Valuing Companies

Learning Objectives

Upon completing this chapter, readers should be able to:

- summarise why valuations of entities or equity are needed;
- outline the inherent problems with valuing companies;
- describe the valuation process and economic rationale for such activities;
- calculate a company's value using asset values, earnings, dividend payout policy, discounted cash flows and market values;
- explain the advantages and limitations of each of the methods; and
- outline typical steps taken by an analyst when valuing an entity.

INTRODUCTION

The majority of businesses, whether private or publicly listed, have to be valued at some point in their existence. Even small private businesses are likely to be valued, with the valuation usually required to assist an individual's decision-making with personal financial wealth management in mind. For example, partners/sole traders may wish to have a valuation undertaken if they are considering succession planning, when refinancing the business or when an individual offers to purchase a share in the business. The tax authorities may require a valuation when the business is being transferred on the death of a sole trader to their next of kin, or when there is a change in a partnership. The courts may require a valuation if a partner/sole trader gets divorced and their ex-partner is claiming a portion of the individual's assets.

Many businesses are not valued by the markets. For example, sole traders, partnerships and private companies will not have a market value for their equity or debt, therefore they require a formal company valuation if the owners are trying to determine the business's value. When a company's shares are publicly traded, a market value for that company's equity already exists. However, even in these circumstances a formal valuation is normally required. The reason for this is now explained. If stock markets are strong-form efficient (discussed in **Chapter 1**), then equity share values would correctly value the equity stake in a company. Research has shown that the UK, Ireland and US stock markets are weak- to semi-strong-form efficient – this suggests that equity value does not always reflect the underlying value of a company.

Therefore, a company valuation can be undertaken to determine if the stock market is correctly valuing a particular company.

Companies usually obtain a valuation for strategic purposes. The valuation may be for the purpose of purchasing or selling a business, for investing in a company, for raising capital on the stock exchange (e.g. an Initial Public Offering (IPO)), for considering a joint venture or merger with another company (when negotiating terms, full information on the entities leads to more informed decision making), for assessing a management buyout, for raising debt by using the business as security, for pricing services (price may be linked to company value, for example the provision of insurance), for securing control of another company, or simply to benchmark the company's business value with that of its competitors. In addition, a company may find itself the target of a predator company that is trying to take over its business. In these circumstances management might have their company valued independently to determine the attractiveness of the purchase offer. All Plcs have to consider any offer made, as they are obliged (by stock exchange regulations) to make decisions with their equity holders' best interests in mind.

Valuing companies is regarded as both a 'science' and an 'art'. It is considered a science as most of the approaches involve a technical approach. It is considered an art because most of the techniques use estimated data and assumptions and are also amended subjectively to take account of factors that are difficult to measure accurately, such as business risk and financial risk. Indeed, each of the techniques used will provide different valuations, though some of the techniques are considered to be more appropriate in some situations than others. The result of the process is not black-and-white either. When valuations are being used to fix a value for the sale or purchase of a company, various techniques provide a range of values. These values inform both sides of the contract and contribute to a bartering process.

There are three main types of approach used to value companies. The first analyses the specific asset values of the company, the second derives company value using multiples obtained from comparable companies, comparable transactions or from past experience, and the final approach uses the time value of money theories to determine the present value of the future stream of cash flows expected from the company. The main techniques are discussed under the three types of approach to company valuation. An example is used to identify the types of adjustment or calculation that are required. The philosophy underlying each technique is explained and the most appropriate conditions in which to use that particular technique are highlighted. In addition, the advantages and limitations of that approach are outlined.

ASSET-BASED APPROACHES

In general, **asset-based approaches** use accounting data – net book value, net realisable value or replacement value – to value a company's assets. The philosophy behind this approach is that the company is considered to be a collection of individual assets that can be sold and company value is the sum of the individual specific assets. This approach would not be suitable if the valuation was for the purposes of buying a company as a going-concern as this technique does not consider the earnings potential of the assets. It is also of limited use where the company being valued is a service-type company, as this type of company will likely have a small proportion of tangible assets making up its value. Most of its value will be intangible intellectual capital, such as employee skills, networks or brand names. This approach is most suitable when a predator company is determining whether it is worth purchasing a target company with the view to dismantling the company and selling off its assets for a quick gain. The predator company will not be interested in the future earnings potential of the current assets, it will only be interested in the net realisable value of the company's assets and will only be willing to pay an amount that ensures the net realisable value of the assets exceeds the purchase price and the costs.

Asset Valuation: Some Issues

There are two main valuation issues that affect company valuation using asset-based techniques. The first is that, as mentioned in **Figure 17.1**, some assets are not recorded in the financial statements. These are typically intangible assets, such as goodwill, employee skills,

FIGURE 17.1: THE ADVANTAGES AND DISADVANTAGES OF ASSET-BASED VALUATION

ADVANTAGES

- **Easy to obtain, simple and understandable.**
- **Asset stripping:** if the purpose of the valuation is to determine whether to purchase a company to make a quick profit by selling its assets, then this approach will provide the best indication of how profitable the purchase may be to the predator company's shareholders.
- **Minimum value:** this approach can provide a value which represents the minimum amount that the company should accept if it is being purchased by an external entity. It can be used to set a floor value for negotiation purposes.

DISADVANTAGES

- **Conservative value:** this valuation is the lowest valuation that should be accepted by any equity holder. It does not take into account the future earnings potential of the company.
- **Valuations:** valuing assets can be complicated. There are a variety of methods for asset valuation.
- **Incomplete:** several assets are not reflected in a company's financial statements, such as brand value or intellectual capital.
- **Accounting treatments:** there is a variety of accounting treatments that impact on the book value of assets, such as depreciation and inventory valuation techniques.
- **Technology:** this approach will seriously understate a company's value, when the company is technology-based or intellectual capital-based.

synergies between assets working together and brands. Purchased intangible assets are capitalised in the financial statements, but home-grown intangible assets are not (the only exception is development costs and these can only be capitalised if they meet stringent preconditions, as laid down in International Accounting Standard 38: *Intangible Assets*). **Intangible assets** are difficult to identify separately from other assets because they may be inert (for example, employee creativity being stifled by a takeover/merger process), changeable and difficult to value. In most cases there is no readily available market for the sale of intangibles, hence valuation of intangible assets is difficult (there are some exceptions, such as quota or franchise licences, where an active market for their sale exists). Therefore, in most instances these assets are ignored when a valuation is being prepared, or a subjective value is placed on them.

The second valuation problem concerns the bases used to value tangible and intangible assets that are recorded in the financial statements of a company. Intangible assets are usually recorded at purchase value and amortised over their useful economic life, unless it is considered that they have an infinite life, wherein they remain valued at historical cost and are not subject to amortisation. The main concern here is that this value is unlikely to reflect the economic value of the asset. The value will be impaired where a permanent diminution in value occurs but cannot be revalued upwards to reflect increases in value. Therefore, it is likely that the statement of financial position value is understating the true value of intangible assets.

Tangible assets in audited financial statements may not reflect economic reality either, as they are typically based on historical cost and are depreciated over the useful economic life of the asset. **Depreciation** is not an attempt by accountants to measure the reduction in the value of an asset. Depreciation is the application of the matching concept wherein the costs of an asset are matched against the revenue generated by the asset, over the life of the asset. Depreciation tries to measure the reduction in the economic life of an asset to the company in a period. The balance remaining (i.e. the net book value) is just the economic life of the asset that has not been allocated yet. When inflation rates are high, the gap between market value and historical net book value is likely to be accentuated.

The alternative accounting method available under International Accounting Standard 16: *Property, Plant and Equipment* is to value tangible assets at their fair value, which equates to market value and to then depreciate this figure. Even if the assets have been revalued to fair value, this is the value at the reporting date, and hence does not reflect current value. Valuations are costly and most companies will only adopt this approach if it is deemed to be beneficial by the management of a company, and companies that adopt this approach usually only revalue property and land. Other tangible fixed assets typically remain valued at historical cost. This is a problem for the individual who is valuing the company as there may not be a readily available market for second-hand plant and machinery, fixtures and fittings or tools. Their market value may only be properly determined if they are put up for sale, which is not feasible. Different accounting bases can also result in different valuations for inventories and trade receivables, which will affect overall company value.

Net Book Value

There are three common types of company valuation, which are based on permutations of asset values. The first is the **net book value approach,** also referred to as the net assets approach. This approach assumes that the company's value is the value of its total assets, as portrayed by the audited statement of financial position:

Company value (total assets) = Non-current assets + Current assets

The equity holder's value is therefore the **net assets**, which is total assets less total liabilities, and the value per equity share is:

$$\textbf{Value of an equity share} = \frac{\textbf{Total assets} - \textbf{Total liabilities}}{\textbf{Number of equity shares in issue}}$$

(***Note:*** preference shares are considered to be debt and are therefore taken away from total assets in the above formula.)

Net Realisable Value (NRV)

A more informative approach is to substitute market values for book values where possible. There are two approaches. Assets can be valued at net realisable value or at replacement cost.

The **net realisable value**, otherwise known as the **liquidation value**, is the value that the company would expect to achieve were the assets to be sold, less the costs of sale. As mentioned above, the net realisable value can be difficult to determine if a readily available liquid market does not exist and can vary depending on the circumstances of the sale. A quick sale will realise a lower price than a managed sale. The value of the company will now change to:

$$\textbf{Company value} = \textbf{Non-current assets at NRV} + \textbf{Current assets at NRV}$$

The equity holder's value is therefore the **net realisable assets**, which is total assets at realisable value less total liabilities at their realisable value, and the value per equity share is:

$$\textbf{Value of an equity share} = \frac{\textbf{Total assets at NRV} - \textbf{Total liabilities at NRV}}{\textbf{Number of equity shares in issue}}$$

Replacement Cost Approach

The final valuation approach, sometimes adopted by companies that are considering setting up a business themselves or buying an already established business, is the **replacement cost approach**. This approach provides a higher company value than the latter two techniques as it assumes that each asset will be replaced and intangible assets will be purchased. The same valuation problems outlined earlier apply. The company is now valued as:

$$\textbf{Company value} = \textbf{Replacement value of non-current assets} + \textbf{Replacement value of current assets}$$

The equity holder's value is therefore the **net replacement value**, which is total assets at replacement cost less total liabilities at their replacement value, and the value per equity share is:

$$\textbf{Value of an equity share} = \frac{\textbf{Total assets at replacement value} - \textbf{Total liabilities at replacement value}}{\textbf{Number of equity shares in issue}}$$

Worked Example 17.1: Calculating Company Value using Asset-based Approaches

Tipex Ltd
Statement of Financial Position
as at 30 June 20X5

	€/£000
ASSETS	
Non-current assets	
Land and buildings	500
Plant and equipment	200
Motor vehicles	50
Investments	100
	850
Goodwill	100
Current assets	
Inventories	150
Trade receivables	150
Short-term investments	20
Bank	15
	335
Total assets	1,285
EQUITY AND LIABILITIES	
Equity and reserves	
Equity share capital (50c/p shares)	400
Reserves	305
	705
Non-current liabilities	
Debentures	200
Preference shares	100
Loan	100
	400
Current liabilities	
Trade payables	130
Taxation	50
	180
Total equity and liabilities	1,285

The directors inform you that the land and premises were valued at €/£750,000, the plant and equipment at €/£140,000, the motor vehicles at €/£35,000 and the long-term investments at €/£120,000. The plant and equipment can be replaced for €/£280,000 and the motor vehicles can be replaced for €/£85,000. The directors also inform you that circa €/£20,000 of the inventory is slow-moving and is only expected to realise 50% of its carrying value, and 10% of trade receivables usually end up as bad debts.

Requirement Prepare valuations per share for Tipex Ltd using the:
(a) net assets valuation approach;
(b) net realisable value approach; and
(c) replacement cost approach.

Solution
(a) Net assets valuation approach:

		€/£000
Total assets		1,285
Less: intangible assets		(100)
Tangible assets		1,185
Less:		
Debentures		(200)
Preference shares		(100)
Loan		(100)
Current liabilities		(180)
Net asset value of equity		605
Number of equity shares		800,000
Value per share	[€/£605,000 ÷ 800,000]	75.625c/p

(b) Share valuation using the net realisable value approach:

	Adjustments to determine NRV	€/£000
Total assets		1,285
Intangible assets		(100)
Revaluation of land and buildings	[€/£750,000 − €/£500,000]	250
Revaluation of plant and equipment	[€/£140,000 − €/£200,000]	(60)
Revaluation of motor vehicles	[€/£35,000 − €/£50,000]	(15)
Revaluation of investments	[€/£120,000 − €/£100,000]	20
Revaluation of inventories	[(€/£20,000 × 50%) − €/£20,000]	(10)
Revaluation of trade receivables	[€/£150,000 × 10%]	(15)
Tangible assets		1,355

Less:		
Debentures		(200)
Preference shares		(100)
Loan		(100)
Current liabilities		(180)
Net asset value of equity		775
Number of equity shares		800,000
Value per share	[€/£775,000 ÷ 800,000]	96.875c/p

(c) Share valuation using the replacement value approach:

	Adjustments to determine NRV	**€/£000**
Total assets		1,285
Intangible assets		(100)
Revaluation of land and buildings	[€/£750,000 − €/£500,000]	250
Revaluation of plant and equipment	[€/£280,000 − €/£200,000]	80
Revaluation of motor vehicles	[€/£85,000 − €/£50,000]	35
Revaluation of investments	[€/£120,000 − €/£100,000]	20
Revaluation of inventories	[(€/£20,000 × 50%) − €/£20,000]	(10)
Revaluation of trade receivables	[€/£150,000 × 10%]	(15)
Tangible assets		1,545
Less:		
Debentures		(200)
Preference shares		(100)
Loan		(100)
Current liabilities		(180)
Net asset value of equity		965
Number of equity shares		800,000
Value per share	[€/£965,000 ÷ 800,000]	120.625c/p

USING MARKET-BASED MULTIPLES

The philosophy behind the **multiples approach** is to value companies by benchmarking them against similar companies that have publicly available data. The analyst tries to determine a common denominator that applies to both the company being valued and a similar company. The common denominator is called the **multiple**. The advantage of this approach to company valuation is that it captures valuation information that is already available in the marketplace. A commonly used multiple is the price earnings (P/E) ratio. The approach is to use the P/E ratio, which is publicly available, for another similar company in the same industry. This is applied to the earnings of the company being valued as it reflects the market's view about risk and return for this type of company, thus providing a valuation. For more information on the P/E ratio see **Chapter 4**.

In some instances, when earnings are not considered to be meaningful, revenue is utilised instead. The multiples approach is usually used when a private company is being valued or when a publicly traded company wishes to benchmark its market value against the market value of its competitors. The multiple chosen by an analyst who is valuing a company is usually based on recent similar transactions, current information available for similar Plcs and the analyst's experience and judgement. Apart from the P/E ratio, other commonly used multiples include the dividend yield ratio, the capital asset pricing model (CAPM) approach and the use of a multiple of adjusted EBIT. The most commonly used multiples are now discussed.

The P/E Ratio

The P/E ratio is calculated as:

$$\textbf{P/E ratio} = \frac{\textbf{Market value}}{\textbf{Earnings per share}}$$

This can be rearranged to find the company's equity market value:

$$\textbf{Market value of a share = Earnings per share} \times \textbf{P/E ratio (similar company)}$$

(***Note:*** **earnings per share** (EPS) is earnings after interest, tax and preference dividends divided by the number of shares in issue. To find the total value of the company's equity, the market value of a share is multiplied by the number of shares in issue.)

The current market price of a share reflects the market's expectations about the future earnings of a company. Therefore, the **price earnings ratio** is a measure of market confidence in a company. A low price earnings ratio suggests that the market sentiment is that a company is unlikely to maintain earnings or have growth in earnings; whereas a high price earnings ratio suggests that the market sentiment is that a company will be able to maintain its performance and indeed improve on it. As with all ratios, care needs to be taken if using the price earnings ratio to analyse two different companies or to value a company. The price earnings ratio also reflects the market's consideration of the risk associated with investing in a company – a risky company with high earnings is likely to have a lower price earnings ratio, compared to a less risky company with the same earnings. The market price will be less for the riskier company. Some factors that influence a company's reported price earnings ratio are outlined in **Figure 17.2**.

Public Limited Companies (Plcs) (Share price)

Though the UK, Ireland and US markets are regarded as being efficient, researchers have noted that they are not strong-form efficient. A company's share price may, therefore, not reflect economic reality, though it may be argued to reflect most of the price-relevant

FIGURE 17.2: INFLUENCES ON A COMPANY'S PRICE EARNINGS RATIO

Influence	Effect
Earnings growth	Where a company has strong growth prospects, this will lead to an increase in the price earnings ratio.
Quality of the company's net assets and earnings	Where the stock market feels that a company's net assets are undervalued, a higher price earnings ratio will be reported. In addition, a stable earnings pattern will also result in a higher price earnings ratio.
Financial risk	The price earnings ratio is inversely related to the gearing of a company. As gearing increases, equity holders' required return increases, hence lowering the price earnings ratio.
Stock market	The current state of the stock market will influence the price earnings ratio. Where the market is bullish, this will push up the price earnings ratio, whereas the price earnings ratio will fall in a bear market.
State of the economy	General economic and financial conditions will impact on a company's price earnings ratio.
Industry	The type of industry is also influential, as is the company's standing within the industry.
Size	Larger companies will be expected to have steadier earnings.
Marketability	Unquoted shares have restricted marketability, hence a higher return is required for investing in them. This is reflected by their having a lower price earnings ratio.

information that is available publicly on the company from the past and about the future. In addition, investors may not act rationally: investors may hold shares in companies that they support because of their environmental policies or because they have held the shares for a considerable period in the past and are loyal to the company, or because they like the products being traded in by the company. Alternatively, investors may not like the ethical policies of a company. This will impact on the demand for a company's shares in the marketplace and its subsequent equity value. The result is that the market price of a company may be different from the company's true economic value. Therefore, the management of a Plc may use this approach to try and determine if their company is undervalued or overvalued by the market.

Private Companies

When valuing a private company using the P/E multiple approach, it is normal to discount the P/E ratio of a similar quoted company by between 30% and 50%, as in the next example.

WORKED EXAMPLE 17.2: CALCULATING COMPANY VALUE USING THE P/E RATIO

In advance of the board of directors' meeting of Pero Plc, the finance manager was asked to provide a valuation for two target companies, one public (Gato Plc) and one private (Pajaro Ltd), using the P/E ratio approach. The companies being targeted are similar in nature to Pero Plc. Pero Plc's shares are currently trading at €/£6.40 and the company's EPS is 40c/p.

Requirement

(a) What market value is the finance manager likely to suggest for the public limited company Gato Plc? Gato Plc has 500,000 equity shares and currently earns €/£300,000 per year (after interest and tax). A preference dividend of €/£50,000 was also paid in the year.

(b) What market value is the finance manager likely to suggest for the private company, Pajaro Ltd? Ten shares are in issue, each share is held by members from two families. Pajaro Ltd has earnings of €/£75,000 per year after interest and tax.

(c) What other issues should the finance manager inform the board about in respect of these valuations?

Solution

(a) Given the information supplied above, the finance manager can calculate the P/E ratio of Pero Plc and apply this to the EPS of Gato Plc to determine a starting value for Gato Plc. The P/E ratio of Pero Plc is:

$$\text{P/E ratio} = \frac{\text{Market value}}{\text{Earnings per share}}$$

$$\text{P/E ratio} = \frac{\text{€/£}6.40}{\text{€/£}0.40} = 16$$

The EPS for Gato Plc is:

$$\frac{\text{Earnings after tax and preference dividends}}{\text{Number of equity shares in issue}} = \text{EPS}$$

$$\frac{\text{€/£}300{,}000 - \text{€/£}50{,}000}{500{,}000} = 50\text{c/p per share}$$

Therefore, an estimated market value for Gato Plc is:

Market value = 16 × 0.50

Market value = €/£8.00 per share

Total market value = €/£8.00 × 500,000 = €/£4,000,000

(b) A similar approach is utilised when the finance manager values the equity of Pajaro Ltd; however, Gato Plc's P/E ratio would be discounted to take into account the lack of marketability of Pajaro Ltd's shares. Selecting the discount factor is subjective – in this instance a discount of 40% is assumed. Therefore the P/E ratio to be applied is now:

$$\text{P/E ratio} = 16 \times 60\%$$

$$\text{P/E ratio} = 9.6$$

The EPS for Pajaro Ltd is:

$$\frac{€/£75{,}000}{10} = €/£7{,}500 \text{ per share}$$

Therefore, an estimated market value for Pajaro Ltd is:
Market value = 9.6 × €/£7,500
Market value = €/£72,000 per share
Total market value = €/£72,000 × 10 = €/£720,000

(c) The P/E ratios are only a starting point. They may have to be adjusted when other factors come to light. Some other factors that may influence the value to be placed on these two companies include the following:

- The book value of Pajaro Ltd's net assets. The values calculated in (a) and (b) can be compared to the book value to determine if they adequately reflect non-recorded assets.
- The market value of Gato Plc's shares will be available. This would allow the finance manager to calculate the current total value of the company as determined by the market. This value could then be compared to the €/£4 million valuation calculated in (a).
- Other factors will influence the decision. Size is important – large companies usually report higher P/E ratios than small companies. This would influence any adjustment that would be required to the P/E ratios in (a) and (b). Gato Plc and Pajaro Ltd are very different in size – Pero Plc would need to determine if Gato Plc was too large for their needs or if Pajaro Ltd was too small. This would influence the P/E ratio adjustment.
- Growth potential is also an influencing factor. It is likely that the smaller private company, Pajaro Ltd, has higher growth potential relative to the larger company, Gato Plc (though this needs to be determined); therefore, the discount applied may be considered to be too high. Where it is considered that Gato Plc has high growth potential, a premium may be added to the P/E ratio to account for this.
- Potential synergies will also impact on the valuations. If there are synergies to be achieved by Pero Plc from investing in either company (e.g. increased profitability, increased growth or the achievement of a strategic objective), then this will mean that Pero Plc should be willing to pay a premium over their reported P/E ratio. This will raise the value that Pero Plc is willing to give for the companies.
- A full review of the accounting policies and management policies of both companies should be undertaken before a valuation using the P/E ratio is relied upon. In particular, Pajaro Ltd may have very different policies in respect of directors' remuneration. Where this is the case, there should be an adjustment to Pajaro Ltd's directors' payment policy to bring it into line with Pero Plc's payment policy before the EPS is calculated.
- Finally, it is assumed that Gato Plc and Pajaro Ltd are two similar companies operating in the same industry as Pero Plc. If they were not, then a P/E ratio of a company in the same industry as the two companies would be more appropriate to use than Pero Plc's ratio.

FIGURE 17.3: ADVANTAGES AND DISADVANTAGES OF THE P/E APPROACH

ADVANTAGES	DISADVANTAGES
• **Straightforward calculations.** • **Market view:** quoted companies are being valued by the market according to the economic conditions at the time of valuation. • **Future economic value:** the market price of a company will include investors' views about future cash flows expected. Investors are experts at analysing company value (it is their job to notice discrepancies in company value and to act in order to make abnormal gains when a discrepancy is noted – only in this way can they beat market returns).	• **Similar company:** finding a similar company to the one that is being valued is not likely in practice. Companies in the same industry are likely to have different cost structures, sizes, management teams, dividend policies and different capital structures. • **Accounting adjustments:** even if a similar company is located, it is very likely that this company will be using different accounting policies and may possibly have a different accounting year-end. • **P/E ratio:** the P/E ratio itself has a number of factors that influence its value, including the risk associated with expected earnings. • **Marketability:** the P/E ratio of a quoted company will always be larger than that which would result for a private company as private company shares have a restricted market (their market is usually restricted to family members). • **Subjective adjustments:** the P/E ratio of a quoted company is usually reduced to take account of the lack of marketability of an unlisted company's shares. The discount used (usually 30–50%) is subjectively determined.

Dividend Yield Ratio Approach

Another method involving a multiple that can be utilised is the **dividend yield method.** Under this approach the dividend yield of a similar quoted company can be utilised to determine the market value of an unquoted company, given its expected maintainable annual dividend. The dividend yield ratio is calculated as follows:

$$\frac{\textbf{Dividend per equity share}}{\textbf{Market price per equity share}} \times 100 = \textbf{dividend yield}$$

The above ratio can be rearranged to find the market value of a private company:

$$\frac{\textbf{Dividend per equity share}}{\textbf{Dividend yield (similar company)}} \times 100 = \textbf{Market value of one share}$$

The dividend per equity share is the maintainable dividend level of the private company. The maintainable dividend level is calculated by multiplying the earnings of the private company by the dividend payout ratio of a similar quoted company.

Figure 17.4: Advantages and Disadvantages of the Dividend Yield Approach

ADVANTAGES

- **Straightforward to calculate:** on the face of it, this approach is simple to calculate.
- **Constant dividend policy**: this approach works best when companies pursue a constant dividend policy. It values the company's shares according to the cash flow benefit expected to be received by shareholders in the form of dividends. This is argued to be the most relevant value to minority shareholders.

DISADVANTAGES

- **Sourcing a similar quoted company.**
- **Dividend policies:** different companies will have different dividend policies. Some companies do not pay a dividend at all and private companies typically have lower payout policies when compared to Plcs.
- **Dividends:** dividends represent a portion of a company's earnings and a valuation based on dividends only may not represent the full value of a company, particularly if the company does not adopt a steady dividend payout policy.

The dividend yield ratio approach is deemed to be more suitable to use when a minority shareholding is being valued, as it is considered that these equity holders do not have control over company decision-making and have to make do with the dividend that the company decides to pay out. Therefore, they are considered to have purchased their share on the strength of the company's dividend policy and will value the share on this basis.

Worked Example 17.3: Calculating Market Value using the Dividend Yield Model

Anika Plc's shares are currently trading at €/£0.40 per share. It has a 40% payout policy. Its most recent dividend was 2c/p per share. Anika Plc is considering the takeover of Obe Ltd, a similar company. Obe Ltd has 500,000 shares in issue and has earnings of €/£100,000 (after tax and preference dividends).

Requirement Using the information provided, calculate the amount that Anika Plc should offer for Obe Ltd.

Solution

Given the information supplied, the dividend yield approach can be used to determine a bid price for Obe Ltd. This involves using Anika's dividend payout policy to determine the expected future dividends to be received from Obe Ltd's earnings and then assuming that this dividend is maintainable into the future. Therefore, discounting the future stream of expected dividend cash flows by Anika Plc's cost of equity (i.e. the dividend yield of Anika Plc) to determine the present value (i.e. the market value).

Estimated expected dividend of Obe Ltd = €/£100,000 × 40% = €/£40,000
Market price = Expected dividend/Dividend yield
Where the dividend yield = Dividend per share ÷ Market price per share
The dividend yield of Anika Plc = 2c/p ÷ by 40c/p = 0.05 = 5%
Market price = €/£40,000 ÷ 5%
Market price = €/£800,000

This should then be discounted for lack of marketability by between 10% and 50%, depending on the size differential between the two companies.

Earnings before Interest and Tax Multiples

In some instances EBIT multiples are used to value a company. Bishopgate Corporate Finance disclosed that it has used multiples of EBIT that range from 4.5 to 9 times. It reports that the multiple selected is influenced by the level of interest shown by prospective buyers. After the multiple is applied to the EBIT, debt and surplus cash are deducted to provide a value for the equity portion of the company.

COMPANY VALUATION USING FUTURE POTENTIAL EARNINGS/CASH FLOWS

The other commonly used approach is to estimate the future stream of benefits that an equity holder will expect to receive and to discount these to their net present value to determine equity value. There are several versions of this approach. The two most common versions are considered in this chapter. The first focuses on dividend cash flows expected and the second forecasts a company's expected free cash flows into the future and discounts these back to find their present value. This present value is the maximum price that should be paid for a company. These two methods are discussed in turn.

The Dividend Valuation Model Approach

In some instances the expected future dividends can be determined and discounted back to their present value to give an equity valuation. This would involve using straightforward discounting and/or the **dividend valuation model** (see **Chapter 15**). The dividend valuation model is rearranged to determine the market value of an unquoted company's equity shares using the cost of equity of a similar quoted company. The formula is as follows:

$$P_0 = \frac{D_0(1+g)}{K_e - g}$$

where D_0 is the last dividend paid, P_0 is the estimated market value of equity, g is a constant growth rate and K_e is an appropriate cost of equity capital. The use of this approach is highlighted in the next example.

Worked Example 17.4: Calculating Market Value using the Dividend Valuation Model Method

Verano Ltd expects to break even in the next two years and therefore is not going to pay a dividend in Year 1 or in Year 2. In Year 3 the finance manager predicts that the company will pay a dividend of 5c/p. It is then expected that the dividend will increase to 8c/p in Year 4 and grow at the rate of 5% each year thereafter.

Requirement Verano Ltd is considering floating on the AIM/IEX and the board of directors has asked you to calculate a market value for Verano Ltd's equity. An analysis of equity holders' required returns in the industry suggests that a return of 14% would be required by equity holders to entice them to buy or sell these shares, were the company to go public.

Solution

Given the information supplied in the question, the only approach that can be utilised to determine a value for Verano Ltd's equity is to calculate the present value of the future stream of dividends that will accrue to an equity holder. As the cash flows are uneven, straightforward discounting will be applied to the expected dividends from Years 1 to 3. Then from Year 3 on, the dividend amount is set and will grow at a constant rate into perpetuity. The dividend valuation model can be used to determine the expected share price, though the resultant figure will represent the value in four years' time, so it will also have to be discounted to the present-day value.

At the end of Year 4 the present value of the future stream of constantly increasing dividends will be worth:

$$P_0 = \frac{8\text{c/p}(1+0.05)}{0.14-0.05} = 93\text{c/p}$$

This is then discounted to determine its value now, along with the present value of the earlier dividends. As this formula provides the value of the future stream of dividends on the first day of Year 5, it is discounted as if it were received on the last day of Year 4.

Year	Cash flow €/£	Discount factor (14%)	Present value €/£
1	0.00	0.877	0.000
2	0.00	0.769	0.000
3	0.05	0.675	0.034
4	0.08	0.592	0.047
4	0.93	0.592	0.551
Net present value			0.632

Verano Ltd should expect to receive 63.2c/p for each share it intends to issue. To ensure a 100% uptake of shares by the market on an IPO, a discount of 10% is allowed off the issue price. Therefore, Verano Ltd should be advised to issue its shares at 56.88c/p.

FIGURE 17.5: ADVANTAGES AND DISADVANTAGES OF THE DIVIDEND VALUATION APPROACH

ADVANTAGES

- **Economic sense:** from an equity holder's perspective, it makes economic sense to value shares based on the present value of the future stream of cash flows that the equity holder should expect to receive from holding the share.

DISADVANTAGES

- **Determining the cost of equity:** it is difficult in practice to find companies that are similar to the company being valued. Therefore, finding a reliable cost of equity can be problematic.
- **Dividend policies:** different companies will have different dividend policies. Some companies do not pay a dividend at all, hence this approach cannot be utilised.
- **Estimating future dividends:** dividends are unlikely to grow at a constant rate into infinity. Estimates of dividends for a period of three or four years may be reliable, but estimates beyond this time period are subject to more risk.
- **Determining the growth rate:** this is difficult to calculate. In some instances, growth in historical dividend payments are utilised as a proxy for growth in prospective dividends.
- **High growth:** if the growth rate exceeds the cost of equity, the model cannot be used as the denominator becomes negative. However, this phenomenon would be rare.

Like the dividend yield approach, the dividend model approach is more appropriate to use when an analyst is trying to value a minority interest in a company. When a minority interest changes hands, this will have little impact on dividend policy. The stage the company is at within its life cycle will also influence the relevance of this method. An emerging (fast-growth) company with many growth opportunities is likely to have a fluctuating dividend policy and is also likely to offer high growth rates in dividends that are unsustainable into infinity. Whereas a mature company in a mature industry will be more likely to have a steady dividend policy, wherein dividends grow in line with company earnings, and the business finance manager pursues a policy of smoothing dividend payouts to achieve a constant growth pattern.

Determining an Appropriate Cost of Equity: CAPM

In some instances the capital asset pricing model (CAPM) is utilised to determine a company-specific cost of equity. As is explained in **Chapter 15**, the CAPM determines a company's cost of equity by measuring the relationship between the risk and return of a company relative to that of the market over time. Historical prices are analysed to determine how the return on a company's shares reacts when there are changes in market returns. The parameter utilised to capture the difference in reaction between the company and the market (the systematic risk) is beta (β). It is then assumed that the equity holders will require a return (r_j) over and above a risk-free investment's return (r_f) to compensate them for thespecific risk attached to this particular company. The additional return to be gained from investing in the market is the average market return (r_m) less the risk-free return (r_f). This additional return is then adjusted to take account of the specific company's risk, in that the market premium ($r_m - r_f$) is multiplied by the beta factor. When a company is not as risky as the market, beta will be a number below one; hence the return required by an equity holder above the risk-free rate will be less than the premium to be gained were the company to have the same risk profile as the market. When a company is riskier than the market, the beta factor will be a number above one; hence the premium required by the equity holder above the risk-free rate will be greater than that of the market. The CAPM formula is as follows:

$$r_j = r_f + \beta(r_m - r_f)$$

The cost of equity can be determined quite easily using the CAPM for any Plc as historical data on returns is readily available. The problem arises when trying to determine the cost of equity for a private company, for use in the dividend valuation model to determine the market value of the company. A similar approach to those mentioned previously is followed. The first step is to find a comparable quoted company with historical data. The company being used as a benchmark should be in the same industry, in the same type of business and, in particular, should be affected by the same economic forces that impact on the private company. Next, the beta for the selected Plc should be determined. Then this beta should be adjusted for financial risk. The adjusted beta should be utilised in the CAPM to determine the equity holders' required return (i.e. cost of equity) and, finally, the value of equity should be determined (using the dividend valuation model) using the calculated cost of equity.

Worked Example 17.5: Equity Value Calculated Using the CAPM

Julio Ltd is a private company with an issued share capital of 1,000,000 equity shares. Half of its financing comes from debt sources. It is planning an IPO wherein 45% of its existing shares will be offered to the public. No new shares will be issued. At present, Julio Ltd pays 40% of its earnings as dividends and reinvests the remainder. Growth in earnings is expected to be maintained at 7%. Earnings in the year just past amounted to €/£800,000.

Requirement You have been asked to suggest an equity share price to the board of directors that will ensure that current equity holders' wealth is maximised and to ensure that the whole issue is taken up in the IPO. The board of directors informs you that the current return on gilts is 6% and the average market return on equity shares is double this.

You have investigated the listed companies that operate in the same industry as Julio Ltd and have identified three that have very similar operations: Mala Plc has an equity beta of 3.5 and is highly geared – 80% of its funding comes from debt sources; Cocina Plc has an equity beta of 1.6 and is geared to 50%; Lampa Plc has an equity beta of 1.1 and 10% of its funding is sourced as debt.

Solution

The first step in the process has already been completed, with companies that have comparable operations already identified. The next step involves looking at financial risk as portrayed by the gearing ratio. Julio Ltd has a gearing level of around 50%; therefore, it would seem that Cocina Plc is the most suitable company to benchmark against as it has similar business risk and similar financial risk. Cocina Plc's beta value will be used to determine a cost of equity for Julio Ltd using the CAPM.

$$r_j = r_f + \beta(r_m - r_f)$$

In this instance r_f is 6%, β is 1.6 and r_m is 12% [6% × 2]. Therefore, the cost of equity (r_j) is:

$$r_j = 6\% + 1.6(12\% - 6\%)$$

$$r_j = 15.6\%$$

And the market value of each share (P_0), before discount, is calculated using the dividend valuation model:

$$P_0 = \frac{D_0(1+g)}{K_e - g}$$

In this instance D_0 is 32c/p [€/£800,000/1,000,000 × 40%], g is 7% and K_e is 15.6%.

$$P_0 = \frac{32\text{c/p}(1+0.07)}{0.156-0.07}$$

$$P_0 = 398\text{c/p}$$

You recommend that the maximum value to offer shares at is €/£3.98 per share. However, to ensure a 100% uptake of shares, a discount of between 10% and 20% should be offered, which means that the share should be issued at a price of between €/£3.18 and €/£3.58.

Free Cash Flow Approach

Free cash flows are cash flows that are available to lenders and equity holders after tax and after investment cash outflows. Interest and dividends are not deducted as they represent financing disbursements, not cash flows from operations. The estimated free cash flows may be as follows:

	20X4	**20X5**
	€/£	**€/£**
Cash flows		
Revenue	6,000,000	6,500,000
Cash paid for operating activities	(4,000,000)	(4,100,000)
Taxation paid	(500,000)	(480,000)
Decreases/(increases) in working capital	100,000	(150,000)
Cash invested in projects	(300,000)	(200,000)
Free cash flows	1,300,000	1,570,000

These free cash flows are estimated into the future and discounted using either the cost of equity (calculated using the CAPM where the purpose of the valuation is to offer a price for a share repurchase/buyout) or the WACC (suitable for project valuation or valuing an entire company for a takeover bid), to provide a valuation for the whole company. Then debt is deducted to find the equity value. The following formula can be used to determine the market price to offer for each equity share:

$$\textbf{Value of an equity share} = \frac{\textbf{NPV of the estimated free cash flows minus debt}}{\textbf{Number of equity shares in issue}}$$

This approach is best suited when the company or project has a finite life. When the company being valued has an infinite life, the above approach combined with an adjusted dividend valuation model can be adopted to provide a valuation for the whole company. In this instance, the free cash flows for the initial years are determined as above and a terminal value is given to the value of the company after this period. This **terminal value** is considered to be the present value of a future stream of free cash flows in perpetuity, which increase at a steady growth rate each year in the same manner as dividends are assumed to increase by a steady rate under the dividend valuation model. The formula for determining this terminal value is:

$$\textbf{Terminal value}_0 = \frac{\textbf{Free cash flows}_0(1+g)}{r-g}$$

Where r can either be the company's cost of equity or its WACC and g is the constant rate of growth in free cash flows. The estimated free cash flows for the early period and the terminal value at the end of the period are discounted to determine the total value of the company. As before, debt should be deducted to find the appropriate value for equity.

WORKED EXAMPLE 17.6: CALCULATING THE MARKET VALUE OF EQUITY USING THE FREE CASH FLOW APPROACH

Gato Plc is considering purchasing a private company called Pero Ltd. Up to this point, Pero Ltd earns about €/£50,000 per year after tax. Its investment in working capital at the end of the year is €/£120,000. Pero Ltd is financed by equity alone and has 50,000 shares in issue. Gato Plc estimates that a sustained investment policy would increase the future profits after tax by the following amounts:

Year	Capital investment in year	Working capital balance at the year end	Cash flow from operating activities
	€/£	€/£	€/£
1	180,000	120,000	70,000
2	150,000	140,000	100,000
3	80,000	150,000	130,000
4	60,000	160,000	150,000
5	50,000	150,000	160,000
6	50,000	140,000	170,000

It is Gato Plc's policy that all investments pay back the initial cost, in discounted terms, within six years. Gato Plc's WACC is 12%.

Requirement As finance manager, you have been asked to determine a bid amount to be tabled at the next board of directors' meeting. This bid should reflect Gato Plc's investment policy.

Solution

Gato Plc's hurdle condition is that investments should be paid back, in discounted terms, within six years (using a discount rate of 12%). Therefore, the maximum that can be offered for Pero Ltd will be the present value of the free cash flows over the six-year period. The first step is to determine the free cash flows:

Year	Cash flow after tax from operating activities	Capital investment in year	Changes in working capital	Free cash flows
	€/£	€/£	€/£	€/£
1	70,000	(180,000)	–	(110,000)
2	100,000	(150,000)	(20,000)	(70,000)
3	130,000	(80,000)	(10,000)	40,000
4	150,000	(60,000)	(10,000)	80,000
5	160,000	(50,000)	10,000	120,000
6	170,000	(50,000)	10,000	130,000

These are then discounted using the company's cost of capital to find the NPV, as follows:

Year	Free cash flows €/£	Discount rate 12%	Present value €/£
1	(110,000)	0.893	(98,230)
2	(70,000)	0.797	(55,790)
3	40,000	0.712	28,480
4	80,000	0.636	50,880
5	120,000	0.567	68,040
6	130,000	0.507	65,910
NPV			59,290

Therefore, Gato Plc should offer a maximum of €/£1.1858 [€/£59,290 ÷ 50,000] per share for the equity of Pero Ltd.

FIGURE 17.6: ADVANTAGES AND DISADVANTAGES OF THE FREE CASH FLOW APPROACH

ADVANTAGES

- **Theoretical justification:** the NPV approach to investment appraisal is regarded as the most appropriate technique to use in investment appraisal. This argument can also be extended to company valuations.
- **Straightforward:** this approach does away with the problems associated with obtaining information from a similar company, as it focuses on the cash returns from the company being valued.

DISADVANTAGES

- **Determining the cash flows:** this involves subjectivity. It is difficult to estimate future cash flows. The further away the cash flow being estimated, the greater the risk that the actual cash flow will be different.
- **Determining the discount rate to use:** there are weaknesses underlying the models used to obtain a discount rate.
- **Amount of investment:** it is difficult to determine in advance the amount that will be invested each period.
- **Determining the terminal value:** the model used to determine the terminal value assumes that earnings grow at a constant rate. This is not likely to happen in practice.

Shareholder Value Analysis

The free cash flow approach has been repackaged as **shareholder value analysis** by Rappaport (1986) and is used by large Plcs. The shareholder value analysis approach strives to link management decision-making and strategy to value creation. It assumes that the primary company objective is equity holder wealth maximisation and that this can be achieved by focusing management attention on value drivers, such as sales growth and gross profit, internal investment, the cost of capital (which is affected by a company's capital structure) and taxation. Under shareholder value analysis, an analyst has to consider the cash flows of the entity being valued over a set time horizon, normally five to 10 years. Once the time period has been set, shareholder value analysis involves four more steps. First, the cash flows for each of the **value drivers** (i.e. sales, investment, cost of capital and taxation) are determined for each year within the specified period. Secondly, discount rates are calculated. Then a terminal value reflecting the value of the resultant company at the end of the specified period is calculated. Finally, the resultant cash flows are discounted to the net present value. This provides an indication of the company's value. The difference between the value based on shareholder value analysis and a free cash flow approach is the focus on strategic value drivers.

The Accounting Rate of Return (ARR) Method of Share Valuation

This approach uses accounting data to determine equity value.

$$\textbf{Equity value} = \frac{\textbf{Estimated future profits}}{\textbf{Required return on capital employed}}$$

In many instances the profits of the company being valued for takeover may have to be adjusted to reflect the expected profits of the company in the future after the takeover takes place. For example, the company may become a Plc. In these circumstances the directors' salaries would be expected to increase, so this should be adjusted for. Where the sale involves any changes to gearing, the resultant expected interest changes should be adjusted for. If the company is going to purchase or sell a property, a rent or interest adjustment may be required and any economies/dis-economies of scale expected should be adjusted for. The resultant profit figure should be the expected equilibrium amount.

Worked Example 17.7: Calculating Equity Value using the ARR Method

The directors of Leonardo Group Plc are considering purchasing Bottecelli Ltd. Bottecelli Ltd has returned a profit after taxation of €/£650,000 per year. The directors of Leonardo Group Plc reckon that, using their own marketing channels, which are already well established, they can increase profits by about €/£150,000 (after tax). At present the owner-manager of Bottecelli Ltd receives a dividend of €/£70,000 each year instead of taking a regular salary. The directors of Leonardo Group Plc consider that they can either replace him with a suitable manager, or encourage him to remain. They think that a salary of €/£80,000 would be required in either case. Tax is payable at 20%.

Requirement What value should Leonardo Group Plc place on Bottecelli Ltd? You are informed that all the subsidiaries within Leonardo Group Plc have to yield an after-tax accounting rate of return of 16% of capital employed.

Solution

The market value should be:

$$\text{Equity value} = \frac{\text{Estimated future maintainable profits}}{\text{Required return on capital employed}}$$

Where the estimated future profits are €/£736,000 [€/£650,000 + €/£150,000 − €/£80,000(0.80)] and the required return on capital employed is 16%.

$$\text{Equity value} = \frac{\text{€/£}736{,}000}{16\%} = \text{€/£}4{,}600{,}000$$

This figure should represent the maximum that Leonardo group Plc should pay for Bottecelli Ltd. This valuation should be compared with valuations prepared using other methods to determine the correct offer amount.

SOME PRACTICAL ISSUES TO CONSIDER

Regardless of the approach taken, there are some issues that will influence the value of a company and the value of its equity.

Control Premium

A premium over the normal price to be paid for equity is usually offered when purchasing equity in an entity, when the intention is to obtain a controlling interest. Some corporate finance houses recommend a **control premium** of up to 20%. A high premium is included when it is assumed that the target company has not been trading at its optimal level. No premium is added when it is assumed that no additional gains can be made over and above the current business model.

Size Discount

In most instances, large companies are valued higher than their smaller counterparts. Large companies are usually regarded as less risky. In general, a **size discount** of between 10% and 40% is applied to large company shares where they are being used as a benchmark to value a smaller, similar company.

Liquidity Discount

When an entity's equity shares are not tradable, or have limited marketability, then this will impact on the valuation that should be placed on the shares. Normally a **liquidity discount** of between 10% and 40% is applied, particularly if the entity is not a Plc and is smaller in size than a similar Plc that is being used to provide a benchmark for the smaller non-quoted company's share price.

Maintainable Earnings

In all instances where earnings are being utilised to determine the market value of equity (and the market value of an entity), it is important that the earnings figure represents normal earnings. Hence any exceptional profits or losses need to be removed. In many instances a multiple calculated from a Plc that has a market value is applied to the earnings of an unquoted entity to determine the unquoted company's value. In these circumstances, adjustments may need to be made to the unquoted company's earnings to reflect expenditure that is normal for a Plc, but not for the unquoted company. The most common example is directors' salaries. In many private companies, the directors are the equity holders and for taxation reasons they may take their yearly earnings from the company in two ways: as a salary and/or as dividends. In addition, directors in Plcs normally command a higher salary and were the valuation to be used to value the unquoted company for the purposes of obtaining a listing on the stock exchange, then the directors' salaries should be added back to earnings and an equivalent salary, which would be payable to the directors were the company a Plc, should be deducted. The multiple can then be applied to the adjusted **maintainable earnings**, when determining equity value.

Terminal Value

In most instances it is assumed that earnings will occur in perpetuity. When earnings forecasts involve specific estimates in the initial years, with more general forecasts beyond a certain point, it is common practice to calculate the exact estimated cash flow forecasts for the initial years and to value the remainder as though they are in perpetuity. This means allocating a residual value to the company/project. This residual value should be accounted for in the cash flows of the final year.

Risk Premium

In all instances, when determining the market value of a company's equity, hence its total market value, it is important to consider risk. Even when a similar Plc is being used to benchmark the value of the company under scrutiny, the analyst should always ask the question: "Is the resultant return on equity suitable for the risk that the company being valued is exposed to?" A **risk premium** may be required if the company being valued is located in a different country, to take account of country risk (e.g. volatility of that country's economy, risk of war, etc.), political risk, structure of the market where the entity is quoted and foreign exchange risk. Risk associated with the structure of a company's markets differs across countries. In some countries only stable, large, diversified companies are listed. The shares in companies quoted on these markets are likely to command a lower premium than shares quoted in markets that allow more risky companies to raise funds. A risk adjustment may also be required if the target levels of business risk.

'Rules of Thumb'

In some industries, the sale of entities is quite common and 'rules of thumb' about company valuation emerge. The valuation methods may involve applying a typical multiple (for example, three times) to historical revenue (commonly used to value service firms, such as accountancy practices), or price per tonne of annual production (commonly used to value mining companies). These common practices should be taken into consideration.

Comparative Transactions

In many industries, where the sale of entities is quite common, a good guide to determining the value of equity – hence the value of the company – is to review the prices that were paid in the past to purchase similar entities (this involves, for example, review takeovers, merger deals, IPOs and acquisitions of similar companies in the past year). Other, more general, factors that may impact on company valuation are included in **Figure 17.7**.

FIGURE 17.7: GENERAL FACTORS THAT MAY IMPACT ON COMPANY VALUATIONS

Exchange rate movements	Become important when a company's operations are spread over several countries.
Interest rate changes	When a company is highly geared and some of its long-term financing is variable rate interest, then changes in interest rates will increase the financial risk associated with the company. Changes in interest rates will also impact on the required return by equity shareholders.
Legislation changes	Most entities are impacted on by legislation changes, but some are more susceptible than others. For example, if the company being valued has high emissions, and legislation changes mean that future expenditure is required to change operations to make them greener, then this will impact on equity value.
The state of the economy	When the economy is booming, growth is assumed to be maintainable and may even be assumed to increase. This will impact on earnings and cash flow projections. When the economy goes into recession, much lower growth rates will be expected – impacting on share valuation.
Takeover speculation	When there is demand for the equity of a company from a variety of sources, this will have a positive impact on expected share price and should be factored into the valuation.
Announcements of results	When the announcements indicate a change in the pattern of the performance of a company, then this will impact on share price. In particular, the growth variable will most likely be affected, resulting in a different expected share price valuation.
Other information	Any information that is regarded as being **value relevant** (i.e. impacts on share price), such as information on management recruitment, on retirement, new products and new strategic decisions, will impact on expected future earnings and growth, hence will impact on share valuation.
Industry information	Information on an industry will also impact on equity valuation. For example, the manufacturing industry in the UK and in Ireland declined as a result of the financial crisis and has impacted on the valuation of a company's shares within that industry.

In addition to all the above underlying factors, the final price agreed when a company is being valued is usually the product of intense negotiation, whereupon the purchasing entity/individuals and the selling entity/equity holders come to an agreement in respect of the price that will ensure the trade takes place and keeps most parties to the transaction happy.

VALUATION PROCESS SUMMARISED

As a general approach to company/equity valuation, an analyst normally considers all the methodologies and decides on the methodology/methodologies that best suit the situation. For example, if the valuation is to obtain a majority shareholding or control, then an assets basis, cash flow or earnings basis might be most appropriate; whereas if the valuation is for the purposes of obtaining a minority shareholding, then a dividend yield basis might be considered to be more appropriate. The next step will involve the analyst reviewing prior IPOs, takeovers, mergers and company sales to determine if a similar company went through this process in the past, and then using the corresponding value agreed as guidance for the current valuation. At this stage the analyst usually tries to identify a number of similar companies that have publicly available data for the purposes of benchmarking. The aim here is to identify multiples (such as the P/E ratio or the dividend yield ratio) that can be applied to the company being valued. These companies should be: in the same line of business, of similar size and affected by similar economic forces. After the most appropriate companies have been identified and suitable multiples noted, the multiples are adjusted to take into consideration the difference in size and marketability/liquidity of the shares between the company being valued and the company being used as a benchmark. In addition, the earnings that the multiples will be applied to should be adjusted to determine the expected future long-run earnings. Therefore, exceptional items should be removed, economies of scale should be predicted and additional expenditure factored in (particularly if the company being valued is a private company). When all the adjustments have been undertaken, it is usual for a number of the approaches to be adopted and a value selected with these in mind. Regardless of the scientific approach, the value of the company will be affected by market demand, market sentiment and other similar transactions.

The difficulties and subjectivity surrounding company valuation are evident from the sale of Uber in 2019, as outlined in **Real World Example 17.1**.

REAL WORLD EXAMPLE 17.1: UBER TECHNOLOGIES INC.

Uber Technologies Inc. (Uber) went public and started trading on 10 May 2019. The company raised $8.1 billion in its first initial public offering (IPO). In 2018, Uber had been valued at $120 billion, but after continued losses and the negative IPO experience of one of its competitors, Lyft, it was considered that $120 billion was over-optimistic. Lyft's stocks fell by 25% over the first quarter after its IPO in March 2019. In terms of Uber, advisors had recommended an IPO price in the range of $44 to $50 and the company elected to place shares at $45. This valued the company at about $80 million, about a third lower than its valuation in the previous year. Moreover, the shares did not begin trading at $45 on 10 May 2019, but at $42, and by the close of business that day they were selling at $41.57. Since this time, the share trading price has fallen by just over 35% of its expected IPO price. This shows the extent of subjectivity in the pricing process.

CONCLUSION

Valuing companies is both a science and an art. There is a variety of quantitative techniques available to help an analyst come up with a variety of different values for a company. Even though these techniques are very black-and-white, there is much subjectivity involved in estimating cash flows, discount rates and multiples to be utilised in the models. Indeed, many analysts will use more than one technique when deciding on a final valuation. In most instances the valuation process involves benchmarking the company being valued to a similar quoted company. Quite a bit of knowledge of the stock market is required if a benchmarking approach is adopted. Benchmarking can provide valuable information, although it comes with the caveat that no two companies are the same and adjustments always need to be made – either to the multiples or to the figure the multiple is being applied to (such as earnings, sales, etc.). These adjustments are usually subjective.

EXAMINATION STANDARD QUESTION: CAPITAL INVESTMENT APPRAISAL AND COMPANY VALUE

Hightech Ltd was established in 20X0 by its owner and managing director, Mr Guage. Hightech manufactures calibration equipment for use in the healthcare industry. The company has grown quickly to date, with its success largely attributable to the quality of its products, to which Mr Guage, an engineer, devotes considerable time and capital in the area of research and development. Extracts from the recently completed management accounts for the year ended 31 December 20X4 are provided in the Appendix. Administration expenses in 20X4 include non-recurring research costs of €/£0.1 million. Retained earnings are budgeted to be €/£0.72 million in 20X5.

Technological developments The high growth rate of the laboratory equipment industry has resulted in an increasing emphasis on quality. Mr Guage has recently been researching Ultra Precision Calibration (UPC), the latest computer-assisted assembly equipment, and its potential impact on production efficiency and quality. Initial research has suggested that the following costs and benefits would accrue to Hightech as a result of investing in such a system.

Costs:

(i) Capital costs of the equipment would be €/£4 million. The equipment would have a useful life of six years, after which its disposal value would be €/£0.4 million.

(ii) Incremental annual maintenance costs of €/£0.2 million would be incurred.

(iii) Changes in the existing plant and production process of Hightech to accommodate the new equipment would mean that both production and sales would be lost in the first two years at an estimated cost (in terms of lost contribution) of €/£0.35 million in Year 1, and €/£0.25 million in Year 2.

Benefits:

(i) UPC would result in shorter lead times and thus a permanent reduction in existing working capital levels from €/£3.0 million to €/£1.8 million.

(ii) The improvement in quality and efficiency would reduce re-work levels and generate production cost savings of €/£1.0 million per annum.

(iii) The UPC equipment requires less floor space than the existing machinery. It is anticipated that one of the existing warehouses could be let at an annual rental of €/£0.15 million, commencing in Year 2.

Mr Guage believes that all investments should generate a minimum return of 15% per annum.

Acquisition Offer Biglab Plc, Hightech's largest UK customer, has recently approached Mr Guage, expressing an interest in acquiring the entire share capital of Hightech. Public information indicates that Biglab has the capacity to complete a purchase from its existing cash balances. Mr Guage has little experience as to methods of valuing companies, and would like some guidance on the matter. Recent publicly available information on Biglab and Medicaid Plc, a competitor of Hightech, is as follows:

	EPS Year ended 31 December 20X4	**Dividend per share**	**Dividend cover**	**P/E Ratio**
Biglab Plc	15.8 pence	2.4 pence	6.6 times	10.5
Medicaid Plc	12.4 pence	1.8 pence	6.9 times	10.0

The market value of Hightech's premises is estimated to be €/£0.3 million in excess of its carrying value in the company's books.

Requirement

(a) (i) Determine whether Hightech should invest in the UPC equipment.
(***Note:*** ignore taxation in making the assessment.)

12 Marks

(ii) Discuss FOUR additional factors that Hightech should consider when deciding to invest in the UPC equipment.

8 Marks

(b) (i) Advise Mr Guage on the probable valuation range of Hightech, both on an earnings and on an assets basis, and comment briefly on FIVE factors which may impact on the valuation.
(***Note:*** ignore the UPC investment proposal in advising on the valuation range for Hightech.)

16 Marks

(ii) Outline two benefits/synergies that could accrue to Biglab if it were successful in its acquisition of Hightech and outline the nature of their impact on the bid price.

4 Marks

Total 40 Marks

(Based on Chartered Accountants Ireland, FAE, MABF, Extract from Autumn 1997, Q1)

Appendix

Hightech Ltd
Statement of Profit or Loss
for the year ended 31 December 20X4

	€/£000
Revenue	12,000
Cost of production	(8,000)
Gross profit	4,000
Selling and distribution expenses	(2,300)
Administration expenses	(1,000)
Interest	(200)
Net income before tax	500
Tax	(50)
Net income after tax	450
Dividends	(60)
Net income retained for the year	390
Revenue reserves brought forward	1,210
Revenue reserves carried forward	1,600

Hightech Ltd
Statement of Financial Position
as at 31 December 20X4

	€/£000
Non-current assets	2,600
Net working capital	3,000
Net debt	(2,400)
	3,200
Financed by	
Equity share capital	1,000
Revenue reserves	1,600
	2,600
Capital grants	600
	3,200

Solution

To: Mr Guage, Hightech Ltd
From: ______________, Company Accountant
Date: XX January, 20X5
Subject: (a) UPC equipment investment
(b) Biglab acquisition offer

(a) **UPC equipment investment evaluation**
(i) Net present value

Year	Capital	Working capital	Maint. costs	Reorg. costs	Saving	Rent	Net flow	Disc. fact.	PV
	€/£m	€/£m	€/£m	€/£m	€/£m	€/£m	€/£m	(15%)	€/£m
0	(4.0)	–	–	–	–	–	(4.00)	1.000	(4.00)
1	–	1.2	(0.2)	(0.35)	1.0	–	1.65	0.870	1.44
2	–		(0.2)	(0.25)	1.0	0.15	0.70	0.756	0.53
3	–	–	(0.2)	–	1.0	0.15	0.95	0.572	0.54
4	–	–	(0.2)	–	1.0	0.15	0.95	0.497	0.47
5	–	–	(0.2)	–	1.0	0.15	0.95	0.432	0.58
6	0.4	–	(0.2)	–	1.0	0.15	1.35		
NPV									0.19

The investment yields a positive net present value of €/£0.19 million when discounted at the required minimum return of 15% per annum. This should be assessed further in the context of (ii) below.

(ii) Additional factors to be considered:

1. All investment decisions should be subject to sensitivity analysis of their key variables, given the inherent uncertainty associated with forecasts. The fact that this investment only yields a positive NPV in Year 6 is an additional imperative for sensitivity analysis.
2. The impact on gearing may be prohibitive given the existing debt position of Hightech. The funding of the initial investment thus needs to be carefully assessed with the availability of grants investigated and the possibility of leasing.
3. The risk of not adopting the new technology should also be considered, e.g. if Hightech's competitors take on UPC, relative quality decline may adversely impact on sales.

4. Other benefits – no allowance has been made for increases in sales due to quality improvements.
5. Other costs – Hightech should consider that loss of sales for two years may make it difficult to recover market share.
6. Labour relations – investing in UPC may lead to redundancies and higher wage costs due to a smaller yet more skilled workforce.
7. Time horizon – with the rapid change in technology the new machinery could well be obsolete in six years, thus impacting on its disposal value.
8. Several suppliers should be contacted to quote and report on the technology. The quality and reliability of the new equipment should be thoroughly investigated and references obtained wherever possible. Any warranties on the system should be carefully evaluated.
9. Any potential tax benefits should be considered.

(b)(i) **Hightech Valuation**

Asset valuation Asset-based valuations see the value of the business as being the value of the underlying assets. Net realisable value is the most common approach used with allowances to be made for disposal costs, including redundancy, if relevant.

	20X4
	€/£000
Non-current assets	2,600
Net working capital	3,000
Net debt	(2,400)
Market value (property uplift)	300
Asset valuation	3,500

Earnings valuation Earnings-based valuations see the value of the business as the present value of its future cash flows. Therefore, the results will only be as good as the estimates of future earnings and the capitalisation rate.

	Historical	**Budget**
	20X4	**20X5**
	€/£000	**€/£000**
Retained profit	390	720
Dividends declared	60	–
Exceptional charge	100	–
Earnings	550	720

Private companies are normally valued at a discount to public companies in the same sector. Therefore, applying a discount of between 15% and 30% of Medicaid Plc's earnings valuation yields the following:

		Profits	
		Historical 20X4	**Budgeted 20X5**
15% Discount	P/E: 8.5	Value: €/£4,675	€/£6,120
30% Discount	P/E: 7.0	Value: €/£3,850	€/£5,040

In determining maximum and minimum prices for a company, the figures are only as good as the techniques employed and the data provided. The final price will be agreed by negotiation and other factors need to be taken into account, such as the following.

1. The high growth nature of the laboratory equipment industry and the relatively good margins.
2. General economic and financial conditions.
3. The size of the undertaking and its status within its industry. Hightech, although a young company, has grown quickly and established a good reputation for quality.
4. An unquoted company is normally valued at a discount relative to a quoted company, due to the lack of a liquid market for its shares.
5. The lack of intention to sell by Mr Guage, the sole equity holder, may cause any approach to be described as hostile, which is likely to put upward pressure on price. This is referred to as a control premium.
6. The reliability of profit estimates and the strong past trading record.
7. The relatively high level of asset backing.
8. The highly specialised nature of the assets may indicate a specialised nature that would detract from their break-up value.
9. Hightech currently has a relatively high level of gearing. The higher the ratio, the greater the financial risk for equity shareholders, who in turn demand a higher rate of return on equity.
10. The extent to which the business is dependent on the technical skills of one or more individuals/key personnel (e.g. Mr Guage).

Conclusion An offer range of €/£5 million (+/− €/£0.25 million) would appear appropriate. This represents a premium of 43% over existing assets, a relatively high multiple of 9.1 times current earnings, but only a multiple of 6.9 times budgeted current year earnings, possibly a more appropriate multiple given the high-growth history and positive trading outlook.

(ii) Possible benefits/synergies to Biglab:
1. Hightech's reputation for quality inputs should enhance the quality of Biglab's outputs, thus increasing the revenue potential for Biglab.
2. Vertical integration by Biglab should achieve cost savings on the inputs to its business. This is most likely to occur by way of reduced selling and distribution costs incurred by Hightech.

3. The acquisition of Hightech may broaden the target markets of Biglab and thus reduce the risk associated with its chosen industry. This may in turn favourably impact on its share price and the rating attached thereto.
4. Biglab's substantial cash balances should enable the acquisition to be funded at a low cost of finance, eliminate Hightech's annual interest charge and result in a higher return on capital employed for itself.
5. Biglab's UK operations may offer opportunities to reduce foreign exchange risk in Hightech's existing operations.

Each, or any, of the above increases the value of Hightech to Biglab. Earnings synergies of €/£0.1 million per annum, where achievable, in theory will add value of €/£1.05 million to the market value of Biglab at its current P/E of 10.5 (ignoring the financing impact of the acquisition on Biglab).

Key Terms

Asset-based approach
Control premium
Depreciation
Dividend valuation model approach
Dividend yield method
Earnings per share
Free cash flows
Intangible assets
Liquidation value
Liquidity discount
Maintainable earnings
Multiple
Multiples approach
Net assets
Net book value approach
Net realisable assets
Net realisable value
Net replacement value
Price earnings ratio
Replacement cost approach
Risk premium
Shareholder value analysis
Size discount
Terminal value
Value drivers
Value-relevant

REVIEW QUESTIONS

(See Suggested Solutions to Review Questions in **Appendix B**.)

Question 17.1

Explain the difference between determining company value and determining the value of a company's equity.

Question 17.2

Carmon Plc has operating profit (after depreciation of €/£7m) of €/£50m. It paid €/£3m in interest, invested €/£6m in capital expenditure and increased its working capital by €/£1m.

Requirement Calculate the free cash flow for Carmon Plc. Assume that the tax rate is 25% and tax is paid in the year it becomes due (capital allowances equal depreciation).

Question 17.3

Greenan Plc has EPS of 25c/p. It retains 80% of its profits for internal investment. It earns about 16% from this reinvestment. The current equity holders have a required return of 14%.

Requirement

(a) Calculate the value of Greenan Plc's equity shares.

(b) Determine the impact on the value of Greenan Plc's equity shares if the company's risk profile changes such that the equity holders now require a return of 16%.

Question 17.4

List the advantages and disadvantages of the dividend yield method of valuing equity shares.

Question 17.5

McKee Plc is an agricultural company. Its equity holders require a return of 14%. An excerpt from its estimated statement of profit or loss for the forthcoming year is as follows:

	€/£000
Revenue	1,500
Operating costs*	(1,000)
Gross profit	500
Tax	(200)
Operating income after tax	300

*Operating costs include depreciation of €/£180,000.

You are also informed that McKee Plc plans to purchase new agricultural equipment worth €/£220,000 in the coming year and will increase its working capital from €/£900,000 to €/£1,000,000. This will give McKee a competitive advantage for the next five years and will increase its free cash flow as follows:

In Year 2 the free cash flow expected is €/£200,000, in Year 3 it is €/£220,000, in Year 4 it is €/£250,000 and in Year 5 it is €/£280,000. At that stage the net assets of McKee Plc are considered to be worth €/£350,000 and terminal value for McKee Plc is predicted to be €/£3,000,000.

Requirement

(a) Calculate the free cash flows for Year 1 from the information provided above. Highlight the value drivers in your calculation.

(b) Calculate the value of McKee Plc now, assuming a shareholder value analysis approach is adopted.

(c) Determine the impact on the valuation if it is assumed that McKee Plc invests €/£500,000 now in order to extend its competitive advantage to nine years. Assume that the free cash flows for Year 6 to 10 are expected to be €/£290,000 per year and the terminal value is predicted to be €/£5,000,000.

Question 17.6

List the valuation stages that an analyst normally takes when valuing a company/shareholding.

CHALLENGING QUESTIONS

(Suggested Solutions to Challenging Questions are available through your lecturer.)

Question 17.1 Hawk (Level 1)

You are a finance manager in Hawk. The company's directors are considering listing the company for an IPO. The company will have to pay after-tax annual fees of €/£500,000 to the stock exchange if listed. You have been provided with the following information.

EXTRACTS FROM HAWK'S FORECAST
Statement of Profit and Loss

	Forecast 20X8 €/£000
Turnover	195,220
Cost of sales	(126,893)
Gross profit	68,327
Expenses (excluding interest)	(38,552)
Interest	(1,502)
Profit before tax	28,273
Tax	(3,534)
Net profit	24,739
Dividend to be paid in 20X8	12,369
Hawk has 100,000,000 shares issued	
Current share price is €/£2.22	

Further information:

1. Price earnings valuation:
   - Expenses in 20X8 include a one-off restructuring cost of €/£1,200,000 relating to an acquisition during the year.
   - The following information relates to two companies that are in the same sector as Hawk and are listed on the stock exchange:

Company	Market	No. of shares in issue (millions)	Net profit (€/£million)	Share price (€/£)
Slider Plc	Main Market	10	32.45	39.75
Hub Manu Plc	Euronext Access/AIM	9	19.26	19.62

2. Dividend valuation:
   - Hawk is expected to maintain the current pay-out ratio indefinitely.
   - Turnover is expected to grow by 10% in each of the next two years and the net profit margin is expected to be 12% and 11% in 20X9 and 20Y0, respectively, after listing costs. After 20Y0, it is expected that dividends would grow at an annual average rate of 3.5% indefinitely.
   - The risk-free rate of return is 2%. Companies listed on the Main Market of the stock exchange, of similar risk to Hawk, have betas of 1.10. The market risk premium is 6%.

Requirement Advise Hawk, using the information provided, on the value it could expect to achieve at an IPO on the Main Market by:
(a) calculating a price/earnings valuation;
(b) calculating a discounted dividend valuation.
(c) Explain which of the two valuation approaches is more appropriate in this context.

13 marks

(Based on Chartered Accountants Ireland, CAP 2, SFMA, Autumn 2018, extract from Q1)

Question 17.2 Thermal (Level 1)

Alf Johnson has informed the shareholders of Thermal that he has been approached by his former employer Matrix Engineering, an international company in the same industry as Thermal, with an offer to acquire 100% of the equity of Thermal. To help assess this offer, you have been tasked with valuing the company. Relevant information includes the following:

EXTRACTS FROM THE FINANCIAL STATEMENTS OF THERMAL

	20X8 Forecast	**20X7**	**20X6**
	€/£000	**€/£000**	**€/£000**
Turnover	4,796	4,944	5,045
Cost of sales	(2,254)	(2,373)	(2,371)
Gross profit	2,542	2,571	2,674
Expenses (excluding depreciation and interest)	(1,331)	(1,358)	(1,345)
Depreciation	(490)	(475)	(460)
Interest	(155)	(155)	(155)
Profit before tax	566	583	714
Tax	(71)	(73)	(89)
Net profit	495	510	625
Dividend paid	198	204	250

	20X8 Forecast	**20X7**	**20X6**
ASSETS	**€/£000**	**€/£000**	**€/£000**
Non-current assets			
Property	3,582	3,222	2,865
Plant and equipment	908	932	965
	4,490	4,154	3,830
Current assets			
Inventory	891	782	765
Trade receivables	562	443	395
Short-term investments	30	22	26
Cash	55	135	188
	1,538	1,382	1,374
Total assets	6,028	5,536	5,204

EQUITY AND LIABILITIES			
Equity			
Ordinary shares	100	100	100
Retained earnings	3,150	2,853	2,547
	3,250	2,953	2,647
Non-current liabilities	1,938	1,938	1,937
Current liabilities			
Bank overdraft	350	265	225
Trade payables	490	380	395
	840	645	620
Total equity and liabilities	6,028	5,536	5,204

Other relevant information

Asset valuation:

Discussions within Thermal have uncovered a number of issues that are **not reflected** in the 20X8 forecast financial statements. These are:

- €/£80,000 of trade receivables is owed by a Belfast customer which is in receivership. It is likely that Thermal will only recover 10% of this sum.
- €/£290,000 of non-current liabilities comprises a 30-year bond held by a pension fund. The trustees of the fund indicate that they would redeem the bond in exchange for a payment of €/£230,000.
- Short-term investments consists of 5,000 shares in a public company. This company has just reported earnings per share of €/£0.96 and trades on a price earnings ratio of 8.3 times.

Free cash flow valuation:

- Thermal has invested an average of 15% of turnover per year in additional investments in non-current assets and working capital historically. This is expected to be maintained in the future. Thermal's financial advisors suggest a long-term average growth rate in free cash flows of 1.5% is reasonable.
- Based on similar companies, a beta factor of 1.6 would apply to Thermal. The risk-free rate is currently 0.75% and the market risk premium is estimated to be 6%. The corporate tax rate is 12.5%.
- The loan rate is 8%.
- The free cash flow valuation of debt and equity should be done **without** reference to any adjustments made for the asset valuation.

Requirement

(a) Calculate an asset valuation of Thermal.
(b) Calculate a free cash flow valuation of Thermal.

10 marks

(Based on Chartered Accountants Ireland, CAP 2, SFMA, Summer 2018, extract from Q1)

Question 17.3 ACA Corporate Finance (Level 2)

Background You have just been appointed manager in a firm of specialist corporate financiers, ACA Corporate Finance. As part of your new role, you specialise in providing recommendations to clients who are considering acquisitions and disposals, as well as other corporate finance activities.

Timber Plc One of your most important clients is Timber Plc, a company that has three sawmills, one each in Dublin, Belfast and Sligo, from which it supplies timber to builders merchants around Ireland. The business is notoriously cyclical and closely follows trends in the construction industry, which uses a lot of timber, particularly for house building.

The directors of Timber are considering a number of new investment projects and the directors have asked you to calculate an appropriate discount rate that could be used to appraise these projects. You have received information on the current financing structure of Timber (see the Appendix to this question).

New Sawmill One of the new projects being considered involves the replacement of an old sawmill, which is causing production problems due to continued breakdowns, etc. A new sawmill would cost €/£25 million and would deliver 25% more efficiency, as well as reduced electricity consumption.

Finefurniture Ltd Another potential investment project involves the acquisition of a furniture manufacturing company called Finefurniture Ltd. The rationale behind this acquisition is that it would provide Timber with a new market for its wood, offering diversification into a new industry and thereby reducing the risk of any downturn within the core timber business. Furniture manufacturing is considered to have a lower level of systematic risk than the timber industry (see Note 5 in the Appendix to this question). Demand for furniture is growing steadily and seems to avoid the peaks and troughs associated with the timber industry.

Potential Disposal While in the process of considering the above expansion options, the directors of Timber have recently received an unsolicited offer to buy the company from its largest competitor, Bigwood Plc. Should the acquisition proceed, the enlarged group would be the largest timber company in Ireland and there would be significant cost and buying power synergies, which would have a very positive impact on profits.

Bigwood's offer includes a substantial takeover premium, which is conditional on the directors of Timber leaving the company, i.e. they would not become directors in the enlarged group going forward. As part of the cost synergies identified by Bigwood, the directors of Timber would be made redundant and would receive termination payments in line with their individual contracts of employment. Given the imminent prospect of redundancy, the directors of Timber are extremely reluctant to contemplate a sale of the company to Bigwood and are proposing to reject the offer outright. Before rejecting the offer, they have asked for your advice as to their responsibilities to the equity holders, under the Stock Exchange rules, in respect of the offer. They have also asked for your views on what potential valuation should be placed on Timber.

Requirement Prepare a report to the board of directors of Timber on the following:

(a) Calculate Timber's cost of equity using the dividend growth model and subsequently calculate the discount rate which should be used to assess the new sawmill project, outlining clearly any assumptions you make.

20 Marks

(b) Calculate the most appropriate discount rate which Timber should use to assess the acquisition of Finefurniture, outlining clearly your reasons.

10 Marks

(***Note:*** assume the company finances the acquisition so that its existing capital structure remains unchanged.)

(c) Compare and contrast the beta factors and P/E ratios associated with the timber and furniture industries, outlining your views as to why they differ so much between these two industries.

8 Marks

(d) Advise the directors of Timber as to their responsibilities to the shareholders, under the Stock Exchange rules, in respect of the offer from Bigwood.

8 Marks

(e) Calculate TWO valuations of Timber, one based on earnings, and the other based on a valuation of assets.

8 Marks

(f) Outline THREE factors which should be taken into account in the valuation when considering the price being offered by Bigwood.

6 Marks
Total 60 Marks

(Based on Chartered Accountants Ireland, MABF, FAE, Extract from Autumn 2005, Q1)

Appendix to Question 17.3

Timber Plc

Statement of Profit or Loss (Extracts)
for the year ended 3l December 20X5

	€/£ million
Net income before interest and tax	125
Interest	(25)
Net income before tax	100
Taxation	(20)
Net income after tax	80

Statement of Financial Position (Extracts)
as at 31 December 20X5

	€/£ million
ASSETS	
Non-current assets	325
Current assets	
Inventories	120
Trade receivables	52
Cash	3
	175
Total assets	500
EQUITY, RESERVES AND LIABILITIES	
Equity and reserves	
Equity share capital	25
Revenue reserves	175
	200
Non-current liabilities	
Long-term bank debt	150
9% debentures	100
	250
Current liabilities	
Trade payables	25
Taxation	25
	50
Total equity and liabilities	500

- The current P/E ratio of Timber is 7, while the standard P/E ratio of companies in the furniture sector is 10.
- Equity share capital comprises 25 million shares at €/£1 each.
- The company is about to pay a dividend, which will result in a dividend yield of 3.5% on its equity shares.
- Dividends are expected to increase at 5% per annum.
- Companies in the timber industry have a beta coefficient of 1.2, while companies in the furniture industry have a beta coefficient of 0.8.
- The 9% debentures are currently trading at 110%. A full year's interest is due immediately and has been provided for in the financial statements.
- The bank debt carries an interest rate of 6%.
- The interest rate on government securities is 7% and, historically, the stock market has given a return of about 5% above the risk-free rate of return.
- Corporation tax is currently 20%.
- Non-current assets have a book value of €/£325 million. However, the market value of the company's property has been independently valued at €/£100 million more than the book value.
- At the beginning of 20X5 the company purchased a new computer system costing €/£20 million, which is being depreciated on a straight-line basis over a four-year period. The net recoverable amount of this asset is currently 50% of its purchase price.

Question 17.4 Qwerty (Level 1)

Growth Opportunities Paul has always been more growth-focused than Joe and for the past year has been exploring various options to expand the company. He has identified a venture capital investor with an interest in small technology companies. The investor has made an offer to invest €/£2 million in Qwerty for 36% of the equity. Paul and Joe agree that this is an attractive offer. Paul is proposing that they use the funds raised from the new investor to part-finance the acquisition of Screen Magic Limited, an Irish company that manufactures computer screens. Paul has had preliminary discussions with the owner (and managing director) of Screen, who is keen to retire after finding the last few years increasingly stressful trying to resolve a complex tax issue affecting Screen and dealing with increasingly onerous regulations on environmental standards in manufacturing. He may be interested in selling Screen and has provided information on the company (see the Appendix to this question).

Requirement

(a) Advise Qwerty on how much it should bid for the equity in Screen based on:
  (i) a net asset valuation;
  (ii) a price earnings valuation;
  (iii) a dividend valuation.

12 Marks

APPENDIX

Screen Magic Limited

STATEMENT OF FINANCIAL POSITION

as at 31 December 20X4

	€/£000	€/£000
ASSETS		
Non-current assets		
Property	1,105	
Plant and machinery	925	2,030

Current assets		
Inventory	860	
Trade receivables	605	1,465
Total assets		3,495
EQUITY AND LIABILITIES		
Current liabilities		
Bank overdraft	360	
Trade payables	480	840
Non-current liabilities		
Debenture		985
Equity		
Ordinary shares		290
Retained earnings		1,380
Total equity and liabilities		3,495

Screen Magic Limited
Statement of Profit or Loss (Abridged)
for the Year Ended 31 December 20X4

	€/£000
Sales revenue	4,110
Cost of sales	(2,466)
Gross profit	1,644
Operating expenses	(965)
Depreciation	(82)
Interest	(30)
Net profit before tax	567
Tax	(74)
Net profit	493
Dividend paid	247

Additional information on Screen:

1. Property consists of two buildings, neither of which has been revalued for several years. Details of the two buildings are as follows:
   - The first building is a manufacturing facility with a book value of €/£640,000. A valuation, two years ago, indicated the manufacturing facility to have a value of €/£760,000.
   - The second building is an office building with a book value of €/£465,000. An identical, adjacent office building is currently rented for €/£95,000 and commercial office buildings in this area generally sell at a net (after-tax) rental yield of 12%.
2. Approximately 15% of inventory is made up of older models, which may not be possible to sell.
3. The debenture has a fixed rate and has 12 years remaining to maturity. It was issued when interest rates were significantly lower than current levels so its market value is considerably less than that recorded in the statement of financial position. Screen estimates its owners would redeem the debenture if offered 85% of the book value.

4. Paul has provided the following details on three publicly listed companies in the same sector as Screen:

	Earnings per share	Share price	Total sales
	€/£	€/£	€/£000
JenTech Plc	0.18	1.44	4,582
Able Systems Plc	0.75	12.00	34,000
Axon Plc	0.50	4.25	2,925

5. A small, listed company in the same sector as Screen (not shown above), has just paid a dividend of €/£0.22 per share. Its share price is €/£2.35 and its dividends are expected to grow at a rate of 4.5%. Paul believes it is reasonable to assume that the cost of equity and growth rate of dividends for Screen will be very similar to this company.
6. If Qwerty acquires Screen, an integration process costing €/£450,000 would be undertaken in the first year. Paul is confident this would yield economies of scale and synergies with a present value of €/£1,200,000.

(Based on Chartered Accountants Ireland, CAP 2, MABF, Autumn 2013, extract from Q1)

Question 17.5 Hexagon (Level 1)

Perform a valuation of Hexagon using the information below.

Hexagon
FORECASTED FINANCIAL PERFORMANCE AND INVESTMENT REQUIREMENTS
for the Next Five Years

	30 June 20X5	30 June 20X6	30 June 20X7	30 June 20X8	30 June 20X9
	€/£000	€/£000	€/£000	€/£000	€/£000
Sales	3,600	3,850	3,900	4,550	4,900
EBIT	900	883	1,362	1,408	1,421
Interest	285	310	310	325	350
Tax	68	60	153	198	155

Additional information:
Use the following definition of free cash flow (FCF).

$$\text{FCF} = \text{EBIT} - \text{Tax} + \text{Depreciation} - \text{Increase in net working capital} - \text{Increase in capital investment}$$

- Depreciation is expected to be €/£285,000 in each of the years 20X5 to 20X9.
- Net working capital is currently €/£1,120,000, which equates to 35% of 20X4 sales. It is expected that this ratio of working capital to sales will be required in the future.
- Annual capital investment has historically averaged 15% of annual sales.
- The three directors believe a growth rate of 4% in FCF could be maintained indefinitely from 20X9.
- Hexagon pays corporation tax at a rate of 20%.
- Hexagon is financed by ordinary equity and traded bonds.
- The bonds were issued eight years ago at a nominal value of €/£100. They currently trade at €/£106.55. The bonds pay an annual coupon of 7.5%. This coupon will be paid in two weeks and the bonds are currently trading cum-interest. These bonds are irredeemable.

- Octagon Plc is a publicly traded company, which is very similar to Hexagon in most respects. Octagon has just paid a dividend of €/£0.09 per share and analysts expect Octagon's dividends to grow at an annual rate of 4.5% in the future. Octagon's share price closed at €/£1.24 yesterday.
- Hexagon's most recent statement of financial position reports values of €/£1,857,000 and €/£2,355,000 for long-term debt and equity, respectively.

Requirement

(a) Estimate the weighted average cost of capital (WACC) of Hexagon. (Explain any assumptions you make.)

6 Marks

(b) Estimate the value of Hexagon using a free cash flow approach. (Explain any assumptions you make.)

9 Marks

Total 15 Marks

(Based on Chartered Accountants Ireland, CAP 2, MABF, Summer 2013, Q4(a),(b))

Question 17.6 Currane (Level 2)

Jim McGee, the Chief Executive of Currane Plc, was shocked last Tuesday morning when Ree Resources Plc announced it had acquired 9% of the shares in Currane and was making a bid for the company.

Currane was founded by Jim McGee's father, Niall McGee, in 1968. It owned several copper and zinc mines throughout Ireland. In 1985 Niall McGee took the company public and the McGee family, the largest shareholder, now owns 8% of Currane and three of the eight directors on the Board are appointed by the family. The remaining 92% of Currane's shares are owned by a dispersed group of shareholders, none of whom owns more than 2% of Currane, other than Ree. Currane's shares are currently trading at €/£1.69.

The offer made by Ree to Currane's shareholders was €/£2.35 cash per share in Currane or 0.45 shares in Ree (currently trading at €/£5.02) per share in Currane.

Requirement Using the information above and that contained in the Appendix to this question:

(a) Estimate the growth rate in dividends for the next five years.

3 Marks

(b) Estimate a valuation range per share for Currane using a discounted dividend valuation approach and a forward price earnings ratio approach.

6 Marks

(c) Highlight any weaknesses of the above approaches to valuation. Advise on whether the offer from Ree should be recommended to shareholders.

3 Marks

Appendix

Currane

Statement of Profit or Loss (Extract)
for year ended 31 December 20X5

	€/£000
Turnover	86,530
Cost of sales	(34,600)
Gross profit	51,930
Operating expenses	(22,980)
Depreciation	(8,000)
EBIT	20,950

Interest	(3,350)
Profit before tax	17,600
Tax	(2,200)
Net profit	15,400

Additional information:

- The sector average forward (prospective) price earnings (P/E) ratio for resource companies in Ireland is 7.
- Currane's shareholders require a return of 12.5%.
- Currane currently retains 50% of earnings and expects to do so for the next three years. After Year 3 the required level of reinvestment is expected to fall and Currane expects to retain 35% of annual earnings indefinitely.
- Currane's return on capital employed (ROCE) is 12%. This is expected to remain stable indefinitely.
- There are 40 million shares outstanding in Currane.

(Based on Chartered Accountants Ireland, CAP 2, Autumn 2012, Q4)

Question 17.7 Inotech (Level 2)

You are a newly qualified Chartered Accountant working in the corporate finance division of a medium-sized practice. Inotech Ltd, a highly reputable sporting goods distributor, has been approached by Geared Plc, a sporting goods manufacturer, with the intention of acquiring the entire share capital of Inotech. Ben Morris, the Managing Director and 90% shareholder at Inotech, has welcomed the approach and needs guidance from you on a potential valuation for Inotech and the nature of any consideration for the acquisition.

Information gathered by you on Inotech in discussions with Ben and following a review of all recent publicly available information on Geared and Compass Plc, a direct competitor of Inotech, is outlined below. Compass is the most suitably quoted company comparison for Inotech. Synergies are expected from the combination, but these are yet to be quantified.

SUMMARY OVERVIEW

	Compass Plc	**Inotech Ltd**
Company age	15 years	3 years
Estimated market share	20%	15%
Market capitalisation	€/£6m	N/A
Number of shares issued	1,000,000	1,000,000
Number of shareholders	Many	3
Cost of equity	12%	18%
WACC	10%	12%
Gearing	29%	67%
ROCE	14%	12%
Asset and Debt Information		
Total asset book value	€/£7m	€/£3m
Total asset realisable value	N/A	€/£2.5m
Total asset replacement cost	N/A	€/£3.8m
Debt	€/£2m	€/£2m
Cash balance	Medium	Low

Market-based Information		
Current share price	€/£6.00	Not available
Historical earnings profile	Stable	Growth
Earnings after tax prior year	€/£750,000	€/£600,000
P/E ratio	8	N/A
Forecasted earnings next year	N/A	€/£630,000
Dividend payout ratio	40%	5%
Dividend prior year	€/£300,000	€/£30,000
Dividend growth	N/A	5%
Free Cash Flow		
Forecast (Year 1 to Year 5)	N/A	€/£800,000
Year 6 +		€/£850,000

Requirement

(a) Determine for Ben a probable valuation range for the entire share capital of Inotech. You are expected to determine any five potential valuations using a variety of approaches and arrive at a recommendation.

12 Marks

(b) Based on the information above, outline any THREE factors that Ben could advance to strengthen his position in negotiating any final price.

3 Marks

(c) Describe, briefly, any THREE factors that Ben should consider in determining the best form of payment for the acquisition (complete this part after studying **Chapter 18**).

3 Marks

Total 18 Marks

(Based on Chartered Accountants Ireland, CAP 2, MABF, Autumn 2011, Q2(b)(c))

18

Mergers and Takeovers

Learning Objectives

Upon completing this chapter, readers should be able to:

- explain the difference between a merger and a takeover;
- describe the different types of merger and takeover;
- explain the motives for mergers and takeovers;
- describe the different methods used by a bidding company to finance a merger/takeover;
- explain the advantages and limitations of each of the finance methods and outline situations where these would be most appropriate;
- distinguish between minority and controlling interests in the context of a takeover situation;
- summarise common defence tactics and comment on their appropriateness;
- describe potential ethical issues that may arise in takeover/merger situations;
- outline the various steps that a bidding company might follow that are likely to improve the chance of making a takeover successful (including post-acquisition measures);
- list and explain the various due diligence work that a bidding company may request when negotiating a takeover; and
- describe the results of research into the success of mergers and takeovers in the past, outlining the stakeholders who have most to benefit from these types of investment activity.

INTRODUCTION

Mergers and takeovers are examples of external growth investment decisions that involve the **amalgamation** (i.e. coming together) of two or more independent companies. A **merger** usually occurs when two companies come together amicably to form a new, larger company. Both sets of equity holders receive shares in the new entity in exchange for the equity shares they held in the original entities. The assets of both companies are transferred to the new company. A **takeover** is different: one company, the **target company**, is absorbed into the other company, the **bidding company**. In general, the bidding company is larger, though this is not always the case. When a small company merges with a large company this is called a **reverse takeover**, though it is sometimes referred to as a **reverse merger**. When a takeover occurs, the target company's assets are transferred to the bidding company and all the shares of the target company are purchased using cash, equity, debt, or a combination of these three forms of consideration. Takeovers can occur amicably, or can be contested by the management of the target company. In the latter scenario they are referred to as **hostile takeover bids**; an example is summarised in **Real World Example 18.1**.

Real World Example 18.1: Hostile Approach

At the time of writing, Naspers, a South African company, made a hostile approach to buy Just Eat. The offer was 710p in cash and meant the bidders had valued the company at £4.9 billion. This was immediately rejected by Just Eat's board. A short time later, a share-for-share exchange rival offer came in from Takeaway.com; however, the shareholders of Takeaway.com reacted negatively and share price fell, with the result that the offer only equated to about 600p per share, with the price still having the potential for more uncertainty. It is expected that Naspers will return with a higher bid, and Just Eat's shareholders are unlikely to reject a cash offer that provides them with a certain return.

Students are advised to research this case to see what happened.

Mergers/takeovers are usually classified according to the relationship that exists between the two companies that are parties to the transaction, as shown in **Figure 18.1**.

Figure 18.1: Types of Amalgamation

Horizontal integration	When the two companies are in the same industry and involved in the same type of activity, for example, both refine crude oil.
Vertical integration	• When the two companies are in the same industry but are involved in different activities, for example one refines crude oil, the other owns a network of filling stations. • When a bidding company takes over an entity that supplies goods to it, this is termed **'backward vertical integration'**. • When a bidding company takes over an entity that it supplies goods to, this is called **'forward vertical integration'**.
Conglomerate merger	When the two companies are in unrelated industries, for example one refines crude oil, the other is in pharmaceuticals.

Many companies also demerge to downsize for a variety of reasons. The three main methods used to downsize are a **leveraged buy-out (LBO)**, the sale of a portion of the company to another company (i.e. a **sell-off**), or a spin-off. A leveraged buy-out describes a variety of methods that are used to explain the sale of a portion of a company to others, wherein the main financing used by the purchasing parties is debt. Examples of LBOs include a management buy-out (MBO), a management buy-in (MBI), a vendor-initiated management buy-out (VIMBO) and sales to private equity investors. A **spin-off** occurs when a large company, with more than one business activity, separates one or more of the business activities and its assets into a separate company. The parent company provides its current equity holders with shares in the new entity. More detail on these methods is provided in **Chapter 5**.

The next section explains the motives for mergers and takeovers, then the methods that are commonly used to finance company mergers/takeovers are discussed and the steps that are usually required during and after this process are outlined. The final part of this chapter links the theory into practice by considering the research on the success of company mergers/takeovers.

MOTIVES FOR TAKEOVERS/MERGERS

As mentioned, mergers and takeovers are investment decisions – hence, the principles and approaches to capital investment appraisal, covered in **Chapter 3**, apply. In brief, the net present value of the expected future incremental cash flows of the company (including those specific to the target company) less the cost of the target company, should be positive when discounted at the company's required rate of return (adjusted for risk, if necessary). The underlying objective of the decision on whether to amalgamate with another business is the same as that for normal capital appraisal decision-making: to maximise equity holder wealth.

As discussed in earlier chapters, each investment undertaken by a company should be aligned with the strategic objectives of the company (maximising equity holder value). The motives for amalgamations that can be considered to increase equity holder value might include: speculative investment, cost reduction, increasing market share, gaining access to markets, increasing production capacity, obtaining intellectual capital, achieving a cost-effective listing, expanding to achieve critical mass so that 'costly' developments can be pursued, and achieving synergies. Other reasons for mergers and takeovers, which may not be consistent with maximising equity holder value, include amalgamating with another company to utilise surplus funds or to diversify risk. The motives are now discussed in more detail.

Motives that Increase Equity Shareholder Value

Speculative Investment

A company may launch a bid to take over another company when it perceives that the other company is undervalued. Where the target company is a public limited company, then the bidding company might be of the opinion that the market is not valuing the target company correctly. The intention of the bidding company in a speculative takeover would be to purchase the target company and sell off its components for an overall premium, a process termed **asset stripping**. The total revenues received for the component parts are expected to exceed the initial purchase consideration, hence increasing the wealth of the equity holders of the bidding company.

Cost Reductions

Economies of scale are cited in many instances as being motivations for amalgamating with another company. Economies of scale might include, for example: the ability to purchase larger quantities, hence negotiate cheaper purchase prices; the ability to reduce costs that are duplicated (typically central costs, such as administrative costs, marketing costs, or research and development costs); the ability to reduce production costs where the company is a manufacturing entity; and/or the ability to negotiate cheaper finance fees when accessing finance from financial institutions and the markets.

Synergies

The term **synergy** is used to describe gains that are not associated with scale economies. Synergies are commonly explained using a mathematical example: assume that the two companies that are merging have earnings of €/£2 each. However, after the amalgamation the combined earnings amount to €/£5. The €/£1 is considered to reflect synergies gained from the amalgamation. Several banks have amalgamated to take advantage of their complementary resources. For example, Lloyds bank merged with the TSB Group and Barclays merged with Woolwich. A recent example is provided in **Real World Example 18.2**.

Real World Example 18.2: Irish Stock Exchange

In 2018, Euronext, the leading pan-European exchange in the eurozone, spanning Belgium, France, Ireland, the Netherlands, Portugal and the UK, took over the Irish Stock Exchange. The takeover is expected to result in significant growth for Euronext as the larger company has more products that can be accessed by Irish-listed companies. In addition, the takeover is expected to reap pre-tax cost synergies of €6 million by 2020.

Increasing Market Share

When a company operates in a competitive industry, where margins are tight and the products are homogenous, it may be possible to gain more earnings by eliminating competition by taking over other companies. This may allow the company to raise prices, which will result in more earnings. **Real World Example 18.3** illustrates increasing market share by merger.

Real World Example 18.3: Gas and Oil

In April 2015, the oil and gas company Royal Dutch Shell bought the BG Group (formerly British Gas) for about $81.5 billion. According to a Bloomberg article, the merger makes Shell the largest producer of liquefied natural gas in the world and as a result of the takeover its gas reserves exceed its oil reserves.

Source: Fox, J., "Stop Calling Shell an Oil Company", 8 April 2015, https://www.bloomberg.com/opinion/articles/2015-04-08/maybe-it-s-time-to-stop-calling-shell-an-oil-company; access July 2020.

Unchecked, horizontal mergers can actually be damaging for the general public who purchase the end products. Therefore, horizontal mergers are policed by governments in both the UK and in Ireland. (This is discussed in detail later in this chapter.) Examples of horizontal mergers/possible mergers that attracted much attention because of the perceived impact on competition include: the proposed takeovers of Safeway by Morrisons, Asda, Sainsbury's and Tesco in the UK in 2005; and the proposed takeover of Aer Lingus by Ryanair in Ireland in 2007. In the UK, the competition watchdog, the Competition and Markets Authority, blocked the Asda, Sainsbury and Tesco bids, but gave the go-ahead to Morrisons. It felt a Morrisons takeover would actually increase competition between the one-stop-shop retail entities as it would produce four large players instead of three. In Ireland, the government (a large equity holder in Aer Lingus) publicly rejected Michael O'Leary's bid for Aer Lingus on the grounds that "it would not be in the best interests of the company, the country, passengers and staff". However, it was the European Commission that considered that the takeover would reduce competition in Europe. It blocked the takeover in 2007 and again in early 2013.

Gaining Access to Markets

In some instances a company will make a takeover bid for another established entity to gain access to its market. The target market may be geographically different, or have a totally different customer base. A current example is provided in **Real Word Example 18.4**.

Real World Example 18.4: Access to New Markets

At the time of writing, a relatively small Chinese company, Jingye, agreed to take over ailing British Steel in a deal worth £50 million. It is speculated that Jingye may see the takeover as a means of gaining access to the UK market for its products, that the takeover will reduce its exposure to the volatile Chinese steel market, or that the steel works will receive raw steel from China, process it and sell it on with a 'Made in Britain' stamp. The reasons are not yet clear. Though the deal is not yet finalised, Jingye has stated that it will invest £1.2 billion in British Steel in the coming years. If this deal goes ahead, it will save 4,000 jobs directly and an estimated 20,000 in the supply chain. It will also avert huge environmental clean-up costs that would arise from dismantling all the steel works. This is the third time that British Steel has changed hands in the past few years. In 2016, Tata (an Indian conglomerate) gave the company to private equity firm, Greybull Capital, for £1.

Students should research this case to see what happened.

Recognising Under-utilisation of Resources

In some instances a bidding company will approach a target company when it perceives that the target company is not utilising its resources to the full potential. An example of an area where under-utilisation may be found is managerial ineffectiveness wherein the bidding company considers that the target company's management team is not utilising the resources of the company to their full potential. When a company reorganisation occurs primarily to change the management team, this is commonly referred to as the **market for corporate control**. This theory suggests that a motivation for mergers/takeovers comes from management, who compete to control company resources. In some instances mergers are agreed to by target companies and used as a tool to selectively remove inefficient staff. The threat of takeover is argued to improve the effectiveness of management teams, and hence will benefit equity holders. Takeovers are considered by some to be a necessary market control that will ultimately benefit equity holders by rooting out ineffective management teams, which are normally replaced after the takeover. Another example of under-utilisation might be where a manufacturing company has excess production capacity. This sort of company may be attractive to a bidding company when it has constraints on its production facility. It may believe that a takeover/merger provides a quicker and better mode of growth, relative to purchasing more factories and more plant and equipment.

Obtaining Critical Mass

In some industries, companies have to undertake extensive research and development to survive, for example, the pharmaceuticals industry, high-tech industries, and the aerospace, weapons and motor industries. Research and development is typically very expensive and in some instances is actually a barrier to entry. Companies in these industries grow either internally or using external means to obtain a critical mass that can then support a significant annual investment in research and development. An example is the Glaxo Wellcome takeover of SmithKline Beecham in 2000.

Obtaining Intellectual Capital

In many instances a large company will purchase a smaller company to obtain rights to its intellectual capital. This approach is used by some entities as part of their research and development strategy. Ireland has seen a number of its home-grown tech companies being purchased by overseas companies just as they reach a certain stage of development, as noted by Shane Dempsey of the Irish Software Association (ISA). "That's almost become a natural trajectory for Irish software companies: they start up, develop a product, then get to a certain stage and are sold or acquired." Examples include the purchase of Xiam, a Dublin-based software developer (for mobile phones) by Qualcomm, a US wireless communications company, for $32 million; and the purchase of Havok, a software company, by Intel for $110 million.[1] An example of a company that is merging to gain access to knowledge is summarised in **Real World Example 18.5**.

Real World Example 18.5: Friendly Approach

In December 2019, the Italian giant Fiat Chrysler (FCA) merged with the French giant Groupe PSA, owners of Peugeot. The merger is said to be worth €40 billion and will create the world's fourth largest car manufacturer. The merger is expected to generate savings and benefits amounting to €3.7 billion. In addition, FCA will gain access to PSA's technology on carbon dioxide emissions. To comply with EU legislation, by 2020 car manufacturers must produce vehicles with CO_2 emissions that average less than 95g/km, with further reductions of 15% by 2025 and 37.5% by 2030. There are fines for every g/km over that amount on each and every car sold.

Source: Tisshaw, M., "Why Fiat Chrysler and PSA Group are merging", 31 October 2019, https://www.autocar.co.uk/opinion/industry/why-fiat-chrysler-and-psa-group-are-merging; accessed July 2020.

Tax Avoidance

A company may take over another company to gain access to advantageous tax treatment in that company's country. This is particularly true in the case of Ireland, as highlighted in **Real World Example 18.6**

[1] Other acquisitions include the purchase of Cape Clear by Workday for an undisclosed sum; the purchase of FotoNation by Tessera for $29 million; the purchase of Allfinanz by Munich Re for €48 million; the purchase of Datacare by Computershare for $12 million; and the purchase of Servecast by Level 3 for €33 million.

REAL WORLD EXAMPLE 18.6: ELAN AND PERRIGO

Elan takeover gives Perrigo Irish tax advantage

In 2013 Perrigo, a US drugmaker, purchased the Irish company Elan for about €6.5 billion. A key motivation for this purchase was tax. After the takeover, Perrigo can move its headquarters to Ireland and take advantage of Ireland's 12.5% corporation tax rate – the corresponding rate in the US being 35%.

Indeed, it is reported that about 40% of S&P 500 companies have subsidiaries in Ireland. Several multinationals have a number of subsidiaries located here, including Apple, Google, Facebook, PepsiCo Global Investment Holdings Ltd and Western Union, to name only a few.

Growth

In some instances, older companies in mature industries target younger companies in industries that have potential to increase their sales/growth figures. Over the last decade a number of companies in mature industries have acquired high-tech companies in the hope that their overall growth performance continues to improve. For an example of this, see **Real World Example 18.7**.

REAL WORLD EXAMPLE 18.7: UBER

In 2019, eight IPOs raising over $1 billion each were listed on the NYSE. Uber's IPO generated $8.1 billion in cash for the company.

To Obtain a Cost-effective Listing

A motivation for merging with another company can be to obtain a listing in a cost-effective manner. This is usually achieved with a reverse merger, wherein a large private company merges with a small listed company. This circumvents the listing process; there is no need to file a prospectus, or to pay the expenses that are required for an IPO. The normal approach in this type of takeover is for the equity holders of the private company to sell their shares to the bidding company (which is the listed company) in exchange for shares in the listed company. This is also known as a **back-door listing**. A practical example of this is outlined in **Real World Example 18.8**.

REAL WORLD EXAMPLE 18.8: REVERSE MERGERS/BACK-DOOR LISTING

In 2017, Alibaba-backed courier YTO Express listed via a $2.7 billion reverse merger with a listed Chinese clothing maker, Dalian Dayang Trands Co. Ltd. Dalian paid for YTO Express using an asset swap and share issue. This resulted in a back-door listing on the Shanghai Bourse for YTP Express.

Source: https://www.reuters.com/article/us-yto-m-a-dayang-trands-idUSKCN0WO1XD; accessed April 2020.

Investment Strategy

In some instances a company will take over another company as part of its investment strategy. When a company has surplus funds it has two options, both of which should lead to the maximisation of equity holders' funds: distribute them to the equity holders, who can subsequently invest the funds to earn their required rate of return; or make an investment that earns a return in excess of the company's costs of capital (adjusted for the risk of the project, etc.). It is under the latter option that a company may elect to purchase a target company for investment.

Taking over another company is a quick way to get an investment up and running. However, additional issues have to be considered when an external investment is being evaluated. Agency theory may apply in this type of decision as managers' lives are usually severely affected by a merger/takeover. Because of the potential personal consequences, directors may pursue sub-optimal decision-making that has their own interests at the forefront. Another problem usually arises due to the sheer size of these external investments, which makes the whole investment appraisal process very difficult and additional steps, using external experts, are usually required (for example, due diligence reports are typically required).

Possible Dysfunctional Motivations for Business Combinations

Bootstrapping

In the 1960s, **bootstrapping** was used by some company managers to boost their earnings per share and growth performance measures. The **bootstrap effect** is a phrase used to describe a merger/takeover that provides no real economic benefit to a company's equity holders. It is best explained using an example.

Worked Example 18.1: The Bootstrap Effect

Financial information for Bidding Group Plc (a fast-growing ungeared company) and Target Company Plc (a slow-growing ungeared company), is as follows:

	Bidding Group Plc €/£000	**Target Company Plc €/£000**
Total net earnings	400	400
Total market value	6,000	3,000
Number of shares in issue	200	200

Bidding can acquire the share capital of Target in exchange for 100,000 shares in Bidding. Therefore, each share of Bidding is regarded as being worth two shares in Target – Bidding's market value being twice that of Target. There are no synergies, economies of scale or any other benefit to be gained from this business combination.

Requirement

(a) Calculate the current market price per share, earnings per share, price earnings ratio and earnings per euro/pound for both companies.

(b) Calculate total earnings, total market value, total shares in issue, the new market price per share, the earnings per share, the price earnings ratio and the earnings per euro/pound invested for Bidding Group Plc, post-acquisition.

(c) Why might this be regarded as an example of financial manipulation? Who stands to gain or lose from this deal?

Solution

(a) Current ratios

		Bidding Group Plc	**Target Company Plc**
Market price per share		€/£6,000,000 / 200,000	€/£3,000,000 / 200,000
	=	€/£30.00	€/£15.00
Earnings per share		€/£400,000 / 200,000	€/£400,000 / 200,000
	=	€/£2.00	€/£2.00
Price earnings ratio		€/£30.00 / €/£2.00	€15.00 / €/£2.00
	=	15 times	7.5 times
Earnings per €/£ invested		€/£2.00 / €/£30.00	€/£2.00 / €/£15.00
	=	6.67%	13.33%

(b) Resultant performance and ratios:

	Bidding Group Plc	**Target Company Plc**	**Bidding (after acquisition)**
Total net earnings	€/£400,000	€/£400,000	€/£800,000
Total market value	€/£6,000,000	€/£3,000,000	€/£9,000,000
Number of shares in issue	200	200	300
Market price per share	€/£30.00	€/£15.00	€/£30.00
Earnings per share	€/£2.00	€/£2.00	€/£2.67
Price earnings ratio	15 times	7.5 times	11.24 times
Earnings per €/£ invested	6.67%	13.33%	8.9%

Workings

Bidding Group Plc

Market price per share $= \frac{€/£9{,}000{,}000}{300{,}000} = €/£30.00$

Earnings per share $= \frac{€/£800{,}000}{300{,}000} = €/£2.67$

Price earnings ratio $= \frac{€/£30.00}{€/£2.67} = 11.24$ times

Earnings per €/£ invested $= \frac{€/£2.67}{€/£30.00} = 8.9\%$

(c) Research has found little evidence to suggest that capital markets are strong-form efficient. Indeed, it has been questioned whether they can be regarded as being semi-strong-form efficient. In a nutshell, it would seem that market price does not reflect the true value of a company because there is information asymmetry, irrational behaviour, etc., in the markets. Therefore, it is possible that market participants do not fully understand the implications of, for example, the above acquisition. It might be interpreted that the growth in earnings per share from €/£2.00 to €/£2.67 (a rise of 33.5%) is sustainable, but it is not. It might be perceived that Bidding Group Plc will improve the performance of Target Company Plc to obtain similar growth as is currently being experienced by Bidding Group Plc, as reflected in its high price earnings ratio. If this sentiment spreads, the share price of Bidding Group Plc will rise in the near future and equity holders will make gains based on their interpretation of the expectations of the performance of Bidding Group Plc. This will fall later as actual results will confirm that this is not the case.

There will be no winners or losers, provided the equity holders of both Bidding Group Plc and Target Company Plc understand the deal.

Companies with high price earnings ratios can actually increase their earnings per share by acquiring companies with a lower price earnings ratio, as in the above example. All things being equal, this should not impact on share price and should bring down the price earnings ratio as the increase in value caused by the short-term growth in earnings will be offset by reduced long-term expected growth. However, if the transaction is interpreted incorrectly by investors, such that they believe the growth prospects of the new company to be higher than it actually is, then this will drive up share price, and the resultant price earnings ratio, in the short term.

Diversification

The motivation between many conglomerate integrations is the wish of the management team of the bidding company to diversify its activities. This is a highly suspect reason for acquiring other businesses. It is argued that management teams that diversify to reduce risk (i.e. portfolio theory – see **Chapter 15**) are not acting in the best interests of their equity holders. Indeed, it could be suggested that this strategy is an example of agency theory, wherein the members of the management team are taking action to diversify the risk associated with losing their main source of income – their salaries. Purchasing another company is a costly exercise. The bidding company normally has to pay a premium for the target company's shares and has to pay substantial costs to consultants and advisors, whereas equity holders can diversify their portfolios at a lower cost, though the shares they purchase will include a premium and they also incur broker fees on each transaction.

Agency Theory

As mentioned previously, managers act as agents for equity holders. They are employed by equity holders to run the company for the benefit of its equity holders. Agency costs occur when management make decisions that are in their own interests, not those of the equity holders. For example, it is argued that some managers pursue acquisitions for self-interest/egotistic reasons. There is a certain amount of status and esteem in being the manager of a large-sized company. Getting a managerial position in a large company is difficult for an individual who only has managerial experience in small-sized entities. One way to open the career door to a large company may be to grow the company the manager works in. In addition to curriculum vitae building, managers of large-sized companies might get satisfaction from the power that they hold over so many resources. Further dysfunctional managerial behaviour may arise if a bidding company gets into competition with other bidding companies. The winners in this scenario are the equity holders of the target company.

PURCHASE CONSIDERATION AND THE EVALUATION OF BUSINESS COMBINATIONS

There are three main sources of finance that are used by a bidding company to purchase a target company – cash, shares, or debt securities. The cash offered by a bidding company can be obtained by an issue of shares to its current equity holders, by issuing debt and/or using cash reserves that have been built up in the bidding company. When the purchase consideration is by share exchange, the bidding company issues equity shares and exchanges these for the target company's equity shares. Finally, the bidding company can issue debt securities to the equity holders in the target company in exchange for their equity shares in that company. Any combination of these is also a possibility. In some instances the bidding company may give the equity holders of the target company an option: shares only, cash only or a combination of shares and cash.

Evaluating an Acquisition where the Purchase Consideration is Cash

When a business finance manager is evaluating the acquisition of an external entity, two key questions need to be positively answered to justify the acquisition in light of the key objective of public companies, i.e. to maximise equity holder wealth. First, will the acquisition of the target company result in a net gain, in present value terms, to the bidding company? Secondly, how much of the overall gain will be attributed to the equity holders of the bidding company, and how much goes to the equity holders of the target company? Though difficult to answer, projections can be utilised to determine answers to these questions. These projections will be used to help justify the proposed acquisition to the equity holders of a bidding company. The following simple example highlights how to approach the calculation of gains and their subsequent split between the two sets of equity holder.

Worked Example 18.2: Evaluating a Business Acquisition – Cash

Pike Plc is considering acquiring all of Minnow Plc's share capital for €/£22 per share. Minnow Plc is a similar company to Pike Plc: they both sell similar items and have no gearing. Relevant details on both companies are as follows:

Statements of Financial Position (Extracts)

	Pike Plc €/£m	Minnow Plc €/£m
Total assets	260	23
Of which:		
Cash	70	4
Other assets (book value)	190	19

Statement of Profit or Loss (Extracts)

	€/£m	€/£m
Revenues	170	25
Costs	125	20
Market value of company	550	48
Number of shares in issue (millions)	11	3

After an extensive review of the potential impact of the merger on the future financial performance of the company, it is considered that the combination will lead to some synergies. Revenues are expected to increase by €/£3 million and costs are expected to fall by €/£2 million. These are the only synergies expected. Pike Plc's cost of capital is 18%.

Requirement

(a) Explain why synergies occur.
(b) Calculate the economic gain to be made from this merger.
(c) Detail who is going to benefit from this gain: the equity holders of Pike Plc, or Minnow Plc?
(d) What are the expected market value, cash balance, total assets, other assets and earnings of Pike Plc post-acquisition?

Solution

(a) Synergies occur when two companies that come together are worth more than they were when on their own. In this example, the increase in revenues may be due to the fact that both companies have complementary products, and the combination may result in the products of, for example, Pike Plc being sold alongside the products of Minnow Plc. Cost savings may be experienced, for example, where the company has similar distribution channels, savings can be made on complementary marketing and administration costs may be reduced.

(b) The economic gains to be made from the business combination are the excess benefits to be made by having one larger company, over the sum of the gains to be made by having two individual companies. The synergies are expected to amount to €/£5 million (an increase in revenues of €/£3 million and a reduction in operating costs of €/£2 million). If it is assumed that these synergies can be maintained into the future (in perpetuity), then the additional economic value resulting from the synergies amounts to €/£27,777,778 [€/£5,000,000 ÷ 0.18].

(c) The current market price of an equity share in Minnow Plc is €/£16.00 [€/£48,000,000 ÷ 3,000,000]. The offer price is €/£22.00. Therefore, the equity holders of Minnow Plc stand to gain €/£6.00 per share, or €/£18,000,000 [3,000,000 × €/£6] in total.

The remaining economic gains will benefit the equity holders of Pike Plc. The expected benefit amounts to €/£9,777,778 [€/£27,777,778 − €/£18,000,000]. Assuming perfect capital markets, this will result in an increase in share price by about 89c/p [€/£9,777,778 ÷ 11,000,000], bringing an individual share's price up to €/£50.89 [(€/£550,000,000 ÷ 11,000,000) + 0.89c/p].

On paper, both sets of equity holders benefit from this business combination. However, the equity holders of Minnow Plc end up with the greatest proportion of the economic gains to be made. In addition, there is no risk associated with their gain, whereas the equity holders of Pike Plc are exposed to the risk that the projected synergy benefits do not materialise, which could mean that the merger makes them worse off.

(d) The expected market value, earnings, cash balance and balance in other assets of Pike Plc after the merger (assuming perfect capital markets) are as follows:

Expected market value of Pike Plc (Working 1)	€/£559,800,000
Number of equity shares in issue	11,000,000
Expected market value of an equity share	€/£50.89
Expected earnings (Working 2)	€/£55,000,000
Expected cash balances (Working 3)	€/£8,000,000
Expected value of other assets (Working 4)	€/£209,000,000
Expected total assets	€/£217,000,000

Workings

1. *Expected market value of Pike Plc post-acquisition*

	€/£m
Market value of Pike Plc prior to business combination	550
Market value of Minnow Plc prior to business combination	48
Present value of synergies expected	27.8
Cash paid to the equity holders of Minnow Plc*	(66)
Expected market value of new larger company	559.8

* The total cash offer is €/£66,000,000 [€/£22.00 × 3,000,000].

2. *Expected earnings of Pike Plc post-acquisition*

STATEMENT OF PROFIT OR LOSS (EXTRACTS)

	Pike Plc	**Minnow Plc**		**Pike Plc post-acquisition**
	€/£m	**€/£m**		**€/£m**
Revenues	170	25	(+3)	198
Cost	125	20	(−2)	143
Net earnings	45	5	(+5)	55

(***Note:*** the synergies are shown in brackets.)

3. *Expected cash balance of Pike Plc post-acquisition*

	€/£m
Cash balance in Pike Plc prior to business combination	70
Cash balance in Minnow Plc prior to business combination	4
Cash paid to the equity holders of Minnow Plc	(66)
Expected cash balance in the amalgamated company	8

4. *Expected other asset values of Pike Plc post-acquisition*

	€/£m
Other assets in Pike Plc prior to business combination (book value)	190
Other assets in Minnow Plc prior to business combination (book value)	19
Expected other assets (book value) balance in the new larger company	209

The economic gain to be made from a business combination by the equity holders of the bidding company can be calculated using a number of different approaches. The gain to the equity holders of the bidding company is expressed using the following formula:

$$\textbf{Gain on business combination} = V_{i+j} - V_i - \textbf{Purchase consideration}$$

where V_i is the value of company *i*, V_j is the value of company *j* and V_{i+j} is the expected value of the combined entity post-acquisition. Therefore, the gain on the business combination for the equity holders of Pike Plc post-acquisition is €/£9,800,000 [(€/£550,000,000 + €/£48,000,000 + €/£27,800,000) − €/£550,000,000 − €/£66,000,000]. Alternatively, an incremental approach to working out the gain attributable to a bidding company's equity holders is possible:

Gain on business combination =
Incremental gain from synergies − Cost of target company

wherein the cost of the target company is calculated using the following equation:

Cost of target company = Cash consideration paid − Market value of target company

Therefore, using the information from the previous example, the cost of purchasing Minnow Plc is €/£18,000,000 [€/£66,000,000 – €/£48,000,000] to Pike Plc and the gain on the business combination to the equity holders of Pike Plc is €/£9,800,000, being the incremental gains from synergies (€/£27,800,000) less the cost of purchasing Minnow Plc (€/£18,000,000).

Evaluating an Acquisition where the Purchase Consideration is a Share Exchange

The second type of purchase consideration considered in this textbook, a **share exchange**, is where a bidding company issues additional equity shares and uses these as currency to exchange for the equity shares of the target company.

Figure 18.2: Advantages and Disadvantages of Cash Consideration

ADVANTAGES

- **Easy to understand:** every party involved in the transaction understands where they stand when the offer is in cash.
- **Reduces price movement risk:** when the offer is in cash. If the offer was a share-for-share exchange, then the offer price would change.
- **Receiving equity holders have more flexibility:** they can easily adjust their portfolios to what suits them best, using the cash received. If they receive shares instead of cash, they would then incur transaction costs liquidating these for reinvestment. If they want to retain their investment in the company, they can purchase shares in the new, larger entity in the market.
- **Bidding company equity holders do not lose control:** as no shares are issued, the current equity holder mix remains unchanged by this transaction; hence there are no shifts in control.
- **Bidding company equity holders reap future rewards:** where the business combination is a success and reaps rewards in excess of those originally anticipated, then the equity holders of the bidding company stand to gain the total reward.

DISADVANTAGES

- **Financing cash:** most bidding companies have to source the cash required for the purchase. They may have some built up in reserves, but it is more likely than not that the bidding company will have to issue debt securities, obtain large bank loans, sell assets, or undertake a rights issue to allow them to finance the purchase of a target company.
- **Deferred payments make the offer unattractive:** one way to spread the cash burden on the bidding company is to spread the purchase payments over a period of time. Though attractive to the bidding company's equity holders, this will not be attractive to the target company's equity holders.
- **Transaction costs:** the equity holders who are receiving cash are going to incur transaction costs when they invest the cash in alternative investments.
- **Taxation:** when shares are sold for cash, the equity holder will be liable to capital gains tax.

The next (simple) example follows on from **Worked Example 18.2**. It is the same in every respect except it assumes that the purchase consideration is in the form of equity shares in the bidding company.

Worked Example 18.3: Evaluating a Business Acquisition – Share Exchange

Pike Plc is considering acquiring all of Minnow Plc's share capital in a share-for-share exchange, as it wants to conserve its cash for future investments. Pike Plc is offering one share in Pike Plc for three shares in Minnow Plc. Minnow Plc is a similar company to Pike Plc. They both sell similar items and have no long-term debt. Relevant details on both companies are as follows:

Statements of Financial Position (Extracts)

	Pike Plc €/£m	**Minnow Plc €/£m**
Total assets	260	23
Of which:		
Cash	70	4
Other assets (book value)	190	19

Statement of Profit or Loss (Extracts)

	Pike Plc €/£m	**Minnow Plc €/£m**
Revenues	170	25
Costs	125	20
Market value of company	550	48
Number of equity shares in issue (millions)	11	3

After an extensive review of the potential impact of the merger on the future financial performance of the company, it is considered that the combination will lead to some synergies. Revenues are expected to increase by €/£3 million and costs are expected to fall by €/£2 million. These are the only synergies expected. Pike Plc's cost of capital is 18%.

Requirement

(a) Calculate the number of shares that Pike Plc will have to issue to purchase the shares of Minnow Plc.

(b) What are the expected market value, cash balance, total assets and earnings of Pike Plc post-acquisition?

(c) Calculate the consideration that the equity holders of Minnow Plc will receive, compare this to the consideration received if the offer were a cash offer of €/£22.00 per share, as in the previous example.

(d) Detail who is going to benefit from this gain – the equity holders of Pike Plc or Minnow Plc? Compare this to the balance of benefit received, when the offer was a cash offer, as covered in **Worked Example 18.2**.

Solution

(a) Minnow Plc has 3,000,000 shares in issue. Pike Plc will be issuing one share for every three held by Minnow Plc. This means Pike Plc will have to issue an additional 1,000,000 shares (3,000,000 ÷ 3), bringing its total issue share capital up to 12,000,000 [11,000,000 + 1,000,000].

(b) The expected market value, earnings, cash balance and balance in other assets of Pike Plc after the merger (assuming perfect capital markets) are as follows:

Expected market value of Pike Plc (Working 1)	€/£625,800,000
Number of shares in issue	12,000,000
Expected market value of an equity share	€/£52.15
Expected earnings (Working 2)	€/£55,000,000
Expected cash balance (Working 3)	€/£74,000,000
Expected value of other assets (Working 4)	€/£209,000,000
Expected total assets	€/£283,000,000

Workings

1. *Expected market value of Pike Plc post-acquisition*

	€/£m
Market value of Pike Plc prior to business combination	550
Market value of Minnow Plc prior to business combination	48
Present value of the synergies expected	27.8
Expected market value of new larger company	625.8

2. *Expected earnings of Pike Plc post-acquisition*

STATEMENT OF PROFIT OR LOSS (EXTRACTS)

	Pike Plc €/£m	Minnow Plc €/£m		Pike Plc post-acquisition €/£m
Revenues	170	25	(+3)	198
Costs	125	20	(−2)	143
Net earnings	45	5	(+5)	55

(***Note:*** the synergies are shown in brackets.)

3. *Expected cash balance of Pike Plc post-acquisition*

	€/£m
Cash balance in Pike Plc prior to business combination	70
Cash balance in Minnow Plc prior to business combination	4
Expected cash balance in the new larger company	74

4. *Expected other asset values of Pike Plc post-acquisition*

	€/£m
Other assets in Pike Plc prior to business combination (book value)	190
Other assets in Minnow Plc prior to business combination (book value)	19
Expected other assets (book value) balance in the new larger company	209

(c) Given Pike Plc's expected share price movement (calculated in (b) above), the total value received for one share is €/£17.38. This is calculated as follows:

The total consideration for the whole of Minnow Plc is €/£52,150,000 [1,000,000 × €/£52.15], this is then divided by the number of shares held by the equity holders in Minnow Plc pre-acquisition to give an individual price of each share of €/£17.38 [€/£52,150,000 ÷ 3,000,000]. The total premium on offer to the equity holders of Minnow Plc is, therefore, €/£4,140,000 [(€/£17.38 − €/£16.00) × 3,000,000].

The cash offer was allowing the equity holders of Minnow Plc a premium of €/£6.00 per share [€/£22.00 − €/£16.00]. This amounted to a total premium of €/£18,000,000 [€/£6.00 × 3,000,000]. Therefore, the equity holders of Minnow Plc are worse off by €/£13,860,000 [€/£18,000,000 − €/£4,140,000].

(d) As was calculated in the previous example, the total economic gain expected is €/£27,800,000. In this example, the equity holders of Minnow Plc stand to benefit from a premium on the transfer of €/£4,140,000.

The current equity holders of Pike Plc stand to gain an increase in their share value from €/£50.00 [€/£550,000,000 ÷ 11,000,000] to €/£52.15 (calculated in (a)). Therefore, the gain to be made per share is €/£2.15 [€/£52.15 − €/£50.00], which equates to a total gain of €/£23,650,000 [€/£2.15 × 11,000,000]. So in this instance, the bulk of the benefit to be gained from this business combination will go to the equity holders of Pike Plc.

On paper, both sets of equity holder benefit from this business combination, but the equity holders in Pike Plc end up with the greatest proportion of the economic gains to be made. In this instance, both sets of equity holders are exposed to the risk that the projected synergy benefits do not materialise.

To summarise, the total economic gain remains the same regardless of the consideration type, at €/£27,800,000, but the balance of gain in this instance has shifted to the equity holders of the bidding company, Pike Plc, as they will now receive 85.11% [€/£23,660,000 ÷ €/£27,800,000] of the gain, whereas the equity holders of Minnow Plc will receive 14.89% [€/£4,140,000 ÷ €/£27,800,000] of the gain.

Figure 18.3: Advantages and Disadvantages of Share Exchange as Consideration

ADVANTAGES

- **Liquidity:** the bidding company's liquidity is not impacted on by the acquisition, except for the costs associated with the transaction.
- **Taxation:** the target company equity holders, who receive shares in the bidding company in exchange for their equity shares in the target company, will not be subject to capital gains tax, as the gain will be rolled over until the equity holders decide to sell their shares.
- **Retain an interest in the company:** the target company equity holders may have an attachment/interest in the company and may want to keep their investment in the company. They also have the ability to reap any additional gains/synergies made by the new combined company.
- **Reduced costs:** where the cash offer involves having to issue debt securities to raise the funds, then a share-for-share exchange may be more cost-effective, with less of an impact on gearing, relative to a cash offer that is financed using debt.

DISADVANTAGES

- **Costly:** equity is the most expensive source of finance. A company has to earn higher returns to keep the equity holders happy, relative to the returns required by debt holders.
- **Control:** there is a dilution in control within the bidding company and possibly a reduction in the earnings per share available for equity holders, if the new larger number of shares is not matched by an equivalent increase in the earnings of the company.
- **Articles of association:** the bidding company may have to approach its equity holders to approve an increase in the number of authorised shares that can be issued.
- **Price risk:** the attractiveness of the offer to the target company is affected by the movements in the share price of the bidding company's shares.
- **Difficulty in evaluating the offer:** connected to the previous point, where the share prices of both companies fluctuate, it is difficult for the equity holders in the target company to accurately evaluate the offer on hand.

Evaluating an Acquisition where the Purchase Consideration is Debt Securities

Sometimes the purchase consideration is an exchange of debt for equity, wherein the bidding company exchanges loan stock for shares in the target company. The advantages and disadvantages of this form of purchase consideration are outlined in **Figure 18.4**.

FIGURE 18.4: ADVANTAGES AND DISADVANTAGES OF DEBT SECURITIES AS CONSIDERATION

ADVANTAGES	DISADVANTAGES
• **Liquidity:** the bidding company's liquidity is not immediately impacted on by the acquisition, except for the costs associated with the transaction. • **Control:** the issue of debt securities will not involve any changes in the control of the company, unless the interest or repayment of the debt falls into arrears, in which case the debt holders have voting rights. • **Capital structure/cost of capital:** where the bidding company has low gearing, the increase in gearing may actually increase the value of the bidding company as equity holders may react positively to this cheaper form of finance, which is tax deductible, being available. • **Lower risk for target company equity holders:** when the target company's equity holders are unsure about the viability of the combined entity, they may be more attracted by a debt-for-share exchange, relative to a share-for-share exchange, as the debt option provides them with guaranteed yearly coupon income and the knowledge that they would rank in front of the equity holders, were the company to go into liquidation.	• **Liquidity:** each year from the date of the acquisition until the maturity of the debt securities, the bidding company will be obliged to make coupon payments and, on maturity of the securities, the capital will have to be repaid. • **Gearing:** the gearing ratio of the bidding company may increase by an amount which increases the financial risk in the company to levels that the equity holders are not happy with. This will increase their required return, resulting in a reduction in share price.

The choice of purchase consideration is impacted on by a number of factors. Research suggests that the bidding company is more likely to offer a share-for-share exchange when the stock markets are performing well (i.e. in a bullish market). The gearing levels of the bidding company will influence the preferred source of finance to fund the acquisition – highly geared companies are more likely to opt for a share-for-share exchange, and companies with low gearing and strong cash flows are likely to opt for a bond-for-share exchange. Companies with high-growth performance are also found to be more likely to use a share-for-share exchange. High-growth companies have a constant funding requirement, as growth requires investment. Any surplus cash made by the company on a yearly basis will be needed to fund this growth. In addition, the company is likely to be less keen to tie itself into the fixed cash outflows that would be required if debt securities were issued in exchange for the target company's shares.

A further reason to explain the preference of high-growth companies for share-for-share exchanges over the use of debt is management's wish to keep a future source of funding in reserve (debt is easier, less costly and quicker to obtain than equity and managers like to keep the option available). Finally, bidding companies that have low-growth potential are less likely to opt for a share-for-share exchange as this form of consideration is less attractive to the equity holders of the target company, who may have invested in the target company primarily for its high growth potential. However, there are exceptions where companies have surplus cash for investment, as noted in **Real World Example 18.9**.

Real World Example 18.9: Wearable Business

In November 2019, Google obtained preliminary agreement to take over Fitbit for $2.1 billion. Google made a $7.35 per share cash offer for Fitbit. This represents a 70% premium over the company's listed price on the day before speculation took place. Google's motivation is to gain access to a watch manufacturer so that it can compete with Apple. Google has its own Fitness tracking app, 'Google fit' – however, it has always relied on third parties to produce Android-compatible watches. Now Google can control its customer. In addition, producing smart watches will extend its product range, which currently includes smartphones, headphones, smart speakers and laptops. The deal is expected to be finalised in 2020, if it gets approval from shareholders and regulators.

Students should research this case to see what happened.

DIFFICULTIES THAT ARISE WHEN EVALUATING A BID

In the last section two acquisition offers were evaluated. In these simple examples everything that could impact on share price was known with certainty. In the real world, things are not so clear-cut. Some of the main issues facing stakeholders who try to evaluate an offer, or who try to come up with an offer price, are now outlined. The examples discussed in this section are by no means exhaustive.

Very few acquisitions take place without there being public knowledge of the event. Therefore, the equity share prices of both parties to the transaction usually change in anticipation of the acquisition happening. For example, when Ryanair made it known that it was interested in purchasing the equity shares of Aer Lingus, there was an immediate response in the markets. Aer Lingus's shares rose by 15%, whereas the value of Ryanair's equity shares fell by 1%. This may be because the bid price disclosed was €2.80, whereas the market was valuing Aer Lingus at €2.20. The immediate 15% increase in the price of Aer Lingus's shares reflects the premium expected from the takeover and does not reflect the market's view of the long-term equilibrium value of Aer Lingus. Also, revisit **Real World Example 18.1** – Takeaway.com's shareholder reaction has effectively knocked the company out of contention in the race to purchase Just Eat. Therefore, determining the equilibrium price of a target company may be quite difficult, especially if the market becomes aware of the impending offer. Indeed, the market may overestimate the expected premium, which may scupper the acquisition as the equity holders in the target company expect too much for their shares.

Deciding on the extent of synergies or economies of scale that will result from a business combination is very difficult. An analyst usually estimates expected future revenues and costs from the amalgamated company and then discounts these back to its present value to determine the expected economic value of the new, larger entity. The current market value of the target company and the consideration are then taken away from this to determine the gains to be made from the business combination. However, any gain that results from this exercise may be due to errors being made in the estimation of the potential additional revenues and reduced costs. These may not be as good as estimated. Conversely, pessimistic estimations of future cash flows may lead to a company not pursuing an acquisition, when in fact gains would arise.

THE REGULATION OF TAKEOVERS AND MERGERS

Regulation in the United Kingdom

At the time of writing, the regulation of business combinations in the UK comes from three sources: under UK legislation, under EU direction and by the City of London (the Takeover Panel). Brexit is likely to have an impact on the extent to which the UK conforms with EU Directives on amalgamations.

1. UK Competition Regulation

The main concern of this first form of regulation is to ensure that the merger or takeover is in the public interest. The Secretary of State for Business, Energy and Industrial Strategy has governmental responsibility for competition regulation. At present the Office of Fair Trading (OFT) uses an asset size measure and a market dominance measure to determine if the merger is in the public interest. Mergers are deemed to be in the public interest when the value of the assets of the target company exceed £70 million, or the combined entities supply, or receive, a minimum of one-quarter of the goods or services of a particular good or service supplied in the UK. In addition, the OFT will assess smaller mergers/takeovers that are brought to its attention, either by complaint or by one of the companies that is party to the merger/takeover. The OFT will investigate the proposed merger/takeover and hear the views of the main interested parties. Where the OFT is happy that the merger/takeover does not harm competition and is in the public interest, then that is the matter ended. However, if it feels that there are competition concerns, it will then refer the proposed merger/takeover to the Secretary of State for Trade and Industry and provide its opinion as to whether the proposed merger/takeover be referred to the Competition and Markets Authority. It may advise actions to be taken to make the merger/takeover more in the public interest and will monitor these actions. The OFT can also refer a proposed merger/takeover to the European Commission (see below).

The Competition and Markets Authority The Competition and Markets Authority investigates any proposed merger/takeover that is referred to it by the Secretary of State for Trade and Industry. It will hear evidence from the main parties and will assess the public's reaction to the proposed business combination. If it thinks that steps can be taken to make the proposed merger/takeover in the public interest, it will outline these and provide its final opinion in a report to the Secretary of State. Recent interventions by the UK regulators are included in **Real World Example 18.9**.

Real World Example 18.9: Takeovers Stopped

In December 2016, Rupert Murdoch bid £11.7 billion for Sky. The takeover was approved by Ofcom and the European Commission. However, in 2018 the Competition and Markets Authority blocked the takeover as it considered that it was "not in the public's interest" – a concern being "media plurality". As Rupert Murdoch owned *Fox News*, the *Financial Times, The Sunday Times* and *The Sun*, the watchdog was concerned that the resulting company could have too much power over public opinion.

In 2016, the Competition and Markets Authority also blocked mobile phone company Three's £10.52 billion bid for O2 over competition concerns.

In 2019, the Government blocked Lloyd TSB's £18.2 billion takeover bid for rival Abbey National after receiving advice from the Competition and Markets Authority and the Director General of Fair Trading that the merger would reduce competition in personal current account markets and banking services for SMEs.

2. European Competition Regulation

The second form of regulation considers competition within an EU context and comes under the jurisdiction of the European Union. Article 82 of the Treaty of Rome prohibits the abuse of a dominant company where it may affect trade between different Member States. The main issues are concerned with: providing general principles for the conduct of the stakeholders in a takeover/merger; providing a regulatory framework to guide bodies that supervise takeovers/mergers in EU Member States; providing basic rules to follow during a takeover/merger; outlining restrictions to barriers that can be placed in the way of takeovers/mergers; requiring minimum disclosure requirements for companies whose shares are traded on regulated markets; and providing guidance on the treatment of minority interests who have not accepted the bidding company's offer (e.g. squeeze-outs and sell-outs).

The underlying issue that is considered under the Directive is whether the merger/takeover will result in a company that has a dominant position, such that it will impede competition across Member States. If this is deemed to be the case, then this merger/takeover will be considered to be incompatible with the common market. The proposed merger between Ryanair and Aer Lingus was ruled to be incompatible under the Directive.

3. Conduct of a Takeover

The first two forms of regulation are more concerned with protecting the public/competition. The third form of regulation, the **City Code**, is not concerned with this issue, and focuses on ensuring that all parties to the takeover/merger act in a manner that is in all the equity holders' best interests. This regulation received statutory backing in 2006 and forms part of the UK's regulatory practices. The City Code is enforced by the **Takeover Panel** – a team of representatives from the main associations who are involved in most takeovers. The panel typically includes a representative from the regulators (for example, the Confederation of British Industry (CBI)), equity holders (a representative from the Stock Exchange represents the views of investors) and advisors (e.g. the Institute of Chartered Accountants in England and Wales (ICAEW)).

The Takeover Panel The Takeover Panel's *City Code on Takeovers and Mergers* is sometimes referred to as the 'Takeover Code', the 'Blue Book' or, as in this textbook, the 'City Code'. Its purpose is to ensure that:

> "shareholders in an offeree company are treated fairly and are not denied an opportunity to decide on the merits of a takeover and that shareholders in the offeree company of the same class are afforded equivalent treatment by an offeror. The Code also provides an orderly framework within which takeovers are conducted. In addition, it is designed to promote, in conjunction with other regulatory regimes, the integrity of the financial markets.
>
> The Code is not concerned with the financial or commercial advantages or disadvantages of a takeover. These are matters for the offeree company and its shareholders. In addition, it is not the purpose of the Code either to facilitate or to impede takeovers. Nor is the Code concerned with those issues, such as competition policy, which are the responsibility of government and other bodies."[2]

The general principles of the City Code are listed in **Figure 18.5**.

FIGURE 18.5: THE CITY CODE: GENERAL PRINCIPLES

Unbiased	The equity holders of the target company should be treated similarly. One offer should be given to all equity holders who hold shares of a similar class.
Sufficient time and information	The equity holders of the target company should be given relevant and adequate information to enable them to reach a properly informed decision on the bid (no information should be withheld).
Maximise equity holder value	Directors should act in the best interests of the whole equity holder body, not in their own interests.
Behaviour of directors	Directors should not encourage or frustrate a bid, without first obtaining the approval of the equity holders.
False market	A false market in the shares of either the bidding company or the target company should not be created. Neither company will be allowed to offer inducements to increase the demand for its equity share capital.

The City Code also provides detailed guidance on timelines and the conduct of the parties to the proposed takeover. These are summarised in **Figure 18.6**.

[2] Panel on Takeovers and Mergers, *The City Code on Takeovers and Mergers* (2016), A2.

FIGURE 18.6: THE CITY CODE: DETAILED RULES

Making a bid	There are specific rules on the approach a bidder has to take when making a bid for a target company.
Going public	The bidding company has to declare its intent to make a takeover bid for the target company publicly.
Conduct	The conduct of both parties is restricted under the City Code. For example, all holdings in the target company of over 3% must be declared to the company, no 'dawn raids' are allowed (i.e. the bidding company cannot acquire equity shares, in any seven-day period, that will bring their holding to above 15%) and when a company amasses over 30% of the shares in a company, it is obliged, under the City Code, to make a formal bid for the remaining shares in the company (the price offered must be at least the maximum price paid for any of the shares acquired in the previous 12 months).
Independent advice	Once an offer comes in, the directors of a target company must seek independent advice from a financial advisor, such as a merchant bank. This serves to protect the interests of the equity holders.
Time limits	There are time limits throughout the whole process, including payment, which should be completed within 95 days from the official offer. In addition, a bidding company cannot make a further takeover bid for the target company within one calendar year of the first offer.

Regulation in the Republic of Ireland

The regulation in Ireland is similar. Competition and public interest are controlled by government departments and the European Parliament, and a framework for proper conduct during a takeover is regulated by the Irish Takeover Panel. The details provided for Ireland are given here in brief as they are similar in many respects to those in the UK.

Irish Legislation on Competition

Prior to a takeover, the parties to the transaction must inform the Minister for Business, Enterprise and Innovation in writing, within one month of an offer being made. It is the Minister's responsibility to monitor takeovers/mergers in Ireland. The report to the Minister must include full details of the proposal. The takeover/merger cannot proceed without the Minister stating that it will not be objected to, or stating it can go ahead with conditions. If the Minister does not respond within three months, the business combination may proceed. If the Minister feels that the proposed takeover/merger is not in the public interest, then he or she can refer it to the **Competition and Consumer Protection Commission** for investigation (the Minister must do this within 30 days of receiving the proposal).

The Competition and Consumer Protection Commission will advise the Minister as to whether the merger/takeover is in the public interest, or not. Alternatively, it may recommend steps that the bidding company can take to make the proposal in the public's interest.

Conduct of a Takeover

The European Communities (Takeover Bids (Directive 2004/25/ EC)) Regulations 2006[3] assigned responsibility for the proper conduct of takeovers to the Irish Takeover Panel (ITP), the Government's designated competent authority. The panel is responsible for making rules to ensure that takeovers, mergers and substantial acquisitions comply with the general principles that are set out in the Irish Takeover Panel Act 1997, the Substantial Acquisition Rules 2007 and Takeover Rules 2013. The rules provide an orderly framework within which takeovers are conducted. The ITP is not concerned with the advantages, disadvantages, or the financial or commercial implications of a proposed business combination. This it considers to be a concern of the relevant companies and their equity holders. The ITP is not concerned with competition as this is regulated by the legislation outlined in the previous paragraphs. Like the Takeover Panel in the UK, it is concerned with the rules of engagement between the parties.

THE TAKEOVER PROCESS

Both the UK's City Code and the Irish Takeover Rules are based on the EU Takeovers Directive (2004/25/EC). The Directive has six general principles to guide the takeover process. These are as follows:

1. All shareholders of the shares of an offeree (i.e. target company) of the same class must be afforded equivalent treatment; moreover, if a person acquires control of a company, the other shareholders must be protected.
2. The shareholders of an offeree must have sufficient time and information to enable them to reach a properly informed decision on the offer. Where it advises the shareholders, the board of the offeree must give its views on the effects of implementation of the offer on employment, conditions of employment and the location of the offeree's places of business.
3. The board of an offeree must act in the interests of the company as a whole and must not deny shareholders the opportunity to decide on the merits of the offer.
4. False markets must not be created in the shares of the offeree, of the offeror (i.e. bidding party) or of any other company concerned by the offer in such a way that the rise or fall of the prices of the shares becomes artificial and the normal functioning of the markets is distorted.
5. An offeror must announce an offer only after ensuring that he or she can fulfil in full any cash consideration, if such is offered, and after taking all reasonable measures to secure the implementation of any other type of consideration.
6. An offeree must not be hindered in the conduct of its affairs for longer than is reasonable by an offer for its shares.

[3] S.I. No. 255 of 2006.

In both the UK and Ireland, the respective Takeover Panels recommend that the acquisition of securities should take place in a timely manner with adequate timely disclosure.

In addition to the general principles, the Directive sets out rules that have been adopted in both the City Code and the Takeover Rules guidance by the respective Takeover Panels. Some of the key rules are as follows:

- When an offeror acquires interests in shares carrying 30% (assumed effective control) or more of the voting rights of a company, they must make a cash offer to all other shareholders, at the highest price paid in the 12 months before the offer was announced.
- When interests in a class of shares carrying 10% or more of the voting rights have been acquired by an offeror in the offer period and in the previous 12 months, the offer must include a cash alternative for all shareholders of that class at the highest price paid by the offeror in that period. Moreover, if the offeror acquires, for cash, any interest in a different class of shares during the offer period, a cash alternative must also be made available at that price at least.
- The offeree company must appoint a competent independent adviser whose advice on the financial terms of the offer must be made known to all the shareholders, together with the opinion of the board.
- Favourable deals for selected shareholders are banned.
- All shareholders must be given the same information.
- Any party issuing takeover circulars (see below) must include statements taking responsibility for the contents.
- Profit forecasts, quantified financial benefits statements and asset valuations must be made to specified standards and must be reported on by professional advisers.
- Misleading, inaccurate or unsubstantiated statements made in documents or to the media must be publicly corrected immediately.
- Actions during the course of an offer by the offeree company which might frustrate the offer are generally prohibited, unless shareholders approve these plans.
- Stringent requirements are laid down for the disclosure of dealings in relevant shares during an offer.
- Employees of both the offeror and the offeree company and the trustees of the offeree company's pension scheme must be informed about an offer. In addition, the offeree company's employee representatives and pension scheme trustees have the right to a separate opinion on the effects of the offer on employment appended to the offeree board's circular (see below) or published on a website.

KEY DOCUMENTS SUPPORTING AN ACQUISITION

Offer Document

A bidding company, the offeror, should prepare an **offer document**, the typical contents of which are outlined in **Figure 18.7**.

Figure 18.7: Offer Document Contents

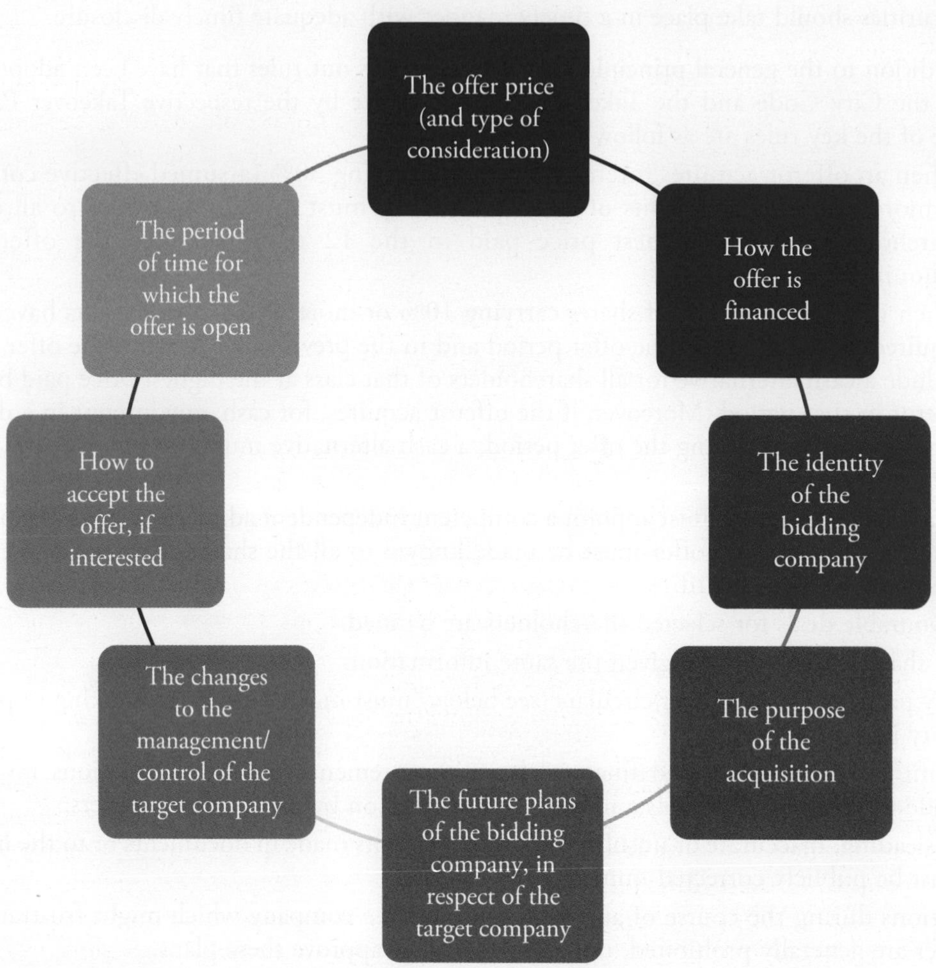

Board Circular

The board of the target company, the offeree, should publish a circular containing its opinion of the offer to its equity holders, employees and pension trustees. If the board of directors is not happy with the offer, this is a **defence document**, stating the reasons for rejection of the offer. The board circular usually refers to guidance from an independent advisor. The board must either agree with this guidance or justify why they do not agree.

Heads of Agreement Document

When a bidding company has identified a target company and justified it as a suitable investment to its equity holders, who accept that the approach should be made, then a 'heads of agreement' is prepared. The **heads of agreement** sets out the proposed terms of purchase/sale between the bidding and target companies and is usually 'subject to contract'. It typically requires that certain conditions are fulfilled (normally in respect of providing information for the due diligence stage). It is not a legally binding agreement, but instead it is more of a moral agreement.

Due Diligence Report

In the context of acquisitions and mergers, **due diligence** is the performance of a voluntary investigation commissioned by the bidding company into the target company. This investigation is performed with a duty of care towards the equity holders of the bidding company. A due diligence audit usually starts with the team obtaining information on the background (history and development) of the company as well as the structure of the company (group, subsidiaries, branches, etc.). It should detail the organisational chart, main people, lines of communication, etc. In terms of financial information, as a minimum the due diligence audit will verify the information provided by the target company to the bidding company directors. The verification will consider the accuracy and integrity of actual information provided. Most target companies provide estimates of future investments and project earnings into the future. The due diligence audit will evaluate the reasonableness of the assumptions used.

Accounting

A due diligence audit will typically cover normal audit practices on accounting information, though it is likely to go deeper. Indeed, the normal audit work will probably help to inform the due diligence report, and may even highlight weak areas that the due diligence team may wish to focus on. The due diligence team will usually request the past three years' financial statements (this will detail the company's accounting policies), the management accounts, projections, copies of trading arrangements with stakeholders (e.g. customers, suppliers), details of the strategic policy in respect of working capital, accounting systems, taxation (e.g. foreign taxation, tax bills, deferred tax). In addition, the team will pay particular attention to the value of tangible assets, particularly land and property (i.e. when last revalued, etc.) and the value of intangible assets held (including patents, trademarks, software, quota, intellectual capital, customer databases). On the potential liability side, any contingent liabilities should be evaluated, and contracts reviewed that may result in an economic outflow from the target company. Risk should also be assessed. Details of the company's perceived risk exposure may be outlined in the annual report (which is attached to the published financial statements). Due diligence work should focus on determining whether the company's risk assessment is appropriate. Other risk areas will also be investigated, including insurance cover, proper recording of intellectual capital, key employee insurance, reliance on a small number of employees, reliance on a few large customers or suppliers, reliance on software systems (including how up-to-date these are), etc.

Legal Documentation

The due diligence team will also review the memorandum and articles of association of the company, any trust deeds for loans issued, loan agreements, contracts with employees (particularly where there are golden parachutes and tin parachutes – discussed later in this chapter) and contracts with suppliers and customers.

Business Compatibility

The due diligence team are likely to investigate the compatibility of various operational aspects of the target company in light of the practices and ethos being followed by the bidding company. The software system in the target company should be assessed to see if it can interface with that in use in the bidding company. The production process, sales, credit control (terms and conditions, etc.), marketing, advertising and management information systems should be investigated to determine how they will integrate within the larger amalgamated company.

Friendly/Hostile

The amount of information that can be captured and verified under the due diligence process is dependent on how the target company reacts to the takeover bid. If the board of directors is happy with the interest, then it is likely that it will provide most, if not all, of the information required by the due diligence team. However, if it considers the takeover interest to be unwelcome, it will only allow the minimum amount of information permissible under the City Code to be made available to the due diligence team. In this instance, the due diligence report will only have limited value.

Sale and Purchase Agreement

The **sale and purchase agreement** will form the legal sale agreement. Its contents will be influenced by the earlier stages. The original offer, detailed on the head of agreement document, may be accepted, though the due diligence work may highlight a few uncertainties that the bidding company will want clarification on, or compensation for, if they turn out to be different or more costly for the bidding company. Any additional warranties or conditions of sale will be included in a disclosure letter.

EQUITY HOLDERS' PERSPECTIVE OF A TAKEOVER

Bidding Company's Equity Holders

Large takeovers cannot proceed without the permission of the bidding company's equity holders at a general meeting. When the equity holders in the bidding company are happy with a proposed takeover, this will be reflected in an increase in the bidding company's share price. If they are unhappy with the takeover, the bidding company's share price will fall. This is most likely to happen when the bidding company's equity holders expect their earnings per share to fall, when they expect the risk profile of the company to increase (possibly due to a reduction in liquidity or a reduction in the proportion of tangible assets held in the company), or if they feel that the offer price is too high.

Target Company's Equity Holders

When a company comes under the scrutiny of other companies, then this can be taken as a signal that the company is undervalued, or is not utilising its resources efficiently. Either way, the equity holders of the target company stand to gain. If the offer provides the equity holders of the target company with a good return, then they are likely to support it. In addition, if they are unhappy with the current management, they are likely to welcome the offer.

The directors of a target company are supposed to act in the interests of their equity holders and should investigate every offer and determine if the company's equity holders would be better off remaining as they are, or accepting the offer. When the target company is unquoted, the directors may also be the dominant equity holders. They simply will not proceed with the takeover unless they are happy with the deal. There is nothing the bidding company can do.

When the target company is a quoted company the situation is different. Sometimes directors resist takeovers for reasons that may be in their own interests, not in the equity holders' interests. This is costly for equity holders as defending a takeover is expensive. The target company will need to hire professional advisors, advertising and marketing specialists, undertake underwriting costs, interest costs of funds used to defend the takeover, loss of management time, and possibly cause a downturn (or a rise) in the company's share price. In most instances, directors will act in the best interests of the equity holders and resist the attempted takeover by adopting defensive tactics to ward off the predator company. In addition, equity holders can refuse to sell their shares. The City Code puts in place certain rules of engagement to allow fairness to all parties to the transaction. It makes it difficult for directors not to act in their equity holders' interests and protects the bidding company once the takeover process has been agreed. As mentioned previously, the bidding company must mount a takeover bid once it has purchased 30% of the target company's equity capital. If the takeover is agreed and 90% of the equity holders sell their shares to the bidding company, then legally the remaining 10% (i.e. the minority interest) must sell their shares to the target company at the price agreed in the offer. This is called a **statutory compulsory acquisition (sell-out)**. The limit is 80% for companies listed on secondary markets, such as the AIM.

DEFENSIVE TACTICS

Several defensive tactics have been utilised in the past to fend off a takeover bid. Some of these are no longer allowed by the City Code as they are considered to negatively impact on equity holder value.

General Defences

As a strategic issue, a company should always consider whether they are susceptible to a takeover bid. Research has shown that an analysis of certain ratios, which record the return earned on shares by equity holders and which monitor a company's growth and resources relationship, can be used to provide an indication of the likelihood of being targeted for a takeover bid. In particular, when the return on shares by equity holders declines steadily over a four- or five-year period or where a company has high growth, but few resources, or low growth and many resources, then this can be seen as a sign of managerial inefficiency and bidding companies may see gains to be made by the takeover. Other ratios that focus on profitability and liquidity are also considered to be predictive.

Efficient Management

The first line of defence for the directors of any company is to maximise the return from a company's resources. The fact that there is an active takeover market in the UK and in Ireland means that company managers always have to 'be on their toes' as inefficiencies/opportunities will be spotted by others.

Employee Share-ownership Schemes

Employees are likely to resist a takeover bid as successful takeovers usually start with the rationalisation of costs – which normally means cutting jobs. If the company can build up the proportion of the equity holders who are employees, then this provides some protection.

Convert to an Unquoted Company/Purchase Own Shares

When a company feels vulnerable, becoming unquoted by delisting will make it more difficult for the bidding firm to obtain a takeover. Another option is for the company to repurchase its own shares. This will drive up demand for the company's shares and hence make the takeover more expensive. This step cannot be taken once the takeover offer is made public.

Create a 'Poison Pill', which will only be Triggered if a takeover is Threatened

A **poison pill** is an anti-takeover measure that can be introduced by a company. An example of a poison pill might be to give existing equity holders rights to buy additional shares, at a discount, if an individual holding exceeds a certain percentage (typically around 15%), or issuing large quantities of convertible debt securities. Another form of poison pill is **golden parachutes**. This is where agreements are reached to pay management (i.e. white collar workers) large sums of money in the event of the company being taken over. **Tin parachutes** are similar, except they are directed at 'blue collar' workers. This is unattractive to bidding companies. These sort of tactics are not supported under the UK's City Code or Irish Takeover Rules and a bidding company can possibly have them removed with the intervention of the respective Takeover Panel and the support of the target company's equity holders.

Aggressive Defences – Usually Undertaken After an Offer is Made

Provide Information to Equity Holders

In many instances the equity holders of a company are not fully aware of all of a company's future plans. Management manages the supply of information to their equity holders and normally does not release every investment option that is being considered, until it is more or less certain, or if it feels the market is not valuing the equity shares of the company correctly. When a takeover is being proposed and the directors feel that the offer is not in the equity holders' interests, the directors may prepare and distribute a circular to the equity holders. This circular will outline their opinion of the offer and may provide the equity holders with information that they did not have beforehand. The price-sensitive information they disclose typically includes profit forecasts, dividend forecasts, investment plans, asset valuations, changes in the management team, etc.

The directors have to be careful with their disclosures. If they issue profit forecasts that cause the takeover to fail and then do not live up to their projections, equity holder confidence in the directors will fall and, in addition, the company will likely be the target of another takeover attempt, possibly at a lower price than beforehand. It is normal for this circular to include increased dividend forecasts. However, the impact of this is limited as this is something that is usually offered by the bidding company. The bidding company can also respond to the circular publicly.

Lobby against the Takeover

The directors of the target company may advertise reasons for staying independent, calling on the loyalty of equity holders and may even attack the bidding company's proposal, or its track record (i.e. its management and financial statements). The bidding company is likely to respond to this.

Competition Authorities/Takeover Panel

The bidding company may petition the competition authorities to get involved if they feel that competition may be severely impacted upon (detailed earlier in this chapter). This technique was successfully used by Aer Lingus to fend off Ryanair's takeover bid. The target company may also petition the respective Takeover Panel if it feels any aspect of the UK's City Code/Irish Takeover Rules has not been adhered to.

Seek a 'White Knight'

Sometimes the management of a company may make it publicly known that it is open to offers from other parties and may enter into friendly takeover talks with another entity, a so-called

white knight. Sometimes the white knight is the management itself and the process is called a **management buy-out (MBO)**. In a similar theme an individual, called a **white squire**, may purchase sufficient shares in the target company to deter the takeover.

Pacman Defence

A **Pacman defence** is where the target company launches a counter-offer to take over the bidding company. This is not common, as the target company is usually much smaller than the bidding company and cannot realistically finance the deal. Related to this, the target company may start to take over another company. This will drive up its value, making it too costly for the bidding company to afford.

Crown Jewels

Another possible defence is to break up the company and to sell off its most valuable portions, its **crown jewels**. This approach may be resisted under the City Code, particularly if it is felt that this will damage the target company's equity holders' wealth.

Leveraged Buy-outs

A **leveraged buy-out (LBO)** is the US term for debt-backed company buy-outs. The most common type of LBO is when the management team from a company backed by external investors (who usually supply some form of mezzanine finance – discussed in **Chapter 14**) purchase a business from its equity holders. This is called an MBO (management buy-out). Most MBOs are financed using management's personal funds, bank finance and venture capital finance. The company becomes a private company after the buy-out, hence is no longer listed. The term LBO also captures MBIs (management buy-ins), BIMBOs (buy-in management buy-out) (discussed in **Chapter 12**), VIMBOs (vendor-initiated management buy-out) and purchases by consortiums of private equity investors.

MANAGEMENT OF THE COMBINED COMPANY POST-MERGER

This is seen as the most important part of a business combination. If this is not given sufficient attention, then the whole exercise may end up being a failure. When a large company takes over a small company that has its own pecking order, organisational structure and communication systems in place, then care has to be taken to ensure that the target company's employees and management team are made to feel that they are an important part of the larger entity and to integrate them into the larger company, in a quick and pain-free manner. A major flaw highlighted in prior studies on the process of mergers is that once the combination has taken place, the management of the large company move their attention on to the next issue and assume the takeover/acquisition has been a success. Meanwhile the directors and employees of the target company become disillusioned and morale and performance drop. The impact of integration costs on company performance is highlighted in **Real World Example 18.10**.

REAL WORLD EXAMPLE 18.10: KRAFT AND CADBURY

Kraft Foods Inc took over British confectioner, Cadbury, in 2010. In the following year, 2011, Kraft reported profits were down by 24% due to integration costs associated with the £11.9 billion purchase of Cadbury.

The integration process that takes place after a business combination is agreed is regarded as the most difficult part of the whole process, particularly where the takeover was not welcomed by the board of directors or employees of the target firm. In these circumstances the bidding company will have less information about the target firm than it would have had the takeover been welcome, as more information would have been included in the due diligence report. Jones (1982, 1986) suggests that the level of integration between the two combining businesses depends on the type of business combination: if it is a conglomerate-type acquisition, then there will be less integration (usually of only the financials), with both companies operating more or less independently of each other. When it is a vertical acquisition, the levels of integration increase (usually integration of the financials, marketing and some elements of manufacturing). When the combination is horizontal in nature, full integration is likely. Several approaches to successful integration have been suggested by a number of academics. The first of these is Peter Drucker's five golden rules for the successful integration of two businesses, as outlined in **Figure 18.8**. These rules are more concerned with conduct and attitude towards a business combination than with actual steps that need to be taken.

FIGURE 18.8: DRUCKER'S FIVE GOLDEN RULES FOR SUCCESSFUL POST-ACQUISITION INTEGRATION

Common core of unity	Both the bidding company and the target company should try for shared technology and markets, not just financial links.
Symbiotic relationship	The bidding company should ask, "What can we offer them?" as well as, "What's in it for us?"
Be respectful	The acquirer should treat the products, customers, etc., of the acquired company with respect, not disparagingly.
Tailored skills for management	The acquirer should provide top management with relevant skills for the acquired company within a year.
Recognition to employees	Cross-company promotions of staff should happen within one year.

Source: see https://www.jstor.org/stable/2486170

Jones (1986) considers that corporate strategy, management accounting and applied psychology all have a role to play in the successful integration of two businesses. He developed an integration sequence that has five key stages (see **Figure 18.9**). He suggests that these be done in turn.

FIGURE 18.9: JONES'S INTEGRATION SEQUENCE

Set up initial reporting relationships	Decide upon and communicate initial reporting relationships (even if temporary). Jones suggests that it is important to do this before managers establish their own informal relationships.
Control of key factors	It is important to quickly gain control of the information flows within the new company. Information assists management to gain control. Financial control should be one of the first areas integrated. At an early stage, agree expenditure limits, investment limits, overdraft limits, etc., and assess the quality of the system supporting the financial decision-making within the acquired company. The system may be good, or it may not. If it is the latter, then implementing a more appropriate system should be a priority.
Resource audit	Investigate the quantity and quality of tangible and intangible assets (including human capital) and gain a clear picture of the quality of management at all levels within the acquired company.
Corporate objectives and plans	Review the corporate objectives and strategic plans of the acquired company and harmonise these with those of the parent company. When the acquired company is in the same industry, harmonisation is easier. When the company is in a different sector, then its objectives may be deemed acceptable and the focus may be on integrating the financing and accountability of the acquired company, to the acquiring company.
Revising the organisational structure	Attention should be afforded to the human capital side of the business combination. The aim should be to keep morale high. This may be achieved, in part, by deciding on any factors that impact on the workforce and communicating these to the workforce promptly and clearly.

Finally, Schuler (2003) outlined five best practices that a parent company should implement in its approach to integrating a newly acquired company. These are listed (in brief) in **Figure 18.10**.

FIGURE 18.10: SCHULER – FIVE BEST PRACTICES FOR INTEGRATING A NEW COMPANY

1. Start planning early.
2. Pay careful attention to leadership selection.
3. Get an insider's view of knowledge networks and information flow.
4. Develop clear, coherent and timely communication strategies.
5. Dedicate adequate resources to the transition management team.

Post-acquisition Audit Procedures

Every company should undertake an audit of the acquisition process and the success of the integration after the acquisition. This allows management to learn lessons from the acquisition process and to adjust its approach and behaviour in future acquisitions. The audit should compare the actual integration with the planned integration. Like any capital investment project, the performance of the combined group after the amalgamation should be compared to what had been predicted at the bidding stage. This will highlight management's investment performance, or lack of performance.

CONCLUSION

Takeovers and mergers have been popular amongst UK and Irish companies for a number of decades (both by home and by foreign bidders). Company acquisitions are complicated. There will be a certain amount of information asymmetry between the quantity of, and interpretation of knowledge that the advisors to the bidding company have of the target company, relative to what is known by the management of the target company. When a takeover is deemed to be hostile, this problem is accentuated. Most takeovers are large and require additional financing. If a takeover is financed using debt, the capital structure and financial risk of the bidding company may be changed. Then integration of the acquired entity is complicated. If this is not carefully managed, the amalgamation may fail.

Research has shown that takeover activity amongst companies in the marketplace happens in waves. There was an increase in the number of takeovers in the early 1970s and in the late 1980s and an increase in the size of the companies being taken over in the period 1995–2000. Several research studies have suggested reasons for the peaks in amalgamation activity in the 1970s and 1980s, including growth in company profitability. This increases the ability of companies to finance large-scale investments of this type as growth in profitability is accompanied by increases in a company's share price. This makes it attractive for companies to offer share-for-share exchanges or to raise cash by issuing equity. In addition, deregulation of the financial services markets has made debt more accessible. It is argued that the rising markets at that time led to larger firms being overvalued relative to smaller companies, making it easier for them to acquire small companies cheaply (in a share-for-share exchange they will be getting a bargain as the larger company's shares are overvalued by more). In the mid to late 1980s the regulatory environment was considered to be relaxed. The large-scale amalgamations in the late 1990s are considered to be companies' responses to the globalisation of the economy. In some countries, governments are hostile to foreign companies entering the domestic market and utilising their resources; a merger with a local-based company reduces this hostility. In addition, advances in telecommunications (i.e. the internet) and transportation have meant that many companies that are located far apart can now effectively work together.

For a takeover to be successful, the price range suggested by the buyer must overlap with the price range deemed to be acceptable by the vendor. Both companies are likely to use a range of the methods outlined in **Chapter 17** and to come up with a price range at which they are willing to deal.

Who Wins?

In terms of who benefits, research suggests that the winners are the equity holders of target companies. When an offer is made, it typically includes a premium over the market price of the shares. The expectation is that the premium is only part of the overall gains expected from the amalgamation; however, research suggests that in most instances the premium reflects the full gains, if not more. Indeed, in some instances it is thought that the equity holders of the bidding company may even be worse off afterwards. Gregory (1997) reported that the performance of amalgamated companies after a large *domestic* acquisition is typically negative, on average, in the longer term. He also noted that takeovers that were financed using share exchanges adversely impacted on the bidding company's equity holders' value, to a greater extent than cash takeovers, as did agreed bids and companies that had not undertaken an amalgamation before. Conversely, he concluded that hostile bids and companies that had experienced an amalgamation previously created more wealth for their equity holders. In addition, he found that conglomerate integrations were the least successful for creating equity holder wealth, and horizontal integrations were the most successful. More recent reported statistics are also negative. KPMG reports that although 82% of mergers are subjectively considered to be successful, only 17% add value and over half damage value. These statistics were backed up in a report by Deloitte, which reported that 50% of mergers fail because of inadequate planning and poor human resource management.

Research by McKinsey & Company on the takeover activity of 1,000 non-banking companies that were involved in 15,000 takeover deals over a 10-year period, identified that larger companies rely more on merger and acquisitions for growth. In general, companies that undertook many small deals performed better than companies that relied solely on organic growth. However, identifying other patterns was difficult. The researchers found that the success of large deals depends on the industry, whereas the success of small deals is associated with the capabilities of the acquiring companies (Rehn, Uhlaner and West, 2012).

EXAMINATION STANDARD QUESTION: EVALUATING AN ACQUISITION

You are the financial advisor to Cushion Plc, and in that capacity you have been asked to assess and report on a proposal that Cushion Plc should acquire Pin Plc (a similar company).

The proposal is to acquire the entire issued share capital of Pin Plc at a valuation of 90c/p per share, to be satisfied by a cash payment of 50c/p per share and the balance in shares of Cushion Plc valued at €/£1.60 per share. The following are summarised statements of financial position and statements of profit or loss of Cushion Plc and Pin Plc as on 31 December 20X4:

STATEMENTS OF FINANCIAL POSITION

	Cushion Plc €/£000	Pin Plc €/£000
ASSETS		
Non-current assets	3,200	3,650
Current assets		
Inventory	1,900	960
Trade receivables	1,720	1,280

Cash	520	20
	4,140	2,260
Total assets	7,340	5,910
EQUITY AND LIABILITIES		
Equity and reserves		
Equity shares of 25c/p each	1,200	900
Capital reserves	1,200	1,500
Revenue reserves	1,520	1,030
	3,920	3,430
Non-current liabilities		
Deferred taxation	–	250
Term loans	660	700
	660	950
Current liabilities		
Trade payables	2,270	920
Hire-purchase commitments	50	–
Short-term loans	200	480
Taxation	240	130
	2,760	1,530
Total equity and liabilities	7,340	5,910

STATEMENTS OF PROFIT OR LOSS

	Cushion Plc €/£000	Pin Plc €/£000
Net income before taxation and interest	1,350	740
Interest	(55)	(120)
Taxation	(495)	(270)
Net income attributable to equity holders	800	350

The following information may be relevant:

1. Both companies are quoted on the stock exchange and have a wide spread of equity holders.
2. The equity share prices of Cushion Plc and Pin Plc were 170c/p and 75c/p, respectively, on 17 April 20X5.
3. Due to a reduction in the demand for the products of Pin Plc in the home market, it is expected that profits in the year to 31 December 20X5 will be the same as in the year to 31 December 20X4.
4. The strength of the export markets for the products of Cushion Plc means that the profit of Cushion Plc in the year to 31 December 20X5 will be 30% higher than in the year to 31 December 20X4.

5. The rate of taxation is 50%.
6. Cushion Plc can borrow funds at 15% per annum.

The managing director of Cushion Plc believes that, with tighter management control and more aggressive marketing, the profit of Pin Plc could be increased by at least 15% in a full year. He is also satisfied that, although there would be overlapping in some product areas, in the event of an acquisition of Pin Plc by Cushion Plc this would be compensated for by other benefits.

Requirement You are required to prepare a report for the board of directors of Cushion Plc to:

(a) indicate whether, on the basis of the information available, it would make financial sense for Cushion Plc to purchase Pin Plc (you are expected to show earnings per share and net assets per share calculations); and

(b) comment on the suitability of the proposed cash and share issue and discuss possible alternatives.

(*Note:* you should make whatever assumptions you consider necessary, but the assumptions that you do make should be clearly indicated in your report.)

Total 50 Marks

(Based on Chartered Accountants Ireland, MABF, *Questions and Solutions Manual 2007/08*)

Solution

To: Managing Director, Cushion Plc

From: Financial Advisor

Date: 30/04/X5

Subject: Acquisition of Pin Plc

Introduction

In accordance with your instructions, I have examined the proposed acquisition of Pin Plc:

1. It is proposed Cushion Plc acquire the issued share capital of Pin Plc at a valuation of 90c/p a share, satisfied by a cash payment of 50c/p per share and an exchange of four equity shares of Pin Plc for one equity share of Cushion Plc. The valuation of 90c/p per share represents a premium of 15c/p over the current market price of the Pin Plc shares.
2. The financing of the acquisition on the proposed terms would require borrowing of €/£1,800,000, which at a rate of interest of 15% would increase the annual interest charges by €/£270,000. In addition, a further 900,000 equity shares will have to be issued, which will result in an increase in the issued share capital to 5,700,000 equity shares of 25c/p each.
3. The principal factors influencing my assessment of the financial viability of the proposed acquisition include the effect on the net assets and earnings per share of Cushion Plc, the calculations of which are outlined at Appendices I and II, respectively.

Net Assets per Share

4. The valuation of 90c/p attached to the Pin Plc shares compares with its present asset value of 95.3c/p per share. The poor trading performance of the company is illustrated by a comparison of the net asset value per share with the market price of 75c/p.

5. The book value of the assets of Pin Plc may not be of particular significance in view of the limited scope for improvement in the company's trading results. However, I have calculated that the proposed acquisition terms would result in an increase in the net assets per share of Cushion Plc from 81.6c/p to 97.4c/p per share. This increase results from the significant variation between the current book value of each company's equity share capital in relation to valuations used in the formulation of the offer terms.

Earnings per Share

6. On the basis of the 20X4 earnings after tax of Cushion Plc and Pin Plc of €/£800,000 and €/£350,000, respectively, the current earnings per share in each company amount to 16.7c/p and 9.7c/p, respectively. The market's view of the poor future trading prospects for Pin Plc is reflected in its present price earnings ratio of 7.7, as compared to Cushion Plc's price earnings ratio of 10.2.
7. On the basis of Cushion Plc's budgeted results for 20X5, I have calculated that the present strength of its export markets may result in an increase in earnings per share to 17.7c/p from the present level of 16.7c/p (see Appendix II below).

   In addition, I have calculated that the effect of the acquisition of Pin Plc on the proposed terms may be to further increase the earnings per share of Cushion Plc to up to 18.9c/p.
8. The effect of the acquisition of Pin Plc on the market valuation of Cushion Plc is difficult to forecast. However, the maintenance of Cushion Plc's present price earnings ratio would result in an increase in the market price of Cushion Plc shares in proportion to the projected increase in earnings per share.

Conclusion and Recommendation

9. On the basis of the offer terms and projected earnings outlined above, the acquisition of Pin Plc may be expected to lead to an increase in earnings per share of Cushion Plc from 17.7c/p to 18.9c/p and an increase in net assets per share from 81.6c/p to 97.4c/p.
10. On the assumption that the market maintains its current price earnings ratio of 10.2 times after the acquisition of Pin Plc, the projected increase in earnings per share will result in an increase in Cushion Plc's equity share price from 180.5c/p to 193.0c/p, with the resulting benefit to its existing equity holders. However, the projected increase in market valuation may be considered to be marginal in view of the degree of uncertainty in respect of the market reaction to the takeover and to the increased quantity of share capital on the market.
11. The effect of an increase in the cash element of the offer terms will be to further increase the projected gearing of Cushion Plc, with a possible adverse effect on its credit rating from the viewpoint of future sources of loan finance. However, it will be noted that a lower proportion of the bid price accounted for by the share capital of Cushion Plc will result in an increase in the anticipated improvement in its earnings per share and market capitalisation.
12. An alternative that should be considered is the inclusion in the offer terms of an element of unsecured loan stock at, for example, a rate of interest of 12%, convertible into equity share capital after five years at a discount against the expected market value of Cushion Plc's equity share capital at that date. This rate of interest is lower than the present rate at which it can obtain loan finance and, in substitution for the equity share capital of Cushion Plc offered to the Pin Plc equity holders, would result in an increase in earnings

per share accruing to Cushion Plc's present equity holders. In addition, such an issue would have a less disadvantageous effect on the capital structure as a result of the fact that the borrowed capital will not eventually have to be directly repaid by the company.

APPENDIX I

ASSETS PER SHARE

(i) *Present assets per share*

	Cushion Plc	Pin Plc
	€/£000	**€/£000**
Equity capital	1,200	900
Capital reserves	1,200	1,500
Revenue reserves	1,520	1,030
Total net assets	3,920	3,430
Equity shares of 25c/p	4,800,000	3,600,000
Net assets per share	81.6c/p	95.3c/p

(ii) *Projected assets per share (Cushion Plc, post-acquisition)*

	€/£000
Net assets	
– Cushion Plc	3,920
– Pin Plc	3,430
	7,350
Less cash paid to equity holders of Pin Plc	(1,800)
Projected total net assets	5,550
Equity shares of 25c/p	5,700,000
Projected net assets per share	97.4c/p

APPENDIX II

EARNINGS PER SHARE

(i) *Present earnings per share*

		Cushion Plc	Pin Plc
Earnings per share		€/£800,000	€/£350,000
		4,800,000	3,600,000
	=	16.7c/p	9.7c/p
Price earnings ratio		170c/p	75
		16.7c/p	9.7c/p
	=	10.2 times	7.7 times

(ii) *Projected earnings per share of Cushion Plc in 20X5*

	€/£000
Trading profits before tax and interest (+30%)	1,755
Interest	(55)
	1,700
Taxation (50%)	(850)
Profits after taxation	850
Equity shares of 25c/p	4,800,000
Earnings per share	17.7c/p

(iii) *Projected earnings per share of Cushion Plc in 20X5 (post-acquisition)*

	€/£000
Trading profit before tax and interest	
– Cushion Plc	1,755
– Pin Plc (+15%)	851
	2,606
Interest – Cushion Plc (+€/£270,000)	(325)
Pin PLC	(120)
	2,161
Taxation (50%)	(1,080)
	1,081
Equity shares of 25c/p	5,700,000
Earnings per share	18.9c/p

Key Terms

Amalgamation
Asset stripping
Back-door listing
Backward vertical integration
Bidding company
Bootstrap effect
City Code
Competition and Markets Authority (CMA)
Competition and Consumer Protection Commission (CCPC)
Conglomerate merger
Crown jewels
Defence document
Due diligence
Economies of scale
Forward vertical integration
Golden parachute
Heads of agreement
Horizontal integration
Hostile takeover
Integration
Leveraged buy-out (LBO)
Market for corporate control
Merger
Offer document
Pacman defence

Poison pill
Post-acquisition audit procedures
Reverse merger
Reverse takeovers
Share-for-share exchange
Statutory compulsory acquisition
Synergy
Takeover
Takeover Code
Takeover Panel
Target company
Tin parachute
Vertical integration
White knight
White squire

REVIEW QUESTIONS

(See Suggested Solutions to Review Questions in **Appendix B**.)

Question 18.1

Outline the steps that a company should take when it decides to take over another company.

Question 18.2

A Plc has 1,000,000 shares in issue. They are currently trading at €/£20 per share. A smaller company in the same industry, B Plc, has 400,000 shares in issue that are currently trading at €/£10 per share. A Plc is considering offering €/£11.25 per share to the equity holders in B Plc for their shares. A Plc has a cost of capital of 20%. It expects a yearly increase in net earnings arising from synergies of €/£140,000.

Requirement

(a) Calculate the NPV of the bid by A Plc for B Plc.
(b) Determine who will get the value of the synergies (i.e. the proportion of the synergies going to the equity holders in A Plc and the proportion going to B Plc).

Question 18.3

Explain the difference between an MBO and an MBI.

Question 18.4

Financial information for Bidding Group Plc (a fast-growing ungeared company) and Target Company Plc (a slow-growing ungeared company) is as follows:

	Bidding Group Plc	**Target Company Plc**	**Bidding (after acquisition) – estimate**
	€/£000	**€/£000**	**€/£000**
Total net earnings	400	400	800
Total market value	6,000	3,000	9,000
Number of shares in issue	200	200	300
Market price per share	€/£30.00	€/£15.00	€/£30.00
Earnings per share	€/£2.00	€/£2.00	€/£2.67
Price earnings ratio	15 times	7.5 times	11.24 times
Earnings per €/£ invested	6.67%	13.33%	8.9%

The above information was calculated in **Worked Example 18.1** and it is assumed that Bidding acquires the share capital of Target in exchange for 100,000 shares in Bidding. Therefore, each share of Bidding is regarded as being worth two shares in Target (Bidding's market value being twice that of Target). There are no synergies, economies of scale or any other benefit to be gained from this business combination. However, there have been concerns in respect of the potential earnings of Target Company Plc and the directors of Bidding Group Plc have commissioned a due diligence audit of Target Company Plc. The results of this audit will be made public and are expected to impact on the share price of Target Company Plc immediately.

The due diligence report predicts that the growth of Target Company Plc is not as strong as was first anticipated and that the equilibrium market price of Target Company Plc should in fact be €/£7.50.

Requirement Recalculate the impact of the acquisition on the number of shares to be issued by Bidding Group Plc and on the performance ratios of both Target Company Plc and the combined company thereafter, in light of the revised information emanating from the due diligence audit.

Question 18.5

Fox Plc makes a cash offer of €/£20.00 per share for the equity shares of Hen Plc. Hen Plc has 500,000 shares in issue and they are currently trading at €/£15.00 per share.

Requirement

(a) In terms of the economic gain to be made from this takeover, what must the directors believe the value of the minimum synergies to be?

(b) Given that Fox Plc has a cost of capital of 20%, what is the expected yearly increase in earnings (from synergies only)?

Question 18.6

Explain how synergy gains impact on the cost of the acquisition to a bidding company, assuming the company elects to offer cash. Compare this to the cost of the acquisition were the company to offer a share-for-share exchange.

CHALLENGING QUESTIONS

(Suggested Solutions to Challenging Questions are available through your lecturer.)

Question 18.1 Pike Plc and Minnow Plc (Level 2)

Pike Plc is considering acquiring all of Minnow Plc's share capital. Two options are being proposed by the management of Pike Plc to its equity holders. The equity holders have to vote on the option to select in a meeting in two weeks' time.

- The first option is to offer €/£20.00 for each share in Minnow Plc.
- The second option is to offer one share in Pike Plc for two shares in Minnow Plc.

Minnow Plc is a similar company to Pike Plc. They both sell similar items and have no long-term debt. The management have informed the equity holders that, after an extensive review of the potential impact of the merger on the future financial performance of the company, they believe that the acquisition will lead to synergies; revenues are expected to increase by €/£4 million and costs are expected to fall by €/£3 million. These are the only synergies expected. Pike Plc's cost of capital is 20%.

Relevant details on both companies are as follows:

STATEMENTS OF FINANCIAL POSITION (EXTRACTS)

	Pike Plc **€/£m**	**Minnow Plc** **€/£m**
Total assets	260	23
Of which:		
Cash	70	4
Other assets (book value)	190	19

STATEMENTS OF PROFIT OR LOSS (EXTRACTS)

	Pike Plc **€/£m**	**Minnow Plc** **€/£m**
Revenues	170	25
Costs	125	20
Market value of company	550	48
Number of equity shares in issue (millions)	11	3

Requirement You are a financial advisor to the equity holders of Pike Plc. You have been asked to write a report explaining the economic consequences of each option and to advise the equity holders of the most favourable option. You will meet the equity holders next week to discuss the finding of your report. The report should cover the following areas and should:

(a) Calculate the value of the synergies expected.

(b) Evaluate the cash offer. This will involve:
   (i) Determining the purchase consideration of the acquisition.
   (ii) Determining the expected new market value, cash balance, total assets and earnings of Pike Plc post-acquisition.
   (iii) Advising the equity holders of Pike Plc on how the synergy gains will be split between the equity holders of Pike Plc and Minnow Plc under the share offer.
   (iv) Highlighting which set of equity holders is exposed to the risk that the synergy calculations may be incorrect.

(c) Evaluate the share exchange offer. This will involve:
   (i) Calculating the number of shares that Pike Plc will have to issue to purchase the shares of Minnow Plc.
   (ii) Determining the expected new market value, cash balance, total assets and earnings of Pike Plc post-acquisition.
   (iii) Determining the purchase consideration of the acquisition.
   (iv) Advising the equity holders of Pike Plc on how the synergy gains will be split between the equity holders of Pike Plc and Minnow Plc under the cash offer.

(v) Highlighting which set of equity holders is exposed to the risk that the synergy calculations may be incorrect.

(d) Advise the equity holders of Pike Plc of which option to support in the forthcoming meeting.

60 Marks

Question 18.2 East-West (Level 2)

Purchase of Supplier At the recent board meeting, the divisional director informed the board that the main supplier of raw materials, Silco Ltd, has been offered for sale. The divisional director expressed the view that the purchase of Silco would not only be a good investment, because it would improve control of the supply line, but it would enable East-West to reduce the cost of materials within its product. The board asked you to investigate the possibility of purchasing Silco and the financial impact the purchase could have on East-West.

Requirement Write a report to the board of East-West setting out the information the board of East-West would need to enable it to evaluate the purchase of Silco. Indicate what factors the Board should consider.

10 Marks

(Based on Chartered Accountants Ireland, MABF, FAE, extract from Autumn 2007)

Question 18.3 Qwerty (Level 2)

Growth Opportunities Paul has always been more growth-focused than Joe and for the past year has been exploring various options to expand the company. He has identified a venture capital investor with an interest in small technology companies. The investor has made an offer to invest €/£2 million in Qwerty for 36% of the equity. Paul and Joe agree that this is an attractive offer. An agreement has been signed and this investment will go ahead within the next three months.

Paul is proposing that they use the funds raised from the new investor to part-finance the acquisition of Screen Magic Limited, an Irish company that manufactures computer screens. Paul has had preliminary discussions with the owner (and managing director) of Screen, who has told him he is keen to retire soon, after finding the last few years increasingly stressful trying to resolve a complex tax issue affecting Screen and dealing with increasingly onerous regulations on environmental standards in manufacturing. He may be interested in selling Screen and has provided information on the company (see the Appendix to **Challenging Question 17.4**). Paul has been pushing a 'growth by acquisition' strategy for several years because he believes that Qwerty is too narrowly focused on one sector and that acquisitions almost always deliver significant value through synergies and economies of scale. He is confident that if Qwerty acquires another company, he and Joe have the management skills required to ensure a successful integration. Paul is eager to agree the terms of the takeover of Screen before the venture capital investor takes his seat on the board as he is not sure if the investor would approve of the takeover. Bridging finance would be available from Qwerty's bank to finance the acquisition, pending receipt of the new equity funds. This facility would be personally guaranteed by Paul and Joe.

Requirement

(a) Critically evaluate Paul's THREE reasons for wanting to pursue an acquisition strategy.

6 Marks

(b) Outline FOUR specific areas Qwerty's due diligence should focus on as part of the acquisition of Screen.

4 Marks

Total 10 Marks

(Based on Chartered Accountants Ireland, CAP 2, MABF, Autumn 2013, extract from Q1)

Question 18.4 Currane (Level 2)

Jim McGee, the Chief Executive of Currane Plc, was shocked last Tuesday morning when Ree Resources Plc announced it had acquired 9% of the shares in Currane and was making a bid for the company.

Currane was founded by Jim McGee's father, Niall McGee, in 1968. It owned several copper and zinc mines throughout Ireland. In 1985 Niall McGee took the company public and the McGee family, the largest shareholder, now owns 8% of Currane and three of the eight directors on the Board are appointed by the family. The remaining 92% of Currane's shares are owned by a dispersed group of shareholders, none of whom owns more than 2% of Currane, other than Ree. Currane's shares are currently trading at €/£1.69.

The offer made by Ree to Currane's shareholders was €/£2.35 cash per share in Currane, or 0.45 shares in Ree (currently trading at €/£5.02) per share in Currane. In its offer document Ree had said that Currane was significantly undervalued given the current buoyant commodities market and that it believed poor management was to blame for this.

Jim's immediate reaction on hearing about the offer was to ring Noel Kennedy, a long-serving independent director and the chair of Currane, and say, "How dare they ... this company has been in the McGee family for more than 40 years ... we have to convene a Board meeting straightaway and strongly recommend a no vote to shareholders". Noel had replied: "I've been a director for 10 years and Currane has always been very well managed in that time. I'll certainly be recommending a no vote." Noel immediately issued a press release saying Currane was considering the offer and would comment following a Board meeting next Friday.

Requirement

(a) Discuss the relative attractiveness of the cash and the share offers for shareholders in Currane.

4 Marks

(b) Outline any ethical issue that arises for the directors of Currane and suggest how this issue could be addressed.

5 Marks

Total 9 Marks

(Based on Chartered Accountants Ireland, CAP 2, Autumn 2012, Q4(b)(c))

Question 18.5 RD and LO (Level 2)

RD Plc has made a takeover bid for LO Plc. RD Plc's share price has been performing well in recent months as the market believes its managing director, Mr Jones, has the ability to improve dramatically the company's earnings. The acquisition of LO Plc, an erratic performer in recent years, seems to be a sensible move in commercial terms. However, the market does not react to the terms of the bid as Mr Jones expected and he finds RD Plc's share price falls.

A summary of the financial data before the bid is as follows.

	RD Plc	**LO Plc**
Number of shares in issue	5 million	15 million
Earnings available to ordinary shareholders	£2.5 million	£7.5 million
P/E ratio	12.5	7.5

Mr Jones' estimated financial data post-acquisition:

Estimated market capitalisation	£125 million
Estimated share price	£8.33
Estimated EPS	£0.67
Estimated equivalent value of an old LO Plc share	£5.55

The offer is 10 RD Plc shares for 15 LO Plc shares. At the time of the bid announcement, no information is related other that the bid terms and the comment by Mr Jones that he hopes to "turn LO round". The expected rate of return on RD Plc's equity capital is 15% per annum constant.

Requirement

(a) Suggest how Mr Jones might have calculated post-acquisition values.

5 Marks

(b) Write a short report suggesting a probable post-acquisition share price and advising shareholders in both RD Plc and LO Plc on whether the bid should proceed.

10 Marks

It is later announced that the proposed merger is expected to result in immediate administrative savings of £5 million. Sales of redundant assets by the end of the first year are expected to realise £10 million. Net income is expected to increase by £7.5 million per annum for the foreseeable future as a result of a more aggressive marketing policy for LO Plc's business.

(***Note:*** you should assume all figures are net of tax.)

Requirement

(c) Explain how this new information would affect your estimate of a probable post-acquisition share price, and comment on how it might affect LO Plc's bargaining position.

10 Marks

Total 25 Marks

Question 18.6 Redbrick (Level 2)

You have recently been appointed financial director of Redbrick Plc, a company that manufactures a traditional range of brick products for use in the construction industry. The company operates from factory premises located just outside a major urban centre, which allows easy access to the large number of construction sites located in the area. The company sources its raw materials (mainly sand and mineral supplies) from a variety of local quarry operators.

Redbrick's main customers include major local residential house-builders and property development companies. However, the company has traditionally found it difficult to break into the cross-border market, due to the strong competition from local manufacturers. One of Redbrick's main competitors across the border is Tarragh Ltd, which, although smaller in size to Redbrick, has experienced significant sales growth due to the success of its unique range of sandstone brick products. Tarragh's main manufacturing plant is located beside its own quarry, from which it is able to extract the unique local sandstone that is the main raw material in the manufacture of its bricks.

Mike Ryan, Redbrick's chief executive, has long admired Tarragh's growth record and its complementary product range, and has asked you to prepare a report commenting on the benefits or otherwise of a possible acquisition of Tarragh. He also asked you to give an indication of the likely price that Redbrick should consider paying for the acquisition.

Tarragh also has a small roof tile distribution operation that is located in separate premises. It is envisaged that this would be disposed of post-acquisition, potentially freeing-up space that, with a small capital investment, could be used to create additional production capacity should this be required at a future date.

On the assumption that the acquisition will proceed, Mike Ryan has also asked you to detail those matters that you would wish to be included in a due diligence report on Tarragh, and to comment on any potential impact on the company's valuation.

The following information is available in respect of shares in Redbrick Plc as at 31 December 20X5:

Share price	€/£2.20
Earnings per share	22c/p

Financial information on Tarragh is provided in the Appendix to this question.

Oldestyle Brick After a long period of product research and development, Redbrick has recently introduced a new range of brick products called 'Oldestyle'. This product gives the appearance of an aged and rougher brick surface, more associated with older houses. The distressed appearance of the Oldestyle range has recently become fashionable again, particularly in the construction of inner-city houses and pubs, and this product is now seen as a way to diversify into a distinct niche market.

The unique texture of the Oldestyle brick is achieved by using a rougher grade of material (which actually costs less than that used in the manufacture of the company's other brick ranges), and increasing the baking time in the kiln.

Redbrick's full product range now includes the following:

- Rustic (standard red brick range, smooth surface texture).
- Mellow (same finish as rustic, slightly lighter colour).
- Oldestyle (more weathered appearance, rougher surface texture).

Requirement Draft a report to the chief executive detailing each of the following matters:

(a) Calculate an estimated valuation range for Tarragh using both an earnings and an asset-based valuation technique.

26 Marks

(b) Detail THREE specific matters that you would want to be included within a due diligence report on Tarragh (other than standard due diligence procedures), and comment on their possible impact on the valuation of the company. Outline two specific matters on which you would seek directors' warranties.

12 Marks

(c) List THREE potential benefits that could arise from the proposed acquisition of Tarragh and list *three* potential difficulties that may arise with the enlarged group (excluding those matters to be examined under the due diligence procedures).

(***Note:*** ignore any foreign exchange issues.)

12 Marks
Total 50 Marks

(Based on Chartered Accountants Ireland, MABF, FAE, Extract from Autumn 2000)

Appendix
Tarragh Ltd
Statement of Financial Position
as at 31 December 20X5

	Note	€/£000
ASSETS		
Tangible assets		
Premises	1	1,300
Quarry reserves	2	700
Plant and machinery		1,000
		3,000
Intangible assets		
Goodwill		200
Current assets		
Inventories		300
Trade receivables	3	700
Cash		50
		1,050
Total assets		4,250
EQUITY, RESERVES AND LIABILITIES		
Equity and reserves		
Equity share capital		300
Revenue reserves		2,450
		2,750
Non-current liabilities		
Long-term bank loan		400
3% debentures	4	300
		700
Current liabilities		
Overdraft		500
Trade payables		300
		800
Total equity reserves and liabilities		4,250

Notes:

1. Premises includes €/£500,000 relating to a small office-block that houses the company's accounting department. It has been established that the accounts function could be managed from Redbrick's existing accounts function, thereby saving salaries of €/£250,000 per annum. In addition, Tarragh's office building could be sold or let post-acquisition. This property has a current rental value of €/£70,000 per annum and could be readily sold to reflect a 10% yield (rental value) to a prospective purchaser. In addition, it is estimated that the remaining Tarragh premises are undervalued by €/£150,000.
2. Quarry reserves are stated at the depreciated historical cost of the sandstone quarry purchased 10 years ago (in 20W5). At the time of purchase it was estimated that the reserves were the equivalent of 25 years' production. No revised valuation survey has since been undertaken to estimate the depth of reserves underground.
3. Trade receivables includes €/£25,000 owing from a small construction company that has now gone into liquidation. It is thought that this amount is likely to be unrecoverable. It would appear that there are potentially a number of other similar trade receivables whose financial position is known to be precarious.
4. The debenture stockholders have agreed to a total redemption consideration of €/£200,000.

Statement of Profit or Loss (Extracts)
year ended 31 December 20X5

	€/£000
Net income before tax	300
Taxation	(75)
Net income after tax	225
Dividend	(75)
Retained income	150

Additional information:

- The non-core roof tiling operation has a net asset value of €/£400,000. It is estimated that the operation generates annual pre-tax profits of €/£100,000, but could be readily sold for €/£600,000.
- If the acquisition proceeds, Mike Ryan has indicated that he would undertake a €/£600,000 capital expenditure programme that would result in other cost savings of €/£120,000 per annum.
- Tarragh's long-standing managing director and its sales director have both indicated their wish to retire if the acquisition is successfully completed. This would save a further €/£130,000 per annum.
- The employee pension fund was last subject to an actuarial valuation three years ago (in 20X2) and, at that time, required no adjustments to annual contributions. The directors of Tarragh now estimate that the fund is currently underfunded to the extent of €/£150,000. It is proposed that this shortfall should be met by increased employer's contributions over the next three years.

- The directors of Tarragh have made reference to ongoing legal action by a former employee who was injured while working in the quarry. They are of the opinion that their case is strong and consequently they have not provided for any contingent liability in the audited accounts.
- Tarragh is under legal obligation to operate the quarry in accordance with the latest EU environmental Directives.
- Both Redbrick and Tarragh have effective tax rates of 25%, which should be assumed to remain unchanged. Some years ago Tarragh was the subject of an investigation by the tax authorities, which resulted in a payment of €/£75,000 to cover unpaid tax and resultant penalties.
- Ignore any foreign exchange issues.

Question 18.7 Pharmacon (Level 2)

Pharmacon Ltd manufactures a range of drugs on long-term licenses from large pharmaceutical companies (Licensed Manufacturing Division). It also has a smaller division that develops and produces original, patented drugs (Original Drug Manufacturing Division). It was founded over twenty years ago by Jim Edwards and Tony Phillips, who retain a 50% shareholding each. Jim is the managing director and Tony is the financial director. For the first decade of Pharmacon's existence growth was strong, driven by the Licensed Manufacturing Division. Over the past number of years, however, Pharmacon has failed to win a number of important manufacturing contracts and growth had slowed considerably. Feedback from the industry analysts has been that Pharmacon is too small to compete with competitors in terms of production capacity and price due to a lack of economies of scale.

At a meeting of the board of directors last week, Jim suggested Pharmacon was at a crossroads. Continuing on its current path would inevitably lead to a slow decline. He suggested that they had two alternatives. They could sell Pharmacon to a competitor, or they could expand the production capacity significantly to enable it to compete successfully for manufacturing contracts.

Pharmacon has recently received several bids, one made by Generic Pharma Ltd. The offer from Generic was €/£37 million for 100% of the shares in Pharmacon, contingent on a satisfactory due diligence process. This offer had not been seriously considered by Jim and Tony at the time. If Pharmacon were sold, Jim and Tony would resign their positions immediately.

Zenith Marketing Consultants produced a growth forecast for Pharmacon last year. This forecasts the long-term earnings growth rate for the Licensed Manufacturing Division (which accounts for 65% of revenues and costs) to be 2% and the long-term growth rate for the Original Drug Manufacturing Division to be 5%. Both Jim and Tony believe these forecasts are reasonable.

Requirement

(a) Advise the shareholders of Pharmacon on the offer received from Generic.

6 Marks

(b) Specify THREE matters you would expect Generic to focus on in its due diligence report on Pharmacon. These matters should be particularly relevant to Pharmacon.

3 Marks

Total 9 Marks

(Based on Chartered Accountants Ireland, CAP 2, MABF, Summer 2012, Extract from Q2)

Appendix

Pharmacon Ltd

Statement of Profit or Loss
for the Year Ended 31 December 20X5

	20X5
	€/£000
Turnover	19,004
Cost of sales	(11,402)
Gross profit	**7,602**
Operating expenses	(2,851)
Depreciation	(1,520)
Profit before tax	**3,231**
Tax	(404)
Net profit	2,827

Additional information:

- Pharmacon's cost of equity is estimated at 11.5%.
- Zenith Marketing Consultants has estimated that, to generate the forecasted growth rates, the Licensed Manufacturing Division would have to reinvest 4% of turnover annually and the Original Drug Manufacturing Division would have to reinvest 7% of turnover annually.
- Creatum Plc, a publicly traded Original Drug Manufacturer, trades at a P/E ratio of 20 times earnings.
- Adams Healthcare Ltd, a privately held Licensed Drug Manufacturer, was recently sold for 12 times earnings.

Question 18.8 Bull (Level 2)

Bull Plc has a strategy of growth by acquisition and is the dominant player in its market. The board recently met to discuss the acquisition of Bear Plc, a small but nimble competitor that is gaining a foothold in this market. The primary motive for the acquisition is the removal of the only real competitive threat. The Directors of Bear view the approach as hostile and have provided the minimum information to Bull permissible under the City Code/Irish Takeover Panel. Both companies have very different cultures and operating styles.

The directors of Bull are determined to proceed with the acquisition and believe their superior size will enable them to extract maximum value from any deal for their shareholders. The current share price of Bull and Bear is €/£40 and €/£15, respectively. Bull has 15 million shares in issue and Bear has 4 million.

The following are the three proposals under consideration, though no formal offer has been made:

1. A full cash offer of €/£70 million.
2. An offer of one share in Bull for every two shares in Bear.
3. An offer of €/£25 million cash in addition to one share in Bull for every four shares in Bear.

Bull expects that at least 40% of the employees in Bear will be made redundant. The employees of Bear own 30% of the company via an employee share-ownership scheme.

Additional annualised post-tax synergy benefits and probabilities of achievement are: €/£12m (25%), €/£8m (50%) and €/£4m (25%). This provides expected post-tax synergy benefits of €/£8m per annum which the Directors expect to continue indefinitely into the future. The cost of capital of Bull is 16%.

Bear is very close to securing a lucrative five-year exclusive contract with a new customer in the market worth €/£2 million profit per annum. The directors of Bear have not yet informed their shareholders or Bull.

There are no white knights or squires on the horizon and Bear will not use poison pills or golden parachutes and does not have the financial capability to launch a counter bid for Bull.

Requirement

(a) Describe briefly any two post-acquisition operational concerns that you would have following the proposed acquisition of Bear.

4 Marks

(b) Based on the known expected post-tax synergy benefits and for each of the three proposals:

(i) Estimate the post-acquisition total market value of the combined entity.

6 Marks

(ii) Evaluate each proposal from the perspective of the equity holders of Bull and Bear. Your answer should include financial and non-financial considerations.

8 Marks

(c) Based on the question facts, prioritise and explain briefly FOUR defensive tactics that the directors of Bear could employ to fend off the approach by Bull.

4 Marks

Total 22 Marks

(Based on Chartered Accountants Ireland, CAP 2, Summer 2011, Q2)

Question 18.9 Electrical (Level 2)

Background Smith Electrical Ireland Ltd manufactures security systems for the domestic and commercial markets in Ireland and sells these directly to end users as well as to retailers. Electrical has a manufacturing plant in Dundalk and has been in business for 30 years. The company is owned by Alex Smith (50% shareholding) and his daughter, Jenny Smith (50% shareholding). Their combined holding in Electrical was recently valued by their advisors at €/£18,500,000. Jenny and Alex have substantial assets outside of their shareholding in Electrical.

Takeover Electrical is in negotiation with the owner of Iris Monitoring Systems Ltd to acquire Iris. Iris was founded three years ago and develops innovative "smart security" systems for domestic users. These include CCTV, fire and burglar alarm systems which can be operated remotely through smartphone apps. Iris is owned by a large multinational security company, Axis. Relevant financial information in respect of Iris is provided in Appendix I. Iris made losses for its first two years, but is forecasting a profit for the current year. Iris competes with major multinational technology companies in the "smart security" sector. Sales have been limited to Ireland to date, but Iris is planning to sell its products in the Asian and US markets in the near future. If an acquisition is agreed, it will take place on 1 January 20Y0. Alex and Jenny Smith have considered several options to finance the acquisition, which are detailed in Appendix II.

Requirement

(a) Based on the information provided in Appendix I:
   (i) calculate a free cash flow valuation for Iris;
   (ii) calculate an earnings based valuation for Iris;
   (iii) critically assess ONE of the assumptions provided in the information for valuations;
   (iv) advise Electrical whether the €/£4,000,000 cash takeover of Iris represents value, based on your calculations above.

16 Marks

(b) (i) Outline the advantages **and** disadvantages of **each** of the THREE financing structures outlined in Appendix II.
   (ii) Advise Alex and Jenny Smith which is the most suitable for the acquisition.

Your answer should include supporting calculations, where appropriate.

11 Marks

(c) Identify TWO significant risks that may arise should Electrical acquire Iris **and** suggest how these may be managed and/or reduced.

6 Marks
Total 33 Marks

(Based on Chartered Accountants Ireland, CAP 2, SFMA, Summer 2019, extract from Q1)

Appendix I

Extracts from Iris 20X9

FORECAST STATEMENT OF PROFIT OR LOSS:

	20X9 Forecast €/£000
Turnover	1,835
Cost of sales	(837)
Gross profit	998
Selling and distribution expenses	(135)
Administrative expenses	(96)
Depreciation	(180)
Other expenses	(320)
Profit before tax	**267**
Tax (15%)	(40)
Net profit	**227**

Further information:

1. Free cash flow valuation:
   - Iris expects investments in working capital to total €/£450,000, €/£490,000 and €/£200,000 in years 20Y0, 20Y1 and 20Y2, respectively. It expects the 20Y2 level of investment to be reflective of the long-term investment requirement.
   - Similar companies to Iris have an average beta factor of 1.8. It is assumed that this is reflective of the risk of Iris. The risk-free rate is currently 2.5% and the market risk premium is estimated to be 5%.
   - Depreciation is expected to remain at the current level for the next three years. Turnover is expected to grow by 10% per year for the three years following acquisition. Net profit margin is expected to increase to 16% of sales in 20Y0 and remain at this percentage for three years. After three years, a long-term growth rate of 3% in free cash flows is expected.
   - Iris is an all equity financed company.
   - Electrical estimates that if it acquires Iris, total synergies with a present value of €/£900,000 will be generated.

2. Earnings valuation:
   - Three publicly listed companies operating in the security sector are:

Company	Sector	Share price €/£	EPS €/£
SeeComm	Smart Security	14.60	0.98
SecurIT	Smart Security	7.81	0.55
Alliance Security	Traditional alarm systems and smart security	12.20	1.03

   - Included in the statement of profit or loss of Iris within "other expenses" is a salary of €/£100,000 for the managing director of Iris. This position would no longer be required in the event of an acquisition and a redundancy payment of €/£14,000 would be payable in 20Y0.

Appendix II

Alternative financing structures for the proposed takeover of Iris

1. **Share exchange:** Axis is prepared to exchange 100% of the equity in Iris for 22% of the equity in Electrical.
2. **€/£4,000,000 cash offer funded by debt:** Electrical could borrow €/£4,000,000 over 10 years at 8.5% on an interest-only basis.
3. **€/£4,000,000 cash offer funded by equity:** Jenny and Alex could liquidate €/£4,000,000 in other personal assets and use the proceeds to capitalise Electrical. This would allow Electrical to acquire Iris without using debt.

Information on Electrical:

- The following information is drawn from Electrical's 20X8 financial statements:
  - o Outstanding debt of €/£2,350,000;
  - o Interest expense of €/£71,500;
  - o Interest cover ratio is 14.6 times.
- You can assume that the recent valuation of €/£18,500,000 is a fair value of equity in Electrical.
- Electrical has no available cash at present to fund the acquisition of Iris.
- The average gearing ratio (debt/equity) in the security sector is 35%.

PART V

RISK MANAGEMENT

CHAPTERS

19. Risk Management
20. Exchange Rate Risk
21. Interest Rate Risk

19

Risk Management

Learning Objectives

Upon completing this chapter, readers should be able to:
- describe the functions performed by a typical treasury department;
- outline the advantages and disadvantages of a centralised and decentralised treasury function;
- identify and describe the key financial risks facing a business;
- summarise how key financial risks can be managed and measured;
- outline how a risk management policy may be set and monitored;
- perform simple calculations to determine the cost of a hedge; and
- determine the financial implications of a derivative position.

INTRODUCTION

In terms of business finance, **risk** is the expectation that actual outcomes (e.g. input and output prices, cash flows, interest rates, foreign exchange rates, etc.) will differ from expected outcomes. The greater the variability in cash flows, the greater the risk and vice versa. In business it is difficult to manage cash flows where there are high levels of uncertainty in respect of costs, revenues and cash flows. To reduce this uncertainty, managers take steps to manage their risk exposures, preferring stable, certain outcomes to gains that may occur when interest rates/commodity prices/exchange rates move in the company's favour. The process of transferring a risky cash flow to a risk-free/risk-reduced cash flow is called **hedging**. Hedging has become more important for most large companies as the globalisation of the economic market over the past two to three decades has resulted in companies being exposed to greater types and, as a result, greater aggregate levels of risk. The financial services sector has responded by developing a sweep of products that are designed to hedge against risk. In the main, these products are paper securities (i.e. contracts) that are attached to underlying assets, such as cash, commodities, or currencies. These paper securities are called derivatives because they derive value from movements in the value of the underlying asset.

A network of financial institutions and exchanges has developed over time to provide derivative products that enable managers to manage their risk exposures. In general, risk management in large companies is undertaken by a specialist department called the treasury department.

This chapter starts off by describing the typical activities undertaken within a treasury function and outlines the advantages and disadvantages of a company having a centralised or a decentralised treasury function. Then the economic environment is examined, with particular emphasis being placed on the globalisation of markets and products and the interaction between microeconomic factors across countries. This sets the scene for introducing the variety of financial risks that a business faces and examining the way in which these risks can be managed. The management techniques used to manage risks include internal structuring and derivative products. In addition, the financial implications of a derivative position are explained.

THE GLOBAL ECONOMY

Many large companies are **multinationals**. This means that they own or control a business unit outside the country in which the head office is located. Multinationals usually position some of their activities in 'tax havens' so as to minimise their worldwide taxation bill. **Tax haven** is a term used to describe a country that has lenient taxation rules designed to attract foreign direct investment (FDI). Another reason for locating business units in foreign countries is to gain access to resources, such as lower labour costs, lower oil costs, etc., products (e.g. by purchasing an already established company), intellectual capital (e.g. purchasing research/technology-based entities), or to move closer to customers, thereby reducing transportation costs (e.g. market seeking). The benefits of being a multinational are outlined in **Figure 19.1**.

FIGURE 19.1: POSSIBLE BENEFITS OF BEING A MULTINATIONAL COMPANY

Economies of scale	Treasury economies	Technology/ intellectual capital
Multinationals are large companies. They can locate certain parts of their processes in countries that have comparative benefits over other countries. For example, the manual parts of production might be located in business units in India or China where labour is cheap, whereas the technical parts of production might be located in a country that has a highly educated workforce, such as Sweden.	Multinationals can reduce their overall interest fees by facilitating the ability of business units to loan to each other. They can hedge their interest and currency exposures by pooling debt and currencies centrally and managing them from one pot. They may source funds in one country, where debt is cheaper, for use in another country, where debt is more expensive.	Most multinationals invest heavily in research and development. Many countries welcome multinationals because they expect multinationals to bring superior technology and expertise into their country.

The global economic conditions at present make it easier and more attractive for companies to become multinationals, or to expand their foreign-based activities. The advances made in technology (e.g. the internet) have resulted in multinationals being better able to control a wider dispersed range of business units. In addition, capital markets worldwide are easier to access and have more sophisticated telecommunications systems that report real-time information. The financial environments in many countries have experienced much deregulation, therefore the financial markets have similar rules and many of the exchanges have signed up to International Financial Reporting Standards. This makes it easier and more cost-effective for an entity to raise funds around the world as one set of financial statements is appropriate for most exchanges. In addition, securities from different countries can be traded on a variety of exchanges. Companies can also access cash in the Eurocurrency markets. This is where local banks do business in foreign currencies; for example, a UK bank may loan US Dollars to its UK client company.

THE TREASURY FUNCTION

Treasury management is concerned with the management of cash flows (e.g. liquidity) and the financial risks surrounding these cash flows. In smaller companies treasury management comes under the remit of the accounting department. In these instances the head of this department is commonly referred to as the chief financial officer (CFO). The CFO's duties usually include risk management, funding management, strategic planning, financial reporting and investor relations. However, most large companies have a separate treasury function, staffed by suitably qualified individuals who have a strong knowledge of derivative products. The head of a treasury department is usually called the **corporate treasurer**. The corporate treasurer's responsibilities may involve managing the capital structure of the company, managing risk and managing relationships with investors/providers of finance. When the treasury department is separate from the accounting department, a close relationship must exist if the two departments are to maximise their potential.

The importance of having a treasury function is dependent on the size of the organisation, the extent of its globalisation, the risk surrounding the value of its inputs and outputs and the attitude of the company's board of directors to risk. For example, most large oil companies have fluctuating oil prices and supply oil all around the world. Commodity price risk and exchange rate risk are real concerns for this type of company. Therefore, the majority of large oil companies have sophisticated treasury functions that are managed by an appropriately qualified corporate treasurer.

Most treasury departments in very large companies have four distinct roles. The first deals with **equity management**, including mergers and acquisitions, the markets, issuing equity and maintaining relationships with investors. The second role usually focuses on **global financial transactions**, including managing currency transactions, hedging interest rate exposures and insurance management. These two roles are sometimes referred to as **treasury management**. The third deals with cash handling (for example, determining the optimum lodgement policy, managing the flow of cash between short-term deposits and the current account to ensure sufficient liquidity is maintained and cash forecasting for operational needs). A fourth role is usually concerned with **corporate finance**. This entails maintaining strong banking relationships, dealing with the bond markets, managing the company's financing, liquidity and working capital. The latter two roles are sometimes referred to as **funding management**. The functions are outlined in **Figure 19.2**.

FIGURE 19.2: TRADITIONAL TREASURY DEPARTMENT FUNCTIONS

Cash management	Controlling cash within the group, determining a cash management policy and implementing a supporting information system (e.g. integrating it with the banks' systems). This also involves considering risk and the willingness of the group to expose cash flows/ liquidity to risk.
Bank relationships	Selecting a bank and the types of account to operate and meeting the information needs of banks.
Cash investment policy	Identifying cash investment opportunities and fostering relationships with brokers and dealers.
Risk management	Credit management, managing contingencies, including possible legal actions, creating business disaster recovery policies, identifying and managing employee risks, and identifying and managing economic risks (e.g. competition, customers).
Insurance management	Treasury management should make sure that all a company's risk exposures are covered in some form or other. This involves considering all a company's insurance needs and selecting appropriate policies to reduce risk.
Hedging	A form of insurance, normally utilised to reduce currency risk, interest rate risk and commodity price risk.
Accounts receivable management	Creating policies and systems for controlling cash receipts, setting up facilities for credit card and debit card receipting, etc., enhancing relationships between customers and the group, and dealing with disputes.
Accounts payable management	Creating policies and systems for controlling cash payments from the company, including maintaining a balance between maintaining liquidity, keeping suppliers happy and availing of discounts. It also involves enhancing relationships between suppliers and the company and dealing with disputes.
Investor relations	Ensuring the company has a competent equity holder service provider. The service provider should manage the flow of information from the company to its equity holder body so as not to breach any listings rules.

Treasury Function: Strategic Policy

The organisational structure, aims and policies of the treasury department (including the working capital and liquidity stance to take) are decided at board of directors level. The board should set out strict controls, such as restricting the use of derivatives to hedging and not allowing their use for speculation, setting authorisation levels on transactions beyond which the board has to be informed of a transaction, and preparing and reviewing control procedures. Trading in derivatives is highly specialised and in some instances dealers working within treasury departments have accumulated huge losses over time unnoticed by others, as highlighted in **Real World Example 19.1**.

Real World Example 19.1: Examples of Trading Losses

Dealing in derivatives is inherently risky. Traders can reap massive returns for their investor clients; however, they can also amass huge losses. Like many hedge funds in the first half of 2019, Bill Ackman's publicly traded Pershing Square Capital Management gained 45% in value. However, other traders were not so successful. For example, Autonomy Capital lost $1.1 billion in August 2019 when the price of Argentina's 100-year bonds fell due to uncertainty around election results; and Option Traders, a US hedge trading company, lost $150 million trading on natural gas. In 2018, Citi Group lost about $180 million on its Asia hedge fund.

In December 2018, Bloomberg uncovered that two Barclay's traders had amassed losses of nearly $400 million in 2011 when trading in the commodities markets. Similarly, Glencore Plc also lost about $172 million in the zinc market in 1982.

Two infamous trading losses were incurred in 1995, the first by Nick Leeson, with losses so great they brought down Barings Bank. While Toshihidi Iguchi, the executive vice-president of Daiwa Bank's New York branch, lost $1.1 billion trading in US Treasury bonds. As the bank did not inform the Securities and Exchange Commission, it was kicked out of the US markets.

Treasury and Sustainability

In 2015, the United Nations agreed on 17 global Sustainable Development Goals (SDGs), designed to be a "blueprint to achieve a better and more sustainable future for all".[1] Treasury departments have a role to play as the UN identified the importance of having a sustainable global financial system that supports the achievement of these goals. Treasury departments not only need to finance the company's transition to a sustainable business model, but also need to be equipped to support and promote the company's strategic sustainability goals. To achieve this, treasury departments should design a sustainable finance framework within their company that issues 'green bonds' when relevant and that integrates environmental, social and governance (ESG) matters into all loans and credit facilities. Treasury should promote consideration of ESG issues when making decisions and should demonstrate how the company is promoting sustainability when communicating with finance providers.

Structure of the Treasury Function

The structure of the treasury department should be decided by the board of directors. The main issues are whether the treasury department should be centralised or decentralised and whether the treasury department operates as a profit centre or a cost centre.

A **centralised treasury department** is where one central treasury department serves the needs of all the companies in a group, regardless of their size and location. The advantages of having a centralised treasury department are outlined in **Figure 19.3**.

[1] See https://sustainabledevelopment.un.org/?menu=1300; accessed May 2020.

FIGURE 19.3: ADVANTAGES OF HAVING A CENTRALISED TREASURY DEPARTMENT

Easy to manage	The corporate treasurer will find it easier to manage the funding and treasury needs of the group as the information will be readily available.
Hedging	Internal hedging is easier. When a group has companies located in different countries, and sources and supplies to different companies, then a centralised treasury department can operate with a variety of accounts in the different currencies. This will reduce both transaction costs and currency risk exposure.
Taxation	The corporate treasurer can expatriate/supply cash from/to foreign countries in the most tax-efficient manner, from the group's perspective.
Scale economies	Overhead and staff costs are likely to be more efficient as costs will not be duplicated.
Expertise/ human capital risk	Treasury management is a highly specialised topic. Having one department enables the group-wide policy to be shared amongst several employees. It also promotes the spread of intellectual capital in respect of dealing with treasury and funding management issues amongst the employees of the department. This reduces a company's exposure to the loss of intellectual capital when a key employee leaves, as others should be knowledgeable enough to continue their work.

When a group has a decentralised treasury function, each subsidiary or division may have its own treasury function, either separately or within the accounts department. The individual treasury functions usually follow group-wide policies and aims, which are set by the board of directors. The advantages of having a decentralised treasury function are set out in **Figure 19.4**.

FIGURE 19.4: DECENTRALISED TREASURY FUNCTION: ADVANTAGES

Cost control and responsibility	When the treasury function is decentralised, the cost centre managers (subsidiaries/branches/divisions/business units) are in control of the cost of running the treasury department. When the treasury function is centralised, its costs are either charged out or allocated to the various business units. The centre manager has no control over these costs, yet the performance of his/her unit is impacted on by the allocation.
Comparative advantage	A decentralised treasury function is more aware of the local opportunities and threats in respect of funding, finance and treasury issues.
Speed of action	A decentralised treasury function can take action quickly to reap rewards, maintain liquidity, or reduce costs (resulting from local opportunities or threats).

Treasury functions can be operated as either cost or profit centres. When they operate as a **cost centre** they do not have profit targets, nor do they charge business units for their services at commercial rates. Instead their costs are allocated to business units. Their aim should be to service the group's needs in the most cost-effective manner. **Profit centres** tend to charge the business units market rates for their services. Indeed, they could also provide services to outside entities. They are more likely to have profit-related performance targets; however, cost minimisation will be a major factor. Most companies operate their treasury function as a cost centre with strict controls on the type of derivative transactions that they can enter into.

Finally, a treasury department usually has the same underlying goal as every other department within an organisation: to maximise equity holder value by providing a quality service/product at minimum cost. Teigen (2001) suggests that a successful treasury function should have certain attributes, which are summarised in **Figure 19.5**.

FIGURE 19.5: TEIGEN'S ATTRIBUTES OF A SUCCESSFUL TREASURY DEPARTMENT

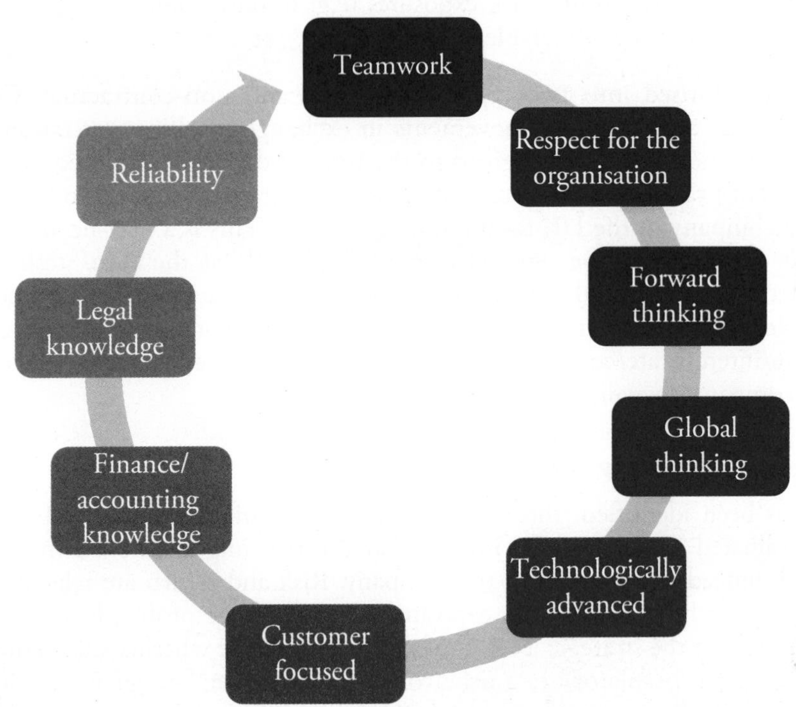

As a director of a corporate treasury, Teigen (2001) suggests that the other departments within an organisation should regard the treasury department as "an internal consultant, with expertise in risk and finance".

MANAGING RISK

Most companies will have policies that specifically relate to risk management. Credit, cash and liquidity management have been covered in other chapters in this text. This section focuses on the specific policies and techniques that a treasury department may take to manage market risk. The three main categories of **market risk** are currency risk, interest rate risk and commodity price risk. Risk can rarely be eliminated fully and most treasury departments aim to minimise the exposure whilst maximising the return expected from a transaction, though this is not always the case. Recognising, evaluating, measuring and balancing the risk and return associated with trading internationally using a variety of different currencies, loan products and commodities are part of a treasury department's risk-management function.

Recognising Risk

Most companies have improved their risk-recognising procedures in the wake of the *Turnbull Report* (1999), wherein it was suggested that the board of directors of a company should focus on identifying its company's risks and should direct its attention to managing the riskier areas. This means that risk is a corporate problem, with corporate-level responsibility for identifying and managing it. The treasury department will be particularly interested in identifying financial and business risk exposures (e.g. imports and exports). **Exposure** is a term used to describe being vulnerable to risk.

Risk can be categorised into two types: contractual and non-contractual. **Contractual risks** are risks that are caused by movements in exchange rates/interest rates/commodity prices from the time a contract is agreed to the time of delivery of the required currency/funds/goods. For example, assume an Irish company purchases supplies on credit (say, 90 days) from a company in the UK for a set Sterling price. This is a non-negotiable contract and the Irish company will be exposed to contractual risk, as the euro/Sterling exchange rate may change over the 90-day period, making the produce either cheaper or more expensive. **Non-contractual risks** occur when no specific contract has been entered but exchange rate/interest rate/commodity price movements have caused the competitive position of the company, overall, to change.

Evaluating and Measuring Risk

Once risk has been identified, the next stage is to determine the extent of the risk. This should be evaluated in light of the impact that the risk might have on the profitability, liquidity and, indeed, the survival of the company. Risk and return are related and a company that accepts a high level of risk exposure can make huge profits; however, it can also make huge losses. At the strategic level, the board must decide whether the company should be a risk taker (i.e. a speculator), or a risk avoider (i.e. a hedger), or agree some level of risk-taking activity that reflects corporate attitude. Cost is also an influencing factor. Hedging has its costs and a company will weigh up whether the cost of hedging outweighs the benefits received from hedging (for example, losses possible from a movement in exchange rates and the likelihood of these happening).

Managing Risks

Several approaches can be taken in respect of the management of market risk. These are now outlined briefly.

Choosing to Do Nothing about Risk

A large company may elect to stay exposed to risk. It may be a risk taker and may have attracted equity holders who support this approach in the hope of making excess gains over normal trading activities. Other large companies may not hedge because they feel that the cost of hedging outweighs the benefits. They may take the view that profits and losses associated with changes in interest rates, currency rates and commodity prices even out in the long term and the company will be no better or no worse off. If a company has a strategy of not hedging, then it needs to ensure that it holds sufficient cash to cover unexpected changes in trading and finance cash flows. This strategy might not be appropriate in companies that have high levels of business and financial risk, as there is less cash flexibility in these types of company.

Avoiding Risk Totally

Companies that avoid risk might only enter into contracts that are risk-free. They may have a policy of only supplying to reputable customers in countries with stable economies and may demand payment in their own currency. Likewise they may purchase locally or from reputable companies in countries that have stable economies. They might only purchase goods if the supplier agrees a price that is denominated in their own currency. This effectively means that currency risk is transferred fully to the third parties in each transaction. Companies with this approach are likely to miss many profit-making opportunities. Suppliers are going to factor the risks accepted into the price they quote for the supplies and customers will be willing to purchase the product only when the exchange rate makes the price favourable.

Policy of Reducing Exposure

A company can adopt a policy of reducing the risk exposures identified, or some of the exposures identified. Non-contractual exposures are difficult to manage; however, a large company may diversify its interests globally in an attempt to diversify away some of the risks associated with currencies and indeed countries. For example, a company may relocate a factory close to the sales marketplace for a particular product and may start to source supplies locally. This will reduce currency risk, which would arise if the product was being manufactured in one country and sold in another. Another example is where a company that is selling goods to one country may start to source supplies in that country. When the sales and the purchases cash flows are the same, the exposure to movements in the exchange rate between the two countries is reduced. Some companies diversify their product range in an attempt to diversify their risk.

Contractual exposures are easier to manage. There are two approaches. The first is to pay a premium to transfer downside risks to another company (e.g. an insurance company/bank) that specialises in diversifying risk exposures. In return for a premium, an insurance company will reimburse the premium holder for losses made if the underlying factor (e.g. interest rate/currency rate/commodity price) moves in such a manner as to cause the company to make losses on a contract. In these instances, the policy-holding company is able to reap the rewards from gains made if the factor price moves in such a way as to benefit the company.

The second approach involves transferring the full risk of the contract to a third party for a fee. The practice of transferring risks is called **hedging**. There are always investors, companies or financial institutions that want to take risks in the hope that they can make a good return. In addition, there may be companies on the opposite end of a similar transaction that wish to reduce their risk and that will enter into a contract to hedge (reduce) their risk exposure. A simple example of a hedged transaction is where one company sells to another company in a foreign country at an agreed price and an agreed exchange rate. In this example, both companies have hedged their positions. Though one will lose and one will gain from this agreement, both will be happy that they are not exposed to the risk of loss, which might occur if the market price of the product or the exchange rate were to change.

HEDGING

Several standard **financial instruments** (paper agreements) are utilised to hedge risks. These are commonly called derivatives (short for derivative financial instruments). In simple terms, a derivative is a contract to buy or sell an asset or liability at an agreed price at some point in the future. Though they are primarily designed to reduce risks, some investors/companies/financial institutions use them for speculative purposes. Speculators do not have the underlying asset. They buy and sell paper assets in an attempt to make a profit on the price movements over the term of the derivative. The advantages and disadvantages of hedging are outlined in **Figure 19.6**.

FIGURE 19.6: ADVANTAGES AND DISADVANTAGES OF HEDGING

ADVANTAGES	DISADVANTAGES
• **Risk reduction:** hedging reduces risk. Currency fluctuations can cut profitability overnight. Changes in interest rates can push up fixed costs, and so hedging can avert bankruptcy risks and can control financial risk. • **Planning made easier:** hedging reduces the uncertainty associated with financial planning as future cash flows are more certain.	• **Speculative profits missed:** a company cannot claim speculative gains when the value of the underlying hedged asset moves in such a manner as would favour the company. • **Costly:** hedging is not free. It is costly to set up a hedging agreement. This agreement is usually a legally binding agreement between two or more parties. • **Additional controls:** treasury departments typically have strong controls in place to ensure that one person does not have full control of derivative transactions. • **Expertise:** to effectively hedge transactions, business finance managers require specialist training in derivatives and in risk management.

DERIVATIVES

Derivatives are commonly used to manage the contractual risks that arise in a company's normal business activities, such as currency risk, interest rate risk and commodity price risk. The most commonly used derivatives are futures contracts, forward contracts, swap contracts and options. These are now explained in turn.

Futures Contracts

A **futures contract** is an agreement between two parties wherein a specified asset will be bought or sold, at a predefined price on a specified date in the future. The underlying asset is typically money, currency or commodities. However, it is possible for the underlying asset to be anything of value. For example, there are futures contracts that have equity shares, stock market indices, gold or bonds as the underlying asset. Indeed, futures contracts are also used to trade EU carbon allowances (EUAs). These contracts are a standard size: 1,000 EUAs. One EUA allows the holder to emit one tonne of carbon dioxide. Financial futures are traded on financial exchanges and are traded in standard sizes (for example, the Sterling/euro and Sterling/dollar futures on the NYSE Liffe exchange have a standard contract size of £10,000; however, depending on the exchange, they can be £62,500 or €125,000); and have standard delivery dates, terms and conditions.

The Mechanics of Trading in Futures Contracts

All futures contracts are traded on a futures exchange. When a finance manager starts trading in futures, he or she **opens** a futures position by either buying or selling a future contract. To **close** the contract the opposite occurs. The company then sells or buys a similar future contract. Most futures contracts are 'closed' before their maturity date. When a finance manager believes that the price of the underlying asset will increase, they usually buy futures **long**. This means the finance manager is going to buy the underlying asset at an agreed higher price on an agreed date. When a finance manager believes that the price of the underlying asset will fall, he or she usually sells futures **short**. This means the finance manager will sell the underlying asset at a lower agreed price on an agreed date.

Exchanges normally disclose two prices for each future contract. The **bid price** is the price at which the exchange is willing to buy futures contracts. The **offer price** is the price at which the exchange is willing to sell a futures contract. The difference between the bid price and the offer price is called the **spread**. Anyone wishing to deal in futures usually approaches a broker (a member of an exchange), who subsequently instructs a market-maker. At the outset the parties to a futures contract have to give an initial **margin** to the exchange. This is a liquidity deposit for the exchange, which is refunded when the futures contract is closed. No money changes hands in respect of the futures contract. Futures contracts are usually **marked-to-market** daily, meaning that the parties to a futures contract must make good any loss, or can withdraw any benefit from movements in the price of the underlying asset from the exchange, on a daily basis. They have to keep the margin at an agreed level. Futures are measured in terms of **ticks**. A 'tick' is one hundredth of a percent (0.01%) and this is the smallest movement allowed by the market in the value of a future. They are traded at a percentage value, e.g. 90.00 means that the future is worth 90% of its nominal value.

How a futures contract can be utilised to hedge risk exposure

The price of a futures contract is normally the current price of the underlying asset plus a premium for financing costs and holding costs less any income receivable from the asset during the futures period. Therefore, to hedge against an asset falling in value, the holder of the asset should sell futures short, then, before the maturity of the futures contract, buy back (close) the futures contract. The losses made on the underlying asset will be compensated for by the profit made on the futures contract. This is shown in **Worked Example 19.1**.

Worked Example 19.1: Commodity Futures Contracts for Hedging

In April 20X5 the futures market for corn was quoting a bid price of €/£2.00 a bushel. A co-operative decides to lock into this price for the benefit of its members, so it sells 100 futures contracts (there are 5,000 bushels in each contract). The futures are due to mature when the harvest season is over in September. The co-operative is hedging against a fall in the potential sale price of corn.

Requirement

(a) Calculate the profit/loss made by the co-operative assuming the market value of each bushel falls to €/£1.20 each.

(b) Calculate the profit/loss made by the co-operative assuming the market value of each bushel rises to €/£2.40 each.

Solution

The actual cash flows are now detailed.

In April 20X5 the co-operative considers that it will have to sell 500,000 bushels of corn for its members at harvest time (i.e. in September) and considers that €/£2.00 (the current market price) is a fair price. Therefore, to hedge against price movements, the co-operative sells 100 corn futures contracts at €/£2.00 for each bushel (€/£1,000,000 in total). The only money to change hands at this stage is the margin that the co-operative will have to post with the relevant exchange. This is refundable at a later stage.

(a) By September the market price has fallen to €/£1.20.

The co-operative now has to take two steps. It will sell the 500,000 bushels of corn in the market place for €/£1.20 each (€/£600,000) and will buy 100 futures contracts at €/£1.20 each (commodity futures contracts usually reflect the current market price of the underlying assets). This closes out its initial futures contract. Therefore, it will make a margin of 80c/p [€/£2.00 – €/£1.20] on each bushel under the futures contract, which amounts to €/£400,000 profit on the futures contract.

Therefore, the co-operative has secured a net sale price of €/£2.00, made up of a cash price of €/£1.20 [in total 500,000 × €/£1.20 = €/£600,000] and a profit on the futures contract of 80c/p a bushel [in total 500,000 × 80c/p = €/£400,000].

The profit on the futures contract will have been received by the co-operative throughout the life of the futures contract as it will have been marked-to-market at the close of business every day and any surplus made over the initial margin withdrawn by the co-operative.

(b) The actual cash flow is as detailed above. The approach is similar to that in (a). By September the market price has risen to €/£2.40.

The co-operative now has to take two steps. It will sell the 500,000 bushels of corn in the market place for €/£2.40 each (€/£1,200,000) and will buy 100 futures contracts at €/£2.40 each (commodity futures contracts usually reflect current market price of the underlying assets). This closes out its initial futures contract. Therefore, it will make a loss of 40c/p [€/£2.00 − €/£2.40] on each bushel under the futures contract, which amounts to a loss of €/£200,000 overall.

Therefore, the co-operative has secured a net sale price of €/£2.00 (€/£1,000,000), as intended. It is now made up of a cash price of €/£2.40 (€/£1,200,000) and a loss on the futures contract of 40c/p a bushel (€/£200,000).

The €/£200,000 loss will already have been paid by the co-operative to the exchange over the life of the futures contract as the contracts are marked-to-market every day. With every increase in price, the corresponding opportunity revenue lost will be paid to the exchange to maintain the margin.

How to Speculate using a Futures Contract

Futures contracts can also be utilised for speculative purposes. In these circumstances the investor does not own the underlying asset; they are gambling on the suspected movement in the value of the underlying asset. This is shown in **Worked Example 19.2**.

Worked Example 19.2: Futures Contracts for Speculative Profits

In April 20X5 the futures market for corn was quoting a bid price of €/£2.00 a bushel. An investor is diversifying his portfolio of investments and decides that he will put a portion of his wealth into the futures markets. He thinks that the price of corn will rise, therefore he buys 100 futures contracts long (there are 5,000 bushels in each contract). The futures are due to mature when the harvest season is over in September. The investor has no corn and has no intention of ever owning the underlying corn!

Requirement

(a) Calculate the profit/loss made by the investor assuming the market value of each bushel rises to €/£2.40.

(b) Calculate the profit/loss made by the investor assuming the market value of each bushel falls to €/£1.20.

Solution

The actual cash flows are now detailed.

In April 20X5 the investor decides to buy 100 corn futures contracts (the underlying price of the corn is €/£2.00 a bushel). The only money to change hands at this stage is the margin, which the investor will have to post with the relevant exchange. This is refundable at a later stage.

(a) By September the market price has risen to €/£2.40.

In September the investor will sell 100 futures contracts at €/£2.40 each (commodity futures contracts usually reflect the current market price of the underlying assets). This closes out their initial futures contract. Therefore, they will make a profit of 40c/p [€/£2.40 − €/£2.00] on each bushel, which amounts to a profit of €/£200,000 overall.

(b) The actual cash flow is as detailed above. The approach is similar to that in (a). By September the market price has fallen to €/£1.20 per bushel.

In September the investor will sell 100 futures contracts at €/£1.20 each. This closes out their initial futures contract. Therefore, the investor will lose 80c/p [€/£2.00 − €/£1.20] on each bushel, which amounts to a loss of €/£400,000 overall.

This deficit on the futures contract will have been paid to the exchange by the investor throughout the life of the futures contract as it will have been marked-to-market at the close of business every day and any deficit made over the initial margin lodged by the investor, or the broker acting on the investor's behalf. The investor can close out the futures contract at any time.

Forward Contracts

Futures contracts are standardised, with set sizes, terms and conditions, and maturity dates. This may not suit some companies that are trying to hedge a value that is different from the standard sizes, or have delivery dates that do not correspond to the standard dates. In these circumstances, a company can buy or sell a forward contract. **Forward contracts** are bespoke futures contracts. Like a futures contract, no cash exchanges hands on inception; however, a margin may be posted by both parties to the contract as collateral. The price agreed for the asset on maturity is calculated in the same way as the price under a futures contract. There are two major differences. First, forward contracts are not traded on an exchange – they are usually administered over-the-counter (OTC) by a bank on behalf of its customer. Secondly, they are not marked-to-market. The overall difference between the spot price and the forward price is determined and settled at maturity. The difference is called the **forward premium** (the profit) or **forward discount** (the loss), as shown in **Worked Example 19.3**.

Worked Example 19.3: Forward Contracts for Hedging Purposes

Ringo Plc wishes to sell a building. Star Plc wishes to purchase the property in two years' time. The current market value of the property is €/£750,000. Ringo Plc has a cost of capital of 10%. Star Plc has a cost of capital of 12%. It costs Ringo Plc €/£10,000 each year to insure and maintain the building, payable at the start of each year.

Requirement

(a) Calculate the minimum forward price that Ringo Plc will accept before signing up to a forward rate contract with Star Plc.

(b) Calculate the profit/loss made by Ringo Plc and Star Plc if the market value of the property:

 (i) rises to €/£1,000,000;

 (ii) rises to €/£850,000.

Solution

(a) The minimum forward price that Ringo Plc will agree to must cover the market value of the building plus the opportunity cost of holding the building for a further two years. This opportunity cost will include the revenue foregone from not investing the funds that the company could receive now and any incidental costs or revenues that are expected to occur in the two-year period.

Therefore, Ringo Plc will only sign up if the forward price agreed is equal to, or greater than €/£930,600, made up as follows:

	Costs €/£	**Cumulative €/£**
Spot price	750,000	750,000
Costs in Year 1 (Insurance)	10,000	760,000
Return foregone in Year 1:		
(€/£760,000 × 10%)	76,000	836,000
Costs in Year 2 (Insurance)	10,000	846,000
Return foregone in Year 2:		
(€/£846,000 × 10%)	84,600	930,600

(b) (i) If the market value of the property in two years' time is €/£1,000,000, then Ringo Plc will have made a loss on the contract of €/£69,400 [€/£1,000,000 – €/£930,600]. Star Plc will have made a profit on the contract of the same amount.

(ii) If the market value of the property in two years' time is €/£850,000, then Ringo Plc will make a profit of €/£80,600 [€/£930,600 – €/£850,000] and Star Plc will make a loss on the forward contract of the same amount.

The advantages and disadvantages of forwards over futures are summarised in **Figure 19.7**.

FIGURE 19.7: FORWARDS VERSUS FUTURES

ADVANTAGES OF FORWARDS OVER FUTURES	DISADVANTAGES OF FORWARDS OVER FUTURES
• **Bespoke:** the dates and amounts in a forward contract can be tailored to suit the needs of the investor, while futures contracts are standardised. • **Perfect hedge:** in a forward contract the amount and timing of the contract can be changed to form a perfect hedge, or as near to a perfect hedge as is possible. • **Assets:** forward contracts can be written in respect of any asset. Futures contracts usually cover set assets. For example, futures are not available for every currency, nor for individual properties.	• **Cost:** forward contracts are usually more costly to set up because they are bespoke. • **Less flexible:** the futures contract can be closed out at any time up until the maturity of the future, and is usually closed out after the sale/purchase of the underlying asset. The futures contract is therefore like an option, which must be exercised by a set date. The forward contract does not have this option period.

Swap Contracts

A **swap** is a written contractual agreement between two counterparties to exchange one stream of cash flows for another stream of cash flows. The two cash flow streams are called the **legs of the swap**. Like both futures and forward contracts, the underlying asset – called the principal amount – is normally not exchanged between counterparties. The five main types of swaps are summarised in **Figure 19.8**.

FIGURE 19.8: TYPES OF SWAP CONTRACT

Total return swap	One party to the contract (A) swaps the total return (e.g. capital gain/loss plus any interest/dividend received) on a notional asset with the other party (B) for periodic interest payments on the capital value of the notional asset, which can be fixed or floating. Therefore, B can get access to the return on the asset, without owning it; whereas A (which has the asset on its balance sheet) has hedged its exposure to a loss in the asset value and income from the notional asset.
Equity swap	A total return swap. The notional principal asset in an equity swap is a particular type of equity share, a basket of equity shares or an equity share index.
Credit default swap	This is like an insurance agreement. In a credit default swap, one party (the buyer) pays the other party a stream of payments in return for credit protection from the swap seller for a particular debt from a third party. If the third party defaults, the seller has to make good the difference between the amount received (the recoverable amount) from the third party and the notional amount noted in the swap agreement.
Plain vanilla swap	A straight exchange of the right to pay a fixed rate of interest on a notional principal amount for the right to pay a variable rate of interest on the notional principal amount.
Currency swap	Involves exchanging both the principal and the repayments (capital and interest) in one currency with the principal and repayments in another currency.

Most swaps are bespoke and are traded OTC, usually through banks, though some can be obtained in the derivatives markets. The extent of trading activity on swaps is detailed in **Real World Example 19.2**.

REAL WORLD EXAMPLE 19.2: GLOBAL SWAP ACTIVITY

The Bank for International Settlements noted that OTC derivatives of $595 trillion were outstanding at the end of June 2018 and the amount outstanding on Credit Default Swaps was $9.4 trillion.

Swaps are typically used to hedge risk exposures (usually interest rate risk or currency risk), though they can be used for speculative purposes. Normally, one leg is variable in nature, the other is fixed. The party with the variable cash flows wants fixed cash flows (hedging their position); the party with the fixed cash flows wants variable cash flows (speculating on changes in the rate to be applied to the underlying asset value). This is normally called a **fixed-to-floating rate swap**. The party that pays floating and receives fixed is said to be *short* in the swap and the party that pays fixed and receives floating is said to be *long* in the swap. The variable rate is usually pegged to an independent source, such as LIBOR, the European Bank's base rate, or the FTSE 100 index.

Valuation of Swap Contracts

A swap is valued as the net present value (NPV) of the expected future cash flows. At the outset, the NPV of a swap agreement is zero as the initial set-up fee that transfers between the counterparties will equal the expected benefit to be derived, otherwise the party with the better expected stream of cash flows will not agree to the swap. It is only when the actual cash flows differ (due to changes in the underlying variable rate) from expected cash flows that either party makes a profit or a loss on the swap.

Swaps are normally arranged by a dealer, who takes a cut on the cash flows that are being exchanged. For example, if a company wishes to change floating for fixed rate debt and they agree to pay a fixed rate of 7.5%, then a broker may agree the exchange but charge them 7.6% for the swap. The dealer will then close out this swap with another company that is looking for variable rate payments, and will also take a margin on the cash flow agreed with that party.

Options

Options are derivative financial instruments that convey the right, but not the obligation, to undertake a transaction at a specified **exercise price** (also known as the **strike price**) on or before a specified date, which is referred to as the **exercise date.** A **call option** is a term used to describe an option that conveys the right to buy a certain quantity of an asset at a set price (the exercise price), on or before the exercise date. The holder of a call option will only exercise it on or before the exercise date, if the market value of the underlying asset to be purchased is worth more than the pre-agreed exercise price. Indeed, the price of the asset would need to move to the exercise price plus the option price before the holder makes a gain. The value of a call option is the difference between the market value of the underlying asset and the exercise price. When the market value of the underlying asset is less than the exercise price, the call option is worthless. For example, when the call option specifies that the exercise price that the holder can buy at is €/£2.00 per share and the option was purchased for 10c/p. Then the transaction will be worthless if the market value of the share price falls below €/£2.00, as the holder will not exercise the option but will just buy the shares at the lower price. If the market value is €/£2.00, the holder may, or may not exercise the option – in this instance, the holder will make a loss that is equal to the price of the option (10c/p). The holder starts to make money when the market value of the share rises above €/£2.10 [€/£2.00 + €/£0.10].

A **put option** is a term used to describe an option that conveys the right to sell a certain quantity of an asset at a predetermined exercise price on, or before, the exercise date. The holder of a put option will only sell on the exercise date if the exercise price of the asset is higher than the market value of the underlying asset. The value of a put option will be the exercise price less the market value of the underlying asset. When the market value of the underlying asset is higher than the exercise price, the put option is worthless as the holder of the asset can sell the asset for a higher price in the marketplace. The holder of a put option will make money when the market value of the asset is less than the exercise price, net of the option price – for example, when the put option specifies that the exercise price that the holder can sell at is €/£2.00 per share and the option was purchased for 10c/p. Then the transaction will be worthless if the market value of the share moves above €/£2.00, as the holder will not exercise the option but will just sell the shares at the higher price. If the market value is €/£2.00, the holder may, or may not exercise the option – in this instance the holder will make a loss that equals to the price of the option (10c/p). The holder starts to make money when the market value of the share falls below €/£1.90 [€/£2.00 − €/£0.10].

Sometimes the holder of equity shares may hedge their position against both upward and downward price movements. To do this they will hold both a call and a put option with the same exercise date and price. This is called a **straddle**. A variety of other combinations are also possible depending on the holder's perception of how share price will move; a **strip** is created when two puts are combined with one call option, a **strap** is combining two calls and one put option. Finally, another commonly used strategy is a **covered call**. This is where a holder buys a stock and sells a call option. If the share price rises, the trader exercises their option if it falls, the trader's loss is reduced by the amount received from the sale of the call option. In all instances the writer of an option will hold an equal, but opposite, position and will make a gain/loss that will be equivalent to the loss/gain being made by the holder. Trading in options for speculative purposes is risky, with the trader likely to make high returns, or to suffer high losses. This is highlighted in **Worked Example 19.4**.

Worked Example 19.4: Trading in Options versus Buying Shares

Pero Plc has €/£500,000 to invest. The company has decided to invest this into either options, or equity shares. The company is strong, has steady returns and has pigeonholed this €/£500,000 for investment in risky-type investments, in the hope that premium returns can be made. This strategy has been agreed at board level.

Assume that the finance manager has decided to invest in one particular company, Zena Plc. At present Zena Plc's share price is €/£2.50 per share and its call options are 40c/p per share with an exercise price of €/£2.40.

Requirement Prepare calculations to show the profits/(losses) that will result if the finance manager elects to purchase shares in Zena Plc, or call options in Zena Plc. In your answer assume two outcomes. By the exercise date, the share price will either:

(a) rise to €/£3.10; or
(b) fall to €/£2.00.

Solution

The finance manager can either decide to purchase shares or call options.

(a) Share price rises to €/£3.10

Assume the finance manager purchases shares in Zena Plc.

Purchase 200,000 [€/£500,000 ÷ €/£2.50] shares	(€/£500,000)
Sale value on exercise date [200,000 × €/£3.10]	€/£620,000
Profit on sale	€/£120,000
Return on investment [€/£120,000 ÷ €/£500,000]	24%

Assume the finance manager purchases call options in Zena Plc.

Purchase 1,250,000 [€/£500,000 ÷ €/£0.40] options	(€/£500,000)
Exercise price [1,250,000 × €/£2.40]	(€/£3,000,000)
Sale at market value [1,250,000 × €/£3.10]	€/£3,875,000
Profit on sale	€/£375,000
Return on investment [€/£375,000 ÷ €/£500,000]	75%

(b) Share price falls to €/£2.00

Assume the finance manager purchases shares in Zena Plc.

Purchase 200,000 [€/£500,000 ÷ €/£2.50] shares	(€/£500,000)
Sale value on exercise date [200,000 × €/£2.00]	€/£400,000
Loss on investment	(€/£100,000)

Assume the finance manager purchases call options in Zena Plc.

Purchase 1,250,000 [€/£500,000 ÷ €/£0.40] options	(€/£500,000)
Loss on investment	(€/£500,000)*

*In this instance, the finance manager will not exercise the option, therefore the loss is restricted to the cost of the options.

Options are traded separately on equity exchanges; however, they can also be arranged OTC, usually through a financial intermediary. **Exchange traded options (listed options)** are standardised agreements that are administered by a clearing house. Exchange traded options include commodity options, bond options, interest rate options, index options (for example, an equity index such as the FTSE 100), options on futures contracts and employee share options. **Employee share options** are options that are issued to employees by a company as a form of compensation. Options can be written into any contract, including mortgages (e.g. the right, but not the obligation, to repay capital each year in lump sums up to a certain amount) and real estate deals (e.g. the right to purchase adjoining land in three years' time at a set price) and bespoke option agreements, or **over-the-counter options** (also called **dealer options**) can be brokered through a dealer. These are not listed on any exchange and typically include interest rate options, currency options and **swaptions** (options on swap agreements).

There are a variety of mathematical models that are used to predict how the value of an option will change in response to changes to the variables that will impact on an option's value. Two models are considered in this chapter: the binomial model and the Black–Scholes model.

Binomial Model

The **binomial model** values an option based on the assumption that share price will be one of two amounts, one a low value, the other a high value. Though the binomial model approach is straightforward, it is constrained by the unrealistic assumption that the share price has only two possible outcomes. This constraint is eliminated by the Black–Sholes model that assumes that the share price return between the period of valuation and exercise date is normally distributed. This is considered to be a more realistic assumption.

Black–Scholes Model

The **Black–Scholes model** is named after its founders – Fischer Black and Myron Scholes.[2] The model assumes that capital markets are in equilibrium and a portfolio of shares and call options can be created that is risk-free (the options hedge the holder against risk). Therefore, the option is priced assuming that the rate of return on the underlying equity assets is equal to the risk-free rate of return. The model assumes that the value of the option is dependent not on the expected return on the share but on the current market price of the asset, the exercise price, the cost of holding the underlying asset (for example, interest and dividends), the time to the exercise date, restrictions on exercise dates and an estimate of the future volatility of market returns of the asset over the term of the option. The first four of these variables are relatively easy to determine. The last is estimated. A typical approach is to view the variability of returns of the asset in the past and to use this as a proxy for the expected variability of returns in the future.

The Black–Scholes model to value a call option is as follows:

$$P_0 = PsN(d_1) - Xe^{-rT}N(d_2)$$

where P_0 is the current value of the option, Ps is the current value of the asset, X is the exercise price, e is the exponential constant (2.7183), r is the risk-free rate of interest for the period and T is the time (in years) remaining in the option contract. $N(d_1)$ and $N(d_2)$ are values of the cumulative normal distribution, defined as:

$$d_1 = \frac{\text{Ln}(Ps/X) + rT}{\sigma\sqrt{T}} + 0.5\,\sigma\sqrt{T}$$

and

$$d_2 = d_1 - \sigma\sqrt{T}$$

where Ln is the natural logarithm and σ is the standard deviation of the return on the share; σ^2 is the variance of the return on the share (i.e. the changes in market value and income). The valuation of an option is shown in **Worked Example 19.7**.

WORKED EXAMPLE 19.7: VALUING AN OPTION

Sherry Plc is offered 100 options by one of the companies that it invests in (Gallagher Plc). The current market price of Gallagher Plc's shares is €/£2.00. The exercise price written into the option agreement is €/£2.40. At the present time, the continuously compound rate of interest is 6%. The option is open for three years.

Requirement Calculate the price that Sherry Plc should pay for the options, given that the return on Gallagher's shares over the past year has a standard deviation of 25%.

[2] Robert Merton and Myron Scholes were awarded a Nobel Prize in Economics in 1997 for their groundbreaking work in relation to this model (Fischer Black passed away in 1995).

Solution

$$P_0 = PsN(d_1) - Xe^{-rT}N(d_2)$$

P_0 is the current value of the option (?)
Ps is the current value of the asset (€/£2.00)
X is the exercise price (€/£2.40)
e is the exponential constant (2.7183)
r is the risk-free rate of interest for the period (6%)
T is the time (in years) remaining in the option contract (3 years)
σ is the standard deviation (0.25)

$$d_1 = \frac{Ln(Ps/X) + rT}{\sigma\sqrt{T}} + 0.5\,\sigma\sqrt{T}$$

$$d_1 = \frac{Ln(200/240) + (0.06)(3)}{(0.25) \times \sqrt{3}} + 0.5(0.25)(\sqrt{3})$$

$$d_1 = 0.2111$$
$$N(d_1) = 0.5832^*$$

* This value is obtained from **Appendix G**.

$$d_2 = d_1 - \sigma\sqrt{T}$$
$$= 0.2111 - (0.25)\sqrt{3}$$
$$d_2 = -0.2218$$
$$N(d_2) = 1 - 0.5871^* = 0.4129$$
$$PsN(d_1) - Xe^{-rT}N(d_2)$$

*This value is obtained from **Appendix G**.

Therefore, the value of the option is:

$$P_0 = 200(0.5832) - 240 \times 2.7183^{-0.06\times3} \times 0.4129$$

$$P_0 = 116.64 - 82.77$$
$$P_0 = 33.86 \text{ (€/£0.34)}$$

Sherry Plc should offer €/£34 for the 100 options (€/£0.34 × 100).

Though the Black–Scholes model is used in practice, it is academic. As such it has a number of assumptions that are also regarded as limitations (see **Figure 19.9**).

FIGURE 19.9: ASSUMPTIONS OF THE BLACK–SCHOLES MODEL

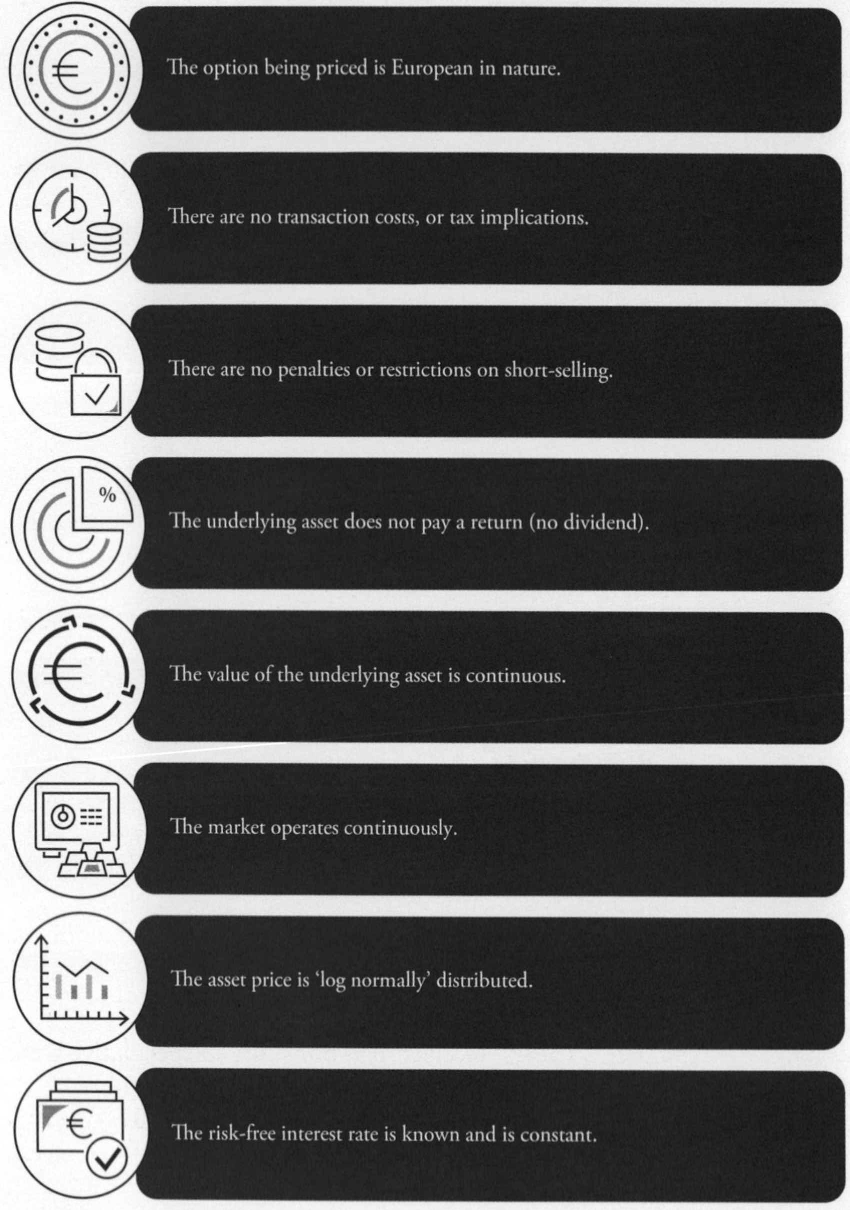

The option being priced is European in nature.
There are no transaction costs, or tax implications.
There are no penalties or restrictions on short-selling.
%
The underlying asset does not pay a return (no dividend).
The value of the underlying asset is continuous.
The market operates continuously.
The asset price is 'log normally' distributed.
The risk-free interest rate is known and is constant.

Regardless of the model that is used to value options, two variables are regarded as influencing the price of an option – both are risk-related: the length of time to the exercise date; and the variability in the returns of the asset. Options with longer exercise times and greater variability in expected returns will be valued higher than options that have short lifespans and lower variability in expected returns.

Options Applied to Financing and Investment Decision-making

It has been argued that managers should apply the principles laid down in the Black–Scholes model to other decisions, such as deciding on whether to invest in a particular venture that may have an option to expand/grow in the future. By using the Black–Scholes model and data for the five key variables, a value can be placed on the option to expand/grow, which should be taken into consideration at the outset. In other instances finance managers may purchase call options on the ability to purchase, for example, land that may be required for expansion in the future. A variety of financial assets also have options (usually call options) written into them. For example, warrants may be issued with equity or debt as a sweetener to entice investors to invest in the company. A **warrant** gives the holder the right to purchase equity shares from the company at a set price before a specified future date. A **convertible bond** is similar. It gives the holder the right to exchange their bond for a specified number of shares on or before a specified future date. A **callable bond** puts flexibility into the hands of the issuer, by allowing them to repurchase the bond back in any period up to the maturity date. These financial products have been discussed in more detail in **Chapter 13**.

CONCLUSION

Advances in technology (e.g. the internet, cloud technology) and improvements in transport have resulted in an active world economy. Most companies that are beyond a certain size are likely to transact with third parties in various countries throughout the world. Some countries have comparative advantage over other countries because of their natural resources, tax status, etc. If a multinational company does not take advantage of country-specific efficiencies, it will be left behind in the profit race game. Companies that wish to be competitive on a worldwide basis have to adopt global strategies.

Dealing globally increases the number and level of risks to which a company is exposed. Increased risk leads to increased uncertainty in planning and controlling an entity's cash flows and profits. Most companies adopt a policy to manage risk. The starting point in this process is the identification of risks. A company can have risks that are hedged internally. The key is to highlight risks that put the company's cash flows and value at risk and to take steps to hedge these. A variety of methods can be utilised, including in-house steps, such as netting, matching, aligning supply purchases in countries where sales take place, etc. Alternatively, financial derivatives can be utilised to hedge risk exposure or to make speculative gains.

Derivatives have, over the past 20 years, received bad press due to speculative trading going wrong for dealers in a number of companies. In these instances, it would seem that procedural error (e.g. lack of control) and fraud were more to blame than the actual derivatives themselves. There is no doubt that derivatives that are used for speculative purposes are risky. Indeed, derivatives work because two parties take bets on what will happen in the marketplace. For example, they may bet on the direction of the movement in interest rates. One bets that they will rise, the other that they will fall. Both parties have to have opposite views, and there will be one winner and one loser. For this reason, derivatives are regarded to be a **zero sum game**. Derivatives reduce risk if they are utilised correctly, but they are costly and a company has to weigh up the costs and benefits of getting involved in these instruments.

KEY TERMS

Bid price
Binomial model
Black–Scholes model
Call option
Centralised treasury department
Contractual risks
Convertible bond
Corporate finance
Corporate treasurer
Cost centre
Covered call
Credit default swap
Dealer options
Derivatives
Employee share options
Equity management
Equity swap
Exchange traded options
Exercise date
Exercise price
Exposure
Financial instruments
Fixed-to-floating rate swap
Forward contract
Forward discount
Forward premium
Funding management
Futures contract
Global financial transactions
Hedging
Legs of the swap
Listed options
Long position
Marked-to-market
Market risk
Multinationals
Non-contractual risks
Offer price
Open position
Options
Over-the-counter options
Plain vanilla swap
Profit centre
Risk
Put option
Short position
Spread
Straddle
Strap
Strip
Strike price
Swap
Swaptions
Tax haven
Tick
Total return swap
Treasury
Treasury management
Warrant
Zero sum game

REVIEW QUESTIONS

(See Suggested Solutions to Review Questions in **Appendix B**.)

Question 19.1

Why do companies use derivative financial instruments?

Question 19.2

A company purchased call options for 10,000 equity shares in ABC Plc at 25c/p per share one year ago when the share price was €/£1.50. The exercise price on the call option is €/£1.80. The current price is €/£2.10.

Requirement

(a) Should the company exercise the call options?
(b) What is the profit/(loss) on the transaction?
(c) What would the profit/(loss) on the transaction be if the current price was €/£1.60?
(d) What could the profit/(loss) be if the monies that were invested in options were utilised instead to purchase shares?
(***Note:*** assume the current price is €/£2.10, then rework assuming it is €/£1.60.)

Question 19.3

What are the determinants of an option's value?

Question 19.4

Determine the value of a call option on an equity share (that does not pay a dividend) using the Black–Scholes model, using the following information:

The current share price is €/£7.50, the exercise price is €/£8.00, the exercise date is six months' time, the risk-free rate of interest (continuously compounded) is 7% and the standard deviation of returns on the share in the past has been 40%.

CHALLENGING QUESTIONS

(Suggested Solutions to Challenging Questions are available through your lecturer.)

Question 19.1 Mega

Mega Plc operates a large chain of supermarkets that are located in several countries worldwide. At present the Supermarket Country Manager is responsible for treasury management at country level.

Given that Mega is part of a worldwide multinational group, advise management on possible ways to optimise the treasury structure.

8 Marks

(Based on Chartered Accountants Ireland, SFMA, Mock Exam 2009, Extract from Q4)

Question 19.2 Agency Theory

Discuss the implications of agency theory using a treasury department's derivative investment manager as an example.

Question 19.3 Sesco (Level 2)

Sesco Plc operates 37 supermarket stores selling food and other household supplies in the domestic market.

There is considerable competition between the various supermarket chains operating in Ireland. In recent years there have been examples of too many supermarkets attempting to operate in some catchment areas, where the size of the customer base was too small to support the number of outlets. Also, there have been examples of national and local price wars breaking out (between Sesco and its competitors) as a result of one or more operators attempting to increase market share.

Requirement

(a) Set out briefly the strategic risks associated with a 'domestic company' such as Sesco expanding its operations into a foreign country.

6 Marks

(b) Discuss the role of management accountants in risk management.

10 Marks
Total 16 Marks

(Based on Chartered Accountants Ireland, CAP 2, SFMA, Summer 2009, Extract from Q1)

Question 19.4 Starling (Level 2)

Mr Jim Starling, the managing director of Starling Products Limited, has become increasingly stressed recently due to the rapid expansion of the company. Starling, which manufactures cleaning products, has grown from a small, domestically focussed producer to a major player in the European market. Sales to the US and Asian markets were also increasing for Starling.

Starling had been founded by Jim's father, Mike Starling, and for the first 25 years of its existence sold all of its output to supermarket chains and hardware shops in Ireland. In 20X4 Jim's nephew, Paul Neilson, developed a new chemical for cleaning windows that was dramatically more effective than any other product on the market. Jim saw an opportunity and offered Paul a 25% shareholding in Starling in return for the sole rights to manufacture and sell this new chemical. Paul had acquired a European patent on the product at this stage.

Revenues had grown from €/£1,600,000 in 20X4 to €/£17,500,000 in 20Y2, but in many ways Starling had not changed as it grew. Its management structure was the same in 20Y2 as it had been in 20X0. Jim's wife, Ellen, was Starling's only other director and worked part-time in Starling with a responsibility for credit control and general working capital management. Ellen was struggling to deal with all of Starling's new debtors, many of whom were overseas. Jim also felt he no longer had a sense for how Starling was performing as it had grown so big and complex.

The priority right now for Jim was expanding production capacity. Starling currently manufactures its products in a factory in the west of Ireland, which is operating at maximum capacity.

Requirement Identify FOUR key risks facing Starling and outline how Starling should address each of these risks (ignore interest rate risk).

8 Marks

(Based on Chartered Accountants Ireland, CAP 2, MABF, Summer 2013, Q3)

Question 19.5 Endeavour (Level 2)

It is 1 June 20X5 and Lincoln Schofield is currently employed as the treasury expert at Endeavour Plc, a listed company that has a policy of hedging all currency and interest rate risk. Endeavour estimates that upwards of €/£250 million worth of transactions are hedged in any one financial year. All derivative transactions are fully controlled by Lincoln, given his specialist knowledge in the area.

Requirement Comment critically on Endeavour's policy of hedging all currency and interest rate risks and the centralisation of control in Lincoln Schofield over all derivative transactions. Your answer should include any recommendations for improvement.

6 Marks

(Based on Chartered Accountants Ireland, CAP 2, MABF, Summer 2010, Q4(a))

Question 19.6 (Level 1)

The details of a call option are as follows: current share price is £100; the exercise price is £95; the risk-free rate of interest is 10% per annum. The standard deviation of returns on the share is 50% and the time to expiry is three months (i.e. 0.25 of a year).

(a) Using this information, determine the value of the call option on the equity share (it does not pay a dividend) using the Black–Scholes Model.

8 Marks

(b) Determine the intrinsic value of the option and, separately, the time value.

2 Marks

Question 19.7 (Level 1)

You are asked to value a European call option RST75 on the stock ABC. It expires in six months with a strike price of 75c/p. The volatility factor is 0.20. The other variables are as follows:

$Ps = 70$

$X = 75$

$T = 0.5$

$\sigma = 0.20$

$r = 0.06$

Requirement Value the call option using the Black–Scholes model.

8 Marks

Question 19.8

Armagh Metals Ltd own several zinc and lead mines throughout Ireland. It sells the zinc and lead ore that it extracts at the daily commodity market price (i.e. the spot market).

Requirement Explain the commodity price risk that Armagh faces in relation to its sales of zinc and lead ore **and** advise on TWO possible approaches to managing this risk (no calculations are necessary).

4 Marks

(Based on Chartered Accountants Ireland, CAP 2, SFMA, Autumn 2018, extract from Q4)

Question 19.9

URHealth Ltd is a large Irish pharmacy company that operates with two subsidiaries, one in Ireland and the other in the UK. It owns and operates a total of 65 pharmacy shops. Some aspects of the Irish and UK subsidiaries are managed separately, notably their treasury functions, which are entirely separate and deal exclusively with their domestic shops.

During the due diligence review of Pharmak's operations, it was discovered that the UK subsidiary pharmacy shops were established and are still evaluated as investment centres, whereas the Irish shops are evaluated as profit centres.

Requirement

(a) Assess the advantages and disadvantages of URHealth's proposal to centralise the treasury functions of the Irish and UK operations.

4 Marks

(b) Outline and briefly explain THREE disadvantages with continuing to evaluate the UK subsidiary shops as investment centres going forward.

6 Marks

Total 10 Marks

(Based on Chartered Accountants Ireland, CAP 2, SFMA, Summer 2017, extract from Q3)

20

Exchange Rate Risk

Learning Objectives

Upon completing this chapter, readers should be able to:

- determine the financial flows resulting from buying and selling currencies;
- explain the influences on exchange rates (including interest rates and inflation rates);
- identify and describe the key currency risks facing a business;
- outline the basic relationships between currencies;
- apply the interest rate parity model and the Open Fisher model to predict forward rates;
- explain different methods of managing currency risk using hedging products; and
- perform simple calculations to determine the financial implications of a currency hedge.

INTRODUCTION

Any company that trades with foreign suppliers or customers or is a multinational will have to have a good knowledge of exchange rates and the influences on exchange rates. This is vital so as to be able to determine with accuracy the cash flows expected by the company. An **exchange rate** is the rate at which one country's currency can be traded in exchange for another country's currency. Currency that is traded and is immediately exchanged is traded at the **spot rate** (i.e. the current rate) and currency that is purchased now at an agreed rate, but which will be exchanged at some time in the future, is regarded as being traded at a **forward rate**. This chapter covers transacting in foreign currencies, influences on foreign currencies, hedging for currency exposure and derivative transactions.

BUYING AND SELLING CURRENCY

Banking institutions form the backbone of the foreign exchange markets and most companies buy and sell currencies through banks. The bank makes money on these transactions by buying currency at one rate (called the **bid rate**) and selling it at another rate (called the **offer rate**). The difference between the buying and selling rate is called the **spread**. The spread is the bank's premium. They may also charge an administration fee. For example, if you went to purchase Sterling, the bank may bid €1.30 for every £1.00 required (plus a set transaction fee). However, if you wanted to exchange Sterling for euro, then the bank may offer €1.22 for every £1.00 exchanged (plus a transaction fee). The difference between the two rates, €0.08, is the spread. Buying and selling currency is shown in **Worked Example 20.1.**

Worked Example 20.1: Buying and Selling Currencies

The bank is quoting the following rates for the US$:

	Offer	Bid
Spot rate (US$)	1.53	1.55
1-month forward rate (US$)	1.55	1.57

Requirement

(a) ABC Plc sold four machines to an American company and has just received in $500,000. How much euro/Sterling will you obtain when you change the dollars at the bank?

(b) ABC Plc has to pay an American supplier for parts. The invoice is now due and $350,000 is to be paid by bank draft today. How much will this cost in euro/Sterling?

Solution

(a) As ABC Plc has the dollars, it will be selling them and the bank will be buying them, so the relevant rate is the bid rate of US$1.55.

The revenue received in euro/Sterling is $500,000 ÷ $1.55 = €/£322,581

(b) As ABC Plc requires dollars it will have to buy them, hence the bank will be selling them, so the relevant rate is the offer rate of US$1.53.

The cost in euro/Sterling is $350,000 ÷ $1.53 = €/£228,758.

The bank may also quote forward rates and may advertise them either as the rate (as shown in **Worked Example 20.1**) or as a movement from the spot rate. The expression **discount on spot** (disc) or **premium on spot** (pm) is used to indicate the direction of movement in the currency. A discount is always added to the spot rate to obtain the future forward price and, conversely, a premium is always deducted from the spot rate to obtain the future forward price. So in **Worked Example 20.1** the one month forward could have been quoted as 2c discount for both the offer and bid price instead of disclosing the 'US$1.55' and the 'US$1.57'.

Exchange rates fluctuate between countries in response to supply and demand for the respective currencies within foreign exchange markets. Both supply and demand are influenced by a variety of factors, as outlined in **Figure 20.1**.

Two of these influences are considered to have a linear relationship to each other and to the currency exchange rate and are discussed after **Figure 20.1**.

FIGURE 20.1: INFLUENCES ON EXCHANGE RATES

- Inflation rate differentials between countries.
- Interest rate differentials between countries.
- Government policy on intervening to influence exchange rates.
- Gross Domestic Product.
- A country's balance of payments.
- Levels of speculation.
- The sentiment of the market participants in respect of the future economic prospects.
- Political stability within a country.
- Government policy on holding currency reserves.
- Natural resources within a country – a country with high levels of natural resources is more likely to have a strong currency relative to a country that has limited natural resources.

THE RELATIONSHIP BETWEEN INTEREST RATES, EXCHANGE RATES AND INFLATION RATES

A multinational might be tempted to borrow funds in one country, which has low interest rates, for use in another country, which has high interest rates. Though this seems like a smart idea, in practice it is not straightforward. It would make sense if interest rates were the only factor impacting on this type of transaction; however, demand for the cheaper debt will actually drive up the price of the currency in that country (causing a shift in the exchange rate). A process of arbitrage is likely to occur until it is no longer beneficial to purchase currency (obtain debt) in the country with the low interest rate – there is a readily available market of investors and companies who are looking to obtain debt/currency cheaply, theoretically it will not be possible to obtain debt cheaper in another country as demand will cause the currency rate to change, thus eliminating the interest rate differential quite quickly. This is known as **interest rate parity** – the difference between the interest rates will equal the difference between the forward and spot rates for the currencies. The spot rate is the exchange rate at present; the forward is the exchange rate the currency is expected to move to in the future, given the difference in the interest rates (r). This is expressed by the following equation:

$$\frac{1+r_{euro}}{1+r_{stg}} = \frac{\textbf{Forward}_{euro/stg}}{\textbf{Spot}_{euro/stg}}$$

This equation can be rearranged to determine the expected forward rate, given the spot rate, and the interest rates in the two different countries.

$$\textbf{Forward}_{euro/stg} = \textbf{Spot}_{euro/stg} \times \frac{1+r_{euro}}{1+r_{stg}}$$

This relationship is best explained with an example:

WORKED EXAMPLE 20.2: INTEREST RATE PARITY

A company in the UK can borrow funds at 9% in the UK and can also get access to funds at 7% in Ireland. Assume the current exchange rate between the euro and Sterling is 1.298, wherein £1.00 will purchase €1.298 and, conversely, €1.00 will purchase 77p Sterling.

Requirement

(a) What is the expected one-year forward rate (assume the interest rate parity theory holds)? Explain the impact of this on Sterling and on the euro.

(b) If a company borrows the equivalent of £500,000, how much euro will it have to borrow now and to repay in one year's time? What is the Sterling equivalent of this repayment (given the movement in the exchange rate predicted in (a) happens)?

(c) What would this debt have cost if it had been sourced in the UK?

Solution

(a) The forward rate can be calculated as follows:

$$\frac{1+0.07}{1+0.09} = \frac{\text{Forward}_{euro/stg}}{1.298}$$

$$1.274 = \text{Forward}_{euro/stg}$$

Sterling will weaken against the euro: €1 will buy 78p, £1 will buy €1.274.

(b) It will borrow £500,000 × 1.298 = €649,000. The bank in Ireland will charge 7% interest: €649,000 × 7% = €45,430. At the end of one year the company will have to pay back: €694,430 [€649,000 + €45,430].

In one year's time the company will have to convert £545,078 [€649,430 ÷ 1.274] into euro to pay the loan back.

(c) Had the debt been sourced in the UK, then it would have cost the company: £545,000 [£500,000 + (£500,000 × 9%)].

The difference between the answer given in (b) and the answer given in (c) is due to rounding. This question does not take into account set-up fees, which may make borrowing in a different currency more expensive.

A company can forward buy a currency to enable it to pay back debt or to pay for supplies that are denominated in another currency. It is argued that buying forwards forces the spot rate to move towards the forward rate, therefore speculators will not be able to make consistent gains on currency speculation about forward rates. This is called the **expectations theory of exchange rates** – the expected spot exchange rate will equal the forward rate and the difference between the forward and spot rate will equal the expected change in the spot rate. This is portrayed by the following formula:

$$\frac{\textbf{Forward}_{\textbf{euro/stg}}}{\textbf{Spot}_{\textbf{euro/stg}}} = \frac{\textbf{Expected spot}_{\textbf{euro/stg}}}{\textbf{Spot}_{\textbf{euro/stg}}}$$

So,

$$\textbf{Forward}_{\textbf{euro/stg}} = \textbf{Expected Spot}_{\textbf{euro/stg}}$$

If this theory applies, then a business finance manager can take comfort from the fact that any currency they forward buy will reflect the spot exchange rate on the maturity of the forward contract. In the above example the spot exchange rate between Sterling and euro is 1.298 and the forward rate is 1.274. This means that the current spot rate is trading at a discount. Any entity holding Sterling now would be tempted to sell its Sterling for euro to obtain the larger quantity. The cumulative impact of companies/investors selling Sterling would eventually drive down Sterling's value until it was no longer economically viable to exchange Sterling (i.e. this value would be the rate 1.274) – so the forward rate becomes the expected spot rate.

Given these theories, why then do countries have different interest rates and why do governments/central banks change interest rates? The answer lies with inflation (i.e. increases in the cost of goods which erode the purchasing value of a currency). Governments/central banks typically use interest rates to control inflation. When inflation is high, interest rates are high and vice versa. Investors are interested in the real rate of return to be earned on a currency; this is the return after inflation is stripped out of the gross reported return. The **International Fisher Effect** theory, otherwise known as the **Open Fisher** theory, suggests that real interest rates in all countries are the same. Where differences arise, then this is due to expectations about inflation. This is portrayed by the following formula (which depicts that the difference in the interest rates between two countries equals the expected difference in the two countries' inflation rates):

$$\frac{1+r_{\text{euro}}}{1+r_{\text{stg}}}=\frac{1+i_{\text{euro}}}{1+i_{\text{stg}}}$$

where r is the interest rate and i is the inflation rate. When this is linked to the interest rate parity equation, the following relationship results:

$$\frac{1+r_{\text{euro}}}{1+r_{\text{stg}}}\times \textbf{Spot}_{\text{euro/stg}}=\textbf{Forward}_{\text{euro/stg}}=\textbf{Spot}_{\text{euro/stg}}\times\frac{1+i_{\text{euro}}}{1+i_{\text{stg}}}$$

The next example examines how changes in inflation rates are likely to result in different interest rates across countries. It also considers the benefits and pitfalls of being part of the Economic and Monetary Union (EMU) of the European Union (EU).

Worked Example 20.3: International Fisher Effect Theory

Assume the base rate charged in the UK in June 20X8 was 5% and the inflation figure for May 20X8 was 3.3%. This had increased from 2.2% in March. The UK Government set an inflation rate target of 2%. The economy had remained within this target for part of 20X7, when the Bank of England base rate was 5.75%; however, there had been a steady increase in inflation rates caused by the impact of increases in the price of oil, and all products that are made using energy.

Assume the inflation rate in Ireland was 5% in April 20X8, up from 4.2% in January and the European Central Bank (ECB) base rate was 4%. The European parliament had set itself an inflation target of 2%. The inflation rate in Ireland was affected by oil in a similar manner to the UK market.

Requirement

(a) Assume that the equilibrium euro inflation rate is 2% and that an interest rate of 5.5% captures the equilibrium real return required by the international markets. Assume that inflation in the UK and in Ireland cannot be controlled because the price of oil cannot be influenced by the governments. What should the interest rates move to, assuming the International Fisher Effect is evident?

(b) Ireland is a member of the EMU. What does this mean?

(c) List the arguments for and against being a member of the EMU.

Solution

(a) Given this information, the interest rate in the UK (r) should move to:

$$\frac{1+0.055}{1+r_{\text{stg}}}=\frac{1.02}{1.033}$$

$$1+r_{\text{stg}}=1.0684$$

$$r_{\text{stg}}=6.84\%$$

wherein 5.5% is the equilibrium interest rate, given 2% inflation and 3.3% is the underlying inflation rate in the UK that cannot be changed.

The interest rate in Ireland (r) should move to:

$$\frac{1+0.055}{1+r_{euro}}=\frac{1.02}{1.05}$$

$$1 + r_{euro} = 1.086$$

$$r_{euro} = 8.6\%$$

wherein 5.5% is the equilibrium interest rate given 2% inflation and 5% is the underlying inflation rate in the UK that cannot be changed.

(b) The point of the European Union (EU), in general, is to provide an unrestricted common market that promotes free trade between member states. To this end, the EU introduced the EMU, which provides for a unified monetary policy for all Member States that signed up to the EMU and introduced a single currency, the euro (not all Member States signed up to the EMU). The ECB was established to issue euro, to establish the monetary policy for the EU, to act as a lender of last resort for Member States and to manage the currency exchange rate for the euro.

(c) The arguments in favour of joining the EMU may include the following:
- **Economic stability**: to remain a member of the EMU a country must adhere to strict economic criteria. For example, the interest rate is set centrally and the Member State government cannot raise it to control inflation.
- **Reduces short-term political policies**: many governments change economic variables as election ploys in the run-up to election time. Though the changes may be popular with the electorate, they may have long-term ramifications for the economy. When a country is a member of the EMU, monetary policy is out of the country's government's hands.
- **Lower interest rates**: the interest rates set by the ECB have been consistently low, indeed they are currently at their lowest level, a respectable 0.25% (April 2020).
- **Free trade**: having a single currency eliminates currency risk in transactions between companies, individuals and governments from different countries. This should save transaction and hedging costs.

The arguments against joining the EMU might include the following:
- **Loss of control**: the government loses control over economic policy – which is now within the hands of the ECB. Governments are unable to raise interest rates to control inflation.
- **Weaker countries**: the stronger countries usually have to loan funds to weaker countries to support them as they try to remain within the EMU
- **Loss of national pride**: some individuals feel that joining the EU and merging everything takes away from a country's identity.

As noted, inflation is considered to impact on interest rates, and vice versa. It is also considered to impact on exchange rates. When a country's inflation rate increases relative to the inflation rate in other countries, then the value of its currency will fall relative to the value of the currencies in the other countries. This is because inflation impacts on the price of goods within a country and price differentials will cause shifts in demand for that country's produce, which will cause a shift in the demand for that country's currency, resulting in a shift in the value of the currency (i.e. a movement in the exchange rate). This theory is termed the **purchasing power parity (PPP)** theory. The PPP theory assumes that the overall cost of living in different countries is the same, because exchange rates adjust to offset inflation differences between countries. A numerical example is best to explain this theory. Suppose inflation in Ireland was such that the price of a Mars bar increased from €1.00 to €2.00. If PPP were to hold, then the value of the euro would fall by a half. So, say a euro is currently worth 84p (Sterling), then at present a Mars bar in Ireland costs 84p (Sterling). After the period of high inflation, PPP theory suggests that the high inflation rate will be counteracted by a fall in the value of the euro, such that a euro will now be worth 42p, hence the Mars bar will cost the same to someone in the UK [€2.00 × 0.42p = 0.84p]. This relationship is reflected in the following equation:

$$\frac{1+i_{\text{euro}}}{1+i_{\text{stg}}}=\frac{\text{Expected spot}_{\text{euro/stg}}}{\text{Spot}_{\text{euro/stg}}}$$

The expected difference in the inflation rate (i) between two countries equals the expected change in the spot rate between the two countries.

IDENTIFYING CURRENCY RISKS

Exchange rate risk is also known as **currency risk**. Exchange rate risk is prevalent in every company that either transacts with a third party (such as a customer/supplier) in a different country, or has assets, or debt, denominated in a foreign currency. There are two main types of short-term currency risk: transaction risk and translation risk. A third type of risk, **economic risk**, occurs when exchange rate uncertainty lasts for a long period of time.

Transaction risk affects the cash flows and profitability of a company. It is another name for **contractual risk** and is prevalent in every credit transaction that involves the conversion of one currency into another currency. For example, an Irish company may agree to purchase 1,000 cars from Charles Hurst in Belfast at £10,000 per car. If it is assumed that the spot rate when the transaction takes place is €1.22 to £1, then this will cost the Irish company €12,200,000. However, three months' credit is agreed. If, in this three-month period, the euro weakens against Sterling so that the exchange rate is €1.45 to £1, then the cost of these vehicles increases significantly to €14,500,000. This is a significant difference that will impact on the profitability and cash flows of the Irish company. Transactions reported in a company's statement of profit or loss and statement of cash flows are subject to transaction risk.

Translation risk does not impact on a company's cash flows. It affects the reported value of assets that are located in a different country or are denominated in a different currency. When currency rates change, these assets will be translated at different values from those previously reported. The result is that statement of financial position values can change significantly, not because the underlying assets have changed but because their reported value has changed. This can impact on a company's overall perceived performance as ratios such as the return on capital employed, or the return on assets will be affected.

Economic risk occurs when the exchange rate movements are long-term. This can be caused by a change in country risk or political risk. Where the exchange rate in a country weakens, more of that country's currency will be required to pay for the importer. The long-term impact of this is that any assets held by a UK or Irish company in that country will be worth less, and any sales made that are translated will produce lower profits. This will be a long-term issue that may impact on the underlying value of the whole company.

MANAGING CURRENCY RISK

As mentioned previously, a company should have a set policy on risk and the management of risk. Currency risk will lie within this policy. If it were assumed that the interlocking theories on inflation rates, interest rates, commodity prices and exchange rates (discussed earlier in this chapter) held true and moved in line with the efficient market hypothesis, then currency risk would not be a concern as the price of products in every country would be the same when converted into one currency. However, these theories do not operate in a totally free market. Government intervention in many countries strives to control inflation rates, interest rates and exchange rates and responses to shifts in inflation and interest rates take time. The result is differences between currency rates that do not conform to the predicted equations' results. This means that speculators can reap rewards from dealing in currencies and companies can gain profits, or hedge against losses, by managing their finances effectively.

Budgeting for Currencies

A starting point in currency management is to forecast the company's need for, and surplus of, different kinds of currencies. The business finance manager should, therefore, try to forecast expected exchange rates for each currency. This approach will allow a business finance manager to determine the steps to take to manage cash flows that are expected to originate and to be paid in other currencies. This enables more accurate cash flow and profit forecasts to be made, which allows better decision-making in respect of pricing goods, working capital management and project appraisal in foreign countries. It also allows a finance manager to determine the impact of exchange rate movements on the value of the company.

When determining the change in expected exchange rates, a finance manager usually takes two approaches. The first, called **fundamental analysis**, considers how the balance of payments on a country's current account will change. It is assumed that the balance of payments impacts on a country's exchange rate. When a country imports more than it exports, then the current account will be in deficit. This will reduce the value of the country's currency as there is less demand for its currency. Changes in inflation rates and interest rates impact on the balance of payments as these factors impact on the demand for exports and imports. A further factor to impact on the demand for a country's currency is the level of investment in the country by foreign entities/individuals. This equates to exporting when the balance of payments is considered – when foreign entities/individuals purchase government bonds and equity shares on domestic markets, they are not only buying the underlying asset but are also purchasing the local currency.

The second approach, called **technical analysis**, is a chartist approach. To determine future changes in foreign currency exchange rates, the finance manager considers patterns in the movement of exchange rates in the past and uses these to predict future movements in exchange rates.

HEDGING

Once currency exposures have been identified, the next step is to determine if they should be hedged, or not. It may be that the finance manager believes that exchange rate movements will benefit the company and he/she may decide exposures should not be hedged. However, this is speculation which, as an approach, would need to be agreed strategically. In many instances currency exposures are hedged internally: for example by arranging for the company to export and import from the same country. Only expected net differences require hedging. Another internal hedge is when a company finances foreign investment using debt denominated in the currency of the foreign investment. Long-term non-monetary investments are not usually hedged because PPP is argued to hold in the long-term but not in the short-term. To recap, PPP suggests that the value of the asset/liability denominated in a foreign currency will rise or fall in value to exactly offset the fall or rise in the value of the foreign currency. Assets that are held for short periods of time are exposed to exchange rate risk as the links between the asset's value (which may change due to inflation) and the exchange rate take time to move to equilibrium. It is also argued that short-term loans do not require hedging as the interest rate is pegged at such a level so as to take currency differences into account. Therefore, the currency issues that a finance manager should manage are monetary assets denominated in another currency and transactions that are not hedged internally but are subject to translation risk (when converting from the foreign currency to the domestic currency).

Hedging Techniques

Centralise the Currency Management Function

This means that **currency netting** can take place centrally and hedging requirements are reduced. Netting will not only reduce the exposure of the company to exchange rate risks but will also reduce transaction costs.

Leading and Lagging Currency Payments

This is cash flow management and involves paying early when exchange rates are favourable and paying late when they are not, or offering a discount for payment to encourage customers to pay their accounts when the exchange rate is favourable and allowing longer credit periods when it is not. All the principles covered in respect of the management of trade receivables and trade payables are still relevant. For example, it may make sense to delay payment for supplies as this will result in cheaper supplies due to expected exchange rate movements. However, discounts may be lost and suppliers may get annoyed with the company, which impacts on future price and even supply.

Factoring

An international factor will absorb exchange rate risk, paying up to 80% of the credit receivable upfront. However, as noted in **Chapter 8**, international factoring is more expensive than domestic factoring because of the transfer of risk from the company to the factor company.

Bills of Exchange

Many exporting companies use bills of exchange when dealing with customers in foreign companies. This allows them to sell the bill at the spot rate, hence passing the exchange rate risk to the holder of the bill.

Matching Currency Flows

This involves being proactive in approach and ensuring that there is both demand and supply for a particular currency. This may be achieved by sourcing supplies from a country that is a customer of the company or investing in a project in that country. In some instances the match can be achieved by investing or supplying to a country that is closely connected economically with the foreign country. Countries that are closely linked economically will experience similar movements in their prospective exchange rates. The most commonly cited example is the US dollar and the Canadian dollar.

Adjusting Price

A company might anticipate exchange rate movements and may, for example, factor the additional expected cost into the price of the good. This effectively transfers a portion of the risk to the customer. However, if exchange rates move beyond what was expected, then the company's profits will be affected. In addition, the increase in price may result in the loss of the sale.

Invoicing in the Domestic Currency

A company might transfer all the risks to customers by denominating its sales prices in the domestic currency and insisting on purchasing goods at prices that are denominated in the domestic currency. However, this may impact on the demand for the company's goods and the price of goods being supplied to the company, as customers and suppliers will prefer to deal with companies that absorb the exchange rate risk.

Risk Sharing

In some instances, a company may be able to enter into an agreement with a customer/supplier in respect of exchange rate movements, which shares the risk between the parties to the transaction.

Using the Money Markets

When a company in Ireland or the UK knows that it will receive a currency in the future, it can borrow the present value of that currency now, convert it to euros/Sterling now (hence locking into the spot rates), and then pay the capital and interest back when the foreign currency funds are received in the future. Similarly, when a company has to pay currency in the future it can invest the present value of the amount required by buying the foreign currency now and then depositing the funds in a deposit account denominated in the foreign currency. When the account matures, the capital and interest (i.e. the future value) will be sufficient to pay off the foreign currency owed. This is shown in **Worked Example 20.4**.

WORKED EXAMPLE 20.4: HEDGING USING THE MONEY MARKETS

ABC Plc sold goods to a US customer for $15,000,000, receivable in three months' time. It has to pay an Australian supplier AU$12,000,000 for parts in two months' time.

The following annual interest rates apply:

	€/£ deposit	**€/£ borrowing**	**AU$ deposit**	**AU$ borrowing**	**US$ deposit**	**US$ borrowing**
2 months	2.5%	5%	4%	6%	1%	4%
3 months	3%	5.5%	4.25%	6.5%	1%	4.5%

The following exchange rates apply:

	AU$ to €/£		**US$ to €/£**	
Spot	1.65	1.70	1.60	1.63
2-month forward	0.5c disc	0.6c disc	0.9c pm	0.8c pm
3-month forward	1.3c disc	1.1c disc	2.1c pm	2.0c pm

(***Note:*** disc refers to discount on spot, pm to premium on spot.)

Requirement Demonstrate how a perfect hedge can be obtained using the money markets for both transactions.

Solution

US dollar transaction US$15,000,000 is receivable in three months' time. To hedge against exchange rate fluctuations, the company could borrow the present value of US$15,000,000 now, convert this to euro/Sterling and then pay off the loan when the funds are received in three months' time.

The amount to be loaned that will result in a gross balance owing in three months' time is calculated using the following formula:

$$\text{Future value} = \text{Present value } (1+r)^n$$

where we know the future value (US$15,000,000), the borrowing rate in US dollars (r) is 4.5% and the time (n) is three months (0.25 years). We want to find the PV to borrow now.

Therefore: PV = US$15,000,000/$(1.045)^{0.25}$ = US$14,835,841.55

This will be borrowed now and converted to euro/Sterling at the spot rate of US$1.63.

So the company will obtain a guaranteed €/£9,101,743.29 [US$14,835,841.55 ÷ US$1.63] (i.e. revenue valued now). This can be put on deposit in an Irish/UK account for three months at 3% and will mature at €/£9,101,743.29$(1.03)^{0.25}$ = €/£9,169,251.57 (revenue valued in three months' time).

In three months' time the bank loan plus interest will equal US$15,000,000 and the receipt from the customer will be used to repay this in full.

Australian dollar transaction AU$12,000,000 to be paid out in two months' time.

In this instance, to lock into the spot rate, the present value of the currency required will be put into an AU$ deposit account for a fixed two-month period.

Therefore: PV is AU$12,000,000 ÷ $(1.04)^{2/12}$ = AU$11,921,814.39

This needs to be purchased now so the bank offer rate is relevant.

AU$11,921,814.39 ÷ AU$1.65 = €/£7,225,342.06 needs to be paid now (cost valued now).

The cost of financing this upfront payment for two months is €/£7,225,342.06 × $(1.05)^{2/12}$ = €/£7,284,335.87 (cost valued in two months' time).

FORWARD CONTRACTS

Currency forward contracts are bespoke agreements that specify that a set amount of currency will be bought/or sold at a pre-agreed exchange rate on a specified date. This is a contractual agreement that has to be fulfilled on the specified date. Both buyer and seller to this contract agree with the terms. The exchange rate agreed is usually influenced by the forward rates being quoted by the markets. When exchange rates on the exercise date are different, one party suffers a loss relative to the market, the other makes a profit.

Worked Example 20.5: Hedging Using Forward Contracts

ABC Plc sold goods to a US customer for $15,000,000, receivable in three months' time. It has to pay an Australian supplier AU$12,000,000 for parts in two months' time.

The following exchange rates apply:

	AU$ to €/£		**US$ to €/£**	
Spot	1.65	1.70	1.60	1.63
2-month forward	0.5c disc	0.6c disc	0.9c pm	0.8c pm
3-month forward	1.3c disc	1.1c disc	2.1c pm	2.0c pm

Requirement Demonstrate how a perfect hedge can be obtained using the forward contracts for both transactions.

Solution

US dollar transaction US$15,000,000 is receivable in three months' time. To hedge against exchange rate fluctuations, the company could enter into a three month forward contract to sell US$ (bank buys, hence the bid rate is relevant) at US$1.61 [US$1.63 – US$0.02].

Therefore, the company is guaranteed €/£9,316,770.18 [US$15,000,000 ÷ US$1.61] in three months' time.

Australian dollar transaction AU$12,000,000 is to be paid out in two months' time.

In this instance, the company can enter into a two-month forward contract to buy AU$ (bank sells, hence the offer price is relevant) at AU$1.655 [AU$1.65 + 0.005].

Therefore, the company has locked into paying €/£7,250,755.29 [$12,000,000 ÷ AU$1.655] in two months' time to buy the required dollars to pay the supplier.

A downside to forward contracts, like the one entered into in **Worked Example 20.5** for US Dollars, is that the currency risk may have been hedged but credit risk is still prevalent (however, the company may take out insurance to cover credit default risk). The US customer may not pay. If this were to happen, the company would still have to fulfil the terms of the future contract. It would have to borrow US$15,000,000 at the market rate to close out the forward contract.

FUTURES CONTRACTS

Currency futures are agreements to buy or sell a specific amount of a specified currency on a set date. Unlike bespoke currency forward contracts, currency futures are standardised and traded in the futures markets. They can be closed before maturity by entering into an opposite agreement. They have all the attributes of a general futures contract, as discussed in the previous chapter, i.e. marked-to-market, margin, set maturity dates, set size, market prices, etc. They can be used, for example, when a company knows that it is going to receive foreign currency in three months' time. It can contract to sell that currency at future rates agreed now, in three months' time. This means that any loss on the currency exchange will be offset, to an extent, by profits on the futures contract.

OPTIONS

Currency options give the holder the right, but not the obligation, to buy or sell a predefined amount of a particular currency at or before a specified date at a pre-agreed exchange rate. This exchange rate is the exercise price. Options can be traded through exchanges. In these instances the contracts are for specific amounts, specific currencies and have specific exercise dates and exercise prices. Options can also be traded over-the-counter (OTC), usually through banks. As these are bespoke, they are more expensive. There are two types of options: **European options**, which restrict exercise of the contract to the exercise date only; or **American options**, which can be exercised at any time up to, and on, the exercise date. The greatest loss that can be incurred in both instances is the cost of the option. This is shown in **Worked Example 20.6**.

Worked Example 20.6: Hedging Using Option Contracts

ABC Plc expects to receive US$1,000,000 on 30 September 20X6.

A US$ option could be purchased now (30 June 20X6) at a premium of €/£500 per $100,000 at a strike rate of US$1.54 to €/£1, effective 30 September 20X6.

US interest rates are 7% on borrowings and 5% on savings.

Sterling/euro interest rates are 5% on borrowings and 3% on savings.

Requirement Demonstrate the financial implications of the option assuming ABC is to proceed with it now.

Solution

The option will allow ABC to sell US$1,000,000 at US$1.54, netting €/£649,351 on 31 September 20X6.

To avail of the option ABC will have to buy the option contracts now (30 June 20X6). This will cost it US$1,000,000/US$100,000 = 10 contracts.

10 contracts × €/£500 per contract = €/£5,000 on 30 June 20X6. This €/£5,000 has to be financed for three months, hence the true cost is €/£5,000$(1.05)^{0.25}$ = €/£5,061.

The net revenue in three months' time is, therefore, €/£644,290 [€/£649,351 – €/£5,061).

SWAP AGREEMENTS

Foreign **currency swaps** involve the exchange of cash flows in one currency for cash flows in another currency. For example, if A Plc (a UK company) purchases goods that cost €100,000 from B Plc (an Irish company) every month and C Plc (an Irish company) purchases goods from D Plc (a UK company) for £82,000 every month, and assuming the exchange rate is €1 to £0.82 (i.e. the two cash flows are worth the same), then a swap contract can be agreed whereby A Plc (a UK company) agrees to pay D Plc (a UK company) £82,000 and C Plc agrees to pay B Plc (both Irish companies) €100,000 each month. This agreement means that exchange rate risk for the four companies is totally hedged. This is a simplified version of a swap. In practice, the stronger, more dominant companies that are involved in the transaction may demand commission. Banks that have branches in different countries may take the place of two of the companies. They will charge a fee for this service. Currency swaps are more likely to be used to hedge debt transactions than operating transactions.

CONCLUSION

This chapter has highlighted the relationships that exist between inflation rates, interest rates and exchange rates between countries. Supporters of the theories outlined in this chapter would argue that the world economy is relatively efficient and that price differentials (i.e. the potential to make abnormal profits on movements in currency, interest rates and product prices) are eventually eroded by arbitrage. They suggest that treasury managers need to be very careful when they source debt, even though a source in a different country may have a lower interest rate tag. The exchange rate and inflation rate movements may actually make the debt more expensive in the long-term.

However, it is considered that these theories only hold true in the long term, not in the short term, and many companies transact in the short-term. In addition, external interference, such as government intervention in the economic system, may thwart the free market's natural progression towards equilibrium – hence global markets are not in equilibrium and speculative profits can be made from dealing across different countries. Therefore, most companies adopt a policy to manage exchange rate risk. The starting point in this process is the identification of exchange rate risks. Exchange rate risk is normally categorised as transaction risk, translation risk and economic risk. A company can take steps to hedge risks. A variety of methods can be utilised, including in-house steps, such as netting, matching, aligning supply purchases in countries where sales take place, aligning finance in the country where the asset is located, etc. Alternatively, financial derivatives, such as forwards, futures, options and swaps, can be utilised to hedge risk exposure, or to make speculative gains.

EXAMINATION STANDARD QUESTION: HEDGING

Alpha Semiconductor Ltd manufactures components for the computer hardware industry. Until recently it has been selling exclusively in the European market. In the last two years it has expanded aggressively and has now begun selling in the US and Japanese markets.

The treasury department in Alpha is small and focussed on managing working capital. Since Alpha had no foreign currency denominated sales or costs until recently, the department did not engage in any foreign exchange risk management. Although 35% of Alpha's sales are now denominated in USD or in JPY, the treasury department continues to pursue a policy of not managing foreign exchange risk.

Alpha recently delivered an order worth US$1,500,000 to a US customer, but adverse currency movements between delivery and receipt of payment meant that the order was loss-making. A second order of US$1,500,000 is expected from the same customer in one month's time. The order will take one month to complete and payment is due two months after completion.

In light of the loss due to currency movements, Fred Halpin, the Financial Director, has decided to investigate further the appropriateness of Alpha's current policy of not actively managing foreign exchange exposure. Fred has engaged Risk Consulting Partners, for whom you work, to draw up a report on this matter. A decision is required whether or not to proceed with hedging.

Market Data

Spot and Forward Exchange Rates

Spot rate	US$1.2316 to €/£1
3-month forward rate*	US$1.250 to €/£1

*A fee of 1% of the covered sum (in €/£) is charged for arranging the forward contract. This is payable at the outset of the contract. (You may ignore the time value of money when considering this alternative.)

Exchange Traded Foreign Currency Options

US$ to €/£ 3-month put option @ US$1.2450 to €/£1
Contract size: US$100,000.
Premium: US$0.02 per US$1 covered.

Requirement

(a) Illustrate how the expected US$ exposure could be hedged using a forward contract *and* foreign currency options. Compare the payoffs if the exposure is:
(i) hedged using a forward contract;
(ii) hedged using foreign currency options;
(iii) not hedged.

In each case show the cash flows in euro/Sterling if the US Dollar appreciates by 15% and if the US Dollar depreciates by 15% between putting the hedge in place and receiving payment. Assume the hedges are put in place once the order is received.

12 Marks

(b) Which instrument would you advise Alpha to use to hedge the exposure? Give reasons for your answer.

4 Marks

(c) Critically compare Alpha's policy of not hedging foreign exchange exposure to a policy of hedging all foreign exchange exposure.

5 Marks

Total 21 Marks

(Based on Chartered Accountants Ireland, CAP 2, MABF, Summer 2012, Q4)

Solution

(a) (i) *Hedging using the Forward Market*

- Alpha Semiconductor Ltd contracts with a counterparty, generally a commercial bank, to sell forward (3 months) $1,500,000 at a rate of US$1.250 to €/£1.
- An arrangement fee of 1% is payable for this contract immediately: (1,500,000 ÷ 1.250) × 0.01 = €/£12,000

Net Proceeds
$1,500,000 ÷ 1.250 = €/£1,200,000
Less cost of hedge €/£12,000
= €/£1,188,000

- Since a forward contract is binding on both parties once entered into, the proceeds of this hedge will be the same regardless of $ to €/£ movements between now and the hedge being completed.

- It should be noted that, because this is an over-the-counter (OTC) contract, there is counterparty risk. Should the counterparty (the bank) with which Alpha Semiconductor Ltd arranged the forward contract not be in a position to fulfil the contract at expiry, Alpha Semiconductors Ltd may be left with an exposure to the exchange rate.
- In order to minimise this risk, Alpha Semiconductor Ltd should put in place a policy of only dealing with counterparties above a specified minimum credit rating.

(ii) *Hedging using Exchange Traded Options*

- Alpha Semiconductor Ltd purchases a US$ to €/£ put option with a 3-month expiry.
- The market data provided indicates that a put option with a strike price of US$1.2450 to €/£1 is available at a cost of $0.02 per $1. The contract size is $100,000.
- Number of contracts required to hedge: $1,500,000 ÷ $100,000 = 15 contracts.
- Cost of hedge:
  Total covered = 15 × $100,000 = $1,500,000
  $1,500,000 × 0.02 = $30,000
  This is payable immediately and is not dependent on whether the option is ultimately exercised or not.

Net Proceeds
@ 15% US$ depreciation:

- Spot rate in 3 months: US$1.2316 × (1 + 0.15)
  = US$1.4163 to €/£1
- Since the strike price is higher than the spot price, the option should be exercised.
- $1,500,000 ÷ 1.2450 = €/£1,204,819
- Less the option premium of $30,000 @ spot rate ($1.2316) = €/£24,358
  = €/£1,180,461

Net Proceeds
@ 15% US$ appreciation:

- Spot rate in 3 months: US$1.2316 ÷ (1 + 0.15) = US$1.0709 to €/£1
- Since the spot price is higher than the strike price, the option should not be exercised and Alpha Semiconductor Ltd should transact on the spot market.
- $1,500,000 ÷ $1.0709 = €/£1,400,699
- Less the option premium of $30,000 @ spot rate ($1.2316) = €/£24,358
  = €/£1,376,333

(iii) *Not Hedging*

In this case Alpha Semiconductor Ltd transacts on the spot market at the prevailing exchange rate

- @ 15% US$ depreciation:
  Spot rate in 3 months: US$1.2316 × (1 + 0.15) = US$1.4163 to €/£1
  = €/£1,059,097 ($1,500,000 ÷ $1.4163)
- @ 15% US$ appreciation:
  Spot rate in 3 months: US$1.2316 ÷ (1 + 0.15) = US$1.04686 to €/£1
  = €/£1,432,856 ($1,500,000 ÷ $1.04686)

Possible net proceeds

	Forward contract	Option contract	No hedge
15% appreciation	€/£1,188,000	€/£1,376,333	€/£1,432,856
15% depreciation	€/£1,188,000	€/£1,180,461	€/£1,059,097

(b) Not one of these approaches to managing foreign exchange rate risk is superior to the others in every respect.
- The forward contract has no variability but has limited upside and no downside.
- The option contract has good upside potential but limited downside potential.
- The forward contract offers certainty at a relatively low price. The arrangement fee of 1% is half the cost of the option.
- The disadvantage with the forward contract is that if the US$ appreciates, the forward contract must be exercised despite the fact that it would be more advantageous to transact on the spot market.
- Forward contracts expose the company to counterparty risk.
- The exchange traded options are more expensive than forward contracts: €/£24,358 versus €/£12,000.
- However, options allow Alpha Semiconductor Ltd to transact at the prevailing spot rate should that be more advantageous.
- A second significant advantage of using options is that they are suitable for hedging 'conditional' exposure, where it is not certain that an exposure will arise. If the expected exposure does not arise, the company is not locked into a hedge.
- Not hedging is the cheapest in terms of transaction risk, but provides no protection against any depreciation in the US$.
- The use of 15% plus or minus in the exchange rate within a three-month period appears very large and may need to be revised.
- Alpha Semiconductor Ltd was clearly concerned about the recent foreign exchange losses. This suggests that the company is relatively risk averse and should use one of the two hedging approaches outlined above.

Since the contract being hedged is not yet certain, options are particularly suitable in this case, despite being more expensive. An option will also allow the possibility of speculative profits.

(c) Alpha Semiconductor Ltd's policy of not hedging foreign exchange rate risk has both advantages and disadvantages:
- Not hedging foreign exchange exposures allows the company to benefit from speculative profits.
- Hedging is expensive and not hedging avoids these costs.
- It is impossible to get a 100% hedge, so the policy may not be fully achievable.
- Since the derivatives used in hedging foreign exchange risk could be misused, this may expose Alpha Semiconductor Ltd to the risk of fraud or mistakes by its treasury employees. It would be essential that adequate controls be put in place should the company decide to pursue a policy of hedging. These controls are expensive.

- It appears that Alpha Semiconductor Ltd does not have the requisite expertise at the moment to manage foreign exchange (FX) risk. If it chooses to manage this risk, it will have to either invest in training its treasury staff or hire experienced staff.
- Hedging will reduce the volatility of Alpha Semiconductor Ltd's cash flows. Adverse currency movements would not cause losses such as the recent loss on the US$ sale.
- Planning and budgeting is simplified because of the greater certainty about future cash flows.
- If the shareholders of Alpha Semiconductors Ltd have not diversified their risk over a number of investments (as is generally the case with owners of private companies), the risk reduction due to hedging will be of value. If, however, they have already diversified their income, then they will not get any additional risk reduction.
- Hedging increases the risk of unauthorised transaction, as can be seen from past financial scandals.

Key Terms

Bid rate
Contractual risk
Currency risk
Currency swap
Discount on spot rate
Economic risk
Exchange rate
Exchange rate risk
Expectations theory
Forward rate
Fundamental analysis
Hedging
Interest rate parity (IRP)
International Fisher Effect (IFE)
Offer rate
Open Fisher
Premium on spot rate
Purchasing power parity (PPP)
Spot rate
Spread
Technical analysis
Transaction risk
Translation risk

REVIEW QUESTIONS

(See Suggested Solutions to Review Questions in **Appendix B**.)

Question 20.1

The price of a pint of beer now in Dublin is €4.50. The price of a pint now in Belfast is £3.50. The exchange rate for euro to Sterling is €1.40 to £1. UK inflation is 4% and inflation in Ireland is 6%.

Requirement

(a) Use the law of one price to predict the relative price of a pint of beer in one year's time in both cities.
(b) Using the results from (a), determine the future Sterling/euro spot rate assuming PPP.

Question 20.2 Forward Rates

(a) What is the one-year forward rate where the spot rate today is US$1.40 to £1 and the interest rates in the US are 3% for savings and 5% for debt, and are 1.5% for savings and 3% for borrowings in the UK?

(b) Using the information in (a) determine the six-month forward rate.
(c) Using the information in (a) determine the three-month forward rate.
(d) Interest rates in the US are expected to move to 4% for savings and 6.5% for debt in the following year and to 2% for savings and 4.5% for borrowings in the UK. What is the two-year forward rate expected to change to?

Question 20.3

Given a spot rate of US$1.65, what are the forward rates if you are told that:
(a) The one-month forward is at a 0.5c premium?
(b) The one-month forward is at a 1.2c discount?

Question 20.4

The base rate charged in Country A (a non-EU country) in June 20X8 was 5% and the inflation figure for May 20X8 was 3.3%. This had increased from 2.2% in March. Country A's Government set an inflation rate target of 2%. The economy had remained within this target for part of 20X7, when the Central Bank of Country A's base rate was 5.75%; however, there had been a steady increase in inflation rates caused by the impact of increases in the price of oil, and all products that are made using energy.

The inflation rate in Country B (an EU country) was 5% in April 20X8, up from 4.2% in January, and the European Central Bank (ECB) base rate was 4%. The European Parliament had set itself an inflation target of 2%. The inflation rate in Country B was affected by oil in a similar manner to Country A's market.

Requirement
(a) Which governing body is likely to be more concerned about inflation and why?
(b) Which governing body is likely to change interest rates?

Question 20.5

The bank is quoting the following exchange rate prices:

	Offer	Bid
Spot rate (US$)	1.63	1.65
1-month forward rate (US$)	1.65	1.67
3-month forward rate (US$)	1.66	1.68

Requirement
(a) ABC has to pay its supplier $500,000 in three months' time. How can ABC hedge against currency risk and what are the financial implications of your advice?
(b) ABC will receive $800,000 from a US customer in one month's time. How can ABC hedge against currency risk and what are the financial implications of your advice?

CHALLENGING QUESTIONS

(Suggested Solutions to Challenging Questions are available through your lecturer.)

Question 20.1 Receiving Foreign Currency (Level 2)

Tartan Plc (a UK company) has been invited to tender for a contract in Ireland with the bid priced in euro. Tartan Plc thinks the contract will cost £1,850,000. Because of fierce competition for the bid, Tartan Plc is willing to price the contract at £2,000,000. Since the exchange rate is currently €2.80 to £1.00, it puts in a bid of €5,600,000. The contract will not be awarded until after six months.

Requirement Outline the cost/profit implications for Tartan Plc assuming the following scenarios:

(a) Tartan Plc hedges the potential contract for currency risk using a forward rate contract, which is priced at the spot rate now, and Tartan Plc does not win the contract. The exchange rate in six months' time has moved to €2.50 to £1.

2 Marks

(b) Tartan Plc does not enter into a forward rate contract. Instead, it waits to see what will happen. In six months' time Tartan Plc is awarded the contract. At this time the value of the euro has fallen to €3.20 to £1.

2 Marks

(c) Tartan Plc takes out a put option costing £40,000 to sell €5,600,000 in six months' time at €2.80 to £1. Evaluate Tartan Plc's position now assuming:
  (i) Tartan Plc fails to win the contract.

  4 Marks

  (ii) Tartan Plc is awarded the contract. Exchange rates move to €3.20 to £1.

  4 Marks

  (iii) Tartan Plc is awarded the contract. Exchange rates move to €2.50 to £1.

  4 Marks

Total 16 Marks

(Based on Chartered Accountants Ireland, MABF, *Questions and Solutions Manual 2007*)

Question 20.2 Paying Foreign Currency (Level 2)

Tartan Plc (a UK company) is trying to purchase a plot of land in Ireland. The closing date for the auction is six months' time. Bids have to be made by closed envelope, which will only be opened in six months' time. Tartan Plc thinks the land is worth £1,850,000. However, it is willing to price the contract at £2,000,000 because of fierce competition. Since the exchange rate is currently €2.80 to £1.00, it puts in a bid of €5,600,000.

Requirement Outline the cost/profit implications for Tartan Plc assuming the following scenarios:

(a) Tartan Plc obtains the Sterling funds (£2,000,000) by way of a loan (at 7%) and converts the funds to euro now and invests the euro in a currency account through the local bank. The bank offers a return of 5% per annum on the euro deposit account. Evaluate Tartan Plc's position assuming:
  (i) Tartan Plc fails to win the contract and has to convert the euro back to Sterling to repay the six-month loan. The value of the euro has remained the same.

  3 Marks

  (ii) Tartan Plc is awarded the contract. The value of the euro has fallen to €3.20 to £1 by this time.

  3 Marks

  (iii) Tartan Plc is awarded the contract. The value of the euro has appreciated to €2.50 to £1 by this time.

  3 Marks

(b) Tartan Plc hedges the potential contract for currency risk using a forward rate contract, which is priced at the spot rate now and Tartan Plc does not win the contract. The exchange rate in six months' time has moved to €2.50 to £1.

3 Marks

(c) Tartan Plc does not enter into a forward rate contract. Instead, it waits to see what will happen. In six months' time Tartan Plc wins the sale at the auction. At this time the value of the euro has fallen to €3.20 to £1.

3 Marks

(d) Tartan Plc takes out a call option costing £40,000 to buy €5,600,000 in six months' time at €2.80 to £1. Evaluate Tartan Plc's position now assuming:

(i) Tartan Plc fails to win the contract.

3 Marks

(ii) Tartan Plc is awarded the contract. Exchange rates move to €3.20 to £1.

3 Marks

(iii) Tartan Plc is awarded the contract. Exchange rates move to €2.50 to £1.

3 Marks
Total 24 Marks

Question 20.3 Hotel (Level 2)

John runs Allens Hotel, which is renowned for its service and frequented by US tourists. He is aware of the recent currency fluctuations in the United States Dollar (USD), but is not sure of what options are available to the hotel to manage the impact on its US customer base.

Requirement Outline the likely impact on the customer base of Allens of the fluctuating trend in USD. What actions, within the control of Allens, could be taken to mitigate this impact?

3 Marks

(Based on Chartered Accountants Ireland, CAP 2, MABF, Summer 2010, Q1(c))

Question 20.4 System (Level 2)

System Technologies Limited manufactures computer chips from its facility in Ireland. A year ago, System acquired a patent from a US company. System financed this payment with a bullet repayment loan (i.e. principal and all accrued interest due at maturity) from a US bank. The loan is due to mature in 12 months and a total of US$10.5 million, being the original principal plus interest, is repayable then.

The US$ to €/£ exchange rate when the loan was drawn down was US$1.1989 to €/£1. This morning, the exchange rate was US$1.3344 to €/£1. System is keen to 'lock in' this favourable exchange rate, which reduces the €/£ cost of redeeming the loan. At a meeting yesterday with National Bank, System's bankers, two alternative strategies were proposed to System. The bank's treasury department suggested using either a 'forward contract hedge' or a 'currency swap arrangement'.

The table below was provided by National Bank and outlines the features of the two alternatives.

Forward contract	1-year forward rate today is US$1.3265 to €/£1. An arrangement fee of 0.85% of the US$ amount covered is payable at the maturity of the contract.
Currency swap	Available in units of US$1,000,000 and €/£ equivalent at current spot rate. No exchange of notional principal and the swap is settled on a cash basis. System will pay National Bank if it makes a currency gain and National Bank will pay System if System makes a currency loss. A fee of 0.5% of the US$ notional principal, in US$, is payable at the outset of the contract.

MARKET DATA

	US$	**€/£**
Spot 1-year base interest rates	1.65%	2.25%

Requirement

(a) Calculate the gain/loss to date that System has made by its failure to hedge the loan when it was obtained last year and briefly critique the policy not to hedge at that time.

5 Marks

(b) Outline the effects of each of the two alternatives suggested by National Bank as well as the effect of not hedging the exposure. Your analysis should include the cash flows arising from each transaction. Show the effect of the transactions both where the US$ appreciates and depreciates, from today's rate, by 10% relative to the €/£ over the next 12 months.

12 Marks

(c) Based on the information provided and your answer to (b), advise System as to whether it should hedge the exposure and, if so, using which of the alternative approaches. Your advice should include a discussion of any TWO factors you consider relevant to the decision.

4 Marks

Total 21 Marks

(Based on Chartered Accountants Ireland, CAP 2, MABF, Autumn 2013, Q3)

Question 20.5 Surgical Solutions (Level 2)

Surgical Solutions Ltd sells its products locally and in the United States (US). In the prior year, sales to the US represented 25% of a total turnover of €/£10,000,000 and delivered a margin of €/£500,000. The company currently avoids all risks related to foreign exchange, payables and receivables and interest rates, with all payments made and received in their own currency (€/£), all purchases and sales from reputable suppliers and to reputable customers and fixing all debt finance.

The newly appointed Finance Director, David Simms, believes that demanding payment in €/£ and supplying only to AAA rated customers has constrained growth into the US and has cited a number of recent tender losses and lost opportunities to support his case. David has recommended that the Board of Surgical Solutions amend its risk management strategy from risk avoidance to active risk management.

Surgical Solutions has recently been invited to tender for a significant US contract with Bingham Products Inc on 1 April 2011. The following are extracts from a conference call between David and Roy McEvoy, the Finance Director of BMP, on 17 March:

Roy McEvoy:

> "Happy St Patrick's Day ... David, this is a big opportunity for both our companies. We have a preference for Surgical Solutions, but need your tender in $ at a competitive price ... we will personally make it worth your while if you can convince your Board ... BMP will pay in full six months from the date of the bid ... I can give you a list of companies as trade references and I will obtain a reference for you from our bankers and send it to you ... no, I don't have the last three years' accounts to hand, but I will send them on. No issues there, I assure you ... ".

David Simms:

> "I'm sure there aren't any issues and thanks for your help with the credit checks. What you propose sounds fine to me. By the way, our current terms with our existing US customers are 60 days."

Roy McEvoy:

> "This is a big contract, David ... and potentially the first of many."

David estimates that the contract will cost €/£585,000 and recommends it be priced in $ on the day of the bid to deliver a profit margin of 10% on the €/£ selling price. On the day of the bid, the spot rate is $1.50 to €/£1. Given recent volatility in exchange rates, David estimates there is an equal probability that the exchange rate could move up or down by 10% in six months' time. David wants you to calculate the net gain or loss of managing such movements in exchange rates under the three options below.

1. Do nothing.
2. Forward contract: a local bank is prepared to offer a six-month forward rate of $1.45 to €/£1.
3. Option: take out a six-month put option, at a premium of 2% on the €/£ contract value at a rate of $1.55 to €/£1.

David can see no reason for disclosing his conversation with Roy and the reference to any personal benefit he may obtain by getting the Board to approve the tender in $. After all, he was going to recommend this anyway. David believes there is a 90% chance of being awarded the contract.

On David's recommendation, the Board decides to make the bid on 1 April. Three weeks later, no news on the bid or credit information has been received from BMP.

Requirement:

(a) Comment critically on the current risk-avoidance strategy at Surgical Solutions and David's recommendation to move to an active risk-management strategy.

4 Marks

(b) (i) Calculate the expected net gain or loss under the BMP contract for the three approaches outlined by David. Your answer should present the expected outcome under each approach for a 10% rise or fall in the current exchange rate and be laid out as follows:

	Not awarded BMP contract Expected gain/(loss)		**Awarded BMP contract Expected gain/(loss)**	
	Spot + 10%	Spot – 10%	Spot + 10%	Spot – 10%
Do nothing				
Forward contract				
Future option				

12 Marks

(ii) Advise, briefly, the board on the most suitable approach and why.

2 Marks

(c) Outline any two ethical and any two credit concerns you would have based on the conference call extract between Roy and David and David's resulting actions.

4 Marks

Total 22 Marks

(Based on Chartered Accountants Ireland, CAP 2, MABF, Autumn 2011, Q4)

Question 20.6 Meridian (Level 2)

Meridian Toys Ltd manufactures and sells toys for the domestic market. One of its products, the Super Scooter, has been extremely successful in the past year and has caught the attention of TOYZ, a large chain of toy shops in the US. TOYZ has ordered 25,000 units of the Super Scooter, to be delivered in six months, in time for the lucrative Christmas market. Meridian has agreed a unit price of $15, with payment due a further six months after delivery. TOYZ has also agreed an option to purchase a further 15,000 units in May 20X9.

Meridian has never dealt with foreign exchange risk before and has sought the advice of its accountant. She has advised that this exposure should be hedged, given its magnitude, and has provided some market data to Meridian related to potential hedges. She advises that the current spot rate of exchange is $1.07115 = €/£1. She also advises that it would be reasonable to assume that when payment is received, the spot rate would be equally likely to be $1.13000 = €/£1 or $1.01982 = €/£1.

Relevant market data:

- Euro/Sterling one-year interest rate is 2.5%.
- US dollar one-year interest rate is 1.0%.
- A bank will charge a fee of 0.5% of the $ amount covered for arranging a $ to €/£ forward contact, payable at the outset.
- Traded currency options are available with a one-year maturity. A call option, allowing the purchase of €/£ for $, with a strike price of $1.05500 = €/£1 and a contract size of $75,000 can be purchased for 1.75% of the $ amount covered, payable at the outset.
- A discount rate of 10% should be used to discount any cash-flows.

Requirement

(a) Compare the present value of cash-flows arising from hedging the order of 25,000 units under **each** of the TWO possible spot rates indicated by Meridian's accountant using:

(i) a forward contract; **and**

(ii) a currency option.

10 Marks

(b) Briefly discuss the hedging of the second order of 15,000 units (no detailed calculations are required).

2 Marks

Total 12 Marks

(Based on Chartered Accountants Ireland, CAP 2, SFMA, Summer 2018, Extract from Q4)

Question 20.7 Instrumedix (Level 2)

Note: in this question, reference is made to a fictitious overseas country, Rotina, and its fictitious currency, the Rotina rot (RR).

Background You are a recently qualified chartered accountant and have just commenced employment as a business finance manager with Instrumedix Ltd. Instrumedix is a prosperous private company whose four directors each own 25% of the share capital. The company is engaged in the distribution of healthcare equipment and acquires and supplies all its products locally.

Future Developments: Finncare A former colleague of one of the directors has opened a clinic, Finncare, in Rotina. Instrumedix has been invited to tender for a contract to supply healthcare equipment to this clinic. All tenders must be quoted in Rotina rot. The equipment can currently be sourced directly from the United States for $500,000. Instrumedix will undertake to re-engineer the equipment in a form suitable for distribution to Finncare. It is estimated that additional engineering, administration and distribution costs associated with this contract will be €/£60,000, incurred and payable in euro/Sterling (€/£).

The directors have agreed that the contract price should be quoted at an amount that will yield a profit of 20% of sales, in euro/Sterling (€/£), based on current exchange rates.

It will take one month for Finncare to determine who should be awarded the contract. If it is successful with its tender, Instrumedix will order the equipment, re-engineer and distribute it to Finncare within a further two weeks. It is expected that payment will be made, and monies received, two months after the contract has been awarded (three months from today).

The banks are quoting the following spot and forward rates:

	US dollar (US$)			Rotina rot (RR)		
	Offer	**Bid**		**Offer**	**Bid**	
Spot rate	1.680	1.700		6.950	6.975	
1-month forward rate	0.020	0.015	pm	0.400	0.450	disc
3-month forward rate	0.030	0.025	pm	0.550	0.600	disc

The following estimates have been made as to what future spot rates and forward contracts will be at various intervals over the next three months:

	US dollar (US$)		Rotina rot (RR)	
	Offer	**Bid**	**Offer**	**Bid**
Spot rates				
1 month's time	1.620	1.630	7.000	7.150
2 months' time	1.575	1.600	7.200	7.300
3 months' time	1.540	1.560	7.600	7.750
Forward rates in 1 month's time				
2-month forward rate	1.600	1.625	7.700	7.875
3-month forward rate	1.580	1.595	7.750	7.928

Three foreign exchange strategies are currently being considered by the directors:

1. Enter into a forward exchange contract immediately.
2. Wait until the contract has been awarded (i.e. one month), before entering into a forward exchange contract.
3. Do nothing.

The directors have expressed concern about the consequences of future exchange rate movements being contrary to predictions when adopting a particular exchange policy and about the fact that they are not guaranteed the Finncare contract.

Requirement Prepare a memorandum for the board of directors dealing with the following:

(a) Determine the price of the contract.

(b) In relation to the Finncare contract, consider the three foreign exchange strategies currently under review by the Board and outline the potential consequences of each strategy. Suggest and describe alternatives, if any, that may be more appropriate in the circumstances.

Total 24 Marks

(Based on Chartered Accountants Ireland, MABF, FAE, Extract from Autumn 1996, Q1)

Question 20.8 Interglaze (Level 2)

Note: in this question, reference is made to four fictitious overseas countries and their related fictitious currencies: Saxonia and the sax; Ruritania and the rur; Kostalonika and the kosta; and Dalmatria and the dal.

Background Interglaze Ltd is a large family-owned company that specialises in the design, manufacture and fitting of glass windows. The company has expanded rapidly over the past five years, due to the unprecedented growth in the Irish construction sector. The company's main customers are Irish construction companies that sub-contract the glazing element of building contracts to Interglaze.

Aware of the possibility of a downturn in the Irish construction market, the directors recently decided to undertake some contracts outside Ireland. Although smaller in size compared to many of its foreign competitors, Interglaze quickly developed a reputation as a high-quality operator. In particular, the company's ability to produce tailormade glass capable of meeting the stringent design requirements of leading international architects led to the award of a number of high-profile contracts, including the glazing of the Louvre museum in Paris.

Over the past number of years, Interglaze has successfully developed long-term trading relationships with all the major Irish construction companies. Interglaze has only recently entered foreign markets and has not yet been able to develop similar relationships with key foreign target customers, most of whom are construction companies operating in their respective countries. Consequently, the directors do not have the same degree of knowledge about potential foreign customers compared to their Irish equivalents.

This lack of background knowledge on foreign customers was recently demonstrated when Interglaze suffered a bad debt on a glazing contract completed in Saxonia. The Saxonian company had sent brochures detailing some of its previous contracts and looked, on paper, to be a very strong company. On this basis no other research was undertaken. However, the Saxonian company was extremely slow in making payment, which was due on completion of the contract. It subsequently transpired that the Saxonian company had incurred a major loss on another building contract, which ultimately caused it to go into liquidation. Eventually, Interglaze received approximately three million sax out of a total four million sax owed.

The directors had considered the foreign markets as having good long-term growth prospects, but in light of the bad debt experience in Saxonia, they are now extremely wary of undertaking any more contracts outside the Irish market, or with contractors with whom they do not have a previous trading/business relationship.

Ruritanian Contract Recently, Interglaze has been offered the opportunity to tender for a large contract in Ruritania. Although the contract would be very lucrative, the directors are unsure as to whether to proceed with this tender, given the concerns regarding possible bad debts. In view of the continued growth in the Irish market, some of the directors are proposing to abandon the expansion into overseas markets and, instead, concentrate on the Irish market. The directors have now commissioned an external review of the company's operations to determine future strategy. You are a senior consultant in a local firm of management consultants that has been appointed to undertake this exercise.

A leading firm of worldwide building contractors, which has heard of Interglaze's reputation for design and quality, has invited the company to tender for this prestigious contract in Ruritania. The tender must be priced in Ruritanian rurs. The contract will be awarded in three months' time, with payment being received nine months after the date on which the contract is awarded.

The sales director has priced the contract at €/£1 million, and the directors have decided to quote a price in rurs based on the current spot rates. Besides their fears over the possibility of another bad debt, Interglaze's directors are concerned about the degree to which the rur has weakened in recent months. In addition, the directors are keen to minimise foreign exchange risk associated with any further weakening in the rur. They are considering the following strategies:

- enter into a forward exchange contract now; or
- enter into a currency option now; or
- wait until the contract has been awarded and then enter a forward exchange contract.

The directors have asked for your recommendation as to the most appropriate strategy. Exchange rate details (€/£ to rur) are shown in Appendix I to this question.

Kostalonikan (Kosta) Loan On 31 August 20X2, Interglaze took out a 200 million kosta loan to pay for a new glass-cutting machine that was purchased in Kostalonika. The loan was taken out in kostas in order to avail of low Kostalonikan interest rates that were available at that time. In addition, the directors negotiated a repayment structure whereby the loan was repayable in a single repayment of 200 million kostas on 31 August 20X8, with interest costs being met on a normal quarterly basis.

However, in the last couple of years, Kostalonikan interest rates have increased sharply and the directors are concerned that Interglaze's higher interest costs are now having a negative impact on profitability. In order to reduce interest costs, the directors are now considering repaying the kosta loan by taking out a new bank facility, possibly in €/£ or Dalmatrian dals. Both Irish/UK and Dalmatrian interest rates are now significantly below Kostalonikan rates (details shown in Appendix II to this question).

If the loan was converted to €/£, the directors would propose increasing the company's existing €/£1 million overdraft facility to accommodate the Kostalonikan loan. As a result of the failure to collect the remaining one million sax (approximately €/£300,000) due from the Saxonian contract, and the continued growth of the business, the overdraft facility has been fully drawn down for the past six months. The company does not have any other bank facilities besides the overdraft and the Kostalonikan loan. The directors have asked for your advice on their proposal to repay the kosta loan, assuming there are no penalties on early repayment.

Appendix I

Ruritanian Contract (€/£ to Rr)

	The Rur	
Current spot and forward rates	**Offer**	**Bid**
Spot rate	1.250	1.300
3-month forward rate	0.050 disc	0.060 disc
9-month forward rate	0.150 disc	0.180 disc
12-month forward rate	0.200 disc	0.220 disc
Estimated forward rates in 3 months' time		
9-month forward rate	1.500	1.535
12-month forward rate	1.515	1.550

Options

12-month options can currently be obtained at the following prices:

Rur put option at €/£1 to rur 1.51 premium €/£500 per 100,000 rur

Rur call option at €/£1 to rur 1.51 premium €/£450 per 100,000 rur

Interest rates It should be assumed that Irish/UK interest rates are currently 6%.

Appendix II

Kostalonikan (Kosta) Loan

	Ireland/UK	**Kostalonika**	**Dalmatria**
Date loan was drawn (31/Aug/20X2)			
Exchange rates	€/£1	Kosta 200	n/a
Interest rates	12%	5%	n/a
Current (31/Aug/20X5)			
Exchange rates	€/£1	Kosta 150	n/a
Interest rates	6%	10%	4%

Requirement Draft a report to the managing director setting out your advice on the following matters:

(a) Advise the directors on whether they should continue the expansion into foreign markets, outlining the reasons for your answer. (***Note:*** ignore any capacity constraints.)

6 Marks

(b) Assuming that Interglaze decides to proceed with the expansion into foreign markets, suggest ways in which the company could minimise the possibility of incurring any further bad debts.

12 Marks

(c) Assuming that Interglaze proceeds with the Ruritanian tender, determine the price (in rurs) that the company should submit for this tender.

4 Marks

(d) Calculate the outcome of each of the three proposed foreign exchange strategies, and recommend which strategy you consider most appropriate in the circumstances.

16 Marks

(e) Advise the directors on their proposal to convert the Kostalonikan (kostas) loan into €/£ by way of an increase to the company's existing overdraft facility, or into a Dalmatrian (dals) facility. Outline any other recommendations you would make regarding the structure of the company's existing bank facilities.

12 Marks

Total 50 Marks

(Based on Chartered Accountants Ireland, MABF, FAE, Extract from Autumn 2002)

Question 20.9 Ziggy (Level 2)

Ziggy Plc has export orders from a company in Singapore for 250,000 ornamental daggers, and from a company in Indonesia for 100,000 ornamental daggers. The unit variable cost to Ziggy of producing ornamental daggers is 55 cents/pence. The unit sales price to Singapore is 2.862 Singapore dollars (SG$) and to Indonesia, 2,246 rupiah (Rp), the currency of Indonesia. Both orders are subject to credit terms of 60 days, and are payable in the currency of the importers. It is considered possible that either payment could be delayed for as long as 90 days.

The Indonesian customer has offered Ziggy the alternative of being paid US$125,000 in three months' time instead of payment in rupiah. The rupiah is forecast by Ziggy's bank to depreciate in value during the next year by 30% (from an Indonesian viewpoint) relative to the US dollar.

Whenever appropriate, Ziggy uses time option forward foreign exchange contracts.

Foreign exchange rates (mid rates)

	US$1 = SG$	**€/£1 = SG$**	**€/£1 = US$1**	**€/£1 = Rp**
Spot	2.1378	3.1780	1.4866	2,481
1-month forward	2.1132	3.1620	1.4963	No forward market
2-month forward	2.0964	3.1545	1.5047	No forward market
3-month forward	2.0915	3.1584	1.5101	No forward market

Assume that in the domestic economy any foreign currency holding must be immediately converted into euro/Sterling.

	Money market rates (% per year)	
	Deposit	**Borrow**
UK/Irish clearing bank	6.5	10.5
Singapore bank	4	7
Indonesian bank	15	Not available
US domestic bank	8	12

These interest rates are fixed rates for either immediate deposits or borrowing over a period of two or three months, but the rates for periods longer than three months are subject to future movement according to economic pressures.

Requirement

(a) (i) Given the information provided, calculate the euro/Sterling receipts that Ziggy can expect from its sales to Singapore and Indonesia, if the foreign exchange risk is hedged using:
(1) the money markets;
(2) forward exchange contracts.

8 Marks

(ii) Advise Ziggy on the optimal foreign exchange hedging strategy in relation to the Singaporean and Indonesian transactions.

(***Note:*** all contracts, including forward exchange and money market contracts, may be assumed to be free from the risk of default. Transaction costs, and any possibility of making arbitrage profits, may be ignored.)

4 Marks

(b) If the Indonesian customer offered immediate payment at a 5% discount on the rupiah unit sales price, calculate whether payment in this form would be advantageous to Ziggy.

4 Marks

(c) Discuss briefly the advantages and disadvantages to a company of invoicing an export sale in a foreign currency.

4 Marks
Total 20 Marks

(Based on Chartered Accountants Ireland, CAP 2, MABF, Summer 2009, Q2)

Question 20.10 Toys for Toddlers (Level 2)

Sean Campbell is the Finance Director at Toys for Toddlers Ltd (TFT), a company specialising in the production and distribution of toys for the UK and Ireland. The company has recently commenced Christmas toy production, a peak period for TFT that requires skilled casual labour. Their current star product is the Gizmo. It is 31 October 20X5.

Following the cancellation of a Christmas order for 50,000 Gizmo units (none of which had been manufactured by TFT), management were excited by an approach by a US company for an immediate USD quote for the delivery of 75,000 Gizmo units for Christmas, to be paid at the end of April 20X6. Sean has determined a minimum price of $25 per Gizmo unit, as outlined in the Appendix to this question.

A preliminary credit review of the US customer has revealed a 10% chance of a late payment or default. Sean is considering two options to manage the foreign exchange and receivable risk:

Option A Take out an insurance policy now with Safe Co. Inc. and utilise a forward contract to guarantee the amount to be received in €/£. The cost of the insurance is €/£52,500 and this provides 100% cover against late payment or default. The insurer will make any payment to TFT on 30 April 20X6 in USD. A local bank is prepared to offer an April 20X6 forward exchange rate of $1.27 to €/£1.00.

Option B Utilise the services of a non-recourse export factor who is willing to guarantee that €/£1,440,000 will be paid in six months, or €/£1,375,000 in nine months if the customer makes a late payment or defaults. The factor is willing to advance an immediate €/£1,000,000 at an interest cost of 6.0%. The costs of the arrangement are included within the guaranteed sum.

TFT can borrow funds in UK/Ireland at 6% per annum.

Requirement

(a) Determine how Sean calculated the relevant cost of packaging and skilled labour on the US order. You can assume that Sean's calculations are correct. All required information is contained in the Appendix to this question.

6 Marks

(b) Other than foreign exchange and receivable risk, briefly outline three key risks for TFT in accepting the US approach.

3 Marks

(c) (i) Assuming the minimum unit price ($25) is charged on the US order, determine the expected net receipts in €/£ that TFT can expect under both options to manage the foreign exchange and receivable risk.

8 Marks

(ii) Briefly outline TWO qualitative factors that TFT should consider for each proposed option prior to deciding which one to employ. You are not required to consider other potential options open to TFT.

4 Marks

Total 21 Marks

(Based on Chartered Accountants Ireland, CAP 2, MABF, Autumn 2010, Q3)

Appendix

Summarised Gizmo per Unit Costs

	TFT current cost	**US customer relevant cost**
	€/£	**€/£**
Variable costs		
Skilled labour costs (Note 1)	4.00	5.00
Packaging costs (Note 2)	3.00	0.70
Other variable costs	13.50	14.30
	20.50	20.00
Fixed costs	5.90	0
Total cost/relevant cost	26.40	20.00
Margin at 7%	1.85	0
Cost	28.25	20.00
Exchange rate		(US$1.25 to €/£1)
USD		$25.00

Note 1: Packaging Costs TFT had already committed to purchase the required 50,000 packaging units required for the UK order at €/£3 per unit. One unit of packaging material is utilised in the production of one unit of the Gizmo. The packaging supplier is now offering a discount of 10% on

all purchases and will honour this discount in respect of the original commitment should TFT increase its order size.

Note 2: Skilled Labour The production of Gizmo requires the use of skilled casual labour to meet annual demand. One unit of the Gizmo requires 30 minutes of skilled labour. TFT have estimated that 25% of the surplus skilled labour hours due to the loss of the UK order could be redeployed to other toy products, generating an additional contribution of €/£10 per labour hour. The remaining 75% is represented by skilled casual labour that would only be hired if the US order were accepted. Any additional skilled casual labour required for the US order would need to be contracted in, specifically for this purpose, from an employment agency quoting €/£13 per labour hour.

21

Interest Rate Risk

Learning Objectives

Upon completing this chapter, readers should be able to:

- explain interest rate risk;
- explain different methods of managing interest risk using hedging products; and
- perform simple calculations to determine the financial implications of a derivative position.

INTRODUCTION

Several factors need to be considered when managing debt, including maturity mix (covered in **Chapter 10**), cash synchronisation (i.e. matching cash outflows to cash inflows), currency mix (covered in **Chapter 20**) and interest rate risk, including whether to opt for fixed or floating rate interest. Interest rate risk arises when market rates change in a manner that was not expected. When a finance manager considers that interest rates will rise, it is likely that he or she will arrange debt that has a fixed rate of interest attached to it. When a finance manager considers that interest rates will fall, he or she is more likely to tie the company into floating rate debt. The problem arises when market rates turn out to be different from what the treasurer predicted. If market rates fall and the company's debt is on fixed interest rate terms, then the company will not benefit from the reduction in interest rates. Alternatively, when market rates rise and the company's debt is variable in nature, then the company is exposed to potential increases in cash outflows. Therefore, a business finance manager can take several steps to hedge against these unexpected interest rate movements or to speculate for financial gain, if it is the company's policy to do so. Common derivative products used to hedge against uncertainty include: interest rate swap agreements, interest rate futures contracts and forward interest rate agreements. In addition, more straightforward over-the-counter (OTC) products can be obtained either from banks, or in some instances the financial exchanges, to hedge interest rate exposures, including interest rate caps, collars and floors. This chapter discusses and provides a worked example on each type of hedging product.

INTEREST RATE SWAP AGREEMENTS

Swap agreements are commonly utilised to manage interest rate risk. Companies wanting to stabilise their cash flows arrange to exchange variable rate debt interest payments for fixed rate debt interest payments. This can be achieved using a **fixed-for-floating rate swap** agreement. An example of this is provided in **Worked Example 21.1**. The principal amounts do not change hands, just the net difference in the interest rates, less commission. The party that pays floating and receives fixed is said to be **short** in the swap; the party that pays fixed and receives floating is said to be **long** in the swap. The variable rate is usually pegged to an independent source, such as LIBOR, the European Bank's base rate (EURIBOR) or the FTSE 100 index. These swap agreements are straightforward and at the start the perceived gain on the swap is zero as one party will have to pay the other party to take the risks – this will typically be that party's best estimate of what they expect the profit on the swap to be. Profits/losses occur when the movement in the market interest rate (or whatever the swap is pegged to) differs from that expected, as shown in **Worked Example 21.1**.

Worked Example 21.1: Swap Contracts for Hedging Purposes

John Plc has €/£2,000,000 of debt on which it pays interest at the rate of 5%. Paul Plc also has €/£2,000,000 of debt on which it pays interest at the rate of LIBOR/EURIBOR plus 100 basis points (equivalent to 1%). LIBOR/EURIBOR is currently 5%. In both instances, the principal amount has to be repaid to the lenders in five years' time.

John Plc expects interest rates to fall and therefore wants to speculate a little by converting his interest payments to floating rate. Paul Plc is quite heavily geared and wants to reduce its financial risk by locking-in interest rates to a fixed rate. Both parties are introduced to each other by their respective banks, who agree to administer the contract.

Requirement

(a) Calculate the fee that Paul Plc will have to pay John Plc to get it to sign up to the swap, at the above rates. John Plc's cost of capital is 7%.

(b) Calculate the profit/loss made by John Plc and Paul Plc if LIBOR/EURIBOR:
  (i) rises to 7%;
  (ii) falls to 3%.

Solution

(a) The minimum fee that John Plc will accept to enter into the swap agreement (given the differential in the interest rates) must cover the cost of the additional interest that John Plc expects to pay over the life of the swap. At the present time John Plc is paying 5%, Paul Plc is paying 6%. Therefore, John Plc will not enter this agreement unless Paul Plc pays it an initial premium to cover the present value of the interest differential, assuming the differential remains for five years. Therefore, the initial fee payable by Paul Plc to John Plc is the present value of a five-year annuity of €/£20,000 [€/£2,000,000 × 1%] at 7%, which is €/£20,000 × 4.10 = €/£82,000.

(b) (i) Assume that interest rates rise to 7%: in this instance, John Plc's interest charge before the deal is €/£100,000 [€/£2,000,000 × 5%].

Paul Plc's interest charge before the deal is €/£160,000 [€/£2,000,000 × 8%].

Because both parties have signed up to a swap agreement, John Plc will have to pay Paul Plc €/£60,000, being the difference between the variable rate interest (€/£160,000) that the company wanted and the fixed rate that the company currently pays (€/£100,000). In the first year Paul Plc will have to pay John Plc the agreement fee of €/£82,000.

(ii) Assume that interest rates fall to 3%: in this instance, John Plc's interest charge before the deal is €/£100,000 [€/£2,000,000 × 5%].

Paul Plc's interest charge before the deal is €/£80,000 [€/£2,000,000 × 4%].

In this instance, Paul Plc will have to pay John Plc the interest differential of €/£20,000 [€/£100,000 – €/£80,000] each year plus the initial fee of €/£82,000.

This example shows a straightforward simple swap. In practice, there are fees and other conditions that can be written into the agreement, in particular, penalties for breaking the agreement can be quite high, possibly the present value of the losses to the company (gain to the counterparty) at current rates or rates that are specified in the original swap contract. The Financial Conduct Authority (FCA) in the UK has acted against banks, considering that they mis-sold these products to small businesses that did not have the in-house expertise available to consider the potential pitfalls that may arise. In many instances the FCA considered that the banks did not make the downside risk clear to the businesses and compensatory payouts have already started – see **Real World Example 21.1**.

Real World Example 21.1: Mis-selling of Swap Products

Interest rate swaps are sold as protection against a rise in interest rates without the customer fully grasping the downside risks. They were marketed as low-cost protection against rising interest rates, often as a condition of a business loan. But businesses, such as small B&Bs and takeaway shops, were left with major bills after the financial crisis caused interest rates to slide. Many faced steep penalties to get out of the deals.

The FCA found that the banks mis-sold the products and ordered banks to pay compensation to those who were deemed to be "unsophisticated" when they entered into the swap agreement. Any business with a turnover of more than £6.5 million is deemed to be sophisticated. Over £2 billion was paid out in compensation to customers.

Swap agreements are also commonly used to hedge both interest rate and currency rate risk in one contract. This typically happens when a company issues bonds or obtains bank debt in a foreign country and wants to convert the whole transaction into the domestic currency, or when a company wants foreign currency for business reasons (to pay for an investment in that country or to pay for supplies that are being received from that country). The whole currency/interest swap agreement is usually arranged through a bank and typically has three stages. In the first instance the principal amounts are exchanged, usually at spot rate, then the interest payments are exchanged (this can be fixed-for-variable, fixed-for-fixed, or variable-for-variable). Finally, the original principal amounts are re-exchanged at an exchange rate that is agreed at the outset. The patterns of cash flows are best explained using an example. Assume that A Plc (a RoI company) requires £40 million and B Plc (a UK company) requires €50 million.

The two companies enter into a currency and interest rate swap agreement through their bank. The three steps to this agreement are outlined in **Figures 21.1**, **21.2** and **21.3**.

FIGURE 21.1: CURRENCY AND INTEREST RATE SWAP (STEP 1): EXCHANGE OF PRINCIPAL AMOUNTS

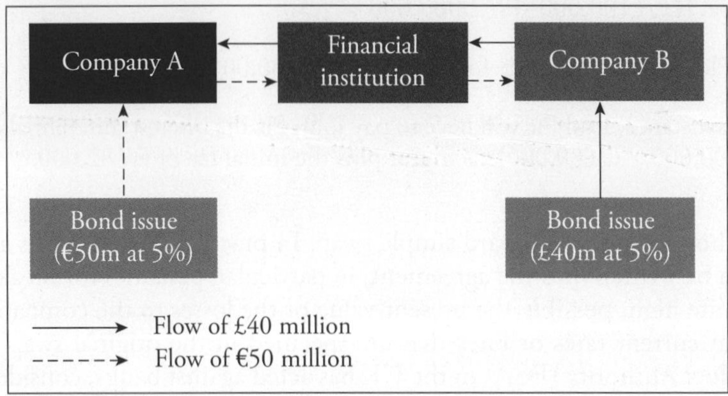

FIGURE 21.2: CURRENCY AND INTEREST RATE SWAP (STEP 2): INTEREST PAYMENTS DURING THE LIFE OF A SWAP CONTRACT

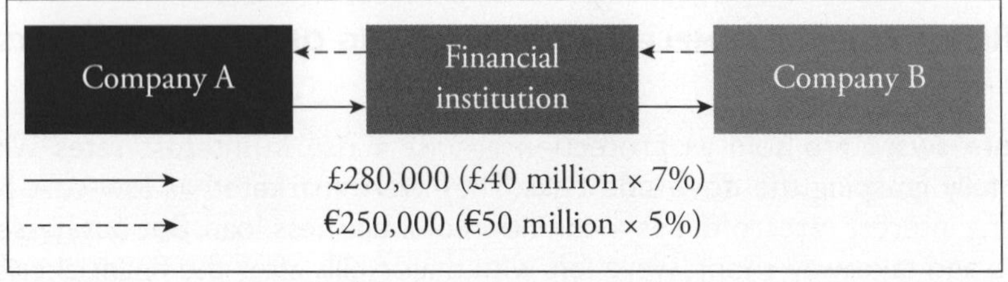

FIGURE 21.3: CURRENCY AND INTEREST RATE SWAP (STEP 3): REPAYMENT OF THE PRINCIPAL SUM

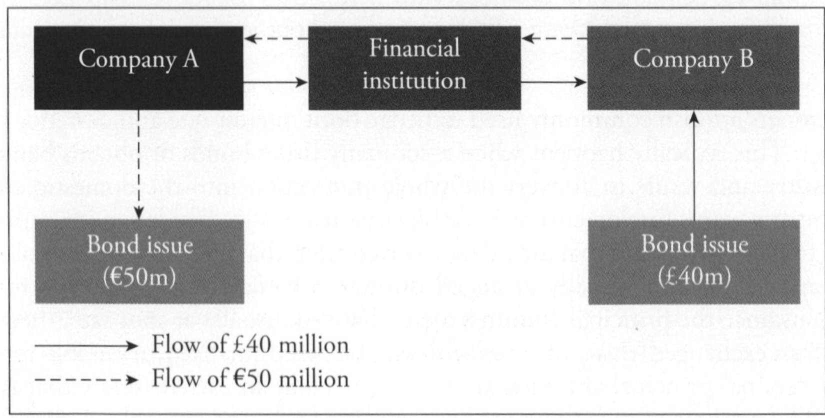

A Plc receives €50 million from a bond issue, which it transfers through the financial institution to B Plc, in return for B Plc transferring £40 million to it. Both parties will pay the financial institution a premium for arranging the swap. The lines represent the flow of cash that will occur each year for the duration of the swap contract. Company A can then use the euro received from B to pay the coupon to the debt holders each year and Company B can use the Sterling received from company A to pay its debt holders.

The financial intermediary that set up this transaction and that administers it will receive a commission on every currency transfer. This makes the swap expensive. The cash flows in relation to the principal amount are fully hedged from the perspectives of both Company A and Company B. However, the interest payments are not. For example, Company A, which is located in the Republic of Ireland, will need to find £280,000 each year to honour its side of the swap agreement. This will probably be obtained using transactions that are exchanged at the spot rate in existence each time the payment is required. The companies can opt to hedge these cash flows separately also using, for example, forward rate contracts.

At the end of the swap contract Company A will return the £40 million to Company B, which will use it to redeem its debentures; and Company B will return the €50 million to Company A, which will also use it to redeem its debentures.

As in all hedging transactions, one of the parties will make a loss and the other a profit when currency rates and exchange rates differ from those built into the swap agreement. Most companies are happy to accept the possibility of making a loss on the agreement, so long as cash flows are certain. Indeed, some companies and financial institutions will enter into these agreements for speculative purposes, not to hedge risk exposures.

Swaptions

A **swaption** is an option to buy an interest rate swap agreement. It gives a company the right, but not the obligation, to enter into an interest rate swap agreement.

INTEREST RATE FUTURES CONTRACTS

An **interest rate futures** contract has two parties: one who agrees to buy or sell a standard quantity of a particular financial instrument on or before a future date at a set price; a futures exchange is typically the counterparty. One of the counterparties will make a profit, the other an equal loss, depending on how market interest rates move. The futures contract is totally independent of the principal debt amount; indeed, the holders of futures contracts do not have to hold or own the financial instrument at all. They just have to agree to pay or receive the difference in the price of the notional amount of principal. When futures are used to hedge interest rate risk, the interest payments are set up in the opposite direction to the interest payments on the underlying principal amount, so when interest rates move in one direction the future's price will move in the opposite direction. A futures price of 98 means an interest rate of 2%. If the interest rates increase to 3%, then futures prices will to move to 97. **Short-term interest rates futures** are called STIRs. They normally have three-month maturities. Long-term products may also be available depending on the market.

Investment: Interest Hedging using Futures Contracts

Futures contracts can be used to hedge returns on deposits, in particular **certificates of deposit (CD)**. A CD is a relatively risk-free savings product that offers a fixed rate of return for a specified period. Any withdrawals from the CD will incur a financial penalty. Hedging will be considered by a company that has funds coming free for investment in the future where it thinks the market interest rates may fall in the period up to the point of the funds being available. The company can buy futures now to lock into the higher interest rates that are currently being offered (lower futures price) and sell them later when interest rates are lower (higher futures price) to close the position. Note, Sterling futures have a notional value of £500,000 and euro of €1,000,000 on NYSE Liffe (London). Futures profits and losses are also assumed to be for three months, not 12 months.

When a company makes a loss on the actual interest being paid in the money markets (relative to the interest rate target), this will be offset by an equal profit being made on the futures contract when the interest rate and futures contract move by the same amount but in the opposite direction. When it comes to hedging against a fall in investment interest income, the rule is always to buy interest rate futures contracts. Companies should only get involved in hedging interest investment income if they consider that interest rates will fall and they will need to consider if the fall will be more than the cost involved in transacting in futures. The costs include broker commission.

Debt Hedging using Futures Contracts

When a company wishes to hedge interest rate exposure on debt, the concern is that interest rates will increase. In general, when a company expects interest rates to rise, it will sell futures. When interest rates rise, the value of futures contracts fall, which means the company will buy futures at the lower price to close the position, making a profit on the future. This profit should offset the higher interest rate being charged in the market place (so long as the future and interest rate movements are exactly the same but in opposite directions).

FORWARD INTEREST RATE AGREEMENTS

Forward interest rate agreements (FRAs) are over-the-counter (OTC) future contracts that are bespoke. They are usually arranged between a company and its bank. In a forward rate agreement, the counterparties to a contract agree to pay or receive interest on a specified nominal sum at a prearranged date. The actual loan/investment is a different contract. Payments made or received on the forward rate contract are due on the maturity of the contract and only the difference between the agreed interest rates and the market rates is either paid to, or received from the bank – depending on whether the forward contract made a profit, or not. The contract normally matures on the date the actual investment or loan is made and the payment or receipt is made on this date. It is typically discounted to its present value to reflect the time value of money at market rates.

An example of a FRA to hedge against falls in investment interest is outlined in **Worked Example 21.2**.

Worked Example 21.2: FRA – Hedging Investment Interest Rate Exposure

ABC Plc is going to receive €/£8,000,000 in three months' time and the finance manager wishes to invest the funds in CDs for a three-month period. The finance manager is concerned that interest rates are going to fall. The bank is offering to provide a forward rate agreement to cover the investment at 4% starting in three months' time for a three-month period.

Requirement

(a) Demonstrate the financial implications of this transaction assuming the market rates of interest move to 3%.

(b) Demonstrate the financial implications of this transaction assuming the market rates of interest move to 6%.

Solution

(a) The fixed interest that is receivable in the marketplace on the €/£8,000,000 in three months available at 3% equates to a cash inflow of €/£60,000 [€/£8,000,000 × 3% × 3/12] receivable at the end of the CD period from the bank.

Under the FRA, ABC Plc will be entitled to a receipt of €/£20,000 [€/£8,000,000 × (4% – 3%) × 3/12] from the bank. If the settlement date from the bank is in six months, then it will receive the full €/£20,000 on that date, making its total income from the hedged transaction €/£80,000 [€/£60,000 + €/£20,000]. However, if the FRA has a settlement date at the start of the FRA (more common), then the bank will pay ABC Plc the present value of the settlement amount discounted at the market rate of interest. This equates to a cash receipt of €/£19,851 [€/£20,000 × (1 ÷ 1.0075*)] on the first day of the FRA.

*3% for three months equates to 0.75%.

(b) The fixed interest rate that is receivable in the marketplace on the €/£8,000,000 in three months available at 6% equates to a cash inflow of €/£120,000 [€/£8,000,000 × 6% × 3/12] receivable at the end of the CD period from the bank.

Under the FRA, ABC Plc will have to make a payment of €/£40,000 [€/£8,000,000 × (4% – 6%) × 3/12] to the bank. If the settlement date from the bank is in six month's time then it will have to pay the full €/£40,000 on that date, making its total income from the hedged transaction €/£80,000 [€/£120,000 – €/£40,000]. However, if the FRA has a settlement date at the start of the FRA (more common), then ABC Plc will have to pay the bank the present value of the settlement amount discounted at the market rate of interest. This equates to a cash payment of €/£39,409 [€/£40,000 × (1 ÷ 1.015*)] on the first day of the FRA.

*6% for three months equates to 1.5%.

Worked Example 21.3 covers the situation where the company wants to hedge against interest rate movements on future debt.

Worked Example 21.3: Forward Rate Agreement – Hedging Debt Interest Rate Exposure

Gato Plc is planning to borrow €/£10 million in three months' time for a three-month period. The finance manager in Gato Plc reckons that interest rates are going to rise steadily over the next year. Therefore, it decided to enter into a forward rate agreement with Pajaro Bank Plc to minimise the company's exposure to fluctuations in interest rates in this period. The current interest rate is 7% and the bank agrees to provide debt at this rate in three months' time. The bank will charge a premium for this, particularly if it feels that interest rates are going to rise.

Requirement

(a) Assume that interest rates in three months' time move to 10% and Gato Plc loans the €/£10 million from Pero Bank Plc on this date for a period of three months. Show how this can be hedged, assuming Gato Plc enters into the forward rate agreement with Pajaro Bank Plc now.

(b) Assume that interest rates fall to 6% and Gato Plc loans the €/£10 million from Pero Bank Plc on this date for a period of three months. Show the cash flows that will result assuming Gato Plc enters into the forward rate agreement with the Pajaro Bank Plc now.

Solution

(a) **Step 1:** to hedge the transaction Gato Plc enters into a forward rate agreement with Pajaro Bank Plc to borrow €/£10 million in three months' time at 7%.

Step 2: in three months' time Gato Plc borrows €/£10 million at the spot rate of 10%. This loan is sourced from Pero bank Plc.

Step 3: at the end of the three months Gato Plc will have to pay Pero Bank Plc €/£250,000 [€/£10 million × 10% × 3/12].

Step 4: at the start of the FRA, Gato PLC will receive €/£73,171 [€/£250,000 – €/£175,000 (€/£10 million × 7% × 3/12) × 1/1.025] from Pajaro Bank Plc.*

*The agreement states that Gato Plc should pay interest of €/£175,000 and Pajaro Bank Plc is guaranteeing this. If Gato Plc has to pay more, the Pajaro Bank Plc will compensate it with the difference discounted at the market rate (10% for three months, which equates to 2.5%).

(b) **Step 1:** to hedge the transaction Gato Plc enters into a forward rate agreement with Pajaro Bank Plc to borrow €/£10 million in three months' time at 7%.

Step 2: in three months' time Gato Plc borrows €/£10 million at the spot rate of 6%. This loan is sourced from Pero Bank Plc.

Step 3: at the end of the three months Gato Plc will have to pay Pero Bank Plc €/£150,000 [€/£10m × 6% × 3/12].

Step 4: at the start of the FRA, Gato Plc will have to pay €/£24,631 [(€/£175,000 (€/£10m × 7% × 3/12) − €/£150,000) × (1 ÷ 1.015)] to Pajaro Bank Plc.*

*The agreement states that Gato Plc should pay interest of €/£175,000. If Gato Plc has less interest to pay, then it has to pay Pajaro Bank Plc the difference discounted at the market rate (i.e. 6% for three months, which equates to 1.5%).

INTEREST RATE OPTIONS

Similar to a currency rate option, an interest rate option gives the holder the right, but not the obligation, to trade at pre-agreed interest rate (the exercise rate) at some predefined date in the future. Interest rate options can be tailormade or exchange traded interest rate options. Interest rate caps, collars and floors are examples of OTC option contracts.

OTC Options: Caps, Collars and Floors

A **cap** is a pre-agreed ceiling interest rate that can be written into variable interest loan agreements. The interest rate charged moves with changes in the base rate (EURIBOR or LIBOR), but only to the ceiling level, the cap rate. The company is only charged the cap rate when the base rates are beyond that level. When the rates are beyond the cap level, the bank suffers a loss. Because the bank takes over this risk, it will charge a set-up fee for this facility, the size of the fee being dependent on how likely the rates are to exceed the stated cap rate. A benefit of a cap is that it reduces a company's downside risk, while allowing the company to reap all the benefits were interest rates to fall. A **floor** is a pre-agreed lower interest rate that the interest charged will not fall below. It can be written into variable interest loan agreements. Like a cap, the interest rate charged floats with the base rate, but does not fall below the floor level. The company absorbs the loss when market rates fall below the floor level, as the company has to pay interest to the bank at the floor level. Because of this the bank is unlikely to charge a fee to set up this type of agreement, or charges a lower fee relative to the other loan products. A **collar** is a combination of a cap and a floor. The interest rate charged by the bank will not exceed the cap level, nor will it fall below the floor level. The fee charged by the bank in a collar transaction will be less than that charged for a cap agreement, but more than that charged for a floor agreement, because the bank has a chance of making excess returns if rates fall below floor level.

Worked Example 21.4: Collar, Cap and Floor Options

Simba Plc wishes to hedge against interest rates increases above the current rate of 8% on its borrowing, which is rolled over every six months. The premium of 1% is quoted by the bank for an interest rate cap of 10%, but this was considered by the treasurer as too high. The treasurer also took the view that interest rates were unlikely to fall during the lifetime of the loan. A bank has offered Simba an interest rate collar with a cap of 10% and a floor of 7% for a premium of 0.5%.

Assume three scenarios, where the market rates on the rollover date are:

(i) 5%;
(ii) 7%;
(iii) 12%.

Requirement Show the overall interest rate, including any premium that Simba will have to pay, for each scenario on:

(a) the interest rate cap;
(b) the interest rate collar.

Solution

(a) Cap

(i) Market rate on the rollover date is 5%

Effective cost	
Premium	1.0%
Interest	5.0%
Net cost	6.0%

(ii) Market rate on the rollover date is 7%

Effective cost	
Premium	1.0%
Interest	7.0%
Net cost	8.0%

(iii) Market rate on the rollover date is 12%

Effective cost	
Premium	1.0%
Interest	12.0%
Cap	(2.0%)
Net cost	11.0%

(b) Collar

(i) Market rate on the rollover date is 5%

Effective cost	
Premium	0.5%
Interest	5.0%
Collar	2.0%
Net cost	7.5%

(ii) Market rate on the rollover date is 7%

Effective cost

Premium	0.5%
Interest	7.0%
Net cost	7.5%

(iii) Market rate on the rollover date is 12%

Effective cost

Premium	0.5%
Interest	12.0%
Collar	(2.0%)
Net cost	10.5%

The cap is best if interest rates are low, but the collar is best if the rates are above the *floor* rate due to the lower premium.

CONCLUSION

Companies are subject to interest rate risk when they have to accept variable rates of interest on investments and on debts. A variety of options are available for companies to hedge this exposure, including OTC bank products such as caps, floors and collars, interest rate swaps, FRAs and exchange traded future contracts and options on future contracts. In all instances commission and fees are required and some downside risk may still be evident. For example, trading in futures contracts rarely provides a perfect hedge as the standard exchange contract sizes may not be an exact multiple of the amount being invested/borrowed and the futures contract price may not move by exactly the same amount as the interest rate movement. In addition, fees are payable. Bespoke hedges, such as FRAs, are normally more expensive to set up due to their tailored specification and a cost–benefit analysis needs to be performed to see if the cost of hedging is likely to be outweighed by the benefit of hedging.

EXAMINATION STANDARD QUESTION: SWAP, COLLAR AND FIXED RATE DEBT

Armagh Metals Ltd own several zinc and lead mines throughout Ireland. It has recently purchased a new mining licence and made a major capital investment to begin mining at the site. The total cost of this investment (€/£3,950,000) was financed with an interest-only 10-year, floating rate loan. The interest rate on this loan is EURIBOR/LIBOR + 5.75%. Armagh is concerned that, although interest rates are very low currently, they may rise and is seeking to protect itself from potentially higher borrowing costs in the future. EURIBOR/LIBOR is currently 2%. Loan interest is payable at the end of each year.

Following a meeting with Armagh's bank, the following three hedging approaches have been suggested.

1. **Swap Contract** A 10-year swap contract, where Armagh will pay fixed 7.3% and receive EURIBOR/LIBOR + 5.7% on a notional principal of €/£3,950,000. An arrangement fee of 0.5% of the notional principal is payable immediately.

2. **Interest Rate Collar** For the full €/£3,950,000 loan, Armagh purchases a cap at 7.9% for a premium payable of 0.25% and sells a floor at 5.9% for a premium receivable of 0.20%.

3. **Refinance Loan at Fixed Rate** Armagh refinances the floating rate loan using a €/£3,950,000 10-year fixed rate loan, interest only at a rate of 8%. An arrangement fee of 0.5% of the borrowed sum would be payable immediately.

Armagh has just agreed to sell a mining operation in Ireland to a competitor. It will receive €/£2,875,000 tomorrow from this transaction. Armagh plans to reinvest this sum in a future acquisition two years from now. In the interim it is seeking a suitable short-term investment for this cash, but is concerned about the very low returns available from bank deposits.

Requirement

(a) For each of the three proposed hedges, calculate the interest and hedging cash flows that would arise in year one if EURIBOR/LIBOR were immediately to:

(i) rise to 3%; and

(ii) fall to 1%.

Ignore the time value of money and taxation. Advise Armagh which hedging approach to use.

13 Marks

(b) Advise Armagh on alternatives to a bank deposit for the €/£2,875,000 and recommend a suitable short-term investment option.

4 Marks
Total 17 Marks

(Based on Chartered Accountants Ireland, CAP 2, SFMA, Autumn 2018, Extract from Q4)

Solution

(a) Information summary:

Current EURIBOR/LIBOR rate		2.00%
Floating	EUR/LIB+	5.75%
Current rate		7.75%
Loan principal		€/£3,950,000
Annual interest at current rate		€/£306,125
Swap fixed rate		7.30%
Swap floating	EUR/LIB+	5.70%
Cap		7.90%
Floor		5.90%
Fixed rate		8.00%

Two interest-rate scenarios

(i)	EUR/LIB rises to	3.00%
(ii)	EUR/LIB falls to	1.00%

If interest rate risk is not hedged

			Time
(i)	EUR/LIB rises by 1%	8.75%	
	Interest payable	€/£345,625	1 Year
(ii)	EUR/LIB falls by 1%	6.75%	
	Interest payable	€/£266,625	1 Year

Three hedging options:

1. Swap Contract

(i)	EUR/LIB rises by 1%	8.75%	
	Interest payable	€/£345,625	1 Year
	Swap interest received (EUR/LIB + 5.7%)	(€/£343,650)	
	Swap interest payable (7.3%)	€/£288,350	
	Net interest	€/£290,325	
	Fees	€/£19,750	Today
	Total cost	€/£310,075	

(ii) EUR/LIB falls by 1%	**6.75%**	
Interest payable	€/£266,625	1 Year
Swap interest received (EUR/LIB + 5.7%)	(€/£264,650)	
Swap interest payable (7.3%)	€/£288,350	
Net interest	€/£290,325	
Fees	€/£19,750	Today
Total cost (7.85%)	€/£310,075	

2. Collar

(i) EUR/LIB rises by 1%	8.75%	
Interest payable (cap @ 7.9%)	€/£312,050	1 Year
Fees: 0.25% paid	€/£9,875	Today
0.2% received	(€/£7,900)	Today
Net fee	€/£1,975	Today
Total cost	€/£314,025	
(ii) EUR/LIB falls by 1%	6.75%	
Interest payable (floor @ 5.9%)	€/£266,625	1 Year
(***Note:*** interest rate does not trigger floor)		
Fees: 0.25% paid	€/£9,875	Today
0.2% received	(€/£7,900)	Today
Net fee	€/£1,975	Today
Total cost	€/£268,600	
Average [(€/£314,025 + €/£268,600)÷2]	€/£291,313	

3. Fixed Rate Refinance

(i) EUR/LIB rises by 1%	8.75%	
Interest payable (fixed)	€/£316,000	1 Year
Fees (0.5%)	€/£19,750	Today
Total cost	€/£335,750	

(ii) EUR/LIB falls by 1%	6.75%	
Interest payable (fixed)	€/£316,000	1 Year
Fees (0.5%)	€/£19,750	Today
Total cost (8.5%)	€/£335,750	

Advice The swap and the fixed rate hedge both have symmetrical pay-offs, that is, the same pay-off regardless of interest rate over the period. The swap is significantly cheaper, however. The fixed rate hedge can therefore be discounted as an efficient hedge. The collar provides protection from interest rate rises at the cost of giving up some of the potential savings of an interest rate fall. In this case it appears to be worth accepting the volatility of the collar hedge as the maximum interest cost is only marginally above the cost of the swap and the collar offers significant upside in interest savings, should rates fall. The collar therefore represents the best alternative in this instance.

(b) Interest rates generally have been extremely low for a decade, to an extent unprecedented in modern economic history. Bank deposits interest rates are close to zero in most cases. Armagh has some alternatives, depending on its risk appetite:

- Government bonds, particularly short-duration bonds (two years), offer very low returns (close to zero); they are currently, however, risk-free.
- Corporate bonds would offer higher returns to Armagh over the two-year investment horizon. The riskier the company (i.e. bonds with a lower credit rating), the higher the return offered.
- Equity investments – a diversified equity portfolio would offer significantly higher expected returns over a two-year investment horizon, however the variance in returns over this short a period would be very large and therefore this type of investment would not be suitable for Armagh.

A diversified portfolio of corporate bonds would offer the best trade-off between risk and return over this time horizon for Armagh.

Key Terms

Cap
Certificate of deposit (CD)
Collar
Custody account statements
Fixed-for-floating rate swap
Floor
Forward interest rate agreement
Interest rate futures
Long position
Short position
Swap agreement
Swaption

REVIEW QUESTIONS

(See Suggested Solutions to Review Questions in **Appendix B.**)

Question 21.1

Explain how an interest rate futures option works.

Question 21.2

ABC Plc wants to borrow €/£5 million in three months' time for three months. The current rate of interest is 3.4% and the company treasurer does not want the borrowing rate to exceed 5%. What product would you advise?

Question 21.3

DEF Plc wants to borrow €/£15 million in three months' time for six months. The current rate of interest is 5% and the company treasurer does not want the rate to exceed 6%. The bank offers a cap at 6% for 0.2% premium of the size of the loan, but will reduce this to 0.1% if DEF Plc agrees to a floor level of 4.5%.

Requirement Demonstrate the financial implications of the arrangement if interest rates move to:

(a) 5.2% for the full duration;
(b) 4% for the full duration;
(c) 7% for the full duration.

Question 21.4

Stimpy Plc, an Irish company, wants to borrow £10 million for seven years at a fixed rate to finance a capital investment in Manchester. The cheapest rate that Stimpy Plc can obtain on the money markets is 10.25% per annum. This is cheaper than borrowing in Ireland. Stimpy Plc can borrow euro at a floating rate of LIBOR + 0.5%.

Stimpy Plc's bankers suggest that one of its UK customers (Wrent Plc) would be interested in a swap agreement that would match the capital value in full. Wrent Plc requires a floating rate euro loan. They have been pricing the market in the UK and the best deal they have been offered is LIBOR + 1.5%. It could borrow in Sterling at the fixed rate of 11.5%. The bank charges a set arrangement fee of 0.15% each year, payable by both Stimpy Plc and Wrent Plc. The current exchange rate is €1.25 to £1.

Requirement Create a swap agreement that would be agreeable to both Stimpy Plc and Wrent Plc.

CHALLENGING QUESTIONS

(Suggested Solutions to Challenging Questions are available through your lecturer.)

Question 21.1 Property Holdings (Level 2) Interest rate protection

Property Holdings has a significant level of long-term bank loans that were used to assist in funding the acquisition of the company's investment property portfolio. The directors are concerned about the possibility that long-term interest rates may increase, which would lead to a significant increase in the interest payable on the company's bank borrowings. You have been asked to outline to the board some possible options for protecting the company from adverse interest rate movements.

Requirement Outline three alternative ways to protect the company against possible increases in interest rates on the company's long-term loans, indicating the merits and demerits of each alternative.

10 Marks

(Based on Chartered Accountants Ireland, MABF, FAE, Extract from Autumn 2003)

Question 21.2 Top Parts (Level 2) Foreign exchange risk management

A Moldovan customer was to be invoiced 51,000,000 MDL in May and 51,000,000 MDL in November for payments at the end of June 20X6 and December 20X6, respectively. The Finance Manager planned to hedge the currency exposure from 1 January 20X6. The expected annual interest rate for 20X6 was 6% locally and 10% in Moldova. The spot rate on 1 January 20X6 was MDL17 to €/£1. Top Parts' local bank offered a forward rate of MDL17.4 to €/£1 for June and MDL17.6 to €/£1 for December.

Requirement Explain (with supporting calculations) how the currency exposure created in June and December on the Moldovan contract could have been hedged, using the forward and money markets from 1 January 20X6, and comment briefly on the results.

6 Marks

(Based on Chartered Accountants Ireland, CAP 2, MABF, Summer 2011, Q1(b))

Question 21.3 Starling (Level 2)

Jim is expanding production capacity. Starling currently manufactures its products in a factory in the west of Ireland that is operating at maximum capacity. An adjacent site has been acquired for a new factory and Jim has now to secure funding for this new factory. Jim's intention is to use debt to fund the factory as Starling is currently an all-equity-financed company, however Jim is worried about interest rate increases in the future. Jim has read a newspaper article recently saying that interest rates "were at an all-time low and could only go in one direction". Starling would need to borrow €/£8 million. The three-month LIBOR/EURIBOR rate is currently 4.5%. Starling's bank was very keen to lend the money and offered two financing alternatives to Jim. The two financing alternatives are detailed below.

Alternatives proposed by Starling's bank:

1. Fixed rate, interest-only loan of €/£8 million for five years, with capital repayable in five years. Interest rate of 6.75%. Payments would be made annually in arrears. An arrangement fee of €/£100,000 would be payable immediately.
2. Variable rate, interest only, loan of €/£8,000,000 for five years. Variable rate will be adjusted on a weekly basis. With capital repayable in five years. Interest rate of three-month LIBOR/EURIBOR + 1.5%. This can be hedged using a swap contract, where Starling would pay a fixed rate of 6.35% and would receive three-month LIBOR/EURIBOR + 1.5%. Payments would be made annually in arrears. A fee of 1% of the principal amount is payable immediately for arranging a swap.

You should ignore any interest rate exposure after the first year. You can also ignore the impact of taxation and the time value of money.

Requirement

(a) Outline the cumulative cash flows that will arise in the first year from each of the two financing alternatives proposed by Starling's bank assuming that:

(i) immediately after borrowing LIBOR/EURIBOR falls to 2.5% and then remains unchanged thereafter; and

(ii) immediately after borrowing LIBOR/EURIBOR rises to 6% and then remains unchanged thereafter.

9 Marks

(b) Advise Starling on which of the two financing alternatives it should choose. In your answer outline the factors you considered in making your decision.

4 Marks

Total 13 Marks

(Based on Chartered Accountants Ireland, CAP 2, MABF, Summer 2013, Extract from Q3)

Question 21.4 Delphi (Level 2)

Delphi Limited provides a range of consulting and outsourcing services in Ireland. Delphi is owned by Helen Hayes and her husband, Jim Hayes. Helen is the managing director and Jim is the financial director. Delphi currently operates from premises in Dublin.

Delphi has recently begun consulting for several new clients in the south of the country and is finding it difficult to maintain the required quality of service without a base near these clients. Helen proposed, at a recent board meeting, that Delphi consider acquiring premises in Cork. Jim has located a suitable office building in a business park outside Cork City that is for sale for €/£3 million.

Delphi has been consistently profitable since being founded 20 years ago and Jim and Helen have reinvested most of Delphi's profits into the business, with the consequence that Delphi is now entirely financed by equity. Delphi has €/£4 million cash on deposit, most of which is from the recent sale of its minority interest in a German consulting firm. Delphi had intended paying a dividend of €/£3.5 million in three months' time with this money. At a recent board meeting the directors decided that if they were to proceed with the acquisition of the Cork premises, they should investigate using debt to finance it. Helen and Jim considered the possibility of buying the Cork premises personally and renting it to Delphi, but decided against this.

Jim and his accountants met a relationship manager from Delphi's bank last week and presented Delphi's proposal to borrow €/£3 million to finance the purchase of the Cork premises. The bank was very supportive of the proposal given Delphi's strong cash flow and the fact that it currently has no debt. The bank has offered a 10-year, interest-only loan facility of €/£3 million and outlined a number of interest rate alternatives below (the bank does not offer fixed rate loans):

1. A floating rate of EURIBOR/LIBOR +1.5%.
2. A loan at the above floating rate and a 10-year swap arrangement where Delphi will pay a fixed rate of 5.25% and receive EURIBOR/LIBOR +1.5%. The counterparty to this swap will be another customer of the bank who the bank does not wish to name for confidentiality reasons. An initial arrangement fee of 2% of the notional principal is payable to the bank for arranging this swap.
3. A loan at the above floating rate and a 10-year interest rate collar arrangement with a cap and floor rate, respectively, of 6% and 4%. An annual premium of 0.5% of the notional principal is payable to the bank for arranging this contract.

(***Note:*** EURIBOR/LIBOR is currently 2.5%. The applicable corporation tax rate is 12.5%.)

Requirement

(a) Advise Helen and Jim Hayes, as the shareholders in Delphi, on whether Delphi should finance the purchase of the Cork premises from cash or pay a dividend and finance the purchase using borrowings.

6 Marks

(b) For each of the three interest rate alternatives offered by the bank, outline the total cash flows (total interest and related costs) for Delphi in the first year of the loan if:
   (i) EURIBOR/LIBOR remains at 2.5%;
   (ii) EURIBOR/LIBOR immediately rises to 4% and remains at that level for the year;
   (iii) EURIBOR/LIBOR immediately falls to 1% and remains at that level for the year.

6 Marks

(c) Outline the advantages and disadvantages of each of the three interest rate alternatives offered by the bank and advise Delphi on which alternative to choose if it decides to borrow to finance the purchase of the Cork premises.

6 Marks
Total 18 Marks

(Based on Chartered Accountants Ireland, CAP 2, MABF, Autumn 2012)

Question 21.5 Galvin (Level 2)

Galvin Industrial Ireland Ltd specialises in the production of oil filters that are used predominantly in commercial aircraft. The company is in the process of moving operations from its current base in Dublin to a new office and factory complex in Cork. Galvin has contracted to pay the developer of the Cork property in full, €/£9,000,000, two months from now. To finance the purchase Galvin has negotiated:

- A floating rate, interest-only loan from United Bank for €/£9,000,000 at EURIBOR/LIBOR + 6.5% for a period of 10 months.

Galvin expects to complete the sale of its current property in Dublin, which it owns, 12 months from now when construction of the Cork property finishes. The sale is expected to realise €/£5,500,000, all of which will be used to partially repay the €/£9,000,000 loan from United Bank. Galvin has also negotiated:

- A 10-year, €/£3,500,000 interest-only loan at EURIBOR/LIBOR + 5%. This will be drawn down in 12 months' time, when the sale of the Dublin property has been completed. This new loan will repay the balance remaining on the loan from United Bank.

Interbank lending markets are highly volatile at present and Galvin is concerned that EURIBOR/LIBOR could move very significantly from its current level of 2% before it draws down the €/£9,000,000 facility. A second bank, Davos Bank, has offered a forward rate agreement (FRA) for the relevant term and underlying amount at a fixed interest rate of 9%, with a fee of 0.25% to be paid on agreement.

Note that all interest rates are quoted on an annual basis.

Requirement

(a) (i) Show the cash flows arising from the €/£9,000,000 loan **combined with** the forward rate agreement (FRA) over the next 12 months at:

(1) A EURIBOR/LIBOR rate of 1.5%;
(2) A EURIBOR/LIBOR rate of 4.0%.

(ii) Advise GALVIN of ONE significant advantage and ONE significant disadvantage of using an FRA to hedge this exposure.

6 Marks

(b) (i) Explain, without calculations, how the €/£3,500,000 long-term loan could be hedged using:
(1) A futures contract;
(2) A swap arrangement.

(ii) Recommend, giving reasons, which alternative would be more appropriate for Galvin.

6 Marks
Total 12 Marks

(Based on Chartered Accountants Ireland, CAP 2, SFMA, Summer 2019 extract from Q3)

Question 21.6 Toys 4 Kids (Level 2)

Toys 4 Kids Plc (T4K) manufactures a range of electronic games and seeks competitive funding to support the ongoing expansion of the business. It currently has borrowings of €/£15 million that are due to mature in one year's time. These borrowings are at a fixed rate of 4% per annum.

Due to the current economic downturn, interest rates have fallen and T4K has set itself the objective of taking advantage of lower interest rates. However, there are significant penalties for early redemption of the above borrowings.

As a way of dealing with this, the company treasurer has discussed with its bankers (Irish Banks Plc) the possibility of an interest rate swap. The bank has identified a company (counterparty) with similar borrowing needs to T4K with variable funding finance but that wishes to switch to fixed rate finance.

The counterparty has borrowed at a variable rate of EURIBOR/LIBOR plus 1.5%.

The terms of the proposed swap are:

- T4K to pay a variable (floating) rate of interest (per annum) of EURIBOR/LIBOR plus 2% to the counterparty;
- T4K will receive a fixed rate of interest of 3.5% from the counterparty.

Irish Banks Plc will charge an arrangement fee of 0.25% on the value of the loan.

The company treasurer is unsure as to whether interest rates will remain low should the economy remain depressed, or rise should the economy begin to recover and inflation begin to rise.

(***Note:*** taxation may be ignored.)

Requirement

(a) Consider the benefits or otherwise of a swap for T4K:
(i) If EURIBOR/LIBOR remains at 1% for the whole year;
(ii) If EURIBOR/LIBOR increases to 2.5% for the whole year.

Your answer should include reference to possible criteria that the company treasurer should use in determining whether or not to enter into the swap.

7 Marks

QUESTIONS – CHAPTER 21

(b) T4K expects to have €/£1 million in surplus funds for three months prior to making a tax payment. Discuss the possible short-term investments for these funds in the current low interest environment.

5 Marks

(c) T4K is considering borrowing €/£5 million in six months' time for a period of six months. The company treasurer is concerned that interest rates may have risen in six months' time. In order to protect itself against a rise, T4K is considering entering into a forward rate agreement. Outline in practical terms how a forward rate agreement might be used in these circumstances.

5 Marks

(d) T4K has a separate loan of US$7 million, which was taken out when the rate of exchange was US$2 to €/£1, but now the US dollar is quoted at US$2.5 to €/£1. Calculate the translation gain arising and explain how currency swaps could be used to convert this translation gain into a realised gain.

5 Marks
Total 22 Marks

(Based on Chartered Accountants Ireland, CAP 2, Autumn 2009, Q2)

Part VI

DIVIDEND DECISION AND SHAREHOLDER WEALTH MAXIMISATION

Chapter

22

Dividend Policy

Learning Objectives

Upon completing this chapter, readers should be able to:

- explain market protocol in respect of the pricing of shares before and after dividend distributions;
- discuss the traditional, residual and irrelevancy dividend theories, highlighting the differences between the three;
- calculate whether a share price is in equilibrium using the dividend valuation model;
- calculate growth using either retentions or the past pattern of dividend distributions;
- discuss the practical factors that influence dividend policy, highlighting influences on low and high dividend payouts;
- explain scrip issues, stock splits and share repurchases and identify reasons for undertaking each and differences between them; and
- comment on empirical research findings in respect of the relevancy of the dividend decision.

INTRODUCTION

In **Chapter 15**, the dividend valuation model is explained. A key assumption to this model is that investors value equity shares based on the future stream of dividends expected to be received. To this juncture in the textbook, this future stream of dividends is taken as given, however in reality the situation is not so clear-cut. This chapter discusses theories on the impact of dividend payout policy on equity holder wealth. There is debate as to whether there is an optimal dividend policy. What is evident from academic literature is that the majority of Plcs choose a stable payout policy and equity holders consider deviations from a chosen policy as signals about a company's future. The chapter explains: dividends; dividend policy; M&M's irrelevancy theory; traditional theory; residual theory; practical issues surrounding the dividend payout decision; and the use of share repurchase as an alternative to distributing dividends.

GENERAL INFORMATION ON DIVIDENDS

Dividends are distributions out of earnings. The most common type is cash dividends, which are declared and paid on each issued share. Scrip dividends, scrip issues or share repurchases are also deemed to be forms of distributions (explained later in this chapter). Dividend distributions are either half-yearly or, as is currently becoming vogue, quarter-yearly – this practice is more common in the US. Indeed, some companies choose not to distribute any dividends at all. Distributions made during a company's accounting year are referred to as **interim dividends**. The **final dividend** is agreed by equity holders at the annual general meeting (AGM), when the financial statements for the year are also presented. Though the final dividend is agreed at the AGM by the equity holders, they only have the power to reduce the distribution, not to increase it. Therefore, the board of directors is the dominant influence on the level of dividends a company distributes. When dividends are declared and agreed at an AGM, they become a liability of the company that has to be accrued immediately. Therefore, they impact on company liquidity.

It is not a simple world and dividends cannot be paid to equity holders at the exact time of being declared. The administrative process behind paying a dividend takes time. In this period the stock market continues to trade the company's shares. This causes confusion as to who gets the dividend, the seller of a share or the buyer, and also causes problems for brokers. Therefore, to deal with this problem, the stock market sets an ex-dividend date, or a cut-off date. This is usually two days before a company's declared date of record. On the **declared date of record** a company lists the equity holders that, according to its records, are entitled to dividends. The two days set by the stock exchanges are to allow companies to update their records in light of the buying and selling transactions that have taken place to the ex-dividend date. The **payment date** is usually a couple of weeks after the declared record date. Around these dates, shares are advertised and traded as either ex-dividend or cum-dividend.

FIGURE 22.1: SHARE DIVIDEND RIGHTS

Ex-dividend	Cum-dividend
• Without dividend. • Shares purchased with this description do not have a right to the impending dividend.	• With dividend. • Shares purchased have rights to the impending dividend.

The distinction is important as it impacts on the value of a share. When a dividend is declared the share price will reflect the company's value, including the amount of the cash dividend that is about to be paid; therefore, it is expected that the value of the share will fall after the dividend distribution. An example of this process is provided in **Real World Example 22.1**.

REAL WORLD EXAMPLE 22.1: MICROSOFT

At the time of writing, Microsoft had just announced details of its forthcoming annual shareholders meeting on 4 December 2019 and its dividend intentions for the quarter. It also stipulated that anyone who was on record as a shareholder by the close of business on 8 October could attend and vote.

On 17 September 2019, Microsoft's board of directors declared a quarterly dividend of $0.51 per share. This reflects 11% or 5 cents increase over the previous quarter's dividend of $0.46. The dividend is to be paid on 12 December 2019 to shareholders on record on 21 November 2019. Therefore, the ex-dividend date is 20 November 2019.

In addition to the dividend, the board of directors is recommending a new share repurchase program that will allow up to $40 billion in share repurchases. This repurchase scheme has no expiration date and can be cancelled at any time.

Source: https://news.microsoft.com/2019/09/18/microsoft-announces-quarterly-dividend-increase-and-new-share-repurchase-program/; accessed November 2019.

DIVIDEND POLICY

Dividend policy refers to the pattern of dividend payments made by a company over time. It encapsulates patterns in the **payout policy**, which is the *percentage of the current year's earnings that are distributed* and consequently the **retentions policy** (*the percentage of the current year's earnings that are retained*) and the actual **dividend paid per share**. An underlying assumption in this textbook is that business finance decisions should be made that maximise equity holders' value (i.e. company value). Dividend policy is considered as one of the three main decisions to be taken by a business finance manager. It is argued by some that dividend policy is a key determinant of company value. Modigliani and Miller (M&M theory, see **Chapter 16**) consider dividend policy to be irrelevant. It is also suggested that dividends only be paid when there are funds available that have no other productive use (i.e. residual theory). These three views are now explained in turn.

Relevancy Theory

The dividend valuation model assumes that the value of a share (hence the value of equity) is related to the future stream of dividends that are receivable. It could be interpreted then that a company with greater dividends would be more highly valued. However, a component of the model is growth in dividends. An analysis of growth (under the traditional theory) shows that it is related to the level of retentions (see **Chapter 15**). When a larger proportion of profits is retained by a company for investment, the growth in earnings, hence dividends, is expected to be higher in the future and share price will increase. In addition, the higher the return from new investments, the higher the growth in earnings. This is reflected in the following example.

Worked Example 22.1: Growth in Dividends

Vienta Plc has a payout ratio of 40%, and retains the rest of the distributable profits for investing in projects that yield 15%.

Trienta Plc has a payout of 80%, and retains the rest of the distributable profits for investment at 15%.

Requirement

(a) What are the estimated annual rates of growth in dividends for both companies?
(b) What would the rates of growth change to if the yield increased to 20%?

Solution

(a) The formula for calculating growth in dividends is:

$$g = br$$

where g is growth, b is the proportion that is retained and r is the expected return on new investments.

Vienta Plc: growth = 60% × 15% = 9%

Trienta Plc: growth = 20% × 15% = 3%

(b) The rate of growth increases in both instances.

Vienta Plc: growth = 60% × 20% = 12%

Trienta Plc: growth = 20% × 20% = 4%

There are various factors that can impact on variables that are used in the dividend valuation model and consequently impact on company value. Under **relevancy theory** (i.e. the **traditional theory**), boards have to choose a policy that maximises equity holders' value and it is assumed that an optimum dividend policy exists. Porterfield (1965) uses a simple formula to apply when determining the level of dividend to distribute, or not. He claims that you should distribute when:

$$D_1 + P_1 > P_0$$

where D_1 is the cash value to the equity holder of the dividend to be paid, P_1 is the expected equity share price value after the dividend has been paid (i.e. ex-dividend) and P_0 is the equity share price before the dividend was paid (i.e. cum-dividend). The value of D_1 to equity holders will be impacted on by their tax status, i.e. an equity holder with surplus personal tax allowance available will value a higher dividend, compared to an equity holder who pays income tax at the higher rate tax band. Therefore, different equity holders will value a company differently. P_0 is the market's perception about the future profitability, growth and consequential dividend payments expected from the company, before the dividend is declared. P_1 will change due to the loss of resources associated with paying the dividend and may also change in light of the level of D_1, which may be different from market expectations, causing the market to revise its expectations of future dividend flows. P_1 and P_0 are derived using the dividend valuation model, as discussed in **Chapter 15**. This model is rearranged to derive P_0, the dividend cum-interest:

$$P_0 = \frac{D_0(1+g)}{K_e - g} + D_0$$

where D_0 is the dividend that is about to be paid, g is growth in dividends and K_e is the cost of equity (i.e. equity holders' required rate of return). When calculating the value of equity ex-dividend (P_1), the formula changes to:

$$P_0 = \frac{D_0\left(1+g\right)}{K_e - g}$$

Worked Example 22.2: Relevancy Theory

Tantrum Plc has achieved earnings of €/£800,000 this year. The company intends to pursue a policy of financing all its investment opportunities out of retained earnings. There are considerable investment opportunities, which are expected to be available indefinitely. However, if Tantrum Plc does not exploit any of the available opportunities, its annual earnings will remain at €/£800,000, in perpetuity. The following figures are available:

Proportion of earnings retained	**Growth rate in earnings**	**Required return on all investments by equity holders**
%	%	%
0	0	14
25	5	15
40	7	16

The rate of return required by equity holders rises if earnings are retained, because of the risk associated with the new investments.

Requirement What is the optimum retentions policy for Tantrum Plc? The full dividend payment for this year will be paid in the near future.

Solution

The question states that the dividend will be paid in the near future. Therefore, the value of equity at present is cum-dividend. The dividend valuation model calculates the value of equity ex-dividend (P_1), therefore the dividend value (D_1) has to be included to find the current cum-dividend value (P_0).

$$D_1 + P_1 > P_0$$

Scenario 1 (Growth is zero, retentions are zero, and the cost of equity is 14%.) In this scenario, equity holders' value will amount to:

$$P_0 = \frac{€/£800,000(1+0)}{0.14-0} + €/£800,000 = €/£6,514,286$$

Scenario 2 (Growth is estimated at 5% per year, retentions are 25% of net earnings, and the cost of equity is 15%.) As 25% of earnings (which are €/£800,000) are retained, then 75% [€/£800,000 × 75% = €/£600,000] are distributed.

In this scenario, equity holders' value will amount to:

$$P_0 = \frac{€/£600,000(1+0.05)}{0.15-0.05} + €/£600,000 = €/£6,900,000$$

Scenario 3 (Growth is estimated at 7% per year, retentions are 40% of net earnings, and the cost of equity is 16%.) As 40% of earnings (which are €/£800,000) are retained, then 60% [€/£800,000 × 60% = €/£480,000] are distributed. In this scenario, equity holders' value will amount to:

$$P_0 = \frac{€/£480,000(1+0.07)}{0.16-0.07} + €/£480,000 = €/£6,186,667$$

The optimum policy is Scenario 2 as this maximises equity holders' overall wealth.

Relevancy Theory and Share Valuation

Under relevancy theory, dividend policy affects share price. This information can be used to value companies (see **Chapter 17**) and to determine if shares are correctly priced (see **Worked Example 22.3**).

Worked Example 22.3: Dividends (Constant) and Share Price

You are the business finance manager of Skit Plc. Its shares are currently trading at €/£2.95. They are about to pay a dividend of 40c/p per share. Future dividends are expected to grow at the rate of 6% per annum. The cost of equity for shares in companies similar to Skit Plc is 25% per annum.

Requirement Would you advise the company to raise funding using a share issue?

Solution

The shares are currently trading cum-dividend as the dividend is about to be paid. The variables required to find the current value are D_0 = 40c/p; g = 6%; K_e = 25%. This information is slotted into the dividend valuation model:

$$P_0 = \frac{€/£0.40\ (1.06)}{0.25-0.06} = P_0 = €/£2.23 \text{ (ex-dividend)}$$

Therefore, P_1 = €/£2.23 + €/£0.40 = €/£2.63 (cum-dividend).

As the shares are currently trading at €/£2.95, they are overvalued; therefore, it is beneficial for current equity shareholders to raise finance using a share issue.

The dividend valuation model assumes that share price is the present value of a constant stream of dividends that have a constant growth rate. However, the pattern of dividends may not be constant for many reasons. For example, the company may have investment planned and so makes no dividends in the first year or two; or the company may have excess cash reserves from the sale of a business unit that it plans to distribute in the next year or two; or it may simply be that the rate of growth is expected to change. When determining if share price is correct in these circumstances, the underlying concept is the same – share price equates to the present value of the future stream of dividends, each dividend may have to be discounted separately. This is shown in **Worked Example 22.4**.

Worked Example 22.4: Dividends (Irregular) and Share Price

You are the business finance manager of Wren Plc. Its shares are currently trading at €/£1.20 per share. Wren Plc has just paid a dividend of 15c/p per share. The directors predict growth in dividends over the next two years of 30%, followed by growth in dividends of 15% in year three and 6% every year thereafter. The cost of equity for shares in companies similar to Wren Plc is 25% per annum.

Requirement Determine whether the company's market share price reflects its underlying value using dividend valuation techniques.

Solution

The shares are trading ex-dividend as the dividend has just been paid. The variables required to find the current value are D_1 = 15c/p; K_e = 25% with growth of 30% in the first two years, 15% in year three and 6% each year thereafter. The present value of this stream of dividends is as follows:

Year	Dividend working	Dividend c/p	Discount factor K_e = 25%	Present value c/p
1	15(1.30)	19.50	0.800	15.60
2	19.5(1.3)	25.35	0.640	16.22
3	25.35(1.15)	29.15	0.512	14.92
3*	$\frac{29.15(1.06)}{0.25–0.06}$	162.64	0.512	83.27
				130.01

*The dividend valuation model already discounts the values to the start of the period, hence the dividend in year 4 is already discounted to day 1 of year 4. Therefore, to get it back to the present value now the amount is discounted for three years, not four.

At present the shares are under-valued. It would be a good time to buy back shares in the company.

Irrelevancy Theory (Modigliani and Miller Theory)

The link between retentions and growth is questioned under M&M's irrelevancy theory (1961). They consider that where investment opportunities are favourable to a company, the funds for this investment can be obtained from new long-term sources; hence, this should not impact on the dividend decision. They consider that company performance and growth is related to the availability and quality of projects undertaken (i.e. projects undertaken should have positive NPVs). The financing of projects does not have to be sourced from retained earnings; indeed, due to the benefit of the tax shield, they consider debt (to a point) to be the optimum source of funds to obtain in order to maximise company value (see **Chapter 16**). Therefore, the use to which surpluses from projects are utilised is irrelevant, so long as the cost of capital is covered.

Worked Example 22.5: M&M Irrelevancy Theory

Setenta Plc is an ungeared company. The directors plan to dissolve the company in three years. The expected cash inflows over the next three years are €/£20,000 per year. Equity holders expect a return of 10% on their investment.

Applying M&M's theory, show that dividend policy is irrelevant. Assume that the current policy is to distribute all available cash flows per year. Compare this to a scenario in which the company decides to distribute €/£30,000 of the total available (€/£60,000) in Year 1 (assume that this distribution does not breach any legal restrictions placed on dividend distributions), €/£20,000 in Year 2, with the remainder in Year 3. In this situation M&M would suggest paying the dividend in Year 1 and obtaining the €/£10,000 shortfall by either issuing equity or loan stock. Assume the extra €/£10,000 is raised by an equity distribution and does not breach any legal restrictions placed on dividend distributions.

Requirement

(a) Calculate the market value of equity based on the current policy.
(b) Calculate the existing equity holders' worth if the new dividend policy is pursued (applying M&M's irrelevancy theory).

Solution

(a) The current policy is to distribute all net cash flows each year (i.e. €/£20,000 per year). Therefore, equity holders will value the company based on the future stream of cash flows, discounted to their present value at the equity holders' required rate of return (10%):

$$(\text{€/£}20{,}000 \div (1.1)) + (\text{€/£}20{,}000 \div (1.1)^2) + (\text{€/£}20{,}000 \div (1.1)^3) = \text{€/£}49{,}737$$

(b) Under the revised policy wherein €/£30,000 is distributed in Year 1 to the current equity holders, a trade-off is taking place and an additional €/£10,000 has to be raised. These new equity holders will require a 10% return also, therefore, in future, the return to current equity holders will fall by the new equity holders' requirements, which is €/£10,000 × 10% = €/£1,000 in Year 2 and Year 3; leaving a future distribution of €/£19,000 to the current equity holders in Year 2 and €/£9,000 in Year 3 (being the €/£10,000 less the dividend to the new equity holders, i.e. 10% of €/£10,000).

The value of the company to the current equity holders based on this future stream of expected cash outflows is as follows:

$$(€/£30,000 \div (1.1)) + (€/£19,000 \div (1.1)^2) + (€/£9,000 \div (1.1)^3) = €/£49,737$$

Therefore, regardless of the pattern of payout, the value of equity after taking account of the time-value of money at the equity holders' required rate of return will remain the same.

The Assumptions

M&M argue that dividend policy can be irrelevant in a world where there are no taxes and no transaction costs; where equity holders have all the information about a company and do not misinterpret it; and where there is a constant interest rate that is equal for companies and investors.

Residual Theory

Residual dividend theory assumes that raising external finance is costly; therefore, retentions should be the first source of funds a company uses when investing in projects. The argument is that before a dividend is considered, all available projects with positive NPVs should be invested in. When these have been exhausted, the residual funds can be distributed. This allows equity holders the option of investing the funds in other companies that can provide their required return. Therefore, this maximises equity holders' value. If the funds were retained and not invested in projects that provide a return over and above the equity holders' required rate of return, then equity holder value would diminish over time. This process is shown graphically in **Figure 22.2**.

As depicted in the graph in **Figure 22.2**, all available earnings should be invested in suitable projects, starting with those considered to have the highest IRR and ending at point A (for clarification of the IRR, see **Chapter 2**). At this point the IRR equals the equity holders' required return (K_e or their marginal cost of capital (MCC)). After this point the available projects' returns are less than the equity holders' current required rate of return. Any surplus funds should be distributed as a dividend. Under this theory, no dividend is an acceptable policy, when appropriate investment opportunities exist. Two famous global giants, Microsoft and Apple, used the residual theory approach to determine their dividend policies. However, they came under pressure to pay a dividend as they accumulated excessive cash with little evidence of potential capital investment opportunities to absorb the quantities being retained.

FIGURE 22.2: THE INVESTMENT AND DIVIDEND DECISION UNDER RESIDUAL THEORY

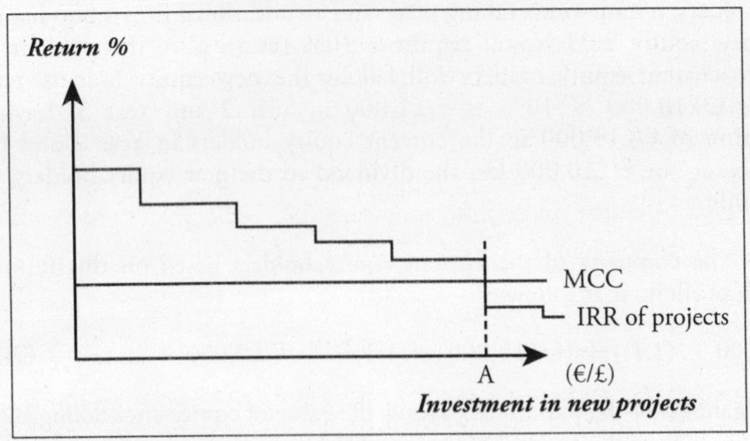

REAL WORLD EXAMPLE 22.2: MICROSOFT AND APPLE

Microsoft

Microsoft used to follow the ethos of the residual dividend theory. For 17 years it did not pay a dividend to its shareholders, retaining funds for research and development. However, cash balances increased and pressure from shareholders caused the company to change its dividend policy and to start paying dividends in 2003. The first dividend paid was 8c per share. By December 2019, the quarterly dividend had increased to 51c.

Source: Microsoft (2019), http://www.microsoft.com.

Apple

From 1990 to 1995, Apple paid a constant quarterly cash dividend of $0.12 per share. It then stopped paying cash dividends from 1995 to 2012 as it was retaining funds for reinvestment, although it did two 2-for-1 stock splits, one in 2000, the other in 2005. However, after pressure from shareholders, sparked by large cash reserves, Apple started paying cash dividends again. In July 2012 a quarterly dividend of $2.65 started, increasing to $3.29 by April 2014. However, in June 2014 the company did a 7-for-1 stock split and continued with a lower quarterly dividend per share of $0.47 in July 2014. Since this time, payout policy has been constant (quarterly) and the dividend per share has been increasing each year. At the time of writing (April 2020) the quarterly dividend was $0.82 per share.

Source: https://investor.apple.com/dividend-history/default.aspx; accessed July 2020.

ISSUES AFFECTING DIVIDEND POLICY

There are many factors that, depending on the company, would suggest that either a low distribution or a high distribution is best for equity holder wealth. These are now explained.

Taxation and Transaction Costs

The two main factors that are argued to support paying either low or high levels of dividend, which are relevant for most companies, are 'taxation rates' and 'transaction costs'. These influences are explained briefly in **Figures 22.3** and **22.4**.

FIGURE 22.3: FACTORS SUPPORTING LOW DISTRIBUTIONS

Taxation levels

- Dividends are subject to income tax, whereas returns on share sales are subject to capital gains tax. When a government's **capital gains tax** rates are lower than their **income tax** rates, low distributions are preferable as this will maximise an equity holder's financial position as low distributions result in higher capital gains.
- Elton and Gruber (1970) report empirical evidence to support the argument that high-income equity holders are attracted to companies with low payout policies.

Transaction costs (company)

- When a company distributes funds to investors, this depletes the funds that are available for investment. In reality, raising new funds, for example issuing shares, is costly and companies that distribute more will have to incur larger costs when they undertake new projects, relative to companies that retain more funds.
- Pecking order theory (see **Chapter 17**) suggests preference by companies to amass retained earnings and use these for investment purposes.

FIGURE 22.4: FACTORS SUPPORTING HIGH DISTRIBUTIONS

Taxation

- When **income tax rates** are lower than **capital gains tax** rates, high distributions are preferable as this will maximise equity holder value as high distributions result in lower capital gains.
- Elton and Gruber (1970) report empirical evidence to support the argument that low income equity holders are attracted to companies with high payout policies.

Transaction costs (investors)

When an equity holder is dependent on the dividend for yearly income, they will incur high transaction costs if they have to sell shares to provide themselves with a steady income if the dividend is reduced. In these circumstances, a high dividend payout policy is preferable.

'Bird in the hand' theory

Gordon (1959) argues that investors value dividends (near cash) at a higher premium than they value distant, more risky, capital gains. Gordon integrated this theory into the dividend valuation model (he added a growth variable), which values equity with higher growth in dividends at a premium, to equity that has lower growth in dividends.

Taxation: Clientele Effects

In the latter sections it is argued that taxation is likely to impact on an equity holder's valuation of equity depending on government taxation policy. However, an individual's personal income position will also influence the value of a particular type of dividend policy to them. Each person is entitled to a tax-free allowance for taxable income and, separately, each person has a tax-free capital gains allowance. Therefore, the attractiveness of a company's dividend policy will depend on the other types of income that an individual receives. The consequence of this is that a company cannot predict a policy to maximise an individual equity holder's return.

It is argued by some (see, for example, Elton and Gruber (1970) and Lewellen, Stanley, Lease and Schlarbaum (1978)) that management decides on a particular policy to attract a particular type of investor and that investors choose companies to invest in because their dividend policy matches their desired income type. This is known as the **clientele effect**. It might be thought that changes in dividend policy, once established, will be penalised by the market; however, M&M argue that theoretically this is not the case, suggesting that it is a matter of supply and demand. So long as the market has sufficient numbers of high payout and low payout policy companies to satisfy current demand, changing dividend policy will not impact on share price. The current equity holders will just sell their shares and purchase shares in a company that suits their preference. However, in the real world, a company that changes policy regularly will be penalised as equity holders will incur transaction costs when they sell shares. This means that most companies will try to keep a stable policy, even if their net earnings fluctuate.

The Signalling Power of Dividends

Hakansson (1982) suggests that dividend payout is used as a means of conveying information to the market. A change in dividend policy is a **signal** to the market in respect of management's view on expected future cash flows. An increase in dividend payout may reflect managerial optimism about future net cash flows, or management's view that the market has not valued the company's investment portfolio correctly. A decline in the dividend payout might reflect pessimism about maintaining net cash flows in the future. However, in most countries, the market is usually well informed in respect of expected dividend distributions. Miller (1986) suggests that it is only variations from an expected dividend policy that can be regarded as signalling. In these circumstances much publicity usually surrounds the diverging dividend payout, making it difficult for management to use this as a means of manipulating company value. Therefore, when divergences from the expected occur, they can be assumed to reflect management's true view on the ability of the company to maintain the new dividend levels into the future.

Other Practical Issues

Legislation

Company legislation typically restricts the maximum dividend that a limited company can distribute to: its accumulated realised profits less its accumulated realised losses. A further restriction is placed on Plcs to ensure that sufficient funds are also retained to cover unrealised losses. Plcs are allowed to make a distribution up to the point at which the company's net assets are equal to the aggregate of its called-up equity share capital and undistributable reserves. A company's **undistributable reserves** include: the share premium account; the capital redemption reserve; the excess of a company's accumulated unrealised profits over its accumulated unrealised losses; and any other reserve identified by legislation as not distributable. A distribution should not reduce the net asset total below the balance on the latter accounts. The reasoning for this restriction is to protect the creditors of a company by ensuring that equity holders cannot get distributions when creditors are owed more than the assets of the company are worth.

Liquidity

As mentioned earlier in this chapter, dividends are payable out of distributable earnings and are usually made in cash. Therefore, liquidity is a key influence on dividend policy. Being profitable may not be synonymous with having cash. Indeed, many growing profitable companies have cash shortages and this will influence the directors' decision in respect of the dividend policy to adopt. As discussed earlier, theoretically it can be argued that a profitable company, with profitable projects, can borrow in the capital markets and pay a dividend. However, in practice, directors prefer to service dividend payments from a company's current resources, as there are costs and control issues associated with raising capital in the markets that are not considered in the theory.

Inflation

Linked to the previous paragraph, inflation may influence dividend policy, because of its impact on the liquid resources of a company. Inflation usually increases the working capital requirements of a company and hence has a direct cash requirement. In a country where inflation rates are low, this issue is not as problematic as in countries where inflation rates are quite high.

Covenants/Debt Capital/Long-term Finance

When a company issues debt capital, it is common practice to include legally binding restrictions, called **restrictive covenants**, into the debt capital agreements. These restrictions serve to protect the prospective purchasers of debt capital from actions that may erode the potential for the debt to be redeemed in the future. Restrictive covenants may limit dividends that can be paid by a company, or may require that certain minimum liquidity ratios are maintained.

Aside from covenants, a company's directors need to ensure that sufficient liquid funds are available to redeem debt capital or pay off other types of long-term finance. In some instances directors may elect to provide for the redemption of loan stock by setting aside a portion of each year's earnings into a **sinking fund** (a separate fund that is invested in to earn a return over the period of the debt. The proceeds of the fund are used to repay the debt). This usually requires that a higher level of earnings is retained, impacting on the level of dividends that can be distributed. Where a company is financed by a long-term loan, it will have yearly, non-negotiable cash outflows, which will impact on the ability to pay cash dividends.

Stability of Profits

Research indicates that equity holders like constant, stable dividend policies and directors try to set their policy so that a constant or increasing level of dividends can be paid (Lintner, 1956). Therefore, the stability of profits from year to year is likely to impact on the level of dividend that directors choose to set: the more volatile a company's profits, the more likely that a company's directors will select a low payout policy.

Investment Potential

Different companies are faced with different investment opportunities. In addition, depending on their standing or age, companies may incur various levels of capital rationing. For example, it is more difficult and costly for a young, emerging company to raise capital for small projects than it is for a large, established company to raise capital for a large project. There are economies of scale associated with capital market costs. Therefore, directors will be influenced by current and predicted cash requirements for investment opportunities when deciding on the dividend payout level. It is more likely and more acceptable by the market for a young, growing company to have higher retention levels.

Ownership and Control

Where a company is controlled by a small number of equity holders, it is likely that they will not be happy if the company issues more share capital, as this may dilute their control. In these circumstances, equity holders would be supportive of a low payout policy, ensuring that investments and future growth are financed from retained earnings.

OTHER DISTRIBUTIONS

Scrip Dividends/Bonus Issues

A **scrip dividend** is a **scrip issue**, or **bonus issue**, that pays a dividend in shares. A scrip dividend capitalises distributable profits, i.e. transfers an amount equal to the scrip dividend from retained earnings or share capital to equity share capital. The equity holders are allocated additional shares and can choose either to add them to their portfolio, or to sell them and release cash. The shares allocated in a scrip issue are not subject to taxation whereas dividends are. A derivation of this is the **dividend reinvestment plan (DRIP)**. Under this scheme shareholders get the company to use the dividends (after tax) to repurchase shares in the company for them. This is not as popular as the scrip dividend as there is a tax cost. Some companies that wish to maintain their liquid resources can offer a choice of either a cash dividend or an enhanced scrip dividend. An **enhanced scrip dividend** is a scrip dividend that is issued at a premium to the cash dividend, as shown in **Real World Example 22.3**.

REAL WORLD EXAMPLE 22.3: SCRIP DIVIDENDS

British American Tobacco and Santander

British American Tobacco (BAT) Industries was the first company to offer either a cash dividend, or shares to the value of 1.5 times the dividend amount (1993); 92% of their equity holders elected to receive the scrip dividend. Scrip issues became increasingly popular during the financial crisis as companies tried to balance the need for liquidity, given the difficulty in obtaining it externally, with the wish to keep shareholders happy, given their dividend expectation.

Most banks offer scrip issues as an alternative to a cash dividend (Barclays, HSBC and Santander). For example, in 2013 Santander offered either a cash dividend or a rights issue, wherein each shareholder who held 41 shares was entitled to a new share with a set value of £6.405. The individual right per share was priced at £0.153. Shareholders could give up their rights for shares, or they could sell their rights back to Santander for cash or they could sell them in the market. This type of dividend was a yearly feature of Santander's dividend policy; however, in 2018 Santander said it would only use cash dividends. It has since backtracked and is continuing to use scrip dividends.

Source: BAT Industries, http://www.bat.com/investorcentre/cgt, accessed November 2019. Santander, https://www.bloomberg.com/news/articles/2019-02-27/santander-does-u-turn-on-scrip-dividend-amid-low-capital-levels; accessed April 2020.

HSBC Holdings Plc

HSBC offer a scrip dividend alternative to its shareholders. The terms of the scrip dividend are that the market value of the ordinary shares under the scrip are as close as possible (but not greater than) to the amount to be received by way of a cash dividend. See https://www.hsbc.com/investors/shareholder-information/scrip-dividend for details of the values attached to shares at each quarterly scrip issue.

The mechanics of a scrip dividend are outlined in **Worked Example 22.6.**

WORKED EXAMPLE 22.6: BONUS ISSUE

At the start of 20X4, Cocina Plc had one million issued equity shares. No new shares had been issued in the prior three years. The company paid a €/£200,000 dividend in 20X2, €/£210,000 in 20X3 and €/£230,000 in 20X4. Assume that Cocina Plc made a 'one-for-two' bonus issue in 20X4. Ms Marido owns 2% of the shares in Cocina Plc.

Requirement Determine the impact the bonus issue in 20X4 will have on Ms Marido's *number of shares, dividend per share* and *total dividend* by considering the dividend she would have received had the bonus issue not taken place, compared to the situation where it has taken place.

Solution

Marido's position prior to the bonus issue was that she owned 2% of the shares in Cocina Plc (1,000,000 × 2% = 20,000 shares). Had the bonus issue not taken place, Marido would have been entitled to 2% of the total dividend distribution [€/£230,000 × 2% = €/£4,600]. This amounts to a dividend of 23.00c/p per share.

After the bonus issue Marido holds 30,000 shares (i.e. for every two shares held, Cocina Plc issued another one). Her dividend will still be 2% of the distributable amount, which has not changed (her dividend entitlement is still €/£4,600); the dividend per share is now 15.33c/p [€/£4,600 ÷ 30,000].

Therefore, though Marido holds 50% more shares, the overall value of her total holding will not increase as there have been no changes to the overall company value, nor will the value of her total dividend.

Stock Splits

A **stock split** is where the number of shares in a company is increased by a set proportion. For example, a 'two-for-one' split, wherein two new equity shares are issued for each old share held. It may seem that this paper transaction is like a bonus/scrip issue, however, unlike a bonus issue/scrip dividend, which involves a transfer from retained earnings to equity share capital, a stock split leaves the statement of financial position accounts unaffected, only changing the number of shares making up the equity share capital account. The value of a stock split can be questioned from a logic perspective, but in practice it usually does increase equity holder wealth, particularly in companies that have very high individual share prices. A split in share value makes the shares more marketable and attractive to more investors. This increases demand for the shares, hence share price. There are costs associated with a stock split and management usually only employs this technique if it considers a positive outcome will result.

Share Repurchases

Share repurchases have increasingly become part of the long-term strategies of some companies. Under legislation, a company can repurchase its own shares, either by buying them in the stock market, making an offer to all equity holders or by approaching individual equity holders. Companies either hold the shares they buy back (as treasury shares), or cancel them. In some instances, companies transfer the repurchased shares into a trust scheme for their employees. It is argued that a share repurchase is another way of distributing earnings to equity holders. As discussed earlier, equity holders are attracted to companies with stable dividend policies; even so, they will penalise companies that hold cash that is not earning a suitable return. From the company's perspective, distributing this cash as a dividend is not a suitable option, if the company is unable to maintain that dividend level in the future. The company has two options: to distribute a well publicised **special dividend** (i.e. a one-off payment) or a share repurchase. A share repurchase, though more costly to a company, has benefits. It reduces the number of shares in issue; this will drive up the earnings per share for the remaining equity holders, a factor that may affect share price.

In other instances management may feel that the market is not valuing the company's cash flows correctly, resulting in the shares being undervalued. In these instances, where the company has surplus cash it may be regarded as a good investment to buy back shares and cancel them. The company will no longer have to pay a dividend on these shares. The result of the additional share activity may be interpreted as a positive signal by the market, hence driving up share price.

Where a company has volatile profits and cash flows, it may use share repurchases in years where the company has excess cash to reduce the risk of being unable to maintain a constant dividend policy in the long term. Share repurchase can also be used to manipulate the capital structure of a company, in instances where the goal is to increase the gearing levels of the company, e.g. by obtaining debt to repurchase equity. It is argued, though, that this may increase the risks pertaining to those remaining equity holders and the existing debt holders due to the increased financial risk. Finally, share repurchases can target individual equity holders; hence can be used to buy out unwelcome equity holders.

Ryanair has used share repurchases and special dividends, in recent years, to distribute surplus funds back to shareholders, without committing to a dividend policy, as highlighted in **Real World Example 22.4**.

Real World Example 22.4: Ryanair Holdings Plc

Ryanair Holdings Plc Annual Report and Financial Statements 2019 (Extract)

15. Issued share capital, share premium account and share options (extract)

Share capital

Other movement in the share capital balance year-on-year principally relates to the cancellation of 37.8m shares relating to share buy-backs (2018: 46.7m; 2017: 72.8m). There were no new shares issued in fiscal year 2019 (2018: nil; 2017: nil). Ordinary equity shares do not confer on the holders thereof the specific right to be paid a dividend out of profit.

For full details, see: https://investor.ryanair.com/wp-content/uploads/2019/07/Ryanair-2019-Annual-Report.pdf, accessed November 2019.

The effect of a share repurchase and a special dividend payment on the returns to shareholders is explained in **Worked Example 22.7**.

WORKED EXAMPLE 22.7: SHARE REPURCHASE VERSUS DIVIDEND PAYMENT

Aseo Plc is an ungeared company with 1,000,000 equity shares that are worth €/£2,000,000 (market value). The company has surplus earnings of €/£100,000 in 20X5 and currently has €/£500,000 in the bank. These funds were accumulated to purchase a competitor; however, this investment has fallen through. The funds earn only 2% per annum and there are no immediate investment opportunities available to the company. The company has a track record of paying a set amount of dividend per share, which increases slightly each year. Earnings fluctuate from year to year.

Requirement

(a) Discuss the options available to the company.
(b) Show, using an example of an equity holder (Ms Mujer) who owns 10% of the share capital of the company, that theoretically her wealth will not alter if the company were to distribute all the surplus cash, either as a dividend or as a capital repurchase (ignore taxation).
(c) Which option would the equity holder prefer if she were a higher rate taxpayer?

Solution

(a) As there are no immediate investment plans, Aseo Plc should consider returning the excess funds to equity holders for them to invest in other companies, allowing them to earn a return that is equal to, or above, their required return. The company is currently earning a return of 2% on the funds, which is low. In the long term, retaining funds that earn such a low premium will damage equity holders' wealth and the value of the company.

The excess cash position is a one-off scenario. The company should treat it as such and should either issue a one-off large, special dividend payment, or repurchase its shares. Both methods will return funds to the equity holders, but will not impact on the required payout ratio expected by the equity holders. Given the volatile nature of the company's earnings, it might be argued that after paying the yearly dividend, a share repurchase is the best option as this reduces pressure on the company to maintain its policy of distributing a growing dividend per share in the future.

(b) **Scenario 1** *In the first scenario it is assumed that Aseo Plc distributes the surplus €/£500,000 by way of a dividend.*

Before the distribution, the value of Ms Mujer's equity will be €/£200,000 [€/£2,000,000 × 10%]. Ms Mujer will receive a dividend of €/£50,000 [€/£500,000 × 10%]. The effect on company value of the distribution will be to reduce it by the resource outflow, i.e. by the

€/£500,000, to €/£1,500,000. Therefore, Ms Mujer's equity will now be worth €/£150,000 [€/£1,500,000 × 10%], though she will also have the €/£50,000 dividend, leaving her overall value unchanged. The difference is that she can take the €/£50,000 and invest it in other companies to earn a return in excess of the return the funds were earning in Aseo Plc.

Scenario 2 *In the second scenario it is assumed that Aseo Plc buys back 25% of its own shares and cancels them. It is assumed that all equity holders are tendered for the buy-back and all accept.*

As in Scenario 1, before the share buyback, the value of Ms Mujer's equity will be €/£200,000 [€/£2,000,000 × 10%]. When the share buyback takes place, 25% of Ms Mujer's shares will be repurchased by the company. This will equate to €/£200,000 × 25% = €/£50,000. The company will experience an outflow of its value equal to the total share repurchase amount, i.e. the €/£500,000, leaving it worth €/£1,500,000. Ms Mujer will be left with shares worth €/£150,000 and will also have the cash received from the sale of her shares (€/£50,000), which she can invest elsewhere.

The difference between the two options is that the number of shares in issue under Scenario 1 will remain the same, and the future dividend payout will keep rising. Under Scenario 2 the number of shares in issue will fall; therefore, there will be large reduction in the next cash outflow that Aseo Plc has to distribute, without the payout policy changing and, therefore, the earnings per share will increase.

(c) If Ms Mujer is a higher rate taxpayer who is paying income tax at the high tax bracket, she may be more interested in the share buyback option. The sale of shares are treated as a capital gain by the tax authorities and the tax payable will be calculated on the difference between the cash received and the amount paid for the shares (indexed for any time allowances relating to the number of years the shares are held). In addition, each individual has a capital gains tax annual exemption allowance. If Ms Mujer has not made any other capital sales in the year, then the whole allowance may be available for her to set-off against any net income made on the sale of these shares.

RESEARCH FINDINGS IN RELATION TO DIVIDEND POLICY

Prior to M&M's theoretical irrelevancy paradigm, the business world operated on the assumption that high dividend payout policies were optimal for equity holder wealth. Even though M&M's irrelevancy paradigm is set in a theoretical world, where there are many assumptions, this theory's and the residual theory's ideals did impact on the attitudes of many in the business world. In particular, management started to question the logic of distributing a dividend, when the funds could be utilised by the company to earn high returns, which in turn would increase equity holder wealth. The result is that some companies adopt a policy of no distributions, claiming that they can invest the monies better than equity holders could (for example, Ryanair, as highlighted in **Real World Example 22.4**).

Theoretical models are usually given credence with empirical results. The impact and relevance of the dividend decision has stimulated many researchers to investigate empirically the relationship between earnings and dividends. A simple overview would suggest that earnings are a key determinant of dividend policy. However, due to the behaviour of management, i.e. maintenance of a constant policy, this relationship is difficult to test appropriately. Risk is considered important with, in general, low-risk companies electing to payout higher dividends and high-risk companies electing to payout lower dividends.

In respect of setting dividend policy, an influential study is Lintner's research, published in 1956. He interviewed 28 companies and reported that management considered the dividend decision to be important. Based on the information obtained from management interviews, he developed a simple model to capture the expected change in dividends from management's perspective. He found that the previous year's dividend provides the basis for the current year's dividend and that management believe equity holders prefer a stable payout policy, which does not reduce the dividend level and, indeed, increases it slightly. The dividend level is a set proportion of current earnings. He also found that management incorporated a safety factor into their calculations to reduce the impact of fluctuations in yearly earnings. The model he suggested is as follows:

Dividend change in year = Annual upward drift + (Safety factor × (Current earnings × Target ratio)) − Dividend of the previous year

Later empirical studies reported findings that support **Lintner's model** (one example is Farrelly, Baker and Edelman 1985). More recently, Brav, Graham, Harvey and Michaely (2005) surveyed 384 executives and conducted 23 in-depth interviews to find the influences on the dividend and share repurchase decision. They found that maintaining the dividend level was considered as important as the dividend decision and that share repurchases were used when companies had residual cash. Share repurchases are more popular as managers find them to be more flexible than committing to the payment of increased dividends. Application of Lintner's model is outlined in **Worked Example 22.8**.

Worked Example 22.8: Target Payout Dividend

Despacho Plc earned €2,000,000 in the year. Last year it paid a dividend of €/£600,000. The annual growth in Despacho Plc's dividend is about 5%. The directors have indicated that they aim to pay out 40% of the company's earnings, though have a safety factor of 80%.

Requirement Calculate the dividend to distribute in the current year using Lintner's model.

Solution

Lintner's model:

Dividend change in year = Annual upward drift + (Safety factor × (Current earnings × Target ratio)) − Dividend of the previous year

Where the annual upward drift is:	€/£30,000 [€/£600,000 × 5%]
The safety factor is:	80%
Current earnings are:	€/£2,000,000
The target ratio is:	40%
The prior year dividend is:	€/£600,000

Therefore:

Dividend change in year = €/£30,000 + (80% × (€/£2,000,000 × 40%)) – €/£600,000
= €/£70,000

The current year dividend = €/£600,000 + €/£70,000
= €/£670,000

CONCLUSION

Dividend policy is a complicated issue that is influenced by various factors which, taken together, result in differing policies being more appropriate for companies depending on their differing situations with, in some instances, a policy of zero payout being considered acceptable. There is support for the ideals of M&M; however, it is recognised that in the real world their assumptions undermine their theory. Residual theory also informs the debate and may, in part, explain why younger companies and research and development intensive companies with greater investment opportunities are expected to have lower payouts. Empirical research on dividend policy has reported that dividend policy does influence company value, and earnings and risk are also considered major influences.

The practicalities of setting a dividend policy are that management has to predict its cash flow requirements for many years in advance. This process separately considers expected cash outflows to service current operations and planned investment (and its corresponding expected cash flows). Other repayments are also factored into the equation. The resultant pattern of cash flows will influence management as to the dividend policy that it can adopt. Underlying the whole process is the belief that a constant dividend policy is most appropriate. The risks associated with the projections, including the variability in net cash flows, will influence management's decision as to the target percentage to set and the safety factor to build into its calculations.

In general, younger companies with many growth opportunities are more able to set a low payout policy; older, more established companies that may have fewer growth opportunities are expected to distribute more each year. As discussed, tax is also important and changes in government policy in respect of the difference between income tax rates and capital gains tax rates may influence dividend policy. However, if a company were to change its policy, it is considered more appropriate to do it gradually over time, or to use other means of manipulating its payout, such as share repurchases, bonus issues or special dividends.

EXAMINATION STANDARD QUESTION: DIVIDEND POLICY

Rex Coverings Ltd is a family-owned business engaged in the distribution of bedroom furnishings and accessories. The company was established 60 years ago and 34 descendants of the founder now own all the equity shares.

The company has recently appointed John Smith as managing director. He is not a member of the family that owns the business and does not have an equity holding in the company.

The family members do not wish to dispose of their equity holdings as they are content with the receipt of annual dividends. There is, however, an internal market for shares in Rex Coverings Ltd between family members. This allows any individual who requires liquidity to dispose of their equity holding.

The equity structure of Rex Coverings Ltd is as follows:

	€/£
500,000 equity shares of €/£1	500,000
450,000 preference shares of €/£1	450,000

The equity shares, which are owned by family members, carry entitlement to vote, participate in a winding up and control the appointment of directors.

The preference shares are owned by a merchant bank, Westbank Plc. Some years ago Rex Coverings Ltd experienced financial difficulties and Westbank Plc provided a loan to the company. This loan was paid off. However, as part of the rescue package, the bank subscribed for preference shares. These shares have no rights, except that an annual dividend of €/£75,000 must be paid. If the dividend is not paid, the preference shares are convertible into 15% of the enlarged equity share capital of the company.

Rex Coverings Ltd has bank funding of €/£4.5 million (overdraft and term loan). The overdraft is used to fund short-term working capital requirements and to enable payment of annual dividends.

Up to now the company distributed its annual profits by way of dividend. In 20X5 the equity dividends totalled €/£2 per share.

John Smith is keen to expand the business and undertake new projects. He is concerned about a number of issues, including the following:

1. Whether he can invest in projects that require significant initial costs and that would, therefore, reduce profits for a period with consequent dividend implications?
2. What discount rates he might use to evaluate projects?

He has retained you to advise him on these matters.

Requirement

(a) Explain why the views of equity holders and John Smith might differ on the growth strategy for Rex Coverings Ltd.

5 Marks

(b) Draft, for John Smith, the key points he should include in a document that he might send to equity holders suggesting a change in dividend policy and the reasons for such a change.

10 Marks

(c) Calculate, assuming absence of any change in existing dividend policy, the discount rate that John Smith should use in evaluating new projects. Assume a required rate of return on equity of 20% and a corporation tax rate of 40%.

5 Marks

Total 20 Marks

(Based on Chartered Accountants Ireland, MABF, *Questions and Solutions Manual 2000/01*)

Solution

(a) In the absence of a remuneration package linked to the achievement of the equity holders' objectives, John Smith is likely to have views on the company's growth strategy that are quite different from those of equity holders.

Significant growth by reinvestment of profits is likely to be favoured by John Smith. This would increase his profile as managing director. This desire is apparent from his desire to expand the business and undertake new projects.

The equity holders appear to be quite content with the sizeable dividend income, and they have no desire to realise capital by obtaining a stock exchange quotation. There is, in any case, an internal market to cater for such a need. The growth envisaged by John Smith, however, will require substantial financing. The company is already heavily borrowed and the equity holders are unlikely to inject capital into the company. A stock exchange quotation therefore seems to be a logical objective as far as John Smith is concerned. This is likely to direct his management decisions towards the expectations of potential institutional investors.

Overall, John Smith will look to investment opportunities as providing the basis for long-term growth. This contrasts sharply with the attitude of the family equity holders, for whom dividends are of primary importance, with reinvestment being a mere residual.

(b) A document addressing possible change in dividend policy should address the following:

- *Ability to pay dividends* The policy of distributing annual profits by way of dividend may cause the company liquidity problems, as profit does not necessarily equate to a cash surplus.
- *Taxation* A reduction in dividends might have the beneficial effect of reducing some equity holders' marginal income tax rate on distributions.
- *Historical pattern of dividends* A policy of paying out all of the current year's earnings as dividends results in an erratic and unpredictable return for equity holders. The policy has also resulted in increased borrowings and interest charges.
- *Impact of a more orthodox dividend policy* A dividend of a fixed amount per share with an annual dividend growth rate would have the following advantages:
  - Stability of income for equity holders.
  - Ability of company to reinvest profits for future growth, thus securing future dividend payments.
- *Raising finance*
  - The cost of debt finance, used to pay dividends, is likely to be higher than borrowings for capital investment purposes.
  - A policy of full dividend payout is unlikely to facilitate a flotation in the future. A flotation might allow family members easier access to a market for their shares and a better price per share.
- *Conversion of loan stock* A full payout policy restricts the ability of management to ensure profitability on an annual basis, thus increasing the risk of conversion of the loan stock.

The annual cost of conversion to the family equity holders could be estimated, based on the 20X5 dividend of €/£1m [500,000 × €/£2], plus the preference dividend saved of €/£75,000:

	€/£
Total dividend	1,075,000
Receivable by family (85%)	913,750
Received by family 20X5 (100%)	1,000,000
Reduction of annual family income on conversion	86,250

(c) Discount rate for new projects – one approach in deriving a discount rate is to calculate a company's WACC:

Valuation

Equity Shares Dividend (D_1): €/£2 per share (assume zero growth)
Required return on equity (K_e): 20%

$$P_0 = \frac{D_1}{K_e}$$

$$\text{Equity value} = \frac{€/£2}{0.2} = €/£10$$

$$\text{Total value} = €/£10 \times 500{,}000$$
$$= €/£5{,}000{,}000$$

Preference Shares On the assumption that the dividend of €/£75,000 represents a reasonable market rate, and that conversion is unlikely, then the nominal value of €/£450,000 can also be taken as the market value.

Term Loan It is assumed in this solution that long-term loans comprise €/£3m of total bank borrowings.

Cost

• Equity shares	20.00%
• Preference shares (€/£75,000 ÷ €/£450,000)	16.67%
• Loans – interest rate of 13% assumed (13% × (1 − 0.4))	7.80%

WACC

	Market value €/£000	Cost €/£000
Equity capital	5,000	1,000
Preference shares	450	75
Loans	3,000	234
	8,450	1,309

$$\text{WACC} = \frac{\text{€/£}1{,}309{,}000}{\text{€/£}8{,}450{,}00} \times 100 = 15.49\%$$

This WACC is only valid for discounting project cash flows that have the same level of risk that is, on average, incurred on the company's existing projects.

Key Terms

'Bird in the hand' theory
Bonus issue
Clientele effect
Cum-dividend
Declared date of record
Dividend
Dividend per share
Dividend reinvestment plan (DRIP)
Enhanced scrip dividend
Ex-dividend
Final dividend
Interim dividend
Irrelevancy theory
Lintner's model
Payment date
Payout policy
Relevancy theory
Residual dividend theory
Retentions policy
Restrictive covenants
Scrip dividend
Scrip issue
Share repurchase
Signal
Special dividend
Stock split
Traditional theory
Undistributable reserves

REVIEW QUESTIONS

(See Suggested Solutions to Review Questions in **Appendix B.**)

Question 22.1

Describe the process companies and markets adopt to clarify who is entitled to a dividend, given that share trading does not cease.

Question 22.2

According to the relevancy theory, should a dividend of 10c/p be distributed if the value of the share cum-dividend is €/£1.80 and is predicted to move to €/£1.68 ex-dividend?

Question 22.3

What are the assumptions underlying M&M's irrelevancy theory?

Question 22.4

Salon Plc has earnings of €/£5,000,000 and a cost of capital amounting to 15%. In the past it has paid out 50% of its earnings as a dividend. In this current year, three investment projects are available as follows:

Project	Cost (€/£000)	Expected return
A	1,500	12%
B	2,000	18%
C	2,500	22%

Requirement Assuming the company is going to apply residual dividend theory, indicate the dividend payout percentage that will result.

Question 22.5

Explain the clientele effect.

Question 22.6

Optimal Ltd currently has a share price of €/£1.25 per share. The board of directors is currently considering the level of dividend that should be proposed in respect of the year ended 31 December 20X5. The board has researched the market's reaction to the dividend levels under consideration, and the resulting expected ex-dividend share prices are estimated as follows:

Dividend	Expected ex-dividend share price
Nil	100c/p
4.0c/p	117c/p
4.5c/p	120c/p
5.0c/p	134c/p
5.5c/p	136c/p
6.0c/p	128c/p

A dividend of 4.5c/p per share was paid in respect of the year ended 31 December 20X4. The average rate of income tax which Optimal Ltd's equity holders will pay on dividend income is estimated at 30%.

Requirement Calculate the level of dividend that should be proposed by Optimal Ltd for 20X5.

Question 22.7

(a) Discuss briefly the factors that might influence a private company's choice as to whether or not to pay a dividend and the amount of such a dividend.

6 Marks

(b) The managing directors of three profitable listed public companies discussed their companies' dividend policies at a business lunch.

- Company A has deliberately paid no dividends for the last five years.
- Company B always pays a dividend of 50% of earnings after taxation.
- Company C maintains a low but constant dividend per share (after adjusting for the general price index) and offers regular scrip issues and shareholder concessions.

Each managing director is convinced that their company's policy is maximising shareholder wealth.

Requirement What are the advantages and disadvantages of the alternative dividend policies of the three companies? Discuss the circumstances under which each managing director might be correct in their belief that their company's dividend policy is maximising shareholder wealth. State clearly any assumptions that you make.

12 Marks

Total 18 Marks

(Based on Chartered Accountants Ireland, MABF II, Summer 2006, Q7)

CHALLENGING QUESTIONS

(Suggested Solutions to Challenging Questions are available through your lecturer.)

Question 22.1 Deakin (Level 1)

(a) The Modigliani and Miller (M&M) dividend irrelevancy theory is based upon a number of assumptions, including the absence of taxation and transactions and flotation costs. Critically discuss the assumptions upon which the irrelevance proposition is based.

6 Marks

(b) Deakin Plc, a quoted textile manufacturer, has followed a policy in recent years of paying out a steadily increasing dividend per share, as shown below:

Year	Earnings per share	Dividend (net) per share	Dividend cover
20X2	11.8c/p	5.0c/p	2.4
20X3	12.5c/p	5.5c/p	2.3
20X4	14.6c/p	6.0c/p	2.4
20X5	13.5c/p	6.5c/p	2.1
20X6	16.0c/p	7.3c/p	2.2

Deakin Plc has recently made the 20X6 dividend payment and, therefore, the shares are currently quoted ex-dividend. The board of directors is considering a change in strategy whereby more of the company's financing will be generated from internal sources. This will involve reducing the dividend payout in 20X7 to 5c/p (net) per share.

The investment projects thus funded will increase the growth rate of the company's earnings and dividends to 14%, although some operating managers have suggested that the rate of growth is unlikely to exceed 12%. The overall return required by the company's equity holders is 16%.

Requirement

(i) Using the dividend growth model, estimate the market price per share for Deakin Plc prior to the change in policy.

4 Marks

(ii) Assess the likely impact of the proposed change on the company's share price.

2 Marks

(iii) Discuss the possible reaction of the equity holders and the market to the proposed change in light of the previous dividend policy.

6 Marks

Total 18 Marks

(Based on Chartered Accountants Ireland, MABF II, Autumn 1998, Q6)

Question 22.2 Botanic (Level 1)

(a) M&M claim that a company cannot affect the market value of its equity by altering its dividend policy.

Requirement Discuss the assumptions necessary to sustain this proposition.

8 Marks

(b) Botanic Plc, a quoted engineering company, has just announced its final results for the year ended 31 December 20X4. Earnings per share (EPS) and dividends per share (DPS) for the past five years are as follows:

	20X0	20X1	20X2	20X3	20X4
EPS (c/p)	61	64	71	73	76
DPS (c/p)	38	40	41	42	44

The board of directors believes that the future annual growth rate in dividends will be consistent with the average growth rate in dividends above.

Botanic Plc's beta factor has been calculated at 1.4.

The risk-free rate of interest is 7% and analysts are forecasting a 12% per annum return on the stock exchange index over the next few years.

Requirement

(i) Using the CAPM and Gordon's dividend growth model, calculate the share price that might be expected.

5 Marks

(ii) Give reasons why the share price might react differently from (i) above.

5 Marks
Total 18 Marks

(Based on Chartered Accountants Ireland, MABF II, Autumn 1997, Q7)

Question 22.3 Modigliani and Miller (Level 1)

Most quoted companies attempt to maintain a relatively stable dividend payout policy, despite Modigliani and Miller's (M&M) contention that dividend policy is irrelevant for company valuation purposes.

Requirement

(a) Critically appraise M&M's argument, suggesting reasons why, in practice, corporate management appear to regard dividend policy as an important financial strategy decision.

10 Marks

(b) Suggest situations in which you would not recommend the pursuance of a stable dividend policy.

5 Marks

(c) Assume that a new system of taxation was introduced that favoured the distribution of profits and penalised retained earnings. Discuss how this development might influence:
   (i) corporate financial management;
   (ii) equity holders.

10 Marks
Total 25 Marks

(Based on Chartered Accountants Ireland, MABF II, Autumn 1994, Q5)

Question 22.4 Bel (Level 1)

Bel Plc was formed in 20W7 as a result of a management buyout by two employees of their former company. The buyout was funded with the assistance of venture capital institutions that were issued with 0% €/£100 convertible debentures while the founders were issued with equity shares.

It was agreed, at the time of the buyout, that the founders would seek a full stock exchange listing within a certain timeframe and the convertible debentures would be converted to fully paid equity shares just prior to the listing. The agreement also precluded Bel Plc from issuing any long-term debt or paying any dividends while the convertible debentures were outstanding.

On 7 December 20X1, Bel Plc obtained its stock exchange listing and on that date the company's issued share capital consisted of 10 million equity shares of €/£1 each. The company's earnings and dividends since the listing have been as follows:

Year ended 31 May	Profits after tax €/£	Dividends per share
20X2	5,066,000	9.7c/p
20X3	6,133,000	12.0c/p
20X4	8,875,000	14.0c/p

The company's profits after tax are expected to be in the region of €/£10 million for 20X5 and are expected to grow by 13% per annum. The company's share price is currently 380c/p. The risk-free rate is 9%, the equity market return is 15% and the company is currently regarded as being 40% more risky than the market.

Requirement

(a) Consider whether Bel Plc's shares are under- or over-valued at 380c/p, using the CAPM and the dividend valuation model.

8 Marks

(b) Comment on Bel Plc's dividend policy since the company went public and suggest factors that should be taken into account by the board in formulating a dividend policy for the future.

6 Marks

Total 14 Marks

(Based on Chartered Accountants Ireland, MABF, *Questions and Solutions Manual 2000/01*)

Question 22.5 Rackett (Level 1)

(a) Recent empirical evidence suggests that dividend decisions in Irish companies are taken with reference to the factor of dividend stability, but some consideration is also given to other factors.

Requirement Outline the main factors involved in the dividend decision and explain why the factor of dividend stability is seen to be most important.

10 Marks

(b) Rackett Plc distributes 20% of all available profits annually. The company is financed by 500,000 €/£1 equity shares and a €/£150,000 10% fixed rate loan. One of the conditions imposed by Rackett Plc is that the loan is to be repaid by a series of equal annual payments (including interest and principal) over three years. Annual payments are to be made at the end of each year.

The profits before interest for the three-year period, for which the loan is being repaid, are as follows:

	Year 1 €/£000	Year 2 €/£000	Year 3 €/£000
Profit before interest	150	170	190

The rate of corporation tax is 18%.

Requirement Calculate the annual average growth rate in dividends payable by Rackett Plc over the three-year period.

8 Marks

Total 18 Marks

(Based on Chartered Accountants Ireland, MABF II, Autumn 2000, Q7)

Question 22.6 Sprinter (Level 2)

Sprinter Ltd was founded in 20X0, after the Sydney Olympics. The company developed a small range of high-tech biomechanical devices targeted at elite and intermediate sprinters in Ireland, which provide critical information to assist them in achieving optimum performance.

On the back of significant investment in research and development, Sprinter is now recognised within the industry as a market leader for innovation, with an upgrade for each product expected every 18 months.

The three company directors recently met to consider the future dividend policy of Sprinter. To date, no dividends had been paid and dividend policies followed by competitors were ignored. The table below summarises the discussions and the proposals for the future dividend policy.

John Coughlan	**Sonia Treacy**	**Eamon O'Sullivan**
Future Dividend Policy €/£0.15 per share with a growth rate thereafter of 5% per annum.	**Future Dividend Policy** A flat 75% of profits per annum.	**Future Dividend Policy** No dividend payout.
Basis for Proposal "It does not reflect well on the company that we have not yet returned any dividends to the shareholders." "A confident company pays dividends." "A steady dividend with low growth is optimal." "Paying low dividends will eliminate the need for additional equity."	**Basis for Proposal** "A company with a high payout policy will have a higher valuation." "We can borrow cash for expansion. Interest rates are low and interest payments are tax deductible." "Paying dividends, I expect, will reduce the cost of equity to 13%."	**Basis for Proposal** "Dividends should only be paid where there are no alternative uses available to us." "Raising debt finance is costly, retained earnings are effectively free."

John holds 70% of the equity and Sonia 5% and a small number of silent partner investors hold the remaining 25%. Eamon was hired as the business development director in 20X6 and has no equity interest. All development projects are financed out of retained earnings. Sonia is particularly keen that the company be taken public in the very near future.

The company currently has an EPS of €/£0.60, which the directors believe is maintainable into the future and is financed by €/£1 million in shares, each share having a nominal value of €/£0.50.

The cost of equity is 15%. The P/E ratio of a similar quoted company is 5.

The directors are keen to set a floor price in advance of any flotation and intend to buy back the shares held by the silent investors, financed with a combination of cash reserves and debt.

Requirement

(a) Evaluate critically the supporting bases made by each director on the future dividend policy of Sprinter. Your answer should also discuss whether each proposal is consistent with the maximisation of shareholder value.

10 Marks

(b) (i) Using the dividend valuation model, estimate the value of Sprinter's equity for the dividend proposals presented by John and Sonia.

4 Marks

(ii) Using the P/E ratio of the similar quoted company, estimate the value of Sprinter's equity.

2 Marks

(iii) Comment briefly on any variability in the estimated equity values in (i) and (ii) above.

3 Marks

(c) Comment briefly on the directors' share buyback proposal.

3 Marks

Total 22 Marks

(Based on Chartered Accountants Ireland, CAP 2, MABF, Summer 2011, Q3)

Question 22.7 Williams (Level 2)

Williams Plc is a company involved in the software industry. The company has been in existence for seven years and has been very successful to date specialising in the development of e-learning educational products. The company makes average annual operating profits of €/£450,000. Income from investments amounts to €/£20,000 per annum. Corporation tax is charged at a rate of 30% per annum. The company is financed by 400,000 €/£0.50 equity shares and €/£20,000 of 8% irredeemable debentures.

The directors are considering the company's dividend policy and the following views emerged from discussions at the recent board meeting.

Director A is concerned that the company has not paid any dividend to the equity holders to date. She is concerned that, if the company does not distribute some profit soon, it will reflect poorly on the company's share price. Director A is proposing a dividend of €/£0.10 per share next year with a growth rate thereafter of 1% per annum.

Director B is of the view that the company should distribute 100% of its profits each year and that, if the company requires additional finance for future investments, such finance could be raised from external sources.

Director C is of the view that the company should eliminate the need to pay dividends by re-purchasing all of its equity and replacing it with debt. She has recently read, in an academic journal, that "to maximise equity holder wealth in a world with tax, a company should gear itself as much as possible".

The company's required rate of return on an investment in the e-learning business is 18%.

Requirement

(a) Discuss each of the proposals that the directors have made in relation to the future dividend policy of the company.

9 Marks

(b) Calculate, using the dividend valuation model, the market price of the company's share under each of the following scenarios:

(i) A dividend of 10c/p per share is paid out in the current year, with annual growth thereafter of 1%.

(ii) A dividend of 100% of the annual profits is paid out annually.

5 Marks

(c) Comment on the results of part (b). Include in your comments an explanation as to why the actual market price of the company's shares may not be the same as the figures calculated above.

4 Marks

Total 18 Marks

(Based on Chartered Accountants Ireland, MABF II, Summer 2002, Q6)

Question 22.8 Dividend Policy (Level 2)

"… dividends … cannot increase shareholder wealth; only good investment decisions increase shareholder wealth." (Shapiro and Barbirer, *Modern Corporate Finance* (2000).)

(a) Discuss briefly the above quotation.

4 Marks

(b) Outline FOUR factors that a company is likely to take into account in deciding on its dividend policy.

4 Marks

(c) Describe whether each of the following is likely to increase, decrease or be irrelevant to the amount of dividends paid by companies. Give brief reasons for your answer in both cases.

(i) An increase in the rate of capital gains tax with no corresponding increase in the rate of income tax.

2 Marks

(ii) The sudden onset of a sharp economic downturn.

3 Marks

(d) Outline the reasons why three different external parties might wish to forecast an organisation's future financial performance.

5 Marks

Total 18 Marks

(Based on Chartered Accountants Ireland, MABF II, Autumn 2004, Q7)

Question 22.9 Sayang (Level 2)

Sayang Plc has earnings available for equity shareholders of €/£2 million and has 500,000 equity shares in issue. The current share price is €/£60 per share. The company is currently considering the payment of €/£2 per share in cash dividends.

Requirement

(a) Calculate the company's current earnings per share (EPS) and price earnings (P/E) ratio.

2 Marks

(b) If the company can buy back its own shares at €/£62 per share, how many shares can be purchased in lieu of making the proposed cash dividend payment?

1 Mark

(c) How much will the EPS be after the proposed buyback? Explain your reasoning.

2 Marks

(d) If the P/E ratio prior to the buyback continues to apply, what will the market price of the shares be after the buyback?

1 Mark

(e) Compare and contrast the EPS before and after the proposed buyback.

2 Marks

(f) Compare and contrast the equity holders' position under the dividend payment and buyback alternatives.

3 Marks

Total 11 Marks

(Based on Chartered Accountants Ireland, MABF II, Autumn 2007, Q6(b))

Question 22.10 Abnormal Times (Level 2)

Abnormal Times Plc has just paid a dividend of 11c/p per share. Because of adverse economic conditions and a rapid decline in profits, the directors have advised shareholders to expect no dividends for the next two years. The directors are confident that dividends of 12c/p per share will be paid in Year 3 and can be expected to grow at a constant 8% per annum after Year 3. The company's required rate of return is 10%. One director, who has previously been keen on a management buyout, suggests it would be inappropriate and reckless to indicate the likely resumption of dividend growth of 8%.

Requirement Calculate the value of a share now in Abnormal Times Plc, with and without the dividend growth information, and comment on whether the directors should disclose the growth estimate.

7 Marks

(Based on Chartered Accountants Ireland, CAP 1, Finance, Summer 2009, extract from Q2)

QUESTIONS – CHAPTER 22

Question 22.11 McMahon (Level 2)

You are the business finance manager in McMahon Plc. The financial accountant has provided the following information.

EXTRACTS FROM MCMAHON'S
STATEMENT OF PROFIT OR LOSS FORECAST

	20X7	**20X6**	**20X5**
	€/£000	**€/£000**	**€/£000**
Profit before tax	872	1,296	1,626
Tax	(262)	(389)	(488)
Net profit	610	907	1,138
Dividend	214	317	398

Additional information:

- The company had 100,000 shares in issue.
- The risk-free rate is currently 1% and the market risk premium is estimated to be 5.5%. A beta of 1.1 is appropriate for McMahon. Net profit is expected to grow by 2% for the next three years and at 2.5% thereafter. McMahon's dividend as a percentage of net profit is expected to remain at the current level indefinitely.

Requirement Determine a share price for the company using the discounted dividend valuation model approach.

5 Marks

(Based on Chartered Accountants Ireland, CAP 2, SFMA, Autumn 2017, extract from Q1)

APPENDICES

Appendix A Financial Mathematics for Assessing the Time Value of Money

Appendix B Solutions to Review Questions

Appendix C Present Value Discount Factor Table

Appendix D Annuity Factor Table

Appendix E Terminal/Future Value Factor Table

Appendix F Future Value Annuity Factor Table

Appendix G Cumulative Probability [N(*d*)] that a Normally Distributed Variable Will be Less than *d* Standard Deviations from the Mean

Appendix A

Financial Mathematics for Assessing the Time Value of Money

An appreciation of the time value of money is crucial for business finance decision-making. Most financial decision-making involves determining the current value of future cash flows. There are several formulae and index tables that can assist in this evaluation. The formulae are used to calculate the present value (PV) of cash flows and the terminal value (TV) of cash flows (otherwise known as the future value (FV)). The tables are reproduced in **Appendices C–F**.

TERMINAL VALUE

The terminal value (TV) of a cash flow represents the future value of that cash flow. It is the actual amount of cash that a company expects to receive. The TV is calculated using the following formula:

$$\mathbf{TV = PV(1 + \mathit{r})^{\mathit{n}}}$$

where PV is the present value, r is the discount rate and n is the number of years the cash flows will be received in the future. For example:

Worked Example 1: TV

Primavera Ltd has just placed €/£500,000 in a four-year fixed interest deposit account earning 6% per annum.

Requirement What is the TV of this investment on its maturity?

Solution

The TV will equal: €/£500,000$(1.06)^4$ = €/£631,238

Worked Example 2: TV

In addition to the €/£500,000 deposited as in **Worked Example 1**, Primavera Ltd plans to put a further €/£500,000 in the same account next year and to leave it deposited for the remaining three years. The bank has guaranteed the fixed rate of interest of the second deposit.

Requirement What is the TV of this investment on its maturity?

Solution

The TV will equal: €/£500,000$(1.06)^4$ + €/£500,000$(1.06)^3$ = €/£1,226,746

Terminal value factors $(1 + r)^n$ are provided in **Appendix E** for rates ranging from 1% to 30% for a 15-year period.

PRESENT VALUE AND PRESENT VALUE DISCOUNT FACTORS

The sooner cash is received, the more it is worth, as cash can be invested to earn a return. Receiving cash in the future is the same as receiving the TV of a current cash flow. Indeed, there is a direct link between present value (PV) and TV, which can be obtained by rearranging the previous formula:

$$\mathbf{PV = TV \div (1 + r)^n}$$

where PV is the present value, r is the discount rate, n is the number of years the cash flows will be received in the future and TV is the expected future cash flow. This formula is commonly split into two parts for ease of calculation, with the TV being separated from the portion of the formula that makes the adjustment for the time value of money. This portion of the formula is commonly referred to as the discount factor and is expressed as follows:

$$\textbf{Discount factor} = \mathbf{1 \div (1 + r)^n}$$

where r is the discount rate and n is the number of years the cash flows will be received in the future. The discount factors for rates ranging from 1% to 30% for a 15-year period are provided in **Appendix C**. Each discount factor is calculated in the following manner:

Worked Example 3: PV Discount Factors

Assume that the annual time value of money is 8%.

Requirement
(a) Calculate the PV discount factor that should be applied to a cash flow expected in one year's time.
(b) Calculate the PV discount factor that should be applied to a cash flow expected in five years' time.

Solution

(a) The PV discount factor is $1 \div (1.08)^1 = 0.926$.
(b) The PV discount factor is $1 \div (1.08)^5 = 0.681$.

These PV discount factors can then be utilised to determine the PV of a future cash flow, as depicted in the next example.

Worked Example 4: PV

Assume that the annual time value of money is 8%.

Requirement

(a) Calculate the PV of €/£500,000 to be received in one year's time.
(b) Calculate the PV of €/£500,000 to be received in five years' time.

Solution

(a) The PV is €/£500,000 × 0.926 = €/£463,000.
(b) The PV is €/£500,000 × 0.681 = €/£340,500.

This example shows the importance of taking into account the time value of money. If €/£340,500 were received by the company now, it could be invested at a discount rate of 8%, which will result in a TV of €/£500,000 in five years' time.

ANNUITIES

An annuity describes a certain pattern of cash flows, wherein a set amount of cash flow is received, or paid, over a set period of time. For example, receiving €/£10,000 every year for five years would be described as a five-year annuity of €/£10,000. In business finance it is important to be able to work out the PV of an annuity. The principles outlined in the previous section can be applied to the cash flows and the PV of each individual receipt calculated and then totalled to give a single PV figure. Alternatively, an annuity factor can be applied to the annuity amount to determine the overall PV. These two approaches are now examined.

Worked Example 5: Annuities

Primavera Ltd's insurance company has agreed to pay the company €/£320,000 each year for the next three years. Assume that the annual time value of money is 8%.

Requirement:

(a) Calculate the present value of the annuity assuming the first payment will be received on the last day of the year using the two approaches:
  (i) each individual cash flow totalled to find the overall PV of the annuity;
  (ii) from the annuity factor table, showing how the annuity factor is determined.
(b) Calculate the PV of the annuity assuming the first payment will be received on the first day of the year (use the quickest approach).

Solution

(a) (i) The PV of the cash flow received at the end of Year 1 is: €/£320,000 × 0.926 = €/£296,320

The PV of the cash flow received at the end of Year 2 is: €£320,000 × 0.857 = €/£274,240

The PV of the cash flow received at the end of Year 3 is: €/£320,000 × 0.794 = €/£254,080

The PV of the annuity is the sum of these outcomes:

€/£296,320 + €/£274,240 + €/£254,080 = €/£824,640

(ii) The annuity factor provided by the annuity factor tables for an annuity of three years at 8% is 2.577. This factor represents the sum of the discount factors for Years 1–3 [0.926 + 0.857 + 0.794]. The annuity cash flow is multiplied by this factor to give a PV of €/£824,640 [€/£320,000 × 2.577].

(b) In this scenario the first receipt does not need to be adjusted for the time value of money, as it is received immediately. Therefore, the cash flows will be €/£320,000 received immediately, followed by a two-year annuity of €/£320,000. The PV will be: €/£320,000 + (€/£320,000 × 1.783) = €/890,560.

Annuity factors are provided in **Appendix D** for rates ranging from 1% to 30% for annual periods up to 15 years.

PERPETUITIES

'Perpetuity' is a term used to describe a pattern of cash flows, wherein a set amount of cash will be received, or paid, at regular, even intervals (usually yearly) indefinitely. The PV of a perpetuity can be determined using the following formula:

$$\textbf{Perpetuity} = \frac{\textbf{Periodic cash flow}}{r}$$

where r is the discount rate.

Worked Example 6: Perpetuity

Primavera Ltd's insurance company has agreed to pay the company €/£320,000 each year in perpetuity. Assume that the annual time value of money is 8%.

Requirement

(a) Calculate the PV of the perpetuity assuming the first receipt will be received on the last day of the year.
(b) Calculate the PV of the perpetuity assuming the first receipt will be received immediately.

Solution

(a) The PV is: €/£320,000 ÷ 0.08 = €/£4,000,000.
(b) The PV is: €/£320,000 + (€/£320,000 ÷ 0.08) = €/£4,320,000.

Some of the models used to estimate a company's share price or bond price are adjustments to the perpetuity formula. They use expected future dividend receipts or interest receipts as proxies for the annual cash flow expected.

INTEGRATED EXAMPLES

Worked Example 7

Primavera Ltd's insurance company has agreed to pay the company €/£320,000 each year for the next three years, commencing one year from now. Primavera Ltd invests these sums immediately to a fund that earns 6% and matures at the end of the three years. Assume that the annual time value of money is 8%.

Requirement:
(a) Calculate the TV of this annuity.
(b) Calculate the PV of this annuity.

Solution

(a) The TV is: (€/£320,000 × $(1.06)^2$) + (€/£320,000 × 1.06) + €/£320,000 = €/£1,018,752.
(b) The PV is €/£1,018,752 ÷ $(1.08)^3$ = €/£808,718.

Worked Example 8

Primavera Ltd's insurance company has agreed to pay the company €/£320,000 each year for the next three years, the first receipt commences one year from now, followed by €/£500,000 in perpetuity, commencing at the start of Year 4 (the first receipt being at the end of the year). Assume a discount rate of 8%.

Requirement Calculate the PV of these cash flows.

Solution

The PV of the annuity is: €/£320,000 × 2.577 = €/£824,640.

The PV of the perpetuity at the start of Year 4 is: €/£500,000 ÷ 0.08 = €/£6,250,000. This has to be discounted to the present time. The first day of Year 4 equates to the last day of Year 3. Therefore, the PV of the perpetuity is: €/£6,250,000 ÷ $(1.08)^3$ = €/£4,961,452.

Therefore, the PV of the total cash flows is: €/£824,640 + €/£4,961,452 = €/£5,786,092.

Appendix B

Solutions to Review Questions

CHAPTER 1

Question 1.1

Strategic management is defined as:

> "a systematic approach to positioning the business in relation to its environment to ensure continued success and offer security from surprises" (Pike and Neale, 2003).

Question 1.2

Typical non-financial objectives pursued by a company might include:

The provision of a service Most utility companies will strive to achieve a particular standard of service to the public as a key objective. Companies such as Viridian Group Plc, British Telecom Plc, Eir and the Electricity Supply Board (ESB) pursue minimum standards of service. These service standards are agreed with government regulators and are monitored by them.

The welfare of employees Many companies pursue a policy of ensuring their employees are treated well. They do this by providing competitive wages, a strong pension policy, adequate training, a clear career development path, perks, a suitable induction programme, good redundancy and retraining initiatives when necessary, comfortable working facilities and by implementing a strong health and safety policy.

The welfare of society Many companies that have the potential to pollute the environment pursue policies to ensure that damage to the environment is minimised as far as possible. Manufacturing companies introduce processes to reduce air and waste pollution; car companies commit resources yearly for research into the creation of more economical vehicles that can run on environmentally friendly sources of energy, such as electricity and bio-fuel; and many retail outlets pursue a policy of recycling plastic bags or providing a 'bag for life'.

The welfare of directors This is otherwise known as 'agency theory'. Some companies may end up taking decisions that are primarily to benefit directors. This usually happens when decisions are made to maximise profits in the short term to the detriment of long-term profitability. Directors' salary bonuses may be pegged to profitability, resulting in this type of sub-optimal decision-making.

The maintenance of strong supplier and customer relationships Some companies will strive to maintain certain quality standards, to advance the products being produced, for the benefit of customers. Dealing ethically with both customers and suppliers may also be an aim. Establishing agreed terms of trade and sticking to them will benefit both customers and suppliers. The government has acted for the benefit of suppliers by allowing them to legally charge interest on overdue amounts that are not paid by an agreed payment date. Even so, withholding cash from small suppliers may cause them severe liquidity problems and many large companies pursue policies of being respectful to their suppliers by paying for supplies on time.

Question 1.3

Non-financial objectives do not replace financial objectives. They are usually secondary objectives, and in most instances place constraints on the extent of achievement of the financial objectives. In business finance, value creation/equity holder value maximisation is assumed to be the primary financial objective, yet all financial decisions have to be mindful of the rights and responsibilities of a company to act ethically towards other stakeholders. When a company is mindful of its responsibilities to the various stakeholders, this will usually restrict short-term profitability; however, in the long term, it is likely to be congruent with value creation. For example, not paying suppliers will leave cash in the company that can be used to earn a quick return; however, this: will not help to ensure the future of that supply; is likely to result in the loss of discounts; and may even push up the price of future supplies. Not providing good working conditions for employees, or awarding pay increases below the inflation rate will increase company profitability in the short term, but is likely to lead to high staff turnover, sickness and lower productivity from the employees – hence lower long-term profitability.

Question 1.4

In Ireland and Britain, the governments use indirect means to influence company decision-making, for example:

Legislation The governments put in safeguards to help promote ethical decision-making within companies. Legislation places a duty of care on companies in respect of their interactions with stakeholders and potential stakeholders. For example, legislation promotes responsible, reliable company reporting, good governance and the ethical treatment of employees, creditors and customers. It also protects the general public by setting environmental requirements and ensuring that companies do not abuse their positions.

Taxation The governments set several taxes, which influence company decision-making. Examples include corporation tax (i.e. tax on company profits), capital gains tax (e.g. tax on share price increases when shares are sold), income tax (e.g. tax on dividends received), value added tax (i.e. tax on supplies, collected by a company on behalf of the government); capital allowances (i.e. tax-allowable deductions for capital expenditure), pay as you earn (i.e. tax on salaries deducted by companies on behalf of government), and national insurance (i.e. tax on salaries deducted by companies on behalf of government). Corporation tax and capital allowances affect the yearly costs and cash flows of a company; income tax and capital gains tax (and allowances) influence equity holder preferences in respect of dividend policy, and salary taxes influence direct company costs and, hence, profitability.

Economic policy The governments and central banks try to control growth in the economy using macroeconomics. For example: inflation influences cash flow requirements; interest rate changes influence company finance costs and options, and hence inflation; foreign exchange rate policy influences exporting and importing costs and, again, inflation.

Grants To encourage new investment in a particular industry, governments might provide grants for capital expenditure or staff training, or might grant accelerated capital allowances that allow a quicker tax deduction for capital expenditure.

Encouraging share ownership The governments in Ireland and Britain have actively encouraged private investment in equity markets by providing tax incentives for individuals who invest in certain types of companies, for example, start-up companies.

Question 1.5

Taxation Taxation is relevant to every decision taken under business finance. When deciding on dividend policy, the business finance manager has to be mindful of changes in the income tax and capital gains tax rates. A change in dividend policy, which does not take equity holders' tax position into account, is likely to result in a detrimental reaction by the markets.

When deciding on the type of finance to obtain, knowledge of tax is also required. Interest is tax deductible by companies, reducing the overall cost of debt, whereas dividends are not tax deductible. Therefore, the level of corporation tax affects the cost of debt (so long as a company is profitable).

When considering a new investment, the profits to be made will be subject to tax, and expenditure on capital is subject to capital allowances. Corporation tax is usually a cash outflow and a business finance manager needs to be able to determine the amount of the expected outflow to find the true net present value of a project. As tax is a real cost to companies, business finance managers need to be aware of any concessions or tax breaks that are available for companies so that the investment decision can be tailored to take advantage of these.

Finally, when a company has overseas branches, or subsidiaries, knowledge is required of any double taxation agreement in existence between the country of the parent company and the country where its branches/subsidiaries are located. Knowledge of taxation in these countries is also required.

Law The business finance manager requires knowledge of several areas of law. These areas are now considered (this list is not exhaustive).

Contract law The law of contract is relevant to all activities involving stakeholders. These include customers, suppliers, employees and financiers.

Civil law Civil law will require that companies observe the terms of their contracts with the various stakeholders.

Company law Company law constrains decisions that can be taken on behalf of a company so that stakeholders are not disadvantaged unfairly. Company law requires that a company's principal activities are consistent with those laid down in its Memorandum and Articles of Association. Company law ensures that: directors do not raise more capital than the limits laid down in these documents without equity holder agreement; distributions are not made out of non-distributable profits (to protect the loan creditors); and responsible reporting is followed by the company.

Environmental law Environmental law places requirements on companies not to pollute or damage the environment beyond certain agreed levels.

Other legislation is also relevant and might be considered in the solution: health and safety law, employment law, law specific to an industry, and equality laws. Mention might also be made of debenture trusts, deeds and covenants.

Mathematics A business finance manager usually has to take account of economic events; quantitative techniques are best placed to analyse such information. For example, time-series analysis can be used for forecasting, correlation and regression analysis can be used to analyse the behaviour of costs, indices may be used to examine the impact of inflation and probability calculations can be used for the assessment of risk and return. In addition, specific mathematical formulae can be used to back up decision-making, for example: the economic order quantity model can be used to determine the optimum inventory order quantity; linear programming can be used in capital budgeting decisions when there are several constraints; and simulation models can be used to determine the outcome when there is variation in inputs.

Economics Business finance decisions usually involve the allocation and use of scarce resources to achieve a desired outcome. Knowledge of economics would greatly assist in decision-making as there are various models and theories on the behaviour of variables when changes are made (for example, the price elasticity of demand) and models to determine the appropriate use of scarce resources. Areas where economics is particularly relevant include investment appraisal and the determination of an appropriate cost of capital.

Having knowledge of macroeconomics improves the quality of forecasting, as the business finance manager is more likely to better predict cash flows based on expectations in respect of inflation rates, interest rates and foreign exchange rates.

CHAPTER 2

Question 2.1

Investment appraisal involves making decisions now on whether to invest in investments that will provide a stream of future cash flows/profits to a company. The fact that the analysis considers *expected* outcomes is an underlying limitation that exists with every appraisal technique. The reliability of the appraisal process is influenced by the reliability of the estimates made.

Another steering influence in the decision-making process is the strategic aim of a company. Only projects that have outcomes that are aligned with the strategic goals of a company should be undertaken.

Only relevant cash flows should be considered when appraising a project. Therefore, sunk costs should be ignored, the focus being on analysing the incremental cash flows relative to the project. This is complicated slightly by the need to include opportunity costs (loss in cash flows elsewhere) due to an investment being implemented.

As the appraisal process considers estimates made about the future, the process should take the time value of money into consideration. This is also problematic, as determining an accurate discount rate is not straightforward. The company's current cost of capital is subject to fluctuation due to the influence of the external economy/markets and the investment being analysed may not be of a similar type to the projects/business undertaken by a company. The new project might be riskier, or less risky and determining an appropriate rate is, to some extent, subjective.

Question 2.2

Advantages of using the ARR for investment appraisal

- The ARR is simple to calculate.
- The ARR is readily understandable by management who are familiar with performance being assessed using ratios calculated from financial statements. These ratios are usually based on profits not cash flows, for example, the ROCE.
- An ARR can be set by management and used as a cut-off point when assessing a number of projects.

Disadvantages of using the ARR for investment appraisal

- This technique ignores the time value of money.
- The ARR ignores the timing of cash flows.
- The size of an investment is not reflected in the resulting rate.
- The duration of the project is not reflected in the resulting rate.
- The ARR is not influenced by the pattern of profits expected.

Question 2.3

Advantages of using the payback period method for investment appraisal

- The payback period method is quick and easy to calculate.
- The method focuses on cash flows, not profit.
- It provides useful information to help a manager decide between projects that have similar ARRs.
- It is a useful screening device for selecting projects for further analysis, particularly where a company has liquidity issues.
- It is regarded as a useful risk screening device. The risk associated with cash flow estimates is deemed to increase with time, i.e. the further away an estimated cash flow, the greater the risk that the actual cash flow will be different.

Disadvantages of using the payback period method for investment appraisal

- This method focuses on cash flows and ignores profitability.
- The payback period method ignores cash flows expected after the payback period, which may be substantial.
- The time value of money is ignored.
- The size of the project does not influence the resultant ranking of the projects.

Question 2.4

In this instance the discount rate should be the company's cost of capital – 12%. As there is no inflation, the current value of the cash flows will equal their future value in money terms.

Year	Sales €/£	Costs €/£	Net cash flow €/£	Discount factor 12%	NPV €/£
0	–	(200,000)	(200,000)	1.000	(200,000)
1	200,000	(120,000)	80,000	0.893	71,440
2	200,000	(132,000)	68,000	0.797	54,196
3	200,000	(145,200)	54,800	0.712	39,018
4	200,000	(159,720)	40,280	0.636	25,618
5	200,000	(175,692)	24,308	0.567	13,783
				NPV	4,055

As the project yields a positive NPV of €/£4,055, the investment should be undertaken.

Question 2.5

There are two approaches to the appraisal of these cash flows. In the first approach, the cash inflows are deflated by the inflation rate (5%) to get the current value of the expected cash flows, which are then discounted at the company's cost of capital (12%). This cost of capital equates to the real rate required, as it does not take into account inflation.

Year	Net cash flow €/£	Deflation of cash flows (5%)	Deflated cash flows €/£	Discount factor (12%)	Inflation-adjusted present value €/£
0	(200,000)	1.000	(200,000)	1.000	(200,000)
1	80,000	0.952	76,160	0.893	68,011
2	68,000	0.907	61,676	0.797	49,156
3	54,800	0.864	47,347	0.712	33,711
4	40,280	0.823	33,150	0.636	21,083
5	24,308	0.784	19,057	0.567	10,805
				NPV	(17,234)

When inflation is taken into account the project becomes unviable, as a negative NPV of €/£17,234 is now reported.

Alternatively, the real rate and the inflation rate can be combined using the formula provided in **Chapter 2**, to give a single nominal/money rate that can then be used to discount the cash flows.

Nominal rate = ((1 + Real rate)(1 + Inflation rate)) − 1
Nominal rate = ((1.12)(1.05)) − 1
Nominal rate = 17.6%

Year	Net cash flow €/£	Discount factor (17.6%)	Present value €/£
0	(200,000)	1.000	(200,000)
1	80,000	0.850	68,000
2	68,000	0.723	49,164
13	54,800	0.615	33,702
4	40,280	0.523	21,066
5	24,308	0.444	10,793
		NPV	(17,275)

Using the formula to calculate the nominal/money discount rate and applying this to the expected actual cash flows yields the same result as is obtained when the cash flows are deflated and then discounted at the real rate of return. The small difference between the two reported NPVs is as a result of rounding in the discount rates.

Question 2.6

The nominal/money discount rate is the resultant rate, after adjustment for expected inflation. This rate will always be greater than the real rate, unless an economy suffers deflation, which is unlikely.

The real discount rate is the rate before being adjusted for expected inflation.

Question 2.7

(a) In selecting a discount rate for project appraisal: the rate chosen should reflect the risk of the investment being appraised and also the financial risk of the business as a whole. The risk of an individual project is a function of operating leverage and the cyclical nature of the cash flows, whereas the financial risk of a company as whole is a function of its capital structure.

- Using a company's overall WACC as the discount rate for evaluating a new project is only appropriate when the new project has the same business risk as existing projects. Thus, if the risk of a new project is different from the risk on existing investments, then the risk of that project will not be adequately captured in the investment appraisal if the overall WACC is used as the discount rate. The advantage, however, to using the existing WACC as its discount rate is that is easily calculated and there is no subjectivity regarding the calculation as it is based on market values and the costs of existing funds.
- Using a system of multiple cut-off rates overcomes the major disadvantage associated with using the WACC. Using a specific rate appropriate to reflect individual project risk usually involves adjusting the WACC upwards or downwards. As the specific discount rate is based on the WACC, the financial risk of a company as a whole is captured in the analysis and, additionally, the risk of an individual project is captured by adjusting the WACC to reflect that risk. This approach is easy to understand, but the difficulty is assessing the risk of an individual project and adjusting the WACC appropriately. One way of calculating the adjustment required to the WACC to arrive at a specific discount rate is to use the CAPM. However, there may be arbitrariness involved in calculating risk premiums and also beta factors are based on historical data and may not reflect future risks.
- Basing a discount rate for a project on the specific cost of funding that project is inappropriate. While the approach may capture the investment risk associated with the individual project, it fails to capture the financial risk of a company. For example, if it were proposed that a new project would be fully financed by debt funding, the cost, and hence the risk to a company as a whole, is not simply the cost of debt finance. It also includes any increase in return required by equity holders who perceive an increase in financial risk due to increased leverage in the company.

For the reasons set out above (in the second bulletpoint), multiple cut-off rates that reflect the risk of each investment should be adopted for appraising new projects.

(b) *NPV calculations*

	Year 0	**Year 1**	**Year 2**	**Year 3**	**Year 4**	**Year 5**
	€/£000	**€/£000**	**€/£000**	**€/£000**	**€/£000**	**€/£000**
Plant	(1,500)	–	–	–	–	40
Equipment	(500)	–	–	–	–	–
Working capital	(40)	–	–	–	–	40
Cash inflows (W1)	–	415	635	975	1,015	–
Tax payable (W2)	–	–	8.5	(13.5)	(47.5)	(55.5)
Net cash flow	(2,040)	415	643.5	961.5	967.5	24.5
Discount @ 18%	1.000	0.847	0.718	0.609	0.516	0.437
Present value	(2,040)	352	462	586	499	11

NPV = (€/£130,000)

As the NPV is negative, the project should be rejected.

W1: Calculation of annual cash flows:

	Year 1 €/£000	**Year 2 €/£000**	**Year 3 €/£000**	**Year 4 €/£000**
Operating cash flows	400	620	960	1,000
Loan interest	15	15	15	15
Relevant cash flows	415	635	975	1,015

W2: Calculation of tax:

	Year 1 €/£000	**Year 2 €/£000**	**Year 3 €/£000**	**Year 4 €/£000**
Relevant cash flows	415	635	975	1,015
Capital allowances	(500)	(500)	(500)	(500)
Balancing charge	–	–	–	40
Taxable profits	(85)	135	475	555
Tax at 10%	(8.5)*	13.5	47.5	55.5
Tax payable (receivable) in	Year 2	Year 3	Year 4	Year 5

* **Note**: the approach taken in this suggested solution with regard to the tax loss is to obtain a refund of the amount. An alternative treatment of this loss would be to carry it forward to the following year to reduce the tax charge of that year.

IRR calculation

To calculate the IRR we need to discount the net cash flows at two discount rates. Therefore, the cash flows are now discounted at 12%:

	Year 0 €/£000	**Year 1 €/£000**	**Year 2 €/£000**	**Year 3 €/£000**	**Year 4 €/£000**	**Year 5 €/£000**
Net cash flow	(2,040)	415	643.5	961.5	967.5	24.5
12% discount factor	1.000	0.893	0.797	0.712	0.636	0.567
Present value	(2,040)	371	513	685	615	14

NPV = €/£158,000

$$\text{IRR} = 12\% + \frac{€/£158{,}000 \times (18\% - 12\%)}{€/£158{,}000 - -€/£130{,}000} = 15.3\%$$

The IRR calculation confirms the decision that the project should be rejected as the IRR (15.3%) is below the cost of the project (18%).

CHAPTER 3

Question 3.1

Both of the terms – risk and uncertainty – refer to the likelihood that actual cash flows and/or discount rates are different from the estimated cash flows and/or discount rates used in the initial project evaluation. Risk occurs when probabilities can be assigned to the various possible outcomes. When the outcomes are regarded as totally uncertain, no probabilities can be assigned to the outcomes.

The two terms are sometimes used interchangeably as the probabilities assigned to possible outcomes are sometimes determined in a very subjective manner, making them quite uncertain. This usually occurs when a project is new to a company and no prior experience is available to allow an objective assessment of the probabilities of various outcomes.

Question 3.2

The margin of safety is a term used to signify the extent of change that can affect a variable, before the project starts to make a negative NPV. It is the point at which the project breaks even. It can be stated either in whole currency units or as a percentage change in the amount by which a variable's cost/price can change.

Question 3.3

Simulation analysis is being more widely used due to advances in computer technology regarding the speed at which computer packages can perform calculations and provide a wide range of possible NPV outcomes for a project. Each project can be modelled (this includes pre-programming impacts of changes in, for example, the relationship between units and price and time – the various potential amounts and probabilities of occurrence are input) and then the computer performs hundreds of separate NPV calculations. The computer uses Monte Carlo Simulation techniques, wherein it randomly selects a variable to change, runs the calculation and plots the resultant NPV and its probability of occurring. At the end of the process, a probability distribution is plotted, which highlights the expected return from the project and its related risk.

Question 3.4

Two steps that might help to reduce country risk when investing in a capital project in a foreign country might include:

- using a foreign manager, a foreign workforce and sourcing materials in the foreign country;
- forging links with the government of the foreign country and involving them in the project; or
- partnering with a local company in the foreign country.

Question 3.5

(a)	**Project Margo €/£**	**Project Trish €/£**	**Project Dymphna €/£**
Profitability index	263,000 / 1,750,000	154,000 / 985,000	201,350 / 1,350,000
	0.15	0.156	0.149
Rank	2	1	3

Divisible projects			*Indivisible projects*	
Capital available	€/£3,000,000		Capital available	€/£3,000,000
Project Trish	(€/£985,000)		Project Trish	(€/£985,000)
Project Margo	(€/£1,750,000)		Project Margo	(€/£1,750,000)
Project Dymphna	(€/£265,000)	19.6%		

(b) Advantages of capital rationing:

- **Budget:** capital rationing introduces a sense of strict budgeting of the resources of a company.
- **No wastage:** capital rationing prevents wastage of resources by focusing on funding the best projects.
- **Fewer projects:** capital rationing ensures that a lesser number of projects are selected by imposing capital restrictions. This helps in keeping the number of active projects to a minimum and thus managing them better.
- **Higher returns:** through capital rationing, companies invest only in projects where the expected return is high thus eliminating projects with lower returns on capital.
- **More stability:** as the company is not investing in every project, the finances are not over-extended. This helps in having adequate finances for tough times and ensures more stability and an increase in the stock price of the company

Question 3.6

(a)

	Year 0	**Year 1**	**Year 2**	**Year 3**	**Year 4**	**NPV**
Initial investment	(750,000)	—	—	—	125,000	
Sales	—	540,000	540,000	540,000	540,000	
Variable costs	—	(264,000)	(264,000)	(264,000)	(264,000)	
Rental costs	—	(20,000)	(20,000)	(20,000)	(20,000)	
Net flow	(750,000)	256,000	256,000	256,000	381,000	
Cost of capital – 8%	1.000	0.926	0.857	0.794	0.735	
DCF	(750,000)	237,056	219,392	203,264	280,035	189,747
Cost of capital – 20%	1.000	0.833	0.694	0.579	0.482	
DCF	(750,000)	213,248	177,664	148,224	183,642	(27,222)

IRR

$$= \text{Rate 1} + \frac{\text{NPV1 (Rate 2 – Rate 1)}}{\text{NPV1 – NPV2}}$$

$$= 8\% + \frac{189{,}747\ (20\% - 8\%)}{189{,}747 + 27{,}222} = 18\%$$

(b) Advantages of IRR for project appraisal:

- The time value of money is taken into consideration.
- All cash flows are considered in the appraisal process.

Disadvantages of IRR for project appraisal:

- Time-consuming calculations.
- Linearity assumption underlies the interpolation process.
- Ignores scale.
- Difficult to use when there are unconventional cash flows.
- Can't be used when projects are mutually exclusive.

(c)

	Year 1	**Year 2**	**Year 3**	**Year 4**	**NPV**
Variable costs	(264,000)	(264,000)	(264,000)	(264,000)	
Cost of capital – 8%	0.926	0.857	0.794	0.735	
DCF	(244,464)	(226,248)	(209,616)	(194,040)	(874,368)

Present value of variable costs = €/£874,368

Sensitivity analysis = $\frac{\text{€/£189,747}}{\text{€/£874,368}}$ = 21.7%

Variable costs could increase by a maximum of 21.7%. Were this to happen, the project would then produce a NPV of zero. ACS Ltd should take steps in advance to ensure that these costs do not escalate dramatically.

Question 3.7

(a) The NPV of the 'most likely' outcome is as follows:

Year	**Cash flows €/£**	**Discount (10%)**	**Present value €/£**
0	(200,000)	1.000	(200,000)
1	110,000	0.909	99,990
2	110,000	0.826	90,860
3	160,000	0.751	120,160
		NPV	111,010

(b) Sensitivity analysis

The first variable being analysed is sales price. There are two approaches – both are covered in this solution.

(i) *Break-even point – sales price*

The first approach uses interpolation to determine the sales price that will result in the investment breaking even. A lower sales price of €/£3.50 is used as the sales price of €/£4.20 gives a positive NPV.

The NPV when sales price is €/£3.50:

Year	**Cash flows €/£**	**Discount (10%)**	**Present value €/£**
0	(200,000)	1.000	(200,000)
1–3	40,000 (W1)	2.486	99,440
3	50,000	0.751	37,550
		NPV	(63,010)

W1: The yearly cash inflow is now:

	€/£	€/£
Sales: [100,000 × €/£3.50]		350,000
Labour	(210,000)	
Materials	(80,000)	
Other direct costs	(20,000)	(310,000)
Net cash flow		40,000

Using interpolation, the break-even sales price is:

$$€/£3.50 + \frac{-€/£63,010\ (€/£4.20 - €/£3.50)}{-€/£63,010 - €/£111,010} = €/£3.75$$

Therefore, the margin of safety is €/£3.75 – €/£4.20 = (€/£0.45).

Sales price can fall by 45c/p before break-even point is reached.

Expressed as a percentage, sales price can fall by 10.7% (45c/p ÷ €/£4.20) before break-even point is reached.

A second approach can also be adopted. The first step is to find the PV of the variable that is changing – in this case, sales.

The PV is €/£1,044,120 [€/£420,000 × 2.486].

The NPV is 10.63% [€/£111,010 ÷ €/£1,044,120] of the PV of the variable; therefore, sales price can fall by 10.63% before the project reaches break-even point.

Sales price can fall by 44.6c/p [€/£4.20 × 10.63%] to €/£3.75 before the project starts to make a loss.

(ii) *Break-even point – labour costs*

A trial cash outflow of €/£270,000 is utilised, as follows:

Year	Cash flows €/£	Discount factor (10%)	Present value €/£
0	(200,000)	1.000	(200,000)
1–3	50,000 (W2)	2.486	124,300
3	50,000	0.751	37,550
		NPV	(38,150)

W2: Yearly cash inflow now:

	€/£	€/£
Sales: [100,000 × €/£4.20]		420,000
Labour	(270,000)	
Materials	(80,000)	
Other direct costs	(20,000)	(370,000)
Net cash flow		50,000

Using interpolation, the break-even labour cost is:

$$€/£270{,}000 + \frac{-€/£38{,}150\ (€/£210{,}000\ -\ €/£270{,}000)}{-€/£38{,}150\ -\ €/£111{,}010}$$

$$= €/£254{,}654$$

Therefore, the margin of safety is €/£44,654 [€/£254,654 − €/£210,000].

Labour can increase by €/£44,654, before break-even point is reached.

Expressed as a percentage, the cost of labour can increase by 21.26% [€/£44,654 ÷ €/£210,000] before break-even point is reached.

The second approach is also adopted. The first step is to find the PV of the variable that is changing – in this case, labour.

The PV is €/£522,060 [€/£210,000 × 2.486].

The NPV is 21.26% [€/£111,010 ÷ €/£522,060] of the PV of the variable. Therefore, labour costs can increase by 21.26% before break-even point is reached.

Labour costs can rise by €/£44,654 [€/£210,000 × 21.26%] to €/£254,646 before the project starts to make a loss.

(iii) *Break-even point – Material costs*

The second method is utilised for the next two variables as it is quicker to calculate:

The PV of the material costs is €/£198,880 [€/£80,000 × 2.486].

The NPV as a percentage of the PV of the material costs is 55.8% [€/£111,010 ÷ €/£198,880].

Therefore, material costs can increase by 55.8% before the project reaches break-even.

Material costs can rise by €/£44,640 [€/£80,000 × 55.8%] to €/£124,640 [€/£80,000 + €/£44,640] before the project starts to make a loss.

(iv) *Break-even point – Other direct costs*

The PV of other direct costs is €/£49,720 [€/£20,000 × 2.486].

The NPV as a percentage of the PV of other direct costs is 223% [€/£111,010 ÷ €/£49,720].

Therefore, other costs can increase by 223% before the project break-even point is reached.

Other costs can rise by €/£44,600 [€/£20,000 × 223%] to €/£64,600 [€/£20,000 + €/£44,600] before the project starts to make a loss.

(v) *Break-even point – Discount rate*

The IRR is utilised to find the sensitivity in the discount rate. A rate of 43% is utilised as an alternative estimate.

Year	Cash flows €/£	Discount factor (43%)	Present value €/£
0	(200,000)	1.000	(200,000)
1–3	110,000	1.530	168,300
3	50,000	0.342	17,100
		NPV	(14,600)

$$10\% + \frac{€/£111{,}010\ (43\% - 10\%)}{€/£111{,}010 - -€/£14{,}600} = 39.16\%$$

The discount rate can increase from 10% to 39.16% before the project starts to make a loss.

The riskiest variable affecting this project is sales price, as a fall of above 10% in sales price will result in the project returning a negative NPV.

CHAPTER 4

Question 4.1

Inflation impacts on various parts of the financial statements in different ways. This can cause distortions when interpreting ratios. For example, inflation will increase the profitability of a company; however, changes to the value of historic assets are not updated. Therefore, the reported return on assets for two companies with identical assets and profits may be quite different, where the companies have purchased the assets years apart. A way round this might be to use the fair values of the assets; however, this information may not be readily available and can be costly to obtain.

Question 4.2

Solvency deals with the ability of a company to meet its debts as they fall due for payment. It covers both the long- and short-term ability of a company to settle its debt and creditor repayments. Information on solvency can be obtained from cash budgets, the statement of cash flows, the gearing ratio and liquidity ratios.

Liquidity deals with the ability of a company to meet its short-term liabilities from its short-term sources of funds. Information on the liquidity position of a company can be obtained from the current ratio and the acid test ratio. Causes of shifts in liquidity can be ascertained from an analysis of the trade receivables period, the trade payables period, the inventory holding period, and changes in cash levels.

Question 4.3

(a)

	Alpha	**Omega**
ROCE	€/£340 ÷ €/£2,000 = 17%	€/£404 ÷ €/£2,160 = 18.7%
Gross profit margin	€/£1,440 ÷ €/£6,000 = 24%	€/£1,584 ÷ €/£7,200 = 22%
Net profit margin	€/£340 ÷ €/£6,000 = 5.66%	€/£404 ÷ €/£7,200 = 5.61%
Total asset turnover	€/£6,000 ÷ €/£2,900 = 2.07	€/£7,200 ÷ €/£4,000 = 1.8
Inventory turnover	€/£4,560 ÷ €/£1,200 = 3.8	€/£5,616 ÷ €/£1,800 = 3.12
Trade receivables period	(€/£720 ÷ €/£6,000) × 365 = 43.8 days	(€/£1,200 ÷ €/£7,200) × 365 = 61 days
Trade payables period	(€/£900 ÷ €/£4,760) × 365 = 69 days	(€/£1,040 ÷ €/£5,916) × 365 = 64 days
Current ratio	€/£2,110 ÷ €/£900 = 2.34 : 1	€/£3,000 ÷ €/£1,840 = 1.63 : 1

Quick ratio	€/£910 ÷ €/£900 = 1.01 : 1	€/£1,200 ÷ €/£1,840 = 0.65 : 1
Gearing ratio	€/£500 ÷ €/£2,000 = 25%	N/A

Note – figures are in millions.

Profitability Given the results of the analysis of the ratios, it would seem that Alpha is more profitable than Omega, as it has a greater gross profit margin (24%) relative to Omega's gross profit percentage of 22%. The sales mix of Alpha may include more profitable lines relative to Omega, or Alpha may be availing of discounts, or may be able to charge a higher price due to better service. More information is required. Alpha also has a higher net profit margin (5.66%) relative to Omega's 5.61%, though the difference in the reported gross profit percentage has fallen. This may signify that Alpha has higher fixed administration and distribution costs relative to Omega.

In contrast, Omega has a greater ROCE than Alpha. This may be down to the accounting policies that are being adopted in respect of the depreciation of non-current assets or may indicate a need for Alpha to invest in new, more up-to-date efficient assets to achieve higher returns. Again, more information is required about the assets before a conclusion can be obtained. At this stage it can be said that Omega is generating more sales from each euro/pound invested in assets.

Efficiency An analysis of the result of the working capital ratios would suggest that Alpha is more efficient in its management of working capital. Alpha gets payment from customers sooner (within 43.8 days compared to 61 days for Omega), pays its suppliers later (every 69 days compared to 64 days for Omega) and turns its inventories over faster (3.8 times per year, or every 96 days compared to 3.12 times for Omega (every 117 days)). As Alpha reports a higher gross profit margin, the efficiencies have not been at the expense of providing discounts to customers, or at receiving discounts from suppliers (the trade payables period is longer).

Liquidity Alpha also has a stronger liquidity position. Its current ratio is 2.34 : 1, compared with 1.63 : 1 for Omega. If the industry average were known, a better conclusion on the current ratio could be reached. If the industry averages were the benchmark for the current ratio of 2 : 1, then it could be concluded that Alpha has too much invested in current assets, whereas Omega has too little. As Alpha only has a small balance in the bank, this would mean that its levels of trade receivables and inventory, though lower than the levels kept by Omega in relative terms, are still too high and need to be reduced. Alpha has a quick ratio of 1.01 : 1, which is close to the benchmark quick ratio of 1 : 1. Omega's reported quick ratio is much lower at 0.65 : 1. Omega has a large bank overdraft and no cash, whereas Alpha has €/£190 million in the bank. This lower ratio seems to be a result of Omega's financing policy, which is discussed next.

Gearing Omega's long-term financing is equity. Omega has no long-term debt. However, Omega seems to be using its overdraft as a source of finance for the company. Working capital is a permanent requirement which should be financed by an equally permanent source of finance; however, Omega is financing it with an overdraft. Alpha seems to be financed in a less risky manner. It has €/£1,500 million in equity and a long-term loan of €/£500 million. Alpha has adopted a policy of financing part of its working capital requirement using long-term sources. This has resulted in Alpha having a more liquid position, with cash in the bank.

(b) Three possible limitations of ratio analysis might include any of the following:
- Ratios do not give the whole picture of a company's condition.
- Ratios cannot be used to interpret non-financial information, such as employee morale or future developments.
- Companies with different accounting policies will end up with different ratios, making comparison meaningless.

- The statement of financial position is only a 'snapshot' of a company at a moment in time, the next day the statement of financial position will be different. The problem is most accentuated when the company's trade is seasonal in nature, as the ratios will not be representative of the year being reported on.
- Ratios do not take into account the changing business environment. For example, an increase in profitability may be below a country's inflation rate, hence in real-terms – profitability has fallen.
- Short-term fluctuations in the market may distort ratios, in particular, the investment ratio – the price earnings ratio.
- The calculation of ratios does not take into account the change in the value of money (inflation).

CHAPTER 5

Question 5.1

Overtrading occurs when a company grows too quickly with insufficient long-term finance to support the increased level of assets that should be held, given the higher level of operational activity.

Question 5.2

Examinerships are court-managed restructuring procedures. The examinership process offers protection from the court to the company for a period of up to 100 days. In this period no creditor can file for bankruptcy. The management and directors remain in post. The examiner contacts its creditors asking them to agree to restructuring the company's debts. The crux of the agreement is usually an extension on the time required to repay the sums owed, an agreement not to charge interest penalties and, in some instances, discounts are negotiated. The discounts may be a reduction in the amount owed by the company, an agreement to charge a lower interest rate, an agreement to take equity shares in exchange for debt repayments, or a combination of these options.

Question 5.3

Formal liquidation is timely, costly and the end result is that the business disappears. The insolvency practitioners have to be paid from the proceeds of any asset realisations before creditors are paid; therefore, they are very unlikely to get what they are owed, in addition all creditors rank in front of the owners when the business is being liquidated and in many instances, the owner ends up with nothing.

Question 5.4

To protect the company from formally receiving a bankruptcy petition, the company may appoint an examiner. Examinerships are court-managed restructuring procedures. The examinership process offers protection from the court to the company for a period of up to 100 days. In this period no creditor can file for bankruptcy.

Question 5.5

A business that has been demerged and purchased by management (a MBO) might be more successful than it had been when it was part of the group, for the following reasons:

- The management team members may be more motivated now that they are the owners (goal congruence, in that gains accrued by the business will directly benefit the management team).
- The management team has total control. It can make decisions quicker and has more flexibility in its decision-making.
- The management team can undertake speculative investments (for example, purchasing supplies at a large discount from a company that is going out of business) and can pursue stricter debt-collection policies, or can write off 'no-hope' debts, rather than chasing them up in the courts (it may have been the group's policy to pursue every debt through the courts regardless of size).
- The business will not have to contribute to central costs.
- If profitable, the business can retain profits for investment, rather than transferring them to the parent.

Question 5.6

A MBO might fail because:

- The price paid for the business was too high.
- The management team does not have the expertise or contacts to run an independent company.
- Key employees may leave the company – this is likely to happen when employees are unsure about their future.
- Employee pension rights agreed in the original company may be crippling for the new company.
- The finance obtained to back the buyout may not have been sufficient. It may have covered the initial purchase price, but not the set-up costs, working capital, capital investment, etc.
- An economic downturn at this embryonic stage may adversely impact on the demerged entity.

Question 5.7

The questions an investor might ask about a management buy-out include:

- Does the management team have sufficient expertise to take the new company forward?
- Is the price being offered for the business good value, or is it too high?
- What exactly is being purchased – shares in a spin-off company, or assets?
- What contribution to the financing of this buyout is coming from the management team?
- What is the expected performance of the demerged business?
- What are key assets in the demerged business?
- Why is the group selling this business?
- What has the performance of the business been like in the past?
- Has the management made sufficient provision for the finance of the new independent company (in terms of capital investment, working capital, etc.)?
- Is the new business reliant on any key employees?

CHAPTER 6

Question 6.1

Working capital is a company's investment in net current assets. It is the difference between a company's operating current assets and its operating current liabilities.

Question 6.2

Over-capitalisation is the over-investment in current assets, while paying suppliers in a timely manner, i.e. an over-investment in working capital. It describes a situation whereby too much inventory is held and credit periods allowed are too long, yet trade payable days are short.

Question 6.3

The solution is split into three parts: the first considers the profitability assumed by the directors; the second identifies the change in overall working capital requirements; and the third considers the changes in each of the components of working capital.

Profitability

	Current year €/£000	**Next year €/£000**
Revenue	500,200	580,000
Cost of goods produced	(420,050)	(500,000)
Profit	80,150	80,000

As is highlighted in the question, it would appear initially that the absolute amount of profit made in the current year will be maintained in the coming year. However, this does not mean that the company is as profitable as the profits are only possible if the increase in revenue is achieved. The gross margin achieved from each euro/Sterling of revenue has actually fallen from 16c/p in the euro/Sterling to 13.8c/p in the euro/Sterling.

$$\textit{Gross profit percentage} = \frac{\text{Gross profit}}{\text{Revenue}} \quad \frac{80{,}150}{500{,}200} = 16\% \quad \frac{80{,}000}{580{,}000} = 13.8\%$$

Change in working capital

The above analysis does not take into account the potential cost/savings from an increase/decrease in working capital requirements. The working capital requirements are as follows:

	Current year €/£000	**Next year €/£000**
Finished goods inventory	60,000	70,000
Work in progress inventory	45,000	80,000
Raw material inventory	80,000	150,000
Trade receivables	62,500	65,000
Trade payables	(42,000)	(60,000)
Working capital requirement	205,500	305,000

An additional cash requirement of €/£99,500 [€/£305,000 − €/£205,500] is predicted based on the budgeted figures for the next year. This will not be without cost. The question does not indicate whether the company has an overdraft. In addition, it does not mention the return that can be made by the company in other investments. However, it is assumed that a finance cost will be incurred due to the increase in working capital requirements. For example, if the company has an overdraft that charges 10%, then the increase in working capital requirements would lead to an additional interest charge of €/£9,950 per year. This reduces profitability by almost 12.4% [€/£9,950 ÷ €/£80,000]. Based on this information, it would seem that the company is not going to perform as well in the next period and equity holders should be made aware of the expected fall in profitability.

Assessment of working capital management

The working capital policy pursued by the company can be evaluated for its efficiency using changes to the operating cycle of each of the components.

$$\textit{Finished goods conversion period} = \frac{\text{Finished goods}}{\text{Cost of goods sold}}$$

Current year €/£000	**Next year €/£000**
$\frac{60{,}000 \times 365}{420{,}050} = 52.14$ days	$\frac{70{,}000 \times 365}{500{,}000} = 51.1$ days

Finished goods are expected to be held for 51 days next year, relative to 52 days this year. This is a sign of improved efficiency and may lead to a reduction in storage costs of finished goods.

$$\textit{Work in progress conversion period} = \frac{\text{Work in progress}}{\text{Cost of goods sold}}$$

Current year €/£000		**Next year €/£000**	
$\frac{45{,}000 \times 365}{420{,}050}$	= 39.1 days	$\frac{80{,}000 \times 365}{500{,}000}$	= 58.4 days

The production period has increased by almost 19 days. This indicates a problem area. Production is expected to be less efficient in the coming year. This may account for the reduction in finished goods days. The company should investigate the production process to highlight reasons for the increase in the work in progress period and take steps to reduce this.

$$\textit{Raw material inventory conversion period} = \frac{\text{Raw materials}}{\text{Purchases of raw materials}}$$

€/£000		**€/£000**	
$\frac{80{,}000 \times 365}{280{,}000}$	= 104.28 days	$\frac{150{,}000 \times 365}{340{,}000}$	= 161.03 days

There has been an increase in the level of raw material held. Now 161 days' worth of purchases are being held, compared to 104 days in the prior year. This is an indication of over-buying and tying up funds unnecessarily. It also suggests that the increase in the work in progress period is not attributable to delays/stock-outs of raw material and is more associated with the other costs of production, such as staff costs and overheads. The purchasing manager may have availed of high discounts – however, this is not clear from the profitability analysis in part (i). This area should also be investigated and the planned expenditure and inventory levels reduced.

$$\textit{Trade receivables conversion period} = \frac{\text{Trade receivables}}{\text{Revenue}}$$

€/£000		**€/£000**	
$\frac{62{,}500 \times 365}{500{,}200}$	= 45.61 days	$\frac{65{,}000 \times 365}{580{,}000}$	= 40.9 days

The trade receivables conversion period has fallen by approximately four days. This means that the credit manager is receiving funds in quicker time than in the prior year. So long as the manager is not giving discounts that adversely affect profitability, this is a sign of efficient credit management, which actually releases funds.

$$\textit{Period of credit granted by suppliers} = \frac{\text{Trade payables}}{\text{Purchases}}$$

€/£000		**€/£000**	
$\frac{42{,}000 \times 365}{280{,}000}$	= 54.75 days	$\frac{60{,}000 \times 365}{340{,}000}$	= 64.42 days

The trade payables conversion period has increased by almost 10 days. This is a source of funds to the company, as credit purchases do not have to be paid for as quickly. This increase in credit period allowed may be as a result of an agreement to purchase larger quantities, if so, then it is a false saving as the funds are just tied up in raw materials that have to be stored at a cost. If the credit period taken is not agreed and is assumed, then the company runs the risk of annoying the supplier, possibly affecting the supply price, discounts and even supply in the long run.

Overall The main area of concern is the level of raw materials being held and work in progress (which reflects the length of time inventory remains in production). These components need to be investigated to determine where the suspected inefficiencies are going to occur and corrective action should be taken.

CHAPTER 7

Question 7.1

In a manufacturing company, it is normal to find four types of inventory: manufactured finished goods; work in progress; raw materials; and consumables. In a retail company, two types of inventory are typical: purchased finished goods and consumables.

Question 7.2

The purpose of inventory management is to minimise the cost of holding inventory and ordering inventory, while ensuring there are no stock-out costs.

Question 7.3

There are several negative consequences associated with not having an appropriate inventory management system. Some key consequences are outlined here:

- The inventory costs and hence production costs may not be properly recorded and therefore the financial information on production and inventory will not be reliable. In addition, where there is no system to record inventory movement accurately, it is harder for managers to monitor and control costs.
- Where an appropriate monitoring system is not used, there may be excessive use of inventory in the production process, resulting in excessive waste.
- If inventories are stored without proper planning, then there may be:
  - stock-outs;
  - time costs associated with searching for inventory;
  - physical deterioration of inventory where there is no system to use older items first, etc.;
  - a higher risk of theft; and
  - a higher risk of hazard where the inventory is of a hazardous nature, for example, the inventory may be flammable or poisonous.

Question 7.4

A company uses the EOQ model to determine the optimum level of inventory to order to minimise the total inventory holding costs and ordering costs. It is used to determine optimum inventory levels.

Question 7.5

JIT is an inventory management system that aims to minimise inventory holding costs. It requires strong quality procedures and is dependent on a company having good relationships with its suppliers and a sophisticated inventory management system to allow fast communication between all the parties involved with the inventories.

Question 7.6

(a) The EOQ is the square root of [(2 × 200,000 × €/£32) ÷ (€/£8 × 10%)] = 4,000 units

The number of orders = [200,000 units/4,000 units per order] = 50 orders

The annual ordering cost = [number of orders × cost per order] = 50 × €/£32 = €/£1,600

Holding cost per annum = average inventory × holding cost per unit = [4,000 ÷ 2] × (€/£8 × 10%) = €/£1,600

(b) To consider the impact of retaining the existing order quantity, we must compare the holding and ordering costs that would be incurred at the existing economic order quantity, to the costs that would be incurred if the order quantity was changed to the new EOQ.

Costs of ordering at the existing order quantity – 4,000 units:

		€/£
Order costs:	[(242,000 units ÷ 4,000 units) × €/£32]	1,936
Holding costs:	[(4,000 units ÷ 2) × €/£0.80]	1,600
Total costs:	[€/£1,936 + €/£1,600]	3,536

Costs of ordering at the new EOQ:

The new EOQ is the square root of: [(2 × 242,000 × €/£32) ÷ (€/£8 × 10%)] = 4,400 units

Costs of ordering in batches of 4,400 units:

		€/£
Order costs:	[(242,000 units ÷ 4,400 units) × €/£32]	1,760
Holding costs:	[(4,400 units ÷ 2) × €/£0.80]	1,760
Total costs:	[€/£1,760 + €/£1,760]	3,520

The impact of retaining the order quantity of 4,000 units when annual demand increases to 242,000 units is an excess of holding and ordering costs of €/£16. For a variation in the demand of 42,000 units from the estimated forecast of 200,000 units, an increase of €/£16 is immaterial. Although the EOQ is based on a precise number, it should be recognised that there is a range within which the total costs of inventory will not vary a great deal: this is known as the economic order range (EOR). The implication of this is that the EOQ model can still be successfully used in situations where demand is not completely certain.

(c) The EOQ model is not appropriate in the following circumstances:

- when ordering costs are not known;
- when fixed inventory holding costs are not known;
- when demand cannot be reasonably forecast;
- where there are discounts for bulk-buying;
- where other inventory systems are used, such as JIT; and
- where goods are manufactured internally (use EBQ).

CHAPTER 8

Question 8.1

The 80/20 rule is a form of credit management wherein the small number of customers who account for the majority of revenue from a company (80%) are identified and given priority attention in the credit-collection process. The aim is not to press them more than other customers for payment and to foster strong customer goodwill.

Question 8.2

This can signal that a customer is starting to become higher risk, particularly if this is a new customer. They may have exceeded their credit periods with other companies that subsequently restrict supply, resulting in an increase in demand. Alternatively, it may signal that the credit limit for this customer is set at too short a time. If an appropriate length of time is not set, then this may cause a customer to seek their supplies elsewhere, resulting in lost contribution.

Question 8.3

The credit **period** is the amount of time customers are allowed before they have to make payment.

Question 8.4

Credit quality refers to the probability that customers will not pay their accounts on time and potentially become bad debts.

Question 8.5

The cost of granting credit includes: the opportunity cost of finance tied up in trade receivables, e.g. these funds could be used to reduce an overdraft or be invested to earn a return; the risk of bad debts; the possibility of having to allow a discount; and the cost of administration time spent chasing up outstanding accounts. The benefit to be gained from granting credit is the contribution earned from the sale. If credit is not awarded, a customer may just take their custom elsewhere.

Question 8.6

The average collection period is calculated as follows:

Collection period		Proportion of good debts	Expected days
36	×	10% ÷ 90%	4
45	×	60% ÷ 90%	30
72	×	20% ÷ 90%	16
			50

The investment in trade receivables that needs to be financed is, therefore:

Credit sales (net of bad debts) × Trade receivables cash conversion ratio

= (€/£5,000,000 − €/£500,000) × 50 ÷ 365 = €/£616,438

Question 8.7

Insight Ltd's proposed expansion into a new market can be evaluated as follows:

Calculation of the direct effect on the income statement:

	€/£000	€/£000
Revenue		10,000
Variable costs	(8,000)	
Bad debts	(500)	
Collection costs	(100)	(8,600)
Net profit before deducting financing costs		1,400

Financing costs:

	€/£000
Increase in trade receivables:	
(sales less bad debts) × 60/365 = (€/£10m − €/£0.5m) × 60/365	1,561.6
Increase in inventory	1,000
Less increase in trade payables = €/£10m × 80% × 30/365	(657.5)
Increase in working capital	1,904.1

Integration of income statement effect and financing costs:

	€/£000
Net profit before deducting financing costs	1,400
Financing costs:	
Increase in working capital × 12% = €/£1.904m × 12%	(228)
	1,172

Conclusion

Expansion into the new market should increase annual net profit by approximately €/£1.2 million. Insight Limited should proceed with its expansion plans.

Question 8.8

(a)

	Jan–June 20X5 €/£000	Jan–June 20X7 €/£000
Interest costs:		
Trade receivables: [€/£700,000 × 8.5% × 0.5]	29.75	
Trade receivables: [€/£1,350,000 × 17% × 0.5]		114.75
Inventories: [€/£420,000 × 8.5% × 0.5]	17.85	
Inventories: [€/£420,000 × 17% × 0.5]		35.70
	47.60	150.45

Interest costs have increased by 3.16 times (€/£150,450 ÷ €/£47,600). The directors' estimate is correct, with interest costs increasing for a number of reasons:

- The annual costs of overdraft finance have doubled from 8.5% to 17%.
- The proportion of revenue on credit terms has increased from 85% to 95%, requiring increased financing.
- Average trade receivables have increased by 93% [(€/£1,350,000 ÷ €/£700,000) – 1].

(b)

$$\textit{Trade receivables conversion period} = \frac{\text{Average trade receivables}}{\text{credit revenue}} \times 365 \text{ days}$$

Six-month period 20X5

$$\frac{\text{€/£700,000}}{[\text{€/£3,300,000} \times 0.85]} \times 365 = 91 \text{ days}$$

Six-month period 20X7

$$\frac{\text{€/£1,350,000}}{[\text{€/£3,600,000} \times 0.95]} \times 365 = 144 \text{ days}$$

$$\textit{Inventory holding period} = \frac{\text{Average inventories}}{\text{Total revenue (Note 1)}} \times 365 \text{ days}$$

Six-month period 20X5

$$\frac{\text{€/£420,000}}{\text{€/£3,300,000}} \times 365 = 46 \text{ days}$$

Six-month period 20X7

$$\frac{\text{€/£420,000}}{[\text{€/£3,600,000} \times 0.95]} \times 365 = 43 \text{ days}$$

Note 1: the cost of sales figure is unavailable for the work in progress and finished goods inventory turnover calculations. The purchases figure is unavailable for raw material inventory turnover calculations. Revenue is used as a proxy for the unavailable information.

The trade receivables cash-conversion period must be reduced: it has increased by over 50% [(144 ÷ 91) − 1], from 91 days two years ago to 144 days now. This results in higher interest costs than when trade receivables were lower.

The inventory holding period has reduced somewhat over the past two years, due to a reduction in the inventory of finished goods. The company should investigate whether levels could be reduced further without significantly influencing customer service. The reasons for the increase in raw materials inventory by 26.3% [(120 ÷ 95) − 1] over the past two years should be investigated, given that revenue levels have only increased by 9% [(€/£3,600,000 ÷ €/£3,300,000) − 1].

The company should look into the feasibility of operating just-in-time (JIT) purchasing for raw material supplies and JIT production in the manufacturing process. Work in progress levels are the most significant component of total inventories and are indicative of, perhaps, poor production control, allowing inventories to build up, or else a long manufacturing cycle time. Both of these factors need investigation by management and the true cause of high work in progress inventory levels should be discovered and addressed.

Question 8.9

The risk assessment checklist could include the following questions:

- Has the customer exceeded the agreed credit limit?
- Has the customer exceeded the agreed credit period?
- Have any of the payments received from the customer not been honoured by its bank?
- Has the customer requested a longer credit period?
- Is the customer in the habit of disputing invoices (a delay tactic used to stall payment of the invoice)?
- Does the customer offer post-dated cheques?

- Have the customer's order quantities reduced with little explanation?
- Have there been any newspaper articles or web stories that would cause questions to be asked in respect of the financial position of a customer?
- Have there been negative rumours from other companies in respect of the customer's payments?
- Does the customer only pay for goods when the invoice for the next sales order is received?
- Is there an increase in the customer's staff turnover, particularly management?
- Does the customer state that the cheque is in the post, when experience dictates that it is not?
- Do the credit control staff have difficulties contacting the customer?

Chapter 8.10

The main aim of creditor management is to obtain good quality, competitively priced supplies using the longest credit period possible, whilst minimising the cost of administering and managing the supplies. These costs are interrelated and a balance has to be obtained that results in the maximisation of equity holder wealth. The following key points should help to ensure that the objective is achieved.

- Foster a strong credit reputation and ethical approach to creditor management.
- Ensure staff are appropriately trained.
- Put in place strong procedures and controls to ensure documentary and computer processes are efficient and effective.
- Ensure the credit period and limit received is formally documented in a credit agreement with each supplier.
- Review the policy and negotiate any changes with each supplier.

CHAPTER 9

Question 9.1

Transaction motive: holding sufficient cash to cover the operational transaction costs of a company.

Precautionary motive: holding a cash buffer to allow payment of unexpected one-off cash outflows.

Speculative motive: holding an additional amount of cash to allow management to take advantage of profitable opportunities when they arise at short notice.

Question 9.2

Transmission delay: delays in the time between a supplier writing a cheque and it reaching a company's premises.

Lodgement delay: delays in the time between receiving a cheque and lodging the cheque to a bank.

Clearance delay: delays in the time between a cheque being presented to a bank and the cash being available for use.

Question 9.3

There are many factors that can result in cash shortages. The answer might include:

- inflation;
- growth;
- losses;
- capital expenditure;

- dividend payments;
- seasonal fluctuations in operations;
- taxation; or
- debt repayments.

Question 9.4

Current policy The cost of the current lodgement policy is the interest saving foregone for each day that takings are not lodged. It is assumed that the company's overdraft rate is higher than its cost of capital/investment return potential; hence this is the appropriate opportunity rate to use when quantifying the cost of not lodging.

Therefore, the cost of not lodging every day is the amount that could be lodged multiplied by the daily overdraft rate. The daily takings are the yearly sales divided by the number of days the shop earns income. It is open six days each week for every week in the year. Therefore, the total income generated is over 312 (6 × 52) days in each year and the daily takings are €/£12,500 [€/£3,900,000 ÷ 312].

The daily overdraft rate is approximated from the yearly rate 0.0329% [12% ÷ 365].

Therefore, the daily interest foregone is €/£4.1125 [€/£12,500 × 0.0329%].

The number of days' interest lost is as follows:

Day sales arise	Days until banked*
Monday	6
Tuesday	5
Wednesday	4
Thursday	3
Friday	2
Saturday	1
Total	21

* The monies are banked on Monday morning, so will be eligible for deduction when that day's interest is calculated.

The total cost for the week is €/£86.3625 [€/£4.1125 × 21].

The total cost each year is, therefore, €/£4,490.85 [€/£86.3625 × 52].

Proposed policy As the takings are lodged at the close of business every day, the only interest foregone is the Saturday takings, which are lodged with Monday's takings at the close of business on a Monday. Therefore, the cost will be: €/£427.70 [2 × €/£4.1125 × 52].

By implementing the accountant's suggested policy, Thomas stands to save €/£4,063.15 [€/£4,490.85 − €/£427.70].

CHAPTER 10

Question 10.1

Disintermediation refers to a move away from the use of intermediaries for bill finance. Intermediaries usually guarantee and sell finance bills in the markets on behalf of a company. Disintermediation refers to a situation where a company arranges the finance bill and approaches the market itself. This reduces the cost of obtaining finance. Only large, listed, reputable companies can successfully cut out the financial intermediaries.

Question 10.2

In a statement of financial position, assets are disclosed according to the length of time a company intends to keep them. Assets the company intends to keep for less than one year are categorised as current assets, whereas assets the company intends to hold for more than one year are categorised as non-current assets. Current assets typically include inventories, trade receivables, short-dated securities, prepayments, bank deposit account balances, current account balances (if positive) and cash. Non-current assets are usually sorted into three categories: tangible (which typically includes land, buildings, plant and machinery, fixtures and fittings, motor vehicles and office equipment); investments (which typically includes shares in subsidiaries, joint ventures, associates, financial investments and derivatives); and intangible assets (which typically includes purchased goodwill, capitalised development expenditure, patents and quota).

Question 10.3

In most companies, current assets are a permanent feature of the statement of financial position. Most companies have to carry inventories and have to sell goods on credit (resulting in trade receivables). This means that all year round the company has to invest in a minimum level of working capital to support its operating activities. This is a permanent requirement and is regarded as the permanent portion of current assets. In addition to the permanent requirement, most companies will have temporary increased demand for additional working capital, termed 'temporary current assets'. The best way to explain temporary current asset requirements is to consider a company that has seasonal sales, such as an umbrella company. Production would be constant all year round, yet sales would take place mostly in the winter months. Therefore, there would be a large inventory build-up during the year, needing short-term financing, and a surplus of cash in the winter when sales would outstrip production.

Question 10.4

There are two types of costs: opportunity costs and shortage costs. An opportunity cost is revenue lost from not investing monies in non-current assets. This can be compared with shortage costs that would result when insufficient levels of current asset are held because a higher proportion of funds are invested in non-current assets. Shortage costs might include: lost sales from stock-outs, lost sales caused by disruptions in production, lost sales from having too aggressive a credit policy or penalty charges from having to cash in securities before their maturities.

Question 10.5

If a company were to pursue a neutral policy in respect of its asset mix, it would hold sufficient levels of current assets to ensure that limited shortage costs occurred, yet not hold too much so as to be regarded as inefficient. A company pursuing a flexible approach would hold high levels of current assets. This would involve holding high levels of inventory, granting long credit periods and holding cash reserves in short-dated securities. A company pursuing a restrictive approach would hold low levels of current assets and high levels of non-current assets. The company would experience many shortage costs. This is a risky strategy as the liquidity of a company is related to the level of its current assets relative to its current liabilities.

Question 10.6

A company adopting a matching approach to the financing of its investments would match the term of the finance to the term of the investment. This adopts a 'self-liquidating loan' approach wherein the investment financed by the finance should be structured in such a manner as to repay the finance requirement, without having to rely on resources from other parts of the company. A company adopting a flexible approach would have sufficient long-term finance arranged to finance all its requirements, both permanent and temporary. When temporary demand reduces, the excess finance funds would be invested in short-term securities. A company pursuing a restrictive policy would finance its short-term requirements solely by short-term means, but would also use short-term sources to finance permanent current assets and possibly some non-current assets.

Question 10.7

In 1970 the economist Eugene Fama suggested that market efficiency be analysed using three levels of efficiency. The ideal situation he termed 'strong-form efficiency'. When a market is operating with strong-form efficiency, all relevant current information, including information that is not available publicly, is reflected in current share price. As all internal information is reflected in share price, there is no scope for gains to be made from insider trading. The second level of efficiency is called 'semi-strong-form efficiency'. This level of efficiency suggests that all publicly available information is reflected in share price; however, insider information is not. This would suggest that insider trading can reap rewards, but market traders cannot make gains as all the gains are reflected in the share price immediately. The final level of efficiency Fama termed 'weak-form efficiency'. This suggests that share price fully reflects all the information contained in past share price movements. As this information is already reflected in share price, there are no gains to be made from charting the share price movements in the past in an attempt at predicting future price movements.

CHAPTER 11

Question 11.1

Any two of the following will suffice: commercial banks will provide short-term finance, as will factor companies, discount houses and acceptance houses. These are normally subsidiaries of commercial or merchant banks.

Question 11.2

Overdrafts, short-term loans, factoring, invoice discounting.

Question 11.3

Factoring is where an outside company, usually a financial institution, provides finance to a company on the strength of the trade receivables of the company. The factor also takes over the administration of trade credit, vets customers, issues invoices and statements and chases up late payers. Customers are normally fully aware of the factor's involvement with the company.

Under a confidential factoring agreement, the factor's involvement is not visible; the company remains responsible for the administration of the trade receivables ledger and issues invoices, statements and letters using its own stationery. The company still sells the invoices to the factor; however, it acts as an agent for the factor company in the collection of the debts.

Question 11.4

Two ways of externally financing trade receivables are:
- the assignment of debts (invoice discounting); or
- the selling of debts (factoring).

Invoice discounting is characterised by the fact that a lender not only has a lien on debts, but also has recourse to the borrower (i.e. the seller of the receivables), i.e. if the person or company who bought the goods does not pay, the selling company must take the loss. In other words, the risk of default on the trade balances pledged remains with the borrower. In addition, the buyer of the goods is not usually notified about the pledging of the debts.

Factoring, on the other hand, is frequently undertaken 'without recourse', i.e. the factor must bear the loss in the event that the customer who bought the goods does not pay.

There are advantages and disadvantages to factoring and invoice discounting as a method of raising funds for an individual company:

- First of all, the flexibility of these sources of finance is an advantage – as the company's sales expand and more financing is needed, the amount of readily available financing increases. The client company of a bank can convert up to 80% of its book debts into cash immediately. The company can be in charge of its funding management, since funds can be drawn down only as required, and it can rely on the invoice discounter to fund quality debts, when the need arises. At the same time, this will enable companies to pay their suppliers sooner and to take advantage of bulk discounts.
- Secondly, trade receivables or invoices provide security for a loan (provided by the discounting bank) that a company might otherwise be unable to obtain.
- Thirdly, factoring provides the services of a credit department that might otherwise only be available under much more expensive conditions. Invoice discounting is particularly beneficial to new companies, where significant equity holder investment is not available, and young companies, where the statement of financial position, or lack of track record, precludes or restricts traditional bank lending. Other potential users include expanding companies, whose growth demands additional working capital, exporting companies where export sales can be funded, and seasonal companies, which experience peaks and troughs in their cash flow requirements.
- Finally, any company that uses the facility prudently will be able to expand and increase profits, without having to increase the capital investment in the company.

Invoice discounting and factoring also have disadvantages:

- When invoices are numerous and relatively small in value, the administrative costs involved may render these methods of financing inconvenient and expensive.
- For a long time, factoring of trade receivables was frowned upon by suppliers and, indeed, was regarded as a confession of a company's unsound financial position, whereas invoice discounting is confidential.

Some companies, such as small and medium-sized enterprises, are unaware of the potential of these forms of finance. Some companies consider that having a good credit management system in place reduces the need to use invoice discounting. In fact, a prerequisite of invoice discounting is that good credit management systems must be in place. A traditional reliance by Irish companies on bank overdrafts and loans has meant that there is often a reluctance to accept other forms of finance.

Although both factoring and invoice discounting can be attractive to companies, particularly small companies, and can give flexibility in terms of the provision of finance and assistance in credit management and credit intelligence, these techniques may impede the overall ability of the company using them to raise overdraft finance, because the prospective lending bank is unable to take a floating charge on the accounts receivable of the company.

Question 11.5

The arrangement that affords the most protection to the exporter, whilst providing credit to the importer while the goods are in transit, is an irrevocable documented letter of credit that has been confirmed. This is a legally binding arrangement that outlines the payment to be made, the documents to be delivered and the dates on which the documents should be delivered. The payment terms should be on a sight draft basis, meaning that the importer's bank has to pay the sum due when the letter is presented and the goods arrive. The contract cannot be altered or cancelled without the consent of all parties. When the arrangement is for payment on sight of the letter, the bill of lading is usually withheld and passed with the confirmed documented letter of credit to the importer's bank when payment is processed.

CHAPTER 12

Question 12.1

A revolving credit facility is a flexible term loan. Repayments made reduce the capital element of the debt; however, the funds are accessible again by a borrower. With notice, a borrower can draw down on the loan again, up to the original agreed level, within the timescale of the initial agreement. This flexibility means that this type of facility is more expensive relative to a straight term loan, as the bank has to keep additional reserves to be able to cater for the additional demand for cash.

Question 12.2

Advantages and disadvantages to a hiree company of using hire-purchase finance:

Advantages	**Disadvantages**
Easy to arrange	Cost
Quick source of finance	Lack of flexibility
Availability	Cancellation is costly
Cash flow certainty/easier budgeting	Maintenance/insurance
Not repayable on demand	Risks of ownership
Cash flow advantage	Underutilisation
Tax relief	
Ownership	

Question 12.3

Main motives for lease finance:

- It is an alternative source of funds that can be obtained when other sources are exhausted.
- It is quick and easy to arrange and obtain.
- The finance house does not require security.
- It has cash flow advantages.
- It may be cheaper than other sources of finance and is tax deductible (the deduction differs depending on whether the lease is an operating or a finance lease).

(See **Chapter 10** for more detail.)

Question 12.4

As the interest rate is the flat rate, it will be applied to the €/£50,000 for three years. Therefore, the total interest, which is calculated at the start of the agreement, will be €/£50,000 × 10% × 3 = €/£15,000. The total repayments per year will be €/£21,667 [€/£16,667 (€/£50,000 ÷ 3) plus interest of €/£5,000 (€/£15,000 ÷ 3)].

Question 12.5

(a)

€/£15,000 × 10% = €/£1,500 = €/£13,500 capital balance

Interest: €/£13,500 × 7.5% = €/£1,012.50 per annum

Capital = €/£13,500/4 = €/£3,375 per annum

Total annual repayment = €/£4,387.50

(b)

$$\frac{€/£13{,}500}{€/£4387.50} = 3.076923$$

Hence, APR lies between 11% and 12% based on an annuity factor of 3.076923.

$$11\% + \frac{3.102 - 3.077}{3.102 - 3.037} = 11.38\%$$

Question 12.6

REPORT

To: A Client
From: A Student, Financial Consultant
Date: 30 May 20XX
Re: Short-term and medium-term sources of finance

As requested, this report offers advice on short-term and medium-term sources of finance. The report will first address factors that should be considered when selecting an appropriate source of finance and will then outline the main features of a number of sources of finance.

The factors that should be considered when selecting an appropriate source of finance may be summed up by a series of questions:

How long is the finance required? Finance that is repayable within one year is regarded as short term, whereas finance repayable between one and seven years is considered to be medium-term financing.

The determination of the period over which finance is required facilitates the choice of short-term or medium-term sources: for example, €/£10,000 required for 10 days until a customer settles an account suggests a short-term source, rather than a medium-term source.

How much finance is required? A company must assess the amount of finance required to facilitate selection of the source of finance. For example, if an amount of €/£75,000 is needed, a medium-term loan for four years may be more appropriate than a bank overdraft for up to a year.

What will it cost? It is important to establish the costs of similar sources of finance so that the most economical source may be selected for the particular circumstances.

For what purpose is it required? This aspect deals with the matching principle, i.e. the purpose of the finance should be matched by the type of financing selected. For example, the purchase of a non-current asset expected to have a useful economic life of five years would be more appropriately matched to a medium-term source of finance than a short-term source of finance.

There are various sources of short-term and medium-term finance; however, this report will outline the main features of four of the main sources:

- bank overdraft (short-term source);
- medium-term bank loan (medium-term source);
- hire-purchase (medium-term source); and
- leasing (medium-term source).

(*The solution should refer to the following key points.*)

1. Bank overdraft
    - Flexible – the lender may borrow as much, or as little, as is required.
    - Relatively cheap – interest is charged only on the amount used.
    - Overdraft interest is deductible for taxation purposes.
    - Variable interest rate applies.
    - Usually requires security or guarantee.
    - In some instances, the bank account must be in credit for 30 days during the year.
    - This financing is repayable on demand.
    - Suitable and commonly used for financing short-term working capital requirements.
2. Medium-term bank loan
    - Usually contract-based.
    - Requires security, which may be a fixed or floating charge on assets.
    - May have to adhere to a financial covenant requiring a specific level of interest cover or a minimum current asset ratio.
    - Repayable in a lump sum or by instalments.
    - Loan may allow 'rest periods' when instalments may not be payable and no penalty applies.
    - Interest rate attaching to the loan may be fixed or variable.
    - Commonly used for purchase of non-current assets.
3. Hire-purchase
    - Commonly used for purchase of non-current assets, such as plant and machinery.
    - A hire-purchase company purchases the asset and, in return for regular instalments, supplies the asset to a hiree.
    - Hiree gains immediate use of asset, without high initial capital payment.
    - Hire-purchase payments include both capital and interest elements.
    - Legal ownership remains with the hire-purchase company until all instalments have been paid.
    - Generally considered to be an expensive source of finance.
4. Leasing
    - A lease conveys the legal right to use an asset in return for payment of a fee.
    - Ownership of asset remains with the owner, the lessor.
    - Lease agreements may be for less than a year or for the entire life of an asset.
    - Lease agreements require that the lessee is responsible for the insurance and maintenance of the asset being leased.
    - Leases are typically used for larger non-current assets, such as vehicles, plant and machinery, etc.

When operating a company, it is very important to ensure that proper financing is in place. It is necessary to consider for how long the finance is required, how much is required, what the associated costs are and why the finance is required. Once these questions have been answered, it should be clear whether a short- or medium-term source of finance is required and it will be possible to make a choice between the various sources available. This report has highlighted the features of the most commonly used sources of short-term and medium-term finance. Each should be considered carefully before making a selection.

I hope that this report has provided all the information that you require. If you have any further questions about any aspect of the report, please do not hesitate to contact me.

A Student

Financial Consultant

Question 12.7

According to Simpson (2001), venture capitalists will base their decision on four fundamental areas of the proposed venture: the strengths of the management team; the entrepreneur leading the team; the product; and market opportunities. Simpson goes on to state that the integrity and quality of the management team is the most significant influence.

Having a clear exit strategy is also very important. Venture capitalists will want a high return and will want to be able to liquidate it within about five to seven years. The most lucrative means is by flotation and venture capitalists are more open to investing in companies with this objective in mind.

CHAPTER 13

Question 13.1

The purpose of a restrictive covenant is to restrict the extent to which management (which acts on behalf of equity holders) can 'engage in opportunistic behaviour' to increase the value of equity at the expense of the other main collective investors in the company – for example, creditors and debt holders. The more restrictive the covenants, the less risky the debt, hence this debt will be valued higher by the market.

Question 13.2

A trust deed sets out the terms of the contract between a company and its bondholders and establishes the identity of a trustee and sets out his/her powers. It contains information such as the coupon rate, date interest should be paid, redemption date, right to receive financial statements and restrictive covenants.

Question 13.3

The company could set up a sinking fund. It could stagger the repayment by issuing a band of redemption dates (for example, redeemable 2030–2035). It could repurchase some of the bonds on the market, or make an offer to repurchase the bonds from the bondholders. It could issue the bonds as irredeemable and buy them back when it suits. It could issue equity capital and use the proceeds to redeem the bonds.

Question 13.4

Fallen angel.

Question 13.5

There will be 15 payments into the sinking fund. The terminal value of the fund should be €/£2,500,000 × 1.05 = €/£2,625,000. The future value of an annuity factor for 15 payments that earn a fixed rate of 15% is 47.580. Therefore, the required yearly repayment *(X)* is:

$$X \times 47.580 = \text{€/£}2{,}625{,}000$$

$$X = \text{€/£}55{,}170$$

So long as the sinking fund earns the target return of 15%, then a transfer of €/£55,170 every year for 15 years will result in the sinking fund having a terminal value of €/£2,625,000.

Question 13.6

The current return on Jock Plc's bonds is:

$$r = \frac{\text{€/£}9}{\text{€/£}90} = 10\%$$

Therefore, this is a very good investment for the investor, as his expected return is 8%.

Question 13.7

The cash flows in relation to each bond are as follows:

Year	Cash flow €/£
0	(95)
0.5	5
1	5
1.5	5
2	5
2	100

This information can then be used to find the exact half-yearly discount rate, which can then be converted into an annual rate.

Period	Cash flow €/£	Discount factor Try 5%	Present value €/£	Discount factor Try 8%	Present value €/£
0	95	1.000	95	1.000	95
1–2 (4)*	(5)	3.546	(17.73)	3.312	(16.56)
2	(100)	0.823	(82.30)	0.735	(73.50)
			(5.03)		4.94

* Though the cash flows occur over a two-year period, it is a four-period annuity that needs to be used at half the rate.

Using interpolation, a more precise estimate of the half-yearly rate is:

$$5\% + \frac{-5.03(8-5)}{-5.03-4.94} = 6.51\%$$

This half-yearly rate is then converted to an annual rate:

$$(1 + 0.0651)^2 - 1 = 13.44\%$$

This rate is gross and can be reduced for the bondholder's tax rate to get the net return to the bondholder.

Question 13.8

The approach is to find the discount rate (i.e. the compound interest rate) (r) that would be achieved if €/£50 were to be invested now to achieve a terminal value payment of €/£100.

This is represented by the following:

$$€/£50(1 + r)^{10} = £100$$

This can be rearranged to:

$$r = \sqrt[10]{100 \div 50} - 1$$

$$r = 0.0718\ (7.18\%)$$

Therefore, an investor is receiving an annual gross return of 7.18% (before tax).

CHAPTER 14

Question 14.1

Book value of equity This represents a combination of the investment made by equity holders and undistributed gains made by the company. It includes the book value of the equity share capital, the share premium account, the capital redemption reserve, the revaluation reserve and revenue reserves. The total of these will equate to the book value of a company's total assets less its total liabilities. It bears little relationship to market value, which will factor in unrecorded items, such as intellectual capital, the quality of the management team and expectations about future earnings.

Nominal value Each share a company issues has a nominal value (otherwise known as par value). The nominal value is established by the directors of a company when it is being incorporated, with the value and number of shares authorised for issue being stipulated in a company's Articles of Association. The nominal value can only be changed using a special resolution at an annual general meeting with the agreement of equity holders.

Market value The nominal value bears no relationship to market value, which is the price that the market places on the equity of the company.

Question 14.2

In the UK the main exchange is the London Stock Exchange. It has two equity trading markets – the Main Market, which is used by very large companies, and an over-the-counter market, the AIM, which is used mostly by small and medium-sized companies. It is mostly financial intermediaries that trade in these markets. In Ireland, the exchange is NYSE Euronext Dublin (formerly the Irish Stock Exchange). It has three markets: Euronext, for large established companies, Euronext Access & Access+ for SMEs listing for the first time and Euronext Growth for high-growth SME companies.

The conditions and rules on prospectuses in the London Stock Exchange may change as a result of Brexit.

Question 14.3

Advantages	**Disadvantages**
Access to growth capital	Market risk
Access to an acquisitions platform	Costs
An exit for equity holders	Agency theory
Increased credibility	Loss of control
Increased public profile	Regulatory burden
Attract, reward and incentivise staff	Managerial time tied up
	Employee demotivation

Question 14.4

Pre-emptive rights refers to a stock exchange rule that became a legal requirement. It requires that companies that want to make a further issue of equity for cash must offer the new shares to the existing equity holders in proportion to their current holding, in the first instance. This gives current equity holders the chance to maintain their percentage holding in a company.

Question 14.5

The net earnings available for distribution to equity holders under both methods of financing are as follows:

	Preference shares €/£000	**Debentures €/£000**
Earnings before interest and tax	2,000	2,000
Interest: [€/£2,000,000 × 14%]	–	(280)
Earnings before tax	2,000	1,720
Taxation @ 40%	(800)	(688)
Earnings available for distribution	1,200	1,032

Therefore, equity holders would be better off if the company were to to issue debentures, as the €/£1,200,000 is distributable to both preference and equity holders. As preference shareholders get a dividend of €/£180,000, this only leaves €/£1,020,000 for the equity holders.

Question 14.6

(a)

	€/£
Before:	
Each lot of two shares is currently worth: [2 × €/£5.00]	10.00
The new issue will be priced at: (1 × €/£4.00)	4.00
The total holding is worth:	14.00
After:	
Therefore, after the issue the theoretical ex-rights share price expected will be:	
[€/£14.00 ÷ 3]	4.67

(b) The value of the right attached to each existing share will be:

€/£5.00 – €/£4.67 = €/£0.33 per existing share.

(c) The value of the right were it assumed to be attached to the new share is: €/£4.67 – €/£4.00 = €/£0.67 per new share. (This can also be found by multiplying the existing shares required to qualify for a new share by the value of the rights per current share: €/£0.67 [€/£0.33 × 2] (rounded).)

(d)

	€/£
Before:	
The equity holder owned 2,000 shares valued at €/£5.00 per share: (2,000 × €/£5.00)	10,000
To receive the 1,000 new shares the equity holder will have to pay the company: (1,000 × €/£4.00)	4,000
After:	
The equity holder will own [2,000 + (2,000/2)] = 3,000 shares valued at €/£4.67 each.	
Total value: [3,000 × €/£4.67]	14,000

Therefore, the equity holders' wealth has not increased, but the company will have €/£4,000 additional cash to invest in projects.

(e)

	€/£
Before:	
The equity holder owned 2,000 shares valued at €/£5.00 per share: [2,000 × €/£5.00]	10,000
After:	
The equity holder decides to sell their rights.	
They are issued with 1,000 rights, which can be sold for €/£0.67 each, so they get cash worth: [1,000 × €/£0.67]	670
They still have their 2,000 shares, though, which are worth €/£4.67 each after the issue: [2,000 × €/£4.67]	9,340
Total equity holder value:	10,010
(The difference is due to rounding.)	

(f) The number of shares the equity holder can purchase is calculated using the following formula:

$$\frac{\text{Rights price} \times \text{Number of shares allotted}}{\text{Theoretical ex-rights price}}$$

(€/£0.67 × 1,000) ÷ €/£4.67 = 144 shares

	€/£
Therefore, the equity holder will have to sell [1,000 – 144] 856 rights	
providing them with cash of: [856 × €/£0.67]	574.00
which will be used to purchase 144 shares at €/£4.00 each: [144 × €/£4.00]	576.00
(The difference is due to rounding.)	

After the sale the equity holder will have 2,144 shares valued at:	€/£
€/£4.67: [2,144 × €/£4.67]	10,012

Equivalent to the original investment of €/£10,000.

(The difference is due to rounding.)

(g) The company will sell the rights at an auction and reimburse the equity holder the proceeds, net of costs incurred selling the rights: €/£670 [€/£0.67 × 1,000]. A cheque for €/£670, less any auction fees, will be issued to the equity holder by the company.

CHAPTER 15

Question 15.1

The value of Enero Plc's shares (P_0) to be used in the calculation of the WACC is €/£900,000 [(€/£2.05 – €/£0.15 – €/£0.10) × 500,000].

Question 15.2

The expected net cash inflow from issuing one share will be €/£2.30 [€/£2.50 – €/£0.20].

The company pays constant dividends of 46c/p per share. Therefore, the cost of equity is 20% [€/£0.46/€/£2.30].

Question 15.3

Abril Plc's cost of equity (K_e) is: $\frac{8c/p(1+0.06)}{90c/p} + 0.06 = 0.1542\ (15.42\%)$

Question 15.4

Mayo Plc's ROCE (r) is 20%. Its retentions (b) are 50%. Therefore, expected growth in dividends (g) is 10% [50% × 20%].

Question 15.5

The market value (P_0) is the earnings per share multiplied by the price earnings ratio of a similar quoted company: €/£900,000 [500,000 × (€/£0.20 × (10 × 90%))].

Question 15.6

The current market value of the debentures is €/£112.00 for each €/£100.00 block. There is no mention of issue costs and the debentures are trading cum-interest. Therefore, the market value of a single debenture to be included in the WACC is €/£102 [€/£112 – (€/£100 × 10%)]. The total market value of the debentures is: €/£1,020,000 [(€/£1,000,000 ÷ €/£100) × €/£102].

The cost of the debentures is as follows:

Year	Cash flows €/£	Discount Try 5%	NPV €/£	Discount Try 10%	NPV €/£
0	102	1.000	102.00	1.000	102.00
1–8	(10(1–0.3))	6.463	(45.24)	5.335	(37.35)
8	(100)	0.677	(67.70)	0.467	(46.70)
			(10.94)		17.95

$$K_d = 5\% + \frac{-€/£10.94(10\% - 5\%)}{-€/£10.94 - €/£17.95} = 6.89\%$$

(b) The WACC can be used as an appropriate discount rate for capital investment appraisal when: the WACC reflects the company's long-term optimal capital structure; the investment being financed is of the same business risk as that of the company; the project is small; the finance being raised is in the same proportion to the current level of debt and equity in the company (this can be achieved over time, so short-term fluctuations are assumed to happen); and all the information is readily available (i.e. there is a market value for the debt capital and the equity capital).

Question 15.7

(a) The after-tax weighted average cost of capital should be calculated.

Equity shares

	€/£
Market value of shares cum-dividend	3.27
Dividend per share: [€/£810,000÷3,000,000]	(0.27)
Market value of shares ex-dividend	3.00

The formula for calculating the cost of equity when there is dividend growth is:

$$K_e = \frac{D_0(1+g)}{P_0} + g$$

where K_e is cost of equity, D_0 is current dividend, g is rate of growth and P_0 is current ex-dividend market value.

In this case, the future rate of growth (g) in dividends is estimated from the average growth in dividends over the past four years.

$$€/£810,000 = €/£620,000\ (1+g)^4$$

$$(1+g)^4 = \frac{€/£810,000}{€/£620,000}$$

$$(1+g)^4 = 1.3065$$

$$(1+g) = 1.069$$

$$g = 0.069\ (6.9\%)$$

The cost of equity is:

$$K_e = \frac{€/£0.27 \times 1.069}{€/£3.27 - €/£0.27} + 0.069 = 0.165\ (16.5\%)$$

7% debentures

In order to find the after-tax cost of the debentures, which are redeemable in 10 years' time, it is necessary to find the discount rate (using interpolation) that will give the future after-tax cash flows a present value of €/£77.10

The relevant cash flows are:

1. Annual interest payments, net of tax, which are €/£60,970 [€/£1,300,000 × 7% × 67%], for 10 years; and
2. A capital repayment of €/£1,300,000 in 10 years' time.

It is assumed that tax relief on the debenture interest arises at the same time as the interest payment. In practice the cash flow effect is unlikely to be felt for about a year, but this will have no significant effect on the calculations.

Interpolation calculation

	€/£000
Try 8%	
Current market value of debentures: [€/£1,300,000 at 77.1%]	(1,002.3)
Annual interest payments net of tax: [€/£60,970 × 6.710]	409.1
Capital repayment: [€/£1,300,000 × 0.463 (8% in 10 years' time)]	601.9
NPV	8.7
Try 9%	
Current market value of debentures: [€/£1,300,000 at 77.1%]	(1,002.3)
Annual interest payments net of tax: [€/£60,970 × 6.418]	391.3
Capital repayment: [€/£1,300,000 × 0.422]	548.6
NPV	(62.4)

$$\text{IRR} = 8\% + \frac{€/£8{,}700\,(9\% - 8\%)}{€/£8{,}700 - €/£62{,}400} = 8.12\%$$

The weighted average cost of capital:

	Market value €/£000	**Weight %**	**Cost %**	**WACC %**
Equity	9,000	90	16.50	14.85
7% debentures	1,002	10	8.12	0.81
	10,002	100		15.66

The above calculations suggest that a discount rate in the region of 16% might be appropriate for the appraisal of new investment opportunities.

(b) Difficulties and uncertainties in the above estimates arise in a number of areas.

The cost of equity: the above calculation assumes that all equity holders have the same marginal cost of capital and the same dividend expectations, which is unrealistic. In addition, it is assumed that dividend growth has been, and will be, at a constant rate of 6.9%. In fact, actual growth in the years 20X1–X2 and 20X4–X5 was in excess of 9%, while in the year 20X3–X4 there was no dividend growth; 6.9% is merely the average rate of growth for the past four years. The rate of future growth will depend more on the return from future projects undertaken than on the past dividend record.

The use of the weighted average cost of capital: use of the weighted average cost of capital as a discount rate is only justified where the company in question has achieved what it believes to be the optimal capital structure (the mix of debt and equity), and where it intends to maintain this structure in the long term.

The projects themselves: the weighted average cost of capital makes no allowance for the business risk of individual projects. In practice some companies, having calculated the WACC, then add a premium for risk. In this case, for example, if one used a risk premium of 5%, the final discount rate would be 21%. Ideally, the risk premium should vary from project to project, since not all projects are equally risky. In general, the riskier the project, the higher the discount rate that should be used.

CHAPTER 16

Question 16.1

The capital structure of a company is its mix of long-term debt and equity.

Question 16.2

The WACC of a company is the return required by a company to cover the average return required by its investors. The investors are the holders of debt and equity capital in the company, i.e. their investment makes up a company's capital structure. In general, equity investors require a higher return relative to debt investors as they face higher risks. Therefore, as the different sources of long-term finance in a company cost different amounts, the level of each type held will impact on the overall WACC.

Question 16.3

Financial risk captures the additional sensitivity in returns available to investors arising due to the level of debt in a company's financial structure.

Question 16.4

(a) The question provides the reader with information on equity share price and earnings for the two companies. This is sufficient to use the dividend-valuation model to calculate the cost of equity. The question states that all earnings after interest are distributed as dividends, hence there is no growth. As share price is given ex-dividend, the only workings required are to find dividends.

	Pero Plc €/£000	Gato Plc €/£000
Earnings	300	300
Interest [€/£1.2m × 10%]	–	(120)
Dividend	300	180

$$\text{Cost of equity} \quad \frac{€/£300{,}000}{[€/£1.40 \times 1{,}600{,}000]} \qquad \frac{€/£180{,}000}{[€/£1.60 \times 800{,}000]}$$

Cost of equity 13.39% 14.06%

(b) Pero Plc is an all-equity-financed company. Its WACC is the same as its cost of equity (13.39%).

Market value of equity and debt:

	Pero Plc €/£000	Gato Plc €/£000
Equity: 1,600,000 × €/£1.40	2,240	
800,000 × €/£1.60		1,280
Debt	–	1,200
Total company value ($D + E$)	2,240	2,480

Gato Plc's WACC is as follows:

$$\frac{€/£1{,}280{,}000}{€/£2{,}480{,}000}(14.06\%) + \frac{€/£1{,}200{,}000}{€/£2{,}480{,}000}(10\%) = 12.10\%$$

(c) Gato Plc has a higher cost of equity (14.06%) compared to Pero Plc (13.39%) as its equity holders require a higher return to compensate them for the financial risk they bear due to gearing. However, Gato Plc has an overall lower WACC because its capital structure includes debt, which is at a lower cost, and the additional premium commanded by its equity holders is more than compensated for by the cheaper debt.

(d) M&M (without taxes) would argue that the WACC in both companies should be the same, as a company's capital structure does not determine its value. The cost of equity in one of the companies is out of equilibrium. As the return/dividend is known, then the only explanation is that the equity is mispriced. It may be undervalued in Pero Plc or overvalued in Gato Plc, or a mixture of both.

Question 16.5

There are two views of the cost of capital. The traditional view states that the cost of capital is a function of a company's capital structure; therefore, a company's overall cost of funds can be reduced by a judicious use of debt finance. The M&M view states that, in a world with no taxes, there is no gearing effect on market value, i.e. the cost of capital is independent of gearing because the advantages of using cheaper debt are exactly offset by the disadvantages (increased financial risk) of that increased debt.

Certain restrictive assumptions govern the M&M view:

- Perfect capital markets exist, wherein companies can borrow unlimited amounts at similar rates of interest.
- There are no taxes or transactions costs.
- Personal borrowing is a perfect substitute for corporate borrowing.
- Companies exist with the same level of business or systematic risk, but with different levels of gearing.

M&M put forward three propositions:

Proposition I The cost of capital and market value of a company are independent of its gearing. This is because the market value of any company is given by capitalising its expected total earnings at the capitalisation rate appropriate to an all-equity company of that risk class. The income generated by a company from its business activities is that which determines value rather than the way in which it is split between the providers of capital. Thus:

$$K_0 = \frac{\text{EBIT}}{\text{MV}}$$

where K_0 is overall cost of capital, MV is market value of the company (which should be independent of capital structure), and EBIT is earnings before interest and tax or net operating income.

Proposition II The introduction of debt into the capital structure immediately increases the financial risk of the equity holders, who require a premium to compensate. This exactly offsets the apparently lower cost of debt and leaves K_0 and the MV of the company constant.

This means that the expected return on the equity of an enterprise is equal to the expected return on a pure equity stream, plus a financial risk premium adjusted by the ratio of debt to equity. The effect on the cost of equity of introducing debt into the capital structure is that the cost of equity rises linearly to offset the lower cost debt directly, giving a constant overall cost of capital irrespective of the level of gearing.

Proposition III To be accepted, projects will have to have a rate of return (*k*) greater than or equal to the overall cost of capital K_0. To achieve this, M&M rests on the arbitrage assumption – if there are two enterprises, X and Y, each with the same EBIT, they must be valued equally, whether the payments are made to equity holders or debt holders. If they are not, then arbitrage profits can ensue.

Question 16.6

(a) Gearing

$$\frac{D}{E} = \frac{5{,}550}{4{,}200 + 100} = 128\%$$

$$\frac{D}{E} + E = \frac{5{,}550}{5{,}500 + 4{,}200 + 100} = 56\%$$

(b) Significance

- Highlights the financial risk of investing in the company; generally, the higher the level of gearing, the higher the financial risk.
- Highlights the potential of the company to raise finance.
- The level of gearing should be compared to industry norms before its significance can be determined.
- Rule of thumb: a company should be able to cover its long-term debt from its equity. This is not the case for Jack.

(c) Practical factors that influence a company's capital structure

- **Tax rates**: the higher the level of corporate taxes, the more attractive debt capital becomes.
- **Asset base**: companies with high levels of tangible assets will find it easier to take on debt as they are in a better position to offer security.
- **Cash flow volatility**: a company with stable cash flows can service debt capital more easily than a company with volatile cash flows.
- **Interest rate levels**: debt capital issues are attractive when interest rates are low.
- **Articles of Association**: This indicates what types of finance are authorised or what covenants are applicable.
- **Issue costs**: debt tends to have cheaper issuance costs than equity.
- **Management preference**: retained earnings are often preferred over debt and equity.
- **Industry norms**: substantial deviations from industry norms may send the wrong signal to investors.
- **Dilution of earnings**: large issuance of equity could lead to the dilution of EPS.

Question 16.7

- A higher cost of capital (either for debt or equity) due to its financial situation.
- Lost sales due to fear of impaired services and loss of trust.
- Managers and employees may take drastic actions to save the firm that might result in some long-term problems.
- Companies might have trouble keeping highly skilled managers and employees.
- Suppliers may cease supplying due to a fear that the company has an inability to pay.

Question 16.8

- **Lending restriction** – for example, security and debt covenants.
- **Gearing level** – is the company currently highly geared and exposed to financial risk?
- **Liquidity implications** – in the case of debt finance, does the company have the ability to service the new debt?
- The impact the financing options will have on the financial statements.
- **Availability** – the availability of finance depends on the creditworthiness of the borrower and the willingness of lenders to extend credit.
- **Effect on control** – will selecting a certain source of finance result in a dilution of control for existing shareholders, which in turn may impact the EPS? This could have an influence on whether potential new shareholders invest in the company.
- Does the company have the appropriate collateral available to secure the debt?

CHAPTER 17

Question 17.1

The value of a company is the value of its total assets (non-current and current). The value of a company's equity is its total assets less all outstanding liabilities, such as current liabilities and long-term liabilities (including preference shares).

Question 17.2

The expected free cash flow is as follows:

	€/£m
Net revenue	50
Depreciation	7
Interest (Note 1)	–
Taxation (Note 2)	(11.75)
Investment	(6.0)
Increase in working capital	(1)
Free cash flow	38.25

Note 1: interest is not deducted when calculating the free cash flows.

Note 2: taxation = (€/£50 – €/£3) × 25% = €/£47 × 25% = €/£11.75.

Question 17.3

(a) The value of Greenan Plc's equity can be calculated using the dividend valuation model.

The dividend (D_0) is 20% [1–80%] of the EPS, which is 5c/p [20% × 25c/p].

Growth (g) is calculated using the formula $g = br$, where b is the retentions percentage (80%) and r is the return earned by the investments (16%). Therefore, g = 12.8% [80% × 16%].

The cost of equity (K_e) is 14%.

$$P_0 = \frac{D_0(1+g)}{K_e - g}$$

$$P_0 = \frac{5\text{c/p}(1+0.128)}{0.14-0.128} = P_0 = \text{€/£}4.70$$

(b) Now K_e is 16%.

$$P_0 = \frac{5\text{c/p}(1+0.128)}{0.16-0.128} P_0 = \text{€/£}1.7625$$

Question 17.4

The advantages of using the dividend yield ratio approach:

- **Straightforward to calculate:** on the face of it, this approach is simple to calculate.
- **Constant dividend policy:** this approach works best when companies pursue a constant dividend policy. This approach will value the company's shares according to the cash flow benefit expected to be received by shareholders in the form of dividends. This is argued to be the most relevant value to minority shareholders.

The disadvantages of using this approach:

- **Sourcing a similar quoted company:** in practice it is difficult to find a company to benchmark against as no two companies are ever exactly the same.
- **Dividend policies:** different companies will have different dividend policies. Some companies do not pay a dividend at all and private companies typically have lower payout policies when compared to Plcs.
- **Dividends:** dividends represent a portion of a company's earnings and a valuation based on dividends only may not represent the full value of the company, particularly if the company does not adopt a steady dividend payout policy.

Question 17.5

(a)

Estimated data for Year 1	**€/£000**	**Value drivers**
Revenue	1,500	Sales growth
Operating costs	(1,000)	
Gross profit	500	Margin
Tax	(200)	Tax rate
Operating income after tax	300	
Depreciation	180	
Capital expenditure	(220)	Investment
Increase in working capital	(100)	Investment
Free cash flow	160	

(b)

Year	Cash flows €/£000	Discount factor 14%	PV €/£000
1	160	0.877	140.3
2	200	0.769	153.8
3	220	0.675	148.5
4	250	0.592	148.0
5	280	0.519	145.3
5	3,000	0.519	1,557.0
		NPV	2,292.9

Using the shareholder valuation analysis approach, a company value of €/£2.2929 million results.

(c)

Year	Cash flows €/£000	Discount factor 14%	PV €/£000
1	(120)*	0.877	(105.2)
2	200	0.769	153.8
3	220	0.675	148.5
4	250	0.592	148.0
5	280	0.519	145.3
6	290	0.456	132.2
7	290	0.400	116.0
8	290	0.351	101.8
9	290	0.308	89.3
9	5,000	0.308	1,540.0
		NPV	2,469.7

* €/£160,000 + €/£220,000 – €/£500,000

Under this scenario, the company is valued at €/£2.4697 million, €/£0.1768 million more than under part (b).

Question 17.6

An analyst usually takes seven to eight steps when valuing a company/share holding. These steps are listed and explained here:

1. Review the valuation methodologies and determine which of these is the most appropriate, given the purpose of the valuation. (For example, if the valuation is for a minority holding, then the dividend yield basis might be considered to be a starting point. If the valuation is for a controlling holding, then an earnings or a cash flow basis, such as the P/E ratio basis, might be first choice. When the purpose of the valuation is to purchase a company for break-up, then the assets basis might be the most appropriate approach.
2. Review any prior IPOs, mergers, takeovers or company sales of similar type companies. This will give a strong guide as to the expected value to place on the entity.
3. Find suitable benchmark companies. These companies should be in the same industry, in the same type of business within the industry and sensitive to the same economic influences to the entity being valued.
4. Select a suitable multiple (influenced by the outcome of Step 1) and adjust it to take into account differences between the entity being valued and the benchmark entity. For example, there may be a size adjustment, or a marketability/liquidity adjustment.
5. Where a factor of earnings is being used to value the entity, adjust these so that they reflect the expected equilibrium earnings from the entity in the future. Exceptional items should be removed, additional expected expenses included and economies of scale deducted.

6. Determine the expected value using the chosen methodology employing the adjusted figures from Steps 4 and 5. Identify a ceiling and floor value to offer and justify the value chosen.
7. Consider market demand, market sentiment and the willingness of the company to enter into sale negotiations when deciding on the value to place on the company.
8. Be prepared to negotiate. Valuations rarely are accepted first time around. Indeed, this knowledge usually influences the first bid.

CHAPTER 18

Question 18.1

The approach to be taken should include:

- Setting out and clarifying the company's strategic aim in respect of pursuing a takeover policy as a means of growing/investing.
- Detail how a takeover can achieve the strategic aims stipulated.
- Identify possible target companies and perform an analysis of each one to determine which would achieve the strategic aim of the takeover.
- Determine how the target company selected will fit within the group and plan for the future integration of the target company.
- Contact the directors of the target company to determine their views on a takeover. This meeting will include an offer for the company.
- Perform a due diligence audit.
- If they are hostile to this, announce the takeover offer publicly.
- If the equity holders accept the offer, then complete the takeover.
- Set up an integration team and act quickly to integrate the new company into the group.
- Perform a post-audit of the whole takeover and integration process.

Question 18.2

(a) Market value of A Plc is €/£20,000,000 [1,000,000 × €/£20].

Market value of B Plc is €/£4,000,000 [400,000 × €/£10].

A Plc offers €/£4,500,000 [400,000 × €/£11.25] for B Plc, giving a premium of €/£500,000 [400,000 × (€/£11.25 − €/£10.00)].

NPV of the project expected (the present value of the synergies):

$$= \frac{\text{Net earnings from synergies per annum}}{\text{Cost of capital}}$$

$$= \frac{\text{€/£}140{,}000}{0.20}$$

= €/£700,000 NPV to A is €/£200,000 [€/£700,000 – €/£500,000]

(b) The proportion of the premium going to the equity holders in B Plc is 71.42% [€/£500,000 ÷ €/£700,000], with the remainder 28.58% [€/£200,000 ÷ €/£700,000] going to the equity holders in A Plc.

Question 18.3

A management buy-out (MBO) is where the current management team of a business purchases that business from the equity holders, usually for cash. The business is normally a subsidiary, branch or small business within a much larger enterprise.

A management buy-in (MBI) is where the management team of a different company (usually in a similar line of business) purchases that part of the company from the equity holders, usually for cash. It normally considers that it can run the business more effectively than it is currently being run by the internal management team.

Question 18.4

To acquire the equity shares of Target Company Plc, Bidding Group Plc will have to issue fewer shares. Bidding Group Plc's shares have a market value of €/£30.00 per share and Target Company Plc's shares now have a market value of €/£7.50, which means that only one share in Bidding Group Plc has to be issued to acquire four shares in Target Company Plc. Therefore, Bidding Group Plc can purchase Target Company Plc for 50,000 shares (200,000 ÷ 4).

Summary of the impact of the changes to the value of Target Company Plc on the acquisition and on the reported performance of the resultant amalgamated company.

	Bidding Group Plc €/£000	**Target Company Plc €/£000**	**Bidding (post-acq.) €/£000**
Total net earnings	400	400	800
Total market value	6,000	1,500	7,500
Number of shares in issue	200	200	250
Market price per share	€/£30.00	€/£7.50	€/£30.00
Earnings per share	€/£2.00	€/£2.00	€/£3.20
Price earnings ratio	15 times	3.75 times	9.375 times
Earnings per €/£ invested	6.67%	26.67%	10.67%

Workings		**Target Company Plc**	**Bidding Group Plc (post-acquisition)**
Market price per share		$\frac{€/£1,500,000}{200,000}$	$\frac{€/£7,500,000}{250,000}$
	=	€/£7.50	€/£30.00
Earnings per share		$\frac{€/£400,000}{200,000}$	$\frac{€/£800,000}{250,000}$
	=	€/£2.00	€/£3.20
Price earnings ratio		$\frac{€/£7.50}{€/£2.00}$	$\frac{€/£30.00}{€/£3.20}$
	=	3.75 times	9.375 times
Earnings per €/£ invested		$\frac{€/£2.00}{€/£7.50}$	$\frac{€/£3.20}{€/£30.00}$
	=	26.67%	10.67%

The impact of a fall in the value of Target Company Plc is to make this company cheaper to purchase by Bidding Group Plc. As the earnings have not changed, this means that the earnings per share of Bidding Group Plc after the acquisition will increase (the total number of shares in issue is now lower than before). This means that an uninformed investor may believe that Bidding Group Plc's earnings per share increased by 60% in the period of the acquisition. The reduction in the price earnings ratio should provide some hints as to the quality of this growth in earnings.

Question 18.5

(a) Fox Plc is offering a premium of €/£5.00 per share for each share held by equity holders in Hen Plc. This amounts to a total premium over market value of €/£2,500,000 [€/£5.00 × 500,000]. Therefore, Fox Plc expects that the synergies to be made have a minimum net present value of €/£2,500,000.

(b) Assuming that Fox Plc's cost of capital is 20%, this means that Fox Plc expects yearly net synergy gains (over and above the combined earnings of Fox Plc and Hen Plc's current earnings) to be a minimum of €/£500,000 per year, calculated as follows:

The present value of the future earnings must at least equal €/£2,500,000. This is equivalent to the synergy gains discounted at 20% into perpetuity. Assume the synergy gains (earnings) are X. They can be found by solving the following perpetuity:

$$\text{Present value} = \frac{\text{Earnings}}{\text{Cost of capital}}$$

$$\text{€/£ } 2{,}500{,}000 = \frac{X}{0.20}$$

$$X = \text{€/£}2{,}500{,}000 \times 0.20$$

$$X = \text{€/£}500{,}000$$

This represents the minimum expected synergy gains, as the equity holders of Fox Plc will not agree to the acquisition unless they also stand to gain a portion of the synergy gains expected.

Question 18.6

When a company elects to purchase another entity using cash, the acquisition price is known with certainty and synergy gains do not impact on the cost – it remains static.

When a company purchases another entity using a share exchange deal, then the cost of the acquisition will be affected by the expected synergy gains to be made, as these will be reflected in the bidding company's share price, post-acquisition (assuming perfect capital markets). They increase the cost of the acquisition.

CHAPTER 19

Question 19.1

Many companies use derivative financial instruments to reduce risk. Most companies trade with a variety of different customers in a variety of different countries. In addition, most companies have debt. Having to deal with third parties, foreign countries and having debt exposes a company to various types of risk, including commodity risk, exchange rate risk, credit risk and interest rate risk. Risk is defined as the chance that actual outcomes will differ from expected outcomes. If there is too much risk in a company's cash flows, it is difficult for it to plan. Therefore, a company will take a variety of steps to reduce risk by hedging transactions using derivative financial instruments to make cash flows more certain.

Question 19.2

(a) The company should exercise the call option as the market value of the share on the exercise date is higher than the exercise price.

(b) ABC Plc should buy 10,000 shares at €/£1.80 and then sell them immediately on the open market for €/£2.10 per share.

Return on the purchase of the call option:

	€/£
Purchase 10,000 call options at 25c/p	(2,500)
Purchase 10,000 shares at €/£1.80	(18,000)
	(20,500)
Sell 10,000 shares at €/£2.10	21,000
Profit on sale	500
Return on investment [€/£500 ÷ €/£2,500]	20%

(c) In this instance, ABC Plc will not exercise the option, so the loss is the price paid for the option.

Return on the purchase of the call option assuming the market price is €/£1.60:

Purchase 10,000 call options at 25c/p	(€/£2,500)
Loss on investment	(€/£2,500)

(d) Assume the company purchases shares in ABC Plc.

Assume current sale price is €/£2.10:

	€/£
Purchase 1,667 shares [€/£2,500 ÷ €/£1.50]	(2,500)
Sale value on exercise date [1,667 × €/£2.10]	3,500
Profit on investment	1,000
Return on investment [€/£1,000 ÷ €/£2,500]	40%

Assume current sale price is €/£1.60:

	€/£
Purchase 1,667 shares [€/£2,500 ÷ €/£1.50]	(2,500)
Sale value on exercise date [1,667 × €/£1.60]	2,667
Profit on investment	167
Return on investment [€/£167 ÷ €/£2,500]	6.7%

Question 19.3

Option value is usually impacted on by three variables.

1. **The exercise price listed on the option** – when the exercise price is low, relative to the market value of the asset, then the option will have a high value.
2. **The length of time to the exercise date** – a call option is a cheap way of obtaining an asset now, but paying for it at some future stage. Therefore, it provides free credit. However, this is factored into the price of the option: the longer the period to exercise date, the more valuable the option.
3. **The variability of returns on the underlying asset** – a call option will only be exercised if the share price rises above the exercise price. In these instances the holder of the option will not exercise the option and the holder will lose the monies paid out to obtain the option. However, if share prices rise above the exercise price, the holder of the option will exercise the option and can avail of unlimited profits. Therefore, an asset with volatile returns is likely to be attractive as the potential for greater profits is higher.

Question 19.4

The value of the option is calculated using the Black–Scholes model:

$$P_0 = PsN(d_1) - Xe^{-rT}N(d_2)$$

where P_0 is the current value of the option (to find), Ps is the current value of the asset (€/£7.50), X is the exercise price (€/£8.00), e is the exponential constant (2.7183), r is the risk-free rate of interest for the period (7%), T is the time (in years) remaining in the option contract (0.5 years) and σ is the standard deviation of returns expected (40%).

$$d_1 = \frac{\text{Ln}(Ps/X) + rT}{\sigma\sqrt{T}} + 0.5\,\sigma\sqrt{T}$$

$$d_1 = \frac{\text{Ln}(7.50/8.00) + (0.07)(0.5)}{0.4 \times \sqrt{0.5}}$$

$$d_1 = 0.037$$

$$N(d_1) = 0.515^*$$

* This value is obtained from **Appendix G.**

$$d_2 = d_1 - \sigma\sqrt{T}$$

$$d_2 = 0.037 - (0.4)(\sqrt{0.5})$$

$$d_2 = -0.3$$

$$N(d_2) = 1 - 0.6179 = 0.3821$$

Therefore, the value of the option is:

$$P_0 = 7.50(0.515) - 8.00(2.7183^{-0.07\times0.5}) \times 0.3821$$

$$P_0 = 3.86 - 2.95 \qquad P_0 = €/£0.91$$

CHAPTER 20

Question 20.1

(a) The expected price of a pint of beer in Dublin in one year's time is €4.77 (£4.50 × 1.06). The expected price of a pint of beer in Belfast in one year's time is £3.64 (£3.50 × 1.04).

(b) The expected forward exchange rate, assuming PPP holds, will be €4.77/£3.64 = €1.31 to £1.00.

Question 20.2

(a) The one-year forward rate is US\$1.40 × (1.05 ÷ 1.03) = US\$1.427 to €/£1

(b) The six-month forward rate is US\$1.40 × ($1.05^{6/12}$ ÷ $1.03^{6/12}$) = US\$1.414 to €/£1

(c) The three-month forward rate is US\$1.40 × ($1.05^{3/12}$ ÷ $1.03^{3/12}$) = US\$1.407 to €/£1

(d) The two-year forward rate is US\$1.427 × (1.065 ÷ 1.045) = US\$1.454 to €/£1

Question 20.3

(a) The one-month forward rate is US\$1.65 − US\$0.005 = US\$1.645

(b) The one-month forward rate is US\$1.65 − US\$0.012 = US\$1.662

Question 20.4

(a) The inflation rates in both countries are increasing and in both instances the inflationary increases are being influenced by oil price increases. The supply price of oil is not controllable by either government, but the tax on oil is.

The inflation rate in Country A is lower (i.e. 3.3%) than that reported in Country B (i.e. 5%) and is closer to its target of 2%. The interest rate in Country A is 5.75%, whereas it is 4% in the Eurozone.

Based on these economic factors, Country B would be more concerned about inflation as its inflation rate is higher and it is further away from the EU target level of 2%. Its interest rates are lower and hence it has greater potential to raise interest rates (to dampen inflation) than Country A without damaging businesses that will have to pay higher funding costs. However, it does not have control over interest rates and high inflation rates usually cause a slowdown in the economy.

(b) County A's Government is more likely to increase interest rates as it has more control over them. However, this is wholly dependent on the state of the economy. If the economy is in boom, then businesses are performing strongly and interest rate increases can reduce demand but should not have a detrimental impact on growth. However, if the economy is in decline, then an interest rate increase would accelerate the rate of the slowdown and may cause businesses to fail as interest costs are increased and demand will fall.

Question 20.5

(a) ABC should enter into a forward contract now to purchase the \$500,000 from the bank. This will mean that ABC can lock into the exchange rate now and hence eliminate any risk of the purchase costing more than anticipated.

As ABC has to buy \$500,000 from the bank in three months' time, the relevant rate is the bank offer rate. ABC requires the funds in three months' time, hence it should enter into a three-month forward rate at US\$1.66 now.

This will cost \$500,000 ÷ \$1.66 = €/£301,205.

Regardless of what the rates are in the marketplace in three months' time, ABC will have to honour the forward contract.

If Sterling strengthens such that in three months' time the exchange rate is greater than $1.66, ABC will make a loss relative to the market rate as it would cost less if the market rate were used. If Sterling weakens or strengthens by a smaller amount such that the exchange rate is less than £1.66, then it will make a profit relative to the market rate as it will get more US dollars under the forward contract.

(b) ABC should enter into a forward contract now to sell the $800,000 to the bank. This will mean that ABC can lock into the exchange rate now and hence eliminate any risk of receiving less from the foreign sale than anticipated over the month.

As ABC has to sell $800,000 to the bank in one month's time, the relevant rate is the bank bid rate. ABC will have the funds in one month's time, hence it should enter into a one-month forward rate at US$1.67 now.

This will result in a cash inflow of $800,000 ÷ $1.67 = €/£479,042.

Regardless of what the rates are in the marketplace in one month's time, ABC will have to honour the forward contract.

If Sterling strengthens such that in one month's time the exchange rate is greater than $1.67, ABC will make a profit relative to the market rate. If Sterling weakens or strengthens by a smaller amount such that the exchange rate is less than £1.67, then it will make a loss relative to the market rate.

CHAPTER 21

Question 21.1

This gives the holder the right, but not the obligation, to enter into a futures contract at a specified exercise price on or before the option expiry date. The option can either be a 'call' option, which gives the holder the potential to buy futures at the exercise price (which will be exercised if interest rates fall as the market price of the futures will rise and a profit will result when the position is closed), or a 'put' option, which gives the holder the potential to sell futures at the exercise price (which will be exercised if interest rates increase as the market price of the future will fall and a profit will result when the position is closed).

Question 21.2

The company treasurer should approach the bank to see if they will agree to a cap product where the upper limit is set at 5%. The bank will charge a fee for this, but the company will still be able to benefit if interest rates fall.

Question 21.3

DEF Plc will have to pay the following:

		Cap	**Collar**
		€/£	**€/£**
Commission	€/£15m × 0.2%	30,000	15,000
Interest under scenario			
Market rates 5.2%	€/£15m × 5.2% × 6/12	390,000	390,000
	Total cost	420,000	405,000

Market rates 4%	€/£15m × 4% × 6/12	300,000	
	€/£15m × 4.5% × 6/12		337,500
	Total cost	330,000	352,500
Market rates 7%	€/£15m × 6% × 6/12	450,000	450,000
	Total cost	480,000	465,000

If the company opts for the cap product, then the bank will take over the downside risk in relation to interest rates that exceed 6%. Therefore, the maximum interest and charges payable by DEF Plc will be €/£480,000. They will be able to reap the reward of lower interest payments when rates go down. If they opt for the collar, then the maximum interest and charges payable will be €/£465,000, but the minimum will be €/£352,000.

Question 21.4

Stimpy Plc wants £10 million. This is the equivalent of €12.5 million at the current exchange rate of £1:€1.25 [£10 million × 1.25].

The interest options open to both are highlighted in the following table.

Can borrow at a:

	Stimpy Plc	**Wrent Plc**
Fixed rate of:	10.25%	11.5%
Variable rate of:	LIBOR + 0.5%	LIBOR + 1.5%

Stimpy Plc wants fixed-rate debt from the swap, but knows that Wrent Plc wants floating-rate debt. Stimpy Plc could borrow in the domestic market at LIBOR + 0.5% for the purposes of swapping. Wrent Plc's interest options are more expensive than Stimpy Plc's options. Wrent Plc could borrow in the UK at the fixed rate of 11.5%, but Stimpy Plc will not agree to pay more than 10.25% (the rate it can currently obtain in the home markets). Therefore, the 10.25% becomes the rate that forms part of the swap agreement. Wrent Plc will have to make up the shortfall. Therefore, Stimpy Plc should borrow the €12.5 million at the variable rate of LIBOR + 0.5%. Wrent Plc should borrow £10 million at the fixed rate of 11.5% and then both parties can swap the capital sums and pre-agreed interest payments.

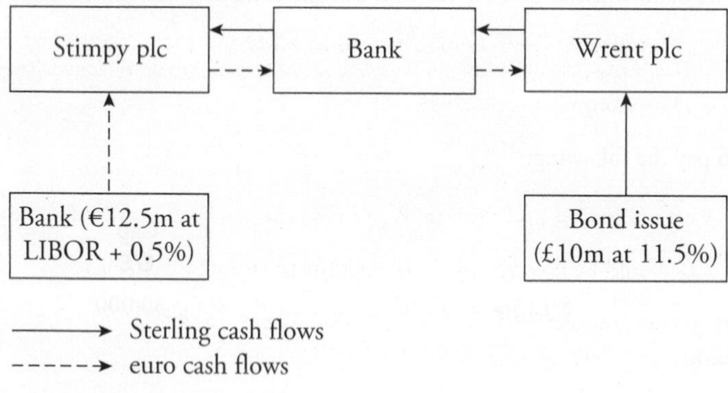

With the above arrangement the following interest payments will result:

	Stimpy Plc	Wrent Plc
Interest on loan to bank	(LIBOR + 0.5%)	(11.5%)
Swap		
Agreed to pay	(10.25%)	(LIBOR + 0.5%)
Receives	LIBOR + 0.5%	10.25%
Net interest cost before commission	(10.25%)	(LIBOR + 1.75%*)
Commission	(0.15%)	(0.15%)
Total interest to pay	(10.4%)	(LIBOR + 1.9%)

* (11.5% − 10.25%) + 0.5% = 1.75%

Finally, in seven years' time Stimpy Plc will refund the £10 million to Wrent Plc, which will use it to pay off the bank, and Wrent Plc will refund the €12.5 million to Stimpy Plc, which will also use it to repay the bank. The capital value of the loan has been hedged 100% in this instance against currency fluctuations.

CHAPTER 22

Question 22.1

It takes time for companies to update their records when share exchanges take place. It is considered that two days is ample time for this administrative process to be completed. Therefore, the market sets a cut-off date that is two days before the company's declared date of record. Buyers before this date are considered to purchase shares cum-dividend, hence are entitled to the distribution. Buyers after this date are trading in the shares ex-dividend (they have no right to the dividend). This process allows brokers to market the shares clearly as either cum-dividend or ex-dividend.

Question 22.2

The dividend should not be distributed, as $d_0 + P_1$ is not greater than P_0. The equity holders will be worse off by 2c/p for every share that they own.

Question 22.3

M&M argue that dividend policy can be irrelevant in a world where there are no taxes and no transaction costs, where equity holders have all company information (and do not misinterpret it), and where there is a constant interest rate (that is equal for companies and investors).

Question 22.4

The company's cost of capital is 15% and Projects B and C's expected returns exceed this target rate.

Therefore, these projects should be invested in. This amounts to an investment of €/£4,500,000 in the year.

The remainder of the year's earnings, €/£500,000 [€/£5,000,000 – €/£4,500,000], should be distributed as a dividend, resulting in a payout ratio of 10% [€/£500,000 ÷ €/£5,000,000].

Question 22.5

The **clientele effect** is where management decides on a particular policy to attract a particular type of investor, and investors choose companies to invest in because the company's dividend policy matches their desired income type. For example, high income taxpayers would be more attracted to a company that pursues a low payout ratio, as increases in that equity holders' value will be reflected in increases in the company's share price. The higher rate taxpayer can then plan the sale of the shares over time, taking into consideration other capital transactions, so as to maximise their net tax income position. Individuals have an annual capital gains tax exemption and high-income tax-paying individuals will be keen to use this yearly exemption.

Question 22.6

Optimal Ltd

Dividend level	Estimated ex-dividend share price	Dividend (net of income tax)	Total value
Nil	100c/p	Nil	100.00c/p
4.0c/p	117c/p	2.80c/p	119.80c/p
4.5c/p	120c/p	3.15c/p	123.15c/p
5.0c/p	134c/p	3.50c/p	137.50c/p
5.5c/p	136c/p	3.85c/p	139.85c/p
6.0c/p	128c/p	4.20c/p	132.20c/p

The optimal dividend level is 5.5c/p. This probably reflects sentiment in the market that a rise in the dividend level will be required to justify an increase in share price. However, too high a dividend may cause the market to view the company as adopting an imprudent dividend strategy.

Question 22.7

(a) As a private company does not need to concern itself with such things as the information content of dividends or the clientele effect, it is freer than public companies to decide whether and how much of a dividend to pay. However, there are certain factors that will tend to influence those decisions:

- *Tax differential* – shareholders may prefer capital gains to dividends due to the lower tax rate on capital gains. In this instance the company may decide to issue low dividends or no dividends at all.
- *Investment opportunities* – if a company has a project or projects that require investment but that will generate returns in excess of the company's cost of capital, then it would make financial sense to use whatever cash is required to pursue these opportunities. This may, in turn, leave a smaller amount of cash for distribution as a dividend.
- *Available cash* – following from the previous point, if a company does not have surplus cash, it will not be in a position to pay a dividend, unless it seeks to borrow the money.
- *External factors* – there may be various other external factors that limit the amount of dividend that a company can pay. Examples of these would be loan terms and conditions, where financial institutions specify limits on the level of dividends declared in order to protect their own interest.

(b) **Company A** This company is espousing the Tax Differential policy. With this approach investors can expect to maximise the capital appreciation of their shareholding at the expense of dividend payouts. The advantage of this is that if they cash in their investment, the gain will be taxed at a lower rate than the dividends would have been taxed at. The disadvantage is that individual investors have to wait to take all their gains at once. They do not get a regular income. Also, if an investor pays income tax at the standard rate, the tax differential is likely to be so small that, after broker's commission and other associated charges, the investor may actually be worse off.

Where a company has an investor base that does not rely on its investments for regular income, and it pays income tax at the marginal rate, this policy may be the most appropriate.

Company B By having a fixed percentage payout policy, this company is sending a very strong signal to investors. Investors can always be sure of where they stand with the company and what their entitlements are regarding dividend payment. The disadvantage is that the company is locked into this level of dividend payment. If an attractive investment opportunity arose that required an investment of more than 50% of retained earnings, the company may not be able to avail of the opportunity.

This policy would be most likely to maximise shareholder wealth where the company is in a stable environment, it knows the level of shareholders' funds it needs to retain and it is not likely to suffer any opportunity losses.

Company C This company is making its main payouts in the form of scrip issues. The shareholders can, if they wish, sell the newly issued shares at market value. While they may not make a large capital profit on the sale, they will also not have to pay much (or any) capital gains tax. The disadvantage is that if they do choose to generate income by selling their shares, their overall percentage holding will decrease and their future entitlement to both dividends and scrip issues will reduce.

This policy is likely to maximise shareholder wealth where the shareholders want control over the timing of the revenue generation of their investment.

pendix C

I ount Factor Table

Present value of 1, i.e. $(1+r)^{-n}$

where r is the discount rate and n is the number of periods until payment.

Periods	Discount rates (r)									
(n)	1%	2%	3%	4%	5%	6%	7%	8%	9%	10%
1	0.990	0.980	0.971	0.962	0.952	0.943	0.935	0.926	0.917	0.909
2	0.980	0.961	0.943	0.925	0.907	0.890	0.873	0.857	0.842	0.826
3	0.971	0.942	0.915	0.889	0.864	0.840	0.816	0.794	0.772	0.751
4	0.961	0.924	0.888	0.855	0.823	0.792	0.763	0.735	0.708	0.683
5	0.951	0.906	0.863	0.822	0.784	0.747	0.713	0.681	0.650	0.621
6	0.942	0.888	0.837	0.790	0.746	0.705	0.666	0.630	0.596	0.564
7	0.933	0.871	0.813	0.760	0.711	0.665	0.623	0.583	0.547	0.513
8	0.923	0.853	0.789	0.731	0.677	0.627	0.582	0.540	0.502	0.467
9	0.914	0.837	0.766	0.703	0.645	0.592	0.544	0.500	0.460	0.424
10	0.905	0.820	0.744	0.676	0.614	0.558	0.508	0.463	0.422	0.386
11	0.896	0.804	0.722	0.650	0.585	0.527	0.475	0.429	0.388	0.350
12	0.887	0.788	0.701	0.625	0.557	0.497	0.444	0.397	0.356	0.319
13	0.879	0.773	0.681	0.601	0.530	0.469	0.415	0.368	0.326	0.290
14	0.870	0.758	0.661	0.577	0.505	0.442	0.388	0.340	0.299	0.263
15	0.861	0.743	0.642	0.555	0.481	0.417	0.362	0.315	0.275	0.239

Periods	Discount rates (*r*)									
(*n*)	11%	12%	13%	14%	15%	16%	17%	18%	19%	20%
1	0.901	0.893	0.885	0.877	0.870	0.862	0.855	0.847	0.840	0.833
2	0.812	0.797	0.783	0.769	0.756	0.743	0.731	0.718	0.706	0.694
3	0.731	0.712	0.693	0.675	0.658	0.641	0.624	0.609	0.593	0.579
4	0.659	0.636	0.613	0.592	0.572	0.552	0.534	0.516	0.499	0.482
5	0.593	0.567	0.543	0.519	0.497	0.476	0.456	0.437	0.419	0.402
6	0.535	0.507	0.480	0.456	0.432	0.410	0.390	0.370	0.352	0.335
7	0.482	0.452	0.425	0.400	0.376	0.354	0.333	0.314	0.296	0.279
8	0.434	0.404	0.376	0.351	0.327	0.305	0.285	0.266	0.249	0.233
9	0.391	0.361	0.333	0.308	0.284	0.263	0.243	0.225	0.209	0.194
10	0.352	0.322	0.295	0.270	0.247	0.227	0.208	0.191	0.176	0.162
11	0.317	0.287	0.261	0.237	0.215	0.195	0.178	0.162	0.148	0.135
12	0.286	0.257	0.231	0.208	0.187	0.168	0.152	0.137	0.124	0.112
13	0.258	0.229	0.204	0.182	0.163	0.145	0.130	0.116	0.104	0.093
14	0.232	0.205	0.181	0.160	0.141	0.125	0.111	0.099	0.088	0.078
15	0.209	0.183	0.160	0.140	0.123	0.108	0.095	0.084	0.074	0.065

Periods	Discount rates (*r*)									
(*n*)	21%	22%	23%	24%	25%	26%	27%	28%	29%	30%
1	0.826	0.820	0.813	0.807	0.800	0.794	0.787	0.781	0.775	0.769
2	0.683	0.672	0.661	0.650	0.640	0.630	0.620	0.610	0.601	0.592
3	0.565	0.551	0.537	0.525	0.512	0.500	0.488	0.477	0.466	0.455
4	0.467	0.451	0.437	0.423	0.410	0.397	0.384	0.373	0.361	0.350
5	0.386	0.370	0.355	0.341	0.328	0.315	0.303	0.291	0.280	0.269
6	0.319	0.303	0.289	0.275	0.262	0.250	0.238	0.227	0.217	0.207
7	0.263	0.249	0.235	0.222	0.210	0.198	0.188	0.178	0.168	0.159
8	0.218	0.204	0.191	0.179	0.168	0.157	0.148	0.139	0.130	0.123
9	0.180	0.167	0.155	0.144	0.134	0.125	0.116	0.108	0.101	0.094
10	0.149	0.137	0.126	0.116	0.107	0.099	0.092	0.085	0.078	0.073
11	0.123	0.112	0.103	0.094	0.086	0.079	0.072	0.066	0.061	0.056
12	0.102	0.092	0.083	0.076	0.069	0.063	0.057	0.052	0.047	0.043
13	0.084	0.075	0.068	0.061	0.055	0.050	0.045	0.040	0.037	0.033
14	0.069	0.062	0.055	0.049	0.044	0.039	0.035	0.032	0.028	0.025
15	0.057	0.051	0.045	0.040	0.035	0.031	0.028	0.025	0.022	0.020

Appendix D

Annuity Factor Table

Present value of an annuity of 1, i.e. $\frac{1-(1+r)^{-n}}{r}$

where r is the discount rate and n is the number of periods.

Periods	Discount rates (r)									
(n)	1%	2%	3%	4%	5%	6%	7%	8%	9%	10%
1	0.990	0.980	0.971	0.962	0.952	0.943	0.935	0.926	0.917	0.909
2	1.970	1.942	1.913	1.886	1.859	1.833	1.808	1.783	1.759	1.736
3	2.941	2.884	2.829	2.775	2.723	2.673	2.624	2.577	2.531	2.486
4	3.902	3.808	3.717	3.630	3.546	3.465	3.387	3.312	3.240	3.170
5	4.853	4.713	4.580	4.452	4.329	4.212	4.100	3.993	3.890	3.791
6	5.795	5.601	5.417	5.242	5.076	4.917	4.767	4.623	4.486	4.355
7	6.728	6.472	6.230	6.002	5.786	5.582	5.389	5.206	5.033	4.868
8	7.652	7.325	7.020	6.733	6.463	6.210	5.971	5.747	5.535	5.335
9	8.566	8.162	7.786	7.435	7.108	6.802	6.515	6.247	5.995	5.759
10	9.471	8.983	8.530	8.111	7.722	7.360	7.024	6.710	6.418	6.145
11	10.368	9.787	9.253	8.760	8.306	7.887	7.499	7.139	6.805	6.495
12	11.255	10.575	9.954	9.385	8.863	8.384	7.943	7.536	7.161	6.814
13	12.134	11.348	10.635	9.986	9.394	8.853	8.358	7.904	7.487	7.103
14	13.004	12.106	11.296	10.563	9.899	9.295	8.745	8.244	7.786	7.367
15	13.865	12.849	11.938	11.118	10.380	9.712	9.108	8.559	8.061	7.606

Periods	Discount rates (*r*)									
(*n*)	11%	12%	13%	14%	15%	16%	17%	18%	19%	20%
1	0.901	0.893	0.885	0.877	0.870	0.862	0.855	0.847	0.840	0.833
2	1.713	1.690	1.668	1.647	1.626	1.605	1.585	1.566	1.547	1.528
3	2.444	2.402	2.361	2.322	2.283	2.246	2.210	2.174	2.140	2.106
4	3.102	3.037	2.974	2.914	2.855	2.798	2.743	2.690	2.639	2.589
5	3.696	3.605	3.517	3.433	3.352	3.274	3.199	3.127	3.058	2.991
6	4.231	4.111	3.998	3.889	3.784	3.685	3.589	3.498	3.410	3.326
7	4.712	4.564	4.423	4.288	4.160	4.039	3.922	3.812	3.706	3.605
8	5.146	4.968	4.799	4.639	4.487	4.344	4.207	4.078	3.954	3.837
9	5.537	5.328	5.132	4.946	4.772	4.607	4.451	4.303	4.163	4.031
10	5.889	5.650	5.426	5.216	5.019	4.833	4.659	4.494	4.339	4.192
11	6.207	5.938	5.687	5.453	5.234	5.029	4.836	4.656	4.486	4.327
12	6.492	6.194	5.918	5.660	5.421	5.197	4.988	4.793	4.611	4.439
13	6.750	6.424	6.122	5.842	5.583	5.342	5.118	4.910	4.715	4.533
14	6.982	6.628	6.302	6.002	5.724	5.468	5.229	5.008	4.802	4.611
15	7.191	6.811	6.462	6.142	5.847	5.575	5.324	5.092	4.876	4.675

Periods	Discount rates (*r*)									
(*n*)	21%	22%	23%	24%	25%	26%	27%	28%	29%	30%
1	0.826	0.820	0.813	0.806	0.800	0.794	0.787	0.781	0.775	0.769
2	1.509	1.492	1.474	1.457	1.440	1.424	1.407	1.392	1.376	1.361
3	2.074	2.042	2.011	1.981	1.952	1.923	1.896	1.868	1.842	1.816
4	2.540	2.494	2.448	2.404	2.362	2.320	2.280	2.241	2.203	2.166
5	2.926	2.864	2.803	2.745	2.689	2.635	2.583	2.532	2.483	2.436
6	3.245	3.167	3.092	3.020	2.951	2.885	2.821	2.759	2.700	2.643
7	3.508	3.416	3.327	3.242	3.161	3.083	3.009	2.937	2.868	2.802
8	3.726	3.619	3.518	3.421	3.329	3.241	3.156	3.076	2.999	2.925
9	3.905	3.786	3.673	3.566	3.463	3.366	3.273	3.184	3.100	3.019
10	4.054	3.923	3.799	3.682	3.571	3.465	3.364	3.269	3.178	3.092
11	4.177	4.035	3.902	3.776	3.656	3.543	3.437	3.335	3.239	3.147
12	4.278	4.127	3.985	3.851	3.725	3.606	3.493	3.387	3.286	3.190
13	4.362	4.203	4.053	3.912	3.780	3.656	3.538	3.427	3.322	3.223
14	4.432	4.265	4.108	3.962	3.824	3.695	3.573	3.459	3.351	3.249
15	4.489	4.315	4.153	4.001	3.859	3.726	3.601	3.483	3.373	3.268

Appendix E

Terminal/Future Value Factor Table

Terminal or future value of 1, i.e. $(1 + r)^n$

where r is the interest rate and n is the number of periods.

Periods	Interest rates (r)									
(n)	1%	2%	3%	4%	5%	6%	7%	8%	9%	10%
1	1.010	1.020	1.030	1.040	1.050	1.060	1.070	1.080	1.090	1.100
2	1.020	1.040	1.061	1.082	1.103	1.124	1.145	1.166	1.188	1.210
3	1.030	1.061	1.093	1.125	1.158	1.191	1.225	1.260	1.295	1.331
4	1.041	1.082	1.126	1.170	1.216	1.263	1.311	1.361	1.412	1.464
5	1.051	1.104	1.159	1.218	1.276	1.338	1.403	1.469	1.539	1.611
6	1.062	1.126	1.194	1.265	1.340	1.419	1.501	1.587	1.677	1.772
7	1.072	1.149	1.230	1.316	1.407	1.504	1.606	1.714	1.828	1.949
8	1.083	1.172	1.267	1.369	1.478	1.594	1.718	1.851	1.993	2.144
9	1.094	1.195	1.305	1.423	1.551	1.690	1.839	1.999	2.172	2.358
10	1.105	1.219	1.344	1.480	1.629	1.791	1.967	2.159	2.367	2.594
11	1.116	1.243	1.384	1.540	1.710	1.898	2.104	2.332	2.580	2.853
12	1.127	1.268	1.426	1.601	1.796	2.012	2.252	2.518	2.813	3.138
13	1.138	1.294	1.469	1.666	1.886	2.133	2.410	2.720	3.066	3.452
14	1.150	1.320	1.513	1.732	1.980	2.261	2.579	2.937	3.342	3.798
15	1.161	1.346	1.558	1.801	2.079	2.397	2.759	3.172	3.643	4.177

Periods	Interest rates (*r*)									
(*n*)	11%	12%	13%	14%	15%	16%	17%	18%	19%	20%
1	1.110	1.120	1.130	1.140	1.150	1.160	1.170	1.180	1.190	1.200
2	1.232	1.254	1.277	1.300	1.323	1.346	1.369	1.392	1.416	1.440
3	1.368	1.405	1.443	1.482	1.521	1.561	1.602	1.643	1.685	1.728
4	1.518	1.574	1.631	1.689	1.749	1.811	1.874	1.939	2.005	2.074
5	1.685	1.762	1.842	1.925	2.011	2.100	2.192	2.288	2.386	2.488
6	1.870	1.974	2.082	2.195	2.313	2.436	2.565	2.700	2.840	2.986
7	2.076	2.211	3.353	2.502	2.660	2.826	3.001	3.186	3.379	3.583
8	2.304	2.476	2.658	2.853	3.059	3.278	3.512	3.759	4.021	4.300
9	2.558	2.773	3.004	3.252	3.518	3.803	4.108	4.436	4.785	5.160
10	2.839	3.106	3.395	3.707	4.046	4.411	4.807	5.234	5.695	6.192
11	3.152	3.479	3.836	4.226	4.652	5.117	5.624	6.176	6.777	7.430
12	3.499	3.896	4.335	4.818	5.350	5.936	6.580	7.288	8.064	8.916
13	3.883	4.364	4.898	5.492	6.153	6.886	7.699	8.600	9.596	10.699
14	4.310	4.887	5.535	6.261	7.076	7.988	9.008	10.147	11.420	12.839
15	4.785	5.474	6.254	7.138	8.137	9.266	10.539	11.974	13.590	15.407

Periods	Interest rates (*r*)									
(*n*)	21%	22%	23%	24%	25%	26%	27%	28%	29%	30%
1	1.210	1.220	1.230	1.240	1.250	1.260	1.270	1.280	1.290	1.300
2	1.464	1.488	1.513	1.538	1.563	1.588	1.613	1.638	1.664	1.690
3	1.772	1.816	1.861	1.907	1.953	2.000	2.048	2.097	2.147	2.197
4	2.144	2.215	2.289	2.364	2.441	2.521	2.601	2.684	2.769	2.856
5	2.594	2.703	2.815	2.932	3.052	3.176	3.304	3.436	3.572	3.713
6	3.138	3.297	3.463	3.635	3.815	4.002	4.196	4.398	4.608	4.827
7	3.798	4.023	4.259	4.508	4.768	5.042	5.329	5.630	5.945	6.275
8	4.595	4.908	5.239	5.590	5.961	6.353	6.768	7.206	7.669	8.157
9	5.560	5.987	6.444	6.931	7.451	8.005	8.595	9.223	9.893	10.605
10	6.728	7.305	7.926	8.594	9.313	10.086	10.915	11.806	12.761	13.786
11	8.140	8.912	7.749	10.657	11.642	12.708	13.863	15.112	16.462	17.922
12	9.850	10.872	11.991	13.215	14.552	16.012	17.605	19.343	21.236	23.298
13	11.918	13.264	14.749	16.386	18.190	20.175	22.359	24.759	27.395	30.288
14	14.421	16.182	18.141	20.319	22.737	25.421	28.396	31.691	35.339	39.374
15	17.449	19.742	22.314	25.196	28.422	32.030	36.063	40.565	45.588	51.186

Appendix F

Future Value Annuity Factor Table

Future value of an annuity of 1, i.e. $\frac{(1+r)^n - 1}{r}$

where r is the interest rate and n is the number of periods.

Periods	Interest rates (r)									
(n)	1%	2%	3%	4%	5%	6%	7%	8%	9%	10%
1	1.000	1.000	1.000	1.000	1.000	1.000	1.000	1.000	1.000	1.000
2	2.010	2.020	2.030	2.040	2.050	2.060	2.070	2.080	2.090	2.100
3	3.030	3.060	3.091	3.122	3.153	3.184	3.215	3.246	3.278	3.310
4	4.060	4.122	4.184	4.247	4.310	4.375	4.440	4.506	4.573	4.641
5	5.101	5.204	5.309	5.416	5.526	5.637	5.751	5.867	5.985	6.105
6	6.152	6.308	6.468	6.633	6.802	6.975	7.153	7.336	7.523	7.716
7	7.214	7.434	7.663	7.898	8.142	8.394	8.654	8.923	9.200	9.487
8	8.286	8.583	8.892	9.214	9.549	9.898	10.260	10.673	11.028	11.463
9	9.369	9.755	10.159	10.538	11.027	11.491	11.978	12.488	13.021	13.579
10	10.462	10.950	11.464	12.006	12.578	13.181	13.816	14.487	15.193	15.937
11	11.567	12.169	12.808	13.486	14.207	14.972	15.784	16.645	17.560	18.531
12	12.683	13.412	14.192	15.026	15.917	16.870	17.888	18.977	20.141	21.384
13	13.809	14.680	15.618	16.627	17.713	18.882	20.141	21.495	22.935	24.523
14	14.947	15.974	17.086	18.292	19.599	21.015	22.550	24.215	26.019	27.975
15	16.097	17.293	18.599	20.024	21.579	23.276	25.129	27.152	29.361	31.772

Periods	Interest rates (*r*)									
(*n*)	11%	12%	13%	14%	15%	16%	17%	18%	19%	20%
1	1.000	1.000	1.000	1.000	1.000	1.000	1.000	1.000	1.000	1.000
2	2.110	2.120	2.130	2.140	2.150	2.160	2.170	2.180	2.190	2.200
3	3.342	3.374	3.407	3.440	3.473	3.506	3.539	2.572	3.606	3.640
4	4.710	4.779	4.850	4.921	4.993	5.067	5.141	5.215	5.291	5.368
5	6.228	6.353	6.480	6.101	6.742	6.877	7.014	7.154	7.297	7.442
6	7.913	8.115	8.323	8.536	8.754	8.978	9.207	9.442	9.683	9.930
7	9.783	10.089	10.405	10.730	11.067	11.414	11.772	12.142	12.523	12.916
8	11.859	12.300	12.757	13.233	13.727	14.240	14.773	15.327	15.902	16.499
9	14.164	14.776	15.416	16.085	16.786	17.519	18.285	19.086	19.923	20.799
10	16.722	17.549	18.420	19.337	20.304	21.321	22.393	23.521	24.709	25.959
11	19.561	20.655	21.814	23.045	24.349	25.733	27.200	28.755	30.404	32.150
12	22.713	24.133	25.650	27.271	29.002	30.850	32.824	34.931	37.180	39.581
13	26.212	28.029	29.985	32.089	34.352	36.786	39.404	42.219	45.245	48.497
14	30.095	32.383	34.883	37.581	40.505	43.672	47.103	50.818	54.841	59.196
15	34.405	37.280	40.417	43.842	47.580	51.660	56.110	60.965	66.261	72.035

Periods	Interest rates (*r*)									
(*n*)	21%	22%	23%	24%	25%	26%	27%	28%	29%	30%
1	1.000	1.000	1.000	1.000	1.000	1.000	1.000	1.000	1.000	1.000
2	2.210	2.220	2.230	2.240	2.250	2.260	2.270	2.280	2.290	2.300
3	3.674	3.708	3.742	3.778	3.813	3.848	3.883	3.918	3.954	3.990
4	5.446	5.524	5.604	5.684	5.766	5.848	5.931	6.016	6.101	6.187
5	7.589	7.740	7.893	8.048	8.207	8.368	8.533	8.700	8.870	9.043
6	10.183	10.442	10.708	10.980	11.259	11.544	11.837	12.136	12.442	12.756
7	13.321	13.740	14.171	14.615	15.074	15.546	16.032	16.534	17.051	17.583
8	17.119	17.762	18.430	19.123	19.842	20.588	21.361	22.163	22.995	23.858
9	21.714	22.670	23.669	24.713	25.802	26.940	28.129	29.369	30.664	32.015
10	27.274	28.657	30.113	31.643	33.253	34.945	36.724	38.593	40.556	42.620
11	34.001	35.962	38.039	40.238	42.566	45.031	47.639	50.399	53.318	56.405
12	42.142	44.874	47.788	50.895	54.208	57.739	61.501	65.510	69.780	74.327
13	51.991	55.746	59.779	64.110	68.760	73.751	79.107	84.853	91.016	97.625
14	63.910	69.010	74.528	80.496	86.950	93.926	101.465	109.612	118.411	127.913
15	78.331	85.192	92.669	100.815	109.687	119.347	129.861	141.303	153.785	167.286

Appendix G

Cumulative Probability [N(*d*)] that a Normally Distributed Variable Will be Less than *d* Standard Deviations from the Mean

(*d*)	0.00	0.01	0.02	0.03	0.04	0.05	0.06	0.07	0.08	0.09
0.0	0.5000	0.5040	0.5080	0.5120	0.5160	0.5199	0.5239	0.5279	0.5319	0.5359
0.1	0.5398	0.5438	0.5478	0.5517	0.5557	0.5596	0.5636	0.5675	0.5714	0.5723
0.2	0.5793	0.5832	0.5871	0.5910	0.5948	0.5987	0.6026	0.6064	0.6103	0.6141
0.3	0.6179	0.6217	0.6255	0.6293	0.6331	0.6368	0.6406	0.6443	0.6480	0.6517
0.4	0.6554	0.6591	0.6628	0.6664	0.6700	0.6736	0.6772	0.6808	0.6844	0.6879
0.5	0.6915	0.6950	0.6985	0.7019	0.7054	0.7088	0.7123	0.7157	0.7190	0.7224
0.6	0.7257	0.7291	0.7324	0.7357	0.7389	0.7422	0.7454	0.7486	0.7517	0.7549
0.7	0.7580	0.7611	0.7642	0.7673	0.7704	0.7734	0.7764	0.7794	0.7823	0.7852
0.8	0.7881	0.7910	0.7939	0.7967	0.7995	0.8023	0.8051	0.8079	0.8106	0.8133
0.9	0.8159	0.8186	0.8212	0.8238	0.8264	0.8289	0.8315	0.8340	0.8365	0.8389
1.0	0.8413	0.8438	0.8461	0.8485	0.8508	0.8531	0.8554	0.8577	0.8599	0.8621
1.1	0.8643	0.8665	0.8686	0.8708	0.8729	0.8749	0.8770	0.8790	0.8810	0.8830
1.2	0.8849	0.8869	0.8888	0.8907	0.8925	0.8944	0.8962	0.8980	0.8997	0.9015
1.3	0.9032	0.9049	0.9066	0.9082	0.9099	0.9115	0.9131	0.9147	0.9162	0.9177
1.4	0.9192	0.9207	0.9222	0.9236	0.9251	0.9265	0.9279	0.9292	0.9306	0.9319

Note: if *d* is 1.23, then [N(*d*)] is 0.8907. This means there is a 89.07% probability that a normally distributed variable will be less than 1.23 standard deviations above the mean.

(*d*)	0.00	0.01	0.02	0.03	0.04	0.05	0.06	0.07	0.08	0.09
1.5	0.9332	0.9345	0.9357	0.9370	0.9382	0.9394	0.9406	0.9418	0.9429	0.9441
1.6	0.9452	0.9463	0.9474	0.9484	0.9495	0.9505	0.9515	0.9525	0.9535	0.9545
1.7	0.9554	0.9564	0.9573	0.9582	0.9591	0.9599	0.9608	0.9616	0.9625	0.9633
1.8	0.9641	0.9649	0.9656	0.9664	0.9671	0.9678	0.9686	0.9693	0.9699	0.9706
1.9	0.9713	0.9719	0.9726	0.9732	0.9738	0.9744	0.9750	0.9756	0.9761	0.9767
2.0	0.9772	0.9778	0.9783	0.9788	0.9793	0.9798	0.9803	0.9808	0.9812	0.9817
2.1	0.9821	0.9826	0.9830	0.9834	0.9838	0.9842	0.9846	0.9850	0.9854	0.9857
2.2	0.9861	0.9864	0.9868	0.9871	0.9875	0.9878	0.9881	0.9884	0.9887	0.9890
2.3	0.9893	0.9896	0.9898	0.9901	0.9904	0.9906	0.9909	0.9911	0.9913	0.9916
2.4	0.9918	0.9920	0.9922	0.9924	0.9927	0.9929	0.9931	0.9932	0.9934	0.9936
2.5	0.9938	0.9940	0.9941	0.9943	0.9945	0.9946	0.9948	0.9949	0.9951	0.9952
2.6	0.9953	0.9955	0.9956	0.9957	0.9959	0.9960	0.9961	0.9962	0.9963	0.9964
2.7	0.9965	0.9966	0.9967	0.9968	0.9969	0.9970	0.9971	0.9972	0.9973	0.9974
2.8	0.9974	0.9975	0.9976	0.9977	0.9977	0.9978	0.9979	0.9979	0.9980	0.9981
2.9	0.9981	0.9982	0.9982	0.9983	0.9984	0.9984	0.9985	0.9985	0.9986	0.9986
3.0	0.9986	0.9987	0.9987	0.9988	0.9988	0.9989	0.9989	0.9989	0.9990	0.9990

Bibliography

Alkaraan, F. and Northcott, D. (2006) 'Strategic Capital Investment Decision Making: A Role for Emergent Analysis Tools? A Study of Practice in Large UK Manufacturing Companies'. *British Accounting Review*, 38 (2), 149–174.

Altman, E. I. (1968) 'Financial Ratios, Discriminant Analysis and the Prediction of Corporate Bankruptcy'. *Journal of Finance*, 23 (4), 589–609.

Arnold, G. and Hatzopoulos, P. (2000) 'The Theory-Practice Gap in Capital Budgeting: Evidence from the United Kingdom'. *Journal of Business, Finance and Accounting*, 27 (5 and 6), 603–626.

Beaver, W. H. (1966) 'Financial ratios are predictors of failure'. *Journal of Accounting Research*, Vol. 4.

Beaver, W. H. (1968) 'Alternative accounting measures as predictors of failure'. *The Accounting Review*, January.

Brown, P., Izan, H. and Loh, A., (1992), 'Fixed Asset Revaluations and Managerial Incentives'. *Abacus*, 28 (1), 36–57.

Donaldson, G., *Corporate Debt Capacity* (Harvard University Press, 1961).

Drury, C., *Management Accounting* (International Thompson Business Press, 1996).

Drury, C., Braund, S. Osborne, P. and Tayes, M. (1993) 'A Survey of Management Accounting Practices in UK Manufacturing Companies'. ACCA, *Research Report No. 32.*

Elton, E. and Gruber, M. (1970) 'Marginal Stockholder Tax Rates and the Clientele Effect'. *Review of Economics and Statistics*, 52 (1), 68–74.

Farrelly, G., Baker, H. and Edelman, R. (1985) 'A Survey of Management Views on Dividend Policy'. *Financial Management*, 14 (3), 78–84.

Financial Reporting Council , 'Internal Control: Guidance for Directors on the Combined Code (Turnbull Guidance)' (1999).

Financial Reporting Council, 'Internal Control: Revised Guidance for Directors on the Combined Code' (October 2005).

Financial Reporting Council, 'The Turnbull Guidance as an Evaluation Framework for the purposes of Section 404(a) of the Sarbanes–Oxley Act' (December 2004).

Financial Reporting Council, *UK Stewardship Code* (2020).

Financial Reporting Council, *UK Corporate Governance Code* (2018).

Gordon, M. (1959) 'Dividends, Earnings and Stock Prices'. *Review of Economics and Statistics*, 41 (2), 99–105.

Henderson, S. and Goodwin, J. (1992) 'The Case Against Asset Revaluations'. *Abacus*, 28 (1), 75–86.

Jensen, M. and Meckling, W. (1976) 'Theory of the Firm: Managerial Behaviour, Agency Costs and Ownership Structure'. *Journal of Financial Economics*, October.

Lefley, F. (1994) 'Capital Investment Appraisal of Manufacturing Technology'. *International Journal of Production Research*, 32 (12), 2751–2756.

Lewellen, W., Stanley, K., Lease, R. and Schlarbaum G. (1978) 'Some Direct Evidence on the Dividend Clientele Phenomenon'. *Journal of Finance*, December, 1385–1399.

Lintner, J. (1956) 'Distributions of Incomes of Corporations among Dividends, Retained Earnings and Taxes'. *American Economic Review*, May, 97–113.

Miller, M. and Modigliani, F. (1961) 'Dividend Policy, Growth and the Valuation of Shares'. *Journal of Business*, Vol. 34, October, 411–433.

Miller, M. and Orr, D. (1966), 'A model of the Demand for Money by Firms', *Quarterly Journal of Economics*, August, 413–435.

Miller, M. (1986) 'Behavioural Rationality in Finance: The Case of Dividends'. *Journal of Business*, 59 (4), S451–S468.

Modigliani, F. and Miller, M. (1958) 'The Cost of Capital, Corporation Finance and the Theory of Investment'. *American Economic Review*, Vol. 48, June, 261–297.

Modigliani, F. and Miller, M., (1963), 'Corporate Income Taxes and the Cost of Capital: A Correction', *American Economic Review*, Vol. 53, June, 433–443.

Morris, R. (1998) 'Forecasting bankruptcy: how useful are failure prediction models?'. *Management Accounting*, May.

Myers, S. and Majluf, N. (1984) 'Corporate Financing and Investment Decisions when Firms have Information that Investors do not have'. *Journal of Financial Economics*, Vol. 13, 187–221.

Pike, R. (1996) 'A Longitudinal Survey of Capital Budgeting Practices'. *Journal of Business, Finance and Accounting*, 23 (1), 79–92.

Porter, M. E., *Competitive Advantage* (Free Press, 1985).

Porterfield, J. T., *Investment Decisions and Capital Costs* (Prentice Hall, 1965).

Rappaport, A., *Creating Shareholder Value: The New Standard for Business Performance* (Macmillan, 1986).

Solomons, D., *Divisional Performance: Measurement and Control* (Richard D. Irwin, 1965).

Taffler, R. J. (1983) 'The assessment of company solvency and performance using a statistical model – a comparative UK-based study'. *Accounting and Business Research*, 13 (52), 295–308.

Taffler, R. J. and Tisshaw, H. (1977) 'Going, going, gone – four factors which predict'. *Accountancy*, March.

Whittred, G. and Chan, Y. (1992) 'Asset Revaluations and the Mitigation of Underinvestment'. *Abacus*, 28 (1), 58–74.

Whittred, G. and Zimmer, I. (1986) 'Accounting in the Market for Debt'. *Accounting and Finance*, 26 (2), 19–33.

Index